EARLY CHRISTIANITY AND CLASSICAL CULTURE

SUPPLEMENTS TO

NOVUM TESTAMENTUM

VOLUME CX

EARLY CHRISTIANITY AND CLASSICAL CULTURE

Comparative Studies in Honor of Abraham J. Malherbe

EDITED BY

JOHN T. FITZGERALD,
THOMAS H. OLBRICHT,
AND L. MICHAEL WHITE

BRILL
LEIDEN · BOSTON
2003

This book is printed on acid-free paper.

Library of Congress Cataloging-in-Publication Data

Early Christianity and classical culture : comparative studies in honor of Abraham J.
  Malherbe / edited by John T. Fitzgerald, Thomas H. Olbricht, and L. Michael
  White.
      p. cm. – (Supplements to Novum Testamentum, ISSN 0167-9732 ; v. 110)
  Includes bibliographical references and index.
  ISBN 90-04-13022-5 (alk. paper)
    1. Bible, N.T.–Criticism, interpretation, etc. 2. Christianity and other religions–
  Greek. 3. Christianity and other religions–Roman. I. Malherbe, Abraham J. II.
  Fitzgerald, John T., 1948- III. Olbricht, Thomas H. IV. White, L. Michael.
  V. Series.

  BS2361.3.E37 2003
  270.1–dc21

BS

2361.3

.E37

2003

2003050225

ISSN   0167-9732
ISBN   90 04 13022 5

PRINTED IN THE NETHERLANDS

Abraham Johannes Malherbe

To

Abraham J. Malherbe

Mentor, Colleague, Friend and Scholar
of
Uncompromising Integrity
and
Uncommon Insight

CONTENTS

List of Contributors xi

Abbreviations xv

Thomas H. Olbricht, *Preface* 1

L. Michael White and John T. Fitzgerald, Quod est comparandum: *The Problem of Parallels* 13

A Bibliography of the Writings of Abraham J. Malherbe 41

Part I. *Graphos*

Dieter Zeller, *The θεῖα φύσις of Hippocrates and of Other "Divine Men"* 49

Harold W. Attridge, *Making Scents of Paul: The Background and Sense of 2 Cor 2: 14–17* 71

Gerard Mussies, *"In Those Days:" Some Remarks on the Use of "Days" in Matthew 2:1, 3:1, and Luke 2:1* 89

David E. Aune, *Distinct Lexical Meanings of ἀπαρχή in Hellenism, Judaism, and Early Christianity* 103

Hans-Josef Klauck, *Compilation of Letters in Cicero's Correspondence* 131

Duane F. Watson, *A Reexamination of the Epistolary Analysis Underpinning the Arguments for the Composite Nature of Philippians* 157

Part II. *Ethos*

Ronald F. Hock, *The Parable of the Foolish Rich Man (Luke 12:16–20) and Graeco-Roman Conventions of Thought and Behavior* 181

Troels Engberg-Pedersen, *Radical Altruism in Philippians 2:4* 197

Luke Timothy Johnson, *Transformation of the Mind and Moral Discernment in Paul* 215

James W. Thompson, *Creation, Shame and Nature in 1 Cor 11:2–16: The Background and Coherence of Paul's Argument* 237

Cilliers Breytenbach, *Civic Concord and Cosmic Harmony: Sources of Metaphoric Mapping in 1 Clement 20.3* 259

Part III. *Logos*

Edgar Krentz, *Logos or Sophia: The Pauline Use of the Ancient Dispute between Rhetoric and Philosophy* 277

Bruce W. Winter, *The Toppling of Favorinus and Paul by the Corinthians* 291

L. Michael White, *Rhetoric and Reality in Galatians: Framing the Social Demands of Friendship* 307

Stanley K. Stowers, *Apostrophe, Προσωποποιία and Paul's Rhetorical Education* 351

Thomas H. Olbricht, *Analogy and Allegory in Classical Rhetoric* 371

Everett Ferguson, *The Art of Praise: Philo and Philodemus on Music* 391

Part IV. *Ethnos*

Carl R. Holladay, *Paul and His Predecessors in the Diaspora: Some Reflections on Ethnic Identity in the Fragmentary Hellenistic Jewish Authors* 429

Leander E. Keck, *The Jewish Paul among the Gentiles: Two Portrayals* 461

David L. Balch, *The Cultural Origin of "Receiving All Nations" in Luke-Acts: Alexander the Great or Roman Social Policy?* 483

E. A. Judge, *Did the Churches Compete with Cult Groups?* 501

Hanne Sigismund Nielsen, *Men, Women and Marital Chastity: Public Preaching and Popular Piety at Rome* 525

Part V. *Nomos*

Johan C. Thom, *"The Mind is its Own Place:" Defining the* Topos 555

J. Louis Martyn, *Nomos Plus Genitive Noun in Paul: The History of God's Law* 575

Benjamin J. Fiore, *Household Rules at Ephesus: Good News, Bad News, No News* 589

Marinus de Jonge and L. Michael White, *The Washing of Adam in the Acherusian Lake (Greek* Life of Adam and Eve *37.3) in the Context of Early Christian Notions of Afterlife* 609

John T. Fitzgerald, *Last Wills and Testaments in Graeco-Roman Perspective* 637

Index of Ancient Sources 673
Index of Modern Scholars 727

LIST OF CONTRIBUTORS

Harold W. Attridge
Dean and Lillian Claus Professor of New Testament
Yale Divinity School
New Haven, CT 06511

David E. Aune
Professor of New Testament
Department of Theology
University of Notre Dame
Notre Dame, IN 46556

David L. Balch
Professor of New Testament
Brite Divinity School
Texas Christian University
Fort Worth, TX 76129

Cilliers Breytenbach
Professor of Literature and Religion of Early Christianity
Institute for Early Christianity and Antiquity
Humboldt University
10099 Berlin, Germany
Visiting Professor
Department of Old and New Testament
University of Stellenbosch
Matieland, Republic of South Africa

Troels Engberg-Pedersen
Professor of New Testament
Institute of Biblical Exegesis
Faculty of Theology
University of Copenhagen
1150 Copenhagen, Denmark

Everett Ferguson
Professor of Church History, Emeritus
Abilene Christian University
Abilene, TX 79699

Benjamin Fiore, S.J.
Professor of New Testament
Department of Religious Studies
Canisius College
Buffalo, NY 14208

John T. Fitzgerald
Associate Professor of Religious Studies
Department of Religious Studies
University of Miami
Coral Gables, FL 33124

Ronald F. Hock
Professor of Religion
School of Religion
University of Southern California
Los Angeles, CA 90089

Carl R. Holladay
C. H. Candler Professor of New Testament
Candler School of Theology
Emory University
Atlanta, GA 30322

Luke Timothy Johnson
R. W. Woodruff Professor of New Testament and Christian Origins
Candler School of Theology
Emory University
Atlanta, GA 30322

Marinus de Jonge
Professor of New Testament and
Ancient Christian Literature
Faculty of Theology
University of Leiden
2318 VE Leiden, The Netherlands

E. A. Judge
Emeritus Professor of History
Macquarie University
Sydney, NSW 2109, Australia

Leander E. Keck
Winkley Professor of Biblical Theology, Emeritus
Yale Divinity School
New Haven, CT 06511

Hans-Josef Klauck
Professor of New Testament & Early Christian Literature
The Divinity School
University of Chicago
Chicago, IL 60637

Edgar M. Krentz
Professor of New Testament, Emeritus
Lutheran School of Theology at Chicago
Chicago, IL 60615

J. Louis Martyn
Edward Robinson Professor of Biblical Theology, Emeritus
Union Theological Seminary
New York, New York 10027

Gerard Mussies
Lecturer in Biblical Greek
Faculty of Theology
University of Utrecht
Utrecht 3508 TC, The Netherlands

Hanne Sigismund Nielsen
Associate Professor of Classics
University of Calgary
Calgary, T2N 1N4, Alberta, Canada

Thomas H. Olbricht
Distinguished Professor of Religion, Emeritus
Pepperdine University
Malibu, CA 90265

Stanley K. Stowers
Professor of Religious Studies
Brown University
Providence, RI 02912

Johan C. Thom
Professor of Classics
Department of Ancient Studies
University of Stellenbosch
Matieland, 7602Republic of South Africa

James W. Thompson
Professor of New Testament
Abilene Christian University
Abilene, TX 79699

Duane F. Watson
Professor of New Testament
School of Theology
Malone College
Canton, OH 44709

L. Michael White
R. N. Smith Professor of Classics and Christian Origins
Director, Institute for the Study of Antiquity & Christian Origins
Department of Classics
The University of Texas at Austin
Austin, Texas 78712

Bruce W. Winter
Director
Institute of Early Christianity in the Graeco-Roman World
Tyndale House, Fellow, St. Edmund's College
Cambridge University
Cambridge CB3 9BA, UK

Dieter Zeller
Professor of Religionswissenschaft des Hellenismus
Johannes Gutenberg University
55099 Mainz, Germany

ABBREVIATIONS

Abbreviations used for titles of modern books, periodicals, translations, and series follow, as far as possible, the guidelines of the Society of Biblical Literature as published in *Journal of Biblical Literature* 107 (1988) 579-96. Other abbreviations follow Liddel-Scott-Jones-McKenzie, *A Greek-English Lexicon with Supplement* (Oxford: Clarendon Press, 1968) or *Dictionary of Bibliographic Abbreviations found in Scholarship of Classical Studies and Related Disciplines*, compiled by Jean Susorney Wellington (Westport and London: Greenwood Press, 1983).

AB	Anchor Bible
ABD	D. N. Freedman (ed.), *Anchor Bible Dictionary*
ABR	*Australian Biblical Review*
AGJU	Arbeiten zur Geschichte des antiken Judentums und des Urchristentums
AJP	*American Journal of Philology*
ALGHJ	Arbeiten zur Literatur und Geschichte des hellenistischen Judentums
ANRW	*Aufstieg und Niedergand der römischen Welt*
ASNU	Acta seminarii neotestamentici upsaliensis
AUS	American University Studies
AV	Authorized Version
BAGD	W. Bauer, W.F. Arndt, F.W. Gingrich, and F.W. Danker, *Greek-English Lexicon of the New Testament* (2nd ed.)
BDAG	W. Baur, F.W. Danker, W.F. Arndt, and F.W. Gingrich, *Greek-English Lexicon of the New Testament* (3rd ed.)
BASP	*Bulletin of the American Society of Papyrologists*
BBR	*Bulletin for Biblical Research*
BEvT	Beiträge zur evangelischen Theologie
BFCT	Beiträge zur Förderung christlicher Theologie
BGU	Berlin Griechische Urkunden (*Ägyptische Urkunden aus den Königlichen Staatlichen Museen zu Berlin*)
BJS	Brown Judaic Studies
BMCR	*Bryn Mawr Classical Review (on-line)*
BNF	Bibliotèque Nationale de France
BNJ	*Byzantisch- Neogriechische Jahrbücher*
BNTC	Black's New Testament Commentaries

BR	*Biblical Research*
BTB	*Biblical Theology Bulletin*
BZNW	Beihefte zur ZNW
CBET	Contributions to Biblical Exegesis and Theology
CBQ	*Catholic Biblical Quarterly*
CCSL	*Corpus christianorum: Series latina*
CEV	Contemporary English Version
CIL	*Corpus inscriptionum latinarum*
CIMRM	M. J. Vermaseren, *Corpus inscriptionum et monumentorum religionis Mitriacae*
CJ	*Classical Journal*
CMG	*Corpus medicorum graecorum*
CNT	Commentaire du Nouveau Testament
ConBNT	Coniectanea biblica, New Testament
COr	Cahiers d'Orientalisme
CP	*Classical Philology*
CRINT	Compendia rerum iudaicarum ad novum testamentum
CSCO	Corpus scriptorum christianorum orientalium
CSEL	Corpus scriptorum ecclesiasticorum latinorum
DBSup	*Dictionnaire de la Bible, Supplément*
DCH	*Dictionary of Classical Hebrew*
EDNT	H. Balz and G. Schneider (eds.), *Exegetical Dictionary of the New Testament*
EKKNT	Evangelische-katholischer Kommentar zum Neuen Testament
EPRO	Études préliminaires aux religions orientales dans l'empire Romain
ET	English Translation
FF	*Forschungen und Fortschritte: Korrespondenzblat der deutschen Wissenschaft und Technik*
FFNT	Foundations and Facets: New Testament
FHJA	Carl R. Holladay, *Fragments from Hellenistic Jewish Authors*
FrGH	F. Jacoby, *Fragmente der griechischen Historkier*
FRLANT	Forschungen zur Religion und Literatur des Alten und Neuen Testaments
GBS	Guides to Biblical Scholarship
GRBS	*Greek, Roman, and Byzantine Studies*
GRS	see SBLGRS
GTA	Göttinger theologische Arbeiten
HAW	Handbuch des Altertumswissenschaft

HNT	Handbuch zum Neuen Testament
HTKNT	Herders theologischer Kommentar zum Neuen Testament
HTR	*Harvard Theological Review*
HTS	Harvard Theological Studies
ICC	International Critical Commentary
ICS	*Illinois Classical Studies*
ICUR	J. B. de Rossi (ed.), *Inscriptiones christianae urbis Romae*
IDBSup	Supplementary volume to G. A. Buttrick (ed.), *Interpreter's Dictionary of the Bible*
IG	*Inscriptiones Graecae*
IGUR	*Inscriptiones graecae urbis Romae*
ILS	H. Dessau (ed.), *Inscriptiones latinae selectae*
JAAR	*Journal of the American Academy of Religion*
JAC	Jahrbuch für Antike und Christentum
JBL	*Journal of Biblical Literature*
JETS	*Journal of the Evangelical Theological Society*
JHS	*Journal of Hellenic Studies*
JR	*Journal of Religion*
JRH	*Journal of Religious History*
JRS	*Journal of Roman Studies*
JSJ	*Journal for the Study of Judaism in the Persian, Hellenistic and Roman Period*
JSNT	*Journal for the Study of the New Testament*
JSNTSup	*JSNT* – Supplement
JSOT	*Journal for the Study of the Old Testament*
JTS	*Journal of Theological Studies*
KAV	Kommentar zu den Apostolischen Vätern
KEK	Kritisch-exegetisches Kommentar über das Neue Testament (Meyer-Kommentar)
LCL	Loeb Classical Library
LD	Lectio divina
LEC	Library of Early Christianity
LSJ	Liddel-Scott-Jones[-McKenzie], *Greek-English Lexicon*
LSJM	Liddel-Scott-Jones-McKenzie, *Greek-English Lexicon*
LXX	Septuagint
MT	Massoretic Text
MTZ	*Münchener theologische Zeitschrift*
NAB	New American Bible
NASB	New American Standard Bible
NEB	New English Bible

NGWG	Nachrichten (von) der Gesellschaft der Wissenschaften (zu) in Göttingen
NICNT	New International Commentary on the New Testament
NIGTC	The New International Greek Testament Commentary
NIV	New International Version
NJB	H. Wansbrough (ed.), *New Jerusalem Bible*
NovT	Novum Testamentum
NovTSup	Supplements to *Novum Testamentum*
NPNFN	Nicene and Post-Nicene Fathers
NT	New Testament
NTAbh	Neutestamentliche Abhandlungen
NTS	*New Testament Studies*
NTTS	New Testament Tools and Studies
OCD	M. Cary et al. (eds.), *The Oxford Classical Dictionary*
OLD	P. G. W. Glare (ed.), *The Oxford Latin Dictionary*
OT	Old Testament
OTP	J. H. Charlesworth (ed.), *The Old Testament Pseudoepigrapha*
OTS	*Oudtestamentische Studiën*
PG	J. Migne, *Patrologia graeca*
PGM	K. Preisendanz (ed.), *Papyri graecae magicae*
Philol	*Philologus: Zeitschrift für das klassische Altertum*
PL	J. Migne, *Patrologia latina*
PW	Pauly-Wissowa, *Real-Encyclopädie der classischen Altertumwissenschaft*
PWSup	*Supplement to PW*
RAC	T. Klauser et al. (eds.), *Reallexikon für Antike und Christentum*
REB	Revised English Bible
REG	*Revue des études grecques*
ResQ	*Restoration Quarterly*
RevExp	*Review and Expositor*
RGG	*Religion in Geschichte und Gegenwart*
RhM	*Rheinisches Museum*
RivAC	*Rivista di archeologia cristiana*
RSR	*Recherches de science religieuse*
RSV	Revised Standard Version
RTR	*Reformed Theological Review*
SacPag	Sacra Pagina
SB	Sources bibliques
SBL	Society of Biblical Literature
SBLDS	SBL Dissertation Series

SBLEJL	SBL Early Judaism and Its Literature
SBLGRS	SBL Graeco-Roman Religion Series
SBLMS	SBL Monograph Series
SBLRBS	SBL Resources for Biblical Study
SBLSBS	SBL Sources for Biblical Study
SBLSCS	SBL Septuagint and Cognate Studies
SBLSP	SLB Seminar Papers
SBLTT	SBL Text and Translation Series
SBS	Stuttgarter Bibelstudien
SBT	Studies in Biblical Theology
SC	Sources chrétiennes
SCHNT	Studia ad corpus hellenisticum Novi Testamenti
SecCent	The Second Century
SD	Studies and Documents
SHAW	Sitzungesberichte der heidelberger Akademie der Wissen-schaften
SIG	W. Dittenberger (ed.), *Sylloge inscriptionum graecarum*
SJT	*Scottish Journal of Theology*
SNTIW	Studies of the New Testament and Its World
SNTSMS	Society for New Testament Studies Monograph Series
SPhA	*Studia Philonica Annual*
StPhilo	*Studia Philonica*
SVF	H. von Arnim, *Stoicorum veterum fragmenta*
SVTP	Studia in Veteris Testamenti pseudoepigrapha
TAPA	*Transactions of the American Philological Association*
TDNT	G. Kittel and G. Friedrich (eds.), *Theological Dictionary of the New Testament* [Eng. ed. of *TWNT*]
TDOT	G. J. Botterweck and H. Ringgren (eds.), *Theological Dictio-nary of the Old Testament* [Eng. ed. of *TWAT*]
TGL	*Thesaurus Graecae Linguae*, ed. H. Éstienne
THKNT	Theologischer Handkommentar zum Neuen Testament
ThViat	*Theologia viatorum*
TLG	Thesaurus Linguae Graecae
TLZ	*Theologische Literaturzeitung*
TRE	*Theologische Realenzyklopäedie*
TSAJ	Texte und Studien zum antiken Judentum
TU	Texte und Untersuchungen
TWAT	G. J. Botterweck and H. Ringgren (eds.), *Theologisches Wörterbuch zum Alten Testament*

TWNT	G. Kittel and G. Friedrich (eds.), *Theologisches Wörterbuch zum Neuen Testament*
TynBul	*Tyndale Bulletin*
TZ	*Theologische Zeitschrift*
UBS	United Bible Societies
UPZ	U. Wilcken, *Urkunden der Ptolemäerzeit*
USFSHJ	University of South Florida Studies in the History of Judaism
VC	*Vigiliae Christianae*
VCSup	Supplements to *Vigiliae Christianae*
WBC	World Biblical Commentary
WUNT	Wissenschaftliche Untersuchungen zum Neuen Testament
ZNW	*Zeitschrift für die neutestamentliche Wissenschaft*
ZPE	*Zeitschrift für Papyrologie und Epigraphik*
ZTK	*Zeitschrift für Theologie und Kirche*

PREFACE

Thomas H. Olbricht

The question of early Christianity's relationship to Classical culture is an ancient one that historically has been answered in a variety of ways. Some observers have stressed the differences, whereas others have emphasized the similarities, yet most agree that the correct answer to the question depends not only on various temporal and geographical factors involved in making the assessment but also on the individuals and institutions compared. The early Christians themselves were well aware of both the similarities and the differences. Tertullian, for example, in battling against heretics who supported their theological claims with arguments drawn from philosophy, can contrast Christian and pagan thought, asking, "What indeed has Athens to do with Jerusalem? What concord is there between the Academy and the Church?"[1] Yet in a different context he himself freely admits the similarity between Christian and pagan thought on certain subjects and can unhesitatingly refer to the Stoic philosopher Seneca as "ever our Seneca."[2]

The essays in this volume thus take up an old question but attempt to examine it in new ways.[3] They originated in part from a special session of the 1998 SBL International Meeting in Krakow, Poland, devoted to the topic of Christianity and Classical Culture. The occasion was particularly auspicious, since it afforded scholars from Europe, Africa, and North America the opportunity to revisit an old issue in a fresh setting. John Fitzgerald was the organizer of the program, and one of the issues that emerged from the beginning stages was the degree

---

[1] *De praescriptione haereticorum* 7.

[2] *De anima* 20.

[3] Previous attempts to address various aspects of the complex relationship between early Christianity and Classical culture include the following: Charles N. Cochrane, *Christianity and Classical Culture: A Study of Thought and Action from Augustus to Augustine* (Oxford: Clarendon, 1940); William R. Schoedel and Robert L. Wilken (eds.), *Early Christian Literature and the Classical Intellectual Tradition: In Honorem Robert M. Grant* (Théologie historique 54; Paris: Éditions Beauchesne, 1979); Jaroslav J. Pelikan, *Christianity and Classical Culture: The Metamorphosis of Natural Theology in the Christian Encounter with Hellenism* (New Haven: Yale University Press, 1993). See also E. G. Weitlin, *Athens and Jerusalem: An Interpretative Essay on Christianity and Classical Culture* (American Academy of Religion Studies in Religion 49; Atlanta: Scholars Press, 1987).

of mutual influence and respect that these scholars from such varied backgrounds—some of whom had never met—were able to use as a basis for fruitful new explorations of the issue at hand. In light of those papers, therefore, this volume was born. Other scholars, many who work with the Hellenistic Moral Philosophy and Early Christianity Section of the SBL, were invited to round out the volume, and the process began.

The process of selecting and editing these articles has been rigorous, primarily because it is often the nature of edited collections of this sort to lack focus or organizing themes. Consequently, the three editors each read and made suggestions on every article. Michael White then compiled these comments and offered them to the authors, who in turn made appropriate revisions and additions. In some cases these were extensive. In every case the exchange proved engaging and productive. We express our gratitude to our colleagues for their patience, their scholarly gifts, and their collaborative efforts. Final revisions, copy editing, and production of the manuscript were completed by Michael White with the admirable editorial assistance of Mr. Michael DeBrauw and Mr. Milton Torres, doctoral candidates in Classics at the University of Texas at Austin. We also express our appreciation to the *Institute for the Study of Antiquity and Christian Origins* (ISAC) at the University of Texas at Austin for its support of the project. In particular, it was a fond vision of the late Professor William Shive, who was instrumental in establishing ISAC, to support the study of early Christianity in its historical context.

We also wish to thank the editors of the *Novum Testamentum* Supplements series, Margaret M. Mitchell and David P. Moessner and the editorial staff under Louise Schouten at Brill who have made this volume a reality.

Among the factors in establishing the common ground for these studies, both in Krakow and in the SBL Hellenistic Moral Philosophy Section, is the work of one scholar, Abraham J. Malherbe, Buckingham Professor of New Testament, Emeritus at Yale Divinity School. Of course, no one would claim—let alone Malherbe himself—that his work was the sole basis for everything being done. Indeed, his awareness of the history and intersections of scholarship is one of the hallmarks of Malherbe's own work. Rather, the common ground came from the awareness that Malherbe's scholarship has so clearly focused the critical issues in dealing with Hellenistic texts and traditions, and that these issues have thus helped to return the comparative study of the interaction of Jews and Christians with Hellenistic and Roman culture to a central position within both Classical and early Christian fields.

Malherbe has spent his career exploring the interlacing of Classical culture with early Christianity. Working closely with students and international colleagues, he introduced a specialized new regimen into the study of social and moral aspects of early Christianity, while not dismissing the religious dimensions. Together they have scrutinized and in some cases translated numerous ancient texts, unknown to or ignored by many scholars, whether in Classics or in New Testament. They have especially focused on contemporary Graeco-Roman texts that shed new light on New Testament writings. These studies reflect this ongoing work, and Malherbe has set out the parameters:

> The whole range of possible ways in which religions react when they meet, extending from opposition or rejection through amelioration to assimilation, conscious and unconscious, should be taken into consideration. This will require the type of empirical investigation that is uncongenial to generalization, and should be pursued despite the bogeyman of "positivism."[4]

The essays in this volume are, therefore, dedicated to Abe Malherbe. They traverse a rich panoply of texts from ancient Mediterranean culture. They are grouped around five Greek terms that reflect key arenas of the cultural interaction of ancient Jews and Christians with their Greek and Roman neighbors: respectively, *Graphos*—semantics and writing, *Ethos*—ethics and moral characterization, *Logos*—rhetoric and literary expression, *Ethnos*—self-definition and acculturation, and *Nomos*—law and normative values. Abe Malherbe's work has touched on each of these areas and on the underlying methodological issue of how to draw comparisons between early Christian materials and classical texts. The volume opens, therefore, with an essay by co-editors Michael White and John Fitzgerald on the use of Classical and Jewish "parallels" in the history of New Testament scholarship. They illuminate the changing perspectives gained from recent trends in social world scholarship to locate these materials in their cultural context by careful analysis of both social conventions and literary function.

---

[4] Abraham J. Malherbe, "Graeco-Roman Religion and Philosophy and the New Testament," *The New Testament and Its Modern Interpreters* (eds. Eldon Jay Epp, and George W. MacRae, Atlanta: Scholars Press, 1989) 11.

PART I. *Graphos*

The essays in Part I focus on ancient writing in terms of semantics, lexicography, and composition. These investigations indicate that much insight is still to be obtained by focusing carefully on key terms, ideas, and modes of expression that place literary and theological formulations in their historical and cultural context.

Dieter Zeller in *The ϑεία φύσις of Hippocrates and of other "Divine Men,"* notes that from the beginning of the twentieth century many New Testament scholars sought to characterize Jesus according to the category of "divine man," a designation well known in the Graeco-Roman world. Recently, however, this depiction has declined in popularity. In contrast, Zeller shows, based upon the use of the adjectival forms of *theios,-a* in several documents, that "divine man" was a valid category in Greek usage and meant excellence above the human level. It may be reflected by extraodinary abilities in artistry, medicine, or the magical arts, but is not primarily concerned with the miracles as previously assumed in New Testament studies. Those considered "divine men" tended to receive these capabilities from the gods at birth, but not as the result of being overcome by the spirit of God as in the Biblical tradition. Zeller ends by exploring the semantic ramifications of *theios* in a little known text about Hippocrates the founder of medicine.

Harold W. Attridge in *Making Scents of Paul* explores the sensual images Paul employs in 2 Corinthians 2:14–17. Attridge surveys the ways that the ancients used scents (perfumes)—for a lover, as healing balms, or for embalming, and he cites numerous texts to establish these uses. He concludes that the importing of sensual images into this passage "can be construed as a consistent development of the imagery of sacred unguents used in religious 'triumphs' in which devotees made known the presence of the deity and also their relationship to the potent power celebrating the triumph." He concludes that this potent metaphor is an expression of Paul's self-understanding.

Gerard Mussies in *"In Those Days:" Some Remarks on the Use of "Days" in Matthew 2:1, 3:1, and Luke 2:1*, examines the phrase from the standpoint of instances contained in the Hebrew Bible, and in Hellenistic Jewish and Roman texts. He concludes that the phrase implies the period of a person's life, that is, the time span in which they lived, or it covers a period, for example, all the days subsumed in the harvest. In Matthew 3:1 "in those days" seems to include all the events from the birth of Jesus.

In his essay, *Distinct Lexical Meanings of ἀπαρχή in Hellenism, Judaism, and Early Christianity*, David E. Aune shows that ἀπαρχή in the Septuagint, despite numerous mistaken word studies, was employed to speak of crops and not of animals or humans. Josephus employed the word in the same manner as the Septuagint, but Philo used it in regard to humans and animals. In Greek usage the word often identifies slaves consecrated to particular deities for temple service. Furthermore, those involved in theological word studies have claimed that with two exceptions the word is employed metaphorically in the New Testament and in the Apostolic Fathers. Aune finds instead that it is used literally in every case, and he concludes with a summons to further lexicographical studies based on careful historical analysis of semantic contexts.

Hans-Josef Klauck discusses the *Compilation of Letters in Cicero's Correspondence*. In this important study he argues that the place for supporting partition theories must be the epistolary collections and that the best corpus for comparison is that of Cicero. He examines the way that the Ciceronian collection attested to the existence of partitions. In the case of Paul's letters, however, each instance must be established upon hard evidence, which is not always forthcoming. If partitions occurred they were likely simple, involving serial additions rather than interpolations. He concludes that it is unlikely that 1 Thessalonians, Philippians and Romans display evidences of partition.

Duane F. Watson, in *A Reexamination of the Epistolary Analysis Underpinning the Arguments for the Composite Nature of Philippians*, addresses the question of whether Philippians is composite or a single letter. After examining the epistolary conventions offered by scholars in support a of tripartite composition of Philippians, Watson concludes that when more carefully scrutinized these conventions are better interpreted as transitions within one letter. He also asserts that Philippians is in the genre of a friendly letter.

PART II. *Ethos*

Scholars have long had an interest in New Testament ethics and their relationship to Graeco-Roman moral perspectives. The essays here all focus on ethical terms, concepts, and paradigms in New Testament and early Christian materials by bringing insights to bear from the Graeco-Roman world. Individually and cumulatively they show that it is important to know Graeco-Roman ideals and conventions in order to discern the nuances and emphases of New Testament morals and ethics.

In *The Parable of the Foolish Rich Man (Luke 12:16–20) and Graeco-Roman Conventions of Thought and Behavior*, Ronald F. Hock has drawn attention to Graeco-Roman perspectives on greed which help clarify the parable of the rich fool. He brings to the fore the role of inheritance in a traditional agrarian economy as depicted in Greek novels, and especially Cynic views on wealth. He concludes that these materials throw light on the parable not only of the failure of the rich man to share his wealth, but also in his neglect of his soul because of his hedonistic style of life.

Troels Engberg-Pedersen in *Radical Altruism in Philippians 2:4*, comments upon the translation of selected passages in 1 Corinthians, Galatians and Romans, in addition to Philippians. He compares Paul's outlooks with two of Cicero's treatises concerning self-sacrifice, which Engberg-Pedersen identifies as "radical altruism." At the close of the essay he reflects on the Pauline concept from the perspective of two contemporary American philosophers, Samuel Scheffler and Thomas Nagel. He concludes that Paul's view is strongly other-directed or communal but is not one of "abject self-sacrifice." Paul and the Stoics, as shown in Cicero, both insisted that humans have a higher and lower self and that the lower or personal self should be allowed for, but that the higher self which takes seriously oneself-as-one-of-the-others must not be diluted. This is the "radical altruism" of Paul.

In *Transformation of the Mind and Moral Discernment in Paul*, Luke Timothy Johnson raises the question as to whether Paul affirms a role for the human *psyche* somewhere between the power which comes from the Holy Spirit and the disposition of the *soma* by human persons. He argues that Romans shows the problem in the sharpest form and then turns to 1 Corinthians, Philippians and Galatians. Furthermore, he is of the conviction that Aristotle's discussion of *phronesis* in the *Nicomachean Ethics* provides a framework that makes Paul's perspectives more coherent. He concludes that Paul's moral logic is remarkably similar to that of Aristotle, but the framework for that logic is tinctured by his religious convictions. Prudential reasoning is not only informed by one's own mind, but also by the mind of Christ, and the outcomes are not only for one's self, but also for the community of believers.

James W. Thompson in *Creation, Shame and Nature in 1 Cor 11:2–16: The Background and Coherence of Paul's Argument*, argues that Hellenistic Judaism perceived creation as a chain of being which in turn determines whether conduct is shameful or fitting for men and women. He establishes his case especially through statements of Philo. Thompson concludes that both Philo and Paul held that nature taught that a distinction between male and female can be drawn based upon hair and hair covering. Furthermore, they both perceived the male as higher in the hierarchy of nature than the female. Paul's argument therefore was not convoluted when assessed against the backdrop of widely shared assumptions among Hellenistic Jewish writers.

Cilliers Breytenbach, in *Civic Concord and Cosmic Harmony: Sources of Metaphoric Mapping in 1 Clement 20.3*, raises the question of whether 1 Clement employs Stoic backgrounds or is more dependent upon traditional Jewish materials. He shows that Werner Jaeger cast 1 Clement against the backdrop of Greek rhetoric and that he employed Stoic arguments. Van Unnik went on to establish that the form of rhetoric in 1 Clement is deliberative and locates his approach against the backdrop of the notion of concord and peace in Dio Chrysostom, Plutarch, Lucian, Dio Cassius, Epictetus and Aelius Aristides. Breytenbach concludes that 1 Clement in 20.3 used the Stoic vision of comic order in the universe as an example of the harmony to be exhibited by the Corinthians in a manner very similar to that of Dio Chrysostom. Nevertheless 1 Clement is highly dependent upon the Jewish Christian monotheistic tradition.

PART III. *Logos*

Discourse studies on the scriptures go back to ancient times. Church fathers, Chrysostom and Augustine for example, reflected upon rhetorical features in various books of the Bible. Rhetorical studies came to the fore in the Renaissance, Reformation and through the eighteenth century in the work of Melancthon and Johann August Ernesti. Such studies continued in the nineteenth century with Christian Gottlob Wilke and Eduard Norden. In the 1970's a renewed interest in rhetorical analysis of the New Testament arose employing both Greek and Roman rhetoric, sparked by Hans Dieter Betz' commentary on Galatians. A concomitant focus upon moral persuasion arose among those involved in the continuing SBL Section on Hellenistic Moral Philosophy and Early Christianity. The essays in this section reflect both ranges of discussion, contending that ancient rhetoric and modes of literary expression provide discrete insights into both the form and the posture of religious outlook and argumentation.

In *Logos or Sophia: The Pauline Use of the Ancient Dispute between Rhetoric and Philosophy*, Edgar Krentz surveys the disparate analyses on Paul's repudiation of rhetoric in 1 Corinthians 2. He examines several ancient philosophers who denigrated rhetoric. He argues that Paul employed the language drawn from the debate between the rhetoricians and philosophers in order to depict himself as a teacher of the true wisdom, rather than that which comes from rhetorical skill and agility. Divine wisdom is therefore superior to that obtained by rhetoric, and Paul's attack was similar to the manner in which the philosophers belittled rhetoric.

Bruce W. Winter in *The Toppling of Favorinus and Paul by the Corinthians* argues that there are significant parallels between the responses of Paul toward his rejection by some of the Corinthians, and that of the orator Favorinus, who was also rebuffed by the Corinthians. Thus, he examines Favorinus' response, as set out in a speech delivered on his third visit to Corinth ([ps-] Dio, *Or. 37*). Winter concludes that Favorinus, though giving the impression of offering an *apologia* in court, nevertheless did not follow the rhetorical conventions in respect to formal divisions, even though his style was "grand." Winter likewise thinks that 2 Corinthians lacks a rhetorical structure. He concludes that this is characteristic of ancient speakers, even of those thoroughly trained in rhetoric. Rather, both Paul and Favorinus employed a variety of responses and forms.

In *Rhetoric and Reality in Galatians: Framing the Social Demands of Friendship*, L. Michael White provides a new reading of the rhetorical character and function of Gal 4:12–20. Whereas traditional readings had taken Paul's plea as an emotional outburst, Hans Dieter Betz showed that the passage was based on the *topos* on friendship. Betz saw this use of the friendship language, however, as a rhetorical ploy only loosely connected to Paul's *apologia*. Based on comparisons with Dio Chrysostom, Favorinus, and the epistolary handbooks, White argues that Paul's use of the rhetoric of friendship in 4:12–20 is much sharper in tone and thus more central to the structure, setting, and purpose of Galatians as a letter of rebuke.

Stanley K. Stowers in *Apostrophe, Προσωποποιία and Paul's Rhetorical Education*, responds to certain criticisms by R. Dean Anderson regarding Stower's observations on Romans. He contends that the ancient approach was based upon ear and voice contrast as opposed to modern silent reading and writing which is dependent upon the visual spatial representation of the text. Using instances from the ancient rhetoricians and others, he shows that ancient readers were better able to make the bodily and oral distinctions necessary to understand texts appropriately.

Therefore it would not have been difficult for Paul's ancient audience to identify the προσοποποιία Stowers pointed out in Romans.

Thomas H. Olbricht has been interested in features of Biblical texts upon which the rhetoricians did not comment. In his essay *Analogy and Allegory in Classical Rhetoric*, he has explored the ancient rhetorical treatises in respect to analogy and allegory. He concludes that the rhetoricians conceived analogical features of discourse as essentially stylistic devices. In the communication of the synagogue and church, however, analogical approaches reflected a fundamental vision of reality. Furthermore, the writings of both Jews and Christians in Alexandria are a fertile field for assessing the rhetorical aspects of analogical discourse.

In *The Art of Praise: Philo and Philodemus on Music*, Everett Ferguson presents a comprehensive study on the topic in Philo and Philodemus. Philodemus' treatise on music is an important but little tapped source for the ancient discussions, while Philo is shown to employ many of the same technical discussions, albeit sprinkled through many works rather than in one systematic treatment. Both writers reflect the ancient view that locates music among the "arts," such as rhetoric and medicine. In keeping with these theoretical assumptions, when giving praises to the divine, carefully crafted words carry power and bring harmony to the soul. It is clear that Philo prized vocal music above instrumentation in his favorable description of the Therapeutae. Since Philodemus likewise gave centrality to words, Ferguson concludes that the educated Greeks focused on the words rather than the musical score as the heart's expression of praise.

PART IV. *Ethnos*

The ethnic nature of various phenomena having to do with Biblical interpretation has been a preoccupation of Biblical critics almost from the beginning. Ethnic considerations especially came to the forefront with the thesis of F. C. Baur that the clashes of Jewish and Gentile versions of Christianity and their resolution explained many aspects of New Testament materials. Scholars since the time of Baur have sifted through the various data to support or question his thesis. Few any longer fully embrace Baur's position, but many aspects of ethnic matters remain unsettled. In recent studies the social ramifications of self-definition, both as process and as language, have come to the fore. The essayists in this section reflect on various non-Biblical materials so as to understand more fully the ways that Jews, Christians, and others articulated self definition and ethnicity.

Carl R. Holladay, in *Paul and His Predecessors in the Diaspora: Some Reflections on Ethnic Identity in the Fragmentary Hellenistic Jewish Authors*, writes about five Hellenistic Jewish authors—Demetrius, Artapanus, Pseudo-Hecataeus, Ezekiel the Tragedian, and. Aristobulus. Although their works are only partially preserved, these five writers serve as precursors to Philo and Josephus, especially in regard to ethnic identity and Diaspora consciousness. As such they also inform our understanding of Paul. Holladay concludes that while Paul envisions much the same bifurcation of Jew vs. Gentile, yet he was an anomalous Diaspora Jew in regard to various outlooks including that on circumcision.

In *The Jewish Paul among the Gentiles: Two Portrayals*, Leander E. Keck argues that there is much about Paul we do not know, for example, why he endured such hardships to plant a string of house churches. Keck sets out to answer this question by comparing and contrasting Romans 9–11 with Acts in regard to Paul's vision of himself, of Israel and of the Gentiles. He argues that Paul and Acts report a consistent view that Paul went first to the Jews, often without success, but that the converted Gentiles were grafted into the Jewish stock. Paul did not abandon his own people.

David L. Balch, in *The Cultural Origin of 'Receiving all Nations' in Luke-Acts: Alexander the Great or Roman Social Policy?* investigates the antecedents for the claim that the "nations" are to be received into the people of God. He contends that there are structural parallels between Dionysius of Halicarnasus, *Roman Antiquites*, Plutarch, and Luke-Acts in regard to a tri-partite history. Further, he searches parallels with "receiving all nations" found in Acts. He concludes that these are not in the Hellenistic materials that narrate the policies of Alexander the Great, as has sometimes been suggested. He argues, rather, that "'Receiving all nations' is a Romanization, not a Hellenization, of the people of God."

In *Did the Churches Compete with Cult Groups?*, E. A. Judge, after examining evidences from the early Christian era, concludes that while associational language from the ancient world was a convenient shorthand for categorizing the churches, the differences were pronounced. He finds that Christianity was different in that it was (1) a movement of ideas, (2) futuristic in outlook, (3) involved in a reconstruction of community life, (4) composed of members gifted by God for the common good, and thereby undercutting the foundations of the public community, and (5) involved in the prospect for a trans-national society.

In *Men, Women and Marital Chastity: Public Preaching and Popular Piety at Rome*, Hanne Sigismund Nielsen, raises the question of whether Christians of the time of Augustine and Jerome lived according to the teaching of the church regarding moral conduct. She concludes that on the normative level or in public expression, at least, married couples adopted these moral ideals because their salvation was thought to depend upon it. For data she analyzes patterns of commemoration of spouses in both pagan and Christian epitaphs from the Roman catacombs. These commemorations show numerous similarities in the way that epithets of piety, affection, and devotion are displayed; however, the Christian epitaphs are more frequent in mentioning terms associated with marital chastity that reflect themes in the Christian preaching of the fourth century.

PART V. *Nomos*

The final section includes several studies of law, regulatory language, and normative values. A reoccurring question is whether ancient contemporary topics and forms are helpful in understanding New Testament and early Christian language in these areas. The history of these questions overlaps to some degree with the previous parts.

In *"The Mind is its Own Place:" Defining the* Topos, Johan C. Thom deals with the role of *topoi* or "commonplaces" as recently employed by contemporary New Testament scholars; the most frequent are friendship, frank criticism, moral progress and the passions. Thom sets out the history of *topos* as a technical term, then makes a few suggestions in regard to the use of *topos* in New Testament and related research, focusing upon logical or rhetorical, literary, moral or philosophical *topoi*. After examining several lists from Graeco-Roman authors he concludes that *topoi* form a part of everyday experience and through them we enter the worldviews of ancient authors.

J. Louis Martyn in Nomos *Plus Genitive Noun in Paul: The History of God's Law*, argues that Paul alone among early Christian authors employed with sophistication *nomos* along with another noun in the genitive case. Martyn discusses the view of H. Räisänen that Paul in four or more cases employs *nomos* in a general way rather than specifically in respect to the Law of Moses. Martyn argues that such a conclusion is based upon the view that Paul's attitude toward the Torah is fundamentally negative. Martyn concludes that by examining the locution *nomos* plus the genitive, it is clear that Paul thinks of the

Law as neither exclusively negative nor positive, and that in every case
he refers to the Torah itself.

In *Household Rules at Ephesus: Good News, Bad News, No News*, Benjamin
J. Fiore notes that editors and translators of Ephesians have been
inconsistent as to where the household rules in Ephesians 5 begin. He
goes on to show that such matters are influenced by concerns external
to textual criticism and accuracy in translation. He concludes that the
household rules in the New Testament epistles are more nuanced than
the charge of either patriarchy or emancipation of women allows.

In *The Washing of Adam in the Acherusian Lake (Greek* Life of Adam and
Eve *37.3) in the Context of Early Christian Notions of Afterlife*, Marinus de
Jonge and L. Michael White state that the surprise in the Greek *Life
of Adam and Eve* is that Adam was washed three times in the Acherusian Lake, a notable feature in the Classical landscape of Hades. This
raises the question of the background of the document. After tracing
the occurances of this motif in other pseudepigraphic literature, they
conclude that no Jewish texts may be found that mention the Acherusian Lake, but that it is found in documents such as the apocalypses
of Peter and Paul. Therefore, *Life of Adam and Eve* and the apocalypses
represent an early Christian tradition concerning the Acherusian Lake.
Based on the evolution of the motif in Classical views of the afterlife,
especially in Plato, they argue that the Christian appropriation of these
elements represents key developments in the Christian view of afterlife.

John T. Fitzgerald in *Last Wills and Testaments in Graeco-Roman Perspective*, provides a prolegomenon to study of the language and form
of testaments in the early Jewish and Christian tradition. Building on
the recent work of Edward Champlin, *Final Judgments*, Fitzgerald surveys the patterns of testation among Greeks and Romans. He examines
both the derivation of key legal terms and the forms of testamentary
language. Next, he examines the underlying moral concerns and social
obligations that operated in the practice of making wills and bequests.
These include discussions of patron-client relationships, slavery, and
friendship motifs in both the practice and the rhetoric of wills. Following three case studies from the Roman period he concludes that a
key component of the wills was the moral judgment of both oneself and
of those who would potentially receive bequests. Wills thus represent
a hitherto untapped resource for looking into the moral judgments of
Graeco-Roman culture, and within it those of Jews and Christians as
well.

QUOD EST COMPARANDUM
THE PROBLEM OF PARALLELS

L. Michael White
and
John T. Fitzgerald

> *Dies irae, that dreadful day,*
> *Heaven and earth shall burn away;*
> *So David and the Sibyl say.*

From Sibyls' Song to Vergil's Tour

The *Dies irae* ("Day of Wrath") officially entered the Latin Mass in 1485 as a sequence for the dead; it had probably been known, at least in Italy, since the thirteenth century. Written in the first person singular, the canticle presents the "prophecies" of the Cumaean Sibyl regarding the day of judgment. Long before, the Sibyl, legendary symbol of Rome's destiny, had already been "baptized." Both Jewish and Christian editors had made extensive additions to the *Sibylline Oracles*, thus turning the sacred texts of pagan Rome's ritual calendar into apocalyptic predictions.[1] So, too, she appears in Michelangelo's composition of the Sistine Chapel (1508–1512), sitting opposite the Delphic oracle. With exaggerated, ambivalent posture, both pivot away from the poignant touch of the Creation scene and toward the Last Judgment at the opposite end of the hall. The Sibyl consults her books; the Pythia looks up from a scroll, as they survey the sweep of human history.[2] By the Renaissance the Sibyl could hardly be read in any other way, than as a divinely inspired visionary of Christian history. So, too, for much of the classical tradition—it must either anticipate the triumph of Christianity or be considered its antithesis.

---

[1] John J. Collins, "The Sibylline Oracles," in *Jewish Writings from the Second Temple Period: Apocrypha, Pseudepigrapha, Qumran, Sectarian Writings, Philo, Josephus*, ed. by M. E. Stone (CRINT 2.2; Minneapolis: Fortress Press, 1984) 357–81; "The Development of the Sibylline Tradition," *ANRW* II.20.1 (1987) 421–59.

[2] Other classical motifs abound. For example, in the Last Judgment scene there is a vignette of Charon ferrying a boatload of the damned to hell. For an early source of

But the Renaissance also began to see a burgeoning of new interests in the classical tradition in art, architecture, and literature. The new "humanism," as it came to be called, would have a profound effect on the understanding of the relation between Christianity and classical culture. The change can already be seen in Dante's *Inferno* (1314), where the poet Vergil—who had also sung the Sibyl's song[3]—becomes the guide for a tour of hell. Who better? Vergil had written about just such a tour in the *Aeneid*. Still, Dante's attitude toward Rome's pagan past is markedly different; noble pagans such as Vergil and Statius often come off far better than popes and prelates.[4] It marks quite a reversal from the earlier medieval version, where the pagans are regularly depicted in the most gruesome torments imaginable; now the lower rungs of Hades are haunted by clerics instead. That is not to say that everything had changed overnight, but the manifold effects of the Renaissance would bring to light once again the magnificence of Roman culture and raise anew the questions both about its demise and about its basic relationship to the Christian culture of western Europe. There were, after all, numerous indisputable parallels.

---

this imagery in Christian views of the afterlife see the article by Marinus de Jonge and L. Michael White in this volume.

[3] *Eclogues* 4.4–5: *Ultima Cumaei venit iam carminis aetas; magnus ab integro saeclorum nascitur ordo* ("Comes now the last age of the song of Cumae; the great order of the ages is born anew"). For discussion of Vergil's poem in Augustan context, and varying interpretations of its supposed "messianic" symbolism, see Karl C. Galinsky, *Augustan Culture* (Princeton: Princeton University Press, 1996) 91–93. By the fourth century, however, the "golden child" predicted by the Sibyl in the *Fourth Eclogue* had come to be understood as Christian prophecy. The first to do so was Lactantius (*Div. inst.* 7.4; cf. 5.5); his interpretation was taken over in a Greek sermon, *Address to the Assembly of the Saints* (323 CE), ascribed by Eusebius of Caesarea to Constantine himself (*Vita Const.* 4.32). In this work the infant was clearly understood to be Christ. Apparently this view was still circulating in Rome at the end of the century, as it was repudiated by Jerome in a letter to Paulinus of Nola (*Ep.* 53.7, dated 394 CE). Twenty-five years later, however, when we get to Augustine's *City of God*, the *Fourth Eclogue* had become a prophecy of Christ's ushering in the new age (10.27). Augustine even says that the opening line (quoted above) means that Vergil was not speaking on his own but from the Sibyl. He also refers to Vergil's prophecies in his letters (cf. *Epp.* 104.3; 137.12; 258.5). Cf. Jaroslav Pelikan, *The Excellent Empire: The Fall of Rome and the Triumph of the Church* (San Francisco: Harper & Row, 1987) 50–51; for the date of Jerome's correspondence with Paulinus, see J.N.D. Kelly, *Jerome: His Life Writings, and Controversies* (San Francisco: Harper & Row, 1974) 292.

[4] Cf. *Purgatorio* 22.64–73 where the Roman poet Statius claims that Vergil's *Fourth Eclogue* had converted him to Christianity. See the previous note.

The Search for Parallels

The question of "parallels" to the language and formulations of the New Testament and other early Christian literature has been a key scholarly issue since the seventeenth century, when a number of linguistic and comparative studies began to appear. These works, largely the product of a new philologically oriented approach to early Christian literature, continued to proliferate during the eighteenth century and included several limited or specialized collections of parallels based on individual authors (e.g., Polybius, Diodorus Siculus, Josephus, and Philo).[5] Best known among these was that of Johann Jacob Wettstein.[6] Wettstein's collection originated out of the burgeoning work of the period on textual criticism. His Η ΚΑΙΝΗ ΔΙΑΘΗΚΗ was primarily a critical edition of the text of the New Testament based on new manuscript readings. Printing the *textus receptus*, Wettstein presented the variant manuscript evidence in a critical apparatus below the text, much as it is to this day. Then, he added a second apparatus (referred to in the title as a *commentario pleniore*, "copious commentary") below the first in which he assembled numerous "parallels" for each passage, primarily to support text-critical judgments on grammatical or stylistic grounds. In the process, however, his collection produced the most extensive assemblage to date for such non-Christian literary parallels running across the entire New Testament. It is really this second apparatus that has long been associated with Wettstein's name as the bell-

---

[5] Most were called *annotationes* or *observationes*, but other terms were occasionally used, including *illustrata* (G.F. Hezel, 1788) and *Παραλληλισμός* (G.W. Kirchmaier, 1725). For a list of these see Jan Ros, *De studie van het Bijbelgrieksch van Hugo Grotius tot Adolf Deissmann* (Nijmegen: Dekker & Van de Vegt, 1940) 49–56; Abraham J. Malherbe, "Hellenistic Moralists and the New Testament," *ANRW* II.26.1 (1992) 274 n. 38b; H. J. de Jonge, *De bestudering van het Nieuwe Testament aan de Noordnederlandse universiteiten en het Remonstrants Seminarie van 1575 tot 1700* (Amsterdam: Hakkert, 1980); Gerhard Delling, "Zum Corpus Hellenisticum Novi Testamenti," *ZNW* 54 (1963) 1–15, esp. n. 1.

[6] *Η ΚΑΙΝΗ ΔΙΑΘΗΚΗ Novum Testamentum Graecum editionis receptae cum lectionibus variantibus ... nec non commentario pleniore* (2 vols.; Amsterdam: Ex officina Dommeriana,1751–52); repr. under the title *Novum Testamentum Graecum* (Graz: Akademische Druck- und Verlagsanstalt, 1962). To give but two examples of Wettstein's pagan parallels, he cites various myths about unique and miraculous births as a parallel to Jesus' birth, and he compares Jesus' wine miracle at Cana (John 2:1–11) to the fable of Bacchus' transformation of water into wine. See William Baird, *History of New Testament Research* (Minneapolis: Fortress, 1992) 106.

wether for the study of parallels.[7] Wettstein himself outlined the key scholarly issues in an essay "on the interpretation of the New Testament" that was included in H KAINH ΔIAΘHKH.[8] He said:

> Two things, above all else, are required of a good interpreter: first, that, so far as possible, he establish the text of the ancient writer with whom he is engaged, and, second, that he bring out the meaning of the words as well as possible.[9]

> We get to know the meaning of words and sentences in the first instance from other passages by the same author, then from the rest of the sacred writings, as well as from the version of the seventy translators, then from the authors who lived about the same time in the same region, and finally from *common usage*. ... And, since the sacred writers invented no new language, but made use of the one they had learned from their contemporaries, the same judgement is also required of their writings. By *"common usage"* I understand the common speech of the apostolic age, but not the usage of medieval writers, and much less that of the scholastic and modern theologians.[10]

> If you wish to get a thorough and complete understanding of the books of the New Testament, put yourself in the place of those to whom they were first delivered by the apostles as a legacy. Transfer yourself in thought to that time and that area where they first were read. Endeavor, so far as possible, to acquaint yourself with the customs, practices, habits, opinions, accepted ways of thought, proverbs, symbolic language, and everyday expressions of these men, and with the ways and means by which they attempt to persuade others or to furnish a foundation for faith. Above all, keep in mind, when you turn to a passage, that you can make no progress by means of any modern system, whether of theology or logic, or by means of opinions current today.[11]

---

[7] Pieter Willem van der Horst, "Johann Jakob Wettstein nach 300 Jahren: Erbe und Anfang," *TZ* 49 (1993) 267–81.

[8] For other aspects of Wettstein's career at Basel and Amsterdam, see C. L. Hulbert-Powell, *John James Wettstein, 1693–1754: An Account of His Life, Work, and Some of His Contemporaries* (London: Society for Promoting Christian Knowledge, 1938); Baird, *History of New Testament Research*, 101–7, and "Wettstein, Johann Jacob," in *Dictionary of Biblical Interpretation*, ed. by John H. Hayes (2 vols.; Nashville: Abingdon Press, 1999) 2:642; and Werner G. Kümmel, *The New Testament: The History of the Investigation of its Problems* (Nashville: Abingdon Press, 1972) 49–50. The translation that follows here of Wettstein's essay on interpretation is taken from Kümmel.

[9] Wettstein, *Novum Testamentum Graecum*, 1:1.

[10] *Ibid.*, 2:876 (italics added).

[11] *Ibid.*, 2:878.

These last two comments speak directly to his sense of how the parallels might be used to bring out the original meaning of New Testament language.

It should be noted in passing that the work of Wettstein and others in the eighteenth century was really the culmination of a mounting trend in New Testament scholarship that had begun with the era of the Reformation as it came out of Renaissance humanism. Textual criticism, whether of the New Testament or Classical authors, came of age beginning in the sixteenth century, and many of the "reform-minded" biblical scholars were also trained in Classical text criticism. In his early career, after studying the law, John Calvin produced a Latin commentary on Seneca's *De clementia* (1532). Seneca, like a number of other classical authors, was traditionally considered very close to Christian thought.[12] The first critical edition of the *Tabula of Cebes* appeared in 1504. Regularly included in editions with Epictetus,[13] it became popular in Christian moral education. By 1522 a Holbein woodcut of the *Tabula* was used as the title page for the third edition of Erasmus' *Novum Testamentum*, and it may have been one of the sources used by John Bunyan in *Pilgrim's Progress* (1678).[14]

Assumptions regarding the affinity of such classical texts to the New Testament also began to produce more critical studies. Joachim Camerarius (1500–1574), a noted classical philologist at Leipzig, published a commentary on selected New Testament epistles, in which he sought to

---

[12] Marcia Colish ("Stoicism and the New Testament: An Essay in Historiography," *ANRW* II.26.1 [1992] 335–79) surveys both the Late Antique through Medieval appropriation of the Stoic tradition and the history of scholarship on New Testament-Stoic "parallels" from the Renaissance to the late 1970's. In part based on the similarities of thought, extensive patristic citations, and the apocryphal correspondence with Paul, Seneca had long enjoyed an exceptional standing in Christian thought. Consequently Tertullian (*De anima* 20) called him "ever *our* Seneca," and later both Jerome (*De vir. ill.* 12) and Augustine (*Ep.* 153.14) considered him a convert. Cf. A. Kurfess, "Zu dem apokryphen Briefwechsel zwischen dem Philosophen Seneca und dem Apostel Paulus," *Aevum* 26 (1952) 42–48; J.N. Sevenster, *Paul and Seneca* (Leiden: E.J. Brill, 1961).

[13] Hieronymous Wolf, *Epicteti enchiridion … , Cebetis Thebani tabula … : Graece et Latine editione* (3 vols.; Basel: Ioannem Oporinum, 1561–63).

[14] John T. Fitzgerald and L. Michael White, *The Tabula of Cebes: Text, Translation, and Notes* (SBLTT 24/GRS 7; Chico: Scholars Press, 1983) 1 and further references cited on 29; cf. Sandra Sider, *Cebes' Tablet: Facsimiles of the Greek Text, and of Selected Latin, French, English, Spanish, Italian, German, Dutch, and Polish Translations* (Renaissance Text Series; New York: Renaissance Society of America, 1979) 2; Reinhart Schleier, *Tabula Cebetis; oder Spiegel des menschlichen Lebens, darin Tugent und Untugent abgemalet ist. Studien zur Rezeption einer antiken Bildbeschreibung im 16. und 17. Jahrhundert* (Berlin: Mann, 1974).

elucidate the meaning of the grammar and vocabulary based on comparison with and citation of classical authors.[15] This work was carried still farther by Hugo Grotius (1583–1645), who had been a student of the eminent French classicist Joseph Scaliger (1540–1609).[16] While in Paris Grotius published an exhaustive series of *Annotationes*[17] on individual words and phrases of the Bible based on copious citations from classical, Jewish, and patristic authors. From this work he made some of the first important moves toward historical-critical analysis of the New Testament.[18] His "notes" on the New Testament were still being used, updated, and republished as late as 1834.[19] It was against the background of Grotius' work and the burgeoning of classical scholarship, when many of the early major editions and studies of the classical "canon" appeared, that Wettstein's work should be understood.

By the nineteenth century, the practice of citing non-Jewish authors in New Testament lexicons and commentaries was customary, and these citations encouraged various comparisons between biblical verses and pagan passages.[20] The prevailing current of usage for these paral-

---

[15] *Commentarius in Novum Foedus: In quo et figurae sermonis, et verborum significatio, et orationis sententia, ad illius Foederis intelligentiam certiorem, tractantur* (Leipzig: Teubner, 1572; repr. Cambridge, 1642); cf. Kümmel, *History of Investigation*, 31–32; Frank Baron (ed.), *Joachim Camerarius (1500–1574): Beiträge zur Geschichte des Humanismus im Zeitalter der Reformation* (Humanistische Bibliothek 1.24; Munich: Fink, 1978); and Stephan Kunkler, *Zwischen Humanismus und Reformation: Der Humanist Joachim Camerarius (1500–1574) im Wechselspiel von pädgagogischem Pathos und theologischem Ethos* (Theologische Texte und Studien 8; Hildesheim: Olms, 2000). Particularly important for future biblical studies was Camerarius' insistence that the linguistic usage of ancient authors was a *conditio sine qua non* for the proper interpretation of the New Testament.

[16] For a brief overview of Scaliger's contributions to both Classics and biblical studies as well as recent treatments of him, see G. E. Schwerdtfeger, "Scaliger, Joseph Justus," *Dictionary of Biblical Interpretation*, 2:440–41.

[17] *Annotationes in libros evangeliorum et varia loca S. Scripturae* (Paris, 1641); *Annotationes in Epistula Philemonem* (Paris, 1642); *Annotationes in Vetus Testamentum* (Paris, 1644); and *Annotationes in Novum Testamentum* (Paris, 1644). The last of these is a massive multivolume work in which Grotius gives great attention to both historical and philological aspects of the biblical text.

[18] Kümmel, *History of Investigation*, 33–38; Baird, *History of New Testament Research*, 7–11; and John H. Hayes, "Grotius, Hugo," *Dictionary of Biblical Interpretation*, 1:470–71. It is also worth noting that Grotius, from Holland, was an Arminian, and it was in the Remonstrants (Dutch Arminians) Seminary of Amsterdam that Wettstein produced his work a century later. Cf. de Jonge, "De bestudering," *passim*.

[19] (rev. ed.; 9 vols.; Groningen: W. Zuidema, 1826–1834).

[20] On the history of New Testament lexicography, see John T. Fitzgerald, "Lexicons, New Testament," *Dictionary of Biblical Interpretation*, 2:62–66. The culmination of nineteenth-century lexical studies was the second edition of the German-Greek New Testament lexicon of C. Grimm (1868), which was translated into English and aug-

lels was nonetheless more mixed than Wettstein's own idealistic goal to understand "common usage." One of the more famous compilations was that of Edmund Spiess, *Logos Spermaticós: Parallelstellen zum Neuen Testament aus den Schriften der alten Griechen*.[21] With the increased awareness of the "parallels," however, came a lively discussion of their significance for understanding the relationship between the New Testament writers and their antecedents and contemporaries from the Hellenistic world. At about this same time, the emergence of the *Religionsgeschichtliche Schule* and radical historiographical criticism, especially as practiced by the so-called "Tübingen School," contributed to the debate. For example, following an observation by Bruno Bauer,[22] Rudolf Steck argued that Paul's catalog of hardships in Rom 8:35 had been derived from Seneca (*Ep.* 85.26–27 and 41).[23] In the previous year, the same sort of intertextual connection between these two passages had been asserted by Johannes Kreyher,[24] who argued conversely that Seneca had borrowed from Paul. Ironically, such debates over direct literary dependence were in some sense the nineteenth-century critics' version of the apocryphal *Correspondence between Paul and Seneca*. Nor were such claims of direct influence restricted to Paul and Seneca. Amédée Fleury had earlier argued that Paul had also been the source of inspiration for both Ps.-Heraclitus (*Ep.* 4.3) and Lucian (*Peregrinus* 32).[25]

Out of the midst of such extravagant claims and counterclaims came the first systematic attempts to explore the relationships of Graeco-Roman authors to the New Testament and early Christian writers. The work of Carl Friedrich Georg Heinrici, especially in his commentaries on the Corinthian correspondence, became pivotal.[26] According

---

mented by Joseph H. Thayer, *A Greek-English Lexicon of the New Testament* (corrected ed.; New York: American Book Company, 1886).

[21] (Leipzig: Engelmann, 1871).

[22] *Christus und die Caesaren* (Berlin: Grosser, 1877) 52–54.

[23] Rudolf Steck, *Der Galaterbrief nach seiner Echtheit untersucht, nebst kritischen Bemerkungen zu den paulinischen Hauptbriefen* (Berlin: Reimer, 1888) 256. Whereas Bauer had adduced the Seneca parallel in relation to 2 Cor 11:23–28 (supplementing the more traditional parallel from ps.-Heraclitus, *Ep.* 4.3), Steck argued for a direct dependence of "Paul" (actually ps.-Paul according to Steck) on Seneca. Cf. John T. Fitzgerald, *Cracks in an Earthen Vessel: An Examination of the Catalogues of Hardships in the Corinthian Correspondence* (SBLDS 99; Atlanta: Scholars, 1988) 7 n. 2.

[24] *L. Annaeus Seneca und seine Beziehungen zum Urchristentum* (Berlin: Gaertner, 1887) 86.

[25] *Saint Paul et Sénèque* (2 vols.; Paris: Ladrange, 1853) 1:36–39; 2:247–49.

[26] *Das erste Sendschreiben des Apostels Paulus an die Korinther* (Berlin: Hertz, 1880); *Das zweite Sendschreiben des Apostels Paulus an die Korinther* (Berlin: Hertz, 1887); *Kritisch-exegetisches Handbuch über den ersten Brief an die Korinther* (KEK 5; 7th ed.; Göttingen: Vanden-

to Heinrici, "there is such an accumulation of analogies with Polybius, … with Epictetus, with Plutarch, with Dionysius of Halicarnassus, and others that it can only be explained by a common spiritual sphere of life."[27] Although criticized by some contemporaries, notably Eduard Norden,[28] for "exaggerating" the Greek element over the Semitic in Paul's letters, Heinrici made it impossible for future New Testament scholars to ignore the Hellenistic character of Paul's letters. With copious examples he made a solid case that Paul both thought and spoke under the influence of Hellenistic culture. He pointed in particular to the diatribe and argued that Paul's style was directly comparable to that of Epictetus.[29] He also compared 2 Cor 10–12 to Plutarch's *On Inoffensive Self-Praise*, noting astutely that Plutarch's advice on the subject corresponded closely to what Paul actually did in these chapters.[30]

Heinrici influenced others, notably Johannes Weiss and Weiss's student Rudolf Bultmann, and through them a new generation of scholars. Bultmann's 1910 dissertation took up the topic of the diatribe following Heinrici's observations on stylistic similarities.[31] About this same

hoeck & Ruprecht, 1888); and *Der zweite Brief an die Korinther* (KEK 6; 7th ed.; Göttingen: Vandenhoeck & Ruprecht, 1890; 8th ed., 1900). See also his *Hellenismus und Christentum* (Biblische Zeit-und Streitfragen V.8; Gr. Lichterfelde-Berlin: Edwin Runge, 1909). For a brief orientation to his life and thought, see Nikolaus Walter, "Heinrici, Carl Friedrich Georg," *Dictionary of Biblical Interpretation*, 1:491.

[27] *Das zweite Sendschreiben*, 594.

[28] *Die antike Kunstprosa* (2 vols.; Leipzig: Teubner, 1898) 493–98. The viciousness of Norden's attack produced a long-running controversy between the two. Cf. Fitzgerald, *Cracks in an Earthen Vessel*, 9 n. 14. Norden stressed Semitic elements in Paul's Greek; on which see below.

[29] *Das zweite Sendschreiben*, 576; *Der zweite Brief*, 438 n.; 439, 442, 448, 451, 454–55. The growing awareness of similarities between Epictetus and the New Testament prompted the Classical scholar Adolf Bonhöffer, an expert on Stoicism, to discuss the relationship; see his *Epiktet und das Neue Testament* (Religionsgeschichtliche Versuche und Vorarbeiten 10; Giessen: Töppelmann, 1911). See also his *Die Ethik des Stoikers Epictet* (Stuttgart: F. Enke, 1894), now conveniently available as *The Ethics of the Stoic Epictetus: An English Translation* (trans. by W. O. Stephens; Revisioning Philosophy 2; New York: Peter Lang, 1996). For Bonhöffer's *Auseinandersetzung* with Rudolf Bultmann on the relationship of Epictetus to the New Testament, see Bultmann, "Das religiöse Moment in der ethischen Unterweisung des Epiktet und das Neue Testament," *ZNW* 13 (1912) 97–110, 177–91, and Bonhöffer, "Epiktet und das Neue Testament," *ZNW* 13 (1912) 281–92.

[30] Heinrici, *Der literarische Charakter der neutestamentlichen Schriften* (Leipzig: Dürr'sche Buchhandlung, 1908) 67 n. 2.

[31] *Der Stil der paulinischen Predigt und die kynisch-stoische Diatribe* (FRLANT 13; Göttingen: Vandenhoeck & Ruprecht, 1910). Cf. Stanley K. Stowers, *The Diatribe and Paul's Letter to the Romans* (SBLDS 57; Chico: Scholars, 1981) 7–25.

time Heinrici began to organize a group of younger scholars for the purpose of producing a "new Wettstein," that is, a new collection of relevant parallels to the New Testament. As co-editors he enlisted the services of Adolf Deissmann (Berlin),[32] Ernst von Dobschütz (Halle),[33] Hans Lietzmann (then at Jena, later at Berlin),[34] and Hans Windisch (Leiden).[35] When Heinrici died in 1915, his place on the team was taken

---

[32] Deissmann's work on newly discovered papyri, inscriptions, and other non-literary materials was intended to demonstrate the colloquial character of New Testament Greek. He labored for many years on a projected Greek-German lexicon of the New Testament in which he hoped fully to exploit these sources for the interpretation of the New Testament, but he never completed the work. Many of his discoveries and insights were incorporated by J. H. Moulton and G. Milligan in their *The Vocabulary of the Greek Testament Illustrated from the Papyri and Other Non-Literary Sources* (1930; repr., Grand Rapids: Eerdmans, 1982). Walter Bauer shared Deissmann's conviction that the New Testament generally represents the Koine of the Graeco-Roman period, but he thought that the Septuagint was the most important influence on early Christian literature. Consequently, he included numerous references to both secular Greek texts and Hellenistic Jewish writings in the various editions of his famous New Testament lexicon, first published in 1928. All subsequent New Testament lexicography has built upon the foundation that Bauer laid; see now Frederick W. Danker (ed.), *A Greek-English Lexicon of the New Testament and Other Early Christian Literature: Third Edition (BDAG)* (Chicago: University of Chicago Press, 2000).

[33] "Der Plan eines Neuen Wettstein," *ZNW* 21 (1922) 146–48; *ZNW* 23 (1924) 312–13; "Zum Corpus Hellenisticum," *ZNW* 24 (1925) 43–51; *ZNW* 25 (1926) 172–73. See also von Dobschütz's treatment of his life and work on the *Corpus Hellenisticum* project in Erich Stange (ed.), *Die Religionswissenschaft der Gegenwart in Selbstdarstellungen* (5 vols.; Leipzig: F. Meiner, 1925–1929) 4:31–62.

[34] Lietzmann had studied Classical philology under both F. Bücheler (1837–1908) and H. Usener (1834–1905), and already in 1902 had created the series *Kleine Texte für Vorlesungen und Übungen* as a means of training theology students to read and interpret non-biblical sources in their original languages. His famous New Testament commentary series, *Handbuch zum Neuen Testament* (which began in 1907), gave emphasis to philological and historical issues rather than theological ones. See Nikolaus Walter, "Lietzmann, Hans," *Dictionary of Biblical Interpretation*, 2:75.

[35] "Zum Corpus Hellenisticum," *ZNW* 34 (1935) 124–25. Windisch had come into close contact with Heinrici while he was a *Privatdozent* at Leipzig from 1908 to 1913, a period during which he contributed commentaries on the Catholic Epistles (1911) and Hebrews (1913) to Lietzmann's *Handbuch zum Neuen Testament* series. He moved to Leiden in 1913 when Kirsopp Lake decided to leave his post at Leiden and accept an appointment at Harvard, and Windisch remained there until 1929, a period during when he wrote two important commentaries, one on Barnabas (1920) for the *Handbuch* series and one on 2 Corinthians (1924) for the *Kritisch-exegetischer Kommentar über das Neue Testament* series founded by H.A.W. Meyer. The latter commentary remains unsurpassed in its utilization of Hellenistic materials for the interpretation of 2 Corinthians. For Windisch's research during his years at Leiden, see Marinus de Jonge, "Hans Windisch als Neutestamentler an der Universität Leiden (1914–1929)," in *Text und Geschichte: Facetten theologischen Arbeitens aus dem Freundes- und Schülerkreis: Dieter Lührmann zum 60. Geburtstag*," ed. by S. Maser and E. Schlarb (Marburger Theologische Studien 50; Marburg: N.G. Elwert

by Johannes Leipoldt (his successor at Leipzig); the chief responsibility
for overseeing the project shifted to von Dobschütz, who was probably
the one who bestowed on it the name by which it was subsequently
known, *Corpus Hellenisticum Novi Testamenti*.[36] During this same period
a similar effort to produce a "new Wettstein" was begun in England
under the leadership of the noted Philo scholar, F. H. Colson (Cambridge). When the leaders of these two initiatives became aware of the
other's work, they initially wanted to collaborate. Unfortunately, a lack
of financial support precluded the two teams from working together.
Convinced that the European project was in a more advanced state
than their own and not wishing unnecessarily to duplicate the labors of
their counterparts on the Continent, the British team decided to dis-
continue their project and magnanimously turned over the results of all
their work to their European colleagues.[37]

Two preconditions made the *Corpus Hellenisticum Novi Testamenti* project both feasible and desirable. First was the burgeoning of new editions of most of the key Hellenistic authors, beginning in 1849 with
the new series of Teubner critical editions. New editions of John Stobaeus, Philo, and Plutarch's *Moralia* also appeared in this period. Second was the interest shown in these authors by Classical scholars and
the fact that many of the German New Testament scholars were classi-
cally trained.[38] As work on the project continued in the period between
the two World Wars, thousands of parallels were assembled for eventual
publication, and two important decisions were made. The first was the
decision to exclude rabbinic materials from the collection because Paul
Billerbeck was assembling those for his massive *Kommentar zum Neuen
Testament aus Talmud und Midrasch*.[39] The second decision was to divide

---

Verlag, 1999) 47–65. On his significance for New Testament scholarship, see Erik Beyer,
"Hans Windisch und seine Bedeutung für die neutestamentliche Wissenschaft," *ZNW*
48 (1957) 22–49.

[36] For a brief history of the project, see Pieter W. van der Horst, "Corpus Hellenisticum Novi Testamenti," *ABD* 1:1157–61.

[37] Von Dobschütz, "Plan," 147–48.

[38] A few examples will suffice: Bultmann also studied with Paul Wendland, just
as Albrecht Ritchl had studied with Gottfried Hermann. On the other side, Karl
Praechter, Karl Müller, and other Classicists of the period were equally interested in the
later Hellenistic authors and adduced similarities with the New Testament materials on
occasions to develop critical arguments on certain works. A good example is Praechter's
1885 dissertation on the *Tabula of Cebes*, which finally laid to rest the tradition that it was
an authentic work of the Socratic circle by showing it to be a product of the later
Hellenistic age. Cf. Fitzgerald and White, *Tabula of Cebes*, 3–4.

[39] Hermann L. Strack and Paul Billerbeck, *Kommentar zum Neuen Testament aus Talmud*

the work, with the Hellenistic Jewish portion of the project remaining at Halle under the direction of Erich Klostermann (who had been von Dobschütz's colleague) and the investigation of the pagan materials moving to Uppsala under the oversight of Anton Fridrichsen (a former student of both von Dobschütz and Paul Wendland).[40] Despite the elimination of rabbinic texts from the project and the division of labor, a "new Wettstein" was never produced during this period. The failure to complete the project in a timely fashion was doubtless due to a variety of factors, including the immense scope of the investigation, research on other projects, the disruptions of the early- to mid-twentieth century, and the deaths of several key participants, including von Dobschütz (1934), Windisch (1935), and Deissmann (1937). With the outbreak of the second World War and conditions in Europe during the post-war years, progress on both branches of the project slowed to a snail's pace.[41]

In the meantime, with the passing of the older generation of scholars and the emergence of new directions in both Classical and New Testament work, the emphasis on examining the parallels between

---

und Midrasch (1926–1928; 7th reprinted ed.; 6 vols.; Munich: Beck, 1978). See also below at n. 79.

[40] Anton Fridrichsen and Erich Klostermann, "Zum Corpus Hellenisticum," *ZNW* 40 (1941) 255.

[41] As far as work on the pagan materials was concerned, the only significant post-war publication was that of Helge Amquist, *Plutarch und das Neue Testament: Ein Beitrag zum Corpus Hellenisticum Novi Testamenti* (ASNU 15; Uppsala: Appelberg, 1946), which was a dissertation produced under Fridrichsen. The latter's own research for the *Corpus Hellenisticum* project resulted in several post-war articles, some of which are included in his *Exegetical Writings: A Selection*, translated and edited by C. C. Caragounis and T. Fornberg (WUNT 76; Tübingen: Mohr, 1994). Unfortunately, Fridrichsen's post-war productivity was severely hindered by a long-lasting illness, so that his most significant contributions to the project were made during the 1920's and 1930's. After his retirement and death in 1953, work on the pagan portion of the project functionally ceased for several years and was only revived in the mid-1950's when the project was transferred to Utrecht under the direction of W.C. van Unnik. The Hellenistic Jewish portion of the project suffered a similar fate. Klostermann, who was born in 1870, had already retired for the first time in 1936 and had to depend on the labors of younger scholars, such as Julius Schniewind and Herbert Preisker. But with the early deaths of Schniewind in 1948 and Preisker in 1952, and with Klostermann's third and final retirement in 1954, work on the project ceased altogether for a short time. Unlike the pagan portion of the project, however, oversight of the Hellenistic Jewish portion was not transferred to another geographical center of research but remained in Halle, where Gerhard Delling assumed responsibility for the endeavor. See Kurt Aland, "Das Corpus Hellenisticum," *TLZ* 80 (1955) 627–28, and "The Corpus Hellenisticum," *NTS* 2 (1955–1956) 217–21.

early Christianity and its Hellenistic environment languished in relative obscurity.[42] Interest in the relationship continued through Bultmann and his students but often drifted more into *Religionsgeschichte*. Out of this period, for example, came Franz Josef Dölger's project, now best known as *Antike und Christentum*, begun in 1909.[43] The project continued through the subsequent leadership of Theodor Klauser, who developed it into both a lexical project (the *Reallexikon für Antike und Christentum*, begun in 1941) and a journal (the *Jahrbuch für Antike und Christentum*, begun in 1958). Further explorations of Graeco-Roman religions were taken up by Richard Reitzenstein (Strassbourg, Freiburg, and Göttingen),[44] Arthur Darby Nock (Cambridge and Harvard),[45] and Franz Cumont (Ghent, Brussels, and Rome),[46] and followed by Cumont's students under the leadership of Maarten J. Vermaseren (Nijmegen and Utrecht).[47]

The *Corpus Hellenisticum Novi Testamenti* project was finally revitalized in the late 1950's and early 1960's largely through the efforts of W. C. van Unnik at Utrecht and Gerhard Delling at Halle.[48] To date six works have appeared exploring the significance of individual non-Christian pagan authors (e.g., Plutarch and Dio Chrysostom) under the general series title *Studia ad Corpus Hellenisticum Novi Testamenti*, begun in 1970 under the leadership of Hans Dieter Betz.[49] At Utrecht van

---

[42] The success of the previous generation in demonstrating the lateness of many works previously listed in the Classical Greek "canon" (such as the *Tabula of Cebes*) caused them largely to be ignored by subsequent Classics scholarship.

[43] E. A. Judge, "'Antike und Christentum': Towards a Definition of the Field," *ANRW* II.23.1 (1979) 3–58.

[44] *Die hellenistische Mysterienreligions* (Leipzig: Teubner, 1926).

[45] See especially his *Conversion* (Oxford: Clarendon Press, 1933) and *Essays on Religion in the Ancient World*, ed. by Zeph Stewart (2 vols.; Oxford: Oxford University Press, 1972).

[46] *Inter alia*, see esp. Cumont's *Les religions orientales dans le paganisme romain* (2nd rev. ed.; Paris: E. Laroux, 1906; ET: London: Routledge & Sons, 1911).

[47] The chief series, developed under Vermaseren, was the *Études préliminaires aux religions orientales dans l'Empire romain*, begun in 1961.

[48] For the non-Jewish portion of the project, see W. C. van Unnik, "Second Report on the Corpus Hellenisticum," *NTS* 3 (1956–1957) 254–59; "Corpus Hellenisticum Novi Testamenti," *JBL* 83 (1964) 17–33; and "Words Come to Life: The Work for the 'Corpus Hellenisticum Novi Testamenti,'" *NovT* 13 (1971) 199–216. Cf. van der Horst, "Wettstein nach 300 Jahren," 274–75. For the Hellenistic Jewish portion of the project, see Delling, "Zum Corpus Hellenisticum Novi Testamenti," 1–15, and "Bemerkungen zum Corpus Hellenisticum Novi Testamenti," *FF* 37 (1963) 183–85. See also n. 41 above.

[49] Gerd Petzke, *Die Traditionen über Apollonius von Tyana und das Neue Testament* (SCHNT 1; Leiden: Brill, 1970); Gerard Mussies, *Dio Chrysostom and the New Testament* (SCHNT

Unnik's work[50] has been carried on by Pieter Willem van der Horst and Gerard Mussies.[51] Recently, M. Eugene Boring, Klaus Berger, and Carsten Colpe have published in English the *Hellenistic Commentary to the New Testament*,[52] which is based on a German edition by Berger and Colpe under the title *Religionsgeschichtliches Textbuch zum Neuen Testament*.[53] To date this is the most like a Wettstein-style assemblage of parallels on a passage by passage basis. A multi-volume collection, begun at Göttingen under the direction of the late Georg Strecker (d. 1994)[54] and continuing under Udo Schnelle (at Halle), will finally carry the title *Neuer Wettstein: Texte zum Neuen Testament aus Griechentum und Hellenismus*.[55]

2; Leiden: Brill, 1972); Hans Dieter Betz (ed.), *Plutarch's Theological Writings and Early Christian Literature* (SCHNT 3; Leiden: Brill, 1975), and *Plutarch's Ethical Writings and Early Christian Literature* (SCHNT 4; Leiden: Brill, 1978); William C. Grese, *Corpus Hermeticum XIII and the New Testament* (SCHNT 5; Leiden: Brill, 1979); and Pieter W. van der Horst, *Aelius Aristides and the New Testament* (SCHNT 6; Leiden: Brill, 1980). See also Hans Dieter Betz and E. W. Smith, "Contributions to the Corpus Hellenisticum," *NovT* 13 (1971) 217–35. Whereas van Unnik and Betz in their leadership of the pagan portion of the *Corpus Hellenisticum* project gave emphasis to ancient authors and texts, Delling directed his energies toward a compilation of modern secondary literature on Hellenistic Jewish authors and writings. As a consequence, the major contribution of this portion of the project has been bibliographic; see Delling (ed.), *Bibliographie zur jüdisch-hellenistischen und intertestamentarischen Literatur, 1900–1970* (2nd ed.; TU 106; Berlin: Akademie-Verlag, 1975).

[50] Willem Cornelis van Unnik, *Sparsa Collecta: Collected Essays* (3 vols.; NovTSup. 29–31; Leiden: E.J. Brill, 1973–1983); see also his *Das Selbstverständnis der jüdischen Diaspora in der hellenistisch-römischen Zeit* (revised and edited by P.W. van der Horst from the papers in van Unnik's estate [Leiden: E.J. Brill, 1993]). [The latter contains an essay by van der Horst on van Unnik's life and work, with a bibliography.]

[51] *Studies on the Hellenistic Background of the New Testament* (Utrechtse theologische reeks 10; Utrecht: Rijksuniversiteit, 1990). See also G. Mussies, "Parallels to Matthew's Version of the Pedigree of Jesus," *NovT* 28 (1986) 32–47. For a more recent contribution from the Utrecht research circle, see Bert Cozijnsen, "A Critical Contribution to the *Corpus Hellenisticum Novi Testamenti*: Jude and Hesiod," in *The Use of Sacred Books in the Ancient World*, ed. L.V. Rutgers, P.W. van der Horst, H.W. Havelaar, and L. Teugels (CBET 22; Leuven: Peeters, 1998) 79–109. It should be emphasized that research at Utrecht has not been confined to pagan texts but has included various kinds of Hellenistic Jewish materials; see n. 58 below.

[52] (Nashville: Abingdon, 1995).

[53] (Texte zum Neuen Testament 1; Göttingen: Vandenhoeck & Ruprecht, 1987).

[54] Georg Strecker, "Das Göttinger Projekt »Neuer Wettstein«," *ZNW* 83 (1992) 245–52.

[55] (3 vols.; Berlin: de Gruyter, 1996–2001). The first two volumes, which were published in 1996 and together form Band II of the collection, cover Romans through Revelation. Band I will be published in three parts; the second of these, dealing with the Gospel of John, was published in 2001. The first part of Band I will cover the Synoptic Gospels and the third part the Book of Acts.

In the United States the most extensive studies in these areas were carried out beginning in the 1970–1990's under Hans Dieter Betz (at Claremont and Chicago)[56] and Abraham J. Malherbe (at Yale). Malherbe studied with both A. D. Nock at Harvard and W. C. van Unnik at Utrecht. His work, and that of his students, has been marked less by a focus on single Hellenistic authors and more on primary *topoi* ("commonplaces") and forms of Hellenistic expression, such as paraenesis and moral exhortation or epistolary conventions, especially as practiced by the Hellenistic moral philosophers.[57] The Hellenistic Moral Philosophy and Early Christianity Section of the Society of Biblical Literature has largely been organized by students of Malherbe and Betz.[58]

One key difference in the recent work from that of the nineteenth century is the inclusion of much more in the way of Hellenistic Jewish and rabbinic parallels along with those from Greek and Roman authors. At work within this change is a greater awareness of the interaction between the Hellenistic and Jewish cultures both before and

---

[56] In addition to Betz's two volumes in the *Studia ad Corpus Hellenisticum Novi Testamenti* series listed above in n. 49, see his *Lukian von Samosata und das Neue Testament: Religionsgeschichtliche und paränetische Parallelen. Ein Beitrag zum Corpus Hellenisticum Novi Testamenti* (TU 76; Berlin: Akademie Verlag, 1961), and "Hellenismus," in *Theologische Realenzyklopädie* 15 (1986) 19–35. Cf. Adela Yarbro Collins and Margaret M. Mitchell (eds.), *Antiquity and Humanity: Essays on Ancient Religion and Philosophy presented to Hans Dieter Betz on his 70th Birthday* (Tübingen: Mohr-Siebeck, 2001).

[57] See especially his articles, "Hellenistic Moralists and the New Testament," 267–333, and "Greco-Roman Religion and Philosophy and the New Testament," in *The New Testament and Its Modern Interpreters*, ed. by E.J. Epp, and G.W. MacRae (Atlanta: Scholars Press, 1989) 3–26. A bibliography of Malherbe's scholarly works follows this article.

[58] The idea for a SBL working group devoted to the exploration of Hellenistic moral philosophy and early Christianity was the brainchild of Abraham Malherbe, who first mentioned it to some former students at the 1988 SBL Annual Meeting. The first informal gathering to discuss his proposal took place the following year, and from 1990 to 1992 the program unit met officially as a Consultation, becoming a standing Group in 1993 and a Section in 2000. From 1990–1996 John Fitzgerald served as Program Chair; from 1997 – present, Michael White has served as Program Chair. Cf. Gregory E. Sterling, "Hellenistic Philosophy and the New Testament," in *Handbook to Exegesis of the New Testament*, ed. by S. E. Porter (NTTS 25; Leiden: E.J. Brill, 1997) 317; Thomas F. Olbricht, "Biblical Interpretation in North America in the 20th Century," *Historical Handbook of Major Biblical Interpreters*, ed. by D. McKim (Carol Stream: Intervarsity Press, 1998) 552. In addition to two volumes of studies on Friendship in the Graeco-Roman and early Christian world (see n. 71 below), this group has produced a text and translation of *Philodemus, On Frank Criticism: Introduction, Translation, and Notes*, ed. by D. Konstan, D. Clay, C.E. Glad, J.C. Thom, and J. Ware (SBLTT 43/GRS 13; Atlanta: Scholars Press, 1998, and a volume of essays on *Philodemus and the New Testament World*, ed. by J.T. Fitzgerald, G. Holland, and D. Obbink (NovTSup; Leiden: E.J. Brill, 2003).

during the emergence of the Christian movement.[59] For comparison, from 1850 to 1875 only three works were published that tried to explore Hellenistic and Jewish interactions;[60] from 1950 to 1975 some 68 works appeared on this subject.[61] As Henry Fischel has observed, even these statistics do not tell the whole story: "There is a pronounced shift from the search for isolated parallel detail to more coherent observation and interpretation. ... Fortunately, an earlier premature exercise of synthesis, a dramatized portrayal of an almost allegorical clash between Judea and Hellas, was now abandoned."[62] More recent work has shown that even further sophistication is needed.[63]

The Problem of Parallels

As this survey shows, the quest for parallels is nothing new, but, as Fischel's astute remark suggests, the issue is how to understand and interpret them. The older view is that espoused by G. Ernest Wright and Floyd Filson in 1949 through a series of joint lectures under the title "The Bible against its Environment."[64] Later published under separate titles, these two studies were the inaugural volumes in a new series

---

[59] W. C. van Unnik was a force in stimulating this change as well, having helped inaugurate also the *Compendia rerum iudaicarum ad Novum Testamentum* (CRINT) series. Cf. Pieter Willem van der Horst, *Essays on the Jewish World of Early Christianity* (Freiborg: Universitätsverlag, 1990), and *Ancient Jewish Epitaphs: An Introductory Survey of a Millennium of Jewish Funerary Epigraphy (300 BCE – 700 CE)* (Kampen: Kok Pharos, 1991); Martin Hengel, *Judaism and Hellenism* (2 vols.; Philadelphia: Fortress Press, 1972), and his presidential address to the *Studiorum Novi Testamenti Societas*, "Aufgaben der neutestamentlichen Wissenschaft," *NTS* 40 (1994) 321–57.

[60] While Wettstein had cited passages from the Hebrew Bible and rabbinic literature it was largely undigested. The first significant study of the phenomenon was that of Michael Sachs, *Beiträge zur Sprach- und Altertumsforschung* (Berlin: Akademie-Verlag, 1852). The pioneering work was that of J. Freudenthal, *Hellenistische Studien: Alexander Polyhistor und die von ihm erhaltenen Reste jüdischer und samaritanischer Geschichtswerke* (2 vols.; Breslau: H. Skutsch, 1874–1879). These statistics and the bibliographical catalogue come from the article by Henry Fischel cited below in note 62.

[61] *Inter alia*, Albrecht Dihle, *Die Goldene Regel* (Studienhefte zur Altertumswissenschaft 7; Göttingen: Vandenhoeck & Ruprecht, 1962); Saul Lieberman, *Hellenism in Jewish Palestine: Studies in the Literary Transmission, Beliefs, and Manners of Palestine in the I Century BCE—IV Century CE* (New York: JTS, 1950; 2nd ed.; 1962).

[62] "Prolegomenon," in *Essays in Greco-Roman and Related Talmudic Literature*, ed. by Henry A. Fischel (New York: KTAV, 1977) xxvi.

[63] See below, nn. 84–85. For a recent effort along these lines, see the essays in Troels Engberg-Pedersen (ed.), *Paul Beyond the Judaism/Hellenism Divide* (Louisville: Westminster John Knox, 2001).

[64] They were originally delivered as the 1949 Haskell Lectures at Oberlin College.

devoted to biblical theology.[65] They concluded that, despite the numerous parallels explored, the Christian gospel was a new and recognizably different religious message. The "*essential* message" of New Testament was *not* the product of a secondary phase of Christian development in the Gentile world; instead it came to the Gentile world as a challenge.[66] In support of this basic premise, Filson said:

> [We do not] ask whether we find in the philosophy and religion of the earlier Gentile world parallels to certain terms and ideas in the New Testament. There are such parallels. It demands attention, however, that almost invariably they are only partial parallels.[67]

> We may see many partial parallels with ancient life and thought, and as a result may wonder how much originality or difference the New Testament really had. The ancient world had no such problem. As far as I can find, they sensed the fact that the Gospel was a different thing from the religious messages they had known. The Jews and later the Judaizers saw that it was breaking the limits of current Judaism.[68]

From his perspective, the Old Testament contained the root ideas carried on in the distinctive Christian message. First-century Judaism was the principal vehicle of transmission; however, it had lost the pure "essence" because of its excessive legalism.[69] So, key theological terms like ἀγάπη or κοινωνία—as found especially in Paul and more generally in Christian usage—could not possibly have the same semantic meaning as in pagan usage.[70] In sharp contrast, recent studies have demonstrated not only that these terms come from the ordinary language of friendship, but also that the usage in early Jewish and Christian writers depends on the semantic fields, social conventions, and cultural ideals that are contained in and cluster around the root social mean-

---

[65] G. Ernest Wright, *The Old Testament against its Environment* (SBT 2; London: SCM, 1950); Floyd V. Filson, *The New Testament against its Environment* (SBT 3; London: SCM, 1950).

[66] Filson, *NT against its Environment*, 28; he also says, "the Hellenistic character of the later books of the New Testament has often been overstated" (30). Specifically, he means James, Hebrews, 2 Peter, and John (31–33).

[67] *Ibid.*, 28–29.

[68] *Ibid.*, 96.

[69] *Ibid.*, 22–23, 29.

[70] Filson does not deal directly with these terms as reflecting the social language of the New Testament, but cf. *NT against its Environment*, 80 (on fellowship) and 83 n. 18 (on love). From such assumptions also came some popular but erroneous modern distinctions between the Greek terms for "love" in contrast to *agape* as a peculiar form of "Christian love," as in the formulation of Anders Nygren, *Agape and Eros* (London: SPCK, 1953) 143 et passim.

ing of friendship within the Graeco-Roman environment. What then becomes important is how these terms can be invested with theological colorations, legitimations, or motivations by different pagan, Jewish, and Christian authors.[71]

This change of view was initiated in part by the work of James Barr, *The Semantics of Biblical Language*.[72] Barr addressed the problem of religious language—and thereby the underlying question of hermeneutics—by examining the transmission of theological meaning and content outside of the original environment in which the language arose. Coming out of generations of scholarship that invariably assumed lexicography as the starting point for biblical exegesis, Gerhard Kittel's *Theologisches Wörterbuch zum Neuen Testament* institutionalized some of these traditional theological notions of language.[73] For Kittel, following the lexicographical work of Hermann Cremer,[74] the theological language of the New Testament has a

> new force and impress and energy given to Greek words as "the horizons of those who spoke and wrote them changed with the point of departure and termination of all thinking." The true aim of the present book is to bring out in our discussions this *new* content of individual terms.[75]

---

[71] See especially David Konstan, *Friendship in the Classical World* (Cambridge: Cambridge University Press, 1997); and the two volumes from the Hellenistic Moral Philosophy and Early Christianity group, edited by John T. Fitzgerald, *Friendship, Flattery, and Frankness of Speech: Studies on Friendship in the New Testament World* (NovTSup 82; Leiden: E.J. Brill, 1996), and *Greco-Roman Perspectives on Friendship* (SBLRBS 34; Atlanta: Scholars Press, 1997). For criticism of Nygren's views see especially the article by Frederick M. Schroeder, "Friendship in Aristotle and Some Peripatetic Philosophers," in *Greco-Roman Perspectives on Friendship*, 38. For a "socially tuned" reading of friendship language as employed in Pauline Christological formulation, see L. Michael White, "Morality between Two Worlds: A Paradigm of Friendship in Philippians," in *Greeks, Romans, and Christians: Essays in Honor of Abraham J. Malherbe* (Minneapolis: Fortress Press, 1990) 201–15, and the article by Engberg-Pedersen in this volume.

[72] James Barr, *The Semantics of Biblical Language* (Oxford: Clarendon, 1961).

[73] (10 vols. in 12; Stuttgart: W. Kohlhammer Verlag, 1932–1979). Kittel studied at Leipzig, Tübingen, and Berlin, receiving his doctorate in 1913 from Kiel. The bulk of his career was at Tübingen (1926–39) and Vienna (1939–1945).

[74] In his preface to *TWNT* Kittel credits Augustus Hermann Cremer's *Biblisch-theologisches Wörterbuch der neutestamentlichen Gracität* (Stuttgart: Kohlhammer, 1866; 9th ed., 1902; 11th ed., revised by J. Kögel, 1923). Cremer, a contemporary of G. Kittel's father, Rudolf, had been Professor of Systematic Theology at Griefswald (retired 1890; died 1903), where G. Kittel also taught briefly in 1921.

[75] From the preface to *TWNT* vol. 1, as translated by G. W. Bromiley in the English edition, *Theological Dictionary of the New Testament*, edited by Gerhard Kittel (10 vols.; Grand Rapids: Eerdmans, 1964–1976) vii. The quote within the quotation is from Cremer's preface. [NB: for the referent of the phrase "point of departure and

Thus, Barr challenged both the neo-orthodox linguistic principles and their underlying theological assumptions as follows:

> We may then sum up these criticisms of *TWNT* by saying that the great weakness is a failure to get to grips with the semantic value of words *in their contexts*, and a strong tendency to assume that this value will on its own agree with and illuminate the contours of a theological structure which is felt to be characteristic of the New Testament and *distinctively contrasting with its environment*.[76]

In this critique, Barr forced the issue of *interpretation* in biblical analysis back to the issue of *context*, more particularly the question of *historical and social context* as the primary locus for meaning. Instead, he argued, the language of the NT employed "the same semantic function as [it] normally had in the usage of Hellenistic speakers," and not even the semantic value found in the most abstract usage of philosophy, but that of more common speech.[77]

Just as Barr was calling for lexical and semantic studies to be more attentive to the ambient environment, others were starting to question the theological assumptions used in traditional studies of Graeco-Roman and Jewish "parallels" to New Testament materials. For example, van Unnik's *Corpus Hellenisticum* project began to speak of "antiparallels," while Samuel Sandmel's 1961 SBL Presidential Address took aim at the problem he termed "parallelomania."[78] He called special attention to the inappropriate use of parallels in Strack-Billerbeck's *Kommentar zum Neuen Testament aus Talmud und Midrasch*.[79] He says:

> I would state here that NT scholars devoid of rabbinic learning have been misled by Strack-Billerbeck into arrogating to themselves a competency they do not possess. Strack-Billerbeck confers upon a student untrained and inexperienced in rabbinic literature not competency but confusion. … The fourth and crowning sin of Strack-Billerbeck involves a paradox. On the one hand, they quote the rabbinic literature endlessly

---

termination of all things," read "Christ."] See also Kittel's Cambridge lectures of 1937, *Lexicographia sacra: The Making of the Theologisches Wörterbuch zum Neuen Testament* (London: SPCK, 1938).

[76] Barr, *Semantics* 231 (emphasis added).

[77] *Ibid.*, 250–51.

[78] Samuel Sandmel, "Parallelomania," *JBL* 81 (1962) 1–13.

[79] See note 39 above. Predecessors included John Lightfoot, *Horae hebraicae et talmudicae* (1658–1674; ET: 4 vols.; Oxford: Oxford University Press, 1859) and J. Christian Schöttgen, *Horae hebraicae et talmudicae in universum Novum Testamentum* (Dresden-Leipzig: C. Hekelii B. Filium, 1733–42).

to clarify the NT. Yet even where Jesus and the rabbis seem to say identically the same thing, Strack-Billerbeck manage to demonstrate that what Jesus said is finer and better. … Why, I must ask, pile up the alleged parallels, if the end result is to show a forced, artificial, and untenable distinction even within the admitted parallels?[80]

As a result of such criticisms, several significant new projects have been launched and groundbreaking studies published that give emphasis to "semantic fields" (as opposed to individual key words).[81] In future studies of this type it will be crucial to investigate such terms, not simply in isolation from one another, but as part of the conceptual "linkage group" to which they belong and with increased attention to the social worlds in which they are used.[82] Similarly, attention will need to be given to combinations of Greek words as well as to equivalent terms and similar expressions in Latin and other languages. While there is thus a need to expand the linguistic horizons of research, the data used in making comparisons must not be restricted to instances of verbal identity or similarity. Some of the most striking parallels between Christian and non-Christian texts are primarily conceptual and involve little or no verbal agreement between the two.[83] Attention must also be given to the dates of the *comparanda*. One of the most recent turns in this discussion as it relates to the Jewish materials concerns the viability of using the later rabbinic collections (the Mishnah and Talmudim) as evidence for either pre-70 Pharisaism or of pre-70 Judaism in general. So, too, this has a decided impact on the way we should consider the "backgrounds" to both Jesus and Paul. Still very much in the traditional mold is the work of E. P. Sanders, even though his concern has been to develop a revisionist orientation toward Pharisaic [rabbinic] terminology and theology.[84] Alan Segal sharpens the point nicely when he suggests that perhaps we have been going about it backwards: instead

---

[80] Sandmel, "Parallelomania," 9–10.

[81] For example, the Macquarrie University lexicography project (also known as the "new Moulton-Milligan"), founded by E.A. Judge and G.H.R. Horsley, which produces the series *New Documents Illustrating Early Christianity* (8 vols.; Grand Rapids: Eerdmans, 1981–1998) or F.W. Danker's study of *Benefactor: Study of a Graeco-Roman and New Testament Semantic Field* (St. Louis: Clarion Press, 1982).

[82] For a treatment of the term "reconciliation" as part of the linkage group to which "friendship" belongs, see John T. Fitzgerald, "Paul and Paradigm Shifts: Reconciliation and Its Linkage Group," in *Paul Beyond the Judaism/Hellenism Divide*, 241–62, 316–25.

[83] Van der Horst, "Corpus Hellenisticum Novi Testamenti," 1159–60.

[84] *Paul and Palestinian Judaism* (Philadelphia: Fortress, 1977).

of using the rabbinic materials to talk about the "backgrounds" to the New Testament, we ought to be using the growth of the early Christian movement as a "background" to the rabbis.[85]

From Parallels to Backgrounds

This discussion reflects more than a century of debate within New Testament scholarship over the nature, function, and benefit of the study of parallels and the so-called "backgrounds" of the New Testament. We may consider two opposing approaches to the study of backgrounds as a way of rethinking the task of studying the parallels for the sake of comparison.

What has sometime been called the first social history of earliest Christianity is Adolf Harnack's *Die Mission und Ausbreitung des Christentums* (or *The Mission and Expansion of Christianity*). It appeared in 1902, the same year as his Berlin Lectures on *Das Wesen des Christentums* (literally "The Essence of Christianity") were published in English under the title *What is Christianity?* It also came out of Harnack's work on the *History of Dogma* (third German edition in 1894).[86] The *Mission und Ausbreitung* subsequently went through three more editions, the last appearing in 1924, the same year as his influential study of *Marcion*.[87]

The place where Harnack does most of his work on the "backgrounds" is in his first volume of *Die Mission und Ausbreitung*, where he sets the stage for the "expansion" by examining the conditions of the world that explain why the Christian message could hold such appeal. Still, for Harnack the truth of the gospel "message"—that is, the very *essence* of Christianity—was independent of the social context and was

---

[85] Segal has made the point in various discussions, *inter alia*, "Universalism in Judaism and Christianity," in *Paul in His Hellenistic Context*, ed. by T. Engberg-Pedersen (Edinburgh: T&T Clark, 1994) 1–2, and *Paul the Convert: The Apostolate and Apostasy of Saul the Pharisee* (New Haven: Yale University Press, 1990) xiv-xvi.

[86] *Die Mission und Ausbreitung des Christentums in der ersten drei Jahrhunderten* (2 vols.; Leipzig: Henrichs, 1902; 2nd ed., 1906; ET: London: Williams & Norgate, 1905; 2nd ed., 1908); *Das Wesen des Christentums* (Leipzig: Henrichs, 1900; ET: London: Williams & Norgate, 1901); *Lehrbuch der Dogmengeschichte* (7 vols.; Tübingen: J.C.B Mohr, 1886; 3rd ed.; 1894; ET: London: Williams & Norgate, 1900).

[87] See L. Michael White, "Adolf Harnack and the 'Expansion' of Christianity: A Reappraisal of Social History," *SecCent* 5 (1985–86) 97–127; "Harnack, Karl Gustav Adolf von (1851–1930)," *Dictionary of Biblical Interpretation*, I:481–83.

constantly being inserted into and stripped away from the "collective syncretism" of each new religious environment, whether Jewish, Greek, or Roman.[88]

Second, then, for Harnack, who was vigorously opposed to the emerging "history of religions" school at the turn of the century, the truly Christian elements were almost completely isolated from their historical environment or "backgrounds."[89] Thus, the "backgrounds"— or what we now tend to call the "social world"—for Harnack was merely a "backdrop" or scenery against which the real action took place. In the final analysis, however, between the Christian actors at center stage and the scenery there was no real interaction.

On the other side of the fence stands the *Religionsgeschichtliche Schule*. In 1909 Franz Josef Dölger inaugurated a new journal entitled *Antike und Christentum: Kultur- und Religionsgeschichtliche Studien* centered on his own personal pursuit of the cultural parallels between Christian expression and action with that of the ancient world. First appearing in 1929, *Antike und Christentum* comprised six volumes, the last appearing in 1950, a full decade after Dölger's death.[90] His work was taken up and continued by Theodor Klauser and others.[91] In sharp contrast to Harnack, their approach was phenomenological.[92]

---

[88] Harnack, *Mission and Expansion* (2nd ed.) I:318. Cf. *What is Christianity?* 190–91; *Lehrbuch der Dogmengeschichte* (1st ed.) I:58–59. Cf. White, "Adolf Harnack and the 'Expansion,'" 99–100.

[89] So his famous 1901 Berlin Lecture, "Die Aufgabe der theologischen Facultäten und die allgemeine Religionsgeschichte: Rede zur Gedächtnisfeier des Stifters der Berliner Universität;" Cf. White, "Adolf Harnack and the 'Expansion,'" 100.

[90] Cf. Theodor Klauser and Adolf Rücker (eds.), *Pisciculi: Studien zur Religion und Kultur des Altertums, Franz Joseph Dölger zum sechzigsten Geburtstage* (Antike und Christentum Ergänzungsband 1; Münster: Aschendorff Verlag, 1939). [Contains a bibliography of Dölger's work compiled by Karl Baus.]

[91] See the discussion of the history and scope of Dölger's work, and that of his successors, by E. A. Judge, "'Antike und Christentum,'" 4–9. In 1955 the enterprise was placed under the auspices of an institute at Bonn named in honor of Dölger. In addition to Klauser, it featured such scholars as J.H. Waszink (Leiden), L. Wenger (Vienna), and Hans Lietzmann (Harnack's successor at Berlin). Under this leadership it oversaw the flowering of the first German *Religionsgeschichtliche Schule* through a careful treatment of the early Christian materials in relation to the classical.

[92] To quote Judge ("'Antike und Christentum,'" 6): "[His] eye is most sharply focused upon a very specific type of phenomenon: the physical signs, symbols, and gestures by which Christians express their beliefs, and the comparable practices in usage in antiquity. He did not in the end move far from his original interest in sacrament and liturgy. But he expanded it to embrace the ritual and customary procedures of the whole of life, and above all he moved beyond the framework of the history of dogma

One of the main difficulties in Dölger's phenomenological approach —which focuses on topics and symbols rather than society and history—is integrating the archaeological and non-literary remains of the classical culture with the predominantly literary tradition used to reflect much of the Christian side. While Dölger and company have certainly been more interested than most in the archaeological and artistic materials from the early Christian world, such materials were often read through the lens of the literary tradition alone, and not in their archaeological (hence, cultural) context. This led to some criticism of their historical method precisely because the phenomenological approach tended to become "a piling up of antiquarian detail without sufficient regard to time and place, which prevented justice being done to concrete historical relationships."[93] In other words, despite the radically different orientation toward the contributions of Graeco-Roman culture to early Christian life and practice, the lack of historical nuance nonetheless created an artificially static view of the culture. Once again we find the parallels have become lifeless scenery, mere "backgrounds" rather than living culture.[94] The discovery of parallels—no matter how striking the similarity—does not exist outside of an historical and social context.

From another perspective we must also be aware that there is often a theological subtext in positing both similarities and differences.[95] Jonathan Z. Smith has shown that the tradition of comparing early Christianity to Graeco-Roman religions emerged since the Enlightenment in an environment dominated by "Protestant anti-Catholic apologetics."[96] He notes that regular comparisons were made between the Pauline "sacraments" and those ostensibly found in the mysteries in order to make the point that post-Pauline Christianity was taking on Greek ideas. The basic assumption being worked out through comparison is that

---

to adopt the more anthropological approach of social and religious history—or rather antiquities."

[93] Judge, "'Antike und Christentum,'" 13, paraphrasing reviews of the *Reallexikon für Antike und Christentum* by E. Peterson in *RivAC* 31 (1955) 275–79 and 33 (1957) 203–4.

[94] Judge ("'Antike und Christentum,'" 13) also notes Klauser's reply to Peterson's criticism and suggests that later approaches in the *RAC* attempted to deal with these issues in some ways.

[95] Colish, "Stoicism and the New Testament," 367–77.

[96] *Drudgery Divine: On the Comparison of Early Christianities and the Religions of Late Antiquity* (Chicago: University of Chicago Press, 1990) 34.

if Christianity is 'unique' with respect to the other religions, then 'apostolic' (or Pauline) Christianity is 'unique' with respect to other (especially later) modes of Christianity. This is a modulation of the Protestant historiographic myth: a 'uniquely' pristine 'original' Christianity which suffered later 'corruptions.'[97]

In this way, the uniqueness of apostolic Christianity is "Protestant," whereas later forms of Christianity, influenced by the ritual practices of the mysteries, become "Catholic."[98] Smith traces these basic ideas back to the work of Isaac Casaubon (1559–1614), a French Heugenot, a Classicist who wrote on Greek and Roman satire, and a contemporary of Joseph Scaliger and Hugo Grotius.[99] From there they came down to some of the more influential theological works of the past half century.[100] More recent work has shown that many of the supposed similarities to "sacraments" are indeed erroneous, while the origins of the mysteries are indigenously Greek.[101] Thus here again, more careful attention to historical detail and cultural context, not to mention theological tendencies, is required on both sides of the comparative equation.

So the "piling up" of parallels is not the only answer. Everett Ferguson, following in the tradition of Arthur Darby Nock, puts it this way:

> What is to be made of these parallels? Do they explain away Christianity as a natural product of its environment? Must they be explained away in order to defend the truth or validity of Christianity? Neither position is necessary. … It is possible to emphasize the similarities of Christianity to elements in its environment, and one may stress these items either to argue *for* the *providential preparation* for Christianity *or* to give a *naturalistic* explanation of Christianity as another *syncretistic religion* of the time. Conversely, it is possible to deny significant similarities in an effort to defend Christianity's uniqueness or to make it out as a fraud. Either approach, from whatever motivation, seems to me to be misguided.[102]

---

[97] *Ibid.*, 43.

[98] *Ibid.*, 47.

[99] *Ibid.*, 56–59.

[100] Smith (*Ibid.*, 34 n. 58) cites Filson, *NT against its Environment*, 94, for using the concept of *ex opere operato* as an encoded anti-Catholic criticism. He also discusses (43 & 48) the way similar ideas are reflected in the treatment of Bruce M. Metzger, "Methodology in the Study of the Mystery Religions," *HTR* 45 (1955) 1–2; revised version reprinted in Metzger's *Historical and Literary Studies: Pagan, Jewish, and Christian* (Grand Rapids: Eerdmans, 1968) 1–24.

[101] Cf. Walter Burkert, *Ancient Mystery Cults* (Cambridge: Harvard University Press, 1987) 3, 31.

[102] *Backgrounds of Early Christianity* (2nd ed., Grand Rapids: Eerdmans, 1993) 1–2.

Upon discovering certain parallels, a key methodological consideration must be what can be understood by analyzing them comparatively. Adolf Deissmann proposed that any case of parallelism might be understood either as *analogy* ("more or less equal religious experiences") or as *genealogy* ("dependence" or "demonstrable borrowings").[103] Once again, Jonathan Z. Smith has called for greater sophistication in thinking about what the task of comparative analysis ought to entail by not limiting the role of parallels to dyadic oppositions or similarities.[104] At the same time, the social location of the ancient materials has undergone considerable reclassification in the light of more recent comparative research.[105]

Perhaps we ought to say it this way: The process of recognizing parallels—like Darwin discovering distinctive but similar species of finches on the various islands of the Gallapagos—is first and foremost the assembly of a data set on and from which new analysis will need to be based. On first sight, the similarities must evoke some appropriate theoretical explanation. But upon reflection and with the collection of each new data set, one will begin to evaluate and analyze not only the data but also the previous theories themselves. Indeed, one of the problems in recent efforts to apply sociological or anthropological theories to the study of the ancient world, and early Christianity in particular, has been inflexibility in the use of theories and models. The process of comparison in the light of new data sets must also cause us to reformulate—or as Smith puts it, to deconstruct and reconstruct[106]—

---

[103] *Light from the Ancient East: The New Testament Illustrated by Recently Discovered Texts of the Graeco-Roman World* (ET from the 4th German edition; London: Hodder & Stauton, 1927) 265. Smith (*Drudgery*, 48–49) also discusses Deissmann's views in the light of the fact that later scholars (notably Metzger) have used "analogy" to discount the similarities, while "genealogy" was a common way of discounting later (i.e., "Catholic") Christianity and Late Antiquity more generally.

[104] *Drudgery*, 47–53.

[105] For criticism of Deissmann's thesis regarding the implications of the papyri for understanding the social location of early Christian literature see Abraham J. Malherbe, "Soziale Ebene und Literarische Bildung," in *Zur Soziologie des Urchristentums*, ed. by W. A. Meeks (Munich: Kaiser Press, 1979) 194–221; ET included in Malherbe's *Social Aspects of Early Christianity* (2nd ed.; Philadelphia: Fortress Press, 1983) 29–59. In general, the non-literary materials have not always been handled well in these discussions. For a critical treatment of the hermeneutical tendencies (akin to those proposed by Smith, nn. 97–98 above) in some older treatments of architectural and archaeological issues see the article by Paul Corby Finney, "Early Christian Architecture: The Beginnings (A Review Article)," *HTR* 81 (1988) 319–39.

[106] *Drudgery*, 52.

the theories themselves.[107] In the case of the ancient world, then, we must constantly be aware of context and culture as dynamic factors in all forms of social interaction within any particular historical sphere, just as in an ecosystem.

From Parallels to Context

Despite all the debates over how to use such parallels in studying the New Testament, there has been a lasting contribution made especially by the investment of New Testament scholars in relation to the late Classical (or Hellenistic-Roman) world out of which it came. We could cite numerous studies that have attempted over the years to detail both the extent and the overall character of this interdependence. Perhaps the most significant contributions have been made in three areas: (1) the rebirth (and reconceptualization) of interests both from Classicists and New Testament scholars in the syncretistic religious environment of the Hellenistic-Roman world (best seen in studies of the Hellenistic mysteries and Diaspora Judaism); (2) the philosophical and intellectual traditions (especially in studies of Philo, the Hellenistic moralists, and the Second Sophistic); and (3) the growth of social world studies (especially those that have brought greater sophistication to our understanding of archaeology, cultural phenomena and symbolic worldview formation). With the advent of greater access and search capabilities in ancient texts through electronic media (e.g., the *Thesaurus Linguae Graecae*), the discovery of parallels seems even more promising. Even so it requires caution and sophistication.

Still the problem exists of what to do with the parallels. In his review article on "Hellenistic Moralists and the New Testament," Abraham Malherbe warned,

> A major problem attending the use of such tools as the "Corpus Hel-lenisticum" is the focus on "parallels." ... Parallels so collected may very well be used in the ways parallels from hellenistic moral philosophical material have been used in the past. These ways range from the rather superficial use of some concept or description from the philosophers to illuminate a New Testament term, for example, the [term] apostle, or the subject of freedom, through citing the parallels in commentaries on books of the New Testament without allowing the exposition of those

---

[107] See L. Michael White, "Social Networks: Theoretical Orientation and Historical Applications," in *Social Networks in the Early Christian Environment: Issues and Methods for Social History*, ed. by L.M. White (*Semeia* 56; Atlanta: Scholars Press, 1992) 31–34.

books to be substantially influenced by the parallels, or a similar use in treatments of such subjects as New Testament ethics. ... Such uncritical use of parallels is particularly unfortunate in light of the fact that the moral philosophers have frequently been approached with conceptions of eclecticism and syncretism which have not always contributed to precision. ... The problem has been accentuated when the philosophical materials have been approached from the Christian side with an agenda set by a New Testament interest, thus offering a Christian organizing principle for "parallels" found in the pagan materials.[108]

In the final analysis, Malherbe argues, one must deal with the nuances and differences among the moralists and other non-Christian writers based on their context, backgrounds, and intentions—in precisely the same way that we need to be aware of the drastic differences among the New Testament writings themselves.

> The problems associated with hunting for parallels is accentuated when we speak of someone, say Paul, and his "background." The next step is then to think of Paul as [merely] taking things from his "background" and adapting them to his own circumstances and purposes. It is potentially fruitful, and certainly more realistic, to place Paul in the context of these discussions ... .[109]

Thus, parallels alone are not enough. The *topoi* and other philosophical conventions that one regularly finds among the Hellenistic moralists and in Paul (as well as other NT writers) are more than mere *clichés*.[110] They, too, were products of socially constructed communities of meaning. There is a need for more nuanced treatment of social-historical as well as archaeological-cultural data in order to provide contextual grounding and correlation for the parallels. We need to discover both the social realities and the cultural understanding of their day.

To take but one example of the difficulties, we may look briefly at the recent *Hellenistic Commentary to the New Testament*, edited by Boring, Berger, and Colpe.[111] For the entire Galatian letter, it lists a total of 31 parallels, comprised of 22 pagan texts, 5 pre-70 Jewish texts, 2 rabbinic texts, and 2 later Christian texts from Nag Hammadi. Despite the fact that Betz's commentary has shown quite convincingly that Gal 4:12–20 is replete with allusions to the friendship *topos*,[112] the *Hellenistic*

---

[108] "Hellenistic Moralists and the New Testament," 275–76.
[109] Malherbe, "Hellenistic Moralists and the New Testament," 299.
[110] *Ibid.*, 320 n. 252 and 324.
[111] See notes 52 and 53 above.
[112] Hans Dieter Betz, *Galatians* (Hermeneia; Philadelphia: Fortress Press, 1979) 220–21. Betz cites a number of the parallels in the footnotes.

Commentary lists no parallels of any sort for this passage.[113] In fact the *Hellenistic Commentary* lists only one parallel (at Rom 7:22) in all of Paul's letters to an example of the friendship *topos*, but even that is not about friendship.[114] This omission is the more striking, then, in light of recent work on friendship in the Graeco-Roman and early Christian world.[115] At the same time due caution must be observed when we try to assess the possible implications for Paul's use of the cultural ideology of friendship as applied to Christian social organization over against its use as a foundational value in moral exhortation.[116]

What underlies these backgrounds is a common set of worldview assumptions—a symbolic universe or template of reality—that places Jews and Christians more fully in their cultural context. Paul's use of the semantics of friendship, benefaction, or patronage, various *topoi*, or forms of paraenesis demonstrates his adherence to widely understood assumptions of his time both in the intellectual environment of the moralists and in the socio-economic environment of Roman rule in the Aegean during his day. The use of the same assumptions and traditions by other Jews (such as Philo) or Christians of a later day (such as Clement of Alexandria) must surely allow for subtle differences. In order for us to understand fully how a Paul—or any other writer of the time, whether pagan, Jew, or Christian—might have appropriated these semantic and social conventions, we must continue to examine closely the parallels in their contexts. *Quod est comparandum* ("Thus should it be compared").

---

[113] See the article by L. Michael White in this volume for further discussion of this passage in the light of the friendship *topos* with parallels from Dio, Favorinus, and the epistolary handbooks.

[114] Out of ten parallels on friendship, nine are found in the Gospels and Acts. The only Pauline occurrence is at §591 (*ad loc.* Rom 7:22), citing Plutarch, *Maxime cum principibus philosopho esse disserendum* 2 (*Mor.* 777C), that the aim of the two kinds of speech is friendship. But the point of reference in the parallel to Rom 7:22 seems to be primarily about Paul's internal discourse, compared to what Plutarch seems to call "the speech in the mind," since the preceding entries (§§589–90) list Plato's *Rep.* 588D–589B and *Corpus Hermeticum* 13.7 as parallels to this verse.

[115] See above n. 71.

[116] See the caution of Hans-Josef Klauck ("Kirche als Freundesgemeinschaft? Auf Spurensuche im Neuen Testament," *MTZ* 42 [1991] 3–12) who argues that, despite the parallels, the friendship language is subordinate to fictive kinship language. Cf. Sterling, "Hellenistic Philosophy and the New Testament," 329–30. On the other hand, it may be the case that at the level of ideological value system, the two kinds of language are much more intertwined.

A BIBLIOGRAPHY OF THE WRITINGS
OF ABRAHAM J. MALHERBE

Books

1967   (Editor and Author) *The World of the New Testament*. Austin: Sweet Publishing Co.

1977   *Social Aspects of Early Christianity*. Baton Rouge: Louisiana State University Press.

        (Editor and Author) *The Cynic Epistles: A Study Edition*. Missoula: Scholars Press.

1978   (with Everett Ferguson) *Gregory of Nyssa, The Life of Moses: Introduction, Translation and Notes*. New York: Paulist Press.

1983   *Social Aspects of Early Christianity*. Second, enlarged edition. Philadelphia: Fortress Press.

1986   *Moral Exhortation: A Graeco-Roman Sourcebook*. Philadelphia: Westminster Press.

1987   *Paul and the Thessalonians: The Philosophic Tradition of Pastoral Care*. Philadelphia: Fortress Press. Reprinted: Sigler Press, 2000.

1988   *Ancient Epistolary Theorists*. Atlanta: Scholars Press.

        Paul and the Popular Philosophers. Philadelphia: Fortress Press.

1993   (Editor with Wayne Meeks) *The Future of Christology: Essays in Honor of Leander E. Keck*. Philadelphia: Fortress Press.

1998   (Editor and Author with Frederick W. Norris and James W. Thompson) *The Early Church in Its Context: Essays in Honor of Everett Ferguson*. Leiden: E.J. Brill.

2000   *The Letters to the Thessalonians*. The Anchor Bible 32B. New York: Doubleday.

Selected Articles

1959   "The Corinthian Contribution," *Restoration Quarterly* 3:221–33.

1961   "The Task and Method of New Testament Exegesis," *Restoration Quarterly* 5:169–78.

1963   "Apologetic and Philosophy in the Second Century," *Restoration Quarterly* 7:19–32.

1968   "Towards Understanding the Apologists," *Restoration Quarterly* 12:215–24.

        "The Beasts at Ephesus," *Journal of Biblical Literature* 87:71–80. Reprinted: Pp. 79–89 in *Paul and the Popular Philosophers.*

1969   "Athenagoras on Christian Ethics," *Journal of Ecclesiastical History* 20:1–5. Reprinted: *Studies in Early Christianity, Vol. 16: Early Christian Ethics, Morality and Discipline*, ed. by E. Ferguson. (1993) New York: Garland.

        "The Holy Spirit in Athenagoras," *Journal of Theological Studies* N.S. 20:538–42.

        "A People under the Word." Pp. 207–23 in *The Concept of the Believers' Church*, ed. by James L. Garrett. Scottsdale: Herald Press.

        "The Structure of Athenagoras, '*Supplicatio pro Christianis*,'" *Vigiliae Christianae* 23:1–20. Reprinted: *Studies in Early Christianity, Vol. 2: Literature in the Early Church*, ed. by E. Ferguson. (1993) New York: Garland.

1970   "'Gentle as a Nurse': The Cynic Background to I Thess ii," *Novum Testamentum* 12:203–17. Reprinted: Pp. 35–48 in *Paul and the Popular Philosophers.*

        "Athenagoras on the Poets and Philosophers." Pp. 214–25 in *Kyriakon: Festschrift Johannes Quasten*, ed. by P. Granfield and J. Jungmann. Münster: Ashendorff.

        "The Apologetic Theology of the Preaching of Peter," *Restoration Quarterly* 13:205–23.

        "Athenagoras on the Location of God," *Theologische Zeitschrift* 16:46–52.

1971   "The Household of God," *Religion and Society* 4:17–24.

1972   In *Great Events from History, Ancient and Medieval Series, Vol. 2.*, ed. by F.N. Magill. Salem: Salem Press:

"Inception of Christian Apologetic," pp. 707–11.

"Publication of Celsus' *True Word*," pp. 731–36.

"Emergence of Theology as a Concept," pp. 757–61.

"Crystallization of the New Testament," pp. 779–83.

1976   In *Interpreter's Dictionary of the Bible, Supplement Volume*. Nashville: Abingdon:

"Cynics," pp. 201–03.

"Epictetus," pp. 271.

1977   "The Inhospitality of Diotrephes." Pp. 222–32 in *God's Christ and His People: Studies in Honour of Nils Alstrup Dahl*, ed. by Jacob Jervell and Wayne A. Meeks. Oslo: Oslo Universitetsforlaget. Reprinted: Pp. 92–112 in the second edition of *Social Aspects of Early Christianity*.

"Ancient Epistolary Theorists," *Ohio Journal of Religious Studies* 5:3–77. Revised version: *Ancient Epistolary Theorists*.

1978   "Pseudo Heraclitus, Epistle 4: The Divinization of the Wise Man," *Jahrbuch für Antike und Christentum*. 21:42–64.

1979   "Soziale Ebene und Literarische Bildung." Pp. 194–221 in *Zur Soziologie des Urchristentums*, ed. by Wayne A. Meeks. Munich: Kaiser Press.

1980   "Continuities in Scholarship: The Work of Nils Dahl," *Reflection* 78:8–12.

"Medical Imagery in the Pastoral Epistles." Pp. 19–35 in *Texts and Testaments: Critical Essays in Honor of Stuart D. Currie*, ed. by W. Eugene March. San Antonio: Trinity University Press. Reprinted: Pp. 121–36 in *Paul and the Popular Philosophers*.

"*Me genoito* in the Diatribe and Paul," *Harvard Theological Review* 73:231–40. Reprinted: Pp. 25–33 in *Paul and the Popular Philosophers*.

1981   "Crescens and Justin." Pp. 312–27 in *Christian Teaching: Studies in Honor of LeMoine G. Lewis*, ed. by Everett Ferguson. Abilene: Abilene Christian University.

1982   "Self-Definition among Cynics and Epicureans." Pp. 46–59, 192–97 in *Self-Definition in the Graeco-Roman World*, ed. by Ben F. Meyer and E.P. Sanders. Philadelphia: Fortress Press. Reprinted: Pp. 11–24 in *Paul and the Popular Philosophers*.

"Early Christianity and Society: A Contemporary Academic Interest." Pp. 69–92 in *Freedom, Order and the University*, ed. by James R. Wilburn. Malibu: Pepperdine University.

1983   "Exhortation in First Thessalonians,' *Novum Testamentum* 25:238–56. Reprinted: Pp. 49–66 in *Paul and the Popular Philosophers*.

"Antisthenes and Odysseus, and Paul at War," *Harvard Theological Review* 76:143–73. Reprinted: Pp. 91–119 in *Paul and the Popular Philosophers*.

1984   "'In Season and Out of Season': 2 Timothy 4:2," *Journal of Biblical Literature* 103:235–43. Reprinted: Pp. 137–45 in *Paul and the Popular Philosophers*.

Review Essay: "Helmut Koester, *Introduction to the New Testament*," *Religious Studies Review* 10:112–16.

1985   "Paul: Hellenistic Philosopher or Christian Pastor?" *American Theological Library Association Proceedings* 39:86–98. Reprinted: *Anglican Theological Review* 68 (1986) 3–13 and as pp. 67–77 in *Paul and the Popular Philosophers*.

1985/86 "'Not in a Corner': Early Christian Apologetic in Acts 26:26," *The Second Century* 5:193–210. Reprinted: Pp. 147–63 in *Paul and the Popular Philosophers*.

1986   "A Physical Description of Paul." Pp. 170–175 in *Christians among Jews and Gentiles: Essays in Honor of Krister Stendahl on His Sixty-Fifth Birthday*, ed. by George W.E. Nickelsburg with George W. MacRae. Philadelphia: Fortress Press. Reprinted: *Harvard Theological Review* 79 (1986) 170–75 and as pp. 165–70 in *Paul and the Popular Philosophers*.

1988   "Herakles," *Reallexikon für Antike und Christendum* 14:559–83.

1989   "Graeco-Roman Religion and Philosophy and the New Testament." Pp. 3–26 *The New Testament and Its Modern Interpreters*, ed. by Eldon Jay Epp and George McRae. Atlanta: Scholars Press.

1990   "'Pastoral Care' in the Thessalonian Church," *New Testament Studies* 36:375–91.

"Did the Thessalonians Write to Paul?" Pp. 246–57 in *The Conversation Continues: Studies in Paul and John. In Honor of J. Louis Martyn*, ed. by R. Fortna and B. Gaventa. Nashville: Abingdon.

"Traditions and Theology of Care in the New Testament." Pp. 787–92 in *Dictionary of Pastoral Care and Counseling*, ed. by R. Hunter. Nashville: Abingdon.

1991   "'Seneca' on Paul as Letter Writer." Pp. 414–21 in *The Future of Early Christianity: Essays in Honor of Helmut Koester*, ed. by Birger A. Pearson. Philadelphia: Fortress Press.

1992   "Hellenistic Moralists and the New Testament." Pp. 267–333 in *Aufstieg und Niedergang der römischen Welt* II.26.I, ed. by Wolfgang Haase. Berlin: De Gruyter.

1993   In *The Oxford Companion to the Bible*, ed. by Bruce M. Metzger. Oxford: Oxford University Press:

"Epicureans," p. 190.

"Hospitality," pp. 292–93.

"Stoics," pp. 714–15.

1994   "Determinism and Free Will in Paul: The Argument of 1 Corinthians 8 and 9." Pp. 231–55 in *Paul in His Hellenistic Context*, ed. by Troels Engberg-Pedersen. Philadelphia: Fortress Press.

"*Paulus Senex*," *Restoration Quarterly* 36:297–307.

1995   "God's Family at Thessalonica." Pp. 117–28 in *The First Christians and their Social World: Studies in Honor of Wayne A. Meeks*, ed. by L. Michael White and O. Larry Yarbrough. Philadelphia: Fortress Press.

"Paul's Self-Sufficiency (Philippians 4:11)." Pp. 813–26 in *Texts and Contexts: The Function of Biblical Texts in Their Textual and Situatice Contexts. Fetschrift for Lars Hartman*, ed. by Tord Fornberg and David Hellholm. Oslo: University of Oslo Press.

"The Graeco-Roman Cultural Context of the New Testament." Pp. 12–26 in Vol. 8 of *The New Interpreter's Bible*, ed. by Leander E. Keck *et al*. Nashville: Abingdon.

1996   "The Christianization of a *Topos*: Luke 12:13–34," *Novum Testamentum* 36:123–35.

"Paul's Self-Sufficiency (Philippians 4:11)." Reprinted: Pp. 125–39 of *Friendship, Flattery, and Frankness of Speech: Studies on Friendship in the New Testament World*, ed. by John T. Fitzgerald. NovTSup 82. Leiden: E.J. Brill.

1998   "Conversion to Paul's Gospel." Pp. 30–44 in *The Early Church in Its Context. Essays in Honor of Everett Ferguson*, ed. by Abraham J. Malherbe *et al*. Leiden: E.J. Brill.

1999   "The Apostle Paul as a Pastor." Pp. 97–139 in *Jesus, John and Paul*, ed. by LO Lung-kwong. Chuen King Lecture Series 1. Hong Kong: Theology Division, Chung Chi College, Chinese University of Hong Kong.

"Anti-Epicurean Rhetoric in 1 Thessalonians." In *Text und Geschichte: Facetten theologischen Arbeitens aus dem Freundes- und Schülerkreis Dieter Lührmann zum 60. Geburtstag*, ed. by Stefan Maser and Egbert Schlarb. Marburger Theologische Studien 50. Marburg: Elwart Verlag.

PART I

ΓΡΑΦΟΣ

Graphos

THE ΘΕΙΑ ΦΥΣΙΣ OF HIPPOCRATES
AND OF OTHER "DIVINE MEN"

Dieter Zeller

A Neglected Aspect in Recent Research[1]

In the early decades of the Twentieth century the figure of the θεῖος ἀνήρ or "divine man" was a favorite category among many New Testament scholars for classifying depictions of Jesus and understanding the early development of christology. Arising out of the *Religionsgeschichtliche Schule* (or "History of Religions School") it was proposed that Jesus was portrayed according to an established category of "divine man" well known in the larger Graeco-Roman world. In recent decades of scholarship, however, this assumption has received several heavy blows and, as a result, declined in popularity.[2] There are several reasons for this decline.

To begin with, the attributes and functions thought to be characteristic of the "divine man" figures from antiquity varied by epoch and cultural milieu to such a degree that the root form θεῖος ἀνήρ ceased to be a phenomenologically useful category.[3] Hellenistic Judaism, once regarded as a mediator between the pagan world and the New Testament, was said to ignore the concept because it was foreign to biblical thinking. Some scholars preferred to explain the gospel narratives

---

[1] For revising my manuscript I am much indebted to John T. Fitzgerald and L. Michael White. The latter also supplied much of the Greek text for the primary source quotations and contributed some useful additional footnotes (nn. 16, 20, 39, 44, 45, 53, 54, 80, 85, and 91).

[2] For a review of the most important literature see my article "Mensch, göttlicher," *Neues Bibellexikon* 2 (1995) 764–5. The history of investigation is resumed by E. Koskenniemi, *Apollonios von Tyana in der neutestamentlichen Exegese* (WUNT 2.61; Tübingen: Mohr, 1994) 64–164 and by D. S. du Toit, *Theios Anthropos* (WUNT 2.91; Tübingen: Mohr, 1997) 2–39. See also A. Pilgaard, "The Hellenistic *Theios Aner*—A Model for Early Christian Christology?" *The New Testament and Hellenistic Judaism*, ed. P. Borgen and S. Giversen (Aarhus: Aarhus University Press, 1995) 101–122.

[3] G. P. Corrington, *The "Divine Man"* (AUS 7.17; New York, Bern, Frankfurt/M.: Lang, 1986) tried to save a homogenous phenotype, but could do so only with the help of a concept of δύναμις ("power") shining in various colours.

through Old Testament or Jewish models rather than appeal to a concept that does not explicitly appear in the New Testament.

The protests of classical philologists were even more weighty.[4] They denied that the term θεῖος (the adjective "divine" derived from θεός, the noun "god") signified in Greek literature what New Testament exegetes had regularly associated with it, i.e., the divinity or divine origins of the person so identified. They showed, moreover, that the term is barely connected with the title "Son of God;" it does not necessarily include miraculous activity; and in pre-Christian times θεῖος ἀνήρ does not seem to be used as a *terminus technicus*. At the center of this discussion lay *The Life of Apollonius of Tyana* by Philostratus, from the early third century CE, the principal pagan exponent of the so-called "divine man" biography. Most recently, E. Koskenniemi has called further attention to difficulties in citing Philostratus' work as a source for the "typical" usage in the first century CE. Consequently he has called into question the postulation of H. D. Betz regarding miracle-working philosophers as a common phenotype in the earlier period.[5]

It is true that some scholars have continued to use the term conventionally.[6] "But," as A. Pilgaard rightly remarks, "one still has to ask if the term would not have occured more often if it expressed a well known category. More important, however, is the question whether a specific semantic content ... has determined the definition of the scientific term *theios aner* in an inappropriate way."[7] The recent dissertation of D. S. du Toit now concentrates on this very issue, namely, the semantic task. He wants to elucidate the use of θεῖος ἄνθρωπος ("divine human") and correlated notions, e.g., θεσπέσιος and δαιμόνιος, in imperial times.[8] His statement of the problem and the formulation of his results are determined by the situation in New Testament research. Du

---

[4] See esp. W. von Martitz, "υἱός, κτλ A," *TWNT* 8.335–340, 337–339; du Toit (*Theios Anthropos*, 2–3) uses this article as his starting point.

[5] Koskenniemi, *Apollonios von Tyana*, 233–5; cf. his article "Apollonius of Tyana: A Typical ΘΕΙΟΣ ΑΝΗΡ?" *JBL* 117 (1998) 455–67.

[6] So B. Kollmann, *Jesus und die Christen als Wundertäter* (FRLANT 170; Göttingen: Vandenhoeck & Ruprecht, 1996) 89–115. After a short sketch of the debate, he takes θεῖος ἀνήρ as "Sammelbezeichnung für antike Wundertäter mit übernatürlichem oder göttlichem Status" (58–9: "A collective designation for ancient wonderworkers with supernatural or divine status"). That is exactly the meaning denied in recent investigation.

[7] "The Hellenistic *Theios Aner*," 103.

[8] Cited in n. 2 above. See also my review of this work in *TLZ* 123 (1998) 62–64. The Greek term θεσπέσιος literally means "divinely-sounding" (LSJ) and δαιμόνιος is derived from δαίμων, originally a synonym for θεός ("god").

Toit emphasizes that this terminology is never used for "Gottmenschen oder Göttersöhne,"[9] and that it is missing in the context of divinization and religious veneration. He concludes, therefore, that it does not have an ontological meaning, and that it is generally lacking in passages with miracle traditions.[10]

Also du Toit states his thesis in useful linguistic concepts. Following J. Lyons he distinguishes two classes of adjectives:

(I) Adjectives of quality (or, as I would say, accidental qualities).
(II) Adjectives that denote essential proprieties, which are divided into two subcategories:
    (a) those that assign something to such a class (*adskriptives Klassen-adjektiv*, "ascriptive adjective of class"), or
    (b) those that merely put something in relation to such a class, where these may designate either:
        (1) an active relation to the class (modifier in an objective sense), or
        (2) a passive relation (modifier in a subjective sense).

As a result du Toit affirms that θεῖος ἄνθρωπος or similar expressions in the period under observation almost never function as adjectives that ascribe someone to the class of the gods (category II.a above).[11] Instead, it typically signifies a religious-ethical quality or is applied in an epistemological context to "archegetes" (or founding figures) of knowledge, its sense vacillating between an adjective of quality (category I) and an adjective indicating a passive relation to the gods (e.g. "inspired by the gods," so category II.b.2). This latter type of reference may even constitute technical language ("*phrasales Lexem*").

Certainly, du Toit's work produces some fine analyses and impressive results, but unfortunately, as I have shown in my review,[12] his strictly

---

[9] "God-man" and "Son of God;" because the former term is a Christian coinage, we can pass over it.

[10] du Toit, *Theios Anthropos*, 402.

[11] Except for some ironic uses; so du Toit, *Theios Anthropos*, 195, 272–3. Here one must ask whether the term is applied as univocally as du Toit seems to presuppose. Rather, I would suggest that the adjective is sometimes attributed in an analogous manner, such as when, for example, one applies "male" and "female" to blossoms (*männliche und weibliche Blüten*, an attribution apparently not so typical in English, which may use "staminate" and "pistillate" respectively) according to their biological function. Only this analogous usage does justice to the intermediate position of the "divine man" between gods and humans.

[12] See n. 8 above.

synchronic point of view—with the exception of two excurses—veils
the fact that the language of the imperial period is stamped by Homer
and Plato. Thus, du Toit overlooks a category of traditionally so-called
"divine men"—the oracles or mantic prophets (μάντεις).[13] Their knowledge was not transmitted in the same way that founders of either philosophical schools or scientific disciplines inaugurate a *Wissenstradition* or
"school of thought;" therefore, it is unwise to subsume them under
the category "*archegetes* of knowledge." Like the poets, prophets sometimes are said to owe their ability to foresee the future to their θεῖα
φύσις ("divine nature"). Consequently, it is a regrettable weakness of du
Toit's endeavor that he does not take into consideration this expression,
which may conceal the characteristic feature of the Hellenistic concept
of "divine men." The work of du Toit thus needs to be supplemented
by a further investigation of this important, but largely neglected, concept of "divine nature," as we shall see in the course of this study.

Θεῖα Φύσις: From God-given Faculty to God-like Nature

At first glance θεῖα φύσις seems to comprise an "ontological" meaning,
if their "divine nature" distinguishes such men from ordinary humans.
A survey of the usage of the term in Greek literature will show that
originally this was not the case, but that in imperial times such an
understanding began to lurk behind the term.[14]

Classical Greek Writers[15]

Let us begin with the Boeotian poet Pindar (518–438 BCE), the first to
use not only the word φύσις but also the verb φῦναι and the noun φυά

---

[13] Cf. the seer Teiresias in Sophocles, *OT* 298; the Cretan Epimenides, who (according to Plato, *Leg.* 1.642D) was a θεῖος ἀνήρ performing sacrifices and giving oracles
of salvation to the Athenians; and generally Plato, *Meno.* 99C: χρησμῳδοὶ καὶ μάντεις
alongside of the poets; Pythagoras following Hermippos in Diogenes Laertius, *Vit. phil.*
8.41 (allegedly staying in the underworld, he knew the things happening on earth;
therefore, the Italians looked on him as "divine"—here we even have the predicate
θεῖός τις), not to mention the evidence in imperial times.

[14] Here I want to modify a precipitate sentence in my review (*TLZ* 123:63) where
I said too sweepingly that participation in "divine nature" indicates ascription to the
class of gods.

[15] For the following cf. O. Thimme, Φύσις, Τρόπος, Ἦθος (Diss. Göttingen, 1935,
printed Quakenbrück, without date); W. Marg, *Der Charakter in der Sprache der frühgriechi-
schen Dichtung* (Kieler Arbeiten zur Klassischen Philologie 1; Würzburg: Triltsch, 1938)

in a significant way.[16] In his hymns of triumph he praises victorious men
on the basis of their heroic past and by invoking a god. Thus, man –
hero – god: these are the levels on which he moves (cf. *Olym.* 2.2). These
levels, however, do not remain wholly separated. The beginning of the
sixth Nemean ode marks the unity, but also the difference, between
gods and men:

> But in something we approach nevertheless to the immortals:
> be it through a great spirit, be it through bodily excellence (φύσις)
>
> (*Nem.* 6.4–5).

Athletic constitution as well as spiritual talents are conceived here as
gifts of the gods bestowed on certain men from birth. They enable such
men to godlike achievements (ἀρεταί, cf. *Pyth.* 1.41–2). Beside athletic
achievements it is wisdom and the art of poetry which "grew up" (or
"originated," ἔφυν) from the gods.[17] According to Pindar's first Nemean
ode,

> The origins are laid by the gods together with the superhuman (δαιμό-
> νιος) virtues of that man (*Nem.* 1.8).

Later in the same ode, this god-given disposition (φυά) is divided into
physical power (σθένος) and mind (or reason, φρήν), including the
"inborn capacity to foresee the future" (προιδεῖν συγγενὲς οἷς ἕπεται).[18]
Such an endowment contrasts with the necessity to learn as required of
other mortals.[19]

Whereas in a feudalistic society Pindar wants to legitimate by divine
causality what man possesses by birth, under more democratic circumstances the accent shifts to the actual charisma added to human
nature. Thus, for Plato rather than human wisdom, it is their special
φύσις together with their divine ecstasy (*literally* "enthusiastic state,"

80–99; H. Koester, "φύσις, κτλ.," *TWNT* 9.246–271, 248–250; H. Patzer, *Physis: Grundle-
gung zu einer Geschichte des Wortes* (Sitzungsberichte der Wissenschaftlichen Gesellschaft
der Johann-Wolfgang-Goethe-Universität Frankfurt/Main 30.6; Stuttgart: Steiner,
1993). J. Starr, *Sharers in Divine Nature: 2 Peter 1:4 in Its Hellenistic Context* (ConBNT 33;
Stockholm: Almqvist & Wiksell, 2000) was not yet available to me at the time of writing. All translations from the Greek are those of the author, with the assistance of the
editors, unless otherwise noted.
 [16] The usual translation of φύσις is "nature;" of φῦναι, "to grow up or be by nature;"
and of φυά, "natural capacity."
 [17] Cf. also *Olym.* 9.28–29, 110; 11.10; *Pyth.* 5.25.
 [18] *Nem.* 1.25–8.
 [19] Cf. *Olym.* 2.86–8; 9.100–2; *Nem.* 3.40–3. For the concept of being "self-taught"
(αὐτοδίδακτος) see also below at nn. 82–3.

ἐνθουσιάζοντες)²⁰ that enabled the poets (χρησμῳδοί) and soothsayers
(θεομάντεις) to speak without even knowing (ἴσασιν) what they say (*Apol.*
22C). In his *Meno* Plato further extends the inspiration traditionally
accorded to these "divine" singers and seers to capable politicians
(99CD). Here he perhaps not casually prefers to speak of θεῖα μοῖρα
("divine lot") instead of θεῖα φύσις.²¹ Similarly lawgivers are called θεῖος
because of their being filled with divine inspiration. In the *Laws*, for
example, Lycurgus is described as "some human nature mixed with
some divine power" (φύσις τις ἀνθρωπίνη μεμιγμένη θείᾳ τινὶ δυνάμει).²²
Later on Plato speaks of him as of a "divine being" who delivered his
laws by oracle from a god (Apollo).²³ Thus, the static conception of
an inherent "nature" from earliest childhood on is complemented by a
more dynamic one, the experience of actually being owned by the god.
This notion is familiar to biblical prophets, too, while the former one
seems to be alien to them.

Hellenistic and Imperial Greek Writers

The idea of an ἐνθουσιασμός ("divine possession or inspiration") specific
to poets and prophets continues in Hellenistic and imperial times, and
sometimes is expressed by the possession of a θεῖα φύσις. In this way,
already Democritus (ca. 460 BCE) said of Homer that he could only
erect such a polymorphic building of words because he had "received
a divine nature" (φύσεως λαχὼν θεαζούσης).²⁴ Dio Chrysostom quotes
the passage from Democritus and explains "that without a divine and
superhuman nature (ἄνευ θείας καὶ δαιμονίας φύσεως) it is impossible to
produce verses of such beauty and wisdom."²⁵ Later in the same treatise
on Homer, Dio seems to use "divine inspiration" as the equivalent to
this notion of a divine nature: "Indeed, without divine favour (θεία
τύχης), without inspiration (ἐπίπνοια) of the Muses and Apollo, it is
simply impossible for poetry to be created …"²⁶

---

²⁰ The verb ἐνθουσιάζω is derived from the adjective root ἔνθεος (through the
contract form ἔνθους), meaning "possessed by a god." See also below.
²¹ *Meno* 99E, 100B; cf. *Ion* 534C, 542A with regard to the poets.
²² *Leg.* 3.691E; cf. *Ion* 533D–534C in the context of poetry.
²³ *Leg.* 3.696B: ἃς μὴ τὸ κατ᾽ ἀρχὰς ὑμῖν θεῖον παρὰ θεοῦ διεμαντεύσατό τινος.
²⁴ *Frag.* 68 B 21 in the edition of H. Diels, *Die Fragmente der Vorsokratiker* (ed. W. Kranz;
12th ed.; Zürich- Hildesheim: Weidmann, 1985) II.147.
²⁵ *Or.* 53.1.
²⁶ *Or.* 53.6. Compare *Or.* 36.34; du Toit (*Theios Anthropos*, 157–8) cites only the second
passage.

In other cases simply θειότης ("divinity"), instead of "divine nature," is said to fill the poet-prophet.[27] In such a case, where "human" and "divine" nature are put in contrast, an ontological meaning of θεῖος is undeniable. Yet, the same adjective can be paraphrased as "sent by god;" therefore, in the terminology of du Toit, we have here only a "relational adjective of class in the subjective sense" (category II.b.2). Men with such a divine endowment can be termed "divine by participation and derivation."[28] Such a religious foundation of human "divinity," however, is not as exceptional as du Toit maintains.[29]

It is on the basis of this background that the use of θεῖος in Josephus may be explained. Although as a pious Jew he opposed the divinization of men,[30] he also knows of humans who take part in "divine nature." In his polemic against pagan detractors (*Against Apion*) he quotes a fragment from Manetho (third cent. BCE) purporting to expose the "real" story of Moses and the exodus. According to Manetho's account a key figure in the story was a certain Amenophis, son of Paapis, a seer in the court of the pharaoh who "seemed to partake in divine nature (θείας δὲ δοκοῦντι μετεσχηκέναι φύσεως) according to his wisdom and foreknowlege of the future."[31] It is significant, then, that while Josephus roundly refutes Manetho's account on a variety of "historical" grounds, he does not question the description of the seer's powers or their source, his "divine nature."

---

[27] For example, *POxy.* 1381.164f (hymn on Imuthes-Asklepios). So compare the two versions of the life of Pythagoras: whereas Porphyry, *Vit. Pyth.* 30 says that we can not grasp the harmony of the spheres because of the smallness of our nature, Iamblichus, *Vita Pyth.* 65 stresses the necessity of an ineffable and unthinkable "divinity" to hear it.

[28] Cf. the definition of G.W.H. Lampe, *A Patristic Greek Lexicon* (Oxford: Clarendon, 1961) quoted by du Toit, *Theios Anthropos*, 50 n. 55.

[29] He admits the inspiration-model only for the perspective of Dio Chrysostom; for the bulk of poets or philosophers—according to du Toit—the reason why they are termed θεῖοι is not participation in divine wisdom, but their function as founders of scientific traditions.

[30] In *Ant.* 19.345 he disapproves of flatterers who call Agrippa "god" (θεόν), where they are said to distinguish him in terms of φύσις: "Though until now we feared you as man, now we confess you as one of more than mortal nature (κρείττονά σε θνητῆς φύσεως)." Cf. Philo, *Leg. ad Gaium* 367: Jewish people do not want to believe that Caligula has inherited the nature of a god.

[31] *Contra Apionem* 1.232 Here C. R. Holladay, *"Theios Aner" in Hellenistic Judaism* (SBLDS 40; Missoula: Scholars Press, 1977) 62 even grants an ontological nuance; so compare 59–61 on the signification of θεῖος in Josephus. Heliodorus, *Aeth.* 3.16.4 offers a close parallel: here the astrological wisdom of Egyptian prophets is said to "deal with the gods" and to "take part in the nature of the stronger ones," that is to say, in the immortality of the divinized celestial bodies.

Similarly, Josephus describes the attitude of Herod towards some prophesying Essenes; the king is said to have "thought something greater about them than is worth saying according to their mortal nature (μεῖζόν τι φρονῶν ἐπ' αὐτοῖς ἢ κατὰ τὴν θνητὴν φύσιν εἰπεῖν ἄξιον)."[32] Thus Josephus introduces one of the Essenes, a certain Manaem who was famed for his ability to foretell the future.[33] It was this Manaem that had predicted Herod's future kingship while he was still only a boy. In the end Josephus interprets Manaem's foreknowledge of the future to be the result of these people having "an empirical knowledge of divine things (τῆς τῶν θείων ἐμπειρίας)" which is rooted in their virtue (καλοκαγαθίας).[34] Josephus also implies in this passage that such attributes are not uncommon among the Jews because of their reverence for God. Thus it was also for Daniel, who earned the fame of θειότης ("divinity") even among the Persians, whose *magi* were legendary, because his foretellings proved true.[35]

Is this merely to be construed as pagan language taken over by Josephus and hence typical of the Egyptian Manetho, the half-heathen Herod, and the Persian crowd? I do not think so, because Josephus elsewhere without any scruples gives to the Jewish prophets the same attribute, θεῖος.[36] A. Schlatter rightly takes this as parallel to ἔνθεος.[37] Though one should not "overload the term with metaphysical connotations," as du Toit argues,[38] one should not overlook the fact that such a participation in divinity was recognized among the Jews and inspired religious awe or wonder (θαῦμα).

---

[32] *Ant.* 15.372.

[33] *Ant.* 15.371–79. The opening in 371–2 together with 379 constitutes the redactional, generalizing frame of the particular episode with Manaem; it shows why Herod held the Essenes in esteem and granted them certain exemptions (so note the *inclusio* at 378 *fin*).

[34] *Ant.* 15.379; cf. 373.

[35] *Ant.* 10.268.

[36] *Ant.* 8.243; 10.35; cf. 18.64 where it occurs in the disputed *testimonium Flavianum*, too.

[37] *Die Theologie des Judentums nach dem Bericht des Josefus* (BFCT 26; Gütersloh: Bertelsmann, 1932) 58–60. For ἔνθεος see also n. 20 above. Du Toit (*Theios Anthropos*, 383–6), who does not take the φύσις passages into account, pleads for the meaning "sent by God" here. Cf. now du Toit's recent study, "Die Verwendung von θεῖος als Attribut für Menschen in den Schriften des Flavius Josephus," in *Internationales Josephus-Kolloquium Brüssel 1998*, ed. J. U. Kalms and F. Siegert, (Münsteraner Judaistische Studien, 4; Münster: LIT, 1999) 53–93, which, however, came to my attention too late to be used for this study.

[38] *Theios Anthropos*, 385–6.

Such is the case with Josephus' treatment of Moses, too. Not only did the Egyptians "consider him a wonderful and divine man (τὸν ἄνδρα θαυμαστὸν μὲν ... καὶ θεῖον νομίζουσι),"[39] so also does Josephus himself. In a passage where he refutes the charge of impiety attributed to himself and other Jews—because they do not properly reverence the gods— he shows the Mosaic cultic institutions to be symbols of reverence to the divine realm, i.e., the same elements identified by the Greeks with the Olympian deities. Thus, Josephus wants to compel those doubting his piety to acknowledge "that our lawgiver truly is a θεῖος ἀνήρ."[40] In his discussion of both passages, Du Toit argues that Moses is seen here merely as guarantor of transmitted knowledge.[41] But I think that he is seen more easily in Platonic tradition as divinely inspired lawgiver.

The sense of the often-discussed latter passage is elucidated by another passage not mentioned by du Toit: "Thus, the legislation which seemed to be from God (νομοθεσία τοῦ θεοῦ) led the man [Moses] to be reckoned higher than his own nature (τὸν ἄνδρα πεποίηκε τῆς αὐτοῦ φύσεως κρείττονα νομίζεσθαι)."[42] With this phrasing, "a nature higher than his own," Josephus adopts a Hellenistic concept, but he interprets it as indicating the divine origin of the Law—in the same way that the laws of Lycurgus via the Pythia were said go back to Apollo.[43] Therefore, an ontological meaning of θεῖος ἀνήρ should not be denied, as the synonym "of higher nature" makes evident. Similarly, in a closely related passage, the authority of the Jewish Law, even for non-Jews, is expressed as the "superhuman power (τῆς ὑπὲρ ἄνθρω- πόν ἐστι δυνάμεως)" of Moses which is demonstrated by "many other proofs" (τεκμήρια).[44]

That Josephus' formulation regarding "a higher nature" indicates a state between god and humans, becomes clear from two passages of Plutarch. In his *Life of Alexander* a eunuch consoles the vanquished Darius by reminding him to think of it as being conquered "by a

---

[39] So *Contra Ap.* 1.279. Note here that Josephus actually uses the term ἀνὴρ θεῖος. For the response of "wonder" or awe, see also below at n. 45. It should be noted that the root noun θαῦμα can mean either the reaction of awe or that which causes the awe, i.e., a miracle. Thus, in such cases it is too simplistic to say that the "divine man" terminology is not accompanied by miracles. So see also n. 44 below.

[40] *Ant.* 3.180.

[41] *Theîos Anthropos*, 392, 395.

[42] *Ant.* 3.320. Cf. n. 45 below.

[43] Cf. *Contra Ap.* 2.162-3.

[44] So *Ant.* 3.317-9, the phrase "superhuman power" is from 318. For τεκμήρια signi- fying miraculous demonstrations, in a very similar construction, compare Acts 1:3.

man of higher than human nature (ὑπ' ἀνδρὸς ἡττῆσθαι κρείττονος ἢ
κατὰ τὴν ἀνθρωπίνην φύσιν)" who can only inspire wonder (ἀλλὰ καὶ
θαυμάζειν).[45] Plutarch attributes similar qualities to the Spartan king
Cleomenes III (ca. 260–219 BCE) whose exploits as a Greek nation-
alist during the period of the Hellenistic monarchies were legendary.
His death at the hands of Ptolemy IV Philopator gave rise to commemorations both in his native Sparta and in Alexandria which are the
occasions for Plutarch's comments on his nature. First, after his death
the appearance of a snake on the impaled corpse aroused religious awe
and fear (δεισιδαιμονία ... καὶ φοβός) on the part of Ptolemy, "as if a
man dear to the gods and of higher nature had passed away (ὡς ἀνδρὸς
ἀνῃρημένου θεοφιλοῦς καὶ κρείττονος τὴν φύσιν.)."[46] In turn the people
of Alexandria frequented (φοιτῶντες) the place of his death and suppli-
cated (προσετρέποντο) Kleomenes, addressing him as "hero and son of
the Gods (ἥρωα τὸν Κλεομένη καὶ θεῶν παῖδα προσαγορεύοντες)."[47]

To be sure Plutarch himself treats some of this as superstition, but
he sees in the affair a proof of Cleomenes' abiding virtue.[48] Likewise
Plutarch in other instances follows the Platonic definition of θεῖος and
uses the word with a moral signification. For example, at the end of
the comparison between Kimon and Lucullus, he says that the gods
testified to both of them being "good and divine with regard to their
φύσις."[49] In this instance, φύσις means "character." On this philosophical level, θεῖος denotes a religious-moral quality, as du Toit has shown.[50]
But even so, such men are exalted beyond human measure.[51]

---

[45] *Alex.* 30.10 (in the Teubner ed. of Ziegler, = 30.5 in the LCL ed. of Perrin).
Compare the similar wording in Josephus, *Contra Ap.* 1.279 (n. 39 above); *Ant.* 3.320
(n. 42 above); and 19.345 (n. 30 above). Also in Plutarch, cf. next note.

[46] *Cleom.* 39.2–3 (Ziegler ed., = 39.2, Perrin ed.).

[47] *Ibid.*, 39.4 (Ziegler ed., = 39.2, Perrin ed.).

[48] *Ibid.*, 39.1 (Ziegler ed., = 39.1 Perrin ed.).

[49] *Luc.* 46; compare already Plato, *Rep.* 366C; for a similar use of the τὴν φύσιν as an
accusative of respect see Musonius, *Frag.* 17; Apollonius, *Ep.* 17; Lucian, *Alex.* 61 (here of
Epicurus).

[50] When a Stoic source declares the wise man alone priest, because he is "inside
of the divine nature" (*Stob.* 2.67–8), this could simply mean that he is "at home with
religious things." But the parallel in Diogenes Laertius, *Vit. phil.* 7.119 says that wise
men are "divine, because they have, so to speak, god in themselves." Therefore, one
could surmise that he also takes part in "divine nature" through reason. Cf. *Theios
Anthropos*, 82 n. 73, 85–6.

[51] So compare two passages of Aelius Aristides. In his *Panathenaic Oration* (*Or.* 13.174.
10–11; ed. Dindorf I:285), delivered in 155 CE, he extols an action which exhibits
the admirable character of the Athenians "and should be regarded as greater than
human behavior." So also Aristides in another speech, entitled *Against Leptines on behalf*

Philostratus Reconsidered

With this background of usage among Hellenistic and Imperial writers, the important case of Philostratus' *Life of Apollonius of Tyana*, often thought of as the quintessential "divine man" biography, may now be evaluated more closely. In his biography Philostratus wants to explicate the reasons why the famous Apollonius of Tyana won the reputation of being "supernatural and divine" (δαιμόνιος τε καὶ θεῖος).[52] This claim already precedes him, probably because of his miraculous feats. In general, however, Philostratus subsumes Apollonius' healing powers to his superior "foresight" (called both πρόγνωσις and μαντική), which itself is anchored in his extraordinary purity of heart and a soul filled with an exceptional quantity of aether. He maintains that people who enjoy mantic faculties "become divine on this basis and bring about salvation of humans" (θεῖοί τε ὑπ' αὐτῆς γίγνονται καὶ πρὸς σωτηρίαν ἀνθρώπων πράττουσι).[53]

It is true that Philostratus ascribes such a "participation in divinity" in principle to every noble human (τοὺς ἀγαθοὺς τῶν ἀνθρώπων θεοῦ τι ἔχειν); however, he asserts that, since the cosmos is in disorder, it "needs a man made in likeness to god" (ἀνδρὸς δεῖσθαι θεῷ εἰκασμένου), or, as he continues, "it needs a man who will administer the cosmos that pertains to them [the human souls], who because of his wisdom comes to be a god" (ἀνδρός, ὃς ἐπιμελήσεται τοῦ περὶ αὐτάς κόσμου, θεὸς ὑπὸ σοφίας ἥκων).[54] In this light we may now reconsider the crucial passage *Vit. Apol.* 7.38. While in prison and before the eyes of his

---

of Exemptions (the title taken from Demosthenes *Or.* 20) and delivered presumably on the same visit as the *Panathenaic Oration* (or during his earlier school days) praises the Athenians since through their virtues they seem to be beyond human nature (*Or.* 54.152.8; ed. Dindorf II:696). A similar quality is extolled by Dionysius of Halicarnassus concerning the founder of Rome, who says that Numa "ordered that Romulus himself, as one who had shown a greatness beyond mortal nature, should be honoured under the name of Quirinus" (*Ant. Rom.* 2.63.3).

[52] *Vita Apol.* 1.2.

[53] For this combination of attributes, see esp. *Vit. Apol.* 3.42; cf. the related apologetic passage in 8.7.7–9 (also discussed below). Here θεῖος—*pace* du Toit (*Theios Anthropos*, 302)—is not synonymous with ἀγαθός (meaning "good" or "noble") since it is contrasted with the state of "humans." Instead, as the passage continues, such men are said to be "blessed with the same mysterious power as Apollo," in their euergetic function. The speaker, an Indian sage, perceives Apollonius to possess these qualities because he has "so much aether in [his] soul," and finally concludes that indeed Apollonius is "something δαιμόνιον" (3.43).

[54] *Vit. Apol.* 8.7.7. The final phrase follows the translation of du Toit (*Theios Anthropos*,

beloved disciple Damis, Apollonius miraculously removes his feet from their shackles and then replaces them. Damis confesses that "only at this moment did he accurately comprehend the nature of Apollonius, that it was divine and superior to that of a human" (τότε πρῶτον ... ἀκριβῶς ξυνεῖναι τῆς Ἀπολλωνίου φύσεως, ὅτι θεία τε εἴη καὶ κρείττων ἀνθρώπου).

Du Toit takes Apollonius' statement while removing the shackles, "I'll give you proof of my own freedom," not as a miracle, but merely as a prediction that he will be freed the same day.[55] But the disclosure for Damis happens while they are still in prison and before such a prediction could prove true. Thus, what opens Damis' eyes is the miraculous feat with the shackles. This miracle thus reveals the sovereignty of the philosopher above the situation (ἐφ' ἑαυτῷ εἶναι) due to his superhuman wisdom, as it appears later in the flashback of Damis (Vit. Apol. 8.13). Afterward while on trial he suddenly disappears out of the court, thereby demonstrating that he cannot be kept against his will; because of this fact, the emperor should not ignore his "nature."[56] Thus, even with a moral foundation the "divinity" of Apollonius does not exclude miracles; on the contrary, they conspicuously reveal his superiority in comparison with the rest of mankind. Expressed with the term θεῖα φύσις ("divine nature"), it certainly has an ontological ring, one which is not simply introduced into the discussion by Christian readers such as Eusebius.[57] So we note in another work where Philostratus says of Apollonius, that in wisdom he surpassed human nature.[58]

---

298); however, it may also be translated "since by virtue of wisdom he comes as a god." F.C. Conybeare (in the LCL edition) translates: "a god sent by wisdom."

[55] Theios Anthropos, 309–12. Similarly for θεσπέσιος (in 8.13) du Toit admits only a use as adjective of quality.

[56] Vit. Apol. 8.5. This phrase is not translated by V. Mumprecht in her edition of Philostratos (Sammlung Tusculum; München-Zürich: Artemis, 1983).

[57] As du Toit (Theios Anthropos, 318) asserts. He admits an ontological reading of Philostratus among pagan writers only in Eunapius (319). But his characterization of Apollonius as "something between the gods and men" (Eunapius, Vit. soph. 454) is inspired by what Aristotle said with regard to Pythagoras (cf. Iamblichus, Vita Pyth. 31). In all the inflationary and superlative use of θεῖος by the Neoplatonists one cannot overlook the fact that the philophers are thereby raised above human nature. So compare Eunapius, Vit. soph. 491–2: Prohairesius, who after a declamation is acknowledged as "god" by everybody, is said to have been in all respects "beyond the measure of man;" he entirely "surpassed the ordinary human type (φύσιν);" in 491 Eunapius also speaks of his "genius" (φύσις).

[58] Vit. soph. 521: ὑπερενεγκὼν σοφίᾳ τὴν ἀνθρωπίνην φύσιν.

As we have seen in previous writers, the term θεῖα φύσις does not necessarily indicate divine descent; however, in the case of Apollonius such a notion clearly goes along with it.[59] Another passage from Philostratus, this time in his *Lives of the Sophists*, shows a comparable usage in reference to the giant Agathion from Boeotia. The context is the career and achievements of the Athenian orator and benefactor Herodes Atticus.[60] Agathion was a favorite of Herodes, who came to be known far and wide as "Herodes' Heracles." Herodes had heard Agathion say that his father was the rustic hero Marathon;[61] from such an origin corresponding deeds are to be expected. Because of his knowledge of hidden things Herodes recognized, "that there was a superhuman aura (δαιμονία φύσις) about him."[62]

In these texts, therefore, origin from a god, or at least a hero, and miraculous faculties are connected. The later "divine man" biographies of Pythagoras also incorporate such features. For example, the historian Aelian, a contemporary of Philostratus, provides the following headline for a traditional series of Pythagorean miracles: "Pythagoras taught the people that he was born out of higher semen than corresponding to mortal nature."[63] This formulation may even go back to Aristotle or Theopompus; thus, generation by a god entails a superhuman constitution. This view is also presupposed by Aelius Aristides in his praise of Heracles:

> And it is no wonder that he has so far surpassed human nature, whose father is the first of beings ... So concerned was his father in the matter of his procreation that they say that he slept with her for three days and nights in a row, since he wished to infuse into his offspring the largest and purest possible amount of his nature.[64]

---

[59] So see *Vit. Apol.* 1.6. How important physical descent can be for "divinity" on a lower level is evident in Philostratus, *Vita soph.* 570. There a woman is said to have had intercourse with Apollonius "because of her desire for noble offspring, since he was more divine than ordinary man." Philostratus disclaims this because it contradicts his ascetic image of Apollonius.

[60] *Vit. soph.* 552.

[61] *Ibid.*, 553.

[62] *Ibid.*, 554.

[63] *Var. hist.* 4.17.

[64] *Or.* 5.31.13 (ed. Dindorf I:51). The translation is that of C. A. Behr. In the whole oration Aristides wants to establish the divinity of the hero whose φύσις is above human condition (cf. 33.3–5, ed. Dindorf I:56). For similar claims, compare the prophecy of Tanaquil that a dynasty generated from the royal hearth will be stronger than human nature (Dionysius of Halicarnassus, *Ant. Rom.* 4.2.2).

To return to Apollonius of Tyana: these examples may have shown that his alleged origin from Zeus and his miraculous actions are correlated to his "divine nature," although Philostratus does not attach much importance to them.[65]

A New Semantic Development

Let us summarize our results thus far. In our earliest texts θεῖα φύσις means the inherited constitution granted by the gods to only a few humans; it makes possible exceptional endeavors. It can be combined with actual inspiration. This kind of person is called "divine" because his achievements presuppose an endowment which exceeds human powers. Hence it not only originates from the gods; rather, it also suggests—at least in texts of the imperial era—a divine nature of such men.[66] Philosophers such as Plato and Plutarch, as well as writers like Josephus and Philostratus, try to correct this traditional image of the θεῖος ἀνήρ by affirming that true participation in divinity consists in piety and virtue. Thus, φύσις acquires the meaning of "character." But even in Philostratus and later Neoplatonic writers the ontological meaning is inherent, as the occasional contrast with "human nature" makes clear. Consequently, I think we should differentiate the *denotation* of a term from the reason why it is applied to certain subjects. This distinction will become apparent in the following example.

The Case of the "Divine" Hippocrates

I wish now to illustrate the semantic content of θεῖος in the early imperial period by a little-known text dealing with Hippocrates, the founder of medicine.[67] The text that concerns us here is a kind of encomium found as the second letter in a pseudepigrafic collection of letters under the name of Hippocrates.[68]

---

[65] Cf *Vit. Apol.* 1.4–6.
[66] Cf. on the level of magic, *PGM* IV.220: Through the encounter with the god the magician has acquired a "godlike nature" (ἰσόθεος φύσις).
[67] This text is not known to du Toit, but was mentioned in passing by L. Bieler, *ΘΕΙΟΣ ANHP* (Wien: Oskar Höfels, 1935/6; repr. Darmstadt: Wissenschaftliche Buchgesellschaft, 1967) 16 n. 16.
[68] See the recent edition by W. D. Smith, *Hippocrates: Pseudepigraphic Writings* (Studies in Ancient Medicine 2; Leiden: Brill, 1990) from which I have taken both text and translation used here. However, for the text, the edition of D. T. Sakalis, Ἱπποκράτους Ἐπιστολαί (Ἰωάννινα: Panepistemio Ioanninon, 1989) should be compared.

The Pseudo-Hippocratic Letters

The entire series of letters constitutes a kind of Hippocrates-romance and knits together two basic plots: (1) The Persian king Artaxerxes (which one is not clear) summons Hippocrates; the latter, however refuses to help the enemy of Greece, despite a sizable remuneration (*Letters* 3–9). (2) The people of Abdera call for Hippocrates, because their compatriot Democritus seems have gone mad; again the physician refuses, having come to the conclusion that it is not the philosopher, but the Abderites themselves who are mad (*Letters* 10–21 with 23 as appendix). The two plots are made to interact in *Letter* 11, showing further the symmetrical nature of the composition.

Since parts of the corpus have been preserved in early papyrus copies, a date of origin before Claudius is plausible; there are also indications of at least one prior revision of the text.[69] As a result, the first two letters now form a prelude to the first plot; they clarify how "the fame of the science of the physician Hippocrates of Cos, descendant of Asclepius, has reached even" the Persian King of Kings (so *Let.* 3). *Let.* 1 and 2 are thus addressed as an exchange, between Artaxerxes and a certain physician[70] named Petos or Paitos.[71] It is this Paitos who recommends the "famous Hippocrates" to come to the aid of Artaxerxes.

The name of Paitos is also important to the dating of the romance in its present form. It is the hellenized form of the Latin *Paetus*, a well-known Roman family. Like other names in the correspondence, it might be an actual allusion. Depending on the identification of this Paitos the introduction (*Letters* 1–2) is ascribed to different early editions of the romance: R. Philippson thinks the addressee was a friend of Cicero, the Epicurean Papirius Paetus; therefore, *Let.* 1–2 would have

---

[69] On the development of the ms. tradition beginning in antiquity, see Smith, *Hippocrates: Pseudepigraphic Writings*, 35–43.

[70] This is evident from *Letter* 1, even if σου (line 4) is omitted in some mss.

[71] D. T. Sakalis, "Beiträge zu den pseudo-hippokratischen Briefen," *Formes de pensée dans la collection hippocratique*, ed. F. Lasserre – Ph. Mudry (Genève: Droz, 1983) 499–514, 504–506 accepts the variant *Petos* as the original since it is represented by older mss. He guesses that this Petos was a Persian or, more likely, an Egyptian physician within reach of the King of Kings. This allows him to plead for the unity of the letter-romance written still in the first cent. BCE. Smith (*Hippocrates: Pseudepigraphic Writings*, 18 n. 50) looks upon this proposal as "eminently reasonable," but considers *Let.* 1 and 2 to be later additions.

been added in a second edition after 44 BCE.[72] H. Diels proposed
Caecus Paetus, a proconsul of Asia, who committed suicide in 42 CE;
therefore, Diels argued that a third edition of the Claudian period was
dedicated to him.[73] Only F. Kudlien takes into account the medical
profession of Paetus and identifies him with the physician known to
us from Lucian's *Alexander* 60; therefore, he proposed that the first two
letters are an addition of the second century CE.[74] It is not possible,
therefore, to say definitively whether *Let.* 2, in which Paitos sings the
praises of Hippocrates as saviour, is early first century or of a slightly
later date. Nonetheless, it constitutes an instructive example of praise
with all the traditional topics required for an encomium.[75] Because this
encomium to Hippocrates is so little known, and because of the key
terms employed within it, we will give the entire text here and then
comment below.[76]

Ps-Hippocrates, *Letter* 2: Text and Translation

(48) 2. Παῖτος βασιλεῖ μεγάλῳ Ἀρταξέρξῃ χαίρειν

Τὰ φυσικὰ βοηθήματα οὐ λύει τὴν ἐπιδημίαν λοιμικοῦ πάθους· ἃ δὲ ἐκ
15 φύσεως γίγνεται νοσήματα, αὐτὴ ἡ φύσις ἰῆται κρίνουσα· ὅσα δὲ ἐξ
ἐπιδημίης, τέχνη τεχνικῶς κρίνουσα τὴν τροπὴν τῶν σωμάτων.
Ἱπποκράτης δὲ ἰητρὸς ἰῆται τοῦτο τὸ πάθος· τῷ γένει μὲν | οὖν ἐστι
Δωριεύς, πόλεως δὲ Κῶ, πατρὸς δὲ Ἡρακλείδα τοῦ Ἱπποκράτους τοῦ
Γνωσιδίκου τοῦ Νέβρου τοῦ Σωστράτου τοῦ Θεοδώρου τοῦ Κλεομυττάδα

---

[72] R. Philippson, "Verfasser und Abfassungszeit der sogenannten Hippokratesbrie-
fe," *RhM* 77 (1928) 293–328, 328.
[73] "Hippokratische Forschungen V," *Hermes* 53 (1918) 57–88; but his presupposition
that the Paetus in the letters is assumed to be a satrap of Asia Minor is probably wrong.
[74] "Paetus 3," *PWSup* 10.473–4. He overlooks the fact that the pestilence described in
Let. 1 is briefly mentioned again in *Let.* 11; see Smith *Hippocrates: Pseudepigraphic Writings*,
19. That *Let.* 1 and 2 are lacking in the papyri and in ms. f is not so important because
these mss. are selective in other places too.
[75] Cf. K. Berger, "Hellenistische Gattungen im Neuen Testament," *ANRW* II.25.2
(1984) 1031–1432, 1173f; M. Valloza, "Enkomion," *Historisches Wörterbuch der Rhetorik*,
ed. G. Ueding (Darmstadt: Wissenschaftliche Buchgesellschaft, 1994) 2.1152–1160; R.
Brucker, '*Christushymnen*' *oder epideiktische Passagen?* (FRLANT 176; Göttingen: Vandenhoeck & Ruprecht, 1997) 110–173. Subsequent to the completion of this article I discovered that the text is partially quoted as illustration of the encomium in Phil 2:6–11 by
K. Berger and C. Colpe, *Religionsgeschichtliches Textbuch zum Neuen Testament* (Göttingen-
Zürich: Vandenhoeck & Ruprecht, 1987) 287; cf. ET by Eugene Boring, *Hellenistic Commentary to the New Testament* (Nashville: Abingdon, 1995) 479.
[76] The text printed here is from Smith, *Hippocrates: Pseudepigraphic Writings*, 48 and 50,
with the translation on 49 and 51. The marginal numbers given here are those of the
page and line number from Smith's text. (See also above n. 68.)

20 τοῦ Κρισάμιδος. οὗτος θείᾳ φύσει κέχρηται καὶ ἐκ μικρῶν καὶ ἰδιωτικῶν
εἰς μεγάλα καὶ τεχνικὰ προήγαγε τὴν ἰητρικήν. Γίνεται μὲν οὖν ὁ θεῖος
Ἱπποκράτης, ἔνατος μὲν ἀπὸ Κρισάμιδος τοῦ βασιλέως, ὀκτωκαιδέκατος δὲ
ἀπὸ Ἀσκληπιοῦ, εἰκοστὸς δὲ ἀπὸ Διός, μητρὸς δὲ Πραξιθέας τῆς
Φαιναρέτης ἐκ τῆς οἰκίας τῶν Ἡρακλειδῶν· ὥστε κατὰ ἀμφότερα τὰ
25 σπέρματα θεῶν ἀπόγονός ἐστιν ὁ θεῖος Ἱπποκράτης, πρὸς μὲν πατρὸς
Ἀσκληπιάδης ὤν, πρὸς δὲ μητρὸς Ἡρακλείδης. ἔμαθε δὲ τὴν τέχνην παρά
τε τῷ πατρὶ Ἡρακλείδῃ καὶ παρὰ τῷ πάππῳ Ἱπποκράτει. ἀλλὰ παρὰ
μὲν τούτοις, ὡς εἰκός, τὰ πρῶτα ἐμυήθη τῆς ἰητρικῆς, ὅσα πιθανὸν ἦν
καὶ τούτους εἰδέναι, τὴν δὲ σύμπασαν τέχνην αὐτὸς ἑωυτὸν ἐδιδάξατο
(50) ἐνθείᾳ φύσει κεχρημένος καὶ τοσοῦτον ὑπερβεβηκὼς τῇ τῆς ψυχῆς
εὐφυΐᾳ τοὺς προγόνους, ὅσον διενήνοχεν αὐτῶν καὶ τῇ τῆς τέχνης
ἀρετῇ. καθαίρει δὲ οὐ θηρίων μὲν γένος, θηριωδῶν δὲ νοσημάτων καὶ
ἀγρίων πολλὴν γῆν καὶ θάλατταν διασπείρων πανταχοῦ ὥσπερ ὁ
5 Τριπτόλεμος τὰ τῆς Δήμητρος σπέρματα, τὰ τοῦ Ἀσκληπιοῦ βοηθήματα.
τοιγαροῦν ἐνδικώτατα καὶ αὐτὸς ἀνιέρευται πολλαχοῦ τῆς γῆς
ἠξίωταί τε τῶν αὐτῶν Ἡρακλεῖ τε καὶ Ἀσκληπιῷ ὑπὸ Ἀθηναίων
δωρεῶν. αὐτὸν μετάπεμψαι κελεύων ἀργύριον καὶ χρυσίον, ὅσον ἂν
βούληται, δώσειν αὐτῷ. οὗτος γὰρ ἐπίσταται οὐχ ἕνα τρόπον τῆς ἰήσιος
10 τοῦ πάθους, οὗτος πατὴρ ὑγείας, οὗτος σωτήρ, οὗτος ἀκεσώδυνος, οὗτος
ἁπλῶς ἡγεμὼν τῆς θεοπρεποῦς ἐπιστήμης. ἔρρωσο.

Translation: Paitus to the Great King Artaxerxes. Greetings.

Natural remedies do not get rid of the visitation of the plague epidemic.
Diseases from nature, nature herself judges (brings to a crisis) and heals.
Those from a visitation the science heals, judging scientifically the alterations of bodies. Hippocrates the physician cures this malady. By family
he is Dorian, of the city Cos, son of Heraclides, son of Hippocrates, son
of Gnosidicus, son of Nebros, son of Sostratus, son of Theodorus, son
of Cleomyttades, son of Crisamis. He has a divine nature, and he has
brought forth the healing science from minor, idiosyncratic activities to
great scientific ones. The divine Hippocrates is eighth, you know, from
King Crisamis, seventeenth from Asclepius, nineteenth from Zeus, and
his mother is Phainete's daughter Praxithea, from the Heraclid house.

Hence, by the seed of both sides, the divine Hippocrates is descended
from gods, from Asclepius by his father, from Heracles by his mother.
He learned the science from his father Heraclides and his grandfather
Hippocrates. It seems likely that he was first initiated by them into the
first mysteries of the science, which it is credible that even they knew, but
he taught the total science to himself employing his divine nature, and
surpassing his forebears in the natural quality of his soul by as much as
he has surpassed them in scientific excellence. He cleanses the earth and
sea over wide areas, not of wild beasts but of beastly wild diseases, and as
Triptolemus sowed everywhere the seeds of Demeter, he sows the cures
of Asclepius.

Whence justly he has been given divine honors widely on earth and is accorded the same gifts as are Heracles and Asclepius by the Athenians. Do send for him; and direct that he be given all the gold and silver that he wants. For he knows not just a single manner of healing the affection, he is the father of health, savior, soother of pain. In short he is leader in the divine science. Be well!

Commentary

For purposes of discussion and analysis we shall now take up some key points within this text in the form of a commentary.

a. γένος (48.17–20): The text presents Hippocrates, his tribe, his native place, his father and his ancestors until the seventh generation. The description that follows in lines 20–21 ("He has a divine endowment, and he has brought forth the healing science from minor idiosyncratic activities to great scientific ones") anticipates both his φύσις and his πράξεις. It is certainly by this achievement, which is mentioned again in the last phrase before the greeting ("In short he is leader in the divine science") that Hippocrates earned from his successors the attribute θεῖος, which appears in 48.21 and 25.[77] But his role as *archegete* does not exhaust the meaning of θεῖος in this text. That this is so becomes clear from the amplification of the divine descent of the "divine Hippocrates" (48.21–26). Here, the paternal line is not only traced back to a mythological king of Cos, but in keeping with the principles of an encomium[78] it is extended to Asclepius. Thus via Apollo, Hippocrates descends from Zeus. The maternal line which now is supplemented shows him an offspring of Heracles.[79] Divine origin—even when far removed—can thus contribute to "divinity."

b. ἀνατροφή and φύσις (48.26–50.2): Though being instructed by both his father and grandfather, only he could teach himself medical

---

[77] More precisely, it is the empiricist wing of medicine in Alexandria (between 225 and 50 BCE) which felt confirmed by the works of Hippocrates. Cf. W. D. Smith, *The Hippocratic Tradition* (Ithaca/London: Cornell UP, 1979) chap. 3; see 87 for Hippocrates as "*archegete*." The earliest preserved commentary (Apollonius of Citium, first cent. BCE) calls him θειότατος (*CMG* 11.1.1; 10.5 [p. 12, lines 2–4]). Cf. O. Temkin, "Hippokrates," *RAC* 15 (1991) 466–481, 468.

[78] Cf. Menander (Spengel 371.1): "You will say that he (the king) originates from the gods."

[79] On the whole this is confirmed by the *Vita Hippocratis* of Soranus 1 (CMG 4.175–178), written ca. 100 CE, though there the name of the mother (Phainarete, here the grandmother) and the number of the generations differ slightly. For the legend of Hippocrates cf. L. Edelstein, "Hippokrates," *PWSup* 6 (1935) 1290–1345, 1292–1305.

art[80] as a scientific system. This became possible because he was gifted with a "divine" or "inspired"[81] φύσις ("nature"), which distinguished him even from his ancestors. This term, which we have already discussed, can be further illuminated by the discussion of the role played in pedagogy by inborn disposition, learning, and training. The αὐτομαθής or αὐτοδίδακτος (both meaning "one self-taught") needs neither teachers nor training because of the talent given him by god.[82] Such a θεῖα φύσις ("divine endowment"), as we have seen, can also be a component of the "divine man," though not always so constitutive as in the case of divine seers and minstrels. It enables such a person to do outstanding feats—here the medical skill of Hippocrates. In the case of Hippocrates, these are not miraculous healings, though amazing diagnostic and prognostic knowledge is ascribed to him elsewhere.[83]

c. πράξεις and τιμαί (50.2–8): As with the "divine men" of the old type (Abaris, Epimenides, Pythagoras) Hippocrates' activity is described as "cleansing" (καθαίρειν). By contrast to Pythagoras[84] or still more his own ancestor Heracles, Hippocrates does not cleanse the land of wild beasts. Rather he rids it of something just as wild and beastly, namely disease.[85] The letter next adduces as σύγκρισις ("comparison")

---

[80] Smith's translation ("initiated into the mysteries of the *science*") here should be noted. The reference in 48.27, however, is to ἰητρική "medicine" or "the medical art," since it typically assumes the designation of medicine as one of the learned "arts" (τέχναι). The term ἰητρική occurs again in this sense at 48.21 along with τέχνη. The terms τέχνη and τεχνικῶς also occur at 48.16, 26, 29; and 50.2, where it too is translated "science;" cf. also *Let.* 3 (50.14–15). Medicine as a τέχνη is frequently listed along with rhetoric and music among the moralist writers. So compare Musonius Rufus, *Frag.* 6; see also the article by Everett Ferguson in this volume. It is also worth noting the use of the verb μυεῖν in this context, and to suggest that it may deserve further investigation. So compare the prayer of Apollonius in the Temple of Asclepius (Philostratus, *Vit. Apol.* 1.11), which likewise suggests connotations of mystery language (so note ἄρρητόν τε καὶ συγγενῆ).

[81] The mss. and the editors vacillate between θεῖα and ἔνθεια. The former is clearly attested in 48.20.

[82] Cf. D. Zeller, *Charis bei Philon und Paulus* (SBS 142; Stuttgart: Kath. Bibelwerk, 1990) 84. The earliest testimony is from Homer, so *Od.* 22.347–8: "God let grow (ἐμφύω) the songs in the mind of the self-made singer." Cf. O. Luschnat, "Autodidaktos—eine Begriffsgeschichte," *ThViat* 8 (1961/2) 157–172.

[83] Cf. Athenodorus quoted by Diogenes Laertius *Vit. phil.* 9.42; Maximus of Tyre *Or.* 13.5 lists Hippocrates together with Pherecydes and Timesias of Clazomenae as ἀνθρώπων ὅσοι δαιμόνιοι who can predict natural phenomena. The passage is missing in du Toit's book.

[84] So Iamblichus, *Vita Pyth.* 142.

[85] This combination of metaphors is also found frequently among the moralists, where vice and passion are regularly depicted both as deadly beasts (θηρία) and as

the famous propagator of civilization, the Attic hero Triptolemus.[86]
Following a conviction widespread at that time, such heroes merited
divine honors. So note that 50.6–8 affirms such honors for Hippocrates
as an established fact:[87] "Whence justly he has been given divine honors
widely on earth and is accorded the same gifts as are Heracles and
Asclepius by the Athenians."

Like these two heroes, Hippocrates in part had a human parentage,
but because of his achievements he attained honors due to the gods.
Historically, this may seem exaggerated,[88] but it is significant for "divine
man" tradition. Like heroes, after death their affinity to the gods is
recognized by cultic veneration.[89] For du Toit this is an important
criterion for an "ontological meaning" of θεῖος, but he does not think
it is typical for the founders of philosophical schools.[90] Yet Hippocrates
here is both archegete and "divine" hero. So, the present text concludes
by bestowing a number of hymnic or aretalogical titles on the Coan
physician ("the father of health, the savior, the soother of pain …").

Conclusions

In the light of our previous discussion of "divine nature" the celebration
of the "divine Hippocrates" in a first century romance warrants the
following conclusions:

---

deadly disease (νόσος); so see *Tabula of Cebes* 19.1–5; 22.2–23.1; 26.2–3 (and further
comments and parallels cited in nn. 64, 66–7, 80, and 82–3 in the edition of Fitzgerald
and White) also Plutarch's *Animine an corporis affect.* (Mor. 501B–502A). For a comparable
combination of elements in medicine see Galen, *De sanitate tuenda* 1.8 (Kuhn ed. VI:40).

[86] How traditional this use of comparisons was can be seen from the glorification of
Epicurus in Lucretius, *De rer. nat.* 5.13–21 (comparing him with Ceres and Liber) and
5.22–54 (with Heracles).

[87] So note the use of the perfect tense (ἠξίωται) in 50.7.

[88] Soranus, *Vita Hippocratis* 3, attests only an heroic sacrifice of the Coans on his
birthday. Lucian, *Philops.* 21 concedes to his statue no more honours than was usual
for deceased; but apparently in the private cult this limit was transgressed. Temkin,
"Hippocrates," 470 underscores the fact that we lack secure testimony for a diffused
cult of Hippocrates invoking him for miraculous healings. Also on the grant of divine
honors to heroes see Smith, *Hippocrates: Pseudepigraphic Writings*, 51 n. 1.

[89] For the "classical" figures, cf. Aristeas of Proconnesus (Pindar in Origen, *Contra
Cels.* 3.26); Hermotimus of Clazomenae (Apollonius., *mir.* 3); Epimenides (Diogenes
Laertius, *Vit. phil.* 1.114); Pythagoras (Porphyry, *Vit. Pyth.* 20). Empedocles already in
his life-time was received as a god (Diels-Kranz, *Die Fragmente der Vorsokratiker* 31 B 112).

[90] Cf. *Theios Anthropos*, 86, 92–3, 294–5; there I miss a feeling for secularized forms of
cult, played down like the adjective, too.

1. It is true θεῖος in the literature of the imperial period often refers to founders of a discipline or a philosophical school. But this reference does not constitute the *denotation* of the adjective. It simply means excellence above the human level. This quality is reflected in the Ps-Hippocrates text in 50.1–2.

2. The achievements which manifest such excellence are seen to vary considerably. They include prophecy, artistic works, wisdom, and virtue as well as miracles. The fixation of New Testament scholars on miracles ends in a bottleneck.

3. In many cases such superhuman activity is grounded in a θεῖα φύσις ("divine endowment"). This Greek conception of a permanent disposition given by the gods from birth seems to be alien to the biblical tradition, in which charismatic figures are, by contrast, overcome by the spirit of God. Of course, there is some point of contact in the idea of inspiration. But biblical tradition more typically conceives of relations (they are "men of God"), while Greek thinking characterizes them as being "of divine kind."[91]

4. Finally, on the semantic level divine origin and religious veneration are not necessarily *denoted* in the attribute θεῖος ("divine"). On the other hand, it is possible to say, at the very least, that both divine origin and veneration can be *connoted* by the epithet θεῖος, as the example of Hippocrates clearly shows.

---

[91] Perhaps the one caveat to suggest here in the biblical tradition is the notion of prophetic calling as being set apart "from my mothers womb" (so Jer 1:4; cf. Gal 1:13). Similarly, the prophet Samuel was dedicated to God before birth (1 Sam 1:19–28) and already experienced his legendary mantic gifts (cf. 9:5–10) and divine calling in childhood (so 3:2–20). Both features are at work in the Lukan birth narrative.

MAKING SCENTS OF PAUL

THE BACKGROUND AND SENSE OF 2 COR 2:14–17

Harold W. Attridge*

Introduction

In 2 Corinthians, Paul's most colorful letter, the apostle deploys an array of evocative sensual images to describe his relationship with God, Christ, and his Corinthian Christians. The series begins with the "thanksgiving" of 2:14–15:[1]

> But thanks be to God, who in Christ always leads us in triumphal procession (θριαμβεύοντι), and through us spreads in every place the fragrance that comes from knowing him (τὴν ὀσμὴν τῆς γνώσεως αὐτοῦ). For we are the aroma (εὐωδία) of Christ to God among those who are being saved and among those who are perishing: to the one a fragrance (ὀσμή) from death to death, to the other a fragrance from life to life (NRSV).

* Participants in the International Meeting of the Society of Biblical Literature in Cracow in the summer of 1998, particularly Heinrich von Staden, Dieter Georgi, and David Balch made helpful suggestions about this paper. The editors of the volume, John Fitzgerald and Michael White, and Yale colleagues Margot Fassler and Adela Yarbro Collins, made several more. If the final paper has a better fragance than its original version, it is largely due to their helpful suggestions and critique.

[1] The unity and integrity of the letter has long been a problem. For a survey of the major positions, see Victor Paul Furnish, *II Corinthians* (AB 32A; Garden City: Doubleday, 1984) 30–48, who favors a two-letter solution: 2 Cor 1–9; 10–13, and Margaret Thrall, *The Second Epistle to the Corinthians* (2 vols.; ICC; Edinburgh: Clark, 1994) 3–49, who favors a three-letter solution: 2 Cor 1–8, 9, 10–13. For a five-part division, Günther Bornkamm, *Der Vorgeschichte des sogennanten zweiten Korintherbriefes* (SHAW 2; Heidelberg: Winter, 1961; repr. in Geschichte und Glaube, Gesammelte Aufsätze [Munich: Kaiser, 1971] 4.162–94; English summary in "The History of the Origin of the So-Called Second Letter to the Corinthians," *NTS* 8 [1962] 258–64), Dieter Georgi, The Opponents of Paul in Second Corinthians (Philadelphia: Fortress, 1986) 9–14; and Hans-Dieter Betz, *2 Corinthians 8 and 9: A Commentary on Two Administrative Letters of the Apostle Paul* (Hermeneia; Philadelphia: Fortress, 1985) 3–36, Margaret M. Mitchell, "Rhetorical Shorthand in Pauline Argumentation," in L. Ann Jervis and Peter Richardson, eds., *Gospel in Paul: Studies on Corinthians, Galatians and Romans for Richard N. Longenecker* (JSNT Sup 108; Sheffield: JSOT Press, 1994) 76 n. 36. For an alternative view, skeptical of partition hypotheses, see Paul Barnett, *The Second Epistle to the Corinthians* (Grand Rapids, MI; Cambridge, UK: Eerdmans, 1997). It matters little for the purposes of this paper whether 2:14–7:4 (with or without 6:14–7:1) is a fragment of a letter or an integral part of a unified composition, 1:1–7:16, which I suspect is the case.

The imagery of these verses has long puzzled commentators. Particularly problematic have been (1) the sense in which Paul intends the language of "triumph," (2) the way in which the olfactory images function, (3) the relationship, if any, between the sensory images and the scene of the "triumph."

It is clear that Paul here begins to reflect on his own apostolic ministry, the vast responsibility of which seems to daunt him. He does so for the purposes that this letter fragment serves: to offer an apology for his position vis-a-vis his Corinthian converts, and to celebrate reconciliation with them after a period of difficulty in their relationship. While Paul's strategy is fairly clear, his tactics are debated. Readings of the passage fall into a spectrum defined at one end by scholars who see a set of perhaps colorful but discrete terms and at the other end those who discern a more or less coherent set of interrelated images.

Atomistic Interpretations of the Imagery

Those who see a set of rather discrete terms and images tend to minimize their metaphorical quality. This minimizing tendency is most clear in the case of θριαμβεύοντι. Most commentators agree that the image of the Roman military triumph, in which a victorious general celebrated a victory by leading captives in parade, is somehow involved. Yet some demur, on various grounds. Typical is G. Dautzenberg in the *Exegetical Dictionary of the New Testament*,[2] who argues that the word has nothing to do with the image of a military procession, but that it simply means "make known," both at 2 Cor 2:14 and Col 2:15, its other occurrence in the NT. His reasons for adopting that interpretation are largely an inability to see how the image of a triumph works, since: (1) the verb θριαμβεύω, if not to be taken in some vague or derived sense, must refer to a Roman military celebration; and (2) while it might be possible to contemplate a vague analogy to a triumph, none of the images that such analogies conjure up seems to work. Thus, he concludes:

> If θριαμβεύω, in 2 Cor 2:14 were alluding to the image of the triumphal procession, the passage would be about a triumphal procession of God through the world, in which (a) Paul or the apostles are led along as defeated enemies (Delling 160; Williamson, 325f.). If one takes the analogy to the Roman triumphal processions—*there are no others* (emphasis

---

[2] G. Dautzenberg, "θριαμβεύω," *EDNT* 2 (1991) 155–56.

mine)– less rigorously, it could also mean that (b) God leads Paul or
the apostles in the triumphal procession in the same way that a general would his officers and soldiers (LSJ 806p for a weakened allusion to
the image of the triumphal procession, H. Lietzmann and W. B. Kümmel, *1–2 Cor.* [HNT] 108, 198; R. Bultmann, *2 Cor.* [Eng. tr., 1985] 63).
The image of the triumphal procession also provides the background for
the translation (c): "allow to triumph": God grants the triumph, and the
apostles are the victors …

Considerations against these interpretations are a) they fit poorly in the
context, in which Paul refers not to his victory through God, but rather
to his role as mediator (→ εὐωδία); there are no uses of the term in Greek
literature corresponding to b) and c) (Williamson 322); in c) the role of
the apostle is overrated. *Moreover, the Greeks used θριαμβεύω to describe actual
triumphal processions; there are no texts indicating a figurative use of the term in NT
times.* (emphasis mine)

Dautzenberg goes on[3] to argue for the meaning of "make known," on
the basis of Ctesias *Persica* 13 (θριαμβεύσας τὸν μάγον᾽ cf. 58)[4] and *BGU*
IV.1061.19, noted long ago by Moulton and Milligan (293), although the
passage in question uses ἐκθριαμβεύω.[5] Accordingly, the image
works as follows:

Because God makes the apostles known, he can spread "the fragrance
of the knowledge of him" through them. The "in Christ" that follows
θριαμβεύοντι ἡμᾶς should express the idea that God makes them known
in their relationship to Christ as proclaimers of the gospel of Christ.

The positive evidence for θριαμβεύω /-ειν meaning "to make known"
is in fact quite weak. Most importantly, neither of the passages cited
by Dautzenberg is incompatible with a metaphorical use of "triumph"
language. In both cases, a colorful term is used to describe a situation
where someone or something is "paraded about."[6] Finally, it is not quite
clear what exactly the "fragrance of the knowledge of him" means on
Dautzenberg's reading.

----

[3] Following Lamar Williamson, Jr., "Led in Triumph: Paul's Use of Thriambeuo,"
Int 22 (1968) 317–32, esp. 320–22,

[4] *BAGD* 363 cites this as an example of "cause to triumph" probably in error. See
below.

[5] καὶ πρὸς τὸ μὴ ἐκθριαμβισθῆναι τὸ πρᾶγμα ἀπελύθησαν. Thrall *(Second Corinthians,*
193 n. 31) also notes Rory B. Egan, "Lexical Evidence on Two Pauline Passages," *NovT*
19 (1977) 34–62, who argues that the clause means "in order that the matter not be
noised abroad."

[6] This is, in effect, the third meaning of the term suggested by *BAGD*, based on
Ctesias, *Persica* 58 which speaks of the exhibition in a public procession of the head and
right hand of a slain enemy.

Others at this end of the spectrum, focusing still on θριαμβεύοντι, find other ways to evacuate the term of its metaphorical content, arguing that it means simply "lead about"[7] or in the stronger sense of "make a show or spectacle of," suggestions which, as various commentators note, have rather weak lexical support.[8] Another way of putting the point would be to recognize that θριαμβεύω and its derivatives have a primary referent in the Roman military parade, but that the term can be used metaphorically in various contexts when something or someone is to be "paraded about" in a triumphal fashion.

Without "triumph" imagery in v. 14 serving as a guide or control over the colorful language that follows, scholars are free to speculate on the readings of the "aroma" imagery of vv. 14b, 15 and 16. Bultmann, for instance, denying any connection with triumphs, finds in the olfactory imagery the general and well-attested notion that deities exude a pleasant aroma.[9] The notion is certainly relevant to "the scent of his knowledge" in 14a, but it is not very helpful with the remaining olfactory images.

Quite far removed from the initial triumphal language is the suggestion that Paul is using sapiential imagery, inspired by Sir 24:15: "Like cassia and camel's thorn I gave forth perfume (ἀρωμάτων ὀσμήν), and like choice myrrh (σμύρνα) I spread my fragrance (εὐωδίαν), like galbanum, onycha, and stacte, and like the odor of incense (λιβάνου ἀτμίς)

---

[7] Theodoret PG 82.389 [?] argued for this meaning: θριαμβεύειν = πάντοτε περιάγειν. Hans Lietzmann, *An die Korinther I, II* (4th ed.; HNT 9; Tübingen: Mohr-Siebeck, 1949) 108, notes that the basic meaning is "lead in triumph," as in Plutarch, *Thesei et Rom comp.* 4 (38D): καὶ βασιλεῖς ἐθριάμβευσε καὶ ἡγεμόνας. Then, for the more general meaning, "lead about," which he favors, he cites Anasts. Sinait. *Hexaemeron* 12, PG 89.1052b; *Vita Amphilochii*, PG 39.25c.

[8] Lietzmann (*An die Kor.*) cites Greg Naz. *Or.* 40.27 (712d). Thrall (*Second Corinthians*, 192–93) discusses the possibility of "make public," "make a show or spectacle of," noting Chrysostom PG 61.429. In favor: ἐκθριαμβεύω is attested in the papyri meaning, [see Moulton and Milligan, cited by Dautzenberg] "to make known" and θρίαμβος in *Acts of Paul and Thecla* means "spectacle." Yet, Thrall argues, ἐκθριαμβεύω does not equal θριαμβεύω and Chrysostom's clarification using φανερός indicates that this meaning of θριαμβεύω is not transparent.

[9] Rudolf Bultmann, *The Second Letter to the Corinthians* (trans. Roy A. Harrisville; Minneapolis: Augsburg, 1985) 64: "the ancient idea that fragrance is a sign of the divine presence and the divine life." Bultmann (68) cites the fragrance of Isis in Plutarch *Isis and Osiris* (357B): καὶ τῷ χρωτὶ θαυμαστὴν εὐωδίαν ἐπιπνέουσαν ἀφ' ἑαυτῆς. Euripides *Hipp.* 1391, 1393; Ovid, *Fasti* 5.376. In general, see Ernst Lohmeyer, *Vom göttlichen Wohlgeruch* (SHAW 9; Heidelberg: Winter, 1919) 4–14 for Graeco-Roman and 25–31 for Jewish instances, including 1 Enoch 24:4–25:6.

in the tent."[10] Such a reading works well for the "scent of his knowledge" of v. 14, which is thus the word of the Gospel that Paul preaches.
It may work for the divisive quality of the scent, noted in v. 16.[11] For further support some scholars appeal to the rabbinic description in *Ta'an*
7a, of the Torah,[12] as a סמ, a drug, that gives life to some and death
to others.[13] While not exactly a fragrance, it at least divides. How to
make sense in that context of the affirmation of 15a, that "we are the
εὐωδία of Christ" remains a mystery, unless Paul is simply and shame-
lessly mixing his metaphors.

Triumphal Interpretations of the Imagery

At the other end of the interpretive spectrum stand those scholars who
see a more or less consistent development of some triumphal imagery
in these verses.[14] But how the image is to work is debated. One reading

---

[10] Cf. also Sir 39:13; 50:15. Lietzmann (*An die Kor.*, 108) doesn't see a connection
with the image of the "triumph." So also Édouard Cothenet, "Parfums," *DBSup* 6
(1960) 1296–1331, esp. 1328–29. Cf. Jean-François Collange, *Enigmes de la deuxieme epitre
de Paul aux Corinthiens: Etude exegetique de 2 Cor 2:14–7:4* (SNTSMS18; Cambridge: Cambridge University Press, 1972) 29–30; Gerhard Delling, "ὀσμή," *TWNT* 5 (1967) 493–95.
Delling (495, n. 1) denies any link with the triumph image: "Nor is there any material
link with θριαμβεύοντι (→ III, 160) in v 14."

[11] As Thrall (*Second Corinthians*, 199) notes: "Perhaps Paul takes up this idea. For him,
the life-giving ὀσμή is the product of the knowledge of God revealed by Christ. This
might fit the ὀσμή ... εἰς ζωήν of v. 16b, but is scarcely compatible with the ὀσμή ἐκ
θανάτου εἰς θάνατον of v. 16a."

[12] For the equation of Torah and Wisdom, cf. Sir 24:23.

[13] *b. Ta'an.* 7a; cf. Str-B. 3.498–99. The case is argued by Thomas W. Manson,
"2 Cor 2:14–17: Suggestions towards an exegesis," in *Studia in honorem J. de Zwaan*, ed.
J. N. Sevenster and W. C. van Unnik (Haarlem: De Ehrem F. Bohn N.V., 1953) 155–62;
cf. also Ceslas Spicq, *Théologie morale du NT* (Paris: Gabalda, 1965) 2.728 n. 3;

[14] Johan Jakob Wettstein, Η ΚΑΙΝΗ ΔΙΑΘΗΚΗ [*Novum Testamentum Graecum*] (2 vols.;
Amsterdam: Ex officina Dommeriana, 1751–52; repr. Graz: Akademische Druck- und
Verlagsanstalt, 1962) 2:181–82, and H. A. W. Meyer, *Critical and Exegetical Handbook to the
Epistle to the Corinthians* (5th ed.; Peabody, MA: Hendrickson, 1983) 451–52, cited by Paul
Brooks Duff, "Metaphor, Motif, and Meaning: The Rhetorical Strategy behind the
Image 'Led in Triumph' in 2 Cor 2,14," *CBQ* 53 (1991) 79–92. See also Cilliers Breyten-
bach, "Paul's Proclamation and God's 'Thriambos': Notes on 2 Corinthians 2:14–16b,"
Neotestamentica 24 (1990) 257–71. For general surveys, see John Fitzgerald, *Cracks in an
Earthen Vessel: An Examination of the Catalogues of Hardships in the Corinthian Correspondence*
(SBLDS 99; Atlanta: Scholars, 1988) 160–65, and Scott Hafemann, *Suffering and the Spirit*
(WUNT 2/19; Tübingen: Mohr-Siebeck, 1986; Grand Rapids: Eerdmans, 1990) 16–34
and Thrall, *Second Corinthians*, 190–208.

of 14a would be that God leads his captive, Paul, like a Roman general leading his enslaved enemy to eventual execution.[15] Some scholars find that imagery distasteful and argue for some special or derived
sense of "triumph." Others insist that it is precisely the shameful connotation of the captive's status that appeals to Paul.[16] Commentators
doubtful of the utility of the language have canvassed various possibilities, including a factitive sense, as in the KJV: "Now thanks be unto
God which always causeth us to triumph in Christ." This meaning,
however, lacks lexical support.[17] At times such a reading moves beyond
simple lexical considerations to an alternative construal of the image.
Some argue that Paul conjures up the scene of a victorious general
leading his military associates in triumph along with him,[18] but there is
neither lexical nor cultural support for such a reading.[19] Hence, most
interpreters wrestle with the ways in which God drags along his poor
captive.[20]

These scholars construe the olfactory imagery, at least in v. 14, as
a part of the triumphal scene. The usual move is to see an allusion

---

[15] For details of the triumphal procession, see H. S. Versnel, *Triumphus: An Inquity into the Origin, Development and Meaning of the Roman Triumph* (Leiden: Brill, 1970) and Ernst Künzel, *Der römische Triumph: Siegesfeiern im antiken Rom* (München: Beck, 1988).

[16] Peter Marshall, "A Metaphor of Social Shame: θριαμβεύειν in 2 Cor 2:14," *NovT* 25 (1983) 302–17.

[17] Thrall (*Second Corinthians*, 192) agrees with Williamson, "Led in Triumph," that *BAGD*'s claim that Ctesias, *Persica* 13, attests this sense is mistaken. The verb there should be translated 'denounce,' 'publicly expose,' or 'hold up to ridicule.' Most con-temporary commentators agree. Charles K. Barrett, *A Commentary on the First Epistle to the Corinthians* (HNTC; New York: Harper and Row, 1968) 98: "It can scarcely mean (though some translators take it so) "to cause to triumph." Collange, *Enigmes*, 24: "Malheureusement on ne trouve aucun cas de l'emploi de θριαμβεύω dans ce sens."

[18] Thrall (*Second Corinthians*, 192) notes in favor Calvin, Wendland, and Bruce. Barrett (*Second Corinthians*, 98) likewise approves: "Notwithstanding the lack of supporting lexical evidence it is right to follow L. S., Allo, and Kümmel in taking Paul to represent himself as one of the victorious general's soldiers sharing in the glory of his triumph. But there is a paradox here; Paul did not forget (1 Cor. xv.9; Gal. i. 13, 23) that he had fought on the wrong side, and that his position in the triumphal progress was due to a reversal by grace of his deserts."

[19] Thrall's judgment (*Second Corinthians*, 192): "This would make good sense, but has no lexical support."

[20] For recent examples, see Thrall, *Second Corinthians*, 195: "Whatever the exegetical difficulties, it is surely right to understand the verb in its usual, attested sense when followed by a direct object 'lead (as a conquered prisoner) in a triumphal procession', and to see the image as derived from the Roman triumph. At the same time, one has to ask how much content should be read into it." See also Hafemann, *Suffering*, 35–49.

to incense,[21] which was certainly burned at Roman triumphs,[22] as well
as at other processions.[23] As Thrall remarks, an allusion to the Roman
triumph would continue in the phrase "to death" of 16a, since paraded
captives were regularly executed at the end of the triumph, the fact
which, of course, leads other scholars to discount the triumph imagery
in the first place.

Triumphs and the smell of incense go together, but difficulties
abound. Some commentators find problems even in v. 14. Understanding the direction of incense to be equivalent to that of the savor of
sacrifice, i.e., godward, Thrall, for example, notes:

> The supporting Hellenistic texts, however, are somewhat sparse, and
> even if incense was customarily burned on these occasions it was burned
> as an offering to the gods, whilst the point here is the spreading of the
> fragrance throughout the world of humanity.[24]

Even those who may not be bothered by this problem with incense
usually argue that Paul shifts his imagery between v. 14 and v. 15, moving from incense to the sweet savor of sacrifice, using the Septuagintal[25] expression ὀσμὴ εὐωδίας for the Hebrew ראח נכוח.[26] Paul certainly

---

[21] Thrall, *Second Corinthians* cites Heinrici, 144; Alford, 640, Wordsworth, 151; Windisch, 97; and some who emphasize the pervasive quality of the scent: Schlatter, *Paulus*,
495–96; Plummer, 67; Hughes, 78; Barnett, 151; Barrett, 98: "The best explanation of
the new figure (see Windisch and Lietzmann; also Knox, P.G. [*St. Paul and the church
of the Gentiles*, 1939], p. 129, with important references) is that the use of incense was
customary in triumphal and quasi-triumphal processions, both royal and religious.
Goudge rightly raises the question whether this practice was one that would have
occurred to a Jew, such as Paul, but it is hard to think of a better explanation." Of
v 15 (Henry L. Goudge, *The Second Epistle to the Corinthians* [Westminster Commentaries;
London: Methuen, 1927] 99): "The thought of incense suggested in verse 14 is now
developed as Paul uses a fresh word for odour, which is here rendered as *sweet savour
of sacrifice*. ... Its meaning can hardly be other than sacrificial here, and for this reason
the word sacrifice has been introduced into the translation." Collange, *Enigmes*, 29, n. 2:
cites Windisch, Plummer, Hughes, Filson, Spicq.

[22] Barnett (*Second Corinthians*, 151 n. 23): "The strewing of incense as part of the
victory ceremonial is mentioned at the triumph of Scipio Africanus minor (Appian,
Punic Wars 66)." See Künzl, *Triumph*, 105.

[23] Livy 29.11.7 notes the clouds of incense in perfume burners that welcomed Cybele
to Rome. See Robert Turcan, *The Cults of the Roman Empire* (Oxford: Blackwell, 1996) 37.

[24] Thrall, *Second Corinthians*, 197, citing Furnish 188; Bultmann 68; cf. Collange,
Enigmes, 29: "Toutefois les textes que l'on cite à l'appui de cette thèse sont très peu
nombreux et elle ne correspond pas vraiment au sens que nous avons reconnu dans
θριαμβεύοντι et φανεροῦντι."

[25] Gen 8:21; Num 15:28; 29. Sir 24:15 (split into two parallel clauses) uses the terms
as synonyms, both for the metaphorical fragrance of Wisdom.

[26] Barnett, *Second Corinthians*, 146: "The opening metaphor is a complex combination

knows the phrase,[27] although it is curious that he here separates ὀσμή and εὐωδία.

Thus even those who find a connection between triumph and scent have difficulty in unpacking the metaphorical language in a simple and coherent fashion. The problem is compounded by v. 16 and its suggestion that the aroma has different effects on different groups. Chrysostom and Aristotle provide data that some scents could be harmful to various creatures,[28] and the Rabbinic account of the ambivalent סם surfaces.[29] Integrating v. 16 with what precedes is, in any case, difficult.

Most commentators eventually resort to the notion that Paul does mix his metaphors.[30] The resultant reading, and the play that Paul makes, may be outlined roughly as follows:

	Word	*Image*	*Referent*
a	θριαμβεύοντι	triumph	Paul's itinerant apostolic activity
b.	ὀσμή τ. γ.	incense	The Gospel
c.	εὐωδία Χ.	savor of sacrifice	Paul's suffering
d.	ὀσμὴ ἐκ ζωῆς	savor/**sacred** meat	Redemption for those who accept (b)
e.	ὀσμὴ ἐκ θανάτου	savor/sacred **meat**	Damnation for those who reject (b)

On this reading, these verses paint two overlapping images, that of a triumphal procession and its sweet smell and that of the sacrifice, perhaps at the end of the procession, the smells of which could elicit

---

of a victory procession (v. 14) and the impact of fragrance and aroma on God and people (vv. 15–16). As God leads Paul in his victory procession through Paul's preaching and life, the apostle spreads the fragrance of the knowledge of Christ wherever he goes (v. 14). Yet, the bearer of this fragrance to people suffers in the course of his apostleship, whether in Ephesus or Troas. Hence Paul sees himself—in continuity with "the sufferings of Christ"—as the aroma of an acceptable sacrifice ascending to God (v. 15a)."

[27] Phil 4:18; cf. Eph 5:2, for the gift of the congregation to Paul.

[28] Thrall (*Second Corinthians*, 205) cites Chrysostom PG 61.430 regarding ointment suffocating swine and Aristotle, *Mirab. Auscult.* 147 (845a–b) that vultures are said to die "from the scent of myrrh and beetles from the scent of roses," a passage already noted by Wettstein, Η ΚΑΙΝΗ ΔΙΑΘΗΚΗ, 2:182.

[29] See above.

[30] See Thrall (*Second Corinthians*, 207), commenting on v. 16: "It seems, then, that Paul's image is complex in origin, deriving from ideas of sacrifice, Torah, and Wisdom, and combining motifs from each. These motifs run throughout vv. 14b–16ab and predominate, whether or not subsidiary motifs, such as the triumphal image in v. 14a, also play some part." Cf. Hafemann, *Suffering*, 35–83.

either positive or negative reactions. Paul equates himself both with the members of the procession who provide the incense, i.e., preach the gospel, and with the smell of the sacrifice. In the metaphorical nostrils of those who smell, he can be either a sweet fragrance, if they see his suffering in the light of the Gospel, or an obnoxious odor, if they view his suffering purely on a human level. For them the suffering apostle is neither fragrant incense nor the savor of sacred meat, only the acrid stench of charred flesh. The reading of the imagery is moderately satisfying, and appropriate to the context of 2 Corinthians, but it clearly despairs of a simple, integrated use of Paul's colorful language.

Sniffing Out a Different Background

Before turning to some other interpretive considerations, a brief excursus on v 14 is necessary. There is immediately a grammatical problem in the image here: how is "fragrance" related to "knowledge"? Is "knowledge" an objective or subjective genitive? The NRSV opts for the understanding that the noun γνώσεως is a subjective genitive, or a genitive of source or origin, "the fragrance that comes from knowing him." On none of the readings that we have examined is such a construal likely. Instead, whatever the image, God must "spread out in every place the aroma that makes him known."[31] Whatever else we may say about these verses, the NRSV can hardly be correct.

We have been exploring that end of the interpretive spectrum on 2 Cor 2:14–17 that sees a more or less coherent image being developed around the triumphal procession and two sorts of scents that might be associated with it. The close parallelism between the two unusual and graphic clauses of v. 14 is perhaps the strongest indicator that Paul is trying to paint a verbal picture. The most common reading suggests considerable complexity in the image.

Most recently this end of the interpretive spectrum has found a new anchor, which introduces a possible new simplicity to the exegesis of the text. This position notes, in effect, that while language of "triumph" *stricto sensu* applies to Roman military parades, such language, *pace* Dautzenberg, could be applied to other parades, particularly religious processions, in which a deity became manifest to worshippers.[32]

---

[31] Thrall (*Second Corinthians*, 199): "The genitive is obviously objective, 'knowledge about him,' rather than 'his knowledge,' but does 'him' mean Christ or God?".

[32] This is true whatever one makes of the thesis that the Roman triumphs *derive* from

Although others have suggested a rendering along those lines,[33] the suggestion has been developed in the most comprehensive fashion by Paul B. Duff,[34] who has made the intriguing argument that "epiphanic processions" form the most immediate background for Paul's imagery here and in the following verses.

To make the connection with the Roman triumph, Duff notes examples of the application of military language and imagery to the processions of deities. Duff notes too the fact that Isis was regularly labeled "victrix" or "triumphalis,"[35] whose processions then would be metaphorical triumphs. In the climactic scene of the *Metamorphoses*, Apuleius in fact describes the crowds assembling for the *pompa* of Isis as having triumphal characteristics; so 11:7: *et ecce discursu religioso ac prorsus triumphali turbulae complent totas plateas* ("and now crowds of people filled all the streets, moving to and fro in a religious and altogether triumphant manner"). The myths of Dionysus recorded his "invasion" of India[36] and his subsequent "triumph."[37] Plastic art as well knew the metaphor and sarcophagi often depict Dionysiac processions with the accouterments of military triumphs.[38] In the metaphorical world of Dionysiac triumphs, his devotees would be prisoners led in a comic triumphal procession. Processions of other deities, such as Cybele, could also involve triumphal imagery.[39] In late antiquity religious and civil "triumphs"

Bacchic processions. See H. S. Versnel, *Triumphus*, 245–6. A linguistic connection with Dionysus rests on the word θρίαμβος, which could refer either to a hymn to the god or serve as an epithet of the god (although still associated with ritual hymnody), as in the poem of the fifth or fourth century lyric poet Pratinas, θρίαμβε διθύραμβε κισσό-ζαιτ' ἄναξ (l. 15: "dithyramb-tirumphing ivy-wreathed lord"), preserved in Athenaeus *Deipnosophistae* 14.617B-F; the text is also given by D. L. Page, *Poeti Melici Graeci* (Oxford: Clarendon, 1962) 367 (no. 708).

[33] G. G. Findlay, "St. Paul's use of θριαμβεύω," *Expositor* 10 (1879) 404–5.

[34] Duff, "Metaphor, Motif, and Meaning," 79–92.

[35] CIL 9.3144, 5179; 11.695 for *victrix*; CIL 6.355 for *triumphalis*.

[36] Cf. Apollonius Rhodius, *Argonautica* 2.904; Vergil, *Aeneid* 6.801.

[37] Diodorus Siculus 4.3.1 describes him as καταγαγεῖν δὲ πρῶτον τῶν ἁπάντων θρίαμ-βον ἐπ' ἐλέφαντος Ἰνδίκου. Vallerius Flaccus *Argonautica* 3.538, depicts Dionysus leading the *fercula* or carts in which prisoners would be carried in a Roman triumph. See Versnel, *Triumphus*, 246; Künzel, *Triumph*, 102–106.

[38] Duff, "Metaphor, Motif, and Meaning," 85, citing Friederich Matz, *Die dionysischen Sarkophage* 2 (Berlin: Mann, 1968) no. 129 (pp. 263–67), pl. 144 and Ludwig Budde and Richard Nichols, *A Catalogue of the Greek and Roman Sculpture in the Fitzwilliam Museum Cambridge* (Cambridge: Cambrige University Press, 1964) 98–102.

[39] Turcan, *Cults*, 46, refers to a "triumph" of Commodus and Cybele on the feast of the resurrection of Attis on March 25. Cybele had a procession in the Circus Maximus on April 10. Cf. Macrobius, *Saturnalia* 1.21.10 and Herodian 1.10.5–7 for other

would continue to mingle and develop into the rich symbolic world of medieval processions and their reflections in art and liturgy.[40]

In such religious "triumphs" there would be another source of aromas, the fragrant perfume that devotees would sprinkle along the processional way. Before Duff, some scholars, particularly F. F. Bruce, noted the possibility, although they did not draw any implications from their observation.[41] Apuleius, *Metamorphoses* 11.9 offers a particularly vivid picture of such a procession, set, incidentally, in the environs of Corinth, and its use of fragrances:

> While these amusing delights of the people were appearing all over the place, the procession (*pompa*) proper of the Saviour Goddess was on its way. Women radiant in white garments, rejoicing in different kinds of emblems, which they carried, and garlanded with flowers of spring, were strewing the ground with blossoms from their bosoms along the road where the sacred company (*sacer comitatus*) proceeded. Other women had reversed shining mirrors behind their backs to show respect to the goddess as she moved after them; others carrying ivory combs represented with waving arms and bending fingers the adornment and combing of the queen's hair; others again bespattered the streets with various perfumes and a delightful balm shaken out in drops (*illae etiam,*

---

descriptions of the procession. Cybele would process annually on March 27 from her temple in Rome down the Appian Way to the Tiber for her annual Lavatio or Bath. She would be asked if she would return to Rome and always responded positively.

[40] On this afterlife of the various triumphs of antiquity, see Geir Hellemo, *Adventus Domini: Eschatological Thought in 4th-century Apses and Catecheses* (VCSup 5; Leiden: Brill, 1989); Ernst Kantorowicz, "The King's Advent," *Art Bulletin* 26 (1944) 207–31; Michael McCormick, *Eternal Victory: Triumphal Rulership in Late Antiquity, Byzantium, and the Early Medieval West* (Cambridge: Harvard, 1987); Margot Fassler, "Liturgy and Sacred History in the Twelfth-century Tympana at Chartres," *Art Bulletin* 75 (1993) 499–520; idem, "The Meaning of Entrance: Liturgical Commentary and the Introit Tropes," in Paul Brainard, ed., *Reflections on the Sacred: A Musicological Perspective* (New Haven: Yale Institute of Sacred Music, 1994); Gordon Kipling, *Enter the King: Theatre, Liturgy and Ritual in the Medieval Civic Triumph* (Oxford: Oxford University Press, 1998).

[41] F. F. Bruce, *1 and 2 Corinthians*, 187, "there may be an allusion to the perfumes sprinkled along the triumphal way." Thrall (*Second Corinthians*, 205) notes the comment, but does not pursue it. T. E. Schmidt, "Mark 15:16–32: The Crucifixion Narrative and the Roman Triumphal Procession," *NTS* 41 (1995) 1–18, here p. 5, cites Suetonius *Nero* 25.2, which describes a triumph at the beginning of Nero's reign, in which "All along the route victims were slain [and] the streets were sprinkled from time to time with perfume." Schmidt rightly sees that Paul is drawing on such imagery in 2 Corinthians, but offers a different explanation of how the image works: to "signify the preservation of life to those who celebrated with the triumphator and impending death to the train of captives, some of whom would be killed along the way." Schmidt is not so much interested in how Paul's image works as in establishing a precedent for his reading of the Markan passion narrative as a parody of a triumph.

quae ceteris unguentis et geniali balsamo guttatim excusso conspargebant plateas). A large number of people, besides, of both sexes were seeking the blessing of Her who is the creator of the stars of heaven with lanterns, torches, wax tapers, and other kinds of artificial light. etc.

The text does not indicate the precise significance of the "various perfumes" and the drops of "delightful balm," but the other elements of the procession symbolize the goddess and herald the coming of her image. The fragrance, then, is no doubt something that makes her known.[42]

Duff argues that certain details of Paul's imagery suggest his use of the triumphal metaphor. 2 Cor 5:14a portrays Paul as prisoner of the love of Christ. Paul's image would then parallel that of Ovid as enslaved to the god of love.[43] Duff summarizes:

> Accordingly, in 2 Cor 2:14b, Paul ties the verb φανερόω with an allusion to Graeco-Roman epiphany processions. Just as those processions featured aromatic substances such as incense or scented oil whose function was to indicate to those present the epiphany of the deity, so Paul depicts his evangelizing efforts as the manifestation of the "scent of [god's] knowledge." But Paul is not content merely to portray his role with imagery from the epiphany procession of his time. Rather, he juxtaposes the image of himself as the vehicle for the manifestation of "the scent of [God's] knowledge" with the figure of this same God who "leads him in triumph." By means of the proximate placement of these two images in identical structural settings, Paul urges the reader/hearer to interpret one image in terms of the other. … Paul, in keeping with the rhetoricians' advice on the construction of the *insinuatio*, begins his defense by taking up the theme of his opponents, his "weakness" and suffering, and describing it metaphorically with the image of himself "led in triumph." In other words, he begins where his opponents left off. He describes himself with an image which would be eagerly embraced by his opponents; but throughout the course of the letter fragment he subtly redefines it using metaphors and allusions drawn from the processions of the Graeco-Roman world.

---

[42] For the fragrance associated with the self-disclosure of Demeter, cf. the Homeric *Hymn to Demeter* 2.277, a passage, which as Michael White notes, probably inspired Plutarch *De Iside* 357b and may reflect the practice of an "epiphanic" procession connected with the Eleusinian rites. Compare also the sweet fragrance (called separately ὀδμή and εὐωδία) that attends Dionysus' epiphany in Homeric *Hymn* 7.36–7. For connections of these images to ritual procession and performance see also Michael Lonsdale, *Dance and Ritual Play in Ancient Greece* (Baltimore: The Johns Hopkins Universtiy Press, 1993) 91–8. As Lonsdale notes, the context in Dionysiac ritual is one that also links this epiphanic imagery to the term θρίαμβος; cf. n. 32 above.

[43] *Am.* 1.2.27–30. (Also Propertius 2.14; 3.1; Ovid, *Ars Am.*1.189; *Am.* 2.12.).

While Duff's suggestion about the basic image involved here is quite persuasive, he moves too quickly to an application of the image in the context of Paul's ironic apology to the Corinthians. The image, I suggest, involves a complex series of tropes revolving around the connotations of fragrant unguent.

The Subtle Scents of Fragrant Unguents

The entire passage (vv 14–17) is held together by the subtle interplay of its images of scent and procession. In 14a there are three possible signifiers, the *triumphator* himself, i.e., God, the scent of his knowledge, and "us" through whom that scent is made manifest. On the level of the image, therefore, Paul portrays himself either as a devotee of the deity, like one of the women in the Isis procession described by Apuleius, or like a satyr in the ritualized "triumph" of Dionysus. It is in that sense, rather than in the sense of a captive being led to the slaughter, that he is being "led in triumph." He is indeed a slave to the triumphing deity, but a slave in his ongoing service, heralding the deity's approach. It is even remotely possible that Paul envisions himself here not as an agent, but as a humbler instrument, the vessel in which the fragrant ointment is contained. The image would then parallel his later self-portrait as the earthenware lamp (4:7) containing the light of God's glorious knowledge (4:6).[44] In either case Paul is not concentrating on his abased status[45] but locating himself as an intermediary. There may, moreover, be an element of the burlesque in Paul's self-descripton, whether he imagines himself as a servile devotee or the devotee's cheap vessel.

The image shifts between vv. 14 and 15, as commentators duly note. The word εὐωδία, in which many find the language of sacrifice, signals the shift. Yet the parallels with sacrificial terminology are probably misleading, and the various doubts about a reference to sacrificial aromas are well founded. The mere fact that Paul does not use the technical term ὀσμὴ εὐωδίας should serve as a yellow, if not red, flag, and the passage from Sirach noted earlier in fact indicates that the olfactory terminology can easily be used without a technical allusion to sacrificial smells.

---

[44] Duff notes the presence of processional imagery throughout this portion of 2 Corinthians.

[45] Which Marshall emphasizes. On this Lietzmann (*An die Kor.*) was correct: there is no notion of shame involved.

It is quite possible to see Paul developing and reworking the processional imagery that he has already deployed. The shift in the imagery
begins, in fact, with a suggestion that there is continuity with the image
of the pervasive, revelatory scent. The εὐωδία is, after all, of Χριστοῦ,
the anointed one. Paul's most striking move is to identify himself with
the scent, which, in the imagery of the previous verse, he would simply have carried or spread about. With its emphatic genitive, Χριστοῦ,
the verse also specifies the brand of the unguent, i.e., messianic. The
verse should thus be translated: "Because it is Christ's fragrance that
we are, for God,[46] among both saved and lost." The genitive intimates
something about the referent of the metaphor of the aroma. The verse
thereby hints at how it is that Paul operates as the instrument of making
God known: he does so as as an emissary of Christ.

The third stage of the play on smells continues to exploit the image
of the processional fragrance. At this stage, the ultimate referents of
the image exercise strong control over the image itself. Yet the image
remains at work: different people react differently to the scent. How
can that be?

The Ancient Physiology of Scent

A brief excursus into the ancient physiology of scent is necessary. It
will be brief, since the basic outlines of ancient olfactory physiology
were laid down early. Plato did not spend much time worrying about
smells. He could use them as examples of simple pleasures.[47] When he
turned his attention to natural philosophy he thought that smell was
a rather simple process, moving from putrefying matter into the nasal
passages and producing either pleasure or pain.[48] There is hardly any
room here for a post-modernist notion that the smell is in the nostrils
of the smeller.

---

[46] The phrase τῷ Θεῷ could simply mark the possessor of the fragrance, not the
direction in which the aroma moves.

[47] *Rep* 9.584b: "'Take a look, then,' said I, 'at pleasures which do not follow on pain,
so that you may not haply suppose for the present that it is the nature of pleasure to
be a cessation from pain and pain from pleasure.'—'Where shall I look,' he said, 'and
what pleasures do you mean?'—'There are many others,' I said, 'and especially, if you
please to note them, the pleasures connected with smell. For these with no antecedent
pain suddenly attain an indescribable intensity, and their cessation leaves no pain after
them.'" (Translation by Paul Shorey in *The Collected Dialogues of Plato* [Edith Hamilton
and Huntington Cairns, eds.; New York: Bollingen, 1961] 811). Cf. *Philebus* 51E

[48] *Timaeus* 66D–67A: "But smells always proceed from bodies that are damp, or

Aristotle was far more interested in the subject, as he was in the whole process of sensation. For him "odour is a smoke-like evaporation, and smoke-like evaporation arises from fire."[49] In general he recognized the weakness of the sense, noting in the *De anima*: "*men have a poor sense of smell and our apprehension of its objects is bound up with pleasure and pain*, which shows that in us the organ is inaccurate."[50] Although smells had an objective basis, they could be hard to discriminate.[51] There are, nonetheless, distinctions to be made in the objective basis of the perceived smell. For Aristotle, *There are two classes of odors. For one, (e.g.,*

---

putrefying, or liquefying, or evaporating, and are perceptible only in the intermediate state, when water is changing into air and air into water, and all of them are either vapor or mist. That which is passing out of air into water is mist, and that which is passing from water into air is vapor, and hence all smells are thinner than water and thicker than air. The proof of this is that when there is any obstruction to the respiration and a man draws in his breath by force, then no smell filters through, but the air without the smell alone penetrates. Wherefore the varieties of smell have no name, and they have not many or definite and simple kinds, but they are distinguished only as painful and pleasant, the one sort irritating and disturbing the whole cavity which is situated between the head and the navel, the other having a soothing influence and restoring this same region to an agreeable and natural condition." (Translation by Benjamin Jowett in *The Collected Dialogues of Plato* [Edith Hamilton and Huntington Cairns, eds.; Bollingen Series 71; New York: Bollingen, 1961] 1190–91).

[49] *De sensu* 2, 438b16–28.

[50] *De anima* 2.9, 421a11–13. This statement is part of a larger discussion of sense perception in *De anima* 2.9, 421a7–422a7; the principal passage (421a7–16) runs as follows: "Smell and its object are much less easy to determine than what we have hitherto discussed; the distinguishing characteristic of smell is less obvious than those of colour. The ground of this is that our power of smell is less discriminating and in general inferior to that of many species of animals; *men have a poor sense of smell and our apprehension of its objects is bound up with pleasure and pain*, which shows that in us the organ is inaccurate. It is probable that there is a parallel failure in the perception of colour by animals that have hard eyes; probably they discriminate differences of colour only by the presence or absence of what excites fear, and that it is thus that human beings distinguish smells." (Translation by J. A. Smith in *The Complete Works of Aristotle: The Revised Oxford Translation* [Jonathan Barnes, ed.; Bollingen Series 71.2; 2 vols.; Princeton: Princeton University Press, 1984] 1:670).

[51] *De anima* 2.9, 421a28–421b4: "As flavours may be divided into sweet and bitter, so with smells. In some things the flavour and the smell have the same quality, e.g. both are sweet, in others they diverge. Similarly a smell may be pungent, astringent, acid, or succulent. But, as we said, because smells are much less easy to discriminate than flavours, the names of these varieties are applied to smells in virtue of similarity; for example sweet belongs to saffron or honey, pungent to thyme, and so on." (Translation, *ibid.*, 1:670). Cf. *De anima* 2.12, 424b4–19: "Now a smell is just what can be smelt, and if it produces any effect it can only be so as to make something smell it, and it might be argued that what cannot smell cannot be affected by smells and further that what can smell can be affected by it only in so far as it has in it the power to smell (similarly with the proper objects of all the other senses)." (Translation, *ibid.*, 1:675).

nutrients), *"pleasantness or unpleasantness belongs incidentally"*; … *"the other class of odours consists of those agreeable in their essential nature, e.g. those of flowers."*[52] Yet even for things like fragrant unguents, which may have an essentially pleasurable scent (and thus can incidentally herald the arrival of a deity), it may be possible to make erroneous judgments about their scents, or as he put it in *De anima* 3.3, 428b10–25 *"Sense stimulates imagination, which may be true or false. Immediate perceptions are inerrant, but perceptions of what is incidental to the objects of perception may err."* Things incidental to the scent, such as its source or its significance, may stimulate different imagining and elicit different judgments.

Later followers of Aristotle, responsible for the *Problems*, devoted two whole chapters to issues of the ambiguity of aromas, asking, for instance, "Why is it that the odours of burning perfumes and of flowers are less sweet-scented at a close distance?" or "Why is it that flowers and burnt perfumes smell sweeter at a distance, whereas close at hand they have rather the smell either of vegetation or of smoke?"[53] or again "Why have flowers an unpleasant odour when they are rubbed?"[54]

In sum, for the ancient philosophical tradition, insofar as it reflected on the problems of smell, scents could either give pleasure or pain, but which they offered was a function of various factors, including the judgments made by the smeller about things incidental to the aromas themselves.

Discernment of Aromas

What, then, at the level of the image, could have been the basis for the different judgments in the lost and the saved who witnessed the triumph of God and his apostle? The image of the sacrificial victim offers one possibility. The image of unguent offers another. Some of the fragrant substances that would have been used in processional ointment had many uses and, to use Aristotle's phrase, many incidental characteristics. They could be healing balms, ointments for messiahs, or embalming scents. This is particularly true of myrrh, one of the scents that Wisdom claimed for herself in Sir 24:15. Myrrh was the primary component of the "holy anointing oil" used for Aaron and his sons in

---

[52] *De sensu* 5.443b20–27 (Translation by J. I. Beare in *ibid.*, 1:670). The entire discussion of the chapter, 441b26–445b1 is an interesting treatment of smell.

[53] *Problems* 12, 906a21–907b19 (Translation by E. S. Forster in *ibid.*, 2:1408).

[54] *Problems* 13, 907b21–909a10 (Translation, *ibid.* 2:1410).

Exod 30:23–33. Myrrh was also the perfume of love, with which the hands of the lady of the Song of Songs and the lips of her lover were dripping (Song [Cant] 5:5, 13).[55] Finally, mixed with aloe, it was among the aromatic spices with which Jesus was buried, according to John 19:39. What was true of myrrh was also true of nard, which Pliny treats as "foremost among perfumes."[56] It too could be a lover's perfume,[57] could evoke the scent of paradise,[58] and could, in the hands of Mary of Bethany, betoken the burial of Jesus.[59] Although Pliny did not know John, his comment about the adoption of perfume by the Romans is apt:

> the pleasure of perfume was also admitted by our fellow countrymen as well among the most elegant and also most honorable enjoyments of life and even began to be an appropriate tribute to the dead.[60]

What one person might smell as a reminder of health and the pleasures of life, another could take as a *memento mori*.[61]

Conclusion

The "scent" (ὀσμή) which Paul distributed in God's triumph, the scent with which he identified himself, was the fragrance (εὐωδία) of the Anointed One, anointed in life in anticipation of his death and anointed in a death that brought life to the world.[62] Paul's image of the fragrant unction points finally to his identification with that Anointed

---

[55] Cf. also Prov 7:17 for myrrh, aloes and cinnamon perfuming a bed, and Ps 45:9, for perfumed clothing. It appears with a list of other fragrances at Song [Cant] 4:14. Pliny, *Natural History* 12.33–35.66–71, devotes considerable attention to the sources and processing of myrrh.

[56] Pliny, *Natural History* 12.26.42: *De folio nardi plura dici pr est ut principali in unguentis.*

[57] Song [Cant] 1:12; 4:12.

[58] *Apoc. Mos.* [Greek *Life of Adam and Eve*] 29:6; cf. the Latin in *Vit. Adae* 43:3. For further discussion of this text see the article by M. de Jonge in this volume.

[59] John 12:3, 7.

[60] Pliny, *Natural History* 13.2. The ambiguity of aroma noted by Pliny could be replicated in many spheres. For a treatment of the multivalence of spices and the perfumes derived from them, see Marcel Detienne, *The Gardens of Adonis: Spices in Greek Mythology* (Hassocks, Sussex, UK: Harvester, 1977); ET of *Les Jardins d'Adonis* (Paris: Gallimard, 1972).

[61] It may well be, as John Fitzgerald suggests (*Cracks*, 179, n. 171), that Paul eventually plays on imagery from two types of process, the *pompa triumphalis* at 2:14 and the *pompa funebris* at 4:10, but here the point of the play hinges on the ambiguity of aromas.

[62] Whether Paul knew traditions such as those of the fourth gospel is, of course, uncertain, but he need not have known them in order to make metaphorical mileage on the theme of anointing.

One, an identification that precludes his being identified with a mere huckster (v. 17).[63] A judgment about the apostle is ultimately a judgment about the one he serves and that is the judgment which, in Paul's mind, brings either life or death.

To conclude: Paul's imagery in 2Cor 2:14–17 can be construed as a consistent development of the imagery of sacred unguents used in religious "triumphs" in which devotees made known the presence of a deity and also their relationship to the potent power celebrating the triumph.

Word	Image	Referent
a. θριαμβεύοντι	triumph	Paul's itinerant apostolic activity
b. δι᾽ ἡμῶν	agent/instrument	Paul
c. ὀσμή τ. γ.	unguent	The Gospel
d. εὐωδία Χ.	unguent	Paul's identification with Christ
e. ὀσμὴ ἐκ ζωῆς	healing unguent	Paul/Christ's **fragrance understood by believers**
f. ὀσμὴ ἐκ θανάτου	embalming unguent	Paul/Christ's **fragrance misjudged by unbelievers**

---

[63] Perhaps the contrast evokes another element of the processional scene. However Paul portrays himself, he is part of the procession itself, not on the sidelines working, as a κάπελος for gain.

"IN THOSE DAYS"

SOME REMARKS ON THE USE OF "DAYS"
IN MATTHEW 2:1, 3:1, AND LUKE 2:1

Gerard Mussies

Introduction

In the Gospels one finds several Greek constructions that employ the term "day" or "days" (ἡμέρα/αι) in reference to time or chronology. Three of these will be of special concern in this study:

> Matt 2:1: Τοῦ δὲ Ἰησοῦ γεννηθέντος ἐν Βηθλέεμ τῆς Ἰουδαίας ἐν ἡμέραις Ἡρῴδου τοῦ βασιλέως ... ("Now when Jesus was born in Bethlehem of Judea in the days of Herod the king ..."—RSV).

> Matt. 3:1: Ἐν δὲ ταῖς ἡμέραις ἐκείναις παραγίνεται Ἰωάννης ὁ βαπτιστὴς κηρύσσων ἐν τῇ ἐρήμῳ τῆς Ἰουδαίας ... ("In those days came John the Baptist preaching in the wilderness of Judea ..."—RSV).

> Luke 2:1: Ἐγένετο δὲ ἐν ταῖς ἡμέραις ἐκείναις ἐξῆλθεν δόγμα παρὰ Καίσαρος Αὐγούστου ἀπογράφεσθαι πᾶσαν τὴν οἰκουμένην ("And it happened in those days, that a decree went out from Emperor Augustus that all the world should be registered"—RSV, modified).

Such usages have long been recognized for their interpretive difficulties, and have often been explained in terms of the Semitic background of the New Testament. In order to provide a broader context for understanding, we shall examine both the Semitic patterns of usage and their adaptation into Greek in the Septuagint, the New Testament, and other contemporary literature.

The most conspicuous semantic characteristic of the biblical Hebrew word "days" is the fact that it occurs in passages where one would rather expect to find other terms used—either comprehensive words indicating a specific collection of days, such as "week," "month," or "year," or more general expressions such as "time" or "age."

The use of "day" for "a day and a night" is not so different from modern usage. This is found at Gen 15:18 in "on that day" (בַּיּוֹם הַהוּא) which happens to be equivalent to what has been said in the preceding verse: "when the sun had set and darkness had come" (15:17). Consequently, "that day," here signifies a day and the following night, or rather a night and the preceding day, which more or less equals our present way of reckoning time over a twenty-four hour period. The phrase "the 12th of March" also signifies a day and the following night, as it refers to a span of time, not of twelve, but of twenty-four hours. This seems to be one of the root meanings.

But when the plural "days" occurs in the story of the Flood in combination with "seven" (Gen 8:10, 12), or with the likely rounded "forty" (7:4, 12, 17; 8:4), as also with "one hundred fifty" (8:3), one wonders why the author did not make use of alternative phrases, such as "one week," "for over a month," and "five months," respectively.

Furthermore, in a number of passages the plural "days" is commonly taken to mean as much as "a year" or "yearly:"

(a) Lev 25:29: "his (right of) redemption shall be till the fullness of a year after its (the house's) sale, (for) days shall be his (right of) redemption," is probably a doublet in which "year" and "days" stand as equivalents. The LXX has combined both in ἐνιαυτὸς ἡμερῶν ("a year of days").

(b) Judg 17:10: "and I shall pay you ten pieces of silver for the days" (לַיָּמִים), apparently means "per year," which the LXX renders with εἰς ἡμέρας.

(c) 1 Sam 1:21; cf. 2:19; 20:6: the expression "the sacrifice of the days" (MT: אֶת־זֶבַח הַיָּמִים; LXX: τὴν θυσίαν τῶν ἡμερῶν) is usually taken to mean "the yearly sacrifice," because at 2:19 it is used together with:

(d) the phrase "from days to days" (MT: מִיָּמִים יָמִימָה; LXX: ἐξ ἡμερῶν εἰς ἡμέρας), which is considered to signify "on an annual basis;" cf. Ex 13:10, etc.

(e) 1 Sam 27:7: "and the number of the days (הַיָּמִים) that David stayed in the fields of the Philistines were *days and four months* (יָמִים וְאַרְבָּעָה חֳדָשִׁים)," usually thought to mean "a year and four months." Here the LXX renders it simply as "four months" (τέσσαρας μῆνας). At Judg 19:2, however, the similar Hebrew expression, lacking only the conjunction (וְ), "days four months" (יָמִים אַרְבָּעָה חֳדָשִׁים) is usually taken to mean just "four months," but the LXX renders it more literally as ἡμέρας τετράμηνον.

Finally, where the Hebrew words for "week(s)," "month(s)," and "year(s)" are actually found, they may still be accompanied by the noun "days" without use of a conjunction, preposition, or possessive, for instance in: "three weeks days" (Dan 10:2–3 [bis]; MT: שְׁלֹשָׁה שָׁבֻעִים

יָמִים),[1] "a month days" (Gen 29:14; MT: חֹדֶשׁ יָמִים; but note LXX: μῆνα ἡμερῶν – "a month of days"), and "after two years days" (Gen 41:1; MT: מִקֵּץ שְׁנָתַיִם יָמִים; where LXX has μετὰ δύο ἔτη ἡμερῶν – "after two years of days"). Perhaps the cases already mentioned in Lev 25:29 and Judg 19:2 are also instances of the same redundancy.

Apparently then, the day, as the most immediately graspable unit of time to the mind of primeval humans, was for that reason not always supplanted by the words that express specific multiples of it. The basic units of a person's life-time are also called his "days," as in Gen 3:14 "all the days of your life." In the genealogy in Gen 5:1–20 we are consistently informed about the number of years which amounted to "the days of the life" of each patriarch, from Adam to Noah, and similarly about the "days" of king Solomon's reign (1 Kgs 11:42). As a consequence, "in the days (of)" (בִּימֵי) + a personal name, which occurs frequently in the books of Kings and Chronicles, came to mean "during a person's life-time, reign, or public activity," e.g. 1 Kgs 10:21: "in the days of Solomon" (LXX = 3 Kgdms 10:21: ἐν ταῖς ἡμέραις Σαλωμών; cf. 2 Kgs 15.29).

These uses of "days" for any number of days show its lexical meaning to have been what is usually termed "unmarked," as opposed to the "marked" meanings of such words as "week" etc., which can only indicate a specific number of days. On the other hand, "in the day of the harvest" (Prov 25:13: בְּיוֹם קָצִיר) is not just one or the first harvest-day only, but all the days of the harvest or the entire "harvest season" (as it is rendered in the LXX: ἐν ἀμήτῳ). Similarly, "in the day *of my distress*" (בְּיוֹם צַר לִי) and "in the day when I cry out" (בְּיוֹם אֶקְרָא), both in Psalm 102:3, have the more general meaning of "each such a day" or "whenever;" so, the LXX [= Ps 101:3] translates ἐν ᾗ ἂν ἡμέρᾳ + subjunctive in both cases. This specific use of the singular for all days is usually termed its "generic use," and has its modern parallels in such expressions as "in his day" = "in his time and age," "the press of the day" = "of that period," and the like.

---

[1] Unless one takes this to mean etymologically "three sevens (heptads) of days," which is how the LXX understood it: τὰς τρεῖς ἑβδομάδας τῶν ἡμερῶν ("three weeks of days").

Some Ambiguities in Usage

As these various uses of "day" or "days" occur side by side with their more restricted literal usage, it is not always clear which of these is actually intended in a given context. For instance, Gen 2:17: "in the day you will eat (בְּיוֹם אֲכָלְךָ) from it, you will certainly die" uses the same construction meaning "in the day when" or "whenever," (seen above in Ps 102:3) and is translated with the same Greek equivalent in the LXX (ᾗ δ' ἂν ἡμέρα + subj. [φάγητε]). Here, at first sight, it might be interpreted quite literally. Yet it is evident that the very long life of Adam recorded later (Gen 5:5) did not seem to the composer/redactor of Genesis to militate against the previously announced punishment. In other words, "in the day (when)" in Gen 2:17 was not understood to pronounce instant death for Adam and Eve on the selfsame day of their eating the forbidden fruit. The ensuing exegetical problem is well-known: either "on the day when" is here not taken too literally, or the punishment is considered to have been alleviated in such a way that it would be carried out much later.

The use of the plural can be equally puzzling, especially in the expression "in those days" (בַּיָּמִים הָהֵם). Usually it is possible to fill in the name of a relevant (active, ruling) person or circumstance. So, for instance, in 1 Sam 3:1 the name of Eli can be supplied as the then ruling judge, or in 1 Sam 28:1 the fact that David was then dwelling with the Philistines is to be understood.[2] But in Gen 6:4: "in those days (בַּיָּמִים הָהֵם) there were giants on the earth," the expression probably refers rather broadly to the whole period between the birth of Enos (Gen 4:26) and the Flood (Gen 7:11), a period of some 1,500 years according to the narrative's genealogical reckoning. Equally broad is Ezek 38:17 where "in those days" encompasses the activity of all the prophets of Israel.

If it is interpreted too strictly, the expression can even seem to figure anachronistically in a few texts. This is the case in 2 Kgs 20:1 (= Is 38:1): "in those days Hezekiah fell mortally ill." It would be typical to connect this temporal reference to the time of the preceding episode in the narrative, which in this case is Sennacherib's death (2 Kgs 19:37 = Is 37:38), dated to 681 BCE. But this cannot be the referent since Hezekiah himself died five years before Sennacherib.

---

[2] In the latter instance, "in those days" is understood to refer back to the period specified earlier in 1 Sam 27:7 by the phrase "days and four months" discussed above.

This verse about Sennacherib's demise is a chronological preview, and not necessarily a later interpolation. That being the case, one next looks to the penultimate event in the narrative as the likely referent, i.e., Sennacherib's siege of Jerusalem in 701 BCE (2 Kgs 18:13–19:36); however, this presents a problem, too. Instead, the reference in 2 Kgs 20.1 is probably to events in the years 702–701 BCE, just prior to the siege (cf. 20:12 = Is 39:1),[3] and Hezekiah reportedly reigned for another fifteen years after this illness (20:6 = Is 38:6), till 686 BCE. Thus, "in those / these days" (MT: בַּיָּמִים הָהֵם; LXX: ἐν ἐκείναις ταῖς ἡμέραις) either meant "during the siege of Jerusalem" as described earlier (2 Kgs 18:16–19:36), or "at about the time of the siege." More broadly still, it might simply mean "during the reign of Hezekiah" taken as a whole. In other words, the author of Kings, who wrote at least 120 years later (cf. 2 Kgs 25:27), apparently could not distinguish proximate events seen from such a distance in time or did not use the phrase "in those days" to signify a precise chronological sequence.

In the LXX the renderings of such passages generally contain the word ἡμέρα/αι etc., except in the case of Prov 25:13 (ἐν ἀμήτῳ), as noted above. The generic use of the singular "day" was certainly not absent in non-biblical Greek, but it was not as frequent as in the Hebrew. An example is παλαιᾷ … ἀμέρα (literally, "ancient day") to mean "old age" in Sophocles, *Ajax* 624, where it parallels λευκῷ τε γήρᾳ ("white old age") in the very next line. The use of the plural "days," however, for a king's reign and the like is decidedly a Hebraistic turn, as Wettstein already observed in regard to the construction of Matt 2:1: ἐν ἡμέραις Ἡρῴδου ("in the days of Herod").[4] In Greek a more idiomatic expression would have been ἐν τῷ χρόνῳ / τοῖς χρόνοις ("in the time / times") followed by a genitive. This is found a number of times in the LXX, for instance at Gen 26:1: ἐν τῷ χρόνῳ τῷ Ἀβραάμ (*var. leg.* in some mss.: καιρῷ) where the MT has the more typical formulation "in the days

---

[3] Another notorious exegetical problem. The reference in 2 Kgs 20:12 to Merodach-baladan, who ruled in 703–702 BCE and sent an embassy to Judah, suggests that the illness of Hezekiah actually occurred prior to the siege of Jerusalem by Sennacherib. So, it is often argued that this episode is out of sequence with the events in 2 Kgs 18:16–19:36 (= Is 36:1–37:37) even though the chronology given by the author(s) (cf. 2 Kgs 18:2; 18:13; and 20:6) is internally consistent. This may also be one of several cases (such as Gen 2:17 and 5:5 noted above) where successive redactional layers in the text further complicate matters.

[4] "Hebraismus, tempore Regis Herodis." J. J. Wettstein, *H ΚΑΙΝΗ ΔΙΑΘΗΚΗ* (2 vols.; Amsterdam: Officina Dommeriana, 1751–52; repr. Graz: Akademische Druck- und Verlagsanstalt, 1962) 1:240.

of Abraham." Compare also 1 Esdr 2:12: ἐν δὲ τοῖς ἐπὶ Ἀρταξέρξου τοῦ Περσῶν βασιλέως χρόνοις ("in the times of Artaxerxes king of Persia;" MT: absent). Non-biblical instances are Strabo, *Geogr.* 7.3.8: τοῖς Ὁμή- ρου χρόνοις ("in the times/age of Homer"), and Plutarch, *Numa* 1.1: περὶ τῶν Νομᾶ τοῦ βασιλέως χρόνων καθ᾽ οὓς γέγονε ("concerning the times of king Numa at which he lived"). Still more typically Greek, however, would have been a genitive absolute with a participle of some verb meaning "ruling," as in 1 Esdr 8:1: βασιλεύοντος Ἀρταξέρξου τοῦ Περσῶν βασιλέως ("when Artaxexes the king of Persia was reigning").[5]

Uses of "Days" in the New Testament

As might be expected because of this background in Semitic and Septu- agint usage, we see when we turn to the NT that the Greek use of "day" and "days" is not widely different from that in biblical Hebrew. The singular can occur in the sense of "each day" as in Matt 6:34: literally "sufficient to the day (τῇ ἡμέρᾳ) are its troubles," which means "each day has enough trouble of its own." But it may also be used in the sense of "at that time" or "then" as in Mark 2:20: "But *the days* (ἡμέραι) will come when the bridegroom will be taken from them, and *on that day* (ἐν ἐκείνῃ τῇ ἡμέρᾳ) they will fast." Moreover, the plural can occur instead of "month" as in Matt 4:2: "after fasting forty days" (νηστεύσας ἡμέρας τεσσεράκοντα); elsewhere, instead of "years" or "lifetime," as in Luke 1:7: "and they were both well along in their days" (προβεβηκότες ἐν ταῖς ἡμέραις αὐτῶν ἦσαν; cf. Luke 1:18; 2:36). It can also stand for a specific historical period as in Matt 24:38: "in the days before the Flood" (ἐν

---

[5] Here, the MT of the parallel passage in Ezra 7:1 reads: "in the kingdom/reign (בְּמַלְכוּת) of Artaxerxes, king of Persia," which the LXX (2 Esdr 7:1) renders more literally: ἐν βασιλείᾳ Ἀρθασασθα βασιλέως Περσῶν. These two versions thus show distinctive patterns of rendering the Hebrew into Greek. In the LXX the various constructions are often further combined with a regnal year, e.g. in 3 Kgdms (MT 1 Kgs) 14:25: ἐν τῷ ἐνιαυτῷ τῷ πέμπτῳ βασιλεύοντος Ῥοβοάμ ("in the fifth year of Rehoboam's ruling"); cf. Dan 1:1: ἐπὶ βασιλέως Ἰωακίμ τῆς Ἰουδαίας ἔτους τρίτου ("in the third year of king [? = reign of] Jehoiakim of Judah"). It might also use some other substantive, e.g., Jer 25:20: ἐν ἀρχῇ βασιλεύοντος Σεδεκίου τοῦ βασιλέως ("in the beginninig of the ruling of Zedekiah the king"). The more usual Greek phrase is found, for example, in Dan 10:1 (LXX): ἐν τῷ ἐνιαυτῷ τῷ πρώτῳ Κύρου τοῦ βασιλέως Περσῶν ("in the first year of Cyrus, king of Persia"); cf. the variant reading of the Theodotian text: ἐν ἔτει τρίτῳ Κύρου βασιλέως ("in the third year"), which is closer to the MT in terms of the number of years. With the latter formulation compare also the wording of Luke 3:1: ἐν ἔτει δὲ πεντεκαιδεκάτῳ τῆς ἡγεμονίας Τιβερίου Καίσαρος ("in the fifteenth year of the reign of Tiberius Caesar"); this passage will be discussed below.

ταῖς ἡμέραις ταῖς πρὸ τοῦ κατακλυσμοῦ), or for an unknown stretch of time as in Matt 28:20 "and surely I will be with you all the days (πάσας τὰς ἡμέρας) to the very end of the age." Further senses are "during the activity of," as in Matt 24:37: "as it was in the days of Noah" (cf. 1 Pet 3:20; Rev 2:13), and "during the reign of," as in Matt 2:1: "in the days of King Herod" (cf. Luke 1:5).

Furthermore, "those days" can refer to the more or less remote past as seen from the point of view of the author, for instance, in Acts 7:41, where it indicates Israel's wilderness wanderings. Elsewhere, however, it may refer to the future, as in Luke 21:23 (regarding the siege of Jerusalem) and in Rev 9:6 (where it predicts what will happen when the fifth angel blows his trumpet).

Like the LXX the NT authors also use other, more idiomatic Greek expressions. In addition to "in those days" one finds ἐν ἐκείνῳ / αὐτῷ τῷ καιρῷ, ("at that / the same time") which in Matt 11:25 amounts to little more than "after Jesus' previous statement." Elsewhere, the same narrative sequence is introduced simply by τότε ("then"), as we see only a few verses earlier in Matt 11:20 (cf. 12:1; 14:1; Luke 13:1). One also finds κατ' ἐκεῖνον τὸν καιρόν ("about that same time") in Acts 12:1 and 19:23, referring back to occasions earlier mentioned in 11:30 and 19:22 respectively. Besides "in these days" Luke uses ἐν τῷ καιρῷ / χρόνῳ τούτῳ ("in this time") in Luke 18:30 and Acts 1:6. In the latter case the alternative formulation is probably for stylistic variation after ταύτας ἡμέρας ("these days") in the preceding verse.

In addition to "in the days of" Luke also employs the genitive absolute, e.g., in both Luke 2:2: ἡγεμονεύοντος τῆς Συρίας Κυρηνίου ("when Quirinius was governing Syria") and 3:1: ἡγεμονεύοντος Ποντίου Πιλάτου ("when Pontius Pilate was governing"), etc. Compare also Josephus, *Ant.* 7.103: Ἀχάβου βασιλεύοντος τῶν Ἰσραηλιτῶν ("when Ahab was reigning over Israel"). Elsewhere Luke uses the preposition ἐπί + the genitive, as in Luke 3:2: ἐπὶ ἀρχιερέως Ἄννα ("in the highpriesthood of Annas"). Compare also Acts 11:28: ἐπὶ Κλαυδίου, meaning "at the time of Claudius."

In later times the Hebraism of Matt 2:1 was sometimes imitated by Christian authors such as Palladius (III/IV cent.): ἐν ταῖς ἡμέραις Ἰουλιανοῦ τοῦ δυσωνύμου βασιλέως ("in the days of Julian, the ill named/ famed emperor," *Hist. Laus.* 45.1). Patriarch Photius of Constantinople (IX cent.) not only admits of it in his own personal style: "in the days of Justin the emperor of the Romans" (*Library* p.7b), but also puts it in the mouth of non-Christian authors whose works he epitomizes, such as the historian Olympiodorus (V cent.): "in the days of the emperor Constantius" (p.60a), or the philosopher Damascius (V/VI cent.): "in the days of Leon the emperor of the Romans" (p.340b).

Some Ambiguities in New Testament Usage

As in the MT and LXX the phrase "in those days" may pose problems in understanding the NT. On the one hand it can actually refer to the very time of the story in which it figures. In Luke 4:2 it refers to the forty days of Jesus' temptation in the desert mentioned in the same verse. The story of the Transfiguration in Luke 9:28–36, which immediately precedes Jesus' final journey to Jerusalem, ends with "and in those days they reported to no one anything of what they had seen;" in this case it points to the remaining days up to the Resurrection, as also appears from the parallel versions in Matt 17:9 and Mark 9:9. Luke, however, seems to prefer "before/in/after *these* days" when he refers to the time as implied in the previous story or to actual days earlier mentioned.[6] In fact, with the exception of the author of Hebrews (1:2), Luke is the only NT author to use the words "these days" (αὗται ἡμέραι) at all. In Acts 1:5; 3:24; 5:36; 21:38 they figure in direct discourse and have practically the same meaning as the adverb "now." Only at Luke 6:12 is the expression completely disconnected from the context, and at 21:22 it predicts the future siege of Jerusalem. In the last case, curiously, it is equivalent to "those days" (ἐν ἐκείναις ταῖς ἡμέραις), perhaps a more traditionally biblical or apocalyptic formulation, which occurs in the very next verse (21:23). With these uses in mind we may now turn to some difficult cases that have long plagued NT interpretation.

Matt 3:1: "In those days came John the Baptist preaching"

A problematic instance is Matt 3:1: Ἐν δὲ ταῖς ἡμέραις ἐκείναις παραγί-νεται Ἰωάννης ὁ βαπτιστὴς κηρύσσων. This statement follows the birth narrative proper, which was set "in the days of Herod" (2:1), as already

---

[6] In Luke 1:24 it refers to the days of Zechariah's temple-service (1:8); in 1:39, to Elizabeth's sixth month of pregnancy (cf. 1:26); in 23:7 and 24:18 to the time around Passover; in Acts 1:5, to the days between Passover and Pentecost; in Acts 6:1 to Peter's being brought up before the Sanhedrin (cf. 5:17–42); in 11:27, to the "whole year" (mentioned in 11:26); and in 21:15, to the "several days" mentioned earlier in 21:10.

noted. Matthew then relates in rather rapid succession, Joseph's flight to Egypt (2:14), the Bethlehem murders (2:16), Herod's death and the succession by Archelaus (2:19), Joseph's return to Israel (2:21), and his final settlement in Nazareth (2:23). All of this occurs while Jesus was still a child (παιδίον, 2:21). At first sight this may seem to imply that all these events took place within a relatively short span of time, but this assumption looses much of its probability as soon as one sees that Matthew's next story—about the activity of John the Baptist and the baptism of the grown-up Jesus—has been connected with the preceding events by the introductory formula "and in those days" (3:1). At first sight this phrase seems to recall the time when Joseph settled down in Galilee (2:23), that is, in the early years of Jesus (so 2:21) and during the reign of Archelaus (2:19) from 4 BCE-6CE. On the other hand, the stories of the baptism and the following temptation in the desert show Jesus no longer to be a child, but a young man, at least some twenty years of age.

From the vantage of Matthew, writing at a much later time, all these earlier events—which in reality may have been years or even decades apart—appeared to him as having happened in about the same period, "in those days." Keeping in mind this quite understandable loss of perspective (sometimes called "telescoping") one should also reckon with the possibility that between the flight to Egypt and Herod's death more years might have elapsed than Matthew's fluent narrative now seems to suggest. Of course, this caveat will have implications for the usual dates assigned to the birth of Jesus, as reflected in the passage discussed earlier in Matt 2:1. The classical parallels which Wettstein adduces to Mt 3:1 are not quite to the point.[7] Livy 27.15: *iisdem fer(m)e diebus* is meant very literally, namely "just in those same days" or "just at that very time" Marcellus and Hannibal were fighting one another near Canusium (Northern Apulia) in 209 BCE. The same holds true of Virgil, *Aen.* 2.342: *illis ... forte diebus* ("in those days, as it happened") which implies that the Phrygian Coroebus, who sided with the Trojans against the Greeks, had come to Troy just before the Greeks slipped into the city in their giant wooden horse.

---

[7] *H KAINH ΔIAΘHKH*, 1:254.

Luke 3:1: "In those days a decree went out"

Another problematic case in the NT is Luke 2:1: Ἐγένετο δὲ ἐν ταῖς ἡμέραις ἐκείναις ἐξῆλθεν δόγμα παρὰ Καίσαρος Αὐγούστου ἀπογράφεσθαι πᾶσαν τὴν οἰκουμένην ("and it happened in those days that a decree went out from [was issued by] Caesar Augustus that the whole empire should be registered"). Once again, as in 2 Kgs 20:1 and Matt 3:1, the words "in those days" are in any case anachronistic since they do not link up with the immediately preceding event in the narrative. Here it is Luke's proleptic description of the sojourn of John the Baptist in the desert before his public activity began (Luke 1:80; cf. 4:19–20). As a result, these words are traditionally taken to refer to the penultimate preceding event, i.e., the birth of John the Baptist (Luke 1:57), six months before that of Jesus (cf. Luke 1:26). In this sequence, the phrase "in those days" implies that Augustus' decree was no more than half a year or so earlier than Joseph and Mary's ensuing journey from Galilee to Bethlehem. Yet, the phrase "in those days" refers to the remote past, at least as seen from the author's vantage. It has, however, often been held against Luke that no other historical source attests to such a general decree of Augustus around the year 6 CE. It is thus argued that Luke has erroneously equated the census under Quirinius with a non-existant edict of Augustus. But just as in 2 Kgs 20:1, where "those days" refers to an event some twenty years before the last mentioned event in the narrative—or in Matt 3:1, to one at least twenty years after it—there is no reason why in Luke 2:1 the phrase could not refer to a still more distant past.

Actually, in 28 BCE, after an *intermezzo* of some forty years, Augustus and his colleague M. Agrippa carried out as city-censors the long overdue/postponed census in Rome and Italy in order to assess the number of Roman citizens (*Res Gestae Divi Augusti* II.8). The following year the emperor issued a decree by which he allotted a number of provinces of the empire to the senate, such as Asia and Bithynia, but kept others for himself, notably Gaul, Spain and Syria (Dio Cassius 53.12). The most fitting occasion for him to have issued general instructions about the census to be carried out in these provinces, too, was this decree of 27 BCE.[8] Augustus himself took this provincial census in Gaul in the same

---

[8] In D. W. J. Gill and C. Gempf (eds.), *The Book of Acts in its First Century Setting* (Grand Rapids: Eerdmans, 1994) 2:280 the "constitutional settlement" by Augustus is dated to 23 BCE (for Cyprus only?).

year, and in Spain probably in 26 BCE (Dio Cassius 53.22.5). In the Eastern half of the empire, which he did not visit in 27/26, the measure must have been effected through the emperor's governors. Indeed, when Augustus himself did travel to the East, from 22 to 19 BCE, we are told that he either reduced or raised the tribute in several cities of Asia and Bithynia (Dio Cassius 54.7.4–5). Such corrective measures presuppose that a local census had previously been completed there as well, most likely also in the years 27–26 BCE.

At this time Judea did not form part of the empire; it came under provincial administration only after the removal of Archelaus in 6 CE, when it was annexed to the adjacent province of Syria. Consequently, a provincial census cannot have been held in Judea before this occasion. Luke thus seems to understand the census under Quirinius to be the result of the edict of Augustus, as a kind of "standing order" perhaps, even though it had already been carried out decades earlier elsewhere and in some provinces more than once. It is completely logical, then, that in addition to his remark about the institution of the provincial census as such, Luke can remark that it was taken in Judea for the first time under Quirinius. In this light, the formulation in Luke 3:2: αὕτη ἀπογραφὴ πρώτη ἐγένετο ἡγεμονεύοντος τῆς Συρίας Κυρηνίου may now be translated more naturally: "This first census came about[9] *when Quirinius was governing* Syria." Using the genitive absolute, as we saw earlier, it clearly means "after Quirinius had taken office." Both inscriptions and other historical records confirm that Quirinius became governor of Syria in 6 CE., and he was especially commissioned to confiscate Archelaus' possessions and submit the recently annexed Judea to the census.[10] For Luke at the time when he was writing, then, "in those days" simply means "during the (long) reign of Augustus."[11] Inasmuch

---

[9] That this expression was difficult to understand is further indicated by the fact that a number of mss. insert the definite article ἡ after αὕτη, so that the text reads "this *was the* first census, when …" While scholars have recognized that the definite article here is an interpolation, most modern translations continue to render the passage with this sense. Still others have tried to stretch the construction even farther by allowing the word πρώτη a comparative sense, and thus to refer to a "former" census before that of Quirinius. Neither of these readings is warranted by the Greek.

[10] So Josephus, *Ant.* 18.1–2 (cf. 17.385; 18.26); Tacitus, *Ann.* 3.48. For the inscription, which gives the date and mentions the census, see H. Dessau, *Inscriptiones Latinae Selectae* (Berlin: Weidmann, 1892–1916) no. 2683 (cf. also nos. 3004, 6095, 8150, and 9502–3 for other aspects of Quirinius' career).

[11] Even so, it seems difficult to square Luke's chronology here with the reference in Luke 1:5, which clearly places the general frame of the birth narrative "in the days of

as the pluperfect tense in Koine Greek, as in Latin, came to be used more and more for the pre-past, Luke might well have used it here instead of the aorists ἐγένετο and ἐξῆλθεν, but not necessarily so. Elsewhere he also uses the aorist for actions or events that took place before some other past action, e.g., in Acts 14:27: "and they reported all that God had done (ἐποίησεν; Vulgate: *fecisset*) through them and that he had opened (ἤνοιξεν; Vulgate: *aperuisset*) the door of belief to the gentiles."

Josephus, Ant. Iud. *18.65: "About this same time"*

Such a broad connotation of the various temporal constructions was not limited to the MT, LXX, or NT. A telling instance is found in Josephus' *Ant.* 18. Having related the notorious *Testimonium Flavianum* (18.63–64) about the crucifixion of Jesus under Pilate, Josephus goes on in the very next section (18.65–84) to tell about the simultaneous expulsions of the Jewish community and the Isis-cult from Rome. In reality, however, these expulsions had already happened some years earlier, in 19 CE.[12] As is well known, Pilate only came to Judea in 26 CE, and the death of Jesus occurred some time after this date. Josephus introduces the anachronistic expulsion episode as follows: "And *about this same time* (ὑπὸ τοὺς αὐτοὺς χρόνους) another disaster disturbed the Jews, while there also occurred practices not free of scandal around the Isis-temple in Rome." Even if the *Testimonium Flavianum* (18.63–64) were entirely deleted from the text as an alleged interpolation, the anachronism in Josephus' terminology remains; for the immediately preceding paragraphs (18.55–62) still deal with Pilate's administration of Judea. Moreover, the event preceding this account of Pilate's administration is the death of Antiochus of Commagene and the ensuing assassination of Germanicus (18.53–54); like the expulsions (18.65–84) the latter also occurred in 19 CE. In any case, then, Josephus' narrative does not run in a strictly chronological order. Indeed, it seems that Josephus intentionally placed the events in this order and connected them using the

---

Herod the king" (cf. Matt 2:1), i.e., at least ten years earlier, unless one assumes that this is instead a reference to Archelaus, who appears on his own coinage and elsewhere as "Herod;" see J. D. M. Derrett, "Further Light on the Narratives of the Nativity," *NT* 17 (1975) 83; and G. Mussies, "Lucas 2:1–6 in enig recent onderzoek," *Nederlands Theologisch Tijdschrift* 51 (1997) 89–103.

[12] Tacitus, *Ann.* 2.85; Suetonius, *Tib.* 36; Dio Cassius 57.18.5a.

temporal construction for transition.[13] Thus, the introductory temporal formula at 18.65 simply means "during the reign of Tiberius," as seen from the author's vantage when writing his narrative some 50–75 years later. According to *Ant.* 20.267 Josephus completed the work in 93/94 CE.

To sum up, then, temporal phrases using "day/days" are extremely variable as to meaning in biblical Hebrew as well as in the Greek literature, both Jewish and Christian, that was influenced by it. In these last three cases, temporal phrases such as "in those days" or "at the same time" do not refer to a strict chronological sequence in relation to preceding and succeding episodes within each narrative. In each case the connotation is determined relatively within the surrounding literary context by establishing a general time-frame defined by the reign of a king or kings. In Matt 3.1 it encompasses the perod from Herod to some time well after the removal of Archelaus, but told from a distant perspective that is apparently not able to make fine gradations of time. In the latter two cases, the author's distant vantage point plays an equally important role. Here, moreover, the traditional Semitic and Septuagintal constructions for time have been correlated to reflect Roman imperial rule. In other words, "in those days" the parameters of a given ruler established the broad and relative contextual lines—presumably functioning as common knowledge between author and audience—for establishing narrative referents, but without strict chronological precision, at least not by the standards of "our day."

---

[13] Similarly, the rest of the introductory sentence at 18.65: "another disaster disturbed (ἐθορύβει) the Jews" must also presuppose the two uprisings described previously under the administration of Pilate; these occur in 18.55–59 (the incident with the standards) and 60–62 (the appropriation of temple funds), respectively. So it should be noted that each one ends with some reference to "disturbances" on the part of the local Jewish population: so, θορυβεῖν (18.58) and θορυβοῦντας (18.62). Thus, these two episodes under Pilate provide the context for the reference to "another" disturbance in 18.65. Finally, immediately after completing the description of the expulsion of the Jews in 19 CE (18.84) Josephus resumes with events in 35–36 CE, at the end of Pilate's tenure (18.85–89). This episode, which resulted in Pilate's slaughter of Samaritans (cf. Luke 13.1) and his eventual removal from office (18.89), is also introduced with thematic references to "disturbance" (θορύβου) in 18.85 & 88.

DISTINCT LEXICAL MEANINGS
OF ΑΠΑΡΧΗ IN HELLENISM, JUDAISM AND
EARLY CHRISTIANITY

David E. Aune

Introduction

Despite the many treatments of ἀπαρχή which have appeared in lexical reference works, the semantic problems presented by the usage of this term in the New Testament have not yet been satisfactorily resolved. Three specific problems may be mentioned at the outset. First, though the term ἀπαρχή in the NT and early Christian literature is used only of *people*, ἀπαρχή is used of people just twice in the LXX (Pss. 77:51; 104:36), both in a non-cultic context, though lexical discussions rarely take account of this fact. However, ἀπαρχή is often used of people in a literal sense in Hellenistic usage, suggesting that terms like ἀπαρχή were part of the living, developing language of native Greek speakers. It is methodological problematic to focus exclusively on Graeco-Jewish usage as a context for understanding the semantics of NT and early Christian lexemes. Second, most commentators are convinced that ἀπαρχή is used figuratively or metaphorically in the NT and early Christian literature with the sole exceptions of Rom 11:16 and *Did.* 13:3–7. A close analysis of the contextual meanings of ἀπαρχή, however, does not support this assumption.

Third, lexical discussions of ἀπαρχή by Biblical scholars have been often flawed by inaccuracies. Some lexical discussions of ἀπαρχή by NT scholars, particularly those with a primarily theological agenda, for example, have claimed that the term is used of people in the LXX. Consider the following statement by Alexander Sand:[1]

> The LXX is likewise familiar with ἀπαρχή as a concept in sacrificial vocabulary (Exod 23:19; 25:2; 36:6; Lev 22:12; Deut 12:6, 11, 17; 18:4; 26:2, 10; Ezek 44:30). In this context it has to do with the flawless first-fruits of natural products, the firstfruits of *human beings* [emphasis mine], animals, and plants (in Ezekiel ἀπαρχή several times denotes a piece of farm land

---

[1] Alexander Sand, "ἀπαρχή," *EDNT* 1.116.

which must be turned over to God when the land is purchased), all of which are owed to Yahweh (or the sanctuary).

The problem with this statement is that ἀπαρχή is *never* used in the LXX of "the first-fruits of human beings ... which are owed to Yahweh (or the sanctuary)," at least not in the passages to which he refers. It is therefore problematic that Sand applies the gloss "first-fruits" to human beings. While בְּכֹרָה בְּכוֹר or בְּכוֹר (plural בְּכֹרֹת) can refer to the firstborn of animals or human beings, it *never* refers to inanimate objects and is *never* translated ἀπαρχή in the LXX, but rather is frequently rendered πρωτότοκος (131 times), followed by πρωτογενής (twice: Exod 13:2; Prov 24:70 [MT 31:2]), παιδίον (once: Deut 25:6), and πρεσβύτερος (twice: Job 1:13, 18). The masculine plural form בְּכוּרִים can mean "first-fruits," usually with cultic connotations, but is *never* used of animals or humans in the OT,[2] and is *never* translated ἀπαρχή (or ἀπαρχαί) in the LXX, even though the plural form ἀπαρχαί is perhaps the most logical gloss to use in Greek.

Sand is not alone in making erroneous claims for the meaning of ἀπαρχή. In Gerhard Delling's otherwise excellent discussion of ἀπαρχή, he makes the following statement:[3]

> In the LXX ἀπαρχή is first used in the original sense a. of the "first-fruits" of the field or flocks which is offered to God (Dt. 18:4; 26:2, 10; Nu. 18:8–12; Neh 10:37ff.; cf. Ez. 45:13–16) and thus separated to Him and sanctified (Nu. 5:9). The fiction is maintained that the ἀπαρχαί of men and cattle also belong to God (Nu. 18:15).

The problem with this statement is the fact that ἀπαρχή in the LXX is not used of the "first-fruits" of flocks, nor of men. LXX Num 18:15 actually reads τὰ πρωτότοκα τῶν ἀνθρώπων καὶ τὰ πρωτότοκα τῶν κτηνῶν τῶν ἀκαθάρτων, "the firstborn of humans and the firstborn of unclean animals," *not* αἱ ἀπαρχαὶ τῶν ἀνθρώπων καὶ αἱ ἀπαρχαί τῶν κτηνῶν τῶν ἀκαθάρτων. Similarly, in a theological discussion of first-fruits in the proclamation of the NT, Martin Albertz observed:[4] "Die ἀπαρχή ist nun im Alten Testament die Opfergabe. So ist der Erstling der Erstgeborene einer Ehe, 1. Mose 49, 3; 5 Mose 21, 17." The problem with this statement is that ἀπαρχή does not occur in LXX Gen 49:3 and Deut 21:17, where πρωτότοκος occurs as the translation of בְּכוֹר.

---

[2] M. Tsevat, *TDOT* 2.122.

[3] *TDNT* 1.485.

[4] Martin Albertz, "Die 'Erstlinge' in der Botschaft des Neuen Testament," *Evangelische Theologie* 12 (1952–53) 151.

The core of the problem may be that though these scholars purport to be discussing the meanings of ἀπαρχή, in reality they are primarily concerned with the Hebrew word בְּכוֹר, and are so preoccupied with the religious concept of "first-fruits" that they neglect the specific linguistic data which pertains to the particular lexemes and the semantic fields to which they belong. The statements just quoted by Sand, Delling and Albertz, can be contrasted to the very similar, but accurate, statement made by H.-G. Link and C. Brown:

> ἀπαρχή, used since Sophocles and Herodotus, is a technical term of sacrificial language and denotes the first fruits of any sort, e.g. of natural products of livestock, which were sacred to the deity and had to be consecrated to it before the whole could be given over to profane use (Herodotus 1.92). In religious contexts there is also occasional mention of the offering of individual men or of whole groups to the deity (Plutarch, *De Pythiae Oraculis* 16; *Quaestiones Graecae* 35).

The claims made in this quotation accurately and succinctly summarizes the available literary evidence, for in Greek culture generally (though not in the LXX), ἀπαρχή is used for the first-fruits of the field and the flock as well as of human beings.

Some lexical problems, given the nature of the extant data, are simply insoluble. For instance, as I have observed above, the Hebrew word בְּכוֹר and its feminine plural בְּכֹרֹת refer *only* to the firstborn of animals and human beings,[5] while the masculine plural form בְּכוּרִים refers *only* to the "first-fruits" or "first portion" of cereal and fruit crops which are presented to God in a cultic context.[6] It is not clear why this is so. Neither term is ever translated ἀπαρχή in the LXX.[7] רֵאשִׁית is also used to refer to the "first-fruits" (of the field) in a cultic sense, but again it is not at all clear what difference, if any, existed between רֵאשִׁית and בְּכוּרִים in Israelite sacrificial protocol.[8] The semantic problem is compounded by the rare phrase רֵאשִׁית בִּכּוּרִים, translated as τὰς ἀπαρχὰς τῶν πρωτο-γεννημάτων (Exod 23:19 [cf. Philo *De sacr.* 72]; 34:26; Ezek 44:30), "the firstlings of the firstborn."

---

[5] *DCH* 2.170–72.

[6] *DCH* 2.172. One apparent exception is the *DCH* emendation of Nahum 3:12= 4QpNah [=4Q169] 4:9 to a reading meaning "your people are first-fruits," which appears unlikely given the normal range of meaning of בְּכוּרִים. A second exception is the sole LXX translation of בִּכּוּרִים as τὰ πρωτότοκα πάντων, "the firstborn of everyone," which apparently misunderstands the Hebrew.

[7] Takamitsu Muraoka, *Hebrew/Aramaic Index to the Septuagint* (Grand Rapids: Baker Books, 1998) 27.

[8] Tsevat, *TDOT* 2.122.

Lexical Analyses of ἀπαρχή

In this section I will briefly review and critique some of the existing lexical treatments of ἀπαρχή. One problem which besets the lexicography of ἀπαρχή is the explicit or implicit tendency to adopt a model of the historical development of the various meanings of the word, even though such reconstructions are highly speculative given the paucity of the evidence. Such historical reconstructions often presume a basic meaning or *Grundbedeutung* for ἀπαρχή from which all subsequent meanings are derived. A second problem with assessing the meaning of ἀπαρχή is the possibility of Semitic interference, i.e., to what extent is ἀπαρχή a Greek word with a Hebrew meaning? A third problem is that ἀπαρχή can only occasionally be translated "first-fruits" (the usual gloss for the most common definition of the term), for when it is used of animals the term "firstlings" is obviously more appropriate. When ἀπαρχή is used of people and translated "first-fruits," a metaphorical meaning is clearly presupposed. For other uses of the term it is not always clear what the appropriate alternative definitions and glosses should be.

1. *Henri Éstienne (Henricus Stephanus)*, Thesaurus Graecae Linguae *(1831–65)*

Henri Éstienne (1531–98) was the erratic linguistic genius who published the *Thesaurus Graecae Linguae* in five volumes in 1572, an enormous feat of erudition arranged, in accordance with prevailing lexical fashion, etymologically rather than alphabetically.[9] This work, retaining its original awkward etymological arrangement but interlarded with a mass of additional information, was re-published in nine volumes in London in 1816–28. A massive rearrangement of the work in alphabetical order constituted a third edition which was published in eight volumes by Firmin Didot in 1831–65; it began under the editorship of Karl Benedict Haase with the first volume (covering alpha in two parts), and continued under the co-editorship of Wilhelm and Ludwig

---

[9] The etymological arrangement of lexica remained standard for centuries. See, for example, the NT Greek lexicon produced by Christian Stock, *Clavis Linguae Sanctae Novi Testamenti* (3rd ed.; Jena: Joh. Felicem Bielkckium, 1737) 150, where the relatively extensive (and well-organized) entry under ἀπαρχή is typically buried in the entries following APX.

Dindorf. The second part of the first volume on alpha, in which the term ἀπαρχή is treated, consists of 2,794 columns.

The 1572 edition of the *TGL* contained an eleven-line column entry under ἀπαρχή (buried in a long collection of lexemes sharing the root **APX**) listing the meanings "Primitiae" ["first-fruits"] and "Libamentum" ["drink-offering, first-fruits"] and listing works in which the term appeared but not the more exact locations of books, chapters, and so forth. In the second edition ἀπαρχή continued to be buried in an even longer and more rambling group of lexemes based on **APX**, now expanded to seventeen column lines, with the addition of a few new references and a list of nine new meanings largely uncoordinated with specific texts exhibiting those meanings in Greek literature: "Libamen ['drink-offering, first-fruits'], Primitia [pl. 'first-fruits'], Delibatus ['of first-fruits'], Delibatio ['first-fruit'], Praemetium ['preliminary harvest, first-fruits'], Incoeptio ['beginning'], Inchoatio ['beginning'], Primitiae ['first-fruits'] and Primordium ['beginnings, origin']."[10] The third edition of the *TGL* (fully alphabetized) contains a much expanded entry of 117 column lines (17 devoted to the use ἀπαρχή in early Christian texts), with many new definitions and scores of texts exemplifying usage. The uses of ἀπαρχή catalogued in *TGL*³ served as a data base for examples of usage which were drawn on by LSJM and other western Greek lexica.

2. *The LSJM* Greek-English Lexicon *(9ᵗʰ edition 1925–40; Supplement 1996)*

A short but broad treatment of the meanings of ἀπαρχή in ancient Greek literature, papyri and inscriptions generally is found in the *Greek-English Lexicon* of Liddell-Scott-Jones-McKenzie,[11] which borrowed heavily from *TGL*³).[12] Liddell and Scott produced several editions of their lexicon, the first appearing in 1843, the second in 1845, the third in 1849, the fourth (fully revised) in 1855, the fifth in 1861, the sixth in 1869, the seventh in 1882, the eighth in 1897, and finally the ninth

---

[10] Henricus Stephanus, *Thesaurus Graecae Linguae* (9 vols.; London: Valpian, 1816–28) 3.2293.

[11] Henricus Stephanus, *Thesaurus Graecae Linguae* (8 vols.; Paris: Firmin-Didot, 1829) vols. 1, part 2.1208–9.

[12] H. G. Liddell, R. Scott, H. S. Jones and R. McKenzie, *A Greek-English Lexicon* (9ᵗʰ ed.; Oxford: Clarendon, 1940) 180, now supplemented by P. G. W. Glare and A. A. Thompson, *Greek-English Lexicon: Revised Supplement* (Oxford: Clarendon Press, 1996) 41.

edition was published in ten fascicles from 1925 to 1940, the last fascicle appearing the year following the death of the principal editor, H. Stuart Jones, and three years after the death of Roderick MacKenzie. Seven categories of meaning for ἀπαρχή are proposed in LSJM (the references included are highly selective): (1) *beginning of a sacrifice, primal offering* (of hairs from the forehead), Euripides *Orest.* 96; later a *banquet* held on this occasion (Plutarch 2.40b), (2) *firstlings* for sacrifice or offering, *first-fruits*, both literally (Exod 25:2; Rom 11:16) and metaphorically (1 Cor 15:20; James 1:18), (3) further metaphorical meanings, e.g., ἀπαρχὴ τῆς σοφίας ἀνέθεσαν, Plato *Prot.* 343b [referring to the maxims inscribed on the temple of Apollo at Delphi], (4) *tax on inheritances* (*P. Taur.* 1.7.10; *Stud. Pal.* 4.72J), (5) *entrance fee* (*P. Teb.* 316.10J), (6) apparently *a board of officials* sent by a city to order the affairs of a colony (*IG* 12[8].273, 280, 283, 285 [Thasos]),[13] (7) *birth-certificate* of a free person (*P. Teb.* 316.10), perhaps used metaphorically in Rom 8:23.

The LSJM treatment of ἀπαρχή is typical of that lexicon in that it consists of a catalogue of meanings attested in a variety of ancient texts with little attempt to impose a framework of the historical development of the various meanings listed. The order of meanings begins with the most common meanings and ends with the less common, more peripheral or specialized meanings. Meanings (4) and (5) are very similar and may be defined as payments made, often in currency or precious metals, in a context of subordination or dependency. The common phrase in Attic tribute lists, ἀπαρχὴ τοῦ φόρου, "payment of tribute" (Dittenberger, *Sylloge*, 18,51; 19,8), could be included here. There are, however, several distinct meanings of ἀπαρχή which LSJM has missed (see below), e.g., "sacrifice" (with no connotation of priority), "gift," and the application of the term to human beings as well as to animals and agricultural produce.

3. *J. H. Thayer,* Greek-English Lexicon *(1889)*

In J. H. Thayer's translation and expansion of the German lexicon of C. G. Wilke and C. L. W. Grimm, the basic meaning of ἀπαρχή is "the first fruits of the productions of the earth … which were offered to God," a meaning found in the LXX (Num 15:19–21), but attested

---

[13] Supplemented by Glare and Thompson, *Greek-English Lexicon: Revised Supplement*, 41.

in the NT only in Rom 11:16.[14] He then proposes three categories for
the "transferred use" of ἀπαρχή: (1) "of persons consecrated+ to God,
leading the rest in time" (e.g., 1 Cor 16:15; Rom 16:5; James 1:18; 2 Thess
2:13; 1 Cor 15:20, 23), (2) "of persons superior in excellence to others of
the same class" (e.g., Rev 14:4), (3) those "who have the first-fruits (of
future blessings) in the Spirit" (Rom 8:23).

Thayer, like Bauer-Aland below, proposes a basic meaning for ἀπαρχή, but unlike Bauer-Aland derives it exclusively from the Hebrew
Bible, the LXX and the NT (Rom 11:16). However, most lexemes have
no basic meanings, only distinct meanings which vary from common
meanings to highly marked, peripheral meanings. Since he restricted
ἀπαρχή to Judaeo-Christian literature, the range of meanings of ἀπαρχή proposed is unnecessarily restricted (i.e., those consulting the lexicon
can only choose from the meanings presented, though some which are
not presented may be valid possibilities). When Thayer proposes that
ἀπαρχή can mean "persons superior in excellence to others of the same
class," he cites only Rev 14:4 and a late but instructive scholion on
Euipides *Oresteia* 96 (ἀπαρχὴ ἐλέγετο οὐ μόνον τὸ πρῶτον τῇ τάχει ἀλλὰ
καὶ τὸ πρῶτον τῇ τιμῇ, "ἀπαρχή means not only the first in order but
also the first in honor"). Two definitions proposed by Thayer are significant: "of persons consecrated to God, leading the rest in time," and "of
persons superior in excellence to others of the same class, though it is
doubtful whether either should be considered instances of "transferred
use."

4. *Gerhard Delling*

In the context of an article on ἄρχω, κτλ. in the first volume of the *Theologisches Wörterbuch zum Neuen Testament*, which appeared in 1930, Delling
devoted the equivalent of two pages to ἀπαρχή outside the NT and in
the NT.[15] Despite the errors in Delling's article to which I have called
attention above (see note 3), he provides an otherwise excellent, though
necessarily brief, discussion of the lexical evidence outside the NT. He
points out that the earliest Greek literary evidence indicates that ἀπαρχή has three literal meanings: (1) "first-fruits of natural products," (2)

[14] J. H. Thayer, *A Greek-English Lexicon of the New Testament* (New York: Harper and
Brothers, 1889) 54.
[15] Gerhard Kittel (ed.), *Theological Dictionary of the New Testament*, trans. G. W. Bromiley (9 vols.; Grand Rapids: Eerdmans, 1963–74) 1.484–86.

"proportionate gift" from the earnings or possessions of the pious giver, as well as "thankoffering," and (3) "an 'offering' to the deity or to the servants or sanctuary of the deity, whether as a special or regular offering," e.g., the Jewish tax, firstruits to the state or inheritance tax. Delling then distinguishes three figurative meanings: (1) προσφθεγμάτων ἀπαρχαί, the first greeting to Apollo (Euripides *Ion* 401–2), (2) "beginning," and (3) "certification of birth." He then calls attention to the use of ἀπαρχή when applied to people, e.g., portions of the population of a city who colonize a new region, as well as individuals who dedicate themselves to a deity for service at a sanctuary or children who are dedicated by their parents. This latter meaning of ἀπαρχή is important for understanding Rev 14:4 (see below).

It is striking that much of the material briefly discussed by Delling has apparently not had much of an impact on his own discussion of ἀπαρχή in the NT, nor has it had any discernible influence on the German and English revisions of Bauer's lexicon. Delling presents the various meanings of ἀπαρχή in a way that suggests an implicit notion of their historical development. He refers, for example, to the "original sense" of ἀπαρχή in the LXX as "first-fruits."

5. *Moulton and Milligan (1930)*

An important article on ἀπαρχή was included in the specialized lexicon compiled by Moulton and Milligan.[16] After surveying the papyri, they draw the following important conclusion:

> It is clear that the connotation "*first*-fruits" could·not be pressed in our exegesis of the term when it appears in NT apart from associations wholly outside the field survey in this article; and we are perhaps at liberty to render "sacrifice" or "gift" where it improves the sense.

Though the lexicographical evidence in this reference work is limited to non-literary sources, papyri and inscriptions, it is striking that even inscriptions which go back to the sixth century BCE provide evidence for understanding ἀπαρχή to mean simply "gift" or "sacrifice" with no emphasis on spatial or temporal priority.[17]

---

[16] J. H. Moulton and G. Milligan, *The Vocabulary of the Greek Testament Illustrated from the Papyri and Other Non-Literary Sources* (Grand Rapids: Eerdmans, 1980 [originally published in 1930]) 54.

[17] One striking example is the inscription published by Wilhelm Dittenberger, *Sylloge Inscriptionum Graecarum* (2nd ed.; 3 vols.; Leipzig: S. Hirzel, 1900) 529.21, 35–38.

6. *Walter Bauer (German and English Versions)*

The Bauer-Arndt-Gingrich-Danker lexicon proposes two main categories of meaning for ἀπαρχή with extensive subdivisions within the first category:[18] (1) A technical sacrificial term for "first-fruits" of any kind (including animals, both domesticated and wild), which were holy to the divinity and were consecrated before the rest could be put to secular use" (only pagan Greek literature is cited in support). A. Literally "first-fruits" of bread dough (Num 15:18–21), produce of the wine-press and threshing-floor (*Did* 13:3–6; 1 *Clem* 29:3). b. Figuratively: α. Of persons, first-fruits of Christians (Rom 16:5; 1 Cor 16:15; perhaps 2 Thess 2:13; 1 *Clem* 42:4; James 1:18; Rev 14:4; Philo *Spec. leg.* 4.180). β. Of things (Rom 8:23; Barn 1:7). 2. "Birth certificate" also suits the context of Rom 8:23 (an addition found only in the English translation).

The Bauer-Aland lexicon, which took no notice of any of the changes introduced in the Bauer-Arndt-Gingrich-Danker translation and revision of the fourth edition of Bauer's lexicon, reorganized the categories of meaning of ἀπαρχή.[19] Beginning, like Thayer, with the basic meaning of ἀπαρχή as "Erstlingsgabe jeder Art," a technical sacrificial term, two major categories of meaning are then proposed: 1. Actual or literal meaning, i.e., "Erstlinge" of crops and animals (Rom 11:16; Num 15:18–21; *Did* 13:3–7; 1 *Clem* 29:3). 2. Extended meanings: a. Persons (Rom 16:5; 1 Cor 16:15; 2 Thess 2:13; 1 *Clem* 42:4); more generally (James 1:18). b. Things (Rom 8:23; Barn 1:7).

The Bauer-Aland lexicon, like that of Thayer, falls into the trap of proposing a basic meaning for ἀπαρχή from which the subsequent meanings are supposedly derived. Rather than argue that words have basic meanings (*Grundbedeutungen*) shared by all the specific meanings of a word, it is more appropriate to distinguish between more generic and more specific meanings and between distinct meanings of a word marked by context, some of which are more common than others. In both versions of this lexicon, the English translation of the fourth German edition and the sixth German edition, two qualifications are proposed under 1.b.α (BAGD) and 2.a (Bauer-Aland), respectively for the

---

[18] Walter Bauer, *A Greek-English Lexicon of the New Testament and Other Early Christian Literature*, trans. and rev. W. F. Arndt, F. W. Gingrich and F. W. Danker (2nd ed.; Chicago: University of Chicago, 1979) 81.

[19] Walter Bauer, *Griechisch-deutsches Wörterbuch zu den Schriften des Neuen Testaments und der frühchristlichen Literatur*, hrsg. von Kurt Aland und Barbara Aland (6. Aufl.; New York and Berlin: Walter de Gruyter, 1988) 162.

figurative or transferred meaning of ἀπαρχή when used of persons: (1) a lesser emphasis on chronological sequence than quality is reflected in James 1:18 and Rev 14:4, and (2) the original meaning of ἀπαρχή is weakened so that it becomes almost equivalent to πρῶτος when applied to Christ in 1 Cor 15:20, 23. The first qualification contrasts chronological sequence with quality, though neither of these two aspects of meaning has been mentioned previously. The second qualification implies a historical development of ἀπαρχή which is not confirmed by the data. Finally, the first category of meaning in both versions of Bauer is based on the one common meaning of the term in pagan Greek (ἀπαρχή included both agricultural products and animals), and the limitation of ἀπαρχή to agricultural products in the LXX (a more marked or limited meaning of the term) is not mentioned.

7. *Louw and Nida*

The Greek-English lexicon edited by Johannes Louw and Eugene A. Nida has abandoned the alphabetical listing of Greek lexemes and substituted a complex system of semantic domains.[20] In the brief treatment of ἀπαρχή by Louw and Nida, the word is given three meanings: (1) "first portion," i.e., "the first portion of something which has been set aside and offered to God before the rest of the substance or objects can be used—'first portion, first offering,'" e.g., Rom 11:16 (§53.23), located in the semantic domain of "Offering, Sacrifice" (§53.16–27), within the larger field of "Religious Activities" (§53). (2) "First," i.e., "the first of a set, often in relation to something being given—'first,'" e.g., 1 Cor 15:20 (§61.8), located in the semantic field of "Sequence" (§61), and (3) "Foretaste," a figurative extension of the meaning of (1), "a foretaste and pledge of blessings to come—'foretaste, pledge, foretaste and pledge,'" e.g., Rom 8:23 (§57.171), in the semantic field of "Pay, Price, Cost" (§57.152–171).

Since the construction of semantic domains in the Lous-Nida lexicon is based exclusively on Greek lexemes from the New Testament (from a linguistic perspective, a small, limited, and rather arbitrary collection of Greek linguistic evidence from the early imperial period), it is hardly representative of written Koine (oral Koine is of course inaccessible),

---

[20] Johannes P. Louw and Eugene A. Nida (eds.), *Greek-English Lexicon of the New Testament Based on Semantic Domains* (2 vols.; 2nd ed.; New York: United Bible Societies, 1989).

and so cannot disclose various meanings of ἀπαρχή which a more comprehensive selection of texts might suggest. Nevertheless, approaching
lexicography from the perspective of semantic domains is an important
step forward in assessing the range of meanings represented by individual lexemes.

8. *Lust-Eynickel-Hauspie (1992–96)*

There is a very short entry under ἀπαρχή in the recent lexicon of
the LXX edited by Lust, Eynickel, and Huspie.[21] Though extremely
brief, and restricted to the LXX, it is limited to glosses rather than
definitions (a significant limitation). However, the list of glosses is generally excellent: (1) "offering" (Exod 25:3), (2) "the first (offering)" (Deut
26:10), (3) "portion" (1 Sam 10:4), (4) "first-offerings" (Exod 23:19), (5)
"first-fruits" (Exod 22:28). Meanings (2) and (4), however, do not appear
to be distinct enough to constitute two distinct meanings. In formulating meanings (1) and (3), the editors recognize that ἀπαρχή can be
used without an indication of temporial or spatial prioriy. These usages
are important because they reflect a widespread common meaning of
ἀπαρχή recognized by both Delling and Moulton-Milligan.

9. *Ceslas Spicq*

Perhaps the most detailed and competent lexical discussion of ἀπαρχή
is the article by Ceslas Spicq.[22] Spicq is aware of the variety of ways in
which ἀπαρχή was used in pagan Greek, but in discussing the NT texts
he sees only the influence of the OT, refracted by Philo and the rabbis,
as relevant for understanding those texts. He concludes that ἀπαρχή
in the NT emphasizes less the offering to God than the connection
between the first-fruits and the entire harvest, emphasizing the unity
between the first-fruits and the rest of the harvest.

---

[21] J. Lust, E. Eynickel and K. Hauspie, *A Greek-English Lexicon of the Septuagint* (2 vols.;
Stuttgart: Deutsche Bibelgesellschaft, 1992–96) 45.
[22] Ceslas Spicq, O.P., *Theological Lexicon of the New Testament*, trans. J. D. Ernest (3 vols.;
Peabody: Hendrickson, 1994) 1.145–52.

10. *General Lexical Conclusions*

First, the importance of defining each distinctive meaning of ἀπαρχή, rather than simply providing glosses which fail to convey the nuances of each distinctive meaning is carried through consistently only in the Louw-Nida lexicon, though some helpful definitions are formulated by Thayer and the German and English lexicons associated with the name Walter Bauer. In most of the analyses of ἀπαρχή summarized above, it is far from clear whether the authors attempted to distinguish between the *distinct meanings* of ἀπαρχή, and there are many instances in which no definition is provided at all.

Second, a major problem in the lexicography of ἀπαρχή is that the eight occurrences of the word in the NT are used figuratively, even though all 76 uses of the term in the LXX are used literally. While בְּכוֹר is occasionally used figuratively in the OT in such phrases as "the firstborn of death" (Job 18:13), Israel as the "firstborn of Yahweh" (Exod 4:22), "Ephraim is my [Yahweh's] firstborn" (Jer 31:9), how and why did the figurative extensions in meaning of ἀπαρχή arise?

ἀπαρχή *in Graeco-Jewish Literature*

The term ἀπαρχή occurs 76 times in the LXX (36 times in the plural), while the verb ἀπάρχεσθαι, "to offer (the first-fruits of)" or "to offer first-fruits," occurs six times (2 Chr 30:24 [*bis*]; 35:7, 8, 9; Prov 3:9).[23] ἀπαρχή is used to translate several different Hebrew words: תְּרוּמָה (37 times), רֵאשִׁית (17 times), חֵלֶב (twice: Num 18:12), תְּנוּפָה (once: Exod 39:21 [MT: 38:24]), מִצְעָר (once: Deut 12:16[17]). ἀπαρχή also appears five times in the LXX with no corresponding lexeme in the underlying Hebrew text (Exod 22:29; Num 18:1; 1 Kgs 10:4; Ezek 20:31; 48:12), and eight times in books which do not occur in the Hebrew Bible. Though בִּכּוּרִים can mean "first-fruits," it is inexplicably never translated with ἀπαρχή in the LXX, though it is rather frequently rendered by πρωτογεννήματα (Exod 23:16, 19; 34:26; Lev 2:14; 23:17, 20; Num 18:13; 2 Kgs 4:42), once by ἀρχή (Exod 34:22),[24] once by πρόδρομοι (Num 13:20), and once by τὰ ἔα (Num 28:26).

---

[23] The basic translation "(Erstlings-) Opfer darbringen" is proposed by Friedrich Rehkopf, *Septuaginta-Vokabular* (Göttingen: Vandenhoeck & Ruprecht, 1989) 30.

[24] ἀρχή is used by Philo as a synonym for ἀπαρχή (*Her.* 113–16).

There are just two passages in the LXX in which the term ἀπαρχή is used of human beings, Psa 77:51 (MT: 78:51) and the closely parallel Psa 104:36 (MT: 105:36). In both passages ἀπαρχή is used in the second colon of a synonymous couplet as a term parallel to πρωτότοκος, both lexemes referring to the firstborn of Egypt who were destroyed in the plague narrated in Exod 12:29–36:[25]

Psa 77 (MT 78):51	*Psa 104 (MT 105):36*
καὶ ἐπάταξεν πᾶν πρωτότοκον	καὶ ἐπάταξεν πᾶν πρωτότοκον
And he struck every firstborn	And he struck every firstborn
ἐν Αἰγύπτῳ,	ἐν τῇ γῇ αὐτῶν,
in Egypt,	in their land,
ἀπαρχὴν τῶν πόνων αὐτῶν	ἀπαρχὴν παντὸς πόνου αὐτῶν
the first of their toils	the first of all their toil
ἐν τοῖς σκηνώμασι Χαμ.	
In the tents of Ham	

In both passages (which are literal translations of the underlying Hebrew text) πρωτότοκος is used to translate בְּכוֹר, and ἀπαρχή renders רֵשִׁית. Even though ἀπαρχή is used in both Psa 77:51 and 104:36 of human beings, ἀπαρχή does not have a cultic meaning in these contexts, and is therefore not used figuratively or metaphorically, but simply means "the first (of a series),"[26] i.e., in this case the first or eldest son, ἀπαρχή is closely associated in meaning with πρωτότοκος.

The cognate term ἀρχή is used figuratively in Jer 2:3, where it refers to all Israel and in this instance means "first-fruits":

ἅγιος Ἰσραὴλ τῷ κυρίῳ
Holy is Israel to the Lord

ἀρχὴ γενημάτων αὐτοῦ [רֵאשִׁית תְּבוּאָתֹה]
the first-fruits of his produce.

πάντες οἱ ἔσθοντες αὐτὸν πλημμελήσουσιν
All who eat it will transgress.

The phrase רֵאשִׁית תְּבוּאָתֹה, which underlies ἀρχὴ γενημάτων αὐτοῦ, can be translated "the first-fruits of his harvest," a metaphor which emphasizes the inviolability of Israel. Just as consuming the first-fruits incurs the penalty of the Law (though no specific penalty is mentioned

---

[25] πρωτότοκος and ἀπαρχή occur as parallel terms in Philo *Spec. leg.* 2.134, where πρωτότοκοι is used of the Egyptian firstborn and ἀπαρχαί of the Israelite firstborn.

[26] Louw and Nida, *Greek-English Lexicon* 1.§61.8.

in Torah) so harming Israel will provoke punishment by Yahweh. This metaphor is paraphrastically translated in *Targ. Jer.* 2:3:[27]

> The house of Israel are holy before the Lord in respect of those who plunder them like fruits of heave-offering of harvest, of which whoever eats is guilty of death; and like firstlings of harvest, the sheaf of the heave-offering, of which every one who eats, before the priests the sons of Aaron offer it as a sacrifice upon the altar, is guilty. Even so are all those who plunder the house of Israel guilty: evil shall come upon them, says the Lord.

In the OT and in early Jewish literature, terms meaning "first fruits" occur frequently, most often referring to an actual portion of the agricultural harvest, representing the entire harvest.[28] The term בְּכוֹר ("firstborn") a term often used synonymously with גָּדוֹל ("eldest"), is based on the same root as בִּכּוּרִים ("first fruits"), and the assumption is that the firstborn or firstlings of animals and people (i.e., the first and the best) as well as the first fruits of the field, belong to God.[29] The presentation of the first fruits of the harvest, which could not be consumed by the offerer (Jer 2:3b), represent and thereby sanctify the entire harvest which can then be subject to profane consumption (Lev 23:14; cf. Prov 3:9–10). In the OT the first fruits was an offering reserved for priests and Levites,[30] a practice which continued in some segments of early Christianity according to *Did* 13:3–7. There is evidence in the OT that רֵאשִׁית takes on the meaning "the best."[31]

It is important to emphasize the fact that the term ἀπαρχή is *never* used cultically or literally of the firstborn of animals or people in the LXX or early Graeco-Jewish literature. Therefore the figurative use of ἀπαρχή when applied to people in the NT, whether individually or collectively, is a metaphor drawn from the first fruits of the field, such as barley, wheat, bread, grapes and so forth.

---

[27] Robert Hayward, *The Targum of Jeremiah* (Aramaic Bible 12; Wilmington: Glazier, 1987) 48–48.
[28] Exod 23:19; 34:22; Lev 23:9–14; Num 28:26–27; Deut 16:9–12; Deut 26:1–11; 2 Kgs 4:42; Neh 10:35 [MT v. 36]; Prov 3:9–10; *Ep. Arist.* 158; *T. Levi* 9:7, 14; *T. Judah* 21:5; *T. Iss.* 5:6; 1QS 6.5–6; 1QSa 2.18–19; Josephus *Ant.* 4.70; 9.273; *Apost. Const.* 8.40.2); see *TWAT* 1.644–45; 7.292–93; *EDNT* 1.116–17; J. Milgrom, "First Fruits, OT," *IDBSup*, 336–37; R. O. Rigsby, "First Fruits," *ABD* 2.796–97.
[29] Exod 13:2–16; Lev 27:26–27; Num 3:44–51; 18:13–17; Deut 14:23–26; Neh 10:36 [MT v. 37]; Josephus *Ant.* 4.70; cf. Ezek 20:25–26.
[30] Num 18:12–13; Deut 18:4; Ezek 44:30; Sir 7:31; 45:20.
[31] Num 24:20; 1 Sam 15:21; Jer 49:35; Amos 6:6; see *TWNT* 1.644; 7.293; Rigsby, "First Fruits," *ABD* 2.796.

The Mishnah has two tractates particularly relevant for the present discussion, *Bikkurim* ("first fruits") and *Bekhoroth* ("firstlings") which contain most of the discussion of various aspects of both cultic practices in the Mishnah. All uses of בִּכּוּרִים are both literal and cultic. *M. Bik.* 1.3 refers to the seven types of agricultural products which which first-fruits can be brought, presumably the list of seven found in Deut 8:8: wheat, barley, grapes, figs, pomegranates, olive oil and date honey (cf. *m. Ber.* 6.4). The first fruits must be brought to the temple mount (*m. Bik.* 1.9; 2.10; 3.2; cf. Deut 26:2), and given to the priests (*m. Bik,* 2.1; *m.Maʿaʾś. Š.* 5.6). The rabbis were very conscious of the fact that no specific measure for the amount of first fruits was prescribed in the Torah (*m.Peah* 1.1), and it was apparently possible for a person to designate an entire field of crops as first-fruits (*m.Bik.* 2.4). Philo refers to the practice of giving tithes of agricultural produce as first-fruits (*De virt.* 95).

Philo frequently mentions ἀπαρχή or ἀπαρχαί in his commentaries. He can use ἀπαρχαί in a non-cultic context to mean "samples" of food (*Her.* 253) similar to Dionysius Hal. who speaks of ἐμμέτρων τε καὶ πέζων λόγων ἀπαρχὰς ὀλίγας προχειρισάμενος, "selecting a few examples of poetic and prose passages" (*Comp.* 3). When he refers to ἀπὸ τῶν πρωτοτόκων τὰς ἀπαρχαί, "the firstlings from the firstborn" (*De sacr.* 136), he is departing from the normal use of ἀπαρχαί in the LXX and using it as the virtual equivalent of the firstborn male child (see *Conf.* 124, where, again comparing Cain and Abel, he maintains the LXX distinction by referring to Cain's retention of the ἀπαρχαί and Abel's offering of τὰ πρωτότοκα). Elsewhere he speaks of presenting firstborn males as a kind of ἀπαρχή ("offering") which he designates as χαριστήρια, "thankoffering" (*Spec. leg.* 138), and he speaks of fathers who have many sons presenting one of them as an ἀπαρχή to God, while Abraham has but one son and yet offers him to God (*Abr.* 196). Philo frequently uses the phrase ἀπαρχὴ καρπῶν (*Sacr.* 72). Philo also provides an allegorical interpretation of ἀπαρχαί as a "word of thanksgiving" (*Sacr.* 74; *Somn.* 272; cf. *Pss. Sol.* 15:3, where ἀπαρχή is similarly used metaphorically of speech in praise of God). He uses ἀπαρχαί in other figurative senses also, such as the ἀπαρχαί or tithe of the reason, the first and best thing within us (*Cong.* 98), thus equating the tithe with ἀπαρχή (*Mut.* 191–92). He also interprets the ἀπαρχή of reaping, not of the land but of ourselves (*Somn.* 77, 272).

For Josephus ἀπαρχαί (in the twelve occurrences of this lexeme, the plural form occurs ten times) refers most frequently to ἀπαρχαὶ καρπῶν, literally "first-fruits" (*Ant.*3.251; 4.70; 9.273; cf. 3.235, 250; 4.226), and the ἀπαρχή of wool (*Ant.* 4.71). When referring to the sacrificial offering of firstborn animals, he does not use ἀπαρχή, but maintains the practice of the LXX in limiting the term to agricultural products, and refers to them as τὸ γεννηθὲν πρῶτον, "the first born" (*Ant.* 4.70) and to firstborn human males as ἀνθρώπου πρωτότοκος (*Ant.* 4.71). He uses the singular ἀπαρχή just twice; once for the booty (silver and gold) from Jericho that was to be dedicated to God in his rewriting of Josh 6 (*Ant.* 5.26), and again for David's gift of three thousand talents of gold to help Solomon finance the building of the temple (*Ant.* 7.378).[32] The interesting phrase ἀπαρχὰς ἀναθημάτων, "first-fruits of dedicatory offerings" (using a genitive of apposition meaning "first-fruits, that is, dedicatory offerings") occurs in a putative letter from Ptolemy Philadelphus in the Letter of Aristeas (Josephus *Ant.* 12.50). In *Ant.* 16.173, ἀπαρχαί seems to refer in a general sense to "offerings" which do not include animals intended for sacrifice, nor do the notions of primacy or representation appear to be implied.

ἀπαρχή *in the Greek World*

In the ancient Mediterranean world, there were three primary types of "sacrifice" or gifts to the gods (i.e., commodities withdrawn from regular human use): offerings of food, offerings of objects (votive offerings) and animal sacrifices, all of which could be designated as ἀπαρχαί.[33] The offering of first-fruits (ἀπαρχή or ἀκροθίνια), which belongs to the first category, was regarded by the Greeks as "the simplest and most basic form of uncorrupted piety."[34] The means of offering first-fruits, however, exhibited a wide spectrum: they may be offered to any god; they may be left at a holy place until they decompose or are eaten by animals or scavengers; they may be thrown into ponds, rivers, or the sea; they may be burned.

ἀπαρχή or ἀπαρχαί (the lexeme usually occurs in the plural form) exhibits a number of distinctive meanings in Greek sources. In Euripides *Orestes* 96, Helen refers to her κόμης ἀπαρχὰς καὶ χοάς, "offering of hair and drink offering." However, a more appropriate gloss for ἀπαρχαί in this context might be "representative offering," and a working

---

[32] The text here is problematic.
[33] Stengel, "ἀπαρχαί," *PW* 1.2666–8; Burkert, *Ritual*, 52–54.
[34] Walter Burkert, *Structure and History in Greek Mythology and Ritual* (Berkeley: University of California Press, 1979) 52.

definition of this distinctive meaning of ἀπαρχαί can be: a category of sacrifice in which that which is offered to the deity, though only a small part of a whole, nevertheless carries with it the implication that the whole entity has been sacrificed, i.e., made holy. The cultic meaning of ἀπαρχαί in Greek literature, as in the OT and early Jewish literature, refers most often to agricultural products,[35] in which case the gloss "first-fruits" is more appropriate than "representative offering." In the oldest occurrence of ἀπαρχή in Greek literature, it is very close in meaning to ἀνάθημα, and refers to a "representative offering" by Croesus of the wealth he inherited from his father (Herodotus 1.92). ἀπαρχαί, which tended to be regarded in a universally positive manner (in contrast to animal sacrifices which were opposed by some Greek philosophical traditions such as Pythagoreanism and Neopythagoreanism) could consist of crops, wine or both (Sophocles *Trach.* 183; Euripides *Phoen.* 857) or in a metaphorical sense the speech which greets Apollo (Euripides *Ion* 401–2). The equivalent term in Latin is *primitiae*, which in Roman sacrificial ritual similarly refers to the offering of the first-fruits of a harvest.[36] In Rome, as in ancient Israel, the produce of a new harvest could not be eaten until the offering of first-fruits had been made (Pliny *Hist. nat.* 18.8).

The phrase ἀπαρχὴ ἀνθρώπων or ἀπαρχαὶ ἀνθρώπων occurs frequently in Greek literary and non-literary sources.[37] Here ἀνθρώπων is a genitive of material or content, so that the whole phrase could be translated "offering consisting of people," with no suggestion of primacy. This reflects the Greek custom of dedicating individuals, often prisoners of war, to a deity, such as Apollo, who then become temple servants (Euripides *Ion* 327; Diodorus 4.66.5 [here Daphne is dedicated as an ἀκροθίνιον to the god]; Pausanias 7.3.1).

One example drawn from a story repeated several times in Plutarch is found in *Theseus* 16.2 (LCL trans.):

---

[35] *Odyssey* 14.422 (verb ἀπάρχεσθαι); Herodotus 4.71; Sophocles *Trach.* 183, 761; Euripides *Phoen.* 857, 1524; Thucydides 3.85; Isocrates *Archidamus* 96; Aristotle *Nic. Eth.* 8.11 [1160a]; *SIG,* 83.55; 200.10; 455.2; 502.40; 739.5; see Stephanus, *TGL* I/2.1208–9; Delling, *TDNT* 1.484–85.

[36] Pliny *Hist. nat.* 18.2.8; 18.30.119; Varro *De lingua latina* 6.16; Ovid *Fasti* 2.520; *Metam.* 8.274; Livy 26.11.9; Dionysius Hal. *Ant. Rom.* 7.72.15; Dio Cassius 73.16 [two gold coins are called "first-fruits"]; Georg Wissowa, *Religion und Kultus der Römer,* (2. Aufl.; München: C. H. Beck, 1912), 409–410; *OLD* 1456.

[37] Stengel, "ἀπαρχαί," 2667.

And he [Aristotle] says that the Cretans once, in fulfilment of an ancient vow, sent ἀνθρώπων ἀπαρχήν to Delphi, and that some descendants of those Athenians were among the victims, and went forth with them.

In this LCL translation, Bernadotte Perrin translated the phrase ἀνθρώπων ἀπαρχήν as "an offering of their first-born," though there is no indication (apart from the use of the term ἀπαρχή itself) that these people were in fact "firstborn." The phrase could more appropriately be translated "human offering." Plutarch narrates another version of the same story in *Quaest. Graecae* 298f–299a:

Κρῆτάς φασιν εὐξαμένους ἀνθρώπων ἀπαρχὴν εἰς Δελφοὺς ἀποστεῖλαι,
They say that the Cretans, because of a vow, sent ἀνθρώπων ἀπαρχὴν to Delphi,

τοὺς δὲ πεμφθέντας, ὡς ἑώρων οὐδεμίαν οὖσαν εὐπορίαν,
but when those who were sent saw no means of livelihood there,

αὐτόθεν εἰς ἀποικίαν ὁρμῆσαι
they left there to found a settlement.

Here F. C. Babbitt, correctly, I think, translates ἀνθρώπων ἀπαρχή as "consecrated offering of people," since there is nothing in the context to suggest that this group of men were either the firstborn or constituted part of a larger group.

A similar text is found in Plutarch *De Pythiae oraculis* 401f–402a:

ἐπαινῶ … ἔτι μᾶλλον Ἐρετριεῖς καὶ Μάγνητας,
I applaud … the Eretrians and the Magnesians even more,

ἀνθρώπων ἀπαρχαῖς δωρησαμένους τὸν θεόν
who presented the god with ἀνθρώπων ἀπαρχαῖς,

ὡς καρπῶν δοτῆρα καὶ πατρῷον καὶ γενέσιον καὶ φιλάνθρωπον
as the dispenser of crops, but also as the god of their fathers, and the progenitor and the lover of humankind.

I have translated the last line somewhat paraphrastically to emphasize the contrast in the text between crops on the one hand and people on the other. While in this case F. C. Babbitt translates ἀνθρώπων ἀπαρχαῖς as "with the first-fruits of their people," it would be more appropriate if he had rendered the phrase "with a consecrated offering of people."

A final example of the use of the phrase ἀπαρχὴ ἀνθρώπων is found in Philo *Spec. leg.* 4.180:

διότι τοῦ σύμπαντος ἀνθρώπων γένους ἀπενεμήθη
There it has been rendered of the entire human race

οἷά τις ἀπαρχὴ τῷ ποιητῇ καὶ πατρί
as a sort of offering to the Maker and Father.

Here ἀπαρχὴ is used in a qualitative sense of "best, choice."

Ἀπαρχή *in Early Christian Literature*

The lexeme ἀπαρχή occurs nine times in the NT, seven of which occur in the Pauline corpus,[38] and nine times in the Apostolic Fathers.[39] ἀπαρχή is used seven times in a figurative sense in the NT, while in the Apostolic Fathers just three uses are figurative (*Barn.* 1:7; *1 Clem.* 24:1; 42:4). In Judaeo-Christian literature ἀπαρχή is usually in the collective singular, while in pagan Greek literature it is the plural, though the plural does occur in *Barn.* 1:7 and *1 Clem.* 42:4. Unlike the LXX, ἀπαρχή is used in early Christian literature of human beings, both in a singular way of Christ (1 Cor 15:20, 23; *1 Clem.* 24:1), as well as of initial converts to Christianity from particular regions (Rom 16:5; 1 Cor 16:15; 2 Thess 2:13; James 1:18; *1 Clem.* 42:4). Rev 14:4 presents particularly difficult interpretive problems which require special discussion.

1. *Roman 11:16*

Rom 11:16 is the only instance in the NT in which ἀπαρχή refers to the OT sacrificial ritual of first-fruits, and provides us with a useful definition of the term: εἰ δὲ ἀπαρχὴ ἅγια καὶ τὸ φύραμα, "if the first portion is holy, so is the whole batch of dough" (an allusion to Num 15:20–21, where the phrase ἀπαρχὴν φυράματος occurs).[40] However, nowhere in the OT is it ever made explicit that the offering of the ἀπαρχή makes holy the whole from which it is taken, a fact noted by many commentators. The terms ἀπαρχή and. φύραμα here, the part and the whole, constitute a metaphor, with ἀπαρχή representing Jewish Christians, and φύραμα representing all the seed of Abraham. It is of interest that Philo also interprets Num 15:20–21 allegorically, and understands φύραμα as referring to individuals, while the ἀπαρχαί are the holy impulses of soul or body which are virtuous (*Sacr.* 107–9;

---

[38] Rom 8:23; 11:16; 16:5; 1 Cor 15:20, 23; 16:15; 2 Thess 2:13; James 1:18; Rev 14:4.

[39] *Did.* 13:3 [*bis*], 5, 6, 7; *Barn.* 1:7; *1 Clem* 24:1; 29:3; 42:4.

[40] For Philo (*Spec. leg.* 1.132–34) the ἀπαρχή functions as a means of providing priests, who have no other means of livelihood, with a variety of food necessary to sustain themselves.

cf. 117). Rather than regarding ἀπαρχή as fulfilling a cultic obligation which renders the rest of the agricultural produce as free for profane use, Paul extends the notion of holiness from the representative portion to the entire entity from which it was derived. A working definition of the meaning of ἀπαρχή in Rom 11:16 is this: a category of sacrifice in which that which is offered to the deity, while only a fraction of the whole, nevertheless carries with it the implication that the whole entity has been sacrificed, i.e., made holy.

2. *Christ as* ἀπαρχή

There are three passages in early Christian literature in which the term ἀπαρχή is used of Christ (1Cor 15:20, 23; *1Clem.* 24:1), and all of them require lexical reassessment. In 1Cor 15:20 the following statement is made:

> νυνὶ δὲ Χριστὸς ἐγήγερται ἐκ νεκρῶν,
> But now Christ has been raised from the dead,
>
> ἀπαρχὴ τῶν κεκοιμημένων.
> as ἀπαρχή of those who have died.

Here ἀπαρχή is a nominative of apposition, and the two clauses are essentially parallel. In 1Cor 15:23, the subject is still the final resurrection:

> Ἕκαστος δὲ ἐν τῷ ἰδίῳ τάγματι·
> But each in his or her own order;
>
> ἀπαρχὴ Χριστός,
> Christ as ἀπαρχή,
>
> ἔπειτα οἱ τοῦ Χριστοῦ ἐν τῇ παρουσίᾳ αὐτοῦ.
> Then those who belong to Christ at his return.

In both passages there is a clear sequential connection between Christ as ἀπαρχή and "the dead" or "those who have fallen asleep" in 1Cor 15:20, and "those who belong to Christ" in 1Cor 15:23. The third passage is found in *1Clem.* 24:1, where the author betrays an awareness of 1Cor 15:[41]

> κατανοήσωμεν, ἀγαπητοί, πῶς ὁ δεσπότης ἐπιδείκνυται διηνεκῶς ἡμῖν
> We know, beloved, what the Lord continually reveals to us

---

[41] Andreas Lindemann, *Die Clemensbriefe* (HNT 17; Tübingen: Mohr-Siebeck, 1992) 86.

τὴν μέλλουσαν ἀνάστασιν ἔσεσθαι,
what the coming resurrection will be like,

ἧς τὴν ἀπαρχὴν ἐποιήσατο τὸν κύριον Ἰησοῦν Χριστὸν
of which he made the Lord Jesus Christ the ἀπαρχή

ἐκ νεκρῶν ἀναστήσας.
by raising him from the dead.

Here ἡ μέλλουσα ἀνάστασις, "the coming resurrection" refers to the eschatological resurrection of all believers, and the resurrection of Christ provides the model for what that will be like.

The conventional interpretation of all three passages understands ἀπαρχή as a metaphor for the first portion of the harvest which guarantees the rest of the harvest.[42] On reflection, however, there is nothing in the literal cultic ritual of dedicating the ἀπαρχή to God which provides a comprehensible basis for such a metaphor, for the ἀπαρχή in no way "guarantees" the remainder of the harvested crop from which it is taken. Rather, the presentation or dedication of the ἀπαρχή releases the rest of the crop for profane use. In all three passages, ἀπαρχή can be glossed "first," but should be defined as "the first of a set, often in relation to something being given,"[43] i.e., "the first [in a series]," a relatively common meaning of ἀπαρχή in pagan Greek usage. It is inappropriate to claim that the "original" meaning is greatly weakened so that ἀπαρχή almost equals πρῶτος.[44] It is therefore inappropriate to translate ἀπαρχή in any of these passages as "first-fruits" which would suggest a metaphorical understanding of the term.[45] In all three passages, ἀπαρχή is not used metaphorically, but literally.

---

[42] I give just three examples: Johannes Weiß, *Der erste Korintherbrief* (9. Aufl.; Göttingen: Vandenhoeck & Ruprecht, 1977) 356; Archibald Robertson and Alfred Plummer, *A Critical and Exegetical Commentary on the First Epistle of Paul to the Corinthians* (ICC; 2nd ed.; Edinburgh: T. & T. Clark, 1914) 351–51; Gordon Fee, *The First Epistle to the Corinthians* (NICNT; Grand Rapids: Eerdmans, 1987) 749.

[43] Louw and Nida, *Greek-English Lexicon* 1.§61.8.

[44] Bauer-Aland, *Wörterbuch*, 162.

[45] Hans Conzelmann recognizes the problem when he observes that "The history of the concept ἀπαρχή, 'firstfruits,' is of little help in regard to the meaning" (this observation is quite wrong), but nevertheless concludes that "Here [1 Cor 15:20] Paul is stating in the first instance that Jesus is the first of a series" (*1 Corinthians* [Hermeneia; Philadelphia: Fortress, 1975] 268), yet he translates ἀπαρχή as "firstfruits" in both 1 Cor 15:20 and 23. ἀπαρχή is translated "firstfruits" in 1 Cor 15:20, 23 in nearly all modern English translations (RSV; NRSV; NEB; REB [both the NEB and REB render 1 Cor 15:20 as "first fruits of the harvest of the dead"]; NAB; NIV).

Closely parallel phrases include πρωτότοκος [ἐκ] τῶν νεκρῶν, "first-born from the dead" (Col 1:18; Rev 1:5),[46] and ὁ Χριστός εἰ πρῶτος ἐξ ἀναστάσεως νεκρῶν, "Christ, [the] first of the resurrection from the dead," i.e., "Christ, the first to rise from the dead" (Acts 26:23). In this latter passage, πρῶτος means "the first in a series," and therefore over-laps in meaning with ἀπαρχή in 1 Cor 15:20, 23; *1 Clem.* 24:1.

3. *Christians as* ἀπαρχή

There are five occurrences of the term ἀπαρχή in the NT and the Apostolic Fathers in which it is applied to converts (Rom 16:5; 1 Cor 16:15; 2 Thess 2:13; James 1:18; *1 Clem.* 42:4). In three of these passages, ἀπαρχή is followed by a partitive genitive: (1) in Rom 16:5, Paul refers to Epaenetus "who is the ἀπαρχή of Asia in Christ." (2) In 1 Cor 16:15 he refers to the household of Stephus as the ἀπαρχή of Achaia. (3) Finally, In James 1:18, the author tells the recipients that God "brought us forth by the word of truth that we should be a kind of ἀπαρχή of his creatures."

In two other passages, ἀπαρχή is used absolutely: (1) in 2 Thess 2:13, the author tells the recipients that "God chose you as ἀπαρχή for sal-vation by sanctification of the Spirit and by faith in the truth." (2) According to *1 Clem.* 42:4, κατὰ χώρας οὖν καὶ πόλεις κηρύσσοντες καθί-στανον τὰς ἀπαρχάς αὐτῶν ... εἰς ἐπισκόπους καὶ διακόνους, "Preach-ing throughout districts and cities, they appointed their τὰς ἀπαρχάς as bishops and deacons." The plural possessive pronoun αὐτῶν can refer either to the apostles or to the districts and cities. It is inappropriate to translate ἀπαρχαί in this context as "first converts," for it makes little sense to suppose that Clement thought that the apostles appointed their first converts to serve as bishops and deacons. Rather, ἀπαρχαί should be understood to mean something like "outstanding converts," i.e., the term is used in a qualitative rather than temporal sense.

4. ἀπαρχή *and the Eschaton (Rom 8:23 and* Barn. *1:7)*

One of the more difficult ἀπαρχή texts in the New Testament is found in Rom 8:23: ἀλλὰ καὶ αὐτοὶ τὴν ἀπαρχὴν τοῦ πνεύματος ἔχοντες, ἡμεῖς καὶ αὐτοὶ ἐν ἑαυτοῖς στενάζομεν υἱοθεσίαν ἀπεκδεχόμενοι, τὴν ἀπολύτρω-

---

[46] The term πρωτότοκος is too problematic to be discussed in this context.

σιν τοῦ σώματος ἡμῶν, "But we ourselves—who have the ἀπαρχή of the Spirit—we groan within ourselves in expectation of our adoption, the redemption of our bodies." Even though ἀπαρχή here is typically translated "first-fruits" in this passage (AV, RSV, NRSV, NEB, REB, NAB, NIV), it is obviously not a question of a gift by humans to the deity, but rather a gift by God to humans. Many commentators have pointed this out, but they err in assuming that ἀπαρχή here is a metaphor drawn from the cultic language of the LXX. In OT cultic usage, the ἀπαρχή may represent the remainder of the harvested crop, but it does not "guarantee" the rest of the crop nor can it be considered a "downpayment" which will be followed by the rest of the crop, for the ἀπαρχή is the representative portion of the crop which belongs to God, so that the rest of the crop may be consumed or disposed of by the farmer. The genitive τοῦ πνεύματος can be construed as either a genitive of apposition, i.e., "the ἀπαρχή, that is, the Spirit," or "the ἀπαρχή consisting of the Spirit," or it can be construed as a genitive of possession, i.e., "the ἀπαρχή belonging to the Spirit" (probably the former).[47] The contrast in this verse is between the present situation in which Christians have the ἀπαρχή of the Spirit (with a strong contextual element of inwardness indicated by the phrase ἐν ἑαυτοῖς στενάζομεν) and the future situation, i.e., the full realization of eschatological salvation, described as the attainment of υἱοθεσία, which Paul then explains with an accusative of apposition, τὴν ἀπολύτρωσιν τοῦ σώματος ἡμῶν.

It seems clear that ἀπαρχή in this context constitutes a "down payment," and is thus overlaps in meaning with ἀρραβών ("first installment, down payment, pledge, deposit") used similarly in 2 Cor 1:22 and Eph 1:4. As we have seen above, ἀπαρχή can be used of various financial transactions in which a representative portion of a larger amount is paid as a fee, tax or gift, and thus ἀπαρχή in Rom 8:23 can be glossed "pledge, first installment," without making it necessary to consider it a figurative extension of a literal cultic meaning of ἀπαρχή. It is instructive to observe that ἀπαρχή is also juxtaposed with the notion of redemption in Rev 14:4 (ἀπολύτρωσις and ἀγοράζω belong to the same semantic field).[48]

---

[47] C. E. B. Cranfield, *A Critical and Exegetical Commentary on the Epistle to the Romans* (ICC; 2 vols.; Edinburgh: T. & T. Clark, 1975–79) 1.418.

[48] Louw and Nida, *Greek-English Lexicon*, 1.§ 37.128 (ἀπολύτρωσις); § 37.131 (ἀγοράζω), both in the semantic domain of "Release, Set Free (§ 37.127–138)."

According to *Barn.* 1:7, "the Lord made known to us through the prophets what has happened and what is happening and has given us the ἀπαρχαί of a taste of what will happen." The phrase ἀπαρχαὶ γεύσεως, is often, and I think appropriately, translated "foretaste."[49] Here ἀπαρχή means "sample, example," a meaning found in Philo *Her.* 253 and Dionysius Hal. *Comp.* 3, discussed above and also categorized as a distinct meaning of ἀπαρχή by Louw-Nida.[50] While it is not completely clear just was the author of *Barnabas* means by τῶν μελλόντων ἀπαρχαί γεύσεως, "a foretaste of what is coming," it is likely that he means knowledge derived from the prophets, i.e., partial knowledge of the future.

5. *Revelation 14:4*

One of the more problematic occurrences of ἀπαρχή in the NT is found in Rev 14:4, where the 144,000 are referred to as οὗτοι ἠγοράσθησαν ἀπὸ τῶν ἀνθρώπων ἀπαρχὴ τῷ θεῷ καὶ τῷ ἀρνίῳ, "these were ransomed from humanity as ἀπαρχή to God and the Lamb." Here ἀπαρχή is a collective singular functioning as a nominative of apposition modifying οὗτοι, and gives the appearance of being a gloss on the text. This possibility is suggested by a parallel text in Rev 5:9 (part of a hymn addressed to the Lamb) where the term ἀπαρχή is missing: καὶ ἠγόρασας τῷ θεῷ ἐν τῷ αἵματί σου, ἐκ πάσης φυλῆς καὶ γλώσσης καὶ λαοῦ καὶ ἔθνους, "and you redeemed for God by your blood [people] from every tribe and language and people and nation." The parallelism between these two passages becomes even clearer when it is noted that ἀπὸ τῶν ἀνθρώπων is a summary of the more typical and expansive expression ἐκ πάσης φυλῆς καὶ γλώσσης καὶ λαοῦ καὶ ἔθνους. The connection between οὗτοι ἠγοράσθησαν and ἀπαρχή is far from clear. οὗτοι ἠγοράσθησαν is a metaphor drawn from the practice of manumission, i.e., the release of a person from slavery, while ἀπαρχή very likely refers to the dedication of these "freed slaves" to the service of God and the Lamb.

---

[49] Robert A. Kraft, *Barnabas and the Didache*, Vol. 3 of *The Apostolic Fathers: A New Translation and Commentary*, ed. R. M. Grant (New York: Thomas Nelson, 1965) 82; Ernst Baasland and Reidar Hvalvik, *De apostoliske Fedre* (Oslo: Luther Forlag, 1984) 167 ("en forsmak"); J. B. Lightfoot and J. R. Harmer, *The Apostolic Fathers*, ed. Michael W. Holmes (2nd ed; Grand Rapids: Baker Book House, 1989) 162; Andreas Lindemann and Henning Paulsen, *Die apostolischen Väter* (Tübingen: Mohr-Siebeck, 1992) 29 ("Vorgeschmack").

[50] Louw and Nida, *Greek-English Lexicon*, 1.§57.171.

In this context, ἀπαρχή represents 144,000 people who are part of a much larger group, all humanity. The problem, however, is to determine the intended relationship between the ἀπαρχή and all humanity. It makes little sense, however to construe ἀπαρχή as the first of a set, the remainder of which will follow, i.e., all humanity, for the modern concept of universal salvation was unknown to our author. It is rather appropriate to understand ἀπαρχή here in terms of the widespread Greek understanding of the term as reflected in the phrase ἀπαρχὴ ἀνθρώπων, i.e., as a "consecrated offering of people," i.e., "servants devoted to" God and the Lamb (cf. Plutarch *Quaest. Graecae* 298f–299a; *De Pythiae oraculis* 401f–402a).

6. ἀπαρχή in the Didache

The term ἀπαρχή occurs five times in a single context in Did. 13:3–7, and is used exclusively of parts of various categories of possessions which are surrendered to God (i.e., a prophet or the poor), presumably as an expression of thanksgiving:

> 3 Therefore, taking every ἀπαρχήν of the produce of the winepress and of the threshing floor, and of cattle and of sheep, you will present τὴν ἀπαρχήν to the prophets, for they are your high priests. 4 But if you have no prophet, give it to the poor. 5 If you make bread, take τὴν ἀπαρχήν and give it in accordance to the commandment. 6 Similarly when you open a jar of wine, take τὴν ἀπαρχήν and give it to the prophets. 7 Also take[51] τὴν ἀπαρχήν of silver and of clothing and of every possession, as seems best to you, give it in accordance with the commandment.

This passage reflects the prescriptions of Num 18:12: "All the best of the oil, and all the best of the wine and of the grain, the first fruits of what they give to the Lord, I give to you." A close parallel is occurs in Deut 18:3–4:

> And this shall be the priests' due from the people, from those offering a sacrifice, whether it be ox or sheep: they shall give to the priest the shoulder and the two cheeks and the stomach. The first fruits of your grain, of your wine and of your oil, and the first of the fleece of your sheep, you shall give him.

---

[51] The firstlings of animals which belong to the Lord is mentioned in Lev 27:26 (see 11QT 60:3–4), while the tithe of herds and flocks is mentioned only in Lev 27:32 and 2 Chron 31:6, and thereafter in Jub. 32:15.

There are several striking features of these cultic uses of ἀπαρχή some of which go well beyond the halakahic prescriptions found in the Torah.[52] First, unlike the LXX, the term is used both for agricultural products as well and for the firstlings of livestock. Second, tithing is not mentioned (neither here nor elsewhere in the Didache), though tithing and ἀπαρχή are very closely linked in the OT. Third, just as vv. 3–4 presuppose a rural situation,[53] vv. 5–7 apparently applies the obligation to present ἀπαρχή to an urban situation. Fourth, while money is mentioned, this form of property never occurs in the OT as a basis for ἀπαρχή.[54] Fifth, the ἀπαρχή of cattle for the surrogates of the high priest is mentioned once in the Torah in Lev 27:26, and then also in 11QT 60:3–4. Sixth, nowhere in the Torah is the first portion of the products of grain and grapes, namely, bread and wine.

John M. Court has argued that the Didache's use of ἀπαρχή, a term drawn from LXX language of sacrifice, is used in a figurative or spiritual rather than literal way.[55] His proposal is unconvincing for two reasons. First, actual sacrificial commodities are involved, even though they are presented to surrogates of the OT priests. Second, the halakic features of Did. 13:3–7 reflect a development well beyond the prescriptions of the Torah, indicating that they are drawn from a living and developing halakic tradition.

Conclusions

After calling attention to a number of inaccuracies in modern lexical assessments of the meaning of ἀπαρχή in the LXX on the part of NT scholars, some major lexical treatments of ἀπαρχή were reviewed, from the three editions of *Thesaurus Graecae Linguae* founded by Henri Ésti-

---

[52] The comments on the problems of this passage by Kurt Niederwimmer are remarkably unhelpful in that no attempt is made to situate the halakic prescriptions of Did. 13:3–7 within the context of analogous halakic developments in early Judaism and early Christianity (*The Didache* [Hermeneia; Minneapolis: Fortress, 1998] 191–93).

[53] W. Rordorf and A. Tuilier, *La doctrine des Douze Apôtres (Didachè)* (SC 248; Paris: Les Éditions du Cerf, 1978) 98, 190, n. 3.

[54] According to *Jub.* 32:2, Jacob tithed everything which came with him, man, beast, gold, all sorts of vessels and clothes. Cf. Luke 18:12, where the Pharisee claims to give tithes of all that he gets. See Gedaliah Alon, "The Halacha in the Teaching of the Twelve Apostles," *The Didache in Modern Research*, ed. Jonathan Draper (AGJU 37; Leiden: Brill, 1996) 191–94. The conversion of the second tithe or *terumah* into money is mentioned in Deut 14:24–27; cf. Tob 1:7.

[55] John M. Court, "The Didache and St. Matthew's Gospel," *SJT* 34 (1981) 116–17.

enne (1572), to the *Greek-English Lexicon of the Septuagint* edited by Lust, Eynickel and Hauspie (1992–96). Some of the problems in these analyses include failed attempts to trace a historical developments of the meanings of ἀπαρχή and related attempts to identify a basic meaning of the term from which all secondary meanings are derived. Another problem is the assumption that the use of ἀπαρχή in the NT and early Christian literature is based almost exclusively on the LXX, whereas it is clear that the meanings of such lexemes cannot be properly assessed apart from general Greek usage.

Thereafter the meanings of ἀπαρχή in Graeco-Jewish literature and pagan Greek were surveyed. While the notion of representation is often explicitly or implicitly present in the uses of ἀπαρχή or ἀπαρχαί, that is not always true and each context needs careful examination. One common meaning of ἀπαρχή in the LXX and Josephus relates to the representative offering of agricultural products, appropriately translated as "first-fruits," but never applied to human beings (LXX Pss. 77:51 and 104:36 are not exceptions). Philo, on the other hand understands ἀπαρχή-sacrifices more broadly, in line with pagan Greek usage, of animals and humans as well as agricultural products. An important use of ἀπαρχή or ἀπαρχαί in pagan Greek usage is its application to humans who are consecrated to particular deities as slaves for temple service, with no trace of explicit representation whatsoever, either as "first-fruits" or "first-born" used either literally or metaphorically.

Finally, all the passages in which ἀπαρχή or ἀπαρχαί occurs in the NT (nine times) and the Apostolic Fathers (nine times) were reviewed, and it was concluded that while ἀπαρχή or ἀπαρχαί are frequently thought to be used metaphorically in all contexts with the exception of Rom 11:16 and *Did.* 13-3–7, in reality the terms are used literally, in one or another of its distinctive meanings in all of its occurrences in these two bodies of literature. This is particularly striking in 1 Cor 15:20, 23 and *1 Clem.* 24:1, where the identification of Christ as ἀπαρχή from the dead is not a metaphorical use of a cultic term from the LXX in which the ἀπαρχή ("first-fruits") guarantees the rest of the harvest, but rather is a common use of ἀπαρχή with the distinctive meaning "first of a set."

Perhaps the major lesson to be learned from this survey of the meanings of ἀπαρχή in Graeco-Jewish and pagan Greek literature, inscriptions and papyri as linguistic contexts for understanding the language of early Christianity is that the lexicographical task is far from over. In a very real sense it is entering into a new and significant phase.

COMPILATION OF LETTERS
IN CICERO'S CORRESPONDENCE

Hans-Josef Klauck

Defining the Task[1]

Scholars in the twentieth century have divided most of the authentic Pauline letters into two or more independent parts, arguing that these were combined to form one canonical letter only at the stage of a post-Pauline redaction. This has been postulated in the case of 1 Thessalonians,[2] the Corinthian correspondence,[3] Philippians[4] and Ro-

---

[1] This theme takes up a line of investigation into ancient letters and their relation to New Testament epistolary literature, for which our esteemed colleague, Abraham J. Malherbe, set the path; see his *The Cynic Epistles: A Study Edition* (SBLSBS 12; Atlanta: Scholars Press, 1977); *Ancient Epistolary Theorists* (SBLSBS 19; Atlanta: Scholars Press, 1988), esp. 20–27 (on Cicero). For Cicero, see also Hans-Josef Klauck, *Die antike Briefliteratur und das Neue Testament: Ein Lehr- und Arbeitsbuch* (Uni-Taschenbücher 2022; Paderborn: Ferdinand Schöningh, 1998) 126–33, with further literature (in the following notes I take the opportunity to add some new titles on ancient epistolography which have not yet been given in my book). Special thanks are due to Dr. Brian McNeil, Munich, for correcting my English, and to John T. Fitzgerald and L. Michael White for editing the manuscript.

[2] Walter Schmithals, "The Historical Situation of the Thessalonian Epistles," *Paul and the Gnostics* (Nashville: Abingdon, 1972) 123–218; Christoph Demke, "Theologie und Literarkritik im 1. Thessalonicherbrief. Ein Diskussionsbeitrag," *Festschrift für Ernst Fuchs*, ed. Gerhard Ebeling, et al. (Tübingen: J.C.B. Mohr, 1973) 103–124; Rudolf Pesch, *Die Entdeckung des ältesten Paulus-Briefes* (Herder-Bücherei 1167; Freiburg i.Br.: Herder, 1984); Earl J. Richard, *First and Second Thessalonians* (SacPag 11; Collegeville: The Liturgical Press, 1995) 29–32.

[3] Walter Schmithals, *Die Briefe des Paulus in ihrer ursprünglichen Form* (Zürich: Theologischer Verlag, 1984) 19–85; Rudolf Pesch, *Paulus ringt um die Lebensform der Kirche. Vier Briefe an die Gemeinde Gottes in Korinth* (Herder-Bücherei 1291; Freiburg i.Br.: Herder 1986); Gerhard Sellin, "Hauptprobleme des Ersten Korintherbriefes," *ANRW* II.25.4 (1987) 2940–3044. esp. 2965–68; Gerhard Dautzenberg, "Der zweite Korintherbrief als Briefsammlung," *ANRW* II.25.4 (1987) 3045–3066.

[4] See the overview of David E. Garland, "The Composition and Unity of Philippians. Some Neglected Literary Factors," *NovT* 27 (1985) 141–73 and e.g. Günther Bornkamm, "Der Philipperbrief als paulinische Briefsammlung," *Geschichte und Glaube. Zweiter Teil. Gesammelte Aufsätze Band IV* (BEvT 53; München: Christian Kaiser Verlag, 1971) 195–205; Joachim Gnilka, *Der Philipperbrief* (3rd ed., HTKNT 10.3; Freiburg i.Br.: Herder, 1980) 6–18.

mans,[5] Philemon obviously being much too short for partition theories
and Galatians (somewhat surprisingly) being spared.[6] At the turn of the
century, the pendulum seems to have swung around. The integrity of
the letters is defended by most, and the adherents of partition theories
find themselves a minority, except perhaps as regards 2 Corinthians. It
is, nevertheless, rather astonishing that the question of the technical
possibilities and difficulties of the compilation of several letters into one
has seldom been posed;[7] the search for comparable processes or for
analogies in non-biblical epistolary literature from antiquity seems to
have been completely neglected. It is of course true that the result of
such an investigation, whether positive or negative, decides nothing in
the exegetical discussion, but at least it makes possible a somewhat pre-
ciser evaluation of the plausibility or implausibility of partition theories.

One reason for this neglect may be the difficulty of identifying material suitable for comparison. It is obvious that we cannot use single
letters for this task. The papyrus letters, to which New Testament exegesis since Deissmann's days[8] has rightly paid so much attention, will
not assist us here. What we need are letter collections. The process of
collecting individual letters into one corpus is the natural place where
compilations of letters could have been made. Unfortunately, we do
not possess many letter collections from Hellenistic and early imperial
times, even if many more certainly once existed. For example, a collection of letters of Aristotle, alluded to by Demetrius, *De elocutione* 223
("Artemon, the editor of Aristotle's *Letters*, says ..."), is lost. Of the thirteen letters ascribed to Plato, most are spurious; only the sixth, the

---

[5] Junji Kinoshita, "Romans—Two Writings Combined: A New Interpretation of
the Body of Romans," *NovT* 7 (1964) 258–77; Walter Schmithals, *Der Römerbrief. Ein
Kommentar* (Gütersloh: Gerd Mohn, 1988).

[6] No partition theories are discussed or listed in the exhaustive new commentaries
of Richard N. Longenecker, *Galatians* (WBC 41; Dallas: Word Books, 1990); J. Louis
Martyn, *Galatians. A New Translation with Introduction and Commentary* (AB 33A; New York:
Doubleday, 1997). But there is of course the thesis of J. C. O'Neill, *The Recovery of Paul's
Letter to the Galatians* (London: SPCK, 1972), whose arguing for massive interpolations is
akin to a partition theory.

[7] This is now very ably done in an article by Alistair Stewart-Sykes, "Ancient
Editors and Copyists and Modern Partition Theories: The Case of the Corinthian
Correspondence," *JSNT* 61 (1996) 53–64; he thinks that it is possible for the redactor
and the scribe to handle two or three roles at the same time, but not more, and that
therefore "simple" partitions of a letter into two earlier writings remain a possibility,
whereas more complicated theories, which run up e.g. to nine letter fragments for the
Corinthian Correspondence, face serious difficulties.

[8] See now Hans-Josef Klauck, "Deißmann, (Gustav) Adolf," *RGG⁴* 2 (1999) 623.

seventh (with important biographical information) and the eighth may be authentic, but this is not undisputed.[9] Epicurus and the Epicureans would make an excellent case. We know that frequent letter writing was one of their means of propagating their teaching and holding the school together, but the three lengthy protreptic letters of Epicurus, which are given in Diogenes Laertius 10.35–135 (the authenticity of the second one, *To Pythocles* [10.84–116], being doubted), do not constitute a real collection. So, too, the Epicurean letters collected in the Herculaneum papyri[10] and in the inscription of Oinoanda[11] are in a much too fragmentary state to yield convincing results. The Pythagorean,[12] Socratic,[13] Cynic,[14] and similar[15] letters are transmitted in collections, but there we have the problem that they are not only very short in most cases, but, more importantly, that they are fictitious from the outset. This makes them very interesting for New Testament exegesis as examples of pseudepigraphic letter writing and of the technique of *ethopoiïa* or *prosopopoiïa*, but not suitable for the elucidation of partition theories. Seneca himself made the edition of his *Epistulae morales ad Lucilium*— if these texts were intended as real letters at all. More probably, he consciously chose the letter form only to give a more dialogical frame

---

[9] See Norman Gulley, "The Authenticity of the Platonic Epistles," *Pseudepigrapha I: Pseudopythagorica—Lettres de Platon—Littérature pseudéphigraphique juive*, ed. Kurt von Fritz (Entretiens sur l'antiquité classique 18; Vandœuvre-Genève: Fondation Hardt, 1972) 103–30; Victoria Wohl, "Plato avant la lettre: Authenticity in Plato's Epistles," *Ramus* 27 (1998) 60–93.

[10] Anna Angeli, "La scuola epicurea di Lampsaco nel PHerc. 176," *Cronache Ercolanesi* 18 (1988) 27–51; "Frammenti di lettere di Epicuro nei papiri d'Ercolano," *Cronache Ercolanesi* 23 (1993) 11–27.

[11] Martin F. Smith, *The Philosophical Inscription of Diogenes of Oinoanda* (Titulae Asiae minoris. Ergänzungsbände 20; Wien: Österreichische Akademie der Wissenschaften, 1996) Fr. 62–96.

[12] Alfons Städele, *Die Briefe des Pythagoras und der Pythagoräer* (Beiträge zur klassischen Philologie 115; Meisenheim am Glan: Hain, 1980).

[13] Josef-Friedrich Borkowski, *Socratis quae feruntur epistolae: Edition, Übersetzung, Kommentar* (Beiträge zur Altertumskunde 94; Leipzig: B.G. Teubner, 1997).

[14] Besides Malherbe, *Cynic Epistles*, see now Eike Müseler, *Die Kynikerbriefe. 1. Die Überlieferung; 2. Kritische Ausgabe mit deutscher Übersetzung* (Studien zur Geschichte und Kultur des Altertums. Neue Folge 1.6–7; Paderborn: F. Schöningh, 1994), who follows a more restricted definition of "cynic" and only deals with the letters of Diogenes and Crates, whereas Malherbe includes those of Heraclitus, Anacharsis and Socrates and the Socratics too.

[15] See e.g. Wesley D. Smith, *Hippocrates: Pseudepigraphic Writings. Letters, Embassy, Speech from the Altar, Decree* (Studies in Ancient Medicine 2; Leiden: E.J. Brill, 1990). See also the article by Zeller in this volume.

to his philosophical and ethical reasoning.[16] The case is similar with
Pliny the Younger, who for the first nine books of his letters—the tenth,
containing his official correspondence with the Emperor Trajan, was
added later—reworked letters he actually had written and added others, which he specially composed for his collection of "Kunstbriefe."[17]
With Alciphron and his four books of mimetic letters[18] we not only
reach the realm of pure literature, but also the late second or early
third century.

Who is left? Only the one author who is the most important letter
writer of Graeco-Roman antiquity, who unintentionally gave a decisive
stimulus to the collection and publication of private letters, and whose
extensive literary production time and again proves to be most fruitful for comparison with the New Testament writings: Marcus Tullius
Cicero.

Cicero's Correspondence and its Collection: Introductory Remarks

Some introductory remarks are necessary.[19] Cicero's correspondence
consists mainly of private letters, not intended for publication at all,
though some open letters are included (e.g. *Ad fam.* 1.9; *Ad Quint. fratr.*
1.1), and in his later years Cicero tentatively played with the idea of
having some of his letters edited by his secretary Tiro (cf. *Ad Att.* 16.5.5).
In any case, Tiro remains the decisive figure, at least if we follow what
amounts to a scholarly consensus regarding the circumstances of the
collection. Immediately after the death of his master, Tiro, out of piety
and loyalty, began not only to write a biography of Cicero, but also
to edit his letters, where he presumably found useful information for
the biography as well. For this task he could use copies which had
been made from outgoing letters and kept in Cicero's (or Tiro's own)

---

[16] See now, *inter alia*, Beat Schönegg, *Senecas* epistulae morales *als philosophisches Kunst-
werk* (Europäische Hochschulschriften XX.578; Bern: P. Lang, 1999); Hildegard Cancik-
Lindemaier, "Seneca's Collection of Epistles: A Medium of Philosophical Communication," *Ancient and Modern Perspectives on the Bible and Culture: Essays in Honor of Hans Dieter
Betz*, ed. Adela Yarbro Collins (Antlanta, Ga.: Scholars Press, 1999) 88–109.
[17] Matthias Ludolph, *Epistolographie und Selbstdarstellung: Untersuchungen zu den 'Parade-
briefen' Plinius des Jüngeren* (Classica Monacensia 17; Tübingen: Gunter Narr, 1997).
[18] Cf. B.P. Reardon, *Courants littéraires grecs des IIᵉ et IIIᵉ siècles après J.-C* (Annales
littéraires de l'université de Nantes 3; Paris: Les Belles Lettres, 1971) 180–185.
[19] See Karl Büchner, "M. Tullius Cicero, Briefe," PW A.7 (1948) 1192–1235; Hermann Peter, *Der Brief in der römischen Literatur: Literargeschichtliche Untersuchungen und Zusam-
menfassungen* (1901, repr. Hildesheim: G. Olms, 1965) 29–100.

archive. Where items were missing or copies had not been made, he asked the addressees for the original, or got it back from them even without asking. From the archive again he added a number of letters not authored by Cicero but addressed to him. Those were collected in the *volumina* or *libri epistularum acceptarum*, Cicero's own letters in the *volumina* or *libri epistularum missarum*.[20]

Tiro first produced collections, each in several books, with letters to a single person, to Caesar, to Pompey, to Octavian, to Cato, to Cicero's son Marcus, to name just a few. Only a fraction of these collections has survived: the *Epistulae ad Quintum fratrem* in three books and the *Epistulae ad M. Brutum*. The epistles to and by Brutus are now in two books, but these contain only the letters of the ninth and last book of the original collection,[21] and the order has to be changed: First comes *Ad Brut.* 2.1–5, then *Ad Brut.* 1.1–18. Another collection in sixteen books, which was given the name *Ad familiares* ("To his Friends") in medieval times, was made by Tiro to save the rest of Cicero's vast correspondence that did not fit into the individual collections. Book 13 of *Ad familiares* consists entirely of letters of recommendation, and the last book fittingly assembles letters addressed to Tiro.

The case looks different with the letters to T. Pomponius Atticus, Cicero's best friend, who often received a letter a day, sometimes more. Copies were not made, nor were Atticus' answers preserved. But Atticus kept Cicero's letters in his personal archive. If Shackleton Bailey is right, he had many of them, but not all, copied in eleven papyrus rolls.[22] Their publication took place only a hundred years later, between 55–60 CE, at the time of Nero, which saw a renewed interest in the period

---

[20] On these two categories, cf. Paolo Cugusi, "L'epistolografia. Modelli e tipologie di comunicazione," *Lo spazio letterario di Roma antica*, vol: II: *La circolazione del testo* (Rome: Salerno Editrice, 1989) 379–419: 381; for conservation of official and private correspondence see ibid., 413–17, with an instructive bibliography. For another modern overview, see Michaela Zelzer, "Die Briefliteratur," *Neues Handbuch der Literaturwissenschaft*, vol. IV: *Spätantike* (Wiesbaden: AULA-Verlag, 1997) 321–53; compare too Catherine Salles, "L'épistolographie hellénistique et romaine," *Paul de Tarse. Congrès de l'ACFEB (Strasbourg, 1995)*, ed. Jacques Schlosser (LD 165; Paris: du Cerf, 1996) 79–87, for Cicero esp. 86–88.

[21] Shown by Ludwig Gurlitt, "Der Archetypus der Brutusbriefe," *Jahrbücher für classische Philologie* 31 (1885) 561–76.

[22] D.R. Shackleton Bailey, *Cicero: Letters to Atticus*, vol. I (LCL 7; Cambridge: Harvard University Press, 1999) 2, a summing up of his *Cicero's Letters to Atticus*, vol. I (Cambridge Classical Texts and Commentaries 3; Cambridge: Cambridge University Press, 1965) 69–73, and based on his reading and understanding of Cornelius Nepos, *De viris illustribus* 25.16.3: "XI volumina epistularum," with XI, which is given in the manuscripts, instead of Aldus' conjecture XVI, taken up in modern editions.

of the Civil War and the beginning of the principate. Then the "loose" letters may have been combined with those in the eleven rolls to form one collection in sixteen books.

The manuscript status of Cicero's letters is a rather poor one, because they obviously were not read very much in the medieval age (Petrarch rediscovered them for modern times).[23] *Ad familiares* is represented completely only in one manuscript (M = Mediceus 49.9) from the 9th or 10th century, but there are later manuscripts from the 12th to 15th centuries which contain portions of either books 1 to 8 or books 9 to 16. The most important witness for *Ad Atticum*, which contains also *Ad Quintum fratrem* and *Ad M. Brutum* 1.1–18[24] and represents a family of its own, is a manuscript (M = Mediceus 49.18, not identical with M = Mediceus 49.9 above), comes from the late 14th century. Together with eight or nine manuscripts of the second family, equally late and not always complete, it goes back to a single archetype which is lost. That makes it very difficult, if not impossible, to trace anything like a tradition history of the letter collections.

Unfortunately, working with Cicero's letters is not easy for other reasons too. Nearly each edition introduces its own numbering and divides letters, as we will see in one instance, into several parts, sometimes located at different places. Additional addressees and dates are introduced in the headings, more than once without any indication that these are missing in the manuscripts. The editors and translators often try to establish a chronological order of the letters against the manuscript order. In some cases they are not content with reordering the letters within one of the collections, but extend this procedure to the letter corpus as a whole. Then we may find under running numbers two letters from *Ad familiares*, followed by one from *Ad Brutum* and another one from *Ad Atticum*.[25] That makes excellent reading if your

---

[23] Cf. Peter L. Schmidt, "Die Rezeption des römischen Freundschaftsbriefes (Cicero—Plinius) im frühen Humanismus (Petrarca—Coluccio Salutati)," *Der Brief im Zeitalter der Renaissance*, ed. Franz Josef Worstbrock (Mitteilung der Komission für Humanismusforschung 9; Weinheim: Acta humaniora, 1983) 25–59.

[24] *Ad Brut.* 2.1–5 has a very special history. The letters are known today only from the edition of Cratander (Basel 1538). The "old codex" which he used seems to have been lost. Only book 2 is dealt with by Wilhelm Sternkopf, "Die Blattversetzung in den Brutusbriefen," *Hermes* 46 (1911) 355–375.

[25] See for example the last two volumes of the French edition: Jean Beaujeu, *Cicéron: Correspondance*, tome X (Collection des Universités de France; Paris: Les Belles Lettres, 1991), and tome XI (1996); *Ad Brut.* 1.3.1–3 is given there as number 866 in X:241–2, *Ad Brut.* 1.3.4 as number 868 in XI:37–8 and *Ad Brut.* 1.2.1–3 as number 896 in XI:75–

interests are primarily historical, but it is a real burden if you want to apply critical and analytical tools.

Letter Partitions in Cicero: An Overview

We continue with some simple statistical observations. I have checked two authoritative modern editions of Cicero's letters, the one by W.S. Watt in the Oxford series,[26] and the other by D.R. Shackleton Bailey in the Teubner series.[27] These have the advantage of sticking more closely to the order of the letters in the manuscripts than most other editions (in Shackleton Bailey's case more closely than he himself does in his numerous other volumes on Cicero's letters) and of following the numbering of the so-called *Vulgata*, but letters are divided into a, b, etc. Sometimes these divisions are based on the testimony of a subgroup of the manuscripts (we shall return to this point); more often they reflect the decisions of early editors or modern critics. What follows are the basic findings in the modern critical editions, grouped by the traditional collections of the materials.

The Letters to his Brother, Quintus: Ad Quintum fratrem

2.4 (= 2.4.1–2) // 2.5 (2.4.3–7); this division affects the whole numbering which is doubled in this second book.

3.7(9) is counted as a single letter in some of the manuscripts and in the editions, but combined in others with 3.6(8) to form one letter.

6, interspersed with letters from *Ad familiares* and *Ad Atticum*. The still indispensable older edition by Robert Yelverton Tyrell and Louis Claude Purser, *The Correspondence of M. Tullius Cicero, Arranged according to Its Chronological Order, vol. I–VI* (2nd ed. [vol. I 3rd ed.], 1904–1932, repr. Hildesheim: G. Olms, 1969), with its massive commentary follows the same policy.

[26] W.S. Watt, *M. Tulli Ciceronis Epistulae, vol. I: Epistulae ad familiares* (Scriptorum classicorum Bibliotheca Oxoniensis; Oxford: Clarendon Press, 1982); *M. Tulli Ciceronis Epistulae*, vol. II: *Epistulae ad Atticum, pars prior, libri I–VIII* (Scriptorum classicorum Bibliotheca Oxoniensis; Oxford: Clarendon Press, 1965); *pars posterior, libri IX–XVI* (1988); *M. Tulli Ciceronis Epistulae, vol. III: Epistulae ad Quintum fratrem, Epistulae ad M. Brutum, Fragmenta epistularum* (Scriptorum classicorum Bibliotheca Oxoniensis; Oxford: Clarendon Press, 1958).

[27] D.R. Shackleton Bailey, *M. Tulli Ciceronis Epistulae ad Quintum fratrem, Epistulae ad M. Brutum* (Bibliotheca scriptorum Graecorum et Romanorum Teubneriana; Stuttgart: B.G. Teubner, 1988); *M. Tulli Ciceronis Epistulae ad familares* (Bibliotheca scriptorum Graecorum et Romanorum Teubneriana; Stuttgart: B.G. Teubner, 1988); *M. Tulli Ciceronis Epistulae ad Atticum, vol. I–II* (Bibliotheca scriptorum Graecorum et Romanorum Teubneriana; Stuttgart: B.G. Teubner, 1987–8).

3.5 (= 3.5 + 3.6 + 3.7); here we have a rare case: three letters separated in the tradition are combined to form one single new letter in the editions.[28]

The Letters to his Friends: Ad familiares

1.5a (4 §§)	// 1.5b (2 §§)	
5.10a (3 §§)	// 5.10b (1 §)	// 5.10c (1 §)[29]
6.10a (3 §§)	// 6.10b (3 §§)	
10.21 (6 §§)	// 10.21a (1 §)	
10.24 (2 §§)	// 10.24a (1 §)	
10.34 (2 §§)	// 10.34a (2 §§)	
11.6 (1 §)	// 11.6a (2 §§)	
11.13 (4 §§)	// 11.13a (2 §§)	// 11.13b[30]
12.15a (§ 1–6)	// 12.15b (§ 7)[31]	
12.22 (2 §§)	// 12.22a (2 §§)	
12.24 (2 §§)	// 12.24a (1 §)	
12.25 (5 §§)	// 12.25a (2 §§)	
13.6 (5 §§)	// 13.6a (1 §)	
13.28 (3 §§)	// 13.28a (2 §§)	

The Letters to Marcus Brutus: Ad Brutum

1.2 (3 §§)	// 1.2a (3 §§)
1.3 (3 §§)	// 1.3a (1 §)
1.4 (3 §§)	// 1.4a (4§§)

The Letters to Atticus: Ad Atticum

4.4 (1 §)	// 4.4a (2 §§)
4.8 (2 §§)	// 4.8a (4 §§)
7.13 (5 §§)	// 7.13a (3 §§)
8.9a (3 §§)	// 8.9b (2 §§)

---

[28] Another example is *Ad Att.* 13.35 + 13.36, which is numbered as 334 in Shackleton Bailey.

[29] Shackleton Bailey counts §3 of Watt's 5.10a as a third letter.

[30] Of 11.13b only the first two words *Parmenses miserrimos* ... are given (from the index of manuscript M) to indicate the beginning of a lost letter.

[31] Not in Watt or Shackleton Bailey, but in Tyrell and Purser, *Correspondence, vol. VI*, 226–36, 251–2; §7 is a typical postscript which can be dealt with in different ways, see below.

9.2 (1 §)   // 9.2a (3 §§)
9.13 (7 §§)   // 9.13a (1 §)
9.15 (5 §§)   // 9.15a (1 §)

10.1 (3 §§)   // 10.1a (1 §)
10.3 (1 §)   // 10.3a (2 §§)
10.12 (4 §§)   // 10.12a (4 §§)

11.4 (1 §)   // 11.4a (1 §)
11.17 (1 §)   // 11.17a (3 §§)

12.5 (1 §)   // 12.5a (1 §)   // 12.5b (1 §)   // 12.5c (1 §)[32]
12.6 (2 §§)   // 12.6a (2 §§)
12.18 (4 §§)   // 12.18a (2 §§)
12.31.1–2   // 12.31.3 + 12.32
12.34 + 12.35.1   // 12.35.2
12.37 (3 §§)   // 12.37a (1 §)
12.38 (2 §§)   // 12.38 (2 §§)
12.42.1–3a   // 12.42.3b + 12.43
12.44 + 12.45.1   // 12.45.2–3
12.46 + 12.47.1   // 12.47.3 + 12.48.1a   // 12.48.1b + 12.49

13.2 (1 §)   // 13.2a (1 §)   // 13.2b (1 §)
13.6 (3 §§)   // 13.6a (1 §)
13.7 (1 §)   // 13.7a (1 §)
13.13 + 13.14.1   // 13.14.2 + 13.15
13.21 (3 §§)   // 13.21a (4 §§)
13.24 + 13.25.1a   // 13.25.1b–3
13.28 + 13.29.1   // 13.29.23 + 13.30.1   // 13.30.2–3
13.33 (3 §§)   // 13.33a (2 §§)
13.37 (3 §§)   // 13.37a (1 §)
13.47 (1 §)   // 13.47a (2 §§)

14.14 + 14.15.1   // 14.15.2–4

15,1 (5 §§)   // 15.1a (2 §§)
15.4 (4 §§)   // 15.4a (1 §)
15.13 (4 §§)   // 15.13a (3 §§)
15.16 (1 §)   // 15.16a (1 §)

16.13 (2 §§)   // 16.13a (1 §)   // 16.13b (2 §)

All together there are some fifty to sixty cases—on 864 letters in all—
where editors feel compelled to divide letters. Certainly, an extreme
instance is *Ad Att. 12.5*, where a not very long letter of four paragraphs is
divided into as many independent letters. And so far we have assembled

[32] These four letters are numbered in Shackleton Bailey as 242, 307, 316, 241; in
Kasten as 12.5, 13.12, 13.20, 12.3.

only part of the evidence. There are instances where partitions of letters
are not reflected in the numbering at all, because they were already
introduced against the manuscripts by the very first editions. That is
the case, if we concentrate on the letters to Atticus, in *Ad Att.* 1.2, 1.3,
1.7, 1.9, 1.10, 1.12, 4.2, 4.10, 4,18, 7.9, 7.17, 9.4, 9.6, 9.13, 10.5, 10.7, 13.12,
13.29–34, 13.38, 13.42, 13.45, 13.46, 13.48, 13.52, 14.13, 14.15, 14.17. With
few exceptions the letters in book 15 and in book 16 form a running
text in the manuscripts, most of the identification of individual letters
had therefore to be done by editors.

There is still another side to it. We have already said that the splitting
of letter numbers may be based on the manuscripts where one group
does divide and the other group keeps the letters together. If the early
editions followed that subgroup which divides, the fact that there is
another group which combines does not show in the numbering at
all. If you are lucky, you may find the information in the critical
apparatus (more often in Shackleton Bailey than in Watt). No effort
has been made here to collect and present this evidence too, but one
may compare *Ad Att.* 1.14, 3.27, 4.2, 4.19, 7.9, 7.18, 7.26, 9.3, 9.11, 9.12,
9.16, 9.18, 9.19, 10.6, 10.9, 10.11–18, 14.7, 14.8, 14.9, 14.10, 14.19, 14.20,
14.21, 14.22, with the notes in Shackleton Bailey's Teubner edition.

It is clear (and what has just been said confirms it) that the tradition
history of Cicero's letters is the real reason for this state of affairs, but
it is not clear at which stage of this process compilations were made.
They may have been produced by scribes through the centuries, they
may result from mechanical accidents like the damage and loss of pages
or the displacement of pages in a codex. But the possibility remains that
at least in a few instances we have to go back to the moment when the
collections were produced, or even to the archives, though we can no
longer prove this. And another question is how compilations can be
detected and reversed by later readers.

To deal more thoroughly with these questions would mean writing
the monograph on this subject which is so badly needed. Here we can
only discuss some examples, not only of compilations and their reversal,
but also of other topics linked to this and of interest for New Testament
exegesis.

Analysis of Some Key Examples

From the Letters to His Friends[33]

1. The Example

We must be clear from the outset that the first letter which we shall discuss in more detail, *Ad fam.* 8.6.1–5, is not a conflation.[34] It is taken from book 8 of *Ad familiares*, which contains seventeen letters sent to Cicero in 51/50 BCE by Marcus Caelius Rufus, aged thirty-five to thirty-seven at that time and very eager to promote his political career, which had already led him to the position of an curule aedile. Cicero is serving as proconsul in Cilicia in Asia minor during this period, and he needs Caelius as a correspondent to inform him about the political development in the capital in the crucial time of Civil War.

The main theme of letter 6 from February 50 BCE is the case of Appius Claudius Pulcher, Cicero's predecessor as proconsul in Cilicia. Through the marriage of one of his daughters to Gnaeus Pompeius, he was related to Pompey, the father of Gnaeus (cf. the allusion to this fact in §3). Appius is now being prosecuted, perhaps because of mismanagement in his province, by P. Cornelius Dolabella. There is a subtle undercurrent to the whole letter, which we grasp only if we know that secret negotiations are on their way to win Dolabella, who has just divorced his wife (cf. end of §1), as a third husband for Cicero's daughter Tullia. Dolabella's prosecution of Appius, to whom Cicero in 52–50 BCE addresses the letters in *Ad fam.* 3.1–13, therefore brings Cicero into a rather precarious situation.

Having dealt with Appius and Dolabella, Caelius adds some afterthoughts in §3 and 4 about the incompetent consuls of that year, about his own doings as aedile, about the hapless Bibulus, proconsul

---

[33] For editions and translations in addition to Watt and Shackleton Bailey, see Helmut Kasten, *Marcus Tullius Cicero: An seine Freunde* (4th ed.; Tusculum Bücherei; München-Zürich: Artemis, 1989); W. Glynn Williams, *Cicero*, vol. XXV–XXVII: *The Letters to His Friends, vol. I–III* (LCL 205; Cambridge: Harvard University Press, 1927, repr. 1979); (LCL 216; 1929, repr. 1983); (LCL 230; 1926, repr. 1979); D.R. Shackleton Bailey, *Cicero: Epistulae ad familiares, vol. I–II* (Cambridge Classical Texts and Commentaries 16–17; Cambridge: Cambridge University Press, 1977).

[34] From the perspective of literary criticism, this letter is treated by G.O. Hutchinson, *Cicero's Correspondence: a Literary Study* (Oxford: Clarendon Press, 1998) 141–8; for the whole book, see Alberto Cavarzere, *Marco Celio Rufo, Lettere (Cic. fam. l. VIII)* (Testi classici 6; Brescia: Paideia Ed., 1983) esp. 120–5 (text and translation of 8.6), 277–98 (commentary).

in Syria, who had lost his first cohort, centurions and tribune included, in a local skirmish. With ironic understatement, Caelius speaks of his *cohorticulae*[35] and about "our Curio, whose tribuneship is frozen" (*Curioni nostro tribunitas conglaciat*). This Scribonius Curio (cf. *Ad fam.* 2,1–7), an intimate friend of Caelius and quite similar to him in age, character, and ambition, was still considered as a member of the party of Pompey and the optimates.

But the letter does not end here. In §5 we find repetitions and contradictions, which could be used to build up a partition theory: Caelius returns to Appius and his process, to Dolabella and the secret marriage plans, to the Greek panthers, which form a running gag in this correspondence,[36] and to Curio: "If I wrote you above that Curio was very cold—now he is warm enough (*iam calet*)! He is even pulled to pieces in a most fervent way. Because he did not succeed in matters of intercalation,[37] he simply went over to the popular side and is starting to argue publicly for Caesar ..."[38]

There is a simple explanation for this surprising feature. Caelius continues: "This he had not yet done when I wrote the first part of this letter" (*dum priorem partem epistulae scripsi*). Curio's change of fronts took place between §§1–4 and §5; in other words, §5 is a postscript, written some days later.[39] We might even suspect that, whereas the letter was dictated as usual, the postscript was written in Caelius' own hand. This finds a brilliant confirmation in Cicero's answering letter, which is preserved in *Ad fam.* 2.13: we hear in §3: *extrema pagella pupugit me tuo chirographo* ... , "The last page in your own handwriting gave me a pang! What are you saying? Curio is defending Caesar now!?" Exegetes of 2 Corinthians will recall Lietzmann's "one sleepless night"

---

[35] Cf. Hutchinson, *Cicero's Correspondence*, 145: "... his failure is ironically presented as a laudable, if slight, success in the circumstances. Even without the Parthians he achieved some small loss."

[36] Cf. *Ad fam.* 13.2.2, 13.4.5, 13.8.10, 13.9.3; Greek panthers are panthers from Asia minor as opposed to African panthers which Curio had presented for the games he gave when becoming popular tribune. Caelius urged Cicero to get him these panthers for his own games he had to organize for his aedileship, because he wanted to be able to rival and overcome Curio, but Cicero did not react.

[37] As one of the pontiffs, Curio tried to intercalate a month after February 50 BCE, which would have given him a longer term of office.

[38] Actually Caesar had bribed him by paying his huge debts. In his epic on the Civil War, Lucan (*Pharsalia* 4.819–20) saw the defection of Curio as decisive in tilting the scales against Pompey and the Senate.

[39] Cf. Shackleton Bailey, *Epistulae ad familiares, vol. I* (1977), 414: "The postscript (§5) may have been added a day or two later."

as the explanation of the change of tone between 2 Cor 1–9 and 2 Cor 10–13,[40] or of the less well known proposal of Bahr that we should see 2 Cor 10–13 as an extended postscript in Paul's own hand.[41]

2. *Further issues: The Use of Postscripts*

The postscript and the writing of a letter over a longer period deserve some further remarks. First the postscript, which prompts a methodological reflection of some importance. In *Ad Att.* 9.14 from March 49 BCE, Cicero says in §3: "This letter had already been written (*scripta epistula*) when I received before daybreak a letter from Lepta in Capua … ," and the content of Lepta's letter is briefly mentioned. Here we have a real postscript, added to the already finished letter and dispatched together with it as one writing. We may call that an author-composed letter. The next letter, *Ad Att.* 9.15, gives a slightly different picture. There we are told in §6: "After I had dispatched my letter on March 25, the boys I had sent with Matius and Trebatius brought me a letter running like this … ." Cicero then quotes the letter co-authored by Gaius Matius, a faithful supporter of Caesar, and Gaius Trebatius Testa, a friend of Cicero, and at the end adds again: *Epistula conscripta nuntiatum est nobis*, "When this letter was finished, we got the news," with a brief information about Caesar's movements following. Strictly speaking, these are two letters: the one (9.15.1–5) already having been on its way when the other (9.15.6) was composed. In turn, the latter (9.15.6) again has a real postscript of its own. The distinction between these two instances may be a fine one, but it does exist, and has consequences. In 9.15.1–6 a conflation of two separate letters has been made, maybe by later scribes, maybe by the first-century CE editor, or maybe even already in the archives of Atticus. The reasons for this conflation are understandable, but a compilation it remains.[42] Other examples could be multiplied.

---

[40] Hans Lietzmann, *An die Korinther I/II* (5th ed., HNT 9; Tübingen: J.C.B. Mohr, 1969) 139: "Mir genügt z.B. die Annahme einer schlaflos durchwachten Nacht zwischen c. 9 und c. 10 zur Erklärung." On similar lines for 1 Cor, Martinus C. De Boer, "The Composition of 1 Corinthians," *NTS* 40 (1994) 229–245, who postulates a break in time and the incoming of new information between the writing of 1 Cor 1–4 and 1 Cor 5–16.

[41] Gordon J. Bahr, "Paul and Letter Writing in the First Century," *CBQ* 28 (1966) 465–77, esp. 467.

[42] Shackelton Bailey in his translations therefore counts 9.14.1–3 as no. 182, but 9.15.1–5 as no. 183 and 9.15.6 as no. 184.

A solid case for the composing of a letter over a longer period—
longer than "one sleepless night"—combined with responses to several
letters, is represented by the extended letter from September 54 B.C.E.
in *Ad Quint. fratr.* 3.1.1–25. In §8 Cicero writes: *Venio nunc ad tuas litteras*
("I come now to your letters"), which reminds us a bit of 1 Cor 7:1:
Περὶ δὲ ὧν ἐγράψατε ("Now concerning the matters about which you
wrote"). He deals first with a longer letter of Quintus (§§ 9–10) and then
with a shorter letter (§ 11), thus: *Rescripsi epistulae maximae. Audi nunc de
minuscula* ("I have answered your very long letter; hear now about the
very short one"). Next, he goes on to a third one (§ 12), which he had
received together with the first two; with a fourth one (§ 13) that arrived
on a different day. Then in § 14, he reacts to "a very old letter, but late in
its delivery," and after an interlude (§ 17) we hear: "I was just folding this
letter, when today, September 20, letter-carriers from you and Caesar
arrived, twenty-six days after their departure." Their arrival makes a
continuation necessary, and it is given in § 17–18 as an autograph: *Cum
scripsissem haec infima, quae sunt mea manu* ("After I had written the last
lines in my own hand, your son Cicero came in and had dinner with
us," § 19, beginning). Young Cicero, the nephew, brings another letter
from his father Quintus that is discussed during the meal, so Cicero dictates this ending as a postscript: *Hoc inter cenam Tironi dictavi, ne mirere alia
manu esse* ("I dictated this to Tiro during dinner, lest you be alarmed by
the different hand," § 19, end). So far the letter had been composed in
Cicero's country estate near Arpinum, the home-town of the Cicerones
in Latium. In § 21 we are back in Rome again, and Cicero comments
on the curious features of this letter: "This letter I had in my hands
many days, because of the delay of the letter-carriers. Therefore many
themes crept in at different times, and now e.g. the following too …"
(§ 23). Three more paragraphs with allusions to still more letters are
added, before this "letter on letters" comes to a close. This is a composite letter, no doubt, but composed by the author himself.

From the Letters to Marcus Brutus[43]

1. *The Situation*

The extant letters of the original book 9 of the correspondence between
Cicero and Brutus (one letter, 1.17, is addressed by Brutus to Atticus)

---

[43] For editions and translations in addition to Watt and Shackleton Bailey, see Hel-

were all exchanged in the few months of March to July 43 B.C.E., and
we must keep in mind the following scenario, if we are to understand
the items we will discuss: Marcus Brutus stayed with his troops in
Greece. The camp (e.g. 1.6.4: *ex castris*) and Dyrrhachium (1.2.2), today's
Durazzo, the port just opposite Brindisi, where the *Via Egnatia* began,
are mentioned as the places where he stays. In upper Italy, Marcus
Antonius besieged the city of Mutina (Modena), where Decimus Brutus,
another member of the *gens Brutii*, commanded the troops of the senate
party. The consuls Hirtius and Pansa came from Rome with their army,
Octavian brought in his private legions, Decimus Brutus made a sortie,
and together on April 21 they overcame Marcus Antonius and forced
him to retreat with his troops to Gallia. But the price for this victory
was high: both consuls died, and Octavian did not pursue and crush
Marcus Antonius, whom he secretly may already have considered a
potential ally. In Rome, Cicero is the head of the opposition to Marcus
Antonius and his two brothers (and he will very soon have to pay for
this with his life).

2. *The Example: A Dislocation?*

Numbering is becoming more and more complicated now. Near the
beginning of the collection, often counted as no. 6, we find a letter
from April 17, 43 BCE without an opening, in which Cicero confirms
his utter dislike of the Antonii. The traditional numbering of this text is
given as *Ad Brut.*1.2.(3)4–6 (§3 only consisting of one sentence). What
about §1–2 and the beginning of §3? Much later, often counted as
no. 14, there is a letter dating from May 20, with an opening that
is familiar by now: "My letter had already been written and sealed,
when your letter full of new information arrived." This letter suddenly
breaks off at the end of §3. Here we have the beginning of our text,
since the traditional numbering of this piece is *Ad Brut.* 1.2.1–3. The

mut Kasten, *Marcus Tullius Cicero: An den Bruder Quintus, An Brutus, Über die Bewerbung*
(Tusculum Bücherei; 2nd ed., München: Heimeran, 1976); Marion Giebel, *M. Tullius
Cicero: Briefwechsel mit M. Brutus* (Reclam-Universalbibliothek 7745; Stuttgart: Reclam,
1982); M. Cary, in: W. Glynn Williams, M. Cary, and Mary Henderson, *Cicero, vol.
XXVIII: The Letters to His Brother Quintus, The Letters to Brutus, Handbook of Electioneer-
ing, Letter to Octavian* (LCL 462; Cambridge: Harvard University Press, 1972) 613–717;
D.R. Shackleton Bailey, *Cicero: Epistulae ad Quintum fratrem et M. Brutum* (Cambridge Classical Texts and Commentaries 22; Cambridge: Cambridge University Press, 1980). See,
too, Ulrike Blank-Sangmeister, *Marcus Tullius Cicero: Epistulae ad Quintum fratrem* (Reclam-
Universalbibliothek 7095; Stuttgart: Reclam, 1993).

reason for dislocating 1.2 in such a way, the first half of the text now forming the later letter and the second half, the earlier one,[44] is the movements of Brutus and Dolabella, which are reflected in the text and can be retraced. Why the later joining of the two pieces? In this instance displacement of pages or loss of a page may be the solution,[45] but we should not overlook the fact that a voice has been raised in support of the unity of *Ad Brut.* 1.2.1–6.[46]

3. *Conflated Letters*

But displacement or loss is no valid explanation (although this has been proposed) in the case of *Ad Brut.* 1.3.1–3 // 1.3.4 and 1.4.1–3a // 1.4.3b–6. In §1–3 of 1.3 from April 21 (date reconstructed) Cicero, referring to a slightly earlier successful battle at Forum Gallorum, rejoices: "Our case looks much better now … The consuls (i.e. Hirtius and Pansa) truly showed their character … But the boy Caesar (i.e. Octavian) proved marvelously well endowed …" (§1). He cannot yet have heard that both consuls had died in the next battle. This information did not reach Rome earlier than April 25. In addition Cicero tries to convince Brutus in this letter (1.3.1–3) that the Antonii should be declared public enemies of Rome by the Senate. That indeed did happen, but later, on April 26.

For §4 of 1.3 April 27 is given as a date at the end (*v. Kal. Maias*). The first sentence reads: "We have lost two consuls, both loyal men," i.e., Hirtius, who died on the battle field, and Pansa, who died of his wounds. Cicero continues: "The remaining troops of the enemy are pursued by (Decimus) Brutus and Caesar (Octavian)," but that is only a vain hope. And Cicero adds on a note of triumph that Marcus Antonius and all his followers have been declared public enemies by the Senate and that this is true also of the captives taken by Marcus Brutus, among them Gaius Antonius, a brother of Marcus Antonius. It is obvious that some days must have passed between 1.3.1–3 and 1.4; hence the dividing of the letter into two. What about a composition over several

---

[44] We may feel compelled to compare the "letter of reconciliation'" in 2 Cor 1–9 and the earlier "letter of tears" in 2 Cor 10–13 (if Hausrath was right).

[45] Proposed by Tyrell and Purser, *Correspondence*, vol. *VI*, 133–4; see now M.M. Willcock, *Cicero: The Letters of January to April 43BC* (Warminster: Aris & Phillips Ltd., 1995) 128: "Probably one page of the archetype was omitted, perhaps helped by the similarity of the subject matter at this point … ."

[46] By Edmund Ruete, *Die Correspondenz Ciceros in den Jahren 44 und 43* (Diss. phil. Straßburg; Marburg: N. Elwert, 1883) 81–4.

days and a postscript? That should be reflected more clearly in the text, as it usually does. Here we have not the slightest indication for this process. So it is better to reckon with two individual letters and their later conflation, more likely at a very early, rather than later, date.[47]

4. A Case of Interpolation?

Otto Eduard Schmidt has proposed a different solution for 1.3[48]: Only the first half of §4, from *Consules duos, bonos quidem ...* to *... Brutus persequitur et Caesar*, has to be classified as a fragment of another Ciceronian letter that was interpolated into the earlier document consisting of §1–3 and the second half of §4. This thesis did not find a following,[49] and rightly so. Schmidt took note of the different statements regarding the consuls, but not of the development of the public enemy issue. But nevertheless, structurally his proposal looks like a miniature model of more complex partition theories in New Testament exegesis, which see e.g. the "apology" at 2 Cor 2:14–6:13 sandwiched between two halves of the "letter of reconciliation" in 2 Cor 1:2–2:13 and 7:2–16.

5. Another Look in the Light of Brutus' Response

The two letters of Cicero in *Ad Brut.* 1.3 are answered by Brutus in 1.4, presumably by two letters, 1.4.1–3a and 1.4.3b–6. In the letter from May 7 (date reconstructed), Brutus first expresses (§1–3a) his delight at the success of his namesake Decimus Brutus and the consuls, but he is not willing to see the Antonii as public enemies as long as the Senate has not spoken. He cannot yet know about the death of the consuls, and his lack of information is confirmed by his hesitation about the status of Marcus Antonius and his partisans. Letters between Rome and Dyrrhachium will have taken nine to twelve days to be delivered, sometimes even more. So there is nothing improbable in the fact that Brutus still shows himself uninformed.

---

[47] Cf. the analogous case in *Ad fam.* 12.25.1–5: Pansa is still acting, while in 12.25.6, Hirtius and Pansa are dead.

[48] Otto Eduard Schmidt, "Zur Kritik und Erklärung der Briefe Ciceros an M. Brutus," *Jahrbücher für classische Philologie* 30 (1884) 617–44: 624; Id., "Beiträge zur Kritik der Briefe Ciceros an M. Brutus und zur Geschichte des Mutinensischen Krieges," *Jahrbücher für classische Philologie* 36 (1890) 109–38: 112–115.

[49] See the critique in Tyrell and Purser, *Correspondence, vol. VI*, 142, who opt for a postscript.

Things are different in the second part, firmly dated on May 15 (§6, at the end: *Idibus Maiis, ex castris*). We only have to hear the beginning, to notice the changing of gesture: "Now, Cicero, now we must act, or our rejoicing about the defeat of Antonius will prove delusive ..." (§1). Nor is it by chance that these two conflated letters, one by Cicero, one by Brutus, which run parallel, form a pair in the tradition. Indeed, this looks like editorial work. But could there also be other compositional activities involved?

6. *The Matter of Forgeries*

When writing his biography of Marcus Brutus at the end of the first century CE, Plutarch already knew of a letter that was probably forged in the name of Brutus.[50] There was a time in the 18th and 19th centuries when the genuineness of Cicero's whole correspondence with Brutus was called into question, but this position is no longer upheld. One of its main opponents was Ludwig Gurlitt,[51] who convincingly demonstrated the authenticity of the corpus, but with some exceptions. Two letters—1.16 from Brutus to Cicero and 1.17 from Brutus to Atticus[52]—are considered inauthentic by him and other modern critics, and their doubts seem well founded.[53] The addition of two inauthentic letters to a corpus of authentic correspondence is already an interesting feature in itself, one that does not look so strange to New Testament critics.

The whole collection *Ad Brutum* once closed with 1.18 as the last letter of the ninth book, written by Cicero to Brutus on July 27, 43 BCE. Why were the two inauthentic letters 1.16 and 1.17 interpolated exactly at this place, before 1.18, when they might have been simply added at the end? Gurlitt in his earlier publication thought that this was done on purpose by the forger, who inserted his products near the end of the collection, but wanted to have it framed by authentic letters so that his

---

[50] Plutarch, *Brutus* 53.6–7. A letter by Brutus to Cicero is referred to in *Brutus* 22.4.

[51] Ludwig Gurlitt, "Die Briefe Cicero's an M. Brutus. In Bezug auf ihre Echtheit geprüft," *Philol* Sup 4 (1884) 551–630; see also his "Handschriftliches und Textkritisches zu Ciceros epistulae ad M. Brutum," *Philol* 55 (1896) 318–340.

[52] Letters (plural) of Brutus to Atticus are indeed mentioned in Plutarch, *Cicero* 45.2.

[53] Cf. Gurlitt, "Die Briefe Cicero's an M. Brutus," 614–628; Peter, *Der Brief*, 95, and now especially Shackelton Bailey, *Epistulae ad Quintum fratrem et M. Brutum* (1980), 10–14; the authenticity is defended e.g. by Ruete, *Die Correspondenz Ciceros*, 97–9; Büchner, "Briefe," 1199.

intervention could not so easily be detected afterwards.[54] Later, Gurlitt changed his position. He no longer spoke of the malice of a forger, but argued that pages had been displaced at the end of the manuscript.[55] This recourse to mechanical devices like dislocations, mutilations or loss of pages was especially popular in the 19th century. I feel that there was more wisdom in Gurlitt's earlier intuition.

While defending the genuineness of most of the correspondence, Gurlitt had his doubts about 1.15.1–13 too. But here he develops a more intricate solution. He maintains that this text is made up of two authentic but independent letters of Cicero (§1–2 and §12–13, resepectively), between which an inauthentic middle piece was inserted in §3–11. This would make a compilation of letters plus interpolation plus forgery. Schmidt, on the other hand, energetically defended the unity and authenticity of 1.15,[56] which left an impression on Gurlitt too.

From the Letters to Atticus[57]

1. *The Example*

We come to the letters to Atticus and single out only one example (8.9) for more detailed treatment.[58] It is a compilation again, where the later letter and the earlier letter have changed places: the second half (8.9.3–4) is from February 25, 49 BCE, while the first half (8.9.1–2[3a]) is from March 29 or 30 of the same year. For the earlier letter the date is given by chance in the text, in §4: *sed cum haec scribebam v Kal., Pompeius iam Brindisium venisse poterat* ("When I write this today, on the 25th, Pompey might already have reached Brindisi"). The date of the later letter is deduced from allusions in the text. In Shackelton Bailey they carry the numbers 160 (for 8.9.3–4) and 188 (for 8.9.1–2) respectively.

---

[54] Gurlitt, "Die Briefe Cicero's an M. Brutus", 627: "Der echte brief I. 18 ist den gefälschten nachgesetzt worden, damit er den betrug verbergen sollte."

[55] Ludwig Gurlitt, "Nochmals der Archetypus der Brutusbriefe," *Jahrbücher für classische Philologie* 38 (1892) 410–16: 412–3.

[56] Schmidt, "Beiträge zur Kritik," 117–138.

[57] For editions and translations in addition to Watt and Shackleton Bailey, see Helmut Kasten, *Marcus Tullius Cicero: Atticus-Briefe* (Tusculum Bücherei; 4th ed., München-Zürich: Artemis, 1990); D.R. Shackleton Bailey, *Cicero's Letters to Atticus, vol. I–VII* (Cambridge Classical Texts and Commentaries 3–9; Cambridge: Cambridge University Press, 1965–70), Id., *Cicero: Letters to Atticus, vol. I–IV* (LCL 7, 8, 97, 491; Cambridge, Ma.: Harvard University Press, 1999).

[58] Cf. Shackleton Bailey, *Cicero's Letters to Atticus, vol. I* (1968), 394–5.

We are in the time of the Civil War again. In the earlier letter, the ending in §4 is noteworthy. After having discussed Pompey's movements, Cicero adds: *sed hoc* τέρας *horribili vigilantia, celeritate, diligentia est. Plane quid futurum sit nescio* ("But this monster is terribly awake, fast and careful; I simply do not know what will happen"). With the term τέρας, drawn from portents in mythology, he means Gaius Julius Caesar. This brings us to another trait of Cicero's letter writing: he likes to intersperse his texts with terms, quotations, proverbs and sentences given in Greek, most often so in the letters to Atticus, who lived in Athens from 86–65 BCE and was enthusiastic about Greece and Greek. Thus Cicero displays the superior culture common to his addressees and himself, and he does so with irony and urbanity.[59]

More instructive for us is the later letter in 8.9.1–2(3a).[60] In §3a (one sentence only) Cicero expresses his hope to be in his villa near Arpinum very soon, *pr. Kal.*, which means the end of the month, but which month? Here we must consider the beginning of the letter, where Cicero says: "You write that my letter has been published. I feel not sorry at all to hear that, indeed I have myself had a number of people making copies of it." Atticus obviously wanted to inform Cicero that a letter of his had been broadcast in Rome by the notable addressee, and he may have commented on the rather unfavorable reception this letter found. Cicero does not feel disturbed by this because he wanted his letter to be circulated and had himself made efforts to that end.[61] In §2 he asks: "Why should I not wish that my letter be openly recited *in contione*?," that is, in a gathering of the people of Rome. Cicero also compares his procedure with that of Pompey, who had a letter to this same individual posted in public. Of course, this is all slightly

---

[59] For the use of Greek in the letters, cf. Michael von Albrecht, "M.T. Cicero, Sprache und Stil II A 3 in den Briefen," PWSup 13 (1973) 1271–86: 1274–5; Hutchinson, *Cicero's Correspondence*, 13–16.

[60] See Shackleton Bailey, *Cicero's Letters to Atticus, vol. I* (1968), 394–5; Tyrell and Purser, *Correspondence, vol. IV*, 90–92.

[61] We must bear this in mind, when confronted with the often-quoted other examples where Cicero shows aversion against the publication of private letters, like *Ad fam.* 15.21.4 (but this passage is not so clear) or esp. *Phil.* 2.7. There Cicero heavily criticizes Marcus Antonius for having publicly recited a letter allegedly sent by Cicero, which should never be done with letters among friends (!). But here we have to take into account the rhetorical situation of the Second Philippic, which might by the way never have been held, but only circulated as a pamphlet among Cicero's friends; see Manfred Fuhrmann, *Marcus Tullius Cicero: Die politischen Reden, vol. III* (Tusculum Bücherei; München-Zürich: Artemis, 1993) 626–7.

reminiscent of the public reading of one of Paul's letters in the ἐκκλησία (cf. 1 Thess 5.27), but what might it also say about the circulation of a single letter to different house churches?

We know the contents of this "open letter." It is addressed, as we may already suspect, to none other than Julius Caesar and dates from March 19 or 20, 49 BCE. A certain amount of time must have elapsed since then; for Caesar, who was on his way from Brindisi to Rome, must have received it and sent it on to Rome where it was disseminated. Atticus must have heard of it, and his own letter with his comments must have reached Cicero in the meantime. That is why the end (*pr. Kal.*) of the month can only mean the end of March, and that still seems rather quick, if we take into account what must have happened in the meantime. This in turn is not compatible with the dating of 8.9.3–4, hence the partition.

2. *Enclosed Copies*

One question remains: How do we know about this "open letter"? And, more importantly, do we possess it? Yes, because Cicero has enclosed a copy of it in a letter he wrote to Atticus on March 20, i.e., at about the same time he sent the letter to Julius Caesar. This he announces in 9.11.4 with the words: "I send you a copy of my letter to Caesar. I think that it will bring some good." Then the letter to Caesar follows. In the modern critical editions, these enclosed copies are indicated in the numbering system by using capitals; in this instance 9.11A(§1–3), or in Shackleton Bailey, no. 178A. Other instances from *Ad Atticum* (this trait is missing in the other collections) are:

8.11 with 11A, B, C, D
8.12 with 12A, B, C, D
8.15 with 15A

9.6 with 6A
9.7 with 7A, B, C
9.13 with 13A

10.8 with 8A, B
10.9 with 9A

14.13 with 13A, B
14.17 with 17A

16.16 with 16A, B, C, D, E, F

Sometimes copies of other letters of Cicero that were otherwise not preserved, are found. These include, for example, his letters to Pompey (8.11B and 8.11D), his letter to Marcus Antonius (14.13B), and a small collection of his own letters (16.16A-F). Sometimes matters get even more complicated. On one occasion Oppius and Balbus wrote jointly to Cicero (9.7A); then Balbus wrote again (9.7B) and included a copy of a letter by Caesar to Oppius and Cornelius (9.7C). We know all this only because Cicero transmits copies of the first two letters (9.7A and B) and a copy of the copy of Caesar's letter (9.7C) to Atticus, all as an addendum to 9.7. In 9.13A we have another enclosure; however, the modern numbering obscures the fact that, once again, it contains not one, but two enclosed letters: the first is a copy of another letter of Balbus to Cicero, in the middle of which Balbus inserted the copy of a short letter of Caesar to Balbus. In other words, when Cicero sent the the letter (9.13) to Atticus, it contained not only a copy of a letter (Balbus to Cicero), but also a copy of a copy of another letter (Caesar to Balbus). Trying to untangle such "letter compositions" nearly takes one's breath away.

There is nothing in the New Testament similar to this way of assembling letters—unless perhaps we try to discover how the letter to Colossae (if genuine) and the letter to Laodicea were to be exchanged between the two communities, so that they could be read in each assembly (cf. Col 4:16). On the other hand, this might shed new light on the traditional debate over Phil 3.1: τὰ αὐτὰ γράφειν ὑμῖν ἐμοὶ μὲν οὐκ ὀκνηρόν ("to write the same things to you is not troublesome to me").[62]

A tour de force of a special kind is *Ad Att.* 9.10.4–10 from March 18, 49 BCE, only a day or so before he wrote the "open letter" to Caesar (9.11A, cf. 8.91–2[3a]) and sent a copy of it in a letter to Atticus (9.11), as we saw above. In 9.10.4–10 Cicero wants to prove that Atticus had consistently advised him to stay in Italy. For that reason he tells Atticus at the opening of §4: *evolvi volumen epistularum tuarum* ("I have unrolled the roll of your letters") and then in a real staccato he barrages Atticus with his own comments from, if I have correctly counted, thirteen different letters. That shows that he has a grip on his material, that he collected Atticus' letters, and that he had at least some of them or parts of them transcribed in a roll at this earliest possible stage (a species of a *volumen epistularum acceptarum*, see above).

---

[62] See also the article by Watson that follows.

Results

Reading Cicero's correspondence is a pleasure of its own, for which no excuse is needed, and much can be learned from it for dealing with New Testament letters in general terms.[63] But we set out to find some elucidation for controversial partition theories in New Testament exegesis, so we are bound to gather some results. We may be sure of this: it no longer suffices to assert (as is sometimes done) that there are no analogies in ancient epistolary literature, so that partition theories are invalidated a priori. At the very least, such a statement needs very careful qualification.

On the other hand, of course, our comparison does not necessarily prove that partition theories are correct. Each case has to be evaluated on its own merits. A problem with Cicero's correspondence is its tangled and complicated tradition history and the small manuscript basis with which we have to work. Compilations of letters no doubt did occur, and to quite a large extent, but we simply cannot be sure when and how they were made. It may have been done by medieval scribes, or it may have happened by accident; but such a development would not be so interesting for us, because compilations of letters of Paul must have been made, if at all, for the first edition of the Corpus Paulinum or even earlier, when the letters were stored in the archive of a community (at Ephesus? at Corinth? in the house of the business people Prisca and Aquila?). But the other option, viz. that letters of Cicero where combined very early, by Tiro or by Atticus or by an editor in the first century CE, who joined the loose letters with the eleven rolls produced by Atticus, cannot be excluded a priori, and that is enough for us to open up possibilities.

Two points in particular strike me in Cicero: first, the composition of a letter over several days or an even longer period, and second, the fine line that exists between affixing a postscript to a letter which is finished but not yet sent off, and writing a new letter as reaction

---

[63] Cf. the résumé in the excellent monograph by Hutchinson, *Cicero's Correspondence*, 199: "Some impression has also perhaps been given of the extraordinary range of the collection, and some glimpse, at least, of the numerous avenues of interest that they offer for exploration. … On a hedonistic note, a liking for letters, once acquired, opens up an immense and irreplaceable source of literary pleasure. Worse still, the eloquence, vitality, and attractiveness of late Republican letters can absorb even the more or less dutiful at the busiest times, and actually detain them (by deplorable irony) from the demands of more utilitarian correspondence."

to incoming new information when the earlier letter already is on its way. The content may be the same, but the procedure is different. If afterwards we have one single letter in each case, then one is an authorial composition and the other a redactor's compilation. To be sure, 2 Cor 10–13 is much too long for an authorial postscript; but on the other hand, Romans was hardly written in a day. Maybe we should reflect more carefully on the significance of the fact that it took Paul some time to dictate a letter, and on the traces this might have left in the finished product. The composition of longer letters might then be seen more as an evolving process, and not so much as the result of an instantaneous decision.

Compilations found in Cicero's correspondence usually seem to follow rather simple rules: letters were added, one after the other, so that prescripts and sometimes endings too were lost. Now and then letters changed place, the earlier one being found as the second part and vice versa. More complicated theories that postulate interpolations of fragments into letters are unsatisfactory, and have not won agreement. This we can take as warning not to look for too complicated models in our dealing with letter partition in the New Testament.

Today, conflated letters in the corpus Ciceronianum are separated again by editors. What are their criteria? Inherent reasons and traces in the texts, that is true, but in the case of Cicero's correspondence we have some hard evidence, too. The dates given at the end of quite a few letters help enormously. We are then able to correlate these dates and the content of the letters with our knowledge of late republican Roman history, which we get from other sources too, and not only from the letters themselves. We look in vain for help of this kind in New Testament exegesis, but we do nevertheless have tiny pieces of hard evidence. I think of the mention of an earlier letter in 1 Cor 5:9 and of a tearful letter in 2 Cor 2:4. Since the identification of either of these with 1 Corinthians seems a desperate solution, we can at least be certain that two more letters existed and that we are not looking for a phantom.

To sum up: the comparison of exegetical theories concerning New Testament letters with the evolution of the collections of Cicero's correspondence strengthens a position which might be arrived at by other means, too. Partition theories are not a priori implausible, but they should be kept rather simple, serial addition being more probable than interpolation of fragments. Additional hard evidence should be looked for, and that is missing in the case of 1 Thessalonians, Philippians and Romans. We have some clues for the Corinthian correspondence, but there it is inadvisable to search for more letters than the four about which there is some certainty: the earlier letter (1 Cor 5:9) and the answering letter (1 Cor); the tearful letter (2 Cor 2:4) and reconciliatory letter (2 Cor 1–9). By the way: What happened to the questioning letter from the Corinthians (1 Cor 7:1)? Did Paul or Prisca and Aquila at Ephesus keep a *volumen epistolarum acceptarum*? And *ceterum censo*: There is still much additional insight for dealing with New Testament epistolary literature from a more thorough study of Cicero's correspondence.

A REEXAMINATION OF THE EPISTOLARY ANALYSIS UNDERPINNING THE ARGUMENTS FOR THE COMPOSITE NATURE OF PHILIPPIANS

Duane F. Watson

Epistolary Conventions and Partition Theory

It is well-known that the structure and coherence of Paul's Epistle to the Philippians is continually debated. Contributing to this debate are the epistolary conventions and formulae that are found earlier or later than expected in a single letter. In other words, epistolary conventions indicative of the letter body-opening, middle, or closing are found scattered throughout the letter. These conventions are observed in concert with 1) the abrupt shift at 3:2 from a friendly to an agitated tone, from concern about the Philippians to invective against opponents, 2) the interruption of the flow of the letter by 3:2–4:3, with 4:4 seeming to be the natural conclusion of 3:1 and its reference to joy, and 3) the unusual placement of thanks to the Philippians for their gift at the end of the letter in 4:10–20, and seemingly after a delay from the reception of the gift, for Epaphroditus who brought the gift has had time to recover from a subsequent illness (2:25–30). These and other features have led many scholars to affirm that Philippians is a composite of three letters. With subtle variations, these three letters are labeled Letter A, a letter of thanks (4:10–20); Letter B, the letter sent to the Philippians with Epaphroditus (1:1–3:1; 4:4–9, 21–23) and Letter C, a polemical letter (3:2–4:3).

It is not my purpose to rehearse all the arguments for the unity and disunity of Philippians, for there are many recent reviews of this issue.[1]

---

[1] For recent discussion of the composition of Philippians, see Gordon D. Fee, *Paul's Letter to the Philippians* (NICNT; Grand Rapids: Eerdmans, 1995) 21–23; John T. Fitzgerald, "Philippians, Epistle to the," *ABD* 5.320–22; David E. Garland, "The Composition and Unity of Philippians: Some Neglected Literary Factors," *NovT* 27 (1985) 141–73; Timothy C. Geoffrion, *The Rhetorical Purpose and the Political and Military Character of Philippians: A Call to Stand Firm* (Lewiston, NY: Mellen Biblical Press, 1993) 1–22; Gerald F. Hawthorne, *Philippians* (WBC 43; Waco, TX: Word Books, 1983) xxix-xxxii; Peter T. O'Brien, *The Epistle to the Philippians* (NIGTC; Grand Rapids: Eerdmans, 1991) 10–18; Berthold Mengel, *Studien zum Philipperbrief* (WUNT 2/8; Tübingen: Mohr Siebeck, 1982) 286–316; Jeffrey T. Reed, *A Discourse Analysis of Philippians: Method and Rhetoric*

It is also not my purpose to provide a complete epistolary analysis of Philippians. No consensus has been reached about the coherence and structure of Philippians using Hellenistic epistolography. This is due particularly to the difficulty of identifying the epistolary conventions of the letter body which constitutes the bulk of a Pauline letter.

It is the more focused purpose of this article to examine how the important epistolary conventions used to support the composite nature of Philippians are often misidentified or identified in restricted ways when other identifications are equally possible or more probable.[2] These misidentifications and restricted identifications are perpetuated in the literature and need to be reexamined. The epistolary conventions found at what have been identified as the seams between the fragments of the three letters used to create our current form of Philippians have been the focus of the unity-disunity debate. They will be our focus as well. I will rely mainly upon the work of scholars who have carefully analyzed Philippians according to epistolary conventions and the papyri. I hope to show that when the epistolary conventions usually noted to support the composite nature of Philippians are more carefully analyzed they are better interpreted as transitions within one letter and support the unity of Philippians.

A word of caution. We need to acknowledge that the epistolary conventions and formulae in the letter body, especially the body-middle, are not easily defined with certainty. The letter body was less subject to epistolary conventions than the letter opening or closing. In letters which give evidence of literary and rhetorical skill, such as those of Paul, the letter body is subject to the contingencies of the situation

---

in the Debate over Literary Integrity (JSNTSup 136; Sheffield: Sheffield Academic Press, 1997); Johannes Schoon-Janssen, *Umstrittene "Apologien" in den Paulusbriefen: Studien zur rhetorischen Situation des 1. Thessalonicherbriefes, des Galaterbriefes und des Philipperbriefes* (GTA 45; Göttingen: Vandenhoeck and Ruprecht, 1991) 119–36; Philip Sellew, *"Laodiceans* and the Philippians Fragments Hypothesis," *HTR* 87 (1994) 17–28; Duane F. Watson, "A Rhetorical Analysis of Philippians and its Implications for the Unity Question," *NovT* 30 (188) 80–83.

[2] This study emerges from another presented at the London Conference on the Rhetorical Analysis of Scripture in 1995 and subsequently published as "The Integration of Epistolary and Rhetorical Analysis of Philippians," *The Rhetorical Analysis of Scripture: Essays from the 1995 London Conference*, eds. S. E. Porter and T. H. Olbricht (JSNTSup 146; Sheffield: Sheffield Academic Press, 1997) 398–426. Not only Professor Malherbe's own fine work in epistolary studies, but his kind remarks after the London presentation led me to pursue the epistolary form of Philippians further. This article is the result of that pursuit and I dedicate it in his honor.

addressed and the rhetorical artistry of the author.[3] Loveday Alexander observes: "It must be recognized that the 'body' of the hellenistic letter cannot be subject to such rigorous formal analysis as the opening and closing sections of the letter. The 'body' is fluid, flexible, and adaptable to a wide variety of situations and subjects."[4]

The epistolary studies of Philippians that I am using rarely refer to Letters A, B, or C. However, the divisions of the letter they give correspond to the typical divisions of Letters A, B, and C and allow us to address the issues involved in these divisions using epistolary analysis. For the sake of clarity, complete epistolary outlines offered by these studies are given below:[5]

John L. White

Letter Opening (1:1–2)
Thanksgiving (1:3–11)
Letter Body (1:12–2:30)
Body Opening (1:12–18a)
Body Middle (1:18b–2:18)
Body Closing (2:19–30)

(Another Letter)
Body Opening (4:10–13)
Body Closing (4:14–20)

---

[3] David E. Aune, *The New Testament in Its Literary Environment* (LEC 8; Philadelphia: Westminster, 1987) 183; William G. Doty, *Letters in Primitive Christianity* (GBS; Philadelphia: Fortress, 1973) 35–36; Stanley K. Stowers, *Letter Writing in Graeco-Roman Antiquity* (LEC 5; Philadelphia: Westminster, 1986) 22–23; John L. White, *The Form and Function of the Body of the Greek Letter* (SBLDS 2; Missoula, MT: Scholars Press, 1972) 102 n. 5; "Introductory Formulae in the Body of the Pauline Letter," *JBL* 90 (1971) 91 n. 2; "New Testament Epistolary Literature in the Framework of Ancient Epistolography," *ANRW* II.25.2 (1991) 1742–43; "Saint Paul and the Apostolic Letter Tradition," *CBQ* 45 (1983) 439; "The Structural Analysis of Philemon: A Point of Departure in the Formal Analysis of the Pauline Letter," *SBL 1971 Seminar Papers*, 1.25.

[4] "Hellenistic Letter-Forms and the Structure of Philippians," *JSNT* 37 (1989) 90.

[5] For epistolary analyses of Philippians, see Alexander, "Structure of Philippians," 87–101; Gregory L. Bloomquist, *The Function of Suffering in Philippians* (JSNTSup 78; Sheffield: Sheffield Academic Press, 1993) 97–118; Doty, *Letters*, 43; Ronald Russell, "Pauline Letter Structure in Philippians," *JETS* 25 (1982) 295–306; White, *Body*, 69–70, 73, 75, 77–79, 84, 85, 87–88. Reed (*Philippians*, 153–295) provides extensive observations on epistolary conventions in Philippians, but resists outlining the letter in light of them.

Ronald Russell

Letter Opening (1:1–2)
Thanksgiving (1:3–11)
Letter Body (1:12–2:30)
Body Opening (1:12–18)
Body Middle (1:19–2:18)
Body Closing (2:19–30)
Exhortation (3:1–4:20)
Letter Closing (4:21–23)

William G. Doty

Letter Opening (1:1–2)
Thanksgiving (1:3–11)
Letter Body (1:12–2:30)
Body Opening (1:12–18)
Eschatological Conclusion (2:14–18)
Travelogue (2:19–24)
Letter Closing (4:20–23)

L. Gregory Bloomquist

Letter Opening (1:1–2)
Thanksgiving (1:3–11)
Letter Body (1:12–4:20)
Body Opening (1:12–14)
Body Middle (1:15–2:18)
Body Closing (2:19–30)
Body Middle (3:1–4:7)
Body Middle (4:8–20)
Letter Closing (4:21–23)

Loveday Alexander

Address and greeting (1:1–2)
Prayer for the recipients (1:3–11)
Reassurance about the sender (1:12–26)
Request for Reassurance about the recipients (1:27–2:18)
Information about the movements of intermediaries (2:19–30)
Sermon at a distance (3:1–4:9)
Expression of thanks (4:10–20)
Exchange of greetings with third parties (4:21–23)
Closing wish for health (4:23)

Epistolary Conventions and Letter B (especially 2:14–3:1)

In current divisions of Philippians, Letter B is composed of 1:1–3:1, 4:4–9, and 4:21–23. The epistolary conventions at the close of the first portion of Letter B (2:14–3:1) are important to our discussion, especially the conventions of 3:1. We will examine these closely and note that neither the closing of a letter body-middle or a letter body-closing is indicated by these conventions.

2:14–18 as a Closing of a Letter Body-Middle

Although its beginning point is debated, there is agreement that the body-middle of Philippians has certainly begun by 2:1. "The body-middle—once the basis of common concern has been introduced—carries the message forward; either by developing its relevant details, introducing new and equally important matters of mutual concern, or by introducing new but less important matters."[6] Many scholars consider 2:18 to be the conclusion of the body-middle of Philippians.[7] They argue that the conclusion of the body-middle is indicated by the eschatological reference to the day of Christ in 2:16–18.[8] In addition, the eschatological conclusion precedes the apostolic parousia and the reference to the movement of emissaries in 2:19–30 which are incorrectly understood as indicating the body-closing (see below). However, in the Pauline letters the eschatological references to the Day of Christ are not restricted to the close of the letter body (e.g., 1:10; 2 Cor 5:10). For that matter, neither are references to the apostolic parousia or movement of emissaries limited to the body-closing of the Pauline letters (see below).

More specifically it is thought that the conclusion of the body-middle begins with the transitional imperative of purpose ποιεῖτε ... ἵνα ... ("do ... so that ...") in 2:14–15, and ends with the transitions in 2:17–18. In 2:14–15 the imperative ποιεῖτε ("do") is a transition in the letter

---

[6] White, *Body*, 39. For further discussion of the body-middle, see Bloomquist, *Philippians*, 77–79; Doty, *Letters*, 35–36; White, *Body*, 31–38, 96–97; "Epistolary Literature," 1736–38; *Light from Ancient Letters* (FFNT; Philadelphia: Fortress, 1986) 211–13; "Structural Analysis of Philemon," 21, 37–38.

[7] Bloomquist, *Philippians*, 107–109; Russell, "Pauline Letter Structure," 303; White, *Body*, 77–79.

[8] Bloomquist, *Philippians*, 107–109; Russell, "Pauline Letter Structure," 303; White, *Body*, 77; cf. Doty, *Letters*, 36, 43.

body, a modification of the petition.[9] Here the imperative is intensified by πάντα, a standard epistolary formula.[10] In 2:17 the conditional
clause ἀλλὰ εἰ καί ("but even if") is a minor, general transition of a
non-formulaic nature, usually confined to the body-middle and closing,
rarely found in the body-opening.[11] Also in 2:17 the two references to
rejoicing in χαίρω καὶ συγχαίρω ("I am glad and rejoice") are transitions. References to joy are used as transitions or for emphasis, acting
as punctuation anywhere in the letter body.[12] In 2:18 the construction
δὲ ... καὶ ("and ... also") and imperatives incorporating a rejoicing formula in χαίρετε καὶ συγχαίρετέ μοι ("you must be glad and rejoice with
me") are transitions.

As noted above, however, the transitions in 2:14–18 are minor and
not typical transitions for a major shift like the one from the body-
middle to the body-closing. The imperative and the joy-rejoicing formula are minor transitions that can be a found anywhere in a letter
body. The conditional clause is a minor transition unless it is in the
body-closing pointing back to previous material on which the sender
wants the recipients to focus, especially requests and commands.[13] In
2:17 the conditional is a minor transition within the body-middle, focusing on the possibility of Paul being poured out as a libation, and does
not pertain to requests or commands.

2:19–3:1 as the Body-Closing of Letter B (1:1–3:1; 4:4–9, 21–23)

Identifying 2:14–18 as the conclusion of the body-middle of Letter B
is even less persuasive when it is noted that epistolary conventions
do not necessarily indicate that 2:19–3:1 (or 2:19–30) is a letter body-
closing as some scholars have concluded.[14] However, many epistolary
elements have been misidentified or identified in a restricted fashion

---

[9] Henry A. Steen, "Les clichés épistolaires dans les lettres sur papyrus grecques,"
Classica et Mediavalia 1 (1939) 153–72; White, "Epistolary Formulas and Cliches in Greek
Papyrus Letters," *SBL 1978 Seminar Papers*, 1.309–12.
[10] Steen, "Les clichés épistolaires," 153–68.
[11] Steen, "Les clichés épistolaires," 126–28; White, *Body*, 13–15.
[12] Terence Y. Mullins, "Formulas in New Testament Epistles," *JBL* 91 (1972) 386–88;
White, *Body*, 77–78.
[13] White, *Body*, 13–15.
[14] Bloomquist, *Philippians*, 109–11; Funk, *Language, Hermeneutic, and Word of God: The
Problem of Language in the New Testament and Contemporary Theology* (New York: Harper and
Row, 1966) 265; Russell, "Pauline Letter Structure," 303; White, *Body*, 84, 85, 87–88; cf.
Doty, *Letters*, 36.

in order to arrive at this conclusion. These misidentifications include the motivation for writing formula in 2:19–23, the visit talk or apostolic parousia of 2:19–30, the confidence formula of 2:24, the reference to the transfer of intermediaries in 2:19–30, the transitions of 3:1a (τὸ λοιπόν, ἀδελφοί, and χαίρετε), and the motivation for writing formula in 3:1b. It is my contention that all these epistolary elements are misidentified or can be identified more appropriately. By no means is it necessary to conclude that 2:19–3:1 (or 2:19–30) is a letter body-closing.

John White has identified the motivation for writing formula, confidence formula, and apostolic parousia (visit talk) as a threefold Pauline body-closing, and others have agreed.[15] These three epistolary elements are thought to be found together in Phil 2:19–30 and create a strong case that this is a body-closing.[16] However, in his study of the confidence formula, Stanley N. Olson writes, "I found no confidence-formulas outside of Paul that are part of such three-part body closings as White outlines."[17] It is my further contention that these three elements have been misidentified or understood in a restrictive fashion and thus their convergence in Phil 2:19–30 is not a case for this section being identified as a body-closing.

1. The Presumed Motivation for Writing Formula in 2:19–23

One general transition usually found within the body-closing is the motivation for writing formula, a type of disclosure formula. In the body-closing this formula finalizes the reason for writing.[18] Phil 2:19–23 has been identified as a motivation for writing formula indicating that 2:19–30 is a letter body-closing.[19] Paul's motivation for writing is assumed to be to inform the Philippians that Timothy is coming: "I hope in the Lord Jesus to send Timothy to you soon, so that I may be cheered by news of you …" (2:19).[20] Since the entire section of 2:19–30

---

[15] White, *Body*, 84, 85, 87–88, 97–99; "Structural Analysis of Philemon," 38–45; Bloomquist, *Philippians*, 79–82, 109–11; Doty, *Letters*, 36–37.

[16] Bloomquist, *Philippians*, 79–82, 109–11; Doty, *Letters*, 36–37; White, *Body*, 84, 85, 87–88, 97–99.

[17] "Pauline Expressions of Confidence in His Addressees," *CBQ* 47 (1985) 287 n. 10.

[18] Bloomquist, *Philippians*, 79–80; White, *Body*, 3, 5, 27, 33, 41, 84–86, 97–98; "Epistolary Formulas and Cliches in Greek Papyrus Letters," *SBL 1978 Seminar Papers*, 1.302; Light, 204–205; "Structural Analysis of Philemon," 38–40.

[19] Bloomquist, *Philippians*, 109–10; White, *Body*, 84, 85, 87–88.

[20] All biblical quotations are from the NRSV.

is not located in the body-closing of the received form of Philippians, the current location of this motivation for writing formula seems to be secondary.

However, Phil 2:19–23 is not properly identified as a motivation for writing formula indicative of the body-closing. These verses do not refer to preceding information as is the case of motivation for writing formulae in the body-closing.[21] More importantly, these verses do not exhibit the three formal elements of the motivation for writing formula: statement of authorship, reference to the act of writing (usually using the verb γράφω), and reiteration of the reason for writing usually introduced by ἵνα, ὅτι, or ὡς ("in order that").[22] John White acknowledges this when he writes of the reference to writing in 2:19–23: "Dissimilarity of formal items notwithstanding, the passage functions structurally in a way comparable to the motivation for writing formula in the other letters."[23] White shows that elsewhere Paul does utilize the motivation for writing formula in its three formal elements in the body closing to refer to preceding information (Rom 15:14–15; Gal 5:2; Phlm 19).[24] Phil 2:19–23 is not analogous to this usage.

2. The Visit Talk or Apostolic Parousia of 2:19–30

The expression of a desire to make a personal visit or a promise of such a personal visit is a transitional device coming near the end of the body-closing. It helps maintain personal relationships in spite of the correspondents being physically apart.[25] In the Pauline letters talk of a visit takes the form of an apostolic parousia, that is, Paul's announcement that he personally plans to visit the recipients and/or dispatch emissaries (e.g., Rom 15:14–33; Phlm 21–22).[26] Phil 2:19–30 has

---

[21] White, *Body*, 25–27.

[22] White, *Body*, 84–86; "Structural Analysis of Philemon," 40 n. 17. White (*Body*, 5, 27) cites the following papyri: *P. Mich.* 10.13–14 (257 BCE), *P. Tebt.* 747.16–17 (243 BCE), *P. Par.* 43.4 (=UPZ 66.4) (154 BCE), *P. Mich.* 512.6 (early III CE). For further examples, see White, "Epistolary Formulas and Cliches," 317 n. 38; *Light* 204 n. 66.

[23] *Body*, 87. Bloomquist calls 2:19–23 a "substitute" for the motivation for writing formula (*Philippians*, 109).

[24] "Structural Analysis of Philemon," 38–40.

[25] White, *Body*, 29–31, 41, 97–99; *Light*, 202. White (*Body*, 30–31) cites *P. Hib.* 66.4ff (228/27 BCE); *P. Oxy* 113.27–28 (II CE); *P. Oxy.* 1216.17ff (II/III CE); *P. Oxy.* 1666.11–14 (III CE). For further examples, see White, *Light*, 202 nn. 61, 62.

[26] For a discussion of the apostolic parousia, see Bloomquist, *Philippians*, pp. 79–82; Doty, *Letters*, 12, 36–37, 43; Robert W. Funk, "The Apostolic *Parousia*: Form and Significance," *Christian History and Interpretation: Studies Presented to John Knox*, eds. W.R. Farmer,

been identified as an apostolic parousia indicating a body-closing, for in this section Paul announces that he will be sending Timothy to Philippi and that he desires to visit as well.[27] However, the apostolic parousia in other Pauline letters is by no means restricted to the body-closing (e.g., Rom 1:8–15; 1 Cor 4:14–21; Gal 4:12–20; 1 Thess 2:17–3:13). As R. Alan Culpepper remarks, Paul "speaks of his co-workers and travels in the body of a letter when these matters are relevant to the problems of the church or the agenda of the letter,"[28] that is, where it is rhetorically appropriate. Mention of a visit in the non-literary papyri occurs throughout the letters and is not restricted to the body-closing.[29]

3. *The Confidence Formula of 2:24*

Ancient letters often contain expressions of the sender's confidence in the audience to do as he or she asks, or confidence in the gods to respond as requested.[30] John White describes a confidence formula in Pauline letters as comprised of the emphatic form of the pronoun ἐγώ, the perfect form of the verb πείθω, specification of the basis of confidence, and the matter of confidence introduced by ὅτι (e.g., Rom 15:14; Gal 5:10; Phlm 21).[31] He also argues that Paul often closes the body of his letter with a confidence formula expressing his confidence that the recipients will undertake what he has proposed in the motivation for

C.F.D. Moule, and R.R. Niebuhr (Cambridge: Cambridge University Press, 1967) 249–68; *Language, Hermeneutic, and Word of God*, 263–70; T.Y. Mullins, "Visit Talk in New Testament Letters," *CBQ* 35 (1973) 350–54; Franz Schnider and Werner Stenger, *Studien zum Neutestamentlichen Briefformula* (NTTS 11; Leiden: E.J. Brill, 1987) 92–107; M. Luther Stirewalt, *Studies in Ancient Epistolography* (SBLRBS 27; Atlanta: Scholars Press, 1993) 5; Klaus Thraede, *Grundzüge griechisch-römischer Brieftopik* (Zetemata 48; Munich: Beck, 1970) 95–106; John White, "Apostolic Mission and Apostolic Message: Congruence in Paul's Epistolary Rhetoric, Structure and Imagery," *Origins and Method: Towards a New Understanding of Judaism and Christianity: Essays in Honour of John C. Hurd*, ed. Bradley H. McLean (JSNTSup 86; Sheffield: Sheffield Academic Press, 1993) 151–53; *Body*, 60–62, 97–99; *Light*, 205, 219–20; cf. 202; "Structural Analysis of Philemon," 38–45.

[27] Bloomquist, *Philippians*, 110; Doty, *Letters*, 36–37; Funk, "The Apostolic *Parousia*," 261–62, 263 n. 1; *Language, Hermeneutic, and Word of God*, 265, 270–71; Russell, "Pauline Letter Structure," 303; White, *Body*, 84–86.

[28] "Co-Workers in Suffering: Philippians 2:19–30," *RevExp* 77 (1980) 350.

[29] Mullins, "Visit Talk," 350–54. *P. Mich.* 8.481.14–15 (early II CE), *P. Oxy.* 1666.11–14 (III CE).

[30] White, *Light*, 205–206.

[31] White, *Body*, 64, 89; "Structural Analysis of Philemon," 40–41.

writing formula (e.g., Rom 15:14; Phlm 21).[32] White asserts that this formulaic use of the confidence formula by Paul is rarely paralleled in the papyri.[33]

However, Stanley N. Olson found that expressions of confidence are *non-formulaic* and *frequently* found in the papyri and literary letters. Pauline confidence expressions conform to these. The two most common types of confidence expressions are self-confidence expressed by the sender and expression of confidence in the recipients that they will comply with his or her wishes.[34] Pauline confidence expressions conform to these. Expressions of confidence in the papyri and New Testament have the following three functional (not formulaic) elements: 1) an indication of a first person subject in verb or pronoun, or in the antecedent to the participle, 2) a confidence term(s), 3) a reference to the addressees as the object of the confidence, using the second person pronoun.[35] Such expressions have functional parallels, but are not formulaic as White suggests, not even in Pauline letters.[36] The sender's expressions of self-confidence can occur anywhere in a letter, especially in the context of apologetic or self-commendation.[37] The senders expressions of confidence in the addressees' compliance are usually found in the closing section of the letter, often adjacent to the letter's request, but cannot be limited to the body-closing per se.[38] In both the papyri and Pauline letters the expressions of confidence in the audience undergird the purpose for which the letter was written.[39]

Phil 2:24 has been identified as a confidence expression indicating a body-closing: "And I trust in the Lord that I will also come soon."[40] This verse is an expression of confidence, here in God. This confidence expression is one of self-confidence rooted in the Lord as is often the case in Pauline expressions of self-confidence (e.g., Rom 15:17; 1Cor

---

[32] White, *Body*, 64, 89, 99; "Epistolary Formulas and Cliches," 306; "Structural Analysis of Philemon," 40–41; Bloomquist, *Philippians*, 80.

[33] *Body*, 64, 99; "Epistolary Formulas and Cliches," 306; "Structural Analysis of Philemon," 40.

[34] "Epistolary Uses of Expressions of Self-Confidence," *JBL* 103 (1984) 585–97; "Pauline Expressions of Confidence," 282–95.

[35] Olson, "Pauline Expressions of Confidence," 295.

[36] Olson, "Expressions of Self-Confidence," 585–86; "Pauline Expressions of Confidence," 282 n. 1, 283, 295.

[37] Olson, "Expressions of Self-Confidence," 587.

[38] Olson, "Pauline Expressions of Confidence," 284, 287.

[39] Olson, "Pauline Expressions of Confidence," 283–284, 287, 295.

[40] Bloomquist, *Philippians*, 110; White, *Body*, 90.

7:40; 2 Cor 1:12). Expressions of self-confidence are found anywhere in the letter. There is no reason to understand 2:24 as indicative of a letter body-closing.

4. *The Reference to the Transfer of Intermediaries in 2:19–30*

One important epistolary feature in 2:19–30 that is often overlooked is the mention of the receipt and transfer of goods, supplies, messengers, and intermediaries. This is a non-formulaic transitional device of a general nature found especially in the body-middle and rarely in the body-opening or closing. The transfer function usually employs the verbs of sending, πέμπῶ or ἀποστέλλω.[41] Paul's many references to sending Timothy and Epaphroditus to Philippi (vv. 19, 23, 25, 28) may be transfer statements, especially since all four references use the verb πέμπω to refer to messengers and intermediaries. As just observed, transfer statements are usually found in the body-middle. These four transfer statements in 2:19–30 further indicate that this section is part of the body-middle, not the body-closing.

5. *The Transitions Τὸ Λοιπόν, Ἀδελφός, and Χαίρετε in 3:1a*

There are several transitions in 3:1 that have been understood to indicate a seam where Letter B (1:1–3:1; 4:4–9, 21–23) and Letter C (3:2–4:3) are sewn together. In 3:1a these transitions include the adverbial construction τὸ λοιπόν ("finally"), the vocative ἀδελφοί ("brothers and sisters"), and the expression of joy, χαίρετε ἐν κυρίῳ ("'rejoice' or 'farewell' in the Lord"). These transitional features have been interpreted to mean that 3:1a is part of the conclusion of the body of Letter B (1:1–3:1). We will examine each one of these transitions.

Any vocative, especially ἀδελφοί in a Pauline letter, is a general, non-formulaic transition that marks major transitions anywhere in the letter.[42] In Philippians ἀδελφοί marks transitions in 2:12; 3:1, 17; and 4:1, 8. In the non-literary papyri the τὸ λοιπόν formula commonly introduces the last item of the letter body, and does so in a Pauline

---

[41] White, *Body*, 10–12, 38, 41; "Epistolary Formulas and Cliches," 304–305. White (*Body*, 10–12) cites *P. Hib.* 41.2ff (ca. 261 BCE); *P. Fay.* 113.3–4 (100 CE); *P. Oxy.* 1293.4–5, 23–24 (117–38 CE); PSI. 841.2ff (IV CE). White ("Epistolary Formulas and Cliches," 304–305) also cites *P. Oxy.* 2.300.3ff (late I CE); *P. Mich.* 8.481.5ff (early II CE); *P. Mich.* 8.499.12–14 (II CE), *P. Oxy.* 12.1488.3ff (II CE); and *P. Mich.* 8.490.5ff (II CE).

[42] White, *Body*, 15–16, 37–38.

letter (2 Cor 13:11; cf. Phil 4:8).[43] However, in Pauline letters, the τὸ λοιπόν formula can occur well before the letter closing (1 Thess 4:1; 2 Thess 3:1). Margaret E. Thrall argues that λοιπόν in post-classical Greek was a transitional particle introducing a logical conclusion or a new beginning in the flow of thought, often used like οὖν ("therefore").[44] Jeffrey T. Reed has found λοιπόν as a discourse marker at the beginning, middle, and end of Hellenistic letters. In the middle of a letter it usually concludes previous narrative or a list of commands. In 3:1a τὸ λοιπόν indicates the middle of a letter, for it is used with a command (χαίρετε), follows two commands (προσδέχεσθε, ἔχετε, 2:29), and follows the narrative about Epaphroditus (2:25–30). It should be translated "in the future," "from now on," or "the remaining time" as in 1 Cor 7:29, rather than as "finally."[45]

Typically the imperative χαίρετε ("rejoice" or "farewell") in 3:1a is assumed to signal the body-closing. Expressions of joy using the verb χαίρω and the noun χαρά are often found in the body-opening or closing to maintain contact between parties, and usually in the body-opening where joy is expressed about the arrival of a letter and its significance for the letter sender (e.g., Phlm 7).[46] However, such joy expressions are used throughout the papyri wherever the receipt of a letter is mentioned.[47] It is used as a transition or for emphasis, acting as punctuation.[48] Loveday Alexander notes that while the imperative χαίρετε means "farewell" in conversation, she did not find any example of χαίρετε in a letter closing meaning "farewell." When χαίρω is used in a letter the infinitive form χαίρειν is found, and found at the beginning of the letter in the sense of "greeting."[49] Harry Gamble found no use of

---

[43] Bloomquist, *Philippians*, 111; White, *Light*, 206–207. White (*Light*, 207 n. 81) cites *P. Col.* 3.6.14–15 (early March 257 BCE); *P. Oslo Inv.* 1475.11 (Mid I CE), and PSI 5.500.8–9 (257 BCE).

[44] *Greek Particles in the New Testament* (NTTS 3; Leiden: Brill, 1962) 25–30.

[45] "Philippians 3:1 and the Epistolary Hesitation Formulas: The Literary Integrity of Philippians, Again," *JBL* 115 (1996) 82–84; *Philippians*, 258–60. In particular he cites *POxy.* 12.1480.13 (32 CE); 1.119.8.8, 13 (reading λυπόν [a spelling of λοιπόν] in line 13 rather than λυρόν as in published editions); 48.3400 (359–65); 17.2154.15 (IV CE); 48.3408.19 (IV CE). τὸ λοίπον is found at the beginning of *POxy.* 17.2149.5 (II/III CE) meaning "for the rest" and at the end of *P. Oxy.* 4.709.12 (50 CE) meaning "finally."

[46] Doty, *Letters*, 35; Mullins, "Formulas," 384–85; White, *Body*, 22–23, 40–41; "Epistolary Literature," 1735; "Introductory Formulae," 95–96; *Light*, 201.

[47] Alexander, "Structure of Philippians," 98.

[48] Terence Y. Mullins, "Formulas," 386–88; White, *Body*, 77–78.

[49] "Structure of Philippians," 97. Reed ("Philippians 3:1," 81 n. 72; *Philippians*, 242 n. 315) has confirmed this with his own search.

the verb χαίρω as a final greeting in ancient letters or in Paul's letters.[50] Paul's usual closing is ἡ χάρις τοῦ κυρίου … , not χαίρετε ἐν κυρίῳ … (1 Cor 16:23; 2 Cor 13:13, Gal 6:18; Phil 4:23; 1 Thess 5:28; Phlm 25; cf. Eph 6:24; Col 4:18; 2 Thess 3:18).[51] Here χαίρετε is another example of the joy *topos* found throughout the letter (1:4, 18, 25; 2:2, 17–18, 28, 29; 3:1; 4:1, 4, 10). It is motivated by the epistolary situation, for Paul wants the Philippians to rejoice that Epaphroditus has recovered and is returning to them. It restates this purpose from the immediate context in 2:28 where Paul mentions that he is sending Epaphroditus back to them "in order that you may rejoice at seeing him again."[52]

6. *The Reference to Writing in 3:1b*

As previously noted when discussing 2:19–23, the motivation for writing is a general transitional or disclosure formula. It is usually found within the body-closing and rarely in the body-middle. It is by nature explanatory and takes the form of the statement of authorship, reference to the act of writing (usually using the verb γραφῶ), and reiteration of the reason for writing usually introduced by ἵνα, ὅτι, or ὡς εἰδῇς. It finalizes the reason for writing or requests information which necessitates further correspondence. It is the only disclosure formula used in the body-closing and usually calls attention to preceding information, often to previous correspondence or the some aspect of the letter being written.[53] The identification of 2:19–3:1 as a body-closing is partially based on the misidentification of 3:1b as a motivation for writing formula: "To write the same things to you is not troublesome to me, and for you it is a safeguard." This reference to writing has been understood to refer to previous correspondence (like Letters A or C) and indicate the body-closing of Letter B.[54]

However, the reference to writing in 3:1b is not explanatory, does not have the standard form of a motivation for writing formula found in the body- closing, nor does it finalize the reason for writing or request information. It is not a motivation for writing formula at all. Rather it is a *reference to writing*, a non-formulaic descriptive transitional device of

---

[50] *The Textual History of the Letter to the Romans* (SD 42; Grand Rapids: Eerdmans, 1977) 146.

[51] Garland, "Composition," 149–50.

[52] Reed, "Philippians 3:1," 81–82; id., *Philippians*, 256–60.

[53] White, *Body*, 27.

[54] See sources in Garland ("Composition," 155) that begin Letter C with 3:2.

a general nature used throughout the letter body to describe the past or future act of writing,[55] often in the body-middle.[56] The reference to writing in 3:1b is non-formulaic and descriptive, referring to the past and present act of writing. Paul describes his writing as a safeguard, but he does not explain how it functions as a safeguard. In its role as a reference to writing, 3:1b can refer to previous correspondence (like the motivation for writing formula does) but by nature is indicative of the body-middle, not the body-closing.

Stanley K. Stowers argues that 3:1b is a hortatory idiom of parenetic letters, assuring the recipients that they really do not need the advice being given. It is similar to the Pauline expressions "you remember" or "you know" used throughout 1 Thessalonians (1:5; 2:1, 2, 5, 9, 11; 4:1, 2, 6; 5:2). It assures the Philippians that the contrasting models in 3:2–21 are familiar to them and contain nothing new.[57] As such there is no need to understand 3:1b as referring to previous correspondence (such as Letters A or C) or classifying it as a motivation for writing formula. It simply introduces the exemplars of 3:2–21.

Jeffrey T. Reed discusses 3:1b in the context of the epistolary hesitation formula, a transitional device. The formula uses the often negated verb ὀκνέω ("hesitate") and related forms plus a dependent clause using the infinitive (often a form of the verb γράφω). Hesitation formulas are to two types: 1) *requests* in which the sender commands the recipients not to hesitate with regard to writing about their situation and needs, or to carry out something mentioned in the letter, and 2) *notifications* in which senders assert that they do not hesitate to take some course of action in relation to the recipients and assure them that they are not negligent towards them. As a *request* the hesitation formula is found in

---

[55] White, *Body*, pp. 12–13, 33–35, 38, 41; "Epistolary Formulas and Cliches," 303–304; Mullins, "Visit Talk," 354–55. White (*Body*, 12–13) cites *P. Mich.* 36.1–2 (254 BCE); *P. Oxy.* 297.3–4 (54 CE); *P. Oxy.* 1068.4–5 (III CE), and *P. Mich.* 58.29–30 (248 BCE). For further examples, see White, *Body*, 33–35. In earlier work White makes a distinction between formulaic and non-formulaic references to writing (cf. *Body*, 12–13, 33–35, 38, 41). However, in later work he admits that these references to writing, other than the reference to writing that is a disclosure formula, "do not submit to formal analysis" ("Epistolary Formulas and Cliches," 303).

[56] Bloomquist, *Philippians*, 78–79; White, *Body*, 33–35, 38, 41. White (*Body*, 13) cites the following examples in the body-middle: *P. Oxy.* 1757.19 (II CE), BGU 846.9–10 (II CE), and *P. Oxy.* 1160.12–13 (IV CE).

[57] "Friends and Enemies in the Politics of Heaven: Reading Theology in Philippians," *Pauline Theology. Volume 1: Thessalonians, Philippians, Galatians, Philemon,* ed. J. M. Bassler (Minneapolis: Fortress, 1991) 115–16. For other examples of similar phraseology, Stowers cites Cicero, *Ep. ad Fam.* 1.4.3; 2.4.2 and Isocrates, *Philip.* 105.

the letter closing immediately preceding the greetings when is concerns having the recipients write about their situation and needs. However, it is found throughout the letter when used to persuade the recipients to carry out an immediately preceding set of instructions. As a *notification* the hesitation formula can be found anywhere in the letter.[58]

Reed argues that the reference to writing in 3:1b, τὰ αὐτὰ γράφειν ὑμῖν ἐμοὶ μὲν οὐκ ὀκνηρόν, ὑμῖν δὲ ἀσφαλές, is a modified hesitation formula using the adjective ὀκνηρόν with the negative οὐκ in conjunction with the infinitive γράφειν. This modified hesitation formula is a notification which can be found anywhere in the letter. In 3:1b the formula refers to preceding matters (2:19–30) rather than future correspondence, and follows commands (2:29–3:1a) and a narrative (2:25–30). This kind of notification often occurs in the middle of the letter.[59] Reed translates 3:1b as "To write the same things [viz., to rejoice] to you is, with respect to me, not a cause of hesitation and is, with respect to you, a cause of steadfastness."[60] The body-middle, not closing, is indicated by 3:1b.

Epistolary Conventions and Letter C: 3:2–4:3

As argued in the preceding section, there are no epistolary conventions in 2:19–3:1 which necessitates identifying it as a letter body-closing. Also there are no transitions in 3:2 indicating the beginning of a new letter, Letter C, defined either as 3:2–4:3 or 3:2–4:9. It is thought by some that Letter C interrupts Letter B, with the commands to rejoice in 3:1 and 4:4 originally belonging together, with the conclusion of Letter B continuing in 4:4–9.[61] However, as noted above regarding 3:1, rejoicing is a minor epistolary transition found throughout the letter body so that the references in 3:1 and 4:4 need not have been originally connected in the same letter.

If Letter C is defined as 3:2–4:3 as it is by some,[62] there are significant transitions in 4:1–3, especially in 4:1: "Therefore, my brothers and sisters, whom I love and long for, my joy and crown, stand firm in the Lord, my beloved." This verse contains a string of transitional elements

---

[58] "Philippians," 63–72; *Philippians*, 228–38.
[59] Reed, "Philippians," 72–80, 88–90; *Philippians*, 246–56, 263–65.
[60] Reed, "Philippians," 89.
[61] For a listing of scholars, see Garland, "Composition," 155.
[62] For a listing of scholars defining Letter C as 3:2–4:3, see Garland, "Composition," 155.

in ὥστε, the vocative, a reference to joy, οὕτως, the imperative, and
the vocative (ὥστε ἀγαπητοί μου ... , χαρά ... , οὕτως στήκετε ... ,
ἀγαπητοί). This transitional verse is followed by two petitions which
function as transitions to new material or a change in subject anywhere
in the letter body.[63] In 4:2 there is the twice repeated personal petition
using the verb παρακαλέω ("urge, appeal") for Euodia and Syntyche "to
be of the same mind in the Lord." In 4:3 there is the familiar petition
using the verb ἐρωτάω ("ask, request") for the Philippians "to help these
women." These, like most petitions, are composed of the background of
the petition, the verb of petition (ἐρωτάω or παρακαλέω), the vocative of
address, the content of the request, and mention of the benefit that will
result from fulfilling the request.[64] None of the transitions and petitions
in 4:1–3 are themselves indicative of the body-closing of a letter as they
would be if 3:2–4:3 was identified as a letter.[65]

If Letter C is defined as 3:2–4:9 as it is by some,[66] there are no
indications of a letter closing in 4:4–9 as well. The imperative χαίρετε
("greetings" or "rejoice") is not used in the body-closing as noted above,
so its twofold use in 4:4 does not indicate a body-closing. As noted
above regarding 3:1, the adverbial expression τὸ λοιπόν and the vocative
ἀδελφοί in 4:8 are transitions found throughout letters. The "God of
peace" expressions in 4:7, 9 could be considered indicative of a letter
closing.[67] Paul often concludes a letter with a "God of peace" expression
(Rom 16:20; 2 Cor 13:11; cf. Rom 15:33), sometimes as a benediction
(1 Thess 5:23; cf. Rom 15:33). However, such an expression is also found
in Pauline letters in places other than the end (1 Cor 14:33), as are

---

[63] Doty, *Letters*, 34; Mullins, "Formulas," 386–87; J. T. Sanders, "The Transition from
Opening Epistolary Thanksgiving to Body in the Letters of the Pauline Corpus," *JBL*
81 (1962) 349, 351–52.

[64] For further discussion of petition, see C. J. Bjerkelund, *Parakalô: Form, Funktion und
Sinn der parakalô-Sätze in den paulinischen Briefen* (Bibliotheca Theologica Norvegica, I;
Oslo: Universitetsforlaget, 1967); Doty, *Letters*, 34; Mullins, "Formulas," 380–81; "Peti-
tion as a Literary Form," *NovT* 5 (1962) 46–54; Sanders, "Transition," 349–57; Steen,
"Les clichés épistolaires," 133–38; White, "Epistolary Formulas and Cliches," 301–302;
"Epistolary Literature," 1743–44; *The Form and Structure of the Official Petition: A Study in
Greek Epistolography* (SBLDS 5; Missoula, MT: Scholars Press, 1972); "Introductory For-
mulae," 93–94; *Light*, 193–96, 204; "Structural Analysis of Philemon," 23–25.

[65] *Contra* Wolfgang Schenk, *Die Philipperbriefe des Paulus* (Stuttgart: Kohlhammer, 1984)
256–59.

[66] For a listing of scholars, see Garland, "Composition," 155.

[67] Schenk, *Philipperbriefe*, 244. For discussion of 4:9 as a peace benediction, see Jeffrey
A. D. Weima, "Pauline Letter Closings: Analysis and Hermeneutical Significance,"
BBR 5 (1995) 177–97, esp. 183–87.

Pauline benedictions in general (Rom 15:5–6, 13; 1 Thess 3:11; 2 Thess 2:16). Again, none of the transitions in 4:4–9 are themselves indicative of the body-closing of a letter.

The transitions in 4:1, the petitions in 4:2–3, the imperative χαίρετε in 4:4, the adverbial expression τὸ λοιπόν and the vocative ἀδελφοί in 4:8, and the "God of peace" expression in 4:7, 9 are all explained as transitions within an originally unified letter and do not necessitate identifying any part of 4:1–9 is a letter closing. In their current position at the close of the canonical form of Philippians they may be transitions in the body-closing. It is primarily their current position in the canonical form of Philippians, not their function as epistolary elements, that gives these transitions a closing function. Any argument that 4:1–9 is somehow indicative of a letter closing of a once independent letter is muted because this material is now found in the closing of the canonical form of Philippians which may be its original position.

Epistolary Conventions and Letter A: 4:10–20

Many interpreters identify 4:10–20 as Letter A, Paul's note of thanks to the Philippians for aid received. It is assumed that it is unusual to place a thanksgiving at the close of a letter, so 4:10–20 must have been a separate note of thanks.[68] The close of a letter is an unusual place to put a discussion of the receipt of aid. As discussed above, the receipt and transfer of goods and supplies and intermediaries is a non-formulaic transitional device of a general nature. It is commonly found in the body-middle and only rarely in the body-opening or body-closing. However, as Peter Artz remarks, "Formulations of thanks to people derive from a writer's personal intention and may appear in various parts of a letter and in various contexts."[69] Loveday Alexander found thanksgivings coming at the end of family letters and coming somewhat begrudgingly, as in Philippians.[70] John White says, "…the expression of appreciation will gravitate toward the letter

---

[68] Funk, *Language, Hermeneutic, and Word of God*, 272; White, *Body*, 69–70, 75; "Introductory Formulae," 95; Schenk, *Philipperbriefe*, 57–61. For a listing of other scholars, see Garland, "Composition," 155.

[69] "The 'Epistolary Introductory Thanksgiving' in the Papyri and in Paul," *NovT* 36 (1994) 36.

[70] "Structure of Philippians," 97–98. She cites *P. Oxy.* 12.1481.7–9 from White, *Light*, 158–59.

closing, regardless of the epistolary setting."[71] Craig Wansink notes that Cicero's letter to his brother Quintus (QFr. 1.3) contains many similarities to Philippians.[72] In both the sender is accused of a crime and acknowledges having received financial aid from friends and family while in need, but without giving explicit thanks for the aid received. Most important for our discussion, this thankless thanks comes at the end of the letter. Thus there is no need to consider 4:10–20 as a separate letter on the grounds that it contains thanks and concludes the canonical form of Philippians.

White defines the letter opening of Letter A as 4:10–13. A key reason is that 4:10 contains a joy expression often found in the body-opening and is found once in the body-opening of a Pauline letter (Phlm 7).[73] The joy expression exhibits three formal characteristics: a classic form of the verb χαίρειν (ἐχάρην), an adverb of magnitude (μεγάλως), with the object of joy introduced by ὅτι: Ἐχάρην … μεγάλως ὅτι.[74] However, as noted above, the joy expression is a general transitional device in the letter body, usually in the body-opening or closing. When the expression is found in the body-opening, it usually refers to the sender's joy in receiving a letter and/or relief about the health and welfare of those who contacted the sender and the significance of their correspondence for the sender (as in Phlm 7).[75] This is not the focus of the joy expressed in 4:10. In Philippians this joy expression is yet another example of the joy *topos* which punctuates the letter (1:4, 18, 25; 2:2, 17–18, 28, 29; 3:1; 4:1, 4, 10).[76] It can be understood as an element of the body-closing of a unified Pauline letter (cf. Rom16:19).

Another reason White describes 4:10–13 as a body-opening is his identification of 4:14–20 as a body-closing. The latter roughly corre-

---

[71] "Epistolary Formulas and Cliches," 301.

[72] *Chained in Christ: The Experience and Rhetoric of Paul's Imprisonments* (JSNTSup 130; Sheffield: Sheffield Academic Press, 1996), 129–32.

[73] White, *Body*, 69–70, 75; "Introductory Formulae," 95.

[74] White, "Introductory Formulae," 95–96.

[75] Doty, *Letters*, 35; White, *Body*, 22–23; "Introductory Formulae," 304; Reed, *Philippians*, White (*Body*, 22–23) cites *P. Elephant.* 13.2–3 (III BCE), *P. Lond.* 42.7ff (168 BCE), *P. Lond.* 43.3–4 (II BCE), *P. Mich.* 483.3ff (Reign of Hadrian), *P. Giss.* 21.3–4) (II CE), and BGU 332.6–7 (II/III CE).

[76] I do not agree with Weima that 4:10–20 in its entirety is a "lengthy joy expression." Other than the initial reference to joy in v. 10, there are no other such references in these verses. Weima's identification is due in part to his questionable assessment that all 4:8–23 is a letter closing (Jeffrey A. D. Weima, *Neglected Endings: The Significance of the Pauline Letter Closings* [JSNTSup 101; Sheffield: Sheffield Academic Press, 1994] 191–94).

sponds to an apostolic parousia which often occurs in body-closing of a Pauline letter.[77] However, this identification is difficult to sustain since there is no talk of a visit in 4:14–20, just a review of Paul's past acquaintance and subsequent relationship with the Philippian church. Also, this identification is muted because in its context in the canonical form of Philippians this section is already in a body-closing which can just as easily be its original position in an originally unified letter. As White says of 4:14–20, "The body-closing of the truncated letter in Phil. 4:10–20 … lacks the formal items which could be subjected to analysis."[78] If 4:10–20 was once an independent letter, and 4:10–13 was the body-opening and 4:14–20 a body-closing, the current form is severely truncated.[79] It would lack the body-middle which in a Pauline letter is the main component. It is easier to see 4:10–20 as part of the body-closing of a single letter that is our current form of Philippians than a disemboweled note of thanks. Also, this identification of 4:14–20 as a body-closing is muted because in its context in the canonical form of Philippians this section is already in a body-closing that can just as easily be its original position in an originally unified letter.

Philippians as a Letter of Friendship

Due to the many similarities of the content of Philippians and letters of friendship, many have classified Philippians as a letter of friendship.[80] This classification, or at least the recognition in Philippians of the *topoi*

---

[77] White, *Body*, p. 75, 84. On the apostolic *parousia*, see above n. 23.

[78] White, *Body*, 84.

[79] As admitted by Funk, *Language, Hermeneutic, and Word of God*, 272; White *Body*, 75.

[80] See Fee, *Philippians*, 2–14; Fitzgerald, "Philippians," 320. For the debate about whether or not Philippians is a letter of friendship, and whether "friendship" is a letter genre as well as letter *topos*, see especially the four articles in "Part Two: Friendship Language in Philippians" in John T. Fitzgerald, ed., *Friendship, Flattery, and Frankness of Speech: Studies on Friendship in the New Testament World* (NovTSup 82; Leiden: E.J. Brill, 1996) 81–160. These include John Reumann, "Philippians, Especially Chapter 4, as a 'Letter of Friendship': Observations on a Checkered History of Scholarship," 83–106; Ken L. Berry, "The Function of Friendship Language in Philippians 4:10–20," 107–24; Abraham J. Malherbe, "Paul's Self-Sufficiency (Philippians 4:11)," 125–39, and John T. Fitzgerald, "Philippians in the Light of Some Ancient Discussions of Friendship," 141–60. Stowers classifies Philippians as a "hortatory" letter of friendship ("Friends and Enemies," 107–114). He apparently has more fully embraced this identification since writing, "Although there are no letters of friendship in the New Testament, some letters employ commonplaces and language from the friendly letter tradition" (*Letter Writing*, 60). While discussing Philippians in the context of Hellenistic virtues and moral paradigms, L. Michael White notes the many topics related to friendship in Philippians

of friendship and approaches typical of friendly letters, also clarifies some of its epistolary features and has bearing on the issue of the unity of the letter.

Stanley Stowers points out that a common hortatory strategy of the friendly letter is the use of the language of opposition and contrastive models. Reference is made to enemies common to both the writer and his or her friends. In 1:11–3:21 Stowers demonstrates how Paul uses his own example and that of Timothy and Epaphroditus as models to contrast the behavior of enemies and promote behavior akin to his own.[81] Thus 2:19–3:1 and 3:2–17 do not need to be understood as originally parts of separate letters. They are just as easily explained as components of Paul's strategy of contrasting models that runs throughout 1:11–3:21.

Gordon Fee notes that the core ideals of friendship included mutual giving and receiving of benefits, often goods and services.[82] This being the case, it is likely that Paul would include a thanksgiving (4:10–20) within a larger friendly letter as just one of the many *topoi*. Philippians 4:10–20 does not need to be identified as a once separate letter of thanksgiving. As John Fitzgerald and Ken Berry rightly argue, the distribution of the language and topics of friendship throughout Philippians points to its unity as well.[83] It is likely that future comparison of Philippians with the letters of friendship will produce further support for its unity from an epistolary standpoint.

Conclusion

The epistolary features of Philippians need to be reevaluated. Many of the epistolary conventions and formulae that are identified as indicating a composite letter are misidentified or understood in an unnecessarily restricted sense. 1) Regarding the epistolary conventions of Letter B (especially 2:19–3:1), no features indicate the body-closing of Letter B,

---

and classifies Philippians as a friendly hortatory letter of reconciliation appealing to reestablish the bonds of friendship ("Morality Between Two Worlds: A Paradigm of Friendship in Philippians," *Greeks, Romans, and Christians: Essays in Honor of Abraham J. Malherbe*, eds. D. L. Balch, E. Ferguson, and W. A. Meeks (Minneapolis: Fortress, 1990] 206, 214–15).

[81] "Friends and Enemies," 114–17.

[82] *Philippians*, 5.

[83] Fitzgerald, "Philippians," 321–22; "Friendship," 148; Berry, "Philippians 4:10–20," 121–23.

but rather a body-middle: a) The reference to sending Timothy to the Philippians in 2:19–23 is not a motivation for writing formula restricted to the body-closing; b) The visit talk or apostolic parousia of 2:19–30 can be found anywhere in a letter; c) The reference to the transfer of intermediaries as in 2:19–30 is usually found in the body-middle; d) The confidence formula of 2:24 is one of self-confidence which can be found anywhere in a letter; e) None of the transitions of 3:1a (τὸ λοιπόν, ἀδελφοί, and χαίρετε) indicate the body-closing. The vocative ἀδελφοί is found anywhere in a letter, the specific use of τὸ λοιπόν after a narrative and commands is usually found in the body-middle, and imperative χαίρετε is not found as a greeting in a body-closing; f) The mention of writing in 3:1b is not a motivation for writing formula, but rather a reference to writing often found in the body-middle. It may be a modified hesitation formula of notification which, when following narrative or commands, usually occurs in the body-middle. 2) Regarding epistolary conventions and Letter C (3:2–4:3), there are no epistolary conventions at either the beginning or ending which clearly indicate the beginning or ending of a letter. 3) Regarding epistolary conventions and Letter A (4:10–20), thanks to the letter recipients can occur anywhere in a letter. The joy expression of 4:10 is not typical of a letter opening and there are no epistolary conventions in 4:14–20 indicating a body-closing.

I hope that this article will spur further investigation into the epistolary form of Philippians, especially as a friendly letter. When reevaluated, the epistolary features of Philippians which occur at the supposed "seams" of the letter support its unity, not its composite nature. They indicate a letter with many conventional transitions, not seams where three letters have been poorly sewn together.

PART II

ΗΘΟΣ

Ethos

THE PARABLE OF THE FOOLISH RICH MAN (LUKE 12:16–20) AND GRAECO-ROMAN CONVENTIONS OF THOUGHT AND BEHAVIOR

Ronald F. Hock

Introduction

Abraham J. Malherbe, universally admired for his studies of Paul,[1] has also written with equal learning and insight on the gospels. One such study focuses on Luke's warning against πλεονεξία, or "greed" (Luke 12:15), within its larger literary framework (12:13–34).[2] His study relates this warning more coherently than previous scholarship to the literary context, and he bases this coherence, in turn, on Luke's use of the *topos* on greed as it was developed especially among the Hellenistic moralists, such as Dio Chrysostom. Dio's seventeenth oration, which is titled "On Greed" (Περὶ πλεονεξίας), is representative of the *topos* and thus is used to set out the themes that appear regularly in various philosophical treatments of the vice of "greed." Like Dio, Luke warns against greed because it involves a desire for superfluities (12:15); is associated with a hedonistic lifestyle, as reflected in the parable that follows about the example of the rich man who utters the slogan "eat, drink, and enjoy yourself" (12:16–20, esp. v. 19); is foolishly ignorant of the uncertainty of wealth (12:20), not to mention the unnecessary daily anxieties that come with it (12:22–23); and in the end is punished by God (12:21).[3]

Malherbe also points out that Luke's use of materials from the Hellenistic moralists is not restricted to this *topos*.[4] It will be my purpose in this article to continue the effort to interpret Luke's gospel in terms of this broader cultural horizon.[5] I will limit myself, however, to that

---

[1] See the collection of his studies, *Paul and the Popular Philosophers* (Minneapolis: Fortress Press, 1989).
[2] Abraham J. Malherbe, "The Christianization of a Topos (Luke 12:13–34)," *NovT* 38 (1996) 123–35.
[3] *Ibid.*, 125–27.
[4] For Luke's awareness of other Hellenistic *topoi*, particularly in Acts, see Malherbe, "Christianization of a Topos," 130. For a thorough introduction to the Hellenistic moralists and their importance for New Testament studies, see Abraham J. Malherbe, "Hellenistic Moralists and the New Testament," *ANRW* II.26.1 (1992) 267–333.
[5] For such an attempt with the Lukan parable of the rich man and Lazarus, see

portion of Luke's passage that deals with the question by someone from the crowd regarding inheritance (Luke 12:13) and Jesus' response to it (12:14–21), especially as he tells the parable of the rich fool (12:16–20)— or, as I prefer to call it, the parable of the foolish rich man.[6]

In this study, more specifically, I will propose two widely attested Graeco-Roman intellectual conventions for the interpretation of the parable—one a rhetorical form and the other a habit of thought. In addition to these intellectual conventions, I will try, more briefly, to clarify several social features in the parable that have been neglected or even misinterpreted by scholars because their ancient context has been overlooked. To accomplish these tasks will require moving beyond the moralists to other genres of Graeco-Roman literature, but especially the Greek novel.[7] Finally, as a variety of observations will be made, it is perhaps best to proceed verse by verse, taking up my proposed intellectual conventions when they appear in the course of the narration of the interlocutor's question and Jesus' response.[8]

Ronald F. Hock, "Lazarus and Micyllus: Greco-Roman Backgrounds to Luke 16:19–31," *JBL* 106 (1987) 447–63.

[6] Admittedly the change is slight, but by switching the word "rich" from an adjective (as in "rich" fool) to a noun phrase (as in "foolish rich man") we remain truer to the characterization of the principal person in the parable, who is explicitly called πλούσιος or "rich man" (Luke 12:16). As is well known, the names for parables in the gospels are secondary and hence may be inaccurate or even misleading (see further Joachim Jeremias, *The Parables of Jesus* [trans., S.H. Hooke; New York: Charles Scribner's Sons, 1963] 128 n. 63). In addition, the more literal "foolish rich man" also makes it less possible to universalize the meaning of the parable, since foolishness may be a far more common human failing, while being rich was decidedly limited in the first century, a tendency particularly noticeable in the interpretation of Joseph Fitzmyer, *The Gospel according to Luke X–XXIV* (AB 28A; Garden City: Doubleday, 1985) 972–73.

[7] See further my "Why New Testament Scholars Should Read Ancient Novels," in *Ancient Fiction and Early Christian Narrative*, ed. R.F. Hock, J.B. Chance, and J. Perkins (SBLSS 6; Atlanta: Scholars Press, 1998) 121–38.

[8] My interest is in this exchange as Luke presents it, not in the form and tradition history of the materials that may have been used by Luke, except to say that I regard these materials as stemming, not from Q, as some think (so, e.g., I. Howard Marshall, *The Gospel of Luke: A Commentary on the Greek Text* [NICNT; Grand Rapids: Eerdmans, 1978]521–22), but from Luke's *Sondergut* (so Walter Grundmann, *Das Evangelium nach Lukas* [THKNT 3; Berlin: Evangelische Verlagsanstalt, 1961] 256, and François Bovon, *Das Evangelium nach Lukas* [EKK 3.2; Neukirchen-Vluyn: Benziger/Neukirchener Verlag, 1996] 2.273–74). For detailed tradition historical analyses of these verses, see Bovon, *Lukas*, 272–74, and especially Bernhard Heininger, *Metaphorik, Erzählsstruktur und szenisch-dramatische Gestaltung in den Sondergutgleichnissen bei Lukas* (NTAbh n.f. 24; Münster: Aschendorff, 1991) 107–21.

The Occasion for the Parable of the Foolish Rich Man

VERSE 13. The immediate occasion for the parable of the foolish rich man, as already noted, is a question put to Jesus by someone from the crowd regarding a dispute he has with his brother over an inheritance (v. 13; cf. 12:1). Scholars have tended to focus on the legal rules regarding inheritance and have tried to discern the implicit nature of the dispute between the brothers,[9] but little has been said about the social role of inheritance and popular attitudes about it.[10]

In a traditional or agrarian economy like that of the Graeco-Roman world inheritance had a greater role than it does in ours, because wealth was far more likely to be inherited than earned, making disputes about inheritance far more frequent and important. Hence the man's request of Jesus to adjudicate a dispute precisely over an inheritance would not be unusual.[11]

VERSES 14–15. But, perhaps surprisingly, so was Jesus' refusal to accept the role of judge (v. 14), which he coupled with a warning against greed (v. 15). Malherbe has aptly related this warning to that of moralists like Dio, but such an attitude is also found outside the moralists and even among the wealthy themselves. One example of the latter, which involves brothers and an inheritance, appears in Longus' novel *Daphnis and Chloe*. Daphnis, who has been exposed as an infant and raised by a goatherd, is eventually reunited with his parents and a brother.[12] Shortly thereafter, the father, Dionysophanes, sits his two sons down

---

[9] Scholars point especially to the laws regarding inheritance as found in Deut. 21:15–17, which prescribes a double portion to the first born son (cf. also Num. 27:1–11; 36:7–9). According to Bovon (*Lukas*, 276–77) what is said fits in well with a Jewish context in Palestine of the first century: A father who had two sons has died, but the younger brother complains about the refusal of the older brother to carry out the distribution prescribed by law, leading to the complaint before a judge, a mediator, in order to settle the dispute. Cf. also John Nolland, *Luke* 9:21–18:34 (WBC 35B; Dallas: Word Books, 1989) 685: it is likely that the situation concerns the younger brother's attempt to gain access to a withheld inheritance. Still, as Fitzmyer (*Luke*, 969) says, "given Jesus' reply, the details of the dispute are unimportant."

[10] For wills and testamentary bequests as occasions for moral judgment, both on oneself and on others, see the article by Fitzgerald in this volume.

[11] It is also not that unusual to have someone approach Jesus in order to have him assume an informal role as judge. For various people, both fictional and real, assuming an informal judicial role, see, e.g., the cowherd Philetas in Longus (2.15.1), the aristocratic husband of Melite in Achilles Tatius (6.9.2), and the sophist Polemo in Philostratus (*VS* 532).

[12] Longus, 1.2.1–3.2.

and speaks to each about the consequences of Daphnis' being found alive. He first apologizes to Daphnis for his earlier decision to expose him.[13] Then, he turns to Daphnis' brother Astylos, and the matter of inheritance is the first one addressed. Dionysophanes says: "Nor should you, Astylos, be distressed since you are now going to receive only a portion instead of all my property, for there is no better possession than a brother … . Rather, love one another … . I will leave to you much land, many skilled slaves, gold, silver, and many other possessions of the rich."[14]

In other words, Dionysophanes tries to head off any dispute between his sons over inheritance by stressing the greater value of brotherly love, as does Luke himself in a very parallel situation with the return of the prodigal son (15:20–24); the father of the prodigal tries to calm his angry elder son with assurances about his future inheritance and hence to remove any reason for him not to rejoice at his brother's return (15:25–31).

The Parable of the Foolish Rich Man

VERSE 16. In addition to the warning against greed, Jesus adds a παρα-βολή, or parable (vv. 16–20). Scholars tend to dismiss the Lukan author's identification, preferring instead the modern technical term *Beispielerzählung*, or example story.[15] Functionally, of course, it is exemplary in its Lukan context, but, formally at least, it is still a parable according to ancient systems of classification, for it has no proper names and deals with everyday events. Instruction in writing such parables was received at the rhetorical stage of education, particularly at the level of compositional instruction from textbooks known as *Progymnasmata*. Extant examples of *Progymnasmata* begin with Theon of Alexandria in the late first century CE,[16] so that a contemporary like Luke and doubtless many of his readers may well have understood the word in this

---

[13] Longus, 4.23.2–24.2
[14] Longus, 4.24.3–4.
[15] See John Dominic Crossan, "Parable and Example in Jesus' Teaching," *NTS* 18 (1972) 285–307, esp. 296–97. Cf. Also Grundmann, *Lukas*, 257; Fitzmyer, *Luke*, 971; Heininger, *Sondergutgleichnisse*, 117–19; and Bovon, *Lukas*, 273.
[16] The best introduction to the *Progymnasmata* is Herbert Hunger, *Die hochsprach-liche profane Literatur der Byzantiner* (HAW 12.5.1–2; Munich: C.H. Beck, 1978) 1.92–120. Besides Theon, we have *Progymnasmata* by Hermogenes of Tarsus (late second century), Aphthonius of Antioch (late fourth century), and Nicolaus of Myra (fifth century), on whom see also Ronald F. Hock and Edward N. O'Neil, eds., *The Chreia in Ancient Rhetoric*.

formal sense.[17] At all events, the parable conforms to this formal definition. It concerns an unnamed πλούσιος, or rich man, and it involves the
recurring event of a harvest, even if it is one with the unusual prospect
of a bumper crop (v. 16).[18]

Scholars are often confused about the social status of this unnamed
rich man. He is clearly not a farmer,[19] nor a relatively rich farmer
who still works his own land,[20] but rather an aristocrat, as is clear not
only from the word πλούσιος[21] itself but also from the man's decision
later in the parable to live a hedonistic life (v. 19)—a lifestyle that
is characteristic of an urban setting and of aristocrats in particular.
In addition, the rich man's rural properties (v. 16: χώρα) are never
described in any detail, but they might be imagined to look somewhat
like those about twenty miles from Mytilene belonging to Longus'

Vol. 1. The Progymnasmata (SBLTT 27; Atlanta: Scholars Press, 1986) 63–66, 155–60, 211–16, and 237–39.

[17] For the role of the παραβολή, or analogy, in composition, see Hermogenes, *Progymn.* 3 (Rabe, p. 8,1–4). Neither Hermogenes nor any of the other writers of the *Progymnasmata* explicitly identify the formal features named above. For that we must turn to the Byzantine commentators on Aphthonius' *Progymnasmata*. John of Sardis (*Comm. in Aphth.* 3 [Rabe, p. 8,13–15]) says: "A parable (παραβολή) differs from an example (παράδειγμα) in that the parable is made up of unidentified people (ἐξ ἀορίστων [scil. προσώπων]), whereas the example is made up of specific people (ἐξ ὡρισμένων)." John Doxapatres (*Hom. in Aphth.* 3 [Walz, 2.273,4–10]) says: "A parable differs from an example insofar as the parable is made up of events that occur daily (καθ' ἑκάστην), as in 'Just as those who till the land ... ,' whereas an example is made up of events that have happened once (ἅπαξ), as in 'Consider, if you will, the life of Demosthenes ... '." With this distinction in mind, the word "once" in Fitzmyer's translation of v. 16 (*Luke*, 970: "There was once a rich man ...") should be deleted, as the Greek more literally reads: "The country estate of a certain rich man bore abundantly." See further below.

[18] Surpluses are anticipated in treatments of household management (see, e.g., Xenophon, *Oec.* 3.5; 17.6; 20.1–2; 21.9) and imagined in a literary settings, even to the use of a form of Luke's εὐφορεῖν (so Alciphron, *Ep.* 2.3.3: εὐφορία).

[19] So, e.g., Fitzmyer, *Luke*, 972, and Charles W. Hedrick, *Parables as Poetic Fictions: The Creative Voice of Jesus* (Peabody, MA: Hendrickson, 1994) 143.

[20] So, e.g., Halvor Moxnes, *The Economy of the Kingdom: Social Conflict and Economic Relations in Luke's Gospel* (Philadelphia: Fortress Press, 1988) 56–58, esp. 57. Cf. also Joel B. Green, *The Gospel of Luke* (Grand Rapids: William B. Eerdmans, 1997) 489.

[21] The word πλούσιος, to judge, say, from Longus, can describe those with a range of levels of wealth, including some peasants who, in comparison with their neighbors, are regarded as πλούσιοι (see Longus, 1.16.4; 3.25.4; 26.4), but the word typically characterizes the urban elite (see Longus, 2.12.1; 3.21.1; 4.11.1; 13.2.; 33.4).

character, the aristocrat Dionysophanes: "mountains that bore wild game, plains that grew wheat, hills that were covered with vineyards, and pastures that grazed sheep … ."[22]

VERSES 17–19. The rich man's abundant harvest required him, as owner of these properties, to take responsibility for managing the situation and hence to decide on a course of action, not unlike the way that Chariton's Leonas, the διοικητής, or manager, of Dionysius' estates,[23] defers to his master's authority when he says:

> Master, it's been a great while since you've been to your properties by the sea and matters there require your presence. It's necessary for you to look over the herds and the fields, and the harvest of the crops draw near.[24]

Presumably, the rich man can be imagined as having journeyed from the city to his rural properties in order to make a decision regarding his extraordinary harvest.[25]

At any rate, the rich man's actual deliberations about his situation are provided by Luke, who uses here a literary technique that Philip Sellew has called "interior monologue," a technique that gives the hearer (or reader) of the parable direct access to the rich man's thoughts about his situation.[26] This monologue dominates the parable, as it accounts for sixty percent of the words, and hence requires our attention, both formally and materially.

Formally, Sellew's term "interior monologue" is accurate enough, but he seems to have derived it from modern discussions of this literary device in ancient and modern literature.[27] A better term, especially in an analytical sense, is an ancient one, taken from the schoolroom, from the *Progymnasmata* and specifically from the exercise known as ἠθοποιία, or a speech that reveals ἦθος, or character.[28]

---

[22] Longus, 1.1.2.

[23] Chariton, 1.12.8.

[24] Chariton, 2.3.1.

[25] On aristocrats journeying to their rural properties to make decisions or handle the problems, see, e.g., Chariton, 3.8.2–9; Xenophon, 2.1.2; Achilles Tatius, 5.17.2–10; and esp. Longus, 4.13.1–2.

[26] See Philip Sellew, "Interior Monologue as a Narrative Device in the Parables of Luke," *JBL* 111 (1992) 239–53. As Sellew points out, this technique, rarely used elsewhere in the gospel tradition, is used in five other Lukan parables: Unfaithful Slave (12:42–46), Prodigal Son (15:11–32), Crafty Slave Manager (16:1–8a), Unjust Judge (18.1–5), and Owner of the Vineyard (20:9–16).

[27] See Sellew, "Interior Monologue," 240 and n. 3.

[28] On the ἠθοποιία, see Hunger, *Literatur*, 1.108–16.

In this exercise students were taught to compose a speech that might have been spoken by someone on a certain occasion—for example, what words Achilles might have said over a fallen Patroclus as he was deciding to go to war.[29] Writers of *Progymnasmata* classified ἠθοποιίαι in various ways. Two of them are of interest to us. First, Theon classifies ἠθοποιίαι according to whether they are composed for a ὡρισμένον or a ἀόριστον πρόσωπον, that is, for a definite or indefinite character.[30] The former would be an Achilles, as in the above example,[31] the latter, a husband, a general,[32] a farmer,[33] a rich man.[34] Second, Hermogenes classifies ἠθοποιίαι according to whether they are ἁπλαῖ or διπλαῖ, meaning "single" or "double."[35] The former are ἠθοποιίαι that are spoken to oneself (καθ᾽ ἑαυτόν), the latter, to other(s) (πρὸς ἄλλον). Hermogenes illustrates as follows: "To oneself—for example, what words a general might say on return from a victory; to others— for example, what words a general might say to his troops after a victory."[36]

To return to Luke: It now is possible to classify the rich man' words in vv. 18–19 as an ἠθοποιία,[37] one whose πρόσωπον is ἀόριστον, namely a πλούσιος, and as an ἠθοποιία that is καθ᾽ ἑαυτόν, spoken to himself. In other words, we can describe what Luke is doing as though it were a classroom exercise as follows: what words a rich man might say on learning of an extraordinary harvest.

But the formal considerations do not end with classification, for there is also a formal structure to an ἠθοποιία, and the structure of this *progymnasma* is temporal, as an ἠθοποιία is supposed to move from

---

[29] See Aphthonius, *Progymn.* 11 (Rabe, p. 35, 6–10).

[30] See Theon, *Progymn.* 10 (1.235, 13–18 Walz). Cf. Also Hermogenes, *Progymn.* 9 (Rabe, p. 20,19–20).

[31] Hermogenes also cites Achilles in this connection: what words Achilles might say to Deidameia when he was about to go forth to war (*Progymn.* 9 [Rabe, p. 20,20–21]).

[32] Theon proposes these ἠθοποιίαι: what words a husband might say to his wife as he is about to go on a journey, and what words a general might say to his troops in the face of dangers (*Progymn.* 10 [Walz 1.235, 13–15]).

[33] See Hermogenes, *Progymn.* 9 (Rabe, p. 21,12–13): what words a farmer might say on first seeing a ship.

[34] See Quintilian, 3.8.51; 10.1.71.

[35] See Hermogenes, *Progymn.* 9 (Rabe, pp. 20,24–21,2).

[36] Hermogenes, *Progymn.* 9 (Rabe, p. 21,2–5).

[37] On occasion scholars use the term ἠθοποιία in this context (so Bovon, *Lukas*, 282 and n. 74, and Heininger, *Sondergutgleichnisse*, 78–80) but not in the analytical sense proposed here.

the present to the past and, finally, to the future.[38] A brief example will illustrate the structure. Severus of Alexandria, a fourth century student of Libanius,[39] composed the following ἠθοποιία for Achilles' beloved captive Briseis:

> What words Briseis might have said as she was being led away by the heralds.[40]
>
> "After the destruction of my country, after the slaying of my king, after so great a series of misfortunes I am being made (γίνομαι) a captive again for the second time."
>
> "The Greeks waged war (ἐστρατεύοντο) against us, and I became (γέγονα) a captive. Greeks turned (γεγόνασι) against Greeks, and so I am being led away to slavery."
>
> "And if, it seems, only death will liberate (ἐλευθερώσει) me, my life as a slave will never cease (παύσεται)."[41]

The temporal structure of this ἠθοποιία is evident from the sequence of present, past and future verbs. Briseis mentions her present circumstance of being led away as a slave (γίνομαι) by the heralds, then she reflects on what in the past has brought her to her present strait (ἐστρατεύοντο, γεγόνασι), and then she concludes by imagining a future of slavery ended only by death (ἐλευθερώσει, παύσεται).

Ἠθοποιίαι were not only classroom exercises, however, but also popular features of literature, especially of the Greek novels,[42] showing that ἠθοποιίαι could be incorporated into a narrative context. Accordingly, the use of this rhetorical form in a parable by Luke is not precluded, and an analysis of the rich man's thoughts suggests that Luke is fol-

---

[38] For this formal structure, see Aphthonius, *Progymn.* 10 (Rabe, p. 35,13–14), and Hunger, *Literatur*, 1.108–9.

[39] On Severus, see Hunger, *Literatur*, 1.110, and Paul Petit, *Les Étudiants de Libanius* (Paris: Nouvelles Éditions Latines, 1956) 25, 62, 64, 81, 155, and 187.

[40] Briseis' speech comes on the occasion when the heralds of Agamemnon, Talthybius and Eurybates, arrive at Achilles' tent to take her away to become Agamemnon's concubine (cf. *Il.* 1.320–48).

[41] For the text of this ἠθοποιία, see Fr. P. Karnthaler, "Severus von Alexandreia: Ein verschollener griechischer Schriftsteller des IV. Jahrhunderts n. Chr.," *BNJ* 9 (1929–1930, 327–30, esp. 327.

[42] On the ἠθοποιία as central to the Greek novels, see the remarks of Erwin Rohde, *Der griechische Roman und seine Vorläufer* (3rd ed.; Leipzig: Breitkopf und Hartel, 1914) 353–56. Cf. also my "The Rhetoric of Romance," in *Handbook of Classical Rhetoric in the Hellenistic Period 330 B.C.-400 A.D.*, ed. S.E.Porter (Leiden: E.J. Brill, 1997) 445–65, esp. 455–59 (for analyses of ἠθοποιίαι in Xenophon, 2.5.6–7; 5.5.5; and Chariton, 5.1.4–7).

lowing the temporal structure prescribed for ἠθοποιίαι. The rich man begins with his present situation, as the question τί ποιήσω in v. 17b means "What should I do *now*?" He then continues: for I have (ἔχω) nowhere to store my harvest" (v. 17c).

The section on the past, admittedly, is missing, although the situation —a bountiful harvest, described with an aorist verb (εὐφόρησεν)—was just narrated at the beginning of the parable (v. 16), and even the present situation of having insufficient storage capacity (v.17c) implies reflection on past circumstances, either past harvests or inadequate planning. The rich man's thoughts turn next to the future. At first, he ponders his immediate future saying: "I will do (ποιήσω) this; I will tear down (καθελῶ) my barns and I will build (οἰκοδομήσω) larger ones (v. 18a). Incidentally, being an aristocrat, the rich man would not be doing this construction himself, despite the first person singular verbs. Rather, he would have his slave or tenant peasants do the work, much as Chariton's Dionysius did, as we learn from a comment of his slave-manager Leonas about an upcoming visit by Dionysius to his rural properties: "... And use the costly lodgings which we built (ᾠκοδομήσαμεν) when you gave the order."[43]

At any rate, the rich man continues with his reflections on the future: "I will gather (συνάξω) there all my grain and my goods" (v. 18b). Then he ponders the long-term change in his lifestyle that this harvest will make possible: "I will say (ἐρῶ) to my soul, 'Soul, you have many good things laid up for many years; take it easy; eat, drink, and enjoy yourself'" (v. 19).[44]

The formal features of the rich man's reflections (vv.17–19), therefore, conform rather well to the classifications and structure of the rhetorical ἠθοποιία, suggesting that this term is more analytically useful than Sellew's "interior monologue" or other terms, such as "soliloquy."[45] In any case, the contents of these reflections also require some clarification. One way to approach the contents is to focus on those words whose repetition gives them prominence in this ἠθοποιία: τὰ ἀγαθά, or "good things" (vv. 18–19), and ψυχή, or "soul" (v 19).

---

[43] Chariton, 2.3.1.

[44] On the words "eat, drink, and enjoy yourself" as shorthand for a hedonistic life, see Abraham J. Malherbe, "The Beasts at Ephesus," *JBL* 87 (1968) 71–80, esp. 79–80 (repr. in *Paul and the Popular Philosophers*, 79–89, esp. 84–85), and Walter Ameling, "ΦΑΓΩΜΕΝ ΚΑΙ ΠΙΩΜΕΝ: Griechische Parallelen zu zwei Stellen aus dem Neuen Testament," *ZPE* 60 (1985) 35–43.

[45] So, e.g., Marshall, *Luke*, 523; Fitzmyer, *Luke*, 973; and Hedrick, *Parables*, 153.

In a narrow sense the words τὰ ἀγαθά point to other products of the rich man's χώρα, as is apparent from its first appearance when it is paired with "all my grain" (v. 18). Τὰ ἀγαθά are often used in this sense,[46] but one text is especially apt in the light of the rich man's decision to lead a hedonistic life. Athenaeus compares the daily symposia of Larensis, the host of the *Deipnosophistae*,[47] with the extraordinary productivity of the χώρα of Lusitania, or Spain. Its abundance results in the easy availability of wine, rabbits, lambs, pigs, sheep, figs, and calves, and in Rome Larensis provides similarly Lusitanian symposia filled with all kinds of good things (παντοῖα ἀγαθά).[48] In other words, everything served at Larensis' symposia is lumped together as ἀγαθά, and the rich man of the Lukan parable likewise says that he has many good things (πολλὰ ἀγαθά) with which to live a life of eating, drinking, and enjoyment (v. 19).

And yet, the words τὰ ἀγαθά may also have a broader and more significant meaning within this parable, especially since it is juxtaposed with ψυχή (v. 19). A characteristic habit of thought in Graeco-Roman intellectual life was διαίρεσις (classification), and one such classification was the tripartite διαίρεσις of τὰ ἀγαθά that contribute to happiness, into those of the soul (ψυχή), the body (σῶμα), and externals (τὰ ἐκτός).

This convention of intellectual culture was thought to go back to Aristotle or perhaps Plato[49] but it was hardly restricted to these philosophical traditions[50] or to philosophy itself. Instead, it was part of the general intellectual currency of the Graeco-Roman world, thanks to its incorporation into the rhetorical curriculum. At any rate, the "good

[46] See, e.g., Xenophon, *Oec.* 5.4; 12.7; Alciphron, *Epp.* 2.11; 4.18.5; and Athenaeus, 8.335b. Cf. also Grundmann, *Lukas*, 257: "Vor allem ist an Getreide und an Wein zu denken."

[47] On Larensis and his symposia, see my "A Dog in the Manger: The Cynic Cynulcus among Athenaeus' Deipnosophists," in *Greeks, Romans, and Christians: Essays in Honor of Abraham J. Malherbe*, ed. D.L Balch, E. Ferguson, and W.A. Meeks (Minneapolis: Fortress Press, 1990) 20–37, esp. 21–26.

[48] See Athenaeus, *Deip.* 8.330f–331c.

[49] See Aristotle, *EN* 1098b 12–15, cf. *Rhet.* 1.6.3–17, but according to Diogenes Laertius, Aristotle attributed this classification to his teacher Plato (Diogenes Laertius, 3.80). Note, however, that Aristotle and the Peripatetics are especially associated with this classification (see, e.g., *Rhet. ad Alex.* 1422a 7–11; Lucian, *Vit. auct.* 26; Alciphron, *Ep.* 3.19.7; Sextus Empiricus, *Adv. math.* 11.45–46; and Diogenes Laertius, 5.30).

[50] Among Stoics, e.g., we find it as early as Zeno (so Diogenes Laertius, 7.106) and later in such writers as Epictetus (so *Diss.* 3.7.2; cf. 1.2.36–37). Outside the philosophical tradition we find it, significantly, in discussions of household management (so, e.g., Xenophon, *Oec.* 1.13, 23).

things" of the soul, according to Plato, are virtues like justice, wisdom, courage, and self-control; those of the body are beauty, vigor, health, and strength; whereas the "good things" classified as externals include friends, the prosperity of one's country, and wealth.[51]

This classification was inculcated during instruction in one of the *progymnasmata*, specifically the ἐγκώμιον, or encomium.[52] Students were taught to organize an ἐγκώμιον precisely around this classification. Indeed as early as Theon we read: "Since the good things (τὰ ἀγαθά) about a person are especially to be praised and since we have good things with regard for the soul and character, others for the body, and still others that are external, it is clear that these three kinds of good things can be an abundant source of *topoi* when composing an encomium."[53] Then the usual examples follow:

> External goods (τὰ ἔξωθεν) are, first, good birth ... then, education, friendship, reputation, office, wealth, many children, and an easy death. Goods of the body (τὸ σῶμα) are health, strength, beauty, and keen sense of perception. Goods of the soul (ψυχικὰ ἀγαθά) are excellent ethical qualities and deeds that are consistent with them—for example, that the person is wise, self-controlled, courageous, just, pious, free, generous, and so forth.[54]

With the inclusion of this classification both in the philosophical tradition and in the rhetorical curriculum we can assume it to have had a widespread currency. Consequently, it is not surprising to find the classification worked into literature, as is illustrated, for example, at the beginning of Xenophon's *Ephesian Tale* where this classification is used to characterize Habrocomes, the hero of the romance. Xenophon tells the reader that Habrocomes is the son of Lycomedes of Ephesus, a man who belonged to the most powerful class in the city, thereby establishing Habrocomes' εὐγένεια (good birth), the first item in Theon's list of externals. Habrocomes himself is then described briefly in terms of body and soul: he is a marvel of beauty (κάλλος) such as has never occurred before in Ionia or in any other land. Beauty is, of course, a prime ἀγαθόν of the body, being listed first by Plato, and is, moreover, especially appropriate in a romance. At any rate, Xenophon continues:

---

[51] See Diogenes Laertius, 3.80–81.
[52] For a survey of this *progymnasma*, see Hunger, *Literatur*, 1.104–6.
[53] Theon, *Progymn.* 8 (Walz, 1.227,5–9).
[54] Theon, *Progymn.* 8 (Walz, 1.227,8–17). See further Hermogenes, *Progymn.* 7 (Rabe, p. 16,3–13); Aphthonius, *Progymn.* 8 (Rabe, p, 22, 5–9); and Nicolaus, *Progymn.* 8 (Felten, p. 50,1–9).

growing apace with the beauty of his body (τοῖς τοῦ σώματος καλοῖς) are
the virtues of his soul (τὰ τῆς ψυχῆς ἀγαθά), including, as we later find
out, σωφροσύνη (self-control), which was his σύντροφος (boyhood companion) and serves as the principal virtue in the romances.[55] Xenophon
is clearly trading on this classification of τὰ ἀγαθά when providing the
reader with an introductory and brief characterization of Habrocomes
as praiseworthy and hence fit to be the protagonist.

Accordingly, it should be no more surprising to discover that Luke,
too, might have had this classification of τὰ ἀγαθά in mind in order to
reveal the ἦθος of the rich man, by characterizing him as focusing only
on his external ἀγαθά, that is, on his wealth: "I have many good things
(πολλὰ ἀγαθά) stored up for many years" (v. 19).

That Luke actually has this classification of ἀγαθά in mind receives
support from the juxtaposition of ἀγαθά with ψυχή in v. 19. The word
ψυχή, despite its repetition, is usually dismissed by commentators by
being identified as a synecdoche, or the use of a part for the whole, so
that ψυχή comes to mean "self," not unlike the use of ἐν ἑαυτῷ λέγων
("saying to himself") in v. 17.[56] But in v. 19 Luke does not use the same
language as in v. 17, suggesting that the two may not be equivalent after
all. Indeed, in terms of the classification of τὰ ἀγαθά the use of ψυχή
may be taken literally. The rich man is saying that the πολλὰ ἀγαθά,
the many good things produced on his χώρα, are τὰ ἀγαθά of his ψυχή
(v. 19). But, as all would immediately know, the ἀγαθά of the ψυχή do
not include externals such wealth, but the virtues. In other words, the
rich man would be viewed as having mistaken one category of ἀγαθά
for another, and as having made a rather foolish mistake at that.

VERSE 20. No wonder, then, that in the next verse God addresses the
rich man, presumably in a dream,[57] as ἄφρων ("you fool," v. 20). And
with this authoritative judgment of the rich man as foolish we begin to
detect the point of view of the parable. This point of view conforms
closely to the Cynic condemnation of the wealthy and their hedonism,
a view already signaled by Luke with the woes on the wealthy (6:24–26;
cf. 9:25; 16:19–31).

----

[55] See Xenophon, 1.1.1–2; 2.1.4.
[56] So, e.g., Grundmann, *Lukas*, 257; Fitzmyer, *Luke*, 973; and Hedrick, *Parables*, 156.
For the figure, see Herbert Weir Smyth, *Greek Grammar* (rev. by G.M. Messing; Cambridge: Harvard University Press, 1956) § 3047.
[57] On dreams as the medium of revelation, see, e.g., Longus, 1.7.1–2. Cf. Fitzmyer,
Luke, 973.

This Cynic condemnation can likewise be cast in terms of the classi-fication of τὰ ἀγαθά. Aristotle had argued that all three kinds of ἀγαθά are necessary for happiness, although he added that the ἀγαθά of the ψυχή—that is, the virtues—are the most important.[58] In contrast, Cyn-ics saw happiness almost entirely in terms of the ἀγαθά of the ψυχή, as is succinctly stated in an epistle attributed to Crates. This epistle reads as follows:

> Crates to his students.
>
> Take care (μελέτω) of your soul (τῆς ψυχῆς), but take care of your body (τοῦ σώματος) only as much as necessary and your externals (τῶν ἔξωθεν) not even that much. For happiness is not pleasure (ἡδονή), on account of which we need externals (τῶν ἐκτός), whereas virtue (ἀρετή) is complete without any externals (μετ' οὐδενὸς τῶν ἐκτός).[59]

God's judgment on the rich man as foolishly thinking that his wealth was an ἀγαθόν of his soul, whereas such external goods can care only for the body, thus parallels the Cynic point of view.[60] Comparisons with Cynic philosophy, however, do not end with a common use of this classification of ἀγαθά and a rejection of externals. The rest of God's judgment of the rich man parallels Cynic critiques of wealth and its attendant hedonism and immorality—that is, a lack of self-control evident from his eating, drinking, and enjoying himself. The emphatic position of "this night" in God's announcement of the rich man's death (v. 20) underscores the foolishness of storing up wealth for a life of hedonism because sudden death was all too frequent. This argument appears in Lucian's *Cataplus*,[61] where the wealthy tyrant Megapenthes dies suddenly one night after being poisoned while drinking earlier at a symposium.[62]

Likewise, the rhetorical question that concludes the parable: "What you've prepared—to whom will it belong?" (v.20), is again nicely illus-trated by Lucian's *Cataplus*. On his way down to Hades, Megapenthes pleads with one of the Fates, Clotho, to return to life in order to tell his wife where he had hidden a large horde of gold. Clotho refuses the

---

[58] See Diogenes Laertius, 5.30.

[59] Ps.-Crates, *Ep.* 3 (Malherbe, p. 54). Cf. also ps.-Crates, *Ep.* 10.3 (Malherbe, p. 62).

[60] A Cynic interpretation at this point thus entails a harsher judgment on the rich man and on wealth than is envisioned by, e.g., Heininger, *Sondergutgleichnisse*, 118–19.

[61] On the importance of this Cynic attack on wealth and hedonism for another parable of Luke (16:19–31), see my "Lazarus and Micyllus," 457–61.

[62] See Lucian, *Cat.* 11. On the suddenness of death and hence the futility of amassing wealth, see also Lucian, *Cont.* 17; *D. Mort.* 1.3; and Seneca, *Ep.* 101.4–9.

request, however, saying that the gold will not be lost since his cousin
Megacles will receive it. At this information Megapenthes says: "What
an insult! He's my enemy, one I did not murder earlier out of laziness."
Clotho adds to his misery: "That's the man. And he will survive you
by forty years and then some, having gotten your concubines, clothing,
and all your gold."[63] Then she informs him: "Midas, your slave, will
have your wife … . Your daughter will be numbered among the concubines of the present tyrant, and your images and statues which the
city set up for you will all be overturned."[64] Here, then, is one example
of what happens to a rich man's externals—his wealth, his slaves, his
family, his reputation—and hence is an answer to the question "what
you've prepared—to whom will it belong?" (v. 20).

VERSE 21. Jesus' final response to the dispute on inheritance is a
generalizing conclusion to the parable: "And so it is for the one who
stores up treasures for himself and is not rich in the sight of God"
(v. 21). This statement is often thought to have been tacked onto the
parable secondarily as a moralizing interpretation, perhaps by Luke
himself.[65] But, even if secondary, it is nevertheless an apt summary of
the parable.[66] Moreover, in its present context this summary is also
reminiscent of the ἐπιμύθιον, or "moral of the story," that concludes
many fables.

Adding an ἐπιμύθιον to a fable was one of the conventions of composition that students learned in the very first progymnasma, the μῦθος,
or fable.[67] Indeed, one way to formulate an ἐπιμύθιον is to begin with
οὕτω(ς), just as Luke does in v. 21. For example, Aphthonius' sample
fable, the fable of the crickets and ants,[68] concludes with this ἐπιμύθιον:
"Thus (οὕτω) youth that is not willing to toil suffers in old age."[69] In

---

[63] See Lucian, *Cat.* 8.
[64] See Lucian, *Cat.* 11.
[65] See, e.g., Jeremias, *Parables*, 110–12; Fitzmyer, *Luke*, 971; Heininger, *Sondergutgleich-nisse*, 108, 110, 119; and Bovon, *Lukas*, 273.
[66] See, e.g., Marshall, *Luke*, 524; Nolland, *Luke*, 687; and Bovon, *Lukas*, 287.
[67] See Aphthonius, *Progymn.* 1 (Rabe, pp. 1,15–2,2). It was also possible to announce the point of a fable at the beginning, the moral now being termed a προμύθιον (see Rabe p. 2,2) Hermogenes does not use the terms προμύθιον or ἐπιμύθιον, but he is aware of the convention, for he says: "The sentence that discloses the benefit of the fable is sometimes placed before it and sometimes after it" (Hermogenes, *Progymn.* 1 [Rabe, p.4,1–2]). In this compositional context we might want to consider the warning against greed in Luke 12:15 as a προμύθιον, since it is often regarded as illustrated by the parable that follows.
[68] See Aphthonius, *Progymn.* 1 (Rabe, p. 2,5–10).
[69] Aphthonius, *Progymn.* 1 (Rabe, p. 2,11–12).

other words, by including a generalizing conclusion to the parable of the foolish rich man Luke is following a habit of thought, learned early in life, that makes explicit the point or moral of a story—whether fable or parable.

The usual understanding of this conclusion and, in a sense, the entire passage is that the rich man was judged as poor before God because he did not share his wealth with "the poor, widows, orphans, sojourners in the land," as Joseph Fitzmyer puts it, echoing Deut. 24:17–22.[70] Similar interpretations abound.[71] While this interpretation gets some support from Jesus' later advice to give alms (12:33), it is too narrow, for it overlooks the logic of the parable. By foolishly thinking that the goods for his body were the goods for his soul, the rich man thereby neglected his soul which thus became impoverished, impoverished in the sense of lacking in virtue—self-control certainly, given his hedonistic lifestyle, but also perhaps in justice, wisdom and courage. He has thus fallen victim of the vice of greed (πλεονεξία) about which Jesus warned in the moralizing προμύθιον (v. 15). In the Cynic view, only the minimum care of the body is required, rather than such hedonistic indulgence. It calls for constant care of the soul and its virtues and, after death, entrance to the Isles of the Blessed[72] or, in Luke's terms, real treasure in the sight of God (v. 21; cf. vv. 33–34).

Conclusion

Abraham Malherbe, in his article on Luke 12:13–34, has proposed a broader cultural context for gospel interpretation, just as he has in greater detail for Paul's letters. He focused on Luke's use of the *topos* on greed that informs and unifies Jesus' teachings in this passage. In this article I have tried to build on this proposal by drawing attention to various other Graeco-Roman conventions of thought and behavior that can clarify the parable of the foolish rich man. Such attention focuses on the role of inheritance in a traditional agrarian economy,

---

[70] Fitzmyer, *Luke*, 974.

[71] See, e.g., Green, *Luke*, 491: the rich man is one whose disposition is "not toward the needs of those around him;" Nolland, *Luke*, 688: the rich man does not use his wealth "for the relief of real needs in the world;" and Bovon, *Lukas*, 287: the rich man must live "ein verantwortliches Leben im Dienst der anderen."

[72] See, e.g., Lucian, *Cat.* 23–29; ps.-Crates, *Ep.* 7 (Malherbe, p.58); and my "Cynics," *ABD* 1 (1992) 1221–26, esp. 1224–25.

the actual look of the χώρα, the characterization of the rich man
through ἠϑοποιία, the use of the convention regarding τὰ ἀγαϑά, the
Cynic point of view that sets the virtues of the soul above wealth and
hedonism, and the habit of drawing a moral through an ἐπιμύϑιον.

RADICAL ALTRUISM IN PHILIPPIANS 2:4

Troels Engberg-Pedersen

Reading Paul: Comparisons and Context

One of Abraham Malherbe's many enduring contributions to Pauline scholarship is his constant insistence on contextualization: that Paul must be seen as sharing a discourse of, broadly speaking, paraenesis with the Hellenistic "popular philosophers." Malherbe has adopted a two-pronged strategy in this insistence. First, he has emphasized the extent to which Paul made use of just those paraenetic motifs and practices that one also finds in the other participants in the shared context. Here the emphasis is on similarity and on seeing Paul as one among the others. But the focus remains on Paul: to use the non-Pauline contextual material to elucidate ideas or practices in the Pauline letters themselves. Second, he has constantly insisted that there are also dissimilarities, features where Paul distinguishes himself from his contextual partners. These too must be noticed—but as part of the strategy of contextualization. For the two prongs in the overall strategy are, of course, perfectly consistent. Paul was not the only one to distinguish himself from the others. All the co-partners did the same, in their own ways. Therefore, to bring out differences is an intrinsic part of seeing Paul as one among the others.

In this study, I shall adopt and try to extend his strategy of employing contextual material to elucidate Paul's meaning in a few select passages in some of the letters (Philippians, 1 Corinthians, Galatians and Romans) that speak about how the individual should relate to himself and to others. The starting-point is a philological one, of how to translate a Pauline verse that is most often mistranslated: Phil 2:4 (section 1). But some other passages (Phil 2:21, 1 Cor 10:24, 33; 13:5, Gal 5:14 and select verses from Rom 12:11–15:6) will also be discussed (section 2). The contextual material is Stoic, deriving from two sources for orthodox Stoicism: book III of Cicero's *De Finibus* and ch. IX §8 (fragments 625–636) of von Arnim's *Stoicorum Veterum Fragmenta* III, which deals with the relationship of wise people with themselves and others. I shall employ this material to bring out a certain kind of "radical altruism" that I argue is to be found in the Pauline passages too, including

Phil 2:4 (section 3). Towards the end of the paper (section 4), I shall take a step which Abraham Malherbe has, perhaps wisely, never attempted to take: that of relating the Pauline and Stoic ideas to certain relevant modern ideas, in this case concerning the relationship between self-directedness and other-directedness in a modern view of human morality. As representatives of these ideas I shall take two contemporary American philosophers, Samuel Scheffler and Thomas Nagel.

The overall focus of the paper comes out in the following two or three questions: Do we find in Paul a form of "radical altruism"? If so, exactly how should the specifically Pauline form of radical altruism be defined? In particular, does it fit the description of it as a matter of "abject self-sacrifice" that is sometimes made?[1] My answers will be: Yes, we find a form of radical altruism in Paul, including Phil 2:4, which in its usual, wrong translation yields another impression. But also: No, it cannot count as a matter of "abject self-sacrifice." Rather, when Paul speaks for radical altruism, he is making a point—which he shares with the Stoics—that cannot be written off just like that.

The idea of finding radical altruism in the sense of "abject self-sacrifice" in Paul may be said to belong at one end of a continuum, the end or pole of nothing but other-directedness. In moving away from this pole, I certainly do not intend to end up at the other pole, that of nothing but self-directedness. Indeed, I shall take issue with an explicit position on this matter that has been well formulated in a stimulating paper by Abraham Malherbe's Pauline co-worker and friend, J. Paul Sampley on "Faith and Its Moral Life: A Study of Individuation in the Thought World of the Apostle Paul."[2] A few quotations from this paper may help to set the scene.

Sampley asks—in relationship to Paul's advice in 1 Thessalonians 5:21: "Test out/discern all things; retain the good"—how one should decide what is good. He suggests that this may be seen from Paul's actual practice in the letters. "What is good is weighed out first as to whether it is good with respect to its impact on oneself, that is, whether an action is appropriate to the individual.[22] Then a con-

---

[1] I take this phrase from Thomas Nagel's book *The Possibility of Altruism* (Oxford: Oxford University Press, 1970) 79, the beginning of chapter 9 on "Altruism: The intuitive issue." Nagel is not here explicitly concerned with any specifically Christian view.

[2] In *Faith and History: Festschrift for Paul W. Meyer*, ed. J.T. Carroll, C.H. Cosgrove, and E.E. Johnson (Atlanta: Scholars Press 1990) 223–38.

templated action is evaluated with regard to its impact on others" (232). Sampley's note 22 runs as follows: "Evidence such as 1 Cor 10:24 and Phil 2:4 may be adduced to support a concern first with another and then (if ever) a concern with oneself. But those verses appear in letters written to believers who have the most basic fundamentals and whose relationships with others are at issue. Those two passages bear on a situation in which an individual might be weighing out his or her rights as over against those of others." On the last page of the paper Sampley further states: "To live the proper life before God [according to Paul] … was to monitor a delicate balance regarding self and others at every point in one's life" (238). And he ends his article like this: "Paul never settles for an eclipsed individuation in favor of retaining a semblance of unity. … For Paul, individuation is not one Christian option among others. Paul's thought world requires individuation."

This, I shall argue, is too close to the pole of self-directedness even when Sampley speaks of a need to "monitor a delicate balance regarding self and others." Paul's own perspective is far more strongly other-directed or communal. But it is not one of "abject self-sacrifice" either. So what is it?

The Translation and Meaning of Phil 2:4

The Options and the Linguistic Issue

Phil 2:4 runs: μὴ τὰ ἑαυτῶν ἕκαστος σκοποῦντες ἀλλὰ [καὶ] τὰ ἑτέρων ἕκαστοι. Here are two different translations of the verse:

(1) "One should look out not only for one's own interests but for what is good for the others."[3]
(2) "… not looking out for your own interests, but for the interests of others."[4]

The former rendering is by far the most common. The latter is the correct one. The linguistic issue concerns the rendering of the καί

[3] Nils A. Dahl, "Euodia and Syntyche and Paul's Letter to the Philippians," in *The Social World of the First Christians: Essays in Honor of Wayne A. Meeks*, ed. L.M. White and O.L. Yarbrough (Minneapolis: Fortress 1995) 3–15, esp. 10. Compare also P.T. O'Brien, *The Epistle to the Philippians: A Commentary on the Greek Text* (NIGTC, Grand Rapids: Eerdmans/Carlisle: Paternoster, 1991) 163.
[4] D. A. Black, "The Discourse Structure of Philippians: A Study in Textlinguistics," *NovT* 37 (1995) 16–49, esp. 36.

just after ἀλλά. The editors of the 27th edition of the NesteAland text placed καί in square brackets to indicate that they were undecided as to whether the text with or without the καί is the more original one. That view is not so easy to understand. First, the best manuscripts (𝔓46, Sinaiticus, Alexandrinus,Vaticanus, etc.) include the καί. Second, it is excluded in the "Western" text, which is often derived from codex D (Claromontanus). Now, the scribe of D often thought for himself. He may very well have found that a meaning like the one given in translation 1 above (call it the "both-and" translation) does not fit the context. And since he did not realize that the καί could have any other meaning, he just excised it. This possibility is supported in part by the fact that a corrector of D restored the καί at a later date. In any case, the καί constitutes a *lectio difficilior* and should therefore be retained.

But the original scribe of D was wrong. The καί can indeed carry another meaning than in the "both-and" translation, namely the one given, or at least implied, in translation 2 above. Call this the "not that-but this" translation. Here καί has the following senses: "not … , (but) *rather* (this:) … ;" "not … , (but) *first of all* (this:) … ;" "not … , (but) *instead* (this:) … ;" or "not … , (but) *precisely* (this:) … ." What καί does here is to focus. The speaker figuratively turns his or her back on possibility A, wishing instead to focus on possibility B. Indeed, one may suggest that the καί here functions in the way that *italics* may be used in modern type-written texts. In this special kind of use, καί is a sign to the reader: "Emphasize the next word(s)!"

The Evidence from Denniston

J. D. Denniston's invaluable book on *The Greek Particles* provides all the material that is needed to see how we should understand the disputed Pauline verse.[5] But he has not developed this material completely in a correct way. Under the general entrance ἀλλά, Denniston in I.iii.a discusses the familiar phrase οὐ μόνον … ἀλλὰ καί. He here mentions three instances where, as he says, "καί is retained and μόνον omitted" (3): Sophocles, *Ajax* 1313; Plato, *Phaedrus* 233B; and *Lysias* 6.13. In the last text, says Denniston, "καί, if sound, perhaps means 'actually'" (3). The last point is entirely right. What is problematic, however, is including these passages under the οὐ μόνον … ἀλλὰ καί construction.

---

[5] (2nd ed.; Oxford University Press, 1954).

Instead, since they do not actually contain a μόνον (which is not just "omitted"), they all three fall under a different construction that carries a "not that-but this" sense.

One example must suffice. In the Sophocles' *Ajax*, Teukros, the brother of the dead Ajax, is challenging King Agamemnon to let Ajax be properly buried. Here is a paraphrase of the crucial parts of Teukros' speech:

> 1308: You must know that if you just throw him aside somewhere, there are three more to whom you must do the same (meaning Teukros himself and Ajax' wife and son).

> 1310: For it would be better for me (καλόν μοι) to die in open defence of him—than to die for your or your brother's wife (that is, Helen).

> 1313: In addition (πρὸς ταῦθ') do not think of *my* case (ὅρα μὴ τοὐμόν) [for that is in fact none of Agamemnon's business, but Teukros' own], but *rather* or *first of all* of your *own* (ἀλλὰ καὶ τὸ σόν).

> 1314: For if you hurt me, you would even (καί!) prefer having been a *coward* in relation to me to being insolent towards me.

Clearly, the force of the ἀλλὰ καί is to turn the attention *away from* A and *instead* towards B. And of course—as in Paul—there *is* no μόνον in the text.

It is curious that Denniston has not himself seen this. For later in the book, in his account of καί as a "particle of emphasis" (316–23), he provides a whole number of examples that bring this meaning of καί out with all clarity. Even here, however, Denniston succumbs to his own reasoning. This is how he introduces the use of καί as a particle of emphasis: "… the sense of addition sometimes recedes into the background, while the sense of climax predominates, a ladder of which only the top rung is clearly seen. 'Even' then passes into 'actually,' and καί is little more than a particle of emphasis, like δή" (316–17). However, Denniston's own examples do not bear out that there is a ladder beneath the supposed "top rung."

Plato, *Alcibiades* I, 103A6 runs: οὗ σὺ τὴν δύναμιν καὶ ὕστερον πεύσῃ. Denniston comments: "'you shall hear *afterwards*': 'there will be an opportunity later, as well as now'" (319, his italics). But the point is precisely that Socrates does *not* intend to speak to Alcibiades *now* of the thing he has just mentioned, but *precisely* to do it later. There is absolutely no warrant, therefore, for Denniston's "as well as now," the "ladder" that supposedly leads to the "top rung." The same is true of a number of Denniston's other passages: Plato, *Symposium* 175E7–

9 and *Republic* 347E2 (Denniston, 319); *Lysias* 25.13 (Denniston, 320); Plato, *Philebus* 25B7 (σὺ καὶ ἐμοὶ φράσεις, entirely rightly: "'*You* shall tell *me*': instead of vice versa," with Denniston's own italics [Denniston, 320]). Finally Denniston discusses a usage in which "καί [of all things:] contrasts" (321–23). That is precisely the point! In short, Denniston provides all the material that is needed for developing the sense "not that-but this" for the Greek οὐ … ἀλλὰ καί, but he does not himself quite see it.

That, then, is the meaning we should also find in Paul's verse—if, that is, it suits the context. In that case we should not take it that a μόνον has been "omitted." We should contrast Phil 2:4 with Phil 2:27, in which Paul does include a μόνον: ἀλλὰ ὁ θεὸς ἠλέησεν αὐτόν, οὐκ αὐτὸν [sc. τὸν Ἐπαφρόδιτον] δὲ *μόνον ἀλλὰ καὶ* ἐμέ ("But God had mercy on him, and *not only* on him [Epaphroditus] *but also* on me"). Instead, we should connect Phil 2:4 with Phil 2:21, in which Paul precisely speaks of certain people who "seek their own, (and) *not* the things of Jesus Christ" (τὰ ἑαυτῶν ζητοῦσιν, οὐ τὰ Ἰησοῦ Χριστοῦ). Here it is clearly not a matter of "both-and," but of "either-or."

The Evidence from the Context

It is obvious that the "not that-but this" reading fits the context of Phil 2:4 best. In the immediately preceding verse Paul enjoins the Philippians to do nothing out of self-directedness (ἐριθεία) nor based on a false view of their own individual accomplishments (κενοδοξία). Instead (! ἀλλά), they must in lowliness or self-abasement (ταπεινοφροσύνη) consider the others *above* themselves (ὑπερέχοντας ἑαυτῶν). Clearly, Paul intends a strong contrast here focused on the idea of giving up *any* consideration for oneself. When one considers the others *above* oneself, one does not give *anything* to *oneself*.

That too is of course the idea expressed in the Christ model that Paul goes on to introduce in the verses immediately following 2:4. Christ too gave up his exalted status, set himself to naught, took the form of a slave, abased himself and so forth. In doing this, did Christ have any concomitant thought for himself? No. To judge from the context, therefore, the idea Paul has in mind in 2:4 is this: *Leave behind* any thought about your own things; *instead*, care for those of the others.

We may bring out the exact force of this by comparing it with Stoicism. Elsewhere, I have argued that the center piece of Stoic ethics—their theory of *oikeiôsis* (Greek οἰκείωσις, lit. "appropriation as one's own")—may be encapsulated in the idea of a movement of self-identifi-cation "from I to we." The child and the unreformed adult basically identifies with him- or herself as a bodily individual. However, through a reform that makes the individual see him- or herself as fundamentally a rational being, (s)he may come to identify instead with the others, who are rational beings too. That movement leaves behind the original focus on oneself as a bodily individual and makes one focus instead on the we-group.[6] The movement takes place within what I have elsewhere called the I→X→S-model, where "S" stands for "*Socii*" (the "compan-ions" or "friends" or members of the we-group), and "X" stands for whatever acts as the focal point or "node" of self-identification that generates the movement.[7]

This model may be directly applied to Phil 2:4. In that verse we have the two poles, the I-pole and the S-pole. We do not have the X-pole, which in Paul's case is of course represented by Christ (as against reason in the Stoic case). But then it is particularly noteworthy that just after the "Christ hymn," which does bring in the Christ figure with full force, we get Paul's pessimistic remark that all his co-workers (apart from Timothy) "seek their own and not the things of Jesus Christ" (2:21). Clearly, were they really to seek the things of Christ, they would by the same token *give up* seeking their own things and *instead* seek those of the others. In short, the I→X→S-model is fully in place in these few pages of Philippians.

This observation may help us to identify the exact content of Paul's point about "not that-but this" in 2:4. On the one hand, he is decidedly not saying that the Philippians should care about *both* their own things *and* each other's. On the other hand, as we can see from comparing him with the Stoics, we should not necessarily take him to be making a positive point to the effect that they must never think about themselves at all. On the Stoic picture, there is more to be said about a person's relationship with him- or herself than what is brought out in the move-ment "from I to we." That movement has the force we have just seen. But the Stoics added to this a number of subsidiary complications that

---

[6] I gave the basic argument for this reading of Stoicism in *The Stoic Theory of Oikeio-sis: Moral Development and Social Interaction in Early Stoic Philosophy* (Studies in Hellenistic Civilization 2; Aarhus: Aarhus University Press, 1990) chs. 3–4. For a summary account see my *Paul and the Stoics* (Edinburgh: T&T Clark/Louisville: Westminster John Knox, 2000) ch. 3.

[7] See *Paul and the Stoics*, ch. 2.

did not, however, change the basic point of the movement itself.[8] As we shall see, Paul does not in fact follow them in explicitly making these additions. But he does not reject them either. He simply does not address them. The point is that in our passage Paul is *just* delineating the movement "from I to we." He does not give a full account of all aspects of the relationship between the individual Christ-believer and the others, e.g., one that would incorporate into some kind of theory his actual handling of that relationship in the letters themselves. What we get in Phil 2:4 is only, as it were, the ideology: the movement *from* I as a normative center of attention *to* a we-perspective that pays no attention whatever to the I-perspective. It is the movement towards seeing oneself just as one among the others, an "objectifying" move that transcends the local I-perspective altogether.

Other Pauline Passages

Are there other passages in Paul that move further in the direction of giving some special place to oneself within a more comprehensive theoretical framework that also incorporates the movement from I to we? Recall Paul Sampley's claim that "Paul never settles for an eclipsed individuation in favor of retaining a semblance of unity."[9] That may or may not be correct if one considers Paul's handling of oneself and others in his actual practice. But has he given this kind of concern for oneself a place within his overall theory?

A number of passages in 1 Corinthians suggest that the answer should be negative. Take 1 Cor 10:24, to which Sampley himself referred: "Let nobody seek his own, but (instead) that of the other person." The verse is highly relevant to a comparison with Stoicism, coming as it does just after a verse that is normally—and rightly—taken to have a Stoic origin: "Everything is allowed—but not everything benefits. Everything is allowed—but not everything builds up" (1 Cor 10:23). The (Stoic) notion of benefit is taken up a few verses later when Paul brings in himself as a model for the practice he is enjoining the Corinthians to adopt: " … just as I too please everybody in everything, not seeking what benefits myself, but what benefits the many [= all the others], in order that they may be saved" (10:33). There is also another relevant Stoic idea involved in these verses, or in fact a whole cluster of them: first, whether

---

[8] For these additions see *The Stoic Theory of Oikeiosis*, chs. 5–6.
[9] "Faith and its Moral Life," 238.

or not one should act in the way that is under dispute—namely of eating meat that may have been consecrated to heathen gods—is up to oneself; it is an issue that falls under one's own "freedom;" second, that is because eating or not-eating is in itself an *adiaphoron* (Greek ἀδιάφορον, lit. "an indifferent thing"), whose genuine value depends entirely on the meaning given to it by the person him- or herself; third, the person who *sees* it as an *adiaphoron* would therefore in principle be completely free to do *what (s)he wishes* (for social or other reasons) *for him- or herself*, that is, *individually*; fourth, *nevertheless*, this freedom to act as one individually wishes must give way to a concern for others where *their* perspective becomes at all relevant—even where what they see from that perspective is *wrong*!

All of Paul's logical moves here could be backed up by Stoic references. In particular, as hinted above, Stoicism allows the individual I-perspective to remain in place once a person has gone through the movement from I to we. That is what accounts for the Stoic notion that certain things—like in Paul's case eating meat for social reasons at a dinner where meat is served—may be "preferable" (though in principle "indifferent"). Paul implicitly reflects the same idea in the present passage, which is another proof that he has imbibed the Stoic idea of *oikeiôsis* to the full. But his explicit and emphatic point, which he brings in at the beginning (10:24) and end (10:33) of the passage, is that the basic perspective expressed in the movement from I to we *must always win*. It is, in the terminology of modern ethics, "overriding," as indeed it is in Stoic ethics. Understood in that way, it does seem that Paul settles very explicitly for "an eclipsed individuation in favor of retaining"—not just "a semblance of unity," but precisely that: genuine unity.

Another passage in 1 Corinthians may just be quoted here: 13:5, that *agapê* "does not seek its own." This is in the middle of Paul's famous praise of *agapê*, indeed in four verses (13:4–7) whose point is that *agapê* excludes a range of types of emotion and behavior that are all based in the individual I-perspective. Thus *agapê* is magnanimous (13:4, cf. Gal 5:22), it is good (same references), it does not envy (13:4, cf. Gal 5:20) and so forth. Clearly, Paul is simply rehearsing here the basic idea in the movement from I to we.

From 1 Corinthians we may move to Galatians, which is interesting because superficially at least Paul here seems to give a larger role to the I-perspective. For the Galatians to avoid "biting" and "devouring" one another (5:15), they must act in a way that is in conformity with the

(Mosaic) law when this is summed up in the injunction to "love your neighbor *as yourself*." Here, it seems, the I is at least given some value, neither more *nor less* than that of the others.

That is a false interpretation, however. Let us leave on one side what the injunction to love one's neighbor as oneself may have been taken to mean in Leviticus, from which Paul quotes. Paul himself at least understood it in complete conformity with what we have already seen. Thus the point made in Gal 5:14 is given in explanation of the injunction of verse 13 that the Galatians must "be slaves to one another through *agapê*." That, surely, brings us directly back to our earlier passages from 1 Corinthians and Philippians. Also, it can be argued— as I have done elsewhere—that the basic contrast in the whole section that Paul appends (5:16–26) in order to spell out what he meant in 5:13– 15 (cf. λέγω δέ in 5:16: "What I mean is this: … ") is between a whole range of vicious act-types that are all based in the I-perspective and a contrasting set of virtues that are all precisely social, headed, of course, by *agapê*.[10] Thus the whole point of 5:16–26 is, once more, to overcome altogether the local I-perspective in favor of the shared we-perspective.

If, then, Paul basically sticks in the whole passage to the picture we know, how will *he* (as opposed to some more original reader of Leviticus) have understood the injunction to "love one's neighbor as oneself"? Answer: that one must see oneself as *one among the others* and *not* love *oneself* at their expense. In other words, in the present passage Paul construes the injunction from Leviticus in such a way that it *just* expresses the movement from I to we—and no more.

From these passages in Galatians, 1 Corinthians, and Philippians one might go on to Romans, in particular chapters 12–15.[11] There are clear reminiscences of Philippians in Rom 12: for example, 12:3 on not having "high thoughts (ὑπερφρονεῖν) among yourselves … , but rather … moderate thoughts (σωφρονεῖν);" 12:10 on "preferring (προηγεῖσθαι) one another in honor;" 12:16 on "having the same thoughts towards one another, not thinking highly (ὑψηλά) but letting oneself move along with the lowly ones (ταπεινοί)." In Rom 13 there is a clear reminiscence of Galatians, when Paul once more quotes Lev 19:18 and relates *agapê* to the Mosaic law (Rom 13:8–10): "for the one who loves his neighbor has fulfilled the law" (13:8). Finally, the overall topic and some of the

---

[10] For the general reading of Gal 5:13–26 that lies behind these remarks see *Paul and the Stoics*, ch. 7.

[11] For another discussion of these passages see the article by Johnson in this volume.

relevant details of Rom 14:1–15:6 reflect the passage in 1 Cor 10 that we looked at. In particular, the strong contrast in 15:13 between "pleasing oneself" and "pleasing one's neighbor" (with Christ acting as a model for the latter behavior) falls immediately into place.

We may conclude that all through Paul is intent on reminding his addressees of the movement from I to we. He is not in the least concerned about the perspective of the self or of "weighing," as Sampley had it, any opposed claims in the "delicate balance regarding self and others." His only concern is to bring to mind the we-perspective as one that must always win. Nor is that interest of his at all difficult to understand. For his aim is, as he himself says, to "build up" (οἰδοδομεῖν). His whole focus is on the S-pole of the model.

This, I suggest, is where we shall eventually end. But we may clarify the goal by trying to reach it through a different route that takes its starting-point from the following questions: Is Paul's view of the relationship between the self and the others one that is best captured under the notion of "self-sacrifice"? And should we even add the predicate "abject" to this characterization? Is that, in fact, what Paul's ταπεινο-φροσύνη (Phil 2:3; cf. Rom 12:16)—which one might well translate more or less literally as "self-abasement"—is all about?

Two Types of "Radical Altruism"

We should distinguish between two senses of "radical altruism." If Paul in Phil 2:4 is understood in the way I have suggested as urging his addressees to leave behind any local I-perspective and to adopt instead an objectifying we-perspective according to which the individual is just one among others, then there is one sense of "radical altruism" in which Paul's meaning in that verse may well be said to fall under the phrase. But there also is another sense in which it may not.

Let us begin from the latter. If by "radical altruism" we mean an attitude of explicit self-denial that one may also term "abject self-sacrifice," then Phil 2:4 does not express radical altruism. There is no *principled* denial of the *self* in the passage, neither in 2:4 nor in the injunction in 2:3 to ταπεινοφροσύνη and considering the others *above* oneself. What I mean is this: There is no *positive* rule directed *against* the self to the effect that *de*basing oneself is the attitude to be adopted always and everywhere. Such a rule might be backed in two different ways. (i) It might be claimed that the very act of self-denial is in one way or another *enjoyable, fulfilling* or whatever—a position of *masochism*. (ii) Or the suggestion

might be that conscious self-denial is the attitude to be adopted because
one *must* adopt it, that is, because one is, and should see oneself as, *just*
being a *slave* to somebody else. In either case, one might well be justified
in speaking of a call for self-sacrifice that is properly "abject."

That, however, is not what Paul has in mind. Instead, there is an
idea—of the movement from I to we—that has two sides to it. One
is the idea that the person who undergoes this movement remains
formally in place as an individual, namely the individual who more or
less self-consciously does undergo the movement.[12] To the extent that
this person also has substantive beliefs and desires that are *not* covered
by the movement (and as we saw, this is in no way excluded), Paul's
account of the movement may be said to be *deficient* since it does not
pay any attention whatever to those remaining features. But to call
Paul's account deficient is very far from saying that the attitude he is
identifying is also an "abject" one.

This point is strengthened by considering the other side of Paul's
idea, which is a strongly positive one: that of *developing* the perspective
of oneself-as-one-of-the-others and insisting on the "fulfilling" character
of *that*. Now that perspective may well be said to define the notion
of altruism. And therefore, to the extent that Paul's line of thought is
intended to insist on just that perspective (and nothing but that) and to
evoke the sheer joy of belonging to the community (of the spirit, cf. Phil
2:12) where *all* will act on the maxim of 2:4—to that extent one may
well find the idea of radical altruism in Phil 2:4.

It is worth insisting on this point. Paul, I am suggesting, is concerned
in our passage (and the other passages too) to *develop and establish the perspective of oneself-as-one-of-the-others*, which the individual may then apply
to his or her own actions in relation to others. He is establishing the *perspective* of altruism (and of radical altruism insofar as he is talking about
that perspective *alone*). Now that is a perspective that cannot be written off just like that. It is present in Stoicism too, where it constitutes
the essence of the Stoic doctrine of *oikeiôsis*. And it is present in most
major ethical positions in philosophy since antiquity. There is nothing
"abject" about that perspective. The most one can criticize Paul for is
that he may have left his account deficient, namely if one thinks—in
itself reasonably enough and here, too, in company with the Stoics—

---

[12] Compare Paul's account in Gal 2:19–20. Even where the Pauline "I" has died
together with Christ, the "I" remains in place as a being who now lives in the faith of
Jesus Christ and so forth.

that in spite of the validity of establishing the perspective of altruism, there is something more to be said about the local I-perspective and how to relate it to the other one.

I have suggested that what Paul does in a passage like Phil 2:4 is just to insist—and evidently for paraenetic purposes—on the perspective of oneself-as-one-of-the-others. I have also claimed that in so doing he is in the company of the Stoics and a major later tradition in ethics. To strengthen the point further, it is worth quoting a few Stoic passages that show how they combined the perspective of oneself-as-one-of-the-others that they had derived from their account of *oikeiôsis* with a pair of notions that are also highly relevant to the Paul of Philippians: friendship (φιλία) and love (τὸ ἀγαπᾶν). Two consecutive fragments in von Arnim (*SVF* 3.630–631, from Stobaeus and Diogenes Laertius) ascribe the following views to the Stoics:

> (630) They ascribe friendship to wise men only, since in those alone is there unanimity (ὁμόνοια) concerning the things pertaining to life. And unanimity is knowledge of *shared* (κοινά) goods. … And they also say that loving (τὸ ἀγαπᾶν), having warm feelings towards (τὸ ἀσπάζεσθαι), and being friendly towards (τὸ φιλεῖν) belong to wise men only.

> (631) They also say that friendship is found among morally good people only, because of their similarity (ὁμοιότης). They say that it is a kind of sharing (κοινωνία) of the things pertaining to life *when we treat our friends as ourselves* (χρωμένων ἡμῶν τοῖς φίλοις ὡς ἑαυτοῖς).

That is the context in which we should also situate the Paul of Phil 2:4. Philippians as a whole is—as is now generally recognized—a paraenetic letter of *friendship*.[13] Paul's aim in 2:1–4 is to spell out for paraenetic purposes the full import of *love*. And in 2:4 he formulates a paraenetic rule or maxim, the content of which is identical with the Stoic idea of *treating one's friends as oneself*: not paying any (special) attention whatever to one's own matters, but caring *instead* for those of the others equals seeing oneself as just one of the others, which again equals treating them as having just as much value as oneself.

So much for the predicate "abject" in the phrase "abject self-sacrifice." But what about "self-sacrifice"? Is that idea not to be found in Paul? Yes, of course. That is precisely the idea that Paul celebrates

---

[13] See e.g. John T. Fitzgerald, "Philippians in the Light of Some Ancient Discussions of Friendship," in *Friendship, Flattery, and Frankness of Speech: Studies on Friendship in the New Testament World*, ed. J.T. Fitzgerald (NovTSup 82, Leiden: Brill, 1996) 141–60, and other literature cited therein.

in the Christ hymn.[14] And it is present in many other places, e.g., in
the idea of Paul himself possibly having to give up his own life for the
sake of the Philippians (cf. Phil 2:17) or the pervasive one of Christ's
having died "for our sake" (e.g. Rom 5:6–8). But is that idea *itself* not
somewhat "abject"? Is it not *just this* idea that should lead us to speak of
"abject self-sacrifice"?

Of course, if one considers the matter from a perspective that is
nothing but I-local, *any* kind of self-sacrifice may appear inherently
"abject" and "despicable." But the point is that there is nothing peculiar, distinctly Pauline—or for that matter "Christian"—about the idea
of self-sacrifice as we meet it in Paul too. On the contrary, it is just
part and parcel of the perspective of altruism that Paul too is trying to
establish.

This may be seen from a single quotation from Cicero's *De Finibus*
III (§64), which comes just after Cicero has stated the part of the Stoic
theory of *oikeiôsis* which grounds the other-regarding side of Stoic ethics.
The text runs like this:[15]

> They hold that the universe is governed by divine will; it is, as it were,
> a city or state of which both men and gods are members, and each one
> of us is a part of this universe; from which it is a natural consequence
> that we should prefer the common advantage to our own. For just as the
> laws set the safety of all above the safety of individuals, so a good, wise
> and law-abiding man, conscious of his duty to the state, cares for the
> advantage of all (*utilitati omnium*) more than that of any single individual
> including himself (*aut suae*). The traitor to his country does not deserve
> greater reprobation than the man who betrays the common advantage
> or security for the sake of his own advantage or security. This explains
> why praise is owed to one who dies for the commonwealth, because it
> becomes us to love our country more than ourselves.

No more eloquent claim for self-sacrifice for the shared cause could
clearly be made. But as is transparent, it is just part of the objectifying
perspective of oneself-as-one-of-the-others that the Stoics were the first

---

[14] L. Michael White ("Morality between Two Worlds: A Paradigm of Friendship
in Philippians," in *Greeks, Romans, and Christians: Studies in Honor of Abraham J. Malherbe*,
ed. D.L. Balch, E. Ferguson, and W.A. Meeks [Philadelphia: Fortress, 1990] 201–15)
argues that the hymn of Phil 2.6–11 is meant to present Jesus' death as a selfless act of
friendship, following the Stoic maxim that a "friend is one who will die for his friend."
In that sense, it is entirely consistent with the point of 2:4, which it is intended both to
illustrate and to ground (2:5) in the lives of the believers.

[15] The translation is the excellent one of H. Rackham in the Loeb edition of the
De Finibus (Cicero, LCL 17; Cambridge: Harvard University Press 1914), with a few
changes and additions of Latin words by myself.

to develop with all clarity. Self-sacrifice is not intrinsically "abject." Nor is there anything distinctly Pauline (or "Christian") about the idea of self-sacrifice—one that we meet in Paul, too.

Well and good. We may conclude, as we suggested already at the end of section 2, that Paul aims only to develop and establish the radical altruist perspective of oneself-as-one-of-the-others. In particular, he does not speak for any distinctly "abject" form of self-sacrifice, nor any distinct form of "self-abasement." But still: is a perspective that contains even the idea of self-sacrifice not in the end too stringent, in Paul as well as the Stoics? If it is not, perhaps, "abject," if it only includes the idea of self-sacrifice as part of a universally recognizable perspective of altruism, nevertheless should we not in the end give some more value to the local I-perspective than is allowed here and so settle for a more moderate, a more human morality, one that does perhaps institute "a delicate balance regarding self and others at every point in one's life"[16] (to quote Sampley for the last time)?

A More Moderate and Human Morality?

This is not the place to address this (huge) issue in the required detail. But it is worth giving the gist of two answers that have recently been made by two modern philosophers and to suggest a third answer that to some extent retains more of the original inspiration from Paul and the Stoics while also being open to the modern concerns for finding room for the local I-perspective too. A redacted string of quotations from the two philosophers may serve us well here.

The most radical departure from the ancient view—though one that nevertheless remains in appreciable contact with it—is that of Samuel Scheffler. Throughout his book on *Human Morality*[17] he argues that morality need not be construed as being so "stringent" and demanding as it has normally been taken, at least in the Kantian tradition in ethics. Instead he wishes to argue for a more "moderate" understanding of morality that gives *two* standpoints"—the moral standpoint and the standpoint of prudence, or individual well-being—the degree of autonomy and mutual independence that they actually have in our thinking" (117). Scheffler does recognize the "appeal of a purely impersonal con-

---

[16] "Faith and its Moral Life," 238.
[17] (New York: Oxford University Press, 1992).

strual of the moral standpoint," which is why his account is directly
relevant to our concerns in this study. He admits that an impersonal
construal is "directly responsive to one important strand in our substantive thinking about morality. In particular, it answers to a conviction that what morality most importantly represents is a form of radical
self-transcendence. The moral point of view, according to this strand of
thought, is a standpoint that one attains by renouncing any distinctive
attachment to oneself, and by acting instead from a thoroughly selfless
concern for all"—which is an almost literal rendering of Paul's point
in Phil 2:4; thus "morality may be very demanding, since it is true by
definition that such extreme self-transcendence requires a willingness to
sacrifice the ordinary interests and concerns of the self" (120). Against
this, however, Scheffler sets an alternative construal, which holds that
"morality attaches unmediated significance to each of two basic propositions. The first proposition is that, from an impersonal standpoint,
everyone's life is of equal intrinsic value and everyone's interests are of
equal intrinsic importance. The second proposition is that each person's interests nevertheless have a significance for him or her that is
out of proportion to their importance from an impersonal standpoint.
On the alternative construal [Scheffler's own], moral norms reflect and
attempt to balance these two fundamental propositions" (122).

   Scheffler himself distinguishes this position from one suggested by
Thomas Nagel in his book *The View from Nowhere*.[18] Nagel's position,
however, is at least inspired by the same aim of generating some "modification in the demands of impersonal morality" (201). Thus Nagel
too is concerned to "take into account the kind of complex beings
for whom it [morality] is being devised. The impersonal is only one
aspect of their nature, not the whole of it. … We must so to speak
strike a bargain between our higher and lower selves in arriving at an
acceptable morality" (202). The way this may be done, according to
Nagel, is by seeing that the objective standpoint, which to begin with
has generated the demands of impersonal morality, will also itself recognize the legitimacy of applying the subjective standpoint with all its
personal motives—to a certain degree which is, admittedly, "hard to
define" (202). Thus one may well conclude on the basis of the objective
standpoint itself that "it is unreasonable to expect people in general to
sacrifice themselves or those to whom they have close personal ties to

---

[18] (New York: Oxford University Press, 1986).

the general good" (202). Or in other words, "there is impersonal sanction for striking the balance between personal and impersonal reasons
in a certain way" (202).

Where Nagels's proposal differs from Scheffler's is that the former's
contains, in the latter's words, the idea of "a concession by morality
to motivational reality: a compromise whereby the requirements of
morality are reduced or relaxed so as to make them more accessible
to human beings with all their flaws and imperfections" (Scheffler, 125).
On Scheffler's own view, by contrast:

> morality is addressed from the outset to human beings as they are.
> It affords them the prospect of integrating two different motivational
> tendencies, and it has no 'prior' content [the one generated by the
> impersonal standpoint, in Nagel's theory] that must be 'reduced' or
> 'modified' when it is brought into contact with human nature (125).

This correct point well explains how Scheffler's proposal is further than
Nagel's from the one we have met in Paul and the Stoics. Like them,
Nagel after all does begin from the impersonal viewpoint and allows
that to define morality. Paul and the Stoics would have agreed. On
another point, however, Nagel shares with Scheffler an aim that makes
them both differ from a third and final position that I wish to sketch,
one that is again closer to the Pauline and Stoic view, but also allows for
some of the modern concerns. The point shared by Nagel and Scheffler is their concern to construe a view of morality that allows for some
form of "integration" in the human being. Thus Nagel's question is
"how personal and impersonal motives are to be integrated" (Nagel,
202). And one of Scheffler's arguments for his alternative construal is
that it "answers to the idea [to be found in 'the underlying strands in
our thinking about morality'] that morality makes possible an important form of personal integration" (Scheffler, 124).

The third position rejects the possibility of such integration and
insists that the moral point of view be defined in exclusively impersonal
terms. To that extent it is completely in line with the Pauline and Stoic
view. This side of the third position is in fact allowed for as a possibility
by both Nagel and Scheffler. Nagel:

> One might take the severe line that moral requirements result from a
> correct assessment of the weight of good and evil, impersonally revealed,
> that it is our job to bring our motives into line with this, and that if
> we cannot do it because of personal weakness, this shows not that the
> requirements are excessive but that we are bad (202).

And Scheffler:

> [It may be argued that] it is no objection to this way of understanding
> morality [namely, as "a form of radical self-transcendence"] to say that
> such self-transcendence may be difficult or impossible for most people—
> or, indeed, for any human being—to achieve or sustain. An ideal may
> inspire us even if it is unattainable, and striving to achieve it may uplift
> and improve us even if our efforts fail. If, by contrast, we take the
> unattainability of the ideal as a reason to modify it to fit our limitations,
> then all we will manage to do is to degrade the ideal, and to ensure that
> the motivational status quo is not improved upon (120–21).

The third position will agree with this and maintain the understanding
of morality as a form of radical self-transcendence. But in rejecting
the idea of integration it will not just give up the personal viewpoint.
On the contrary, it will insist that human beings do have "higher
and lower selves" and that the personal viewpoint must be allowed
to have a say too. In particular, nothing can force us to adopt the
impersonal viewpoint *alone*. But neither can anything allow us to follow
the personal viewpoint alone. We just are beings with a double identity.
Any worthwhile account of how human beings should live must allow
for that. But there is little hope that our two sides may ever be fully and
harmoniously integrated.

This third position—which I have only sketched very briefly here—
may or may not be found attractive. But we may conclude this discussion by noting one thing about it, which is that it does not align
itself with the recent attempts at discovering a morality that is more
"human" (Scheffler) or "reasonable" (Nagel). On the contrary, even
while making its own attempt to allow for the modern concerns, it takes
quite seriously the impersonal standpoint or perspective of oneself-as-
one-of-the-others that Paul was aiming to formulate in his maxim in
Phil 2:4. It applauds that aim and insists that in spite of its deficiencies,
Paul's verse expresses an important idea of radical altruism that should
neither be rejected nor diluted.

TRANSFORMATION OF THE MIND
AND MORAL DISCERNMENT IN PAUL

Luke Timothy Johnson

In this essay I examine the possible connection between two kinds of language in Paul's letters about the way human behavior is directed. The first kind of language is explicitly and obviously religious in character. It aligns human agency with a transcendental spiritual power. The second kind is moral or paraenetic in character.[1] It advocates the practice of virtue and the avoidance of vice. Is there an intrinsic link between these two modes of discourse? Does Paul himself indicate such a link? Is a connection to be inferred from language that Paul himself does not explicate?

To put the question another way: Does Paul allow his readers (whether ancient or contemporary) to appreciate any role for the human ψυχή ("soul") between the power of the πνεῦμα ("spirit") that comes from God and the disposition of the σῶμα ("body") by human persons?[2] The question concerns consistency in Paul's thought, the way in which he did or did not think through his convictions concerning human relatedness to God (expressed in the symbols of Torah) and his directives concerning human moral behavior. The question is also critical to the appropriateness of speaking of "character ethics" in Paul.[3]

As always when asking such questions of Paul, the shape of the Pauline corpus makes methodology an issue impossible to avoid. The occasional character of Paul's correspondence means that we have in each composition only so much of his thinking on any subject as has been raised by the circumstances he considered himself to be addressing. The fact that many of the letters traditionally ascribed to Paul are

---

[1] No one in our generation has done more to make us aware of this dimension of Paul's letters than Abraham J. Malherbe, among whose students I am proud to be included; see especially *Paul and the Popular Philosophers* (Minneapolis: Fortress, 1989).

[2] For the use of these terms in Paul's anthropology, see R. Bultmann, *Theology of the New Testament*, trans. K. Grobel (2 vols.; New York: Charles Scribner's Sons, 1951) 1:191–220, and J.D.G. Dunn, *The Theology of Paul the Apostle* (Grand Rapids: Eerdmans, 1998) 70–78.

[3] An earlier draft of this essay was delivered to the Character Ethics in the Bible Consultation of the Society of Biblical Literature's Annual Meeting, New Orleans, Louisiana, November 1996.

also regarded by the majority of contemporary scholars as pseudonymous means that discussions of "Paul's thought" are bound to be either
conventional or contentious.[4] The best way to overcome the problem of
fragmentation is to embrace it. In this essay I take a single letter and try
to figure out its logic. Such a procedure allows other Pauline letters—
and, as in the present case, other ancient compositions—to serve as
intertexture that might inform both ancient and present day readers as
they try to fill those gaps that might have "gone without saying" for
Paul, but may not have to his first readers and certainly do not to us.[5]

I argue a threefold thesis in this essay. First, Paul's Letter to the
Romans both presents the problem in the sharpest form and also
provides clues to its solving. Second, placing Paul's clues against the
backdrop of Aristotle's discussion of φρόνησις in the *Nicomachean Ethics*
provides a framework that makes them more coherent. Third, the
hypothesis thus derived from Romans is supported by evidence drawn
from other Pauline letters and is disconfirmed by none of them.

A First Look at Romans

How can we account for the fact that the language about the Holy
Spirit, which dominates the theological argument in Romans 5–8, is
virtually absent from the moral instruction in chapters 12–14? To appreciate the difficulty, it is helpful to review the language in some detail.
The "spirit of holiness" (πνεῦμα ἁγιωσύνης) is introduced in 1:4 in connection with that power (δύναμις) designating Jesus as Son of God
because of his resurrection from the dead. In 5:5 this Holy Spirit is
given to those who have been made righteous, pouring out the love of
God into their hearts. In chapter six, Paul shows the irreconcilability of
"walking in newness of life" and continuing in sin (6:1–23). He does not
speak here of the Holy Spirit, but, as we see in 7:6, the power of the
Spirit in this newness of life has been assumed; for Paul states there that
they are now able to serve God "in the newness of the Spirit and not
the oldness of the letter."

---

[4] My own position on these matters—that all letters ascribed to Paul could well
have been written during his lifetime in a complex process of composition that already
involved his "school"—is sketched in *Writings of the New Testament: An Interpretation* (2nd
enl. ed.; Minneapolis: Fortress, 1999) 271–73; 393–95; 407–12; 423–31.

[5] For the notion of "intertexture," see V.K. Robbins, *The Tapestry of Early Christian
Discourse: Rhetoric, Society, and Ideology* (London: Routledge, 1996), 96–191.

The power of the Holy Spirit to direct human behavior is most extensively elaborated in Romans 8. The "law of the Spirit of life" has freed them (8:2) and enables them to "walk according to the Spirit" (8:4–5). As in 5:5, the presence of this Spirit is expressed by terms of astonishing intimacy: they are "in" the Spirit, the Spirit of God "dwells in" them, and they "have" the Spirit of Christ (8:9). The Spirit who raised Jesus from the dead—note the echo of 1:4—"dwells in" them" (8:11). As a result, they have received a "spirit of adoption" making them children of God (8:15). As children of God, furthermore, they are "led about" by the Spirit (8:14), who testifies with their own spirit concerning their identity as God's children (8:16), comes to their assistance when they are weak (8:26), prays for them when they are unable (8:26), so that God, who knows the "intention of the Spirit" (8:27) heeds their prayer. Finally, as Paul begins his long exposition concerning Jews and Gentiles in God's plan, he begins by invoking the "shared witness" of his own and the "Holy Spirit" to the truth concerning his loyalty to his own people (9:1).

Reading Romans to this point one could easily conclude that God's Holy Spirit was most actively and intimately involved in the moral life of believers. Everything in Paul's argument leads the reader to this expectation. Yet when Paul turns in 12:1 to the moral consequences of his argument (note the οὖν, "therefore"), such language about the Holy Spirit virtually disappears.[6] Especially intriguing is 12:1–2, the statement by which Paul makes a transition from the indicative to the imperative mood—often in the participial form frequently used in paraenesis (see especially 12:10–13).[7] Paul says his readers should present their bodies to God as a living sacrifice, their "reasonable worship" (λογικὴ λατρεία). He spells out this general imperative in three discrete stages. Negatively, they are not to "conform themselves" (συσχηματίζεσθε) to this world. Instead, they are to be "transformed by the renewal of mind" (μεταμορφοῦσθε τε ανακαινώσει τοῦ νοός). The purpose of this renewal is to enable the "testing (δοκιμάζειν) of what is God's will, the good, the pleasing, and the perfect."

---

[6] For taking the οὖν at its full weight, see D.J. Moo, *The Epistle to the Romans* (NICNT; Grand Rapids: Eerdmans, 1996) 748.

[7] For discussion of the use of the participle as imperative, see W.T. Wilson, *Love without Pretense: Romans 12:9–21 and Hellenistic Jewish Wisdom Literature* (WUNT 2.46; Tübingen: Mohr-Siebeck, 1991) 156–165.

I note at once that each stage is assumed to be under their control. It is done, the reader might assume, by their own capacities, not under the control of another, such as God's Holy Spirit. Observe further that there is an emphasis on the readers' cognitive capacities rather than affective dispositions: they are to offer reasonable worship (or the worship of their minds), they are to avoid one way of measuring, they are to change their "mind," and they are to test. These are all mental activities. And here, where we most might have expected it, we find no role at all assigned to the Holy Spirit

Indeed, the next part of the letter (12:3–13:14), which is usually considered to be a classic example of paraenesis in the proper sense of the term, that is, a set of exhortations or maxims of a traditional character joined together without any obvious line of argumentation,[8] the only mention of spirit is in a threefold exhortation, "do not be lacking in zeal, be fervent in spirit, serve the Lord" (12:11). This may or may not refer to the Holy Spirit; it may equally likely refer to simple spiritual fervor. Likewise in Paul's subsequent discussion of differences in worship and diet (14:1–15:12), he makes only one reference to the Holy Spirit, when he declares, "For the kingdom of God is not food and drink, but rather righteousness and peace and joy in the Holy Spirit" (14:17). Only at the very end of this discussion does Paul revert to language about the Holy Spirit, when he prays: "May the God of hope fill you with all joy and peace in your believing, so that you may overflow in hope in the power of the Holy Spirit" (15:13). Finally, turning to his own work as an apostle, Paul mentions the "power of signs and wonders, in the power of the Holy Spirit" that has accompanied his preaching among the Gentiles (15:19).

It seems, therefore, that Paul's language in Romans about the work of the Holy Spirit is restricted to what might be called *religious* relationships. It does not appear to affect, except in the most formal and tangential fashion, his language about *moral* behavior among believers. Between pneumatology and ethics there is no obvious connection. That is, unless we are missing something.

---

[8] For discussion and literary parallels, see Wilson, *Love without Pretense*, 71–81, 91–125.

A Second Look at Romans

What we may be missing are subtle connections Paul establishes at the level of the Greek text which have largely escaped translators into English, but which may have been recognized by ancient readers.

1. The use of the noun νοῦς in 12:2 deserves attention. What does Paul mean by "mind" or "intelligence" here? The question is made more pertinent by the omission, in the best manuscripts and the Nestle-Aland 27th edition, of the personal possessive pronoun, "your" (ὑμῶν).[9] The absence of the pronoun leaves some ambiguity about whose mind Paul means. We remember that νοῦς also appeared in 7:23–25, with Paul declaring in 7:23 that his inner self agrees with God's law, but that he also sees another law in his members warring against "the law of my mind" (τῷ νόμῳ τοῦ νοός μου). In 7:25, he states, "Therefore with my mind (τῷ νοΐ) I serve the law of God, but with my flesh (τῇ σαρκί) the law of sin." As a Jew, Paul has the proper understanding of the relationship with God (2:18–20) but, under the influence of the flesh, lacks the capacity to live it out.

Even more pertinent is the way 12:2, addressed to Gentile believers (see 11:13), reverses the situation of the Gentiles that Paul had developed in 1:18–32. There he had argued that idolatry had rendered Gentiles foolish in their ways, and he mocked their self-proclaimed wisdom; each stage of alienation from God, in fact, leads them to a further corruption of understanding: "Whereas they refused (or 'de-tested,' οὐκ ἐδοκίμασαν) to hold God in recognition (ἐν ἐπιγνώσει), God handed them over to an undiscerning mind (or "untesting mind," ἀδόκιμον νοῦν), doing what they should not (τὰ μὴ καθήκοντα), filled with every sort of wickedness, evil …" (1:28–29). Paul concludes with the list of Gentile vices that flow from such perverted understanding (1:29–32).

2. Note further that the *renewal* of the mind in 12:2 has as its purpose that Paul's Gentile readers will be able to discern or test the will of God (compare 2:17) in practical circumstances. The phrase εἰς τὸ δοκιμάζειν ἡμᾶς τί τὸ θέλημα τοῦ θεοῦ is surely an intentional echo

---

[9] The pronoun is read by Codex Sinaiticus (ℵ), the first corrector of Codex Bezae (D¹), the Mt. Athos codex 044 (ψ), Paris ms. BNF Gr. 14 (33), the Koine tradition (𝔐), some old Latin mss., and the Syriac. It is absent from 𝔓46, Alexandrinus (A), Vaticanus (B), the original hand of Bezae, F, G, and many other witnesses.

and response to the ἀδόκιμος νοῦς ascribed to the Gentiles who did *not* "present their bodies as living sacrifice that is pleasing to God, a rational worship," but whose preference for the creature over the creator led to the darkening of their own minds and hearts. Paul shares the logic of ancient moralists, who assume that moral behavior follows upon right perception, enabling ancient polemic to argue that just as good perceptions lead to proper behavior, so also wicked deeds suffice to demonstrate a derangement in thinking.[10] Thus, just as the "untested mind" of idolators led inevitably to vice, so the "renewed mind" of the Gentile believer is to lead to virtue. The link between this understanding and specific attitudes and actions is a process of mental testing (δοκιμάζειν).

3. The connection between νοῦς and δοκιμάζειν, in turn, allows us to take with full seriousness the remarkable incidence of φρον- cognates in this section of Romans: φρόνιμος occurs in 11:25 and 12:16; φρόνημα in 8:6, 7, and 27; ὑπερφρονεῖν in 12:3, and φρονεῖν in 8:5; 11:20; 12:3; 12:16 (twice); 14:6 (twice), and 15:5. The threefold usage in 12:3 is especially striking, since it picks up directly from δοκιμάζειν in 12:2: λέγω γὰρ διὰ τῆς χάριτος τῆς δοθείσης μοι παντὶ τῷ ὄντι ἐν ὑμῖν μὴ ὑπερφρονεῖν παρ' ὃ δεῖ φρονεῖν, ἀλλὰ φρονεῖν εἰς τὸ σωφρονεῖν, ἑκάστῳ ὡς ὁ θεὸς ἐμέρισεν μέτρον πίστεως.

The statement is difficult to translate. Standard translations miss the important play on words represented by φρονεῖν εἰς τὸ σωφρονεῖν. The Douay version has "Let him rate himself according to moderation;" The Jerusalem Bible, "Let him judge himself soberly;" the New American Bible, "estimate himself soberly;" the Revised Standard Version, "think with sober judgments;" the New Revised Standard Version, "think with sober judgment;" the New International Version, "think of yourself with sober judgment."[11]

The problem with the translations is twofold. First, they miss the link to Graeco-Roman moral philosophy established by σωφρονεῖν.[12]

---

[10] See L.T. Johnson, "II Timothy and the Polemic Against False Teachers: A Reexamination," *JRS* 6/7 (1978–79) 1–26, and, "The New Testament's Anti-Jewish Slander and the Conventions of Ancient Polemic," *JBL* 108 (1989) 419–41.

[11] A glance at several standard commentaries shows a similar consistency: E. Käsemann, *Commentary on Romans*, ed. and trans. G.W. Bromiley (Grand Rapids: Eerdmans, 1980) has "think with soberness;" J.A. Fitzmyer, *Romans* (AB 33; Garden City: Doubleday, 1992) "think of yourself with sober judgment;" J.D.G. Dunn *Romans 9–16* (WBC; Dallas: Word Books, 1988), "observe proper moderation;" D.J. Moo, *The Epistle to the Romans* (NICNT; Grand Rapids: Eerdmans, 1996), "think with sober thinking."

[12] The commentaries recognize the allusion, but give it scant attention. They invari-

Second, by translating εἰς τὸ σωφρονεῖν adverbially, they miss the parallelism to εἰς τὸ δοκιμάζειν in 12:2. Both constructions are final clauses expressing purpose and/or result.[13] Just as εἰς τὸ δοκιμάζειν is correctly rendered, "in order to test/discern," or "so that you can test/discern," so should εἰς τὸ σωφρονεῖν be translated as "so that you can think rightly/moderately." Among recent scholars, Stanley Stowers has correctly suggested the importance of this statement within Paul's argument as a whole.[14] Paul's language points us to discussions of practical reason, and the role of prudence (φρόνησις), in moral discernment. The solemn warning not to overestimate oneself, but to φρονεῖν εἰς τὸ σωφρονεῖν is programmatic for Paul's entire moral argument concerning life in the community.

A Glance at Aristotle

No extended justification is required for a turn to Aristotle in any discussion of "character ethics," nor for the use of his *Nicomachean Ethics* as the main point of reference.[15] It may be helpful, however, to recall the key role played by prudence in Aristotle's discussion of moral virtue. For example, Aristotle concludes in *NE* II, 5, 6 that "if virtues are neither emotions (πάθη) nor capacities (δύναμεις), it remains that they are dispositions (ἕξεις)," and he states briefly concerning prudence (φρόνησις): "Virtue then is a settled disposition (ἕξις) determining the choice of actions and emotions, consisting essentially in the observance of the mean relative to us, this being determined by principle (λόγῳ), that is, as the prudent man would determine it (ὡς ἂν ὁ φρόνιμος ὁρίσειεν)" (*NE* II, 6, 15).[16]

---

ably refer in passing to the article by U. Luck, "σώφρων, κτλ" in *TDNT* 7: 1097–1102.

[13] Moo (*Epistle to the Romans*, 760 n. 12) recognizes that the construction could indicate purpose, but prefers to see it functioning adverbially.

[14] See S.K. Stowers, *A Rereading of Romans: Justice, Jews, and Gentiles* (New Haven: Yale University Press, 1994) 42–82. Given the weight he has assigned to the entire theme of σωφροσύνη, however, Stowers gives little specific attention to the actual verses where Paul's argument becomes explicit on the point. Likewise, Wilson (*Love without Pretense*, 141) provides some comparative passages but does not develop the theme.

[15] Käsemann (*Romans*, 331) certainly saw the connection: "Thereby he falls back surprisingly on Greek ethics. For Aristotle, σωφροσύνη is in *Nicomachean Ethics* 1117b.13 one of the four cardinal virtues." Cf. Fitzmyer, *Romans*, 645.

[16] Throughout this discussion, I use the translation of H. Rackham, *Aristotle: The Nicomachean Ethics* (LCL; Cambridge: Harvard University Press, 1912).

Aristotle delays a direct discussion of prudence until *NE* VI, 5, 6. Here he characterizes ὁ φρόνιμος as ὁ βουλευτικός (VI, 5, 2), so it may be useful to note how he speaks of "deliberation" in III, 3, 10–11:

> Deliberation (τὸ βουλεύεσθαι) then is employed in matters which, though subject to the rules that generally hold good, are uncertain in their issue; or where the issue is indeterminate ... and we deliberate not about ends (περὶ τῶν τελῶν) but about means (περὶ τῶν πρὸς τὰ τέλη).

This statement is particularly important for its distinction between means and ends, and for its recognition of the element of "indeterminacy" that calls for deliberation or prudence: between the general rules and the specific applications, some mediation is required.

Aristotle's explicit discussion of φρόνησις begins in *NE* VI, 5, 1. He observes that the definition of prudence is best learned by observing "the persons whom we call prudent" (τίνας λέγομεν τοὺς φρονίμους)." Distinguishing prudence from science and art, he considers it "a truth-attaining rational quality, concerned with action in relation to things that are good and bad for human beings" (VI, 5, 4; see also VI, 5, 6). It is therefore preeminently a form of *practical* reasoning, the ability to discern what is good and bad for oneself (and, in the case of statesmen like Pericles, for others as well) amid the complexity of changing circumstances (VI, 5, 6).

Aristotle can speak of deliberative excellence as "correctness in deliberation" (ὀρθότης βουλῆς εὐβουλία) in the sense of "arriving at something good" (ἡ ἀγαθοῦ τευτική) [VI, 9, 4]. At the start of his treatise, Aristotle places prudence among the intellectual rather than the moral virtues (I, 13, 20), but by the end of his discussion, he recognizes that "prudence is intimately connected with moral virtue, and this [viz. moral virtue] with prudence, inasmuch as the first principles (ἀρχαί) which prudence employs are determined by the moral virtues, and the right standard (ὀρθόν) for the moral virtues is determined by prudence" (X, 8, 3).

Four aspects of Aristotle's rich discussion of φρόνησις are of particular pertinence for the reading of Romans:

1. Like Paul in Rom 12:3, Aristotle connects φρόνησις to σωφροσύνη. Having declared that prudence is the faculty for discerning what things are good for the self and (for statesmen like Pericles) for humankind, he says, "This accounts for the word temperance (σωφροσύνη) which signifies 'preserving prudence' (σωζοῦσαν τὴν φρόνησιν) (VI, 5, 6). We may question the etymology and wince at the pun, but his point is serious:

temperance does in fact keep intact the apprehension (ὑπόλεψιν) that is critical for moral discernment. Vice will not destroy one's capacity to perceive mathematical truths, says Aristotle, but love of pleasure or fear of pain can disable the ability to perceive clearly the moral ἀρχή (first principle), and therefore the person thus corrupted "cannot see that he ought to choose and do everything as a means to this end and for its sake; for vice tends to destroy the sense of principle" (VI, 5, 6). This, I submit, sounds a great deal like Paul's view of how the Gentiles' corruption of mind disabled them from seeing clearly and led them ever deeper into darkness and vice (Rom 1:18–32).

2. The resemblance is not accidental, for Aristotle also establishes an explicit if complex link between the νοῦς and φρόνησις, just as Paul does in Rom 12:2–3. In *NE* VI, 6, 2, Aristotle says that the νοῦς is that which apprehends the first principles (ἀρχαί) by which prudence is guided in its decision making. "Intelligence (νοῦς) apprehends definitions, which cannot be proven by reasoning, while prudence deals with the ultimate particular thing, which cannot be apprehended by scientific knowledge" (VI, 8, 9; see also VI, 11, 4). Since prudence depends on experience, it cannot be asked of the young: "Prudence includes a knowledge of particular facts, and this is derived from experience, which a young man does not possess, for experience is the fruit of years" (VI, 8, 5). On the other hand, "Intelligence (νοῦς) is both a beginning and an end (ἀρχὴ καὶ τέλος), for these things are both the starting point and the subject matter of demonstration" (VI, 11, 6).

Aristotle distinguishes cleverness and prudence by making one a natural facility and the other a virtue: "True virtue cannot exist without prudence. Hence some people maintain that all the virtues are forms of prudence." (VI, 8, 3). This is because "…it is a disposition (ἕξις) determined by the right principle; and the right principle is the principle determined by prudence" (VI, 13, 4). Does this sound convoluted? It must have to Aristotle as well, for he tries once more, "Virtue is not merely a disposition conforming to right principle but one cooperating with right principle, and prudence is right principle in matters of conduct" (VI, 13, 5).

If I understand this rather tangled exposition correctly, Aristotle is struggling to express the dialectical relationship between the "mind" (νοῦς) that can understand "first principles"—which in his thought is the realm of properly human action having to do with moral virtue, and which here stand as the "end" toward which specific actions ought

to tend—and the form of practical intelligence (φρόνησις) which is able
in specific complex circumstances to determine rightly those "means"
that tend toward the desired "ends"—namely the ways of acting that
"cooperate" with or conform to those first principles of morality apprehended by the mind (ἢ μὲν γὰρ τὸ τέλος, ἢ δὲ τὰ πρὸς τὸ τέλος ποιεῖ
πράττειν, VI, 13, 7). Understanding makes judgments, and prudence
issues commands, "since its end is a statement of what we ought to do
or not to do" (VI, 10, 2).

3. Aristotle recognizes that prudence "is commonly understood to
mean especially that kind of wisdom which is concerned with oneself, the individual," leading people to use the term "to mean those
who are wise in their own interest" (VI, 8, 3). At the same time, he
notes that the term has wider application, as in the case of statesmen
like Pericles, who have the capacity to discern "what things are good
for themselves and for mankind" (VI, 5, 5), and notes that "prudence
is indeed the same quality of mind as political science, though their
essence is different" (VI, 8, 1). Indeed, the two realms cannot entirely
be separated: "Probably as a matter of fact a man cannot pursue his
own welfare without domestic economy and even politics," although
"even the proper conduct of one's own affairs is a difficult problem and
requires consideration" (VI, 8, 4). For the present analysis, it is sufficient
to note that Aristotle's understanding of moral (or prudential) reasoning includes consideration for others, under the category of "what is
equitable," for "equitable actions are common to all good men in their
behavior toward each other" (VI, 11, 2–3). We see the same tension
between the individual and the community concern in Paul's discussion.

4. Finally, for Aristotle, the role of prudence in moral discernment is
to hit the "mean" between two extremes wherein Aristotle thinks virtue
is to be found, and doing it well: "Hence, while in respect of its substance and the definition that states what it really is in essence virtue is
the observance of the mean, in point of excellence and rightness it is
an extreme" (II, 6, 17). And finding this mean "is determined by principle (λόγῳ), that is, as the prudent man (φρόνιμος) would determine it"
(II, 6, 15). The point I make here is that the determination of virtue is
with reference to a measure or framework. Prudence itself is guided by
those moral "first principles" (ἀρχαί) perceived by the νοῦς and seeks
to express them in action. In this light, Paul's otherwise obscure references to a "measure of faith" (μέτρον πίστεως) in 12:3 and "proportion
of faith" (ἀναλογίαν τῆς πίστεως) in 12:6 might appear more intelligible.

We note that in each case, it is a question of standard: φρονεῖν εἰς τὸ σωφρονεῖν ἑκάστῳ ὡς ὁ θεὸς ἐμέρισεν μέτρον πίστεως, and, εἴτε προφη-τείαν κατὰ τὴν ἀναλογίαν τῆς πίστεως. It will be remembered how criti-cal the concept of "proportionality" (ἀναλογία) is to Aristotle's notion of the "mean between two extremes" that is justice (δικαιοσύνη) [see *NE* V, 3, 1–12].

I do not suggest that Paul was writing with a copy of the *Nicomachean Ethics* in hand, or that Aristotle was a direct influence.[17] I am suggesting that Paul's language about moral discernment follows a strikingly simi-lar kind of logic. In Paul as in Aristotle, the capacity to "test" or "esti-mate" morally derives from the νοῦς, not simply intelligence as a capac-ity, but perhaps something closer to what we would call a "mind-set," that is, a moral intelligence that grasps certain fundamental principles or values. In Paul and in Aristotle, The corruption of the νοῦς makes moral discernment impossible rather than simply difficult. In Paul and Aristotle, prudence or discernment involves what is good for the indi-vidual but inevitably involves as well what is good for other humans. And in both writers, moral deliberation takes place within a framework that enables it to be measured.

To this point, my exposition of Romans 12:1–6, especially in its emphasis on the relationship between νοῦς in 12:2 and the language of φρόνησις has shown an impressive resemblance to Aristotle not least in the way both authors lack any transcendental referent when speaking of moral decision-making, which appears in both to be entirely rational in character. I seem to have failed in my effort to link Paul's religious and moral discourse, his language about Holy Spirit and his language about virtue. Unless still something else has been missed.

The Measure of Faith and the Mind of Christ

What I have missed is that although Paul shares with Aristotle the terms and understandings of νοῦς and μέτρον and ἀναλογία, he gives each of them a distinctive turn. Here is the first way in which Paul's religious and philosophical language can be seen as merging.

1. Paul could not be clearer in 12:3 that the framework for pru-dence/discernment is not a theory of virtue—a matter of hitting the

---

[17] See Stowers (*Rereading Romans*, 58–65) for a good discussion of the widespread theme of self-mastery in Hellenistic Jewish literature; cf. Wilson, *Love without Pretense*, 137.

mean between two extremes, for example—but "the measure of faith," (μετρον πιστεως) and that this measure comes not from human calculation but from God: φρονεῖν εἰς τὸ σωφρονεῖν ἑκάστῳ ὡς ὁ θεὸς ἐμέρισεν μέτρον πίστεως. Each phrase has its own difficulty. Does ἑκάστῳ ("each or that one") refer back to the act of discerning, so that Paul's readers are to exercise moral discernment appropriately *toward each one* according to the measure of faith? In that case, the dative ἑκάστῳ refers to other members of the community. Or does it anticipate the second clause: "as God has given *to each one* (ἑκάστῳ) a measure of faith." The word order suggests the first option, and I consider it the more likely reading. Commentators, however, have tended to take ἑκάστῳ as referring to the recipient of the measure of faith.[18] In either case, however, the rule for measuring moral deliberation is that of faith.[19]

Similarly in 12:6, the phrase κατὰ τὴν ἀναλογίαν τῆς πίστεως should be taken as referring not simply to the exercise of prophecy, but to the measurement of all the χαρίσματα διάφορα of vv. 6–8 according to the gift given to them[20] by the gift-giver, understood as God—although we can note once more in passing that Paul does not use the explicit language of the Holy Spirit here either.

If μέτρον can be understood as a measure, then what are we to understand by Paul's use here of the term "faith?" Rather than repeat the several opinions offered by the commentators—ranging from faithfulness as charismatic gift to community creed[21]—we should proceed exegetically by observing the way Paul speaks of faith in this part of the letter. If we take as a hypothesis that πίστις serves as a measure for moral discernment, we can make good sense of Paul's otherwise odd usage in 14:1. Discussing diversity of practice in the community, Paul instructs his readers to "receive those who are weak in faith." Since the context concerns believers who eat everything and the weak who

---

[18] See Fitzmyer, *Romans*, 645–46; Dunn, *Romans 9–16*, 721; Moo, *Romans*, 760; Käsemann, *Romans*, 331.

[19] For the different possible understandings of "measure of faith," see Moo, *Romans*, 760–761; Käsemann, *Romans*, 335; Fitzmyer, *Romans*, 645–46. Since my own reading resembles Fitzmyer most, but moves in another direction, I will not try to adjudicate between the opinions. But I take vigorous exception to Dunn's view (*Romans*, 721) that "it is very unlikely here that μέτρον has sense of 'standard by which to measure, means of measurement.'" That is precisely what it means.

[20] See especially Käsemann, *Romans*, 333–334.

[21] e.g. Käsemann, *Romans*, 335; Moo, *Romans*, 761; Dunn, *Romans*, 722; Fitzmyer, *Romans*, 647.

eat only vegetables (14:2), the clear implication is that "weakness" here means an inability to live according to the measure given by faith. This becomes even clearer in 14:22–23:

> The faith you hold, hold according to yourself before God. Happy is the one who does not condemn himself in (by?) what he tests (ἐν ᾧ δοκιμάζειν). But the one who is doubting yet eats has already condemned himself, for it was not out of faith. And everything that is not out of faith (ἐκ πίστεως) is sin (ἁμαρτία).[22]

2. The obvious question raised by making faith the measure for moral discernment is, "whose faith?" In one sense Paul clearly refers to the faith and the mind of the individual believer: "the faith that you hold" (14:22).[23] So he says also in 14:5, "One person judges a day over a day; another judges all days [alike]. Let each one be fully assured in his or her own mind (ἐν τῷ ἰδίῳ νοΐ). The one who is mindful (φρονῶν) of the day is mindful (φρονεῖ) toward the Lord." But can Paul also mean more than the individual's personal faith? Can there be another Mind involved here and functioning as a measure beyond that of the individual believer?

It is at this point that Paul's way of speaking of Jesus with reference to the moral behavior of believers in this part of Romans becomes pertinent. Immediately after the statement in 12:3 warning against self-overestimation and calling for φρονεῖν εἰς τὸ σωφρονεῖν according to the measure of faith, Paul draws the comparison between a body with many parts and many functions, and the community: "in the same way we are one body in Christ, individually members related to each other" (12:4–5). Depending on how strongly we take this metaphor of "the Messiah's body," we might ask whose νοῦς is directing it.[24] The link between the dead and raised messiah Jesus and this specific human community is for Paul very real (see also 1 Cor 6: 15–20; 10:16–17; 12:12–31; Col 3:15; Eph 4:4, 15). The one who lives by the rule of God in righteousness and peace and joy in the Holy Spirit is "one who serves Christ in this way" and is pleasing to God as well as approved by humans (14:18, compare the language of 12:1). Even more emphatically, Paul states in 14:7–9:

---

[22] Among commentators, Käsemann in particular notes the pertinence of 12:3 for the understanding of πίστις in this statement (*Romans*, 379).

[23] Or is it "the faithfulness that you have"?

[24] The use of σῶμα in 12:5 is particularly intriguing only four verses after Paul tells his readers to present τὰ σώματα ὑμῶν to God as living sacrifices.

> None of us lives for oneself and no one dies for oneself. For if we live, we live for the Lord, and if we die, we die for the Lord. Whether we should live or die, we are the Lord's. Because it was for this reason that Christ died and came back to life, that he might be Lord over the dead and the living.

Two aspects of this intense and intimate relationship between the risen Christ as Lord and the believer as obedient servant deserve special attention.

A. In a statement that connects moral activity and the bond between believers and Jesus in the most explicit fashion, Paul reminds his readers that they should no longer "walk" as in the night but "decently" (εὐσχημόνως) as in the day (Rom 13:13)—no more revelry, drunkenness, debauchery and licentiousness, contention and jealousy. The vice-list reminds us of the one in Rom 1:29–32 that condemned Gentile behavior as directed by an ἀδόκιμος νοῦς. Instead, they are to "put on the Lord Jesus Christ, and make no provision (πρόνοιαν μὴ ποιεῖσθε) for the desires of the flesh" (13:14). The metaphor of "putting on" a quality as one puts on clothing is not uncommon in Paul; just before this, Paul says that they must "put on" the weapons of light (14:12; compare 1 Thess 5:8; Col 3:10, 12; Eph 6:11, 14; 2 Cor 5:3; 1 Cor 15:53–54). But what does it mean to "put on" a person? At the very least, it suggests that the qualities found in that person are to be the qualities adopted by them. So Paul speaks in Eph 4:24 of "putting on the new person," and in Gal 3:27, he says that those who have been baptized into Christ have "put on Christ." Certainly, such language allows the inference that the same "mind" that was in Christ should also be in the believers. Paul's statement in 14:14 would seem to support this suggestion: "I know and have become fully convinced (οἶδα καὶ πέπεισμαι) in the Lord Jesus that nothing is common (κοινὸν) by itself, but for the person reckoning it as common, for that person it is common." The grammatical relationship between Paul's mental conviction and the phrase "in the Lord Jesus" can be construed in such fashion as to pointing to just such an adoption of the "mind of the messiah" as I am suggesting.

B. Paul invokes the example of Jesus himself as a guide to the moral behavior of his readers. Thus he warns those who consider themselves free to eat any food: "Do not by your eating destroy that one for whom Christ died" (14:15b; compare 1 Cor 8:11). Explicit in the statement is the mutual relatedness of all in the community to the one Lord Jesus (see 14:7–9). But the exhortation also implies that just as Jesus died for another, so should their behavior follow a similar pattern: they should walk according to love and not grieve a brother or sister by their behavior (14:15a).

The exemplary role of the human Jesus is manifest in 15:1–3. Paul says that those who are strong should bear with the weaknesses of those who are not strong, *and not please themselves*; rather "each one should please the neighbor unto the good thing for the sake of building up the community,"

> For Christ also did not please himself, but as it is written, "the reproaches of those who reproach you have fallen upon me" … may the God of patience and comfort give to you so that you might think the same way (τὸ αὐτὸ φρονεῖν) toward each other, according to Christ Jesus … therefore accept one another, just as Christ accepted you unto the glory of God (15:3–7).[25]

If we place these pieces against the backdrop of Aristotle's discussion in the *Nicomachean Ethics*, we can at least entertain the possibility that Paul understands the process of moral discernment within the community to be exercised not only within the measure of faith, but specifically within the "faith of Christ" (see 3:21–26, 5:12–21) that was demonstrated by Jesus' obedience to God and loving self-disposition toward others.[26] The transformation of believers "in the renewal of mind" means therefore their "putting on" the mind of Christ, so that the process of φρόνησις is aligned with the ἀρχαί apprehended by their νοῦς thus renewed and informed.

The Role of the Holy Spirit

We have seen that Paul's religious and moral language do coincide in Romans 12–14, but the role of the Holy Spirit remains elusive. If we read only Romans 8, we might conclude that the Spirit completely took over the direction of human freedom, yet Romans 12–14 has shown

---

[25] See R.B. Hays, "Christ Prays the Psalm," in *The Future of Christology: Essays in Honor of Leander E. Keck*, ed. W.A. Meeks and A.J. Malherbe (Minneapolis: Fortress, 1993) 122–136.

[26] In the ever-growing literature devoted to the question of the faith/faithfulness of Jesus, see R.B. Hays, "*Pistis* and Paul's Christology: What's at Stake," *SBLSP* 30 (1991) 714–29; S.K. Stowers, "ἐκ πίστεως and διὰ τῆς πίστεως in Rom 3:30," *JBL* 108 (1989) 665–74; L.T. Johnson, "Romans 3:21–26 and the Faith of Jesus," *CBQ* 44 (1982) 77–90.

that moral discernment is very much an exercise of the human νοῦς. I have suggested that Paul implies that this human νοῦς is itself shaped by the νοῦς Χριστοῦ. But Paul does not draw an explicit connection between the Spirit given to humans and this process of moral testing and decision-making. Closer examination, however, reveals a number of important but implicit connections.

1. The Holy Spirit empowers moral choice in accord with God's will (8:1–3), so that human φρόνημα can be "according to the Spirit" and not simply "according to the flesh" (8:5–8). This power of the Spirit comes to the assistance of human "weakness" (ἀσθένεια), so that when "we" don't know how to pray, the Spirit prays and God who knows the hearts (of humans!) knows the φρόνημα τοῦ πνεύματος! Here, Paul brings this Spirit of God into the closest possible connection with the disposition of human freedom. Note also that Paul concludes the moral instruction of 12:1–15:12—so otherwise devoid of language about the Spirit—with a prayer that concludes, "in the power of the Holy Spirit" (ἐν δυνάμει πνεύματος ἁγίου).

2. The Holy Spirit "leads" humans who are "children of God" (8:14), and Paul's readers have "not received a spirit of slavery leading you again into fear, but a spirit of sonship by which we cry 'Abba, Father'" (8:15). Shortly after declaring how the Spirit assists them in their weakness (8:27), Paul asserts that God has set aside those whom God has chosen "to be conformed (σύμμορφους) to the image of his Son, so that he can be the first-born of many brothers" (8:29). Here, the close identification of believers and Christ is mediated by the Spirit. The Spirit itself testifies "to our spirit" (or "with our spirit") that "we are children of God" (8:16). Those who call out to God as "sons" can be said to have "the mind of Christ."

3. Indeed, the Spirit "dwelling" in them is at work to replicate the same pattern of dying and rising as in Jesus: "If the Spirit of the one who raised Jesus from the dead dwells in you, the one who raised Jesus from the dead will also give life to your mortal bodies through his spirit which dwells in you" (8:11). We remember the first appearance of the "spirit of holiness" in Rom 1:4, in connection with the resurrection of Jesus and his demarcation of Son of God in power.

4. Paul uses "newness" language only three times in Romans. The first instance speaks of the "newness of life" (καινότης τῆς ζωῆς) in which those baptized were supposed to "walk" (that is, conduct their moral lives): "We were buried therefore with him by baptism into death, so that as Christ was raised from the dead by the glory of the

father, we too might walk in newness of life" (6:4).[27] The second speaks
of the "newness of the Spirit" (or "that comes from the Spirit") that
enables service of God: "now we are discharged from the law, dead
to that which held us captive, so that we may serve not under the old
written code but in the new life of the Spirit (καινότητι τοῦ πνεύματος)".
Finally, in 12:2, Paul tells his readers to be transformed "in the newness
of mind" (ἐν ἀνακαίνωσει τοῦ νοός).

5. Paul declares that the one thing owed to each other is love (13:8),
since love "fulfills the other law" by doing no harm to a neighbor (13:9–
10).[28] Paul follows this with the command to "put on the Lord Jesus
Christ" (13:14). We remember that the "love of God" was said to be
poured into the hearts of believers "through the Holy Spirit which has
been given to us." Once more, the connections between the work of the
Spirit, the model of Christ, and more discernment, are intricate.

In Romans as in Aristotle, then, moral discernment (φρόνησις/δοκι-
μάζειν) is a fully rational exercise of the human intelligence (νοῦς) that
operates within a certain framework and according to certain first
principles. But in Romans, the measure is faith rather than virtue, and
the human νοῦς is in process of renewal by the mind of Christ, so that
the expression of φρόνησις within the community that is the body of the
Messiah is to act according to the pattern of life demonstrated above
all in the obedient faith and self-disposing love of Jesus. In a shorthand
that is anachronistic but also useful, the Holy Spirit may be seen as the
effective cause of this transformation, and the messianic pattern as the
formal cause.

Evidence from Other Letters

The *Nicomachean Ethics* proved helpful in filling what appeared at first
to be some logical gaps in Paul's moral exhortation in Romans 12–14.
Even more support is offered by three of Paul's letters—1 Corinthians,

---

[27] In his response to the original form of this paper, Professor Stephen Fowl helpfully
pointed out that Paul also anticipates chapter 12 by his heavy use of cognitive language
in Romans 6; see ἢ ἀνοεῖτε ὅτι (6:3), τοῦτο γιγνώσκοντες (6:6), πιστεύομεν (6:8), εἰδότες
(6:9) and οὕτως καὶ λογίζεσθε (6:11).

[28] I follow the minority view by translating ὁ γὰρ ἀγαπῶν τὸν ἕτερον νόμον πεπλή-
ρωκεν in this fashion. For the more common translation of ἕτερον as referring to the
neighbor ("the one who loves the other has fulfilled the law") see Dunn, *Romans*, 776–
777 and Fitzmyer, *Romans*, 678.

Philippians, and Galatians—which bring together in the same combination the elements we have identified in Romans.

1. Paul's attempt in 1 Corinthians 1:18–2:16 to rectify his readers'
perceptions concerning their call and identity is of particular interest,
not least because of his flat affirmation in 2:16, "we have the mind
of Christ" (νοῦς Χριστοῦ), which makes implicit what I suggested was
implicit in Rom 12:2. The νοῦς Χριστοῦ in this case is explicitly connected to the revelatory work of the Holy Spirit (2:10–11). In a contrast
not unlike that in Rom 12:2, Paul opposes the "spirit of the world" to
the "spirit of God" (πνεύμα τοῦ θεοῦ) which the believers have been
given (2:12a), and the function of this Spirit is to enable them to know
the things given to them by God (2:12b), in other words, to exercise
discernment. Paul insists that such discrimination is not available to
the "natural person" (ψυχικός) because they are "spiritually discerned"
(πνευματικῶς ἀνακρίνεται, 2:14).

Paul's presentation of Jesus in 1 Cor 1:18–30 is directly pertinent to his
discussion of spiritual discernment, for the cross is the supreme example of that which was "given by God" but could not be "spiritually
discerned" by those lacking God's Spirit (1:18; 2:8), whereas for believers the crucified messiah is "Christ the power of God and the wisdom
of God" (1:24). The "hidden wisdom" in Christ that the rulers of this
world could not see is the way in which God chooses to exercise power
through weakness; but this is both the message Paul proclaims and the
manner of his proclamation (2:2–4), in order that their faith be based
not in human wisdom but in the power of God (2:5). And as the rest of
1 Corinthians as well as 2 Corinthians makes abundantly clear, this same
pattern of exchange based on the obedient death and self-disposing
love of Jesus (foolishness for wisdom, weakness for strength, sin for righteousness, poverty for wealth, death for life) is to be the pattern that
structures their moral thinking within the community (see, e.g. 1 Cor
6:7; 8:11–13; 9:19–22; 10:31–11:1; 11:23–29; 13:1–7; 14:1–5; 2 Cor 4:7–12;
5:16–21; 8:9; 13:3–10).

2. In Philippians 2:2, Paul appeals to his readers to "think in the
same way" or "think one thought" (τὸ αὐτὸ φρονῆτε, τὸ ἓν φρονοῦντες).
He uses the same language for moral discernment that we found in
Aristotle and Romans (see also the use of φρονεῖν in Phil 1:7; 3:15; 19;
4:2, 10).[29] He joins this manner of moral reasoning to the comfort that

---

[29] Other studies have shown that the use of τὸ αὐτὸ φρονεῖν has a strong social
grounding in the Roman world, both in terns of consensual partnership (so J. Paul

is "in Christ" (ἐν Χριστῷ) and the fellowship that is "of the Spirit" (κοινωνία πνεύματος, 2:1). This link is unsurprising, since in Phil 1:19, Paul speaks of the πνεῦμα Ἰησοῦ Χριστοῦ that is at work among them.

In Rom 12:16, Paul warned his readers against thinking too highly of themselves and recommended associating with the lowly (ταπεινοῖς). Here in Phil 2:3, their φρόνησις is likewise to avoid overestimation of the self: "in lowliness (ταπεινοφροσύνη) reckon others as having it over yourselves." The use of "reckon" (ἡγέομαι) is important both because it will run through Paul's argument in chapters 2 and 3,[30] and also because it suggests once more the genuinely *rational* character of moral discernment. We note further that as "putting on the Lord Jesus Christ" in Rom 13:14 was opposed to "contention and jealousy" (Rom 13:13), so here the attitude of considering others more than oneself is contrasted to the measurement of strife and vainglory (Phil 2:3).

Aristotle recognized that prudence inevitably involved looking to the common good as well as that of the individual, but he agreed with the common recognition that φρόνησις had as its main task seeking what was good for the individual. As in Rom 12:4–5, Paul reverses the priority: they can look to their own interest, but must *prefer* that of others: μὴ τὰ ἑαυτῶν ἕκαστοι σκοποῦντες ἀλλὰ καὶ τὰ ἑτέρων.

Finally, as we know, Paul presents to them the pattern of the obedient servant who did not "reckon" (ἡγήσατο) his own interest in being equal to God but emptied himself out in an obedient death (Phil 2:6–11), introducing the example with the exhortation: τοῦτο φρονεῖτε ἐν ὑμῖν ὃ καὶ ἐ Χριστῷ Ἰησοῦ, a phrase almost impossible adequately to translate. The RSV does not do badly when it supplies, "Have this mind among yourselves, which is yours in Christ Jesus," but the substantive

---

Sampley, *Pauline Partnership in Christ* [Philadelphia: Fortress, 1980] 51–78) and in terms of friendship (so L. Michael White, "Morality between Two Worlds: A Paradigm of Friendship in Philippians," in *Greeks, Romans, and Christians: Essays in Honor of Abraham J. Malherbe*, ed. D.L. Balch, E. Ferguson, and W.A. Meeks [Philadelphia: Fortress Press, 1990] 201–15). That this language connotes a kind of "social consciousness of others" governed by the ideals of friendship, see also John T. Fitzgerald, "Philippians in the Light of Some Ancient Discussions of Friendship," in *Friendship, Flattery, and Frankness of Speech: Studies on Friendship in the New Testament World*, ed. J.T. Fitzgerald (NovTSup 82; Leiden: Brill, 1996) 141–62, esp. 145–46 (on the typicality of the language) and 157–60 (in relation to Aristotle's definitions of friendship). See also the article by Engberg-Pedersen in this volume.

[30] See W. S. Kurz, "Kenotic Imitation of Paul and Christ in Phil 3 and 2," in *Discipleship in the New Testament*, ed. F. Segovia (Philadelphia: Fortress, 1985) 103–126. So also it appears as an attribute of Christ in the hymn (Phil 2.6).

"mind"—however appropriate and accurate an echo of 1 Cor 2:16 and
Rom 12:2—misses the dynamism of the present imperative ("keep on
discerning"), and more important, the phrase ὁ καὶ ἐν Χριστῷ Ἰησοῦ
should be rendered, "which is also in Christ Jesus." The τοῦτο and ὁ
connect: the "way of thinking" that they should pursue is the "way of
thinking" that is found in Jesus.[31]

That Paul intends the Christ-hymn to be understood as exemplary[32]
is demonstrated by the way he proceeds to offer three other examples to the Philippians of a "moral reckoning" that gives up an individual's interest for the sake of the greater good: Timothy (2:19–24),
Epaphroditus (2:25–30), and Paul himself (3:1–16). Having given these
moral examples, he says in 3:15–16, "therefore let us think this way
(τοῦτο φρονῶμεν) whosoever are perfect (τέλειοι). And if you are thinking in another way (εἰ τι ἑτέρως φρονεῖτε), God will show you this way
(τοῦτο). But we should stay in line with what we have reached." And he
concludes, "Brethren, become imitators together and pay attention to
those who walk thus, just as you have us for a model" (3:17).

3. In Galatians 5:13–6:5, we find the same elements as in the other
letters. Most striking here is the way Paul's moral instruction is folded
almost entirely into his religious language. The struggle to act according to one's perception of what is right is now described as a battle
between the flesh and the spirit (5:17). The vice list of 5:19–21 has the
"works of the flesh" that exclude people from inheriting the "kingdom
of God" (5:21). In contrast, the virtue list of 5:22–23 is described as the
"fruit of the Spirit" (5:22). And the moral life is defined directly in terms
of the Spirit's guidance: "If you are led by the Spirit, you are not under
the law" (5:18), and "if we live by the Spirit, let us also walk by the spirit
(or: align ourselves with the Spirit)" (5:25).

Yet there is also the very clear sense that the Galatians have the
freedom to dispose of themselves in a manner not in accord with
the Spirit: they can "provide opportunity for the flesh" (5:13).[33] It is
striking that, as in the other letters we have examined, Paul does not

---

[31] For a different way of construing the syntax and theology, see White, "Morality
between Two Worlds," 208–13, who translates it: "have this mind with one another as
you also have this mind with Christ Jesus" (213).

[32] See M.D. Hooker, "Philippians 2:6–11," in *Jesus und Paulus* ed. E.E. Ellis and
E. Grasser (Goettingen: Vandenhoeck & Ruprecht, 1975) 151–64; cf. White, "Morality
between Two Worlds," 209–15.

[33] Note the similarity between Gal 5:13, μὴ τὴν ἐλευθερίαν εἰς ἀφορμὴν τῇ σαρκί and
Rom 3:14, καὶ τῆς σαρκὸς πρόνοιαν μὴ ποιεῖσθε εἰς ἐπιθυμίας.

define such fleshly behavior primarily in terms of bodily excess but in terms of anti-social and solipsistic behavior: the rivalry that leads to snapping and biting at each other to their mutual destruction (5:15), the vices of enmity, rivalry, jealousy, rage, party spirit, divisiveness, sect-forming, envy (5:20–21), the attitude of vainglory, the practice of mutual provocation, the presence of mutual envy (5:26).

Paul tells his readers that those elevating themselves are self-deluded (6:3). Rather, each person is to "test" one's own deeds (6:4) and each person is to carry one's own burden (6:5). Against solipsistic tendencies Paul proposes "serving one another through love, for the entire law is fulfilled in this one saying, you shall love your neighbor as yourself" (5:13–14). This means in practice that those who are "spiritual" (οἱ πνευματικοί) will look after a fellow-member in trouble; they will not use the failure as a basis to build themselves up, but (looking to themselves and knowing that they too can be tested) they tend to such a one in the spirit of meekness (6:1).

They are in fact to "bear one another's burdens and thus fulfill the law of Christ" (νόμος τοῦ Χριστοῦ, 6:2). Paul's constant punning makes such language hard to render. Surely here he means much the same as he meant by the νοῦς Χριστοῦ in 1 Cor 2:16, or the "way of thinking that was in Christ Jesus" in Phil 2:5, namely that pattern of life revealed in the Messiah Jesus, obedient faith toward God and loving service to others. That Paul intends his readers to reach just this conclusion is supported by 5:24: "Those who belong to Christ Jesus have crucified the flesh with its passions and desires."

Conclusion

This investigation into the connection between Paul's religious and moral language, between his pneumatology and ethics, has shown that while Paul's moral logic is remarkably similar to the character ethics of Aristotle—so much so that some of the assumptions that Paul leaves unexpressed can helpfully be supplemented by reference to the *Nico-machean Ethics*—the framework for that logic is pervasively colored by his religious convictions. Human prudential reasoning and testing is demanded, but it is informed not only by one's own mind but also by the mind of Christ. The capacity to see truly and to act appropriately is enabled by the Holy Spirit. The point of prudence is not only one's own interest but above all the good of the community that is the body of Christ. The measure of sound moral reasoning is not hitting the mean which is virtue but corresponding to the faith of Christ which is spelled out in lowly service to others. In short, the habits Paul seeks to shape in his readers are the habits of Jesus, the character he seeks to mold in his communities is the character of Jesus Christ.[34]

---

[34] It is perhaps worth noting that in the character ethics of Thomas Aquinas, which depends so heavily on Aristotle, we find in at least two places the effect of reading Paul. In *Summa Theologica* II, II, 47, 10, Thomas explicitly departs from Aristotle with respect to the private nature of prudence, using Paul—specifically 1 Cor 13:5 and 10:33—to argue that prudence must include concern for the neighbor as well as the self. And in II, II, 52, 1–2, Thomas argues that the human virtue of prudence is helped by the divine gift of the Holy Spirit, specifically the Gift of Counsel.

CREATION, SHAME
AND NATURE IN 1 COR 11:2–16.
THE BACKGROUND AND COHERENCE OF PAUL'S ARGUMENT

James W. Thompson

Locating Paul's Argument: A Scholarly Conundrum

Just as the Balkans have "produced more history than they can consume locally,"[1] the two passages in 1 Corinthians on the roles of men and women (1 Cor 11:2–16; 14:33b–36) in the Christian assembly have produced more than their share of debate. The intensity of the debate reflects not only the importance of the contested territory for resolving contemporary issues, but also the difficulty of this terrain. Almost every line in these passages is contested territory. Because the information available to us is fragmentary at best, we face numerous unresolved exegetical issues: the apparent inconsistency between the instructions for women 11:4–6 and 14:34–36 and the meaning of "head" (κεφαλή, 11:3), of the head covering (κατὰ κεφαλῆς ἔχων, 11:4), of "because of the angels" (διὰ τοὺς ἀγγέλους, 11:10), and of "custom" (συνήθεια, 11:16).

My primary concern is not to resolve the specific exegetical issues, but to determine how—or if—Paul's argument in 1 Corinthians 11:2–16 actually works. He introduces the advice on appropriate head coverings of men and women with an appeal to the created order (11:3) and then lays out his advice in 11:4–6 with an appeal to shame, indicating that the man or woman who does not dress in a manner appropriate to his/her sex "shames his/her head" (καταισχύνει τὴν κεφαλήν). A similar argument from shame is made in 1 Cor 14:35: "it is a shame" (αἰσχρόν) for a woman to speak in the assembly. In 11:7–16, Paul brings together the argument from creation in verse 3 with the instruction for differences in attire, arguing that the created order is the basis for conduct; one "ought" (ὀφείλει, vss. 7, 10) to dress in accordance with the created order. He concludes with an appeal to what "is fitting" (πρέπον, v. 13) and to nature (φύσις, v. 14), arguing that it is a "dishonor" (ἀτιμία)

---

[1] See George F. Will, *The Leveling Wind: Politics, the Culture and Other News, 1990- 1994* (New York: Viking, 1994) 355.

for a man to have long hair. In a church that has been splintered by factions, Paul ultimately to "custom" (συνήθεια) to foster harmony within the Corinthian church (11:16).

Commentators commonly remark that the argument is confusing and convoluted. Some suggest that the argument is so inconsistent with the rest of 1 Corinthians and other undisputed Pauline letters that one must assume that it is an interpolation.[2] Others argue that the passage is authentic but not coherent. According to Robin Scroggs, "In its present form this is hardly one of Paul's happier compositions. The logic is obscure at best and contradictory at worst."[3] Hans Conzelmann suggests that the section stands out from its context and that "the arguments within it are somewhat confused."[4] According to Gordon Fee, "The passage is full of notorious exegetical difficulties, including … the 'logic' of the argument as a whole."[5] Troels Engberg- Pedersen suggests that

> up to v. 11, Paul's argument is (to modern ears, at least) strange but intelligible. The underlying idea is this: there is a certain ontological hierarchy with God at the top and with men being closer to Christ and (through him) to God than women, who are one step farther down in the hierarchy.[6]

Engberg-Pedersen argues that Paul moves from a "religious" response to the issue of head coverings to a "social norm" in terms of what is "fitting" (πρέπον) or in keeping with the teaching of nature (φύσις).[7] He suggests that Paul moves from one argument to the other because the religious argument did not work. Hence Paul resorts to another strategy based on social norms, leaving the argument as a whole largely unintelligible.

Others have argued that the key to understanding Paul's argument is to recognize the problem he is facing. The problem is the real-

---

[2] See William O. Walker, "1 Corinthians 11:2–16 and Paul's Views Regarding Women," *JBL* 94 (1975) 94–110, and "The Vocabulary of 1 Corinthians 11.3–16: Pauline or Non- Pauline?" *JSNT* 35 (1989) 75–88; Lamar Cope, "1 Cor 11:2–16: One Step Further," *JBL* 97 (1978) 435–36.
[3] Robin Scroggs, "Paul and the Eschatological Woman," *JAAR* 40 (1972) 297.
[4] Hans Conzelmann, *A Commentary on the First Epistle to the Corinthians* (Hermeneia; Philadelphia: Fortress, 1975) 182.
[5] Gordon Fee, *The First Epistle to the Corinthians* (NICNT; Grand Rapids: Eerdmans, 1987) 502.
[6] Troels Engberg-Pedersen, "1 Corinthians 11:16 and the Character of Pauline Exhortation," *JBL* 110 (1994) 681.
[7] *Ibid.*

ized eschatology of some part of the Corinthian community that has resulted in their interpretation of the baptismal confession "there is no longer male or female" (Gal 3:28) as the transcending of sexual distinctions. According to Wayne Meeks, the Corinthians interpreted Paul's echo of Gen 1:27 ("male and female he created them") in the baptismal confession as the restoration of the androgynous image and demonstrated this conviction by erasing the conventional sexual distinctions in head coverings.[8] Jerome Murphy-O'Connor and Richard Oster have argued that Paul is facing a problem from both men and women who have blurred the accepted sexual distinctions.[9] Murphy-O'Connor suggests that, while Paul was not entirely comfortable with his own reasoning, it nevertheless is a coherent, "multi-pronged argument against hair arrangements which tended to blur the distinction between the sexes."[10] Paul has rejected the patriarchalist interpretation of Genesis, insisting that "Christ is the source of every (believing) person's being, but man is the source of the woman's being, and God is the source of Christ's being as savior."[11]

Recent discussion of 1 Corinthians demonstrates the problem of determining the coherence of 1 Cor 11:2–16. In what literary and historical context would the argument from creation, shame, and nature have been persuasive? The argument from nature and what "is fitting," which is echoed in Rom 1:26–27, would have been persuasive in a Stoic context, as numerous scholars have shown.[12] Popular philosophers commonly appealed to nature in determining the roles and the appropriate appearances of men and women.[13] The appeal to shame

[8] Wayne A. Meeks, "The Image of the Androgyne: Some Uses of a Symbol in Earliest Christianity," *History of Religions* 13 (1974) 189–208; Meeks discusses 1 Cor 11:2–16 on 199–203.

[9] Jerome Murphy-O'Connor, "Sex and Logic in 1 Corinthians 11:2–16," *CBQ* 42 (1980) 483; Richard Oster, "When Men Wore Veils to Worship: The Historical Context of 1 Corinthians 11:4," *NTS* 34 (1988) 502–5.

[10] Murphy-O'Connor, "Sex and Logic," 498.

[11] *Ibid.*, 499.

[12] On τὸ πρέπον in Stoic thought, see Max Pohlenz, "Τὸ πρέπον. Ein Beitrag zur Geschichte des griechischen Geistes," *NGWG* (1933) 53–92. On the Stoic argument from nature cf. Musonius Rufus, *frag.* 17. Musonius equates the life of virtue with living according to nature. See also Epictetus, *Diss.* 2.14.12; Cicero, *Leg.* 1.8.25; Seneca, *Ep.* 75; and Ps-Diogenes, *Ep.* 6.26; 7.11; 1.25; 16.25. See Abraham J. Malherbe, *The Cynic Epistles* (Missoula: Scholars Press, 1977) for the text of Ps-Diogenes.

[13] Scholars have drawn attention to numerous parallels between Paul's argument in 1 Cor 11:13–16 and the ethical appeals in popular philosophy. Dio Chrysostom applauds the evidence of appropriate customs in Tarsus, which prescribe that women should be

also has an important role within the honor-shame codes of antiquity, and it was sometimes associated with sexual codes of conduct, as in 1 Corinthians.[14] Nonetheless, the distinctive feature of Paul's argument here is the combination of the appeal to Scripture, shame, and nature. This argument would have been functional primarily within the context of Hellenistic Judaism, where philosophical and scriptural arguments were often combined. Consequently, I shall place Paul's argument in its Hellenistic-Jewish context in order to determine its coherence. I shall also raise questions about the assumed difference between the argument here and elsewhere in the Pauline corpus.

Paul's Argument in Context: Appeals to Honor and Shame

Paul's concluding statement to the discussion of the head coverings of men and women, "If anyone is disposed to be contentious (εἰ δέ τις δοκεῖ φιλόνεικος) ..." (11:16), places the discussion in the larger context of the dominant purpose of 1 Corinthians: the call for the Corinthi-

---

arrayed in such a way that no one could see any part of them (*Or.* 33). In the same oration Dio insists that men should follow the guidance of nature and refrain from shaving their beards and other hair. Such shaving is "shameful and unseemly" (αἰσχρᾷ καὶ ἀπρεπεῖ, *Or.* 33 61). On the other hand, it must be remembered that Dio himself was sometimes criticized for having long hair, which he attributed to his "Cynic" calling. The entire twenty-seventh fragment of Musonius Rufus is devoted to the cutting of the hair. He argues from nature (φύσις) that one might cut the hair to be free from a burden, but that one should not do so in order to look attractive. Such men are to be seen as "androgynes and womanish" (ἀνδρόγυνοι καὶ γυναικώδεις). See the discussion in Robert Grant, "Neither Male Nor Female," *BR* 37 (1992) 12–13. Epictetus also wrote about the way people wore their hair, arguing that young men should not attempt to make themselves beautiful by plucking out their hair. Instead, they should live in accordance with nature. (*Diss.* 3.1.14, 42–45; 3.22.10, 30; 4.1.115). Musonius Rufus (*frag.* 14) argues that marriage is ordained by creation and in accordance with nature. See the discussion in Raymond F. Collins, *First Corinthians* (SacPag 7; Collegeville: Liturgical Press, 1999) 396–98.

   [14] See Elizabeth A Clark, "Sex, Shame, and Rhetoric: Engendering Early Christian Ethics," *JAAR* 59 (1991) 221–45; Halvor Moxnes, "Honor and Shame in the Greco-Roman World," *BTB* 23 (1993) 167–76. Moxnes rightly indicates (175) that honor and shame are not static qualities. Many characteristics of the ancient honor and shame codes are not present in early Christian writings; however, a commonplace in Mediterranean societies was the association of honor and shame with sexual roles. Plutarch, for example, says that the proper woman "puts on modesty" (αἰδώς) and is deferential to her husband (*Mor.* 139C). Similarly, in 1 Tim 2:9, modest attire (μετὰ αἰδοῦς) is fitting (πρέπει) for women (cited in Moxnes, 171). Augustine argues that it is a shame for Christian women to wear make-up. *De doctr. chr.* 4.21.49–50 (cf. Clark, "Sex, Shame, and Rhetoric," 224).

ans to "speak the same thing" (1:10) and to overcome the factions and rivalry that threaten the community (1:10–11; 3:1–5). In response to the reports from Chloe's people (1:11), the visits from some Corinthians (16:17–18), and the letter from the Corinthians (1 Cor 7:1), Paul addresses numerous problems that must be overcome if unity is to prevail. Some of their questions may be requests for clarification of Paul's previous instructions (cf. 1 Cor 5:9), while other questions may reflect matters of major conflict within the church.[15] Behind these issues of sexuality and marriage (5:1–13; 6:12–7:40), Christian interaction with idolatry (8:1–11:1), and corporate worship (11:2–14:40) is the underlying problem of the arrogance of some Corinthians who celebrate wisdom, rhetoric, and individual freedom in a way that undermines the unity of the community.[16] With their slogan πάντα ἔξεστιν ("everything is permissible," 6:12; 10:23), they declare their independence from others, challenge Paul's leadership (4:1–13), and claim the right to do as they please.[17] The issues originate primarily from the socially-pretentious members of the congregation who claim honor and status for themselves and their teachers, create jealousy and strife among some members (1:11; 3:1–5) and take less fortunate members before pagan courts (6:1–11). As people of privilege, they claim the right (ἐξουσία, 8:9) to attend banquets with pagans (8:1–11:1). At the Lord's Supper, this influential minority shames those who have nothing (11:22). These issues reflect less a coherent theological position than the arrogance and anti-communal outlook of some of the Corinthians.[18] Paul's ironic comments in 4:8 ("Already you have all you want! Already you have become rich! Without us you have become kings!") is aimed not at their "realized eschatology" but at their arrogant conduct.[19]

Paul responds to this crisis with a call for unity. Following the appeal in the *propositio* to "speak the same thing" (τὸ αὐτὸ λέγειν, 1:10),[20] he

---

[15] See Jerry Sumney, *Identifying Paul's Opponents: The Question of Method in 2 Corinthians* (JSNTSup 40; Sheffield: JSOT, 1990) 97–113, on the method for reconstructing Paul's opponents and analyzing the nature of Paul's opposition. Sumney argues correctly for caution in the exercise of mirror reading of Paul's letters.

[16] Stephen M. Pogoloff, *Logos and Sophia: The Rhetorical Situation of 1 Corinthians* (SBLDS 134; Atlanta: Scholars Press, 1992) 113–19.

[17] See Peter Marshall, *Enmity at Corinth* (WUNT 2.23; Tübingen: Mohr-Siebeck, 1987) 189.

[18] Pogoloff, *Logos and Sophia*, 104.

[19] See the discussion of Marshall, *Enmity at Corinth*, 180–89.

[20] See Margaret Mitchell, *Paul and the Rhetoric of Reconciliation* (Louisville: John Knox, 1991) 198. See also Elisabeth Schüssler-Fiorenza, "Rhetorical Situation and Historical

develops his case for harmony. He proceeds with a series of arguments in which he elaborates on traditions that are already known to the Corinthians.[21] In chapters 1–4 his restatement of the content of his preaching of the cross (1:18- 25) becomes the basis for his subversion of the Corinthians' insistence on honor and status. God has chosen the foolish things of the world in order to "shame" (καταισχύνῃ) the wise (1:27). In adopting the demeanor that exemplifies the shame of the cross (4:6–13), he challenges their understanding of honor and shame. In his discussion of the relationship between the church and the world (5:1–11:1), he again presents arguments based on the traditions that he has communicated previously in order to shame the offenders (6:5; cf. 5:1–13) and to address the issues of sexuality, idolatry, and lawsuits with the emphasis on subordination to others within the community.[22] In his discussion of the assembly in 11:2–14:40, he again appeals to the community's traditions (11:2, 23–26; 12:13) as the foundation for community solidarity. Similarly, his discussion of the resurrection in chapter 15 is an elaboration on the traditions of the community. These traditions are both *halakhic* and confessional statements that Paul teaches "in all of the churches" (cf. 4:17). They are the premises he expects the Corinthian community to share. Thus in anticipation of the argument in 11:2–14:40, Paul has appealed to the community's traditions to reorient the values of the Corinthians, including their ideas about honor and shame, and he has called for conduct that conforms to these val-

·

Reconstruction in 1 Corinthians," *NTS* 33 (1987) 393. Mitchell argues correctly that 1 Corinthians is deliberative rhetoric intended to alter the behavior of the quarrelsome readers and to provide the basis for unity. My understanding of the rhetorical structure of 1 Corinthians as described here and below is indebted to Mitchell, *Rhetoric*, 200–295.

[21] For the use of traditions as rhetorical proof, see Anders Eriksson, *Traditions as Rhetorical Proof: Pauline Argumentation in 1 Corinthians* (ConBNT 29; Stockholm: Almqvist and Wiksell, 1998) 86–134. Eriksson isolates the traditions that are central to Paul's argument and demonstrates their central place in numerous units in 1 Corinthians. Important traditions include 1 Cor 8:6, 11b; 10:16; 11:23–25; 12:3, 13; 15:3–5; 16:22. These traditions are confessional statements articulating "the core commitments of the Christian faith" (p. 301). Eriksson does not list *halakhic* passages as part of the tradition, nor does he treat the only reference in 1 Corinthians that actually uses the term "tradition" (παράδοσις), i.e., in 11:2. E. Earle Ellis ("Traditions in 1 Corinthians," *NTS* 32 [1986] 481–502) demonstrates that the traditions also include Jesus traditions 1 Cor 7:10; 9:14; 11:23–26), OT *midrashim* (1 Cor 2:6–16; 10:1–13), congregational regulations (11:3–16; 14:34–36), and other aspects of Christian teaching Paul expects his readers to know (cf. οὐκ οἴδατε in 1 Cor 3:16; 5:6; 6:3, 9).

[22] On the theme of subordination to others within the community, see 1 Cor 6:7; 7:1–7; 8:11–13; 9:19–23; 11:27–34; 14:26–36.

ues. His consistent appeal to the community's traditions suggests that the argument from tradition in 11:2–16 fits well within the context of 1 Corinthians.

Following the Argument: Paul's Elaboration of the Tradition

Section 11:2–16 is a unit within the larger context of Paul's discussion of conduct in the assembly that extends through 14:40. The instructions for women form an *inclusio* for the entire discussion (11:2–26; 14:33b–36).[23] This unit is linked closely to 11:17–34 by the appeal to tradition (cf. 11:23–26), the introductory phrases "I praise" (ἐπαινῶ, 11:2) and "I do not praise" (οὐκ ἐπαινῶ, 11:17), and the appeal to shame (11:4–6, 22; cf. 12:23; cf. also ἀτιμία in 11:14). Thus the opening statement in 11:2, which forms the *exordium* to Paul's argument in this unit,[24] suggests the continuity between Paul's instructions and his conversation about the traditions elsewhere in 1 Corinthians. With the opening praise of the listeners and the introductory reference to their traditions,[25] Paul initiates the discussion by making the audience favorably disposed and by introducing the topic for discussion.[26] Verse 16, with its reference to συνήθεια ("custom"), forms an *inclusio* with v. 2. These references to the community's traditions and common practices indicate that Paul is attempting to establish common Christian practice in Corinth.[27]

---

[23] Schüssler-Fiorenza, "Rhetorical Situation," 395.

[24] See Huub van de Sandt, "1 Kor 11,2–16 als een retorische eenheid," *Bijdragen* 49 (1988) 410–25.

[25] Paul expresses his praise for the readers with the twofold ὅτι clause: "that you remember me in every way (πάντα μου μέμνησθε)" and "that you keep the traditions, just as I delivered them to you (καὶ, καθὼς παρέδωκα ὑμῖν, τὰς παραδόσεις κατέχετε)". The first clause links the new unit to the concluding line of the preceding section ("Become imitators of me"). The second clause is epexegetical, signifying the close relationship between Paul's personal example and the traditions that he has handed on (cf. 4:17). See the discussion of Wolfgang Schrage, *Der erste Brief an die Korinther* (EKK; Neukirchen: Neukirchener Verlag, 1995) 497.

[26] Praise of the audience is one dimension of the task of the *exordium* to make the audience favorably disposed. See H. Lausberg, *Handbook of Literary Rhetoric* (Eng. trans. from the 1973 German edition; Leiden: Brill, 1998) §275–77. For the importance of praise as the introduction to the oration, see the portrayal of the orator Tertullus in Acts 24:2; cf. the portrayal of Paul's oratorical skills in Acts 17:22. On epideictic letters that mix praise and blame as forms of exhortation, see the discussion of Stanley Stowers, *Letter Writing in Greco-Roman Antiquity* (LEC; Philadelphia: Westminster, 1986) 77–78; see also the article by White in this volume.

[27] See Ben Witherington, *Conflict and Community at Corinth* (Grand Rapids: Eerdmans, 1995) 236–39.

One may assume that Paul's introduction of the community's traditions here, as elsewhere in 1 Corinthians, is a response to the questions raised by the community (1 Cor 7:1). Previous references to sexual matters in 5:1–13 and 6:12–7:40 suggest that unresolved issues on sexual matters in both the private and community life of the Corinthians still prevent the harmony that Paul calls for in 1:10. Paul introduces the traditions with the confessional statement in 11:3 that will serve as the *propositio* of the argument.[28] "I want you to know" (θέλω δὲ ὑμᾶς εἰδέναι) functions as a transition marker and introduces the community's traditions (cf. Rom 1:13; 1 Cor 10:1; 11:3; 12:1; 2 Cor 1:8; Col 2:1; 1 Thess 4:13).[29] The tradition consists of an ontological hierarchy drawn from reflections on the creation story,[30] which Paul develops further in 11:7- 9, 12. The opening phrase, "The head of every man is Christ" (παντὸς ἀνδρὸς ἡ κεφαλὴ ὁ Χριστός ἐστιν), anticipates the comment in v. 7 that the man is the "image (εἰκών) and glory (δόξα) of God." The second phrase, "the head of the woman is the man" (κεφαλὴ δὲ γυναικὸς ὁ ἀνήρ), anticipates the statement that the woman is the δόξα of the man (v. 7). In 11:12, Paul summarizes the content of the *propositio* with the phrase "all things are from God" (τὰ δὲ πάντα ἐκ τοῦ θεοῦ). The third phrase of the *propositio*, "the head of Christ is God" (κεφαλὴ δὲ τοῦ Χριστοῦ ὁ θεός), with its elaboration in 11:12, resumes the articulation of the community's creation traditions, which he first employed in 8:6, using both Stoic and Platonic categories, including a "prepositional metaphysics" to distinguish the father and the son.[31] One may note also the earlier

---

[28] Van den Sandt, "1 Kor 11,2–16 als een retorische eeinheid," 411.

[29] Except for the phrase in Col 2:1, these disclosure formulae are normally stated in the negative form. In each case the disclosure form is used to take up a new topic. The nature of the transition in 11:2–3 is disputed. Schüssler-Fiorenza ("Rhetorical Situation," 395) and Engberg-Pedersen ("Pauline Exhortation," 681) interpret δέ in 11:3 as the introduction of a contrast ("but I want you to know") in which Paul corrects the Corinthian understanding. Δέ is commonly used as a simple connective and is best understood in this way here. Paul commonly cites traditions in order to begin with premises he shares with the congregation, as I have shown above.

[30] The content of the tradition has been the subject of some debate. E. Earle Ellis ("Traditions in 1 Corinthians," 492) suggests that 11:3–16 and 14:34–36 are variations on the domestic code that Paul handed on to his churches. Peter Tomson, (*Paul and the Jewish Law* [CRINT; Minneapolis: Fortress, 1990], 132–33) argues that the traditions are the common *halakhic* norms of the synagogue. In view of the parallels between 11:3 and 8:6, one may conclude that the tradition includes the order of creation.

[31] Gregory E. Sterling, "Prepositional Metaphysics in Jewish Wisdom Speculation and Early Christian Liturgical Texts," *SPhA* 9 (1997) 235. The text appears to make a distinction between the Father and the Lord through the use of different prepositional phrases (ἐξ οὗ versus δι᾽ οὗ).

claim in 3:23, "And you are of Christ, and Christ is of God" (ὑμεῖς δὲ Χριστοῦ, Χριστὸς δὲ θεοῦ). These earlier statements of the order of creation suggest that 11:3 is the elaboration of the creation traditions that Paul has already given the community. Here, however, he extends this order of creation to include sexuality. As in 1 Cor 6:16–17, Paul's supports his instructions on sexuality with an appeal to the creation traditions, which evidently derive from his earlier catechetical instruction.[32] The new dimension of the tradition in 11:3 is that, instead of listing the threefold order of God, Christ, and the community (cf. 3:23), Paul lists God, Christ, man, and woman (sequence here is Christ, man, woman, Christ, God), thus introducing the specific topic of discussion: the place of man and woman in creation. Moreover, instead of the "prepositional metaphysics" of 8:6, Paul employs the term κεφαλή ("head") to indicate the relationship between beings in anticipation of the discussion of head coverings. Κεφαλή, therefore, functions as the converse of "image" (εἰκών) and "glory" (δόξα) in 11:7 and the equivalent of the phrases "from whom" (ἐξ οὖ) and "through whom" (δι' αὐτοῦ) of 8:6.[33] Paul employs "head" (κεφαλή) in a metaphorical sense in anticipation of the topic of head coverings in 11:4–16. He is likely appealing to the interpretative tradition of Genesis 1 and 2[34] in establishing the foundation of his argument. Inasmuch as the traditions function regularly in Paul's argument as the premise he shares with the community (cf. 1 Cor 11:23–26; 15:3–5), the tradition in 11:3 is most likely the common ground he expects the Corinthians to accept.[35]

---

[32] See W. Schrage, *Der erste Brief an die Korinther*, 500. Jervis, "'But I Want You to Know ... ,' Paul's Midrashic Intertextual Response to the Corinthian Worshipers (1 Cor 11:2–16)," *JBL* 112 (1993) 231.

[33] See also 3:23.

[34] W. Schrage, *Der erste Brief an die Korinther*, 500. Gregory E. Sterling ("'Wisdom among the Perfect': Creation Traditions in Alexandrian Judaism and Corinthian Christianity," *NovT* 37 [1995] 355–86) has shown that creation traditions, especially those mediated by Philo, are important in the argument of 1 Corinthians at several places, including 1 Cor 15:44–49; 2:16–3:4; and 11:7–12.

[35] Compare the exegetical tradition that has emerged in the last generation, according to which 11:3 is Paul's correction of the Corinthians' interpretation of his own baptismal traditions. According to this view, Paul is responding to the "realized eschatology" expressed in the phrase "no longer male and female" (Gal 3:28). Robin Scroggs ("Paul and the Eschatological Woman," 291–3) argued for a pre-Pauline appropriation of this baptismal tradition, according to which the eschatological community recognizes the equality of the sexes. Wayne Meeks ("Image of the Androgyne," 165–208) argues that the baptismal reunification formula in Gal 3:28 was familiar to the congregations associated with Paul. The formula reflects an awareness of the myth of the androgynous progenitor of the human race. Later Gnostic groups, in fact, attest to the

The tradition that Paul restates in 11:3 has some parallels with Philo's interpretation of Genesis and his view of sexuality within the created order. In his interpretation of Gen 1 and 2 in *Opif.* 134–50, Philo describes the order of creation. Here as elsewhere (cf. *Leg.* 2.31; *Alleg. Gen.* 1.31), Philo distinguishes the man created from clay (Gen 2:7) from the man who is made in the image of God. The man who is made in the image of God is "incorporeal" (ἀσώματος), neither male nor female (οὔτ᾽ ἄρρεν οὔτε θῆλυ),³⁶ and in nature incorruptible (ἄφθαρτος φύσει), while the man made of clay is the empirical man, whose life of solitude and inner harmony is interrupted by the formation of the female (*Opif.* 149–51). Thus, it appears that here and elsewhere Philo

existence of those who celebrated the renewal of the bisexual image through corporate rituals. The Corinthians, according to Meeks, had accepted Paul's use of the Adam-Androgyne symbolism in the eschatological ritual of baptism but had sought to implement this new reality in practice as a part of their realized eschatology. Antoinette Wire (*The Corinthian Women Prophets* [Minneapolis: Fortress, 1990] 116–34) follows the view that the women prophets had interpreted the baptismal confession to validate their new status. Jervis ("'I Want You to Know,'" 231–38) argues that Paul had originally taught the Corinthians the creation story of Genesis 1:27, which the Corinthian "spirituals" have interpreted "in the context of a Jewish-Hellenistic understanding of restoration of the original (genderless) image of God." Paul now counters, according to Jervis, with an intertextual reading of Gen 2:4b–25 in order to emphasize that the divine image is in two genders.

I find this argument unconvincing for the following reasons: 1) it assumes far more than one can demonstrate about the Corinthian "spirituals" and their realized eschatology; 2) it is based on the assumption that the formula "no longer male and female" in Gal 3:28 was the common property of all of the Pauline churches (whereas the "reunification formula" [cf. 1Cor 12:13; Col 3:11], like other Pauline traditions, might well take numerous forms); 3) neither the Gnostic nor Rabbinic texts provide direct or indirect information about the situation in Corinth, even if they do show that similar interpretations of Gen 1–2 were later commn; and 4) [contral Jarvis] the fact that Paul appeals to the second creation story in 1Cor 6:12–20 indicates that he has also interpreted Gen 2:4b–25 for them in his prior instruction (οὐκ οἴδατε, 6:15–16); it was probably already part of the midrashic tradition that had formed the basis of his/their *paradosis* in 1Cor 11:2–3, as argued also by Meeks ("Image of the Androgyne," 196, 202). We are not certain precisely what questions evoked Paul's response in 1Cor 11:2–16. The move toward liberation in Corinth is very likely reflected in Paul's response. In 11:3 Paul is probably not correcting the Corinthians' exegesis of Genesis, but establishing a common ground for his argument. To suggest that is opposing a coherent theological perspective or interpretation of the tradition goes beyond the evidence.

³⁶ For this phrase elsewhere in Philo, see also *Somn.* 2.184; cf. *Ebr.* 212 for the phrase οὔτ᾽ ἄρρην … οὔτε θῆλεια. In both instances the reference is to a eunuch in contrast to a whole man or woman. Thus the passage refers to asexuality rather than bisexuality. See Richard Baer, *Philo's Use of the Categories Male and Female* (ALGHJ; Leiden: Brill, 1970) 32.

also uses the Adam-Androgyne myth in interpreting the creation story (including Gen 1 & 2).[37] Thus, according to Philo, the polarity of male and female belongs to that part of the created order that is corruptible and subject to change. This polarity becomes the basis for his numerous comments about the roles of men and women.[38]

Κεφαλή ("head") is an unusual term in Paul's description of the order of creation. Although the term is clearly metaphorical here, the signification of the metaphor is disputed. Some have suggested, largely on the basis of the argument in vv. 7–9, that it has the meaning of "source" rather than preeminence.[39] This argument is supported by the claim that κεφαλή is not a metaphor for rule or superiority in the LXX or in the Graeco-Roman world.[40] That κεφαλή can mean "source" may also be suggested by the statement in 11:8, that woman is "from the man," and parallel expressions in 3:23 and 8:6. A review of the relevant literature suggests, however, that one cannot easily divorce κεφαλή as source from κεφαλή as a term for ontological preeminence.

---

[37] Although Philo's language has echoes of the myth of the androgynous being (cf. Plato, *Symposium* 189C–193D), "neither male nor female" in Philo is to be understood as "asexual" rather than androgynous, at least when applied to the heavenly human (ἄνθρωπος). However, in *Opif.* 151–52 (cf. *Q.Gen.* 1.25) Philo's language suggests that he employs the myth of an androgynous primal human to interpret Gen 2:21–25, the story of Eve's creation and the origination of marriage as a reuniting "as it were, divided halves of a single living creature" (καθάπερ ἑνὸς ζῴου διττὰ τμήματα). Cf. Meeks, "Image of the Androgune," 186; Baer, *Philo's Use of Male and Female*, 38. Baer (83–84) also argues that *Opif.* 136–70 was derived from an even earlier Jewish source that contained this interpretation of Genesis. It is noteworthy, however, that Philo does *not* use the term "androgyne" (ἀνδρόγυνος) itself in these contexts, since he gives it a more negative connotation (so *Spec. leg.* 3.37–50). Philo elsewhere (*Contemp.* 63) speaks of "myths of double-bodied men" (δισωμάτους) in such a way to suggest that he also knew, but vigorously disapproved, of the Platonic version and its implications.

[38] *Ibid.*, 35–44.

[39] See Scroggs, "Paul and the Eschatological Woman," 298; Murphy-O'Connor, "The Non-Pauline Character of 1 Corinthians 11:2–16?" 492–93.

[40] *Ibid.*, 503. See Joseph Fitzmyer, "Another Look at ΚΕΦΑΛΗ in 1 Corinthians 11.3," *NTS* 35 (1989), for numerous examples of κεφαλή in the OT and in Philo as a term for preeminence or authority. A. C. Perriman ("The Head of a Woman: The Meaning of ΚΕΦΑΛΗ in 1 Cor 11:3," *JTS* n.s. 45 [1994]), in response to Fitzmyer, argues that none of the texts adduced by Fitzmyer from the OT and Philo connotes authority of one person over another. Perriman, however, draws a narrow distinction between authority and preeminence, acknowledging that the latter is commonly associated with κεφαλή in the relevant texts.

The Use of κεφαλή ("Head") in Philo

Philo of Alexandria offers an especially useful comparison to Paul at this point. Scholars have observed that Paul's christological statements in 1 Corinthians, especially in 8:6 and 11:3 (cf. 10:4), are parallel in numerous respects to Philo's description of God's relation to the world.[41] Philo also offers an important parallel in his metaphorical use of κεφαλή. When he describes the nature of the universe, he speaks of heaven as the κεφαλή (*Post.* 53.5–6) and earth as the "foot" (*Somn.* 1.145). In several instances, Philo describes the head as the governing part of the body of the human. According to *Opif.* 119, "It is the most princely [or ruling] part of the animal" (τὸ ἡγεμονικώτατον ἐν ζῴῳ); words issue from it, undying laws of an undying soul, by means of which the life of reason is guided. It is the seat of reason (λογικός, *Leg.* 1.70.6; 171.6) and the "first and highest part of the reasoning creature" (πρῶτον τοῦ ζῴου καὶ ἀνωτάτο, *Leg. all.* 1.71.6; cf. *Leg.* 3.116; 4.92).[42] Nature confers sovereignty of the body (τοῦ σώματος ἡγεμονίαν) and "the possession of the citadel as the most suitable position for its kingly rank" (τόπον οἰκειότατον ὡς βασιλεῖ τὴν ἄκραν) to the head (*Spec.* 3.184). Because of the preeminence of the head to the body, the head may rightly be called "king" (*Leg.* 3.115). This metaphorical usage, drawn largely from Platonic terminology, indicates that for Philo the head is both the source and the ruler of the organism.

Philo places the head at the top of the hierarchy of being in which all other parts of the body are subordinate to the head. This use is clearly indicated in Philo's allegorical comments on Deut 28:13 ("The Lord will make you the head and not the tail: you shall be always at the top and never at the bottom"). Philo concludes from the passage, "For as in an animal the head is the first and the best part and the tail the last and meanest, ... so too, the virtuous one, whether single man or people, will be the head of the human race (κεφαλὴν μὲν τοῦ ἀνθρωπείου γένους) and all the others like the limbs of a body which draw their life from the forces in the head and at the top" (*Praem.* 125). In this context, κεφαλή expresses both sovereignty and source of life.

---

[41] See Sterling, "Prepositional Metaphysics," 219–238. Sterling demonstrates the relation of both Philo and Paul to Stoic and Platonic formulations.

[42] Translation of Philo, unless otherwise noted, is by F. H. Colson and G. H. Whitaker (LCL; Cambridge: Harvard University Press, 1962).

Philo's allegorical treatment of biblical texts demonstrates how easily he can move between the text's literal meaning and his own metaphorical understanding of κεφαλή. The anointing of the head of the priest with oil signifies that "his ruling faculty (τὸ ἡγεμονικόν) is illumined with a brilliant light" (*Fug.* 110). According to the allegorical interpretation of Num 6:5 ("Holy, suffering the hair of his head to grow"), Philo says that "this means that he must foster the young growth of virtue's truths in the mind which rules its being" (*Deus.* 88). Philo refers to the "uncovering of the head" as the symbol of shame. He refers to shame of the captured woman whose head is shaved (*Virt.* 111), and in two instances he treats the trial of the suspected adulteress (Num 5:18), who comes before the priest with her head uncovered (cf. *Spec. leg.* 3.60; *Cher.* 17). In *Cherubim* 17, he indicates that this action involves the stripping of the dominant principles of one's being. These biblical references provide the occasion, therefore, for Philo to treat κεφαλή as a metaphor for the highest part of one's being.

Philo also uses κεφαλή as a term for the preeminence among people. Esau is the κεφαλή of all members of his clan (*Congr.* 66.1). Philo speaks in glowing terms of Ptolemy Philadelphus, saying, "As the head is the highest of the body, so is he head of the kings" (καθάπερ ἐν ζῴῳ τὸ ἡγεμονεῦον κεφαλὴ τρόπον τινὰ τῶν βασιλέων, *Mos.* 2.30).

This usage in Philo suggests that κεφαλή in 1 Cor 11:3 is intelligible against the background of the order of creation that is known in Philo. Κεφαλή signifies both source and sovereignty in a hierarchical relationship that is grounded in creation. A similar understanding of subordination is reflected in 1 Cor 15:28, where Paul anticipates the time when the son "will be subjected to the one who has put all things in subjection to him" (ὑποταγήσεται τῷ ὑποτάξαντι αὐτῷ τὰ πάντα). This usage in 1 Cor 11:3 anticipates the elaboration of that image in Colossians and Ephesians, where Christ is both the head of the body, the church (Col 1:18), and the head over "every rule and authority" (Col 2:10).

The hierarchy of being expressed in the *propositio* in 11:3 is the foundation for the *probatio* in 11:4–16. In the first part of the *probatio*, 11:4–6, it becomes the basis for the argument about head coverings. In parallel statements Paul says of men who wear head coverings and women who do not wear head coverings that each "disgraces the head" (καταισχύνει τὴν κεφαλήν, 11:4–5a), and in 11:5b–6 he supports this claim. The fact that the additional comment in 11:5b–6 applies only to women suggests that their attire is actually Paul's concern. For Paul, the woman without the head covering disgraces her head insofar as "it is one and the same thing as being shaved" (τῇ ἐξυρημένῃ). This claim becomes intelligible against the background of the midrashic reading of OT texts, according to which the woman's shaved head is the symbol of shame (cf. Deut 21:12; 2 Sam 10:4; 1 Chron 19:4; Isa 7:20). Paul's equation of the uncovered head with the shaved head in 11:5b is probably based on Num 5:18 (LXX), according to which the priest "will uncover the head" (ἀποκαλύψει τὴν κεφαλὴν) of a woman suspect of adultery. This reading lies behind the conclusion in 11:6, which is expressed in parallel but antithetical terms: "If a woman does not cover herself, let her be shorn (κειράσθω); but if it is a shame (αἰσχρόν) for a woman to have her hair cut off (κείρασθαι) or to be shaved (ξυρᾶσθαι), let her be covered." Here Paul appeals to what is self-evident to the readers (ἐν ὑμῖν αὐτοῖς κρίνατε) by means of two rhetorical questions: "Is it fitting (πρέπον) for a woman to pray to God with her head uncovered?" And "Does not nature (φύσις) teach you that if a man wears long hair, it is degrading (ἀτιμία) for him, but if a woman has long hair it is her glory (δόξα)?" Here, as in 14:35, Paul argues for gender distinctions based on an appeal to shame. This appeal to shame is consistent with Paul's subversion of the honor/shame values in chapters 1–4 (cf. 6:5). Antoinette Wire has correctly noted that Paul's appeal to shame is intended to subvert the values of those who insist on honor.[43] He assumes that the Corinthians will acknowledge the force of this argument, which has moved from the order of creation to the shamefulness of conduct that violates this order.

Honor/Shame in Paul and Philo

Paul also associates the order of creation with both shame and gender distinctions in Rom 1. In Rom 1:24 Paul goes on to describe the "unnatural" use of sexuality. Men and women turned to their own "to dishonor their bodies" (τοῦ ἀτιμάζεσθαι τὰ σώματα αὐτῶν, 1:24) insofar as their "uses" [or "needs"] were "contrary to nature" (τὴν φυσικὴν χρῆσιν εἰς τὴν παρὰ φύσιν, 1:26). Paul speaks here of a break with the order of the world that becomes visible in social life,[44] and he speaks of

---

[43] Wire, *Corinthian Women Prophets*, 119. Note also the reference to δόξα om 11:7.

[44] Moxnes, "Honor, Shame, and the Outside World in Romans," 209.

women who violate their sexual roles (1:26). It is for men, however, that he reserves his harshest indictment, speaking of their "indecency" (τὴν ἀσχημοσύνην, 1:27).[45]

Anthropologists appear to be unanimous that honor and shame are sexually coded in the Mediterranean society.[46] The literature of Hellenistic Judaism, however, provides the background that is most helpful in our understanding of Paul's argument. One may observe the argument in Ps-Phocylides, who wrote possibly between 30 BCE and 40 CE.[47] He advised parents, "If a child is a boy, do not let locks grow on his head. Braid not his crown nor make cross-knots on the top of his head. Long hair is not fit for men, but for voluptuous women" (ἄρσεσιν οὐκ ἐπέοικε κομᾶν, χλιδαναῖς δὲ γυναιξίν). This author also employs the argument from nature to instruct his pupil on the exercise of sexuality within the constraints of nature. "Transgress not for unlawful sex the natural limits of sexuality."[48]

Philo of Alexandria offers the best parallel to Paul's transition from hierarchy of being to the appeal to shame. He uses the term αἰδώς ("shame") for the awareness of one's position in the greater scheme of things in the cosmic order.[49] "Shame" here is the feeling of the human in the presence of God (*Mut.* 201, *Mos.* 1.84; *Legat.* 293), of pupils for teachers (*Spec. leg.* 4.140; *Legat.* 5), of youth for elders and parents (*Post.* 181, *Mut.* 217, *Prob.* 87, *Ios.* 257), and of subjects for rulers (*Ios.* 107, *Mos.* 1.161, *Praem.* 97; *Legat.* 276, 352). It is also the attitude Philo prescribes for women.[50]

Philo is significant for our purposes insofar as he combines Graeco-Roman appeals to shame with the allegorical interpretation of Scripture. One may observe that Philo moves easily from the head as metaphor of sovereignty to the woman's uncovered head as the symbol of shame. His treatment of the suspected adulteress in Num 5:18 is of special significance. According to the LXX, as part of the ritual the priest will "uncover the head" (ἀποκαλύψει τὴν κεφαλήν) of the woman. In *Cher.* 17.3 Philo interprets the passage allegorically as a reference to the

---

[45] *Ibid.*, 213.
[46] Clark, "Sex, Shame, and Rhetoric," 227.
[47] P. W. van der Horst, *The Sentences of Pseudo-Phocylides with Introduction and Commentary* (SVTP 4; Leiden: Brill, 1978) 81–83. See also Murphy-O'Connor, "Sex and Logic in 1 Corinthians 11:2–16," 485.
[48] van der Horst, *Pseudo-Phocylides*, 190.
[49] Dorothy Sly, *Philo's Perception of Women* (BJS 209; Atlanta: Scholars Press, 1990) 204.
[50] *Ibid.*

fate of the soul that has been stripped bare, resulting in the exposure
of the nakedness of the soul. Philo gives a more extended discussion
of the passage in *Spec.* 3.56–60: "The priest taking the offering hands
it to the woman and removes her kerchief (ἐπίκρανον),[51] in order that
she may be judged with her head bared and stripped of the symbol
of modesty (αἰδοῦς), regularly worn by women who are wholly innocent" (ἀναιτίοις, 3.56).[52] Philo's emphasis on her lack of head covering
is suggested when he repeats the comment that she comes before the
priest "with uncovered head" (ἀκατακαλύπτῳ τῇ κεφαλῇ, *Spec. leg.* 3.60).
When he describes the treatment of captive women in *Virt.* 111, he again
associates the uncovered head with shame: "And you will give this alle-
viation if you shave the hair of her head (τὰς ... τῆς κεφαλῆς τρίχας
ἀποκείρας) and pare her nails."

Philo's view must be seen in the larger context of his views on modesty, shame, and appropriate dress. Dorothy Sly has shown that, "Of
the four traditional Greek virtues, σωφροσύνη,[53] with its sister virtue αἰδώς, is the only one Philo explicitly expects of women."[54] Conversely,
he associates shame with the inappropriate dress of the harlot (*Spec. leg.*
3.51), "that stranger to decency and modesty (κοσμιότητος καὶ αἰδοῦς)
and temperance and the other virtues." He says that "she casts shame
upon the undying beauty of the mind (τὸ μὲν τῆς διανοίας ἀθάνατον
κάλλος αἰσχύνει) and prefers in honour the short-lived comeliness of the
body."

One may also note Philo's argument that appropriate dress for men
involves maintaining sexual distinctions. He is vitriolic in his denunciation of men who transgress the boundaries set by nature. In *Spec.
leg.* 3.37–50, Philo describes pederasty as a "shame" (ὄνειδός) even to

---

[51] Ἐπίκρανον, which can mean the top of a wall, can be used for any kind of
headdress or hat. See LSJ, s. v.

[52] Literally, "in order that she may be judged with her head being naked, having
been stripped of the symbol of modesty, which it is a custom to use by those who are
innocent in every way."

[53] Σωφροσύνη is used in classical texts for "soundness of mind," "temperance," or
"moderation." See LSJ., s.v.

[54] Sly, *Philo's Perception of Women*, 206. Some examples of Philo's application of the
term ἰδώς to women include the following: "The maiden Virtue possesses modesty,
and it also follows in her train (*Sac.* 26f.); the blushes of the Hebrew midwife include
her modesty (*Heres.* 128); despite her outward appearance, Tamar has inward chastity
and modesty (*Cong.* 124); the daughters of Zelophedad approached the ruler 'in the
modesty appropriate to maidens' (*Mos.* 2.234); brothers should not insult the modesty of
maidens: "maidens must blush, why drive the hue from their cheeks?' (*Spec. leg.* 3.25)."

mention (3.37, 49). Those who adopt the role of the passive partners
succumb to the "disease of effemination" (νόσον θήλειαν, 3.37). They
transform the male nature to the female, "counterfeiting the law of
nature" (τὰ φύσεως νόμισμα παρακόπτοντα), thus violating the law that
ordains that the ἀνδρόγυνος should be put to death (3.38). For Philo
"androgyne" here is synonymous with the "effeminate" male as a passive sexual object. He speaks of "how conspicuously they braid and
adorn their heads, and how they scrub and paint their faces with cosmetics and pigments and the like" (3.37). In *Contempl.* (52), he makes a
similar denunciation of the use of slave boys in the symposium, noting
that the slave boys use cosmetics and elaborate hair styles associated
with women to enhance their beauty.[55] Such people are a disgrace to
themselves, their house, and the whole human race (*Spec. leg.* 3.38).

When Paul instructs the women to limit their speech to the home,
arguing in 1 Cor 14:35 that it is "shameful (αἰσχρόν) for a woman to
speak in church," he is again consistent with Philo's views. In *Spec. leg.*
3.169, Philo writes,

> Market-places and council-halls and law-courts and gatherings and
> meetings where a large number of people are assembled, and open-air
> life with full scope for discussion and action—all these are suitable to
> men both in war and peace. The women are best suited to the indoor
> life which never strays from the house, within which the middle door is
> taken by the maidens as their boundary, and the outer door by those who
> have reached full womanhood.

Even when she goes to the temple, "she should take pains to go, not
when the market is full, but when most people have gone" (*Spec. leg.*
3.171). To exceed the limits nature has given her by being outside the
home—at the marketplace, in war, or at gymnastic events—exposes her
to shame (αἰσχύνη, *Spec. leg.* 3.173).

The Argument from Creation in Paul and Philo

Philo's concerns illuminate the issues that Paul faces in 1 Corinthians.
For Philo, the order of creation requires a distinction between the
sexes that is demonstrated in the appropriate covering of the head. In
his midrashic treatment of Pentateuchal laws, Philo demonstrates that
women violate the order of creation when they appear without a head

---

[55] On long hair as one of the distinguishing characteristics of men who adopted a
feminine appearance, see H. Herter, "Effeminatus," *RAC* 4.632.

covering, while men violate the order of creation when they "braid
and adorn their heads." To violate nature's dictates is to engage in
shameful conduct. Both Philo and Paul indicate that it is a shame for a
woman to appear "with uncovered head" (ἀποκατακαλύπτῳ τῇ κεφαλῇ,
Spec. leg. 3.60; 1 Cor 11:5). The similarity of wording between Philo and
Paul suggests that both are following the same midrashic traditions in
interpreting the Torah's mandates on the appropriate head coverings of
men and women. The similarity between Philo and Paul also clarifies
the situation Paul is facing at Corinth. He is not addressing men who
wear veils, nor is he addressing the problem of women who let their
hair down. Like Philo, he assumes that the dictates of Torah demand
that women wear head coverings and that men avoid any associations
with homosexuality.

For Philo, the demands of God that are given in the Torah are
rooted in the laws of nature.[56] Philo speaks in Stoic terms of the "right
reason of nature" (τῆς φύσεως ὀρθός λόγος) as the "constitution" of the
cosmos viewed as a city (*Ios.* 31; cf. *Mos.* 1.48).[57] In keeping with this
equation is Philo's portrayal of the true cosmopolitan as the one who
acts according to the will of nature.[58] According to *Opif.* 3, "The world
is in harmony with the law, and the law with the world, and … the
man who observes the law is constituted thereby a loyal citizen of the
world, regulating his doings by the purpose and will of nature." Indeed,
many individual laws are presented as laws of nature (*Praem.* 108; *Spec.
leg.* 2.129f; 3.112; *Decal.* 132; *Sobr.* 25).[59]

Philo insists that nature gives humanity moral instruction. According
to *Q.Gen.* 3.27, nature wipes out and cleanses the wrong kind of learning, while at the same time it "offers an abundance of instruction and
guidance." According to *Q.Gen.* 3.54, virtues are "being taught beforehand by nature what is sovereign and what is unservile."

Philo, following the Stoics,[60] speaks of the "use prescribed by nature"
(κατὰ φύσιν χρῆσις) of the seven natural capacities of the human: sexual
potency, speech, and the five senses (*Mut.* 111f.). Hence Philo insists that
the laws governing sexual distinctions are founded on the law of nature.

---

[56] See Hindy Najman, "The Law of Nature and the Authority of the Mosaic Law,"
SPhA 11 (1999) 55–73 and Richard Horsley, "The Law of Nature in Philo and Cicero,"
HTR 71 (1978) 35–59.
[57] Helmut Koester, "Φύσις," *TDNT* 9.269.
[58] *Ibid.*
[59] *Ibid.*
[60] Chrysippus, *Fr* 389 in von Arnim, *SVF* 3.94; cited in Koester, "Φύσις," 269.

He consistently describes sexual aberrations as a violation of the natural law. According to *Abr.* 135, the inhabitants of Sodom "threw off their necks the law of nature" (τὸν τῆς φύσεως νόμον). In his discussion of sexual laws in *Spec. leg.* 3, he consistently interprets the law of Moses to demonstrate that the dictates of nature provide the norm for human existence. Those who quench the life of the seed as it drops to the ground are the "enemies of nature" (ἐχθροὶ τῆς φύσεως, 3.36). The "man-woman" (ἀνδρόγυνος) debases "the sterling coin of nature" (3.38) by engaging in pleasures that are against nature (παρὰ φύσιν, 3.39 [my translation]).[61] The harlot has "corrupted the gifts of nature" (τὰς τῆς φύσεως διαφθείρασα χάριτας, 3.51, [my translation]).

Philo's argument from nature is the basis for his appeal to shame in his description of women who lack the head covering as a symbol of modesty and men who adorn their hair. He also appeals to nature when he indicates that women should avoid the sporting arena (*Spec.* 3.176), where the modesty required of women is violated. Related to Philo's appeal to modesty to justify the sequestering of women and his equation of law and nature is his reliance on arguments about what is fitting and suitable, which are expressed with the synonymous use of ἁρμορτεῖν ("to be appropriate"), πρέπειν ("to be fitting"), and ἀκόλουθον τῇ φύσει ("in conformity with nature").[62] One may note this synonymous use in *Spec. leg.* 3.48, where he describes the laws prohibiting that which is παρὰ φύσιν ("contrary to nature") and requiring that which is ἀναλόγως τοῦ πρέποντος καὶ ἀκολούθου τῇ φύσει ("what was in accord with decency and in accordance with nature"). One who does not live in accord with nature "cares nothing for seemliness" (*Spec. leg.* 3.50: μέλει τοῦ πρέποντος οὐκετʼ). Women do not enter wars or even fights because of "the fitness of things" (τὸ πρέπον, *Spec. leg.* 3.172), which is based on what nature permits (*Spec. leg.* 3.173).

Philo's comments about the attire and place in society that are fitting for men and women belong to the larger context of reflections on the place of men and women. Whereas he devotes an entire treatise, *De congressu*, to a reasoned account of male education, he says that girls should have "education as befits maidens" before entering a "suitable

---

[61] For the meaning of ἀνδρόγυνος in Philo, see Holder Szesnat, "'Pretty Boys' in Philo's *De vita comptemplativa*," *SPhA* 10 (1998) 98. He argues that the term was used not only for congenital hermaphrodites but also for a man who transgressed gender boundaries: "For Philo, the connotations are, then, both gender-transgressions in the form of dress, hairstyles, cosmetics, gait, *and* the passive role in sexual intercourse."

[62] Sly, *Philo's Perception of Women*, 206.

marriage" (γάμου τοῦ πρέποντος *Spec. leg.* 2.125). The world of business, government, war, and action "are suitable" (ἀνδράσιν ἐφαρμόζουσι) for men, whereas women "are suited" to life behind closed doors (*Spec. leg.* 3.169).[63]

Conclusion

Philo's perspective offers helpful insights for our grasp of the dynamics of Paul's argument in 1 Cor 11:2–16. Although they address very different issues—the case law for prostitutes and adulteresses in Philo and the proper head covering in Paul—both argue in similar ways. Both Paul and Philo regard the created order as the basis for the specific conduct of men and women in a public place. The violation of the order of creation, which is evident in the specific laws, is the source of shame. The appropriate conduct, according to both writers, is to conduct oneself as "nature teaches," that is, in accordance with what is fitting. Thus Paul's argument in 1 Cor 11:2–16 would not have been perceived as convoluted to one who was schooled in a tradition similar to that of Philo. The argument works within the assumptions of one who was schooled in the exegetical traditions of Hellenistic Judaism.

Philo's treatment of the conduct of men and women provides additional insight about the specific requirements that Paul places on the Corinthians. Commentators have debated precisely what Paul means by κατὰ κεφαλῆς ἔχων (11:4) and ἀκατακαλύπτῳ τῇ κεφαλῇ (11:5). Philo, as noted above,[64] uses the latter phrase in the context of his midrash on Num 5:18 to refer not to the woman's hairdo but to the head-dress that was the symbol of the woman's modesty. His midrashic treatment of Scripture, combined with his Stoic perspective, leads him also to argue that long hair for men is the sign of the ἀνδρόγυνος. This background suggests that Paul is following a similar midrashic tradition drawn from OT texts that describe the head coverings of women. He is not addressing Roman customs in which men wore veils to worship. Nor is his argument especially unusual in 1 Corinthians, where he elsewhere argues from the community's traditions and from creation. Like Philo, he is concerned that men and women not blur sexual distinctions by their attire and conduct.

---

[63] *Ibid.*
[64] See above at n. 43

One may observe the continuity between Paul's argument in 1 Cor 11:2–16 and later discussions in the disputed Pauline letters. The basis of Paul's argument in 1 Cor 11:2–16—that Christ is the κεφαλή of the man, who is the κεφαλή of the woman in an order of creation—is developed in Colossians and Ephesians, where Christ is the head of the church (Eph 1:23; Col 1:18), of every principality and power (Col 2:10), and of the husband (5:22), who is the head of the wife. Although the language of Colossians and Ephesians reflects cosmological and theological interests that are not present in 1 Cor 11:2–16, these epistles express a hierarchy of being that is a development of, but not a radical departure from, the earlier instructions. This hierarchy is the basis for social relations within the church and family.

Although Paul's argument is convoluted to modern readers and his conclusions disturbing to contemporary sensibilities, ancient readers most likely would have regarded the argument as neither convoluted nor disturbing. The argument reflects an interpretative tradition within Hellenistic Judaism, according to which the order of creation establishes a hierarchy of being that determines the conduct that is either shameful or fitting for men and women. The argument in 1 Cor 11:2–16 demonstrates that Paul is not a first-century egalitarian whose pronouncements were quickly undermined by followers who retreated to the hierarchical views that were prevalent in their own society. Paul's argument rests on hierarchical assumptions that were widely shared among Hellenistic Jewish writers.

CIVIC CONCORD AND COSMIC HARMONY
SOURCES OF METAPHORIC MAPPING
IN *1 CLEMENT* 20:3

Cilliers Breytenbach

Introduction

In his Carl Newell Jackson Lectures on "early Christianity and Greek *paideia*," delivered at Harvard in 1960, Werner Jaeger briefly analysed *1 Clement* against the background of the Greek rhetorical tradition, comparing Clement to Demosthenes.[1] By drawing on the topos that internal discord had overthrown great kings and powerful states, Clement had reverted to classical Greek tradition. Jaeger reminds us:

> "…Concord (*homonoia*) had always been the slogan of peacemaking leaders and political educators, of poets, sophists, and statesmen in the classical age of the Greek *polis*. In the Roman period, Concordia had even become a goddess. … Philosophers had praised her as the divine power that yokes the universe and upholds world order and world peace. So we are not surprised, and yet again we are, when we see Clement refer in that wonderful twentieth chapter of his letter to the cosmic order of all things as the ultimate principle established by the will of God, the creator, as a visible model for human life and peaceful cooperation."[2]

Jaeger, who suggested that Clement used a Stoic source for his argument,[3] was not the first and the only one to investigate the Stoic background of *1 Clement* 20. Long before Jaeger, G. Bardy and Louis Sanders followed Rudolf Knopf's commentary,[4] and drew the attention to the parallels, especially between chapter 20 and several authors.[5] It was Jaeger, however, who stressed the importance of the notion of ὁμόνοια. He argued that *1 Clement* stands in the tradition of promoting concord

---

[1] W. Jaeger, *Early Christianity and Greek Paideia* (Cambridge: Belknap, 1962) 12–26.

[2] *Ibid.*, 13–4.

[3] Cf. *ibid.*, 15 with note 8.

[4] Cf. R. Knopf, *Die Apostolischen Väter. Die Lehre der zwölf Apostel. Die zwei Clemensbriefe* (Tübingen: Mohr, 1920) 75–6.

[5] Cf. G. Bardy, "Expressions stoïciennes dans la 1ª Clementis," *RSR* 12 (1922) 73–85; L. Sanders, *L'Hellénisme de Saint Clément de Rome et le Paulinisme* (Studia Hellenistica; Louvain: Peeters, 1943) 121–30; Ch. Eggenberger, *Die Quellen der politischen Ethik des 1. Klemensbriefes* (Zürich: Zwiingli-Verlag, 1961).

using the genus *symbouleutikon*.[6] In an unsurpassed study published in Dutch only, Willem van Unnik followed Jaeger in classifying *1 Clement* as a letter using symbouleutic (deliberative) rhetoric in order to bring about peace and concord in the strife torn Corinthian church.[7] Following the line of argumentation of the letter, he demonstrated the parallel use of the notion of concord and peace by Dio Chrysostom, Plutarch, Lucian, Dio Cassius, Epictetus and Aelius Aristides.

Because Van Unnik ventures to prove his case that *1 Clement* should be classified as συμβουλή, he does not analyse the specific use of ὁμόνοια in 20:3. The use of the term concord to refer to cosmic harmony is less usual than its combination with peace in reference to civic unanimity. To use the word ὁμόνοια ("oneness of mind", "unanimity", "concord")[8] to refer to the ἁρμονία in the universe is clearly a metaphor. I shall pursue this line of thought further.

In this regard, Van Unnik's suggestion that *1 Clement* be studied against the background of the symbouleutic rhetoric of Dio Chrysostom and Aelius Aristides deserves to be followed. A survey of the use of ὁμόνοια in the Hellenistic and early Roman periods[9] has confirmed that in the use of the example of cosmic concord, Dio Chrysostom and Aelius Aristides, *inter alia*, prove to be the closest to *1 Clement* 20:3.[10] Since the origin and development of the notion of concord have been studied elsewhere,[11] we can thus turn our attention to those cases where ὁμόνοια was associated with cosmic harmony.

---

[6] Cf. W. Jaeger, "Echo eines unbekannten Tragikerfragmentes in Clemens' Brief an die Korinther," *Rheinisches Museum für Philologie* 102 (1959) 330–40.

[7] Cf. W.C. van Unnik, *Studies over de zogenaamde Eerste Brief van Clemens* (I Het Litteraire Genre; Amsterdam: Noord Hollandische Uitg., 1970).

[8] Cf. LSJ, *s.v.*

[9] For semantic reasons I confined the search (using the TLG, CD Rom #D) to the Greek expression. The editions cited are those in the canon of the TLG. For the use of *concordia* cf. P. Jal, "Pax civilis" – "concordia," *Revue des Études Latines* 34 (1961) 210–31.

[10] Incidentally, the linguistic evidence has pointed in a direction where I could follow the example of Abraham Malherbe's oeuvre.

[11] Cf. J. de Romilly, "Vocabulaire et propagande ou les premiers emplois de mot ὁμόνοια," in *Mélanges de Linguistique et de Philologie Grecques offerts à Pierre Chantraine* (Paris: Klinksieck; 1972) 199–209; A. Moulakis, *Homonoia, Eintracht und die Entwicklung eines politischen Bewusstseins*, (Schriften reihe zur Politik und Geschichte; Munich: P. List, 1977); C. Breytenbach, "Harmonie im All und Eintracht in der korinthischen Gemeinde. Beobachtungen anhand von 1 Klem 20" (paper submitted to the "Harnack-Runde der Berliner Wissenschaftlichen Gesellschaft," 10 February 2000). To be published in the yearbook of the society.

Cosmic Concord in Hellenistic Thought

The expansion of the Greek concept of concord since Alexander the Great might have enhanced the use of the notion in order to describe relationships in other fields than those normally associated with ὁμόνοια, i.e. the πόλις[12] and household.[13] In the *De universi natura* of Ps-Ocellus of Lucania, the binding power of harmony in the cosmos was compared to concord holding the household and the city together (*Frag.* 1):

Συνέχει γὰρ τὰ μὲν σκάνεα τῶν ζῴων ζωά,
ταύτας δ' αἴτιον ψυχά·
τὸν δὲ κόσμον ἁρμονία,
    ταύτας δ' αἴτιος ὁ θεός·
τὼς δ' οἴκως καὶ τὰς πόλιας ὁμόνοια,
ταύτας δ' αἴτιος νόμος.
τίς ὧν αἰτία καὶ φύσις τὸν μὲν κόσμον ἁρμόχθαι διὰ παντὸς
καὶ μηδέποτ' ἐς ἀκοσμίαν ἐκβαίνειν,
τὰς δὲ πόλιας καὶ τὼς οἴκως ὀλιγοχρονίως ἦμεν;

Because it holds intact:
    Through spirits, ways of life the tents of living things,
    Through god, harmony the cosmos,
    Through law, concord the households and the cities.
Which is the cause and the natural ground holding the cosmos permanently together that it never may fall into chaos, whilst the cities and the households are temporary?[14]

The similarity ends at this point. In the last part of the fragment Ps-Ocellus contrasts the temporality of civic and household concord with the permanence of the harmonious movement in nature. Households and cities are creations, formed from material; they are steered, caused by change and misery. In contrast, permanent movement steers, it is θεῖος, possessing reason and intelligence.[15] It is noteworthy that Ps-Ocellus does not use the term ὁμόνοια to refer to the cosmic harmony. He merely compares civic concord with cosmic harmony.

[12] Cf. Polybius, 2.40 1; 42.6; 3.3.7; 4.46.7; 23.11.7; Aristophanes of Byzantium, *Nomina aetatum* 15.5 (cf. *Frag.* 37); 279.5; Posidonius, *Fragmenta*, Fragment 247F (= Edelstein-Kidd 253,29 = FrGH 36).
[13] Cf. W. W. Tarn, *Alexander the Great. II Sources and Studies* (Cambridge: Cambridge University Press, 1948) 409–17.
[14] *De universi natura*, Frag. 1 (ed. R. Harder = Stobaeus *Ecl.* 1.13.2 [= Wachsmuth, 139–40]).
[15] *De universi natura* Frag. 1 (= Stobaeus *Ecl.* 1.13.2).

Stobaeus has left us an extract from the third century Pythagorean philosopher Ps-*Ecphantus*, in which it is said that friendship in the πόλις shares in perfection when it imitates the concord of the universe.[16] The language used is peculiar, especially the phrase τὰν τοῦ παντὸς ὁμόνοιαν. One does not expect the word "oneness of mind" referring to relations in the universe. The word ὁμόνοια originated in connection with unanimity between the members of a household or the citizens of a city-state.[17] Its use in reference to the cosmos is metaphoric. In this expression, the conceptual domain of cosmic relations is understood in terms of the conceptual domain of "oneness of mind" within the πόλις. Theoretically, the entities, relations, knowledge, *et cetera* of the source domain, i.e. civic concord, are mapped unto the target domain, namely cosmic harmony.[18] To imply that friendship in the city shares in perfection when it imitates cosmic concord is to redirect concord to its domain of origin, the city. The fact that Ecphantus speaks of the "unanimity" of the universe, using language from the domain of the city as an example for friendship in the πόλις, shows us that civic concord has become a conceptual metaphor, which can be successfully applied to other domains.[19]

The Stoic *Chrysippus* wrote a treatise περὶ ὁμόνοιας.[20] The work is no longer extant, but was presumably on political matters. Extracts from his other works transmit a definition of ὁμόνοια: "Concord is knowledge of common goods, through which the morally good are unanimous amongst one another, because they are in harmony with the things of life."[21] In a fragment from Chrysippus' work περὶ θεῶν transmitted by Philodemus, he identified good order, righteousness, concord, peace

---

[16] (Ps) Ecphantus *Frag.* 81 (= Stobaeus *Flor.* 4.7.64 [= Hense, 275]): ἃ δ᾽ ἐν τῇ πόλει φιλία κοινῶ τινος τέλεος ἐχομένα τὰν τῶ παντὸς ὁμόνοιαν μιμᾶται.

[17] For the latter, cf. Moulakis, *Homonoia*.

[18] I here draw on the theory of metaphor developed by G. Lakoff and M. Johnson, *Metaphors We Live By* (Chicago: 1980) and G. Lakoff and M. Turner, *More Than Cool Reason: A Field Guide to Poetic Metaphor* (Chicago: University of Chicago Press, 1989). For an introduction and application on metaphors in the Jesus tradition, cf. J. Liebenberg, *The Language of the Kingdom and Jesus* (BZNW; Berlin: Töpelmann, forthcoming), Chapter 2.3.

[19] Clement speaks of the smallest of living beings co-operating in peace and concord (20:10) and the unanimity with which the living beings went into Noah's ark (9:4). Aelian uses the term to refer to relations amongst fishes (*De natura animalium*, 3.9; 12.2).

[20] Cf. *SVF* 3.353.2 (= Athenaeus, *Deipnosophistae* 6.267b).

[21] *SVF* 3.625.3: Τήν τε ὁμόνοιαν ἐπιστήμην εἶναι κοινῶν ἀγαθῶν, δι᾽ ὅ καὶ τοὺς σπουδαίους πάντας ὁμονοεῖν ἀλλήλοις διὰ τὸ συμφωνεῖν ἐν τοῖς κατὰ τὸν βίον. Cf. also *SVF* 3.630.8–9; *SVF* 3.292.9; *SVF* 3.661.17.

and the universe with one another.[22] Posidonios,[23] Musonius Rufus[24] and Epictetus[25] also know the political overtones of the concept of ὁμόνοια, but it can be fairly said that Stoicism took the idea of household or civic concord from popular tradition. As far as I can see, the notion was never introduced to express their teaching on cosmic order.[26]

Cosmic Concord in Civic Rhetoric under the Empire

From the first century CE onwards, the use of the ὁμόνοια-terminology increased. Although the majority of occurrences refer to civic or household concord,[27] there is some interference between civic concord and cosmic harmony.[28] Because Stoicism understood the cosmos to be a body permeated by one will,[29] it became all the more possible to speak of cosmic harmony in terms of "oneness of mind", thus using ὁμόνοια metaphorically. This can be exemplified by referring to Dio Chrysostom, Aelius Aristides and Ps-Aristotle's *De mundo*. None of these authors can be said to be Stoics,[30] but as far as their cosmology is concerned,

---

[22] *SVF* 2.1076.9–10: Χρύσ(ι)ππος ... φη(σὶν εἶναι) ... καὶ τὴν αὐτὴν εἶναι καὶ εὐνομίαν καὶ δίκην (κ)αὶ ὁμόνοιαν κα(ὶ ε)ἰρήνην καὶ τὸ παρ(α)πλήσιον πᾶν.

[23] Frag. 247F (= Edelstein-Kidd 253.29 = FrGH 36).

[24] Cf. [*Dissertationes*], 8.50 (= ed. Hense, 37 = Stobaeus *Flor.* 4.7.67 [= Hense, 283]):
Καθόλου δὲ τὸν μὲν βασιλέα τὸν ἀγαθὸν ἀνάγκη πᾶσα καὶ λόγῳ καὶ ἔργῳ
εἶναι ἀναμάρτητον καὶ τέλειον·
εἴ περ δεῖ αὐτόν, ὥσπερ ἐδόκει τοῖς παλαιοῖς νόμον ἔμψυχον εἶναι,
εὐνομίαν μὲν καὶ ὁμόνοιαν μηχανώμενον, ἀνομίαν δὲ καὶ στάσιν ἀπείργοντα,
ζηλωτὴν δὲ τοῦ Διὸς ὄντα καὶ πατέρα τῶν ἀρχομένων, ὥσπερ ἐκεῖνον.

[25] Cf. *Dissertationes*, 4.5.35: δόγματα ἐν οἰκίᾳ φιλίαν ποιεῖ ἐν πόλει ὁμόνοιαν, ἐν ἔθνεσιν εἰρήνην, πρὸς θεὸν εὐχάριστον, πανταχοῦ θαρροῦντα, ὡς περὶ τῶν ἀλλοτρίων, ὡς περὶ οὐδενὸς ἀξίων.

[26] The Stoic teaching on cosmic order seems to stand in the tradition of Plato and Aristotle. Cf. D. E. Hahm, *The Origins of Stoic Cosmology* (Columbus: Ohio State University Press, 1977) 185–99.

[27] Cf. Breytenbach, *Harmonie*.

[28] Plutarch's *Vita Agesilai* compares the opinion of some physicists that cosmic harmony (ἡ πρὸς πάντα πάντων ἁρμονία) would set in when the heavenly bodies would stand still, with an erroneous conception that concord means (τὴν ... οὐκ ὀρθῶς ὁμόνοιαν λέγεσθαι) to yield too easily (*Agesilaus* 5:3). In the *Moralia* he compares the harmony in a body made possible through the concord and agreement (τῇ ὁμονοίᾳ καὶ συμφωνίᾳ) between moist and dry, hot and cold to goodwill and concord between brothers (*De fraterno amore* 2:28 = *Moralia* 478F–479A).

[29] Cf. M. Lapidge, "Stoic Cosmology," in J.M. Rist, *The Stoics* (Berkeley: University of California Press, 1978) 161–85, 172–9.

[30] Dio and Aristides could fairly be classified as Sophists and the author of *De mundo* as an Aristotelian.

Dio, a pupil of Musonius Rufus, stands in Stoic tradition,[31]whilst Aelius Aristides and the anonymous author behind *De mundo* are known to have been influenced by popular Stoicism.[32]

In line with rhetoric tradition since Antiphon, Dio Chrysostom treated the subject of concord several times. Intercity rivalries and civic conflicts, often called στάσις ("factionalism or discord"), were rife in the bustling cities of the eastern provinces during the first to third centuries CE. It was such a problem that Dio, employing a critique heard at Rome itself, bemoaned it as typical of "Greek failings" (Ἑλληνικὰ ἁμαρτήματα).[33] We cannot go into detail here.[34] What is of interest, however, is how Dio uses the notion of cosmic order within some of his speeches. Reference is made to cosmic relations to further the social politics of concord. When Dio had to speak on concord in his native city Prusa, he said a good deal not only about human, but also about celestial experiences, using them as examples. He thereby depicts cosmic relations in terms of ὁμόνοια … καὶ φιλία.: "These divine and grand creations, as it happens, require concord and friendship; otherwise there is danger of ruin and destruction for this beautiful work of the creator, the universe."[35] The same would happen to a strife torn city. In his 38th

---

[31] Cf. Louis François, *Essai sur Dion Chrysostome. Philosophie et Moraliste cynique et stoïcien* (Paris: Libraire Delagraves, 1921); for the later discussion, cf. B. F. Harris, "Dio of Prusa: A survey of recent work," *ANRW* II.33.5 (1991) 3853–81, 3873–4.

[32] Cf. A. Boulanger, *Aelius Aristide et la Sophistique dans la province d'Asie au IIe siècle de nôtre ère* (Paris: Bocard, 1923; 2nd ed., 1968) 197–8; H.B. Gottschalk, "Aristotelian Philosophy in the Roman World, from the Time of Cicero to the End of the second century AD," *ANRW* II.36.2 (1987) 1079–1174, esp. 1137–8.

[33] *Or.* 38.38; with reference to the civic discord in the context of diseases of the soul, cf. Plutarch, *Animine an corporis affectionis sint peiores* 4 (*Mor.* 501E–502A). For the social and political context of civic competition in relation to Roman rule and the imperial cult see also S. R. F. Price, *Rituals and Power: The Roman Imperial Cult in Asia Minor* (Cambridge: Cambridge University Press, 1984) 127, 132; S. Friesen, "The Cult of the Roman Emperors in Ephesos: Temple Wardens, City Titles, and Interpretation of the Revelation of John," in *Ephesos, Metropolis of Asia*, ed. H. Koester (HTS 41; Valley Forge: TPI, 1995) 230–9; A. D. Macro, "The Cities of Asia under the Roman Imperium," *ANRW* II.7.2 (1980) 682–3; and S. Mitchell, *Anatolia: Land, Men, and Gods in Asia Minor* (2 vols.; Oxford: Clarendon, 1993) 1:206. For the impact on the social life of the cities and on the public rhetoric see L. M. White, "Counting the Cost of Nobility: The Social Economy of Roman Pergamon," in *Pergamon, Citidel of the Gods*, ed. H. Koester (HTS 46; Harrisburg: TPI, 1998) 336–341 and U. Kampmann, "*Homonoia* Politics in Asia Minor: The Example of Pergamon," in *ibid.*, 373–93.

[34] Cf. Breytenbach, *Harmonie*; C.P. Jones, *The Roman world of Dio Chrysostom* (Cambridge: Harvard University Press, 1978) 83–94; A.R.R. Sheppard, "Homonoia in the Greek cities of the Roman Empire," *Ancient Society* 15–17 (1984–6) 229–52.

[35] *Or.* 48.14: ὅτι τὰ θεῖα ταῦτα καὶ μεγάλα ὁμονοίας τυγχάνει δεόμενα καὶ φιλίας· εἰ δὲ

oration Dio addresses the Nicomedians on concord, advising them to achieve unanimity with the Nicaens.[36] He starts by telling them where concord comes from and what it achieves, trying to persuade them, that "… concord has been proved to be beneficial to all mankind."[37] Delving into the origin of concord, Dio traces "… its very beginning to greatest of divine things (τὰ μέγιστα τῶν θείων πραγμάτων)." He then continues (*Or.* 38.11):

ἡ γὰρ αὐτὴ καὶ φιλία ἐστὶ καὶ καταλλαγὴ καὶ συγγένεια, καὶ ταῦτα πάντα περιείληφεν. καὶ τὰ στοιχεῖα δὲ τί ἄλλο ἢ ὁμόνοια ἑνοῖ; καὶ δι' οὗ σῴζεται πάντα τὰ μέγιστα, τοῦτό ἐστι, καὶ δι' οὗ πάντα ἀπόλλυται, τοὐναντίον.[38]

Dio's verdict that concord unites the basic elements (air, earth, water and fire) and that they are preserved through mutual concord echoes Stoic tradition. In Stoic tradition he was taught to compare the orderly constitution of the universe with the arrangement and orderliness of the administration of a πόλις[39]—provided the city-state is governed in accordance with law in complete friendship and concord.[40]

The Stoic influence on the way he deals with the topic of cosmic concord can also be seen from his 40th oration. Here he uses cosmic order as an example to urge his fellow citizens to foster good relations with the Apameians. Drawing on the tradition of political rhetoric, he uses the expressions ὁμόνοια and ἁρμονία to refer to the eternal orderly relationship between the elements. Should they fall into discord, the universe itself will be destroyed (*Or.* 40.35):

οὐχ ὁρᾶτε τοῦ ξύμπαντος οὐρανοῦ καὶ τῶν ἐν αὐτῷ θείων καὶ μακαρίων αἰώνιον τάξιν καὶ ὁμόνοιαν καὶ σωφροσύνην, ἧς οὔτε κάλλιον οὔτε σεμνό-τερον οὐδὲν οἷόν τ' ἐπινοῆσαι; πρὸς δὲ αὖ τῶν λεγομένων στοιχείων, ἀέρος καὶ γῆς καὶ ὕδατος καὶ πυρός, τὴν ἀσφαλῆ καὶ δικαίαν δι' αἰῶνος ἁρμο-νίαν, μεθ' ὅσης εὐγνωμοσύνης καὶ μετριότητος διαμένειν πέφυκεν αὐτά τε σῳζόμενα καὶ σῴζοντα τὸν ἅπαντα κόσμον;[41]

μή, κίνδυνος ἀπολέσθαι καὶ φθαρῆναι τῷ καλῷ τούτῳ δημιουργήματι τῷ κόσμῳ.

[36] Cf. *Or.* 38.6–7.
[37] *Or.* 38.8 (translation LCL).
[38] *Or.* 38.11 (translation LCL): "For the same manifestation is both friendship and reconciliation and kinship, and it embraces all these. Furthermore, what but concord unites the elements? Again, that through which all the greatest things are preserved is concord, while that through which everything is destroyed is its opposite."
[39] Cf. M. Schofield, *The Stoic idea of the city* (Cambridge: Cambridge University Press, 1991) 75–92; Cicero, *De natura deorum*, 2.3.154; Clemens Alexandrinus, *Stromata*, 4.26.
[40] Cf. *Or.* 30:30.
[41] *Or.* 40.35 (translation LCL): "Do you not see in the heavens as a whole and in the divine and blessed beings that dwell therein an order and concord and self-

The conflation of Stoic cosmology and rhetorical tradition can also be seen when Dio elaborates on the predominant role of the ether, in which the ruling and supreme element of the spiritual power lives: He stresses the friendship and concord in which the air holds its sway (*Or.* 40.37[42]):

ἡ μὲν γὰρ λεγομένη παρὰ τοῖς σοφοῖς ἐπικράτησις αἰθέρος,
  ἐν ᾧ τὸ βασιλεῦον καὶ τὸ κυριώτατον τῆς ψυχικῆς δυνάμεως,
  ὃν οὐκ ἀποτρέπονται πῦρ ὀνομάζειν πολλάκις,
  ὅρῳ τε καὶ πρᾴως γιγνομένη ἔν τισι χρόνοις τεταγμένοις,
  μετὰ πάσης φιλίας καὶ ὁμονοίας ἔοικε συμβαίνειν.[43]

He also urges those who do not share this cosmology to observe, "... that these things [sc. the basic elements], being by nature indestructible and divine and steered by the powerful will of the first and greatest god, want to be preserved as a result of their mutual friendship and concord at all times."[44] The metaphoric use of civic concord in this regard is clear. Dio speaks of cosmic harmony in a language (e.g. ὁμόνοια καὶ φιλία, εὐγνωμοσύνη καὶ μετριότης) borrowed from the domain of civic concord. He does this because in his speeches he advises his audiences to come to an agreement with their fellow citizens or partner cities. Cosmic harmony is used as paradigm, the example itself, however, is portrayed in the language of the overall topic of the oration.

The theological motive is even stronger in Aelius Aristides' treatment of cosmic harmony. According to him "Concord alone preserves the order of the seasons given by Zeus."[45] In his symbouleutic orations, e.g. the 23rd (*De concordia*), Aristides uses nature to illustrate civic concord.

---

control which is eternal, than which it is impossible to conceive of anything either more beautiful or more august? Furthermore, do you not see also the stable, righteous, everlasting concord of the elements, as they are called—air and earth and water and fire—with what reasonableness and moderation it is their nature to continue, not only to be preserved themselves, but also to preserve the entire universe?"

[42] Cf. *SVF* 2.601(= Chrysippus, *Fragmenta logica et physica* 601).

[43] *Or.* 40.37; I have arranged the lines in such a way as to emphasize the rhetorical nature of the formulation. Translation (LCL): "For the predominance of the ether of which the wise men speak—the ether wherein the ruling and supreme element of its spiritual power they often do not shrink from calling fire—taking place as it does with limitation and gentleness within certain appointed cycles, occurs no doubt with entire friendship and concord."

[44] *Or.* 40.36: ὅτι ταῦτα πεφυκότα ἄφθαρτα καὶ θεῖα καὶ τοῦ πρώτου καὶ μεγίστου γνώμῃ καὶ δυνάμει κυβερνώμενα θεοῦ τὸν ἅπαντα χρόνον ἐκ τῆς πρὸς ἄλληλα φιλίας καὶ ὁμονοίας σῴζεσθαι φιλεῖ ...

[45] *Or.* 24.42 (Keil; = Dindorf 44.567.17–18): μόνη [sc. ὁμόνοια] μὲν γὰρ τὰς ἐκ Διὸς ὥρας βεβαιοῖ, μόνη δὲ ἅπαντα ἐπισφραγίζεται.

In introducing his example, he utilises the term ἁρμονία to refer to city administration. In government and in association between groups it is best to strive for harmony, imitating cosmic harmony (*Or.* 23.76–7):

ἐπεὶ καὶ τὸν πάντα οὐρανὸν καὶ κόσμον,
    ὃς τὸ κάλλιστον ἁπάντων σχῆμα καὶ πρόσρημα εἴληφεν,
μία δή που γνώμη καὶ φιλίας δύναμις διοικεῖ·
καὶ μετὰ ταύτης ἥλιός τε πορεύεται τὴν αὐτοῦ χώραν φυλάττων δι᾽ αἰῶνος
καὶ σελήνης φάσματα καὶ ἀστέρων φορὰ χωρεῖ
καὶ ὡρῶν περίοδοι καὶ τάξεις ἑκάστων πρὸς ἄλληλα καὶ ἀποστάσεις τε αἱ
καθήκουσαι
καὶ πάλιν ἁρμονίαι φυλάττονται, νικώσης τῆς ὁμολογίας,
    διαφορᾶς δὲ οὐδεμιᾶς ἐνούσης οὐδὲ ἐγγιγνομένης,
    ἀλλὰ τῷ θεσμῷ πάντων συγκεχωρηκότων
    καὶ μιᾷ γνώμῃ περὶ παντὸς τοῦ προσήκοντος χρωμένων.[46]

Although Aristides does not use the term ὁμόνοια in this example, he describes his example, cosmic ἁρμονία, in human terms (cf. the use of μία … γνώμη καὶ φιλίας δύναμις and νικώσης τῆς ὁμολογίας). He actually propagates civic concord. He turns in his next example to human paradigms and thus to the notion of concord.[47] Like the cities, whose greatest protection and greatest glory is the harmony with which they are administered, the concord and zeal (ὁμόνοια καὶ σπουδή) which the kings have towards one another, is their fairest possession. Like Dio, Aristides uses cosmic harmony as a metaphor to illustrate civic concord. What is mapped from the cosmic realm onto the city administration, is the one power with which everything is kept harmoniously together.

One may also speak of cosmic harmony in terms of the concord so typical of a successful city. Our next author does this. With the unknown author (ps-Aristotle) of *De mundo*, one might ask the question why the cosmos, composed from opposite principles (dry and wet, hot and cold), has not been destroyed long ago and why it did not perish.

---

[46] *Or.* 23.76–77 (Keil; = Dindorf 42.537.12–18), arrangement mine. Translation Behr: "Indeed, one will together with the power of friendship administers all the heavens and Universe, which itself has received the greatest glory and title of all. And in conjunction with this power the sun proceeds in its course ever preserving its proper place, and the phases of the moon and the motion of the stars go on, and the revolutions and the positions of each in respect to one another and their proper distances, and again their harmonies are preserved, since agreement prevails among them, and there are no differences present, nor do they arise, but all things yield to the law of nature and they use one will concerning all their duties, …"

[47] Aristides makes ample use of the notion of civic concord, cf. Breytenbach, *Harmonie*.

The cosmic harmony between opposing forces finds a parallel in civic concord. Why is it that a city does not perish? Ps-Aristotle uses civic concord as an example to illustrate cosmic harmony. He maps some qualities and relations associated with the domain of civic concord unto the cosmos (*De mundo* 396b):

> Ἀγνοοῦσι δὲ ὅτι τοῦτ᾽ ἦν πολιτικῆς ὁμονοίας τὸ θαυμασιώτατον,
> λέγω δὲ τὸ ἐκ πολλῶν μίαν καὶ ὁμοίαν ἐξ ἀνομοίων ἀποτελεῖν διάθεσιν
> ὑποδεχομένην πᾶσαν καὶ φύσιν καὶ τύχην.
> Ἴσως δὲ καὶ τῶν ἐναντίων ἡ φύσις γλίχεται καὶ ἐκ τούτων ἀποτελεῖ τὸ
> σύμφωνον, οὐκ ἐκ τῶν ὁμοίων,
> ὥσπερ ἀμέλει τὸ ἄρρεν συνήγαγε πρὸς τὸ θῆλυ καὶ οὐχ ἑκάτερον πρὸς τὸ
> ὁμόφυλον,
> καὶ τὴν πρώτην ὁμόνοιαν διὰ τῶν ἐναντίων σηνῆψεν, οὐ διὰ τῶν ὁμοίων.[48]

Like a πόλις, the universe is a complex of opposites. Heaven, earth, and the whole cosmos, albeit a mixture of opposite elements, are organised by one harmony, a power that reaches right through everything (μία [ἡ] διὰ πάντων διήκουσα δύναμις). The cosmos is preserved through the agreement between the elements (ἡ τῶν στοιχείων ὁμολογία) and "… nature teaches us that equality is the preserver of concord, and concord is the preserver of the cosmos, which is the parent of all things and the most beautiful of all."[49] Nothing can be compared to the arrangement of the heavens, the movement of the stars and sun and moon or the consistency of hours and seasons. Even the unexpected changes brought about by winds, thunderbolts and violent storms bring the whole into concord and keep it intact.[50] In this respect the cosmic harmony can be compared to civil concord, although it surpasses the latter.

A range of other authors from the second century CE illustrates that the association between civic concord and cosmic harmony found

---

[48] *De mundo* 396b (translation LCL): "They do not recognise that the most wonderful thing of all about the harmonious working of a city-community is this: that out of plurality and diversity it achieves a homogeneous unity capable of admitting every variation of nature and degree. But perhaps nature actually has a liking for opposites; perhaps it is from them that she creates harmony, and not from similar things, in just the same way as she has joined the male to the female, and not each of them to another of the same sex, thus making the first harmonious community not of similar but of opposite things."

[49] *De mundo* 397a (translation LCL): ὅτι τὸ ἴσον σωστικόν πώς ἐστιν ὁμονοίας, ἡ δὲ ὁμόνοια τοῦ πάντων γενετῆρος καὶ περικαλλεστάτου κόσμου.

[50] Cf. *De mundo* 397a.23: Διὰ δὲ τούτων τὸ νοτερὸν ἐκπιεζόμενον τό τε πυρῶδες διαπνεόμενον εἰς ὁμόνοιαν ἄγει τὸ πᾶν καὶ καθίστησιν.

in Dio Chrysostom, Aristides, and Ps-Aristotle was not uncommon. Philostratus refers in his *Vita Apollonii* to the ὁμόνοια τῶν πόλεων and metaphorically to the ὁμόνοια τῶν στοιχείων.[51] Marcus Aurelius describes the reason of the universe as a spirit of fellowship promoting concord:

Ὁ τοῦ ὅλου νοῦς κοινωνικός.
πεποίηκε γοῦν τὰ χείρω τῶν κρειττόνων ἕνεκεν
καὶ τὰ κρείττω ἀλλήλοις συνήρμοσεν.
ὁρᾷς πῶς ὑπέταξε, συνέταξε, καὶ τὸ κατ' ἀξίαν ἀπένειμεν ἑκάστοις
καὶ τὰ κρατιστεύοντα εἰς ὁμόνοιαν ἀλλήλων συνήγαγεν.[52]

According to the first century philosopher Heraclitus in his *Quaestiones Homericae*, Anaxagoras of Clazomenae, disciple and sucessor of Thales, connected the earth as δεύτερον στοιχεῖον with water, the first element: "… in order that wetness mixed with dryness from its opposing nature would remain in single concord."[53] Heraclitus, who is familiar with the normal use of the ὁμόνοια-terminology,[54] uses it here in a metaphoric manner. Theon of Smyrna, who wrote his *De utilitate mathematicae* during the reign of Hadrian, elaborates on music. For him God is the one who fits together (συναρμοστής) disagreeing things (*De utilitate mathematicae*, 12.16–22):

καὶ τοῦτο μέγιστον ἔργον θεοῦ κατὰ μουσικήν τε καὶ κατὰ ἰατρικὴν τὰ ἐχθρὰ φίλα ποιεῖν.
ἐν μουσικῇ, φασίν, ἡ ὁμόνοια τῶν πραγμάτων, ἔτι καὶ ἀριστοκρατία τοῦ παντός·
καὶ γὰρ αὕτη ἐν κόσμῳ μὲν ἁρμονία, ἐν πόλει δ' εὐνομία, ἐν οἴκοις δὲ σωφροσύνη γίνεσθαι πέφυκε·
συστατικῆς γάρ ἐστι καὶ ἑνωτικῆς τῶν πολλῶν·[55]

---

[51] Cf. *Vita Apollonii* 5.41; 4.34.

[52] *Meditationes* 5.30, (trans. A.S.L. Farquharson; Oxford: Oxford University Press, 1944): "The mind of the Whole is social. Certainly it has made the inferior in the interests of the superior and has connected the superior one with another. You see how it has subordinated, co-ordinated, and allotted to each its due and brought the ruling creatures into agreement one with another."

[53] *Quaestiones Homericae* 22.8: ἵνα ξηρῷ μιχθὲν ὑγρὸν ἐξ ἀντιπάλου φύσεως εἰς μίαν ὁμόνοιαν ἀνακραθῇ.

[54] Cf. *Quaestiones Homericae* 32.4; 69.8.

[55] Theon, *De utilitate mathematicae* 12.18–24: "The greatest work of God is to reconcile things that are foes, in music and in medicine. In music, they say, is the concord of things, and even the aristocratic rule of the universe. For concord herself, by nature, becomes harmony in the cosmos, sound government in the polis, and temperance in the household. For all things, it is a force for bring together and unifying."

For Theon, the concord of things (ἡ ὁμόνοια τῶν πραγμάτων) seems to entail cosmic harmony, civic order and peace in the family.[56]

Our review so far has shown that the conflation of the notions of civic concord and cosmic harmony to differ. Some authors still distinguish between the two concepts. The author of *De mundo* and Aelius Aristides show a preference for the term ἁρμονία when referring to the cosmos. Philo of Alexandria, familiar with the civic notion of concord,[57] seems to refer to cosmic harmony by using the term ἐναρμόνιος[58] or ἁρμονία.[59] Texts influenced by Stoic cosmology map particularities of cosmic harmony onto civic concord. In doing so, they use the terminology of their target field, civic concord, to speak about cosmic harmony. This is quite clear from Dio Chrysostom's speeches and Marcus Aurelius' *Meditationes*. A text from a Jewish author transmitted under the name of Phocylides, however, illustrates that this practice of giving ethical instruction by appealing to cosmic concord was not unfamiliar to Greek-speaking Jews. In the case of Pseudo-Phocylides the example is again depicted in the language of what is to be illustrated:

70 μὴ φθονέοις ἀγαθῶν ἑτάροις μὴ μῶρον ἀνάψῃς.
71 ἄφθονοι Οὐρανίδαι καὶ ἐν ἀλλήλοις τελέθουσιν.
72 οὐ φθονέει μήνη πολὺ κρείσσοσιν ἡλίου αὐγαῖς
73 οὐ χθὼν οὐρανίοισ' ὑψώμασι νέρθεν ἐοῦσα
74 οὐ ποταμοὶ πελάγεσσιν. ἀεὶ δ' ὁμόνοιαν ἔχουσιν
75 εἰ γὰρ ἔρις μακάρεσσιν ἔην οὐκ ἂν πόλος ἔστη.[60]

The enduring unanimity in creation is used as an example to urge the listeners not to envy. Envy in the universe would make it perish. This would apply even more to human relations.

---

[56] For the use of the ὁμόνοια-terminonlogy in connection with music, cf. also Philodemus, *De musica*, 85.28

[57] Cf. e.g. *Abr* 243; *Heres* 183; *Spec Leg* 1.138; *Mut* 200. See also the article by Ferguson in this volume.

[58] Cf. e.g. *Agri* 51.

[59] Cf. e.g. *Vit. Mos.* 2.120.

[60] *Sententiae* 70–5 (Translation P.W. van der Horst [OTP II:576]):
"(70) Do not envy (your) friends their goods, do not fix reproach (upon them).
(71) The heavenly ones also are without envy toward each other.
(72) The moon does not envy the much stronger beams of the sun,
(73) nor the earth the heavenly heights though it is below,
(74) nor the rivers the seas. They are always in concord.
(75) For if there were strife among the blessed ones, heaven would not stand firm."

Cosmic Concord in 1 Clement

We can now return to those instances of the text of *1 Clement* 20 where the notion of concord is taken up again.[61] Up to chapter 20 Clement did not use the expression in reference to cosmic relations. The occurrence of ὁμόνοια in *1 Clement* 20:3 is thus of particular interest to us. Here Clement stands in the tradition we have sought to reconstruct in part II.[62] What Clement borrowed from the Stoic idea of agreement (συμφωνία), affinity (συμπάθεια), harmony (ἁρμονία) in the universe, is the unanimity with which the sun, the moon and the dancing stars circle within the bounds assigned to them.[63] "For the Stoics, the final goal in life was to live harmoniously with nature."[64] Clement uses the cosmic order as example that has to be imitated by the Corinthians. In 20.3, however, he draws upon the tradition of political rhetoric and he uses the notion of ὁμόνοια in describing the cosmic order.[65] Similar to the civic orations of Dio and Aelius Aristides,[66] Clement's letter aims to convince the Corinthian church to live in concord.[67] Cosmic harmony is used as an example to forward concord in the community. The domain of cosmic harmony is thereby, as in the case of Dio Chrysostom, depicted in terms of civic concord:

> Ἥλιός τε καὶ σελήνη, ἀστέρων τε χοροὶ κατὰ τὴν διαταγὴν αὐτοῦ
> ἐν ὁμονοίᾳ δίχα πάσης παρεκβάσεως
> ἐξελίσσουσιν τοὺς ἐπιτεταγμένους αὐτοῖς ὁρισμούς.[68]

The text ends with a combination of concord and peace (εἰρήνη),[69] the latter seeming to be the overarching concept.[70] This is because the notion of cosmic concord has been integrated into Clement's Jewish-

---

[61] Previously 9:4; 11:2.

[62] Cf. e.g. the text from Aristides 23rd oration at note 46 above.

[63] Cf. Cicero, *De natura deorum* II 101; Sanders, *L'Hellénisme*, 109–30.

[64] Lapidge, *Stoic Cosmology*, 161.

[65] Because H. Lona (*Der erste Clemensbrief* [KAV; Göttingen: Vandenhoeck und Ruprecht, 1998] 255) does not note the difference between cosmic harmony and civic concord, he sees the background of Clement's utterances in the Hellenistic synagogue. Philo, however, does not speak of cosmic concord, but talks about cosmic harmony (cf. *supra*).

[66] Cf. section two above.

[67] Cf. 21:1; 30:3; 63:2; 65:1.

[68] 1 Clement 20:3 (Translation adapted from Lightfoot): "The sun and the moon and the dancing stars according to his appointment circle in concord within the bounds assigned to them, without any swerving aside."

[69] Cf. 20:10–11.

[70] Cf. its prominent position in 19:2.

Christian conviction that God is the creator.[71] Van Unnik rightly noted
the differences between *1 Clement* 20 and Stoicism: "The tinge of Stoic
language is unmistakable, but this conception of the universe is subjected to another, biblical idea of God."[72] Just by glancing at the text
one can see this clearly. The father and creator (ὁ πατὴρ καὶ κτίστης
– 19:2), the great creator and ruler (ὁ μέγας δημιουργός καὶ δεσπότης
– 20:8,11) dominates the whole text as can be inferred from the recur-
rence of the third person pronoun αὐτός in 19:1,3; 20:1–4,6 and the
relative ᾧ in 20:12 Although the great creator and ruler is introduced
(19:2) as patient, without anger (19:3) and finally praised for the mercies
he bestowed on the readers (20:11–12), the passage focuses on the order
he bestowed on his creation.[73] The peace and concord,[74] brought about
by this order, result from his will[75] and command.[76]

It is undisputed that Clement, and this is also true for the 20th
chapter of the letter,[77] is heavily dependent on his Jewish Christian
monotheistic tradition. The universe is the creation of the one and
only God, the Father who is portrayed to be merciful. As far as the
reception of Stoic tradition is concerned, one can subscribe to Jaeger's
view: "Clement has here … blended stock Stoic ideas with his Jewish-
Christian belief in creation in order to illustrate and substantiate the
latter in detail."[78] Does this also apply to his use of the notion of
ὁμόνοια among the planets? The notion of cosmic order and harmony
is well known in Stoicism. Clement, however, used it in a letter whose
argumentative strategy stands in the tradition of symbouleutic rhetoric.
He urges the church in Corinth to overcome their internal strife, caused

---

[71] As A. von Harnack underlined throughout his last publication: *Einführung in die
Alte Kirchengeschichte. Das Schreiben der Römischen Kirche an die Korinthische aus der Zeit Domitians
(1.Clemensbrief)* (Leipzig: Hinrichs, 1929). Drew's suggestion, however, that Clement used
a liturgical text from Rome (cf. Knopf, *Väter*, 76) is unconvincing; cf. A. Lindemann, *Die
Clemensbriefe* (Tübingen: Mohr-Siebeck, 1992) 76.
[72] W. C. van Unnik, "Is 1Clement 20 purely Stoic?," *Sparsa Collecta III* (NTS 31;
Leiden: Brill, 1983) 52–58, 56.
[73] Cf. the use of -τάσσω κτλ. in 20:1–8,11: ὑποτάσσονται, τὸν τεταγμένον, τὴν διαταγὴν,
ἐπιτεταγμένους, προστάγμασιν, διέταχεν, ταῖς αὐταῖς ταγαῖς, προσέταξεν.
[74] Cf. 19:2; 20:1,3,9–11.
[75] Cf. 20:4 (κατὰ τὸ θέλημα αὐτοῦ).
[76] Cf. 20:1 (τῇ διοικήσει αὐτοῦ), 4 (τι τῶν δεδογματισμένων ὑπ᾽ αὐτοῦ), 6 (κατὰ τὴν
δημιουργίαν αὐτοῦ), 7.
[77] Cf. the review of the research by Lona, *Clemensbrief*, 267–72.
[78] Cf. W. Jaeger, "Echo," 335: "Clemens hat hier … stoisches Gedankengut mit
seinem jüdisch-christlichen Schöpfungsglauben verschmolzen, um diesen im einzelnen
zu veranschaulichen und zu substanziieren."

by the conflict between the younger men and the elders. When he takes up the notion of concord in this respect,[79] he links up with a rhetoric tradition dating back to Antiphon, Isocrates and Demosthenes.[80] The specific example of 20:3, where cosmic order is depicted in terms of concord, draws on this rhetorical tradition in a manner very similar to Dio Chrysostom. The notion of cosmic concord, however, is integrated into Jewish belief in the only God, the Creator.

---

[79] Cf. 21:1; 63:2; 65:1.
[80] For more detail cf. Breytenbach, *Harmonie.*

PART III

ΛΟΓΟΣ

Logos

LOGOS OR *SOPHIA*:
THE PAULINE USE OF THE ANCIENT DISPUTE
BETWEEN RHETORIC AND PHILOSOPHY

Edgar Krentz

Introduction: Paul and Rhetoric[1]

Two outstanding books discussing Paul's use of and attitude toward rhetoric have appeared in recent years. R. Dean Anderson's *Ancient Rhetorical Theory in Paul* appeared in 1996, followed by Bruce W. Winter's *Philo and Paul Among the Sophists* in 1997.[2] They reflect the recently burgeoning of interest in Paul and rhetoric.[3] But they come to divergent interpretations of Paul's evaluation of rhetoric. Anderson concludes his examination of 1 Corinthians 1–4 with the statement that "These chapters say virtually nothing concerning Paul's views on rhetorical theory and practice."[4] He bases this, in part at least, on his conviction that the controversy between philosophy and rhetoric was absent in the first century, following J. Wisse, who argues that the controversy

---

[1] Abraham Malherbe through his own writings and a series of students has contributed immensely to interpreting the New Testament within the social and cultural milieu of the Graeco-Roman world. I am delighted to offer this slight token of respect and affection to him.

[2] R. Dean Anderson, Jr. *Ancient Rhetorical Theory and Paul* (CBET 17; Kampen: Kok Pharos Publishing House, 1996; rev. ed. 1999); Bruce Winter, *Philo and Paul among the Sophists.*(SNTSMS 96, Cambridge: Cambridge University Press, 1997). There are two significant reviews of Anderson's book: Johan D. F. van Halsema in *NovT* 39 (1997) 292–94, and C. Clifton Black in *BMCR* 00.05.13 (online). Also for a response to Anderson, see the article by Stowers in this volume.

[3] Some of the key volumes are George A. Kennedy, *New Testament Interpretation Through Rhetorical Criticism* (Chapel Hill and London: University of North Carolina Press, 1984); *Persuasive Artistry: Studies in New Testament Rhetoric in Honor of George A. Kennedy*, ed. D. F. Watson (JSNTSup 50; Sheffield: JSOT Press, 1991); *Rhetoric and the New Testament: Essays from the 1992 Heidelberg Conference*, ed. S. E. Porter and T. H. Olbricht (JSNTSup 90; Sheffield: JSOT Press, 1993); *Rhetoric, Scripture and Theology: Essays from the 1994 Pretoria Conference*, ed. S. E. Porter and T. H. Olbricht (JSNTSup 131; Sheffield: Sheffield Academic Press, 1996); *The Rhetorical Analysis of Scripture*, ed. S. E. Porter and T. H. Olbricht (JSNTSup 146; Sheffield: Sheffield Academic Press, 1997). Space prohibits listing individual articles or the volumes dealing with the rhetoric of individual books.

[4] Anderson, *Rhetorical Theory*, 239–248; rev. ed., 265–76; the quotation is on 248; rev. ed., 276.

between rhetoric and philosophy did not last beyond the 40's of the first century BCE.[5]

Winter, on the other hand, examines the evidence for the presence of sophists in Corinth in the first and second centuries CE. He holds that Epictetus (ca 55–135 CE) was known in Corinth, and that *Discourses* 3.1 and 3.23 show that the debate between philosophy and rhetoric was still alive.[6] Moreover, Dio Chrysostom (ca 40–112 CE) delivered his eighth oration, "Diogenes," on his visit to Corinth, while Favorinus (ca 80–150 CE), Dio's pupil, visited Corinth three times and delivered a Corinthian oration (no. 37).[7] Herodes Atticus (ca 101–77 CE), Favorinus' pupil, who decorated the Peirene Fountain at Corinth, erected a statue to his wife there.[8] Its inscription describes him as "great" (μέγας) and "preeminent" (ἔξοχος ἄλλων).[9] Finally, Plutarch (ca 50–120 CE) notes the presence of *rhêtores* and sophists at the Isthmian Games.[10] Winter discusses Paul's views of sophistic rhetoric against this background, concentrating on his initial proclamation (2.1–5) and his work in Corinth (1 Cor 9), his critique of the Corinthian Sophistic Tradition (1 Cor 1–4), and his attitude to the Christian Sophists in Corinth (2 Cor 10:10, 11:6, and 12:16). He concludes that Paul regards the sophistic tradition as an inappropriate qualification for church leadership, and that he censures "Christian admiration for rhetorical skill."[11]

The earlier works by Margaret Mitchell[12] and Laurence L. Welborn[13] are valuable contributions to the rhetorical analysis of these letters, but do not address the question raised by Anderson and Winter's variant

---

[5] Jacob Wisse, "Welsprekendheid en filosofie bij Cicero. Studies en commentaar bij Cicero, *De Oratore* 3,19–37a; 52–95" (Unpublished Dissertation. University of Amsterdam, 1994) 17.

[6] Winter, *Philo and Paul*, 16–25.

[7] *Ibid.*, 126–37. See also the articles by Winter and White below.

[8] J. H. Kent, *Corinth. Inscriptions 1926–1960* (Princeton: The American School of Classical Studies at Athens, 1966) no. 128.

[9] Winter, *Philo and Paul*, 137–41.

[10] Plutarch, *Quaetiones Conviviales (Mor.)* 676c, 723–4.

[11] Winter, *Philo and Paul*, 201–20. There is extensive modern literature on Paul and rhetoric, which will not be taken up here. See Anderson and Stephen M. Pogoloff, *Logos and Sophia: the Rhetorical Situation in 1 Corinthians* (SBLDS 134; Atlanta: Scholars Press, 1992) for an overview of this literature and useful bibliographies.

[12] Margaret Mitchell, *Paul and the Rhetoric of Reconciliation: An Exegetical Investigation of the Language and Composition of 1 Corinthians* (Tübingen: Mohr-Siebeck, 1992; Louisville: Westminster/John Knox, 1993).

[13] Laurence L. Welborn, *Politics and Rhetoric in the Corinthian Epistles* (Macon: Mercer University Press, 1997).

conclusions: Was there a debate between rhetoric (λόγος) and philosophy (σοφία) in Paul's world? Recent significant scholarship dealing with aspects of rhetoric and the second sophistic in the Early Roman Empire may aid us in answering this question and evaluating its significance for understanding Paul. Maud Gleason's *Making Men* details the significance of physical appearance and deportment for rhetoricians by discussing the contrast and contest between Favorinus of Arelate and Polemo of Laodicea.[14] Dimitrios Karadimas discusses the conflict between philosophy and rhetoric in the second century in a recent volume discussing Sextus Empiricus and Aelius Aristides.[15] Graham Anderson's recent studies dealing with the Second Sophistic suggest that Paul would have been hesitant to use all the rhetorical resources of that movement, yet ranks him along with the "holy men" of the Roman world.[16] Simon Swain's *Hellenism and Empire*, in some respects a corrective to Graham Anderson,[17] details the interrelationship of language and power in the years 50–250 CE.[18] Rhetorical ability and correct Greek (Ἑλληνισμός) were status marks that conferred prestige and power. Although her main interest is in Dio Chrysostom's portrayal of women, Karin Blomqvist provides significant information on Dio's attitude toward rhetoric and philosophy after his exile.[19] There is a

---

[14] Maud Gleason, *Making Men: Sophists and Self-Presentation in Ancient Rome* (Princeton: Princeton University Press, 1995).

[15] Dimitrios Karadimas, *Sextus Empiricus against Aelius Aristides: The Conflict between Philosophy and Rhetoric in the Second Century A.D.* (Studia Graeca et Latina Lundensia 5; Lund: Lund University Press, 1996).

[16] Graham Anderson, *The Second Sophistic: A Cultural Phenomenon in the Roman Empire* (London and New York: Routledge, 1993) 205; *Sage, Saint and Sophist: Holy Men and their Associates in the Early Roman Empire* (London and New York: Routledge, 1994) passim. His earlier work, *Philostratus: Biography and Belles Lettres in the Third Century A.D.* (London: Croom Helm, 1986) does not discuss New Testament figures.

[17] See the recent *BMCR* 98.6.18 (online) review of Thomas Schmitz, *Bildung und Macht: Zur sozialen und politischen Funktion der zweiten Sophistik in der griechischen Welt der Kaiserzeit* (München: Beck, 1997) by Heinz-Guenther Nesselrath, who writes: "In 1996, Simon Swain's much more thorough and solid *Hellenism and Empire* (see next note) most of all looked into the question how the enormous literary activity on the Greek side between 50 and 250 AD grappled with the all-perevasive effects of Roman domination in Greek affairs." Schmitz's book was not available to me.

[18] Simon Swain, *Hellenism and Empire: Language, Classicism, and Power in the Greek World, AD 50–250* (Oxford: Clarendon Press, 1996).

[19] Karin Blomqvist, *Myth and Moral Message in Dio Chrysostom: A Study in Dio's Moral Thought, with a Particular Focus on His Attitudes Towards Women* (Lund: Studentlitteratur, 1989) 223–239.

debate over the question whether Dio did or did not convert from
rhetoric to philosophy—a matter of some interest for the question
before us.

The Key Pauline Texts

1 and 2 Corinthians are the Pauline texts that most explicitly repudiate
rhetoric as useful for Paul's message. The fundamental Pauline passages
are well known. 1 Cor 1:17 is an explicit rejection of wisdom conveyed
by rhetoric (σοφία λόγου) in favor of proclamation of the good news
(ἀπέστειλέν με Χριστὸς … εὐαγγελίζεσθαι) that the cross of Christ not be
nullified (ἵνα μὴ κενωθῇ ὁ σταυρὸς τοῦ Χριστοῦ). 1 Cor 2:1–5 is a fuller
statement of the same. Here Paul describes his initial proclamation as
follows (key terms underscored): Κἀγὼ ἐλθὼν πρὸς ὑμᾶς, ἀδελφοί, ἦλθον
οὐ καθ᾽ ὑπεροχὴν λόγου ἢ σοφίας καταγγέλλων ὑμῖν τὸ μυστήριον τοῦ
θεοῦ. (2) οὐ γὰρ ἔκρινά τι εἰδέναι ἐν ὑμῖν εἰ μὴ Ἰησοῦν Χριστὸν καὶ
τοῦτον ἐσταυρωμένον. (3) κἀγὼ ἐν ἀσθενείᾳ καὶ ἐν φόβῳ καὶ ἐν τρόμῳ
πολλῷ ἐγενόμην πρὸς ὑμᾶς, (4) καὶ ὁ λόγος μου καὶ τὸ κήρυγμά μου οὐκ
ἐν πειθοῖ[ς] σοφίας [λόγοις] ἀλλ᾽ ἐν ἀποδείξει πνεύματος καὶ δυνάμεως,
(5) ἵνα ἡ πίστις ὑμῶν μὴ ᾖ ἐν σοφίᾳ ἀνθρώπων ἀλλ᾽ ἐν δυνάμει θεοῦ.

1 Cor 2:1–5 has long been regarded as Paul's rejection of rhetoric as
a means of promoting the Gospel. Advisedly so. Here the terms πειθός,
σοφία, λόγος, ἀπόδειξις and πίστις are all drawn from rhetoric and so
deserve attention. As v. 4 makes clear, in the phrase "ὁ λόγος μου καὶ τὸ
κήρυγμά μου," the word λόγος the must here mean speech; therefore
I translate the phrase σοφία λόγου as "wisdom of speech," not as
"wisdom of argument," and the phrase πειθοῖ[ς] σοφίας [λόγοις] as "in
persuasive speeches of wisdom," both referring to persuasive rhetoric.[20]
Paul is thus arguing that "not rhetoric, but the Spirit and power" (a
hendiadys?) provide the proof (ἀπόδειξις). And so their allegience (ἡ
πίστις) should rest in the power of God, not the wisdom of humans.
The heaping up in this paragraph of terminology at home in Greek
rhetoric is impressive.

Paul rejects this rhetoric, called the "wisdom of humans" (v. 5) in
favor of another wisdom in 1 Cor 2:6–16; σοφία is a key term in this
paragraph (see vv. 6, 7, 13). Commentators generally do not tie this

---

[20] Raymond F. Collins, *First Corinthians* (SacPag 7; Collegeville: The Liturgical Press,
2000) 115 translates 2:1, οὐ καθ᾽ ὑπεροχὴν λόγου ἢ σοφίας, as "not with the advantage of
rhetoric or wisdom," which catches the nuance well.

paragraph to Paul's rejection of rhetorical persuasion, generally considering it under the major category of wisdom.[21] Paul opposes the "wisdom of this age," i.e. the wisdom of speech, to the "wisdom of God" (2:6–7). It is a wisdom tied to the Spirit, which investigates the "deep things of God" (τὰ βάθη τοῦ θεοῦ, 2:10). It is communicated in arguments taught by the Spirit (2:13). Only those endowed with Spirit can plumb this wisdom(cf. 2:12, 14), since "the deep things of God" (τὰ βάθη τοῦ θεοῦ, 2:10) are can only by examined in a manner congruent with Spirit (πνευματικῶς, 2:14). Paul makes use of the Greek idea ὅμοια δι' ὁμοίων, literally "similar things through similar things," a *topos* with a long history in Greek thought.[22] Many other passages throughout the Corinthian letters also relate to this issue. Key terms or issues in the larger context include judgement and judge (κρίνειν/κρίσις/κριτής), terms drawn from dicastic rhetoric.[23] Paul's self-evaluation, his attack on his opposition for its false standards of judgment, and his promotion of a wisdom tied to the cross all relate to this superior wisdom.

In spite of this apparent rejection of rhetoric, Paul himself clearly made use of rhetorical techniques and devices in the Corinthian letters. Gary S. Selby holds that Paul presented himself as an apocalyptic seer in 1 Cor 2.[24] Fred Danker recently argued that Paul was highly indebted to Demosthenes' *De Corona* in 2 Corinthians.[25] Glenn Holland argues that Paul's use of "foolishness" in 2 Cor 10–13 is a rhetorical ploy, using contrast (σύγκρισις) to advance his argument.[26] Mario DiCicco

---

[21] See, for example, Gordon Fee, *The First Epistle to the Corinthians* (NICNT; Grand Rapids: Eerdmans, 1987) 98–120; Collins, *First Corinthians*, 121–39.

[22] It first appears in Homer *Od.* 17.218: ὡς ἀεὶ τὸν ὁμοῖον ἄγει θεὸς ὡς τὸν ὁμοῖον ("As ever, the god is bringing like and like together." Unless otherwise indicated, translations of classical authors are taken from the Loeb Classical Library.) Plato *Sym.* 195B cites it as an old statement: ὅμοιον ὁμοίῳ ἀεὶ πελάζει ("Like and like strike together."). Similar expressions in *Rep.* 329A, Aristotle *EN* 1155a34. See LSJ s.v. 1 and R. G. Bury, *The Symposium of Plato* (Cambridge: W. Heffer and Sons, 1909) 73 for additional references.

[23] Cf. 1 Cor 2:2; see Paul Shorey, "Φύσις, Μελετή, Ἐπιστήμη," *TAPA* 40 (1909), 198 on the distinction of criticism from creative powers.

[24] Gary S. Selby, "Paul, the Seer: The Rhetorical Persona in 1 Corinthians 2.1–16," in *The Rhetorical Analysis of Scripture: Essays from the 1995 London Conference*, ed. S.E. Porter and T. H. Olbricht (JSNTSup146; Sheffield: Sheffield Academic Press, 1997) 351–73.

[25] Frederick W. Danker, "Paul's Debt to the *De Corona* of Demosthenes: A Study of Rhetorical Techniques in Second Corinthians," in *Persuasive Artistry: Studies in New Testament Rhetoric in Honor of George A. Kennedy*, ed. D. F. Watson (JSNTSup 50: Sheffield: JSOT Press, 1991) 262–80.

[26] Glenn Holland, "Speaking Like a Fool: Irony in 2 Corinthians 10–13," in *Rhetoric and the New Testament: Essays from the 1992 Heidelberg Conference*, ed. S. E. Porter and T. H. Olbricht (JSNTSup 90; Sheffield: JSOT Press, 1993) 250–64.

has examined Paul's use of Aristotle's three modes of persuasion in
2 Cor 10–13.[27] There is thus quite a variety of interpretations of Paul's
rhetoric and Paul as rhetorician in the Corinthian letters.[28] Paul shows
rhetorical ability in the Corinthian letters, which makes his rejection of
the wisdom of speech even more surprising.

In this essay I suggest that Paul makes use of language drawn from
the debate between rhetoricians and philosophers as teachers of wisdom in the *polis*. He uses the language to identify himself as a teacher
of wisdom and his message as the true wisdom—though not claiming
to be a philosopher. Thus the wisdom he urges on the reader in 1 Cor
2:6–16 is antithetical to the wisdom that comes via good speaking or
persuasive rhetoric alone; rather it is a wisdom that is Spirit taught
and Spirit received. In short, Paul argues for a wisdom superior to that
taught by rhetoric, in a fashion similar to that argued by the proponents
of philosophy over against rhetoric.

Rhetoric in the Early Roman Empire

Recently there has been a burgeoning of interest in rhetoric in the
late republic and the early Roman Empire. Interest has risen in the
resumption of the conflict between rhetoric and philosophy. It is here
that Winter's work becomes very important. He demonstrates that first
century Corinth was well acquainted with the conventions of sophistic
rhetoric.

Anderson cites Hans von Arnim's work on Dio Chrysostom to argue
that the separation of philosophy from rhetoric meant that they no
longer had the same aims.[29] Von Arnim goes on to point out that a controversy arose between rhetoric and philosophy when Romans became
interested in the Greek philosophic schools.[30] The rivalry arose from
the burgeoning of rhetoric in the early Roman Empire alongside the
popularization of Greek philosophy beginning with Cicero. Consider,

---

[27] Mario M. DiCicco, *Paul's Use of Ethos, Pathos, and Logos in 2 Corinthians 10–13* (Mellen
Biblical Press Series 31; Lewiston, Queenston, Lampeter: Mellen Biblical Press, 1995).
[28] Other contributions include Bruce Winter, "Is Paul Among the Sophists?" *RTR*
53 (1994) 28–38; R. A. Horsely, "Wisdom of Word and /Words of Wisdom in Corinth,"
CBQ 39 (1977) 224–239; Johannes Munck, *Paul and the Salvation of Mankind* (London:
SCM Press, 1959) 135–67.
[29] Hans von Arnim, *Leben und Werke Dio von Prusa, mit einer Einleitung: Sophistik, Rhetorik,
Philosophie in ihrem Kampf um die Jugendbildung* (Berlin: Weidmann, 1898) 4–114, especially
68, cited by Anderson, *Rhetorical Theory*, 53.
[30] Von Arnim, *Leben und Werle*, 92.

for example, What are the criteria for evaluating the value of rhetoric? Two questions dominated the discussion: (1) Is rhetoric practically useful? (2) What is the proper field for rhetoric over against philosophy?[31]

1. *The Criterion of Utility*

One answer given by philosophers was that the major criterion for evaluating rhetoric was utility: Did it serve a useful function? An art may be either useful or harmful. The Epicurean philosopher Philodemus questioned its utility. In his treatise *On Rhetoric* he defines the usual or preconceptive meaning of *techne* ('art') as a

> faculty or disposition arising from observation of certain common and fundamental things which extend through most particular instances, a faculty which grasps and produces an effect such as only a few who have not learned the art can accomplish, and doing this firmly and surely, rather than conjecturally."[32]

He comes to the surprising conclusion that sophistic rhetoric is an art, while forensic and political rhetoric are not. Thus Philodemus distinguishes a useful art (forensic and political rhetoric) from one that is useless or even harmful (sophistic rhetoric), a layman's knowledge from technical knowledge.[33] Philodemus' criteria for distinguishing these arts is clear:

> … the Epicurean recognizes *technai* in areas where there are things which can be necessary, useful, or pleasant, although each *techne* itself—or at least one of its forms—may not be helpful in getting these good things, since it has become too specialized, theoretical, or technical. What will get the good things will be, in some instances a lower form of the *techne*, in others a non-technical competence, and in others philosophy itself.[34]

The skeptic Sextus Empiricus devoted book II of *Adversus Mathematicos* to a critique of rhetoric.[35] He argued that one can become a good

---

[31] *Ibid.*, 90–92.

[32] David Blank, "Philodemus on the Technicity of Rhetoric," *Philodemus and Poetry: Poetic Practice and Theory in Lucretius, Philodemus, and Horace*, ed. D. Obink (New York: Oxford University Press, 1995) 179 n. 3, quoting from Philodemus, *On Rhetoric* 2 (*P.Herc.* 1674 col. xxxviii [Longo, 123]): ἕξιϲ ἢ διάθ[ε]ϲι[ϲ] ἀπὸ | παρ[α]τηρή[ϲ]εω[ϲ τιν]ῶν | κοινῶν καὶ [ϲ]τοι[χειω][ˊ]δῶν, ἃ διὰ πλειόν[ω]ν δι| |ήκει τῶν ἐπὶ μέ[ρ]ο[υϲ], κα|ταλαμβά-νουϲά [τ]ι καὶ |[ϲ]υντελοῦϲα τοιοῦτον,| οἷον ὁμοίωϲ τῶν μὴ | μαθόντων ἔ[νιοι], ἐϲτη|κό-τωϲ καὶ βε[βαι]ωϲ οὐ[δ]ὲ ϲτοχαϲτι[κωϲ]ˊˊ.

[33] Blank, "Philodemus," 179.

[34] Blank, "Philodemus," 180.

[35] *Adv. Math.* book II is thus separately titled *Adversus Rhetores*, which opens (§2) with

speaker without knowing the art of rhetoric (*Adv. Rhet* 16–19). In summing up the arguments he credits to the Academy (*Adv. Rhet* 20–42),
Sextus also distinguished two kinds of rhetoric:

> Such then are the arguments used by the men of the Academy concern-
> ing rhetoric, by way of running it down, so that, if it is useful (ὠφέλιμος)
> neither to its possessor nor to his neighbors, it will not be an art. But
> in reply to all this some assert that as there are two forms of rhetoric,
> the one refined (ἀστεῖα) and in use among the wise (σοφοῖς), the other in
> use among inferior people (μέσοις ἀθρώποις), the accusation is not made
> against the refined kind but against that of the baser sort (μοχθηροί).[36]

Sextus also argues that rhetoric is not useful for either the orator or the
city. It forces the orator to associate with evil and untrustworthy people,
to lose his modesty (αἰδῶς), to practice deceit, etc. (*Adv. Rhet* 27–30).[37]
And it does not benefit the city, since rhetoric opposes the laws that
bind a city together in community (*Adv. Rhet.* 31–42).

Thus philosophers of at least two philosophic schools, Epicurean and
Skeptic, distinguish two types of rhetoric on the basis of utility. Such
lay rhetoric may enable one to achieve things that are necessary, useful
or pleasant, that is a rhetorical layman may be able to speak or write
well, without benefit of the formal study of rhetoric—but not satisfy an
upper class, educated audience.

2. *The Proper Areas for Rhetoric and Philosophy*

The areas with which each of these intellectual pursuits deals is an area
of controversy. Philodemus defines the goal of rhetoric as persuasion:
τό τε διὰ [λόγου] | ῥητορικοῦ πειθεῖν [τ]έ | λ[ο]c ἐστὶ τῆc ῥ[ητορι]ικ[ῆ]c.[38]
The role of rhetoric is to speak well, i.e. with persuasive force. Thus
rhetoric does not deal with truth; that is the role of philosophy. "It is
when rhetoric tries to do the job of philosophy that Philodemus con-
demns it."[39] The Epicurean tradition made a sharp distinction between

---

the definition of Plato from *Gorgias* 453a (see also below). Karadimas (*Sextus Empiricus
against Aelius Aristides*, 50–161) has a useful discussion of Sextus on rhetoric.

[36] *Adv. Rhet.* 43. The translation by R. G. Bury, *Sextus Empiricus IV: Against the Professors*
(LCL; Cambridge: Harvard University Press, 1949) 209–11.

[37] Karadimas points out that Aelius Aristides contests each of Sextus' points in
defense of rhetoric—without ever naming Sextus. That suggests that the debate is more
wide ranging than between these two men.

[38] Philodemus, *Rhet.* 2 col i.26 (Longo, 47), cited by Blank, "Philodemus," 186 n. 32.

[39] Phillip H. and Estelle Allen Delacy, *Philodemus, On Methods of Inference* (La Scuola

the areas that philosophy and rhetoric properly occupy. Rhetoric is concerned with persuasion, and can only claim what is likely. Philosophy deals with truth.

3. *The Controversy Between Philosophy and Rhetoric*

The controversy between philosophy and rhetoric goes back to Classical Athens and the beginning of the sophistic movement. The term σοφιστής ("sophist") appears first in the fifth century BCE in reference to a *wise man* (σοφός) who was *skilled* (τεχνικός, τεχνίτης) in a particular discipline or activity. "Sophist" thus came to mean a particular profession related to teaching and rhetoric, usually done for a fee. Of course, the best known of the sophists was Socrates himself, but in Plato's hands Socrates becomes a critic of the sophists. Plato's *Gorgias* 462b3–465e6 has Socrates draw a sharp distinction between genuinely scientific skills or arts (τέχναι) that aim at excellence from "empirical" description that is not really rational and meant mainly to please. The latter are deceptive imitators of the real τέχναι, such as philosophy, which produce moral betterment rather than just rhetoric. Hence in Plato's discussions, "sophist" is usually used with this negative connotation, and Aristotle retains this basic distinction between true wisdom (philosophy) and "apparent wisdom, but not real" for making money.[40]

R. Dean Anderson, following Jacob Wisse, holds that the controversy between rhetoric and philosophy died down after the early 40's BCE because there was "a general demise of philosophical schools." Therefore we should be cautious against all too easily referring Paul's negative comments on persuasion to a contemporary *philosophical* animosity to rhetoric.[41] But there is evidence that this debate had not disappeared from the intellectual landscape. In fact, if anything it was a smoldering ember waiting to burst forth again, as it did in the second

---

de Epicuro 1; Naples: Bibliopolis, 1978) 199, cited by Blank, "Philodemus," 184 n. 20. I did not find this citation in the earlier edition of this work (Philadelphia: American Philological Association, 1941), though there is an extensive discussion of rhetoric. They do say, "Rhetoric, like poetry, must be avoided by the philosopher and the scientist" (152).

[40] Cf. Plato, *Soph.*; Aristotle, *Sophis. Elench.* 165a22; *Meta.* Γ 1004b25. For a revisionist history of the classical sophists, see Gerald B. Kerferd, *The Sophistic Movement* (Cambridge: Harvard University Press, 1981) 4–19.

[41] Anderson, *Rhetorical Theory*, 55–56; rev. ed., 65, citing Wisse, "Welsprekendheid en filosofie bij Cicero," 17.

century CE in what is commonly called the "Second Sophistic."[42] In fact, it is primarily to Flavius Philostratus, the third century chronicler of the sophists (both earlier and later), that we owe the principal definition of *sophists* as "*rhêtores* of surpassing eloquence."[43] He also then distinguishes between those who were truly philosophers and the rest: thus, those "who, though they pursued philosophy, ranked as sophists, and also the sophists (i.e., rhetoricians) properly so called."[44]

The quarrel between rhetoric and philosophy has to do with wisdom and goodness. Both claim to teach goodness. But rhetoric was suspect because it could persuade people to accept something that was untrue or evil. This attack has a long history. One of the earliest is found in Aristophanes *Clouds*. Here just speech and unjust speech (δίκαιος καὶ ἄδικος λόγος) debate each other. But it perdures. Sextus Empiricus argues that rhetorical precepts (τὰ τῆς ῥητορικῆς θεωρήματα) lead one to practice evil deeds, e.g. to mislead judges, to defend adulterers and temple-robbers, etc. (*Adv. Rhet.* 11). Certainly Dio Chrysostom did not view his own civic orations in this way. Yet, in *Or.* 38.1–3, Dio employs the distinction between the rhetoric of civic "flatterers," who titilate the masses with mere "demagogery" (κολάκων ἀνδρῶν, ἵνα δημαγωγοῦσιν αὐτοῖς ἥδωνται) versus his own, in which he dispensed sage "advice" for civic betterment (συμβούλων, ἵνα σῴζωνται ταῖς πολιτείαις).[45]

Paul's Self-Presentation

Winter calls attention to Epictetus' attitude to sophists.[46] Epictetus faults a student of rhetoric for his highly decorated dress and for his "hairdo" (3.1.1). He contrasts this concern for appearance with the beauty that is achieved when a person achieves moral excellence through the practice of the virtues (δικαιοσύνη, σωφροσύνη, ἐγκράτεια, 3.1.7–9).[47] Epicu-

---

[42] See especially Glenn Bowersock, *Greek Sophists in the Roman Empire* (Oxford: Clarendon, 1969) 11; cf. the bibliography cited above in n. 16.

[43] Philostratus, *VS* 1.8.4 (Olearius-Kayser 484): σοφιστὰς ... ἐπωνόμαζον οὐ μόνον τῶν ῥητόρων τοὺς ὑπερφωνοῦντας ... ἀλλὰ καὶ τῶν φιλοσόφων. See also C. P. Jones, "The Reliability of Philostratus," in *Approaches to the Study of the Second Sophistic*, ed. G. Bowersock (University Park: American Philological Association, 1974) 11–16.

[44] *VS*, from the preface (479).

[45] *Or.* 38.2; cf. *Or.* 32.7–11 (also n. 55 below). See the discussion of *Or.* 38 in the article by White in this volume.

[46] Winter, *Philo and Paul*, 116–125.

[47] In 3.1.31 he speaks of the σωμάτιον, the "bodylet," a disparaging term. Oldfather (LCL) translates it "paltry body" (cf. 3.1.31, πραγμάτιον).

rus contrasts the good achieved by philosophy with rhetoric's desire for public approval.[48] He also rejects the rhetorician's avid desire for adulation and the use of rhetoric to attain to public office (3.1.34–36). Therefore the young man is urged to go into philosophy and leave rhetoric. Epictetus 3.23 reinforces this position; here Epictetus discusses epideictic oratory. One must have the correct objective. He asks whether one wishes "to be good or to be praised."[49] Epictetus thus distinguishes between admiration for rhetorical ability in a speaker and ethical activity, clearly opting for the latter over rhetorical excellence.

Maud Gleason stresses that rhetoric was a process involving interaction between the *rhêtor* and the audience, in which rhetoric functioned as an instrument of self-presentation. "One reason that these performances were so riveting was that the encounter between orator and audience was in many cases the anvil on which the self-presentation of ambitious upper-class men was forged."[50] Developing competence as a *rhêtor* required education or training (παιδεία). And that necessitated time, money, effort, and some social position. Language demarked the elite as a "culturally and politically superior group."[51] To speak well in public competition led to the prize in status competition.[52] And it entailed much more than the putting together of words. It included

> … physical control of one's voice, carriage, facial expression, and gesture, control of one's emotions under conditions of competitive stress—in a word, all the arts of deportment necessary in a face-to-face society where one's adequacy as a man was always under suspicion and one's performance was constantly judged.[53]

Thus society in terms of status maintenance for the speaker was constantly agonistic, where a speaker was measured against others. Maud Gleason details this procedure by describing at length the conflict between two second century stars of the Second Sophistic, Favorinus of

---

[48] He cites the case of Polemo, converted by Xenocrates to philosophy from a dissolute life (3.1.14–15).

[49] ὠφεληθῆσαι θώλεις ἢ ἐπαινεθῆναι (3.23.7).

[50] Gleason, *Making Men*, xx.

[51] Gleason, *Making Men*, xxi, citing Lucian, *Somnium* 1: παιδεία μὲν καὶ πόνου καὶ χρόνου μακροῦ καὶ δαπάνης οὐ μικρᾶς καὶ τυχῆς δεῖσθαι λαμπρᾶς ("Higher education required great labor, considerable expense, and conspicuous social position").

[52] Swain, 409. Swain, 17–64, discusses the role of language, especially correctness of speech (Ἑλληνισμός), as a "badge of elite identity" (64). This went beyond Atticism's concern for the use of correct vocabulary; it also included language that was fitting to the subject (πρέπον), expressed with clarity (σαφηνεία), as the case of Galen makes clear.

[53] Gleason, *Making Men*, xxii.

Arelate and Polemo of Laodicea. Polemo sought to put Favorinus down
because he was by nature a eunuch, with high voice, feminine softness,
and a mincing walk; Favorinus countered with a self-presentation that
claimed that his physical condition was a gift of the gods.

Paul does not engage in this agonistic attitude. He stresses that he
does not rely on the wisdom that is dependent on persuasive speech;
but he does not reject all wisdom. Rather he urges the λόγος τοῦ
σταυροῦ as the wisdom that avails. It is a wisdom that is not concerned
with power and status (1 Cor 1:18–31). But it is wisdom, as 2:6–16 makes
clear, a wisdom that is πνευματικός and so corresponds to its subject
matter and to people endowed with Spirit. Small wonder that Paul is
concerned about his own self-presentation in the Corinthian letters. In
1 Cor 2:3 he makes a virtue of his "weakness, fear and great trembling"
(ἐν ἀσθενείᾳ καὶ ἐν φόβῳ καὶ ἐν τρόμῳ πολλῷ) in which he began his
proclamation in Corinth. That demonstrated where the real power
of his message lay, not in rhetoric, but in God and, thus, in truth.
In 2 Cor 11:6 Paul describes himself as an untrained speaker (ἰδιώτης
τῷ λόγῳ), not a professional rhetorician. This reminds one of Sextus'
and Philodemus' rejection of sophistic rhetoric in favor of "natural
rhetoric." He found it necessary to boast because he was under attack
(2 Cor 11:16–12:13). His bragging is done in a situation of self-defense
(2 Cor 12:19: πάλαι δοκεῖτε ὅτι ὑμῖν ἀπολογούμεθα.), a situation that
Plutarch says justifies self-promotion. When one is attacked, one may
praise oneself in defense. You do it well when you let "part of it rest
with chance and part with God."[54]

Paul claims that his personal presence would evidence power as part
of his self defense (2 Cor 13:1–4). This concern for language was already
present in the early first century, as the works of Dionysius of Halicarnassus make evident. The second century simply brings to fullness
what was present earlier. It is clear that there is an opposition in some
thinkers between sophistic rhetoric, done primarily for epideictic purposes, and philosophy. One aims at popular response, the other at benefit for the hearer. One seeks applause, the other change. Paul falls
into the latter group of thinkers. To this we may also compare the
exordium of Dio Chrysostom's Alexandrian Oration, in which he calls on
his audience to be "dull in speech, but right in discernment" (βραδὺ
μὲν φθεγγομένους … ὀρθῶς δὲ διανοουμένους).[55] Later, he will say that,

---

[54] Plutarch, De se ipsum citra invidiam laudando (Mor.) 542E.
[55] Or. 32.2.

unlike the run-of-the-mill "flatterers, charlatans, and sophists" who give philosophers a bad name, he will even risk the "ridicule and uproar" of his audience by "dispensing frank criticism purely and without guile" (καθαρῶς καὶ ἀδόλως παρρησιαζόμενον) in order to make them better (*Or.* 32.11). Dio then goes on in 32.12 to say that he has not chosen this role of civic counselor as a mere profession. Instead, he himself was chosen by the divine (ὑπὸ δαιμονίου); the gods are the ones who supply him with "words that are appropriate and beneficial" (λόγους ἐπιτηδείους καὶ ξυμφέροντας) for the hearer. Referring to benefits (συμφέρειν, σύμφορον), Paul speaks of his teaching and spiritual gifts in much the same way (1 Cor 10:33; 12:7).

Dio Chrysostom describes his conversion to philosophy and its effects in his thirteenth oration (*In Athens on His Exile*).[56] In exile he dressed humbly, and so was often taken for a philosopher, and asked questions about good and evil (πόλλοι γὰρ ἠρώτων προσιόντες ὅ τι μοι φαίνοιτο ἀγαθὸν ἢ κακόν· ὥστε ἠναγκαζόμην φροντίζειν ὑπὲρ τούτων, ἵνα ἔχοιμι ἀποκρίνεσθαι τοῖς ἐρωτῶσιν, *Or.* 13.12).[57] Later he mentions how Socrates questioned the ability of orators "to deliberate and that of their craft (τέχνη) to make men good" (*Or.* 13.22) and urged them study philosophy (*Or.* 13.28). He himself pursued the same course, urging people to practice the great virtues.[58] D. A. Russell describes Dio's style as follows:

> We have to remember both Dio's fame as an improviser, and his self-representation as a mere talker, an ἀδολέσχης, because that is what philosophers in the Socratic tradition were supposed to be. The rigid limit and structures imposed by the law courts and the rhetoricians were alien both to his talents and to his professed stance and technique.[59]

Mutatis mutandis, such a description applies also to Paul's self-presentation in the Corinthians letters. Much of 2 Corinthians 10–13 is an implied σύγκρισις between Paul and the polished speakers admired by the Corinthians. When he accuses the Corinthians of looking at

---

[56] On Dio's conversion see J. L. Moles, "The Career and Conversion of Dio Chrysostom," *JHS* 98 (1978) 80–100.

[57] "For many would approach me and ask what was my opinion about good and evil. As a result I was forced to think about these matters so that I might answer."

[58] See C. P. Jones, *The Roman World of Dio Chrysostom* (Cambridge and London: Harvard University Press, 1978) 45–55, and von Arnim, *Leben und Werke Dio von Prusa*, 223–308, esp. 227–29, *et passim*.

[59] Dio Chrysostom, *Orations VII, XII, and XXXVI*, ed. D. A. Russell (Cambridge: Cambridge University Press, 1992) 12.

appearances (2 Cor 10:7), he rejects part of the rhetorician's stock in trade. Paul both carefully distinguishes his proclamation of the gospel from sophistic speech[60] and contrasts his person with that of the super-apostles (οἱ ὑπερλίαν ἀπόστολοι, 12:11). He differs from the speakers whose power lies in rhetorical competence. His δεινότης lies neither in personal presence—a strong body—nor impressive rhetoric. The power of his good news lies in the God who raised Jesus from the dead. That position, first enunciated in 1 Cor 2:1–5, receives confirmation in 2 Cor 12:1–10, where he describes his physical weakness, to say nothing of his repeated stress on his weakness (2 Cor 4:7–15, 6:1–10). Dio, in *Or.* 13, describes the suffering in his exile as a good, because it turned him to philosophy. Paul in analogous fashion describes his suffering and weaknesses as the occasion for God to demonstrate power in his weakness. He uses a *topos* known elsewhere as part of the philosophic tradition to reject rhetorical flourishes in favor of message whose content is Spirit driven. Having thus established his divine source, his pure message, and his lofty aims, Paul's rhetorical expression can only be for the benefit of his Corinthian audience.

---

[60] Winter, *Philo and Paul among the Sophists*, is fundamental in a consideration of this aspect of Paul's ministry.

THE TOPPLING OF FAVORINUS
AND PAUL BY THE CORINTHIANS

Bruce W. Winter

> *Trust not a Corinthian, and make him
> not your friend.*[1]

What Menander had said of the Greek Corinthians, the famous Roman orator, Favorinus, would certainly have endorsed with respect to their Roman successors.[2] The unexpected and humiliating treatment metered out to him by the leading citizens of Corinth on his third visit there, contrasted starkly with that accorded to him by those who had presented themselves as his Corinthian "friends" on his first two illustrious visits in the second decade of the second century CE. Favorinus was "the best known western sophist." He was born in Arles and, according to Philostratus in his *Lives of the Sophists*, he had created a sensation with his Greek declamations in Rome. Even those who knew no Greek were "charmed by the sound of his voice, the significance of his glance, and the rhythm of his tongue."[3] He stunned the Corinthians with the charm of his eloquence. On a third visit, however, he discovered that the ruling class, living in the most prestigious Roman colony in the East, had no compunction in toppling those whom they had previously put on a pedestal.

Some sixty years prior to that incident, Paul also found his trust undermined and his reputation in tatters in Corinth. This time it was not the actions of its leading citizens, but of those who were "brothers" in the nascent Christian community. Relationships had been made uncertain when the Corinthian Christians indicated they wanted

---

[1] μὴ Κορινθίῳ πίστευε μὴ χρῶ φίλῳ (Menander, *Unidentified Minor Fragments* 763K).

[2] He was a virtuoso orator of the Second Sophistic who was born *c*. C.E. 90 in Arles and died in the middle of the next century. He was among the élite of Rome who moved in the imperial circle until sent into exile to the East by Hadrian and was attacked by another significant orator, Polemo. He was restored to imperial favor by Antonius Pius and was to secure his status and influence in the capital where he remained until his death.

[3] G.A. Kennedy, *The Art of Rhetoric in the Roman World* (Princeton: Princeton University Press, 1972), 591, cit. *Lives of the Sophists*, 491.

Apollos, and not Paul, to return to guide the affairs of their meetings
(1 Cor 16:12) after they had "played" the two former teachers off against
each other (1 Cor 4:6). Paul's attempt to heal the breach on a second
visit failed. Some adversaries would level charges against him which
questioned the integrity of his previous labors among them and would
call into question his ability to minister adequately ever again in this
center of *Romanitas*.

There are some significant parallels between the responses of the two
men. Favorinus delivered his oration ([Dio] *Or.* 37)[4] on his third visit to
Corinth where, in a mock court setting, he "charged" the Corinthians
with acting unjustly towards him. Paul wrote 2 Corinthians as he was
about to make a third visit and warned, in effect, of a "trial", for
he wrote that "in the mouth of two witnesses or three every word
will be established", *i.e.*, the allegations made against him would be
investigated (13:1).[5]

Professor Malherbe has, in his distinguished academic career, traversed an important aspect of the beginning of Paul's defense with his
examination of the military imagery of 2 Cor 10:3–6.[6] This chapter will
pursue in part the discussion that followed. The purpose of this contribution to his Festschrift is to undertake an examination of the mistreatment by the Corinthians of these two men. The nature of the *"apologia"*
that they made in response to unilateral actions taken against those who
were led to believe that they were "friends" of the Corinthians will be
explored. This will provide an opportunity to comment on how apposite the rhetorical or forensic terms "apology" or "defense" are when
applied to their responses.[7]

---

[4] The speech has traditionally been preserved in manuscripts of the speeches of Dio
Chrysostom, hence the designation [Dio] *Or.* 37. Hereafter, we shall simply refer to it
as *Or.* 37 and its subsections by using the siglum §. See also the article by White in this
volume for discussion of this speech.

[5] Its forensic allusions are clear, Deut 19:15; Num 35:30, cf., A. Borkowski, *Textbook
on Roman Law*, 2nd ed., (London: Blackstone, 1997), 77, 81, 107.

[6] "Antisthenes and Odysseus, and Paul at War", *HTR* 76 (1983) 143–73; repr. in *Paul
and the Popular Philosophers* (Philadelphia: Fortress Press, 1988) 91–119.

[7] Unlike the Pauline corpus where there are only fragmentary negative comments
about him to which he refers (2 Cor 10:10, 11:6 and 12:14ff.) we do possess sustained
criticisms of Favorinus by Polemo who engaged in a bitter and highly personal attack
on him. (For the text see G. Hoffmann, *Scriptores physiognomonici* 1.93–294, and Galen
who devoted a work on the best education in which he is critical of the teaching method
of Favorinus, Περὶ ἀρίστης διδασκαλία").

The Reactions of the Corinthians

Favorinus

The established convention of a city honoring generous or famous men, whether benefactors, athletes or orators, involved the passing of a formal resolution by the Council and the People.[8] In exceptional cases they not only engraved in stone a resolution of the "Council and the People" but also erected a statue and allocated a seat of honor in the prominent part of the theatre. Favorinus draws attention to the erecting of "a full length" (τὴν εἰκὼ τοῦ σώματος) bronze statue of himself (*Or.* 37, §10)—it should be remembered that "Corinthian" bronzes were highly prized in the ancient world so that a statue, not in stone but in bronze, was the greatest honor that could be given. He also draws attention to its place of honor—"you took this and set it up in your Library, a front row seat as it were (προεδρία)" (§8). The seats to which he refers were those in the theatre which, unlike others, could have armrests and were often made of expensive marble. They were placed closest to the stage so that all could see who these honored persons were as they took their set place at performances and any civic occasions held at the theatre. His "seat of honor" was in a seat of learning.

The statue had been erected after his second visit when he declined the offer to settle in Corinth to set up a school and play a role in the intellectual and political life of the city. He was originally judged to be such a shining example to the young men of Corinth who entered the library for the purposes of παιδεία that the statue was considered to be the next best thing to him residing there. All this visual "praise" which leading citizens had heaped on Favorinus on his second visit had established his *dignitas* for all in Corinth to see.

On his third visit he noted the fickleness of the Corinthians, "this one (οὗτος) is in jeopardy of being set up as the noblest of Greeks [even though he was a Roman from Gaul] and then being cast down as the worst, all in a brief span of time" (§22). He went on to argue that "each one of these statues … is at once invested with the attributes of sanctity, and the city should defend it as a votive offering" (§28). It has to be remembered that when the Corinthians looked on a statue of Athena

[8] See my *Seek the Welfare of the City: Early Christians as Benefactors and Citizens* (Grand Rapids: Eerdmans; Carlisle: Paternoster, 1994), 26–33.

they did not say "that is a statue of Athena" but "that Athena is visible in her statue."[9] It would seem that Favorinus' statement concerning the "attributes of sanctity" indicates that his statue made him "visible" though absent, hence the use of "this one" (οὗτος), and his subsequent comment, "O thou mute semblance of my eloquence, art thou not visible" (§46).[10] Therefore the casting down of a statue of one designated by the Corinthians as a "cherished friend" (§9), was calculated to inflict maximum disgrace and injury to that which Romans protected and prized most in public, *i.e.*, *dignitas*. The statue of Favorinus was toppled from its pride of place outside the library at the end of the long Stoa in the magnificent Roman forum of Corinth. Its removal signaled the public withdrawal of Corinth's friendship so visibly expressed by the statue erected in his honor.

Paul

When the Corinthians wrote to Paul about various matters,[11] they made it clear at the same time that the church had judged it preferable to have Apollos rather than him return as its teacher. The latter's role as the founding apostle was not in question for they sought rulings from him on critical issues they were facing (1 Cor 7:1ff.).[12] Other matters to which Paul responded came by way of reports, and clearly would have alienated some whose conduct he challenged in his reply.[13] His approach to the use of the grand style of oratory for preaching and his defense of his policy of working with his own hands, would have distanced him further from those whom E. A. Judge described as the "rhetorically fastidious" Christians of Corinth.[14] His censure of moral conduct without fear or favor was alien to the two-tier stan-

---

[9] Robin Lane Fox, *Pagans and Christians* (London: Penguin, 1988), 115.

[10] M.W. Gleason (*Making Men: Sophists and Self-Presentation in Ancient Rome* [Princeton: Princeton University Press, 1995] 13) suggests that the referent of the masculine demonstrative pronoun is ambiguous, i.e., the statue or Favorinus. If however he is present in his statue, no ambiguity arises.

[11] For an example of a περὶ δέ construction in responding to matters raised in a letter, see *BGU* 1141, *ll.* 31, 40 cf. *l.* 14 μοι τοῦτο ἔγραψας, and in 1 Cor 7:1, 25, 8:1, 12:1, 16:1, 16:12.

[12] 1 Cor 1:11, 5:1, 6:1, 12, 11:18, 15:12.

[13] For a detailed discussion of the origins of many of these issues see my *After Paul Left Corinth: The Impact of Secular Ethics and Social Change* (Grand Rapids: Eerdmans, 2000).

[14] E.A. Judge, "Paul's Boasting in Relation to Contemporary Professional Practice", *ABR* 16 (1968) 37–50.

dard that operated among Roman citizens and lower status inhabitants in Corinth.

Detractors who came subsequently to the church appeared to have fuelled the situation by judging Paul's defense of his conduct in 1 Corinthians to be nothing more than a sham. It was seen to be a theological rationalization of personal inadequacies (1:17–2.5, 9:1ff.; 2 Cor 10:10) and a subterfuge for a collection. Protestations about providing his ministry free of charge and not seeking back pay would fall on incredulous ears in subsequent days (9:15–18, 16:1; cf., 2 Cor 12:16).

Paul later learnt of criticisms and charges against him by some of the Christians. Adversaries who were teachers denigrated him by pointing to his inability to present well as was expected of a public speaker in his day.[15] In an age when "delivery" was critical and debarred some from speaking in public, Paul's bodily presence was described as weak and his speech or oratory as ineffectual. There was a long history of writing orators who simply lacked either "the presence" or oratory for public presentation. He was a "layman," i.e., a non-practicing but trained rhetorician, when it came to rhetoric, and he operated with deceitful motives in sending others to them, presumably for the collection (2 Cor 10:10, 11:6, 12:16–7).[16]

It was somewhat paradoxical that Favorinus was toppled, not because his considerable rhetorical ability had been eclipsed by an even greater than he visiting Corinth, but because of the imperial displeasure he incurred for alleged sexual misconduct elsewhere with a senator's wife, even though he had been a eunuch from birth. Paul, on the other hand, was toppled not only because he lacked the rhetorical delivery now sought by Christians in Corinth in their preachers but also on the basis of his *apologia* concerning his anti-rhetorical or anti-sophistic stance which he mounted in 1 Corinthians.

The move against both would have been made by members of an ἐκκλησία, in the case of Favorinus by the leaders of the βουλὴ καὶ δῆμος of the city and in the case of Paul, by the ἐκκλησία τοῦ θεοῦ

---

[15] For a discussion of "delivery" in 2 Cor 10:10 see my forthcoming article "Philodemus and Paul on Rhetorical Delivery (ὑπόκρισις)" in *Philodemus and the New Testament World*, ed. J.T. Fitzgerald, G. Holland and D. Obbink (NovTSup; Leiden: E.J. Brill, 2003).

[16] For a full discussion of this see my "Paul among the Christian Sophists", *Philo and Paul among the Sophists*, 2nd ed., (Grand Rapids: Eerdmans, 2002), ch. 10.

ἐν Κορίνθῳ. Neither man emerged unscathed emotionally from his humiliating experience at the hands of the Corinthians, and neither let the matter rest.

Their responses have been preserved for us. Both are somewhat un-Roman in their tenor, for the public disclosure of personal feelings about the insults inflicted on them was not necessarily the response of the Roman gentleman. The Corinthian Christians clearly did not want Paul back, any more than their secular counterparts would later want to welcome Favorinus back, but both were determined to return.

The Nature of the Defenses

The Apologia of Favorinus

When Favorinus addressed the audience as "gentlemen of the jury" (§22), is it right to conclude that we have a forensic defense (ἀπολογία)? If that were the case then we would expect the *encomium* with its *captatio benevolentae*, commending the particular qualifications of the judges to hear this specific case. Such a speech would contain an *exordium, narratio, confirmatio* and *peroratio* as recommended by the textbooks of the ancient world. While it is true that the actual official proceedings of the court case did not include an *exordium*, official petitions seeking to initiate an action did.[17] His oration has none of the markers that indicated the transition from one section of the forensic speech to the next, although clearly the florid nature of the conclusion of the speech is a *peroratio*.[18]

The oration can be divided into two sections: §§1–19 and §§20–47. In the first, Favorinus recollects the uniqueness of his statue with distinctions, which no one else had had before, bestowed on him. The Corinthians, so upright and glorious in their past history, are authors of an outrage in which they overthrew this particular statue. In the second part, the orator has recourse to an artifice, *i.e.*, a deceit: he feigns a lawsuit by the statue (δίκη ἀνδριάντος) and makes himself the advocate of its cause, delivering an oration before a "tribunal."

The two sections can then be subdivided as follows. In section one he argues that neither Arion, nor Solon, nor Herodotus had the distinction of a statue in Corinth, §§1–8, and he expresses astonishment at the

---

[17] See my "The Importance of the *Capitatio Benevolentiae* in the Speeches of Tertullius and Paul in Acts 24:1–21," *JTS* (n.s.) 42 (1991) 505–31.

[18] *Ibid.*, 508–11.

disappearance of the statue and the supposed cause for it, §§9–19. In the second section he outlines the personal merits which constitute evidence for the right to the honor received, §§20–27, the sacred nature of the honor to have a statue of oneself erected, §§28–31, and the outrage he felt because it was slander, which is the particular problem of great men, §§32–36. He reflects also on the transitory nature of human things, §§37–43, the superiority of the intellect and the eternal nature of its works, §§44–47.[19]

It has been suggested that because the manuscript title is Κοϱινθι-ακός this "would usually mean an encomium" and as a result it has been designated by Maud Gleason as Favorinus' oration in "Praise of Corinth."[20] She argues that he does this by combining "the activity of apology and invective without appearing to perform either," and further suggests, "He does this by burying ironic mockery of Corinth inside historical and literary allusions and by adopting the identity of imaginary *personae* in order to cover his tracks when he is actually prais-ing himself."[21] It is not that they were unaware of his gifts as an ora-tor and a paradigm for the younger generation of rising scholars that he needed to praise himself. They did that at the time of the erect-ing of the statue designating him, a Roman, as "the noblest among the Greeks" (ἄϱιστο Ἑλλήνων, §22). Although Gleason has provided important background information to ancient references and illusions of situations in his speech, she has not taken into account the role that shame played in Roman society and especially the humiliating effects this stinging public rebuke would have had on the Corinthians.[22] Favor-inus' approach could never bring about reconciliation but only widen the rift between him and his audience, and the latter was clearly his intention. If this is correct, then the whole speech is full of irony. He does comment "Now these remarks have been offered in the interest of the city, which must not suffer disgrace in the eyes of the Greeks, seeing that all men not merely welcome with delight him whom you have banished, but even send for him and dispatch him on missions here and there and, among other things, show him honor by actually

---

[19] For the division of the speech see A. Barigazzi, *Favorino di Arelate: Opera Introduzione, Testo Critico e Commento* (Florence: Lelice Le Monnier, 1966) 301.

[20] Gleason, *Making Men*, 10 points out that the manuscript title is Κοϱινθιακός (sc. Λόγος) "which would usually mean an encomium."

[21] Gleason, *Making Men*, 9.

[22] R.A. Kaster, "The Shame of the Romans" *TAPA* 127 (1997), 1–19. See the article by L.M. White that follows, esp. 317 and 321.

erecting statues of him" (§37). The reality is that Corinth, like Athens,[23]
is left with no other choice than to remove his statue, and even more
so in the case of the former because their status as a Roman colony
demanded that they show solidarity with the emperor. His friends are
their friends and his former friends are now their enemies. On the surface it is a mock trial on behalf of a statue, but as it unfolds it is a
stinging rebuke to a city that prided itself on its justice and which is
now being publicly denigrated step by step by the one whom they have
so unjustly humiliated.

This is not the first time Favorinus has experienced rejection. He
wrote of that painful experience and perhaps others as well in *De
Exilio*.[24] The place of his "relegation," rather than "exile" was apparently Chios (14.39ff.). He noted, "For me, even before my enforced exile
(ἐμοὶ δὲ ᾧ καὶ πρὸ τῆς ἀναγκαίας φυγῆς), the majority of my life was
spent throughout many parts of land and sea, in the company of foreign
people, away from home" (11.8ff.). "Missing one's family and friends,"[25]
on top of loving one's country, is set out as a second battle in addition
to that one, as it recalls one's origin and one's common nurture, "going
to school together and spending time in the same ways in the gymnasi-
ums, good times with one's contemporaries and close friends, these are
like a spell, a bait alluring the soul' (12.39ff.). Even making allowances
for the Stoic and Cynic motifs in the treatise[26] and his speech to the
Corinthians, he behaves in a rather un-Roman way in that he discloses
publicly the depth of his personal indignation.

In the "*peroratio*" he develops a theme aimed at further rebutting
the Corinthians by indicating that the everlasting nature of his fame
is not diminished in any way by their action. Having already noted the
absence and immortality of the soul which "is not present when the
body is outworn nor is it concerned for it" (§44)—an allusion to what
they have done to his body, *i.e.*, his statue[27]—he affirms that he "would

---

[23] Philostratus, *VS* 490.

[24] This is a more recently discovered treatise which provides much autobiographical
details. *P.Vat.Gr. II* (early 3rd century A.D.). For a critical edition see A. Barigazzi,
Favorino di Arelate, 375–409.

[25] Another personal detail that emerges from this work is his personal devotion to
his sister who is mentioned in a reference to his parents (*De exilio* 11.22–24).

[26] L. Holford–Strevens, *Aulus Gellius* (London: Duckworth, 1988), 78.

[27] It will probably be melted down (§21) and "recycled," as was also the custom with
stone statues, where the usual provision called for replacing one head with another
when the benefactor died.

not desert a friend, though void of life,"[28] unlike the Corinthians for whom friendship proverbially could mean nothing.[29]

As a result he wants to speak "words of comfort to my friend, the statue, as to one possessing sensation: 'O thou mute semblance of my eloquence, art thou visible?'" Referring to the study of the repeated disappearance and reappearance of Aristeas, whom the men of Proconnesus asserted "was not to be seen, either living or dead," Favorinus declared he "was alive then, lives now, and will live always," as indeed he himself will, but in what sense? Hesiod's statements, along with those of Homer which were used as proof texts for orators and authors, provided the answer, "But fame is never utterly destroyed which many people voice: a goddess she."[30] Favorinus declares that "I will raise you up and place you in the precinct of the goddess [presumably of Fame]" knowing that nothing could tear the statue down there.[31] He enumerates that, in addition to the elements neither "open hostility (φθόνος)[32] nor an enemy" can do this, and that "judgement plays no tricks on good men [public benefactors (ἀνδρῶν ἀγαθῶν)]."[33] Therefore the statue can stand "upright for me like a man."[34] With this "sung" *peroratio* Favorinus declares that he will be vindicated and find himself in other places in "the hall of fame, but even now I find you [standing] in your place" (ἀλλὰ καὶ νῦν σε καταλαμβάνω ἑστηκότα, §47). The implication is clear but it really only emerges at the end of the oration: he now cares little for an official declaration of the Council and People of Corinth, neither does he care what they have done to him subsequently, for a right judgement has already been passed, he is already standing erect, a famous man.

---

[28] A possible allusion to Menander's comment about the reputation of the Corinthians' proverbial disloyalty to friends, *Unidentified Minor Fragments* 763K.

[29] Cit. Euripides, *Laodameia*, Nauck, *Trag. Graec. Frag.* 565.

[30] Hesiod, *Works and Days*, 763–4.

[31] Gleason, *Making Men*, 20 rightly notes that "we do not need to postulate a second unveiling" in Corinth.

[32] For a discussion of this term see K.M.D. Dunbabin and M.W. Dickie, "Invidia runpantur pactora: Iconography of Phthonos/Invidia in Graeco-Roman Art," *JAC* 26 (1983) 7–37.

[33] For epigraphic evidence see my *Seek the Welfare of the City*.

[34] It is not certain if the reference is to his congenital disorder of Reifenstein's syndrome, which meant that he had a penis but no testicles and hence was incapable of being a "man" according to Roman thinking. See Gleason, *Making Men*, 3 citing H. Mason, "Favorinus' Disorder: Reifenstein's Syndrome in Antiquity?" *Janus* 66 (1979) 1–13.

This oration was intended for a highly sophisticated audience with
the endless number of apposite allusions to ancient persons and situations in the past. It can, therefore, be assumed that the élite of Corinth
were listening to a dressing down, unlike "the women and children"
who were entranced by the magic of his oratory on previous visits to
Corinth.

What can we learn about the nature of this speech? An orator of
this standing provides no "structure" to his oration and it basically
defies a form critical analysis. It therefore is a warning to those who
would rush in to "tag" the text according to the so-called canons of
rhetoric, however much it has all the hallmarks of the grand style of
oratory. Favorinus was clearly seen as an important sophist operating in
the full flow of the Second Sophistic and his oration was no set piece
declamation for "gentlemen of the jury" but a presentation aiming to
shame publicly the Corinthians.

The Apologia of Paul

What are we to make of Paul's response to the Corinthians? It is, of
course, no oration but clearly his most impassioned letter, being full of
surprising self-disclosure and unparalleled in his corpus by reason of
that fact. In the context of the extant literature of his day it is amazing
for these two reasons. Its tone is a far cry from the studied *dignitas* of the
first-century gentleman and "memorable" incidents relating to Paul,
such as those reported in 2 Cor 2 or 11. They certainly would not have
made it into the *Memorable Doings and Words* of Valerius Maximus who
wrote in the Principate of Tiberius.[35]

In 2 Cor 12:19 Paul declared, "You think that all this time we are
defending ourselves to you (ὅτι ὑμῖν ἀπολογούμεθὰ)?" He went on to
indicate that he would "establish every word" on the basis of two or
three witnesses and that "if I come again I will not spare" those who
made allegations (13:2–30). This threatening language is reminiscent
of a choice he placed before the Corinthians in a previous context—
"shall I come to you with a rod?" (1 Cor 4:21)—the references replicate

---

[35] See the recent translation in the Loeb series (2000), the first in English since
1678 and C. Skidmore, *Practical Ethics for Roman Gentlemen: The Works of Valerius Maximus*
(Exeter: University of Exeter, 1996).

imperial threats or those of governors who exercised their *imperium* at the criminal assizes to order beatings.[36]

H. D. Betz took the discussion of 2 Corinthians in a new direction when he built a substantial case based on the use of the term, ἀπο-λογία. He argued that Paul was consciously imitating the Socratic tra-dition by refusing to defend himself, having been tried *in absentia* by the Corinthian church.[37] He expanded further on his theme in "The Problem of Rhetoric and Theology according to the Apostle Paul" undaunted by the challenges that had been mounted to his thesis.[38] E.A. Judge had already subjected this proposal to a substantial critique and concluded that "Paul's pseudo-apology is remote from the spirit of Socrates."[39] If Socrates was not the precedent for Paul, is there one? He did use a *terminus technicus* in a cognate of ἀπολογία in 12:19. In spite of his denial did he himself engage in some form of "forensic defense" in much the same way a superficial reading of Favorinus' oration and his comment on "gentlemen of the jury" might suggest?

Paul uses the term ἀπολογία in two other settings. In Philippians 1:7 and 16 he refers to himself as being in "bonds" for the "defense of the gospel." The *Sitz im Leben* is clearly his imprisonment awaiting an actual trial. In his self-description as to why he was there he does not enunciate any charge of *maiestas* as a Roman citizen or any breach of criminal law, but he connects the term with the gospel. It is true that he would make his legal defense and Luke summarizes one such defense before Felix and Festus at Caesarea Maritima.[40] That Paul was capable of mounting his own legal defense is not the point under discussion. Here we have the use of the term, ἀπολογία—that has been plundered for a theological purpose and was a double entendre.

The other use is found in 1 Cor 9:3 where he indicates in the stron-gest terms that "this is my defense to those who examine me" (ἡ ἐμὴ ἀπολογία τοῖς ἐμὲ ἀνακρίνουσίν ἐστιν αὕτη).[41] He is emphatic that this

---

[36] E.M. Larsen, "The Use of the Father Image in Imperial Propaganda 1 Corinthi-ans 4:14–21," *TynBul* 42.1 (1991) 133–36.

[37] H.D. Betz, *Der Apostel Paulus und die sokratische Tradition: eine exegetische Untersuchung zu seiner 'Apologie' 2 Corinther 10–13* (Tübingen: J.C.B. Mohr, 1972.).

[38] In A. Vanhoye (ed.), *L'Apotre Paul: Personnalité, Style et Conception du Ministere* (Leuven: Leuven University Press, 1986) 16–48.

[39] E.A. Judge, "St. Paul and Socrates," *Interchange* 13 (1973) 106–16.

[40] See my "The Importance of the *Captatio Benevolentiae*".

[41] The use of the demonstrative pronoun as the end of the sentence indicates its emphatic role.

is a "defense" and the verb used has clear forensic allusions.[42] On the
basis of Betz' suggestion, one might argue that Paul had been "tried"
in absentia by the Corinthians and declared unfit to lead the church into
the next phase of its life. One might also expect that something of a
forensic or pseudo-forensic presentation could be expected from Paul
in 9:3ff. and therefore a form critical approach would unlock the significance of his argument. Should we not expect to find something of
an *exordium* if not a *narratio, confirmatio* and *peroratio*? After all, Paul has
already declared that he has used a rhetorical device called a covert
allusion in 4:6 with respect to Apollos and himself, even if he has given
it his own peculiar twist by making that which was normally "covert"
very much overt.[43] Rather, we find Paul beginning his ἀπολογία with
eleven questions prefaced with an additional three before the declaration of a defense, (9:1–12a). While it is true that, as Witherington notes,
Quintilian saw a role for questions, nowhere does his discussion envis-
age such a barrage of questions as that to which Paul resorts.[44] Attempts
to divide this passage according to a form critical analysis based on
rhetorical handbooks simply fail. It is not an ἀπολογία in the technical
sense of the term.

What are we to say then concerning Paul's "defense" in 2 Corinthians? Witherington defends the view that "*2 Corinthians taken as a compositional whole is an example of forensic or judicial rhetoric.*"[45] He divides
the whole letter into an *exordium, narratio, propositio, probatio* and *refu-
tatio,* and *peroratio.*[46] As neat as that division is, does it do justice to
Paul's method of letter writing and the *Sitz im Leben* that gave rise to
it, and in which he was to become so personally involved? The struc-
turing of some of his letters is somewhat enigmatic, in spite of recent
interest in subjecting them to form critical analyses. In 1 Cor 1–4 the
immediate reason for tackling the issue raised by reports on the divisions in the church does not emerge until 16:12 when the matter about
which they wrote is revealed and concerns the return of Apollos, and
not Paul, to minister in their congregation. Of course these divisions

---

[42] See for example the references in the entry in LSJ.

[43] For a discussion of his use of irony and exposing the significance of the allusion
so that the Corinthians were left in no doubt as to what he was doing, see my *Philo and
Paul Among the Sophists*, 196–201.

[44] B. Witherington III, *Conflict and Community in Corinth; A Socio-Rhetorical Commentary
on 1 and 2 Corinthians* (Grand Rapids: Eerdmans, 1995) 205. Quintilian, 9.2.6–16.

[45] Witherington, *Conflict and Community*, 333. The italics are his.

[46] Witherington, *Conflict and Community*, 335–36.

also emerge in various places in the community's life, but it is significant that it was not until the end of the letter that the lengthy discussion in 1 Cor 1–4 emerges in spite of a reference to personages such as Peter, Paul and Apollos in the opening section and a reference in 4:6 to some being "puffed up" on behalf of Paul against Apollos.

Paul's letter to the Philippians adopts a similar strategy. The questions of the behavior of some within the church is dealt with in 2:1–18. The seeking for primacy and the presence of a hostility towards other members of the community indicates that there are real internal problems but, unlike 1 Cor 4:21 which ends with a threat, the section in Philippians ends with a call that explicates 1:27 about living worthily of the gospel. It is not until 4:2–3 that names emerge and the statement repeated, "the same mind" (2:2), where it was followed by a description of motive and actions (2:3). It is only here that Paul asks the church to help the two women, Euodia and Syntyche, who had labored with him in the gospel while he was there.[47] In 2 Corinthians there is no clear structure and he rightly asserts this is no ἀπολογία (12:19).

There has been value in comparing these two visitors to Corinth. Favorinus is a great orator, publicly acknowledged to be, in fact, "the noblest of all Greeks" although a Roman, speaking at a time of the revival of "Greek" culture and oratory not only in Rome but also in Corinth. His own speech, although giving the impression of an *apologia* in court, turns out to be a mock trial lacking the hallmarks of the formal divisions of such presentations. His oration alerts us to the fact that, in the context of the Second Sophistic, a leading sophist of the caliber of Favorinus is not restricted by the divisions of the handbooks on rhetoric. The "grand style" is present in his oration but it lacks "the form."

The same has proved to be no less true for Paul who writes on the other side of the cultural divide in Corinth where *Romanitas* was the dominant force in the Roman colony. 2 Corinthians lacks the formal structure we have come to believe was typical of letters of the first century. While he may use rhetorical devices, there is an absence of a rhetorical structure. Issues discussed early in the letter are resumed and, such has been the lack of a readily identifiable structure, some have concluded his second letter consists of two or more letters.

---

[47] See my *Seek the Welfare of the City*, ch. 5.

What is sometimes overlooked is the fact that, while formal education in Greek and Latin was an education in rhetoric at the primary, secondary and tertiary levels, those who experienced such an education were not bound to speak and write on all occasions in the grand style of oratory, or indeed to write within the narrow confines prescribed for forensic briefs or set pieces to be memorized for public declamations. The *Sitz im Leben* determined the personal nature of the response. This is seen even in the case of a polished orator such as Favorinus especially where it effected him personally, as his Corinthian oration reveals.

A clue as to the possible influence on the way that Favorinus framed his oration may be found from a comparable oration of his distinguished teacher, Dio Chrysostom. The latter delivered an oration to his fellow citizens of Prusa *c.* C.E. 102. The reason for it arose over his disappointment and frustration because his political opponents had persuaded certain civic benefactors to withdraw their promises of financial contributions towards his scheme to beautify Prusa. It was a project on a grand scale to which he had committed his own resources. When he stood up to deliver his speech he told his fellow citizens that he would produce a discourse that was not "extraordinary" or "remarkable" or "composed to produce a kind of pleasure" [to his audience] or to "exhibit wisdom." He who was so renowned for his oratory that he was called "golden tongued" pleads that he had forgotten how to declaim. All his previous efforts had been purely good luck, and as a result he was able to deceive cities and citizens alike, he said. However he could do that no longer and the citizen body gathered before him could only expect something amateurish and commonplace, certainly not anything "high-minded" or "wise."[48] As a result of the pettiness and inglorious conduct of his opponents, he denied the assembled gathering that which they longed to hear, *i.e.*, a declamation from the golden tongued Dio. He was not alone in doing this for Aristides refused to declaim altogether in public because of the ingratitude of the young men who paid lip-service to his greatness but neglected to come to his lectures.[49]

Given the possession of a number of letters written by Paul, it seems feasible that the different situations called forth a variety of responses

---

[48] *Or.* 47.1, 8 and for a full discussion see C.P. Jones, *The Roman World of Dio Chrysostom* (Cambridge, Mass.: Harvard University Press, 1978) ch.12.

[49] Aristides, "To those who criticize him because he does not disclaim," *Or.* 33.24–25.

and forms from him. When we come to 2 Corinthians we are faced with Paul having escaped from a "near-death" experience, writing to a congregation which contains some who may still be mildly sympathetic to him, but most of whom are simply hostile to him or are at best indifferent. Paul wrote for the purpose of informing them of his projected visit and preparing the congregation for his return, both encouraging and rebuking them. More than that he sought reconciliation, *i.e.*, restoration of his relationship with a largely disaffected congregation not on their terms for his letter contains stern rebukes.[50] His willingness "to bare his soul" in such an extended way suggests that the situation and difficulties largely determined the intensity and flow of the letter.

Quintilian would have agreed that this should actually be the case for both men, for he believed that personal arguments should be derived from a consideration of circumstances. He acknowledged that each case had its own particular features. These suggest a line of argument which "should spontaneously follow the orator's thoughts." He was not uncritical of Greek rhetorical tradition for its somewhat "mechanical" approach.[51]

Much work has been done on rhetoric by New Testament scholars and, given that the discipline is coming of age, some errors of judgement will naturally have been made.[52] Perhaps at this stage the study of Paul's use of rhetoric would be well served by an extensive comparison with the role it played in the corpus of Philo. He was a fellow Jew and contemporary whom we know trained in this discipline.[53] In response to particular situations both developed their arguments on the basis of the Old Testament scriptures. Philo's work could provide a helpful yardstick against which Paul's ability in this area could be carefully assessed.

One of the abiding influences on Biblical scholarship of the person honored in this volume is his caution and scholarly acumen in the use of ancient sources and literary forms. His enduring friendship expresses itself in his mild correction with a note scribbled as he listens to a

---

[50] For a discussion of the dichotomy and a form critical analysis of 2 Cor 10–13 based on epistolary theory see J.T. Fitzgerald, "Paul, the Ancient Epistolary Theorists, and 2 Corinthians 10–13," in *Greeks, Romans and Christians: Essays in Honor of Abraham J. Malherbe*, ed. D.L. Balch, E. Ferguson and W.A. Meeks, (Minneapolis: Fortress, 1990), 190–200.

[51] Quintilian, 5.10.119–25.

[52] See R. Dean Anderson, Jr., *Ancient Rhetorical Theory and Paul* (2nd ed.; CBET 17; Kampen: Kok Pharos, 1999) for a recent assessment.

[53] M. Alexandre, Jr., *Rhetorical Argumentation in Philo of Alexandria*, (StPhilo Monographs 2; Altanta: Scholars Press, 1999).

paper which was patently defective, or his jovial and gentle interactions afterwards over a meal. He might suggest that a comparison between the oration of Favorinus and Paul's 2 Corinthians was an inappropriate one given the different literary genres. However, this essay has sought to undertake some soundings as we seek to map two extant literary sources directed at the Corinthians some sixty years apart. The nature of Corinthian "fickleness" had not changed from Paul's time nor had the tenacity of the two who visited the colony with reputations now in tatters from inhabitants as they formulated vigorous responses to those who no longer saw themselves as "friends".

RHETORIC AND REALITY IN GALATIANS
FRAMING THE SOCIAL DEMANDS OF FRIENDSHIP

L. Michael White

Paul's "Personal Appeal" in Gal 4:12–20

I am afraid I have labored over you in vain. Brethren, I beseech you,
become as I am, for I also have become as you are. … My little children,
with whom I am again in travail until Christ be formed in you! I could
wish to be present with you now and to change my tone, for I am
perplexed about you. (Gal 4:11–12 & 19–20, RSV)

Galatians is perhaps Paul's harshest letter; well known are the bitter
irony and stinging condemnations that run throughout it. But in Gal
4:11–20[1] Paul turns to address his audience in a direct and very personal way—too personal for some. The passage seems to begin with
trepidation and end with panged exasperation. The question is what to
make of this emotional outburst in the context of a letter whose theological argument and rhetorical sophistication are so central to contemporary Pauline studies. For the most part, it has been ignored. "Es ist
ein Argument des Herzens, das mit starkem Affekt vorgetragen wird,
wie der sprunghafte Gedankengang verrät," said Heinrich Schlier,[2] following Oepke and others.[3] This traditional view is still followed in some
recent commentaries. As a result this passage is taken as an emotional

---

[1] Almost all commentators delimit the passage as 4:12–20, assuming (with text
editors at least since Tischendorf, following the Vulgate and the Koine) that 4:11 is
properly taken as the ending of the preceding section. A few commentators have
noticed, however, that 4:19–20 pick up the same sentiment found in 4:11, and that
these verses form a kind of *inclusio* around the passage. We shall return to affirm this
view later; see n. 111 below.

[2] *Der Brief an die Galater* (KEK; Göttingen: Vandenhoeck & Ruprecht, 1949; 14th [5th]
ed., 1971) 208: "It is an argument of the heart, that was expressed with strong emotion
[*or* emotional disturbance], as the disjointed train of thought betrays" (my translation).

[3] Albrecht Oepke, *Der Brief des Paulus an die Galater* (THKNT 9; Berlin: Evangelische
Verlagsanstalt, 1937; 3rd ed., by J. Rohde, 1973) 140–42; Oepke said that there's no
rationality in the passage as Paul has lost the argument and resorted to a passionate
plea. Compare Pierre Bonnard, *L'Épître de Saint Paul aux Galates* (CNT; Neuchâtel:
Delachaux, 1953) 91, who argues that the elliptical syntax further betrays the inner
agitation of Paul.

and even desperate appeal by Paul and thus out of step with the sophisticated theological argument that dominates the rest of the letter.[4]

Alternatively, Hans Dieter Betz observes that the language of 4.12–20—while still very personal in tone—was predicated on the ancient *topos* on friendship.[5] In support Betz amasses a number of parallels from pagan authors to elucidate the language of friendship in the passage. Betz concludes that Paul employed the *topos* here merely as a rhetorical device to support his argument; the passage even ends with a rather dramatic rhetorical ploy. Says Betz:

> Paul *pretends* to be at the end of his wits—a rhetorical device well-known by the name of *dubitatio*. Thus, the strongly emotional plea ends with a confession of helplessness and the admission of defeat in the argument. Paul *acts* as if he has run out of arguments. Of course, this rhetorical device must be seen for what it is.[6]

Thus, Betz sees the friendship language and the emotional tone in 4.12–20 as rhetorical artifice, a pretense. Consequently, it remains in large measure disconnected both from the actual historical situation and from the theological argument of the letter.

More recent commentaries on Galatians have not generally followed up on Betz's argument, and the passage has received little further attention.[7] James D.G. Dunn admits that the friendship language is there but argues that simply treating it as a "string of *topoi*" (*pace* Betz) "does not clearly bring out the emotional intensity of the passage;"[8] nor does he think the emotion is in any way feigned. J. Louis Martyn accepts the basic observations of Betz regarding the friendship backgound to at least some of the language in Gal. 4.12–20, but opts for another interpretation of the symbolism and intent of the "birthpangs" (ὠδίνω) based

---

[4] So Ronald Fung, *The Epistle to the Galatians* (NICNT; Grand Rapids: Eerdmans, 1988) 195: "this section as Paul's personal appeal to his Galatian converts has little doctrinal content." Cf. Ernest de Witt Burton, *A Critical and Exegetical Commentary on the Epistle to the Galatians* (ICC; Edinburgh: T&T Clark, 1921) 235, who says that Paul had dropped argument in favor of begging and appealing.

[5] Hans Dieter Betz, *Galatians* (Hermeneia; Philadelphia: Fortress, 1979) 220–21. See also Betz, xiii for other comments on Schlier's "ingenious misinterpretation" of the letter.

[6] *Ibid.*, 236–37 (emphasis mine).

[7] It is little discussed in many recent treatments, e.g., F.F. Bruce, *The Epistle to the Galatians* [NIGTC; Grand Rapids: Eerdmans, 1982] 207–13; and Philip F. Esler, *Galatians* (NT Readings; London: Routledge, 1998), 37, 69, 71, 91, 209, 214 (mostly regarding Paul's founding visit).

[8] *The Epistle to the Galatians* (BNTC; Peabody: Hendrikson, 1995) 231.

on Jewish apocalpyticism.[9] Even so, Martyn finally views 4:12–20 more in the vein of an emotional and introspective aside on Paul's part rather than furthering the overall argument or reflecting the social situation of the letter.[10]

Few scholars besides Betz have taken 4:12–20 to have any argumentative force in the overall rhetorical structure of the letter. Reading it as a rhetorical device (*dubitatio*), Betz thus argues that it functions rhetorically in alternation with the heavier theological abstractions of the preceding and following sections. "The argumentative force," he says, "lies in the topic [read *topos*] itself, the marks of 'true' and 'false' friendship," because the Galatians themselves would have recognized the *topos*.[11] He also argues, therefore, that the passage serves as a hinge to the paraenetic section beginning in 5:1. Thus, this "lighter" passage (4:12–20) is setting up the Galatians for Paul's last major argument (4:21–31) of the *probatio* (or "proof"), at least as Betz understands the structure of the letter. He thus identifies the rhetorical function of the letter as *apologia*, a defense of Paul's apostleship and theology.[12]

Other scholars have questioned Betz's classification of the rhetorical form of Galatians.[13] Notably George A. Kennedy made Galatians

---

[9] *Galatians* (AB33A; New York: Anchor/Doubleday, 1997) 418–31. See esp. 420–22 in approval of Betz (but with no citation of the Hellenistic materials), but 427–31 for his alternative reading, following Beverly Roberts Gaventa, "The Maternity of Paul: An Exegetical Study of Gal 4:19," in *The Conversation Continues: Studies in Paul and John in Honor of J. Louis Martyn*, ed. by R.T. Fortna and B.R. Gaventa (Nashville: Abingdon Press, 1991) 189–201.

[10] Martyn, *Galatians*, 430: "Paul understands his suffering by drawing on the apocalyptic image of birth pains. He therefore sees in the Teachers' persecuting activity an instance of the last-ditch effort by which God's enemies hope to thwart the eschatological redemption of the elect."

[11] Betz, *Galatians*, 221 argues that its "personal appeal to friendship" has an argumentative force and is not inconsistent with the rest of the letter, since alternating between heavy and light periods was considered good style. Betz classifies Gal as an example of forensic rhetoric according to the three traditional "species" of Classical rhetoric—forensic (juridical), deliberative (persuasive), and epideictic (praise & blame).

[12] *Ibid.*, 14, and esp. 24: "The apologetic letter, such as Galatians, presupposes the real or fictitious situation of the court of law, with jury, accuser, and defendant. In the case of Galatians, the addressees are identical with the jury, with Paul being the defendant, and his opponents being the accusers. The situation makes Paul's Galatian letter a self-apology, delivered not in person but in a written form." It is, in other words, a speech with epistolary trappings, rather than a letter with rhetorical elements. Generally speaking, Betz has a hard time fitting the paraenetic sections of the letter into his forensic form, and so the link to 4:12–20 is more important since it ties the exhortation more directly to a point in the persuasive arguments.

[13] A good summary of the various ways that rhetorical analysis might outline the

a test case for an alternative view of rhetorical criticism that was less concerned with form than function.[14] Kennedy thus takes Gal as deliberative rhetoric, whose goal is to persuade or dissuade the audience of some future action;[15] however, 4:12–20 plays no significant part.

Following Walter G. Hansen,[16] Richard N. Longenecker[17] proposed instead that Galatians was a "mixed" rhetorical form, beginning as forensic but ending as deliberative. He then argued that 4:12–20 was the major shift between these two parts of the letter. From 4:12 on, says Longenecker, "Paul is no longer so much concerned to accuse or defend as to persuade his Galatian converts to adopt a certain course of action."[18] John L. White[19] and James Hester[20] have instead identified

---

letter is offered by Stanley E. Porter, "Paul of Tarsus and his Letters," in *Handbook of Classical Rhetoric in the Hellenistic Period, 330 BC- AD 400*, ed. S.E. Porter (Leiden: Brill, 1997) 541–47.

[14] *New Testament Interpretation through Rhetorical Criticism* (Chapel Hill: University of North Carolina Press, 1984) 36, 144–51; cf. Porter, "Paul and his Letters," 543 (since Kennedy does not actually provide an outline of the letter according to his analysis of the form).

[15] Kennedy (*NT Interpretation*, 145–46) also allows for some affinities to epideictic; however, he takes the persuasive function of the letter to fit it into the "species" (i.e., form) of deliberative rhetoric. This move is to allow the *rhetorical strategy* to be equivalent to the *rhetorical form*. But in all types of ancient literature such an equation is not a given; in many cases, the *rhetorical strategy* may be intentionally set against the form in which it is employed. This is especially the case in works whose message is conveyed through irony or satire. We shall turn to the issue of *rhetorical strategy* in the next section of this study. For a discussion of Kennedy's method, see Philip H. Kern, *Rhetoric and Galatians: Assessing an Approach to Paul's Epistle* (SNTSMS 101; Cambridge: Cambridge UP, 1998), 137–41. Also Kennedy's critique of Betz has been extended by Robert G. Hall ("The Rhetorical Outline for Galatians: A Reconsideration," *JBL* 106 [1987] 277–87) who offers a different outline of the letter as deliberative rhetoric. For Hall, the section 3:1–6:10 is simply classed as "further headings" within the *probatio*.

[16] *Abraham in Galatians: Epistolary and Rhetorical Contexts* (JSNTSup 29; Sheffield: JSOT Press, 1989) 56–59.

[17] *Galatians* (WBC 41; Dallas: Word Publishing, 1990) 184–5; cf. Hansen, *Abraham in Galatians*, 59 and 224 n. 80. The extensive epistolary elements in this section are important in this shift to deliberative speech and are more in keeping with the exhortation section of the letter.

[18] *Galatians*, 184.

[19] "Apostolic Mission and Apostolic Message: Congruence in Paul's Epistolary Rhetoric, Structure, and Imagery," in *Origins and Method: Towards a New Understanding of Judaism and Christianity: Essays in Honour of John C. Hurd*, ed. B.H. McLean (JSNTSup 86; Sheffield: JSOT Press, 1993) 145–61.

[20] "Placing the Blame: The Presence of Epideictic in Galatians 1–2," in *Persuasive Artistry: Studies in New Testament Rhetoric in Honor of George A. Kennedy*, ed. D.F. Watson (JSNTSup 50; Sheffield: JSOT Press, 1991) 281–307.

Galatians as epideictic rhetoric that offers blame and an educational corrective to Paul's audience.[21] Meanwhile, Philip H. Kern has questioned whether Galatians can be made to fit any of the classical rhetorical types, including the so-called "mixed" type.[22] He argues rather that one must look to the *rhetorical posture* of the letter without recourse to rhetorical form as such.[23] He concurs with the judgements of others who have seriously questioned whether Paul had any formal rhetorical training or that his letters should be evaluated strictly on grounds of rhetorical formalism.[24] Kern also suggests that the inordinate focus on rhetorical artifice has led many of the biographical statements of Galatians to be treated with less seriousness than they might deserve.[25] The emphasis on rhetoric has led to a distortion of the reality in the letter, if not ignoring it altogether.

All of this leaves us in something of a quandary what to make of 4:12–20. In the remainder of this study I shall argue that Betz is indeed correct in identifying the passage as coming from the friendship *topos*, but has missed the way that it thus fits into the overall rhetorical strategy of the letter. Rather than being an aside, an emotional outburst, or a rhetorical artifice, this passage constitutes one of the principal charges that Paul brings against his Galatian converts for failing to live up to the social demands of friendship and patronage. As such, it becomes one of the more important framing elements in the entire letter. What is needed is a way of understanding how the friendship *topos* might actu-

---

[21] The recent book by Mark D. Nanos, *The Irony of Galatians: Paul's Letter in First-Century Context* (Minneapolis: Fortress Press, 2002) was not yet available when this article was written. While some key differences remain, Nanos agrees with my basic contention that Galatians should be viewed as ironic rebuke (32–61), and he also takes note of the friendship motif in setting up the irony (53). In most discussions of classical rhetoric, especially that of the Second Sophistic, epideictic is generally associated with only its positive side, i.e., praise, and is seen predominantly in encomiastic speeches and funeral orations. Very little discussion is given to forms of rebuke in the rhetorical tradition. See George A. Kennedy, *A New History of Classical Rhetoric* (Princeton: Princeton UP, 1994) 225–26; *Greek Rhetoric under Christian Emperors* (Princeton: Princeton UP, 1983) 23–26.

[22] *Rhetoric and Galatians*, esp. 131–66 for his review of these different approaches to typological classification of Galatians. See also now Nanos, *The Irony of Galatians*, 323–31.

[23] *Ibid.*, 259–61.

[24] *Ibid.*, 244–55. Cf. Abraham J. Malherbe, *Social Aspects of Early Christian* (2nd ed.; Philadelphia: Fortress, 1983) 47–49; Porter, "Paul and His Letters," 535–38; 562–70; and the article by Stowers in this volume.

[25] Kern, *Rhetoric and Galatians*, 260.

ally fit into Paul's rhetorical strategy. Here we shall need to examine both how Paul frames this section of the letter and how the friendship motifs are being used.

To do this we shall first need to look at how friendship motifs might be used for rhetorical purposes by comparing two other works from antiquity; both are speeches that were actually delivered on identifiable historical occasions.[26] By using speeches, however, I do not mean to suggest that we reenter the formalist debates already discussed. Rather, I want to demonstrate how both speeches use and adapt friendship motifs as a strategy within the speech, and how, in turn, this strategy reflects on the overall form *and* function of the speech, but quite apart from strictly formalist considerations.

Friendship as Rhetorical Strategy in Dio Chrysostom

In the year 101 CE, a famous traveler, recently returned to his native Aegean from Rome, came to the capital city of Bithynia—his name, Titus Flavius Cocceianus Dion, a citizen of the smaller city of Prusa. Better known to us as Dio Chrysostom (the "golden mouth"), he was by this time one of the most famous orators of his day. Here is the opening of his speech to the *boule* or assembly of Nicomedia when he was invited to become a citizen there (*Or.* 38):[27]

> Men of Nicomedia, when I try to tally the reasons why you have given me citizenship …[28] For I do not see that I have such great wealth so that I should think I have been earnestly sought after by you for some

---

[26] Because the subject of friendship, with its associated motifs and expressions, has been covered in Betz's citation of parallels to Gal 4:12–20 and more recently by several extensive treatments, I shall not attempt here to outline the main components of the *topos* or discuss the principal classical texts. Excellent discussions of these matters may be found now in the following works: David Konstan, *Friendship in the Classical World* (Cambridge: Cambridge UP, 1997); John T. Fitzgerald, ed., *Friendship, Flattery, and Frankness of Speech: Studies on Friendship in the New Testament World* (NovTSup 82; Leiden: Brill, 1996) and *Greco-Roman Perspectives on Friendship* (SBLRBS 34; Atlanta: Scholars Press, 1997). On the other hand, none of these studies has provided a detailed treatment of friendship motifs in the two ancient authors here under discussion. To my knowledge at least, Favorinus (see next section) has not been discussed at all in this connection.

[27] For the historical situation on Dio's return after his exile see Chrisopher P. Jones, *The Roman World of Dio Chrysostom* (Cambridge: Harvard UP, 1978) 49–55; for this speech see esp. 83–89.

[28] In the Greek the first sentence intentionally breaks off at the end. Apparently, Dio here made some sort of gesture to display his sense of "emptyhandedness." We can only guess what the gesture might have been in that culture, perhaps a shrug with hands turned out and empty. Another possibility might have been for Dio to remove

mercenary reasons. Nor am I conscious of being known for treating the masses in a friendly way. So it does not seem that you want me even for the purpose of readily serving your every whim (as a public speaker). No, the fact is that I am not even very good company at a banquet or a sociable person at gatherings of that sort. But if I am not mistaken regarding your intentions concerning me—how I am able to be of service to you—it only remains that I understand the reason why I have been made a citizen by you is nothing other than that I, more so than others, am both willing and able to offer advice (συμβουλεύειν) on those things that are profitable for the common good.

… But, if on the other hand, all cities, or rather the great cities, need the wealthy, both to finance the public spectacles and to make benefactions (φιλοτιμῶνται) for customary expenses, if they need flatterers (κολάκων ἀνδρῶν) to afford pleasure by their demagogery (δημαγωγοῦσιν), and if they also need advisers (συμβούλων) to provide salvation by their (acts of) citizenship (ταῖς πολιτείαις), then I myself shall not shrink from benefiting (ὠφελεῖν) your city to the best of my ability by giving you *advice* (συμβουλεύων) on matters of greatest importance.[29]

The civic leaders of Nicomedia must have been a little disappointed, for such cities were trying to attract wealthy and powerful benefactors by offering grants of citizenship. Dio has turned the tables on them, it seems, by using the style and form of a public speech at which he *should* have graciously accepted their offer of citizenship and announced some public benefaction in return.[30] Instead, Dio turns it into an occasion for something else—a public rebuke. Thus, he continues:

Now then, there are, indeed, some other matters pertaining to your city that deserve correction, and I will render treatment to each according to its own measure, provided that I first persuade you by speaking truly about even greater matters. …[31]

---

his wallet (actually a leather pouch, usually worn looped around one's belt-cord) and dangle it upside down or wringing it out. The point of such a display using money or possessions becomes clear with the next words. That Dio had adopted Cynic ways during his exile, and often spoke of Diogenes, may give further support to the wallet as image, since it was one of the characteristic trappings of the Cynic; so Epictetus, *Diss.* 3.22.50; cf. Dio, *Or.* 13.10–12 for his adoption of the Cynic dress during his exile. Jones (*Roman World of Dio*, 53–54) suggests that *Or.* 13 was delivered just before Dio's return to Bithynia in 101. Also for his comments on his philosopher's garb during speeches see *Or.* 12.15; 32.22; 33.15; 34.2–3; 35.2–4, 11–12.
    [29] Dio Chrysostom, *Or.* 38.1–2., my translation.
    [30] Jones (*Roman World of Dio*, 85) suggests the Nicomedeans had made the honorific grant of citizenship not only because of his fame as an orator but also because he had influence with the emperor Trajan.
    [31] *Or.* 38.3, my translation.

The irony was not lost on the Nicomedians. What follows then is his mildly rebuking speech about the ills of στάσις ("public discord") and his exhortation to them to develop ὁμόνοια ("concord or harmony"), especially with the neighboring city of Nicaea. What I am interested in is the way the rhetorical posture of his speech both reflects a concrete social and political situation and encodes key cultural and social values from their symbolic universe (or what some would call their "moral world"). In the process it summons these values in service to his corrective. On both levels, then, it reflects the *realities* of Dio's day, but the task for the modern reader is often in discerning where these *realities*, both social and symbolic, are operative.

In this light we may consider how Dio employs friendship motifs in this speech. First, he starts by offering himself as an adviser; this is to be his benefaction to the city (§2, quoted above). Already, this places Dio as a "friend of the city," for that is what benefactors are regularly called. Next, the friendship motifs continue when he commences his advice, as he now adopts the posture of the philosopher/friend who delivers reproof with frankness; he renders medical treatment (θηραπείαν) by speaking the truth (τὰληθῆ λέγων, §3, quoted above).[32] He will return to the medical imagery later in the speech as a physician who offers a healing drug (φάρμακον) for the ills of their city (§7). Also, when he begins to define ὁμόνοια he does so in terms of the opposites enmity (ἔχθρας) and friendship (φιλία).[33] Later (§11) he says:

> For even if someone wished to be inquisitive concerning its [concord's] origins, he must trace its beginning to the greatest of divine matters. The self-same [concord] is both friendship (φιλία), and reconciliation (καταλλαγή) and kinship (συγγένεια), and it encompasses all of these. And what else but concord (ὁμόνοια) unites the elements (στοιχεῖα).

---

[32] Compare Gal 4:16. Apparently Dio's reputation as a philosopher/orator, reinforced by his long-haired Cynic demeanor, was as one who often dispensed censure in his speeches. So, compare *Or.* 33.15, 44; 34.2–4, and 35:4. In the last, in particular, he contrasts his willingness to be harsh with the flattering and fawning of charlatans. On the philosopher's frankness (παρρησία) as a motif in Isocrates and Dio see David E. Fredrickson, "ΠΑΡΡΗΣΙΑ in the Pauline Epistles," in Fitzgerald, *Friendship, Flattery, and Frankness of Speech*, 168 and n. 47 (with ref. to *Or.* 38).

[33] So §6 and esp. 8: "Now I wish to break up my speech and to speak first about concord (ὁμόνοια) itself in general, telling both whence it came and what is its cause, and then to distinguish by opposition strife (στάσις) and enmity (ἔχθρας) from friendship (φιλία)." See also below n. 58 and the article above by Breytenbach (264).

In the end, he calls for the Nicomedeans to reconcile their differences with Nicaea and to stop the envy and rivalry that gave these Greek cities such a bad reputation with the Roman authorities.[34] So the rhetoric here is clearly a friendly rebuke and a call for correction, even though he also gives positive advice on how to effect the reconciliation with Nicaea.[35]

The friendship motifs here are very much in the vein of epideictic, dispensing praise and blame to call for a corrective of past actions. Even so, the actual rhetorical form of this speech should be classified as deliberative, or (using the Greek) *symbouleutic* speech, since he is using persuasion to produce a future effect.[36] Thus, he concludes the proemium of his speech by saying: "So, then, if you will endure my advice (συμβουλίαν) you will be persuaded by me concerning the matters on which I am here to offer advice, and indeed I am extremely confident [you will]. ..." (*Or.* 38.4). The *function* of the friendship language, even the ironic twist in accepting their citizenship honors with a frank rebuke, is all part of a rhetorical stance that makes the persuasion work.

---

[34] Notice especially 38.38, where he refers to their inter-civic rivalries and discord as an object of laughter and scorn among the Romans, who in a humiliating way, call it "Greek failings" (Ἑλληνικὰ ἁμαρτήματα). Dio (*Or.* 38.28) also goes on at length about their wrangling over civic titles, especially focusing on the pettiness in seeing who can inscribe title "first" in their civic inscriptions; cf. Jones, *Roman World of Dio*, 87.

[35] Compare Dio's *Or.* 31 and 32, which use a similar rhetorical ploy to offer civic advice. This motif as rhetorical strategy in both Dio and Paul is also discussed in the article by Krentz in this volume.

[36] Several scholars of ancient rhetoric have cautioned against using the three *species* or forms derived from Aristotle as rigid categories. Often overlooked is the fact that Aristotle also says that symbouleutic and epideictic actually overlap; so *Rhet.* 1.9.35 (1368a): "Praise and counsel have a common aspect; for what you might suggest while offering *advice* (ἐν τῷ συμβουλεύειν), with a change of phrase becomes *encomium* (ἐγκώμια γίγνεται)." This is especially true for the imperial period more generally, and the so-called Second Sophistic orators in particular. Much of the public rhetorical display of this period was in the form of either panegyric or civic advice, and in both cases there were ample rhetorical twists. So compare the opening of Aelius Aristides' *Roman Oration*, a panegyric in form, which opens by denouncing panegyrics (or *encomia*) as mere flattery (another ironic use of the friendship motif). On the dominance of *symbouleutic* rhetoric in the Roman period see especially Jeffrey Walker, *Rhetoric and Poetics in Antiquity* (New York: Oxford UP, 2000) 113–17. Walker also argues that the so-called "decline" of rhetoric in the Roman period was itself a rhetorical commonplace (99–109) having more to do with a shift away from the law courts as the principal seat of rhetorical display. This, too, suggests that the traditional forms of classical rhetoric are not so applicable for the rhetorical practice of the imperial period.

Friendship as Rhetorical Strategy in Favorinus

Favorinus was a disciple of Dio's and one of the two most famous Sophists during the reign of Hadrian. Originally from Arelate (Arles) in Roman Gaul, he had moved to Ephesos where he became its pre-eminent rhetorician. His principal rival was M. Antonius Polemo, a Laodicean who served as chief rhetorician and public advocate for Smyrna. As with Dio, the major cities courted these orators for their fame, their influence with Emperors and governors, and their wealth. Most of the famous sophists were also important civic bene-factors. In turn, the orators could expect adulation, respect, and public honors of the sort that only the leading citizens and noble Romans could normally achieve.

This is the situation lying behind Favorinus' *Corinthian Oration* (or Κορινθιακός).[37] As we can see (in §§ 1 & 8) Favorinus had visited Corinth on two previous occasions and had been met with undaunted adulation by the populace, so much so that on the second trip the magistrates tried to convince him to take up residence there instead of Ephesos. When he declined, they erected a bronze statue of him and placed it in front of the library. Now, on his third visit, he faces a different response: he has fallen into disfavor and his statue has been torn down. Delivered during the latter half of Hadrian's reign, this speech is his response to these shifting fortunes.[38]

---

[37] See Appendix B, where I have provided a new translation of the key framing sections. This speech has traditionally been preserved (along with one or two others) among the *Orations* (as number 37) of Dio Chrysostom. But for many years scholars have suspected that it really came from Favorinus. Favorinus' speech in praise of Fortune is preserved as Dio's *Or.* 64; however, the majority of Favorinus's speeches are lost or known only by the title (cf. Aulus Gellius, *Noc. Att.* 17.21.1). A Vatican ms. discovered in 1931 may be an authentic speech of Favorinus reflecting on his exile; see Maude W. Gleason, *Making Men: Sophists and Self-Presentation in Ancient Rome* (Princeton: Princeton UP, 1995) 147–57. The traditional translations of this speech (such as in the LCL) have missed much of its barbed irony and even its basic rhetorical strategy, as reflected in numerous unwarranted emendations. Key examples will be indicated in the following notes as well as in Appendix B.

[38] It dates from after ca. 125/6, perhaps around 130 when Hadrian made his second visit to Greece. Among other momentous events, the Olympieion at Athens was dedicated at this time, and Polemo delivered the dedicatory address. A statue of Favorinus at Athens was also removed at about this time; cf. Philostratus, *Vitae Sophistarum* 1.8 (489–492).

Maude Gleason[39] does a great deal with this speech and with the competition between Favorinus and Polemo in terms of their respective constructions of masculinity. And this is fitting, since the speech shows Favorinus adopting the rhetorical ploy of defending his now missing statue (§23) as a way of indirectly defending himself against the calumnies of the Corinthians. In so doing, he also rebukes them.[40] The point is that Favorinus accuses the Corinthians of being fickle friends who have mistreated his "friend," the poor statue. In this way, he effectively defends and praises himself without doing so directly, while rebuking them for a serious breach of social etiquette that borders on moral turpitude.

Now we may observe how Favorinus couches these ideas rhetorically in terms of the reciprocal bonds of obligation that should attend friendship. He begins (§1):

> When I sojourned (ἐπεδήμησα) in your city the first time, … and shared a measure (μετέδωκα) of my speeches with your demos and magistrates, I seemed to be an intimate friend (ἐπιτήδειος εἶναι)[41] to you to a degree not exceeded even by Arion of Methymne. Yet you did not make a figure (τύπον) of Arion …

Then, after a digression on Arion and other famous "visitors" of old, he comments on his second visit to Corinth (§8):

> you experienced such gladness (ἀσμένως ἐπείδετε) that you tried very hard to keep me, but then, seeing that to be impossible, you instead made a physical likeness (τὴν εἰκὼ τοῦ σώματος), and taking this you set it up (ἀνεθήκατε, or dedicated it) in the library, in a front seat (προεδρίαν), where you thought it might especially summon (προκαλέσασθαι) the youth to follow the same pursuits as we do. For you bestowed such honors not as one of the many who annually disembark at Cenchreai as merchants, or festival-goers, or ambassadors, or travelers, but rather as a beloved friend (ἀγαπητόν), who at last appears after much time.

So, notice that he starts by rehearsing his own prior experiences with them, and their displays of friendship and honor toward him. He is a "beloved friend" who produces the joy of true friendship in their

---

[39] *Making Men*, 3–20.

[40] So also Gleason, *Making Men*, 9. Gleason argues that beneath the Corinthians' contempt in removing the statue runs an undercurrent derived from Polemo's denigration of his masculinity. The article by Bruce Winter in this volume also examines the similarities of Paul's language in 2 Cor.

[41] I have not followed Capps (also Crosby in LCL) here in emending the text with οἰκεῖος before ὑμῖν.

hearts when they see him return.[42] His honored status is signaled by the placement of the statue in a προεδρία ("front seat") in the library. He must mean just outside the entrance to the library in the portico, where, one should guess, he was also standing while delivering this speech. The Corinthians had thereby honored him with the status of a "first man," i.e., a leading citizen and civic benefactor. Yet, paraphrasing Homer,[43] he notes ironically that such civic honors may be fickle and fleeting (§9).

Next he begins to turn the screws (§9), and here we should take special note of the similarity in wording to Gal 4.20:

> So that I stand *perplexed* (ἐν ἀπόρῳ καθεστάναι) both in regard to my own case and now, by Zeus, in regard to that of yet another man too, wondering whether I did not see truly—the things taking place were not a waking appearance but a dream—or whether the things taking place were accurate in every detail, the zeal of the crowd and the judgement of the council … .

Favorinus is saying I, the orator (i.e., the one who brings words to a visual reality), now doubt my own vision of these events.[44] He adds that it is not only his case that is perplexing but that of "another man." At this point he starts to shift the rhetorical ploy of the speech, for the entire rest of the speech—well over half—will now focus on the experience of this "other man," namely the statue of Favorinus, which has itself now disappeared from sight, like the mythical, magical works of Daedalus (§10).

Next he will play with this idea of magically endowed statues in a kind of ring composition from §§11–21,[45] which allows him to propose that, in fact, even if the statue could flee the city, why would it choose to do so, seeing that Corinth is such a beautiful place. So if "he" [the statue] fled, there must be something wrong with the city, or more

---

[42] Compare Gal 4:15–16 where Paul rehearses their former joyful attitude (μακαρισμός) toward seeing him; cf. Betz, *Galatians*, 226–28.

[43] See Appendix B, n. 147.

[44] Compare also the element of "seeing" truly and "with his own eyes" with the references to seeing in both Gal 4.15 (a long-debated passage in Paul) and Gal 3.1—a reference to Paul's earlier preaching. We shall discuss both of these below. Also note the use of "parenthetic" insertions to heighten the irony, also to be discussed below at nn. 119 and 125.

[45] Notice how Favorinus uses the framing addresses in relation to the mythical/historical digressions. The latter carry the bulk of the speech in terms of space, but the former are the key points. The digressions help him to make and illustrate his key arguments, while also showing off his rhetorical artistry. One may wish to rethink the function of Paul's use of the Abraham allegories in the light of this pattern.

precisely with its inhabitants. But, "No," he concludes (in §§20–21), the statue did not flee at all, nor ever intended to leave the city; therefore, something else must have gone wrong. He must have been banished instead. This allows Favorinus to turn the rest of his speech into a defense of the "accused" [i.e., the statue] as if in court, where the audience now takes the role of the jury.[46] In a forthcoming study, I shall argue that this speech was actually delivered in the Forum at Corinth, where the library was also located.[47] Favorinus was standing either in or in front of the library beside the now empty marble base that once supported his bronze statue. It is about and for his "invisible" friend that Favorinus speaks, no doubt gesturing dramatically throughout, just as we see him speaking directly to the absent statue in the final scene.

Having set up the Corinthians rhetorically by implying that they must have been the ones to banish the statue, Favorinus, like a true friend, now leaps to the defense of his friend:

> Then if some sort of decree that statues be called to account were passed by you [Corinthians]—or rather, if you will, supposing that such has been decreed and a trial (ἀγῶνος) has begun—permit me, yes *permit me* to make a [defense] speech before you as though in court on behalf of this very man (αὐτοῦ)[i.e., the statue].[48]

> Men of the jury, they say one must expect anything in the course of time; but this man (οὗτος) is, in a brief span, at risk of being put up (τεθῆναι), on the one hand, as the noblest of the Greeks, and on the other of being put down (ἐκπεσεῖν), as the vilest. Now then to prove that he was put up (ἐστάθη) well and justly and profitably for your city and all the Greeks, I have much to say … (§§22–23)

---

[46] From §§23–47 the speech pretends to be a real forensic defense, but this too is a rhetorical ploy.

[47] L.Michael White, "A Piqued Panorama of the Hadrianic Forum: The View from Favorinus' *Korinthiakos*," in *Urban Religion in Roman Corinth: Archeological & Historical Studies*, edited by D. Showalter and S. Friesen (HTS; Cambridge: Harvard UP, forthcoming). For an effort to read issues of Roman and Greek "identity formation" at Corinth from Favorinus' speech, see Jason König, "Favorinus' *Corinthian Oration* in its Corinthian Context," *Proceedings of the Cambridge Philological Society* 47 (2002) 141–71. König does not attempt to discuss the location of the speech or the statue in Corinth, however.

[48] Here I am reading ὑπὲρ αὐτοῦ ("on behalf of him") following the original ms., as opposed to ὑπὲρ αὑτοῦ ("on my own behalf") as emended by Crosby (LCL). Here and throughout the speech such emendations have Favorinus speaking about himself, but that is not the rhetorical strategy. He is speaking about "the other man," i.e., the statue. Gleason (*Making Men*, 13 and n. 51) observes the same problem in the patterns of erroneous emendation in earlier editions. See also below n. 150.

He begins his case with irony by creating a double entendre: "he" [the statue] was, indeed, *put up* worthily but *banished* (or *put down*) unjustly.[49] In the process, Favorinus adopts two further rhetorical ploys through the friendship *topos*. In §37 he says it is out of his own sense of friendship for the Corinthians that he is pointing out their errors of judgement in "banishing the statue." Here again is the motif of frankness; a friend who is willing to rebuke. In §36 he even uses the term παρρησία ("frank criticism") in this regard. Then in §§46–7 Favorinus concludes the speech by offering consolation to the statue as to a friend, and he calls for the "right" verdict in his "case."[50] So Favorinus, not the Corinthians, is the true friend after all. Of course, the "jury" [i.e., the audience] is supposed to see its previous error and shout its acclamation in favor of the statue. Whether this was the outcome and they returned to favor Favorinus is unfortunately not recorded.[51]

Now I want to return for a moment to Favorinus' expression of disbelief and perplexity at the beginning of this section; for this is what I think Betz is referring to as the rhetorical device of *dubitatio*, even though he never mentions this oration of Favorinus.[52] But here is the point, even if the "perplexity" is in some sense feigned as a rhetorical device, nonetheless it (a) reflects a concrete situation of social tension, and (b) facilitates the ironic rebuke. It does so precisely because such perplexity in relationships is the exact opposite of how true friends ought to deal with one another. It, too, forms part of the friendship *topos* and the rebuke, both here and for Paul. In other words, Favorinus is saying that his "emotional state" of perplexity is the direct result of their breach of the obligations of friendship. *Pace* Betz, then, it is far more than mere *device*; it is a moral judgement on the audience

[49] There's a word play here on the two verbs τιθέναι and ἐκπίπτειν, since both can be used of public or legal actions (meaning "to award or vote in favor of at trial" and "to banish," respectively) and of setting up and taking down a statue as in a temple ("to dedicate or set up" and "to tear down," respectively). This wordplay will continue to the end of the speech, cf. §37, 47.

[50] See the notes to Appendix B for discussion of several key word plays. There is, of course, no "case" in the sense of an actual law suit or court trial; it is merely part of Favorinus' rhetorical strategy.

[51] Crosby, in the introduction (p. 2) to the LCL edition (Dio Chrysostom, vol. 4) proposes that the occasion was an unveiling / dedication for a new statue, but this seems most unlikely. Favorinus' final words are entirely metaphorical (so Gleason, *Making Men*, 20) and rhetorical; see my analysis of its final rhetorical flourish below at nn. 55–58.

[52] See above n. 6 referring to Betz, *Galatians*, 236–37.

for their past actions. He charges them with having turned friendship into enmity. Then in a deliciously satirical twist, Favorinus says that if he himself is perplexed, imagine how the poor statue must feel. In contemporary vernacular, he is the one who has really been "jerked around."

Although Favorinus' speech has an apologetic function, it should be labeled as epideictic with a high degree of irony as he blames the Corinthians for having transgressed the social and moral obligations of friendship by removing his honorific statue.[53] Even the title, Κοϱινθια-κός ("The Corinthian Oration"), is an ironic form of epideictic, since such a title would usually imply a speech in praise of the city.[54] The ostensible court speech (§§23–47) is not the real form or setting, but a rhetorical ploy in order to make the rebuke effective.[55] The framing elements (as given in the selections in Appendix B) are the real key to understanding the speech and its rhetorical strategy.

To the very end Favorinus plays his rhetorical strategy based on friendship motifs. For example, when he turns to console his friend [the statue] at the end of his speech, he concludes with these words addressed to the missing statue:

> Accordingly, I wish now to offer consolation (παϱαμυθήσασθαι) to him [the "friend" i.e., the statue], as to one possessing sensation:
>
> "O silent image of my oratory, will you not show yourself? (§46) ...
>
> I myself will raise you up (ἀναστήσω) before the goddess [Fame], whence nothing will cast you down (καθέλῃ)—*neither earthquake nor wind, neither snow nor rain, neither envy* (φθόνος) *nor enmity* (ἐχθϱός); but even now do I discover you risen up (ἑστηκότα)." (§47)

---

[53] So also Gleason, *Making Men*, 9: "In effect, he has to combine the activities of apology and invective without appearing to perform either." Gleason also discusses the rhetorical problems of self-praise, as reflected in Plutarch's *De se ipsum citra invidiam laudando* (*Mor.* 539A–547F).

[54] Compare Aelius Aristides, *Or.* 43, Ῥοδιακός ("The Rhodian Oration"); however, Dio Chrysostom uses the same title for his customary form of corrective symbouleutic speech (as discussed above) in *Or.* 31, Ῥοδιακός (which also deals with mistreatment of statues, §§95–97) and *Or.* 33, Ταϱσικός A.

[55] Favorinus' speech in praise of Tyche [Fortune] ([ps-Dio] *Or.* 64) is epideictic but couched in terms of *apologia* (i.e., defending her against charges of fickleness); so also Gleason, *Making Men*, 150 n. 73. Compare also Dio, *Or.* 65. Tyche's fickleness was a well-known trope; see *Tabula of Cebes* 7–8 and the discussion in John T. Fitzgerlad and L. Michael White, *The Tabula of Cebes: Text and Translation with Introduction and Notes* (SBLTT 24/GRS 7; Chico: Scholars Press, 1983) 141 nn. 23–28.

This is actually a double use of friendship motifs. In form, it is consolation, as to a friend. Then near the end (in §47), in saying "I'll raise you ... and nothing will cast you down [again]," he describe the dangers that have been overcome in the process: earthquake, wind, snow, rain, etc. The central pair ("*neither snow, nor rain*") is an allusion to Herodotus' famous tribute to the Persian couriers, now better known as the "motto" of the postal service.[56] Presumably the audience was supposed to catch the allusion as well as Favorinus' irony; now the flighty statue will become as steadfast as a Persian courier. But to this Favorinus adds two more pairs of "dangers," one at the beginning and one at the end. At the beginning he refers to *earthquake* and *wind*; these two "dangers" come from an earlier point in the speech as Favorinus muses ironically on what could possibly have made the statue go away.[57] Then comes the Persian courier allusion, a lighter piece of irony. Finally, Favorinus adds two more—"*neither envy nor enmity*" (οὐ φθόνος, οὐκ ἐχθρός)—and these are the real point. Rather than natural disasters that can knock a statue over, they are pitfalls that destroy friendship—and in this case, a statue too.[58] On the basis of the structure and allusions within this line, then, one can imagine how it was delivered rhetorically by pairs—the first pair earnest but soft, the second whimsically, and the last with biting intensity. Favorinius has now twisted the knife against the Corinthians and his detractors for betraying their former friendship through envy and enmity.[59]

---

[56] Favorinus' version goes "οὐ σεισμός, οὐκ ἄνεμος, *οὐ νιφετός, οὐκ ὄμβρος*, οὐ φθόνος, οὐκ ἐχθρός" whereas the passage in Herodotus (8.98) reads "τοὺς *οὔτε νιφετός, οὐκ ὄμβρος*, οὐ καῦμα, οὐ νὺξ ἔργει μὴ οὐ κατανύσαι τὸν προκείμενον αὐτῷ δρόμον τὴν ταχίστην." The snippet from Herodotus (as italicized) is no more than an allusion, but it is meant to be recognizable and thus humorous. Favorinus mentions Herodotus (who is listed as one of the famous visitors to Corinth) by name at several points in the speech; cf. §§7, 18. Notice the precise parallelism created by careful word selection (all masculine nouns ending in -ος, beginning with and without consonants) so that it yields an alternating pattern of οὐ and οὐκ in three pairs.

[57] So §20: "But then did someone overturn the dedication [i.e., the statue] of the city? Well if it were a whirlwind (στρόβιλος), or a hurricane (πρηστήρ), or a thunderbolt falling on it (σκηπτὸς ἐμπεσών) ..."

[58] For envy as a cause of enmity, and enmity as the opposite of friendship see Plutarch, *De capienda ex inimicis utilitate* 1 & 9 (*Mor.* 86C, 91B) and *De invidia et odio* (*Mor.* 536C–38E). The latter may be dependent on Aristotle, *Rhet.* 2.4.30–32. See also Dio, *Or.* 77/78.32–39 and *Or.* 38.22 (enmity as the opposite of friendship and concord between cities, as discussed above). Compare also Gal 4:16; in relation to the use of "enemy" there Betz (*Galatians*, 229 n. 102) cites the definition of Ammonius, *De adfinium voc. diff.* 208: "the 'enemy' is the one who was formerly a friend."

[59] In §35 Favorinus seems to make an allusion to Hadrian and some unnamed

Friendship in the Rhetorical Strategy of Gal 4:12–20

Like Favorinus' speech, then, Paul's address to the Galatians in 4:12–20 is not a desperate appeal but a rebuke couched in terms of friendship. The list of elements from the friendship *topos* in the passage, as identified by Betz, runs the gamut. They include:

(1) the appeal for reciprocity (v. 12);
(2) the "epistolary cliché" that friends do not wrong one another (v. 12);
(3) how they responded to his illness (vv. 13–14);
(4) their former praise of him and willingness to sacrifice for him (v. 15);
(5) the theme of enmity (v. 16);
(6) the theme of frank criticism in "telling the truth" (v. 16);
(7) portrayal of his opponents as flatterers (v. 17);
(8) the constancy and loyalty of true friends, even when apart (v. 18); and
(9) the metaphor of the loving mother (v. 19).[60]

To this list we should add one more item, not identified by Betz in conjunction with the friendship *topos*:

(10) Paul's "tone" of perplexity as a sign of endangered friendship (v. 20).[61]

Hans-Josef Klauck agrees that the friendship motifs are central to the passage, but argues that the source is to be found in earlier appropriations of the *topos* among Hellenistic Jewish writers.[62] In particular he notes parallels with Sir 6:5–17 for terms reflecting enmity (ἔχθρας) as

---

"accuser," possibly even Polemo himself.

[60] Betz, *Galatians*, 221–29. Alan C. Mitchell, ("'Greet the Friends by Name': New Testament Evidence for the Greco-Roman *Topos* on Friendship," in Fitzgerald, *Greco-Roman Perspectives on Friendship*, 227) provides a convenient list of tropes in Betz's commentary similar to this; however, he omits items 4 and 6 above; they are discussed by Betz, *Galatians*, 227–28.

[61] As we saw above in Favorinus' speech (§9).

[62] "Kirche als Freundesgemeinschaft? Auf Spurensuche im Neuen Testament," *MTZ* 42 (1991) 3–12. Klauck finds some useful parallels to the language in Gal 4:12–20 in Philo, Wisdom of Solomon, and especially Sirach. He argues (10–11), however, that such friendship language is actually subordinate in Paul to fictive kinship language, and that this is more in keeping with Paul's Jewish roots.

an alteration or betrayal of friendship.[63] Similarly, Peter Marshall[64] has stressed the theme of enmity in the passage (4:16) to argue that Paul's principal attack is against his opponents, who (in light of 1:6–10) have made disparaging remarks about Paul's inconsistency. That is to say, they have accused Paul of being a false friend. Thus, Paul replies in kind by arguing that the friendship he had formerly enjoyed with the Galatians—and they with him—had been disrupted by his opponents. Then in the next verse (4:17) he portrays these opponents as flatterers rather than true friends.

Both Klauck and Marshall are partially correct on how the language is working, but there are, in fact, two distinct clusters of friendship motifs interwoven within the passage. The first, as seen by Klauck and Marshall, is the theme of enmity, a broken friendship; it corresponds to items 2, 3, 4, 5, 7, and 10 in the list above. The second, is the theme of Paul's frankness in rebuking them as a sign of friendly affection and concern; it corresponds to items 1, 6, 8, 9, and, as we shall see, 10. Thus, the two threads are actually woven together in important ways. In key verses, both threads are found together (e.g., at the center of the passage in 4:16), and it is especially telling that both are found in the beginning and ending verses (4:12 & 20). In using these two main lines of friendship motif, Paul's rebuke is very much like the rhetorical strategy of Favorinus: (1) his rebuke with frank criticism is a sign of true friendship as opposed to flattery, and (2) the Galatians are accused of being false or hypocritical friends. As with Favorinus, both themes are rhetorically charged and often laced with irony; both are also directly connected to the actual situation of the letter.[65] We shall now look at these two interwoven lines of Paul's strategy more closely.

---

[63] *Ibid.*, 8–9. The key terms are πειρασμός ("trial, temptation," Gal 4:13 & Sir 5:7), ἐχθρός ("enemy," Gal 4:16 & Sir 5:9, 13), and μετατιθέναι ("exchange, change, transfer" not in Gal 4 [but see 1:6!] & Sir 5:9). The last, as Klauck notes, is associated with the change from friendship to enmity, and he thinks it is reflected here. On this point, Klauck follows Peter Marshall's discussion of the theme of enmity in v. 16, which I shall discuss next.

[64] *Enmity in Corinth: Social Conventions in Paul's Relations with the Corinthians* (WUNT 2.23; Tübingen: Mohr-Siebeck, 1987) 152–56.

[65] Marshall (*Enmity*, 153) also argues that the passage, and especially the enmity motif in v. 16, is "not simply rhetorical, but points to a serious breakdown in his relations with the Galatians." The place where Betz sees the closest proximity of the rhetoric to the social reality of the situation comes only in his discussion of v. 18b (*Galatians*, 232).

Galatians as a Rebuke of Failed Friendship

Paul's use of the frankness motif in Gal, and especially in 4:12–20, has largely been overlooked by scholars.[66] J. Paul Sampley has recently sought to rectify this problem and sees frank speech functioning in four key passages of Gal—2:11–15 (the rebuke of Peter), 3:1–5; 4:8–11; and 4:12–20 (esp. v. 16)—while other reverberations are to be found in 1:6, 5:19–26, and 6:1–5.[67] Sampley says further:

> At the letter's heart and at the epicenter of Paul's friendship and frankness with the Galatians lies a rich and crucial passage (Gal 4:12–20) that can fully be appreciated only in the context of frank speech.[68]

He then goes on to suggest how the passage fits into the situation of the letter. First, he argues that Paul's "exculpatory declaration" of 4:12 ("you did me no wrong") shows no sense of reprisal for a past wrong. Instead, Paul calls for the Galatians to reevaluate their behavior towards him in conjunction with the solicitations of the outside opponents. For the latter, however, Paul spares no opprobrium, since they are both flatterers and slanderers. So, Paul's frank speech here is intended to call the Galatians "back from the precipice that lies directly ahead of them in the form of the outsider's understanding of circumcision and the law."[69] Later, Sampley argues that the tone of Paul's criticism in Gal is far less severe than that in 2 Cor 10–13. The latter he sees as a severe form of blame, lacking any praise, while Gal mixes praise and blame. Paul views the Galatians as potentially recoverable, while the Corinthians at this juncture are virtually a lost cause.[70]

---

[66] Fredrickson, "ΠΑΡΡΗΣΙΑ in the Pauline Epistles," does not discuss Gal at all because the term is not actually used in the letter. He does (p. 179) appropriately observe the use of the same motif of "speaking the truth" as a feature of frank speech in 2 Cor 6:6.-7 (so ἐν ἀγάπῃ ἀνυποκρίτῳ, ἐν λόγῳ ἀληθείας). The latter of these is very close to the formulation in Gal 4:16, even though given as a verbal construction (ἀληθεύων). The passage in 2 Cor is indeed a close parallel in other respects to the one in Gal, especially in Paul's "labors" or "hardships" on behalf of his converts, as a sign of his friendly affections for them. So, compare Gal 4:11 and 20.

[67] "Paul's Frank Speech with the Galatians and the Corinthians," in *Philodemus and the New Testament*, ed. by J.T. Fitzgerald, G. Holland, and D. Obbink (NovTSup; Leiden: E.J. Brill, 2003). I thank Prof. Sampley for providing me with a copy of the ms. for inclusion in this discussion.

[68] *Ibid.*, 9 (ms.).

[69] *Ibid.*, 13, cf. 5 (ms.).

[70] *Ibid.*, 30 (ms.). On this count Sampley's reading of the function of these letters is closest to the formalist understanding of Margaret Mitchell (*Paul and the Rhetoric of Reconciliation* [Louisville: John Knox, 1991] 198, 200–5), who classifies the Corinthian

Of all recent treatments of the Galatian letter, Sampley's seems to me
to come the closest to giving a full and accurate sense of how 4:12–20
fits into the overall structure as well as the actual situation of the letter.
The similarities with the language in 2 Cor are also aptly drawn.[71] One
further addition will round out the picture. As with Peter Marshall's
treatment, the difficulty is that Sampley's discussion focuses on only
one of the two main streams of the friendship language in Gal, namely
the frankness motif.[72] Sampley himself cites Plutarch in differentiating
two different types of frank speech: one for reclaiming a wrongdoer;
the other, for stirring a person to positive action.[73] He thinks Gal falls
into the latter category, most clearly reflected in 4:12 ("you did me no
wrong"). On the other hand, a closer look now at the enmity motif as it
interweaves with the frankness motif may paint a slightly darker picture
both of Paul's rhetorical strategy and of the situation.

Sampley astutely observes that the frankness motif runs throughout
the letter and comes to a climax in 4:12–20. The same may now be suggested for the enmity motif, especially as it coincides with blaming language in the letter. (For a text and translation of these framing units see
Appendix A.) At several points in the letter Paul accuses them of turning their backs on him and his gospel. So, Gal 1:6 opens the letter both
formally and rhetorically with bitter irony by exchanging Paul's usual
thanksgiving formula (εὐχαριστῶ) for the cacophonous θαυμάζω ("I am
amazed"). This is the first note in the letter of the theme intoned again
at 3:1 and 4:20, with Paul's expression of perplexity. As with Favorinus it is the language of rebuke for a past action, as Paul even says in
the following words: "I am astonished that you are so quickly deserting [literally *transferring* or *exchanging*, Gr. μετατίθεσθε] from the one who
called you in grace to a different gospel" (Gal 1:6). Notice it is not
the gospel they are said to be deserting, but "the one who called" them,
namely Paul.[74] The term μετατιθέναι is the one recognized by Klauck as

correspondence as deliberative rhetoric, because it is meant to be persuasive; however,
she notes the extensive use of epideictic (praise and blame) as well as friendship
language.

[71] Mounting recognition of the similarities of language and tone between 2 Cor and
Gal lead me to suspect that the date and situation of the Galatian letter need to be
reconsidered.

[72] In fact, Sampley gives little attention to Marshall's stress on the enmity motif in
v. 16 (so. "Paul's Frank Speech," 11 [ms.]).

[73] *Ibid.*, 5 (ms.), citing Plutarch, *Quomodo quis suos in virtute sentiat profectus* 74A.

[74] This mode of referring to himself occurs also in Gal 3:5 & 5:8, and extensively in
2 Cor 10–13. Like Favorinus, it seems, Paul tends to refer to himself in the third person

belonging to the enmity motif; it signals the change from friendship to enmity.[75] It is reinforced in the passage by two further terms that reflect deception and betrayal in 1:7: "were there not some who are *troubling* (ταράσσοντες) you and who wish *to pervert* (μεταστρέψαι) the gospel."[76]

Framing Rebuke in the Epistolary Handbooks

It is worth noting here that the language and tone of Gal 1:6 is quite consistent with friendly rebuke as defined by the handbooks on epistolary form and style. There are in fact several different types of rebuke mentioned in the handbooks. Ps-Libanius,[77] for example, lists the following: μεμπτική (blaming, §§6 & 53), ἀπειλητική (threatening, §§13 & 60), ἐλεγκτική (reproving, §§32 & 79), ἐπιτιμητική (censuring, §§34 & 81), εἰρωνική (ironic, §§9 & 56), and ὀνειδιστική (reproaching, §§17 & 64), plus a few more. The terms reflect gradations in tone and severity as depicted in the wording of the sample letters, but even the harshest employ friendship motifs in framing rebuke.

The last two deserve some special attention. Ps-Libanius' sample for the ironic type (§56) goes as follows:

> I wonder greatly (λίαν ἄγαμαι) at your reasonableness (ἐπιείκεια), that you have so quickly changed (οὕτω ταχέως μεταβάλλῃ)[78] from a well-ordered life to the opposite—for I hesitate to call it wickedness. It seems that you

---

at the key moments of the rebuke where he himself is the injured party.

[75] See above n. 64.

[76] One key meaning of ταράσσειν is to "trouble" the mind, i.e., to *disturb* or *agitate* and to *cause confusion*. It is this loss of right thinking that produces rash action and looks ahead to 3:1–5. Similarly, μεταστρέφειν can mean to "turn away," but also carries the sense of turning things "upside down" or "misrepresenting" the truth. It is this last sense that gets to the heart of Paul's charge (cf. 2:14; 4:16). Both notions will show up again later; so compare Gal 5:10 & 12 where ὁ ταράσσων is paralleled by οἱ ἀναστατοῦντες ("to drive into confusion").

[77] Ps-Libanius, *Epistolary Types*. The text may be found in Abraham J. Malherbe, *Ancient Epistolary Theorists* (SBLSBS 19; Atlanta: Scholars, 1988) 66–81. For each type listed, the author has given a brief description of the type and then later gives a sample of wording that fits the type; thus, each type has two references within the letter as noted here. I have chosen to use Ps-Libanius' list rather than that of Ps-Demetrius, *Epistolary Types* (also available in Malherbe, *Ancient Epistolary Theorists*, 31–41) only because the former actually gives a few more types of rebuke. Most of the main terms for rebuke also occur in Ps-Demetrius, although it does add the type called νουθετητικός (admonishing, §7). For the two that we focus on below, compare the parallel passages in Ps-Demetrius, §§20 and 4, respectively.

[78] My translation. Compare Gal 1:6: οὕτως ταχέως μετατίθεσθε. The two verbs μετατιθέναι and μεταβάλλειν are synonymous; both refer to a sudden change of course,

have contrived not to make friends out of your enemies, but enemies out
of your friends (ἀλλὰ τοὺς φίλους ἐχθρούς). For your action has shown
itself to be unworthy of friends (φίλων ἀνάξιον), but entirely worthy of
your own drunkenness (τῆς σῆς παροινίας ἐπάξιον).

The tone and language are strikingly similar to those in Gal 1:6.[79]
For Ps-Libanius what yields the irony is principally the use of ἐπιείκεια ("reasonableness") to describe the character of the addressee, since
his actions betray just the opposite, namely foolishness or rashness
(ἀνόητος, cf. Gal 3:1 & 3).[80] Thus, this ironic opening is what delivers the point of the rebuke at the end. Plutarch discusses the need for
harsher forms of frank criticism in precisely those cases where "rashness" (ἀνόητος) seems to be carrying someone toward the precipice of
error or vice. Plutarch says:

> In which circumstances, then, is it necessary for a friend to be severe
> (σφοδρὸν) and when to employ the *tone* of frank speech (πότε τῷ τόνῳ
> χρῆσθαι τῆς παρρησίας)? [It is] when circumstances summon him [the
> friend] to check an impulsive rush (ἐπιλαβέσθαι φερομένης) into pleasure,
> wrath, or arrogance, or to curtail greed, or to recover from an *inattentive
> rashness* (ἀπροσεξίαν ἀνασχεῖν ἀνόητον).[81]

Next comes Ps-Libanius' sample for the reproachful (ὀνειδιστική) type
of letter (§64); it reads:

---

position, or opinion. So note that John Chrysostom's *Commentary on Galatians* employs
μεταβολή to describe the Galatians' change to enmity in 4:16. For the text of Chrysostom's commentary see PG 61.659.47 and n. 112 below.

[79] In both cases the main verb (ἄγαμαι and θαυμάζω) can have either positive or
negative connotations of "astonishment;" in a pejorative sense, ἄγαμαι can also mean
"to envy." This may be part of the ironic play going on in this particular example.

[80] The term ἐπιείκεια occurs in Paul at 2 Cor 10:1 in the context of Paul's harsh
rebuke; it is usually translated as "gentleness" of Christ (RSV, NRSV). In legal contexts
it is better rendered as "clemency;" its opposite is not "harshness" but "oathbound"
(ὅρκος), i.e., unyielding or strict. But given the context here and elsewhere, its antithesis
is probably better taken as "rashness or heedlessness" (ἀνόητος), the same word found
in Gal 3:1 and 3 as "foolish." This sense is further supported by the connection to
drunkenness.

[81] *Quomodo adulator ab amicis internoscatur* 69E-F, my translation. Compare also Epictetus, *Diss.* 4.12, which deals with attention and "inattentiveness." For other terms that
reflect this heedless "rush" into vice see *Tabula of Cebes* 8.1: ἀπροβούλευτοι ("without
forethought") and 14.3: ἀφροσύνη ("foolishness"). Compare also the wording of the censuring (ἐπιτιμητικός) letter in Ps-Demetrius 6: "For not against your will did you commit
grievous and hurtful acts to many people. It is fitting, therefore, that you meet with
more severe rebuke, since in the present case it so happens that others have also been
wronged." (καὶ γὰρ οὐκ ἄκων μεγάλα καὶ πολλοῖς βλαβερὰ διαπέπραξαι. προσήκει μὲν
οὖν σε μείζονος ἐπιτυχεῖν ἐπιπλήξεως, εἰ δὴ κατὰ τὸ παρὸν συντετύχηκε καὶ ἐπὶ ἑτέρων
τῶν ἀδικηθέντων. My translation).

Since you have received many favors (πολλὰ καλὰ) from us, even I am amazed in the extreme (θαυμάζω καθ᾽ ὑπερβολήν) at how you give no remembrance for any of them, but rather speak evil of us. Such is the mark of an ungrateful disposition. For the ungrateful forget good men [or good deeds] and mistreat (κακῶς ... διατίθενται) their benefactors as though they were enemies (τοὺς εὐεργέτας ὡς ἐχθρούς).

In both samples from Ps-Libanius we have not only the rebuke but also a corrective couched in terms of friendship. It is also noteworthy that the failure stems from not showing proper gratitude to a bene-factor/patron, which is then defined as creating enmity, i.e., a failed friendship. We may also compare the reproachful letter from the bilin-gual copy-book known as the Bologna Papyrus 5:

> That Licinius, once our mutual friend, should have slighted your gen-erosity [toward him] in his will, I would be amazed (ἐθαύμαζον) had I not come to the realization that whichever be ascribed (προσγέγραπται)[82] to mortals—better circumstances or worse—they are not in your con-trol.[83]

Here, of course, the criticism is leveled at the deceased for leaving the addressee out of his will, i.e., he has not treated the latter like a good friend. So the letter functions both as friendly consolation (for the addressee) and reproach (for Licinius). Once again, we find matters of patronal relations intruding into the concerns over friendship.[84] A number of the other sample letters dealing with rebuke in these various ancient handbooks deal with failing to fulfill one's obligations to a friend or patron/benefactor. The leveling of blame is to charge the person with enmity.[85]

---

[82] The meaning is quite clear since the Latin here reads *adsc[riptae] sunt*; both the Latin and Greek terms usually mean to write an addendum, as to a will or a registry. The intent may be a pun, playing on the notion of an added codicil to a person's will for someone who is not a natural heir, as in the case of legacies. This understanding is supported by the fact that the two preceding sample letters in the text also deal with "advice about legacies" (III/IV.1); one of these (III/IV.3–13) also employs the fictional Licinius as the deceased. Thus I would be inclined to translate the wordplay of the last lines as follows: "whichever be bequeathed to mortals ...".

[83] III./IV.26–V/VI.11, my translation. The text is found in Malherbe, *Ancient Episto-lary Theorists*, 48–9; for its background and use (perhaps a student's exercise book), cf. *ibid.*, 4–5.

[84] For the use of friendship language and patronage in relation to wills and legacies see also the article by John Fitzgerald in this volume.

[85] Compare Ps-Demetrius, *Epist. Types* 3, where blame is being given for not return-ing proper thanks for favors.

Framing the Rebuke in Galatians

In Gal 1:6–9 Paul opens the first framing section[86] of the letter by
signaling the enmity of the Galatians in rebuking terms. He further
sanctions the rebuke by imposing magical curse formulas on anyone
(human or angel) who dares to preach (or to follow) a different gospel.[87]
The use of incantations here fully anticipates the next major framing
section of the letter, Gal 3:1–5. But as Sampley rightly notes, it also
sets the stage for Paul's encounter with Cephas (Gal 2:11–15) as a
display of frank rebuke. By rehearsing this episode Paul thus shows
his consistency and clear-headedness, "resolutely standing firm against
one even so preeminent."[88] At the same time, we should recognize that
Paul's account also portrays Peter as the one who fosters enmity by
behaving inconsistently with his Antioch hosts: whereas he formerly
"gave Paul and Barnabas the right hand of fellowship" (2:9) and "ate
with Gentiles," after the people from James arrived, "he drew back
and removed himself" (ὑπέστελλεν καὶ ἀφώριζεν ἑαυτόν) out of fear
(2:12). This is rash action, which Paul says was compounded by making
the other Jews "act hypocritically together with him (συνυπεκρίθησαν
αὐτῷ) ... so that even Barnabas was *carried away* likewise by their
hypocrisy" (ὥστε καὶ Βαρναβᾶς συναπήχθη αὐτῶν τῇ ὑποκρίσει, 2:13).
It is Paul who stands for the truth (2:14) by opposing Peter "face to
face" (κατὰ πρόσωπον, 2:11) to rebuke and condemn him for his breach
of etiquette and friendship. The condemnation (κατεγνωσμένος ἦν)[89] is

---

[86] I use the notion of "framing sections" to focus on the rhetorical strategy rather
than form. I have provided the text and translation, reflecting this discussion, of the
main framing sections of Gal in Appendix A.

[87] Betz (*Galatians*, 50–52) rightly shows that the force of the curses in 1:8–9 sets an
ominous, magical tone for the letter. Betrayal of Paul's gospel is sanctioned by oaths
and divine retribution. Betz also notes that this functions as a framing device as it is
completed by the "blessing" formula in 6:16. I would add in here 6:17 as well: καὶ ὅσοι
τῷ κανόνι τούτῳ στοιχήσουσιν, εἰρήνη ἐπ᾽ αὐτοὺς καὶ ἔλεος καὶ ἐπὶ τὸν Ἰσραὴλ τοῦ θεοῦ.
Τοῦ λοιποῦ κόπους μοι μηδεὶς παρεχέτω· ἐγὼ γὰρ τὰ στίγματα τοῦ Ἰησοῦ ἐν τῷ σώματί
μου βαστάζω. Thus, if, as Betz suggests, the letter has an overall magical tone to it, I
wonder why he does not see the reference to the "evil eye" in 3:1 or to the Galatians'
"blessing" of Paul in 4:15 as also carrying this sanction, since both passages are part of
the charge that the Galatians had betrayed Paul and his gospel. So compare the double
affirmations in 5:2–4 and 6:17–18 where these ideas are continued in later framing
sections [see Appendix A].

[88] Sampley, "Paul's Frank Speech," 8 (ms.).

[89] The periphrastic construction here is well-known, cf. Betz, *Galatians*, 106; but
the full sense of the word-play is often overlooked (so Martyn, *Galatians*, 232; Dunn,
Galatians, 117). Since γνώμη in legal usage means the vote of the assembly to render a

graver for "leading" (ἀπάγειν)[90] Barnabas and the others into the same error of hypocrisy. In a sense, the portrayal of the episode at Antioch functions as a biographical digression to set the stage for Paul to charge the Galatians and the opponents with similar errors—the Galatians for being hypocritical friends and the opponents for misleading them into it.

The next framing section is Paul's charge of enmity in 3:1–5.[91] For Paul now addresses his audience with some of the harshest language in the letter as he twice calls them "foolish" or "rash" (ἀνόητοι, 3:1, 3). It is, as Sampley points out, also a key expression of Paul's frank rebuke.[92] Several features also make it a charge that the Galatians had abandoned Paul, and had thus forsaken the bonds of friendship and obligation. First, Paul asks if they have somehow been "bewitched" (ἐβάσκανεν, 3:1), or more literally had the "evil eye" put on them. Most commentators have taken this in a figurative sense, in reference to the effects of the opponents' teaching.[93] But the force of calling them "rash" combined with the reference to their "eyes" (by which they had

---

verdict at trial, καταγνώμη thus means a "vote against" or a "vote of guilty." (See my comments on the use of γνώμη in this sense in Favorinus *Kor.* 47 at Appendix B n. 153.) Hence, the periphrastic construction here aptly captures the sense, "he was one who had received the guilty verdict." But as Betz points out, this does not constitute Paul's "victory" in the argument; rather, it reflects Paul's charge that Peter was culpable for the "blowup" at Antioch. In the next sentences he will outline what constitutes this guilt: both his own drawing back and his leading others into hypocrisy. Thus, Paul portrays himself as having frankly rebuked Peter by telling him he was "guilty" of a grievous error. In terms of the grades of rebuke in the epistolary handbooks, this very direct charge of guilt should likely be classed as "censuring" (ἐπιτιμητική), one of the harsher forms; cf. Ps-Demetrius, *Epist. Types* 6 (which calls it a "more severe rebuke" [μείζονος ... ἐπιπλήξεως]); Ps-Libanius, *Epist. Types* 34 & 81. Even so, the gradations are subtle; Ps-Libanius' "reproving" or "inculpating" (ἐλεγκτική) letter (§§32 & 79) involves a sharp rebuke, since the offender denies culpability (§32), and the sample letter (§79) refers to "proofs" (ἐλέγχους) of the guilt.

[90] The word ἀπάγειν means to lead away, divert, or to perplex. Consequently, it implies here that the object of the verb has gotten caught up and carried away rashly in an action. Compare Plutarch, *Quomodo adulator* 69E (quoted above), where the term φέρεσθαι (pass. of φέρειν) is used in this sense, and in the same passage the term ἀνέχειν is used of restraining rash behaviors that lead a person off the right path.

[91] Marshall (*Enmity in Corinth*, 154–55) refers to both Gal 1:6–9 and 3:1–5 in his discussion of the enmity motif.

[92] For use of ἀνόητος in connection with severe forms of frank speech in the episto-lary handbooks see also nn. 80–81 above, contra the discussion of Betz (*Galatians*, 130), who takes it as a milder commonplace of diatribe literature.

[93] So Betz, *Galatians*, 131; cf. Martyn, *Galatians*, 282–83. Compare John Chrysostom's *Homily on Galatians* 3:1.

received the gospel from Paul, both in 3:1), one must wonder about a more sinister tone.[94] This comes through especially when Paul again tars them with "rashness" in 3:3 because they had "begun in the spirit" but have ended "in flesh." Here again we have the charge[95] that they had changed their allegiance from Paul to the opponents, parallel to the rash, hypocritical behavior of Peter and Barnabas at Antioch. But here their rashness may have a diabolical origin.

The "spirit" here is more than a theological metaphor for Paul's gospel. It is a palpable reality to their lives that has been dispensed as a gift (χάρις, 1:6), i.e., as a benefaction. So, notice 3:2 where he asks the leading question of their culpability: "I only want to learn this from you: Did you *receive the spirit* (τὸ πνεῦμα ἐλάβετε) from works of law or from hearing of faith." It is this reception of the spirit that they have now rashly abandoned by "ending with the flesh" (3:3). But

---

[94] That the "the eyes are the window of the soul" was a commonplace in the Greco-Roman world, but it had a far more direct meaning than may be recognized today. For as sense organs, the eyes were thought of as conveying information or perceptions directly to the soul. This is why the "evil eye" was considered such a real threat. Also, because rhetoric was a performative genre of display, both the sights and the sounds (words) were thought of as conveying the meaning and power of a speech. Consequently, orators were sometime viewed with some suspicion. So in 3:1, it is the magical power of the opponents who have caused the Galatians to become rash by abandoning the gospel that Paul himself had displayed "before their eyes" (κατ' ὀφθαλμούς) when he "publicly proscribed" (προεγράφη) Jesus as crucified. The term προγράφειν here is unusual and a double entendre. On the one hand, it refers to the vividness of the orator's art to bring things to life before the audience (so also Betz, *Galatians* 131); on the other hand, it is the literal translation of the Latin *proscribere*, which means to mark for death. On βασκανία as the "evil eye" see Matthew W. Dickie, "Heliodorus and Plutarch on the Evil Eye," *CP* 86 (1991) 17–29. For malicious laughter as magically inciting enmity, see Hendrik S. Versnel, "Κόλασαι τοὺς ἡμᾶς τοιούτους ἡδέως βλέπον-τες 'Punish those who rejoice in our misery': On curse texts and *Schadenfreude*," in *The World of Ancient Magic*, ed. D.R. Jordan, H. Montgomery, and E. Thomassen (Papers from the Norwegian Institute at Athens 4; Bergen: Paul Ålstroms, 1999) 143. For rhetor-ical display as a means of arousing passions, through sound, word, and sight, see Ruth Webb, "Imagination and the Arousal of the Emotions in Graeco-Roman Rhetoric," in *The Passions in Roman Thought and Literature*, ed. S.M. Braund and C. Gill (Cambridge: Cambridge UP, 1997) 112–27. On the powerful effects of rhetoric see Lucian's *Nigrinus* 35–6.

[95] John Chrysostom (*Comm. in Gal* 3:1 [PG 61.6487.52–58]) uses both "vehemence" (σφοδρότητι) and "censure" (ἐπιτίμησις) to describe Paul's charges here, but he adds that "they deserved far more severe words" (καὶ γὰρ πολλῷ χαλεπωτέρων ἦσαν ἄξιοι ῥημά-των) than these. Similarly, in 2:11, when Paul "opposed" Peter, Chrysostom describes as "censured vehemently" (ἐπετίμησαν σφόδρα). Chrysostom also takes the "evil eye" language not in the magical sense, but to show envy and jealousy were the causes of enmity in this situation.

the real sting comes in 3:5, when Paul asks the follow-up question: "Now, does *the one who supplies you with the spirit* and who works miracles among you [do so] from works of law or from hearing of faith? (ὁ οὖν ἐπιχορηγῶν ὑμῖν τὸ πνεῦμα καὶ ἐνεργῶν δυνάμεις ἐν ὑμῖν, ἐξ ἔργων νόμου ἢ ἐξ ἀκοῆς πίστεως;)." Again, most commentators take this as a reference to God as "the one who supplies the spirit" and miraculous powers,[96] and surely Paul would say God is the ultimate source (so 4:6). Yet, three factors suggest a different referent here: (1) the context is the charge that they had changed allegience; (2) the parallelism with 3:2 (ἐξ ἔργων νόμου ... ἢ ἐξ ἀκοῆς πίστεως) in reference to their "receipt" of the spirit; and (3) the parallelism with the participial constructions of Gal 1:6 (τοῦ καλέσαντος ὑμᾶς ἐν χάριτι) and 5:8 (ἐκ τοῦ καλοῦντος ὑμᾶς) where Paul is clearly referring to himself. Taken together, these elements point to Paul declaring himself as the benefactor (or "broker," perhaps)[97] for their reception of the spirit through his own presentation of the gospel in their hearing. Their defection is now placed as a battle between magical powers and gifts, and Paul excoriates them for turning their backs on him, when he had given them the very spirit of God. This claim on Paul's part is connected to his understanding of their moment of "adoption as sons" that gave them freedom from slavery to the elements of the universe (4:3–6). In other words, Paul is charging them with having failed to show proper honor toward him not only as friend, but as their spiritual benefactor. Thus, this passage sets up the discussion of Abraham and the law (3:6–22) and the alternative through faith and baptism (3:23–29) that follows.

Next, in 4:1–11 he will return to the attack. In 4:1–7 he opens with benefaction language: the grant of "adoption" (υἱοθεσίαν) afforded by Paul through baptism (3:26–29) has given them freedom from slavery to the "elements" of the cosmos (4:3 & 7). Then, in 4:8–11 he charges them with turning their backs on him and his gospel and returning to a form

---

[96] So Betz, *Galatians*, 135; Martyn, *Galatians*, 285–6.

[97] For ἐπιχορηγεῖν as benefaction language, see Frederick W. Danker, *Benefactor: Epigraphic Study of a Graeco-Roman and New Testament Semantic Field* (St. Louis: Clayton Publishing, 1982) 331; for the phrase τοῦ καλεσάντος ἡμᾶς as reference to benefactor see *ibid.*, 452. Even if Paul views God as the ultimate source of these benefits, this still puts Paul in a position of supplying benefaction. It is parallel to a situation found especially in Roman inscriptions to designate the civic benefactor who secures a favor for the city from the emperor. These are especially common in connection with the imperial cult in the Greek cities. See L. Michael White, "Counting the Costs of Nobility: The Social Economy of Roman Pergamon," in *Pergamon: Citadel of the Gods*, ed. H. Koester (HTS 47; Valley Forge: Trinity Press International, 1998) 331–71.

of "slavery" to the law as one of the elements of the cosmos.[98] Again, it is their defection from Paul that constitutes the basis of his charge of enmity compounded by the fact that they should behave so ungratefully for such a gift. After all, he is the one who *introduced* them to God and "adoption" through baptism into Christ (cf. 3:26–29).[99] Thus he

---

[98] Betz (*Galatians*, 216) argues that Paul's question in 4:9 (πῶς ἐπιστρέφετε πάλιν ἐπὶ τὰ ἀσθενῆ καὶ πτωχὰ στοιχεῖα οἷς πάλιν ἄνωθεν δουλεύειν θέλετε;) is meant to parallel and pick up the question he ostensibly posed to Peter in 2:14 (πῶς τὰ ἔθνη ἀναγκάζεις ἰουδαΐζειν;). On what "elemental spirits of the cosmos" means in Gal 4:3 and 9 see the discussion by Martyn *Galatians*, 393–406 and his article "Christ, the Elements of the Cosmos, and the Law in Galatians," in *The Social World of the First Christians: Essays in Honor of Wayne A. Meeks*, ed. L.M. White and O.L. Yarbrough (Minneapolis: Fortress Press, 1995) 16–39.

[99] The nature of Paul's own "brokering" role in 4:8–9 has been overlooked: Betz (*Galatians*, 213–15) takes 4:9 to be framed in "gnosticizing" terms; Martyn (*Galatians*, 413) instead makes it an apocalyptic formulation. That the Galatians "came to know God" (γνόντες θεόν—noting the aorist) must refer to their conversion and baptism (so also Dunn, *Galatians*, 225), but rather than "gnosticizing" language this is more in the vein of "initiation into the mysteries," which would be entirely consistent with Paul's way of describing baptism in Gal 3:27–28. For Pauline baptism as a "ritual of initiation" see Wayne A. Meeks, *The First Urban Christians: The Social World of the Apostle Paul* (New Haven: Yale UP, 1983) 153–57. For the sense of "knowing with the mind's eye" as a reflection of initiation into the Greek mysteries, see Arthur Darby Nock, "Hellenistic Mysteries and Christian Sacraments," in *Essays on Religion in the Ancient World*, ed. by Zeph Stewart (2 vols.; Oxford: Clarendon, 1972) II:799–801, where he also notes that "initiation" into philosophy uses the same motifs; cf. Abraham J. Malherbe, *Paul and the Thessalonians* (Philadelphia: Fortress, 1987) 21–33. Compare also the use of ἰδιώτης (meaning "outsider" or "uninitiated") in 1Cor 14:16 &23–24, where the root sense means "unlearned" and thus the opposite of τελετή ("perfecting" and, thus, "ritual of initiation"). In Gal 4:9, Paul portrays himself as their mystagogue. But then he makes a reversal on the idea of "knowing," as it is really God who "came to know" them (μᾶλλον δὲ γνωσθέντες ὑπὸ θεοῦ—again using the aorist). This, too, places Paul in a mediating position, as it portrays the relationship of the Galatian gentiles as ones who were previously unacquainted with the God of Israel; it was Paul who provided the "introduction," as if he had written a letter of recommendation for them. So, compare Ps-Demetrius' description of the "letter of recommendation" (§2) he says: "The 'recommending' (συστατικός) type is that which we write on behalf of one person to another … while also speaking to those who were formerly *not known* as though they were *known*" (ἅμα καὶ τοὺς πρότερον ἠγνοημένους λέγοντες ὡς ἐγνωσμένους). The function of the one providing the recommendation is very important, since he/she relies on a relation of friendship to both parties. It also implies some degree of obligation, as if to a patron, both for the one who is receiving the recommendation (obligation *from* the recommender) and for the one being recommended (obligation *to* the recommender). If Paul is saying something like, "I made the introductions for you Galatians to come to 'adoption' as children of God," then he is also saying that they owe him a debt in response, since he is thus their spiritual patron. Hence, both forms of "knowing" in 4:9 point to a "brokering" role on Paul's part. On letters of recommendation as operating within the friendship and patronage orbits see also Marshall, *Enmity in Corinth*, 147–50, 259–71.

concludes this section, at least as it is usually framed,[100] with another claim on his spiritual patronage toward them by saying, "I fear for you, lest somehow I have labored over you in vain (φοβοῦμαι ὑμᾶς μή πως εἰκῇ κεκοπίακα εἰς ὑμᾶς)."[101]

Paul regularly uses terms associated with labor in reference to his missionary activities;[102] however, there is an often overlooked connotation from the realm of benefaction and patronage. So we may compare 1 Thess 5:12 where the linking of the three verbs κοπιᾶν, προϊστάναι, and νουθετεῖν establishes a context of patronal leadership in the house church.[103] Paul accords his house church patrons—male and female—appropriate honors for their "labors," that is, their service and benefaction to the congregation.[104] Use of terms referring to labor, dan-

---

[100] See below n. 111.

[101] Cf. Betz, *Galatians*, 219 for the translation. Betz thinks this is the beginning of the *dubitatio* that continues in 4:12–20.

[102] So Rom 16:6, 12; 1 Cor 4:12; 15:10; 16:16; Phil 2:16; 1 Thess 5:12; cf. Betz, *Galatians*, 219.

[103] So note that giving acknowledgement to "those who labor among you" (εἰδέναι τοὺς κοπιῶντας ἐν ὑμῖν) is supplemented with the additional descriptors "who preside over you and admonish you in the Lord" (καὶ προϊσταμένους ὑμῶν ἐν κυρίῳ καὶ νουθετοῦντας ὑμᾶς). In particular, προϊστάναι can mean to "stand before" or "preside over" and especially in the middle voice where it means "to take as leader or guardian." The term "patroness" (προστάτις) found in reference to Phoebe, the house church leader at Cenchreae (Rom 16:2), is a cognate of this same verb. Compare also Rom 12:8 where προϊστάμενος occurs in the context of other financial services (μεταδιδούς, ἐλεῶν) to the congregation. This may mean that some of the other uses of this terms for service (διακονία) and labor (κόπος) likely refer to the patronage of the house church community, as seems to be the clear context in 1 Cor 16:16. Perhaps the women mentioned in Rom 16:6 & 12 should also be considered house church patrons rather than just missionary helpers.

[104] The sense of "presiding" here does not imply a heirarchical office of elder or bishop; that is a later develpment to be seen in the Pastoral Epistles. Rather, here it is a functional designation for service within the congregation; so Abraham J. Malherbe, *The Letters to the Thessalonians* (AB32B; New York: Doubleday, 2000) 311–13. Malherbe elsewhere (*Paul and the Thessalonians*, 15) suggests that this might likely be a person of some means, like Jason in Acts 17:6 & 9, who posted bond and hosted the congregation in his house, but argues that the root meaning is "care." I suspect, however, that there is additional symbolic weight to these terms referring to patronage of the community even in Paul (as in 1 Thess 5:12, Rom 12:8, and 16:2). Rom 12:8 also uses the term σπουδή ("zeal") in this connection; it implies the steadfast earnestness of a benefactor and is closely connected to friendship language. The term ἐπιμελεῖσθαι is used in tandem with προϊστάναι in 1 Tim 3:5. With its cognates and close synonyms (such as πρόνοια in Greek or *curare*-cognates in Latin) ἐπιμελεῖσθαι occurs frequently in building inscriptions for the one who has charge over a particular building project. There it usually denotes the cost or effort and prestige of the patron in leading the project to completion. It is analogous to the "zeal" (σπουδή) of the benefactor. For cases see my *Social Origins of*

ger, or struggle occur frequently in benefactor inscriptions. Called the "endangered benefactor" motif by Danker, such terms are a standard means of acknowledging and honoring benefactors.[105] Thus, in Gal 4:11 Paul is referring to his laborious service in terms that demand an honorific response from his beneficiaries.[106] As part of his charge of enmity, it escalates the symbolic weight being heaped on their desertion from Paul. Moreover, this verse now sets the stage for the most stinging criticism of all (4:12–20), which will end with a variation on the same theme of Paul's "labor" over them (4:19). Verses 11–12 and 19–20, therefore, form an *inclusio* around this passage to give it further rhetorical weight.

A New Frame for Gal 4:11–20

The two lines of the friendship motif now merge in Gal 4:11–20.[107] With the frankness of a friend Paul charges the Galatians with enmity on account of their hypocrisy, false friendship, and failure to show due honor to him as their spiritual benefactor.[108] It is a powerful charge

---

Christian Architecture (2 vols.; HTS 42; Valley Forge: Trinity Press, 1996–7) 2:117, 119, 140!, 175, 308, 363, 416–17 and Danker, *Benefactor*, 359–61.

[105] *Benefactor*, 417–35. Also, for "zeal" as one of the standard virtues of a benefactor see *ibid.*, 320, 459; others include ἐπιείκεια ("clemency, reasonableness"), *ibid.*, 351; cf. n. 80 above.

[106] As noted by Betz (*Galatians*, 219 n. 58), 𝔓46 uses the aorist form of the verb (ἐκοπίασα) instead of the perfect (κεκοπίακα), thus suggesting past action rather than Paul's on-going labors on their behalf. Given the sense of their betrayal (4:9: οἷς πάλιν ἄνωθεν δουλεύειν θέλετε), bolstered by Paul's reference to "again being in travail" (4:19: πάλιν ὠδίνω) over them, may suggest that the aorist of 𝔓46 is in keeping with Paul's tone and strategy.

[107] For the text and translation of these framing units see Appendix A below.

[108] The recent study of Stephan Joubert, *Paul as Benefactor: Reciprocity, Strategy, and Theological Reflection in Paul's Collection* (WUNT 2.124; Tübingen: Mohr-Siebeck, 2000) should be mentioned here, since he also sees Paul using the ideology and language of benefaction, especially in formulating ideas about the collection for Jerusalem. However, Joubert draws a sharper distinction between the "systems" of patronage and benefaction as "related but distinct." In general, he takes patronage to operate more on an interpersonal basis and with a higher degree of asymmetry, while benefaction operates on a communal basis with less asymmetry (66–69, et passim). In keeping with this distinction, he finds Paul using the language of benefaction, not patronage, in discussing the collection. A key point in making the distinction is the use of friendship language, which, he supposes, only occurs in connection with personal patronage (29–31). He also argues that Roman patronage terminology is not much found in the Greek east (65), so that Greek "benefaction" concepts were the norm. Here his citation of evidence is too limited; he does not take into account Greek uses of benefactor terminology (especially εὐεργέτης) in reference to acts of personal patronage. For example, he does not discuss uses such as the one noted above in Ps-Libanius, *Epist. Types* 64. In this case the explicit

in the light of the moral weight placed on these relationships in Roman society of the Greek provinces.

The entire passage 4:8–20 should be seen as a framing unit linked to the two other principal framing sections in 1:6–10 and 3:1–5 (see Appendix A).[109] In each of these three passages Paul addresses the audience directly and frankly; the same rebuking tone and theme of enmity appear in each one. These framing sections are punctuated and illustrated by intervening digressions where Paul talks in autobiographical, "historical" (i.e., from scripture), or abstract terms about key theological arguments. The *inclusio* of 4:11–20, then, serves as the climax of this rhetorical strategy.

The passage opens in 4:8–10 with Paul turning from his more abstract discussion of freedom and adoption (3:23–4:7) to address the Galatians directly with the implications of the Christ event in their own lives. Beginning with their former condition as Gentiles he outlines a "then/now/how-could-you" sequence of changes.[110] He himself had brokered their new "acquaintance" with God, but they had sub-

<hr />

opposition of benefactors vs. enemies is made; therefore, benefactor is equal to friend in a context of one-to-one patronal relations. Numerous other examples could be cited. For example, Joubert does not seem to take note of the several Latin inscriptions from Corinth in which *patronus* is used for patronage of a whole tribe, the colony itself, or of a civic project (cf. *Corinth* 8.2 nos. 16, 56, 57, 66, 68, 71, and 106); *patronus Corinth[i]* (as clearly found in no. 71) should be read as the Latin equivalent of εὐεργέτης τῆς πόλεως (cf. *Corinth* 8.1 no. 84). The use of "benefactor" in cases where personal patronage is clearly indicated in the sample letters of the epistolary handbooks (see above nn. 80–81) also support this view. So, in practice there was considerably more overlap among the three semantic fields of friendship, patronage, and benefaction than Joubert wants to admit. In this regard, Marshall's study (*Enmity in Corinth*) provides a useful counterbalance. On the other hand, Joubert (73–115) appropriately locates the origination of the collection as reported in Gal 2:1–10 within the realm of benefaction, and he sees the "blowup" at Antioch as seriously threatening this enterprise (117–19). Unfortunately, he does not follow up the benefaction [and/or patronage] language in the rest of Gal. In my view, he misses much of Paul's use of the patronage/benefactor language in Gal and elsewhere; such language seems to be increasing during the later stages of his Aegean mission (where I would tend to locate the Galatian letter), and, no doubt, in conjunction with his efforts to complete the collection for Jerusalem.

[109] In Appendix A I have also provided what I consider to be the last of these framing units, Gal 5:1–13, where Paul addresses the audience directly. I shall not take time to discuss the passage in this study, although I have alluded to some of the parallels of language in the notes. I have included it in the Appendix to demonstrate its similarities to the earlier passages, especially its use of an *inclusio* (5:1 & 13) similar to that in 4:11–20 and a double affirmation that parallels the one in 1:8–9. See n. 131 below.

[110] Rhetorically, the break from the preceding passage is signaled by the adversative conjunction (ἀλλά), followed by a shift to second person address, and the parallel τότε μέν – νῦν δέ structure of the contrast he sets up. I have already discussed

sequently abandoned it. Verses 8–10 read as a single sentence, which
he turns into a rhetorical question of the audience: "how can you
turn again to the weak and beggarly elementals to whom you once
again wish to be enslaved, since you observe days, months, seasons, and
years?"[111] This rhetorical question focuses on their desertion from Paul
and thus sets the tone for Paul's sharper rebuke that follows in 4:11–20.

Like the introductory verses (4:8–10), the structure of 4:11–20 hinges
on the "then/now" contrast, but here it is the contrast between their
earlier friendly feelings toward Paul and their present enmity. In other
words it corresponds to the last two parts of the change sequence given
in verses 8–9, and hence, on the *fact* that they had turned their back on
Paul. The *inclusio* is framed by verses 11–12a and 19–20 respectively, with
their parallel references to Paul's past "labors" on their behalf and his
solicitous expression of doubt about their present stance. Verses 13–15
offer his review of his the prior state of friendship, while verses 17–
18 deal with the present state of enmity created by the opponents'
flattering insincerity. At the center stands verse 16: "so that I have
become your enemy by telling you the truth? (ὥστε ἐχθρὸς ὑμῶν γέγονα
ἀληθεύων ὑμῖν;)." Its meaning is clear enough as it anchors both the
enmity motif and the frankness motif in the passage. It represents
Paul's charge against them. This tradition of interpretation goes back to
early patristic commentators. For example, John Chrysostom read this
sentence as a rhetorical question in the light of the radical change of
disposition from their prior friendship, and rightly makes it anticipatory
of Paul's expression of perplexity in v. 20.[112] Chrysostom's rendering of

---

the implications of the language of "knowing" and "being known" by God as part of
Paul's rebuke; see above n. 99.

[111] The majority reading of verse 10 has παρατηρεῖσθε, and most modern editors take
this sentence with verse 11 (see n. 1); however, 𝔓⁴⁶ has παρατηροῦντες. This reading
makes verse 10 a subordinate explanatory clause going with the preceding question, as
translated above. Even if one were to opt for the majority reading here, the punctuation
between verses 9 and 10 should be a medial stop so that the question carries through to
the end of v. 10, thus: πῶς ἐπιστρέφετε πάλιν ἐπὶ τὰ ἀσθενῆ καὶ πτωχὰ στοιχεῖα οἷς πάλιν
ἄνωθεν δουλεύειν θέλετε· ἡμέρας παρατηρεῖσθε καὶ μῆνας καὶ καιροὺς καὶ ἐνιαυτούς; It
thus sets off the next sentence (4:11) as a sharper, more judgmental statement to open
the *inclusio* of 4:11–20. Even so, it must be reiterated that I veiw all of 4:8–20 as a
"framing section."

[112] *Comm. in Gal.* 4:16 (PG 61.659.46–54): Ἐνταῦθα διαπορεῖ καὶ ἐκπλήττεται, καὶ παρ'
αὐτῶν ζητεῖ τὴν αἰτίαν τῆς μεταβολῆς μαθεῖν. Τίς γὰρ ὑμᾶς ἐξηπάτησε, φησὶ, καὶ ἔπεισεν
ἑτέρως διατεθῆναι πρὸς ἡμᾶς; ... τί τοίνυν γέγονε; πόθεν ἡ ἔχθρα; πόθεν ἡ ὑποψία; ὅτι
τἀληθῆ πρὸς ὑμᾶς εἶπον; Διὰ τοῦτο μὲν οὖν μειζόνως ἐχρῆν τιμᾶν καὶ θεραπεύειν ("Here
he is perplexed and amazed, for he also seeks to learn from them the cause of their

Paul's rebuking tone in this verse nicely catches the irony as well as the implications of the enmity/friendship opposition. Yet the syntax of 4:16 remains a notorious problem, since it seems to be an asyndetic or elliptical question of which only the apodosis (beginning with ὥστε) remains.[113] It is also this elliptical quality that has led some to see it as overly agitated or emotional.[114] What most readers seem to have missed is that we have a natural protasis for this ὥστε-clause in 4:12c, and a further clue to Paul's rhetorical posture in this passage.

Paul's leading statement in this passage is "you have done me no wrong" (4:12c),[115] and virtually all commentators, including John Chrysostom, have taken it as an exculpatory statement of fact.[116] This assumption regarding its sense is also reflected in the standard punctuation of the sentence in modern critical editions, which separate it by a full stop from verse 12a–b (ending with δέομαι ὑμῶν).[117] Because of its terseness (no particles or other connectors) οὐδέν με ἠδικήσατε is then attached to the following sentence (4:13–14) by a medial stop. Thus, the opening of verse 13 (οἴδατε δέ) is taken as approbation of the statement, since Paul affirms their earlier hospitality towards him. This reading has put some strains on the text. Betz notes that the wording of 4:12c is "asyndetic" and "puzzling," but writes it off as an "epistolary cliché"

---

desertion. 'Who has deceived you,' he says, 'and persuaded you to be of a different disposition toward us? … What therefore has happened? Whence this enmity? Whence this jealous suspicion? [Is it] because I told you the truth? Why, on this account you ought to have showed [me] far greater honor and care!'" My translation).

[113] So also Betz (*Galatians*, 228): "ὥστε ('therefore') introducing a question is odd. It draws a conclusion from the preceding but leaves open whether that conclusion is true or not." It is punctuated as a question in all major editions of the NT since Tischendorf, though some translators have preferred to punctuate it with an exclamation in recognition of its ironic sense (so Dunn, *Galatians*, 250 n. 5, following Burton and Longenecker). Compare Schlier (*An die Galater*, 212) who calls it "sarcasm;" however, others have taken it as "poignant" (so Martyn, *Galatians*, 421).

[114] See nn. 2–3 above.

[115] οὐδέν με ἠδικήσατε—more literally, "you have wronged me in nothing;" however, see below at n. 124.

[116] Chrysostom (*Comm. in Gal.* 4:16 [PG 61.658.47–659.7]) takes this as Paul mixing praise with blame. Only Friedrich Sieffert (*Der Brief an die Galater* [KEK; Göttingen: Vandenhoeck, 1899) seems to have held out the possibility that the statement hints at some "wrong" being suffered. Since Schlier's refutation of his view (*An die Galater*, 209), however, there has not been much thought given to this possibility; cf. Betz, *Galatians*, 223 and n. 42.

[117] Only Betz (*Galatians*, 223) argues that the phrase δέομαι ὑμῶν, (4:12b) as a standard epistolary phrase, "does not need a firm connection with the preceeding or following," that is to say, it is asyndetic.

reflecting the friendship *topos*.[118] It forces all translations to gloss over the potentially adversative δέ at the opening of v. 13.[119]

It is worth noting, however, that John Chrysostom did not read the passage quite this way. Instead, he read verses 11 and 12a together as follows: φοβοῦμαι ὑμᾶς μή πως εἰκῇ κεκοπίακα εἰς ὑμᾶς· γίνεσθε ὡς ἐγώ, ὅτι καγὼ ὡς ὑμεῖς.[120] This makes verse 11 the charge and 12a a call to return to Paul's side, "as if extending his hand to them," says Chrysostom.[121] Also, the use of γίνεσθαι here in 12a already anticipates the enmity charge in verse 16 (ἐχθρὸς ὑμῶν γέγονα), so it will have a further ironic twist that pushes toward Paul's final expression of perplexity in verse 20. Next, Chrysostom clearly reads verse 12b–c as follows: ἀδελ-φοί, δέομαι ὑμῶν, οὐδέν με ἠδικήσατε, i.e., as one conciliatory or horta-tory statement;[122] therefore, he takes verses 13–14 as the approbation of this statement, as do most modern commentators.[123] But this is where it seems to me that Chrysostom may point us to another reading of verse 12b–c, now as the missing protasis of verse 16. So, Paul's elliptical question should now read: ἀδελφοί, δέομαι ὑμῶν, οὐδέν με ἠδικήσατε, … ὥστε ἐχθρὸς ὑμῶν γέγονα ἀληθεύων ὑμῖν; Not only is this grammatically superior for construing the ὥστε-clause of verse 16, but it also turns the entire sentence into a rhetorical question, thus: "Brothers, I beg you, did *you* do me no wrong, … so that I have become *your* enemy by telling *you* the truth?" Rather than taking οὐδέν με ἠδικήσατε as a statement of fact, it now becomes an ironic question that sets up the reversal (further strengthened by chiasm) in the apodosis.[124] The opening of the verse in

---

[118] *Galatians*, 223.

[119] Usually the δέ is dropped or read as if it were γάρ (as in numerous other Pauline formulations with οἴδατε), thus creating the sense that v. 12b leads seamlessly into v. 13. For the use of parenthetic insertions to heighten irony, and in the context of "perplexity," compare Favorinus *Kor.* 9 [*Or.* 37.9], quoted above at n. 44.

[120] *Comm. in Gal.* 4:11–12 (PG 61.658.17–30). The syntax of these two clauses seems to me to fit this reading better, since it now alternates and balances between the "I" (Paul) and the "you" (the audience), thus: "I–you" (φοβοῦμαι ὑμᾶς), you–I (γίνεσθε ὡς ἐγώ), "I–you" (καγὼ ὡς ὑμεῖς). This is rhetorically stronger than the traditional punctuation. Also, this pattern of alteration as a rhetorical device will be used in central rhetorical question of verses 12c & 16. See below n. 124.

[121] *Comm. in Gal.* 4:11–12 (PG 61.658.28–9): Εἶτα, ὥσπερ χειμαζομένοις χεῖρα ὀρέγων, ἑαυτὸν εἰς μέσον ἄγει, λέγων, γίνεσθε …

[122] *Comm. in Gal.* 4:12 (PG 61.658.46; 659.7 and 18). He actually quotes the verse three times in this form, although he omits ἀδελφοί in the last two.

[123] *Comm. in Gal.* 4:13 (PG 61. 659.13–17).

[124] While I translate 12c as interrogative here my argument does not absolutely depend on it; it could be declarative in form and still carry the ironic rhetorical force I am describing. The key is the way that the two parts (vv. 12c & 16) once again balance

4:12b (ἀδελφοί, δέομαι ὑμῶν) sets up this rhetorical question while also anticipating Paul's wish "to be present" in verse 20.[125]

Now, 4:13–15 comprise a parenthesis that interrupts the two halves of the rhetorical question, not unlike the way Favorinus frames a key point to heighten the irony (§9, above). It is set off by οἴδατε δέ and punctuated with the emphatic μαρτυρῶ γὰρ ὑμῖν sentence in verse 15. Instead of reaffirming that the Galatians "did no wrong," verses 13–15 "prove" the opposite, by showing how they have abandoned their former friendly treatment. The use of μαρτυρῶ in v. 15 may thus carry the sense of presenting the evidence against them.[126] Then, in verses 17–18 Paul will turn again to argue that his opponents are the real enemy after all, by showing them to be flatterers who only court the Galatians for base reasons. Again, the shift is very abrupt from the "I-you / you me" balance of 4:11–16, as verse 17 opens without particles or connectives by shifting to the third person (ζηλοῦσιν).[127] The very fact that Paul does not even bother to identify "them" descriptively (as he does in 1:7 and 5:7–12) is further indication that "they" are already implicit within the charge he has laid against the Galatians beginning with οἴδατε δὲ ὅτι (4:13). So, verses 17–18 must, in effect, be carrying on the "proof" already begun in verses 13–15.

The overall structure here then is B-C-B'-C', where B-B' is the rhetorical question (verses 12b–c & 16, respectively), while C is the

---

the "I–you" relationship, but now both rendered ironically. So it goes "me-you" [object-subject] (οὐδέν με ἠδικήσατε) then "your-I" [predicate+possessive-subject] (ἐχθρὸς ὑμῶν γέγονα), thus forming a chiasm. Again, this strengthens the rhetorical force of the ironic question. If οὐδέν με ἠδικήσατε is read as an interrogative, the grammar is nonetheless correct, since the use of οὐδέν demands an affirmative answer: "You wronged me, didn't you?"

[125] Paul uses δέομαι as a form of petition six times in the genuine lettes. Three of these (Rom 1:10, 1 Thess 3:10, and 2 Cor 8:4) are as participles. The first two are in the context of prayers to God and reflect Paul's desire to visit. In this sense, here it may be anticipatory of the two references to Paul's "presence" in 4:18 and 20. The reference in 2 Cor 8:4 refers to the Macedonians' "pleading" to participate in the collection for Jerusalem; here note Paul's use of μαρτυρῶ in praise of them (compare Gal 4:15). In only three cases does Paul use the finite verb form δέομαι (Gal 4:11; 2 Cor 5:20 [δεόμεθα] and 10:1). In each of the latter instances δέομαι is the opening of the clause or sentence, just as we propose for Gal 4:11. All the cases from the papyri cited by Moulton-Milligan, where the finite form is used in the sense of petition, supplication, or demand, occur at the beginning of the sentence or clause.

[126] The presentation of "proof" (ἔλεγχος) in the context of rebuke is a feature of letters of reproof (ἐλεγκτική); cf. Ps-Libanius, *Epist. Types*, 79.

[127] As noted also by Betz, *Galatians*, 229.

proof of their change from friendship (4:13–15) and C' is the proof of
the opponents' insincerity (4:17–18) that led them astray.[128] In this vein,
the use of ζηλοῦν (three times in verses 17–18) conveys an important
resonance. The opponents' "zeal" is insincere and selfish, like that of
the flatterer instead of a true friend. It is thus closer to "envy" (φθόνος),
the partner of enmity, than proper "earnestness" (σπουδή).[129] That it
carries a sense of rashness about it is also suggested by Paul's use of it to
describe his former life as a persecutor (Gal 1:14, περισσοτέρως ζηλωτής;
cf. Phil 3:6, κατὰ ζῆλος). This distinction over good and bad "zeal"
helps to explain Paul's comment in 4:18, where he links "good zeal"
with his own apostolic parousia. It once again signals Paul's role in
bringing them the gospel as a benefaction, which now sets the stage for
his closing comments (in verses 19–20). The *inclusio* is now completed by
Paul adopting the stance of the mother in travail, resuming the theme
of his "labors" on behalf of the Galatians from 4:11.[130] The new travail
is their desertion from his gospel, which he takes to be an abandonment
of Christ himself.[131] In other words, he is having to repeat the actions
that brought Christ's death to reality "before their eyes" in the first
place (so Gal 3:1 & 4:13–14). His perplexity (4:20), as noted earlier, is a
sign that the friendship has been broken by their failure to show him
due loyalty and honor for his spiritual benefaction toward them.

---

[128] See also n. 130 below for the structure of the entire frame.

[129] Compare Rom 13:13 and 1 Cor 3:3 where ζῆλος is paired with ἔρις as "strife and
jealousy." Contrast Rom 12:8 where σπουδή is used in the sense of patronage/bene-
faction and in conjunction with 'sincerity" (ἁπλότης) and "cheerfulness" (ἱλαρότης) in
giving. These combinations place ζῆλος squarely within the enmity motif. For the use
of the term in connection with friendship see also Betz, *Galatians*, 229. In addition
compare Plutarch's *Quomodo adulator* 53D and 54C where the true friends' emulation
of one another is "sincere" (σπουδή), versus the covert "jealousy" and "envy" (ζῆλος &
Φθόνος) of the flatterer. Also, whereas σπουδή is regularly found in conjunction with
benefaction as describing the benefactor's enthusiasm and earnestness, ζῆλος is not (cf.
Danker, *Benefactor*, 320–23 and n. 103–104 above). Compare also the use of σπουδή in
2 Cor 8:7–8 in conjunction with the collection for Jerusalem.

[130] Thus, in keeping with the arrangement suggested above for the middle verses, the
overall pattern of the *inclusio* is as follows: A (11–12a) – B (12b–c) – C (13–15) – B' (16) –
C' (17–18) – A' (19–20).

[131] So he will return to this point in the next framing section (5:1–13), which replicates
the adamant double curse of 1:7–8 (5:2–4), picks up the use of μαρτυρεῖν from 4:15 (5:3),
charges them with abandoning "the one who calls them" as in 1:6 & 3:5, cf. 4:13–15
(5:7–8), and accuses the opponents of leading them into rash behavior by confusing
them as in 1:6–7, cf. 2:11–14 and 4:17 (5:7, 10, 12). See Appendix A.

In the final analysis, then, the overall tone of Gal, and especially 4:11–20, is that of rebuke. In terms of rhetorical types, it fits far better with epideictic speech[132] than either forensic or deliberative, even though Paul employs both apologetic and persuasion in his argument. Even so, one wonders whether these formalist typologies from classical rhetoric are quite apt to Paul's epistolary style. From the perspective of the epistolary handbooks, one might instead suggest *oneidistic* (rebuking) or *epitimetic* (censuring)[133] types of letters as closest to Pauline style. This is not to deny the rhetorical strategy and force with which Paul frames the letter, but to place it in a more realistic context. Around the framing units in which Paul addresses the Galatians directly and frankly [see Appendix A] he builds his autobiographical and scriptural digressions to support his theological argument, namely that the Galatians' abandonment of Paul and his gospel is theologically perverted. Far from an emotional outburst or a rhetorical device, Paul's rhetorical strategy should be seen for what it is. Gal 4:11–20 weaves together the friendship themes of frankness and enmity as the climax of Paul's rebuke of the Galatians for having deserted him and his gospel. Much like Favorinus's speech to the Corinthians, he employs friendship and benefaction language to charge them with morally shameful behavior in their treatment of him.[134]

---

[132] This seems to be the way John Chrysostom took the overall tone, as mixing praise and blame, mildness and severity, in order to reprove and correct the Galatians. So, *Comm. in Gal.* 1:1 (PG 61.611.20–25). This mixture of praise and blame shows up especially in Chrysostom's discussion of 4:11–20. For example, he describes 4:11 as "compassionate" (Εἶδες σπλάγχνα ἀποστολικά), and "vehemently shaming" (σφόδρα ἐντρεπτικῶς) [*Comm. in Gal.* PG 61.658.17–19], and of 4:12 he says: "See how again he he addresses them with a name of honor ... For after he assailed them vehemently (σφόδρα καθήψατο), and made comparative (συνέκρινε) judgements of the case from all sides, and showed them their lawlessness, and hit them all about, he again turns and gives them medical attention (θεραπεύει), applying more gentle words (προσηνεστέροις κεχρημένος λόγοις)" [*Comm. in Gal.* 61.658.47–52, my translation]. It should also be noted here that John Chrysostom applies technical terms from the vocabulary of frank criticism and rebuke:, notably comparison (σύγκρισις) and medical treatment (specifically, the "application of opposites" as a curative). But see also the following note.

[133] See n. 81 above for Ps-Demetrius' sample of this type of letter and n. 95 above for John Chrysostom's use of this term to describe Paul's rebuke.

[134] What remains, then, is to probe further the implications of this strategy for understanding the real situation of the Galatian letter. I plan to take up this issue in a subsequent study.

Appendix A

The Framing Sections of the Galatian Letter
(Text and Translation by L.M. White)

1 ⁶ Θαυμάζω ὅτι οὕτως ταχέως μετατίθεσθε ἀπὸ τοῦ καλέσαντος ὑμᾶς ἐν
χάριτι [Χριστοῦ] εἰς ἕτερον εὐαγγέλιον,
⁷ ὃ οὐκ ἔστιν ἄλλο, εἰ μή τινές εἰ-
σιν οἱ ταράσσοντες ὑμᾶς καὶ θέλοντες
μεταστρέψαι τὸ εὐαγγέλιον τοῦ Χριστοῦ. ⁸ ἀλλὰ καὶ ἐὰν ἡμεῖς ἢ ἄγγε-
λος ἐξ οὐρανοῦ εὐαγγελίζηται [ὑμῖν]
παρ᾽ ὃ εὐηγγελισάμεθα ὑμῖν, ἀνάθεμα
ἔστω. ⁹ ὡς προειρήκαμεν καὶ ἄρτι πάλιν λέγω· εἴ τις ὑμᾶς εὐαγγελίζεται
παρ᾽ ὃ παρελάβετε, ἀνάθεμα ἔστω.

1 ⁶ I am astonished that you are so quickly transferring from the one who called you in grace to a different gospel—⁷ which is not another gospel, were there not some who are confusing you and wishing to misrepresent the gospel of Christ. ⁸ But even if we or an angel from heaven should proclaim a gospel contrary to that which we proclaimed to you, let him be accursed! ⁹ As we have said before, so now I say again: if anyone proclaims to you a gospel contrary to that which you received, let him be accursed!

⟦1:10–11 open Paul's defense of his gospel as "not of human origin," which leads to the historical and autobiographical interlude 1:12–2:21, culminating with the confrontation with Peter at Antioch.⟧

3 ¹ Ὦ ἀνόητοι Γαλάται, τίς ὑμᾶς ἐβάσκανεν, οἷς κατ᾽ ὀφθαλμοὺς Ἰησοῦς
Χριστὸς προεγράφη¹³⁵ ἐσταυρωμένος;
² τοῦτο μόνον θέλω μαθεῖν ἀφ᾽ ὑμῶν·
ἐξ ἔργων νόμου τὸ πνεῦμα ἐλάβετε
ἢ ἐξ ἀκοῆς πίστεως; ³ οὕτως ἀνόητοί
ἐστε, ἐναρξάμενοι πνεύματι νῦν σαρκὶ
ἐπιτελεῖσθε; ⁴ τοσαῦτα ἐπάθετε εἰκῇ; εἴ
γε καὶ εἰκῇ. ⁵ ὁ οὖν ἐπιχορηγῶν ὑμῖν τὸ
πνεῦμα καὶ ἐνεργῶν δυνάμεις ἐν ὑμῖν,
ἐξ ἔργων νόμου ἢ ἐξ ἀκοῆς πίστεως;

3 ¹ O foolish Galatians! Who has cast a spell on you—you, to whom Jesus Christ was publicly displayed before your very eyes as being crucified? ² Only one thing do I want to learn from you: Did you receive the spirit from works of law or from hearing of faith? ³ Are you so foolish that having *begun* with the spirit you now *finish*¹³⁶ with the flesh? ⁴ Did you experience so much in vain—if indeed it is in vain? ⁵ Accordingly, does the **one**¹³⁷ who supplies you with the spirit and who works miracles among you do so from lawful works or faithful hearing?

⟦In 3:6–14, Paul gives the first digression on Abraham, followed by a discussion of the value of the Law (3:15–22) and the new opportunity for "adoption" as heirs of Abraham by baptism into Christ. Then in 4:1–7 he returns to the idea of "adoption" constituting freedom from slavery to the "elemental spirits of the cosmos."⟧

---

¹³⁵ A word play, since προγράφω means both "to announce publicly" and "to pro-scribe" (= Latin *proscribere*, i.e., "to sentence to death"). The reference is to Paul's preaching in which he made them "visualize" the crucifixion.

¹³⁶ Both words have technical meaning in sacrifical ritual as the starting and ending actions.

¹³⁷ A reference to Paul himself; *pace* Betz, *Galatians*, 128, 135.

4 ⁸ Ἀλλὰ τότε μὲν οὐκ εἰδότες θεὸν ἐδουλεύσατε τοῖς φύσει μὴ οὖσιν θεοῖς· ⁹ νῦν δὲ γνόντες θεόν, μᾶλλον δὲ γνωσθέντες ὑπὸ θεοῦ, πῶς ἐπιστρέφετε πάλιν ἐπὶ τὰ ἀσθενῆ καὶ πτωχὰ στοιχεῖα οἷς πάλιν ἄνωθεν δουλεύειν θέλετε, ¹⁰ ἡμέρας παρατηροῦντες¹³⁸ καὶ μῆνας καὶ καιροὺς καὶ ἐνιαυτούς;

¹¹ φοβοῦμαι ὑμᾶς μή πως εἰκῇ κεκοπίακα εἰς ὑμᾶς· ¹² γίνεσθε ὡς ἐγώ, ὅτι καγὼ ὡς ὑμεῖς. Ἀδελφοί, δέομαι ὑμῶν. οὐδέν με ἠδικήσατε, — ¹³ οἴδατε δὲ ὅτι δι' ἀσθένειαν τῆς σαρκὸς εὐηγγελισάμην ὑμῖν τὸ πρότερον, ¹⁴ καὶ τὸν πειρασμὸν ὑμῶν ἐν τῇ σαρκί μου οὐκ ἐξουθενήσατε οὐδὲ ἐξεπτύσατε, ἀλλὰ ὡς ἄγγελον θεοῦ ἐδέξασθέ με, ὡς Χριστὸν Ἰησοῦν. ¹⁵ ποῦ οὖν ὁ μακαρισμὸς ὑμῶν; μαρτυρῶ γὰρ ὑμῖν ὅτι εἰ δυνατὸν τοὺς ὀφθαλμοὺς ὑμῶν ἐξορύξαντες ἐδώκατέ μοι. — ¹⁶ ὥστε ἐχθρὸς ὑμῶν γέγονα ἀληθεύων ὑμῖν; ¹⁷ ζηλοῦσιν ὑμᾶς οὐ καλῶς, ἀλλὰ ἐκκλεῖσαι ὑμᾶς θέλουσιν, ἵνα αὐτοὺς ζηλοῦτε· ¹⁸καλὸν δὲ ζηλοῦσθαι ἐν καλῷ πάντοτε καὶ μὴ μόνον ἐν τῷ παρεῖναί με πρὸς ὑμᾶς. ¹⁹ τέκνα μου, οὓς πάλιν ὠδίνω μέχρις οὗ μορφωθῇ Χριστὸς ἐν ὑμῖν· ²⁰ ἤθελον δὲ παρεῖναι πρὸς ὑμᾶς ἄρτι καὶ ἀλλάξαι τὴν φωνήν μου, ὅτι ἀποροῦμαι ἐν ὑμῖν.

4 ⁸ But formerly, when you did not know God, you were enslaved to things which by nature are not gods. ⁹ However, now that you have come to know God—or rather to be known by God—how can you return again to the weak and cowering elemental spirits, to whom you wish yet again to be enslaved, ¹⁰ since you observe days and months and seasons and years?

¹¹ **I fear for you, lest somehow I labored**¹³⁸ **over you in vain.** ¹² Become as I am, for I have become as you. **Brothers, I beg you, did *you* do *me* no wrong,** — ¹³ Now, you know that it was on account of an infirmity of the flesh that I originally proclaimed the gospel to you; ¹⁴ and your test in my flesh you did not reject; nor did you despise [me]; instead, you welcomed me as an angel of God, as Christ Jesus. ¹³ Where then is your blessing [now]? For I testify to you that, if possible, you would have plucked out your *own eyes*¹³⁹ and given them to me. — ¹⁶ **so that *I* have become *your* enemy by telling *you* the truth?** ¹⁷ [And you know that] *They* zealously court [*or* pander to] you, but not for good; instead, they exclude you so that you will pander to them. ¹⁸ It is always good to be pandered after in a good way, and not only when I am present with you. ¹⁹ My little children, with whom I am once again in travail until Christ takes shape in you. ²⁰ **I wish I were present with you now and could change my tone, because I am *perplexed* by you.**

⟦Paul next invokes the second allegorical digression on the Abraham story (4:21–31), ending with the statement: "So, brethren, we are not children of the slave but of the free woman."⟧

5 ¹ Τῇ ἐλευθερίᾳ ἡμᾶς Χριστὸς ἠλευθέρωσεν· στήκετε οὖν καὶ μὴ πάλιν ζυγῷ δουλείας ἐνέχεσθε. ² Ἴδε ἐγὼ Παῦλος λέγω ὑμῖν ὅτι ἐὰν περιτέμνησθε, Χριστὸς ὑμᾶς οὐδὲν ὠφελήσει. ³ μαρτύρομαι δὲ πάλιν παντὶ ἀνθρώπῳ περιτεμνομένῳ ὅτι ὀφειλέτης ἐστὶν ὅλον τὸν νόμον ποιῆσαι. ⁴ κατηργήθητε ἀπὸ Χριστοῦ, οἵτινες ἐν νόμῳ

5 ¹ For freedom Christ has set us free. Stand firm, therefore, and do not submit again to a yoke of slavery. ² Behold, I, Paul, say to you that if you let yourselves be circumcised, Christ will be of no benefit to you. ³ Once again I testify to every man who lets himself be circumcised that he is obliged to keep the whole law. ⁴ You are set free from Christ, you who would be justified by law, you have fallen

---

¹³⁸ The reading above is that of 𝔓⁴⁶. The majority reading is παρατηρεῖσθε.

¹³⁹ 𝔓⁴⁶ reads ἐκοπίασα.

¹⁴⁰ Implied: *the very same eyes before which I displayed the crucified Christ!* Cf. 3:1.

δικαιοῦσθε, τῆς χάριτος ἐξεπέσατε. **5** ἡμεῖς γὰρ πνεύματι ἐκ πίστεως ἐλπίδα δικαιοσύνης ἀπεκδεχόμεθα. **6** ἐν γὰρ Χριστῷ Ἰησοῦ οὔτε περιτομή τι ἰσχύει οὔτε ἀκροβυστία ἀλλὰ πίστις δι᾽ ἀγάπης ἐνεργουμένη. **7** Ἐτρέχετε καλῶς· τίς ὑμᾶς ἐνέκοψεν [τῇ] ἀληθείᾳ μὴ πείθεσθαι; **8** ἡ πεισμονὴ οὐκ ἐκ τοῦ καλοῦντος ὑμᾶς.[141] **9** μικρὰ ζύμη ὅλον τὸ φύραμα ζυμοῖ. **10** ἐγὼ πέποιθα εἰς ὑμᾶς ἐν κυρίῳ ὅτι οὐδὲν ἄλλο φρονήσετε· ὁ δὲ ταράσσων ὑμᾶς βαστάσει τὸ κρίμα, ὅστις ἐὰν ᾖ. **11** Ἐγὼ δέ, ἀδελφοί, εἰ περιτομὴν ἔτι κηρύσσω, τί ἔτι διώκομαι; ἄρα κατήργηται τὸ σκάνδαλον τοῦ σταυροῦ. **12** Ὄφελον καὶ ἀποκόψονται[142] οἱ ἀναστατοῦντες ὑμᾶς. **13** ὑμεῖς γὰρ ἐπ᾽ ἐλευθερίᾳ ἐκλήθητε, ἀδελφοί· μόνον μὴ τὴν ἐλευθερίαν εἰς ἀφορμὴν τῇ σαρκί, ἀλλὰ διὰ τῆς ἀγάπης δουλεύετε ἀλλήλοις.

from grace. **5** For by spirit from faith we await the hope of righteousness. **6** For in Christ Jesus neither does circumcision have any power nor uncircumcision, but faith being worked out through love. **7** You were running well; who has hindered (*lit.* cut in on) you that you not be persuaded of the truth? **8** This persuasion is not from *the one who called you*. **9** A little leaven leavens the whole. **10** I am confident about you in the Lord that you will have no other mind; but *the one who is troubling you*,[143] whoever he may be, will *bear his judgement*.[144] **11** But, brothers, if I still proclaim circumcision, why am I still persecuted? Why then the scandal of the cross has been set free. **12** O, that *those who are driving you to confusion* would just castrate themselves! **13** For you were called to freedom, brothers; only do not [use] your freedom for an opportunity in flesh, but rather through love be servants of one another.

⟦The section 5:1–6:11 constitutes the paraenetic section of the letter framed in terms of a vice and virtue list, the "desires of the flesh" vs. the "fruits of the spirit." In 6:11–18, Paul gives his final salutations and benedictions, ending with the following:⟧

6 **16** καὶ ὅσοι τῷ κανόνι τούτῳ στοιχήσουσιν, εἰρήνη ἐπ᾽ αὐτοὺς καὶ ἔλεος καὶ ἐπὶ τὸν Ἰσραὴλ τοῦ θεοῦ. **17** Τοῦ λοιποῦ κόπους μοι μηδεὶς παρεχέτω· ἐγὼ γὰρ τὰ στίγματα τοῦ Ἰησοῦ ἐν τῷ σώματί μου βαστάζω.

6 **16** As for those who will follow this rule, peace and mercy be upon them, also upon the Israel of God. **17** For the rest, let no one cause me [more] labors; for I bear the marks of Jesus in my body.

---

[141] Paul himself, compare 1:6 and 3:5.
[142] A wordplay on circumcision as well as obstruction language; cf. 5:7.
[143] Compare 1:7 and 5:12.
[144] A contrast to Paul's labors, cf. 6:17.

Appendix B

Favorinus of Arelate

The Corinthian Oration (Κορινθιακός), ca. 125–138 CE
(The Framing Sections, translated by L.M. White)[145]

1. When I sojourned (ἐπεδήμησα) in your city the first time, nearly ten years
past now, and shared a measure (μετέδωκα) of my speeches with your demos
and magistrates, I seemed to be an intimate friend (ἐπιτήδειος εἶναι)[146] to you
to a degree not exceeded even by Arion of Methymne. Yet you did not make a
figure (τύπον) of Arion.

[There follows a digression (through §7) on Arion, Periander, and Adeimantus, ancient
heroes who were honored by Corinth.]

8. But when we sojourned (ἡμᾶς δὲ ἐπιδημήσαντας) [with you] a second time,
you experienced such gladness (ἀσμένως ἐπείδετε) that you tried very hard to
keep [me, as a citizen], but then, seeing that to be impossible, you instead
made a physical likeness (τὴν εἰκὼ τοῦ σώματος), and taking this you set it up
(ἀνεθήκατε, or dedicated it) in the library, in a front seat (προεδρίαν), where
you thought it might especially summon (προκαλέσασθαι) the youth to follow
the same pursuits [or professions] as we do. For you bestowed such honors
not as one of the many who annually disembark at Cenchreai as merchants,
or festival-goers, or ambassadors, or travellers, but rather as a beloved friend
(ἀγαπητόν), who at last appears after much time.

9. *"But Honor, like a dream, has taken wing and flown away." (Od. 2.222)*[147]

So that I stand perplexed (ἐν ἀπόρῳ καθεστάναι) both in regard to my own
case and now, by Zeus, in regard to that of yet another man too, wondering
whether I did not see truly—the things taking place were not a waking appearance but a dream—or whether the things taking place were accurate in every
detail, the zeal of the crowd and the judgement of the council—but the statue
chanced to be a work of Daedalus, and escaped us unnoticed.

11. But even granting that he [the statue] were of the ancient craft of Daedalus,
what is amiss that he should have fled your city … ?

---

[145] The speech is preserved as (ps-)Dio Chrysostom, *Or.* 37. These selections represent
the framing passages for the entire speech. In between, as noted, are rhetorical periods,
mostly ring compositions, where Favorinus digresses into classical illustrations to help
make his point.

[146] I have not followed Capps (as in LCL) here in emending the text with οἰκεῖος
before ὑμῖν.

[147] This is a paraphrase of Homer. Favorinus has replaced ψυχή with τιμή. In keeping
with his rhetorical theme—his fame has disappeared along with his statue—this alteration is also proleptic. At the end of the speech, Favorinus will begin to address the
statue as "a man possessing sensation" (§46 below), i.e., having a soul and feelings.

[There follows a digression (through §15) on the divine foundations of cities in myth and history. What lovelier a place than Corinth for a statue to dwell?]

16. Well then, no: neither has he [the statue] run away, nor attempted to, nor even had any intention to do so; therefore, it yields the conclusion (καταλεί-πεται) that the Corinthians themselves banished him, without even holding a trial or having any kind of charge to bring against him.

[There follows a digression (through §19) on the legendary justice of the Corinthians, and (§§ 20–21) on trials conducted against statues at Syracuse.]

22. Then if some sort of decree that statues be called to account were passed by you [Corinthians]—or rather, if you will, supposing that such has been decreed and a trial (ἀγῶνος) has begun—permit me, yes permit me to make a [defense] speech before you as though in court on behalf of this very man [the statue].[148]

"Men of the jury, they say one must expect anything in the course of time; but this man is, in a brief span, at risk of being put up (τεθῆναι), on the one hand, as the noblest of the Greeks, and on the other of being put down (ἐκπεσεῖν),[149] as the vilest. 23. Now then to prove that he was put up (ἐστάθη)[150] well and justly and profitably for your city and all the Greeks, I have much to say …

[There follows a series of digressions by returning to the trial at Syracuse (see above §20).]

35. But I hold frankness of speech (παρρησίαν) to be two-sided: one that of the person who has a glimpse [of the situation]; the other, that of the agonothete. …"

37. Now these foregoing remarks have been offered on behalf of the city, which ought not to bring disgrace on itself before the Greeks, since[151] not only would all [the Greeks] welcome with delight (ἄσμενοι καταδέχωνται)[152] this one who has been banished (τὸν ἐκπεπτωκότα) by you, but they would also summon him and send out embassies and would grant him honors of this sort and that and, what is more, even by the dedication of statues (τῇ τῶν εἰκόνων ἀναθέσει) …

---

[148] Here I am reading ὑπὲρ αὐτοῦ ("on behalf of him") following the original ms., as opposed to ὑπὲρ αὑτοῦ ("on my own behalf") as emended by Crosby (LCL).

[149] There's a word play here on the two verbs τίθημι and ἐκπίπτω, since both can be used of public or legal actions (meaning "to award or vote in favor of at trial" and "to banish," respectively) and of setting up and taking down a statue as in a temple ("to dedicate or set up" and "to tear down," respectively). This wordplay will continue to the end of the speech, cf. §37, 47.

[150] Crosby (LCL) inexplicably reverts to ἐστάθην (first person) despite earlier correction to third person by Emperius (1844), Von Arnim (1893), and De Budé (1919).

[151] The Greek here is ὅταν, but the sense seems to be causal (as a contraction for ὅτι ἄν) more typical in later Hellenistic Greek, so LSJ, s.v. ὅταν 1.b., cf. Dio Chrysostom, Or. 7.105.

[152] Compare the wording in §8 above.

[There follows a digression on the fate of statues in other cities, followed by a digression on stories of punishment with some speculation about the fate of body and soul.][153]

46. Then, shall we yet not present the statue for melting, even though it might possess sensation? No, while he is now superior to sensation, yet I, in the words of Euripides' *Laodameia*,

would not abandon my friend, though devoid of soul.

Accordingly, I wish now to offer consolation (παραμυθήσασθαι) to him [the "friend" i.e., the statue], as to one possessing sensation:

"O silent image of my oratory, will you not show yourself? …

47. I myself will raise you up (ἀναστήσω) before the goddess [Fame], whence nothing will cast you down (καθέλῃ)—neither earthquake, nor wind, nor snow, nor rain, nor envy (φθόνος), nor enmity (ἐχθρός); but even now do I discover you risen up (ἑστηκότα). *Aye, for now Oblivion has tripped and cheated sundry others, but judgement* (γνώμη)[154] *does no harm to good men,*[155] by which [judgement] to me you stand aright like a man (ἦ κατ' ἄνδρα μοι ὀρθὸς ἔστηκας)."[156]

The End

---

[153] Compare Dio Chrysostom, *Or.* 31.95–97 for similar examples.

[154] A wordplay, since γνώμη can mean both the mental faculty of judgement and the vote of the assembly.

[155] Apparently a paraphrase from Sappho, so Crosby (LCL) following Edmonds, *Lyra Graeca* I, 236 (LCL).

[156] Another word play, since ὀρθός can mean both the affirmative verdict in court ("to be judged right" and thus meaning "just") and standing erect or "upright."

APOSTROPHE, ΠΡΟΣΩΠΟΠΟΙΙΑ AND PAUL'S RHETORICAL EDUCATION

Stanley K. Stowers

Introduction

In the 1970's at Yale, Abraham J. Malherbe led an ongoing and remarkably productive seminar on "The Hellenistic Moralists and the New Testament." Much of Abe's own insightful work in this area was tested there first, and the list of dissertations, books and articles that have been stimulated by that seminar is impressive.[1] It was during this seminar that I was first put on to the topic of the diatribe, which became the focus of my dissertation.[2] I find it appropriate then, in honoring Abe, to revisit the diatribe and Romans in order to clarify some interpretations for which I have argued and to make some points about Paul's rhetoric. I can perhaps best do this by responding to the recent book by R. Dean Anderson, *Ancient Rhetorical Theory and Paul.*[3]

Anderson's work is helpful just because it is the kind of book that challenges Pauline scholars to be aware of complacency and carelessness in the use of ancient rhetoric. I have some agreements with major points of the work that will emerge later in this essay and have learned from Anderson's erudite scholarship. But the book argues that almost all of the scholars who have invoked ancient rhetoric in interpreting Paul's letters have misinterpreted the primary sources on rhetoric. In my case, he argues that a correct understanding of προσωποποιία (or "speech-in-character") in rhetorical theory and in practice invalidates

---

[1] So, to name but a few examples, his articles on "Hellenistic Moralists and the New Testament," *ANRW* II.26.1 (1992) 267–33 and "Self-Definition among Epicureans and Cynics," in *Jewish and Christian Self-Definition*, vol. 3: *Self-Definition in the Graeco-Roman World*, ed. by. B. F. Meyer and E. P. Sanders (Philadelphia: Fortress, 1982); his collected essays on *Paul and the Popular Philosophers* (Minneapolis: Fortress, 1989); and his anthologies *The Cynic Epistles* (SBLSBS; Atlanta: Scholars, 1978), *Moral Exhortation: A Graeco-Roman Sourcebook* (Philadelphia: Westminster, 1986), and *Ancient Epistolary Theorists* (SBLSBS 19; Atlanta: Scholars, 1988). The list of works by students of that seminar, many of whom have contributed to this volume, is far too lengthy to rehearse here.

[2] *The Diatribe and Paul's Letter to the Romans* (SBLDS 57; Atlanta: Scholars, 1981).

[3] (Kampen: Pharos, 1996).

my claims for the use of the figure in Rom 2:1–4:2 and 7:7–8:2.[4] Anderson's critique centers on attempting to show that my discussion of identification of the figure is unsupported by the sources:

> [Stowers] argues that προσωποποιία normally had to be identified in literature by means of stylistic and grammatical considerations, that is to say, that examples of προσωποποιία were *not* normally formally introduced. This is, naturally important to Stowers, given that Paul has no formal introductions indicating προσωποποιία in his letter to the Romans. But it is at this point that his argument is quite weak.[5]

First, Anderson places a greater and quite different emphasis on identification of speaker than I do. He makes it seem as if my main point is that προσωποποιία was generally not introduced "formally," a claim that I do not make. As I will show, this claim is absurd in the face of what I do argue about προσωποποιία in Romans. Second, Anderson removes my discussion of the technique from its larger context. I will take up this last point first.

I introduce προσωποποιία in the context of arguing for an approach to interpreting Paul's letters that emphasizes two closely connected points: (1) interpretation or reading is not fully determinate even at the level of word division, punctuation, or textual arrangement, and (2) historical interpretation should focus on readers and reading rather than on some metaphysical conception of the author. These points are not just intensively discussed and generally accepted principles in most fields of literary study and philosophy; they are equally important to my project. I argue, for example, that even the manuscript and printing traditions have facilitated "readings" of Paul's letters that people in Paul's own time—including Paul himself—could not have undertaken or understood. Reading with προσωποποιία is my strategy for beginning to break through the "obvious" received readings. The several points, and not one (as Anderson claims, viz. that transition to the figure was sometimes without formal introduction), that I make about identifying characters in ancient reading and education are part of this larger context of trying to imagine how ancient readers read and heard texts. Writing and reading Greek in Paul's era differed greatly from the

---

[4] So in my article "Romans 7:7–25 as Speech-in-Character (προσωποποιία)," in *Paul in His Hellenistic Context*, ed. by T. Engberg-Pedersen (SNTIW; Edinburgh: T&T Clark, 1994) 180–202; and in my book *A Rereading of Romans: Justice, Jews, and Gentiles* (New Haven: Yale University Press, 1994) 16–21, 36–7, 100–4, 143–5, 232–3; 264–78, etc.

[5] *Ibid.*, 179.

modern way of reading and writing Greek or English, even to the point of exercising different neuro-physiological and psychological processes.[6] The ancient approach was based on ear and voice in contrast to modern silent reading and writing that is based on the visual spatial representation of a text. These points, I believe, are not controversial, but at the same time they have not made the impact that they should have on New Testament scholarship.

Thus I have two major reasons for pointing out that προσωποποιία was sometimes identified in a passage by the form of the characterization and not only with some language that said, in effect, "now I am going to shift into προσωποποιία." The reasons are the larger question indicated above about text, reading, and determinacy and in order to provide a context for my discussion of Romans 7:7–8:2. But as I will argue, it is misleading merely to characterize this passage as unintroduced. Thus I will begin with the rather minor question of evidence about "formal introductions."

Προσωποποιία and Formal Introductions

Anderson claims that the texts I appeal to do not show evidence for a lack of these and that "in both rhetorical and philosophical texts we find that a formal introduction and identification of the speaker is invariably present."[7] I will briefly go over these disputed passages from ancient writers on rhetoric and then show that Anderson is simply wrong about what he calls formal introductions being invariably present. Anderson writes:

> Firstly, he cites Quint, *Inst.* 1.8.3 where Quintilian is speaking of the appropriate use of the voice when reading out loud. At *Inst.* 1.8.3 he notes that προσωποποιία ought not to be declaimed/pronounced (*pronuntiari*) in the way of comic actors. The unfortunate use of the word "indicate" used to translate *pronuntiare* in the *Loeb* translation of H. E. Butler has lead Stowers to surmise that *identification* of προσωποποιία is also implied by the passage. The question of identification is simply not addressed by Quintilian here.[8]

In attributing this error to me, Anderson has confused two issues. The issue of the kind of character or person that the writer (or speaker, in

---

[6] For this and for excellent bibliography, see Paul Saenger, *Space Between Words: The Origins of Silent Reading* (Stanford: Stanford University Press, 1997).

[7] *Ibid.*, 181.

[8] *Ibid.*, 179.

PART THREE – LOGOS

this case) identifies by various rhetorical-grammatical-syntactical means *is not the same as* the issue of whether an instance of the latter has a formal introduction. I cite the passage from Quintilian in a paragraph that begins, "The identification of the speaking voice and characters formed another aspect of elementary education in reading."[9] Here is my translation (not Butler's) of Quint. *Inst.* 1.8.3 that I give in the book:

> Neither is it good, like some teachers, to indicate speech-in-character [προσωποποιία] in the manner of a comic actor, even though one ought to make use of some modulation of voice [when reading] in order to distinguish speech-in character from where the poet is speaking in his own person [*persona*].[10]

Regardless of whether or not the figure has a formal introduction, προσωποποιία or ἠθοποιία was created and signified by writing or speaking words that imitate a particular person or a recognized character type. The context of the passage in Quintilian is the basic education of boys in reading and writing. My point is that people with some education in Paul's world were trained to "read" for—meaning to listen for—speech according to character, and they composed their writings accordingly. Anderson is wrong. Quintilian says that the poet's voice was read in one way and the character in another so as to distinguish them. The rhetorician objects to adding excessive dramatization of the character on top of adequately expressive reading that would portray the person or indicate a type. He thus assumes that the reader understood when to modulate his voice according to the "person speaking," whether or not there was a formal introduction.

What Anderson takes as my second argument for "lack of formal introductions" actually continues the previous line of thought and concerns the principle of the "person speaking" in Homeric exegesis and textual criticism. Again I emphasize both the skills in analyzing and identifying characters and the problem cases, which would include instances that were not "formally introduced." Anderson is dismissive and seems to deny that this sort thing occured in Homer or was discussed in Homeric exegesis of the Hellenistic and later periods. Two examples will suffice to show that such discussion did indeed take place. The first, as I cite in the book,[11] is the discussion by Aristarchus of

---

[9] *Rereading of Romans*, 18.

[10] *Ibid.* Hereafter I will refer only to Quintilian seeing that the *Institutio* is his only extant work.

[11] *Rereading of Romans*, 18–9.

Byzantium of solving contradictions and restoring excised "interpolations" in Homer by distinguishing the poet's voice from the voice of
his characters. The second is a passage from "Longinus" (*On the Sublime*
27.1) which could not be clearer on this point:

> Again sometimes a writer, while speaking of one of his characters, sud-
> denly turns and changes into the actual character. A figure (εἶδος) of this
> kind is a sort of outbreak of emotion (ἐκβολή τις πάθους):
>
>> Hector lifted up his voice and cried afar to the Trojans
>> To haste them back to the galleys and leave the blood spattered booty.
>> *Whomsoever I spy of his own afar from the galleys,*
>> *death for him will I plan.*" [*Il.* 15.346–9].
>
> There the poet has assigned the narrative (διήγησιν) to himself as his
> proper share, and then suddenly without any warning (ἐξαπίνης οὐδὲν
> προδηλώσας) attached the abrupt threat to the angry champion. To
> insert "Hector said so and so" would have been frigid (ἐψύχετο).[12]

Ps-Longinus understands this as a recognized figure of speech that
makes the writing more sublime, i.e., stylistically superior. The shift is
sudden and not "formally introduced," but clear. This unintroduced
shift from the narrator's voice to imitation of Hector (in italics), here
would have typically been described as προσωποποιία in the era in
which *On the Sublime* was written, the first century CE. Indeed, in the
following passage the author refers to this figure as "changing from one
character to another" (μεταβαίνειν ἐκ προσώπων εἰς πρόσωπα)[13] where
the Greek clearly signifies the literary "character" by the term πρόσωπον. Only a few decades earlier, Dionysius of Halicarnassus employs
the technical terminology in writing about Thucydides' skill with dialogue: "At the beginning he tells in his own person (πρόσωπον) what
was said by each side, but after one exchange of discussion in this form
of reported speech, he dramatizes and writes the ensuing dialogue with
speech-in-character (προσωποποιεῖ)."[14] It will be important for my later
argument to note that Dionysius speaks of προσωποποιία as a skill for
composing dialogue.

Only with my discussion of Quint. 9.2.37 do I begin to discuss
directly the issue of προσωποποιία without formal introductions. I owe
Anderson a debt in showing that Emporius, the fifth-century writer,

---

[12] Translation of W. Hamilton Fyfe, *Longinus, On the Sublime* (LCL; Cambridge:
Harvard University Press, 1927) 249–51. Italics added.

[13] *On the Sublime* 27.2.

[14] Dionysius of Halicarnassus, *Thuc.* 37, commenting on Thuc. *Hist.* 5.84–5.

does not treat the issue of unintroduced characters. I admit that readers
would have no ambiguity in recognizing the direct speech in the examples that Emporius gives. I misinterpreted the passage. But Anderson, I
believe, is wrongly dismissive of Quint. 9.2.37:

> We may also introduce some imaginary person without identifying him,
> as when we say, 'here someone says' (*hic aliquis*) and 'someone will say'
> (*dicat aliquis*). Or the words may be inserted without the introduction of
> any speaker at all, as in, 'Here the Dolopian force fought; here fierce
> Achilles held forth.' [Virg. *Aen.* 2.29] This is a mixture of figures, since
> to προσωποποιία is added ellipse, which here consists in omitting any
> indication of the one speaking."[15]

The two introductory phrases tell the reader that someone is about to
speak, but they do not identify who this speaker is. The reader must
infer an identity from the words of the imaginary speaker themselves in
light of clues from the preceding discourse. The third example is like
the technique discussed by "Longinus" and consists of a sudden shift to
the words of the character with no introduction.

Anderson objects that the latter rarely if ever occurs, I think that
instances are not difficult to find, but agree that there was normally little room for misunderstanding by ancient readers. Although I believe
that there is in general more room for indeterminacy in interpretation than Pauline scholars seem to admit, my point is not that most
instances of προσωποποιία were difficult for ancient readers to detect. I
do not think that they were for readers in the periods in which the texts
were written. These readers or better, hearers, were equipped with the
largely oral/aural skills to make sense of the ancient texts. The problem
is with later and modern readers. Ancient readers were accustomed,
as my discussion tries to show, to read/hear προσωποποιία and related
techniques, but that we are not. Furthermore, readers in later periods
who did not share the same background knowledge, beliefs and practices as the first readers, might encounter difficulties. The discussion
in *A Rereading of Romans* attempts to illuminate the kind of interpretive
habits and skills that various ancient readers might have employed. The
problem comes with modern readers of the Bible who see as significant
only theological propositions about sin, salvation, the nature of Judaism

---

[15] Using a rhetoric of rhetorical purity, Anderson dismisses Quintilian's example
as true προσωποποιία because it is mixed with the figure detractio according to the
rhetorician. (*Rhetorical Theory*, 180)

and so on. I argue that taking seriously Paul's discussions with these imaginary persons changes the "message" in certain ways.

Above all I do not believe that it would have been difficult for Paul's ancient audience to have understood the προσωποποιία that I find in Romans. Quite the opposite of what Anderson assumes, moreover, I argue that the προσωποποιία in Romans *is introduced*. That Anderson refuses to take my reading seriously seems clear from his failure to see this point. In my view, his own reading of Romans merely paraphrases a modern western King James Version-interpretation by adding rhetorical terms and atomistic rhetorical observations on that interpretation without seriously considering that later Christian history and ideas might have been imposed upon it.[16] My basic claim has three parts: (1) instances that I identify as προσωποποιία are a unity; (2) historical interpreters should read in a linear fashion building on the previous knowledge that the text supplies; and (3) that the apostrophes in Rom 2:1–16 and 17–29 function as introductions to προσωποποιία. Here the function of apostrophe (an "aside" addressed, in this case, to an imaginary interlocutor) is important, since its appearance at the beginning of a period would have made reasonably clear what follows. I devote much ink to attempting to discredit an atomistic approach that simply assumes a traditional reading underneath the exterior form of the text. Ignoring or missing all of this, Anderson writes, "Of Stowers' five examples in the letter to the Romans, the fist two may be readily dismissed. As he himself indicates, both 2:1–5 and 17–29 are examples of ἀποστροφή. No speech is put into the mouth of another party, and thus no προσωποποιία can be spoken of."

Apostrophe and προσωποποιία

Perhaps I can make the argument clearer than I did in the book by returning to the discussion of Quintilian 9 and by adding more illustrative evidence of similar patterns. Here, I began with my translation of Quint. 9.2.30–33:[17]

A bolder figure, which Cicero thinks more difficult, is *fictiones personarum* or προσωποποιία. This technique adds wonderful variety and anima-

---

[16] The fact that Anderson might have worked from the Greek text is irrelevant and would not prevent reading a King James-like interpretation into whatever text was used.

[17] *Rereading of Romans*, 20.

> tion to oratory. With this figure we present the inner thoughts of our
> adversaries as though they were talking with themselves ... Or with-
> out diminishing credibility we may introduce conversations between our-
> selves and others, and of others among themselves, and give words of
> advice, reproof, complaint, praise or pity to appropriate persons ... peo-
> ples may find a voice ... or pretend that we have before our eyes things,
> persons or utterances.

about which, I then said:[18]

> This variety of forms persuades me that not only the first person speech
> of Rom 7 but also the apostrophes in 2:1–16 and 2:17–29 and the dia-
> logue in 3:1–8 and 3:27–4:2 ought to be considered types of speech-in-
> character. Quintilian places all these kinds of speech involving imagi-
> nary speakers, interlocutors, or addressees under *prosopopoiia*. According
> to Quintilian, almost all of the dialogical techniques of the so-called dia-
> tribe would be types of speech-in-character.

Contra Anderson, therefore, Quintilian tells us that apostrophe, dialogue, and simulating the words of another person, including imaginary objections, were seen as related phenomena and could all be
included in the category of προσωποποιία. This is easy to understand
in light of the close association between προσωποποιία and dialogue in
narratives and discursive discourses (e.g., forensic speeches, diatribes)
that also contain an authorial voice. I will first discuss evidence for
the association of προσωποποιία with dialogue and then with apostrophe.

What Quintilian identifies as "conversations (*sermones*) between ourselves and others, and of others among themselves," include what both
we and the ancients call dialogue.[19] Quintilian goes on to associate
προσωποποιία explicitly with dialogue; in the process he also reveals
that there were disputes about such terminology and categories among
rhetoricians.

> There are some who call προσωποποιία only instances in which both per-
> sons and words are invented, and choose to call imaginary conversations
> of [real] people διαλόγους, which some translate by the Latin *sermocina-
> tio*. I, at least, call both by the same generally accepted term. For one is
> not able to invent a conversation and not invent a person to speak it (lit.
> conversation of a person).[20]

---

[18] *Ibid.*

[19] The Greek term is not an exact equivalent of the English, but includes what we
call dialogue.

[20] Quint. 9.2.31–32.

The passages from Longinus and Dionysius above also provide examples of ancient rhetoricians associating and, in the case of Dionysius, explicitly describing speeches and dialogue in the direct speech of the characters as προσωποποιία.

Quintilian places *sermocinatio* within the category of *fictio personae*, i. e., προσωποποιία. Among rhetoricians of his time, the former usually meant attributing imaginary speeches, soliloquy, dialogue, or even voiced questions/objections to a real person. The concern with the real derives from the judicial context in which a rhetor might create words of wretched pleading for his defendant to arouse pity or invent the callous thoughts of the one prosecuted before he committed the crime to arouse indignation. One can find a related concern in writing history, for which inventing wholly imaginary persons had no place, but creating imagined speeches that plausibly fit the person was accepted. This limitation, however, made little sense for other types of rhetoric (e. g., of philosophers and moralists) in whom we find the frequent creation of fictitious persons often representing character types and imaginary conversation partners used to advance the argument. There has been much confusion among interpreters, especially New Testament scholars, because the late antique and medieval rhetorical tradition about προσωποποιία and ἠθοποιία developed differently. The terms *fictio personae* and προσωποποιία were later confined to speech given to inanimate objects or abstract concepts (e.g., virtue speaks; a wild olive shoot) and *sermocinatio* and ἠθοποιία came to include the speech of real living (at the time of speaking) people with occasional concessions to imaginary types. Thus scholars who depend on Heinrich Lausberg's *Handbook*,[21] for example, easily get the impression that this categorization was normative in Paul's day. The confusion is compounded by the misunderstanding that προσωποποιία is what we call personification.[22] While it came to mean a figure that included aspects of personification, it is not at all equivalent to personification.

By contrast, Quintilian seems to claim that his inclusion of all of these dialogical techniques under προσωποποιία and *fictio personae* was the customary usage, even though he knows of dissenting opinions

---

[21] Recently edited by David Orton and R. Dean Anderson, *Handbook of Literary Rhetoric* (Leiden: Brill, 1998).

[22] For an example of this misunderstanding, see Lauri Thurén, *Derhetorizing Paul: A Dynamic Perspective on Pauline Theology and the Law* (Tübingen: Mohr Siebeck, 2000) 118–20. I owe this reference to Christopher Matthews.

that are more like the later view.[23] Theon, the earliest of the progymnasmata, supports the idea that Quintilian's categorization was
widespread in his day based on his understanding of the technique.
At any rate, for the purposes of Pauline exegesis, such terminology is
only important in helping us to grasp the rhetorical concept and to
get clear on the history of the theoretical discussions. Whatever the
terms employed, what is most useful for this discussion is what distinguishes Quintialian from other theorists on this figure, namely his
phenomenological/conceptual reasons for placing these techniques in
the same family. He says that they all involve fiction or invention in
creating the speech and the person that must necessarily be evoked
(9.2.32). The way that I would put it is this: that the whole family of techniques involves depicting the "presences" in a dialogical
exchange (either speaking or being addressed) and something of their
individual identity or character, whether as a person or personified
thing.

On this point, however, Anderson instead chooses to *correct* Quintilian: "Quintilian's own interpretation of the figure is rather broad and
one is inclined to say that he sidetracks somewhat, e.g., at *Inst.* 9.2.36
where he refers to the possibility of introducing an imaginary objector.
That is really another figure altogether (cf. s.v. ἐπερώτησις)."[24] Quintilian clearly thinks that an imaginary objection in the words of the
person objecting is προσωποποιία. (Anderson does not even mention
the objection in the form of προσωποποιία of Rom 11:19 introduced
with "you will say.") I find Thomas M. Conley's comment to be more
insightful of the actual use of these figures in our extant evidence. He
notes the helpfulness of Quintilian's acknowledgment of family relations
instead of making him conform to later tradition and rigid definitions,
thus: "… Quit. *Inst.* 9:2:37ff., who holds *sermocinatio* and *prosopopoeia* to
be inseparable. Related to these, functionally, are 'prayer' and 'apostrophe', both important for achieving presence and community."[25] Conley
translates προσωποποιία as "speaking in character" and *sermocinatio* as
"dialogue."

---

[23] So Quint. 9.2.32: *Ego iam recepto more utrumque eodem modo appellavi* ("For my part, I
call both by the same generally accepted term").

[24] *Rhetorical Theory*, 312. Here ἐπερώτησις means the interlocutor or rather his ques-
tion/objection.

[25] "Philo of Alexandria," in *Handbook of Classical Rhetoric in the Hellenistic Period (330
B.C. – A.D. 400)* ed. S. E. Porter (Leiden: Brill, 1997) 701 n. 11.

The narrowness and rigidity of Anderson's approach becomes apparent when one notes that Quintilian gives exactly the same example from Cicero for *interrogatio* (Anderson's ἐπερώτησις) that he does for apostrophe: "What was that sword of yours doing, Tubero, in the field of Pharsalus?" (Cic. *Pro Lig.* 3.9).[26] Rhetorical theorists, of course, could and did distinguish and attempt to define distinctly different types of speaking in the character of another, including real, imaginary, and dead people; soliloquies and interior dialogue; and dialogue of various sorts. In practice, however, such sharp distinctions are often difficult and the boundaries between these figures were fluid. Anderson himself by close reading notes that Theon includes dialogue under προσωπο-ποιία.[27]

Apostrophe or *exclamatio* also has a natural relation to speech-in–character and dialogue. The former makes present an imaginary person and the latter has an imaginary person speaking with someone. In apostrophe, the writer or person actually giving the speech participates by addressing an imagined person. The ancient discussions emphasize that apostrophe is a sudden and unexpected turning from the audience (usually the judge in forensic rhetoric) to the imagined person or personified thing. Quintilian discusses apostrophe immediately after he treats προσωποποιία. This suggests the affinity of the two figures. Moreover, he says that in προσωποποιία, "we may introduce conversations between ourselves and others" (9.2.30). This obviously involves addressing this person who is imagined to be present and is, therefore, akin to apostrophe as he defines it, although perhaps without the element of sudden turning. Quintilian's example noted above of the address to Tubero might be considered not only an instance of apostrophe and rhetorical question, but also προσωποποιία; each seen from a different, but related, angle. Little is at stake in deciding if apostrophe to imaginary persons might be called προσωποποιία, but much in understanding that they are related figures.

Apostrophe, Προσωποποιία, and Dialogue in Romans

In my reading of Romans, I argue that all of these related techniques are used together to form a dialogical unit in 2:1–4:2. Paul's development of these figures, I believe, would have also prepared the ancient

---

[26] In Quint. 9.2.7 and 38.
[27] *Rhetorical Theory*, 313.

reader for the προσωποποιία in 7:7–8:2. Anderson argues that 3:1–4:2
cannot be a dialogue between Paul and a Jewish teacher because such
προσωποποιία was always introduced with words that formally introduce an imaginary speaker. As I have shown in my work on the diatribe, in the book on Romans and in the examples here, this is simply
not true. On the other hand, I agree that ancient speech and texts
normally gave clear indications of a conversation with an imaginary
person even though ancient readers of *scriptura continua* faced greater
textual ambiguity than modern readers do.[28] My argument is that the
apostrophes of 2:1–16 and 17–29 are introductions for the dialogue that
follows and would have made the προσωποποιία clear for the ancient
reader. In the book, I provided analogies from ancient literature. I want
to stress here that this evidence can be much expanded and the issues
sharpened. The power of the case lies in the evidence from actual practice. So-called rhetorical theorists like Quintilian can be very helpful,
but for several reasons, chiefly their focus on forensic speeches, the prescriptions of the theorist do not correspond well to the range of actual
practice in extant literature.

Apostrophe, προσωποποιία and dialogue appear in many forms of
ancient literature and in literature and writings of people from various
social, economic and ethnic contexts. It is a vast illusion to think that
the few extant rhetorical handbooks and so-called theorists adequately
represent this literary and rhetorical complexity. Different forms of literature use these techniques variously, in ways consonant with their
own generic requirements and rhetorical strategies. A thinker as sharp
as Quintilian shows an awareness of this fact and reveals it with occasional comments. But he is so focused on forensic rhetoric and more
generally on the types of speaking customarily practiced by Roman
and Greek aristocrats that the *Institutio* does not reflect the actual variety in the use of such techniques. From Quintilian, for example, one
would never guess that the majority of instances of προσωποποιία (later
called ἠθοποιία) among the papyri, and they are numerous, are poetic
efforts in hexameter.[29] Teachers in Egypt, at least, made the technique a
favorite practice for learning to study and write poetry. Theon mentions
(*Prog.* 20–22) that exercises in προσωποποιία provide training for pane-

---

[28] Saenger, *Space Between Words*, 1–17.
[29] For many examples and discussion of hexameter, see J. L. Fournet, "Une éthopée
de Caïn dans le Codex des Visions de la Bodmer," *ZPE* 92 (1992) 253–66.

gyric, protreptic and writing letters. The figure appears in the moralizing of Hesiod and for the first time regularly in forensic speeches already among the Attic orators.[30] The latter set a pattern for later judicial oratory of employing προσωποποιία in epilogues, although one also finds other uses. They also make apostrophe a standard figure in forensic oratory.[31]

I find four points about the use of these figures in extant literature to be particularly helpful for reading Paul's letter to the Romans. First, apostrophe, προσωποποιία and dialogue often appear in combinations. Second, προσωποποιία can be indicated in the discourse in a number of ways; these indicators usually appear in the immediately preceding text and context of at least the first instance in the particular discourse. Third, apostrophe makes an excellent introduction to προσωποποιία because it involves naming and/or characterization in the invocation of a real or fictitious person. Fourth, earlier instances of προσωποποιία may prepare the reader for recognizing later appearances of the figure and related techniques. Thus Anderson's criticism to the effect that what I identify as the προσωποποιία (in the form of dialogue) of 3:1 and following is unintroduced, neglects my argument. The apt question for Romans is whether in ancient practice, not προσωποποιία, but apostrophe needed to be introduced with some explicit words that said, in effect, "now I am going to call up and address so-and-so as if he stood before me." The answer is "no," because the apostrophe itself performed this function and the dramatic sudden turning was a rhetorically valued feature of the technique.

By "combinations," I mean that these techniques work together as parts of larger dramatic units. These units involve an exchange of speech between the author portrayed in the text and an imagined person or persons whose words are invented. Such combinations can take a variety of forms according to the inventive powers of the speaker or writer. Already in the Athenian orator Aeschines, one finds an interesting and complex case. In *Against Ctesiphon* 21, he "formally" introduces words of an imaginary person: "Oh Heracles! (someone may reply) Because I held a public office, I cannot leave the country?" Then Aeschines apostrophizes this person until (§22), where the imaginary

---

[30] On both figures in the orators see the subject index of Stephen Ussher, *Greek Oratory* (Oxford: Oxford University Press, 1999).

[31] *Ibid.*, index, s.v. apostrophe.

speaker says, "Yes, but there is a certain man who has neither received nor spent public funds, but has only had some involvement in government." Here one knows that these are the words of the person introduced in §21 because of the orator's initial "someone may reply" and the character of those first words of apostrophe that fit the later objection. Another unintroduced example of προσωποποιία by the person occurs at the end of §22.

Such combinations may also begin with an apostrophe. In *The Worse Attacks the Better* 150, Philo suddenly addresses Cain, "What are you saying, noble sir? If you have been exiled from the whole earth, can you still hide? How? Would you be able to live?" This long apostrophe to Cain continues until §§156–7 when Cain reacts with a speech in which he characterizes himself as an Epicurean. Philo responds in §158 with an indignant apostrophe. Later in §§163 and 166 Philo breaks into apostrophes in the second person singular, and because of what went before, Cain is clearly the addressee. The point is that these combinations allow for a kind of "running" dialogue using apostrophe or προσωποποιία that is simply resumed without introduction in order to break up the author's prose. The reader is expected to understand these asides based on the context.

Epictetus provides numerous examples of complex combinations that begin with unintroduced apostrophe and προσωποποιία. *Diss.* 2.6.16 initiates a sudden unintroduced apostrophe. Epictetus has just said that people blame their circumstances and then turns to an imaginary speaker: "What sort of circumstances, man (ἄνθρωπε)?" The apostrophe in the second person singular continues until προσωποποιία in the form of an objection from the man occurs in §21: "I am in danger of my life in Caesar's presence." Epictetus answers and the pattern continues with the imaginary speaker interjecting, "But I risk my reputation in court" (21); "But I am in danger of being exiled" (22); "Yes" to a question from Epictetus (22); "What if I am sent to Gyara?" (22). Neither the apostrophe nor any of the five instances of speech-in-character have any sort of "formal introduction" whatsoever, and yet the figures are clear. The apostrophe of the "man" establishes the presence of the imaginary person and the interlocutor's words make no sense as Epictetus' own, but characterize a person who makes petty excuses for not acting with moral courage. The words of the "I" fit the man introduced in the apostrophe. Likewise in *Diss.* 3.20.4, the philosopher suddenly turns in apostrophe to someone who is addressed twice with ἄνθρωπε. A little dialogue follows (9–10), like that in Rom 3:1, with a question from the addressee followed by further questions and answers. I have elsewhere provided many examples of unintroduced apostrophes that introduce προσωποποιία of various sorts.[32]

Sudden, unintroduced apostrophe is very common and seems to be the norm in moral and philosophical literature. It already occurs in the Attic Orators. Aeschines (*Timarchus* 29) turns toward an addressee after a "Why?" (τί δή ποτε;) that follows a statement about the enactment of a law forbidding certain people from speaking in the assembly: "Man (ἄνθρωπε), if you do not take up arms on behalf of the city or if you cannot defend the city due to cowardice, you must not claim the right to advise the city." The "why" is ambiguous. Is it προσωποποιία representing a question of the "man" or is it merely the orator's rhetorical question to set up the apostrophe? Even so, the apostrophe is unambiguous; it is speech directed to an imaginary person. A quick and very incomplete survey of Philo finds twelve instances of sudden unintroduced apostrophes.[33] Numerous examples occur in Epictetus.[34] Instances can be found in Seneca, Dio Chrysostom, Plutarch and other writers.[35] Philo's "I ask you sir money-lender …" (*Spec. Leg.* 75) or apostrophes to an unnamed "man" typically depict a certain moral or religious type in a critical way that dramatically illustrates and urges some lessen for the audience while advancing an argument.

Thus, contrary to Anderson's criticisms, Romans 2–4 contains absolutely typical usage of apostrophe to introduce προσωποποιία. Richard Hays has complained that my reading of the dialogue in 3:1–9 lacks "methodological controls."[36] I find this to be a somewhat silly criticism. The only criterion is sense. When something that looks exactly like a dialogue follows the apostrophe of the Jewish teacher of gentiles in 2:17–29 and certain words make excellent sense as words of that character, in light of the previous discourse, then it probably is a dialogue. There is

---

[32] *The Diatribe and Romans*, 161 and n. 36. For further examples and examples of other combinations including those introduced with προσωποποιία, see also *ibid.*, 86–92, 158–60.

[33] *Spec. Leg.* 1.294, 320; 2.75, 82, 247; 3.166; *Quod deterius potiori* 150, 156, 158, 163, 166; *De virt.* 133; *Quod deus immutabilis* 147.

[34] *Diss.* 1.2.29; 1.3.5; 1.7.31; *The Diatribe and Romans*, 86–91.

[35] *The Diatribe and Romans*, 86–93; Dio Chrys. *Or.* 16.10.

[36] "'The Gospel is the Power of God for the Gentiles Only'? A Critique of Stanley Stowers' *A Rereading of Romans*," *Critical Review of Books in Religion 1996* (Atlanta: Scholars Press, 1997). I would like to point out that the title of the review very much distorts my position. The book does not claim that salvation was for gentiles only, but rather for both Jews and gentiles.

simply no good (i.e., historical and non-theological / ecclesiastical) reason why the letters of Paul should be treated differently by modern translators, editors and exegetes than the texts of Philo, Epictetus and other ancient writers. In these, quotation marks and textual arrangement regularly set off dialogue and προσωποποιία in texts very much like the Pauline passages. One could, of course, formalize rules or criteria, and to some extent I have in previous work, but these quickly become laboring the obvious. A more helpful suggestion would be for interested scholars to study the analogous passages in Epictetus, Philo, and other writers in order to get a sense of the oral rhetoric of ancient reading and writing that is so different from our own by the visual articulation of the spatial arrangement of words with cues of punctuation.

The question of προσωποποιία in 7:7–8:2 is, I admit, more difficult and requires a discussion that goes beyond what is possible here. Anderson thinks that there is more to my claim than with the earlier passages, but finally disagrees with the ancient commentators who found it there.[37] Again he appeals to the—what I hope is now shown to be the baseless—issue of non-introduction. Here I simply want to sharpen a few of the points about the kind of argument that I have and would make for reading chapter 7 with the figure. First, my case rests very heavily on my reading of 1:18–2:16, which gives, in my view, an account of gentile idolatry that produced bondage to passion and desire or ἀκρασία ("weakness of will" or "incontinence") and an apostrophe to precisely one of these *akratic* gentiles (i.e., 2:1–16).[38] I will not repeat my argument for the way that the text very strongly identifies the "man" as one of the gentile idolaters of chapter one.[39] But I will say that I consider the argument/evidence to be about as decisive as an exegetical argument can be.

The person in Rom 7 forms a classic depiction of an *akratic* person as many commentators from Origen onwards have recognized.[40] Much of my case, then, rests on the idea that ancient readers/listeners were attuned to listening for the reappearance of characters introduced

---

[37] *Rhetorical Theory*, 181–83.

[38] *Rereading of Romans*, 100–142, 251–84. I have not transliterated the term as *akrasia* here, although one frequently sees it transliterated in scholarship and even used as an English loan word that can be morphed to the adjective *akratic*.

[39] *Ibid.*, 103–4. In addition see also the portrayal of the character type in *Tabula of Cebes* 28.2; cf. 19.5.

[40] Recently reaffirmed strongly by Troels Engberg-Pedersen, *Paul and the Stoics* (Louisville: Westminster John Knox, 2000) 243–46.

earlier in the discourse through apostrophe and/or προσωποποιία. But
here is the rub: The type of the *akratic* person does not exist for modern
readers, whereas it was one of the most widely discussed and represented figures in Graeco-Roman antiquity.[41] Thus we cannot easily see
a connection that was probably obvious to them.

Although he does not read chapter two as I do, Troels Engberg-
Pedersen has recently produced a convincing interpretation of Rom
2:15 that, I believe, adds weight to my understanding of the person
addressed in 2:1–16 as an akratic gentile. He has shown that the description of the divided mind or conscience of 2:15 is that of *akrasia*.[42] Thus
it is not only the way that 1:32–2:3 identifies the person as one of the
people described in 1:18–31, but also a reference in 2:15 that tags the
issue as that of ἀκρασία. When Rom 7:7 raises a question introduced
with "what shall we say?" and a speaker begins talking about his ἐπιθυμία ("sexual desire" or "lust") and later his ἀκρασία, ancient readers, I
suggest, would have likely heard the *akratic* man of 2:1–16 whom Paul
had chastised for his presumptuous arrogance and self-delusion about
his bondage to passion and desire (cf. 1.24–32). The source of the person's judging of his fellow gentiles becomes clear, he is a gentile who
has tried to find self-mastery in moral teachings from the Judean law.
(Other arguments from the immediate context and 7:7–8:2 itself can be
found in my book.[43]) In my view, then. it is not quite correct to say that
the speech in 7:7–8:2 is without introduction.

Rhetorical Figures and Paul's Rhetorical Education

The larger purpose of Anderson's discussion of my work and that of
many other scholars is to argue against the idea that Paul was versed
in rhetorical theory such as that represented in the famous writings
on the subject by Aristotle, Cicero, Quintilian and so on. Anderson's
conclusion is a strong negative on the question. But as I have argued,
Paul was undoubtedly skilled in apostrophe and προσωποποιία, and in
ways typical of many extant writers from antiquity.[44] Yet I agree that
Paul's letters show few if any signs of the kind of rhetorical education

---

[41] For references to some of this literature and to theme, see *Rereading of Romans*, 260–64.

[42] *Paul and the Stoics*, 203, 208 and 360 n. 43.

[43] *Rereading of Romans*, 258–84.

[44] Anderson does not even mention the προσωποποιία of Rom 11:19 introduced with "you will say."

advocated by such theorists. Anderson's way of posing the issue of
Paul's rhetorical knowledge makes it difficult for him to deal with the
seeming anomaly of the last two sentences. Anderson tends to take the
normative stance of the theorists themselves, so that their prescriptions
come to represent all rhetoric. The actual picture requires a larger
critical view in which the theorists are taken merely as one, albeit
very important, set of evidence for the varied and complex rhetorical
culture of the early Roman empire. Thus Anderson's argument is set
up in terms of a false alternative: Paul either knew rhetorical theory as
represented by the extant canon that Anderson surveys or he had no
rhetoric at all. Anderson, of course, knows better, but his formulation of
the issue misleads his project.

Frankly, I am mystified that Anderson takes my work as supporting the idea that Paul was trained in the elite culture of rhetoric. My
study of the diatribe, focusing on its dialogical and pedagogical features, illuminated just such an alternative tradition of rhetoric nour-
ished by moral teachers and philosophers who may or may not have
had high rhetorical educations. My work on letter writing tried to show
the limited and complex relationship between epistolography and the
dominant rhetorical tradition.[45] Yet Anderson misrepresents this position.[46] My comparison of types of letters to the broad functional categories of three rhetorical genres is phenomenological and certainly
not an attempt to claim that the rules for speeches were considered
generally applicable to letters.[47] I write that "letter writing remained
only on the fringes of formal rhetorical education throughout antiquity," (34); "the letter writing tradition was essentially independent of
rhetoric" (52); and that moral "exhortation was never systematically
treated by rhetoricians" (91). I conclude that Christian letters in the
first two centuries were largely paraenetic and hortatory and that the
hortatory moral tradition "was only tangentially related to rhetorical
theory" (52). I have consistently maintained that Paul's letters do not
follow the rhetorical parts of speeches or other rules for speeches.

Near the beginning of my discussion of προσωποποιία I write, "Paul's
Greek educational level roughly equals that of someone who had primary instruction with a *grammaticus*, or teacher of letters, and then

---

[45] *Letter Writing in Graeco-Roman Antiquity* (Philadelphia: Westminster, 1986).
[46] *Rhetorical Theory*, 102–104.
[47] Of course, as Anderson himself admits, letters were sometimes treated as speeches.
He has a whole section on what he calls "letter-speeches." (*Rhetorical Theory*, 104)

studied letter writing and some elementary rhetorical exercises."[48] This clearly excludes the higher rhetorical theory. It is not wrong, however, then to go to Cicero and Quintilian in an attempt to understand the figure of προσωποποιία. Paul's education may have been outside of typical Greek schools so that I write "roughly equals." Paul also studied the Septuagint somewhere and in a tradition that read it partly through categories and terms that came from Greek philosophy. The same teacher who taught him the skills in letter writing that make his letters literarily and rhetorically far above the common papyrus letters may also have trained him in some progymnastic exercises useful to letter writers. Among these were προσωποποιία and its first cousins, apostrophe and dialogue.

---

[48] *Rereading of Romans*, 17. The way the sentence is written and punctuated one might misleadingly get the impression that the *grammaticus* and the teacher of letters were the same. The former was of a much higher educational level and could take students far beyond the early stages of reading and writing.

ANALOGY AND ALLEGORY
IN CLASSICAL RHETORIC

Thomas H. Olbricht

For a long time I have been interested in how rhetoric functions in different contexts, especially in the synagogue and church.[1] This interest is obviously related to Biblical criticism, especially in these times in which rhetorical criticism has once again come to the fore among Biblical scholars.[2] In a somewhat parallel endeavor Professor Malherbe and his students have scrutinized styles of exhortation in the Graeco-Roman world and in early Christianity.[3]

In my opinion, it may be as important to give attention to what the ancient rhetoricians failed to expound upon as to what they encompassed. One area they did not pursue in any depth was the rhetorical function of analogical and allegorical materials in religious discourse.[4]

---

[1] Thomas H. Olbricht, "An Aristotelian Rhetorical Analysis of 1 Thessalonians," *Greeks, Romans, and Christians, Essays in Honor of Abraham J. Malherbe*, ed. by D. L. Balch, E. Ferguson, W. A. Meeks (Philadelphia: Fortress Press, 1990) 216–236. The latest is "Anticipating and Presenting the Case for Christ as High Priest in Hebrews", to appear in a volume of essays ed. by Walter Überlacker, Anders Eriksson and Thomas H. Olbricht (Harrisburg: Trinity Press International, 2002).

[2] Duane F. Watson and Alan J. Hauser, *Rhetorical Criticism of the Bible: A Comprehensive Bibliography with Notes on History & Method* (Leiden: E.J. Brill, 1994); see also the bibliography in R. Dean Anderson, Jr., *Ancient Rhetorical Theory and Paul* (Kampen: Kok Pharos Publishing, 1996); Thomas H. Olbricht, "Biblical Interpretation in North American in the 20th Century", *Historical Handbook of Major Biblical Interpreters*, D. K. McKim, editor, (Carol Stream: InterVarsity Press, 1998) 555–556 (on Malherbe and his students see 552). See also Gregory E. Sterling, "Hellenistic Philosophy and the New Testament," *Handbook to Exegesis of the New Testament*, ed. S. E. Porter (Leiden: Brill, 1997) 317.

[3] Abraham J. Malherbe, *Moral Exhortation, A Graeco-Roman Sourcebook* (Philadelphia: Westminster Press, 1986); Abraham, J. Malherbe, "Hellenistic Moralists and the New Testament," *ANRW* II.26.2 (1992) 267–333; Stanley K. Stowers, *The Diatribe and Paul's Letter to the Romans* (SBLDS 57; Chico: Scholars Press, 1981); Stanley K. Stowers, *Letter Writing in Graeco-Roman Antiquity* (Philadelphia: Westminster Press, 1986); Stanley K. Stowers, *A Rereading of Romans: Justice, Jews, & Gentiles* (New Haven: Yale University Press, 1994).

[4] Many useful works have been published on the definition and characteristics of analogy and allegory some of them focusing specifically on Alexandria, including: Sayre N. Greenfield, *The Ends of Allegory* (Newark: University of Delaware Press, 1998); Marc Mastrangelo, "The Psychomachia of Prudentius: A Reappraisal of the Greek Sources and the Origins of Allegory" (Unpublished Ph.D. Dissertation; Brown Uni-

They focused upon speeches in the court (forensic), the political assembly (deliberative) and ceremonial occasions in the cities (epideictic).[5] They did not comment on the special contours of rhetorical approaches in the synagogues or churches because they knew nothing of these contexts.

In this essay I shall scrutinize the comments of the Graeco-Roman rhetoricians upon the analogical aspects of discourse. But I shall also suggest that some early Jewish and Christian settings for religious discourse were fertile grounds for the contributions of classical rhetoric, while, in contrast, others were seedbeds for analogical discourse of the sort unnoticed by the rhetoricians.

Rhetoricians and the Analogical

While Greek and Roman writers on rhetorical theory and practice commented on similes and metaphors, that is, analogical figures of speech, they discussed only to a limited extent the larger metaphorical constructs in discourse. We therefore need to explore the way in which the rhetoricians took up these figures and determine in what manner they thought rhetorical power was attained thereby. The rhetoricians

---

versity, 1997); Roger Travis, *Allegory and the Tragic Chorus in Sophocles' Oedipus at Colonus* (Lanham: Rowman & Littlefield, 1999); John Gwyn Griffiths, *The Tradition of Allegory in Egypt* (Vendome: Imprimerie des Presses Universitaires de France, 1969); Christoph Bloennigen, *Der Griechische Ursprung der Juedisch-Hellenistischen Allegorese und ihre Rezeption in der Alexandrinischen Patristik* (Frankfurt am Main: Peter Lang, 1992); David Dawson, *Allegorical Readers and Cultural Revision in Ancient Alexandria* (Berkeley: University of California Press, 1992); Henry Chadwick, *Antike Schriftauslegung: Pagane und Christliche Allegorese; Activa und Passiva im Antiken Umgang mit der Bibel* (Berlin: de Gruyer, 1998); I. Christiansen, *Die Technik der allegorischen Auslegungswissenschaft bei Philon von Alexandrien* (Beiträge zur Geschichte der biblischen Hermeneutik 7; Tübingen: Mohr, 1969); Naomi G. Cohen, *Philo Judaeus: His Universe of Discourse* (Beiträge zur Erforschung des Alten Testaments und Antiken Judentums 24; Frankfurt: Peter Lang, 1995); David Daube, "Alexandrian Methods of Interpretation and the Rabbis," *Festschrift Hans Lewald* (Basel: Helbing und Lichtenhahn, 1953) 27–44; Gerhard Delling, "Wunder—Allegorie—Mythus bei Philon von Alexandreia," *Studien zum Neuen Testament und zum hellenistischen Judentum* (Göttingen: Vandenhoeck und Ruprecht, 1970) 72–129; David M. Hay, *Both Literal and Allegorical: Studies in Philo of Alexandria's Questions and Answers on Genesis and Exodus* (Brown Judaic Series 232; Atlanta: Scholars Press, 1991); Burton Mack, "Weisheit und Allegorie bei Philo von Alexandrien," *Studia Philonica* 5 (1972) 57–105; Jean Pépin, *Mythe et allégorie: Les origines grecques et les contestations judéo-chrétiennes* (Paris: Aubier, 1958); E. Stein, *Die Allegorische Exegese des Philo aus Alexandria* (Beihefte zur ZNW 51; Giessen: Töpelmann, 1929).

[5] Aristotle, *Rhetoric*, 1,3.

examined here are Aristotle, *The Rhetoric* (ca. 335 B.C.E); [ps-]Demetrius *On Style* (ca. second century, BCE—first century CE); The *Rhetorica ad Herennium* (ca. 85 BCE); Cicero, in *De inventione* (ca. 89 BCE) and *De oratore* (55 BCE.); Longinus, in *On the Sublime* (ca. First Century, CE); and Quintilian, in *Institutio oratoria* (ca. 92 CE)

While something may be learned from rhetoricians prior to Aristotle regarding analogies, it is with Aristotle that clear guidelines have come down to us.[6] The two major terms employed by Aristotle in regard to comparison are παραβολή ("parable, semblance")[7] and εἰκών ("image, figure").[8] In discussing forms of proof Aristotle highlighted two kinds: examples and enthymemes.[9] The examples are further divided into two kinds: those that have happened, which we may designate historical, and those invented, that is, comparisons (παραβολή) or fables (λόγοι).[10] It is the latter that is of interest to us here. Aristotle, though providing examples from Aesop, does not state wherein lies their power.[11] He argued that even though fables are easier to come upon than historical comparisons, "…those derived from facts are more useful for deliberative oratory, because as a rule the future resembles the past."[12] He further argued that enthymemes have more power than examples, though the two should be employed to support each other.

One of Aristotle's fables invites further reflection on its power.

> Aesop, when defending at Samos a demagogue who was being tried for his life, related the following anecdote. "A fox, while crossing a river, was driven into a ravine. Being unable to get out, she was for a long time in sore distress, and a number of dog-fleas clung to her skin. A hedgehog, wandering about, saw her and, moved with compassion, asked her if he should remove the fleas. The fox refused and when the hedgehog asked the reason, she answered; 'They are already full of me and draw little blood; but if you take them away, others will come that are hungry and will drain what remains to me.' You in like manner, O Samians, will

---

[6] Marsh H. McCall, Jr., *Ancient Rhetorical Theories of Simile and Comparison* (Cambridge: Harvard University Press, 1969) 1–23.

[7] Aristotle, *Rhetoric*, 3,19,5; 2,20,4.

[8] *Ibid.*, 3,4,3. Cf. Quintilian, *Institutio Oratoria*, 8,6, 8, 9.

[9] *Ibid.*, 2, 20, 1.

[10] *Ibid.*, 2, 20, 3.

[11] *Ibid.*, 2, 20, 5–8.

[12] *Ibid.*, 2, 20, 8. Unless otherwise noted, translations from Aristotle are those of John Henry Freese in the Loeb Classical Library (Cambridge: Harvard University Press, 1959).

suffer no more harm from this man, for he is wealthy; but if you put him
to death, others will come who are poor, who will steal and squander
your public funds."[13]

The fable in this case shifts the focus away from the demagogue against
whom much animosity persisted to the fox, a neutral entity loosely
analogous to the demagogue's "victims." The plight of the fox stirs
compassion, while her sagacity elicits respect because of the grounds
upon which she rejected help in removing the fleas. The point is simply
and vividly made without stirring the inflammatory passions that arise
in respect to the demagogue: should the demagogue be deposed he will
be replaced by others whose needs are unfulfilled. The power of the
fable therefore, lies in its ability to make a persuasive point that elicited
the plaintiffs' interests while simultaneously waylaying rancor against
the one being defended.[14]

Aristotle discussed εἰκών in Book III ("on style and arrangement") in
chapters 2,4, 10, 11. The word εἰκών is here translated "simile," though
Aristotle stated that it is difficult to distinguish simile from metaphor.
As a stylistic devise Aristotle thought that metaphor was crucial: "It is
the metaphor above all that gives perspicuity (σαφές), pleasure, and a
foreign air, and it cannot be learnt from any else; but we must make
use of metaphors and epithets that are appropriate."[15] In this case
Aristotle declared that what gives analogical devices power are their
resultant clarity and liveliness. Because they do so they increase the
ease of learning.

> Easy learning is naturally pleasant to all, and words mean something, so
> that all words which make us learn something are most pleasant. Now we
> do not know the meaning of strange words, and proper terms we know
> already. It is metaphor, therefore, that above all produces this effect; for
> when Homer calls old age stubble, he teaches and informs us through
> the genus; for both have lost their bloom.[16]

---

[13] *Ibid.*, 2, 20, 6, 7.

[14] Chaim Perelman and L. Olbrechts-Tyteca (*The New Rhetoric: A Treatise on Argumentation* [South Bend: University of Notre Dame Press, 1969] 371–410) provide useful
comments on analogy, metaphor, and simile and deal schematically with aspects of
argumentative and stylistic power; however, they do not really take up the rhetorical
power, that is, how or why rhetorically analogical materials enhance the argument.

[15] Aristotle, *Rhetoric*, 3, 2, 8–9.

[16] *Ibid.*, 3, 10, 2–3. See also Richard Moran, "Artifice and Persuasion: the Work
of Metaphor in the *Rhetoric*". *Essays on Aristotle's Rhetoric*, ed. Amèlie Oksenberg Rorty
(Berkeley: University of California Press, 1996) 385–398.

Clearly then for Aristotle allegories, fables, and metaphors, that is, all types of analogies, serve to clarify and imbue liveliness, and to a lesser extent, augment substance. The purpose is not, as with Philo and Clement to penetrate into a more fundamental level of reality.[17] The chief end is pragmatic, that is, to win the case in the law court, to persuade the citizens of the polis, or to praise and blame the forefathers of cities and states.

The discourse of [ps-]Demetrius, *On Style* was famous for setting out four levels of style: the grand, the elegant, the plain and the forceful.[18] The author argued that metaphors particularly were the driving force of the grand style:

> The diction in the grand style should be distinguished, distinctive and the less usual. It will then have weight, while the normal, usual words may always be clear but are in certain cases unimpressive. In the first place, we should use metaphors, for they more than anything make prose attractive and impressive, but they should not be crowded together (or we write a dithyramb instead of prose), nor yet far-fetched but from the same general area and based on a true analogy.[19]

He further argued that if a metaphor seemed too bold it could be turned into a simile, for example, "instead of saying 'the orator Python was then a rushing torrent against you,'" expand it and say 'was like a rushing torrent against you.'"[20] He also believed that metaphors were suitable for the forceful style, if they were to the point and not extended comparison.[21] In this case metaphors create "force." Clearly

---

[17] John Dillon, *The Middle Platonists 80 B. C. to A. D. 220* (Ithaca: Cornell University Press, 1977) 141. Other studies include: Christoph Riedweg, *Mysterienterminologie bei Platon, Philon und Klemens von Alexandrien* (Berlin: Walter de Gruyter, 1987) and Raoul Mortley, *Connaissance Religieuse et Herméneutique chez Clément D'Alexandrie* (Leiden: E.J. Brill, 1973); Thomas M Conley, *Philo's Rhetoric: Studies in Style, Composition and Exegesis* (Berkeley: Center for Hermeneutical Studies, 1987); Thomas H. Olbricht, "Greek Rhetoric and the Allegorical Rhetoric of Philo and Clement of Alexandria," *Rhetorical Criticism and the Bible: Essays from the 1998 Florence Conference*, ed. by S. E. Porter and D. L. Stamps (Sheffield: Sheffield University Press, 2001).

[18] Most scholars think the attribution to Demetrius of Phalerum in the manuscript tradition is erroneous. For the problems of dating and authorship see G. M. A. Grube, *The Greek and Roman Critics* (London: Methuen, 1965) 110–21; W. Rhys Roberts in the earlier Loeb edition (London: Heinemann, 1932) 270–310, followed by Doreen C. Innes in the revised Loeb edition (Cambridge: Harvard University Press, 1995) 312–21; and D. M. Schenkenveld, *Studies in Demetrius on Style* (Amsterdam: Hakkert, 1964) 135–48.

[19] Demetrius, *On Style*, 77–78. The translation is that of Innes.

[20] *Ibid.*, 80.

[21] *Ibid.*, 272–274.

[ps-]Demetrius believed that analogical devices make discourse arresting and provide force, but they have more to do with attractiveness and understanding than with substance.

For a thousand years the *Rhetorica ad Herennium* was attributed to Cicero, but now almost universally it is considered to be by an unknown author of about the same time (ca. 85 BCE). It is the first complete work on rhetoric in Latin that has come down to us.[22] The *ad Herennium*, in the first part, much as Aristotle, discussed the employment of comparisons in juridical situations, but mostly those that are nonfigurative. The work was, in fact, a handbook addressed to Gaius Herennius for instruction in the techniques of forensic rhetoric. In Book II the author discussed embellishment (*exornatio*) as one of the five parts of a complete argument: (1) the proposition, (2) the reason, (3) the proof of reason, (4) the embellishment, and the résumé.[23] Similes, along with examples, amplifications, and previous judgments are discussed as components of embellishment.[24] As with Aristotle, however, it is in the discussion of style that the *ad Herennium* took up the analogical features of discourse, but unlike Aristotle, who discussed metaphor and comparison together, the *ad Herennium* took them up separately.

Under metaphor the author undertook observations on allegory.

> It [that is, an allegory] assumes three aspects: comparison, argument, and contrast. It operates through a comparison when a number of metaphors originating in a similarity in the mode of expression are set together, as follows: "For when dogs act the part of wolves, to what guardian, pray, are we going to entrust our herds of cattle?"[25]

In none of the examples set forth in the *ad Hernneium*, however, is there an effort to identify allegory as a means of communicating the fundamental meaning of reality. The contributions of similes to style are to embellish, clarify and make vivid, much as declared by Aristotle.

In his two treatises, *De inventione* (ca. 89 BCE) and *De oratore* (55 BCE), Cicero scrutinized comparisons only in the context of forensic rhetoric; therefore, he contributes little to understanding metaphor as a means of penetrating ontological realitiy. As McCall says, "Cicero makes frequent use of terms of comparison but never really undertakes any

---

[22] McCall, *Ancient Rhetorical Theories*, 57.
[23] Harry Caplan, *Ad C. Herennium de Ratione Dicendi (Rhetorica ad Herennium)* (Cambridge: Harvard University Press, 1954) 2, 27–30.
[24] *Rhetorica ad Herennium*, 2, 29.
[25] *Rhetorica ad Herennium*, 4, 34.

detailed treatment of them. In fact, only the youthful and incomplete *De Inventione* does more than give random attention to comparison."[26] Cicero does not associate comparison at any point with metaphor.[27] In a section in *De Oratore* he considers metaphors as employed for "adornment and dignity" and in service to "entertainment."[28] To Cicero, it is clear, the employment of metaphor is for embellishment rather than argumentative power. Metaphors convey brilliance and should be employed insofar as they make the meaning clearer either in action or thought. In some cases they may also achieve brevity.[29]

Longinus' *On the Sublime* (first century CE) essentially followed the classical rhetorical tradition. Of interest in this light is his discussion of the use and proper number of metaphors, as he cites the views of Caecilius, Demosthenes, Aristotle, and Theophrastus.[30] He concludes that what is most expressive is a "sustained series of metaphors."[31] He cites as an example the generation of vivid comparisons for the various anatomical parts of the body. He pointed out that both Xenophon and Plato had employed metaphorically an extended itemization of bodily parts. Metaphors of this type he argued have a natural grandeur and sublimity, and exude emotion. Though metaphors are effective, he concluded that they tended to lead to excesses. He reminded his readers that some criticized Plato for "harsh and intemperate metaphor and allegorical bombast."[32] For Longinus then, analogical materials capture attention, and provide sublimity, as well as, emotional force, as they "sweep everything along in the forward surge of their current."[33]

According to Marsh McCall, Quintilian's, *Institutes* (ca. 92 CE) "… offers the most complete and perceptive discussion of comparison in antiquity."[34] Many of Quintilian's comments, however, have to do with historical or literal comparisons; however, he was aware that what he called "the fictions of poets" might be of use, even though they were

---

[26] McCall, *Ancient Rhetorical Theories*, 87.

[27] Ibid., 98.

[28] Cicero, *De Oratore*, 3, 38, 155–43, 172.

[29] Ibid., 3, 39. 158.

[30] Longinus, *On the Sublime*, 32. See the discussion of the date and authorship questions by Donald Russel, revising the earlier work of W. Hamilton Fyfe, in the Loeb edition (Cambridge: Harvard University Press, 1995) 145–48.

[31] Ibid., 32.5.

[32] Ibid., 32.7.

[33] Ibid., 32.3.

[34] McCall, *Ancient Rhetorical Theories*, 178.

less effective as proofs.[35] In discussing "fictions," that is, the fables of
Aesop, which he thought more properly belonged to Hesiod,[36] Quintilian declared that they have to do with eloquence, more than with
proof.[37]

In regard to metaphor Quintilian felt that they added special dimensions to discourse.

> Let us begin, then, with the commonest and by far the most beautiful of
> *tropes*, namely, *metaphor*, the Greek term for our *translatio*. It is not merely
> so natural a turn of speech that it is often employed unconsciously or
> by uneducated persons, but it is in itself so attractive and elegant that
> however distinguished the language in which it is embedded it shines
> forth with a light that is all its own. For if it be correctly and appro-
> priately applied, it is quite impossible for its effect to be commonplace,
> mean or unpleasing. It adds to the copiousness of language by the inter-
> change of words and by borrowing, and finally succeeds in accomplish-
> ing the supremely difficult task of providing a name for everything. A
> noun or a verb is transferred from the place to which it properly belongs
> to another where there is either no *literal* term or the *transferred* is bet-
> ter than the *literal*. We do this either because it is necessary or to make
> our meaning clearer or, as I have already said, to produce a decorative
> effect.[38]

Later Quintilian wrote that the "metaphor is designed to move the
feelings, give special distinction to things and place them vividly before
the eye ... ."[39]

Quintilian also discussed allegory, but focused more on the metaphorical rather than allegorical if one has in mind allegory as employed
by Philo and Clement of Alexandria.

> *Allegory*, which is translated in Latin by *inversio*, either presenting one
> thing in words and another in meaning, or else something absolutely
> opposed to the meaning of the words. The first type is generally pro-
> duced by a series of metaphors. Take as an example:

---

[35] Quintilian, *Inst.* 5, 11, 17.

[36] *Ibid.*, 5, 11, 19.

[37] Frances M. Young (*Biblical Exegesis and the Formation of Christian Culture* [Cambridge:
Cambridge University Press, 1997] 176) observed, "The word *allegoria* is derived from a
Greek verb meaning 'to speak in public' compounded with the adjective *allos*, meaning
'other.' Ancient definitions all ring the changes on the same theme: allegory is 'to mean
something other than what one says'. It is discussed in the rhetorical text books on style
as a *trope*, a 'turn' or figure of speech, and lies on a spectrum with metaphor and irony."

[38] Quintilian, *Ins.* 8, 6, 4–6.

[39] *Ibid.*, 8, 6, 19.

"Oh ship, new waves will bear thee back to sea. What dost thou? Make the haven, come what may,"[40]

Orators, he avowed, make frequent use of allegories, but oratory chiefly exhibits plainness of speech. He described the following statement from Cicero as a pure allegory. "What I marvel at and complain of is this, that there should exist any man so set on destroying his enemy as to scuttle the ship on which he himself is sailing."[41] An obscure allegory, he declared is a riddle, for example, "Say in what land, and if thou tell me true, I'll hold thee as Apollo's oracle, Three ells will measure all the arch of heaven."[42] It is not clear from Quintilian exactly what special power allegories possess. For him, if they are of value, their meaning is relatively clear. They seem to be a more cryptic form of metaphor and function with the same end in mind.

From this perusal of the rhetoricians, the power of analogical materials first of all lies in clarity, especially in regard to literal or historical comparison. Fictional or allegorical analogies supply vivacity, liveliness and emotion. They function both to enhance style, and to contribute toward proof by way of πάθος ("affect"). As such, however, rhetoricians fail to discuss the manner in which analogies provoke profounder meanings that lie beneath the surface. Rhetoricians did not reflect upon the employment of analogy in the exposition of texts that occurred in ancient moral and religious discourse since they essentially ignored rhetoric endemic in exposition.

The Analogical in Exposition

Another major interest in analogy and allegory in the ancient world revolved about the explication and utilization of texts. The Stoic philosopher Cleanthes (third century BCE) may be the first person known to use the word ἀλληγορία. Frequent use of the term did not come about until the first century BCE. In the first century CE, Heracli-

---

[40] Ibid., 8, 6, 44. Greenfield commented (The Ends of Allegory, 40–50), "Quintilian's description in his Institutio Oratoria (8.6) concerns rhetorical allegory, but he admits that his whole rhetorical discussion of tropes has parallel applications 'given by the teachers of literature as well,' and his examples derive from both oratory and literature. His definition of 'Allegoria' as one thing in words and another in meaning" includes the idea of reading allegory, Maureen Quilligan notes, as does Quintilian's point that allegory functions by 'a series of metaphors' (continuatis translationibus)."

[41] Ibid., 8, 6, 47.

[42] Ibid., 8, 6, 52.

tus in *Quaestiones Homericae*, (22) defined the term: "That is called allegory which, as the name implies, says one things but means something other than what it says."[43] Hansen asserts that Philo and Heraclitus were the first authors to use "the noun in the meaning of 'figurative interpretation of an authoritative text' and not long after them Josephus."[44] Plutarch and others of his day gave attention to various forms of analogy. In his treatise *That the Young Should Study Poetry* he provides information about the development of the word allegory by saying that "what used to be called 'deeper meanings' (ὑπονοίαις) are now called 'allegories' (ἀλληγορίαις)" (*Quom. adolescens poetas audire debeat* 4 [19E]).[45] Other authors reflecting on these matters are Ps.-Plutarch, *De Homero* and Cornutus, *Theologiae Graecae compendium*. To follow through on these analyses provides an additional avenue for understanding the employment of analogical approaches in explication in addition to that of the rhetoricians.

The Setting for Analogical Discourse

Analogical and allegorical rhetorical approaches are in some sense endemic in synagogue and church contexts, but more in some than in others. The ancient rhetoricians did not scrutinize these sorts of materials.[46] For that reason we may presume that they may have more in common with another type or setting of discourse for which the rhetoricians provide limited help in assessing the role of analogical speech as stylistic and communicative features. For sake of discussion we may tentatively call this "religious discourse." Indeed, some examples of religious discourses, may be found in the Hellenistic world, for example, Dio Chrysostom, *Oration* 36 (on Zeus), Aelius Aristides *Oration* 6 (praising Asclepius), and Epictetus, *Dissertations*, all of which date from the late first through the second century CE. Unfortunately, extant homilies from either Jewish or Christian contexts prior to the second century CE are few. But enough material survives so that some work has been

---

[43] On the date and authorship see Felix Buffière, *Héraclite, Allégories d'Homère* (Coll. Budé; Paris: Société d'Édition «Les Belles Lettres», 1962) vii-x.

[44] R. P. C. Hanson, *Allegory and Event* (London: SCM Press, 1959) 39.

[45] See also Jon Whitman, *Allegory: The Dynamics of an Ancient and Medieval Technique* (Oxford: Clarendon Press, 1987) Appendix I: "On the History of the Term 'Allegory'" (263–68).

[46] D. A. G. Hinks, "*Tria Genera Causarum*," *Classical Quarterly* 30 (1936) 170–176.

done, even though identification of actual sermons has proven notoriously difficult.[47]

Noting that there is no technical term for "sermon" in either Greek or Latin usage, Folker Siegert has recently proposed a further gradation of such religious discourses. Thus, he distinguishes "speeches on religious matters" from "speeches explaining sacred doctrines or texts in a liturgical setting."[48] Only to the latter would he ascribe the term "sermon" in the more restrictive sense. For example, he classes Dio's *Or.* 36, Aristides' *Or.* 6, and 4 Maccabees as the former type, while Ps-Philo *On Jonah*, Melito's *On the Pascha*, and Origen's *Homilies* are properly "sermons." Whereas most of the ancient religions employed the broader forms of religious discourse, Siegert argues that only Jews and Christians developed the "sermon" (in the restrictive sense) in the context of a liturgical discourse setting.[49] He also locates the roots of this tradition, at least in part, in the Alexandrian Jewish community.[50]

This observation, brings us back to a classic suggestion regarding the role of religious discourse in the development of distinctive "schools" of Christian interpretation. As it is traditionally articulated, the analogical is much more obvious in the discourses of Alexandria than in Antioch. I am intrigued by the fact that rhetoric flourished in Antioch, but not so much in Alexandria. Alexandria had its share of sophists, as Bruce

---

[47] One of the earliest was the study of Hartwig Thyen, *Der Stil der Jüdisch-Hellenistischen Homilie* (Göttingen: Vandenhoeck and Ruprecht, 1955), which was written in large measure as a response to Bultmann's dissertation comparing Paul's "preaching" to the Cynic-Stoic diatribe (*Der Stil der paulinischen Predigt und die kynisch-stoische Diatribe* [FRLANT 13; Göttingen: Vandenhoeck & Ruprecht, 1910]). Thyen attempted to argue that Paul's dependence on the Hellenistic moralist tradition, as seen in Epictetus, was at most indirect, since there was already a fully developed use of comparable preaching forms in the synagogue. His arguments were not persuasive, however; cf. the review of Thyen by Gerhard Delling in *TLZ* 82 (1957) 352–54; Malherbe, "Hellenistic Moralists and the NT," 313–20 and esp. n. 228; and Stowers, *The Diatribe*, 41. More recent efforts to identify actual Jewish synagogue homiles has been somewhat more restrained. Cf. W. R. Stegner, "The Ancient Jewish Synagogue Homily", *Graeco-Roman Literature and the New Testament*, D. E. Aune, ed. (Atlanta: Scholars Press, 1988) 51–69; J. I. H. McDonald, *Kerygma and Didache* (SNTSMS 37; Cambridge: Cambridge University Press, 1980); C. Schneider, *Geistesgeschichte des antiken Christentums*, II (Munich: Beck, 1954).

[48] Folker Siegert, "Homily and Panegyrical Sermon" *Handbook of Classical Rhetoric in the Hellenistic Period 330 B. C.—A. D. 400*, ed. by Stanley E. Porter, Leiden, Brill, 1997) 421–443.

[49] *Ibid.*, 422.

[50] *Ibid.*, 433–37.

Winter argues persuasively.[51] But according to Robert W. Smith, no
major rhetoricians taught there, and it is difficult to locate information
about specific teachers.[52] Why was this the case? Let us pose the question another way: was there something in the mindset of Antioch that
was more compatible with the foci of the ancient rhetoricians than that
of Alexandria.

Robert M. Grant and David Tracey wrote in regard to Scripture
interpretation in Alexandria and Antioch:

> The school of Antioch insisted on the historical reality of the biblical
> revelation. They were unwilling to lose it in a world of symbols and
> shadows. They were more Aristotelian than Platonist. Where the Alexan-
> drines use the word *theory* as equivalent to allegorical interpretation, the
> Antiochene exegetes use it for a sense of scripture higher or deeper
> than the literal or historical meaning, but firmly based on the letter.
> This understanding does not deny the literal meaning of scripture but
> is grounded on it, as an image is based on the thing represented and
> points towards it.[53]

The major ancient rhetoricians reflected upon discourse in the rumble
tumble world of the law courts, the assemblies of the polis and larger
governmental entities, as well as eulogistic discourse on festivals and
ceremonial days. Their discourse was pragmatic and literalistic. It was
in this sort of climate that church and synagogue rhetoric flourished in
Antioch.

In contrast, decisions affecting the polis in Alexandria tended to be
made from afar, not at the grass roots level. It is of significance to note
that rhetoric, as well as those who theorized about rhetoric, flourished
in contexts in which the citizenry debated policy and practical matters
such as in Greece, Rome, Great Britain and America.[54] It is true
that Alexandrians sometimes spoke and wrote on political matters, for
example Philo in his famous *Embassy to Gaius*.[55] But these discourses

---

[51] Bruce W. Winter, *Philo and Paul among the Sophists* (Cambridge: Cambridge University Press, 1997) 19–112.

[52] Robert W. Smith, *The Art of Rhetoric in Alexandria: Its Theory and Practice in the Ancient
World* (The Hague: Martinus Nijhoff, 1974).

[53] Robert M. Grant with David Tracy, *A Short History of the Interpretation of The Bible*
(Fortress Press, 1984) 66.

[54] Dawson, *Allegorical Readers and Cultural Revision*, 113–126 discusses the context from
which the various ethnic groups addressed each other and their Roman overseers.

[55] Philo, "On the Embassy to Gaius: The First Part of the Treatise on Virtues,"
trans. F. H. Colson in LCL X (Cambridge: Harvard University Press, 1962).

were presented neither to Alexandrian courts nor to legislative assemblies; they were addressed to Roman officials.

The Alexandrian authors discoursed extensively on philosophical and religious matters in which analogical meanings were pervasive.[56] The interests of the intellectuals of the city centered not so much in politics and legal affairs, but in metaphysical matters. As Johannes Quasten observed,

> The school of Alexandria is the oldest centre of sacred science in the history of Christianity. The environment in which it developed gave it its distinctive characteristics, predominant interest in the metaphysical investigation of the content of the faith, a leaning to the philosophy of Plato, and the allegorical interpretation of Sacred Scripture.[57]

It may not be accidental that in contrast with Alexandria, rhetoric flourished in Antioch in the third and fourth centuries with Malchion (third century), Lucian of Antioch (d. 312), Libanius (314–395?), and John Chrysostom (347–407). Part of the reason for the vitality of rhetoric in Antioch is that local administration continued longer.[58] By the fourth century, the predominant culture was Christian so that discourses of the preachers were much more significant in forming public opinion than earlier in Alexander.[59]

The foci of the classical rhetoricians upon argument and literalistic narrative dovetail with the celebrated contours of Antiochian hermeneutics.[60] As Francis Young has observed,

> Antiochene exegesis, then, is grounded in the exegetical activities of the rhetorical schools. The objection to Alexandrian allegory is that it treats texts as a collection of arbitrary tokens, not as 'mirroring' in its narrative coherence the truths which may be discerned within it. *Mimesis* was a key term in ancient literary criticism, and the Antiochene approach was

---

[56] On the use of analogy in philosophy see: G. E. R. Lloyd, *Polarity and Analogy: Two Types of Argumentation in Early Greek Thought* (Cambridge: Cambridge University Press, 1966) and James S. Measell, "Development of the Concept of Analogy in Philosophy, Logic, and Rhetoric to 1850" (Unpublished Ph.D. Dissertation; University of Illinois at Urbana-Champaign, 1970).

[57] Johannes Quasten, *Patrology* (3 vols.; Utrecht: Spectrum, 1975) II:2.

[58] J. H. W. G. Liebeschuetz, *Antioch: City and Imperial Administration in the Later Roman Empire* (Oxford: Oxford University Press, 1972) 10–20.

[59] Robert L. Wilken, *John Chrysostom and the Jews: Rhetoric and Reality in the Late 4ᵗʰ Century* (Berkeley: University of California Press, 1983) 95–127.

[60] Several documents were written against allegory by those of the Antiochene school including the five books *Against the Allegorists* by Theodore of Mopsuestia, according to D. S. Wallace-Hadrill, *Christian Antioch: A Study of Early Christian Thought in the East* (Cambridge: Cambridge University Press, 1982) 35.

to understand the wording and content of the scriptures as 'mimetic' of divine truths, thus providing moral and doctrinal teaching, and also prophecy.[61]

In classical rhetoric, little attention is given to analogy except as a stylistic device as we have observed. Likewise interest of the rhetoricians in narrative had little to do with the power of stories, but was limited to what the orator needs to convey so as to provide as historical perspective on his position or argument. Especially in forensic rhetoric, narrative was focused upon the pertinent facts of the case. Aristotle wrote:

> ... for narrative only belongs in a manner to forensic speech ... From some facts a man may be shown to be courageous, from others wise or just. Besides, a speech of this kind is simpler, whereas the other is intricate and not plain. It is only necessary to recall the famous actions. Again, the narrative should be introduced in several places, sometimes not at all at the beginning. In deliberative oratory narrative is very rare, because no one can narrate things to come; but if there is narrative, it will be of things past, in order that, being reminded of them, the hearers may take better counsel about the future.[62]

In epideictic, narrative is of some use in eulogy or funeral oratory, but the rhetoricians were more interested in amplification in this regard than narrative technique. Little attention was given to narrativity as a means of telling one's own story, or that of others.

The classical rhetoricians likewise commented little on symbol or metaphor except as a figure of speech. They did not reflect on allegory or larger metaphorical means of conveying truths. Of course, the classical philosophers, for example, Plato, employed myths, but the rhetoricians did not discuss these in their rhetorical essays.[63] The Antiochene fathers, mirroring in turn the interests of the rhetoricians, eschewed metaphor and allegory as the grounds of inculcating deeper insight into reality. Young astutely observed,

> They were not adverse to allegory as a figure of speech. You might say they rejected the word *allegoria* because it had been misappropriated by a particular tradition of exegesis which had a different background, and

---

[61] Young, *Biblical Exegesis*, 175. Also, Frances M. Young, "The Rhetorical Schools and their Influence on Patristic Exegesis" in Rowan Williams, ed., *The Making of Orthodoxy. Essays in Honour of Henry Chadwick* (Cambridge: Cambridge University Press, 1989) 182–199.

[62] Aristotle, *Rhetoric*, 3, 13, 5; 16. Cf. *Rhetorica ad Herennium*, 1. 8–9. Quintilian, *Institutio Oratoria*, 4, 2.

[63] J. A. Stewart, *The Myths of Plato* (London: McMillan, 1905).

which shattered the narrative coherence of particular texts, and the Bible as a whole.

> I have argued, then, that Antiochene exegesis is not simply according to the letter, nor was it an anticipation of historical criticism. Rather they used the standard literary techniques in use in the rhetorical schools to protest against esoteric philosophical deductions being made in what they regarded as an arbitrary way.[64]

In Antioch considerable communication took place for immediate practical reasons. Early Christian examples are the *Didache*, and Ignatius.[65] So in the context of the Antiochian mindset, classical rhetoric is of more help than the sort of discourse incorporating allegory and myth such as did Philo, Clement of Alexandria, Origen and various other Platonists. In Alexandria, in contrast with Antioch, allegory and metaphor flourished, and classical rhetoric generally took a back seat. The orientation in Alexandria tended to be philosophical and few discourses addressing immediate situations are extant. My point is not that rhetoric conditioned the mind-set of Antioch, or that by focusing upon rhetorical approaches we can pinpoint the salient features of the differences between Antioch and Alexandria. I am prepared to argue, however, that Antiochian discourses are more representative of the sort that rhetoricians analyzed than those of Alexandria.

Analogy in Synagogue and Church

A fruitful contrast with the approach of the classical rhetoricians to analogical aspects of discourse is a study of Philo (ca. 20 BCE.-50 CE) and Clement of Alexandria (ca. 150–215 CE), who communicate in a different context and culture from that of Antioch in which rhetoric flourished. David Dawson argues that the objective of allegorical interpretation in Alexandria was cultural revision.

> Although allegorical readers of scripture in ancient Alexandria sought to convince their audience that they were interpreting the text itself, they were actually seeking to revise their culture through their allegorical readings ... Allegory is not so much about meaning or lack of meaning

---

[64] Young, *Biblical Exegesis*, 182.

[65] Raymond E. Brown and John P. Meier, *Antioch and Rome: New Testament Cradles of Catholic Christianity* (New York: Paulist Press, 1983) 11–86. Also, Christoph Schäublin, *Untersuchungen zu Methode und Herkunft der Antiochenischen Exegese* (Köln-Bonn: Peter Hanstein, Verlag, 1974); Glanville Downey, *A History of Antioch in Syria from Seleucus to the Arab Conquest* (Princeton: Princeton University Press, 1961).

in texts as it is a way of using texts and their meanings to situate oneself and one's community with respect to society and culture. We have seen that ancient allegorical readers used their readings of scripture to reinterpret the world and the other cultural classics that helped sustain and legitimate that world.[66]

From a study of Alexandrine documents, I have come to the conclusion that in some types of religious discourse, analogical approaches serve a different purpose and possess a different power than that which we have tracked in the Graeco-Roman rhetorical tradition. The details of such a study are published elsewhere but I here present the conclusions.[67] These differences are of importance for the rhetorical analysis of certain Biblical materials.

In his discourse *On the Creation of the World* it is clear that for Philo the privileged text of Scripture, properly understood, discloses a reality beyond the immediately transparent sense.[68] The focus is larger than the tropes and figures of classical rhetoric. Underlying the Scripture is a meaning that both incorporates the insights of the philosophers, especially Plato, but at the same time modifies and corrects Platonic and other philosophical perspectives. This analogical interpretation, therefore, does not simply clarify or vivify a point of view. Rather it locates a reality behind the discrete, and this underlying dimension of reality is the more fundamental because it provides the foundation for the discrete. For example, in respect to the tree of life and the knowledge of good and evil, Philo wrote:

> This description is, I think, intended symbolically rather than literally; for never yet have trees of life or of understanding appeared on the earth, nor is it likely that they will appear hereafter. No. Moses evidently signifies by the pleasance the ruling power of the soul which is full of countless opinions, as it might be of plants.[69]

The text thus sets forth a true account of creation but must be read in such a manner that another primary reality also becomes transparent.

Philo's rhetoric proceeds in the following manner. The Septuagint text is the beginning point for discourse because in it fundamental insight is set forth. Such fundamental insight, however, is not located in the discrete details of the text. Rather, it lies behind these details

---

[66] Dawson, *Allegorical Readers and Cultural Revision*, 235–236.
[67] Olbricht, "Greek Rhetoric and the Allegorical Rhetoric of Philo and Clement of Alexandria."
[68] *De opificio mundi*, trans. F. H. Colson, LCL I (London: Heinemann, 1929).
[69] *On the Creation 154*

either by way of express declaration, or in words as symbols, or words in the etymological roots of words, or in some cases in number symbolism. For Philo, the rhetoric of allegorization has its own rules, and even allegorization has its limits. But fundamental meanings from basic Biblical visions take priority over the views of the philosophers. Dawson concluded,

> And when the connection between literary revision and social practice is kept in view, it becomes unmistakably clear that for Philo allegorical interpretation is an effort to make Greek culture Jewish rather than to dissolve Jewish identity into Greek culture. Philo's concern for the specific practice of Judaism in Alexandrian society reveals that for him allegorical interpretation is central to Jewish communal identity and survival in a hostile environment.[70]

Analogy for Philo therefore communicates an ontology, the aim for which is considerably different from that of the rhetoricians, for whom analogy is essentially mere vivacity of style.[71]

Clement, likewise employs allegory, not so much to clarify, or vivify a point of view, but so as to establish that his arguments are grounded in the Scriptures allegorically. On occasion Clement identified a person or object in scripture as a type, which Philo seldom did, for example, that Isaac is a type of Christ.[72] Typology posits a world in which that which comes afterward brings to fruition what is declared earlier. Such interpretation has a time line; it is horizontal. For Philo there was more of a vertical sense of allegorization. Philo believed that Scripture adumbrated fundamental reality when one searched for basic truths by probing the mysteries and symbols of the text. The allegorization pointed upward (that is, beyond sense experience) and downward (that is, probing the foundational bedrock).

The allegorization of Clement of Alexandria was essentially horizontal and immediate. Texts and persons in history adumbrated positions and persons about whom Clement set out to establish a theological ground point. These points had mostly to do with practical affairs

---

[70] Dawson, *Allegorical Readers and Cultural Revision*, 74.

[71] Manuel Alexandre, Jr., *Rhetorical Argumentation in Philo of Alexandria* (Atlanta: Scholars Press, 1999) has written an exemplary work on Philo employing the insights of the classical rhetoricians. But in my judgment he has missed some of the major features of Philo's discourses, that is, structure dependent upon Scripture, and the rhetorical features of analogical and allegorical materials. He was dependent on the rhetoricians and the rhetoricians provide no guidelines for commenting on these significant features.

[72] Clement of Alexandria, *Stromateis I–III*, trans. John Ferguson (Washington: The Catholic University of America Press, 1991) 31.

and in that sense were more in line with allegorization as discussed
by the rhetoricians. But whereas the example of allegories offered by
the rhetorician needed little elucidation to make them understandable,
Clement had to explain why most of his allegories were suitable to his
purpose. He employed Scriptures, in effect, more by way of allusion
than proof. But he intended Scripture texts as proof inasmuch as he
explicated them in such a manner that he presumes he has established
solid evidence for his conclusions.

Dawson scrutinized allegorical usage not only in Philo and Clement
but also in another Alexandrian—Valentinus. He concluded in regard
to the approaches of the three,

> Philo read scripture allegorically on the assumption that Moses was an
> original author who had re-inscribed cultural and philosophical wisdom
> in the form of the Pentateuch. Valentinus read his precursors (especially
> Gnostic myth) allegorically, expressing his revision of culture in the form
> of his own creative allegorical composition. Clement illustrates yet a third
> mode of allegorical reading and cultural revision. He specialized in what
> he called the tradition of the "elders"— teachers who were thought to
> have transmitted by word of mouth the inner secrets of the Christian
> gospel, derived ultimately from Jesus himself.[73]

From an examination of the allegorical interpretation of Scripture in
Philo and Clement of Alexandria we have a new vision of the manner
in which analogies have rhetorical power. Their rhetorical effects are
rich in textures that are especially endemic to the author and audience.
There is still much work to be done. In the New Testament, for example, Old Testament texts are employed so as to convince the auditors
that they have come to fruition in the last days of this age that is passing
away. The interpretation is typological. And typological interpretation
must also be examined for how it functions rhetorically.

The rhetorical features of ancient discourse are far more varied
than the classical rhetoricians recognized. It is therefore important for
those involved in rhetorical criticism of the Scriptures to give attention
to what the Graeco-Roman rhetoricians commented upon as well as
what they did not. The rhetoricians conceived analogical features of
discourse as essentially stylistic devices. In the communication that took
place in the church and synagogue, however, analogical approaches
reflected a fundamental vision of reality. It is for this reason that increased attention needs to be given to how these features of religious

---

[73] Dawson, *Allegorical Readers and Cultural Revision*, 184.

discourses work as well as the manner in which they possess rhetorical power. The writings of both Jews and Christians in Alexandria are a fertile field for assessing and constructing the rhetorical aspects of analogical discourse.

THE ART OF PRAISE
PHILO AND PHILODEMUS ON MUSIC

Everett Ferguson

Introduction: The Silence of Ancient Sounds

Of all the cultural expressions of the early Jewish and Christian world, perhaps the least heard by modern scholars has been music. But music was all around in the classical world—from the streets to the imperial salon. It was also the subject of extensive technical discussions, especially among philosophers. Two of these, those of Philodemus and Philo, will be the focus of this study. Both give attention to music: Philodemus by a treatise on the subject and Philo by numerous scattered references, but neither author's treatment has attracted extensive analysis. While Abe Malherbe has professed little affinity for Philo, I hope he will accept this study as a melodius tribute, by allowing the tenor of Philo to harmonize with the bass of Philodemus, one of the favorites in his classical chorus.

The neglect of music by scholars may be a result of where one typically encounters it in the extant literary sources. Music, like medicine, grammar, and rhetoric, was considered a τεχνή, a learned "skill" or "art." From the classical Greek tradition it was given stature by its connection to the poetic composition of odes and hymns. Even so, by the Roman period it was not considered an appropriate profession for a person of noble birth. Poetry was now a separate literary art, and music had largely become the province of slaves or women. Unlike rhetoric, elite men were not expected to study music for use in daily life, even though many show substantial awareness of its technical aspects. Jewish and Christian texts give even less attention usually, perhaps because music was often associated with less wholesome activities of the after-dinner entertainment at a symposium. Such carousing with female musicians was to be avoided. Among the moralist philosophers, however, one frequently finds allusions to music and its technical skills as a metaphor or illustration of the precision and practice of pursuing a harmonius moral life. In the arts, skill and training are required to become proficient, as Musonius Rufus said:

Virtue is not theoretical knowledge (ἐπιστήμη θεωρητική) alone but it is practical application as well, just like medicine and music (ἥ τε ἰατρικὴ καὶ ἡ μουσική). Therefore, just as it is necessary for the doctor or the musician respectively not only to master the theoretical principles of his art (τὰ θεωρήματα τῆς αὐτοῦ τέχνης), it is also necessary for him to exercise (γεγυμνάσθαι) at acting according to the principles; so too, a man who wishes to become good should not only learn the precepts which are conducive to virtue, but should also exercise earnestly and strenuously (γυμνάζεσθαι … φιλοτίμως καὶ φιλοπόνως) in accordance with them.[1]

Thus music frequently is found alongside two of the more prominent moral *topoi* that liken philosophy to medical treatment and the virtuous life to an athletic contest.

Philo's frequent statements about music have not drawn much study, perhaps because, as with Musonius, they often occur in discussions of other subjects,[2] but Philo was clearly interested in music and had some knowledge of the technical as well as practical aspects of both instrumental and vocal music. The importance of music for Philo is shown by his abundant use of musical illustrations.[3] Musical ratios and harmonies provide illustrations for his number symbolism, to which he gave much attention.[4] Similarly he elucidates peculiarly Jewish rituals

---

[1] *Frag.* 6. Compare also *Frags.* 2, 5. The text is from C. Lutz, *Musonius Rufus, the Roman Socrates* (Yale Classical Studies 10; New Haven: Yale University Press, 1947) 52; the translation is that of the author, adapted from that of Lutz.

[2] The major study is the valuable article by Louis H. Feldman, "Philo's Views on Music," *Journal of Jewish Music and Liturgy* 9 (1985–86) 36–54, reprinted in *Studies in Hellenistic Judaism* (Leiden: Brill, 1996) 504–528. The neglect is illustrated by Karl Erich Grözinger, *Musik und Gesang in der Theologie der frühen jüdischen Literatur: Talmud, Midrasch, Mystik* (TSAJ 3; Tübingen: Mohr-Siebeck, 1982), which includes the Apocrypha, New Testament, and Qumran in its index of passages but omits Philo altogether. The importance of Philo in music history because of his influence on the church fathers is recognized by Herbert M. Schueller, *The Idea of Music: An Introduction to Musical Aesthetics in Antiquity and the Middle Ages* (Kalamazoo: Medieval Institute Publications, 1988) 130–133.

[3] Feldman, "Philo's Views" 511–513.

[4] *Op. mun.* 15.48 ("the number four contains the ratios of the musical harmonies"); 31.96 ("most musical is the proportion of these numbers"); 37.107–110 (seven is "most harmonious and in a certain way the source of the most beautiful scale"); *Spec. leg.* II.32.200 (ten "is the most perfect fullness of musical theories"); *Cong.* 17.89; *Q. Gen.* 4.27. See Feldman, "Philo's Views" 520–522. For the musical ratios in Greek philosophy, cf. Porphyry, *Commentary on the Harmonics of Ptolemy* 107.15f. on the Pythagoreans (tr. Andrew Barker, *Greek Musical Writings*, Vol.2: *Harmonic and Acoustic Theory* [Cambridge: Cambridge University Press, 1989] 34–35).

with musical metaphors: the thank-offering "is divided into parts in the same manner as are the lyre and other instruments of music."[5]

Philo, it seems, has an illustration for nearly everything, and a large share of his references to music occur in illustrations: the perfect man like the master of music or of grammar requires no instruction.[6] In other cases the physical aspects of hearing and sense perception offer a natural opportunity for comment: the pleasures of the "eyes, ears, stomach, and the parts below the stomach" charm us like musical sounds ringing in the ears.[7]

The majority of Philo's illustrations occur in references to philosophy and paraenetic instruction: "let the whole chorus of philosophers chime in, expounding their customary themes;"[8] or "as the things pertaining to music are apprehended through the science of music … so that which is wise is perceived through wisdom;"[9] and God gives his blessings to a righteous man "just as he gives to the musician the instruments that pertain to music."[10] So, like Musonius, he likens habituation in virtue to practicing at music or the other arts: knowledge without practice is unprofitable, for "What profit is the beautiful voice when it is silent, or of the aulos player if he does not play, or of the kithara player when he does not play?"[11] Even in such metaphorical uses Philo's

---

[5] *Sac.* 20.74. Translations of Philo are for the most part my own but with reference to those in the LCL, whose Greek text I use.

[6] *Leg. all.* I.30.94. As often, the musical comparison accompanies an illustration from medicine or grammar; here the vowels of the alphabet like the notes of music are adapted to produce harmony with one another. Compare *Det. pot.* 9.18: the exercise of a virtue in an exaggerated or improper way is like practising "music unmusically or grammar ungrammatically;" *Det. pot.* 21.75: even as music and grammar remain after the death of a musician or grammarian, virtue survives the death of a virtuous man (cf. Plato, *Phaedo* 86); *Post.* 43.142: not giving to someone according to his needs is as absurd as giving "a lyre to a physician or surgical instruments to a musician."

[7] *Post.* 45.155. Compare *Leg. all.* II.3.7: the mind uses a helper, as it does the sense of hearing in recognizing a musician's voice as sweet or out of tune. When Philo thinks about the sense of hearing, he does so in terms of musical sounds (*Leg. all.* III.18.57— whether "melodious and rhythmical or out of tune and in discord").

[8] *Agr.* 31.139.

[9] *Mig.* 8.39. Cf. *Leg. all.* II.8.26: when occupied with the tunefulness of a voice it cannot exercise its reasoning power; *Leg. all.* II.7.21: "power" expresses a singer's power in singing; *Leg. all.* III.41.121: a false statement is like naming incorrectly a mode of music or a note on the scale; *Sac.* 5.22 and 29: pleasure takes her stand among various evils "like the leader of a chorus" and her "sound sings in the ears;" *Sac.* 7.37: "that which is pleasing to God and virtue is like a tightly strung and robust harmony" (further on the harmony of the soul, see below).

[10] *Mig.* 21.120.

[11] *Cong.* 9.46. Cf. *Cong.* 25.144: each skill deals with some part of reality—"geometry

technical interests show through, as when he employs notions of harmony: the moderation of Moses' laws is like the blending of high and
low notes on a musical instrument to produce a life of harmony and
concord.[12] Similarly, Moses is called God's special instrument and the
Torah his "music": "The sound, moreover, comes when the plectrum,
his Logos, melodiously and skilfully strikes a harmony, through which
legislation is made known."[13] Elsewhere he compares body and mind
to musical instruments: the body is not to be worn out by continuous
labor; as musicians loosen the strings of their instruments "lest they
snap through unrelieved tension," and as music and voices are adapted
to various intensities and relaxations, "so too is it with the mind."[14]

Apart from the seasoning provided by his Jewish heritage and context, Philo's allusions reflect a solid awareness of technical discussions of
music in the Greek philosophical thought represented by Pythagoreans,
Platonists, Aristotelians, and Stoics,[15] as we would expect from his general use of Platonic and Stoic thought. This kinship is seen especially
in regard to the relations between music, the human soul, and cos-

---

has its lines, and music its sounds;" *Mut.* 21.122: "habits are superior to the persons
practising them, as music is superior to the musician;" *Spec. leg.* II.44.246: we do not
punish the servants rather than the actual authors of an act any more than we would
praise the instruments instead of the musician who performed on the aulos or lyre; *Spec.
leg.* II.47.259: virtue is its own reward as holiness is the most beautiful in the chorus;
Gaium 11.75: Macro became "like the leader of a chorus" (the same comparison for
Helicon in 26.166); *Prob.* 7.49: "just as the law of music gives equality with regard to
this art to all those practised in music, so also does the law of human life to those
experienced in the matters of living" (for the reverse application see 8.51); *Prob.* 21.157:
the declaration that one is a "grammarian, geometrician, or musician" no more makes
it so than the declaration that one is free; *Provid.* 2.20: "as it is the height of folly to
make the blind judges of color or the deaf of musical sounds, so is it to make evil men
the judges of the truly good."

[12] *Spec. leg. IV.17.102.* The same illustration of "the harmony which includes a heightening and lowering of the notes as in a musical instrument for the skilful blending of
melody" is applied to individual human beings in *Mut.* 13.87. For other illustrations
from "harmony" cf. *Spec. leg.* II.28.157: God "wished to effect a harmony as on a musical instrument;" *Virt.* 27.145: one law "sings together" with others (is in agreement with
others), "just as in an all harmonious chorus."

[13] *Q. Gen.* IV.196; I use the translation of Ralph Marcus in LCL (*Philo Supplement*
I:486). Compare *Mut.* 24.139: the prophet Hosea's words were "the voice of the Invisible
One whose invisible hand plays on the instrument of the human voice;" *Conf.* 11.41: the
words of Gen 42:11 are a "harmonious symphony."

[14] *Q. Gen.* IV.29 (*Philo Supplement* I: 305). Cf. *Q. Gen.* IV.76 (*Philo Supplement* I: 354): the
one ignorant of the art of a musician has trouble with instruments but to the musician
they are "fitting and suitable."

[15] For the views of these philosophical schools on music, Barker, *Greek Musical Writings.* The Pythagoreans posited that "the 'harmony' of the universe (and sometimes

mic harmony. These relations were especially emphasized by Damon (fifth century BCE) and Diogenes of Babylon (c. 240–152 BCE). But there was another tradition in Greek philosophy in regard to music, represented by some Sophists,[16] the Skeptics,[17] and the Epicureans. For this other tradition, we may take Philodemus as a foil against whom to array Philo.

Philodemus

Philodemus (ca. 110 – ca. 40/35 BCE) was originally from Gadara in the Decapolis, but moved to Athens where he became one of the leading Epicurean philosophers of his day. Sometime between 75–55 BCE he moved to Italy where he wrote and taught under the patronage of L. Calpurnius Piso Caesoninus, the father-in-law of Julius Caesar. Philodemus seems to have divided his time between Rome and Piso's luxurious resort villa (now usually called the "Villa of the Papyri") at Herculaneum, where his teaching and literary activities took place.[18] The result was an extensive library of texts on various aspects of philosophy, especially the doctrines of Epicurus and practical ethics, as well as treatises on poetry, rhetoric, and music.[19]

The treatise *On Music* is partially preserved among the charred rolls of papyri (*P Herc* 1497) found at the villa after it was destroyed in the eruption of Vesuvius in 79 CE. Most, if not all, of the fragments belong to the Fourth Book,[20] devoted to a refutation of Stoic views on music,

---

those of the microcosms of state and soul) were rooted in mathematical relations of the sort that this musical structure displays" (*ibid.*, 2.28). Platonists, Aristotelians, and Stoics developed this perspective in different ways.

[16] The Hibeh Papyrus (c. 280–240 B.C.), containing an attack on the musical theories of Damon, written c. 390 B.C. English translation in Warren D. Anderson, *Ethos and Education in Greek Music* (Cambridge: Harvard UP, 1966) 147–149.

[17] Sextus Empiricus, *Math.* 6 ("Against the Musicians").

[18] In general see Marcello Gigante, *Philodemus in Italy: The Books from Herculaneum*, trans. by D. Obbink (Ann Arbor: Univ. of Michigan Press, 1995) 1–28; Elizabeth Asmis, "Philodemus' Epicureanism," *ANRW* II.36.4 (1990) 2370–73. See also now John T. Fitzgerald, D. Obbink, and G. Holland (eds.), *Philodemus and the New Testament* (Leiden: Brill, 2003) passim.

[19] Gigante, *Philodemus in Italy*, 29–37.

[20] Michael Erler, "Die Schule Epikurs," *Die Hellenistische Philosophie*, Vol. 4.1 of *Die Philosophie der Antike* (Basel: Schwabe, 1994) 1.313. The fullest discussion of the contents in English is Anderson, *Ethos and Education*, 153–176. I use the edition of Annemarie Jeanette Neubecker, *Philodemus Über die Musik IV. Buch: Text, Übersetzung, und Kommentar* (Naples: Bibliopolis, 1986) and for other fragments Ioannes Kemke, ed., *Philodemi De musica librorum quae exstant* (Leipzig: Teubner, 1884). The view put forward by Kemke,

especially those of Diogenes of Babylon.[21] Philodemus did not concern himself with the technical and aesthetic features of music but with ethos, the supposed effects of music on its hearers and their theoretical basis. Philodemus' approach of taking up arguments and refuting each one by one results in a less than logically organized counter position.[22] The absence of an English translation for more than selected short passages justifies a fairly full treatment of the contents, even though the fragmentary state of the text leaves many uncertainties.

Philodemus (or his source) summarizes musical activities as "to sing, to play the kithara, and to dance,"[23] or "singing and playing the kithara."[24] He refers to the principal instruments, "auloi and lyres,"[25] and names the percussion instruments—"tympana, rhombi, and cymbals."[26] Philodemus, like Philo, occasionally refers to three elements of music: "harmonies, melodies, and rhythms,"[27] "voice [or sound], pitch, and rhythm,"[28] or in citing Cleanthes, "measures, melodies, and rhythms,"[29] and referring to Archestratus, "the philosophy of music concerns voice, the nature of tone, intervals, and the like."[30] Most often he uses a twofold summary, "melodies and rhythms."[31] He speaks of the "kinds of harmonies,"[32] but when he refers to specific scales he names

---

that some of the fragments belonged to books 1 and 3, is no longer held. See John T. Fitzgerald, "Philodemus and the Papyri from Herculaneum: An Introduction," in *Philodemus and the New Testament* (n. 18 above), which gives a full summary of the contents.

[21] Diogenes is named in Book IV, col. 7, l. 24; col. 21, l. 19; col. 23, l. 28; (Neubecker, 46, 66, 69).

[22] Annemarie J. Neubecker, "Beobachtungen zu Argumentationsweise und Stil Philodems in der Schrift 'Über die Musik', Buch IV," *Cronache ercolanesi* 13 (1983) 85. The article develops other features of Philodemus' style in the treatise.

[23] Kemke,17, VIII 142, ll. 4–6 and Book IV, col. 16, ll. 27–28 (Neubecker,60). The translations of Philodemus are my own.

[24] Kemke, 7, IX 70, ll. 11–12; 55, VIII 7, ll. 13–14.

[25] Kemke, 28, XI 89, ll. 1–2.

[26] Kemke, 49, VII 190, ll. 3–4. Description of these instruments in M. L. West, *Ancient Greek Music* (Oxford: Clarendon, 1992) 122–126.

[27] Kemke, 23, XI 92, ll. 3–5; cf. 1, IX 69, ll. 11–13.

[28] Kemke, 22, VIII 22, ll.12–13.

[29] Book IV, col. 28, ll. 10–11 (Neubecker, 75).

[30] Book IV, col. 23, ll. 14–19 (Neubecker, 69).

[31] E.g., Book IV, col. 18, ll. 15–16; col. 22, l. 14; col. 26, ll. 6–7, 16–17; col. 27, ll.18–19; col. 29, l l. 42–43 (Neubecker, 62, 68, 72, 73, 74, 78); Kemke, 49, VII 190, ll. 4–5; cf. "to know rhythm and harmony," Kemke, 2, IX 69, ll. 31–31; 7, XI 80, ll. 9–11; cf. "meters and melodies," Book IV, col. 17, l. 11 (Neubecker, 60). Sextus Empiricus, *Math.* 6.38, too, considers music the science of melodies and rhythms.

[32] Book IV, col. 27, ll. 2–3.

only the "enharmonic and chromatic."[33] In addition there is a reference to "making the rhythmic and orderly movements of the hands, feet, and other members of the body."[34]

Occasions for Music

A large part of what survives of Book 4 concerns occasions when music was used in Greek life, which were appealed to as part of the arguments for the effects on music on human behavior. The types of activities and songs related to them include encomia, wedding songs, love songs, laments, war songs, athletic songs, dramatic choruses, and women's dances.[35] Philodemus denies that the music accomplishes its alleged usefulness in these areas. The use of music by those launching ships, harvesting grain, trampling grapes, and rowing ships makes the work easier by relaxation and the admixture of pleasure but does not set the work in motion, present the actions to the mind, nor cause them.[36]

Occasions from literature and history with which music was associated are given attention because they were already cited by Philodemus' opponent. The erotic drive, with reference to several authors, is declared to be "a great evil" that is stimulated "by the voice and eyes, not melodies." One is corrupted by thoughts, not melody, although music may "distract and make a person heedless just as sexual pleasure and drunkeness do."[37] Music is no more connected to the symposium than it is to erotic vice, for Philodeumus does "not consider there to be a so-called banquet virtue [or excellence]." Homer indeed indicates

---

[33] Book IV, col. 2, ll. 15–16 (Neubecker, 39). Sextus Empiricus, who generally follows Philodemus rather closely, in *Math.* 6.39–51 has a fuller discussion of the technical elements of music.

[34] Kemke, 30, XI 88, ll. 4–7. See also below in Philo's description of the Therapeutae.

[35] Book IV, col. 5, l. 13 – col. 7, l. 22 (Neubecker, 43–46); cf. Kemke, 14, XI 74, ll. 5–46 for the bridal song, music for war (trumpet, auloi), gymnastics, athletics (for the pentathlon, aulos). Cf. Ps. Plutarch, *Mus.* 26–27 (*Mor.* 1140b–f) for music in education, war, athletic contests, and the theater. Athenaeus, *Deip.* 620a–631c also takes up the occasions when music was employed in Greek life. The similar topics (hymns, private and public celebrations, war, travel, sailing, rowing, and other manual labors, and mourning) in Aristides Quintilianus, *Mus.* 2.6.61 suggest a common topos in reference to music. Cf. Philostratus, *Vita Apol.* 5.21.

[36] Book IV, col. 8, ll. 4–25, 32 (Neubecker, 47–48). See below on the acceptance of pleasure as an effect of music. Cf. Sextus Empiricus, *Math.* 6.21–24 on music diverting the mind but not causing the benefits claimed for it.

[37] Book IV, col. 13, l. 4 – col. 15, l.44 (Neubecker, 55–59).

that there is a kinship of music with symposia, but this is because there is "a need to relax and play at symposia."[38] Incidents in history when music was claimed to overcome civil discord are cited below.

The approach taken in dealing with the argument for a likeness of music to friendship is typical—to affirm that music produces pleasure, to deny its essential relationship to the topic, to give priority to thoughts and words, and to grant that even if music contributes something to the topic, it does not have the benefits the opponent claims: "Music is useful for pleasure but not for friendship." "Melodies and rhythms do not relax and cheer, but the thoughts combined with them." "Even if [music] should make us relaxed and joyful, … , we would not consider it alone to be the cause of friendship and harmony."[39]

The place of music in education receives only passing mention in the surviving fragments. "[The argument that] music was received by the ancients for the training of children in a model of virtue has produced a discussion …" The effect of a musical culture or its absence happens for some persons, but not for others. "They were formed beforehand into the virtue they would have later as men."[40] A detached fragment refers to the main elements of Greek education: "gymnastics for the body and music for the soul."[41] Philodemus' opponent regarded musical speculation as "almost equal to the literary critic" and the "writing of music to be almost equal to the art of poetry and grammar." Philodemus disputes this but even allowing a similarity to acting and the art of delivery, since "all these things have an obvious likeness to wit and intellect," more is to be said on behalf of the arts of painting and sculpture.[42] His own viewpoint is expressed in this statement: "To attain theoretical musical knowledge of excellent and bad, or of fitting and unfitting melodies does not itself educate, but philosophy working through musical training does."[43]

---

[38] Book IV, col. 16, l. 1 – col. 17, l. 35 (Neubecker, 59–61); symposia are discussed also in col. 11, l. 4 – col. 12, l. 10 (Neubecker, 51–53); cf. Kemke, 16, XI 72, ll. 1–36 on love-making and banquet virtue. Ps. Plutarch, *Mus.* 43 (*Mor.* 1146e–f) argues that Homer did not mean that music is useful only for pleasure.

[39] Book IV, col. 17, l.35 – col. 18, l. 33 (Neubecker, 61–62).

[40] Book IV, col. 12, ll. 12–35 (Neubecker, 54); cf. Kemke, 7, XI 80, ll. 9–12, "professing an understanding of harmony and rhythm to be useful for education [or culture]." See references below for Philo on music in education.

[41] Kemke, 3–4, IX 73, ll. 8–10; cf. Plato, *Leges* 795d; in *Resp.* 410, 441–442 the view is advanced that both are for the benefit of the soul.

[42] Book IV, col. 22, l. 10 – col. 23, l.13 (Neubecker, 68–69).

[43] Kemke, 42–43, VII 187, ll. 5–11.

Music for the Gods

Philodemus refers to his fuller treatment in book three of the theme "Concerning Music for Divinity" and refers to one [Plato? Aristotle? Diogenes?] who says, "Lawful and excellent music was appointed first for the sake of honor to the divine and then for the education of the freeborn."[44] He gives a fair amount of attention in *On Music* to the argument for the usefulness of music from its presence in religion. Happy to claim a thought shared by others, he affirms right off that "the divine has no need of any honor, but it is natural to us to honor it, especially with holy thoughts." If music profits any group, it is the populace, but the musical practices vary in different places and circumstances, and the music is now performed by hired persons. Many other things besides music are involved in cult, so there is no essential connection of the divine with music.[45] Diogenes had claimed that the hymns sung in Ephesus and by the choruses in Sparta were more impressive because accompaniment was added and so showed the power of music to move us, but Philodemus responds that for one person the addition of accompaniment added "only the pleasure of hearing" without pious or rational significance and for another person was impressive because of the honor to the gods or men and not on account of the melody.[46]

Diogenes also argued that since the divine is honored by many people through music there is a kinship between music and religion. Philodemus replied that on this premise "magic, the art of making crowns, preparation of unguents, breadmaking, even agriculture, construction, writing, art, and most occupations" would have to be considered as having a kinship with religion. "Honor occurs rather through the poems, and melody provides a triffling addition."[47] "No god was the inventor of music." Music was not a gift of the gods but was a dis-

---

[44] Kemke, 12–13, IX 64, ll. 3–4, 8–13; Kemke cites as a parallel Ps. Plutarch, *Mus.* 27 (*Mor.* 1140d–f); note also Ptolemy, *Harm.* 3.7.100, "The gods are invoked with music and melody" (Barker, *Greek Musical Writings*, 2.379). Cf. Kemke, 25–26, XI 90, ll. 1–8 on the gods. Anderson, *Ethos and Education*, 162f. refers to Plato, *Laws* 670 and 803 but considers the main opponent here to be Diogenes, not Plato. Sextus Empiricus, *Math.* 6.18 similarly refers to arguments on behalf of music based on its presence in worship of the gods, its incitement to emulate the good, and its presence in rejoicing and in times of grief.
[45] Book IV, col. 4, l.3–41 (Neubecker, 41–42); the language is similar to that in the fragment cited in the preceding note.
[46] Book IV, col. 10, ll. 2–28 (Neubecker, 50).
[47] Book IV, col. 20, l. 28 – col. 21, l.23 (Neubecker, 65–66).

covery by human beings, "indeed it was learned gradually," belonging to the last phase of cultural development.[48] "Let it be said that no god is a musician," nor do the gods "stand in need of such things," "for barbarians suppose to honor the gods through these things," which are "out of place among the Greeks" and "have no kinship with religion."[49]

Debates over the Value of Music

The points made by his opponent that are controverted by Philodemus show not only his style of argument but also philosophical concerns. A weighty argument in the Graeco-Roman world was what was honored by the ancients. Philodemus claims that although this is "to be regarded as allowable proof of the useful to the uneducated, to the educated and even more to the philosopher it was a reproach. Divination is esteemed by the Stoics, as are thousands of other things that provide nothing good."[50] Democritus, "most learned of the ancients in natural phenomena," "says music to be comparatively recent, and he gives the cause saying that what is necessary is not put off but it comes into being out of superfluity." "Nevertheless, even if it be granted that [music] was most ancient, ... it seems that the foulest things were honored at the beginning."[51]

Another argument by the Stoic Diogenes is that "melody has by nature something stimulating and arousing to action." But, Philodemus replies, music is not like fire, "which has the nature to burn." "To be disposed to action means to set oneself in motion and to choose deliberately, but melody does not urge in the way a word [or reason] does nor is it understood to cause a deliberate choice."[52] Musical instinct does

---

[48] Book IV, col. 34, ll. 23–28 (Neubecker, 84); Erler, "Die Schule Epikurs," 314 (with reference to *De Poem.* book IV, col. 7, ll. 22–25), 315. Cf. Ps. Plutarch, *Mus.* 14 (*Mor.* 1136b) on music as an invention of the gods; specifically Apollo in 1135f.

[49] Book IV, col. 35, ll.15–28, 36–39 (Neubecker, 85, 86).

[50] Book IV, col. 10, ll. 28–40 (Neubecker, 50–51).

[51] Book IV, col. 36, l. 29 – col. 37, l. 3 (Neubecker, 87).

[52] Book IV, col. 7, l. 22 – col. 8, l. 3 (Neubecker, 46–47); cf. the view that "melody by nature is capable of moving and disposing to action"–Kemke, 15, XI 73, ll. 7–9. Kemke, 48, VIII 9, ll.16–20 refers to "pleasant things that are sought after naturally, not from teaching or custom but as it were automatically." Sextus Empiricus, *Math* 6.19–20 also denies that melodies are by nature stimulating or repressive, "but they are supposed to be such by us ourselves." Aristides Quintilianus, *Mus.* 2.4.55–56 is a response to those (such as Philodemus and Sextus Empiricus) who doubt whether everyone is moved by

not come by nature.[53]

Because of music's natural affinity with human beings, the claim was made that "Music has power for virtue and vice." Philodemus declares this view "unpersuasive," because "tunes are irrational" and irrational powers influence only irrational things.[54] Those philosophers who learned music did not do so because it was necessary to the attainment of the virtues.[55] On the other hand, Philodemus disputes the possibility that certain melodies are harmful to the composers, performers, and hearers "as if they were not becoming accustomed to shameful words, forms, and thoughts."[56]

Behind Diogenes of Babylon stood Damon, teacher of Pericles, whose ethical theory of music influenced Plato. A fragment from Philodemus has Damon advance the view that "music brings with it both virtues and pleasures."[57] Philodemus' opponent in the *De musica*, furthermore, affirms that music "somehow affects the disposition not only of the body but also of the soul." Philodemus disputes even the effect on the body, for the face of singers causes the ode rather than the ode causing the appearance, and the melody does not move the body, unless the melody is the pretense for this.[58] Much less was he prepared to accept that "some melodies arouse the understanding and stretch it for instruc-

---

melody; in 2.17.86 he overlooks them: "The fact that the soul is naturally stirred by the music of instruments is one that everybody knows" (Barker, *Greek Musical Writings*, 2.489).

[53] Erler, "Die Schule Epikurs," 314.

[54] Kemke, 38, VII 187, ll. 5–11; 55, VIII 7, ll. 15–17 associates singing and playing the kithara with courage, prudence, and justice; on the whole subject see L.P. Wilkinson, "Philodemus on *Ethos* in Music," *Classical Quarterly* 32 (1938) 174–181. Ps.Plutarch, *Mus.* frequently affirms the ethos theory of music. Even musical theorists, such as Aristoxenus, accepted the view that music makes persons morally better—*Elementa Harmonica* 2.31.15–30; cf. Ptolemy, *Harm.* 3.5.96–3.7.100 on the elements of music attuned to the different parts and activities of the soul and Aristides Quintilianus, *Mus.* 2.6.61, "The aim set for music is to help us towards virtue" (Barker, *Greek Musical Writings*, 2.465).

[55] Book IV, col. 25, ll. 12–31 (Neubecker, 71–72).

[56] Book IV, col. 32, ll. 4–21 (Neubecker, 81).

[57] Kemke, 7, IX 70, ll. 4–8; on Damon, see Anderson, *Ethos and Education*, 42, 74–81, 147–153, 161–162, 189–191 and Barker, *Greek Musical Writings*, 1.168–169. Aristides Quintilianus, *Mus.* 2.14.80 attributes to the followers of Damon the demonstration that melodies both instill a character previously absent and draw out a character previously hidden. Plato was concerned with the influence of music–*Leges* 669–670.

[58] Book IV, col. 9, ll. 1–15 (Neubecker, 48). Anderson, *Ethos and Education*, 165–166 examines the passage and considers "Less pardonable … his claim that music has no effect on the body."

tion and the fitting mode of life."⁵⁹ Rather, "We have the causes of our own proper habits not from without but from within."⁶⁰ Different persons react in different ways to the same melodies:

> It happens that according to certain predispositions there are received varied perceptions, but in regard to what is heard there is not any difference at all; but all perceive alike the same melodies and receive comparable pleasures.

Then citing different opinions of the enharmonic and chromatic scales, Philodemus observes, "Both sides import ideas that belong to neither scale," for "None of the attributed qualities belongs to either scale by its nature."⁶¹ Then comes a strong denial of the ethos theory of music:

> No melody as melody, being irrational, arouses that which is sluggish and at rest and leads it to its natural ethical disposition, nor does it calm into a quiet condition the soul carried away with disturbances. It does not turn it from one impulse to another nor bring an increase or diminution in an existing disposition. For music is not imitative, as some imagine, nor, as Diogenes thinks, does it have non-imitative similarities to ethical qualities and manifest such qualities as magnificence and humility, manliness and unmanliness, orderliness and rashness, any more than cookery. The different types of music do not contain different ethical qualities … in so far as the auditory perceptions are concerned.⁶²

The last part of the quotation refers to another viewpoint contradicted by Philodemus, the imitative theory of music.⁶³ No melody has its character by nature, only by convention.⁶⁴

To the claim that music improves the intellect because musicians in creating harmonies set boundaries, Philodemus answers that on the

---

⁵⁹ Book IV, col. 12, ll. 6–11 (Neubecker, 53).
⁶⁰ Kemke, 8, IX 70, ll. 3–6; Anderson, *Ethos and Education* 169.
⁶¹ Book IV, col. 2, ll. 5–36 (Neubecker, 38–39); the passage is studied favorably by Wilkinson, "Philodemus on *Ethos*," 177. Aristides Quintilianus, *Mus.* 2.4.56 also says music affects people differently, but Philodemus uses this against the ethical influences of music.
⁶² Book IV, col. 3, ll.10–41 (Neubecker, 40–41); Anderson, *Ethos and Education*, 163–165, 167–168. Cf. Kemke, 33, VIII 17, ll. 8–15, "One would consider as exceedingly foolish those who say that we are made mild by music, our souls being softened and their savagery taken away, for only the word that teaches … does this." On the other side, Athenaeus, *Deip.* 623f–624a cites the view that music "educates characters and calms people of turbulent disposition and those whose thoughts are wayward."
⁶³ Wilkinson, "Philodemus on *Ethos*" 176; Anderson, *Ethos and Education*, 82, 88, 95–103; cf. Kemke, 45, XI 82, ll. 3–10 and Book IV, col. 32, ll. 30–33 (Neubecker, 81).
⁶⁴ Erler, "Die Schule Epikurs," 314.

basis of the argument, all things would improve the intellect, for other arts in a similar manner undertake classifications.[65]

Another passage refuting an association of music with virtue leads into a discussion of justice and so the relation of music to community life.

> It has turned out now that the notion of some concerning justice is ridiculous. For it is unthinkable that sounds which stimulate only the hearing of what is irrational contribute something to a disposition of the soul that speculates on the things profitable and unprofitable for the political life shared with one another and of the things that one chooses and another avoids.

Philodemus then corrects the appeal to Plato as saying music is of service to justice. Rather Plato said that justice is analogous to music, not that music is just or the just is music, nor does either contribute to the special knowledge of the other.[66] Since on the Stoic view all the virtues are inseparable, a refutation of the usefulness of music to one virtue means it contributes nothing to all.

Philodemus thus attacks the prevalent philosophical ideas of a kinship between music and the soul and between music and the political community. He also challenges the theory that there is a correlation between music and celestial powers.

> They talk nonsense who speak concerning the likeness of music to astronomical phenomena. For let it be granted that the movement of the sun and moon and the distance between them are analogous to the distribution of notes and the zodiac is analogous to the distribution of the chords. But this is not a proof of kinship on account of the fact that many things offering such an analogy differ to an even greater extent. To perceive the differentiated arrangement that exists in heaven seems to supply nothing profitable for the possession itself of virtues and the correction of character.[67]

---

[65] Book IV, col. 21, l.24 – col. 22, l. 9 (Neubecker, 67).

[66] Book IV, col. 24, ll. 9–35 (Neubecker, 70–71); see also below on the argument in regard to music bringing an end to civil discord. Plato, *Resp.* 432–433, 441–444. Justice was part of the discussion that music theorists gave to the correlation between the soul and music—Ptolemy, *Harm.*3.5.97–98.

[67] Book IV, col. 30, ll. 6–24 (Neubecker, 78); cf. Sextus Empiricus, *Math.* 6.30, 37 for the denial of a correlation between celestial phenomena and ethical theory. The viewpoint opposed here is well preserved in later theorists of music–Ptolemy, *Harm.* 3.8.100–111 (he does not suppose, as some others did, that the celestial bodies emit sounds, but they are arranged in accord with harmonic ratios like those in music); Aristides Quintilianus, *Mus.* 3.9.107–27.133.

Philodemus proceeds to claim "no one of the musicians themselves recognized these things," which derived from the utterances of "some Pythagoreans."[68]

Philodemus labelled melody "irrational" (ἄλογος).[69] Music, like other things perceived by the senses, brings no cognitive content. Originally "music" to the Greeks was a unity of word, tune, and dance (or gestures),[70] but by Philodemus' time "musician" was commonly used of instrumentalists.

> Not only myself, but also common usage and even Aristoxenos, to name the model of the musician, use the word musicians for those who produce sounds that have no meaning, such as those made by instruments and by humming … Simonides and Pindar were both musicians and poets; as musicians they composed what has no signification but as poets they composed words … Therefore, one calls such a person a musician, since everything profitable is made from the thoughts; the bare melodies and rhythms I say to be useful for nothing.[71]

This narrowing down of music to the melody and rhythm explains, according to Philodemus, why some in his time attributed to tunes what properly belonged to another element of "music," namely the words. For Philodemus, one must distinguish what someone did as a poet and what as a musician. The things said concerning virtue "are of service to the thoughts, not to the melodies and rhythms. These things are drawn in superfluously, even more as a diversion, being blended together so that the audience may pay attention to the thoughts."[72]

Different Types of Music and their Effects

Not everyone agreed with the limitation of the word musician to those who dealt only with instruments.

---

[68] Book IV, col. 31, ll. 13–19 (Neubecker, 80). See below for Philo on the Pythagorean origins of this common idea.

[69] Book IV, col. 3, l. 12; col. 19, l. 15; col. 24, l. 12 (Neubecker, 40, 63, 71); Wilkinson, "Philodemus on *Ethos*," 178.

[70] Neubecker, "Beobachtungen," 86; Wilkinson, "Philodemus on *Ethos*," 175.

[71] Book IV, col. 29, ll. 14–43 (Neubecker, 76–78); cf. col. 26, ll. 27–35 (Neubecker, 73). Contrast Ps. Aristotle, *Prob.* 19.27, "Even if there is a melody without words, it has ethical character." Sextus Empiricus, *Math.* 6.1 gives three senses of the word music: "science of melodies, notes, and rhythm-making," instrumental skill, or figuratively correctness in any performance.

[72] Book IV, col. 26, ll. 1–14 (Neubecker, 72–73).

> I have heard of some who say we are stupid for thinking some philoso-
> phers or learned musicians to say melodies and rhythms without ver-
> bal significance encourage to virtue, when (actually) men consider the
> words set to melody and rhythm to contribute to this, while indeed Plato
> expressly battles with philosophers as uneducated; and they marvel if we
> should say the composer of instrumental music is a musician, claim musi-
> cians to teach things that do not have verbal significance, or do not wish
> to call Pindar, Simonides, and all the other composers of songs musi-
> cians.[73]

Later in the passage Philodemus deals with the appeal to the Stoic
philosopher Cleanthes, who was quoted as saying that

> Poetic and musical examples are better than the word of the one who is
> capable to proclaim the divine and human things of philosophy, since the
> bare word does not have kindred speech with the great gods, but mea-
> sures, melodies, and rhythms especially touch the truth of speculations
> about the divine—of which it is not easy to find something more laugh-
> able [according to Philodemus]. [Cleanthes says] The thoughts [alone]
> are not helpful, but when they are set to music, the incitement comes
> from both, for fitting things come not by thoughts about them but are
> greater with the melodies.[74]

Philodemus explains what truth there is in this claim is due to the
pleasure and distraction afforded by the words exhibited in this way
and to other circumstances. "There is no one who would not die
laughing upon hearing advice or consolation to those grieving being
given with an ode and some instruments."[75]

Philodemus repeatedly asserts that it is not the musical aspects that
produce the effects attributed to it, but the texts, the words.[76] For
instance, out of the various arguments, he says that it is "the word
alone," not the music, that effects "upright conduct" or "bad practices" in love.[77] With regard to religion, one of the fragments raises the
question, "Are some of those possessed by the gods who are charmed
by the aulos somehow brought to a certain condition, somewhere and
in some way indeed, to quit their frightful fancies by the impact of the
voice alone, since the melody does not exhibit such power?"[78] Or again,

---

[73] Book IV, col. 26, ll. 14–35 (Neubecker, 73).
[74] Book IV, col. 28, ll. 1–22 (Neubecker, 75); cf. col. 11, ll. 14–24 for the association of
enjoyment with persuasion in poetry and music.
[75] Book IV, col. 28, ll.22–41 (Neubecker, 75–76). Literally, "poured out with laughter."
[76] Neubecker, "Beobachtungen" 86.
[77] Book IV, col. 15, ll. 1–5 (Neubecker, 58); cf. col. 13, ll. 16–21 (Neubecker, 55).
[78] Kemke, 49–50, VIII 154, ll. 7–15.

Philodemus' opponent had appealed to occasions when civil strife at Sparta were allayed by the music of Thaletas, Terpander, and others. Philodemus had reservations about the historical details, but

> Even if we allow that the god [Apollo] commanded the Spartans to be of the same mind with those who attended them, it is much easier to find more persuasive that the one who chose to divert them with stirring music and who gave them the commands concerning these affairs was also the one persuading them through the words that were sung. ... If indeed each episode happened, they persuaded through words well-arranged poetically, not through melodies, and they would have attained their purpose better if they had tried to change minds without use of musical accompaniment.[79]

When other considerations are removed, there remains one function for the melodic and rhythmic aspects of music to which allusion is made in the above passages–to give pleasure. This, of course, was a good Epicurean perspective.[80] Epicurus himself was known to have gone to the theatre to hear singers to the kithara and performers on the auloi, but he discouraged the study and discussion of the technical aspects of music, especially at symposia.[81] Philodemus did the same. His slogan was "Everything for rest and enjoyment."[82] With reference to Damon, Philodemus declares that "They speak falsely who say that music alone of the arts is altogether beneficial," for other skills are truly beneficial and helpful to those in need, while music "only brings pleasure physically, not of necessity."[83] He considered the practice required for musi-

---

[79] Book IV, col. 18, l. 33 – col. 20, l. 27 (Neubecker, 63–65). The last phrase may be translated "by prose" but "without musical accompaniment" (as suggested here) ia another meaning of the phrase. In view of the larger context, I consider the latter to be the more likely meaning. Cf. Sextus Empiricus, *Math.* 6.28—melody only gives pleasure, but poetry, which is concerned with thoughts, is able to benefit and to teach prudence.

[80] Sextus Empiricus, *Math.* 6.27 invokes Epicurus as denying Plato's contention that music contributes to happiness. Plato, with everyone else, conceded that music brings pleasure (the art of aulos and lyre playing seeks only pleasure—*Gorgias* 501–502; "pleasure is the characteristic of all music"—*Leges* 802), but wanted it to be the music that delights men of virtue and education—*Leges* 657–659; cf. Aristotle, *Pol.* 1339a. Aristides Quintilianus, *Mus.* 2.6.61 summed up the non-Epicurean philosophical viewpoint: "Not all delight is to be condemned, but neither is delight itself the objective of music" (Barker, *Greek Musical Writings*, 2:465).

[81] Plutarch, *Non posse vivi* 13 (*Mor.* 1095c–1096c); cf. Diogenes Laertius 10.120, quoting Epicurus' advice to converse about music and poetry but not to engage in the work of writing poems.

[82] Kemke, 37, VIII 148, ll. 6–7.

[83] Book IV, col. 33, ll. 11–22 (Neubecker, 82–83).

cal contests and the effort involved in having something to say about music at symposia as involving too much pain ("For I allow that the pleasure is not necessary, nor is the learning and study that we might enjoy ourselves"). He too considered the speculative aspects of music to be a labor to be avoided. Enjoyment and reputation can be found in other pursuits.[84]

Philo

Philo the Alexandrian Jewish philosopoher (ca. 25/20 BCE – ca. 45/50 CE) comes from the next generation after Philodemus and so might have been well-versed in the kinds of technical issues and debates that had gone before.

Occasions for Music and the Types Used

Philo in several passages takes note of the occasions in which music had a place in human life, both pagan and Jewish. Some of those passages not discussed in other connections below will be noted here. Since Philo often uses ὑμνέω to mean "to praise" or "to extoll" with no musical connotation, "song," "ode," or "hymn" are used with it where the musical sense is intended, such as happiness results in "hymning a hymn of joy".[85]

In Roman Alexandria, social entertainment afforded many opportunities for different types of music; often these include forms of instrumental accompaniment. Philo mentions his own presence in a theater, observing the exciting effect on the audience of "a single tune sung by the tragic actors on the stage or played by the kitharodists."[86] The emperor Gaius enjoyed dancers, the singers to the kithara, and choruses.[87] The torture of Jews in Alexandria under the prefect Flaccus was accompanied by "dancers, mimes, aulos players, and other entertainments of theatrical competitions."[88] The description of the incident

---

[84] Book IV, col. 37, l. 8 – col. 38, l. 30 (Neubecker, 88–89); on music speculation, cf. col. 23, ll. 13–27 (Neubecker, 69); cf. the observation that those who lack natural capacity are not made better by music—col. 33, ll. 27–40 (Neubecker, 83).

[85] *Leg. all.* II.21.82. Cf. *Det. pot.* 43.157: the truly good things of life include the pleasure of hearing "all kinds of melodious sounds;" *Post.* 47.163: the poets "sing."

[86] *Ebr.* 43.177; cf. *Leg. all.* 2.18.75, quoted below.

[87] *Gaium* 7.42. See further below on music as bringing pleasure.

[88] *Flacc.* 10.85.

of the golden calf (Ex 32:6, 17–19) includes reference to the wine song of revelry and in contrast the funeral chant.[89] Instruments also had their place in pagan religious festivals. A long description of activities includes "musical contests, … nightlong celebrations with auloi and kitharas."[90] In reference to the ruler cult, Philo notes "the well trained choruses singing paeans to Gaius" and "honoring him with hymns" when he assumed the appearances of Apollo and Dionysus.[91] Philo also refers to the mythological basis of this religious use of music among Greeks, the birth of hymnody from Memory.[92] Music occurred in Jewish religious activities, of which more below, but we note now references to the use of trumpets to announce Rosh Hashanah,[93] to music in victory celebrations, particularly a "victory hymn,"[94] and the association of hymns with thanksgiving.[95]

Philo's knowledge of and interest in music came from its place in the educational curriculum.[96] In a first person passage about his own education, Philo mentions that as preliminary to philosophy he studied grammar, geometry, and music.[97] Philo considered philosophy the crown of human intellectual activity by bringing "knowledge" (ἐπιστήμη),[98] but its study was preceded by "the preliminary studies," the *enkyklios paideia* or general education that one received before profes-

---

[89] *Ebr.* 24.95; other references to singing and choruses in this episode in *Mos.* II.31.162; II.49.270; *Spec. leg.* III.22.125.

[90] *Gaium* 2.12.

[91] *Gaium* 13.96.

[92] *Plant.* 30.129.

[93] *Dec.* 30.159; *Spec. leg.* II.31.188, 192; its use in war is noted in 190. The trumpet "was not used for musical purposes but only for giving signals, especially for battle and in certain ritual and ceremonial contexts;" so West, *Ancient Greek Music*, 118.

[94] *Ebr.* 28.110; "victory song" in 30.115; "the victory and thanksgiving hymn" contrasted with the dirge of defeat in 31.121; *Mos.* 1.51.284; *Agr.* 17.79, quoted below.

[95] *Ebr.* 27.105–"thanksgiving hymn"; *Somn.* II.5.38—"the thankful person takes in hand praises, encomia, hymns, blessings both in speech and song"; *Somn.* II.41.268—"to give thanks and to hymn"; *Plant.* 33.135. For the theme of thanksgiving in Philo, see J. LaPorte, *Eucharistia in Philo* (New York: Edwin Mellen, 1983).

[96] H. I. Marrou, *A History of Education in Antiquity* (New York: Sheed and Ward, 1956) 188–198; Plato, *Leges* 812d–e for his recommendations on musical education; cf. *Resp.* 401d for the potency of musical training because rhythm and harmony penetrate the innermost parts of the soul; Aristotle, *Pol.* 1339b assigns music a place in education for purposes of instruction, amusement, and proper conduct of life; Ps. Plutarch, *Mus.* 26 (*Mor.* 1140b); Aristides Quintilianus, *Mus.* 2.3.55, "The very young could not be educated through bare words, which contain instruction but no pleasure."

[97] *Cong.* 14.74–76; cf. *Agr.* 31.136–139 for philosophy following grammar, music, and geometry.

[98] *Cong.* 25.142.

sional or specialized training. Philo gave a positive value to this general education in spite of his awareness of the dangers Greek culture posed to Jewish faith.[99] He described general education by saying that parents are benefactors of their children, for "they benefitted the body through gymnastic and athletic training ... and the soul through letters, numbers, geometry, and music, and the whole of philosophy."[100]

Another summary of the educational curriculum gives the benefits of the different branches of study: grammar interprets poetry and history; geometry produces a sense of equality according to proportions; "excellent music by rhythm, meter, and melody, heals what is disproportionate, immoderate, and discordant in us"; rhetoric teaches critical thinking and fluency of speech.[101] Moses received this kind of education, and more: "Arithmetic and geometry, rhythmic, harmonic, and metric theory, the whole subject of music through the use of instruments and textbooks, ... and philosophy"; Greeks taught him the rest of the *enkyklios paideia*, and those from other nations taught him other languages and astrology.[102] Philo sometimes summarized the content of education as "grammar, geometry, and music,"[103] but for him "grammar and music [are] the most excellent branches of learning,"[104] and not just grammar, as most would have said. Particularly significant for Philo's evaluation of music is that he ranks it with philosophy as representing those elements of culture that are "like truly divine images of the Godly soul."[105]

His study of music in the educational curriculum gave Philo his knowledge of the technical aspects of music.[106] "She was called music— beautiful in rhythm, harmony, and melody—and from her I begat diatonic, chromatic, and enharmonic scales, conjunct and disjunct melodies, having harmonies of the fourth, fifth, and octave intervals."[107]

---

[99] Alan Mendelson, *Secular Education in Philo of Alexandria* (Cincinnati: Hebrew Union College, 1982) 83.

[100] *Spec. leg.* II.40.230. For this division, see above on Philodemus.

[101] *Cher.* 30.105; cf. *Cong.* 4.15–18 and *Spec. leg.* I.62.343, from which parts are quoted below.

[102] *Mos.* I.5.21–24.

[103] *Mut.* 11.80; 26.146, in varying orders; cf. *Agr.* 31.136–138 and "letters, numbers, and music" in *Spec. leg.* I.61.336.

[104] *Op. mund.* 42.126; cf. *Cong.* 25.142; Ps. Plutarch, *Mus.* 2 (*Mor.* 1131d) takes music as the second skill after grammar.

[105] *Cher.* 27.93.

[106] Mendelson, *Secular Education in Philo*, 15; Feldman, "Philo's Views," 517–519.

[107] *Cong.* 14.76; almost the same classifications in *Agr.* 31.137, except that the three

Rhythm is the one constant in a threefold classification of the components of music; melody, meter, and harmony, in that order of frequency,
vie for the remaining two places.[108] The different types of scales or
melodies and harmonies to which Philo refers are discussed in ancient
Greek technical works on music.[109]

Effects of Music

Music was important in shaping culture because of its effects. "Music
will lead the discordant into concord, charming the unrhythmic with
its rhythms, the inharmonious with its harmony, and the out of tune
and unmelodious with its melody."[110] Here Philo espouses the "ethos
theory" favored by Stoics and Platonists but repudiated by Philodemus,
as we saw above.[111] The positive effects of music resulted in harmony
of the soul and of the whole person. Music contributed both to the
realization of this harmony and serving as a comparison for its presence or absence.[112] Music can influence how human nature comes to
expression.

---

main parts are "rhythm, meter, and melody" (see note after next); in more summary
fashion *Somn.* I.5.28; I.35.205; and *Spec. leg.* I.62.342; cf. *Leg. all.* III.41.122; *Post.* 31.104;
Somn. II.4.27–28. On the three kinds of "scales" or *genera*, cf. Archytas (in Ptolemy, *Harm.*
30–31), Aristoxenus, *El. Harm.* 2.44.20ff. (conjunct and disjunct tetrachords in 3.1); and
Ps. Plutarch, *Mus.* 32 (*Mor.* 1142d).

[108] Philo has various formulations of the three main elements usually using three out
of the following four—rhythm, harmony, meter, and melody. See *Cong.* 4.16; cf. Plato,
Resp. 398, "a song or ode has three parts—the words, the melody, and the rhythm"; so
also *Leges* 669a; "harmony and rhythm" in *Leges* 670b. Cf. Ps. Plutarch, *Mus.* 35 (*Mor.*
1144a) for the note, time, and syllable striking the ear together. Cf. *Cher.* 30.105; *Spec. leg.*
I.62.342; *Sob.* 8.36; *Vita cont.* 3.29; "melodies, meters, and rhythm" in *Spec. leg.* I.62.342–
343 (where "harmonies and consonances" have a different reference); *Spec. leg.* I.5.28;
Mos. I.5.23.

[109] Feldman, "Philo's Views," 518–519 gives references; West, *Ancient Greek Music*, 160–
189.

[110] *Cong.* 4.16. An almost identical passage says, "Song and speech are healthful and
curative medicines, song charming the passions and controlling the unrhythmic in
us with its rhythms, the unmelodious with its melodies, and the immoderate with its
measures ... Belief in the musicians and poets becomes habitual in those well educated"
(*Spec. leg.* I.62.343).

[111] For another statement of the ethos theory of music, cf. *Cher.* 30.105 cited above;
cf. Plato, *Prot.* 326a–b; *Resp.* 401d; Aristotle, *Pol.* 1340a–b; Athenaeus, *Deip.* 623f–624a
(including a reference to Theophrastus as saying music cures diseases).

[112] For the Greek theory of musical ethos, Anderson, *Ethos and Education in Greek Music.*
Plato, *Phaedo* 85–86 on the soul as a *harmonia*; Ps. Plutarch, *Mus.* 42 (*Mor.* 1146d) on
music as first giving thanks to the gods and second making the soul harmonically well

The almost magical power of music to calm and harmonize a person also made it dangerous. It was a commonplace to recognize that music brings pleasure:

> The aulos, the kithara, and every kind of instrument please the hearing; so do the tuneful sounds of creatures without reason—swallows, nightingales, and other birds that make music—and the euphony of rational beings, singing to the kithara in comedy, tragedy and other theatrical productions.[113]

But music was also associated with unworthy pleasures: myriads every day fill up the theatres where they honor "those who play the kithara and sing to its accompaniment and all the effeminate and unmanly music, approving the dancers and other mimes."[114] In contrast to Jewish festivals, the seductive power of such types of music "through the ears arouse ungovernable lusts"[115] and advance idolatry.[116]

More often than speaking of the effects of music on a person's inner well being, Philo uses music to provide the illustration for harmony or the lack thereof in an individual. Human beings are mixtures of the divine and the mortal, "blended together and harmonized according to the proportions of perfect music."[117] As with Plato this inner harmony is achieved by the reason ruling and guiding the senses.[118] Choral imagery describes the internal harmony that Philo considers the human ideal:

---

adjusted. Cf. *Plant.* 38.159: At one time poets and others inspired by the Muses "did not sweeten and enfeeble their hearers with rhythmic sounds, but they revived any faculty of the mind that was weakened and broken and they harmonized with the instruments of nature and virtue whatever of the mind that was out of tune."

[113] *Leg. all.* II.18.75; for the exciting effects of music, cf. *Leg. all.* 3.78.221. See above on Philodemus for music bringing pleasure. Compare *Abr.* 29.148, 150: "We get pleasure from hearing very melodious sounds, and this can be good, being linked with philosophy."

[114] *Agr.* 8.35. A tradition of classifying music as male or female was worked out extensively by Aristides Quintilianus, *Mus.* 2.8.66–19.92; Barker, *Greek Musical Writings*, 2.470 n. 71.

[115] *Spec. leg.* II.32.193.

[116] *Spec. leg.* I.5.28–29. See above on occasions when music was employed in pagan society.

[117] *Mut.* 34.184. Cf. *Q. Ex.* 2.38 (trans. by Ralph Marcus in LCL, *Supplement* II: 81).: "Disonance from decency [virtue] and disharmony are death to the soul. Therefore ... as in an all-musical chorus with the blended voices of all one should play music in harmonious measures of modulation and with skilled fingers, seeking to show (the harmony) not so much in sound as in mind;" *Fuga* 3.22.: Gen 31:27 is applied to the person who does not share in the good things of God: his music is unmusical, and "his kitharas, not instruments but the deeds of life, lack melody and harmony."

[118] E.g., *Resp.* 431, 439–441; Aristotle and the Stoics agreed.

> When the soul enters the intellectual, divine, and truly holy place, the senses aided by virtue and indeed our whole being may join in the hymn just as when a large and melodious chorus sings together one harmonious melody from the different voices blended together, the thoughts of the mind inspiring the preludes—for the leaders of this chorus are the thoughts of the mind—while the senses sing along together the subsequent parts, which resemble the role of the individual chorus members.[119]

Musical language provides the words to describe the union of the gifts of king, lawgiver, high priest, and prophet in Moses.[120] For ordinary human beings, this harmony pertains to the agreement in good between thoughts, words, and deeds. Observance of the Ten Commandments with "good intentions, wholesome words, and diligent actions" result in the soul being "an instrument that makes music harmoniously in all its parts for a melodious life and blameless concert."[121] Similarly, "If, like tuning all the good sounds of a lyre, one succeeded in bringing speech into harmony with the mind and the mind with the deed, such a person would be considered perfect and in harmony with the truth."[122]

Harmony in Human Nature and the Cosmos

Philo used instrumental analogies for all elements of human nature. "The soul harmonized musically is like a lyre … ; [the wise man] keeping it in equal tension strikes and plucks it (ἐπιψάλλειν) melodiously. For the soul is the most perfect instrument fashioned by nature, the archetype (ἀρχέτυπος) of those made by hands."[123] Similarly, Philo con-

---

[119] *Mig.* 18.104; cf. *Ebr.* 30.116–117 and *Deus imm.* 6.24–25 below on the harmony of the soul. This passage is relevant to the discussion below of the manner in which songs were sung.

[120] *Mos.* II.1.7.

[121] *Spec. leg.* IV.25.134; cf. *Deus imm.* 6.25 for this inner harmony expressed in deeds and *Ebr.* 30.117 for it expressed in words; cf. Plato, *Lach.* 188d for harmony of words and deeds better than the harmony of the lyre.

[122] *Post.* 24.88. Cf. *Q. Ex.* 2.20, For God "wishes him who philosophizes in accordance with Him to be a harmony of all sounds like a musical instrument with no discord or dissonance in any part but with one and the same consonance and harmony, of will with word and of word with deed and of deed with both of these" (LCL, *Philo Supplement* II:59–60); *Mos.* 1.6.29.

[123] *Deus imm.* 6.24–25; for the comparison of the soul to a lyre cf. *Cher.* 31.110; *Ebr.* 30.116. The quotations above show that Philo often compared the soul to a chorus; the analogy of a human being to a lyre found expression in Greek musical theorists like Aristoxenus—Annie Bélis, "La théorie de l'âme chez Aristoxène de Tarente," *Revue*

sidered both the mind and the senses as instruments, and the goal was proper harmony of the two.[124] Hence, the confusion of tongues at the tower of Babel offered Philo much opportunity to consider the human condition.[125]

The harmony of the self was extended to the harmony of the community. Indeed, in Gen 11 the primary reference is to the peoples of the earth. As in persons without the gift of music the vocal organ is tuned to disharmony, so the people of Babel were in harmony and agreement, with no discordant voice, in the doing of iniquity.[126] But this is not the way things should be. The city is like a soul, and the best constitution is like a hymn to God.[127] The unity of the whole people is a symphony.[128]

Corresponding to human harmony was cosmic harmony. The Pythagoreans, followed by Plato and then by musical theorists, spoke of the "music of the spheres" and posited the mathematical correspondences of the relations of the heavenly bodies with the ratios of musical intervals.[129] In some passages Philo combines human harmony with the celestial concert. In a striking statement about the created

---

de philologie, de littérature et d'histoire anciennes 59 (1985) 239–246. Note below for heavenly bodies and the human voice as archetypes of music and of instruments.

[124] *Agr.* 17.80, quoted below. Cf. *Ebr.* 30.116: The soul is like an instrument in which a single note out of tune can destroy the harmony, but "it is a symphony when all the keys of courage and every virtue are combined and produce one harmonious melody."

[125] He took the words of Gen 11:6, "the earth was all one lip and one voice," as referring to the peoples' agreement (*symphonia*) in evil deeds, but he then applied it to the multitude of evils in individuals: "especially when the symphony [or unison of voice] within is disharmonious, dissonant, and discordant"; "the symphony of our self-chosen evils"; or in contrast "the symphony of virtues, all harmonious and musical." See *Conf.* 5.15. (cf. 15.67); 7.21 (cf. 18.83); 11.43.

[126] *Conf.* 19.150

[127] *Conf.* 23.108, following the reading of the manuscripts, but see the note in LCL, Vol. 4, 68. On the place of music in establishing and sustaining community, see Plato, *Resp.* 424c; *Leges* 701a–b.

[128] *Conf.* 13.55, 58: "We like musical instruments with all the notes perfectly in tune echo with our voices all the lessons we have heard, speaking no word and practising no deed that is out of tune or out of harmony;" cf. *Somn.* II.41.270: When wisdom is discovered, "all the people will sing not with one part of music but with all its harmonies and melodies."

[129] Plato, *Resp.* 530d–531b; cf. *Tim.* 34b–36d on the musical structure of the soul of the universe; Ps. Plutarch, *Mus.* 44 (*Mor.* 1147a) says Pythagoras and Plato claimed that the movement of the stars came about through the influence of music; Ptolemy, *Harm.* 3.4.95 found harmony in all things that are perfect in their nature but most fully revealed through human souls and through the movements in the heavens; Aristides

order as musical combined with a remarkable tribute to the importance he attached to music, Philo says that the creation is the "true music, the original (ἀρχέτυπον) and model (παραδειγματικήν)" of everything from which human beings derived "this most necessary and beneficial art."[130] He moves from human concord to harmony of the cosmos.[131] The same Logos that ordered the cosmos and created the nine intervals of music is also the leader of the human chorus.[132] Following Aristotle Philo makes a parallel between heavenly music and human music.[133]

Quintilianus *Mus.* 2.8.66–68, 14.79–82, 16.84–89; and 3.7.105, 9.107–27.133 developed an elaborate system of the soul as corresponding to the elements of music and of the cosmic harmony to which earthly music is an imperfect imitation.

[130] *Op. mund.* 25.78. Nicomachus, *Enchiridion* 3.241–242 expressed the view that music among human beings is an imitation of the music of the planets.

[131] *Conf.* 13.56: "the whole world, which is the instrument of him who is the All, may make melody musically with its harmonies." Also on the world as God's instrument cf. *Virt.* 11.74 quoted below.

[132] *Q. Gen.* 4.110 (*Philo Supplement* I, 393–394): the Logos is "the leader and ruler of harmony" so that "melodies and songs sound as one"; the number ten trumpets "the theme of forgiveness in concordant and antiphonal chants leading to one and the same mixture of harmony." For the place of the "divine Logos" in achieving the universal harmony, cf. *Plant.* 2.10, and the human being in tune with nature, cf. *Plant.* 38.159 quoted above. The Armenian fragment of *De Deo* contains the statement, "The Being has ordered the universe by his Word, and [the universe] has been made vocal and rational by his providence" (section 5); see F. Siegert, "The Philonian Fragment *De Deo*: First English Translation," *SPhA* 10 (1998) 5. For the seven planets and two spheres corresponding to the number nine in music, Aristides Quintilianus, *Mus.* 3.6.102 (Philo, however, may have counted the sun and moon with the planets—see quotation at n. 137 below) and 12.112; for the number ten, ibid. 3.6.103 and 23.124–125.

[133] *Q. Gen.* 3.3 (*Philo Supplement* I, 181): "Birds are singers," and Moses alludes "to the music which is perfected in heaven and is produced by the harmony of the movement of the stars. For it is an indication of human skill that all harmonic melody is formed by the voices of animals and living organs through the mechanism of the intelligence. But the heavenly singing does not extend" to the earth, because "that most harmonious and truly heavenly music, when it strikes the organ of hearing" would drive human beings to madness. For Aristotle, see *De caelo* 290b, which explained that humans cannot hear the music of the spheres because the sound is there from our birth and so has no contrasting silence by which it may be discerned; the Pythagorean Archytas offered several possibilities why our nature could not discern the heavenly music— the weakness of its impact, its distance from us, or the very loudness too great to be received (Porphyry, *Comm.* 56–57; for the last explanation cf. Cicero, *Rep.* 6.18–19); Aristides Quintilianus, *Mus.* 3.20.120 said we could not hear it because of the distance and the debilitating influence of the body, but men of virtue can hear it (as Philo said Moses did, see below).

Praise of God and the Music of the Cosmos

In keeping with this theme of the continuity between the harmony of the cosmos and that of the soul, Philo makes numerous brief references to the theme of cosmic music.[134] Second only to seeing God is seeing "the visible heaven and the harmonious and all musical order of the stars truly like a chorus."[135]

Philo considered a principal function of music to be for praising God. *On Dreams* I.6.35–37 is an important passage that brings together several themes under the heading of praise to God:

> Both heaven and the mind have the capacity to declaim praises, hymns, and blessings to the Father who is the One who brought them into being. For the human being was assigned the excellent reward above all other living things to worship the One who is, while the heaven is always melodious, producing all-musical harmony by the movements of its parts. If its sound ever reached our hearing, there would be mad, ceaseless frenzies … [Such] inspired songs of perfect music Moses heard [when he fasted forty days and nights] … The heaven, then, the archetypical instrument of music, appears to have been tuned perfectly for no other purpose than that the hymns being sung to the honor of the Father of all might be accompanied (ἐπιψάλλωνται) musically.[136]

---

[134] *Cher.* 31.110: The reciprocity of the whole created order, earthly as well as heavenly, is like "a lyre, harmonized out of unlike notes, and comes into fellowship and concord." Cf. *Det. pot.* 33.125: In God's creation there are "no meters, rhythms, and melodies of sound attracting the ears through music but the most perfect works of nature itself allotted its own beautiful harmony;" *Op. mund.* 17.54: The human faculty of vision observed the harmonious movement of the stars and "their rhythmic dances, ordered by the harmonious laws of perfect music;" *Spec. leg.* I.18.61: "Evil has been excluded from the divine choir" (for the phrase "divine choir" see Plato, *Phaedrus* 247A.); *Cher.* 7.23: "The fixed stars dance as in a truly divine choral order;" cf. *Mos.* I.38.212: "the choral dance of the planets and fixed stars;" II.49.271, "the chorus of the stars;" *Spec. leg.* I.6.34, "the choral movements of the planets, fixed stars, and the whole heaven;" *Aet.* 2.4, "the cosmos [is] the choric movements and revolutions of the stars." See also *Mig.* 32.178: That "the most harmonious symphony of the universe" is "like the laws of music" was the basis of Chaldean astronomy; cf. *Abr.* 17.77.

[135] *Cong.* 10.51.

[136] *Somn.* I.6.35–7.37. For the heavenly music producing madness in human beings, see *Q. Gen.* 3.3 cited above; for the heavenly bodies as the archetypical music, see *Op. mund.* 25.78 cited above. Ἐπιψάλλω meant "to play on a lyre," then in 2 Macc 1:30 "to sing," and in patristic literature "to sing responses" (e.g., Clement of Alexandria, *Str* 5.8). All three meanings are possible here. Philo reflects classical Greek musical terminology; therefore, he avoids ψαλμοί as the title of the Psalms and calls them ὕμνοι (e.g. *Cont.* 3.25; *Plant.* 7.29; *Mig.* 28.157; *Somn.* II.37.245), ὑμνῳδία (as in *Plant.* 9.39), or ᾆσμα (as in *Somn.* II.37.246; *Mut.* 20.115). Rather than the "Psalmist" David is the ὑμνῳδός in *Deus imm.* 16.74 and "the one who hymns" in *Conf.* 28.149. Consequently,

Similarly, a long passage on the end of Moses's life brings together a number of these themes regarding heavenly music and the praise of God:

> He began to praise God in song [Deut. 32:1–43], rendering thanksgiving … Gathering together a divine assembly, the elements of the universe and the most essential parts of the cosmos, the earth and heaven, one the home of mortals and the other the house of the immortals, in their midst he sang his hymn of praise with all harmony and every kind of symphony so that both men and ministering angels might hear … , the angels themselves skilful in music observing lest there be any discordant note in the song and doubting that someone bound in a corruptible body [Moses] was able like the sun, moon, and the all holy chorus of the other stars to harmonize his soul so as to make music in accompaniment with God's instrument, the heaven and all the cosmos. Having taken his position in the presence of the ethereal chorus, the hierophant blended with his thanksgiving hymns his genuine feelings for the well being of the nation.[137]

The one duty of human beings is to honor God with thanksgiving, voiced with or without melody.[138] In response to the magnificent blessings of God, Philo asks rhetorically, "What is more fitting for one to do than to return to the Benefactor words, and songs, and hymns?"[139] or more fully, "to return to him in a pure manner hymns, blessings, prayers, and other thanksgivings, in a word, praise."[140] Thus it is natural that Philo includes song as typical of Jewish worship[141] and especially in the religious festivals. Moses "called the people to the sanctuary to share in hymns, prayers, and sacrifices";[142] at Passover those gathered for the banquet "fulfill the custom handed down from the fathers with

---

here I have opted for a translation alluding to instrumental accompaniment.

[137] *Virt.* 11.72–75; cf. *Spec. leg.* IV.24.177 for Moses as the "hierophant who hymned the excellencies of Him who is."

[138] *Plant.* 31.131; for "to speak" and "to sing" praise to God, cf. *Somn.* 1.43.256; 2.5.38; and the correction adopted in LCL (V, 562) at 2.41.268.

[139] *Sob.* 11.58.

[140] *Spec. leg.* I.41.224; cf. II.32.199, "to reverence, worship, and honor the Giver with harmonious hymns and blessings" and II.33.209, "they honor God for the good things of the present with songs and words." Cf. Plato, *Leges* 800–802, "hymns, prayers, and encomia."

[141] *Somn.* II.5.34: the allegorical interpretation of Judah as "songs and hymns to God." Also in an expository vein, compare *Mos.* I.46.255: "The people loved by God [Israel] in their gladness and joy set up choruses in a circle around the well and sang a new song to God;" cf. Balaam "singing the most exalted hymns to God" in *Mig.* 20.113 and Jacob "singing and hymning" in *Ios.* 42.253.

[142] *Spec. leg.* I.35.193.

prayers and hymns";[143] at Tabernacles the worshipper brings baskets from the fruit-harvest to the priest, reciting "a beautiful and marvellous song."[144] While Philo has various combinations of words to formulate the response of praise to God,[145] he affirms that "the best and most perfect product of all right actions brought to birth is the hymn to the Father of the universe."[146] Yet from an ultimate standpoint, Philo considered it impossible to render adequate praise to God.[147]

The Therapeutae and Choral Music

Although Philo does not describe music at the temple in Jerusalem nor specifically speak of any musical practices in synagogues,[148] he tells us a great deal more about how the vocal music he preferred was performed among the Jews than is usually acknowledged. Bare references to actual singing, however, are not always informative on the manner of performance.[149] He frequently uses several words for vocal music without any apparent sharp distinction in meaning; e.g., "praise, hymns, and songs fitting for God."[150] Like other ancient writers, Philo recognized the differences in human voices. The parts of the human self and the different members of the people correspond to these different kinds of voices. So too with the celestial music, the combination of different sounds makes a more complete melody: "For if there had not been produced in the world the harmonious blending into a symphony of antiphonal voices as if of a choir sounding as one, it would not have

---

[143] *Spec. leg.* II.27.148.

[144] *Spec. leg.* II.35.216 and 220; cf. *Virt.* 18.95 for "hymns composed to God," which are preserved in the sacred books, accompanying the offerings.

[145] *Heres* 22.110, 111: As the "mind should think of nothing else than God and his excellencies, speech should honor the Father of all with unbridled mouth, with encomia, hymns, and blessings," "hymning with the voice's instrument the world and its Creator;" cf. "sing with sweet melody the excellencies of Him who is" (*Somn.* I.43.256); for hymning God's excellencies (virtues) see *Spec. leg.* 4.34.17.

[146] *Plant.* 33.135.

[147] *Mos.* II.43.239: "O Master, how can one hymn you? With what mouth, what tongue, what organ of speech, what leading part of the soul? If the stars become one chorus, what melody will they sing that is worthy?"

[148] Feldman, "Philo's Views," 527.

[149] E.g., *Cong.* 21.115, "sing a refrain."

[150] *Leg. all.* III.8.26. Given Philo's avoidance of the word "psalms," the statement is a close parallel to Eph 5:19, "psalms, hymns and spiritual songs."

received its full perfection."[151] Philo refers to "precentors" (ἔξαρχοι) or "leaders" (ἡγεμόνες) of the chorus who led the singing."[152]

More significant with regard to the practice of choral music within the Alexandrian synagogue communities is the account of their response to the news, which arrived during the Feast of Tabernacles, of the arrest of the prefect Flaccus, who had allowed the pogrom against the Jews in 37 CE. "Extending their hands to heaven, they sang hymns and songs of victory to God," and "all through the night they continued in hymns and odes." At dawn they went to the beach, since their synagogues had been taken from them, and offered prayer to God.[153] Doubts have been raised about the presence of psalmody or any kind of singing in synagogues during New Testament times.[154] Such a conclusion requires a discounting of the account by Philo, who had immediate knowledge of the events. Even if a sharp distinction were maintained between what was done "in synagogue" and other religious activities, based on the wording of the passage,[155] it testifies nonetheless to a rich experience of vocal religious music among Alexandrian Jews.

This testimony is extended by Philo's fullest and most informative account of the musical activities of some Jews, namely that found in his description of a sectarian community known as the Therapeutae, who lived together not far from Alexandria.[156] An introductory summary

---

[151] *Q. Ex.* II.120 (*Philo Supplement* II, 172); cf. II.38, with reference to inner harmony, quoted above, "In an all-musical chorus" there is "the blended voices of all."

[152] *Ebr.* 31.121; cf. 29.112. We should not think of the "leader" as a modern director of a chorus but perhaps more like a lead singer whom the chorus joined as the song began or to whom it responded. Cf. *Mig.* 18.104 quoted above. West (*Ancient Greek Music*, 339) notes that the pattern of a leader (*exarchos*) and an answering chorus was well established in Greek cultic practice; the practice of a solo singer who leads off and a chorus that answers was widespread throughout the Near East (388).

[153] *Flacc.* 14.121–122.

[154] J. A. Smith, "The Ancient Synagogue, the Early Church and Singing," *Music and Letters* 65 (1984):1–16; J. W. McKinnon, "On the Question of Psalmody in the Ancient Synagogue," *Early Music History* 6 (1986):159–191.

[155] It might be argued, for example, that the setting of the singing is a public, "outdoor" festival (Succoth), to be distinguished from the act of praying, which is said to have taken place at the beach because their "prayerhalls" (προσευχαί) had been confiscated. On the other hand, prayer for the Jews was not as distinct from song as in modern usage, and the festival cycle was closely tied to scripture readings and prayers usually associated with synagogue activity. We should see the first-century synagogues as integral to the total community life of the Jewish residents of Alexandria. The concerted group participation described by Philo with formal acts of song and prayer suggest joint religious activity with which the whole community was familiar.

[156] F. C. Conybeare, *Philo about the Contemplative Life* (Oxford: Clarendon, 1895); Jean Riaud, "Les Thérapeutes d'Alexandrie dans la tradition et dans la recherche critique

of their musical interests states, "They not only engage in contempla-
tion, but they also compose songs and hymns to God in all kinds of
meters and melodies, which they mark with rhythms necessarily more
solemn."[157] The description of their actual singing occurs in the account
of their celebration on the fiftieth day, presumably Pentecost, a description which because of its fullness of musical information deserves to be
quoted extensively.

> [Following a discourse by the president,] The president having stood up
> sings a hymn addressed to God, either a new one composed by himself
> or an old one by poets of an earlier time [one of the Psalms?], for
> they have left behind in many meters and melodies verses in trimeters,
> hymns for processions, at libations, and at the altars, and careful metrical
> arrangements for the stops and varied movements of choruses.[158] After
> him the others [sing] in proper order according to their rank, while all
> the rest listen in great silence except when they must sing the closing
> phrases or refrains, for then all, both men and women, lift up their
> voices. [When each has finished his hymn, the meal is served.]

> [Then came an all-night vigil of the community that was spent in song.]
> They all rise together in the midst of the dining room and first form
> two choruses, one of men and one of women. For each chorus the most
> honored and most musical is chosen as precentor and leader. Then they
> sing hymns to God composed in many meters and melodies, sometimes
> singing together and at other times with antiphonal harmonies, motion-
> ing with their hands and dancing, inspiring in turn processional odes and
> then performing the stops, turnings, and movements of a choric dance.
> Then when each of the choruses has taken its own part in the feast, ...
> they combine and out of the two become one chorus, a copy of what
> was constituted at the Red Sea on account of the marvellous things done
> there ... [At that time] filled with divine enthusiasm, the men together
> with the women, becoming one chorus, sang thanksgiving hymns to God
> their Savior, the prophet Moses leading the men and the prophetess
> Miriam the women. On this model the male and female members with
> responsive and antiphonal strains, blending the bass sound of the men
> with the treble of the women, perform a harmonious and truly musical
> symphony. Truly beautiful are the thoughts, truly beautiful the words,
> reverent are the chorus members. The goal of the thoughts, the words,
> and the choruses is godliness.[159]

---

jusqu'aux découvertes de Qumran," *ANRW* II.20.2 (1987) 1189–1295; Joan E. Taylor
and Philip R. Davies, "The So-Called Therapeutae of *De Vita Contemplativa*," *HTR* 91
(1998) 3–24.

[157] *Cont.* 3.29.

[158] Alternatively, instead of referring to the dances, "the stationary choral songs well
arranged with versatile strophes."

[159] *Cont.* 10.80; 11.83–85, 87–88.

By employing technical vocabulary, Philo intends for the reader to be reminded of the choral music and dances of the Greek theater and religious festivals. Philo describes solo, responsorial (when the leader's text is followed by the others singing a refrain), and unison singing by the Therapeutae. Whether the "antiphonal harmonies" (84) and "antiphonal strains" (88) are to be thought of as yet another style of singing with the choruses of men and women responding to each other antiphonally (suggested by the context of the former statement) or as indicating the contrasting pitches of male and female voices (indicated by the latter statement) is not clear. Philo closes the description with a statement recalling his concern for the harmony of thoughts, words, and actions, and he brings it all under the umbrella of religious piety.

There might be a suspicion that Philo invented the whole account of the Therapeutae, including their musical activities, in order to advance his philosophical ideas or to claim a Jewish version of a Pythagorean-like community; but on the matter of musical practices, there is too much concurrence with other passages in Philo to think that these are made up, even if this specific community did not exist.[160] Perhaps the most surprising feature of this account is its emphasis on antiphonal choruses of men and women. Male and female choruses were common in the Greek world, but not among Jews (see below), another indication that most of what Philo writes about music reflects his Greek education and social world. A specifically Jewish setting is provided by the parallel with the account in Exod 15:1–21 of the celebration by the Israelites of their escape from Egyptian bondage.

In addition to the book of Psalms, which he calls "Hymns,"[161] Philo refers to a number of other songs in the Bible, for example the "song sung by Hannah."[162] There are frequent references to Deut 32, "the

---

[160] For a defense of the historicity of the group, see David M. Hay, "Things Philo Said and Did Not Say about the Therapeutae," *SBLSP* (Atlanta: Scholars Press, 1992) 673–83. For Philo's account as a fabricated story, see Troels Engberg-Pedersen, "Philo's *De vita contemplativa* as a Philosopher's Dream," *JSJ* 30 (1999) 40–64. My own opinion is that there was such a group, however much idealized Philo's account might be. On the other hand, if it were fabricted, it becomes all the more significant as evidence for what Philo thought religious music ought to be. The agreements especially concern his treatment of Exod 15, a particularly important passage for him, judging by the frequency of his references to it, although oddly enough not in his *Questions and Answers on Exodus*.
[161] See note 136 above.
[162] *Mut.* 25.143 (1 Sam 2).

Greater Song" (μείζων ᾠδή) by reason of its length.[163] But the most important Biblical song in its influence on Philo in regard to musical performance was the Song of Victory sung after the crossing of the Red Sea in Exod 15.[164] It is "the Song (τὸ ᾆσμα) in which Moses hymns God."[165] Although the passage was important for Jews generally,[166] it made a significant impression on Philo, who made a distinctive use of it. It is not clear whether this passage occasioned the practice of the Therapeutae or their practice influenced Philo's interpretation of what happened in Exod 15.[167] The separate statements of Exod 15:1 and 21 gave the possibility of presenting separate choruses of men and women as doing the singing.[168] Philo seems to emphasize particularly that the women participated. This sets him at odds with later rabbinic literature, which disapproved of mixed choirs.[169]

---

[163] *Post.* 35.121; 48.167; *Plant.* 14.59; *Sob.* 3.10; *Mut.* 34.182; *Somn.* II.29.191; "Great Song" in *Leg. all.* III.34.105; *Det. pot.* 30.114; simply "a Song" in *Virt.* 11.72.

[164] Judah Goldin, *The Song at the Sea* (New Haven: Yale University Press, 1971) 248 gives a commentary on this passage, *Shirta*, in the *Mekilta de-Rabbi Ismael.* He makes frequent reference to Philo in his notes and offers other evidence for this song sung antiphonally.

[165] *Leg. all.* II.25.102–26.103; *Sob.* 3.13 reverses the verb and noun, "sings the hymn to God"; other references to the song in Exod 15–*Plant.* 12.48; *Ebr.* 19.79; 29.111; *Conf.* 10.35–36; *Somn.* II.41.269 ("we sing the most sacred ode").

[166] Ex 15 provided the wording for the benediction following the recitation of the Shema—Lewis N. Dembitz, "Ge'ullah," *Jewish Encyclopedia*, ed. I. Singer (New York: Funk and Wagnalls, 1910) 5.648; text translated in Martin McNamara, *Targum and Testament* (Shannon: Irish University Press, 1972) 39. See *m.Sota* 5.4 for Exod 15 in temple worship.

[167] Perhaps both considerations were present, the Biblical account taken by the Therapeutae as authorizing their activity and that activity in turn filling in details in Philo's understanding of the text.

[168] *Mos.* I.32.180: "Seeing the total destruction of their enemies in a moment, they set up on the shore two choruses, one of men and one of women, and sang thanksgiving hymns to God, Moses being the precentor for the men and his sister for the women, for these became the leaders of the choruses." Earlier Greek choruses were either male or female, but sources contemporary with Philo mention men and women singing in unison (Ps. Aristotle, *Mund.* 399a; Seneca, *Ep.* 84.9); see West, *Ancient Greek Music*, 40.

[169] *b.Sotah* 48a: "Rabbi Joseph [a third-century Babylonian Amora] said: 'When men sing and women join in it is licentiousness; when women sing and men join in it is like fire in town.' For what practical purpose is this mentioned? To abolish the latter before the former." The footnote to the translation in the Soncino edition, ed. I. Epstein (London: Soncino, 1936) explains that the men joining in is more serious because it is a wilful act by the men to listen to female voices. Feldman, "Philo's Views," 525 cites the opinion of the third-century rabbi Samuel that "A woman's voice is a sexual incitement" (*b.Ber.* 24a) to support the conclusion that a man was not permitted to hear her sing and so women did not sing in the synagogue.

Whatever the actual practice Philo's allegorical expositions on Exod
15 develop the musical aspects of the episode rather fully and bring in
themes already identified. In the first[170] we find the union of song by
heavenly powers with human beings, the harmony of the self (mind
and senses), which is an instrument to be played in praise to God, song
associated with thanksgiving, vocal praise proceeding from the mind,
both women and men singing, each with their own leader to start the
hymn and responding to each other in harmony.

Similar motifs occur in the exposition from the *Life of Moses*;[171] however, here Philo emphasizes the harmony of the people instead of the
harmony of the individual. In this connection, the different qualities of
male and female voices are highlighted. Otherwise, the same manner of
singing is described: a leader beginning, the chorus joining in, and the
separate choruses of men and women either alternating antiphonally,
responding with the refrain together, or perhaps doing both at different
times.

Evaluating Different Types of Music

Philo followed philosophical thought in the evaluations he gave to different kinds of music. A further preference derives from the goal of
praise to God and the continuity of the human soul with the cosmos. The different types of music, therefore, are graded accordingly:
stringed instruments over wind and percussion instruments, the voice
over instrumental music, and "silent singing" (the thoughts of the mind)
over vocal music.

Philo often refers in summary fashion to the different ways of making music, "to play on the aulos, to play on the kithara, to sing, or

---

[170] *Agr.* 17.79–18.82: Ps. Aristotle, *Prob.* 19.39 says the correspondence of different
voices is pleasanter than unison singing and gives the example of the blending of
children's with men's voices.
[171] *Mos.* II.46.256–257. "[Moses] appropriately honors the Benefactor with thanksgiving hymns. He divided the nation into two choruses, one of men and one of women,
and he himself leads the men and he appoints his sister precentor of the women in
order that responding together they might sing hymns to the Father and Creator with
answering [or concordant] harmonies, a blending of temperaments and melodies, ...
a symphony of the combination of bass and treble. For the voices of men are deep
and the women's high, and when their blending occurs in proper proportion there is
produced the sweetest and most harmonious melody. He persuaded these myriads of
people to be of one mind and to sing together the same hymn ... He led off the song,
and his hearers assembled in two choruses and sang together the words spoken above."

any similar kind of performance,"[172] and to the principal instruments: "aulos, kithara, and every kind of instrument,"[173] "aulos, lyre, and other instruments of music,"[174] or "psalterion and kithara" as standing for "all music."[175] Of these instruments, Philo considered the lyre the best and the standard for other instruments: "In music the seven-stringed lyre is generally regarded as the best of instruments, because the enharmonic mode, which is the most dignified of all the classes of melodies, is considered somehow best when rendered by it."[176] Again, "The seven-stringed lyre, which corresponds to the choir of the [seven] planets, produces notable harmonies, and is (one might say) the chief of all the instruments for making music."[177] Philo was particularly negative about percussion instruments, since they did not make music but "noises inarticulate and meaningless."[178]

Vocal music is related to the harmony of a person in which reason rules the senses, and, moreover, instruments are hand-made, but the voice is nature's instrument: "The musician accommodates meters, rhythms, and all kinds of melody to the auloi, kitharas, and other instruments, and he is able apart from the handmade instruments to use the instrument of nature through the voice attuned to all the notes."[179] Interpreting Jubal allegorically as "sounding speech," Philo finds it fitting that he is called the "father of music and all musical instruments" (Gen. 4:21). And he proceeds to declare the organ of sound the most perfect of all instruments and the pattern for artificially fashioned instruments:

> Nature, fashioning for living creatures the vocal organ as the chief and most perfect instrument, granted to it immediately all the harmonies and

---

[172] *Sob.* 8.36; cf. *Leg. all.* 3.78.221.

[173] *Leg. all.* II.18.75.

[174] *Sac.* 4.18; ccf. *Post.* 32.105.

[175] *Post.* 32.111.

[176] *Leg. all.* I.5.14; the preference of the lyre over the aulos was Pythagorean according to Aristides Quintilianus *Mus.* 2.19.91f. (but Sextus Empiricus, *Adv. Math.* 6.7–9, 23 relates a story about Pythagoras that gives a positive evaluation to the aulos); cf. Plato, *Resp.* 397a, 399c–e; there was an association of the lyre with the rational and the aulos with emotional frenzy—*Leges* 790e–791b; so also Aristotle, *Pol.* 1339a, 1341a–b, hence he rejected the aulos from his educational curriculum; he reports Socrates' disapproval of the instrument in 1342a–b.

[177] *Op. mund.* 42.126.

[178] *Fuga* 3.22.

[179] *Sob.* 8.36. Plato, *Resp.* 398d, 400a,d and *Leges* 669 subordinated melody and rhythm to the words. "Music is the sound of the voice that reaches and educates the soul"—*Leges* 673a.

kinds of melodies so that it might become the pattern made beforehand for those instruments going to be fashioned by (human) skill … Nature made for living creatures the rough windpipe, stretching it like a musical scale [or chord], harmonizing the enharmonic, chromatic, and diatonic classes according to the various kinds of conjunct and disjunct melodies, and established it the pattern of every musical instrument.[180]

The passage continues with a praise of natural music over instrumental, of the voice over all other kinds, including a contrast of what is pleasing to the ear (instrumental music) with what is pleasing to both the ear and the mind (vocal music):

Whatever melodious sounds auloi, lyres, and other such instruments produce, they fall as much short of the music of nightingales and swans as a copy and imitation does of an original pattern … None of the other kinds of music is worthy to be compared to that of the human voice, since it has the incomparable privilege, for which it is honored, of articulate expression. By using the modulation of sound and successive changes of tones the other types please only the hearing, but the human being, having been given articulation by nature for speaking and singing, wins over both the hearing and the mind, charming the one by the melody and leading the other by the thoughts. For just as an instrument given to an unmusical person is tuneless but becomes tuneful according to the skill of the musical person, in the same way speech set in motion by a worthless mind is without harmony but by a diligent mind is found altogether melodious. A lyre or any similar instrument, unless it is struck by someone, is quiet, and speech also unless struck by the ruling faculty of necessity remains silent. …[181]

---

[180] Post. 31.103–104; cf. Deus imm. 6.25 below for the soul as the archetype of manmade instruments. The same view was expressed by Nicomachus (beginning of second century A.D.): sounds of stringed, blown, and percussion instruments are imitations of the sounds we ourselves make—Enchiridion 2.240.20ff. Ptolemy, Harm. 1.20.9 has the reverse comparison that the windpipe is something of a natural aulos.

[181] Post. 32.105–108. In classical Greece instruments accompanied song but by Philo's time they were used independently; Ps. Aristotle, Prob. 19.39 still subordinates the accompaniment to the song. Ps. Plutarch, Mus. 2 (Mor. 1131d) offers a comparable statement to Philo: "For it is an act of piety and a principal concern to human beings to hymn the gods, who have given articulate speech to them alone." Ibid., 34 (Mor. 1143f) for the ear and the mind working together (so also Aristoxenus, El. Harm. 2.33.2–10—vocal and instrumental music involve hearing and reason) and 37 (Mor. 1144f) for Pythagoras saying the excellence of music is to be apprehended by the mind and not judged by sense perception. For the voice having the twofold capacity "for speaking and singing" cf. Spec. leg. I.62.342; for articulation as making sound "truly rational" cf. Q. Gen. II.3 and III.3 (the melody of voices comes by means of the intelligence). "Swallows, nightingales, and other birds"—Leg. all. 2.18.75; even grasshoppers have a song—Cont. 4.35. Cf. Aristotle, An. 420b–421a on "voice" in some animals (but not all sounds they produce are from a "voice") and Gen. animal. 788a on rough and smooth

Since speech can proceed from a "worthless mind" and can be itself soulless,[182] Philo ascribed to the proper thoughts of the mind the highest level of praise, the philosophical concept of "silent singing."[183]

> The loudest cry is not with mouth and tongue … but with the all musical and loudest sounding organ of the soul, which is not heard by anyone mortal but only by the uncreated and imperishable One. For only the mind's Musician, not anyone entangled in sense perception, is capable of apprehending the beautiful and symphonic melody of the mind's harmony.[184]

In one of his noblest passages, Philo expressed the basis for this concept of spiritual sacrifice. "God is in need of nothing, but he rejoices in God-loving thoughts and in the human exercise of holiness," and from such worshippers he accepts simple grain offerings, "holding the things of least cost as most precious more than than those things of highest price." He continues:

> Although the worshippers bring nothing else, in offering themselves they bring the best sacrifice–the full and most truly perfect sacrifice of noble living–as they honor their Benefactor and Savior, God, with hymns and thanksgivings, sometimes with the organs of speech, sometimes without tongue or lips when within the soul alone their minds recite or cry out. These expressions one ear alone receives, the divine ear.[185]

---

voices. *Det. pot.* 34.126: The Creator "has made speech like a compound instrument, the articulate utterance of our whole being," and it has its excellence because it is a "brother of the mind," whose thoughts it brings to expression. Cf. Theophrastus (in Porphyry, *Comm.* 61) on the soul turning the voice (itself wordless or non-rational) as it wishes. *Dec.* 9.33: God's voice at Sinai was declared to be "more marvellous than all instruments." It might be nothing remarkable for this to be said of God, but the explanation seems to reflect Philo's general estimate of voices in relation to instruments: "it was fitted with perfect harmonies, not soulless, … but a rational soul full of clarity and distinctness." Aristotle had said, "Nothing that is without soul utters voice"—*An.* 420b; for the description of instruments as "soulless" cf. 1 Cor 14:7.

[182] *Det. pot.* 34.130.

[183] On this concept see Apollonius of Tyana, *De sacrif.* quoted in Eusebius, *Praep. Evang.* 4.13; *Corp. Herm.* 1.31; 13.18–19; from Nag Hammadi *Disc. 8–9* (VI, 58,20–60,5); and Porphyry (building on Theophrastus), *De abst.* 2.34.

[184] *Heres* 4.14–15; cf. without the musical analogy *Leg. all.* 3.14.44. Compare also *Plant.* 30.126: "It is not possible genuinely to give thanks to God through those things most people consider—buildings, offerings, and sacrifices—for the whole world would not be an adequate temple for his honor; but through praises and hymns, not which the spoken voice sings but which the formless and purest mind resounds in uplifted strains;" *Ebr.* 23.94, "those who sing the thanksgiving hymn not with the spoken voice but rather with the understanding" and *Somn.* I.6.35 quoted above for hymns coming from the mind. Cf. *Leg. all.* 2.15.56 for sacrificing the whole mind.

[185] *Spec. leg.* I.50.271–272. For parallels in Greek and Roman poets and philosophers,

Conclusion

Philo and Philodemus provide the philosophical thought in regard to music that sets the context in which to see the references to music in the NT[186] and the development of Christian music in the church.[187] Philo's preference for vocal music and his description of the musical practices of the Therapeutae provide close parallels to early Christian practice. His philosophical observations are also significantly similar to the comments found in patristic literature, but that is another subject.[188] Rabbinic literature agrees with Philo on the centrality of words and on music as "performative."[189] Philodemus too agrees with Philo on the centrality of words. It appears that there was a common cultural assumption, at least among the educated, on the priority of words and so a special regard for vocal music.

---

see the passages collected in my article "Spiritual Sacrifice in Early Christianity and its Environment," *ANRW* II.23.2 (1980) 1152–1156.

[186] W.S. Smith, *Musical Aspects of the New Testament* (Amsterdam: Ten Have, 1962).

[187] James McKinnon, ed., *Music in Early Christian Literature* (Cambridge: Cambridge University Press, 1987); Edward Foley, *Foundations of Christian Music: The Music of Pre-Constantinian Christianity* (Collegeville: Liturgical Press, 1996).

[188] Everett Ferguson, "Towards a Patristic Theology of Music," *Studia Patristica* 24 (1993):266–283.

[189] Grözinger, *Musik und Gesang*, 335, "At the center of the [rabbinic] evaluation of music stands the human voice, which is esteemed as the living medium and organ of the call and encounter between God and men," and this voice is "performative music.

PART IV

ΕΘΝΟΣ

Ethnos

PAUL AND HIS PREDECESSORS IN THE DIASPORA
SOME REFLECTIONS ON ETHNIC IDENTITY IN THE
FRAGMENTARY HELLENISTIC JEWISH AUTHORS

Carl R. Holladay

Before Philo and Josephus

It has long been known that Philo and Josephus stand not at the beginning but at the end of a long tradition of Second Temple Jewish writers who seriously interacted with the Hellenistic-Roman world. Philo is often thought to embody the intriguing tensions and possibilities that come with living in the Diaspora. The sheer volume of his writings, to say nothing of his level of engagement with Hellenistic tradition, makes it impossible to ignore him as a major voice speaking from the Jewish Diaspora. To what extent he was typical of Diaspora Jews has long been debated. Josephus, by contrast, spoke from Palestine, at least initially, and while Greek was his second language, his equally voluminous writings have been preserved largely in Greek. For this reason, he belongs among the company of Hellenistic Jewish writers.

If Philo is a voice speaking primarily from the Diaspora and Josephus is in the first instance a Palestinian voice that nevertheless speaks from the Diaspora back to the homeland, each had his own predecessors. Many of the writings traceable to this period survive more or less in tact; at least, they survive as entire documents. Others were less fortunate, surviving only in scattered quotations in later writers, such as the first century BCE pagan writer Alexander Polyhistor and later Christian writers, mainly Clement and Eusebius. They have acquired the equally unfortunate designation "Fragmentary Hellenistic Jewish Authors."[1] Their brevity and the scattered nature of the quotations make it difficult to generalize about them, but also to place and date them. Those most likely to have a Palestinian provenance are Eupole-

---

[1] For texts and translations, see C. R. Holladay, *Fragments from Hellenistic Jewish Authors* (4 vols.; SBLTT; Atlanta: Scholars Press, 1983–96). English translations are available in J. H. Charlesworth, ed., *The Old Testament Pseudepigrapha* (Garden City, NY: Doubleday, 1985) 2.775–918. German translations are available in *Jüdische Schriften aus hellenistisch-römischer Zeit* (Gütersloh: Mohn 1980–83) 1,2; 3,2; 4,3.

mus, Pseudo-Eupolemus, Theodotus, and Philo the Epic Poet. Others
are more confidently placed in a Diaspora setting, most likely Alexandria: Demetrius, Artapanus, Pseudo-Hecataeus, Ezekiel the Tragedian,
Aristobulus, and the pseudonymous Orphic writings. Most of the others are very difficult to place, primarily because of their brevity. These
include Cleodemus Malchus, Aristeas, Theophilus, Thallus, and Justus
of Tiberius.

It is difficult to know the extent of the lost writings of these fragmentary authors. Some of them appear to have been quite productive. Ezekiel is said to have written "tragedies."[2] Aristobulus' exegetical work is referred to as "commentaries on the Mosaic legislation."[3]
According to Alexander Polyhsitor, one of the fragments from Philo
the Epic Poet was taken from the "fourteenth book," which suggests a
work of considerable length.[4] Few indicators of length are found in the
historians Demetrius, Artapanus, Eupolemus, and Pseudo-Eupolemus,
but these works appear to have covered large portions of the biblical
story and could easily have been large in scope. These fragmentary
remains, then, reinforce the picture we have from other sources: that
this was a period of prodigious literary activity among Greek-speaking
Jews.

The importance of the fragmentary Hellenistic Jewish authors for
reconstructing our understanding of Judaism in the Hellenistic-Roman
period has long been recognized. They figure prominently in major
historical treatments of the nineteenth century, such as Dähne, Dubnow, and Herzfeld, to name only a few. Schürer's extensive treatment
acknowledges their importance.[5] Since they reflect various degrees of
interaction with Hellenistic culture, they occupy a central role in the
overall argument of Hengel's *Judentum und Hellenismus*.[6] In his *Jews in
the Mediterranean Diaspora*, John Barclay draws primarily on Ezekiel the
Tragedian, Aristobulus, and Artapanus for his reconstruction of the
Egyptian Diaspora because their fragmentary remains are the most

---

[2] Clement *Strom.* 1.23.155.1.
[3] Eusebius-Jerome *Chronica* Olymp. 151 (T 8 in *FHJA* 3.119–20). See *FHJA* 3.92–93
n. 151.
[4] Eusebius *P.E.* 9.24.1 (see *FHJA* 2.206–207).
[5] E. Schürer, *The History of the Jewish People in the Age of Jesus Christ* (3 vols. in 4;
Edinburgh: T. & T. Clark, 1973–87) 3.1.509–93.
[6] (WUNT 10; 3rd ed. Tübingen: (Mohr – Siebeck, 1988). English translation *Judaism and Hellenism: Studies in Their Encounter in Palestine During the Early Hellenistic Period* (2
vols.; Philadelphia: Fortress, 1974).

substantial in length and most certainly locatable in Egypt.[7] In spite of their fragmentary state, Barclay incorporates their perspectives throughout his analysis, allowing these texts to enter dialogue with other, better preserved authors, including Paul. Erich Gruen's recent book *Heritage and Hellenism: The Reinvention of Jewish Tradition* takes them into full account, where they serve to illustrate the literary ingenuity of Hellenistic Jews in coming to terms with new social, political, and religious realities during the Hellenistic period.[8]

They have also figured in discussions relating to the New Testament and Christian origins. Because of their preoccupation with Jewish heroic figures and the fascinating ways they re-interpret and re-present many biblical figures, they have become obvious sources for Christological discussions, especially the *theios aner* debate.[9] The treatment of biblical narrative by the historians has caused them to figure prominently in discussions of Luke-Acts. John O'Neill clearly saw the significance of some of these connections and developed them in *The Theology of Acts in Its Historical Setting*.[10] Gregory Sterling developed these insights more fully in *Historiography and Self-Definition: Josephos, Luke-Acts, and Apologetic Historiography*, where the historians serve as examples of apologetic historiography.[11] Fewer connections have been made with Paul, although Barclay's chapter on Paul the "anomalous Diaspora Jew" makes explicit connections with these authors.[12] William Horbury's investigation of δωρήματα in Ezekiel the Tragedian, v. 106, illustrates the exegetical payoff that close analysis of these texts can produce. He convincingly argues that Ezekiel's use of "gifts" is an early witness for characterizing the covenantal privileges of Israel this way and sees it anticipating Paul's thinking in Rom 11:29 and 9:4–5.[13]

In this essay, I explore some of the ways these fragmentary Hellenistic Jewish authors might inform our understanding of Paul. I do so primarily by looking at indications of ethnic identity and Diaspora con-

---

[7] (Edinburgh: T. & T. Clark, 1996). See esp. chapter 6, "Cultural Convergence," 125–80.

[8] Hellenistic Culture and Society, 30; Berkeley: University of California Press, 1998.

[9] They figured prominently in D. Georgi, *The Opponents of Paul in Second Corinthians* (Philadelphia: Fortress, 1986). Also, see C. R. Holladay, *THEIOS ANER in Hellenistic Judaism* (SBLDS, 40; Missoula, Mont.: Scholars Press, 1977). See also the article by Zeller in this volume.

[10] (London: SPCK, 1961). See chapter 6, "The Debt to Hellenistic Judaism," 146–65.

[11] (Leiden: Brill, 1992). See chapter 5, "The Hellenistic Jewish Historians," 136–225.

[12] Barclay, *Jews*, 383.

[13] W. Horbury, "Ezekiel Tragicus 106: δωρήματα," *VT* 36 (1986) 37–51.

sciousness among five of these authors who are most reliably placed in
a Diaspora setting: Demetrius, Artapanus, Pseudo-Hecataeus, Ezekiel
the Tragedian, and Aristobulus. The questions I put to these texts are
these: How do these authors construe ethnic identity? What are the
terms they use to describe the people of Israel whose deeds they recount
in their Jewish writings? Do their treatments of various themes provide
any clear indications that they were living in the Diaspora? If so, how
do they negotiate this reality? Having asked these questions, I then ask
whether these authors' construals of ethnic identity and life in the Diaspora provide useful analogues to Paul. How does their construal of the
Jewish people compare with Paul's? How does his construal of his social
world compare with theirs? Are there useful points of comparison?

Demetrius the Chronographer[14]

Some 200 lines, representing six separate fragments, are preserved from
the works of Demetrius the Chronographer. The first two fragments
treat events from Genesis, Frgs. 3–5 events from Exodus, and Frg. 6
provides a chronological summary based on information from 2 Kings.
Demetrius is reliably placed in Alexandria from the late 3rd to the early
2nd century BCE. He is familiar with Hellenistic historiographical traditions, chronography in particular. One of his overarching concerns in
reading the biblical text is to calculate dates and establish chronological
connections between biblical events. In doing so, he places the biblical story within a larger chronological framework of his own making.
He is one of the earliest writers to delineate periods of biblical history
and calculate their length in years.[15] His interest, however, is not solely
chronological. He also addresses other cruxes in the text and attempts
to provide rational explanations for them.

This Diaspora Jew appears to be very much at home in the intellectual world of Alexandria, and there is reason to believe that he is
seriously engaging that world. But because so few lines of his work are
preserved, it is difficult to ascertain his attitudes about his Alexandrian
setting or his own self-understanding within that setting. The difficulty
is not only the brevity of the material, but the very narrow bore through
which he reads the biblical text. Apart from the chronological calcula-

---

[14] See *FHJA* 1.51–91.
[15] Frg. 2.18. See B. Z. Wacholder, *Eupolemus: A Study of Judaeo-Greek Literature* (Cincinnati: Hebrew Union College-Jewish Institute of Religion, 1994) 103–4.

tions he makes based on the biblical text, Demetrius departs very little from the biblical story. Events of otherwise enormous import, such as Abraham's sacrifice of Isaac, he summarizes in brief compasss. If anything, he renders major biblical characters smaller than life. He exhibits no tendencies to embellish that often characterize other Hellenistic Jewish authors.

His frame of reference is biblical. The place names he mentions are those he finds in the biblical account: Canaan, Shechem, Bethlehem, Hebron, and Bethel. When his field of vision extends beyond Palestine, it is because the biblical story takes him there: Mesopotamia, Haran, and Egypt. Among these, he is most preoccupied with Egypt, which is only natural given his Alexandrian setting. The travels of the patriarchs and the events of their lives find their natural culmination in Egypt.[16] He mentions Joseph's marriage to Asenath, describing her as the daughter of Potiphera, priest of Heliopolis,[17] but here too he is reporting what he finds in the LXX.[18]

We do not learn much from Demetrius' use of designations for the people whose story he relates. Nowhere does he use the terms (οἱ) Ἰουδαῖοι or (οἱ) Ἑβραῖοι. In Fragment 2.7 and 10, he reports Jacob's name change to Ἰσραήλ, and then uses this as a proper name for Jacob in his report of the rape of Dinah.[19] He does not use the term to refer to the people of Israel. His one use of οἱ Ἰσραηλῖται may reflect the perspective of outsiders. Fragment 5 opens, "But someone asked how the Israelites obtained weapons, seeing that they departed from Egypt unarmed …" He proceeds to provide an explanation. Conceivably this is an outsider's question, although it could easily reflect Demetrius' own reading of the LXX.

A glimpse of his own view of outsiders may be seen in the way he refers to Abraham's call. Twice he uses the phrase, "from the time when Abraham was chosen from among the nations (ἀφ' οὗ ἐκλεγῆναι Ἀβραὰμ ἐκ τῶν ἐθνῶν), once describing the migration of Jacob's sons to Egypt,[20] and again in a chronological summary.[21] Even though his use of τὰ ἔθνη for non-Jews is well documented in the Bible, it tends not

---

[16] Frg. 2.
[17] Frg. 2.12.
[18] Gen 41:45, 50–52. LXX: Πετεφρη; Demetrius: Πεντεφρη.
[19] Frg. 2.9.
[20] Frg. 2.16.
[21] Frg. 2.18.

to be used this way in the Genesis account of Abraham's call. Whether
this way of paraphrasing the biblical account reflects Demetrius' own
view of non-Jews is not at all clear.

For all of his preoccupation with Egypt, Demetrius reflects no hostility to Egyptians. This is in keeping with the dry, unemotional tone
of his narrative as a whole. He records the movement of the patriarchs
to Egypt, notes Joseph's rise to power, but is mostly interested in the
length of time the patriarchs spent there. Egypt is simply a fact of life
for Demetrius. It is not an alien society to which one must grow accustomed, nor does it pose a serious threat to one's ethnic identity.[22] Like
other geographical locations, it is little more than a location on the
map, a way of locating events in the biblical story.

Artapanus[23]

Twice Eusebius characterizes Artapanus' work as περὶ Ἰουδαίων.[24]
Whether this is a generic description or a title supplied by Eusebius or
Artapanus himself is not clear. In Fragment 1 Eusebius gives a variant
title τὰ Ἰουδαϊκά, a more unusual form.[25]

In the fragments themselves, which presumably represent Artapanus'
own wording even though they are twice removed from Artapanus
(quoted first by Alexander Polyhistor, then copied by Eusebius), the
most common way of referring to those whom the LXX designates
as "the sons of Israel" (υἱοὶ Ισραηλ, Exod 1:7; τὸ γένος τῶν υἱῶν Ισραηλ,
1:9; similarly, 1:12, 13) or the "Hebrews" (Exod 1:15, 16, 19, 22; 2:6, etc.)
is οἱ Ἰουδαῖοι, which occurs some eleven times (Frg. 1.1 (2x); Frg. 3.2,
3, 21, 22, 31 (2x), 34, 35, 37). He does not refer to them as "Israelites,"
although he does refer to the Arabs as "descendants of Israel" (ἀπογό-
νους Ἰσραήλ, Frg. 2.1), where "Israel" may refer to Jacob himself or his
descendants, the people.

The term "Hebrews" occurs only once—in Eusebius' intriguing
summary that introduces Fragment 1: "Artapanus, in his work *Judaica*,
says that the Jews were named Hermiouth, which means 'Jews' when
translated into the Greek language; and he says that they were called
Hebrews from the time of Abraham" (Ἀρτάπανος δέ φησιν ἐν τοῖς Ἰου-

---

[22] Though, cf. the Egyptian hostility to shepherds in Frg. 2.13.
[23] See *FHJA* 1.189–243.
[24] Frg. 2.1; 3.1.
[25] See 2 Macc 13:21.

δαϊκοῖς τοὺς μὲν Ἰουδαίους ὀνομάζεσθαι Ἑρμιούθ, ὃ εἶναι μεθερμηνευθὲν κατὰ τὴν Ἑλληνίδα φωνὴν Ἰουδαῖοι· καλεῖσθαι δὲ αὐτοὺς Ἑβραίους ἀπὸ Ἀβραάμου). The mystifying designation "Hermiouth" has prompted numerous explanations. Artapanus himself may be responsible for the neologism, whatever it might signify.[26] Whether the explanation of its Greek equivalence as "Jews" is Eusebius' or Artapanus' is not clear. But the claim that the name "Hebrews" is traceable to the time of Abraham must be traceable to Artapanus himself.[27] This may illuminate the otherwise puzzling reference in Gen 14:13 where the MT calls Abraham "the Hebrew" (לְאַבְרָם הָעִבְרִי), but which the LXX renders Αβραμ τῷ περάτῃ. Perhaps it represents an early form of the tradition that later occurs in Symmachus, which reads τῷ Ἑβραίῳ.[28]

Once Artapanus calls Joseph's family who settled and multiplied in Egypt "Syrians" (τοὺς Σύρους).[29] Earlier he had reported Abraham's return from Egypt to "the regions of Syria" (εἰς τοὺς κατὰ Συρίαν … τόπους, Frg. 1). The biblical counterpart is "land of Canaan" (ἐν γῇ Χανααν, Gen 13:12). Since the LXX uses "Syrian" (ὁ Σύρος) to render "Aram" (אֲרָם, Gen 22:21) or "Aramaean" (אֲרַמִּי, Gen 25:20), this is an understandable extension of the term.[30]

Artapanus frequently refers to οἱ Αἰγύπτιοι, the inhabitants of Egypt with whom Abraham, Joseph, and Moses have their dealings. Here his use corresponds to that of the LXX.[31] His familiarity with Egyptian traditions extends well beyond what can be surmised from the biblical text. He knows Heliopolis from LXX Gen 41:45, but also Egyptian sites not mentioned in the Bible, such as Sais[32] and Hermopolis.[33] Moses' activity is placed in the vicinity of Memphis,[34] which is mentioned in the prophetic writings,[35] but Artapanus did not derive its use from those

---

[26] See *FHJA* 1.226 n. 4.

[27] Rather than tracing the name "Hebrews" to the time of Abraham, Artapanus may mean that Ἑβραῖος derives from Ἀβραάμ etymologically . I owe this obsevation to Derek Olsen.

[28] See J. W. Wevers, *Notes on the Greek Text of Genesis* (SBLSCS, 35; Atlanta: Scholars Press, 1993) 193.

[29] Frg. 2.3.

[30] See *FHJA* 1.227 n. 9.

[31] Gen 12:12,14; Exod 1, etc.

[32] Frg. 2.3; see *FHJA* 1.229 n. 24.

[33] Frg. 3.8.

[34] Frg. 3.3, 12, 17.

[35] Isa 19:13; Jer 2:16; Ezek 30:13, 15; Hos 9:6.

writings. He attributes alternative explanations of the crossing of the
Red Sea to the Memphians and the Heliopolitans.[36]

Artapanus reports several conflicts with Egyptians recorded in the
Bible, most notably Moses' confrontation with Pharaoh, the plagues,
and the exodus. But his hostility towards Egypt is not appreciably
intensified beyond the biblical perspective. In fact, his Moses declines
Raguel's proposal to wage war against the Egyptians because "he had
regard for his own people," presumably a reference to the Jews.[37] It
takes a "divine voice" appearing in a sudden fire springing from the
earth to convince Moses to "wage war against Egypt."[38] Interestingly,
his mission is described as one of rescuing the Jews and returning them
"to their ancient fatherland" (εἰς τὴν ἀρχαίαν ... πατρίδα). This is one
of the few glimpses in Artapanus suggesting that Egypt was an alien,
temporary space for Jews to occupy, and thus one of the few indications
that he regards Egypt as part of the Diaspora.

If Artapanus's biblical characters—Abraham, Joseph, and Moses—
are any indication of his own status within the Diaspora, and reflect
at all his self-understanding as a Diaspora Jew, he must have felt very
much at home there. Each conforms to the image of cultural benefactor
that functioned as a widespread *topos* during the Hellenistic period. His
portraits of Joseph and Moses are particularly well developed in this
regard. In both cases, they endear themselves to the Egyptians because
of the numerous improvements they bring to Egyptian life. Egyptian
response to Moses is especially excessive. His efforts to stabilize their
economic and political lives gains the favor of the Egyptian crowds,
prompting their priests to honor him as divine.[39] He acquires the name
of Hermes because of his ability to interpret the sacred writings.

So overwhelming is Moses' popular appeal that he even wins the
favor of those whom he defeats in battle, most natably the Ethiopians,
whom he and a scruffy army of warriors defeat in a ten-year battle!
Eventually they too came to love Moses and even adopted the practice
of circumcision from him. The Egyptians priests followed suit as well.[40]

Especially worth noting is the absence of derogatory comments
about non-Jews or the use of pejorative categories, such as τὰ ἔθνη, in

[36] Frg. 3.35.
[37] Frg. 3.19.
[38] Frg. 3.21.
[39] Frg. 3.6.
[40] Frg. 3.10.

the fragments. Artapanus distinguishes between Egyptians and Greeks, noting, for example, that when Moses reached adulthood, he was honored with the name Musaios "by the Greeks" (ὑπὸ τῶν Ἑλλήνων).[41] Then, reversing the usual relationship between Musaios and Orpheus, Artapanus reports that Moses became the teacher of Orpheus. He does not operate from a position of cultural superiority that allows him to call outsiders "barbarians" (βάρβαροι). To be sure, his Abraham, Joseph, and Moses are responsible for civilizing Egypt in fundamental ways, and the Egypt they benefit is presented as otherwise disorganized, unstable politically, somewhat benighted. But this too should be seen as part of a genre where outsiders rise to positions of prominence and eventually make significant contributions to the land they adopt as native. Through it all there emerges respect for Egypt. Artapanus knows the benefit of presenting Abraham as the one who taught Pharethothes astrology,[42] or showing that Joseph eventually becomes "lord of Egypt,"[43] or that Moses won the favor of Egyptians, priests and people alike. After all, Joseph marries Asenath, the daugther of an Egyptian priest, and Egypt was attractive enough to cause his family to migrate there. The Egyptian king Palmanothes is said to have dealt meanly with the Jews,[44] but this simply reflects the outlook of Exodus 1. The rivalry between Moses and Chenephres should be seen as reflective of the novelistic tradition where kings, princes, and leaders vie for power, fighting among themselves to establish supremacy. Plots to overthrow the hero merely serve as a means for establishing his ability to endure, as is the case here. Hostilities taken by the Egyptians against Jews, such as Chenephres' ordering them to wear linen that would identify them and make them easier subjects for harassment, are harder to assess.[45]

Pseudo-Hecataeus[46]

The fragments that go under the name Pseudo-Hecataeus are more firmly included among Jewish writings from the Diaspora, now that Bezalel Bar-Kochva's 1996 monograph *Pseudo-Hecataeus, "On the Jews"*:

---

[41] Frg. 2.3.
[42] Frg. 1.
[43] Frg. 2.4.
[44] Frg. 3.2.
[45] See 3 Macc 2:29 where Jews are branded with the Dionysiac ivy leaf.
[46] See *FHJA* 1.277–335.

Legitimizing the Jewish Diaspora has appeared.[47] An exhaustive work devoted exclusively to the 130 or so lines from Josephus *Against Apion* that summarize and cite the fragments, Bar-Kochva's book addresses the much-debated question of their authenticity; that is, whether this material relating to the migration of Palestinian Jews to Egypt after the battle of Gaza in 312 BCE and positively portraying their devotion to Torah is attributable to the eminent Hellenistic scholar Hecataeus of Abdera who flourished around 300 BCE, or whether it comes from the hand of an unknown Jewish author. It is a tangled question, complicated by the fact that Hecataeus' work *On the Egyptians* contains an informed, sympathetic treatment of the Jews whose authenticity is not disputed.

Without rehearsing the debate, we may simply note that Bar-Kochva provides detailed examination of the question. The presence of historical anachronisms, as well as other considerations, cause him to date the material between 107 and 93 BCE, around the time of John Hyrcanus and Alexander Jannaeus and the subsequent Jewish expansion into Trans-Jordan.[48]

Bar-Kochva firmly identifies the author as "a Diaspora Jew living in Egypt" and further characterizes him as belonging to the "moderate conservative stream."[49] This distinguishes him from the "allegorists," whom Bar-Kochva describes as the "typical representatives of Hellenistic Jewry."[50] His summary characterization of Pseudo-Hecataeus is worth quoting in full:

> Pseudo-Hecataeus demonstrates a profound knowledge of Jewish tradition, particularly of the cult in the Jerusalem Temple, but his Hellenistic education is incomplete and suffers from significant lacunae. His Greek is a mixture of different styles, and in at least two paragraphs is rather poor. He evidently did not have any philosophical education, and probably avoided reading poetical-mythological literature. There are no traces of allegorical, moral, or philosophical interpretations of Jewish traditions, even when such are badly needed. The author was probably brought up with the Hebrew Bible and went on to use it in religious services, to the exclusion of Septuagint versions. The treatise strictly adheres to Jewish practices and Torah precepts, and advocates intolerance toward pagan cult and beliefs, even violence when possible. The author resides

[47] (Hellenistic Culture and Society, 27; Berkeley: University of California Press, 1996.)
[48] Bar-Kochva, *Pseudo-Hecataeus*, 249.
[49] Bar-Kochva, *Pseudo-Hecataeus*, 249.
[50] Bar-Kochva, *Pseudo-Hecataeus*, 249–50.

in Egypt, but his heart is given to the Holy Land, demonstrating constant interest in current events there as well as loyalty and reverence for the Jerusalem Temple.[51]

The main purpose of Pseudo-Hecataeus' work, according to Bar-Kochva, was "to legitimize and justify Jewish residence in Egypt."[52] The work was composed at a time when Palestinian Judaism was experiencing consolidation and expansion, thereby offering economic and political stability. Egyptian Jews could no longer justify their remaining in the Diaspora on those grounds. Nor could they easily resist Hasmonean overtures for them to return to Palestine to provide much-needed manpower. There was also the matter of the "implicit prohibition of the Torah against returning to Egypt."[53]

Legitimation of the existing Egyptian Diaspora was not enough. Egyptian Jews "needed a justification for remaining in Egypt."[54] Pseudo-Hecataeus responds by showing how Egyptian Jews can exert influence on the Ptolemaic court, thereby benefiting their compatriots in Palestine. What emerges is a "manifesto of conservative Judaism in Hellenistic Egypt."[55]

Though brief, the Pseudo-Hecataeus fragments present us with a strong Jewish voice speaking from the Egyptian Diaspora around 100 BCE. The narrative setting is much earlier, from the late fourth to the early third century BCE, beginning with Ptolemy's defeat of Demetrius Poliorcetes at Gaza in 312. Attributing the work to the third-century polymath Hecataeus of Abdera makes this a plausible setting, since he would be writing as a roughly contemporary witness. Like many such writings, Pseudo-Hecataeus bends history in portraying Ptolemy as a humane ruler, kindly disposed towards the Jews.[56] So impressed are they with his "kindness and humanity," that they wish to accompany him back to Egypt. Singled out for initiating the emigration to Egypt is Hezekiah, "high priest of the Jews," who was highly regarded among his Palestinian contemporaries. We are told that, "having obtained this authority (τῆς τιμῆς) and being well acquainted with us (Greeks), [he] assembled some of the men and pointed out to them the advantage (διαφοράν, presumably of emigration) and read to them the whole

---

[51] Bar-Kochva, *Pseudo-Hecataeus*, 250.
[52] Bar-Kochva, *Pseudo-Hecataeus*, 251.
[53] Bar-Kochva, *Pseudo-Hecataeus*, 251.
[54] Bar-Kochva, *Pseudo-Hecataeus*, 251.
[55] Bar-Kochva, *Pseudo-Hecataeus*, 252.
[56] Frg. 1.186.

{decree? letter?}. For he possessed in writing their settling and constitution (τὴν κατοίκησιν αὐτῶν καὶ τὴν πολιτείαν γεγραμμένην)."⁵⁷ Those
willing to emigrate see an opportunity to participate in "the affairs [of
the kingdom]." Imagined here are highly respected Palestinian Jews
who would be in positions of social prominence and influence in early
Ptolemaic Egypt.

For Pseudo-Hecataeus, exchanging the homeland for the Diaspora
poses no threat to Jewish fidelity. Jews have a history of resisting social
pressure from neighbors and standing up to powerful kings who abuse
their subjects. Faced with tortures and horrible forms of death, they
refused to "change their way of thinking" (οὐ δύνανται μεταπεισθῆ-
ναι τῇ διανοίᾳ) or "repudiate the faith of their forefathers" (ἀρνούμενοι
τὰ πατρῷα).⁵⁸ Ostensibly this describes the situation of Palestinian Jews
under Persian rule, but probably reflects the realities of life in the Eyg-
ptian Diaspora. As an instance of resolute resistance, he cites the case
of Babylonian Jews whose refusal to obey Alexander's order to bring
materials to restore the ruined temple of Bel brought them "severe
chastisement" and heavy fines.⁵⁹ Finally Alexander relented and agreed
to grant them indemnity!

Equally impressive is their willingness to take the initiative against
competing forms of worship that threatened their homeland. They
destroyed "temples and altars" (νεὼς καὶ βωμούς) built by foreign invad-
ers, willingly paying fines to their sponsoring satraps and in some cases
obtaining their forgiveness! Such actions, Pseudo-Hecataeus notes, are
admirable. The story of Mosollamus, the Jewish archer who bested a
native seer by shooting the bird whose flight was expected to guide
the expedition, serves to illustrate the unreliability of popular religion.
Fidelity to the Jewish faith thus remains steadfast at home or abroad.
These specific examples cited by Pseudo-Hecataeus can be taken as
typical of what one might expect of the "tens of thousands" of Jews
living in Babylon, as well as Egypt and Phoenicia.⁶⁰

According to Pseudo-Hecataeus, there is no reason to fear that Jews
living in Egypt will forget the homeland, which is depicted in highly
idealized form. Judea is portrayed as a land of vast fertility, with villages
and fortresses scattered throughout its three million *arourae* (approxi-

---

[57] Frg. 1.189.
[58] Frg. 1.191.
[59] Frg. 1.192.
[60] Frg. 1.194.

mately 8,300 square kilometers!). Its centerpiece is Jerusalem, its only fortified city, inhabited by 120,000 people. At its center is the walled area enclosing the temple, a "great edifice," with its gilded altar and lampstand, and an eternal flame. To distinguish it from other shrines, Pseudo-Hecataeus sketches its distinctive features: it is devoid of statues, votive offerings, and plants of any kind. Its priests are in attendance around the clock, engaged in purification rites, all the while abstaining from wine.

This description, however embellished, serves to locate the loyalties of Pseudo-Hecataeus and the Jewish constituency he represents in Egypt. They may reside in Egypt, but they have not forgotten the homeland. The temple, the city of Jerusalem, and the surrounding land of Judea still capture their imagination and give content to their dreams. These are the things that would impress a distinguished Greek such as Hecataeus.

Pseudo-Hecataeus' language is explicitly and pervasively "Jewish." Even if we set aside Josephus' summarizing comments and look exclusively at the excerpts he cites from Pseudo-Hecataeus, this becomes clear. Hezekiah is designated "high priest of the Jews (ἀρχιερεὺς τῶν Ἰουδαίων)," and he is assisted by more than 1,500 "Jewish priests (οἱ ἱερεῖς τῶν Ἰουδαίων)," all of whom (interestingly enough) "receive a tithe ... and administer public matters."[61] The language describing those Jews who stood alone (μόνους τοὺς Ἰουδαίους) against Alexander the Great may be that of Josephus rather than Pseudo-Hecataeus. But it is Pseudo-Hecataeus who speaks of the many fortresses of the Jews (τῶν Ἰουδαίων ... πολλὰ ὀχυρώματα)[62] to be found throughout Judea (Ἰουδαία).[63] His portrait of Mosollamus is also drawn in unmistakably Jewish language. The central figure is "Mosollamus the Jew" (Μοσόλλαμος ὁ Ἰουδαῖος), marching along with "the escort of Jewish cavalrymen" (ἱππέων Ἰουδαίων). To distinguish his superior gifts of marksmanship, Pseudo-Hecataeus calls him the "best archer among Greeks and barbarians" (τῶν Ἑλλήνων καὶ τῶν βαρβάρων).

For Pseudo-Hecataeus, then, humankind comprises Jews, Greeks, and barbarians. Of the three, Jews occupy center stage. Jewish behavior remains the focal concern, portrayed on the larger canvas of Ptolemaic

---

[61] Frg. 1.187.
[62] Frg. 1.197.
[63] Frg. 1.195.

affairs. When kings and satraps, such as Ptolemy I and Alexander, come on stage, they serve as figures for defining commendable Jewish behavior.

Interestingly enough, Pseudo-Hecataeus uses no other language to designate Jewish identity. The peaple about whom he reports are called neither Hebrews nor Israelites. From start to finish, "Jews" is the preferred term. When Josephus reports that Hecataeus "wrote a book entirely about the Jews themselves (περὶ αὐτῶν Ἰουδαίων)," he may be reporting the actual book title. If not, he properly captures the essence of the work. But neither does he employ τὰ ἔθνη of non-Jews.[64]

For Pseudo-Hecataeus, Jewish identity, whether in Palestine or the Diaspora, is defined in terms of fidelity to Torah[65] and commitment to "the ancestral [laws] (τὰ πάτρῷα, Frg. 1.191)" which take the form of openly resisting competing forms of worship, even destroying non-Jewish temples and altars. Positively, it consists of loyalty to the land of Judea, the city of Jerusalem, the temple, its priesthood, and ongoing rituals of worship. All of these are set in sharp contrast to non-Jewish forms and places of worship. No mention is made of circumcision as a defining rite of membership. But, given the overall perspective of the fragments, one could hardly expect it to be ignored or interpreted allegorically.

Ezekiel the Tragedian[66]

Of the three Hellenistic Jewish poets whose works survive in fragmentary form, Ezekiel the Tragedian is the most certain representative of the Jewish Diaspora.[67] An Alexandrian setting is almost certain, and he can be reliably dated from the middle to late second century BCE.[68] As the most extensively preserved Hellenistic tragedian, his importance has been increasingly recognized by scholars from various disciplines, including classics, biblical studies, and Jewish history.

---

[64] The one use of τὸ ἔθνος in Frg. 2 belongs to Josephus and this single reference is to the Jews.

[65] Whether "the laws" in Frg. 1.190 is Josephus' or Pseudo-Hecataeus' term is uncertain.

[66] See *FHJA* 2.301–529.

[67] The provenance of the epic poets Theodotus and Philo is uncertain but more likely to be Palestine than Egypt.

[68] See H. Jacobson, *The Exagoge of Ezekiel* (Cambridge: Cambridge University Press, 1983) 6, 177–78.

Seventeen fragments comprising 269 lines of iambic trimeter verse have been preserved. Like many of the other fragmentary authors, they were first preserved by the pagan author Alexander Polyhistor, who flourished in the mid-first century BCE, and were later copied from him by Eusebius in *Praeparatio Evangelica*, Book IX. A portion of the fragments is also preserved in Clement's *Stromateis*.

The title of the work given by Polyhistor and Clement is Ἐξαγωγή. Its genre is clearly indicated when witnesses refer to it as δρᾶμα and τραγῳδία. As the title suggests, the major focus of the drama is the story of Moses and the exodus as narrated in Exod 1–15. Although the opening lines allude to Jacob's migration to Egypt as described in Gen 46–49 and the transition under the "new Pharaoh" (Exod 1), the birth and infancy of Moses (Exod 2:1–10) are prominently featured at the beginning (Frg. 1). The final biblical episode mentioned in the undisputed fragments (Frgs. 16–17) is the arrival of Israel at Elim (Exod 15:27).

Given the focus of the work, certain things are understandable. The Jews in Egypt are Ezekiel's central concern, although there are occasional references to the Palestinian homeland. Worth noting for our purposes is the language Ezekiel uses to talk about this period of Jewish history, especially as it compares with the LXX, which he uses throughout and to which he adheres quite closely. As with the other authors, it is important to distinguish between Polyhistor's (and Eusebius') introductory comments and the lines of poetry attributed to Ezekiel himself. Here again, we assume that the way Ezekiel characterizes the Jewish people in his drama might offer some insight into his own self-understanding as a Jew living in the Egyptian Diaspora in the second century BCE.

The primary term Ezekiel uses throughout the fragments is Ἑβραῖος. In some instances, his use reflects what is found in the biblical account. At other times, he uses the term when the biblical text uses a descriptive phrase such as the "sons of Israel." It serves as Ezekiel's preferred term to describe the people of Israel.

In Fragment 1, in a speech by Moses (v. 12), Pharaoh is reported issuing a proclamation "for the Hebrew race (Ἑβραίων γένει) to throw its male children into the deep-flowing river." Here Ezekiel reflects LXX Exod 1:22, "Every male who is born to the Hebrews (τοῖς Ἑβραίοις) throw into the river." Further on in Fragment 1 (v. 22), Moses reports Pharaoh's daughter coming to the river and finding him: "And she knew that I was a Hebrew child (ἔγνω δ' Ἑβραῖον ὄντα)." This reflects LXX Exod 2:6, where Miriam says to Pharaoh's daughter, "This child is from the Hebrew children (ἀπὸ τῶν παιδίων τῶν Ἑβραίων)."⁶⁹ Miriam asks Pharaoh's daughter, "Do you want me quickly to find you a nurse for this child from the Hebrews (ἐκ τῶν Ἑβραίων, vv. 24–25)?" The same language occurs in Exod 2:7: "from the Hebrews (ἐκ τῶν Ἑβραίων)."

In Fragment 2, Clement's introductory remarks report: "after relating the fight between the Hebrew and the Egyptian (τὴν διαμάχην τοῦ ϑ᾿ Ἑβραίου καὶ τοῦ Αἰγυπτίου)." The language is from LXX Exod 2:11, "Moses saw an Egyptian beating a Hebrew (ἄνϑρωπον Αἰγύπτιον τύπτοντά τινα Ἑβραῖον)." Later on, in the poetic text of Fragment 2 (v. 43), Moses is speaking. He says that he saw two men fighting, "the one a Hebrew, the other an Egyptian (τὸν μέν γ᾿ Ἑβραῖον, τὸν δὲ γένος Αἰγύπτιον)." As before, this reflects LXX Exod 2:11b: τινα Ἑβραῖον.

Fragment 9 (v. 107) describes God's appearance to Moses at the burning bush: "I have come to save my people, the Hebrews (πάρειμι σῶσαι λαὸν Ἑβραίων ἐμόν)." Here Ezekiel draws on LXX Exod 3:7, "Behold, I have seen the misfortunes of my people in Egypt," but the biblical text does not use the term "Hebrews." Further on in the same fragment (v. 110), God speaks to Moses, saying, "Go and declare … first to all the assembled Hebrews themselves (αὐτοῖς πᾶσιν Ἑβραίοις ὁμοῦ)." This reflects LXX Exod 3:14–15, "thus you will say to the sons of Israel (τοῖς υἱοῖς Ἰσραηλ)."

In Fragment 13 (v. 152), God speaks to Moses, saying, "… to all the Hebrews together (πᾶσιν Ἑβραίοις ὁμοῦ) you will speak these words …" This describes God's proclamation of Passover, reported in Exod 12:1–20. In Exod 12:3 it is reported, "Speak to all the gathering of the sons of Israel (πρὸς πᾶσαν συναγωγὴν υἱῶν Ἰσραηλ) saying … ." Further on (vv. 154–55), God says in the same speech, "… I will lead the people to another land which I set aside for the fathers of the Hebrew race (εἰς ἄλλην χθόνα, εἰς ἥν ὑπέστην πατράσιν Ἑβραίων γένους)." Here Ezekiel depends on Exod 12 and 13. In 12:17 it is reported: "For on this day will I lead your power (τὴν δύναμιν ὑμῶν) from the land of Egypt." In 13:5, it says, "… when the Lord brings you into the land of the Canaanites … , which he swore to your ancestors (τοῖς πατράσιν σου δοῦναι σοι)." Once again, Ezekiel supplies "Hebrews" where it is absent in the biblical text.

---

⁶⁹ Similarly, Philo V. Mos. 1.15; Josephus Ant. 2.9.5 par. 225–26.

In Fragment 14 (v. 175), it is not clear who is speaking, God or Ezekiel. In either case, someone is giving instructions about Passover observance: "And on the tenth day of this month, let the Hebrew men (ἀνδρῶν Ἑβραίων) according to families take unblemished sheep and young bulls ... ." Here Ezekiel is summarizing LXX Exod 12:3, "Speak to all the gathering of the sons of Israel, saying ..." (see above). Later in the same fragment (v. 187), God gives instructions about the Passover: "Dip them in blood and smear the two door posts, so that death may pass the Hebrews by (ὅπως παρέλθῃ θάνατος Ἑβραίων ἄπο)." This is based on LXX Exod 12, which gives instructions for Passover. In 12:21, Moses called together "all the elders of the sons of Israel (πᾶσαν γερουσίαν υἱῶν Ισραηλ) and said to them ... ." In 12:27 instructions are given about how to respond to children: "for (the Lord) passed over the houses of the sons of Isreal in Egypt when he struck down the Egyptians (τοὺς οἴκους τῶν υἱῶν Ισραηλ ἐν Αἰγύπτῳ)."

In Fragment 15 Eusebius' introductory remarks report that Ezekiel introduces a messenger who relates the conditions of the Hebrews (τήν τε τῶν Ἑβραίων διάθεσιν) and the destruction of the Egyptians (καὶ τὴν τῶν Αἰγυπτίων φθοράν). In Fragment 15 itself (v. 204), the (Egyptian) messenger reports that there were a million men altogether, "when our army encountered the Hebrews" (Ἑβραίων). Later on (v. 223), the messenger reports seeing a great pillar of cloud rising from the earth "midway between our camp and that of the Hebrews (παρεμβολῆς ἡμῶν τε καὶ Ἑβραίων μέσος)."

To summarize, Ezekiel's account is based on a close use of LXX Exodus. He has found the term "Hebrews" in Exod 2 and repeated it in his poetic rendering of the birth of Moses and the slaying of the Egyptian. But as the story unfolds, "Hebrews" becomes his standard term for describing the people of Israel. When the biblical text uses other terms, such as "sons of Israel,"[70] Ezekiel uses "Hebrews" as a substitute. Or, when there is no explicit term in the biblical text, Ezekiel supplies "Hebrews." Unlike the biblical text, where the term tends to be used by outsiders to describe the people of Israel or as a term Israelites use to distinguish themselves from foreigners,[71] in Ezekiel the term acquires a broader sense. Reflecting Exod 2, Ezekiel reports Miriam's conversation with Pharaoh's daughter using the language of

---

[70] Exod 3:14–15; 12:3, 27.
[71] See G. von Rad, "Israel," *TDNT* 3.358–59; also N. P. Lemche, "Hebrew," *ABD* 3.95.

the LXX. Miriam uses "Hebrews" to designate her people, but she is speaking to an Egyptian princess. Similarly, Ezekiel describes the fight between the Egyptian and the Hebrew much like the LXX. Here, again, the term appropriately distinguishes the Hebrews from another people. But as the story unfolds, Ezekiel is quite prepared to depart from the LXX. Where it refers to "the sons of Israel," Ezekiel alters this to "Hebrews." He also places the term on the lips of God who, in speaking to Moses at the burning bush, says that the time has now come to "save my people, the Hebrews." This reflects the language of Exod 3:18, where God instructs Moses to tell Pharaoh that he has been commissioned by "the Lord, the God of the Hebrews."[72] When God gives Moses instructions about observing Passover, God speaks of the "Hebrews" to whom Moses would speak. In fact, Frg. 13.28–29 states that God has set aside "another land ... for the fathers of the Hebrew race (πατράσιν Ἑβραίων γένους)." Here is a clear instance where the term is being used as an ethnic designation. Then, as a way of reporting the actual crossing of the Red Sea dramatically, Ezekiel places the event on the lips of an Egyptian "messenger," one of Pharaoh's soldiers. As one would expect, he describes the Egyptians' enemies as "the Hebrews."

For Ezekiel, then, the term "Hebrews" does more than point to Israel as a distinctive people. That they are, but it serves more as a general descriptor occurring on the lips of Moses, God, and the Egyptian soldier. Indeed, as the one instance in Fragment 13 (v. 155) makes clear, Ezekiel thinks of Hebrews as a "race" (γένος).

Nowhere in the poetic verses themselves does Ezekiel employ the terms "Jews" or "Israelites." In fact, the only time "Jewish" language is used at all is in Clement's description of Ezekiel as the "poet of Jewish tragedies (ὁ Ἐζεκίηλος ὁ τῶν Ἰουδαϊκῶν τραγῳδιῶν ποιητής)." Before drawing too many conclusions about Ezekiel's sense of ethnic identity from his exclusive use of Ἑβραῖος, it must be asked whether he preferred it because it was better suited for composing iambic trimeters than its alternatives, e.g., Ἰουδαῖος or Ἰσραηλίτης.[73]

The fragments from Ezekiel yield very little sense of how ethnic identity of "the Hebrews" is defined over against other peoples. The storyline requires that the Egyptians serve as the adversaries, and Ezekiel's

---

[72] Exod 3:18; similarly, 5:3; 7:16; 9:1, 13.
[73] See J. Strugnell, "Notes on the Text and Metre of Ezekiel the Tragedian's *Exagoge*," *HTR* 60 (1967) 449–57.

account of the story does not appreciably intensify the hostitily between Hebrews and Egyptians beyond what is reported in the Bible.

To determine whether any sense of "Diaspora" emerges in Ezekiel is difficult since the story is, after all, about the exodus. Several indications in the poem simply repeat the biblical perspective. Even so, these are worth reporting. Fragment 1 opens by referring to "the time when Jacob left the land of Canaan and came down to Egypt bringing with him seventy souls" (vv. 1–3). In the same speech, Moses refers to "our descendants" (ἡμῶν γένναν) who became numerically strong in Egypt. In Fragment 2, Moses recalls his mother's telling him about "the race of our fathers and the gifts of God (γένος πατρῷον καὶ θεοῦ δωρήματα, v. 35)." The "Hebrew" Moses rescues from the attacking Egyptian is called his "brother" (ἀδελφόν, v. 45). His departure from Egypt after killing the Egyptian prompts him to say, "Now I am wandering to a foreign land (καὶ νῦν πλανῶμαι γῆν ἐπ' ἀλλοτέρμονα, v. 58)." His flight to Midian becomes a flight to Libya (v. 60), which is inhabited by "Ethiopians, dark-skinned men" (vv. 61–62). In Moses' remarkable dream vision where he sees God enthroned and himself summoned to take a seat on God's throne, he is assured by his father-in-law Raguel, who interprets the dream, that he will judge all humankind (βροτῶν, Frg. 7, v. 86). In the dream, he surveyed "the whole inhabited earth (ὅλην τ' οἰκουμένην, v. 87)." In the burning bush episode, God addresses Moses as "the God of your ancestors (ἐγὼ θεὸς σῶν ... γεννητόρων, v. 104)." Following the biblical account, he identifies God as the God of Abraham, Isaac, and Jacob, whom God has remembered, "as well as my gifts to them (ἐμῶν δωρημάτων)." God instructs Moses to "lead my people forth from the land (ὅπως σὺ λαὸν τὸν ἐμὸν ἐξάγοις χθονός, v. 112)." As already noted, in God's instructions concerning Passover, God speaks of "another land which I set aside for the fathers of the Hebrew race" (vv. 154–55). God later says to Moses, "Whenever you have entered into your own land (ὅταν δ' ἐς ἴδιον χῶρον εἰσέλθηθ', v. 167)."

Ezekiel's poem reinforces the perspective of the Bible—Jacob's descendants left the land of Canaan to come to Egypt, but Egypt never becomes their home. Moses becomes the instrument by which they are able to return to the land that God had set aside for their ancestors. Canaan, not Egypt, is their "own land."

If the sentiments of the poem reflect Ezekiel's own views, he can be said to operate with a strong sense of ethnic identity. Given his use of language in the poem, he would call it "Hebrew" identity, even as he refers to his ancestors as "the Hebrew race (Ἑβραίων γένει, v. 12; also v. 155)" or "the race of our fathers (γένος πατρῷον, v. 35)." Similarly, he would view Egypt as a place of temporary residence, perhaps even exile, but certainly not the Hebrews' "own land."

Aristobulus[74]

Some 250 lines are attributed to Aristobulus who is remembered in the tradition as a Jewish Peripatetic philosopher who wrote commentaries on the Mosaic law dedicated to Ptolemy VI Philometor.[75] He is also identified as the addressee of the letter from Palestinian Jews mentioned in 2 Macc 1:10, where he is said to be of priestly descent and a "teacher of King Ptolemy."

He is an early representative of allegorical exegesis among Jewish writers. In Fragment 2 he provides allegorical explanations for several anthropomorphic expressions in the biblical text. Eusebius' title for Fragment 3 aptly expresses one of Aristobulus' main concerns: "How Aristobulus the Peripatetic, of the Hebrews before us, also shows that the Greeks borrowed from the philosophy of the Hebrews; from the addresses of Aristobulus to King Ptolemy." With enviable confidence, he argues that Greek translations of the Hebrew Scriptures existed early enough for Socrates, Plato, and Pythagoras to draw on them for their wisdom. Equally important for Aristobulus is the resonance between Jewish and Greek tradition. The Jewish conception of the one, transcendent God is seen to reverberate with the teachings of Orpheus and Aratus, and the respectability of Sabbath observance is seen by the sacred reverence for the number "seven" reflected in Homer, Hesiod, and Linus.

Clement's testimony that his commentaries on the Pentateuch were addressed to Ptolemy VI Philometor is widely accepted,[76] as is the testimony of 2 Macc 1:10 which firmly locates him in Egypt and portrays him as an influential figure within the Jewish community there. Thus a mid-second century BCE Egyptian setting for Aristobulus can be confidently assumed.

As with the other fragmentary authors, Aristobulus' views on life in this Disapora setting must be deduced indirectly from what he writes.

---

[74] See *FHJA* 3.
[75] See T 2, 4, 8, 10, 12, 13, 14, 15 in *FHJA* 3.114–25.
[76] See T 3, *FHJA* 3.115.

Two features invite attention: (1) the language he uses to describe the Jewish people, and (2) his frame of reference in speaking about the Jewish tradition.

The term occurring most frequently in the Aristobulus materials is "Hebrew" (Ἑβραῖος), although, interestingly enough, it is used more frequently *of* Aristobulus than *by* him.

Fragment 1 is introduced with Anatolius' introductory remarks about Passover observance, where he says that Aristobulus was numbered among the 70 who translated "the sacred and divine scriptures of the Hebrews (τὰς ἱερὰς καὶ θείας Ἑβραίων ... γραφάς)."[77]

Eusebius introduces Fragment 3 with these words, "I will quote first the words of the Hebrew philosopher (ἐξ Ἑβραίων φιλοσόφου) Aristobulus ... ." This identification is also repeated in the title Eusebius supplies: "How Aristobulus the Peripatetic, of the Hebrews before us (ὁ πρὸ ἡμῶν ἐξ Ἑβραίων), also shows that the Greeks borrowed from the philosophy of the Hebrews (παρ' Ἑβραίοις φιλοσοφίας); from the addresses of Aristobulus to King Ptolemy." Both of these uses anticipate Eusebius' introductory comments to Fragment 5e, where he refers to Aristobulus as "another wise man of the Hebrews (ἄλλος Ἑβραίων σοφὸς ἀνήρ, 13.7)."

The only instance where the term is actually attributed to Aristobulus himself occurs in Fragment 3 §12.1, where both Eusebius and Clement attribute to Aristobulus the following words: "others had translated accounts of the events surrounding the exodus from Egypt of the Hebrews, our countrymen (ἐξαγωγὴν τὴν ἐξ Αἰγύπτου τῶν Ἑβραίων, ἡμετέρων δὲ πολιτῶν)." All of the other instances in the Aristobulus material occur in introductory matter from Eusebius and Clement.[78]

Aristobulus' nomenclature for ethnic identity tells us very little. Nowhere does the term Ἰουδαῖος or Ἰσραηλίτης occur in Aristobulus.[79] His sole use of Ἑβραῖος (Fragment 3 §12.1) could easily be explained on the basis of its occurrence in Exod 1 and 2. Aristobulus' additional com-

---

[77] Frg. 1.16.

[78] In one instance, the term is used in connection with the Hebrew language. In Clement's version of Fragment 3, we are told that "the Scriptures both of the law and the prophets were translated from the dialect of the Hebrews" (ἐκ τῆς τῶν Ἑβραίων διαλέκτου εἰς τὴν Ἑλλάδα γλῶτταν). In Fragment 5d, Clement gives a slightly altered version of Fragment 5, reporting, "... not only the Hebrews (οἱ Ἑβραῖοι) but also the Greeks (οἱ Ἕλληνες) recognize the seventh day as sacred."

[79] The only occurrence of Ἰουδαῖος is in Anatolius' introductory material in Frg. 1.16.

ment, "our countrymen (ἡμετέϱων δὲ πολιτῶν)" is, however, revealing of his own solidarity with his ancestors.

This mention of the way he aligns himself with his ancestral tradition is an appropriate transition to the second feature of his work: his consistent practice of claiming ownership of the Jewish tradition. When referring to the Mosaic law, Moses the legislator, or related aspects of the tradition, Aristobulus typically claims them as "ours."

In Fragment 2, §10.1 he refers to "our Law (τοῦ νόμου τοῦ παϱ ἡμῖν);" in §10.3 to "our lawgiver Moses (ὁ νομοθέτης ἡμῶν Μωσῆς);" in §10.8 Moses is said to indicate something "through our law" (διὰ τῆς νομοθεσίας ἡμῶν); in §10.13, he refers simply to ἡ νομοθεσία, but we are expected to read "our law code."

In Fragment 3, §12.1 Aristobulus claims that Plato followed "the tradition of the law that we use (τῇ καθ' ἡμᾶς νομοθεσίᾳ)," and he reports that Pythagoras "… borrowed many of the things in our traditions (πολλὰ τῶν παϱ' ἡμῖν)."

Fragment 4 §12.3 refers to what Moses said "in our lawcode (διὰ τῆς νομοθεσίας ἡμῖν)." In §12.8 he refers to "our school (ἡ καθ' ἡμᾶς αἵϱεσις)" and the "whole structure of our law (ἡ δὲ τοῦ νόμου κατασκευὴ πᾶσα τοῦ καθ' ἡμᾶς)." He refers in Frg. 5 §12.11 to "Solomon, one of our ancestors (τῶν ἡμετέϱων πϱογόνων τις εἶπε Σολομοῶν)," and in §12.11 to "our code of laws (διὰ τῆς νομοθεσίας)." In §12.13 we are told that Homer and Hesiod took their information "from our books (ἐκ τῶν ἡμετέϱων βιβλίων)."

The cumulative effect of these references is to underscore the assertive form of Aristobulus' stance towards the tradition. Yet it is precisely what one would expect from a work couched in the form of an address to King Ptolemy. It is, after all, the stance of Aristobulus, the exponent of the tradition, set over against an opposing point of view. Nevertheless, some of the occurrences are quite revealing, especially his reference to "our school (ἡ καθ' ἡμᾶς αἵϱεσις, §12.8)." Since he is operating out of a philosophical outlook, this might well refer to a Jewish school of allegorical exegesis in existence in the mid-second century BCE. If so, this would suggest a much more formalized social setting within which these "Hebrew" traditions were being studied, taught, and transmitted.

This is worth noting, since Aristobulus is often regarded as a Hellenistic Jew who meets Greek thought more than half way. We detect none of the supercilious, acerbic tone found, for instance, in the Wisdom of Solomon or the Sibylline Oracles. He is much closer in spirit to the *Epistle of Aristeas* in the way he shows implicit respect for the Greek tradition. Only if it were genuinely admirable would it make sense to claim that Greek wisdom were derived from Moses. His commitment to allegorical exegesis further attests his indebtedness to the Greek tradition.

Even though Aristobulus does not use Ἑβραῖος as a term of self-description, he would doubtless be pleased that the tradition remembered him that way. The biblical story he allegorizes is unabashedly "our law" given to us by "our lawgiver Moses." He solidly identifies with its characters, the Hebrews, as "our countrymen." The distinctive practices of the tradition, especially Sabbath observance, are worth investigating, and they drive him to find echoes of this noble tradition in the most famous of the Greek poets from Homer and Hesiod onward. But equally important is the lofty conception of God found in the Bible. Look far enough, Aristobulus insists, and the industrious student will find this view of God also echoed in Orpheus and Aratus. Aristobulus is much more interested in looking for connections and continuities between the Jewish and Greek traditions than in contrasting them. He is not willing, however, to retain Ζεύς and Δίς in the texts he quotes, substituting θεός instead, which suggests that there are lines he will not cross.[80]

Is Aristobulus at home in Egypt? The answer has to be yes. There is little, if any, reference, much less nostalgia, for the homeland. The images of Jerusalem and Judea, the temple and its worship, do not inspire him the way they do Pseudo-Hecataeus. He seems much more resigned to Diaspora existence and has made concerted efforts to come to terms with a life of mutual co-existence with Greek tradition. In this respect, he is Philo's worthy predecessor.

Paul

The term Ἰουδαῖος occurs 25 times in the undisputed letters, once in the disputed letters (Col 3:11). Of the 25 times it occurs in the seven undisputed letters, it occurs fifteen times as a member of a pair, either with "Greek(s)" or "Gentiles": "Jew first and also (to the) Greek" (Rom 1:16; 2:9, 10); "Jews and Greeks" or its equivalent (Rom 3:9; 10:12; 1 Cor 1:22, 24; 10:32; 12:13; Gal 3:28; similarly in Col 3:11, though the order is reversed); "Jews and Gentiles" (Rom 3:29; 9:24; 1 Cor 1:23; Gal 2:14–

---

[80] See Frg. 4 §7 and comments in *FHJA* 3.222 n. 112.

15 [2×]). Of the other ten times, it is used five times in the singular.[81] Three of the five usages in the plural are articular. Generally, plural uses are undifferentiated—"Jews" as a whole (1 Cor 9:20; 2 Cor 11:24; Gal 2:15; 1 Thess 2:14); one appears to refer to Jewish Christians (Gal 2:13).

Clearly, Paul thinks of humanity dichotomously. One half is comprised of Jews, the other half of people whom he variously designates "Greeks (οἱ Ἕλληνες)" and "Gentiles (τὰ ἔθνη)." That these latter two categories are synonymous is clear from 1 Cor. 1:22–24 and Rom. 3:9, 29; 9:24. The basis for this fundamental distinction appears not to be based on language. "Greeks" are not those who speak Greek, nor are "Jews" those who speak Aramaic or Hebrew. The contrast in Gal 2:14 between "living as a Gentile and living as a Jew (ἐθνικῶς καὶ οὐχὶ Ἰουδαϊκῶς)" doubtless signals distinctive lifestyles, in this case, those resulting from differences in eating practices and social interaction.

Twice he uses the term Ἰουδαϊσμός (Gal 1:13–14). In both cases, it clearly refers to a way of life that is identifiably "Jewish." In 1:14 he identifies the "traditions of my fathers (τῶν πατρικῶν μου παραδόσεων)" as one of its central elements.

Rom 2:17–24 underscores the Mosaic law as a central ingredient of Jewish identity: relying on it, being instructed in it, and regarding it as the "embodiment of knowledge and truth" (v. 20). His exposition of "true circumcision" in Rom 2:25–29 only serves to emphasize how determinative this rite of initiation was for establishing male Jewish identity. Indeed, as Rom 3:29–30 shows, "the circumcised" and "the uncircumcised" are but alternative labels for Jews and Gentiles. When Paul speaks of "being a Jew (Ἰουδαῖος ὑπάρχων)" or elaborates on its significance and implications as he does in Rom 2:17–29, he clearly has in mind an ethnic identity whose distinctive elements include Jewish parentage, male circumcision, Torah observance in its many dimensions, and a distinctive lifestyle that results from all of these. Such a profile of behavior must be presupposed for his designation of Titus as "being a Greek (Ἕλλην ὤν)" to have any meaning at all (Gal 2:3).

His infrequent use of Ἑβραῖος offers a sharp contrast to Artapanus and Ezekiel the Tragedian, for both of whom it had special significance. The polemical description of his opponents in 2 Cor 11:22 doubtless employs terms they themselves proudly used to establish their cre-

---

[81] On Paul's use of Ἰουδαῖος in the singular, see W. Gutbrod, "Ἰσραήλ," *TDNT* 3.380–82.

dentials: Ἑβραῖοι, Ἰσραηλῖται, σπέρμα Ἀβραάμ. Yet Ἑβραῖος is used by Paul approvingly in his self-description in Phil 3:5, which encapsulates as well as any other single passage the essence of Paul's self-understanding as a Jew: περιτομῇ ὀκταήμερος, ἐκ γένους Ἰσραήλ, φυλῆς Βενιαμίν, Ἑβραῖος ἐξ Ἑβραίων, κατὰ νόμον Φαρισαῖος. That this depicts his *former* way of life may be significant, although the persona reflected in his letters continues to be informed by some of these categories (Rom 11:1).[82]

Yet another aspect of ethnic identity is signified by Paul's use of "Israel," which occurs sixteen times in the undisputed letters. Most often, he is thinking of "Israel after the flesh," the people of Israel whose deeds are narrated in the OT (Rom 9:27, 31; 10:19, 21; 11:2, 7–10; 1 Cor 10:18; 2 Cor 3:7, 13; cf. Phil 3:5). Yet "Israel" continues to be a present, theological reality whom he doubtless, although not explicitly, identifies with the Jews of his own time (Rom 9:6; 11:25–26). This becomes especially clear in those instances where he uses "Israel" and "Gentiles" as contrasting ethnic categories (Rom 9:30; 11:25). It is also seen in the close affinity Paul feels with "Israelites," whom he calls his "own people, [his] kindred according to the flesh" (Rom 9:3). The extent of its theological significance is reflected in his speaking of the church as the "Israel of God" (Gal 6:16).[83]

As important as the terms Ἰουδαῖος, Ἑβραῖος, Ἰσραήλ and their cognates are as markers of ethnic identity for Paul, they must be considered along with his use of the categories "circumcised/uncircumcised," "circumcision/uncircumcision." The sheer frequency of his use of περιτέμνω (8x, 1x in Col 2:11), περιτομή (25x in the undisputed letters, 6x in the disputed letters), and ἀκροβυστία (16x in the undisputed letters, 3x in the disputed letters) is itself an important indication of how basic these terms were in the configuration of Paul's world. The heavy concentration of uses in Romans and Galatians reinforces the point even further.

Quite often, Paul has in view the physical act itself, either the state of having the foreskin intact—being uncircumcised, or the physical act of having the foreskin removed (Rom 2:25, 26; 3:1; 4:10, 11, 12; 1 Cor 7:18–19; Gal 2:3; 5:2, 3, 6, 11; 6:12, 13, 15; Phil 3:5). Yet his description of the physical act easily merges with his understanding of

---

[82] Nor does Paul use the cognate forms of Ἑβραῖος, including Ἑβραΐς, Ἑβραϊκός, Ἑβραϊστί.

[83] This idea is further developed in Eph 2:12.

these terms as ethnic labels. This is seen especially well in Rom 4:12 where Paul says that Abraham is "the ancestor of the circumcised (Jews – πατέρα περιτομῆς) who are not only circumised (the physical act – ἐκ περιτομῆς) but who also follow the example of the faith that our ancestor Abraham had before he was circumcised" (the physical act – ἐν ἀκροβυστίᾳ). Not surprisingly, these terms also function as ethnic labels, where "the circumcised" or "(the) circumcision" means "Jews" and "the uncircumcised" or "(the) uncircumcision" means "Gentiles" (Rom 2:26, 27; 3:30; 4:9, 12; 15:8; Gal 2:7; also Col 3:11; 4:11; Tit 1:10).

This alignment of categories is also reflected in the way Paul substitutes "Gentiles (τὰ ἔθνη)" for "the uncircumcision (ἡ ἀκροβυστία)" in Gal 2:7–9.[84]

"Circumcision" and "Jewishness" become most closely aligned in Rom 2:25–29, where Paul expounds on the meaning of Ἰουδαῖος by drawing on the spiritual understanding of circumcision in Deut 10:16. This allows him to distinguish between "outward" (ἐν τῷ φανερῷ) and "inner" (ἐν τῷ κρυπτῷ) dimensions of Jewishness. In this discussion "keeping/breaking the law" also functions as a central ingredient of the definition. Interestingly, this passage seems to imply that "being Jewish (Ἰουδαῖος)" is the broader category of ethnic identity and that "circumcision" and "keeping the law" are subsets, or constituent components, of this larger category. Even so, in the aforementioned references, where "circumcision" and "uncircumcision" serve as shorthand expressions for Jews and Gentiles, this subtle distinction vanishes.

The two exceptions to Paul's general pattern of usage are Gal 2:12, where "those of the circumcision (οἱ ἐκ περιτομῆς)" almost certainly are Jewish Christians, and Phil 3:3, where Paul insists that "we are the circumcision (ἡ περιτομή)." The latter probably recalls Rom 2:25–29, and thus Paul would be insisting that he (and his co-workers) are "true Jews" who worship in Spirit.

As for the other half of humanity, Paul's primary descriptive term is "Gentiles (τὰ ἔθνη)." The term occurs 45 times (and one in 1 Cor 10:20 v. l.) in his undisputed letters. About half of these uses, most of which cluster in Romans and Galatians, are quite general. They are the people to whom Paul has been sent as an apostle (Rom 1:5; 11:13; 15:16–18; Gal 1:16; 2:2), and through his ministry they gain access to God's hidden mystery (Rom 16:26). As beneficiaries of God's promise

---

[84] A similar equation is reflected in Eph 2:11.

through Israel, they have shared in "spiritual blessings" (Rom 15:27) and can be expected to share their material blessings with their bene- factors. Accordingly, Paul can designate his churches as "churches of the Gentiles" (Rom 16:4). Gentiles are also the "nations" mentioned in the OT (Rom 15:9–12) to whom God's promise to Abraham extended (Gal 3:8, 14). The term also describes concrete realities in Paul's world. When Jews behave inconsistently, God's name is "blasphemed among the Gentiles" (Rom 2:24). Paul's apostolic afflictions include "danger from Gentiles" (2 Cor 11:26). Incest among the Corinthians is a prac- tice not even found "among Gentiles" (1 Cor 5:1). 1 Cor 12:2 suggests a pattern of distinctive practices left behind by Gentile converts, most notably worshipping idols. The discussion in Galatians 2 sharply dis- tinguishes Gentiles as those with whom Peter freely dined until James's people came (Gal 2:12) and those whom Peter apparently wished to be circumcised, or at least, live as Jews (Gal 2:14).

In a few cases, τὰ ἔθνη seems best rendered as "nations" (Rom 4:17– 18; 10:19).

Some dozen times the term is used as one part of a binary oppo- sition to signify people other than Jews (Rom 3:29; 9:24; 30–31; 1 Cor 1:23; 1 Thess 2:14–16), Israel (Rom 11:11–12, 25), or "the circumcised" (Rom 15:8–9; Gal 2:8–9). This oppositional use serves to reinforce Paul's use of "Jews," "Israel," and "the circumcised" as virtually syn- onymous terms.

From Paul's pattern of usage there emerges a fairly distinctive pro- file of his understanding of Gentile ethnic identity. They do not "know God" (1 Thess 4:5), which explains why they are incapable of moral behavior on their own. Similar moral superiority is reflected in Paul's distinction in Gal 2:15 between being "Jewish by birth" and "Gentile sinners." From 1 Thess 4:5 one might conclude that the latter is a redun- dant expression. Probably the most distinctive practice Paul associates with Gentile identity is "being enticed by idols and worshipping them" (1 Cor 12:2). According to Rom 2:14 they are defined by "not having the law." Each of these characterizations has deep roots in the OT and extra-biblical Jewish writings.

There is a slight possibility that Paul links "Gentiles" with geograph- ical locales. In Rom 1:13 he expresses the desire to bear fruit among the Romans as he has "among the rest of the Gentiles." Whether this means non-Jews everywhere else, or non-Jews in other regions out- side Palestine, is unclear. When he says in Rom 16:4 that "all the churches of the Gentiles [give thanks]," presumably he is referring to the churches in the Aegean among whom he has ministered for the past 6–7 years.

As already noted, Paul often uses the term "Greeks" (Ἕλληνες) as a synonym for "Gentiles." It occurs twelve times in the undisputed letters, ten of which are members of the binary opposition "Jew(s) and Greek(s)" (Rom 1:16; 2:9, 10; 3:9; 10:12; 1 Cor 1:22, 24; 10:32; 12:13; and Gal 3:28; also in Col 3:11, although in inverted order). The only time he uses the term alone is when he describes Titus as "being a Greek" (Gal 2:3). The other use is Rom 1:14, where he links the term with "barbarians," and as the next phrase makes clear, "Greeks" are understood as "wise," barbarians as "foolish." As 1 Cor 14:11 shows, "barbarian" signifies a non-Greek—someone whose language would be unintelligible to the Greek-speaking Corinthian church. Col 3:11 may give further precision to the term by its apparent equation of βάρβαρος and Σκύθης, although this is by no means clear. Worth noticing perhaps is how rarely Paul uses the term "barbarian." His use of the phrase "Greeks and barbarians" may be usefully compared with its occurrence in Pseudo-Hecataeus.

There are, of course, other dimensions of Paul's understanding of ethnic identity, but these terms identify some of the main contours of how he constructed this part of his social world. Obviously, Paul operates with a very strong sense of Jewish identity. Anyone with the lineage outlined in Phil 3:5 could hardly do otherwise. Jewish parentage, circumcision, and Torah observance all figure prominently in his understanding of what it means to be Jewish. He also operates with many of the cultural assumptions about Gentiles drawn from his Jewish heritage. His contrast between being "Jewish by birth" and being a "Gentile sinner" (Gal 2:15) aptly captures this spirit of moral superiority (also see 1 Thess 4:5).

Yet, to use John Barclay's term, Paul is an "anomalous Diaspora Jew" in some fundamental ways.[85] Would any of his five predecessors discussed earlier ever be inclined to say, "Circumcision is nothing; uncircumcision is nothing; what matters is keeping God's commandments" (1 Cor 7:19; Gal 5:6; 6:15)? Certainly not Pseudo-Hecataeus, even though he never mentions circumcision directly. And probably not Aristobulus, for all of his willingness to allegorize Torah. If Ezekiel's fondness for "Hebrew" identity is any indication, he too would prob-

---

[85] Barclay, *Jews*, 381–95.

ably dissent. Too little of Demetrius' theological convictions emerge to enable us to say. Of the five, Artapanus would most likely emerge as Paul's ally, although, if Erich Gruen is correct, he would be far more whimsical than Paul in his discussion of it.[86]

Certainly Paul shares with these predecessors a conviction of the law's centrality and the importance of Torah observance in establishing and maintaining Jewish identity. Here, especially, would Paul find a close ally in Pseudo-Hecataeus, although they would doubtless construe differently what this entailed. We see in Paul none of Pseudo-Hecataeus' fascination with Judea, Jerusalem, and the temple. For that matter, it is not clear at all that Paul works with a clearly articulated sense of "Diaspora" the way Pseudo-Hecataeus does. While he mentions "Judea," he never speaks of returning there. Nor is there ever the sense that while he travels throughout the Mediterranean is he in alien territory.

While each of his five predecessors reflect different senses of what it means to be "Jewish," none of them reflects the levels of subtlety found in Paul. Distinctions between "inner" and "outer" Jewishness made in Rom 2:25–29 are absent in any of these authors, as is the complex, midrashic interpretation of Torah reflected especially in Romans and Galatians.

The degree to which these six Hellenistic Jewish authors were willing to meet Hellenism half-way invites comparison. Paul does say that he is "indebted both to Greeks and barbarians, to the wise and foolish" (Rom 1:14), and the extent of his indebtedness remains a matter of debate. Compared with Aristobulus, Paul has engaged Hellenistic tradition far less, at least in the sense that he has been immersed in Greek *paideia*. The display of Greek learning reflected in Aristobulus sets him apart from Paul. His knowledge of the Greek poetic tradition, his familiarity with Plato and Pythagoras, albeit slight, even his commitment to allegorical exegesis as a way of interpreting Torah—all of these are absent in Paul. Paul's use of allegory in Gal 4 places him in a tradition of Jewish exegesis that goes back as early as Aristobulus and reaches full flower in Philo, but it is exceptional rather than typical for him. Nor is there in Paul evidence of the kind of learning and formation in Greek *paideia* that we find in Ezekiel the Tragedian, and the other poets Theodotus and Philo Epicus, for that matter. Their mas-

---

[86] See Gruen, *Heritage*, 155–60.

tery of poetic composition is far more impressive than once thought. At the very least, their works show close familiarity with highly regarded Greek models, from Homer onward. A good case can be made that Demetrius' chronographical concerns reflect a serious level of engagement with Hellenistic historiographical traditions that began to emerge early in the Hellenistic period. But even though Paul does not exhibit his engagement with Hellenistic culture in these same ways, it does him injustice to portray him as a Hellenistic minimalist.

On a final note, it is worth asking whether Paul actually operated with a sense of "Diaspora." He never employs the term or its cognates (see James 1:1; 1 Pet 1:1). He mentions "Judea" four times (Rom 15:31; 2 Cor 1:16; Gal 1:22; 1 Thess 2:14) and "Jerusalem" ten times (Rom. 15:19, 25, 26, 31; 1 Cor 16:3; Gal 1:17–18; 2:1; 4:25–26), but, unlike Acts, the Pauline letters do not yield a clear picture of Paul as a native Palestinian who leaves the homeland to travel in the Diaspora and periodically returns. In his letters, Paul offers no clear indications that when he travels to and from Jerusalem and Judea that he sees himself moving back and forth between his "homeland" and the Diaspora. Several times, Paul reports trips to Jerusalem or Judea (Rom 15:25; 1 Cor 16:3; 2 Cor 1:16; Gal 1:18; 2:1), but he does not employ the language of "returning." In fact, the only place to which he says he "returns" is Damascus (Gal 1:17). The closest he comes to suggesting a view of the world with Jerusalem at its center is Rom 15:19, "from Jerusalem and as far around as Illyricum I have fully proclaimed the good news of Christ." Nowhere does Paul locate a place he calls home, unless it is heaven, where he claims to have citizenship (Phil 3:20).

When Paul refers to people in the Diaspora, he does so by referring to their city or province: "Corinthians" (Κορίνθιοι, 2 Cor 6:11); "Macedonians" (Μακεδόνες, 2 Cor 9:2, 4); "Philippians" (Φιλιππήσιοι, Phil 4:15); "Thessalonians" (Θεσσαλονικεῖς, 1 Thess. 1:1). He constructs his territorial world using Roman provincial names: Achaia, Macedonia, Asia, Arabia, Judea, Illyricum, etc.

It is unclear whether Paul correlates ethnic and geographical categories. Does he, for example, think that Gentiles live primarily, or even exclusively, outside Palestine, or that Jews are primarily associated with Judea? In addressing the Romans, he expresses hope in reaping fruit among them "as I have among the rest of the Gentiles" (Rom 1:13). This may suggest that he thinks of places like Rome and the other regions where he ministered, primarily in the Aegean, as places where "Gentiles" live. Similarly, when he speaks of "all the churches of the

Gentiles" (Rom 16:4), presumably he means all of the churches he established in his mission to the Gentiles, which obviously fall outside Palestine. In 1 Thess 2:13–16 (assuming it is authentic), Paul speaks of the Thessalonians imitating the churches in Judea, suffering "the same things from your own compatriots as they did from the Jews." Is he referring to their fellow Thessalonians, Greeks, or Gentiles?

A Note on Theodotus, Fragment 4

The patriarch Jacob figures centrally in the fragments from Theodotus the epic poet. Of particular interest is the rape of Dinah and its implications for Jacob's family. Theodotus' recasting of the biblical story in the form of epic poetry heightens the differences between the families of Jacob and Shechem, emphasizing in particular the importance of circumcision as an identifying rite in Jewish life. Theodotus underscores the necessity of circumcision and the impermissibility of intermarriage among Jews and non-Jews. Every indication is that he is drawing the lines of ethnic identity quite emphatically.

Introducing Fragment 4 are two paragraphs where Alexander Polyhistor summarizes Theodotus' account of the rape of Dinah. It is difficult to know the extent to which Polyhistor's summary utilizes Theodotus' own language. In the summary, he reports that Hamor came with his father Shechem to Jacob in order to obtain Dinah as his wife. We are told, "But her father said that he would not give her until all those living in Shechem became Jews by being circumcised" (τὸν δὲ οὐ φάναι δώσειν, πρὶν ἂν ἢ πάντας τοὺς οἰκοῦντας τὰ Σίκιμα περιτεμνομένους Ἰουδαῖσαι). Then follows Fragment 4 where Jacob insists on the necessity of circumcision.

This use of Ἰουδαῖσαι is worth comparing with the single use of the term by Paul in Gal 2:14, where he reports having said to Cephas, "If you, though a Jew, live like a Gentile and not like a Jew, how can you compel the Gentiles to live like Jews?" (εἰ σὺ Ἰουδαῖος ὑπάρχων ἐθνικῶς καὶ οὐχὶ Ἰουδαϊκῶς ζῇς, πῶς τὰ ἔθνη ἀναγκάζεις ἰουδαΐζειν). In commenting on the New Testament hapax ἰουδαΐζειν, scholars regularly note its single use in the LXX, Esther 8:17, where it is reported that in response to the Jews' celebration of the king's edict, καὶ πολλοὶ τῶν ἐθνῶν περιετέμοντο καὶ ἰουδάϊζον διὰ τὸν φόβον τῶν Ἰουδαίων. Here, the NRSV follows the MT in its translation: "... many of the peoples of the country professed to be Jews, because the fear of the Jews had fallen upon them." "Professed to be Jews" renders מִתְיַהֲדִים, the hithpael participle of יהד, which itself is a hapax. The LXX, however, is more graphic and emphatic by its double translation of this obscure Hebrew term: "... many of the peoples had themselves circumcised and became Jews because of their fear of the Jews."

Apart from the fact that περιτέμνω and Ἰουδαΐζω occur together in Esther 8:17 and Theodotus, suggesting that they are used synonymously, both of these usages, if taken seriously as parallels, would require ἰουδαΐζειν in Gal. 2:14 to be rendered not as "live as a Jew," but "become a Jew," that is, be circumcised. This would suggest that the issue is not keeping Jewish customs, such as food laws and fellowship requirements, but circumcision itself. On this reading, Paul would appear to be accusing Peter not of being inconsistent in the ways he relates to Gentiles in social settings, but of requiring Gentiles to be circumcised.[87]

---

[87] Other uses noted by *BDAG* include: Plutarch, Cicero 7:6, mentions a "freedman named Caecilius, who was suspected of Jewish practices" (ἔνοχος τῷ ἰουδαΐζειν); Josephus *Wars* 2.454: Metilius, commander of the Roman garrison at the siege of Jerusalem, escapes being massacred by the rebels by promising "to turn Jew, and even to be circumcised" (καὶ μέχρι περιτομῆς ἰουδαΐσειν); 2.463: τοὺς ἰουδαΐζοντας; *Acta Pilati* A 2.1; Ignatius, *Mag.* 10:3. Also, see H. D. Betz, *Galatians* (Hermeneia; Philadelphia: Fortress, 1979) 112.

THE JEWISH PAUL AMONG THE GENTILES
TWO PORTRAYALS

Leander E. Keck

The Apostle to the Gentiles

What "everybody knows" often conceals how much is not known. So it is with Paul: "everybody knows" that this ardent Jew was Christ's apostle to non-Jews; that he traversed much of Anatolia as well as Macedonia and Achaia, leaving in his wake house churches in key cities; and that to do so he endured, by his own count, 195 lashes from fellow Jews, unspecified beatings by rods during three arrests by civil authorities, multiple imprisonments, three shipwrecks and stoning, as well as hunger, hypothermia, and persistent anxiety over the well-being of the volatile house churches with whom his relationship was strained repeatedly (2 Cor 11:23–28). What was he trying to accomplish? And why was it so important that he willingly endured such hardships? These are some of the things that are not known, at least not very well. To be sure, we know that he believed he had this task from God, "who had set me apart before I was born and called me through his grace … so that I might preach him among the Gentiles" (Gal 1:15–16). Still, that does not answer the first question, partly because the function of Paul's statement is to account for his apostleship, not to characterize its goal, and especially because the statement does not disclose God's purpose for preaching Christ among the Gentiles.[1]

Not until a pivotal juncture, when he could look back on his activity while also anticipating its next phase (Rom 15:14–32), does he put in writing what he sought to achieve, and this quite apart from the astounding claim that he preached from Jerusalem to modern Albania (Rom 15:19), is rather cryptic: "Now I am speaking to you Gentiles. [Why does he say this when Rom 1:13–15 indicates that he has been writing to Gentiles all along?][2] Inasmuch as I am apostle to the Gentiles

---

[1] For a thorough discussion of Paul's understanding of his Gentile mission, see Terence L. Donaldson, *Paul and the Gentiles: Remapping the Apostle's Convictional World* (Minneapolis: Fortress Press, 1997).

[2] The fact that in 2:17 Paul addresses the Jew reveals little, if anything, about the

[literally, "of the Gentiles, (εἰμι ἐγὼ ἐθνῶν ἀπόστολος)"], I glorify my ministry in order to make my own people jealous and thus save some of them" (Rom 11:13–14).[3] Surely there was more to it than this! Is being "the Gentiles' apostle," and the sufferings that go with it, but a means to a more important end, whose expected result, however, is rather meager ("some of them")? To grasp this intriguing self-portrayal one must see it in the context of Romans 9–11.

There is, of course, another portrayal of Paul, the Jewish apostle among the Gentiles—that found in the Book of Acts. Its portrayal has been pummeled repeatedly by critics, to be sure, and not without reason because at important points it diverges markedly from what Paul himself says or implies (particularly about the council in Jerusalem and its aftermath; Acts 15 and Gal 2). Actually, however, it is precisely the many differences that make the agreements fascinating, and potentially significant. It is Paul's statement in Rom 9–11, however, that gets attention first.

Paul's Self-Presentation in Romans 9–11

Especially significant is Paul's remarkable, sudden, intense personal involvement in the subject matter of these chapters.[4] After the resounding positive peroration at the end of ch.8 ("nothing can separate us from the love of God in Christ Jesus our Lord"), he suddenly insists that he is not lying when he claims to have "great sorrow and unceasing anguish"—exaggerating perhaps but not lying. Yet he does not say exactly what causes such agony, though his insistence that he is not lying suggests that he knows he is being accused of turning his back on his people.[5] The reader also sees that Paul is troubled by the disparity between Israel's privileges—itemized—and the fact that his own "kindred according to the flesh" have refused the gospel of God's righteous-

---

readership, for this is a rhetorical strategy. Bell's claim that Paul addresses Jewish Christians, Gentile Christians, non-Christian Jews, and non-Christian Gentiles goes beyond the evidence. Richard H. Bell, *Provoked to Jealousy: The Origin and Purpose of the Jealousy Motif in Romans 9–11* (WUNT 2.63; Tübingen: J.C.B. Mohr-Siebeck, 1994) 71.

[3] So NRSV. Unless noted, all quotations of scripture use this version for the sake of convenience.

[4] For a discussion of the new authorial voice and personal tone that mark chaps. 9–11, see Stanley K. Stowers, *A Rereading of Romans: Justice, Jews and Gentiles* (New Haven and London: Yale University Press, 1994) 289–93.

[5] This is emphasized by Francis Watson, *Paul, Judaism and the Gentiles: A Sociological Approach.* (SNTSMS 56; Cambridge: Cambridge University Press, 1986) 161.

ness which brings salvation "to the Jew first" (Rom 1:16). So painful is this disjunction between what is theologically true and what has become historically actual that he would be willing to forfeit his own salvation (being "cut off from Christ" is the antithesis of being inseparable from God's love in Christ) if doing so would reverse the situation (Rom 9:1–5). A bit later (10:1) he insists that it is his "heart's desire and prayer that they may be saved."[6] Manifestly, Paul is not writing as a puzzled observer who is fascinated by someone else's self-contradiction, for those in view are his "own people." Being involved with Christ has not severed him from them. To the contrary, it has made his relation to his people painful, comparable to the way the presence of the Spirit in the yet-unredeemed body exacerbates the groaning shared with the yet-unredeemed creation (Rom 8:19–23).

What accounts for the obvious pathos with which this self-involvement is expressed? It is unlikely that it reflects an uncertainty when he began because he did not know where he would come out, i.e., "all Israel will be saved." Romans 9–11 is too carefully crafted to warrant the inference that Paul is recording the flow of his thinking as he struggled toward a solution not yet reached.[7] Instead, in trying to persuade the readers, step by step, to accept the solution to which he has already come, he emphasizes his agony as part of the rhetorical strategy for eliciting an empathetic reception for his argument. This does not imply, however, that it is sheer rhetorical flourish. Were that the case, he would hardly have insisted (twice!) on the truth of what he says. The more one takes Paul seriously here, the more one wants to know what generated this agony and what keeps it alive ("unceasing") in the heart of one who identifies himself as "the Gentiles' apostle."

Might Paul be grieved over the failure of the comity agreement reached a decade before in Jerusalem, according to which the "pillar apostles" would go to the Jews, while he and his associates go to the Gentiles (Gal 2:9)?[8] E.P. Sanders has, in fact, argued that Paul is in

---

[6] For no apparent reason, Stowers adds "from God's anger." *A Rereading of Romans*, 311.

[7] So, e.g., Nikolaus Walter, "Zur Interpretation von Römer 9–11," *ZTK* 81 (1984) 176, and Calvin J. Roetzel, *Paul: The Man and the Myth* (Columbia: University of South Carolina Press, 1998) 130.

[8] It is difficult to discern from Paul's terse formulation just what the participants thought they agreed to. That agreement was inherently flawed because it could be carried out only if the division of labor were essentially geographic (which most interpreters rightly deny). Besides, even if urban Jews lived in well-defined Jewish quarters, their synagogues attracted Gentiles.

anguish because, whereas his mission had been largely successful, that
of the pillar apostles had largely failed. In addition, Sanders proposes
that in Romans 9–11 Paul "rearranges the eschatological sequence so
that it accords with the facts"[9] (non-Jews are saved first, not last). It
is more likely that Paul knew how the gospel fared among Jews, and
that his agony reflects, at least in part, his own experience even though
he does not write with a sense of pique (they rejected me!). If so, this
implies that in going to Gentiles he did not ignore totally his own
people. Part II will return to this.

Though deeply involved in the subject matter, Paul is not writing a
journal in which he deposits his reflections; he is writing a letter to the
believers in Rome, and their interpretation of the widespread Jewish
refusal of the gospel too is a factor in what he writes. Paul has learned
that the refusal has produced (or might well produce) arrogance in
Rome, where the Gentile believers infer that they have taken the Jews'
place in the plan of God. Some such reconstruction is implied in what
Paul says explicitly to the Gentiles in Rom 11:17–32. In other words,
the Jews' unbelief is a problem for Paul because he is a Christian
Jew; simultaneously the Christian Gentiles' arrogance is a problem for
him because he is their Jewish apostle. Paul writes about his people
to Christian Gentiles because they do not truly understand how God
deals with them until and unless they also understand how God deals
with Israel.

Running through the whole discussion, from Rom 9:6 to 11:32, is
the theme of a cleavage in Israel, brought about by God and used by
God. In support of the claim that "it is not as though the word of God
has failed," Paul states the principle that governs the whole: "not all
Israelites truly belong to Israel, and not all of Abraham's children (τέκνα) are his true descendants" (σπέρμα, 9:7). This has always been the
case, first in the distinction between Isaac and Ishmael, then between
Jacob and Esau, so that in each generation "God's purpose in election

---

[9] E. P. Sanders, *Paul, the Law, and the Jewish People* (Philadelphia: Fortress Press, 1983)
185. Donaldson (*Paul and the Gentiles* 188), however, points out that "in the eschatological
pilgrimage tradition [on which Sanders relies for the background of Paul's thought], the
salvation of the Gentile follows the restoration of Israel as a matter not simply of *sequence*
but of *consequence*: it is because they see the redemption of Israel and the glorification of
Zion that the Gentiles abandon their idols and turn to worship the God of Israel. The
inversion of the sequence represents not a simple modification of the tradition, but its
evisceration. Without the restoration of Israel in some form, the hypothesis is deprived
of its explanatory power" (his italics).

might continue." Without the non-elect, there would be no elect; with-out the elect, no grace. The pivotal factor in this electing is neither what humans will nor what they achieve but God who "has mercy on whomever he chooses, and he hardens the heart of whomever he choos-es" (Rom 9:8–18). The God who as potter makes two kinds of vessels from one lump of clay (vv. 20–21) also distinguishes the mass from the remnant (vv. 27–29). The remnant motif is essential for the argument,[10] because by definition the whole has not been rejected so long as the remnant remains. Accordingly, Paul's being "an Israelite, a descendant of Abraham, a member of the tribe of Benjamin" itself shows that God has not repudiated *"the people"* (ὁ λαός), in the sense of *das Volk* (cf. 11:1). In fact, as in Elijah's day, "so too at the present time there is a remnant, chosen by grace"—namely, the Christian Jews, like Paul. Paul presses the cleavage theme relentlessly: Israel [as a people] failed to obtain what it was seeking, the elect [the Christian Jews] attained it, but the rest were hardened" (11:7), indeed by God's own action (11:8–10).

But even so, that God has not rejected his λαός is shown also by the role the non-remnant, the hardened, plays. This majority "stum-bled" but did not fall down—imagery drawn from the racetrack.[11] This "stumbling" picks up from 9:33, according to which God[12] will "lay in Zion the stone that will make people stumble." Just as God caused the hardening, so he caused the stumbling—but for a pur-

---

[10] Donaldson (*Paul and the Gentiles*, 239) notes that statements about the remnant "increase in significance as the argument develops."

[11] Paul's use of the racetrack imagery is discussed both by Stowers, who relates it to the "jealousy" motif (*A Rereading of Romans*, 303–6, 312–16), and by Roetzel, *Paul*, 12–31.

[12] In 9:31–32 Paul explains that Israel did not attain the law of righteousness because they did not strive for it properly (on the basis of faith) but "stumbled (προσέκοψαν) over the stumbling stone (τῷ λίθῳ τοῦ προσκόμματος)," and cites scripture in support (Isa 28:16): "See, I am laying in Zion a stone that will make people stumble (λίθον προσκόμματος), a rock that will make them fall (καὶ πέτραν σκανδάλου), and whoever believes in him [or it] will not be put to shame." The first part of Paul's quotation differs from MT and LXX, both of which refer to a foundation stone (τὰ θεμέλια Σιων λίθον), which is a cornerstone; the second part follows LXX. The first part appears to rely on Isa 8:14 which says that the LORD will "become a sanctuary (ἁγίασμα) and not as a stone for stumbling (οὐχ ὡς λίθον προσκόμματι) nor as a stone of falling (οὐδὲ ὡς πέτρας πτώματι). " Here LXX introduced the negatives οὐχ and οὐδέ. The origin of Paul's form of the quotation is not known. Nor is the referent of the stone self-evident. Although most interpreters think that for Paul it refers to Christ or the gospel, e.g., Joseph A. Fitzmyer, *Romans* (AB 33; New York: Doubleday, 1993) 579–80, Paul Meyer has argued that it refers to the law in "Romans 10:4 and the 'End' of the Law," in *The Divine Helmsman: Studies in God's Control of Human Events, Presented to Lou H. Silberman*, ed. J.L. Crenshaw (New York: Ktav, 1980) 59–78.

pose: "through their stumbling salvation has come to the Gentiles, so
as to make Israel jealous" (11.11). Looking ahead to the salvation of all
Israel (11:26), Paul adds, "Now if their παράπτωμα (RSV and NRSV:
'transgression')[13] means riches for the world, and if their ἥττημα (RSV
and NAS: 'failure')[14] means riches for the Gentiles, how much more
will their πλήρωμα (RSV and NRSV: 'full inclusion')[15] mean!"[16] The
idea that through Israel's tragic action salvation came to Gentiles is so
important for Paul that he restates it in vv. 30–31: "Just as you were
once disobedient to God but have now received mercy because of their
disobedience, so they have now been disobedient in order that, by the
mercy shown to you, they too may now receive mercy."[17]

Having mentioned Israel's "inclusion," Paul now brings the statement with which this essay began: he glorifies his ministry to the Gentiles to provoke his people's jealousy, and so save some of them (11:13–
14). Since this "jealousy" picks up the quotation (in 10:19) from Deut
32:21 ("I [God] will make you jealous of those who are not a nation,"
etc.),[18] Paul implies that *he* is the instrument through which God pro-
vokes this jealousy. Returning to the cleavage motif, Paul adds, "if part
of the dough offered as first fruits is holy, then the whole batch is holy,
and if the root is holy, then the branches are also holy" (11:16).

---

[13] REB renders παράπτωμα as "false step"; NRSV as "stumbling" in order to express
the flow of thought more clearly; NJB has "failure," and CEV reads "sin." Bell (*Provoked
to Jealousy*, 108–10), having reviewed the options, agrees that "transgression" is Paul's
meaning.

[14] NRSV translates ἥττημα as "defeat," NIV and CEV as "loss," REB as "falling
short," and NJB as "fall."

[15] NAS has "fulfillment," NIV "fullness," REB reads "coming to full strength," and
NJB has "when all is restored to them!"

[16] CEV renders v. 12 as follows: "But if the rest of the world's people were helped
so much by Israel's sin and loss, they will be helped even more by their full return,"
thereby shifting the benefit of Israel's inclusion to the Gentiles!

[17] In v. 31 most mss. read αὐτοὶ νῦν ἐλεηθῶσιν, but אBD* 1506 bo omit "now" and
so imply that Israel's receiving mercy will occur in the future, not in the present.

[18] The heart of Bell's monograph, *Provoked to Jealousy*, traces the uses of Deuteron-
omy 32 (the Song of Moses) through early Jewish and early Christian literature, and
concludes that it was an important text for the development of Paul's theology (since
he uses it elsewhere also), not only for the jealousy motif here (284). According to Bell's
interpretation, "Israel would come to see that the Gentiles have received *her* covenant
privileges [by extension not replacement] ... that the Gentiles were playing *her* role in
history," and that they "are now a light to Israel" (199, his italics). This is more likely
than the claim that Paul aimed "to make some Roman Jews jealous of *his* ministry," as
proposed by Mark Nanos, "The Jewish Context of the Gentile Audience Addressed in
Paul's Letter to the Romans," *CBQ* 61 (1999) 302.

Mentioning the root and the branches gives Paul the springboard for his allegory of the olive tree (11:17–24), by which he can now relate the Christian Gentiles to the cleavage in Israel. The main points are fairly clear. (a) Although "some" branches have been broken off (hardened Israel),[19] the root continues with the remaining branches (the elect, the believing Jews).[20] (b) Christian Gentiles, the wild olive, are grafted into the root, alongside the remaining/remnant/branches (ἐν αὐτοῖς), *not* "in their place" as RSV and NRSV have it (v. 17).[21] Not only does this mistranslation nullify the next clause ("sharer of the root," συγκοινωνὸς τῆς ῥίζης), but it makes Paul affirm precisely the line of thought in Rome that produced the arrogance he opposes. Here REB is accurate: "grafted in among them, and have come to share the same root and sap [πιότητος; RSV: 'riches'] as the olive." Both the remnant branches and the grafted branches are related to the root on the same basis: faith. If the grafted Christian Gentiles think otherwise, and lapse into "unfaith" (ἀπιστία) they will be cut off as were the other branches, and for the same reason. In this regard, one may paraphrase 2:11—God is no respecter of branches. (c) If the broken branches do not persist in their "unfaith" God will retrograft them into the root, *not* into the grafted wild olive (i.e., Jewish believers will not enter the Gentile church). Not a word is said about those who are not restored to the root.

In the concluding paragraph (11:25–32) Paul both repeats the "hardening" theme and carries the thought forward: "a hardening has come upon part of Israel,[22] until the full number (πλήρωμα) of the Gentiles has

---

[19] Does "broken off" (ἐξεκλάσθησαν) imply more than what Paul wants to say? Although "broken off" clearly implies total severance, two considerations suggest that this exceeds Paul's point. First, Paul's other references to unbelieving Israel carefully avoid complete separation. In Rom 11:11 he insists that while Israel "stumbled" it did not "fall" (i.e., drop out of the race altogether); in v. 22, saying they are "fallen" allows Paul to refer to God's severity toward them (i.e., the consequences are serious but not fatal); in 11:27 (Isa 27:9) God refers to "my covenant with them, when I take away their sins;" in 11:28 "as regards election, they are [still] beloved." Second, the branches must be "broken off" if they are to be retrografted into the root, a more unnatural, marvelous event than the grafting of the wild olive (v. 24). This imagery would be impossible if the natural branches were merely bent out of shape.

[20] Gaston denies that Paul refers to Christian Jews anywhere in Romans 9–11, and so takes the remaining branches to be Christian Jewish missionaries. This is quite unconvincing. Lloyd Gaston, "Israel's Misstep in the Eyes of Paul," in *The Romans Debate: Revised and Expanded Edition*, ed. K.P. Donfried (Peabody: Hendrickson, 1991) 317.

[21] Donaldson emphasizes the distortion that this mistranslation creates, noting that had Paul thought of displacement he would have written ἀντὶ αὐτῶν not ἐν αὐτοῖς.

[22] Gaston's ("Israel's Misstep," 318) translation of πώρωσις ἀπὸ μέρους τῷ Ἰσραήλ as "a partial blindness has come on Israel" (apparently reading πήρωσις instead of

come in. And so all Israel will be saved, as it is written, 'Out of Zion will come the Deliverer, he will banish ungodliness from Jacob.' And this is my covenant with them when I take away their sins."[23] Corresponding to "all Israel" is the "fullness" of the Gentiles. The hardening of non-remnant Israel will have served its purpose when the πλήρωμα of the Gentiles have "come in" (i.e., been grafted into the root);[24] then the hardening will cease and all Israel will be saved. Together, "the full number of the Gentiles" and "all Israel" (the remnant plus the retro-grafted) constitute the olive tree.

Four inferences are to be noted. *First*, although Paul does not say *when* God's purpose will be achieved, there can be little doubt that he assumes it will be at the Eschaton. *Second*, the conjunction of the cited biblical texts implies that the Deliverer who will take Israel's sins away is God, the doer throughout.[25] This removal of sins/ungodliness fulfills the condition for the broken branches' retrografting—the end of unbelief (v. 23). *Third*, not before then will the cleavage between hardened Israel and the remnant be overcome. Until then, it remains the case that "not all Israelites truly belong to Israel and not all of Abraham's children are his true descendants" (9:7). *Fourth*, the identity of the root is implied in vv. 28–29. By introducing the declaration that "the gifts and calling of God are irrevocable" with "for" (γάρ), Paul identifies this as the validating basis for the previous statement: "as regards the gospel they [hardened Israel] are enemies [NRSV adds 'of God'] for your sake, but as regards election they are beloved, for the sake of their ancestors"—i.e., the patriarchs. In other words, the root is the patriarchs as elected by grace, *not* the empirical Israel.[26] The irrevocability of God's calling and gifts will be manifest at the Eschaton

πώρωσις) distorts the meaning, for Paul is not referring to partial vision, but the unenlightened zeal of 10:2.

[23] NRSV puts v. 27 in quotation marks, implying that it is another quotation. However, only the last line is from a different part of Isaiah (27:9); the first three lines are from Isa 59:20. There the text says that the deliverer will come "for the sake of Zion" (ἕνεκεν Σιων).

[24] Gaston ("Israel's Misstep," 318) thinks this "coming in" alludes to "the eschatological pilgrimage of the Gentiles." Donaldson rightly rejects this interpretation; *Paul and the Gentiles*, 187–97; see also note 6 above.

[25] When Nanos claims that since Jesus the Deliverer has come *to* Zion, Paul is now responsible for bringing this good news *from* Zion to the Diaspora in order to complete the restoration of all Israel, ingenuity has replaced sober exegesis, for this virtually makes Paul the Deliverer. Mark D. Nanos, *The Mystery of Romans: The Jewish Context of Paul's Letter* (Minneapolis: Fortress Press, 1996) 284.

[26] So also Nikolaus Walter, "Zur Interpretation von Römer 9–11," 180–85.

when the root nourishes all Israel and the fullness of the Gentiles. Then the purpose of God's calling and covenanting with Abraham will be achieved: he is to be the father of uncircumcised believers and circumcised believers alike (4:11–12).

There is an inevitable ambiguity about the olive tree. On the one hand, the eschatological retrografting of the branches into the root alongside the wild olive clearly implies that the olive is an eschatological tree. As with other eschatological entities, however, it already exists in the mind of God as the goal of divine activity. Paul had already hinted as much when, in the analogy of the potter and the two kinds of pots, he wrote of "the riches of his glory for the objects of his mercy, which he had prepared beforehand for glory—including us whom he called, not from Jews only but also from the Gentiles" (9:21–24). On the other hand, the tree is not wholly future, for currently wild olive branches are being grafted into it alongside the remnant branches. This ambiguity stems partly from the limited capacity of the tree image to express the full range of Paul's thought, and partly from the already/not yet dimension of his eschatology. When these two factors are not given their due, interpreters readily see deep contradictions between Romans 9 and 11.

The distinction between the root and the tree is, however, essential particularly in light of Paul's letter to the Galatians. It struggled with the same question: How do Gentiles become part of Abraham's "seed"? This became a burning issue because some "Teachers," as Martyn's commentary calls them, insisted that male believers must be circumcised—i.e., become proselytes and so become incorporated fully into the historical, ethnic children of Abraham. In this light, it is apparent why the distinction between the root and the tree is essential: whoever takes the olive tree to be ethnic Israel has Paul espouse exactly the position he opposed in Galatia. That he would have reversed himself so completely on such a basic matter may not be out of the question but inferring that he did requires a very powerful imagination—as well as evidence.

This overview of Romans 9–11 has exposed three things that are pertinent to Paul's understanding of his vocation. The first concerns Paul himself; the second pertains to his people, and third to Christian Gentiles. *First*, as "the Gentiles' apostle" he recognizes that some of his people have accepted the gospel, but he agonizes over the majority that refused it. Moreover, on the one hand, though he does not say, "Despite my best efforts … ," this agony reflects his own experience, at least in part, while on the other, even as the instrument by which God will provoke Israel to "jealousy," he does not expect the situation to change drastically as a result of his mission, for he hopes to save only "some," presumably because he labors during the time of the hardening.[27] *Second*, the painful current cleavage in his people, the distinction between the hardened and the remnant, does not annul God's grace in history but manifests it. It is through hardened Israel's refusal of the gospel that salvation has come to the Gentiles. *Third*, currently, the Christian Gentiles are being linked to the Abrahamic root alongside the remnant branches; in due course, at the End, all Israel will be saved because God will end the hardening and forgive.

Given the uniqueness of Romans 9–11 within a unique letter, it is appropriate to ask whether, and to what extent, these three conclusions appear also in Paul's previous letters.[28] In doing so, however, one must bear in mind that each of the other six uncontested letters responds to situations in Paul's churches, none of which (except perhaps Galatians) required him to reflect thematically on the topic of this essay. Consequently, what evidence there is will be allusive and indirect, for the evidence sought pertains to what Paul did as well as to what he says.

Paul's Self-Presentation in Other Letters

While Paul's other letters give ample evidence of his "unceasing anguish," consistently it is evoked by developments within the house churches, not by the Jews' negative response to the gospel. He does, of course, point out that the gospel of the crucified is a "stumbling block" to Jews and foolishness to Greeks (1 Cor 1:23). While this could well reflect his experience in preaching to both, it could also express his knowledge of how the gospel was viewed by those who did not find it to be God's power and wisdom. In any case, since here the Jews' refusal simply serves as the foil for Paul's positive point, there is no hint that their action causes him pain. Nor does Paul show any anguish when

---

[27] This interpretation differs from that of N.T. Wright, who, denying that Paul predicted "a large-scale, last-minute salvation of Jews" at the *parousia*, claims that Paul saw historical continuity between the "some" saved by his Gentile mission and the salvation of "all Israel" at the end, indeed, that Paul envisioned "a steady flow of Jews into the church." See Wright's *The Climax of the Covenant: Christ and Law in Pauline Theology* (Edinburgh: T & T Clark, 1991) 250–51. Were that the case, there would have been little basis for Paul's agony in Rom 9:1–2.

[28] 1 Thess 2:14–16 will be bracketed out of this discussion because its genuineness remains in doubt.

he interprets the story of the veil that Moses put over his face lest the Israelites see the glory it acquired during the rendezvous with God on the mountain. Of the biblical Israelites Paul says, "Their minds were hardened." Of contemporary Jews he says, "Indeed, to this very day, whenever Moses is read, a veil lies over their minds, but when one turns to the Lord, the veil is removed" (2 Cor 3:12–16). There may be sorrow in this comment, but no sign of "unceasing anguish." Nor, it should be noted, does he say that the minds in the synagogue are veiled because they have been hardened.

Moreover, Paul's knowledge that only a few Jews accept the gospel is built into the way his letters refer to his readers. Compared with the frequent references to their turn from idolatry and to warnings against returning to it unwittingly (1 Thess 1:9; 1 Cor 6: 9–11; 10:14–22; 12:1–2; Gal 4:9–11), apart from the passage just noted, there are no other passages in which Paul writes unambiguously about Jewish readers' "turn to the Lord." Indeed, Sanders notes that "of those definitely known to have been won by Paul, not a single one can be identified *from his letters* as being Jewish."[29] That may be accidental, of course. Be that as it may, the same observation holds true for the problems he addressed in the letters; they have their roots in Gentile ("pagan") values and sensibilities, including the problems connected with "idol meat" (1 Cor 8, 10). Likewise, none of Paul's critical comments about the law in general or about circumcision in particular read like responses to questions Jewish converts raised because of his message. Indeed, it is Paul who raises questions about the role of the law because those on whom it was being imposed apparently didn't have any questions that went to the heart of the matter. Nonetheless, it would be rash to infer from these observations that Paul's churches were completely Gentile, though with an occasional Jew. Such a conclusion would require one to regard 1 Cor 7:18–20 as purely hypothetical—a consequence hard to verify. Here he writes that all should remain what they were when called by God, and that "this is my rule in all the churches,"—namely, the circumcised should "not seek to remove the marks of circumcision" and the uncircumcised should not attempt to acquire them. In short, fragmentary though the evidence is, it is likely that Paul's churches were composed predominantly of Gentiles, and that their Jewish component was indeed but a "remnant" of Israel.

[29] Sanders, *Paul, the Law, and the Jewish People*, 182–3 (italics added).

One need not speculate long on how they came to be included, for two passages point to Paul's own efforts to persuade them to accept the gospel. The first is 1 Cor 9:19–23, where he writes that his mode of life was flexible for the sake of his mission. "To the Jews I became as a Jew, in order to win Jews … . To those outside the law, I became as one outside the law so that I might win those outside the law. I have become all things to all people, that I might by all means save some." It is doubtful that all this is hyperbolic, as Sanders claims.[30] But even if this is true of the last sentence, it does not hold for what preceded it. Rather, since Paul was convinced that food laws and circumcision were *adiaphora*, he could be observant or not observant without jeopardizing his salvation. By being Jewish among Jews and non-Jewish among Gentiles, he could show that in Christ such matters were indeed *adiaphora*: he could also show Jews that, in Sanders' apt phrase, "Jews who enter the Christian movement renounce nothing."[31] Understandably, to those who did not share his standpoint, he surely appeared to be a man without principle.

The other passage is 2 Cor 11:24, where Paul mentions the five times he received thirty-nine lashes from the Jews. That is, he was subjected to synagogue discipline (he assumes he need not explain this), which he could easily have been spared by simply avoiding the Jewish community altogether and living as a Gentile among Gentiles. Had he done that, it is hard to see why synagogue officials would have taken action. They might have been dismayed or disgusted, but would they have cared what this traveling Jew told Gentiles about Jesus? The text, however, clearly implies that there were five occasions—perhaps in more than one place—when he was punished for violating what the Jewish community deemed sacred.[32] The fact that he accepted the lash shows that he did not deny the synagogue's right to discipline him, for he still saw himself as part of the Jewish people. He was not disciplined by outsiders, nor did his arrival in a given city imply that he was the

---

[30] *Ibid.*, 186–87; equally hyperbolic according to Sanders is Paul's claim that he had preached all the way from Jerusalem to Illyricum (Rom 15:19); the latter is more likely than the former.

[31] *Ibid.*, 176. Might this observation account, at least in part, for the fact that Paul's letters do not address problems of Jewish converts?

[32] While this statement may be taken to suggest that Paul continued to visit synagogue communities during his Aegean mission (as reflected in Acts), it must be noted that no explicit time-frame is given. It might be the case, for example, that all of these events came from the 11 to 14 years during which he was based in Antioch and working in the regions of Syria and Cilicia (Gal 1:21–2:3), which would have included his "hometown" of Tarsus.

outsider. In short, both passages show that Paul did not construe his apostleship to Gentiles to entail ignoring fellow Jews. The implications of the five disciplinary acts may well have been part of the experiences that generated the "sorrow and unceasing anguish" he pointed out to the Romans.

Another cluster of material shows that his mission indeed grafted the wild olive into the Abrahamic root. This material is of two closely-related kinds: Paul's use of scripture as a self-evident authority, and the naturalness with which he uses the vocabulary of biblical-Jewish self-understanding to express the identity of his predominantly Gentile churches. This discussion concentrates on the latter. Paul's usage can be called "natural" because he does not find it necessary to explain it or justify using it, even though, historically speaking, using it this way was indeed quite unnatural.[33]

To begin with, Paul repeatedly refers to believers in his orbit as "saints" (ἅγιοι, e.g., 1Cor 1:2; 2Cor 2:1; 13:13; Phil 1:1; 4:22; Phlm 5). That "saints" was an established term designating faithful Jews (often implying a contrast with others) in both biblical and post-biblical apocalyptic texts needs no documentation. What is to be noted, however, is that Paul uses this same term when he refers to the Jewish believers in Jerusalem who are to receive the offering from his Gentile churches (1Cor 16:1; 2Cor 8:4; 9:4; Rom 15:26,31). One would not distort Paul by saying that for him the offering was a mark of their being ingrafted into the Abrahamic root, for it was to be given to fellow believers, not to the temple. Moreover, in 1Cor 1:2 Paul refers to his largely Gentile readers as "called saints" (κλητοῖς ἁγίοις, not "called to be saints" as often translated); they are not saints because they are faithful Jews but because God has "called" (e.g., elected) them. So too, Paul is a "called apostle" (κλητὸς ἀπόστολος), not "called to be an apostle" (1Cor 1:1). Similarly, Paul appropriates ἐκκλησία, used repeatedly in LXX to refer to the gathered people of God. Though the word is used also by non-biblical writers to refer to a civic assembly, Paul's usage derived from scripture. This is implied by the fact that when he refers to his early opposition to Christian Jews, he says he persecuted the ἐκκλησία τοῦ θεοῦ (1Cor 15:9; Gal 1:13; Phil 3:6 omits "of God")—the same expres-

---

[33] There is no reliable way to detect the extent to which such usage simply resulted from his upbringing and life as an erstwhile Pharisee, and to what extent it shows that Paul had warranted this language as part of his on-site teaching. Moreover, the former need not exclude the latter.

sion he uses to address his readers (1 Cor 1:2; 2 Cor 1:1) and to refer to them (1 Cor 10:32; 11:16, 22).[34] Nor should we overlook the fact that Paul does not refer to Christian groups as "synagogues."

In Gal 6:16 he writes of the "Israel of God." Unfortunately, it is any-thing but clear whether he uses the phrase to refer to wholly Gentile Galatian churches or to the Jewish people.[35] No such ambiguity, how-ever, surrounds Phil 3:3, where in a warning against "Judaizers," Paul says flatly, "it is we who are the circumcision" (RSV: "the true circumci-sion").[36] At first glance, Paul comes close to the boasting against which he warns the readers in Rom 11:18, 20. But there the problem was Christian Gentile pride vis-à-vis unbelieving Jews; here, as in Galatia, he is agitated by the insistence that without circumcision the Chris-tian Gentile males are not part of God's people, but at best on the way to becoming Israel. In rejecting this, Paul insists that the Chris-tian Gentiles are already grafted into the root. The same reasoning lies behind his calling the Israelites at the exodus "our fathers" (1 Cor 10:1)—completely apart from physical descent.

Paul's earlier letters contain no statement comparable to Rom 11:26 ("all Israel will be saved")—nor (lest it be overlooked) do they say or hint that Israel will not be saved. Nor do they suggest that he saw in the Jews' refusal of the gospel the turn of events through which salvation came to the Gentiles. That motif appears only in Romans, written when circumstance afforded him the occasion to put both the gospel and his apostleship's meaning in a context that began with Adam and arcs to "the judgement seat of God" at the Eschaton (Rom 14:10).

---

[34] In 1 Cor 14:33 we find "all the churches of the saints;" however, the genuineness of the paragraph is in doubt.

[35] The phrase appears in the autograph appended to the dictated text. Here Paul writes that what amounts to anything (τί) is neither circumcision nor uncircumcision but new creation. To this he adds a rather Jewish blessing: "As for those who follow this rule—peace be upon them, and (καί) upon the Israel of God." Is καί used as a conjunction ("and"), as in NRSV, or is it used epexegetically ("even," or "namely")? If the former, the "Israel of God" would refer to those who do not follow Paul's rule, i.e., the ethnic People (so, e.g., Mussner's commentary), indicating that despite the letter's harsh words about the law, Paul is not disdaining or rejecting his (and God's) People, for his argument is not *with* Judaism but with Judaizing Teachers about Israel (Abraham's "seed"). If the latter, Paul would be using "Israel of God" to refer precisely to the Chris-tian Gentiles insofar as they adhere to his teaching. This is how REB and RSV take it, for they render the καί with a comma, indicating an appositional phrase. The issues and important literature are discussed in the commentaries by Betz, Dunn, and Martyn.

[36] REB paraphrases: "Be on guard against those … who insist on mutilation— 'circumcision' I will not call it; we are the circumcision."

In short, the data (admittedly sparse) do not warrant the claim that Romans 9–11 marks a change in Paul's thought and practice. Such an inference assumes all too readily that, despite the individuality of each letter, what Paul says for the first time he also thought for the first time.

The Presentation of Paul in Acts

Although Paul himself pointedly says that he is "the Gentiles' apostle," the portrayal of his apostolic mission in Acts is more complex. For one thing, the mission responds to the word of the Holy Spirit, asking that Barnabas and Saul be "set apart" not for a mission to Gentiles but "for the [unspecified] work to which I have called them" (Acts 13:2). Moreover, the account of that mission begins and ends with Paul speaking to Jews (13:5; 28:23–31). It is within this framework that Paul goes to the Gentiles, claiming to be commanded by the Lord to be their light (citing Isa 49:6 in support).

According to Acts 28:23–31, on a specified day many Roman Jews arrived at Paul's lodging, where for the entire day he spoke of the kingdom of God and tried "to convince them about Jesus" in light of scripture.[37] "Some were convinced by what he had said, while others refused to believe (ἠπίστουν). So they disagreed with each other." Paul then tells them one more thing: "the Holy Spirit was right (καλῶς) in saying to your[!] ancestors through the prophet Isaiah, 'Go to this people and say, *'You will indeed listen but never* (οὐ μή, or *in no way*) *understand … For this people's heart has grown dull … And they have shut their eyes, so that they might not look … and understand … and turn—and I would heal them'*'" (Isa 6:9–10, LXX). To this he adds the comment, "Let it be known to you that the salvation of God has been sent to the Gentiles; they will listen." A major problem in the interpretation of Acts emerges from the juxtaposition of Paul's comment and Luke's final sentence: for two years Paul "welcomed all who came to him, proclaiming the kingdom of God and teaching about the Lord Jesus Christ … without hindrance" (Acts 28:24–31). Is the reader to infer that "all" includes Jews[38] (some of whom believed), or that it refers only to

---

[37] For a recent analysis of the end of Acts, see Alexander Prieur, *Die Verkündigung der Gottesherrschaft. Exegetische Studien zum lukanischen Verständnis von "basileia tou theou"* (WUNT 2.89; Tübingen: Mohr-Siebeck, 1996) 20–83.

[38] At this point a number of mss (but not 𝔓74 אABE etc.) add v. 29, which says that on leaving the Jews were "arguing vigorously among themselves."

Gentiles, so that in effect, Acts "has written the Jews off," as Haenchen put it?[39]

The latter surely goes beyond the evidence, for as Brawley observed, nowhere in Acts "are the Jews definitively rejected."[40] Were that the case here, it would come as a surprise verdict that Luke's protagonist had failed in his mission. To the contrary, by saying that what Paul spent the day telling the Jews (v. 23) he subsequently said to "all," Acts clearly implies that Paul's mission continues as before, and that the Jews are *not* written off, though two things have changed: people now come to him, and he preaches and teaches "without hindrance" (ἀκωλύτος). The latter is commonly thought to be said with an eye to Rome. But in Acts 13–28 Rome never hindered Paul's mission, but either refused to get involved (18:12–16) or took him into protective custody (21:31–36).[41] As Acts tells it, it was Jews who persisted in hindering his mission. The last word in Acts implies, therefore, that although their interference was now ended, they will continue to argue about the gospel while it goes to the Gentiles.

Comparing what Paul says about his mission in Romans 9–11 with what Acts reports requires looking briefly at two previous places where Paul announced that in response to Jewish opposition he goes to Gentiles (13:46–48; 18:6), as well as observing a detail in the first story of his Damascus experience (9:15). All of these, though addressed to persons in the narrative, are really spoken over their heads to the readers.

At Acts 9:15 the Lord tells Ananias that Paul is the chosen instrument "to bring my name before Gentiles and kings and before the people Israel." Although Acts will show how this comes about with reference to each audience, the narrative will not follow the sequence stated here (Gentiles, kings, Israel); that "the people of Israel" comes last for emphasis is borne out by the narrative.[42] In fact, Jews are always the first to hear Paul, beginning with events on Cyprus (Acts 13:5). Even in Athens, the setting for the example of Paul's preaching to sophisticated

---

[39] Ernst Haenchen, "The Book of Acts as Source Material for the History of Early Christianity," in *Studies in Luke-Acts* [Paul Schubert Festschrift], ed. L.E. Keck and J.L. Martyn (Nashville: Abingdon Press, 1966) 278.

[40] Robert L. Brawley, *Luke-Acts and the Jews: Conflict, Apology, and Conciliation.* (SBLMS 33; Atlanta: Scholars Press, 1987) 72.

[41] Even the "magistrates" (στρατηγοί) who punished Paul in Philippi did not prevent him from preaching; in fact, on learning that he was a Roman citizen they apologized (16:19–40).

[42] Israel is not mentioned last "almost as an afterthought," as Barrett says; cf. *A Critical and Exegetical Commentary on the Acts of the Apostles* (Edinburgh: T&T Clark, 1998).

Gentiles, he goes first to the synagogue (Acts 17:17). Just as Acts 25:23–26:32 shows that he brought it before kings,[43] so when the Roman Jews hear Paul, Acts shows that from the beginning to the end of his mission, Paul did what the Lord had in mind for him.[44]

Acts also shows how it came about that Paul brought the Lord's name to the Gentiles, beginning at Pisidian Antioch (Acts 13). In response to rejection by the Jews, Paul and Barnabas make the programmatic pronouncement: "It was necessary that the word of God should be spoken first to you. Since you reject it and [thereby] judge yourselves unworthy of eternal life, we are now turning to the Gentiles. For so the Lord commanded us [!], saying, 'I have set you to be a light for the Gentiles, so that you may bring salvation to the ends of the earth'" (a cross-reference to Acts 1:8). Acts adds that "when the Gentiles heard this, they were glad … and as many as were destined for eternal life became believers" (Acts 13:45–48). Nonetheless, although Paul continued to go first to Jews, his converts now include Gentiles as well. Thereby Acts provides evidence for Paul's report to the Antioch church of "*how* he [God] had opened a door of faith for the Gentiles" Acts 14:27); this also sets the stage for the story of the Jerusalem council in chap. 15. Likewise, in the narrative that follows the council, Acts shows how it came about that Paul brought the gospel to Gentiles after taking it first to the Jews, many of whom rejected him for doing so. As a result, Paul tells the Corinthian Jews, "Your blood be upon your own heads! I am innocent. From now on I will go to the Gentiles" (18:6). He claims to have fulfilled his obligation. From now on, they, not he, are responsible for the consequences of their action.[45] Although this formal

---

[43] The text repeatedly emphasizes that Agrippa is king (25:24, 25; 26:2, 7, 23, 19, 26, 27); Festus, while not a king, represents Caesar, before whom Paul will stand.

[44] Jacob Jervell errs in saying that in Acts Paul "primarily is a missionary to the Jews," for Paul is portrayed as Christ's witness to both Jews and Gentiles; cf. *The Unknown Paul: Essays in Luke-Acts and Early Christian History* (Minneapolis: Augsburg Publishing House, 1984) 16. He is wide of the mark also when he claims that "Paul regards himself primarily and in the long term as a missionary to the Jews" (*Ibid.*, 59, 74–75), for according to Rom 11:13–14 the significance of Paul's mission for the Jews is indirect.

[45] The reference to "your blood" suggests disaster. Does Luke expect the reader to see here an allusion to the disaster that Jesus had predicted would come on "this generation" (Lk 11:49–51), and to which he alluded in his word to the women who bewailed his going to Golgotha (23:27–31), namely, the siege and fall of Jerusalem (Lk 21:20–24)? (If so, Acts would not distinguish diaspora Jews from Palestinian Jews.) So Jack T. Sanders, "The Jewish People in Luke-Acts" in *Luke-Acts and the Jewish People. Eight Critical Perspectives*, ed. J.B. Tyson (Minneapolis: Augsburg, 1988) 74.

declaration implies that Paul's attempts to win Jews for the gospel has
come to an end, the subsequent stories of Paul's mission in Ephesus
show that this was not the case. Perhaps the declaration stands here
instead of in Ephesus because the Jews there did not actually reject
Paul (20:19–21; 19:8–10); as in Philippi, in Ephesus it was pagans who
caused disturbances (16:16–24; 19:23–41). Moreover, Paul does make a
comparable declaration of innocence there, but it was to the church
elders (20:26).

In any case, Acts shows Paul persistently trying to persuade Jews
to accept his message, and having limited success before turning to
the Gentiles. Had Acts not done so, that is, had it reported that after
Pisidian Antioch Paul went only to the Gentiles, his task of taking the
Lord's name to Israel would have been aborted virtually as soon as
it began. Put in terms of Rom 11:11, Israel would then indeed have
"stumbled so as to fall." Then the resulting portrayal of his mission
would have been consistent with the very Christian Gentile arrogance
in Rome that Paul sought to thwart.

Comparing the Portrayals in Acts and Romans

The differences between the portrayal of Paul in Acts and the critics'
portrayal of him, based as much as possible on his undisputed letters
alone, are well known. What is of interest here, however, is something
else—on the assumption that Luke did not use Paul's letters, it is
remarkable that at certain points what Acts *reports* about Paul's mission
coheres with what he *says* in Romans 9–11. To pursue this, the same
three topics used earlier (Paul himself, Israel, and the Gentiles) will be
used here.

To begin with, the anguished Paul of Rom 9:1–3 is almost wholly
absent from Acts. Although Acts repeatedly reports Jewish hostility
toward Paul, only twice does it imply that their actions distressed him.
At 18:9–11, the Lord, in a vision,[46] exhorts Paul not to be afraid and
assures him that he will be with the Apostle, "and no one will lay a
hand on you to harm you, for there are many in this city [Corinth]
who are my people." This vision, however, is only obliquely related to

---

[46] Just as there are three statements about the gospel going to Gentiles, so there are
three visions in which the Lord reassures Paul: 18:9–11 (in Corinth); 23:11 (in Jerusalem);
27:23–25 (en route to Rome). Like the three reports of his Damascus road experience,
they remind the reader that Paul is doing God's will and has God's protection.

its context, and would be much more appropriate psychologically had it occurred after Paul had been expelled from Pisidian Antioch (13:50), nearly stoned at Iconium (14:5), actually stoned at Lystra (14:19), beaten and jailed at Philippi (16:16–40) or taken out of Thessalonica after dark (17:10). Instead it is reported to have occurred between the report of many baptisms (18:8) and Paul's appearance before Gallio (18:12–17). The other reference to Paul's personal response to problems created by Jews occurs in his farewell to the Ephesian elders; here he mentions his "humility and tears, enduring trials (πειρασμῶν) that came to me through the plots of the Jews" (20:18–19). Even so, endurance is not agony over the refusal of the gospel. However, Acts' general lack of interest in Paul's emotional responses, whether to Jewish opposition or to any other external circumstance, accords easily with the Paul of the rest of Romans, for there too Paul writes with measured tones, arguing and not sharing, exhorting and not effusing as in parts of Philippians or 2 Corinthians, for example.

More significant are the agreements between Acts and Romans regarding *Israel* and its response to the gospel. On the one hand, Paul's "to the Jew first" (Rom 1:16), a theological priority grounded in Israel's privileges in Rom 9:4–5, appears repeatedly in Acts as Paul's missionary practice in going first to the synagogue (or at Philippi to a Sabbath congregation meeting outdoors, 16:13). Moreover, while both Paul and Luke find this priority to be self-evident, only Acts has Paul say that "it was necessary that the word of God should be spoken first to you" (13:46). On the other hand, Paul's letters do not say what Luke shows— that his mission consistently began in the synagogues. Nonetheless, the Lukan Paul's persistence in going to synagogues where he is rejected before going to the Gentiles puts into narrative what Paul says in Rom 10:20–21 (citing Isa 65:1–2): "'I [God] have been found by those who did not seek me'" [the Gentiles]. But of Israel he says, 'All day long I have held out my hands to a disobedient and contrary people.'"

Especially important is the fact that Paul's emphasis on the cleavage in Israel, currently manifest as the believing remnant and the refusing majority, appears in Acts as narrative comments that Paul's preaching divided his Jewish hearers (Acts 14:1–2; 17:1–4, 10–12; 18:8; 19:8–9; 28:24,29 [if part of the text; see above]). Only in Beroea and Athens does this division not occur (17:11–12, 17). Thereby the narrative *shows* what Paul says: "a hardening has come on part of Israel" (Rom 11:25). Acts does not, however, imply that this was God's doing. To the contrary, in the programmatic declaration of Acts 13:46 the Jews excluded themselves ("judge yourselves unworthy of eternal life"). Moreover, by having Paul apply Isa 6:9–10 to the Jews in Rome, it suggests that God foresaw what would happen.[47]

Finally, according to the Paul of Romans, the salvation of the Gentiles is intertwined with that of Israel, because the once disobedient Gentiles have received God's mercy (and so became obedient) because of Israel's current disobedience (Rom 11:30); stated more tersely in 11:11, "through their transgression [in refusing the gospel] salvation has come to the Gentiles." As noted, this idea is strikingly similar to the ending of Acts, where Paul, having quoted Isa 6:9–10, adds, "Let it be known to you then that this salvation of God has been sent to the Gentiles." Acts 13:46 is explicit about the connection: "Since (ἐπειδή) you reject it [God's word] and show yourselves to be unworthy of eternal life [virtually the equivalent of Paul's "transgression"], we are now turning to the Gentiles." Yet the Lord's word to Ananias (9:15), as well as what Paul reports in Jerusalem (22:17–21; 26:15–18), shows that taking the gospel to the Gentiles has been God's plan all along. What Acts portrays, then, is not that the Gentile mission was completely contingent on the Jews' refusal but that the latter was the historical circumstance by which God's purpose was actually achieved. And that is precisely Paul's point in Romans.

In its own way, what Acts reports is consistent also with what Paul says about the olive tree. First, just as the wild olive is grafted into the root alongside the remnant branches (believing Jews), so Acts assumes that Paul's churches consist of both Jews and Gentiles, some of whom were Godfearers (Acts 14:1; 16:14 together with vv. 30–34; 17:1–4; 17:11–12; 18:4,7).[48] Acts also implies that Paul's Gentile converts were grafted into the root, for the message they hear from Paul (when assembled from various passages) is virtually identical with that preached by Peter to Jews. Even more noteworthy is the fact that when Paul defends himself against Agrippa, he not only claims that he is on trial on

---

[47] In Acts 13:45 and 17:5, the Jews are "jealous," but not in Paul's sense in Rom 11:14, for what it precipitates in Acts is the turn to the Gentiles, not the salvation of the Jews.

[48] Jacob Jervell ("The Church of Jews and Godfearers," in *Luke-Acts and the Jewish People*, ed. Tyson, 11–20) has argued that in Acts Paul's churches contain no former "pagans" (direct converts from paganism) because for Luke "Gentiles" always means Godfearers. Consequently, the ending of Acts means that now Paul has completed his mission to Jews, and that from this point on the mission will go "solely to the Gentiles"—the Godfearers. (He regards also the "Gentiles" in 13:46 and 18:6 to be Godfearers.) This interpretation is quite unconvincing.

account of God's promise to the patriarchs pertaining to "our twelve tribes" (Paul's "all Israel"!), but also says that Christ sent him to the Gentiles "to open their eyes so that they may turn from darkness to light and from the power of Satan to God [as in 1 Thess 1:9], so that they may receive forgiveness of sins and a place among those (ἐν τοῖς) who are sanctified by faith in me" (26:18)—a virtual paraphrase of the grafting of the wild olive among (ἐν αὐτοῖς) the remnant branches (Rom 11:17).

Opening the Door

Given the persistent interest in reconstructing "Christian origins," it is understandable that the comparison of the Paul of Acts and the Paul of the letters has concentrated on the differences between them, especially with regard to "what really happened." Important as it is to ascertain reliable information about Paul, which entails accounting for the divergences between Acts and the letters, the agreements between them present an equally important historical phenomenon that must be accounted for, especially if one holds that Luke did not rely on the letters or doubts that he is the author of the "we" sections. Obviously, that cannot be undertaken here.

The task can, however, be brought a bit more into focus by asking this question: Why is it that Luke, writing three or four decades later, still finds it necessary to have Paul make much the same point that the Apostle himself had made—that in going to the Gentiles he did not turn his back on his people, that his mission grafted the Gentiles into the patriarchal root alongside the believing remnant; that in the mystery of God's ways it was through Israel's hardening that the gospel actually came to the Gentiles? Might it be because neither the accusation to which Paul responds nor the Gentile arrogance disappeared but rather continued, perhaps intensified as the Christian movement became ever more Gentile? Indeed, is Luke-Acts itself evidence of a struggle to keep the wild olive grafted into the root?

Perhaps this essay has pried open the door for the pursuit of such questions, even though this is not the time to walk through it. In any case, such might well have been among the most important questions in the history of early Christianity in its Graeco-Roman context.

THE CULTURAL ORIGIN OF "RECEIVING ALL NATIONS" IN LUKE-ACTS

ALEXANDER THE GREAT OR ROMAN SOCIAL POLICY?[*]

David L. Balch

The ancient historian who is the author of Luke-Acts argues for the reception of all nations into the people of God, a social policy that is a radical contrast with the attitude toward foreigners expressed by the Priestly editors of the Pentateuch and by the Maccabean books.[1] This paper investigates the antecedents of this social policy. There are structural parallels between Dionysius of Halicarnassus, *Roman Antiquities*, and Luke's history that involve this social policy. I will very briefly set out some of those similarities and then ask another question: can we trace the origin of the language and the social inclusiveness involved back to Alexander the Great, i.e., back to a cultural impulse of Hellenism?

Dionysius and Plutarch on Romulus Accepting Foreigners

Without going into detail, Dionysius of Halicarnassus, *Roman Antiquities*,[2] and Luke-Acts both divide history into three periods: First, they each inform about ancestors, second, they narrate a central period of history in which the Founder(s) teach(es); and third, they tell of the successors.[3]

---

[*] I offer this essay in gratitude to Abraham Malherbe, a mentor whose ideas and approach to exegesis has been generative for me. This contribution builds on the sort of question he discusses in "'Not in a Corner': Early Christian Apologetic in Acts 26:26," in *Paul and the Popular Philosophers* (Minneapolis: Fortress, 1989) 147–63. John Fitzgerald's suggestions as an editor have also been very helpful.

[1] See my article "Attitudes toward Foreigners in 2 Maccabees, Eupolemus, Esther, Aristeas, and Luke-Acts," in *The Early Church in its Context: Essays in Honor of Everett Ferguson*, ed. A. J. Malherbe, F. W. Norris, and J. W. Thompson (NovTSup 90; Leiden: Brill, 1998) 22–47.

[2] Dionysius of Halicarnassus, *Roman Antiquities*, trans. E. Cary (LCL; Cambridge: Harvard, 1978).

[3] I set out this argument most fully in "ΜΕΤΑΒΟΛΗ ΠΟΛΙΤΕΙΩΝ: Jesus as Founder of the Church in Luke-Acts: Form and Function," in *Contextualizing Acts: Lukan Narrative and Greco-Roman Discourse*, ed. T. Penner and C. Vander Stichele (Symposium Series; Scholars Press and E.J. Brill, in press).

A social policy that the Founder of Rome and the Founder of the church have in common is the policy of receiving foreigners into the citizen/church body. In a key apologetic passage, Dionysius argues that Rome is the most hospitable (κοινοτάτην) and friendly of all cities (*Rom. Ant.* 1.89.1), having intermixed Aborigines, Arcadians, and Peloponnesians, a mixture of barbarians. But this reception (ὑποδεξαμένη) of Samnites, Umbrians, Iberians, and Gauls with innumerable other nations (ἔθνη), who differed from each other in language and habits, did not cause innovation in the ancient order (1.89.2–3). This mixture, the intermingling with many nations, only results in Romans not pronouncing Greek properly (1.90.2)!

The second book of Dionysius' history sets out Romulus' constitutional policy (*Rom. Ant.* 2.15–17). From the very beginning, Romulus made the city large and populous by welcoming (ὑποδέξεσθαι) fugitives, making the power of Rome grow (αὐξῆσαι; 2.15.4). With these additions (προστιθέντες) Rome became inferior in numbers to no other nation (2.16.3). Greek customs, especially those of the Athenians, who pride themselves on their noble birth, grant citizenship to none or few, and who even expel foreigners, are not advantageous and not to be praised (2.17.1). Through a single defeat [by Philip II at Chaeronea in 338 BCE], Athenians lost the leadership of Greece and their liberty. Later in the narrative, an Alban charges the Romans with admitting (ὑποδεξάμενοι) the homeless, vagabonds, and barbarians in great numbers, so that most are of an alien race (ἀλλοφύλου; 3.10.4). The kings are outsiders, and senators are newcomers (3.10.5). Rome is a city without order and discipline (πόλις ἀδιακόσμητός ... καὶ ἀδιάτακτος), a conglomeration of many races (ἐκ πολλῶν ... ἐθνῶν; 3.10.6). The Roman respondent to the charges, however, takes pride in Rome being a mixture of foreigners (ἐπιμιξίαις τοῦ ἀλλοφύλου; 2.11.3–4), a policy that has made Rome great, in contrast to Greek Alba (3.11.7). Factional strife makes Rome grow (αὐξήσει; 3.11.8).

Not only Dionysius, but also Plutarch uses this language when writing of Romulus.[4] Plutarch's first sentence is that Rome is famous among all mankind (διὰ πάντων ἀνθρώπων; *Romulus* I.1). Plutarch tells alternative legends of Rome's origin; one involves the descendants of Aeneas reigning as kings in Alba. According to well-known legends, Romulus and Remus are born. Later, to the displeasure of Numitor, king

---

[4] Plutarch, *Theseus and Romulus*, trans. B. Perrin (LCL; Cambridge: Harvard University, 1967).

of Alba, the two boys accept into their company many needy and slaves (προσεδέχοντο πολλοὺς μέν ἀπόρους, πολλοὺς δὲ δούλους; VII.1). Whereas Alba would not give fugitives the privilege of intermarriage (οὐκ ... ἀναμιγνύναι) with them or receive them as fellow-citizens (οὐδὲ προσδέχεσθαι πολίτας; IX.2), Romulus and Remus received all (ἐδέχοντο πάντας; compare Acts 28:30) who came, delivering none up, neither slave to master, nor debtor to creditors. They made their city the asylum secure for all (πᾶσι), so that the city was soon full of people (IX.3). The city filled up with aliens (ἐποίκων), the greater part of them a mixed rabble (μιγάδες ἐξ ἀπόρων) and obscure persons. Romulus hoped for a blending and fellowship (συγκράσεως καὶ κοινωνίας) with the Sabines (XIV.2). Later, he demanded that the Sabines accept community of marriage (τὴν κοινωνίαν δέχεσθαι; XVI.2), and this more than anything gave growth (ἤυξησε) to Rome, that it united and incorporated those conquered (XVI.5). The city doubled in numbers (XX.1), so that its neighbors sought to check its growth (XXV.1).

Plutarch's *Theseus* modifies this language:[5] the Founder of Athens settled all the residents of Attica in one city (XXIV.1). Wanting to enlarge (αὐξῆσαι) the city, he invited everyone (ἐκάλει πάντας) on equal terms, but did not allow his democracy to become disordered or confused (οὐ μὴν ἄτακτον οὐδὲ μεμιγμένην; XXV.1). In Dionysius (*Rom. Ant.* 3.10.6; 11.3), this is precisely the language that the Greek Alban uses to accuse Rome.[6]

When Plutarch compares the two Founders, he praises Rome for rising to eminence from the smallest beginnings, from slaves and sons of swineherds (IV.1). Romulus was the benefactor of men without homes who wished to become a people and citizens of a common city (IV.2). He mixed and blended two peoples together (συνέμιξεν ἀλλήλοις ... τὰ γένα; VI.3). Comparison of the two kings favors Romulus.

> In this way he [Romulus] intermixed (συνέμιξεν) and blended the two peoples with one another, and supplied his state with a flowing fountain

[5] Discussing similar language in Libanius, A. D. Nock, "The Praises of Antioch," *The Journal of Egyptian Archaeology* 40 (1954) 78 suggests that praising a city for receiving strangers must originally have been Roman, not Athenian.

[6] But Theseus is himself an immigrant and a stranger (*Theseus* XIII.1), an origin resented by the great grandson of Erechtheus (XXXII.1). His tomb becomes a sanctuary for runaway slaves and all the humble (XXXVI.1). This same ambiguity is present in sources about Alexander: many did not consider Macedonians to be Greeks (see Brunt's introduction to his LCL ed. of Arrian, *Alexander*, vol. 1, xxxvii; also Diodorus XVII.100).

of strength and good will ... [T]he two peoples [Romans and Sabines shared] the rights and duties of citizenship, because of that intermarriage; whereas from the marriages of Theseus the Athenians got no new friends at all, nor even any community of enterprise whatsoever, but enmities, wars, slaughters of citizens ... (VI.3–4).

Luke-Acts

The author of Luke-Acts employs similar language. Our historian constructs a programmatic sermon for the Founder that supplies basic themes for the whole two-volume history. Luke pictures Jesus reading scripture: "the Spirit has anointed me to bring good news to the poor" (4:18 quoting Isa 61:1–2; 58:6). Luke adds a "parable" and two illustrations of prophetic miracles from 1 Kings 17 (Elijah) and 2 Kings 5 (Elisha). The eschaton is now: "today this scripture has been fulfilled in your hearing" (4:21). The last phrase that Luke quotes from Isaiah 61 is, "to proclaim the year of the Lord's favor" or acceptance (δεκτόν; 4:19). This verbal adjective recurs in the one sermon in Acts that summarizes the gospel: Peter begins his sermon to Cornelius' household (and to the Jewish Christians whom he has brought with him): "I truly understand that God shows no partiality, but in every nation anyone who fears him and does what is right is acceptable (δεκτός) to him" (Acts 10:35).[7] This verbal adjective is crucial in Luke 4:19, 24, the programmatic, inaugural speech in the gospel, and in Acts 10:35, one of the most important speeches in Acts. Luke employs the compound verb to observe that Jesus "welcomes" sinners (Luke 15:2; see 9:11) and that Paul "accepted all" who came to him (Acts 28:30), the fitting conclusion to the two-volume work! This verb is the very one that Dionysius and Plutarch employ when narrating that Rome "received" many nations into citizenship (*Rom. Ant.* 1.89.2–3; 3.10.4–5; see 3.11.3–4; Plutarch, *Romulus* VII.1; IX.2; *Alex.* IX.3). Members are also "added" to the church (Acts 2:47; 5:14; 11:24) as foreign nations are "added" to Rome (Dionysius, *Rom. Ant.* 2.16.3). And in Acts, the word of God "grows" (Acts 6:7; 12:24; 19:20), a growth that raises the question whether the ancient customs are being "guarded," an accusation at the core of the apologetic of both Dionysius (*Rom Ant.* 1.89–90; 2.17.1; and 7.70–73) and Luke-Acts (see Luke 2:22, 39 and Acts 6:11, 14; 15:5; 21:21). As does Dionysius

---

[7] See Ulrich Wilckens, "Kerygma und Evangelium bei Lukas (Beobachtungen zu Acta 10 34–43)," *ZNW* 49 (1958) 223–37.

(1.60.3; 89.2–3), Acts 2:9–11 lists the nations added. Reading Luke 4 with Acts 10 and 28, Isaiah prophesies God's acceptance of all nations, which Jesus announces in Nazareth, Peter preaches in Caesarea and argues in Jerusalem, and Paul accomplishes in Rome. By Acts 10 in the narrative, readers understand Jesus' announcement. For Luke, Isaiah's prophecy concerns God's providential will revealed both by the Messiah's death, resurrection, and ascension and, second, by the reception of all nations into God's people, the burden of the Cornelius chapters. Luke's innovative interpretation of Isaiah does not correspond with the social values of the Priestly editors of the Pentateuch or with those of the epitomizer who wrote 2 Maccabees. By comparison with Dionysius, at least, it would appear that Luke has assimilated a Roman social policy.

Alexander the Great According to Arrian

Can these terms and social practices be traced back to ideas and actions of Alexander the Great? Some of the ancient accounts of Alexander's exploits might suggest so. The primary sources I survey for Alexander include three sources in Greek, Diodorus of Sicily, book XVII[8] (second half of the first century BCE), Plutarch, *Alexander*[9] (second half of the first and early second century CE), and Arrian, *History of Alexander*[10] (first half of the second century CE), as well as one in Latin, Quintus Curtius Rufus, *History of Alexander* (1st century CE).[11]

The latest of these sources, Arrian, has been thought to be the best historian because he depends on more reliable sources, the eyewitnesses Ptolemy and Aristobulus, while Diodorus and Curtius both relied on Clitarchus of Alexandria, an inferior source. Diodorus and Curtius are often referred to as "the Clitarchean vulgate."[12] However, Arrian's source Ptolemy was heavily influenced by the propaganda of the court historian Callisthenes, and his narrative of Alexander cer-

---

[8] Diodorus of Sicily, trans. C. Bradford Welles (LCL; Cambridge: Harvard University, 1970).

[9] Plutarch, *Alexander and Caesar*, trans. B. Perrin (LCL; Cambrige: Harvard University, 1971).

[10] Arrian, *History of Alexander and Indica*, trans. P. A. Brunt (LCL; Cambridge: Harvard University, 1989).

[11] Quintus Curtius, *History of Alexander*, trans. John C. Rolfe (LCL; Cambridge: Harvard University, 1946).

[12] Brunt, in Arrian, *History of Alexander*, vol. 1, xviii-xxxiv.

tainly enhanced his position as satrap and king of Egypt.[13] Nor is the "vulgate tradition" any longer considered a unified and inferior tradition. Each episode must be examined separately and each source considered on its own merits.

One characteristic of Arrian's narrative, however, poses a question about the tradition of "receiving all nations." Arrian usually presents Alexander as seeking to become lord of Europe and Asia, not of "all nations." This radical difference between Arrian and the Clitarchian vulgate concerns the goals Alexander typically articulated. On only two occasions does Arrian use language that goes beyond referring to Europe and Asia, when Alexander unsuccessfully tried to persuade his exhausted Macedonians to fight on to the Ganges and as he approached Babylon a few months before he died. By contrast, this universal language is assumed by the "vulgate tradition" during his entire rule. I will sketch these instances below, but first I want briefly to review other events in Alexander's conquests where some ancient historians used universal language, but Arrian did not.

When Alexander crossed the Hellespont, he thought of himself as reenacting the actions of Agamemnon crossing onto Asian soil (Arrian I.11.5). After defeating Darius' forces at the river Granicus, he set up the inscription, "Alexander and the Greeks except the Lacedaemonians set up these spoils from the barbarians dwelling in Asia" (I.16.7). When Alexander reached Gordium, he was seized with a longing to see Gordius' waggon and the knot of the waggon's yoke, because there was a legend "that anyone who untied the knot of the yoke would rule Asia" (II.3.6). Before he defeated Darius himself near the Cilician Gates, Alexander gave a speech presenting this as a fight of free men against slaves, Europe against Asia, a struggle "to rule the whole of Asia" (II.7.4–6; see 12.5). Arrian narrates correspondence between Darius and Alexander, in which the latter demands to be regarded as "Lord of all Asia," and that Darius address him as "King of Asia" (II.14.7; see VI.29.8 and Plutarch, *Alex.* XXXIV.1). When Alexander is seized with another longing to visit the oracle of Ammon in Lybia, he "made

---

[13] I thank David F. Graf for this insight. See e.g. A. B. Bosworth, *Alexander and the East: The Tragedy of Triumph* (Oxford: Clarendon, 1996) chap. 2 for contemporary evaluation of the sources, including a critique of Arrian (34): "All sources are to some degree unreliable, including, particularly including, those of an 'official' nature. One can therefore operate only by cross-comparison, painstakingly isolating common material, identifying and explaining variants, and arguing from general probability, that is the appropriateness of the recorded details to the overall historical context."

his inquiry of the god" and "received the answer his heart desired" (III.4.5). In Arrian neither the content of the inquiry nor the answer are specified, a contrast to the vulgate, as we will see.[14] At Gaugamela, Alexander gives another speech, proclaiming that the "sovereignty of all Asia" was then and there to be decided (III.9.6).[15] He is repeatedly concerned with the "barbarians" (III.15.2–3; 23.8; IV.4.2).

More interesting is Alexander's later substitution of the dress of the Medes and the tiara of the Persians for the headdress he had worn (VI.7.3). After Arrian introduces this subject, he collects stories of Macedonian opposition to Alexander, his murder of Clitus (IV.8–9), his argument with Callisthenes about the Persian custom of obeisance to superiors (IV.10–12), and the attempt of Philotas to kill him (IV.13–14). Callisthenes, Aristotle's nephew and student, opposed Alexander's adoption of these customs.[16] His speech argues that Alexander should be honored as a man, not a god, and observes that we compose hymns for gods, but eulogies for men; we do obeisance to gods, but kiss humans. He appeals to Alexander to remember Greece, which sponsors this expedition to annex Asia to Greece; the Greeks are the freest of men, and should not be dishonored by doing obeisance, a barbarian honor. Cyrus was the first of men to receive obeisance, but was brought to his senses by the Scythians, and Darius too by Alexander (IV.11). As Arrian presents Callisthenes' argument against giving Alexander divine honors, he is not claiming to be lord of the world, but to annex Asia.

---

[14] E. Badian, "Alexander in Iran," in *The Cambridge History of Iran*, vol. 2, *The Median and Achaemenian Periods*, ed. I. Gershevitch (Cambridge: Cambridge University, 1985) 420–501; cf. esp. 433: "Alexander went … to consult the oracle of Ammon at Siwah, long known and respected in Greece. What he heard there cannot be known."

[15] Brunt observes in this context, that Arrian uses "Macedonians" with a non-ethnic meaning (Arrian, *History of Alexander*, LCL 1:265 n. 3, commenting on III.13.4).

[16] A. B. Bosworth, *From Arrian to Alexander: Studies in Historical Interpretation* (Oxford: Clarendon, 1988) 113–23, 141–42, 145, 150–51. Bosworth denies that Callisthenes' speech in Arrian reflects thought patterns of the principate, arguing that "there was almost total acceptance of the ruler-cult among the aristocracy of Arrian's day" (118). On the contrary, see Dio Chrysostom, *Or.* 1.7; 2.16, 73; 4.19–23, speeches on kingship given before Trajan. Dio uses the analogy of wise herdsmen dealing with a savage, overbearing and insolent bull (the emperor): "when the owners and the herdsmen, I say, have such a bull, they depose and kill him as not being fit to lead the herd nor salutary to it" (2.73). Curtius (VIII.v.5–24) gives the debate a similar setting, but the content differs: Callisthenes is prepared to accept divine honors for Alexander after his death. Compare Hermolaus' speech, Alexander's would-be assassin (Curtius VIII.vii). See Badian, "Iran" 452, 457–60 and Bosworth, *Alexander and the East*, chap. 4.

Fascinating too are the approximately eighty marriages Alexander
sponsored between himself, his "companions," and Persian brides
(VII.4.4), the 30,000 Persian boys whom he trained in Macedonian
warfare (VII.6.1), his calling Persians his "kinsmen" (συγγενεῖς; VII.
11.6), and the public banquet at which he seated Macedonians and Persians "and then any person from the other peoples (τῶν ἄλλων ἐθνῶν)
who took precedence" (VII.11.8). At the banquet Alexander prayed for
blessings, especially for harmony as partners in government by Macedonians and Persians (ὁμόνοιάν τε καὶ κοινωνίαν τῆς ἀρχῆς Μακεδόσι
καὶ Πέρσαις; VII.11.9; contrast e.g. II.7.4–6!)[17] They drank from the
same bowl, poured the same libations with Greek soothsayers and Magi
initiating the ceremony, and gave one victory cry (in two or more languages?). However, all this unity occurred in the context of the continuing power struggle between Alexander and his Macedonian soldiers,
whom he then discharged and sent home–without their wives and children.[18]

As noted earlier, Arrian twice uses more universal language in describing Alexander's goals. The first occurs after Alexander had invaded India,[19] for then "he would at once be in possession of Asia as a
whole" (IV.15.5). But when his Macedonian soldiers' spirits are flagging
(V.25.2), he delivers another speech.[20] He sets no limits (πέρας) to exer-
tions for a man of noble spirit, and there remains no great stretch of
land to the Ganges (V.26.1).

> … the Indian gulf [Arabian Sea] forms but one stretch of water with
> the Persian Gulf, and the Hyrcanian [Caspian] Sea with the Indian gulf.
> From the Persian gulf our fleet shall sail round to Libya, as far as the
> Pillars of Heracles [Straits of Gibraltar]; from the Pillars all the interior
> of Libya then becomes ours, just as Asia is in fact becoming ours in
> its entirety, and the boundaries of our Empire are here becoming those
> which God set for the whole continent (τῆς γῆς ὅρους ὁ θεὸς ἐποίησε).[21]

---

[17] See Richard Stoneman, *Alexander the Great* (Lancaster Pamphlets; London: Routledge, 1997) 78: William Tarn interpreted this passage to mean that Alexander believed
in "the brotherhood of man."

[18] Badian, "Iran" 482–84 and Stoneman, *Alexander* 80.

[19] Badian, "Iran" 463, 466 observes that the Indian campaign covered territory
unknown to the Greek world at that time. Curtius IX.i.3 refers to Alexander's expectation in India of overrunning "all Asia, that they might visit the world's end, the sea."

[20] Bosworth, *From Arrian* 123–34. Again, Arrian and Curtius (IX.2.10–11) are the
sources for Alexander's speech, and once more, the content differs. Bosworth 127 gives
parallels to the Elder Seneca, *Suas.* 1.

[21] Arrian V.26.2; cf. IV.15.5–6. Compare Curtius IX.ii.11, 26, 28; iii.7–8; iv.19 and
Plutarch, *Alex.* XLVII.2. Compare Craterus' and Alexander's speeches after the latter

This view of the known world, however, does not appear as early as Alexander. It is most likely adopted from Eratosthenes (ca. 285–194 BCE), head of the Alexandrian library under Ptolemy III.[22] Even so, the language appears to be more Roman than Hellenistic.[23]

In this speech, Alexander appears more confident than he actually was historically about the possibility of these voyages.[24] After the disaster of returning from India toward Persia via the Gedrosian Desert,[25] he believed that Nearchus' fleet had been destroyed. He even thought Nearchus' reappearance in the Persian Gulf was a false rumor and initially failed to recognize his admiral (Arrian, *Indica* 20.2). He "did not feel so much pleasure at the safe arrival of Nearchus … as pain at the loss of all his force" (*Indica* 35.2–8). Arrian himself confesses that "I cannot determine with certainty what sort of plans Alexander had in mind, and it is no purpose of mine to make guesses." He supposes that "he would not have stopped there quietly, not even if he had added Europe and Asia and the Britannic Islands to Europe, but that he would always have searched far beyond for something unknown …" (Arrian VII.1.4) This speech with its Eratosthenesian geography and its reference to the Britannic Islands cannot be understood to record Alexander's plans.[26]

Alexander had experienced several reversals:[27] a defeat by his own men who at the Hyphasis (Beas) refused to continue to the Ganges, his own all but fatal wound among the Malli from which Peucestas and

---

had been wounded by an arrow while attacking a city of the Sudracae (Curtius IV.vi.7, 20).

[22] So Bosworth, *From Arrian* 130.

[23] So Badian, "Iran," 131: "But it is most unlikely that the ocean featured prominently in his thinking as a boundary of world empire. That seems more a Roman concept." Compare Stoneman, *Alexander* 51–52 for a summary of Alexander's confused geographical conceptions. See n. 25 below.

[24] See John Maxwell O'Brien, *Alexander the Great: The Invisible Enemy. A Biography* (London: Routledge, 1992) 162, 189–90.

[25] Badian, "Iran" 471 and Stoneman, *Alexander* 73 estimate that Alexander lost 45,000 of his 60,000 soldiers, plus non-combatants, a major disaster. Bosworth, *Alexander and the East* 169–80 disputes such heavy loses.

[26] See Brunt, "The Aims of Alexander," *Greece and Rome* 12 (1965) 205–15, at p. 212, n. 3, citing D. Kienast, *Historia* 14 (1965) 180ff., admitting that "the reliability of this speech is called in grave doubt." See Georg Knaach, "Eratosthenes (4)," in *Paulys Real-Encyclopaedie* 6 (1909) 358–89, at 366–77 on geography in general; Knaach (367, 375) also discusses Eratosthenes' critique of Alexander's creation of myth in relation to Asian geographical sites (Arrian, *An.* V.3.1–4 and *Ind.* 5.8–13). On the debate about Britain see *ibid.*, 373. Renzo Tosi, "Eratosthenes (2)," in *Der neue Pauly* (1998) 44–47 dates his birth before 272 BCE and his call to Alexandria after 246 BCE.

[27] Badian, "Iran," 473, 477.

Leonnatus had saved him, followed by his unheroic march across the Gedrosian desert. His attempt to imitate the heroic exploits of Achilles, Heracles, and Dionysius had failed, "and a search for scapegoats began ... The reign of terror among the satraps and commanders that began at Pura and ended only when Alexander reached Susa was inevitably disguised by the king's propaganda ... The reign of terror can be shown to be due to two main causes: failure and fear."[28] Alexander began to substitute his own men for the eminent Iranian and Macedonian satraps and commanders whom he had preferred earlier. Then Menon died in Arachosia, the newly appointed governor of Gedrosia also died, and Philip, his governor in northern India, was killed by rebellious Indian mercenaries. "Alexander had to rethink his whole eastern frontier ... He saw that northern India, on which he had spent so much military effort and administrative thought, could not be securely held after all, without a return in arms, which—in the foreseeable future—was inconceivable. So he decided to cut his loses ... India was best written off."[29] The frontier shifted west.

The second time that Arrian uses universal language occurs just after these events in the final months of Alexander's life: embassies from the Libyans, Italy, Carthage, the European Scyths, Celts and Iberians met him at he approached Babylon. "It was then that the Greeks and Macedonians first came to be acquainted with their names and appearances" (Arrian VII.15.4; compare Diodorus XVII.113.2, cited in the next section). Arrian continues:

> It was then more than ever that both in his own estimation and in that of his entourage Alexander appeared to be master of every land and sea (γῆς τε ʽαπάσης καὶ θαλάσσης κύριον). Aristus and Asclepiades among the historians of Alexander say that even the Romans sent envoys ... This I have recorded as neither true nor wholly incredible, except that no Roman ever referred to this embassy sent to Alexander, nor did the historians of Alexander whom I prefer to follow, Ptolemy son of Lagus and Aristobulus; nor was it suitable for the Roman government ... (VII.15.5).

Given the disasters that Alexander had experienced, including the loss of northern India, this universal language in Arrian is a later (Roman) projection back onto a political situation in which such claims were inappropriate.

---

[28] Ibid., 473, 476–77.
[29] Ibid., 478.

Alexander the Great According to the Vulgate Tradition

With this occasional surfacing of universal language that suggests goals beyond Europe and Asia, one may contrast the vulgate as represented by Diodorus (all references are to book XVII). Diodorus begins realistically by observing that Alexander conquered no small part of Europe and practically all of Asia (1.4). But in an early story, Plutarch says that "whosoever loosed the fastening [of Midas' waggon] was destined to become king of the whole world" (τῆς οἰκουμένης; *Alex.* XVIII.2; contrast Arrian II.3.6 and Curtius III.i.16).[30] In Egypt, when Alexander goes to Ammon, Diodorus gives universal content to the question that Arrian leaves vague. An elderly prophet said:

> "Rejoice, son; take this form of address as from the god also." He replied, "I accept, father; for the future I shall be called thy son. But tell me if thou givest me the rule of the whole earth (εἴ μοι δίδως τὴν ἁπάσης γῆς ἀρχήν)." ... the prophet cried that of a certainty the god had granted him his request ... (Diodorus 51.1–2; compare Curtius IV.vii.26 and contrast Arrian III.4.5)[31]

Plutarch is even more expansive. When Alexander asks whether it was given to him to become lord and master of all mankind (εἰ πάντων αὐτῶ| δίδωσιν ἀνθρώπων κυρίῳ γενέσθαι), the god answers that this was given to him (*Alex.* XXVII.6–7).

After the battle at Arbela,[32] there was a debate whether to accept Darius' offer to cede all the territory west of the Euphrates, resulting in a famous exchange between Alexander and one of his generals, Parmenion (Diodorus 54.4–5; see Curtius IV.xi.13–15 and III.x.5). Diodorus reports that Alexander added the following images: "the earth (ὁ κόσμος) could not preserve its plan and order if there were two suns nor could the inhabited world (ἡ οἰκουμένη) remain calm and free from war so long as two kings share the rule" (54.5). Later, just before trying to persuade his Macedonians to advance to the Ganges, Alexander remembers that "Ammon had given him the rule of the whole world"

---

[30] Curtius reveals his authorial point of view when referring to the colonies of Tyre, "distributed over almost the whole world: Carthage in Africa, Thebes in Boeotia, Gades on the Ocean; ... now at last ... they are under the protection of Roman clemency" (IV.iv.19, 21; see X.viii.3–4).

[31] Diodorus of Sicily, trans. C. Bradford Welles (LCL; Cambridge: Harvard University, 1970).

[32] Plutarch, *Alexander* XXXI.6 insists that the battle was not at Arbela, but at Gaugamela (an agreement with Arrian).

(τὴν ἁπάσης τῆς γῆς ἐξουσίαν; 93.4). Like Arrian, Diodorus reports
the envoys that came to Alexander as he approached Babylon in the
final months of his life. They came from Asia, Europe and Libya, and
even from Gaul, "whose people became known then first in the Greek
world" (113.2; compare Arrian VII.15.4 quoted above).

My suspicion is that the actual source of this universal language
may be seen in Plutarch's biography of Caesar, which he pairs with
the biography of Alexander. Caesar was the first man to cross the
Rhine[33] with an army, and the first man to launch a fleet on the Atlantic
ocean carrying an army to Britain (Plutarch, *Caesar* XXII.6; XXIII.2).
When Arrian (*Alex.* VII.1.4) speculates about Alexander's plans, he
does so in light of Caesar's conquest of Britain. Caesar's actions carried
Roman supremacy beyond the confines of the inhabited world (ἔξω
τῆς οἰκουμένης; *Caesar* XXIII.3). When Caesar crossed the Rubicon, he
knew that great evils for "all mankind" (πᾶσιν ἀνθρώποις) would follow
(*Caesar* XXXII.7). The plan that Arrian (IV.15.5–6; V.26.2) reports in
one of Alexander 's speeches, Plutarch may more realistically assign to
Julius Caesar:

> He planned and prepared to make an expedition against the Parthians;
> and after subduing these and marching around the Euxine by way of
> Hyrcania, the Caspian sea, and the Caucasus, to invade Scythia; and
> after overrunning the countries bordering on Germany and Germany
> itself, to come back by way of Gaul to Italy, and so to complete this
> circuit of his empire, which would then be bounded on all sides by the
> ocean (*Caesar* LVIII.6–7).

Brunt argues that since Alexander thought of himself as divine, emu-
lating and surpassing Heracles and Dionysus, "the allegiance of all
mankind was rightly due" him.[34] Perhaps so, but in Arrian, Alexander
does not argue that way.

One of Alexander's plans at the end of his life was to conquer
Arabia, "on the pretext that they alone of the barbarians in these parts
had sent no envoys" to him in Babylon (Arrian VII.19.6). When Strabo

---

[33] As both Arrian and Diodorus have observed, the Greeks did not know the names
of the peoples beyond this river.

[34] Brunt, "Aims," 211. Bosworth, *Alexander and the East*, chap. 4, argues that Alexander's actions proceeded from his own belief in his divinity, one of the sources of the
assassination plot by the young pages (ibid. 113 citing the speech by Hermolaus in
Curtius VIII.vii.12–15 and Alexander's reply in viii.13–15). Compare Hermolaus' and
Callisthenes' opinions with Acts 12:22–23; 14:15, verses in tension, however, with Luke
3:38 and Acts 17:27–28.

is telling the same story, admittedly with Aristobulus as one source, he adds that "in truth [he] was reaching out to be lord of all" (πάντων εἶναι κύριον; Strabo, *Geog.* 16.11).[35] Again, the absence of this title in Arrian causes suspicion. "What Alexander's further plans were, apart from the Arabian expedition and one or two projects of exploration already in hand, must have been known to some at the time; but we cannot know. Arrian, recognizing this, refused to guess, and modern historians will be wise to follow him."[36]

Alexander is said to have left memoranda for a gigantic plan of conquest in the west that would have encircled the Mediterranean.[37] Diodorus describes plans for 1,000 warships, for a campaign against Carthage and the western Mediterranean, the construction of a military road across North Africa and the appropriate harbors (Diodorus XVIII.4; Curtius X.1.17–19). Some scholars dismiss these future plans for conquest as unhistorical, and others credit them. Bosworth shows that Alexander had made significant preparations for conquest in the Persian Gulf (detailed by Arrian), and argues strongly for the authenticity of further plans against Africa and the southern Mediterranean. The source in Arrian creates problems, however, for at the conclusion he adds that "he [Alexander] was already rather disturbed that Rome's fame was advancing to a great height" (VII.1.3), another anachronism. And to support this Bosworth must argue that, as he had done in India, Alexander did not himself plan to circumnavigate Africa but would have sent someone else.[38] Bosworth's strongest argument is that one of Alexander's Macedonian admirals, Cleitus, commanded 240 ships in the later Lamian war against Athens, ships which Alexander had had built in the harbors of Cilicia and Phoenicia.[39]

---

[35] Strabo, *Geography*, trans. H. L. Jones (LCL; Cambridge: Harvard, 1966), cited by Brunt, "Aims" 212.

[36] Badian, "Iran," 490.

[37] Badian, "Iran," 185–211; Brunt, "Aims," 212, n. 9, citing the Clitarchean vulgate. See Stoneman, *Alexander*, 90–91.

[38] Bosworth, *From Arrian*, 194–95.

[39] *Ibid.*,198–201. See also S. B. Pomeroy, S. M. Burstein, W. Dolan, and J. T. Roberts, *Ancient Greece: A Political, Social, and Cultural History* (Oxford: Oxford University Press, 1999) 425: "Since antiquity, scholars have disagreed about Alexander's plans for the future of his empire. ... No clear evidence exits that might reveal how Alexander envisioned the final form of that autocracy or the roles he expected the various peoples of his empire to play in it. ... Not surprisingly, his papers contained only schemes for grandiose movements and future campaigns, not plans for the governance of his empire."

Diodorus (XVIII.4.4) narrates that the plans for conquest included population transfers from Asia to Europe and vice versa. He explains that concord and international friendship would be created through mixed marriages, which Bosworth understands as a parenthetical remark by Diodorus himself, since there is no evidence that he ever attempted an ethnic blend.[40]

Curtius and the Emperor Claudius

I conclude with some observations on the relation in Quintus Curtius between ethnic blending and "custom," a debate that has surfaced in the narratives of Alexander sketched above. After the death of Darius, Curtius narrates that Alexander gave himself to pleasures, slipping into foreign habits (VI.ii.1–3). There is a list of nations conquered (VI.ii.13; iii.2–3) in relation to which Alexander makes a speech:

> Do you believe that so many nations accustomed to the rule and name of another, united with us neither by religion, nor customs, nor community of language, have been subdued in the same battle in which they were overcome? It is by your arms that they are restrained, not by their dispositons, and those who fear us when we are present, in our absence will be enemies. We are dealing with savage beasts … . All these [Bactrans, Indians, etc.], as soon as they see our backs, will follow them; for they are of the same nation, we are of an alien race and foreigners … . Accordingly, we must either give up what we have taken, or we must seize what we do not yet hold. Just as in ailing bodies, my soldiers, physicians leave nothing which will do harm. (VI.iii.8–11)[41]

With respect to customs, Hermolaus the page, as just seen, brings the accusation: "it is the Persians' garb and habits that delight you [Alexander]; you have come to loathe the customs of your native land" (*patrios mores*; VIII.vii.12). Likewise when his Macedonians rebel and refuse to follow Alexander to the Ganges, the general Coenus explains, "clad in Persian dress, because that of our own country cannot be brought to us, we have degenerated into foreign ways" (*degeneravimus cultum*; IX.iii.10). Then after the battle at a town of the Sudracae in which an arrow nearly killed Alexander, he explains his reckless bravery,

---

[40] *Ibid.*, 201.

[41] On ethnic conflict between "Macedonians" and "Greeks" within Alexander's army, see the story of Dioxippus (Diodorus, XVII.100–01; Curtius, IX.vii.15–26; Bosworth, *Alexander and the East*, 115–17, an historical event, although it is reported only in the Clitarchian vulgate). On the Scythians serving under Alexander attacking the Indians, see Curtius, VII.xiv.5.

receives envoys from the defeated nations, and gives a banquet. The narrator comments:

> a hundred golden couches had been placed at a small distance from each other; the couches he had hung about with purple tapestries gleaming with gold, displaying in that banquet all that was corrupt in the ancient luxury of the Persians or in the new fashions adopted by the Macedonians, thus intermingling the vices of both nations. (IX.vii.15)

Appropriately then, Curtius' final estimate of Alexander offers the critique that he changed his attire to that of foreign nations and imitated those customs of the conquered races which he had scorned before his victory (X.v.33).

Surprisingly, however, Alexander once articulates a qualitatively different view. After having returned from India, he plans to send some soldiers home to Greece while keeping others in Asia, which generates a mutiny among the Macedonians to be left behind. Alexander becomes furious and admits only Asiatic soldiers into his presence (X.iii.5). Through an interpreter he addresses the foreign troops as follows:

> … I have both made a selection from the men of military age among you, and have incorporated them with my soldiers … . It is for this reason that I myself united in marriage with me Roxane, daughter of the Persian Oxyartes, not disdaining to rear children from a captive … and set the example to my nearest friends of begetting children from captives, in order that by this sacred alliance I might abolish all distinction between vanquished and victor. Therefore believe that in my eyes you are soldiers of our blood, not brought in from outside. Asia and Europe now belong to one and the same kingdom; I give you the arms of the Macedonians, I have made you old soldiers instead of new and foreign ones; you are both my citizens and my soldiers (*inveteravi peregrinam novitatem; et cives mei estis et milites*). All things take on the same colour; it is neither unbecoming for the Persians to simulate the manners of the Macedonians, nor for the Macedonians to copy those of the Persians. These ought to have the same rights who are to live under the same sovereign. (X.iii.10–13)

A comparable attitude toward racial mixture and changing customs can be seen in the Table of Claudius (emperor 41–54 CE), in whose reign Curtius may have written his work.[42] There was opposition in the Senate to Claudius' proposed equal treatment of foreign peoples.

---

[42] On Curtius' date in the reign of the emperor Claudius see Ronald Syme and Barbara M. Levick, "Curtius Rufus," *OCD*[3] (1996) 415–16. Robert Porod, "[II.8] Q. C. Rufus," *Der neue Pauly* 3 (1997) 248–49 acknowledges that most scholars have chosen

Rather the Senate should be recruited from native Italians and kindred peoples (*indigenae consanguinei*), not from hordes of *alienigenae* (Tacitus, *Annals* 11.23.3–4).[43] Momigliano's translation includes the following
exhortation by the emperor to the Roman senate:[44]

> Do not be horrified at the idea of introducing this reform on the ground
> that it is new, but consider how many things in this city have been
> changed and renewed, and how many forms and stages our institutions
> have passed through, from the very foundation of the city. Once upon
> a time Rome was ruled by kings, but it was not their fate to hand it on
> to successors of their own line. Strangers, some of them even foreigners,
> took their place: Romulus, for instance, was succeeded by Numa, who
> came from the Sabine country—a neighbor, no doubt, but in those days
> a foreigner … .

Alexander's speech naming his Asian soldiers as citizens, put into his
mouth by Quintus Curtius in X.iii.10–13, has close affinities with Claudius' reasoning, and we may assume that the ideas are those held by
a minority of Romans in the middle of the first century CE, perhaps
not by Alexander three centuries earlier. The ease with which Romans
admitted whole communities of outsiders to citizenship surprised Greek
observers.[45] Claudius' justification of novelty, including the assertion
that foreigners became Roman kings, was certainly startling.

With the establishment of Rome as a world power and its direct government of the provinces, the honorary and individual grant of citizenship first attained an importance outside Italy.[46] Not until the imperial
period, however, Sherwin-White observes, did a man of peregrine origin make use of his status as a Roman citizen without surrendering his
connection with his original home. The emperor Claudius was charged

---

a date in the reign of Claudius, but choses rather Vespasian (69–79 CE), citing J. Stroux,
"Die Zeit des Curtius," *Philologus* 84 (1929) 33–51.

   [43] A. N. Sherwin-White, *Racial Prejudice in Imperial Rome* (Cambridge: Cambridge
University, 1970) 60; see 74, 79–80, 84–85.

   [44] Arnaldo Momigliano, *Claudius: The Emperor and His Achievement*, trans. W. D. Hog-
arth (Westport, CT: Greenwood, 1981) 11–19, who dates the Table to 48 CE. The quotation is from p. 11; the text is in E. Mary Smallwood, *Documents Illustrating the Principates
of Gaius, Claudius, and Nero* (Cambridge: Cambridge University Press, 1967) no. 369. Barbara Levick, *Claudius* (New Haven: Yale University, 1990) 18, discussing this speech,
notes that Claudius himself boasted of a Sabine origin. For comments on the new
understanding of Claudius, see Rainer Riesner, *Paul's Early Period: Chronology, Mission
Strategy, Theology* (Grand Rapids: Eerdmans, 1998) 92–96.

   [45] M. H. Crawford, "Citizenship, Roman," *OCD*[3] (1996) 334.

   [46] A. N. Sherwin-White, *The Roman Citizenship* (2nd ed.; Oxford: Clarendon, 1973)
245.

with being too lavish with such grants of citizenship in the wrong part of the empire, in Achaea.[47] Charges come from contradictory directions, on the one hand that Claudius deprived "unworthy men" of their Roman status because they had no Latin culture, and on the other, that he allowed Roman citizenship to be bought and sold (Dio Cassius 60.17.4–8). Sherwin-White hypothesizes that Claudius first regularized the practice of presenting auxiliary veterans with citizenship upon discharge.[48] Claudius was following a definite plan, establishing groups of Roman citizens in various provinces; if they accepted some degree of Latin culture, Roman citizenship was the reward.[49] Claudius "broke through a prejudice of his time, and shattered the opinion that the Roman state knew boundaries determined by any other consideration than her own power of absorption and attraction … Claudius is a *princeps* who understands and deliberately promotes the unity of the Roman world, Eastern and Western alike …"[50] Under Claudius too, there is the first example of a community petitioning for a grant of citizenship and municipal status.[51] In the cultural context of Claudius' reign, it is neither accidental nor surprising that a traditional ethnic group meeting in Jerusalem (48 CE, the same year as the Table of Claudius)[52] should decide to admit other "nations," "foreigners," into membership without imposing too many "burdens" (Acts 15:23, 28; 10:28). Similar controversies over ethnic inclusion and integration were occurring both in Rome and in Jerusalem in the late 40's.[53]

---

[47] *Ibid.*, 246 (also 408) referring to Claudius Lysias in Acts 22:28 as an example. Claudius also admitted Philo's nephew, Tiberius Julius Alexander, to an imperial procuratorship.

[48] *Ibid.*, 247; cf. 266, 426.

[49] *Ibid.*, 247, n. 4 cites Aelius Aristides, *Or.* 26.64: "many in every city are fellow-citizens (πολῖται) of yours no less than of their own kinsmen (ὁμοφύλων) … [T]he men of greatest standing and influence in every city guard their own fatherlands for you." James H. Oliver, "The Ruling Power: A Study of the Roman Empire in the Second Century after Christ through the Roman Oration of Aelius Aristides," *Transactions of the American Philosophical Society* n.s. 43/4 (1953) 902 and 987. He compares Tacitus, *Annals* 11.24. I would compare Acts 10:28, where Peter tells Cornelius," you yourselves know that it is unlawful for a Jew[ish disciple of Jesus] to associate with or to visit a Gentile (ἀλλοφύλῳ)."

[50] Sherwin-White, *Roman Citizenship*, 249.

[51] *Ibid.*, 257.

[52] See n. 43 for the date.

[53] For a recent review of the status of the Roman Jews as a "foreign superstition" under Claudius see H. Dixon Slingerland, *Claudian Policymaking and the Early Imperial Repression of Judaism at Rome* (USFSHJ 160; Atlanta: Scholars Press, 1997) 131–50.

Unlike Claudius, Luke in his apologetic history did not dare to evaluate novelty in such positive terms. Instead, he defended "Paul," that is, the Christian house churches, against the accusation that they had "changed" Mosaic customs (Acts 6:11, 13–14; 21:21). Already to Abraham as narrated in the ancient Mosaic Torah as well as to the prophet Isaiah, God had spoken of Israel "receiving all nations."

Conclusion

At the end of Alexander's life, stories in some sources suggest that his goal was to become lord of all the earth. Arrian does not support this suggestion, except in two problematic passages. The clear tendency of the tradition is to add universal language to stories that originally did not include it. Alexander was a more effective and brutal conqueror than he was an administrator of the Asian nations that he had defeated. More important for this paper, the language of "*receiving* all nations" (using some form of δέχομαι), so that the empire will "grow" in numbers, without changing ancient customs, occurs in sources that outline Roman policy or reflect later Roman ideas, not in sources that narrate policies of Alexander the Great. When Luke-Acts promotes "receiving all nations" into the church, the author encourages one aspect of Roman social policy promoted in a controversial manner by the emperor Claudius. The social policy advocated by Luke-Acts is a contrast to Maccabean and Athenian values and employs language that goes beyond Alexander's policies. "Receiving all nations" is a Romanization, not a Hellenization, of the people of God.

DID THE CHURCHES
COMPETE WITH CULT GROUPS?

E.A. Judge

How Words Confound Ideas

Why should we talk of "cult-groups"?[1] Our dictionaries do not recognize the term. It is not a good translation for any ancient one.[2] Presumably then we are devising it for modern ends. Our tidy minds, no doubt, seek an analogy for the churches.

But their name, *ekklesia*, already told its own story. For every civilized man in the Roman world *ekklesia* is the meeting of the sovereign body, the citizens assembled to decide things. In each city where Paul established his new *ekklesia*, there was already an old-established one.[3] It was potentially confronting. We have altogether lost the historic force of this replication. "Church" and "Parliament" (or "Congress") seem to have little in common. Even churches that still call themselves "assemblies" may well have lost the point.

It is easy to see why. *Ekklesia* does not go far enough. The origin, range and purpose of the new "assembly" is radically different from that of its civil homonym. The Lord's *ekklesia* is not merely a meeting, but the community itself that is formed through it. Luther did better to trade in the elliptical "church" (*Kirche*, Greek κυριακή) for "community" (*Gemeinde*).[4]

Every German locality has two communities, the municipal *Gemeinde* and the Evangelical (and/or Catholic) one. This matches exactly the

---

[1] This paper retains the rhetorical style of the one read by Dr B.W. Winter on my behalf at the 1998 SBL International meeting in Cracow. The text has been only slightly adjusted, while the footnotes have been added and section four filled out from its previous summary form. It is offered in appreciation of the studies fostered by A.J. Malherbe at Yale on the cultural setting of the NT churches, and in anticipation of the article "Kultgemeinde" for the *RAC*.

[2] P. Foucart, *Des associations religieuses chez les Grecs: thiases, éranes, orgéons* (Paris: Klinck-sieck, 1873) 1–5: θίασος comes closest.

[3] J.Y. Campbell, "The Origin and Meaning of the Christian Use of the Word ἐκκλησία," *JTS* 49 (1948) 130–42, reprinted in *Three New Testament Studies* (Leiden: Brill, 1965) 41–54, for the implausibility of deriving the NT use from that of the LXX.

[4] T. Rendtorff, in *Historisches Wörterbuch der Philosophie* 3 (Basel: Schwabe, 1974) s.v.

New Testament counterpoint. Yet the two "assemblies" have let each other down in German culture and history.[5] The English may live in a terminological muddle, but the "Church" still crowns the monarch, while "Parliament" was once able to insist that the Church stand by its Book of Common Prayer.

As for the term "cult-group," at least that avoids crediting our category of convenience with too profound a "community" value. Not so *Kultgemeinde*. This term is also not to be found in dictionaries. But it goes the whole way. *Kultgemeinde* risks assigning to our construct the full weight of socially constructive experience that is attested for the New Testament "communities."[6]

There is simply no evidence, nor even any conceivable likelihood, that any fresh mode of community life was ever built around ancient cults, at least not in the strict ancient sense of the term. In essence, the first churches are all community and no cult, while so-called "cult-groups" create far more cult than community. Historically, communities may entrench themselves in cult, but it is not cult that engenders community.

This fundamental distinction has been obliterated by our ambiguous use of the word "religion." No Greek or Latin term corresponds with either of the mutually antipathetic senses we have given it. We apply it to utterly different approaches to life without regard to the uniqueness of the historical changes we are trying to unravel, thus defeating our quest before we begin.[7]

At the end of the fifth century, a belated defender of the old order, Zosimus, accurately identified the historical paradox of Constantine's conversion, though he misdated it, and thus gave a false explanation. In 326 Constantine had killed his eldest son, Crispus, and second wife, Fausta, unhinged by the scandalous recriminations between them. He

---

[5] H.J. Hahn, *German Thought and Culture* (Manchester: Manchester University Press, 1995).

[6] E.A. Judge, "Cultural Conformity and Innovation in Paul: Some Clues from Contemporary Documents," *TynBul* 35 (1984) 3–24, on the novelty of "building" (οἰκοδομή) as a social metaphor (not "edification").

[7] E.A. Judge, "The Beginning of Religious History," *JRH* 15 (1989) 394–412, exploring the fundamental observation about the change of meaning during the third century in what we call "religion" made by W. Cantwell Smith in *The Meaning and End of Religion* (New York: New American Library, 1962, repr. Minneapolis: Fortress Press, 1991).

still practised the ancestral *hiera*, says Zosimus, but the priests said they could not absolve him. An Egyptian referred him instead to the *doxa* of the Christians, which made that possible.[8]

The eminent translator renders both terms by "religion." He might of course have translated ἱερά by "rites" or "sacrifices," and δόξα by "dogma" or "creed." One can easily understand the blurring of the two. Both "rites" and "dogma" for us belong to "religion." But Zosimus was certainly not confusing the two incommensurate and mutually alien modes of life that we have conflated.

Under Augustus the great antiquarian, Verrius Flaccus, formulated the classic dictionary definition of *religio*.[9] After compiling 41 books of "human and divine antiquities," his predecessor Varro had admitted it was impossible to trace the origins and meaning of the multitudinous gods of Rome.[10] So Verrius Flaccus defines the "religious" man as the one who decides which cults to practise according to public custom. He adds, "not involving himself in superstition." Thus *religio*, we can see, means "scrupulosity" with reference to what is conventionally thought prudent. You must not do anything inopportune. And you ought not to worry about why.

But is that not precisely what *we* now mean by "superstition"? For Romans *superstitio* meant what *we* now call "religion." You must not involve yourself and Rome in questioning the reality of the gods, or striving for too much consistency in such matters. This is why Tacitus, Pliny, and Suetonius all condemn the Christians for "superstition."

It was not until the Christians became well established in the public community that they began to claim the dignified title of *religio*, or "scrupulosity," for their own practice. But far from shedding their serious doctrinal drive, they began to turn the meaning of *religio* inside out. It now came to stand for their distinctive commitment to community

---

[8] Zosimus, *New History*, trans. R.T. Ridley (Sydney: Australian Association of Byzantine Studies, 1982) 2.29.3–4.

[9] Sextus Pompeius Festus, epitome of Verrius Flaccus, *De verborum significatu*, ed. W.M. Lindsay, *Glossaria latina* IV (Paris: Les belles lettres, 1930; repr. Hildesheim: Georg Olms, 1965) 389: *religiosi dicuntur qui faciendarum praetermittendarumque rerum divinarum secundum morem civitatis dilectum habent nec se superstitionibus implicant* "People are called 'religious' when they show discrimination in performing and passing over divine matters according to the practice of the city, and do not involve themselves in superstition."

[10] M. Terentius Varro, *Antiquitates rerum divinarum*, ed. B. Cardauns (Mainz: Franz Steiner, 1976), frag. 204 = frag. 1 Agahd = Augustine, *De civitate Dei* 7.17.

building on dogmatic principles, leaving "superstition" as the derogatory label for the old cultic customs they abhorred.[11]

This is why the *Macquarie Dictionary* states that "religion" means "a particular system in which the quest for the ideal life has been embodied." It also cites what it calls an "obsolete" sense, "the practice of sacred rites and observances." But this is not obsolete at all. Most people fuse the two senses into an indefinable tangle. They are certainly separate, however, in historical context. It is the obsolete sense we need to have in mind when we speak of the ancient cults as "religions." The making of the modern sense only begins when the Christian quest itself assumes the trappings of a cult. It is not, however, until the 17th century (1614 to be precise) that the category "religion" is systematically applied to a series of such complexes, Christianity, Islam (then called "Mohammedanism"), Judaism, and so-called "paganism." The eastern "religions" are then coupled to it, in defiance of their fundamental incongruity, only in the 19th century.[12]

Please do not dismiss these definitional points as "logomachies." Just as with terms like "Republic" and "Empire," we lock ourselves into an ineluctable grid of anachronism when we take over the Latin words but fail to allow for their changed meanings in English. The trap only complicates itself when both the Latin and our own usage are shifting as the momentum of the times moves on. Where the words *religio* and *superstitio* actually occur in classical texts, we might translate them as "punctilio" and "commitment" respectively. Where they do not occur in the original, we do well not to use their English derivatives in the translation. Taking a second look at what was actually said is always worth the trouble. English habitually pads itself out with abstracts when our sources deal only in particulars. We no doubt owe the term "logomachies" to that ancient campaigner who wanted to get rid of

---

[11] But the proper Latin terms for what we now call "religion," namely *secta* ("commitment") or *lex* ("rule of life") remained standard in Christian Latin until the 16th century and beyond, as shown by E. Feil, *Religio: Die Geschichte eines neuzeitlichen Grundbegriffs vom Frühchristentum bis zur Reformation* (Göttingen: Vandenhoeck and Ruprecht, 1986).

[12] Peter Harrison, *"Religion" and the Religions in the Enlightenment* (Cambridge: Cambridge University Press, 1990) 39: the first example of the plural is "all religions" in R. Hooker, *Lawes of Ecclesiastical Politie* IV xi 2; the four species of the generic "religion" were established by the work of E. Brerewood, *Enquiries Touching the Diversity of Languages and Religions through the Cheife Parts of the World* (1614).

the "puffed up conceit" of the second generation and stick with the "healthy words" of the original. I refer to the author of the Pastoral Epistles.[13]

The Documentation of Cult-groups

The reason why our topic does not have a recognized name, either then or now, is that it was not even formally discussed in antiquity. But in the inscriptions especially there is abundant documentation where we can test what we think we see. Sokolowski has assembled, in three volumes, a corpus of 400 Greek cult-rules, mostly of Hellenistic and Roman times. Since they published their regulations, these cults self-evidently belong in the public domain. But, whether nationally or privately instituted, they are all necessarily localized to the sanctuary that has been created for them.[14]

There are three physical elements that define a sanctuary:

(1) the sacred space (Greek τέμενος, Latin *templum*—not necessarily a building) that marks it out;
(2) the object within it (often a statue) by which the god's presence is anchored to it;
(3) the altar, upon which sacrifices are to be made by qualified individuals.

Although the sacrifices were often made on behalf of the civil or other communities, the temple was not a meeting hall. Private parties or group-meetings were however regularly held in dining-rooms attached to temples. The temple of Demeter and Kore at Corinth had fifty-two of these.[15] The assemblies of the Christians at first had no connection with any sanctuary, being held in houses or other suitable places, such as a lecture hall or (later) covered markets.[16]

---

[13] Apparently an innovation of NT times, we may surely credit "logomachies" in English to 1 Tim 6:4, 2 Tim 2:14.

[14] F. Sokolowski, *Lois sacrées des cités grecques* (Paris: de Boccard, 1969); *Lois sacrées des cités grecques. Supplément* (Paris: de Boccard, 1962); *Lois sacrées de l'Asie Mineure* (Paris: de Boccard, 1955); unless otherwise indicated, references below are to the first of these.

[15] N. Bookidis, "Ritual Dining in the Sanctuary of Demeter and Kore at Corinth: Some Questions," in *Sympotica*, ed. O. Murray (Oxford: Clarendon, 1990) 86–94.

[16] L. Michael White, *The Social Origins of Christian Architecture* (2 vols.; HTS 42; Valley Forge: Trinity Press International, 1996–97) 1:102–10.

Of the 400 cult-rules collected by Sokolowski, only 5% deal with
matters concerning associated groups. The essential purpose of the
rules was to ensure correct access to the sanctuary. They deal with
the selection and qualifications of priests, the calendar of sacrifices, the
ritual cleanliness of those who offer them, and the division of the meat
between those with a claim to it.

An elementary example from the first century (Sokolowski 54) focuss-
es on the last point. A local farmer in Attica has set up a shrine for
Asclepius and Hygieia. He assumes his neighbors will want to use it to
safeguard their health. He does not need to state how they will do this,
since it is well known. His main concern is to specify that both he and
the officiating priest are assigned their share of the meat, and that the
rest is not reclaimed:

Ἱερὸν τὸ τέμενο[ς]		Sacred is the temple
τοῦ Ἀσκληπιοῦ καὶ		to Asclepius and
τῆς Ὑγιείας.		to Hygieia.
θύειν τοὺς γεωργοὺς		Let the farmers sacrifice,
καὶ τοὺς προσχώρους	5	and the neighbors,
τοῖν θεοῖν ἧι θέμις		as is right for the gods.
καὶ τὰς μοίρας νέμειν		They are to assign shares
τῶι τε εἰσαμένωι καὶ		both to the founder and
τῶι θεηκολοῦντι·		to the "god-cultivator."
τῶν δὲ κρεῶν μὴ	10	None of the meat
φέρεσθαι.		is to be taken away.

Presumably the founder will be selling the surplus. He is providing a
community service, and expects to profit from it. No other form of
group activity is called for.

A more elaborate stage is seen at the end of the inscription from
Sunium of the late second century (Sokolowski 53). The first 26 lines
are too badly damaged to read. They will have been in hexameter
verse, as are lines 27–29. There is a "patron" (προστάτης, 34) who will
have founded the cult. It is related to a tomb, the heir to which (39) has
joint responsibility for conducting the cult (38). They have presumably
agreed that an unspecified group of men (28) may collectively provide
for their own burial under the aegis of the cult. The text and translation
are given in the Appendix (no. 2).

What survives is the statute for a "club" (ἔρανος, 28). The men have
formed this on the principle of "friendship" (φιλία, 29). Their office-
bearers will be chosen annually by lot (37), and will determine the
membership jointly with the patron and the tomb-heir (34). Members
must pass a three-fold test before being admitted to the "meeting"

(σύνοδος, 32). I take this to refer not to periodic meetings, since that would not require such an elaborate selection panel, but to membership of the club itself. I therefore translate ἁγνός (33) not as a test of ritual "purity," but (as in the contemporary inscriptions of Ephesus) as one of financial "honesty." The club seeks "benefactions" (φιλοτιμίαι, 40), and no doubt has a membership fee set from time to time, as well as collecting fines (43) from members.

The sting in the tail discloses the true character of the club. Those who are to be flogged rather than paying fines must be the ones held in slavery (43). The penalties are for "stirring up fighting or uproar" (41). So these "friends" are not bonded primarily by any philosophical or "religious" interest. They are those employees and servants of the patron and tomb-heir who wish to maintain the link through to an honourable burial. They are financing this jointly, and in the meantime enjoying a good time at regular drinking or dining parties. Any sacrifices offered will have been safely performed before the fun began.

The second-century inscription of Xanthus, a Lycian apparently in slavery to a Roman (Sokolowski 55), clearly sets out the relations between cult-founder, the general community, and any club that might be formed. Xanthus has a keen sense of the service he is offering. The god is invoked to be merciful to those who cultivate him "in simpleness of soul" (12). In practice this is expressed in strict attention to physical purity. Sacrifices may only be offered if Xanthus himself is present (7/8), or his nominated delegate (14). Xanthus is very explicit about preserving his investment from damage (15) and about the sharing out of the proceeds. He would welcome the creation of a club (ἔρανος, 21), and budgets exactly for the income he would expect from it. The text and translation are given in the Appendix (no. 3).

These are the only two instances of an ἔρανος in the collections of Sokolowski. There are five instances where a θίασος is positively referred to. They are from different cities, honouring different gods. Whereas the ἔρανος is taken to be a social club attached to a cult for convenience (like a trade association) the θίασος is assumed to be one created primarily to maintain the cult itself. In two fourth-century rules (Sokolowski 36 and 145), however, restrictions are placed on any θίασος. The third century provides four of the positive cases, the fifth being from the second century A.D. It seems that the dominant interest of the θίασος members does not differ from that of ἔρανος members.

This may be seen most clearly from the elaborate rule determined for the Bacchic society of Athens in the third quarter of the second century (Sokolowski 51).[17]

The society (presumably a θίασος) is being resuscitated. It is to meet regularly on all the festivals in the Bacchic calendar, attendance is obligatory, and each member must contribute in "word, deed or benefaction" (l.45). No one may address the banquet without permission, however (l.108). The priest delivers a eulogy of Bacchus (θεολογία, l.115), an innovation, says the inscription. Flogging is not required since this is a distinguished citizen body, but the problems of fighting and uproar seem just as great as with the more homely ἔρανοι.

The generic names of these two types of association do not occur in early Christian literature. The ἑταιρεία, notorious in Greek history as a political club or faction (cf. Sokolowski 36), does perhaps leave its shadow. The vocative ἑταῖρε ("partner") is used three times by Matthew as an ironically amiable form of address, from the vineyard boss to the labourer who had the worst of the deal (Matt 20:13), from the king to the guest without the wedding garment (22:12), and from Jesus to Judas at the betrayal (26:50). This is like left-wing politicians in Australia ostentatiously accosting recalcitrants by calling them "comrade" or "mate." A cult-group that uses this term formally, at least for one lot of members, is the Sabbatistai of Elaioussa in Cilicia, from the time of Augustus (Sokolowski, *Asie Mineure*, 80). Their name suggests a spin-off from Judaism.

The infrequency of explicit reference to group structures in the cult-rules means they should not be taken for granted. S.K. Stowers has demonstrated there were good reasons why Barton and Horsley ought not to have assumed that the rules for access to the "house" of Dionysius at Philadelphia in the first century B.C. (Sokolowski, *Asie Mineure* 20) implied a "cult-group."[18] Since in antiquity all types of association, social or burial, trade or professional, family or state, placed themselves under divine protection, and made the necessary sacrifices, it may not

---

[17] A translation of this inscription may be found in M.W. Meyer, *The Ancient Mysteries: A Sourcebook* (San Francisco: Harper and Row, 1987) 95–99.

[18] S. Barton and G.H.R. Horsley, "A Hellenistic Cult Group and the New Testament Churches," *Jahrbuch für Antike und Christentum* 24 (1981) 7–41; S.K. Stowers, "A Cult from Philadelphia. Oikos Religion or Cultic Association?" *The Early Church in its Context: Essays in Honor of Everett Ferguson*, ed. A.J. Malherbe, F.W. Norris, and J.W. Thompson (NovTSup 90; Leiden: Brill, 1998) 287–301; cf. White, *Social Origins of Christian Architecture*, 1:45.

be easy to tell which, if any, existed for the sake of maintaining the cult itself. As with the Bacchic society of Athens, what is begun for that end may well need, as an inducement, to cater for social demands also. It has been argued that the forming of this type of association for the ancient cults of Egypt marks their "secularization" in Graeco-Roman times.[19]

On the other hand, the attraction of first-century Romans to the ceremonial side of Judaism and the public impact of the cult of Isis show that ritual itself was a compelling force. The conversion of Lucius in Apuleius illustrates its power.[20] The elaborate ritual and dress regulations for the mysteries of Andania in Messenia, dated 92 B.C. (Sokolowski 65), are declared "authoritative for all time."[21] Yet Andania, like Oberammergau, is more of a public community than a cult-group.

Of Vidman's 870 inscriptions documenting the cults of Isis and Sarapis only five mention or imply a θίασος and two an ἔρανος.[22] This is exactly the ratio with Sokolowski's corpus and much the same frequency (since half Vidman's texts are Latin). Although the rituals were highly structured and demanded much attention from those officially involved, one may question the degree to which there was a distinctive group structure embracing the whole cult community. The term κοινόν ("fellowship") is occasionally used in this sense. Two of Sokolowski's θίασοι refer to themselves by this term as well, and there are three other documents in his corpus where it has the same implication.[23] In Vidman's collection κοινόν mostly identifies sub-groups (cf. the κοινόν of the διακόνων, 90), but there are four references to the κοινόν of the Sarapiasts. Much the same goes for the use of the Latin *collegium* with the cults of Isis and Serapis: of eight instances, four refer to sub-groups.[24]

The hymns to Isis, however, present her as the guardian of the civilized status quo in general—the public community. She is the universal

[19] W.M. Brashear, *Vereine im griechisch-römischen Ägypten*, (Xenia 34; Constance: Universitätsverlag Konstanz, 1993) 29, alluding to W.L. Westermann, *Journal of Egyptian Archaeology* 18 (1932) 27.

[20] J.G. Griffiths, *The Isis Book: Apuleius, Book XI* (Leiden: Brill, 1975) 51–55.

[21] Tr. Meyer, *Ancient Mysteries*, 57–59.

[22] L. Vidman, *Sylloge inscriptionum religionis Isiacae et Sarapiacae* (Berlin: de Gruyter, 1969), summarizing in addition at least 300 inscriptions of Delos published by P. Roussel.

[23] Sokolowski 51, 135, 181 (+ θίασος), *Supplément* 20, *Asie Mineure* 2 (+θίασος).

[24] Vidman 176, 196, 236, 265: κοινόν of the Sarapiasts; 481a, 677: *collegium* of Serapis; 476, 498: of Isis.

refuge for those who have lost the anchorage of their older local cults.[25] The churches (and the Virgin) in turn took up the visual, musical and processional glamour of Isis (only the cross stands out as their own contribution, claims MacMullen).[26] But their intellectual heritage undercut the naturalistic order that Isis maintained, and was promoted intensively through the ecclesiastical structures.

The case of Mithraism is even less clear. Among the 2377 inscriptions and monuments collected by Vermaseren, there are only two instances where a group may be called a *collegium* (the comprehensive Latin equivalent of the several Greek terms for association, whether public or private).[27] The term *cultus* does not occur at all, and there are no priests, at least not in the normal sense.[28] There can hardly have been animal sacrifices performed anyway within the sunken and enclosed Mithraic chambers. Their barrel ceilings reveal that the whole point of the initiation was astrological. The key image of Mithras slaying the bull has astrological rather than sacrificial significance.[29] We should cease trying to construe these tightly ordered cells in terms of "cult-groups" or "religion." Their combination of strict secrecy and high respectability amongst groups of professional men puts them on a par rather with the Masonic lodges.[30]

[25] G.H.R. Horsley, *New Documents Illustrating Early Christianity* 1 (1981) 12–20, for *SEG* (1976) 821 and 1 Kyme 41. Also translated in Meyer, *The Ancient Mysteries*, 172–4.

[26] R. MacMullen, *Christianity and Paganism in the Fourth to Eighth Centuries* (New Haven: Yale University Press, 1997) 157.

[27] M.J. Vermaseren, *Corpus inscriptionum et monumentorum religionis Mithriacae* (2 vols.; The Hague: Martinus Nijhoff, 1956–1960).

[28] [The term *cultores* (equated with a list of patrons) occurs in only one mithraic inscription, *CIL* XI.5737 = *CIMRM* 688, text and translation also given in White, *Social Origins*, 2 no. 92. Although the term *sacerdos* does occur with some frequency (e.g, Vermaseren, *CIMRM* 273), it also implies status within the group, often resulting from benefaction; cf. White, *Social Origins*, 1:47–59, esp. 57 n. 129. For other terms in mithraic inscriptions reflecting the social aspects of the group see White, *Social Origins*, 2 no. 88 (*syndexi*, "right-handers").—Ed.]

[29] R. Beck, *Planetary Gods and Planetary Orders in the Mysteries of Mithras* (Leiden: Brill, 1988); D. Ulansey, *The Origins of the Mithraic Mysteries: Cosmology and Salvation in the Ancient World* (New York: Oxford University Press, 1989).

[30] R.L. Beck, "The Mithras Cult as Association," *Studies in Religion* 21.1 (1992) 3–13; M. Clauss, *Cultores Mithrae: Die Anhängerschaft des Mithras-Kultus* (Stuttgart: Steiner, 1992); F. Mitthof, "Der Vorstand der Kultgemeinden des Mithras: Eine Sammlung und Untersuchung der inschriftlichen Zeugnisse," *Klio* 74 (1992) 275–90; J.H.W.G. Liebeschuetz, "The Expansion of Mithraism among the Religious Cults of the Second Century," *Studies in Religion* (Rome: Bretschneider, 1994) 195–216.

My purpose in minimizing the terminological evidence for "cult-groups" is tactical. There are of course very many groups that document themselves without using the sort of technical term that might justify the title "cult-group." My point is that they are all comfortably accommodated within the ruling culture. They are part of its support structure, and do not signal their identity as a self-conscious attempt to remodel community life. There is no doctrine of the group.

Were the Christians Seen As a Cult-group?

By contrast, the Christian *ekklesia* was driven by its intellectual challenge to the reigning culture. The primary purpose of the synagogue assembly had been instruction in the law, to enable devout Jews to maintain their distinctive life-style. The Christians carried this over into Gentile territory. Far from lining up in competition with cults, they denounced them all as idolatrous. It was not merely a matter of banning a rival cult, as occasionally done in the cult-rules.[31] The worship system of Israel itself, temple, priesthood and sacrifice, was transposed as a figure of the gospel.[32]

The sole instance of a cultic act performed in a New Testament *ekklesia* is hypothetical. Paul imagines an unbeliever prostrating himself in worship when confronted in his conscience by the prophesying (1 Cor 14:25). The point is that the divine encounter was totally unpredictable for the outsider. None of the standard indicators was present. Two centuries later the same point (in reverse) was made of Aurelian. When the Senate was proving unusually argumentative, he is said to have complained, "One would think you were meeting in a Christian assembly, and not in the temple of all the gods."[33]

In Rom 12:1 Paul speaks of personal commitment ("present your bodies") as a "sacrifice," but one that is "living" rather than culminating in death. This he says is a form of "worship in your mind" (λο-γικὴ λατρεία, "reasonable worship").[34] In Rom 12:2 he spells out what

---

[31] G.H.R. Horsley (n. 25 above) 21–23.

[32] G. Klinzing, *Die Umdeutung des Kultus in der Qumrangemeinde und im Neuen Testament* (Göttingen: Vandenhoeck and Ruprecht, 1971).

[33] Scriptores Historiae Augustae, *Aurelian* 20.5, using the word *ecclesia* of a building; by this time the churches had taken over another associational term for their debates: A. Lumpe, "Zur Geschichte des Wortes σύνοδος in der antiken christlichen Gräzität," *Annuarium Historiae Conciliorum* 6 (1974) 40–53.

[34] [On this terminology, see also the article by Johnson in this volume.—Ed.]

this means: a mental transformation and renewal, enabling one to act as God wills—in other words, to fulfil "the quest for the ideal life" which we now call "religion." By applying to this the term for cultic worship ("obsolete" religion) he (like James 1:26–27) anticipates the re-categorization of terms that is to come. He is not however classifying Christianity as "a religion."

In an extensive recent study, however, H.D. Betz has argued emphat-ically that he is.[35] Betz holds that "all New Testament writings in one way or another assume that Christianity as religion is an entity still in need of definition;" yet, "all New Testament writings assume that the Christian religion must compete with other religions" (316). Although his article starts with acknowledging the problem of defining "religion," these premises presuppose a definition (though they do not give it), and, more seriously, presuppose a series of "religions" in a way that is simply inapplicable in the Graeco-Roman world at that time.

Betz rejects the claim that "the Greeks had no concept of religion." "The final comprehensive term 'religion' gradually emerged as a result of the confluence of Greek and Roman philosophical ideas" (319). He finds a "negative evaluation of religion" in Rom 1–2, so that "it is not surprising that Paul hesitated to discuss the Christian faith in terms of religion" (327). In the "anthropological myth" (5:12–21), which "may be pre-Pauline," "the inner logic of this argument must be seen in the categories of the history of religions" (331–2). But Rom 12:1–2 provides in λογικὴ λατρεία "a comprehensive concept comprising ritual worship and ethics" which defines "the Christian religion" (320). The Greek phrase was chosen "deliberately and programmatically" to show that "Christianity is an enlightened form of religion," "recreated by the renewal of the intellect" (337–8).

Using Albrecht Dihle's work on "the canon of the two virtues" (sc. piety and philanthropy),[36] Betz claims that "Paul's definition of Christianity as religion in a remarkable way resembles definitions of religion in philosophical and religious literature of the time." Yet his "definition of Christian religion does not appear to be an essential part of his understanding of the Christian faith" (343).

---

[35] "The Birth of Christianity as a Hellenistic Religion," *JR* 74 (1994) 1–25; "Chris-tianity as Religion: Paul's Attempt at Definition in Romans," *JR* 71 (1991) 315–44: page references are to this article.

[36] A. Dihle, *Der Kanon der zwei Tugenden* (Cologne: Westdeutscher Verlag, 1968).

The reason why Paul does not find the concept of religion essential is of course rather that it does not exist in the clear way the thesis of Betz seems to require. Nor has Betz allowed for the metaphorical function of λατρεία in Rom 12:1. Instead he has assumed (as virtually all writers on the New Testament do) that "worship" (in the cultic sense) is seriously provided for in the New Testament.

The "canon of the two virtues" is hardly a defined principle either. It can be discerned rather in the conventional language of popular philosophy and does indeed point to the line of contact between the first Christians and their contemporaries. The Christians are not to be aligned however under "religion," with its concentration upon correct procedure in worship. But they do occupy the ground of the philosophers, insofar as they argue for a new doctrine of God and a consequential revolution in life-style. Neither correct belief nor good behavior was part of what we choose to call "religion" in antiquity.

The converse applies with the Latin term *secta* which, like the Greek αἵρεσις, was in contemporary use for a philosophical following, but certainly not for what we now mean by a religious sect. Constantine even speaks of the Catholic αἵρεσις (Eus. *HE* 10.5.21) against which people are wilfully dissenting, while Galerius had used *secta* of the classical tradition.[37]

Secta is used by Tertullian for the followers of Christ, and Diocletian uses it for the Manichaeans.[38] It is not in either case making a comment about the worship of God. So far as I can tell no cult-group could possibly have been called that, and to speak of "religious sects" in antiquity merely swamps the scene with Weberian constructs at the expense of the classical terminology.

The recent work of the French School at Rome on "the Dionysiac association in ancient societies" includes a demonstration by J. Scheid that the vast catalogue (*IGUR* 160) of names in Greek found under this heading at Torre Nova does not (as Cumont thought) represent the invasion of Rome by a new sect (in the modern sense) but is the proud

---

[37] In his edict of toleration, Lactantius, *De mortibus persecutorum* (Creed) 34.1, Galerius complained that the Christians had abandoned the *secta* of their forbears.

[38] In the edict against the Manichees, preserved in the *Codex Gregorianus* (Riccobono, *Fontes* II 580–1), Diocletian accuses them of setting "novel and unheard-of commitments (*sectas*) against older obligations (*religionibus*)." Tertullian had earlier claimed that the *secta* of the Christians deserved milder treatment amongst the unlicensed *factiones* (*Apol.* 38.1 Waltzing).

domestic record of the welfare organization provided for their staff by two eminent Roman families of the second century.[39]

There was no Dionysiac way of life. In spite of the social tumults caused by Bacchic orgies from time to time, nothing changed at the social level, nor was meant to. The god of wine, as always, presided over the momentary suspension of conventional restraints, not over the creation of any new consciousness of life. Even the Pythagorean revival was essentially a personal retreat from social reality.[40]

It is equally clear that the New Testament churches were not likely to be mistaken for a cult-group. They were far too argumentative or intellectual, far too socially activist for that. Although they attempted to protect themselves against provocation by fortifying convention in some respects, their fundamentally innovatory remodelling of life puts them at the opposite end of the social scene from the classical cults.

The term ἐκκλησία made little or no impression upon contemporaries, and its significance was not pressed by the apologists. Its familiarity as the name for the civil assemblies, or those of a private association,[41] does not seem to have been of any consequence—it certainly does not constitute a claim to civil legitimacy, nor was it sensed as provocative. Celsus rather ridiculed the term by making his Christian worms hold their ἐκκλησία in a dung-heap.[42] I can only assume that the term simply seemed irrelevant to both sides in their confrontation. No claim was being made or feared that the church was in any form either a public or a private association of the ordinary kind.

The centrality of the term for Christians was perhaps fortified by their claim to stand in the heritage of the congregation of Israel. By the time it passes into public usage (late in the third century) that is only because the Christians are now applying it to their distinctive buildings, an innovation of the period immediately prior to Diocletian's reaction.

---

[39] J. Scheid, "Le thiase du Metropolitan Museum (IGUR 160)," *L'Association dionysiaque dans les sociétés anciennes* (Rome: École Française, 1986) 275–90; B.H. McLean, "The Agrippinilla Inscription: Religious Associations and Early Church Formation," *Origins and Methods: Towards a New Understanding of Judaism and Christianity* (Sheffield: JSOT Press, 1993) 239–70.

[40] E.A. Judge, "A Woman's Behaviour," *New Documents Illustrating Early Christianity* 6, ed. S.R. Llewelyn (1992) 18–23.

[41] F. Poland, *Geschichte des griechischen Vereinswesens* (Leipzig: Teubner, 1909, repr. Leipzig: Zentralantiquariat 1967) 332.

[42] Cited in Origen, *Contra Celsum* 4.23.

Ammianus is aware of *ecclesia* only as the name of a building. His term for a meeting (as with the Tetrarchs) is *conventiculum*.[43]

The central term Χριστιανοί is bafflingly peculiar. It is a Graeco-Latin hybrid, and must therefore have been coined by Latin speakers in response to the currency of the Greek word Χριστός. Since Acts 11:26 says it was first used at Antioch one must think of members of the Roman administration, army or business community in the Syrian capital. They will have coined it as part of their Latin vocabulary (not for use when speaking Greek, which would have called for Χριστῖται or some other χριστο- compound). The suffix *-ianus* constitutes a political comment. It is never attached to the name of a god, unless one counts the associations of Herculani, whom I assume to be wrestlers. The Roman Jewish synagogues are Αὐγυστησιοί, Ἀγριππησιοί, etc. but never -ιανοί.[44] This is because the devotees of a god do not engage in the type of activity connoted by the suffix.

It classifies people as partisans of a political leader, and is mildly contemptuous. The young knights whom Nero engaged to applaud at his triumph were dubbed *Augustiani*.[45] Closer to Antioch, one may note the Herodians, who question Jesus on the matter of loyalty to Caesar (Matt 22:16, cf. Mark 12:13, also 3:6). One of the disciples at Antioch, Manaen, had presumably been a Herodian—"a member of the court of Herod the Tetrarch" (Acts 13:1).

The very name Χριστιανοί, then, appears to have arisen in the questions posed for Romans over the political loyalty of the followers of Christ. This will explain the sharp reaction of Herod Agrippa II to Paul's challenge, "Do you believe the prophets? I know that you do." "You needn't think you can make a Χριστιανός of me so quickly" (Acts 26:28), retorted the Herodian leader, embarrassed by the presence of the new governor, Festus, in whose audience chamber at Caesarea this exchange took place. He gave Paul a clearance, however, in closed conference with Festus, after the event (Acts 16:32). The writer of Acts was well informed on such hearings, which will have been carefully documented by the new governor's staff.

---

[43] Ammianus 15.5.31, 27.3.13; Lactantius, *De mortibus persecutorum* (Creed) 15.7 (by implication, Constantius), 34.4 (Galerius).

[44] H.J. Leon, *The Jews of Ancient Rome* (Philadelphia: Jewish Publication Society, 1960) 140–42.

[45] Suetonius, *Nero* 25.1: they treated themselves as his soldiers when he celebrated his Olympic victories at singing and acting by entering Rome in a triumphal chariot. Tacitus, *Annals* 14.15.5: they chanted divine compliments on his voice and good looks.

The first letter of Peter shows why the Christians accepted their name. It identified them with Christ, particularly with the misrepresentation he had suffered. "If you are reproached for the name of Christ, you are blessed" (1 Pet 4:14). The false charges are already at hand: "Let none of you suffer as a murderer, or a thief, or a wrongdoer, or as an ἀλλοτριεπίσκοπος" (4:15). Deissmann translated this as "stirrer" (*Aufrührer*) on the strength of a parallel in the papyri.[46]

The first three classical writers to use the term *Christiani* (Pliny, Tacitus, Suetonius) are all Roman, and all from the period of Ignatius, the first Christian known to have taken up the term. They are all very clear about the identity of the Christians, not in any way confusing them with Jews, nor of course with a cult. Pliny must have thought it quaint that they should have treated their criminal leader Christus "as though he were a god" (*quasi deo*).[47] He is certainly aware that the Christians present an obstruction to the orderly conduct of sacrificial offerings. But it may be their criminal activities that he assumes have upset that routine. He is surprised that he could not substantiate any crimes—their oath was "not for the purposes of any crime" (*non in scelus aliquod*), as he assumed it must be—finding instead only a "depraved and immoderate superstition" (*superstitio prava et immodica*). Religion is *not* what he had expected to find.

It is not until the second half of the second century that we have classical Greek writers referring to Χριστιανοί.[48] Galen avoids the term because he wants to treat them as an intellectual tradition, as with the "school" (διατριβή) of Moses.[49] The fact that the voluminous Greek writers of Pliny's day and earlier (Dio Chrysostom, Plutarch) seem

[46] Details s.v. in the *Lexicon* of Bauer, Arndt, Gingrich, and Danker (2nd ed.), who translate it "revolutionist."

[47] Pliny, *Epistles* 10.96.7: this is what the renegades told him. Pliny did not need to explain to Trajan who Christ was. Suetonius, *Nero* 16.2, does not mention him. Tacitus, *Annals* 15.44.3, explains that he had been executed under Pilate in the time of Tiberius, and was the source of the name *Christianus*.

[48] Marcus Aurelius, *Meditations* 11.3.2: the soul must face its departure rationally and without drama, not with bare-faced bravado (παράταξις) like the Χριστιανοί. Lucian, *Peregrinus* 11, relates how Peregrinus mastered the amazing discipline (σοφία) of the *Christianoi*. In *Alexander* 38, they chant, "down with the atheist Χριστιανοί and Epicureans."

[49] Galen, *De pulsuum differentiis* 2.4, 3.3, objects to the medical empiricists who are committed to their positions (αἱρέσεις) and resist his logical method. One might as well be in the school of Moses and Christ, he complains. Texts and translation in M. Stern, *Greek and Latin Authors on Jews and Judaism* (Jerusalem: Israel Academy, 1974–84) vol. II, nos. 377–8.

utterly oblivious of the Christians may be due to the dominating political character that the movement had in their view.

On the Christian side the term remains rare, with Tatian the last to avoid it entirely. Justin accepts it, while Athenagoras still speaks of "we so-called Χριστιανοί." The lack of a stable name confirms the weight of modern opinion against de Rossi (and many others) who held that the churches in law were *collegia funeraticia*. As the fundamental works of Waltzing, Ziebarth and Poland demonstrated, the private associations of the Greeks and Romans were very prescriptively defined, with published membership lists, and mostly on a very small scale, for very specific purposes indicated by their names.[50] In all of these respects the churches fail to correspond. Paul had in any case ruled out using the institutions of the civil order to manage church affairs (1 Cor 6:1–6).

This is not to say that the church might not constitute its own arrangements and that these might not parallel in certain respects the civil ones. Yet the lack of a name or closed membership shows how different in conception the enterprise was. The disciples are dubbed by thirty or more different styles before slowly agreeing with the general opinion that the one the Romans had coined for them at Antioch was the definitive one.[51]

Yet it was well into the 250s (significantly enough in the sequel to Decius' grand effort to standardize everything around the affirmation of classical sacrifice) that the term Χριστιανός first makes an awkward appearance in papyrus documents.[52] I say "awkward" both because of the ambiguity of the readings and because of the strangeness of the usage (if correctly read) in the particular cases—it functions first as an occupational indicator. There is no need to assume Christians were

---

[50] F. Poland, *Vereinswesen*, reviewing the scene historically, treats the size of associations on 282–89: two or three dozen members was typical (p. 287). E. Ziebarth, *Das griechische Vereinswesen* (Leipzig: Hinzel, 1896; repr. Wiesbaden: Sändig, 1969) gives a structural analysis of the system, with *Kultvereine* on pp. 33–69. J.-P. Waltzing, *Étude historique sur les corporations professionnelles chez les Romains* (Brussels: Hayez, 1895–1900, repr. Hildesheim: Olms, 1970), offers a corpus of inscriptions in vol. 3, with classified lists in vol. 4 (incl. *cultores deorum*, pp. 180–202). On the legal position of the churches, see A. Ehrhardt, "Das Corpus Christi und die Korporationen im spätrömischen Recht," *Zeitschrift der Savigny-Stiftung für Rechtsgeschichte: romanistische Abteilung* 70 (1953) 299–347; 71 (1954) 25–40; and F. de Robertis, *Storia delle corporazioni e del regime associativo nel mondo romano* (Bari: Adriatica, 1973), vol. II, ch. IV.

[51] H. Karpp, "Christennamen," *RAC* 2 (1954) 1114–38 sets out all the names systematically.

[52] The earliest certain case is *P.Oxy.* 3035, dated 28 February, 256. Possibly earlier are *P.Oxy.* 3119 and SB 16.12497.

avoiding their name anyway, since it was not their own chosen official title, nor did they even have one. Nor should we assume they were concealing their tracks in other ways. The fact of the matter is that they were not conceived of by themselves as part of the institutional pattern that required constant documentation. The churches were working in a different register (to use a linguistic term).

It was not that the churches were taciturn or secretive—the very opposite. Eusebius makes clear what the vast extant literature of the fathers would anyway, that we are dealing with an intellectual movement of massive proportions and many ramifications. The papyrus fragments tell their own story. There are about 20 Christian texts extant from the second century, all literary, and some 140 from the third century (half biblical).[53]

Yet only a pitifully slight trail of Christian private letters and business documents begins to be traced before the early fourth century, resting for the most part on indirect indications such as the new-fangled Christian names (Peter especially). Attempts to identify letters as Christian on the grounds of their having suitable sentiments all break down on the increasingly shared fashion for vaguely monotheistic language (e.g. allusions to providence) and common ethical ideals.[54]

The great work of Robin Lane Fox, *Pagans and Christians*, makes the point another way. As he explains, he was inspired to write this saga of third-century culture by discovering the lost world of the Greek inscriptions of that epoch. It is a world alive with gods and experience of the divine, which he recreates with leisurely affection for its infinite variety.[55]

But the Christian world he sets alongside it is derived from quite different sources. Lane Fox rightly draws out the differences of outlook. But his very title sets up the false analogy that his work refutes. Nothing prevented the Christians from enshrining themselves as a cult-group replete with monuments like their neighbors. Nothing, that is, from

---

[53] Summary details in E.A. Judge, "Papyri," *Encyclopedia of Early Christianity* (1990) 686–91, and S.R. Pickering, "Papyri, Early Christian," *ABD* 5 143–46.

[54] M. Naldini, *Il Cristianesimo in Egitto: Lettere private nei papiri dei secoli II–IV* (Florence: Le Monnier, 1968), critically tested by E. Wipszycka, "Remarques sur les lettres privées chrétiennes des IIᵉ–IVᵉ siècles," *Journal of Juristic Papyrology* 18 (1974) 203–21, and by G. Tibiletti, *Le lettere private nei papiri greci del III e IV secolo d. C.: Tra paganesimo e cristianesimo* (Milan: Vita e pensiero, 1979). Naldini responded in the 2nd ed. of his book (Fiesole: Nardini, 1998) 425–57.

[55] R. Lane Fox, *Pagans and Christians* (New York: Knopf, 1987).

the Roman side. Indeed it was the solution that was desired, that the Christians should lend cultic weight to the preservation of the common pattern of culture. They of course were at first profoundly antagonistic to that.

When the accommodation was finally made, there was a paradoxical counter-reaction. There had been in fact a lawful incorporation of the churches in the readjustments after Decius. More specifically there were now recognized *corpora Christianorum* that had the capacity to hold property at law. Hence the sudden efflorescence of church building late in the third century.[56]

After the last paroxysm of the Diocletianic persecution the government itself (in Galerius' edict of toleration) imposed upon the churches (*conventicula*) the duty of praying (*orare*) for the commonwealth. Their "divergent communities" (*varios populos*), complained Galerius, had abandoned the *secta* of their forebears (i.e. the classical culture) and "made up laws for themselves to observe." But now they were not even attending to the God of the Christians. So the public interest required them to be legitimized (again).[57]

But this was not at all what other members of the public desired. In the following year (312) Maximinus was petitioned by the cities of the East begging that the Christians be physically excluded. The new Latin text shows this was to have been a literal policy of apartheid, or ethnic cleansing, controlled at the boundaries of each city's territory. With Constantine's victory in the following year the plan collapsed. But it demonstrates how deeply felt on both sides was the incompatibility of the Christian life with the old culture. They could not be a part of it: rather they ran parallel to it on a city by city basis.[58]

From the social point of view it was precisely this that lay at the heart of the New Testament experiment. In claiming for themselves the heritage of Israel, the Gentile converts of Paul (and Peter) were called to live as foreigners in their *own* land. Had they settled for encapsulation,

---

[56] Lactantius, *De mortibus persecutorum* 34; cf. White, *Social Origins*, 1:123–39.

[57] After the death of Valerian (in 260), Gallienus recorded a *subscriptio* (ἀντιγραφή) on the petition of Dionysius of Alexandria "and the rest of the bishops" providing relief "throughout the world" by handing back "places of worship" and cemeteries (Eus. *HE* 7.13.1). This was in force in Egypt by 262 (7.23). See G. Bovini, *La proprietà ecclesiastica e la condizione giuridica della chiesa in età preconstantiniana* (Milan: Giuffrè, 1948), and White, *Social Origins*.

[58] S. Mitchell, "Maximinus and the Christians in AD 312: A New Latin Inscription," *JRS* 78 (1988) 105–24.

as Judaism did, the historical outcome could have been the ethnically-based multiculturalism our governments now espouse.

But by asserting the right to think and live differently within a common state, even to "form associations against the laws for the sake of truth" (as Origen was the first to put it), the New Testament "assemblies" forged vital principles of our historical development. It is to them that we can trace the roots of the engaged, self-criticizing society that has generated the distinctive intellectual and political openness of the West.[59]

The Social Distinctiveness of Christian Belief and Practice

Ancient cult was not generally dependent on group support. Sacrifice was an individual rather than congregational matter, though everyone was expected to offer sacrifice. The innumerable social, funerary or trade associations linked themselves with a sanctuary for patronage, discipline and legitimacy. But their effective purpose is normally not derived from the cult.

The churches as such at first practised no cult (though individuals might do so as Jews, or for that matter Greeks). At the most there was a quasi-cult inasmuch as they transposed the ritual approach to the divine into a studied reconstruction of social relations. In this they met, in a much more drastic way, some of the psycho-social needs typically satisfied in private associations.[60]

Ancient observers, both Christian and others, sometimes found associational life a convenient short-hand for categorizing the churches, though their scale, membership, structure and activities were very different. The more consistently noted and instructive alignment was with the schools of philosophy, whether classical or Jewish.

Both historically and in terms of leading ideas the most influential sources stemmed from the synagogues. From them arose the fostering of a complex textual tradition, and its outworking in daily life, partly at odds with that of the civil community. Yet although the churches

---

[59] Origen, *Contra Celsum* 1.1; E.A. Judge, "Ancient Beginnings of the Modern World,", *Ancient History in a Modern University*, ed. T.W. Hillard, et al. (Grand Rapids: Eerdmans, 1998) II:468–82.

[60] Brashear, *Vereine im griechisch-römischen Ägypten*, 26–32 identifies seven "universal constants" of men's clubs: voluntary membership, family-like bonds, reduction in aggression, distancing from outsiders, hierarchical order, conformity, and drinking together.

insisted on the legacy of Israel, Roman observers did not confuse church with synagogue.[61]

In contrast with the associations (but to a degree in common with synagogues), the New Testament churches show the following major distinctives.

(1) They constitute a movement of ideas, driven by argument and the interpretation of authoritative texts, a kind of adult re-education.

(2) Their intellectual premises are radically different from the naturalistic logic of the philosophical schools, turning on a re-orientation of world history towards the future.

(3) In anticipation of that, they are attempting a fundamental reconstruction of community life, free of much conventional restraint in terms of nationality, status, gender and numbers.

(4) The effective means to this end is the divine gifting of each person, renewed in spirit but for the common good.

(5) Since this presupposes a decisively new start, the movement undercuts the foundations of the public community, operating as an alternative, trans-national society.[62]

No amount of subsequent assimilation to cultic or cultural patterns fully swamped these sources of social and intellectual transformation. The conservation of a static order was abandoned, at least in principle, in favor of new expectations.[63]

Appendix: Three ancient cult-groups

1. Attica, I[p], white marble stele, F. Sokolowski, *Lois sacrées des cités grecques* (Paris 1969) no.54.

Ἱερὸν τὸ τέμενο[ς]	Sacred is the temple
τοῦ Ἀσκληπιοῦ καὶ	to Asclepius and
τῆς Ὑγιείας.	to Hygieia.

---

[61] E.A. Judge, "Judaism and the Rise of Christianity: A Roman Perspective," *TynBul* 45.2 (1994) 355–68.

[62] For a recent assessment of the so-called mystery cults, see W. Burkert, *Ancient Mystery Cults* (Cambridge: Harvard University Press, 1987) 31: "none of them approaches the Christian model of a church;" for this question in relation to associations in general, J.S. Kloppenborg and S.G. Wilson, eds, *Voluntary Associations in the Graeco-Roman World* (London: Routledge, 1996); and from the NT perspective, J.R. Harrison, "Paul's House Churches and the Cultic Associations," *RTR* 58 (1999) 31–47.

[63] W. Kinzig, *Novitas christiana: Die Idee des Fortschritts in der Alten Kirche bis Eusebius* (Göttingen: Vandenhoeck und Ruprecht, 1994).

θύειν τοὺς γεωργοὺς	Let the farmers sacrifice,
καὶ τοὺς προσχώρους 5	and the neighbours,
τοῖν θεοῖν ἧι θέμις	as is right for the gods.
καὶ τὰς μοίρας νέμειν	They are to assign shares
τῶι τε εἰσαμένωι καὶ	both to the founder and
τῶι θεηκολοῦντι·	to the "god-cultivator."
τῶν δὲ κρεῶν μὴ 10	None of the meat
φέρεσθαι.	is to be taken away.

2. Athens, east of the Parthenon, end of II^p, Pentelic marble, Sokolowski, no.53.

> Ἄρχων μὲν Ταυρίσκος, ἀτὰρ μὴν Μουνιχιὼν ἦν
> ὀκτ[ω]καιδεκάτῃ δ᾽ ἔρανον σύναγον φίλοι ἄνδρες
> καὶ κοινῇ βουλῇ θεσμὸν φιλίης ὑπέγραψαν.
> 30   νόμος ἐρανιστῶν
> [μη]δενὶ ἐξέστω ἰσ[ιέν]αι ἰς τὴν σεμνοτά[τη]ν
> σύνοδον τῶν ἐρανιστῶν πρὶν ἂν δοκι-
> μασθῇ εἴ ἐστι ἁ[γν]ὸς καὶ εὐσεβὴς καὶ ἀγ-
> α[θ]ός· δοκιμα[ζέ]τω δὲ ὁ προστάτης [καὶ]
> 35 [ὁ] ἀρχ⟨ι⟩εραγιστὴς καὶ ὁ γ[ρ]αμματεὺς καὶ
> [οἱ] ταμίαι καὶ σύνδικοι· ἔστωσαν δὲ ο[ὗ]-
> [τ]οι κληρωτοὶ κατὰ ἔ[το]ς χωρὶς π⟨ρισπ⟩ροστάτ[ου]·
> ὁμολείτωρ δὲ ἔ⟨ι⟩στω δ[ιὰ] βίου αὐτο[ῦ]
> ὁ ἐπὶ ἡρῴου καταλιφθείς· αὐξανέτω δ[ὲ]
> 40 ὁ ἔρανος ἐπὶ φιλοτεμίαις· εἰ δέ τις μά-
> χας ἢ θορύβους κεινῶν φαίνοιτο
> ἐκβαλλέσθω τοῦ ἐράνου ζημιού-
> μενος ⟨ε⟩ Ἀττ[ι]καῖς κε ´ ἢ πληγαῖς αἰκ⟨αικ⟩ιζ[ό]-
> μενος ταῖς διπλαῖς πέ⟨τ⟩ρα κρίσεως.

Tauriscus was archon, and it was on the 18th of Munichion that men
friends formed a club and by common consent dictated the rule of
friendship. |
30   Members' Law
No one is to enter the solemn meeting of the members before being
tested for honesty, piety and respectability. The test is to be made by the
35 patron and | the club president and the secretary and the treasurers and
the adjudicators. They are to be set up by lot annually except for the
patron. Joint-administrator for life shall be the one left in charge of the
40 tomb. Let the club thrive | on benefactions. But if anyone seems to be
stirring up fighting or uproar he is to be thrown out of the club with a
fine of 25 Attics or double the flogging that has been determined.

3. Attica, II^p, two copies on stones from Sunium, Sokolowski, no.55,
text and translation (adapted) from G.H.R. Horsley, *New Documents
Illustrating Early Christianity* 3 (1983), no.6.

Ξάνθος Λύκιος Γαίου Ὀρβίου καθειδρύσατο ἱερ[ὸν τοῦ Μηνὸς]
Τυράννου, αἱρετίσαντος τοῦ θεοῦ, ἐπ' ἀγαθῇ τύχῃ. καὶ [μηθένα]
ἀκάθαρτον προσάγειν. καθαριζέστω δὲ ἀπὸ σκόρδων κα[ὶ χοιρέων]
καὶ γυναικός. λουσαμένους δὲ κατακέφαλα αὐθήμερον εἰσ[πορεύ-]
5 εσθα(ι). καὶ ἐκ τῶν γυναικέων διὰ ἑπτὰ ἡμερῶν λουσαμένην κ[ατα-]
κέφαλα εἰσπορεύεσθαι αὐθήμερον. καὶ ἀπὸ νεκροῦ διὰ ἡμερῶν δ[έκα]
καὶ ἀπὸ φθορᾶς ἡμερῶν τετταράκοντα, καὶ μηθένα θυσιάζειν ἄνε[υ]
τοῦ καθειδρυσαμένου τὸ ἱερόν. ἐὰν δέ τις βιάσηται, ἀπρόσδεκτος
ἡ θυσία παρὰ τοῦ θεοῦ. παρέχειν δὲ τῶι θεῶι τὸ καθῆκον, δεξιὸν
10 σκέλος καὶ δορὰν καὶ κεφαλὴν καὶ πόδας καὶ στηθύνιον καὶ ἔλαιον
ἐπὶ βωμὸν καὶ λύχνον καὶ σχίζας καὶ σπονδήν, καὶ εὐείλατος
γένοιτο ὁ θεὸς τοῖς θεραπεύσουσιν ἁπλῇ τῇ ψυχῇ. ἐὰν δέ τινα
ἀνθρώπινα πάσχῃ ἢ ἀσθενήσῃ ἢ ἀποδημήσῃ που, μηθένα ἀνθρώπων ἐξουσίαν ἔχειν, ἐὰν μὴ ὧι ἂν αὐτὸς παραδῶι. ὃς ἂν δὲ πολυ-
15 πραγμονήσῃ τὰ τοῦ θεοῦ ἢ περιεργάσηται, ἁμαρτίαν ὀφειλέτω Μηνὶ
Τυράννωι, ἣν οὐ μὴ δύναται ἐξειλάσασθαι. ὁ δὲ θυσιάζων τῇ ἑβδόμῃ
τὰ καθήκοντα πάντα ποιείτω{ι} τῶι θεῶι. λαμβανέτω{ι} τῆς θυσίας ἧς
ἂν φέρῃ σκέλος καὶ ὦμον, τὰ δὲ λοιπὰ κατακοπτέτω (ἐν τῷ) ἱερῶι. εἰ δέ τις
{εἰ δέ τις} προσφέρει θυσίαν τῶι θεῶι, ἐγ νουμηνίας μέχρι πεντεκαι-
20 δεκάτης. ἐὰν δέ τις τράπεζαν πληρῶι τῶι θεῶι, λαμβανέτω τὸ ἥμισ[υ].
τοὺς δὲ βουλομένους ἔρανον συνάγειν Μηνὶ Τυράννῳ, ἐπ' ἀγαθῇ τύ[χῃ].
ὁμοίως δὲ παρέξουσιν οἱ ἐρανισταὶ τὰ καθήκοντα τῶι θεῶι, δε[ξιὸν]
σκέλος καὶ δορὰν καὶ κοτύλην ἐλαίου καὶ χοῦν οἴνου καὶ να[στὸν χοινι-]
κιαῖον καὶ ἐφίερα τρία καὶ κολλύβων χοίνικες δύο καὶ ἀκρό[δρυα, ἐ-]
25 ἂν κατακλιθῶσιν οἱ ἐρανισταὶ καὶ στέφανον καὶ λημνίσ[κον].
καὶ εὐείλατος γένοιτο ὁ θεὸς τοῖς ἁπλῶς προσπορευομένοις.

Xanthus the Lycian, slave(?) of Gaius Orbius, set up the temple of Men
Tyrannus—the god having chosen him—for good fortune. And no-one
impure is to draw near; but let him be purified from garlic and swine
and woman. When they have bathed from head to foot, on the same
5 day they are to enter. | And a woman, having bathed from head to
foot for seven days after menstruation, is to enter on the same day. And
(likewise) for ten days after (contact with) a corpse, and forty days after
abortion; nor is anyone to offer sacrifice without the founder of the
temple (being present). If anyone violates (these provisions) his sacrifice
will be unacceptable to the god. He is to provide what is appropriate for
10 the god, a right | leg, hide, head, feet, chest, oil for the altar, a lamp,
kindling and a libation; and may the god be very merciful to those who
serve in simpleness of soul. But if he (i.e., the founder) dies, or is sick
or travelling abroad no person is to have authority except him to whom
15 he transmits it. Anyone who interferes | with the god's possessions or is
meddlesome, let him incur sin against Men Tyrannus which he certainly
cannot expiate. And let him who sacrifices on the seventh (day of the
month) perform all that is appropriate for the god; let him receive a leg
and shoulder of the sacrifice which he brings, and as for the rest let him
cut it up at the temple. And if anyone offers a sacrifice to the god, let it be

20 from new moon till the fifteenth. | If anyone fills a table for the god, let him receive half (its contents). Those who wish may form a club for Men Tyrannus, for good fortune. Likewise, the club members shall provide what is appropriate for the god, a right leg, hide, a *kotyle* of oil, twelve *kotylai* of wine, a measure's worth of well-kneaded cake, three sacrificial
25 cakes, two measures of small cakes, and hard-shelled fruits, | as well as a wreath and a woollen ribbon, whenever the club members banquet. And may the god be very merciful to those who approach in simplicity.

MEN, WOMEN AND MARITAL CHASTITY
PUBLIC PREACHING AND POPULAR PIETY AT ROME

Hanne Sigismund Nielsen

Introduction[1]

When he was still a young man, Augustine prayed: "make me chaste, make me continent, but not right now."[2] The story of his earlier life and his eventual conversion is familiar to most readers. Augustine had severe problems overcoming his own sexual impulses, but he finally succeeded and later spent much energy preaching on the subject. A proponent of the ascetic life, he also advocated marital chastity in numerous sermons and other writings devoted to the correct behavior of married couples. Similarly, Jerome gave advice to married couples on how to live according to God's demands. Both Jerome and Augustine contended that virginity was preferrable to marriage, but they accepted the facts of human life, viz. that most Christians married and had children. In light of this fact, the question is how their ideal of the married life affected Christians of the day. Did they respond positively to the teaching of Augustine and others by showing a new awareness of their moral conduct or did they remain unaffected?

In this article I will argue that Christian married couples certainly did—at least on the normative level—become concerned about their moral conduct, especially in sexual matters. Their salvation depended on it. How we may determine their compliance is, of course, part of our critical inquiry. For, as one often observes, the formal rhetoric of

---

[1] For their many suggestions and substantial help, I wish to thank John Fitzgerald and Michael White; without the insight, generosity, and tireless enthusiasm of the latter, this article would not have been written.

[2] *Conf.* 8.7: *da mi castitatem et continentiam, sed noli modo.* In the following I have consulted the standard modern translations of the works of Augustine, principally that of The Nicene and Post-Nicene Fathers, ed. P. Schaff (repr. Grand Rapids: Eerdmans, 1956). Other more recent translations will be cited where pertinent. When it seemed necessary, as is often the case with the older translations, I have either brought the translation into agreement with the Latin text or made my own translation. All translations of epitaphs are my own. The Latin found in epitaphs is often not in accordance with Latin literature; therefore, some of my translations are free in order to convey the meaning of the text.

intellectual élites or church leaders does not always convey the faith and practices of ordinary believers. Nor is it entirely clear how much really changed in private life with the growing dominance of Christianity through the fourth century. Nonetheless, in these matters Augustine's legacy for later generations of Latin-speaking Christians was, to say the least, profound.[3] Consequently, I will begin by considering some of the more important passages from Augustine and Jerome on the mores of married couples. Then I will compare the result of this reading with the evidence from contemporaneous epitaphs by Roman Christians in commemoration of their deceased spouses. On the whole, these epitaphs have not been examined closely as a record of the faith and piety of ordinary folks. My aim is thus to present the material available and let it speak for itself.[4]

Two problems ought to be mentioned at the outset. The first is that all the epitaphs used for this analysis come from the city of Rome itself. Augustine and Jerome spent much of their lives, and produced most of their writings, far away from Rome. Augustine's moral treatises and sermons on marriage, for example, come almost entirely from his episcopal see at Hippo Regius. Nonetheless, both Augustine and Jerome spent considerable time in Rome and had many direct contacts there. Jerome's letters, for example, show him corresponding with friends in Rome and advising them on matters of marriage, sexuality, and asceticism.[5] Indeed, both men had extensive correspondence with persons all over the empire, and their works were widely read. Therefore, I see no reason why their opinions should not have influenced or been in accordance with those of the orthodox church in Rome.

---

[3] See Brent D. Shaw, "The Family in Late Antiquity: The Experience of Augustine," *Past and Present* 115 (1987) 3–51, esp. 36.

[4] This implies that references to modern research are somewhat sparse, especially in the section on the inscriptions. For my part, I came to this study through my previous work on Roman family life, with special attention to funerary inscriptions from Rome. So see my articles, "The physical context of Roman epitaphs, and the structure of 'the Roman Family,'" *Analecta Romana Instituti Danici* 23 (1996) 35–60; "*Ditis examen domus?* On the use of the term Verna in the Roman Epigraphical and Literary Sources," *Classica et Mediaevalia* 42 (1991) 221–40; and the articles cited in n. 74 below. In light of these patterns of pagan funerary commemoration, social aspects of the Christian inscriptions from Rome seemed to me to merit closer analysis. As a Classicist, however, I make no claim to deal with all the theological issues that arise in connection with this topic.

[5] On Jerome's correspondence see J.N.D. Kelly, *Jerome: His Life, Writings, and Controversies* (San Francisco: Harper, 1975) 91–101; Elizabeth A. Clark, *Jerome, Chrysostom, and Friends: Essays and Translations* (Lewiston: Edwin Mellen, 1979) 35–79.

The other problem is dogmatic, and more than difficult to overcome. When reading a Christian epitaph from Rome we cannot be certain that the persons commemorated there were adherants of the "orthodox" Christian doctrines propounded by Jerome or Augustine. Indeed, Jerome and Augustine themselves were often on different sides of key doctrinal issues.[6] Many Christians at Rome, especially among the aristocracy, followed the teachings of Pelagius, while other sects, later condemned as heretics, were operating there, too.[7] Fortunately for our purposes, these heretics were known to be very concerned about personal morals and were, so far as I can see, in basic agreement with Augustine and Jerome on the issue of proper conduct in married life.[8]

Marriage and Chastity: The View from the Pulpit

With the growth of the ascetic tradition, married life was assigned lowest rank in the moral hierarchy of the early Christians. In his *De civitate dei* Augustine explicates the various meanings of the three levels of the ark by using the parable of the sower (Matt 13:8). He takes the "harvests" as levels of rewards to be expected from different types of Christian life:

> It is possible to interpret [the levels of the ark] as those three virtues which the apostle commended: "faith, hope, and charity" [1 Cor 13:13]. Or yet even more suitably, it is possible [to interpret them] as those three rich harvests mentioned in the gospel—the thirty fold, sixty fold and hundred fold—so that the chastity of marriage (*pudicitia coniugalis*) would occupy the lowest level, that of widowhood (*vidualis*) the next above, and that of virginity (*virginalis*) the highest.[9]

---

[6] See Peter Brown, *The Body and Society: Men, Women, and Sexual Renunciation in Early Christianity* (New York: Columbia UP, 1988) 366–86; Elizabeth A. Clark, "Elite Networks and Heresy Accusations: Towards a Social Description of the Origenist Controversy," in *Social Networks in the Early Christian Environment: Issues and Methods for Social History*, ed. L.M. White. (*SEMEIA* 56; Atlanta: Scholars Press, 1991) 79–120. I shall not attempt to make subtle analytical distinctions between Augustine and other writers on these matters.

[7] See Peter Brown, "The Patrons of Pelagius: The Roman Aristocracy between East and West," in *Religion and Society in the Age of St. Augustine* (San Francisco: Harper, 1972) 208–26. See also below at n. 89.

[8] In other words, the differences may not lie in the behaviors advocated but in the philosophical and theological arguments used to support them. Another problem is how deeply Augustine was influenced by his Manichaean past. See Elizabeth A. Clark, "Vitiated Seeds and Holy Vessels: Augustine's Manichean Past," in *Ascetic Piety and Women's Faith: Essays on Late Ancient Christianity* (Lewiston: Edwin Mellen, 1986) 291–349.

[9] 15.26: ... *possunt hic intelligi et tria illa quae commendat apostolus, fides, spes, caritas. Possunt*

This means that married couples had to face the fact that even if they lived their lives according to the strict rules of the church they would still be placed behind continent widows and virgins both on earth and in heaven. Consequently much attention was given to guidelines for remaining chaste within marriage and the definition of – roles for wife and husband.

Pudicitia *("Chastity") in the Ideal and in Practice*

From pagan times *pudicitia* ("modesty" or "chastity") was defined as the fundamental virtue of the Roman *matrona*. The pagan notion of the word implied that the wife should be faithful to her husband and bear him children,[10] but *pudicitia* did not imply sexual continence within the marriage, either for husband or wife.[11] Nor does this change in the Christian usage. Yet, there was, as is well known, a dual standard in traditional Roman household morality. Marriage provided men with sexual property and sexual access, and not to the wife alone. For women, however, *pudicitia* meant becoming the exclusive sexual property of her husband, at least in the ideal. Yet married women were just as much sexual prey.[12] A woman caught having sex with another, whether inside or outside her own household relationships, could be paraded by her husband in public as *impudica* ("unchaste"). No such shame awaited the husband,[13] even though Stoic moralists had long decried the different

---

etiam multo convenientius tres illae ubertates evangelicae, tricena, sexagena, centena, ut in infimo habitet pudicitia coniugalis, supra vidualis atque hac superior virginalis … Jerome uses the passage in a similar way; *Commentarii in evangelium Matthaei* 2: *et nunc breviter perstringimus, centesimum fructum virginibus, sexgesimum viduis et continentibus, tricesimum sancto matrimonio deputantes* ("and now let us summarize briefly, the hundred fold is the harvest for virgins, the sixty fold is that for widows and (sexual) continents, and the thirty fold is that for those abiding in holy marriage"). For references and other interpretations of the three harvests see the comments by E. Bonnard, *Saint Jérome, Commentaire sur S. Matthieu* (2 vols.; SC; Paris: Editions du Cerf, 1977) 1:274–5.

[10] See Livy 1.58 on Lucretia as the paradigm of pagan Roman matronal *pudicitia*. Compare the *Laudatio Turiae* 1.1.30–1 (ed. E. Wistrand; Lund: Berlingska-Boktrykkeriet, 1976) and Seneca, *Cons. ad Helviam* 16.3–4 for praises of chaste Roman matrons, with comments on attendant attributes.

[11] See for example Apuleius, *Apol.* 69 for the case of a widow who reportedly became ill due to lack of sex.

[12] B. Shaw, "The Family in Late Antiquity," 30. Monica warned the young Augustine about married women in *Conf.* 2.3.7.

[13] B. Shaw ("The Family in Late Antiquity," 29) also cites Augustine's comments on these aspects of family life: esp. *Serm.* 82.11 (PL 38.511); 153.5.5–6 (PL 38.828); 224.3 (PL 38.1094–5).

demands of "chastity" for women.[14] At times, at least, the evocation of *pudicitia* for men, too, had become more prominent in the earlier empire.[15] Yet even in the fourth century Ambrose found it necessary to admonish the men in his congregation against sexual "intemperance" within the household.[16] At the end of the century Augustine was still railing against such practices and thereby challenging prevailing norms of male prerogative.[17] Nor should it go unnoticed that many, if not most, of these situations described with opprobrium by Ambrose or Augustine likely reflect the practices of Christian families. On some level at least, not much had really changed.

Despite these realities of married life, matrimony had always been defined by the dictum *liberorum (pro)creandorum causa*, that is "for the purpose of begetting children."[18] This dictum regularly appeared on marriage tablets and had also been used as the philosophical basis for a long tradition of calls for moderation and control of the passions among the Stoics and other moralists.[19] But in reality it had little force

---

[14] So, for example, Seneca, *Ep.* 94.26, which gives traditional exhortation on the subject: *Scis improbum esse, qui ab uxore pudicitiam exigit, ipse alienarum corruptor uxorum; scis ut illi nil eum adultero, sic tibi nil esse debere cum paelice, et non facis* ("You know that a man is wicked who demands chastity of his wife while he himself is a corruptor of the wives of others; you know that, just as a wife should not be with an adulterous man, so also you ought not be with a mistress; and yet you do not act accordingly.")

[15] Hans-Friedrich Mueller, "*Vita, Pudicitia, Libertas*: Juno, Gender, and Religious Politics in Valerius Maximus," *TAPA* 128 (1998) 221−63.

[16] See his *De Abrahamo* 1.4.25−6: *ergo advertistis quid debeatis cavere, ne quis sacramenti se indignum praebeat. Accipite etiam illud, quia huiusmodi intemperantia soluit caritatem coniugii, superbas ancillas facit, iracundas matronas, discordes coniuges, concubinas procaces, inverecundos maritos. Simul ut de domino conceperit ancilla, spernit dominam suam tamquam ditior partu, domina se despici dolet, maritum auctorem iniuriarium suarum arguit* ("Now, take note of what you must avoid lest you should be rendered unworthy of the sacrament. Indeed, you must understand this, since such intemperance ruins conjugal love, makes maids [*ancillae*] arrogant, makes matrons angry, causes spouses to argue, makes concubines impudent, and makes husbands shameless. And what's more, if a maid should bear a child by her master [*domino*] she will look down upon her mistress [*domina*] as if she were more prized for bearing a child; all the while, because it is painful for the mistress [*domina*] to be despised, she will blame her husband as the cause of the injury she has suffered.").

[17] See especially *Serm.* 9.3−4 (CCSL 41.114−15) and 224.3 (PL 38.1095). It is not clear whether the encounter reported in the latter is real or hypothetical, but either way it reflects the normal assumptions of the day, as the accused husband is reported to answer: "Am I not permitted to do what I want in my own household (*in domo mea*)?" Cf. B. Shaw, "The Family in Late Antiquity," 16.

[18] E. Eyben, "Family Planning in Graeco-roman Antiquity," *Anc. Soc.* 11−13 (1980−81) 5−82. Cf. B. Shaw, "The Family in Late Antiquity," 36.

[19] For an excellent summary of the moralist and medical traditions and their devel-

in private sexual practice. On the other hand, by law a man was allowed to divorce a sterile wife; however, this law was hardly ever used. By the time we get to Augustine and Jerome, the definition of a chaste marriage came to be interpreted more strictly than it had been among pagan Romans.[20] Through his sermons and treatises, Augustine idealized the notion of marital chastity for Christians. It may have been Augustine's own experience of officiating at the arrangement and consecration of marriages among his flock that caused him to stress sterner norms of behavior. He apparently thundered the slogan *liberorum (pro)creandorum causa* in his marriage sermons.[21] So, too, in his treatise on marriage and sexual desire, Augustine says:

> In the city of our God, on his holy mountain [Ps 48:2]—that is, in the church of Christ—the duty of this sacrament implies for faithful, i.e., baptized (*fidelibus*), married couples, who are doubtless members of Christ, that even though women marry and men take wives for the purpose of begetting children (*filiorum procreandorum causa*), it is not allowed for the man to divorce a barren wife in order to marry another who is fertile.[22]

It is no accident that Augustine emphasizes that divorce was not allowed. Only in cases of adultery did he allow for divorce, and he strongly recommended that the offended party not remarry. Debates over proper grounds and different possibilities for "legitimate" divorce were extensive in Augustine's day.

Celibacy might be an attractive alternative to marriage, especially for aristocratic women.[23] The case of Melania the Younger was well-

---

opment in Christian ascetic ideology see Teresa Shaw, *The Burden of the Flesh: Fasting and Sexuality in Early Christianity* (Minneapolis: Fortress, 1998) 27–63.

[20] Susan Treggiari, *Roman Marriage: Iusti Coniuges from the time of Cicero to the time of Ulpian* (New York: Oxford UP, 1991) 216–7 and 232–3.

[21] B. Shaw, "The Family in Late Antiquity," 36 and 44, citing *inter alia, De bono coniug.* 17.19; *De nupt. et concup.* 1.10.11; *Serm.* 9.18 (CCSL 41.143); 51.13.22 (PL 38.345); and 278.9.9 (PL 38.1272).

[22] *De nuptiis et concupiscentia* 1.10: *cuius sacramenti tanta observatio est in civitate dei nostri, in monte sancto eius, hoc est in ecclesia christi quibusque fidelibus coniugatis, qui sine dubio membra sunt christi, ut cum filiorum procreandorum causa vel nubant feminae vel ducantur uxores, nec sterilem coniugem fas sit relinquere, ut alia facunda ducatur.* My translation; compare the recent translation in Roland J. Teske, *The Works of Saint Augustine*, vol. 24: *Answer to the Pelagians, II* (Hyde Park: New City Press, 1998) 35.

[23] Clark, "Devil's Gateway and Bride of Christ: Women in the Early Christina World," in *Ascetic Piety and Women's Faith*, 40–3. Whereas widows had for a long time been granted *de iure* control of their lives and fortunes, such an option did not generally exist for younger women of mariageable age or those already married.

known, even to Augustine.[24] Some Christian commentators considered the adoption of a celibate life as viable grounds for seeking divorce. This seems to be the view of a certain Pollentius, who corresponded with Augustine to argue the interpretation of scriptures relevant to the subject. The opposing positions are reflected in Augustine's reply, the two books entitled *On Adulterous Marriages*. In the second book Augustine takes up Pollentius' interpretation of Paul's instructions in 1 Cor 7:10–11:[25]

> On the first of those additional points, I think I ought to reply to you [Pollentius] with the words of the apostle when he says: "But to the rest, I say, not the Lord,[26] that a wife is not to separate from her husband; if she should separate, however, she must remain unmarried or become reconciled with her husband." You do not think that when it says "if she should separate" that it is understood that she has separated from an adulterous husband, which is the only reason allowed for separation.[27]

---

[24] Clark, "Ascetic Renunciation and Feminine Advancement: A Paradox of Late Ancient Christianity," in *ibid.*, 184.

[25] *De adulterinis coniugiis* 2.2.2: *horum primum illud est—cui quidem arbitror me respondere debere—quod in his apostoli verbis, ubi ait: ceteris autem dico, non dominus, mulierem a viro non discedere; quod si discesserit, manere innuptam aut viro suo reconciliari, non putas ita dictum esse si discesserit, ut a viro fornicante discessisse intellegatur, qua sola causa discedere licitum est.* My translation; compare the translations in Charles T. Wilcox, *et al.*, *Saint Augustine: Treatises on Marriage and Other Subjects* (Fathers of the Church 27; New York: Fathers of the Church, Inc., 1955) 102 and Ray Kearney and David G. Hunter, *The Works of Saint Augustine*, I. 9: *Marriage and Virginity* (Hyde Park: New City Press, 1999) 166. On Augustine's quotation from Paul see the following note.

[26] Even allowing for his use of the Vulgate, Augustine has misquoted the text of Paul here. The opening of the quotation (*ceteris autem dico, non dominus*) is actually from 1 Cor 7:12. In the Greek and the Vulgate, 1 Cor 7:10 is actually given as a command of the Lord (*praecipio, non ego sed dominus*) to the married. Augustine quotes the text correctly earlier in this same work (1.4.3), so the reason for the misquotation may be something at work in Augustine's debate with his opponent, Pollentius. For the remainder the text comes from verses 1 Cor 7:10b–11a with only minor changes from the reading of the Vulgate (thus: *mulierem* for *uxorem* in the Vulgate (cf. v. 13); *manere* for *maneat*; and *reconciliari* for *reconcilietur*).

[27] The word *discedere* (here translating χωρίζεσθαι in the Greek) literally means "to depart, leave, or separate," but there is little technical distinction between "divorce" and "separation" in the Roman usage, in contrast to that in modern civil law. In Roman usage, it seems that "separation" (*discedere*) was considered a first step that would result in formal dissolution of the marriage (*divortium* or *matrimonium cessare*) by decree. In fact, the "departure" was the woman's way of signaling the divorce; it was tantamount to a formal divorce decree in lower class marriages where there had been no formal marriage contract. See Ulpian's comment in *Digest* 25.2.17 (ed. T. Mommsen, *et al.*, *The Digest of Justinian* [Philadelphia: University of Pennsylvania Press, 1985] II:734–5) where all three terms are used: *Ulpianus libro trigesimo ad edictum. Si concubina res amoverit, hoc iure utimur, ut furti teneatur: consequenter dicemus, ubicumque cessat matrimonium, ut puta in ea, …*

By linking the passage in 1 Cor 7 with that in Matt 19:3–9, Augustine assumes that "if she separates" means that the husband must have committed adultery, while Pollentius had assumed that it was for the wife to take a vow of sexual continence and was, therefore, approved by Paul. Pollentius argued thereby that scripture had provided other grounds for divorce, even though remarriage was permitted only in cases of adultery. Augustine will have none of this, even though Pollentius was probably closer to the actual meaning of Paul.[28] Thus, earlier in the same work Augustine proposes the hypothetical case of a wife who had separated from her husband to live in continence. Her husband remarried (legitimately, one assumes, at least according to Roman law), but Augustine says he thus became an adulterer. Augustine places the blame on the wife:

> His wife separated from him and began to live in continence; of course she would remain chaste (*casta*), but she would at the same time do what the Lord does not want, namely turn her husband into an adulterer, since he was not able to live in continence (*non continuerit*) and therefore remarried.[29]

In one of his many sermons on marriage, Augustine emphasizes that a wife who had a husband who was *impudicus* did not owe *pudicitia* to him, but to God: "Do you, most chaste women (*pudicissimae feminae*), not imitate your unchaste husbands … A wife does not owe her chastity to an unchaste husband, she owes it to God, she owes it to Christ."[30]

---

cessat matrimonium, cessare rerum amotarum actionem, quia competit furti. Divortii causa res amotas dicimus non solum eas, qual mulier amovit, cum divortii consilium inisset, sed etiam eas quas nupta amoverit, si, cum discederet, eas celaverit … ("Ulpian, *Edict, book 30:*. … Where a concubine unlawfully removes property, we usually hold her liable for theft. Consequently, we say that whenever a mariage is voided, … the action for property unlawfully removed will not stand, since the action for theft does. When we speak of property wrongfully removed, we mean not only the property a woman removes when she decides to obtain a divorce but also that which she removes while she is still married, if when she separates from him, she hides this property."). So notice that Augustine in the passage above says that adultery is the only legitimate ground for the wife to "separate" (*discedere*)—by which he clearly means "divorce" (cf. 1.4.5).

[28] See the discussion of this work by David G. Hunter, "Adulterinis conjugiis, De," *Augustine through the Ages: An Encyclopedia*, ed. A.D. Fitzgerald, *et al.* (Grand Rapids: Eerdmans, 1999) 9–10.

[29] 1.4.4: *discessit ab eo mulier et coepit vivere continenter, ipsa scilicet casta mansura, sed factura, quod dominus non vult, adulterum virum: qui cum se non continuerit, alteram quaeret.*

[30] *Sermo* 392 (PL 39.1712): *nolite autem, pudicissimae feminae, imitari impudicos viros vestros … impudico marito non debet mulier pudicitiam, sed deo illam debet, christo illam debet.*

It is not clear from the text whether the unchaste husband has in fact
been unfaithful to his wife or has insisted on having sex with her in a
"shameful way" or in anywise for reasons other than procreation. For
Augustine, all of them constituted *impudicitia*.

Even though *pudicitia* was primarily a female virtue, for Augustine
it was very important that a husband also show *pudicitia* in relation to
his wife.[31] In *De adulterinis coniugiis* Augustine further discusses what he
means by marital *pudicitia* or *castitas* (both meaning sexual "chastity"):

> You will remember that I have said that this concerned both sexes,
> but it is of special importance to men because they consider themselves
> superior to women and therefore think that they do not need to be their
> wives' equals where chastity (*pudicitia*) is concerned. But they ought to be
> superior to their wives in leading a chaste life, so their wives can obey
> them and consider them their heads.[32]

Male *pudicitia* might, for instance, imply that a man should abstain
from intercourse with his wife if she was already pregnant or past
menopause. In *Contra Iulianum* Augustine says, "This chastity (*pudicitia*)
implies that women who are menstruating, or are pregnant, or past the
age when conception is possible should not be used for sexual intercourse."[33] But a husband was also to blame if he "used his wife intem-
perately," that is in an immoderate or shameful way. In *Enarrationes in
Psalmos*, Augustine says:

> There was a certain catechumen who was superior to many baptized
> in learning and morals. He noticed that many of the baptized were
> quite ignorant, and that many did not live the way he himself lived—
> not nearly so continent (*continentia*), not nearly so chaste (*castitate*)—for
> he did not even take a wife. Then he saw a baptized man, who was
> not adulterous but who used his wife immoderately (*uxore intemperantius
> utentem*). Can the catechumen now raise his head in arrogance and say,

---

[31] In pagan Rome men, especially young men, were in some cases referred to as
pudici. Cicero, *Pro Caelio* is an excellent example of how far a young man could go before
his *pudicitia* suffered. Suetonius, *Iul.* 49 describes how Caesar as a young man had been
the passive partner in a homosexual relationship and had thereby forever damaged his
pudicitia. But still it should be emphasized that sexual continence in general was not part
of the pagan Roman notion of young men's *pudicitia*.

[32] 2.20.21: *haec autem me de utroque sexu memineris dicere, sed maxime propter viros, qui
propterea se feminis superiores esse arbitrabantur, ne pudicitia pares sese dignentur: in qua etiam praeire
debuerunt, ut eos illae tamquam capita sequerentur.*

[33] 3.21.43 (PL 44.724): *talis pudicitia nec menstruatis, nec gravidis utitur feminis, nec eius aetatis
qua certum est eas iam concipere valere* … Compare the translation of Teske, *Answer to the
Pelagians II*, 363.

"Why is it necessary for me to be baptized so that I can receive what he already has—this man to whom I am superior in both life and doctrine?"[34]

In his treatise *On the Good of Marriage*, Augustine makes subtler distinctions on what constitutes this type of "intemperate" behavior between a husband and wife. So, for example, he seems to consider any sex between them done out of lust, where procreation is not the primary goal, to be a venial sin.[35] Other "excessive" or "intemperate" forms of sexual activity, even between husband and wife, were far worse, especially if done with the intent of avoiding conception.[36]

In Christian preaching there were two main reasons why a husband should be at least as *pudicus* as his wife. The first reason was the woman herself, since she was thought by nature to be weaker than the man. Jerome expresses this idea in a letter addressed to the young widow Salvina:

> A woman's chaste reputation *(fama pudicitiae)* is a tender plant; it is like a fair flower which withers at the slightest blast and fades away at the first breath of wind. Especially is this so when she is of an age to fall into temptation, and she lacks the authority of a husband. For the very shadow of a husband is a wife's safeguard.[37]

Augustine added a second reason why husbands ought to be superior to their wives in chastity, since the woman was responsible for the fall of mankind and thus for original sin.[38] In *Sermon* 318.2 Augustine says, "I will quote the holy scripture as evidence of my words; it says, 'by

---

[34] 90.2.6: *exsistit enim aliquando aliquis catechumenus qui forte doctrina et moribus vincit multos fideles; adtendit iam baptizatos multos imperitos, et multos non sic viventes quomodo ipse vivit, non in tanta continentia, non in tanta castitate; iam ille nec uxorem quaerit, et videt aliquando fidelem, si non fornicantem, tamen uxore intemperantius utentem; potest erigere cervicem superbiae, et dicere: quid mihi iam opus est baptizari, ut hoc accipiam quod iste habet, quem iam et vita et doctrina praecedo?*

[35] *De bono coniug.* 11; cf. *Contra Iul.* 3.21.43.

[36] *De bono coniug.* 12. Although Augustine uses a circumlocution to describe what he means, he specifically classes anal intercourse between husband and wife as an "intemperate use," since it meant engaging in sex but avoiding pregnancy. It is likely that Augustine was well aware of this practice as a common form of birth control in antiquity. For discussion see B. Shaw, "The Family in Late Antiquity," 45.

[37] *Ep.* 79.8: *flos pulcherrimus cito ad levem marcescit auram levi que flatu corrumpitur, maxime ubi et aetas tenera res in feminis fama pudicitiae est et quasi consensit ad vitium et maritalis deest auctoritas, cuius umbra tutamen uxoris est.*

[38] We cannot deal with the complex development of Augustine's doctrine of original sin, but two points are worth noting here. First, Augustine's scriptural warrant for the doctrine (Rom 5:12) is a notorious case of his misreading of Paul. So see Rowan A. Greer, "Sinned We All in Adam's Fall?" in *The Social World of the First Christians: Essays in Honor of Wayne A. Meeks*, ed. L.M. White and O.L. Yarbrough (Minneapolis: Fortress,

a woman came the beginning of sin, and because of her we all shall die [Sir 25.24].'"[39] Her punishment was problematic pregnancies and painful childbirths, as Jerome says in *Ep.* 130.8:

> When Jesus was crowned with thorns, bore our transgressions, and suffered for us, it was to make the roses of virginity and the lilies of chastity grow for us out of the brambles and distress that have formed the lot of women since the day when it was said to them, "in anxiety and pain shall you give birth, woman, and your desire shall be to your husband and he shall rule over you [Gen 3:16 *var.*]."[40]

Thus it was the husband's duty, so to speak, to check his wife, his marriage, and himself. Augustine puts it this way in his *De moribus ecclesiae catholicae et Manichaeorum* 1.30.63: "You subject women to their husbands in chaste and faithful obedience (*casta et fideli obedientia*), not to gratify passion, but for the propagation of offspring, and for domestic society."[41] Nonetheless, he admitted that he had not heard any married man say that he never had intercourse with his wife except when hoping for conception.[42]

1995) 382–394, who traces the earlier patristic exegesis of this passage as well as the progressive transformation of it in Augustine's own thought. Second, it is particularly noteworthy for our purposes in this study that one of the key places where Augustine reflects the fully developed form of this doctrine is in his treatise on marriage and sexual desire, *De nuptiis et concupiscentia*, which we have cited earlier. In this text (2.27.45) we also find one of Augustine's erroneous citations of Rom 5:12. We shall return to the issue below at nn. 47–49.

[39] PL 38.1439: *verbi huius mei sanctam scripturam testem citabo: a muliere, inquit, initium factum est peccati, et propter illam morimur omnes.* Compare the recent translation by Edmund Hill, *The Works of Saint Augustine*, III.9: *Sermons 306–340A* (Hyde Park: New City Press, 1994) 149.

[40] *Sed ideo iesus spinis coronatus est et nostra delicta portavit et pro nobis doluit, ut de sentibus et tribulationibus feminarum, ad quas dicitur: in anxietatibus et doloribus paries, mulier, et ad virum conversio tua et ipse tui dominabitur, rosae virginitatis et lilia castitatis nascerentur.* The reference is to Gen 3.16, which is here paraphrased rather than quoted from the Vulgate version: *in dolore paries filios et sub viri potestate eris et ipse dominabitur tui.* Some of the older translations obscure the fact that Jerome, like Augustine, often paraphrases, rather than quotes the scriptures by supplying the text of scripture in English from an authorized version. So, here compare the translation of Fremantle in NPNF, 2nd ser., 6:265.

[41] PL 32.1336: *tu feminas viris suis, non ad explendam libidinem, sed ad propagandam prolem, et ad rei familiaris societatem, casta et fideli obedientia subiicis.* On the family as the nucleus of society, another doctrine derived from earlier Stoicism, note also *Civ. Dei* 15.16.3: "Therefore the coupling (*copulatio*) of male and female, in so far as it pertains to humankind, is the seed-bed (*seminarium*) of the state (*civitas*);" compare Cicero, *De off.* 1.17.54. Cf. B. Shaw, "The Family in Late Antiquity," 11.

[42] *De bono coniug.* 13.15.

On the other hand Augustine recognized that many married women —perhaps the majority—lived a more chaste life than did their husbands. In a recently found letter[43] he writes: "Do you not notice, O men who so dread this burden [of continence], that you are easily vanquished in bearing it by women, that pious multitude of faithful and chaste women which the church fruitfully produces."[44] Augustine does not mention whether these women were married, continent widows, or virgins, but quite a few must have been married.

Marriage or Virginity

Although we hear much about Christian marriage in the writings of Augustine and Jerome, we know very little about how married couples reacted to these ideals of Christian marital behavior. Below I will present an analysis of the early Roman Christian epitaphs; it will become clear from this survey that we know more about how men— especially married men—reacted to the teaching of the church than we know about the women. Until now we have learned that women were weaker than men, and that they all represented Eve who had brought original sin into the world. If they married, childbirth was both a punishment from God and a duty towards their husbands.

Much research has recently been devoted to the growth of female asceticism in late antiquity.[45] This interesting issue is not the subject of my paper, but I find it necessary to mention virginity and its exalted position in the eyes of the church in order to provide a basis for comparing the position of married Christian women. Jerome very briefly says about the Virgin Mary: "If virginity was not preferred to the married state, why did the Holy Spirit not choose a married woman or a

---

[43] J. Divjak, *Sancti Aureli Augustini Opera, epistolae ex duobus codicibus nuper in lucem prolatae* (CSEL 88.2, part 6; Vienna: Brepols, 1981).

[44] *Ep.* 2*.4: *nec attenditis, o viri quicumque istam sarcinam formidatis, facillime in ea portanda vos a feminis vinci, quarum fidelium atque castarum religiosa multitudine fructifera fecundat ecclesia.* Compare the translation by Robert B. Eno, *Saint Augusatine, Letters VI (1*-29*)* (Fathers of the Church; Washington: Catholic University of America Press, 1996) 20.

[45] *Inter alia* Elizabeth A. Clark, "Ascetic Renunciation and Feminine Advancement: A Paradox of Late Ancient Christianity," in *Ascetic Piety and Women's Faith*, 175–208; *Reading Renunciationi: Asceticism and Scripture in Early Christianity* (Princeton: Princeton University Press, 1999) passim; and T. Shaw, *The Burden of the Flesh*, 1–26 and 79–128.

widow?"[46] Augustine goes further; he compares the consecrated virgins with the Virgin Mary herself:

> Indeed both faithful women who are married and virgins dedicated to God—because they do the will of the Father by holy manners and "with charity out of a pure heart, and good conscience, and faith unfeigned" [1 Tim 1:5]—are in a spiritual sense mothers of Christ. But those who in married life give birth to children after the flesh, give birth not to Christ, but to Adam; therefore, they rush to have their offspring become members of Christ by being dipped in the sacrament, because the mothers know to what they have given birth."[47]

Through the teachings of Augustine, even chaste Christian mothers came to believe that the child they had brought into the world was carrying the guilt of original sin, because it had been conceived in sin. Augustine develops this idea in his *Enarrationes in Psalmos* 50.10. The comment concerns Ps 51:5 (50:7 in the Vulgate):

> If infants were born innocent (*innocentes*), why do mothers run to the church with them when they are ill to have them baptized? ... [The infant speaks]: "I was conceived in iniquity, and in sin my mother nourished me in her womb." Christ was born without this stigma of carnal desire by a virgin who conceived by the Holy Spirit.[48]

So, no matter how chastely the married couple had behaved in begetting children, according to Augustine they were still born in sin.[49]

In the letters of Jerome there are examples of women who allegedly lived their lives according to the strict moral ideals described above. Jerome praises his patroness and friend Paula and her family[50] in a

---

[46] *Adversus Iovianum* 1.32: *si non praefertur nuptiis virginitas, spiritus sanctus cur maritatam, cur viduam non elegit?*

[47] *De sancta virginitate* 6.6: *et coniugatae quippe fideles feminae et deo virgines dicatae sanctis moribus et "caritate de corde puro et conscientia bona et fide non ficta,"* [1 Tim 1:5, Vulg.] *quia voluntatem patris faciunt, christi spiritaliter matres sunt; quae autem coniugali vita corporaliter pariunt, non Christum, sed Adam pariunt et ideo currunt, ut sacramentis inbuti christi membra fiant partus earum, quoniam quid peperint norunt.* Compare the translation by Kearney and Hunter, *Works of Saint Augustine,* I.9: *Marriage and Virginity,* 71.

[48] *Si infantes omni modo innocentes sunt, cur matres ad Ecclesiam cum languentibus?* ... [the infant speaks] *sed ego in iniquitate conceptus sum, et in peccatis mater mea me in utero aluit. Praeter hoc vinculum concupiscentiae carnalis natus est Christus sine maculo, ex virgine concipiente de Spiritu Sancto.* The wording of Ps 50:7 in the Vulgate is: *ecce in iniquitate conceptus sum et in peccato peperit me mater mea.* For the tendency to paraphrase the scriptures, see also n. 40 above.

[49] Compare the comment of Ambrose on this same passage in *Apologia prophetae David* 1.11.56.

[50] For Jerome's relationship to Paula and her family see Kelly, *Jerome,* 98–101. On the debates within aristocratic circles at Rome created by Jerome's teaching on celibacy

letter addressed to her daughter Eustochium, who had taken up the
ascetic life:

> Thus nobly born, Paula through her fecundity (*fecunditate*) and her chast-
> ity (*pudicitia*) won approval from all, from her husband first, then from her
> relatives, and lastly from the whole city. She bore five children—Blesilla,
> for whose death I consoled her while in Rome; Paulina, who has left the
> reverend and admirable (*sanctum et admirabilem*) Pammachius to inherit
> both her vows and property, to whom also I addressed a little book
> on her death; Eustochium, who is now in the holy places, a precious
> necklace of virginity and of the church; Rufina, whose untimely death
> overcame the affectionate heart of her mother; and Toxotius, after whom
> she had no more children. You can thus see that it was not her wish to
> fulfil a wife's duty, but that she only complied with her husband's longing
> to have male offspring.[51]

That is, according to Jerome, Paula would have preferred to live in total
continence, but chose to act as a chaste wife and obey her husband. It
was only after his death that she attached herself to Jerome and set
about to establish monasteries for women in the Holy Land. We should
perhaps take special notice of the repute among relatives and friends
that Paula's marital chastity brought her, long before she decided to
become a celibate. A chaste reputation was also an idealized norm, and
chastity and obedience must have been viewed as the burdens as well
as the virtues of the married life.

As mentioned above, with the rise of ascetic piety, virgins ranked
far above married women in the eyes of the church. These attitudes
created something of a dilemma for those who advocated marriage.
Ambrose of Milan, Augustine's mentor, had to walk a thin line: "The
bond of marriage is not thus to be shunned as though it were sinful, but
rather declined as a galling burden."[52] He also wrote a treatise for his

---

see L. Michael White, "Finding the Ties that Bind: Issues from Social Description,"
in *Social Networks in the Early Christian Environment*, 7–14. Whereas Paula stringently
resisted allowing her daughter Eustochium to marry, her son, Toxotius, also a Christian,
married into another aristocratic Roman family and had a daughter, whom he named
Paula.

[51] *Ep.* 108.4: *his, inquam, orta maioribus et fecunditate ac pudicitia probata primum viro, dein
propinquis et totius urbis testimonio, cum quinque liberos edidisset—Blesillam, super cuius morte eam
Romae consolatus sum, Paulinam, quae sanctum et admirabilem virum et propositi et rerum suarum
Pammacchium reliquit heredem, ad quem super obitu eius parvum libellum edidimus, Eustochium, quae
nunc in sanctis locis virginitatis et ecclesiae monile pretiosissimum est, Rufinam, quae immaturo funere
pium matris animum consternavit, et Toxotium, post quem parere desivit, ut intellegeres eam non diu
servire voluisse officio coniugali, sed mariti desiderio, qui mares optabat liberos, oboedisse.*

[52] *De viduis* 13.81 (PL 16.273): *Non ergo copula nuptialis quasi culpa vitanda, sed quasi*

sister Marcellina, who was a consecrated virgin. He mentions among other things the troubled life of a married woman, a life that a holy virgin could avoid:[53]

> Let us compare, if it pleases you, the advantages of married women with that which awaits a virgin. Though the noble woman (*mulier nobilis*) boasts of her abundant offspring, yet the more [offspring] she bears, the more she suffers. Let her count up the comforts of her children, but let her likewise count up the troubles. She marries and weeps (*plorat*).[54] How many vows she makes with tears. She conceives and she grieves (*graviscit*).[55] Her fecundity brings her trouble before offspring. She gives birth and gets sick (*aegrotat*).[56] How sweetly the pledge (*pignus*),[57] which

necessitatis sarcina declinanda. The passage continues: *Lex enim astrinxit uxorem, ut in laboribus et in tristia filios generet, et conversio ejus ad virum sit, quod ei ipse dominetur. Ergo laboribus et doloribus in generatione filiorum addicitur nupta, nonvidua: et dominatui viri sola subditur copulata, non virgo* ("Even the law obligates a wife, so that she must bear children in labor and in sorrow and her desire should be to her man, since she is dominated by him [cf. Gen 3:16; Song 7:10]. Therefore, the bride is bound to labors and pains in the bearing of children, but not widows; and the married [i.e., 'coupled'] woman alone is subjected to a man who exerts dominion over her, but not the virgin.").

[53] *De virginibus* 1.6.25–27: *Conferamus, si placet, bona mulierum cum ultimis virginum. Jacet licet fecundo se mulier nobilis partu: quo plures generavit, plus laborat. Numeret solatia filiorum, sed numeret pariter et molestas. Nubit et plorat. Qualia sunt vota, quae flentur. Concipit et gravescit. Prius utique impedimentum fecunditas incipit afferre quam fructum. Partuerit et aegrotat. Quam dulce pignus quod a periculo incipit, et in periculis desinit, prius dolori futurum quam voluptati in periculis enitur, nec pro arbitrio possidetur. Quid recenseam nutriendi molestias instituendi et copulandi? Felicium sunt istae miserae. Habet mater heredes sed auget dolores. Nam de adversis non oportet dicere, ne sanctissimi morum parentum animi contremiscant. Vide mi soror, quam grave sit pati, quod non oportet audiri. Et haec in praesenti saeculo. Venient autem dies quando dicant: Beatae steriles et ventres qui non genuerunt. Filiae enim huius saeculi generantur et generant: filia autem regni abstinet a voluptate viri, et a voluptate carnis: ut sit sancta corpore et spiritu. Quid ergo famulatus graves et addicta viris servitia replicem feminarum, quas ante jussit Deus servire quam servos.*

[54] A wordplay, since *ploro* ("to weep, wail, or lament") is particularly associated with funerals (rather than weddings). Also virgins were often enlisted for the funeral processions. So compare the lament of Heracles (from Sophocles' *Trachiniae*) as quoted in Latin by Cicero, *Tusc. disp.* 2.9.21: *Heu! virginalem me ore ploratum edere, quem vidit nemo ulli ingemescentem malo!* ("Ah! that my mouth utters virgins' laments, whom no one ere saw groaning over anything ill.")

[55] Another wordplay, since *gravesco* (literally "to become heavy or grave") can mean "to become pregnant" (i.e., the visibly swollen abdomen) and "to be embarrased" or "become grievious."

[56] Another wordplay, since *aegroto* means both "to become sick" (as in morning sickness) and "to become mentally distressed or depressed" (as in postpartem depression). But there may be an even darker side, since maternal mortality in birthing was a serious concern as well.

[57] *Pignus* can mean either a pledge, a wager, or children. Here it probably means the children produced by the sexual union. So see n. 69 below where it is used in this sense in one of the epitaphs. Compare also the use for children in Statius, *Silviae* 2.1.86–7.

begins from danger and ends in danger, brings forth in danger what will bring pain before pleasure, and yet is not possessed at will.[58] Why speak of the troubles of nursing, of childrearing, and of coupling? These are the miseries of those who are fortunate. A mother has heirs, but it increases her sorrows. We dare not speak of the adversities lest the minds of even the holiest (*sanctissimi*) parents should tremble. Consider, my sister, how hard it must be to bear what one ought not even hear about. Yet, this is in the present age. But "the days shall come when they shall say: 'Blessed are the barren, and the wombs that never bore [Lk 23:29].'" For the daughters of this age are conceived, and conceive; but the daughter of the kingdom refrain from lust for a man and the pleasures of the flesh, that she may be holy in body and in spirit (*sancta corpore et spiritu*). Why should I further speak of the painful servitude and slavish duties due to their husbands by wives,[59] to whom God previously gave the command to serve more than slaves.

Ambrose thought it was not only morally superior but far less trouble not to marry at all. Jerome—not to mention Paula or Melania—took a more negative view. Augustine, however, took something of a mediating position on the good of marriage over against the extreme views on both sides of the issue of others in his day.[60] Even so he painted a very dark picture.

Before I turn to the epigraphic material, I shall briefly summarize how the ideal of a Christian marriage was depicted, drawing mostly on Augustine but supplemented from Jerome and Ambrose. Sexual activity in married life was only acceptable for the purpose of begetting children, and both spouses were expected to live a life in chastity based on this norm. It was especially important that the husband lead a chaste life since he was superior to his wife both by nature and according to the Scripture, as it came to be understood in the teaching of the church concerning original sin. Childbirth was considered both a punishment of woman and a duty towards her husband. No matter how chastely a wife and her husband lived, their children would always

---

[58] This is a difficult passage to understand but most likely refers to the high rate of neonatal and infant mortality.

[59] For the wife as the "domestic slave" (*famula*) of the husband in Augustine, see *Contra Faust.* 22.30–1; *De bono coniug.* 6.6; *De coniug. adult.* 2.8.7–8; *Serm.* 332.4.4; 392.4; *Enn. in Psalm.* 143.6. Cf. B. Shaw, "The Family in Late Antiquity," 28–9.

[60] Elizabeth A. Clark, "Heresy, Asceticism, Adam, and Eve: Interpretations of Genesis 1–3 in the Later Latin Fathers," in *Ascetic Piety and Women's Faith*, 362–66. Augustine's *De bono coniug.* was a reply to Jovinian, but without denigrating marriage to the same degree as Jerome; cf. Augustine, *Retractationes* 2.48.1 (CSEL 36.156–7).

be considered conceived in sin. A married couple knew that they always ranked lowest in the moral hierarchy of the church behind continent widows and especially virgins.

Ecclesiastical Prescription and Popular Piety: The Epigraphic Evidence

In the preceding discussion I have attempted to explicate the emerging sexual norms as preached in the Latin church of the late fourth and early fifth century. Despite extreme differences of opinion on the underlying theological questions, the norms themselves are usually expressed or encoded in some key terms that we have seen repeated throughout: *pudicitia* or *castitas* ("chastity"), *casta* ("chaste") and *pudicissima* ("very chaste"), *sanctissima* ("very holy"), *oboediere/ oboedientia* ("obey" and "obedience"), *fidelis* ("faithful," i.e., baptized), and *continentia* ("continent or celibate"). We are now in a position to address the question whether there are any traces of this ideal in popular Christian practice. In order to do so we shall look at early Christian epitaphs commemorating spouses. My analysis of Christian patterns of commemoration is based on two groups of epitaphs from the city of Rome dating to the fourth and fifth centuries CE. The first group of epitaphs comprises 991 inscriptions from the catacombs of Domitilla and Callistus on the Via Ardeatina, published in volumes 3 and 4 of the *Inscriptiones Christianae Urbis Romae* (*ICUR*). The second group comprises another 136 fourth and fifth-century epitaphs from church burials at St. Peter's (the Vatican) and St. Paul's outside-the-walls (on the Via Ostiensis), published in volume 2 of the *ICUR*.[61] Combined the corpus yields a total of 1,127 epitaphs all dating roughly to the era of Augustine and Jerome.

Commemoration and the Christian Ideals of Marriage

Commemoration of the dead using complimentary epithets was a common feature of the epigraphic habit among both pagans and Christians. Yet a survey shows some differences in practice. A typical epitaph for a deceased wife from the pagan corpus at Rome which uses such epithets reads:

---

[61] Edited by G.-B. de Rossi, new series completed and edited by A. Silvagni and A. Ferrua (Rome: Pontifical Institute for Christian Archaeology, 1922–1964).

> To the Divine Shades: [in memory] of Flavia Aphrodite, his dearest (*carissimae*) and well deserving (*bene merenti*) wife, Quintus Memmius Daphnus made [this epitaph].[62]

The commemoration of Christian women from Rome may now be illustrated through a number of characteristic epitaphs, after which we shall return to discuss some patterns in the use of epithets in these commemorations.

The term of relationship *virgineus/a* is not found among the principal epithets which we shall discuss below, but certainly deserves to be mentioned.[63] We meet it in the Christian epigraphic material in epitaphs commemorating spouses as a term of relationship to tell the reader that the spouses had entered marriage when they were still virgins. This term of relationship is likewise found in other pagan epigraphic material from Rome, but only very infrequently. A typical Christian example reads:[64]

> Aurelius Abundantius made this [in memory] of his incomparable (*incomparabili*) wife (*virginea*) of perfect innocence (*innocentiae*) and admirable chastity (*mire castitatis*) Aurelia Melitia. She lived with her husband (*virgineus*) 9 years, 3 months and ? days and lived 23 years 11 months and 20 days. She was buried in peace 17 January.[65]

Here we note that the innocence and chastity of the wife is heavily emphasized, but it is in large measure a comment on the fact that she was fourteen years old, a typical age for women, when they married. In this case and others it is not possible to know for sure if a vow of sexual continence was observed through the course of the marriage. It is noteworthy, however, that no children are mentioned, but she died young during the childbearing years. In an even more interesting epitaph Probilianus is commemorating his *virginea*:

---

[62] *CIL* 6.18280: *D M Flaviae Aphroditae coniugi carissimae bene merenti Q Memmius Daphnus fecit*. See below Table 1 for further information regarding the pagan material used here.

[63] The term is mentioned in 9 epitaphs in the samples from *ICUR* 2–4 analyzed here, but not once in the CIL 6 sample of pagan epitaphs discussed below (cf. Table 1).

[64] All references to Christian epitaphs are to the survey samples from *ICUR* 2–4. Lacunae in the epitaphs are marked by elipsis (…). I have decided not to "fill in the blanks" in the Latin texts by resolving the many standard abbreviations in Latin epigraphic custom. The abbreviations should be understandable from the translations.

[65] *ICUR* 3.9673: *totius innocentiae et mire castitatis incomparabili Aur Melitiae virginiae sue Aur Abundantius fecit q vixit cum virginio suo ann viiii mens iii d xxi … et vixit annos xxiii mens xi d xx d xvi kal fe in pace*. On this use of *virgineus/a* see C. Vogel, "*Facere cum virginia (o) sua (-o) annos*," *Revue de Droit Canonique* 16 (1996) 355–66.

> Probilianus [made this in memory of] his wife (*virginea*) Felicitas(?) whose faithfulness (*fidelitatem*), chastity (*castitate*) and blamelessness (*bonitate*) all the neighbors experienced when she preserved her chastity during her husband's (*virgineus*) 7 years of absence. She was buried in this holy place 30 January.[66]

It is obviously an important point for Probilianus to make that his wife had lived in chastity during his long absence and that all the neighbors knew about it.

Other inscriptions to wives are much shorter than the ones just quoted, but they are nevertheless very concerned to emphasize the chastity and holy mores of the deceased. In his epitaph to his wife Aurelius Ampliatus writes:

> [in memory of] Aurelia Bonifatia his incomparable (*incomparabili*) wife, a woman of true chastity (*castitatis*) who lived 25 years, 2 months, 4 days and 6 hours. Aurelius Ampliatus with their son Gordianus [made this].[67]

About Tertulla it is said that she was obedient to her husband:

> to Tertulla, sweetest (*[dul]cisseme* [sic]) wife who showed obedience (*obsequio*) [towards her husband] in all things. She lived 42 years, 6 months 12 days and predeceased her husband. She was buried in peace 17 June.[68]

The epitaph to Appias(?) stresses that her obedience was the duty of bearing children:

> Appias(?) is lying in this tomb invisible for her relatives, lamented by her children, lamented by her husband. She was chaste and obeyed modestly the duties of married life. She had children, dear pledges (*pignora*) of the marriage bed. She does not live in this sad tomb, but close to Christ in heaven. She was buried 24 August 392. Her husband Restitutus [made this] memorial ...[69]

These examples are fairly typical of the commemoration of Christian wives in the catacomb burials. It seems obvious that the husbands who

---

[66] *ICUR* 4.10953: ... *tati virginiae suae Probilianus queius fidelitatem et castitate et bonitate omnes vicinales experti sunt quae annis n viii absentia virgini sui suam castitatem custodivit unde in hoc loco sancto deposita est iii kal febr.*

[67] *ICUR* 3.7445: *Aureliae Bonifatiae coniugi incomparabili verae castitatis feminae quae vixit ann xxv m ii dieb iiii hor vi Aurel Amplicatus cum Gordiano filio.*

[68] *ICUR* 2.4249: *..lcisseme et omni obsequio ..referende coiugi Tertulle ..ue vixit annos xlii m vi d xii praecessit in pace dep xv kal iul.*

[69] *ICUR* 2.4827: ... *ias hoc tegitur ..uperis invisa ..sepulcro ... bilis haec suboli ..ebilis ista viro ... ta verecundo serbabit iura cubili ... dit et prolem pignora cara tori ..n tamen haec tristes habitat post limine sedes ... sed Cristo sidera celsa tenet ... quae vixit annus p m xxxviii ... Restitu ... maritus com ... ...it.* For *pignus* ("pledges") as children see also n. 57 above.

dedicated these epitaphs were eager to show the world, God, and themselves that they had lived a married life in chastity and obedience. I find it interesting that they all seem to be in accordance with the normative terminology for the married life put forward by Augustine and Jerome. It cannot be overemphasized that epitaphs like these are hardly ever found in the pagan epigraphic material from imperial Rome. In keeping with the preaching discussed earlier, Christian husbands were exhorted to be more chaste than their wives. Therefore there is every reason to believe that husbands by emphasizing their wives' chastity and faithfulness at the same time emphasized their own chastity and honor. This becomes even more clear when we look at the dedications made by Christian wives to their husbands.

Most of the epitaphs dedicated by wives to their husbands are short and modest. A good example is the commemoration of a certain Quiracus, whose wife, not atypically, does not even name herself:

> for her well deserving (*benemerenti*) husband Quiracus with whom she lived 16 years, his wife made [this epitaph]. He lived 40 years, 3 months and ? days and was buried in peace 12 February.[70]

But even a short epitaph may contain important information like the one dedicated to Hermiantis(?):

> The tomb (*locus*) of Hermiantis(?) and Redempta. Redempta made this [memorial] to her husband Hermiantis. You gave me all the comfort I needed.[71]

Two longer epitaphs explain in more detail what a wife expected and had received from her husband:

> Felix of holy faith (*sanctae fidei*) is resting in peace, but his love and care is remembered by his friends forever. He was known as comforting and compassionate towards everybody. Acrippina made this [memorial] to her sweetest (*dulcissimo*) husband with whom she lived for 3 years and 10 months without any wound on her mind. He lived in this world for 32 years and was buried 20 August in the consulship of Valentinian, most noble child, and Victor [i.e., 369].[72]

---

[70] *ICUR* 3.9759: *Quiraco cogiugi venemerenti fec uxor cum quem fecit annos xvi vix … s xxxx mes tres dies vii … ri idus feb in pace.*

[71] *ICUR* 3.7770: *locus Hermi.. ac Redemptae Redempta feci.. coiugi suo He … a quo omne so(laciu habui).*

[72] *ICUR* 2.4165: *Felix sanctae fidei vocitus iit in pace cuius tantus amor et caritas retenetur ab amicis in aevo qui cum esset fuit solacius, misericors omnibus notus Acrippina fecit dulcissimo suo marito cum quem vixit sine lesione animi annos iii et m x fuit in saeculum quod vixit annos xxxii dep xiii kal sept Valentiniano n p et Victori conss.*

Friends also play an important role in the epitaph that Quirilla dedicated to her beloved husband Verus:

> Here lies Verus who always spoke the truth and deserved after his death to be buried in St Peter's. The tomb contains his bones but his soul has been received in heaven. Due to all his virtues his sweet friends miss him. I your lover (*amatrix*) Quirilla dictated these verses, I who after your death wanted to kill myself, but fearing God's demands promised to live a chaste life hereafter. Verus lived 56 years in this world.[73]

Here we notice that Quirilla describes her marriage as a very passionate relationship. She characterizes herself as her husband's *amatrix* ("lover," but it can mean either "beloved," as a sweetheart, or "mistress") and claims that she would have committed suicide had she not adhered to God's demands. This is quite exceptional. Wives obviously expected their husbands to be comforting and compassionate. This is in accordance both with the literary evidence and with the epitaphs dedicated by husbands to their wives. Where husbands expected their wives to be chaste and faithful, wives expected care and comfort from their husbands.

Patterns of Commemoration and the Use of Epithets

These examples are generally representative of Christian commemoration for spouses in our two samples. The major shift in epitaphs for Christian women may now be analyzed in greater detail in comparison with how epithets are used in pagan epigraphic materials.[74] In the pagan epitaphs from imperial Rome the most popular epithets used to characterize the deceased spouse (whether husband or wife) were: *bene merens* ("well deserving"), *dulcissimus/a* ("sweetest"), *carissimus/a* ("dearest"), *sanctissimus* ("very holy"), and *pientissimus/a* ("very

---

[73] *ICUR* 2.4226: *hic Verus qui semper vera locutus / post mortem meruit in Petri limina / sancta iacere ossa tenet tumulus mens est / in celo recepta huius vita bona requirunt dulces amici / hos Quirilla tibi dictabit versus amatrix / quae post morte tua vului me ferro necare / sed dni praecepta timens casta me in futuro promitto / quinquaginta et sex Verus duxit per saecula messes.*

[74] A survey of the uses and patterns in pagan commemoration may be found in my article "Interpreting Epithets in Roman Epitaphs," in *The Roman Family in Italy: Status, Sentiment, Space*, ed. B. Rawson and P. Weaver (Oxford: Clarendon, 1997) 169–204, and in my forthcoming monograph, *Roman Familial Relationships: The Evidence of the Epitaphs* (Rome: "L'Erma" di Bretschneider, forthcoming). The results of these studies were used in Table 1 below.

pious/dutiful").[75] In the Christian epitaphs the picture changes in some significant ways. Here *bene merens* and *dulcissimus/a* are still widely used, but otherwise a new range of epithets such as *virgo* ("virgin"),[76] *innocens* ("innocent"),[77] *fidelis* ("faithful," i.e., baptized), *castissimus/a* and *pudicissimus/a* (both meaning "very chaste")[78] are frequently found. Of the most frequently used Christian epithets only *sanctissimus/a* is also found regularly in the pagan epigraphic material. The differences in choice of epithets between the pagan epitaphs and the early Christian epitaphs from Rome are summarized in Table 1.

Table 1: Distribution of Epithets in Pagan and Christian Epitaphs[79]

	Pagan Epitaphs (CIL 6)[80]		Christian Epitaphs (ICUR 2–4)[81]	
Most Used Epithets	percentage	actual number	percentage	actual number
Bene merens	30	663	30	147
Dulcissimus/a	12	262	19	92
Carissimus/a	12	257	4	21
Pientissimus/a	10	226	1	3

[75] In both pagan and Christian epitaphs it is normal to use the superlative of the characterizing epithet.

[76] *Virgo* here is categorized as an epithet since it is being used this way in the epitaphs.

[77] *Innocens* is often used of children or adolescents; at times it may be synonymous with *virgineus/a*. So see *ICUR* 3.9673 (above at n. 65). It is worth noting that even this usage seems to be contradictory to Augustine's doctrine of original sin, so *Ennar. en Psalm.* 50.10 (quoted above at n. 48); cf. *Sermo* 165. *De civ. dei* 22.22, however, does use the term, with some ambiguity, to refer to baptized infants: *etiam parvulos baptizatos, quibus certe nihil est innocentius, aliquando sic vexant* … ("for so they [demons] sometimes vex baptized infants, than whom surely nothing is more innocent …"). This usage may also be reflected in the epitaphs.

[78] There does not seem to be any appreciable difference in the meaning of the two terms since both mean "marital chastity" and do not imply total sexual continence; so see *ICUR* 3.7445 (above at n. 67). It may well be, however, that the cognates *castus/a – castissimus/a* were favored by Christians because *pudicitia* was a traditional pagan term; cf. below at n. 95. It may also be the case that in later (medieval) usage *castitas* came to be more or less synonymous with *continentia*, but not here.

[79] In this Table only those epithets are listed which occur statistically at a rate of one percent or more of the total in each sample. The findings are reported both as a percentage and in the actual number of occurances. The percentages are based on the total number of epithets in each sample.

[80] The distribution of pagan epithets is based on an analysis of a representative sample of 3,179 epitaphs from *CIL* 6, all from the city of Rome. Among these inscriptions a total of 2,220 epithets are found characterizing the relationship between dedicator and commemorated. For references see above n. 74.

[81] The 1,127 Christian epitaphs from *ICUR* 2–4 contain a total of 483 epithets.

Most Used Epithets	Pagan Epitaphs (CIL 6)		Christian Epitaphs (ICUR 2–4)	
	percentage	actual number	percentage	actual number
Optimus/a	5	113	–	–
Sanctissimus/a	2	52	3	12
Incomparabilis	1	31	1	5
Innocens	–	–	6	30
Virgo	–	–	3	15
Fidelis	–	–	2	8
Castissimus/a	–	–	3	13
Pudicus/a & Pudicissimus/a	–	–	1	5
Aggregates	72%[82]	1,604	73%[83]	351
Total of all Epithets		[2,220]		[483]

In the pagan epigraphic material from Rome *carissimus/a* ("dearest") and *dulcissimus/a* ("sweetest") together with the widely used *bene merens* ("well deserving") are the epithets preferred to characterize a commemorated spouse.[84] These epithets are likewise relatively frequent in the Christian epigraphic material from Rome. In fact, as the statistical survey shows, *bene merens* is used in exactly the same proportion among pagans and Christians, while the affectionate *dulcissimus/a* is actually more frequent among Christians.[85] By contrast, the seemingly religious term *sanctissimus/a*, while common to both, is rather infrequent in the total scheme of commemorative practice with no significant increase among Christians.

More interesting, however, is the fact that epithets connoting chastity and faith (i.e., the terms *virgo*, *pudica/-issima*, and *castissima*) have become more conspicuous in the Christian usage. More importantly, all occurances of these key epithets that I have analyzed from the *ICUR* samples, with but a few exceptions, refer to women, primarily wives. We can see the overall picture when we look at the use of epithets more

---

[82] Examples of other, less frequent epithets found in pagan usage include terms such as: *ingenuosissimus* (*CIL* 6.26112); *infelicissima* (6.26115); and *animae bonae* (6.26473). Given the unusual and even singular nature of some of these epithets, it is difficult to see them as typical of ordinary commemorative notions or practice. The same holds true for the less frequent Christian epithets in n. 83 below.

[83] Examples of other, less frequent epithets found in the Christian samples incude terms such as: *digna* (*ICUR* 4.9415); *ob amorem et affectionem* (4.9422); and *palumba* (4.9762).

[84] I am referring specifically to the sample from CIL 6 used to construct Table 1; see n. 79–80 above.

[85] This term is often used of children who are commemorated by their parents.

generally in the commemoration of women in the *ICUR* samples. In
the samples from *ICUR* 3–4 (the catacomb material) the great majority of commemorations for spouses that employ epithets—73.4% (102
out of 139)—are for wives, while only 26.6% (37) are for husbands.[86]
Over all in the catacomb sample only 58.2% of the commemorations
are for females; therefore, the women receive an inordinate percentage
of the epithets. A similar pattern of epithet usage predominantly for
females is at work in the sample of inscriptions from the two basilicas
(*ICUR* 2). Here 67.7% (21/31) of the spouses commemorated with epithets are female while only 32.3% (10/31) are male, and yet males make
up 57.9% (77/133) of the total of persons commemorated in the basilica
sample.

   This usage of epithets is striking, especially given the fact that men
are generally commemorated more often by far in usual pagan and
Christian practice. Both among pagans and Christians, however, the
use of epithets is more common for women than men.[87] In other words,
the extensive use of these epithets represents a pattern of commemoration by the men—whether pagan or Christian—for their deceased
wives. In the case of the two Christian samples from *ICUR*, however, it
is of additional interest that there is a higher percentage of women commemorated in the catacomb sample, while in the basilica sample, the
ratio of males to females is more typical of pagan epigraphic patterns.[88]
This fact may suggest that there is a socio-economic or class difference
between the two Christian samples, since the basilica group tends to
be associated with more aristocratic circles.[89] Table 2 shows the distribution of the most frequently used epithets characterizing commemo-

---

   [86] For the purposes of the statistical analysis that follows we must distinguish between
the number of epitaphs, the number of commemorations, and the number of epithets,
since a single epitaph (i.e., the inscribed *titulus* placed over or beside the burial *loculus*)
might contain commemorations for more than one individual. Thus, commemoration
here refers to an individual mentioned by name. Similarly, any individual so commemorated might receive zero, one, or more than one epithet.

   [87] In general the ratio of males to females in all epitaphs from the pagan sample of
CIL 6 is 1.28:1 (2,119/1,654). In *CIL* 6 the use of epithets occurs in 932 commemorations
for spouses; of these, 600 (64.4%) are for wives, while 332 (35.6%) are for husbands.
This yields a sex ratio for the use of epithets of 0.55:1 (males:females) which is very low
on the male side compared to pagan epitaphs generally (1.28:1). In other words, pagan
wives tended to be commemorated by the use of epithets more often than husbands.

   [88] See next note (Table 2) for the statistical data on the Christian samples.

   [89] The basilica sample appears to be heavily biased. In general, by the fifth century
only well-to-do Christians or those who were clergy or otherwise closely connected to
the church could obtain the right to burial within these two churches, but especially St.

rated women in these same samples from the Christian catacombs and basilicas respectively.

Table 2: Distribution of the Top Ten Christian Epithets by Gender[90]

	Catacomb Sample[91]				Basilica Sample[92]			
Epithet Used	male	female	tot.	% female	male	female	tot.	% female
Bene merens	53	77	130	60	9	8	17	47
Dulcissimus/a	39	37	76	49	12	4	16	25
Carissimus/a	5	15	20	75	0	1	1	100
Virgo	1	9	10	90	0	5	5	100
Fidelis	0	7	7	100	0	1	1	100
Pudicissimus/a	0	5	5	100				—
Sanctissimus/a	1	7	8	87.5	0	4	4	100
Incomparabilis	0	4	4	100	0	1	1	100
Innocens	10	14	25	56	2	4	6	66.6
Castissimus/a	0	5	5	100	1	7	8	87.5
Totals for Top 10[93]	109	180	290[94]	62.1	24	35	59	59.3

Some important patterns are suggested by this data. Husbands, whether pagan or Christian, tended to commemorate their wives using epithets more often than the reverse. One might suspect that this says something about the cultural value of wives generally—a badge of

---

Peters. On the other hand, it should be noted that a fair number of epitaphs from the catacomb of Callistus (in contrast to Domitilla) represent church hierarchy.

[90] On the Christian side the general sex ratio for all persons commemorated in the catacomb sample (*ICUR* 3–4) is 0.72:1 (426/594), while the ratio for the use of the epithets in this list is 0.61:1 (109/180) i.e., the use of epithets is still higher for femles than males. In the basilica sample (*ICUR* 2) the general sex ratio for all epitaphs is 1.38:1 (77/56), while the ratio among the top ten epithets is 0.69:1 (24/35), i.e., almost the inverse (1:1.46, inverting the fraction as 35/24) of the general ratio. This is not the place to discuss the difference between sex ratio in the pagan and Christian samples, but it should be obvious that wives were commemorated very frequently in all materials using epithets, and that the commemoration of females was very important to the Christians who buried their dead in the catacombs.

[91] From the sample of *ICUR* 3–4.

[92] From the sample of *ICUR* 2.

[93] It should be noted that there are more epithets than the total number of inscriptions that use epithets since many of the epitaphs employ more than one. The samples given in the preceding section illustrate this pattern.

[94] In four instances fragmentation of the inscription means that the gender of the commemorated is indeterminate. Among the epithets in Table 2 this fact is significant only for the term *innocens* (one instance) in the catacomb sample, but it also means that the sum of the columns for males and females does not equal the acutal total.

honor to their husbands—rather than about the nature of the epithets per se. Yet, it should be evident from the distribution that the distinctively Christian epithets connoting holiness and chastity were primarily used to commemorate females, while the epithets used for Christian males remained much more in line with the pagan heritage. If we calculate the use of the three key terms connoting marital chastity (*virgo*, *pudicissima*, and *castissima*) we find that they are used for women in 95% (19/20) of the occurances in the catacomb sample and 92.3% (12/13) of the occurances in the basilica sample, with the aggregate being 93.9% (31/33). Even so these three epithets combined still make up only 6.8% (33/483) of all the epithets used by Christians to commemorate spouses. It is even more noteworthy perhaps that the key epithet complex *pudicus/a*—*pudicissimus/a* does not occur at all in the basilica sample while *castissimus/a* is, if anything, even more conspicuously used of both husbands and wives.[95]

By contrast, the traditional pagan triad of epithets (*bene merens*, *dulcissimus/a*, and *carissimus/a*) still constitutes 53.8% (260/483) of all the epithets used by Christians, the same proportion (53.7%, 1182/2,200) found in pagan usage of these terms. If distributed by gender, however, the Christian usage is even more striking, since these traditional pagan terms make up 66% (142/215) of the top ten epithets for females but 88.1% (118/134) of the top ten epithets for males. At the same time, the two Christian samples show some notable differences in their application of these traditional pagan epithets to men and women. In the catacomb sample, whenever the "pagan triad" is used it is applied to women 57.1% of the time (129/226), but in the basilica sample only 38.2% of the time (13/34). What this means is that among Christians the "pagan triad" of epithets is applied to women roughly half of the time (54.6%, 142/260) when epithets are used; however, when men receive epithets—only 38.4% (134/349) of the occurances—they almost always come from these three traditional pagan terms (88.1%, 118/134).

At this point it does not seem unreasonable to conclude that Christian preaching about marital chastity and ethical mores actually made an impression on married couples at Rome. Or at least it shows what they thought was important to display in their epitaphs. How they actually lived their lives at home they took with them to the grave. Here we must again take note of the fact that the majority of these epithets

---

[95] Although this may be a result of the relatively small size of this sample, but cf. n. 78 above.

come from the husbands and thus reflect what was viewed as normative in their culture. In some ways their cultural values had not changed
much from pagan times, especially in the epithets used to commemorate men. Yet Christian preaching did make an impact, especially in
what had come to be valued about their wives. In epitaphs dedicated
to wives matronal chastity was emphasized by husbands, if for no other
reason than because it simultaneously displayed the chastity of the wid-
owed husbands and thus their married life. It accrued to the husband's
honor to honor his wife. At the same time, this means that the soci-
etal values by which honor was measured were at least beginning to
reflect elements of Christian morality. At least some married couples
were prepared to say by means of their epitaphs that they adhered
to the moral prescripts of the church and could accordingly expect to
obtain salvation—even if only a "thirty fold harvest."

PART V

ΝΟΜΟΣ

Nomos

"THE MIND IS ITS OWN PLACE"

DEFINING THE *TOPOS*

Johan C. Thom

> *The mind is its own place, and in it self*
> *Can make a Heav'n of Hell, a Hell of*
> *Heav'n.*
>
> (Milton, *Paradise Lost* 1.254–55)

Introduction

Topos has become a key term in both classical and New Testament scholarship.[1] Even a superficial survey of articles published by NT scholars will reveal that the term *topos* occurs with increasing frequency in titles, while still more studies are devoted to *topoi* without using the term in the title. Within the context of the Society of Biblical Literature's Hellenistic Moral Philosophers and Early Christianity Group, the *topoi* of friendship, frank criticism, moral progress, and the passions have all been extensively and productively discussed in the last five years, and they remain a central interest for this group.[2]

---

[1] For classical scholarship, see especially Hermann Wankel, "'Alle Menschen müssen sterben': Variationen eines Topos der griechischen Literatur," *Hermes* 111 (1983) 129–54; Laurent Pernot, "Lieu et lieu commun dans la rhétorique antique," *Bulletin de l'Association Guillaume Budé* (1986) 253–84. For a brief, but programmatic survey of the *topos* in New Testament studies see Abraham J. Malherbe, "Hellenistic Moralists and the New Testament," *ANRW* II.26.1 (1992) 267–333, esp. 320–25. This article also contains important references to earlier work on the *topos* in classical literature (320 n. 252).

[2] The work on *topoi* by this group has appeared in several publications: see John T. Fitzgerald, ed., *Friendship, Flattery, and Frankness of Speech: Studies on Friendship in the New Testament World* (NovTSup 82; Leiden: Brill, 1996); John T. Fitzgerald, ed., *Graeco-Roman Perspectives on Friendship* (SBLSBS 34, Atlanta, Ga.: Scholars Press, 1997); David Konstan and others, *Philodemus: On Frank Criticism* (SBLTT 43, Atlanta, Ga.: Scholars Press, 1998). Forthcoming publications include: John T. Fitzgerald, ed., *Passions and Progress in the Hellenistic World*; David Armstrong, *Philodemus: On Death* and *Philodemus: On Anger*; V. Tsouna, *Philodemus: On Household Management* and *On Arrogance* (all four latter books will be published in the SBL Writings from the Graeco-Roman World series). Future *topoi* to be discussed will probably include πλεονεξία (greed), wealth and poverty; φιλοτιμία (love of honor or fame); ὁμόνοια (concord or harmony); piety (εὐσέβεια, *pietas*); and the *topos* on household management.

There is no doubt that much of this interest has been stimulated by Professor Abraham Malherbe, both through his own work and doctoral dissertations directed by him, as well as through his enduring influence on former students and colleagues. This essay is in direct response to some of the observations Malherbe made on the *topos* in his survey entitled "Hellenistic Moralists and the New Testament," originally completed in 1972, updated in 1987, and finally published in 1992, as well as in the "Retrospective Analysis" on the same topic presented at the 1990 SBL Annual Meeting.[3]

Why the interest in *topoi*? There is broad consensus that investigations of ancient *topoi* enrich our understanding of the moral and religious context of the NT and may make important contributions to the interpretation of specific NT passages.[4] There is less clarity, however, about what *topoi* are, and how they function in the NT. The term *topos* is usually used loosely to cover a whole range of phenomena, including rhetorical patterns of argumentation, literary themes, motifs and clichés, as well as conventional treatments of moral and intellectual subjects. As is well known, modern use of the term goes back to Ernst Curtius. In his seminal study *European Literature and the Latin Middle Ages* he asserts that *topoi* originally had a rhetorical function as "intellectual themes, suitable for development and modification at the orator's pleasure ..." They were originally rhetorical aids "towards composing orations," but towards the end of Antiquity they "become clichés, which can be used in any form of literature ..."[5] Curtius' work has stimulated a still-ongoing debate, but there is a growing consensus that his description of the development and nature of the *topos* is both too vague and oversimplistic.[6] Despite progress made by recent scholars, we still lack a

---

[3] Malherbe, "Hellenistic Moralists," 320–25; "Hellenistic Moral Philosophy and the New Testament: A Retrospective Analysis" (Unpublished paper presented at the SBL Annual Meeting, New Orleans, November 1990) 27. The paper gives a brief history of the article; see esp. 23–25.

[4] See, e.g., Malherbe's application of the *topoi* περὶ φιλαδελφίας and περὶ ἡσυχίας to 1 Thess 4:9–12 ("Hellenistic Moralists," 321–24).

[5] Ernst Robert Curtius, *European Literature and the Latin Middle Ages* (tr. Willard R. Trask; Bollingen Series 36; Princeton: Princeton University Press, 1953; reprint 1990) 70; German: *Europäische Literatur und lateinisches Mittelalter* (8th ed.; Bern: Francke, 1973) 79.

[6] Cf. the articles of Wankel ("Alle Menschen müssen sterben") and Pernot ("Lieu et lieu commun") for references to this debate. See also Peter Jehn, ed., *Toposforschung: Eine Dokumentation* (Respublica Literaria 10; Frankfurt: Athenäum, 1972); Max L. Baeumer, ed., *Toposforschung* (Wege der Forschung 395; Darmstadt: Wissenschaftliche Buchgesellschaft, 1973); Dieter Breuer and Helmut Schanze, eds., *Topik: Beiträge zur interdiszi-*

precise description of the *topos* which takes cognizance of all its various meanings and uses. Malherbe correctly identifies "the lack of precision in describing a *topos*" as one of the "problems that have not been addressed."[7]

In this essay I want to consider some of the issues that need to be discussed if we want to obtain greater clarity regarding *topoi*. I should emphasize, however, that this is an exploratory survey, and that I do not intend to give detailed answers to these questions. At most I will attempt to indicate some of the lines of investigation that need to be developed further. Before we look at the issues, it may be helpful to review some recent discussions by NT scholars on this subject.

Views of the Topos *in NT Scholarship*

In a 1953 article entitled "The *Topos* as a Form in the Pauline Paraenesis," David Bradley proposed that the term *topos* be used for "the treatment in independent form of the topic of a proper thought or action, or of a virtue or a vice, etc."[8] According to him, the *topos* is one of "the traditional ethical forms" used in NT paraenesis alongside others, such as the *Haustafeln*, or catalogues of vices and virtues.[9] After considering passages from Greek and Jewish texts on *topoi* such as confidence, wine, and speech, he concludes that as regards *composition*,

> these *topoi* are all self-contained, unitary teachings which have but a loose, and often even an arbitrary, connection with their context. The order in which the passages … appear could be altered without loss of meaning or of value for the teachings of the individual *topoi* involved. They are in reality strung together in much the same way in which the pericopes of the Sermon on the Mount have been joined, sometimes by means of *Stichwörter*, more often without any connection between the adjacent *topoi* being apparent.[10]

---

plinären Diskussion (Kritische Information 99; Munich: Fink, 1981); Lynette Hunter, ed., *Toward a Definition of Topos: Approaches to Analogical Reasoning* (Houndmills, Basingstoke, Hampshire: Macmillan, 1991).

[7] Malherbe, "Hellenistic Moral Philosophy," 24–25. See also his *Moral Exhortation, a Graeco-Roman Sourcebook* (LEC 4; Philadelphia: Westminster Press, 1986) 144; "Hellenistic Moralists," 320 n. 252.

[8] David G. Bradley, "The *Topos* as a Form in the Pauline Paraenesis," *JBL* 72 (1953) 238–46. This article is based on his doctoral dissertation ("The Origins of the Hortatory Materials in the Letters of Paul" [Unpublished Ph.D. thesis, Yale University, 1947]), which was unfortunately not available to me.

[9] Bradley, "*Topos* as a Form," 240.

[10] *Ibid.*, 243.

As to the *form* of the *topos*, Bradley finds "that its distinctive characteristic is that it is composed of more than one sentence dealing with the
same subject. Thus a *topos* may consist of an aggregation of proverbs
or other short teachings on the same topic."[11] On the question of *subject
matter* Bradley observes "that they [sc. *topoi*] include a wide variety of
topics, but have a common denominator in that they are always related
to the problems of daily life and give practical advice on matters of
thought and action which have general, if not universal applicability."[12]
The *topos* has the same *function* as "catalogues of vices and virtues … ;
tables of duties … ; collections of proverbs … ; [and] illustrations from
the lives of great men," namely, to provide the Hellenistic teacher with
"a stock of answers somewhat stereotyped in form and content which
could be used as needed" when confronted with recurrent questions
from hearers or pupils.[13] Finally, according to Bradley a *topos* deals with
a question that is of a general, rather than a specific nature; it is not
addressed to a particular problem facing the community.[14]

I have dwelt on Bradley's article at some length because of the
considerable influence it has had.[15] The main merit of this article lies
in pointing out that NT authors like Paul made use of established
Hellenistic *topoi*, but I believe Bradley is on the wrong track when he
attempts to analyze the *topos* as a "form" among others in keeping with
the principles of Form Criticism.

Bradley's approach was taken still a step further by Terence Mullins.[16] Mullins thinks it is possible to describe the form more precisely
than Bradley does. By analyzing Bradley's examples, Mullins discovers
"four recurring elements":

> There are three essential elements: an *injunction* urging that a certain
> course of behavior be followed or avoided; a *reason* for the injunction;
> and a *discussion* of the logical or practical consequences of the behavior.
> An optional element is the citing of an *analogous situation* to the one dealt
> with in the Topos.[17]

---

[11] *Ibid.*

[12] *Ibid.*, 244.

[13] *Ibid.*, 246.

[14] *Ibid.*, 239–40, 243–46.

[15] See most recently Hermann von Lips, "Die Haustafel als 'Topos' im Rahmen
der urchristlichen Paränese: Beobachtungen anhand des 1. Petrusbriefes und des Titus-
briefes," *NTS* 40 (1994) 261–80, esp. 265 n. 20.

[16] Terence Y. Mullins, "Topos as a New Testament Form," *JBL* 99 (1980) 541–47.

[17] *Ibid.*, 542.

In other examples he finds still another optional element, a *refutation*.[18] Mullins is critical of Bradley's description of the *topos*'s function:

> The Topos as a stereotyped form had a more important function for Paul and the philosophers than to serve up ready-made nuggets for answering common questions. What the Topos supplied was a set of conditions which measured the adequacy of the answers which the user made to common questions. Anyone using the Topos would give a clear indication of the behavior required, would give a reason why that behavior was required, and would indicate one or more consequences which might be expected from such behavior. Its function, therefore, was to assure the speaker or writer that he had given the kind of answer to the question which his audience would be most likely to accept as valid.[19]

As has been pointed out by John Brunt, the characteristics of *topoi* Mullins identified are not true of all *topoi*.[20] Mullins has indeed been misled by Bradley's very narrow selection of examples. The formal elements Mullins listed in fact belong to the rhetorical elaboration of an argument or *thesis* commonly taught and practiced in the Graeco-Roman world;[21] they are not specific to *topoi*. As I shall point out below, it is questionable whether the *topos* should be considered a literary form in the strict form-critical sense. Mullins' recognition of the way *topoi* are often elaborated, however, has merit.

Brunt also criticizes Bradley's idiosyncratic, non-classical, use of the term *topos*. According to him, "the term *topos* does not appear to have been used at all in classical sources for the kind of general teachings that make up the subjects of Bradley's *topoi*."[22] Brunt finally questions Bradley's view that *topoi* did not address a specific situation; whether or not a *topos* is situational depends on the context.[23]

---

[18] *Ibid.*, 547.

[19] *Ibid.*, 546–47.

[20] John C. Brunt, "More on the *Topos* as a New Testament Form," *JBL* 104 (1985) 495–500.

[21] See Burton L. Mack and Vernon K. Robbins, *Patterns of Persuasion in the Gospels* (Foundations & Facets: Literary Facets; Sonoma: Polebridge Press, 1989) 31–67, esp. 51–57; Burton L. Mack, *Rhetoric and the New Testament* (GBS; Minneapolis: Fortress Press, 1990) 41–47.

[22] Brunt, "More on the *Topos* as a New Testament Form," 496–98. He seems unaware, however, of the meaning of the term in rhetorical sources such as the *Progymnasmata*, or its use in philosophical writings; see the discussion below.

[23] *Ibid.*, 499–500.

A different approach, more in line with the rhetorical tradition as represented by Ernst Curtius and Heinrich Lausberg, is taken by Wilhelm Wuellner.[24] He points out that according to ancient views of the *topos*, it has a twofold function: an argumentative-enthymematic function, as well as an elaborative-descriptive one.[25] A similar distinction between "strategic" and "material" *topoi* is used by George Kennedy in his *New Testament Interpretation Through Rhetorical Criticism*.[26]

Other NT scholars deliberately opt for a relatively vague definition of *topoi*, describing them as stereotyped, miniature moral essays,[27] or in Malherbe's words, "as traditional, fairly systematic treatments of moral subjects which make use of common clichés, maxims, short definitions, and so forth, without thereby sacrificing an individual viewpoint."[28]

To summarize the results of this brief survey of the way recent NT scholars suggest we use the term *topos*: It is clear that according to them its use falls into at least two broad categories, namely, the rhetorical or strategic topos, and the moral or substantive topos, although these two categories are sometimes confused. Bradley's *topos* belongs to the latter category. Considering only this type of *topos*, we see that the relationship between its form and content remains problematic, and that there is uncertainty about its function and *Sitz im Leben*. Since many scholars purport to base their own view of the *topos* on ancient usage of the term, we will next briefly consider its terminological history.

History of Topos *as Technical Term*

Although it is difficult to pinpoint its first use, the technical term *topos* appears to have its origin in the Greek *sophistic and rhetorical tradition*.[29] I am not going to discuss the rhetorical *topos* in any detail. This is a complex and well-traversed field, and limitations of space do not allow

---

[24] Wilhelm H. Wuellner, "Toposforschung und Torahinterpretation bei Paulus und Jesus," *NTS* 24 (1978) 463–83. See the description of Curtius's and Lausberg's views below.

[25] "Eine argumentativ-enthymematische und eine amplifikatorisch-darstellerische Funktion" (Wuellner, "Toposforschung und Torahinterpretation," 467).

[26] George A. Kennedy, *New Testament Interpretation Through Rhetorical Criticism* (Chapel Hill: University of North Carolina Press, 1984) 20–22.

[27] Robert W. Funk, *Language, Hermeneutic, and Word of God: The Problem of Language in the New Testament and Contemporary Theology* (New York: Harper and Row, 1966) 255–56; W. G. Doty, *Letters in Primitive Christianity* (GBS; Philadelphia: Fortress Press, 1973) 39.

[28] Malherbe, *Moral Exhortation*, 144.

[29] See Pernot, "Lieu et lieu commun," esp. 255–60, 271–75.

me to make more than a few general observations.[30]

The Greek word τόπος and its Latin equivalent *locus* of course normally mean "place" or "region."[31] *Topoi* in ancient rhetoric thus refer to the "places" in which arguments may be found, that is, the general headings under which one may search for material for one's argument.[32] As such it forms part of the *inventio*. According to Heinrich Lausberg, it has to be kept in mind that

> the *inventio* is not viewed as a creative act … , but as a discovery through remembrance (analogous to the Platonic concept of knowledge): the ideas suitable for the speech are already subconsciously or half-consciously available to the orator as *copia rerum* [material] to draw upon and need only be awoken by the correct memory technique and be kept awake if possible … by constant practice. Memory is thus viewed as a spatial whole, into specific areas ("places": τόποι, *loci*) of which individual ideas are divided. By asking the correct questions … the ideas hidden in the *loci* are called into memory.[33]

It is clear that already in Aristotle the *topos* covered a spectrum of meanings ranging from the more formal to the more substantive.[34] George Kennedy, in discussing Aristotle, distinguishes between "common" or "strategic" *topoi* on the one hand, which provide lines or strategies of argumentation, such as the much used *a fortiori* type of argument, and "material" *topoi*, such as questions of ways and means, war and peace, imports and exports, in deliberative speeches, on the other hand.[35] Even

---

[30] See for a survey Josef Martin, *Antike Rhetorik: Technik und Methode* (Handbuch der Altertumswissenschaft 2; Munich: Beck, 1974) 107–19; Pernot, "Lieu et lieu commun."

[31] LSJ, s.v. τόπος; *Oxford Latin Dictionary*, s.v. *locus*. Most of the other "meanings" listed in these dictionaries derive from the normal meaning.

[32] Cf. Aristotle, *Rhet.* 2.26.1; Theon, *Progymnasmata* (Spengel 106.14–17).

[33] "Die *inventio* wird nicht als ein Schöpfungsvorgang … , sondern als Finden durch Erinnerung (analog der platonischen Auffassung vom Wissen) vorgestellt: die für die Rede geeigneten Gedanken sind im Unterbewußtsein oder Halbbewußtsein des Redners bereits als *copia rerum* vorhanden und brauchen nur durch geschickte Erinnerungstechnik wachgerufen und durch dauernde Übung … möglichst wachgehalten zu werden. Hierbei wird das Gedächtnis als ein räumliches Ganzes vorgestellt, in dessen einzelnen Raumteilen ('Örter': τόποι, *loci*) die einzelnen Gedanken verteilt sind. Durch geeignete Fragen werden … die in den *loci* verborgenen Gedanken in die Erinnerung gerufen" (Heinrich Lausberg, *Elemente der literarischen Rhetorik: Eine Einführung für Studierende der klassischen, romanischen, englischen und deutschen Philologie* [8th ed.; Munich: Max Hueber Verlag, 1984] 24). All translations are my own, unless otherwise indicated.

[34] The term was already in use before Aristotle; see George A. Kennedy, trans., *Aristotle, On Rhetoric: A Theory of Civic Discourse* (New York: Oxford University Press, 1991) 45.

[35] *New Testament Interpretation*, 20–21; *Aristotle, On Rhetoric*, 46 n. 71.

in the latter case, these *topoi* were seen as "topics" to be used, rather
than fully worked out arguments. The tension between form and content in the meaning of *topos* soon gave rise to confusion: Quintilian, for
instance, polemicized against the use of the term to refer to "topics"
such as "against luxury and adultery and so forth;" he wants to restrict
its use to mean "places of arguments, in which arguments lie, and from
which they may be taken."[36] He was, however, fighting a losing battle.[37]

In the later development of rhetorical theory and practice that we
find reflected in the *Progymnasmata* handbooks, the *topos* is defined as "a
discourse [λόγος] elaborating a matter that is agreed upon, whether a
fault or a virtue."[38] As such it may, for example, be contrasted with
a *thesis* (θέσις), because the latter deals with a disputed matter.[39] It
also differs from the *ekphrasis* (ἔκφρασις), since the latter is a "mere"
description of lifeless things, whereas the *topos* is concerned with matters
involving choice, and also demands a moral judgment of the speaker.[40]

In *moral and philosophical writings topos* as a technical term is used in a
sense that can loosely be translated as "topic." I only cite two examples
to illustrate this use. The first comes from the Epicurean philosopher
Philodemus' *On Frank Criticism*:

---

[36] Quintilian, *Inst.* 5.10.20: "locos appello non, ut nunc intellegitur, in luxuriem
et adulterium et similia, sed sedes argumentorum, in quibus latent, ex quibus sunt
petenda" ("By *topoi* I do not mean, as is now understood, 'against luxury and adultery
and so forth,' but places of arguments, in which arguments lie, and from which they
may be taken").

[37] Cf. also Wankel, "Alle Menschen müssen sterben," 131–32.

[38] Theon, *Progymn.* (Spengel 106.5–6): Τόπος ἐστὶ λόγος αὐξητικὸς ὁμολογουμένου
πράγματος ἤτοι ἁμαρτήματος ἢ ἀνδραγαθήματος ("A *topos* is a discourse [λόγος] elaborating a matter that is agreed upon, whether a fault or a virtue"). Cf. also Hermogenes, *Progymn.* 6: Ὁ τόπος ὁ κοινὸς προσαγορευόμενος αὔξησιν ἔχει τοῦ ὁμολογουμένου
πράγματος ("The so-called common *topos* entails elaboration of a matter that is agreed
upon").

[39] Hermogenes, *Progymn.* 11.28–30: Διαφέρει δὲ τόπου ἡ θέσις, ὅτι ὁ μὲν τόπος ἐστὶν
ὁμολογουμένου πράγματος αὔξησις, ἡ δὲ θέσις ἀμφισβητουμένου πράγματος ζήτησις
("The *thesis* differs from the *topos*, because the *topos* is an elaboration of a matter that
is agreed upon, while the *thesis* is an investigation of a disputed matter").

[40] Cf. Theon *Progymn.* (Spengel 119.7–14): διαφέρει δὲ ἀλλήλων πρῶτον μέν, ὅτι ὁ
μὲν τόπος περὶ τῶν ἐκ προαιρέσεώς ἐστιν, ἡ δὲ ἔκφρασις τὰ πολλὰ περὶ τῶν ἀψύχων
καὶ ἀπροαιρέτων γίνεται, δεύτερον δὲ ὅτι ἐν μὲν τῷ τόπῳ τὰ πράγματα ἀπαγγέλλοντες
προστίθεμεν καὶ τὴν ἡμετέραν γνώμην ἢ χρηστὰ ἢ φαῦλα λέγοντες εἶναι, ἐν δὲ τῇ ἐκφράσει
ψιλὴ τῶν πραγμάτων ἐστὶν ἡ ἀπαγγελία ("They differ from one another, in the first place,
because the *topos* is concerned with matters involving choice, while the *ekphrasis* mainly
has to do with lifeless things not subject to choice; and in the second place, in the *topos*,
when we describe things, we also add our judgment, saying whether they are good or
bad, while in the *ekphrasis* we find a mere description of things").

εἰ σοφὸς | τὰ περ[ὶ] αὑτὸν ἀναθή(ε|ται τοῖς φίλοις μετὰ π[αρ|ρη(ίας. *
τὸ τοίνυν ὑπ᾽ ἐνί|ων ἐν [τ]ῶι τόπωι τούτω[ι | ζητούμενον, εἰ σοφ[ὸς τὰ |
π[ερ]ὶ αὑτὸν ἀναθή(εται[ι | το[ῖ]ς φίλοις μετὰ παρ[ρη(ί|ας ...

Whether a wise man will communicate his own {errors} to his friends with frankness.
As for the matter which is explored by some on this topic, {namely}
whether the wise man will communicate his own {errors} to his friends
with frankness ...[41]

The text contains a section heading (italicized in the Greek and both
in the translation), one of twelve in the extant portion of this treatise,
which is then referred to as a "topic." The title of this *topos* is in the
form of a question, as are the other eleven section titles in *On Frank
Criticism*:

(1) Frg. 53: "Whether they will declare things of their own and of one
another to their fellow-students."

(2) Frg. 56: "[Whether it seems to us that one will slip up in accord
with] the [perfection] of reason [by means of what is precon-
ceived.]"

(3) Frg. 67: "Whether he will also speak frankly to those who do not
endure frank criticism, and to one who is [irascible] ..."

(4) Frg. 70: "How will he handle those who have become angry
toward him because of his frank criticism?"

(5) Frg. 74: "Whether he is well-disposed toward us; whether he is
intense in his goodwill; whether he has jettisoned some of the
things charged against him, even if not perfected in everything;
whether toward us and toward [others] [he will be] thankful ..."

(6) Frg. 81 (=83 N): "Whether a wise man will communicate his own
{errors} to his friends with frankness."

(7) Frg. 88 (=94 N): "How will we recognize the one who has endured
frank criticism graciously and the one who is pretending {to do
so}?"

(8) Col. Ia: "...[to distinguish] one who is frank from a polite disposition and one who is so from a vulgar one."

(9) Col. XXa: "...how, [when they recognize] that some of their
number are more intelligent, and in particular that some of them
are teachers, do they not abide frank criticism?"

---

[41] Philodemus, *On Frank Criticism* frg. 81.1–9; ed. and trans. Konstan, et al., *Philodemus:
On Frank Criticism*, 84–85.

(10) Col. XXIb: "[Why does womankind not accept frank criticism with pleasure?]"

(11) Col. XXIIb: "Why is it that, when other things are equal, those who are illustrious both in resources and reputations abide {frank criticism} less well {than others}?"

(12) Col. XXIVa: "Why is it that old men are more annoyed {by frankness}?"[42]

This example illustrates two points I want to emphasize: (a) In the first place, questions are very commonly used in moral and philosophical writings as "titles" of *topoi*, as may easily be demonstrated by, for example, the titles of Philodemus' writings, the diatribes of Musonius Rufus, Plutarch's *Moralia*, the chapters of Epictetus' *Discourses*, and Maximus of Tyre's *Philosophical Orations*.[43] (Whether these titles are original or the work of a redactor, is immaterial for our purpose.) As such, they become important markers for the presence of *topoi*. (b) Secondly, a *topos* such as *frank criticism* (παρρησία) may itself consist of subordinate *topoi*.

My second example comes from Hierocles the Stoic's discussion of marriage:

Ἐν δὲ τῷ περὶ τοῦ γάμου καὶ τῆς παιδοποιίας τόπῳ θετέος ἐστὶ καὶ ὁ τῆς πολυτεκνίας λόγος.

To the *topos* on marriage and the procreation of children also belongs the discussion [λόγος] about having many children.[44]

We may note the following: (a) The *topos* itself may again contain subtopics, such as "having many children" (πολυτεκνία). (b) The *topos* of πολυτεκνία is here referred to as a λόγος, which may simply be translated "subject," but more probably indicates an extensive discussion.[45] (c) The title of the *topos On marriage and the procreation of children* is indicated by the preposition περί, here translated "on." The use of περί (or in the Latin *de*) to indicate *topoi* is even more common than using the interrogative form.

[42] For these headings, see Konstan, et al., *Philodemus: On Frank Criticism*, 8–9.

[43] Cf. also Malherbe, "Hellenistic Moralists," 320–21.

[44] Quoted in Stobaeus, *Anth.* 4.24a.14 = H. von Arnim, *Hierokles, Ethische Elementarlehre (Papyrus 9780): Nebst den bei Stobäus erhaltenen ethischen Excerpten aus Hierokles* (Berliner Klassikertexte 4; Berlin: Weidmann, 1906) 55. For the construction of θετέος with ἐν cf. Philo, *De vita Mosis* 2.235.

[45] For the translation "subject" cf. LSJ, s.v. λόγος VIII ("thing spoken of, subject-matter"); and Malherbe's translation of the passage (*Moral Exhortation*, 103). For λόγος as

In modern literary criticism, the term *topos* has come to be used for any conventional or recurring theme or expression, often in a pejorative sense as "cliché." As we have seen, modern literary study of *topoi* is heavily influenced by Ernst Curtius' work, *European Literature and the Latin Middle Ages*, which is itself a study of the development of various literary *topoi*. Curtius' notion of the *topos* is described by one of his students, Heinrich Lausberg, as follows:

> The *topos* [in the sense of E. R. Curtius] is an infinite ... idea which, through schooling, literary tradition, or similar educational means has become the common possession of at least certain social groups within a cultural circle (for instance, of young people, of poets), and is now applied finitely by an author to his finite ... subject in an extensive ... or short (allusive ...) form.[46]

Examples of *topoi* discussed by Curtius are the *puer senex* ("the aged boy") and the *locus amoenus* ("the ideal landscape").[47] His description of *topoi* as clichés, which now have a pejorative meaning, is unfortunate.[48] As Hermann Wankel proposes, we should rather use the term *topos* in a neutral sense for recurring themes, images, arguments, and so forth—this could cover a spectrum of uses, from the very unimaginative and conventional, on the one hand, to the creative and original, on the other.[49]

Proposals for Using the Term Topos

Against the background given above I wish to make a few suggestions about the use of the term *topos* in NT and related research.

"discussion" cf. LSJ, s.v. III.2, VI.3; also the definition of a *topos* as an elaborated λόγος given by the *Progymnasmata* (quoted n. 38 above).

[46] Heinrich Lausberg, *Handbook of Literary Rhetoric: A Foundation for Literary Study*, ed. David E. Orton and R. Dean Anderson; trans. Matthew T. Bliss, Annemiek Jansen and David E. Orton (Leiden: Brill, 1998) 494 n. 1. The quotation originally comes from Lausberg's abridgment of his larger work: *Elemente*, 38–39, §83.

[47] *European Literature*, 98–101, 183–202.

[48] A strict distinction is made between the rhetorical *topos* and Curtius's "common place" by Pernot, "Lieu et lieu commun," 253–54, 271. He also cites E. Mertner, "Topos und Commonplace," in *Toposforschung: Eine Dokumentation*, ed. Peter Jehn (Respublica Literaria 10; Frankfurt: Athenäum, 1972) 28–34; George A. Kennedy, *The Art of Persuasion in Greece*, vol. 1 of *A History of Rhetoric* (Princeton: Princeton University Press, 1963) 102; George A. Kennedy, *Classical Rhetoric and Its Christian and Secular Tradition from Ancient to Modern Times* (Chapel Hill: University of North Carolina Press; London: Croom Helm, 1980) 71–72.

[49] Wankel, "Alle Menschen müssen sterben," 132–33.

I think it must have become obvious that when modern scholars use
the term *topos*, they do not use it in a strict classical sense (whatever that
may mean).[50] At the same time, it is important to distinguish carefully
between the various denotata of the term when used to describe and
interpret ancient texts. In this regard, I suggest that it would be useful
to keep in mind the Graeco-Roman phenomena associated with this
term in Antiquity, such as we have encountered in the previous section
of this essay. Although the term *topos* is used in different contexts, I suggest that the notion of an ordered cognitive space underlies all these
uses. Some of the principles according to which this space is organized
may be universally valid (such as those underlying the strategic rhetorical *topoi*), but on the whole, the topography of this cognitive space is
culturally determined. Something that is a *topos* in one culture may not
be so in another: a *topos* depends upon, and expresses, a cultural consensus.[51] (This conclusion obviously has important implications for the
problem of determining the cultural roots of the NT.)

Despite this common ground, I think it is useful to distinguish three
types of *topoi*.

The first type may be called the *logical* or *rhetorical topos*: these would
be the "strategic" *topoi*, providing lines of argumentation or schemes
of thought rather than "material" ideas.[52] A very common example of
this type in the NT is the argument *a minore* (e.g., Matt 6:30: "If God
so clothes the grass of the field, which is alive today and tomorrow is
thrown into the oven, will he not much more clothe you?") or *a maiore*
(e.g., Matt 5:44–45: "But I say to you, Love your enemies and pray for
those who persecute you, so that you may be children of your Father
in heaven; for he makes his sun rise on the evil and on the good, and
sends rain on the righteous and on the unrighteous").[53]

The second type would be the *literary topos*. Literary *topoi* consist of
literary themes or motifs that are used over and over again, often only
as an allusion, and not in a worked-out form. Wankel provides an
excellent discussion of the well-known classical example, "Everybody

---

[50] See especially the discussion by Pernot, "Lieu et lieu commun."

[51] Cf. the notion in the *Progymnasmata* that a *topos* is about something that is agreed
upon (references in n. 38 above).

[52] See the valuable survey by Edward P. J. Corbett, *Classical Rhetoric for the Modern
Student* (3d ed.; New York: Oxford University Press, 1990) 94–143. Cf. also Pernot, "Lieu
et lieu commun," 256–71.

[53] All NT translations are from the NRSV.

has to die."[54] Because of the non-literary nature of most NT texts, this type is perhaps not that well-represented in the NT. A possible example may be the younger-son motif in the Parable of the Prodigal Son (Luke 15:11–32).[55] The "gloominess" of the apparently pious person in Matt 6:16 is another example.[56]

The third type is the *moral* or *philosophical topos*. It is a "material" *topos* like the second type, and the difference between them is not always clear-cut. An important difference for our purposes is that although these *topoi* may often function simply by way of allusion or implication, we do find lengthy treatments of them in Hellenistic moral writings. It is on this *topos* that I want to concentrate in the rest of this essay; when I use the term *topos* in what follows, I therefore mean the moral or philosophical *topos*.

A *topos* may be distinguished from another topic by its traditional subject matter, evidenced by the fact that it recurs in the writings of different authors, and by the conventional treatment it receives.[57] If we, for example, just glance at the titles of works representing different philosophical schools such as Philodemus' treatises (Phld.), the diatribes of Musonius Rufus (Mus.), Plutarch's *Moralia* (Plut.), the chapters of Epictetus' *Discourses* (Epict.), Maximus of Tyre's *Philosophical Orations* (Max. Tyr.), and the Hellenistic Pythagorean treatises (Pyth.), we find that the following topics are treated over and over again:

(a) Marriage (Phld., Plut., Mus., Pyth.), sexual love (Phld., Mus., Plut., Max. Tyr.), the household (Phld., Pyth.), parents and children (Mus., Epict., Plut., Pyth.), the role of women (Mus., Pyth.)
(b) Friendship, frank speech and flattery (Phld., Plut., Epict., Max. Tyr.)
(c) Education and training (Phld., Mus., Plut., Epict., Max. Tyr., Pyth.)
(d) Statesmanship (Phld., Mus., Plut., Pyth.)

---

[54] Wankel, "Alle Menschen müssen sterben."

[55] The younger son is often depicted as the cleverer or the hero in folk tales. If this *topos* is indeed at work in the parable, Jesus is using it to confound the audience's expectation: the "hero" is neither the younger nor the elder son, but the father; see J. C. Thom, "Gelykenisse en betekenis," *Scriptura* 9 (1983) 30–43.

[56] See for discussion and references to ancient texts Hans Dieter Betz, *The Sermon on the Mount: A Commentary on the Sermon on the Mount, Including the Sermon on the Plain (Matthew 5:3–7:27 and Luke 6:20–49)* (Hermeneia; Minneapolis: Fortress Press, 1995) 420–21.

[57] See Malherbe, *Moral Exhortation*, 144–45; Malherbe, "Hellenistic Moralists," 320–21.

(e) Anger and other passions (Phld., Plut., Epict., Max. Tyr., Pyth.)
(f) Pleasure and pain (Plut., Max. Tyr.)
(g) Tranquility and equanimity (Epict., Max. Tyr., Pyth.)
(h) Progress in virtue (Mus., Plut., Epict., Max. Tyr.)
(i) Vices (Phld., Mus., Plut.)
(j) Personal adornment (Mus., Epict., Pyth.)
(k) Justice (Pyth. [numerous fragments])
(l) Different ways of life (βίοι) (Phld., Mus., Plut., Epict., Max. Tyr.)
(m) Wealth and poverty (Phld., Plut., Epict.)
(n) Providence, fate and suffering (Phld., Plut., Epict., Max. Tyr., Pyth.)
(o) Piety and the gods (Phld., Plut., Epict., Max. Tyr., Pyth.)

Such lists may easily be extended if we cast our net wider to include other Graeco-Roman writings as well.[58]

Although authors from different traditions may differ in their treatment of a *topos*, there appears to be a common approach which may best be expressed as a shared set of questions. We have already seen how Philodemus discusses the *topos* of παρρησία, *frank criticism*, in terms of a series of questions. Another example is Aristotle's treatment of *friendship* (*Nicomachean Ethics* Bks. 8–9), in which he attempts to answer questions[59] such as:

(a) What is the definition and basis of friendship? (*Eth. Nic.* 8.2.1–4; 9.4.1–9.6.4)
(b) What kinds of friendship are there? (*Eth. Nic.* 8.1.7; 8.3.1; 8.4.6)
(c) What is the perfect form of friendship? (*Eth. Nic.* 8.3.6)
(d) Is it possible for bad people to be friends? (*Eth. Nic.* 8.1.7; 8.3.2)
(e) Is it possible to have many true friends? (*Eth. Nic.* 8.6.2; 9.10.1–6)
(f) Is it possible for people of unequal status to be friends? (*Eth. Nic.* 8.7.1–6)
(g) What are the claims of friendship? (*Eth. Nic.* 8.12.8–8.13.1)
(h) What are the reasons for disputes between friends? (*Eth. Nic.* 8.13.2–9.1.8)
(i) How should a conflict of claims of different friends be handled? (*Eth. Nic.* 9.2.1–10)

---

[58] For a more complete list, see André Oltramare, *Les origines de la diatribe romaine* (Lausanne: Payot, 1926) 301–6. This work was not available to me; it is cited by Malherbe, "Hellenistic Moralists," 321 n. 253. Cf. also the *topoi* treated by Malherbe, *Moral Exhortation*, 144–61.

[59] The term Aristotle uses is ἀπορία.

(j) Under what circumstances may a friendship be dissolved? (*Eth. Nic.* 9.3.1–5)

(k) Is friendship necessary for happiness? (*Eth. Nic.* 9.9.1–10)

(l) Do we need friends more in prosperity or in adversity? (*Eth. Nic.* 9.11.1–6)

In this way, the *topos* becomes a collection of *theses* (θέσεις), that is, issues to be debated.[60] The individuality of an author is perhaps to be found not so much in the questions asked, but in the way they are answered, although there is often substantial agreement between various authors about the answers as well.

The moral universe in the Graeco-Roman world is thus divided into regions or *topoi*, each with its own internal structure, based on the questions it is meant to answer. *Topoi* are also connected to one another in terms of a variety of semantic relationships: the *topos* of friendship, for example, is related to that of frank criticism, but also to *topoi* such as marriage and family, patronage, citizenship, piety, and self-sufficiency,[61] each of which in turn is again linked to other *topoi*. The topical landscape forms a intricate network of relationships. When we speak of the form of a *topos*, we should in the first place think of its internal semantic structure and its interconnectedness with other *topoi*. The textual realization of a *topos*, on the other hand, may differ widely depending on the rhetorical requirements of the context. I would therefore, for example, hesitate to speak of the *Haustafeln* as a *topos*, as some scholars do: the *Haustafeln* is rather a specific literary *form* in which the *topos* of household duties is expressed.[62]

Once the moral world has been mapped out in terms of *topoi*, an author can use these *topoi* as points of reference: he does not have to describe the topic in detail; a few reminders are sufficient. By using *topoi*, an author at the same time embeds his own text in the moral and cultural discourse of his time and evokes a wider sphere of resonance

---

[60] In Philodemus, Περὶ οἰκονομίας col. 12.28 a τόπος is a topic; this topic is then treated as a *thesis*. Cf. Elizabeth Asmis, "Philodemus' Epicureanism," *ANRW* II.36.4 (1990) 2387; see esp. 2394: "[Philodemus'] 'Περὶ παρρησίας' is organized, at least partially, as a series of answers to problems (τόποι)." The relation between a *topos* and a *thesis* is discussed by Pernot, "Lieu et lieu commun," 253–84, esp. 275–83.

[61] See on the latter Abraham J. Malherbe, "Paul's Self-Sufficiency (Philippians 4:11)," in *Friendship, Flattery, and Frankness of Speech: Studies on Friendship in the New Testament World* (NovTSup 82; ed. John T. Fitzgerald; Leiden: Brill, 1996) 125–39.

[62] Contra von Lips, "Die Haustafel als 'Topos,'" 265. Von Lips does not think there is enough evidence to consider the *Haustafeln* a literary form.

than can be explicated in a particular text. A *topos* may thus also provide an underlying coherence to a text that is not immediately obvious on the surface.

Whether or not a *topos* has a contextual or situational relevance, surely depends on the way the author uses the *topos*.[63] A *topos* is clearly not identified with a particular *Sitz im Leben*. As we have seen, a moral *topos* is often amplified in the form of *theses*, questions of a general nature. Just as a *thesis* may be applied to a specific situation and thus become an *hypothesis* (ὑπόθεσις), a *topos* may evidently also be used to throw light on a real-world situation. In the Epistle to the Philippians, for example, Paul can base his depiction of the true Christian community on a topical typology of friendship; in 1 Thess 4:9–12 he uses the topos περὶ ἡσυχίας to warn the church against isolationism.[64]

My final suggestion concerns the value of *topoi* for the interpretation of texts.[65] One obvious benefit is that a good understanding of the *topoi* present in a text helps to identify the issues involved and to locate the text within the cultural and moral discourse of the time. Jerome Neyrey's identification of the *topos* of true deity underlying Heb 7:3 provides a good example from the NT.[66] A Hellenistic example would be the Pythagorean *Golden Verses*. This is an early Hellenistic moralistic text which I have treated in detail elsewhere.[67] Most scholars consider this poem to be a mere compilation of unconnected sayings, but if we consider it from a topical perspective, a different picture emerges. Here I confine myself to two passages.

> τῶν δ' ἄλλων ἀρετῇ ποιεῦ φίλον ὅστις ἄριστος.
> πραέσι δ' εἶκε λόγοισ' ἔργοισί τ' ἐπωφελίμοισι.
> μηδ' ἔχθαιρε φίλον σὸν ἁμαρτάδος εἵνεκα μικρῆς,
> ὄφρα δύνῃ· δύναμις γὰρ ἀνάγκης ἐγγύθι ναίει.

---

[63] Cf. Funk, *Language, Hermeneutic, and Word of God*, 255–56.

[64] John T. Fitzgerald, "Philippians in the Light of Some Ancient Discussions of Friendship," *Friendship, Flattery, and Frankness of Speech*, 141–60, esp. 157–60; Malherbe, "Hellenistic Moralists," 321–24; cf. also 324: "[Paul] was aware of the temptations that faced a group like his Thessalonian church, and ... he used the *topoi appropriate to the situation* to guard against them" (my emphasis).

[65] For the heuristic value of *topoi*, see Baeumer, *Toposforschung*, xiv, 251. An important correction is made by Lothar Bornscheuer, "Bemerkungen zur Toposforschung," *Mittellateinisches Jahrbuch* 11 (1976) 314.

[66] Jerome H. Neyrey, "'Without Beginning of Days or End of Life' (Hebrews 7:3): Topos for a True Deity," *CBQ* 53 (1991) 439–55. See also the examples treated in the articles cited in n. 64 above.

[67] Johan C. Thom, *The Pythagorean Golden Verses: With Introduction and Commentary* (Religions in the Graeco-Roman World 123; Leiden: Brill, 1995).

Among others, choose as your friend him who excels in virtue.
Yield to his gentle words and useful actions,
and do not hate your friend for a small fault,
for as long as you are able to do so. For ability lives near necessity.

(*Golden Verses* 5–8)[68]

Verses 5–8 refer to the *topos* of *friendship*: if we compare these verses
with Aristotle's list of questions regarding friendship,[69] we find allusions
to questions (a) (the definition and basis of friendship); (b) (different
kinds of friendship); (c) (the perfect form of friendship); (g) (the claims
of friendship); (h) (the reasons for disputes); (i) (handling conflicts); and
(j) (the dissolution of friendship). A good understanding of the *topos* thus
helps to identify the issues involved and to locate the text within the
broader moral discourse.[70]

A *topos* may also help us to understand connections within the text
between apparently unrelated material, as in *Golden Verses* 9–20:

Ταῦτα μὲν οὕτως ἴσθι, κρατεῖν δ᾽ εἰθίζεο τῶνδε·
10 γαστρὸς μὲν πρώτιστα καὶ ὕπνου λαγνείης τε
καὶ θυμοῦ. πρήξῃς δ᾽ αἰσχρόν ποτε μήτε μετ᾽ ἄλλου
μήτ᾽ ἰδίῃ· πάντων δὲ μάλιστ᾽ αἰσχύνεο σαυτόν.
εἶτα δικαιοσύνην ἀσκεῖν ἔργῳ τε λόγῳ τε,
μηδ᾽ ἀλογίστως σαυτὸν ἔχειν περὶ μηδὲν ἔθιζε,
15 ἀλλὰ γνῶθι μέν, ὡς θανέειν πέπρωται ἅπασιν,
χρήματα δ᾽ ἄλλοτε μὲν κτᾶσθαι φιλεῖ, ἄλλοτ᾽ ὀλέσθαι.
ὅσσα δὲ δαιμονίαισι τύχαις βροτοὶ ἄλγε᾽ ἔχουσιν,
ἣν ἂν μοῖραν ἔχῃς, ταύτην φέρε μηδ᾽ ἀγανάκτει.
ἰᾶσθαι δὲ πρέπει καθ᾽ ὅσον δύνῃ, ὧδε δὲ φράζευ·
20 οὐ πάνυ τοῖς ἀγαθοῖς τούτων πολὺ Μοῖρα δίδωσιν.

Know the above then, and accustom yourself to be master of the
    following:
10 first of all, of your stomach, of sleep, of lust,
    and of anger. Never do anything shameful, neither with somebody else,
    nor on your own. Feel shame before yourself most of all.
    Furthermore, practice justice both in deed and in word,
    and accustom yourself not to be without thought about anything,
15 but know that death has been destined for all,
    and that property is wont to be acquired now, tomorrow lost.
    But whatever pains mortals suffer through the divine workings of fate,
    whatever lot you have, bear it and do not be angry.

[68] Text and translation for this and the following passage from Thom, *Pythagorean Golden Verses*, 94–95.
[69] See above at n. 59.
[70] For a detailed discussion, see Thom, *Pythagorean Golden Verses*, 119–25.

It is fitting that it be healed as far as possible, and say to yourself as
follows.
20   Fate does not give very many of these sufferings to the good.

(*Golden Verses* 9–20)

Golden Verses 9–20 are based on the *topos* of *cardinal virtues*, which in
turn consists of the smaller *topoi on moderation* (σωφροσύνη, vv. 10–12),
justice (δικαιοσύνη, v. 13), *moral insight* (φρόνησις, vv. 14–16), and *courage*
(ἀνδρεία, vv. 17–20). Simply recognizing these *topoi* already provides us
with an underlying connective framework that is not immediately obvious on the surface. A closer look further reveals meanings suggested by
the juxtaposition and interplay of *topoi*, but not overtly expressed. One
example: the *topos* of *justice* mentioned in line 13 includes as forms of
injustice *hybris* (ὕβρις) (i.e., transgressing one's limits as a human being),
as well as πλεονεξία (greed). The *moral insight* mentioned in the next
three verses (14–16) again refers to the limits of human existence, and
contains an indirect warning against greed.[71] This interaction takes
place on the level of the topical substructure and is only recognized
when one has detailed knowledge of the individual *topoi*.

A better understanding of the *topoi* involved may in the same way
provide insight into the compositional integrity of NT texts such as the
Sermon on the Mount (Matt 5–7), which in the past has often been seen
as a loose concatenation of passages, without strong internal cohesion.[72]
One thinks, for example, of the *topos* of δικαιοσύνη ("righteousness" or
"justice"), which appears to underlie most, if not all of the Sermon (cf.
Matt 5:6, 10, 20; 6:1, 33). This entails, amongst other things, giving both
God and human beings their due (cf., e.g., Matt 5:17–48; 6:9–14, 24;
7:1–12) and the notions of due reward, fairness, balance, proportionality
and reciprocity (e.g., Matt 5:3–11, 19–20, 43–48; 6:1–6, 14–15, 16–18;
7:1–12, 21–27).[73] Another *topos* encountered in the *Golden Verses* that also
plays a role in the Sermon on the Mount is that of φρόνησις ("moral
insight"), which includes an awareness of the limits imposed by the
human condition and a sense of priorities (cf., e.g., Matt 5:3, 6; 6:1,
3–4, 6, 8, 17–18, 19–34; 7:13–14).[74]

---

[71] See ibid., 132–40, for a full discussion.
[72] See, e.g., Bradley, "*Topos* as a Form," 243 (quoted at n. 10 above). The composition
of the Sermon on the Mount is discussed in detail by Betz (*Sermon on the Mount*, 44–66).
[73] An excellent overview of the *topos* is provided by Albrecht Dihle, "Gerechtigkeit,"
RAC 10 (1978) 233–360.
[74] See on this *topos* Thom, *Pythagorean Golden Verses*, 135–39, 155, with the literature

Finally, the point of a passage may lie in its manipulation or adaptation of a *topos* that is assumed. Malherbe recently demonstrated how the *topos* of πλεονεξία is adapted and Christianized in Luke 12:13–34.[75] Another example from Luke illustrates the manipulation of a *topos*: In the Parable of the Prodigal Son (Luke 15:11–32), the apparent issue is δικαιοσύνη, the question of the fairness of the father's treatment of both the younger and the elder son. It becomes clear, however, that both sons' claims to justice are in fact based on πλεονεξία, greed, while the father's boundless love transcends the petty demands of a strict justice.[76]

Conclusion

In the words of Milton, "the mind is its own place" and has the ability to order and make sense of everyday experience by creating its own world of meaning. *Topoi* form part of this process of mental and cultural construction. By gaining insight into ancient *topoi*, we also enter the worldviews of ancient authors.

---

cited there.

[75] Abraham J. Malherbe, "The Christianization of a *Topos* (Luke 12:13–34)," *NovT* (1996) 123–35.

[76] See on this parable also Thom, "Gelykenisse en betekenis."

NOMOS PLUS GENITIVE NOUN IN PAUL
THE HISTORY OF GOD'S LAW

J. Louis Martyn

Translating Nomos *in Paul*

One hardly need mention, much less defend, the point that the word *nomos* (νόμος), usually translated "law," plays a crucial role in the thought of numerous early Christian authors. Paul is alone, however, in using it numerous times and with sophistication in the locution *nomos* plus another noun in the genitive case. Listed in chronological order, the sixteen occurrences are as follows:

Gal 6:2:	ὁ νόμος τοῦ Χριστοῦ ("of Christ")
1 Cor 9:9:	ἐν τῷ Μωϋσέως νόμῳ ("of Moses")
1 Cor 9:21a:	ἄνομος θεοῦ ("of God")
1 Cor 9:21b:	ἔννομος Χριστοῦ ("of Christ")
Rom 3:27a:	[νόμος] τῶν ἔργων ("of works")
Rom 3:27b:	διὰ νόμου πίστεως ("of faith")
Rom 7:2:	ἀπὸ τοῦ νόμου τοῦ ἀνδρός ("of the man/husband")
Rom 7:22:	τῷ νόμῳ τοῦ θεοῦ ("of God")
Rom 7:23a:	τῷ νόμῳ τοῦ νοός μου ("of my mind")
Rom 7:23b:	ἐν τῷ νόμῳ τῆς ἁμαρτίας ("of sin")
Rom 7:25a:	νόμῳ θεοῦ ("of God")
Rom 7:25b:	νόμῳ ἁμαρτίας ("of sin")
Rom 8:2a:	ὁ νόμος τοῦ πνεύματος τῆς ζωῆς ἐν Χριστῷ Ἰησοῦ ("of the spirit of life in Christ Jesus")
Rom 8:2b:	ἀπὸ τοῦ νόμου τῆς ἁμαρτίας καὶ τοῦ θανάτου ("of sin and death")
Rom 8:7:	τῷ νόμῳ τοῦ θεοῦ ("of God")
Rom 9:31:	νόμον δικαιοσύνης ("of righteousness")

In at least seven of these instances the locution is clearly a literal and specific reference to "the Law of Moses," that Law being "the Law of God" (1 Cor 9:9, 21a; Rom 3:27a; 7:2, 22, 25a; 8:7).[1] Some exegetes see the same referent in several or most—or indeed all—of

---

[1] Concerning the expression in Rom 7:2, see now Will Deming, "Paul, Gaius, and 'the Law of Persons': The Conceptualization of Roman Law in the Early Classical Period," *CQ* 51 (2001) 218–30.

the remaining instances.[2] Others, however, confidently find that in a number of cases—usually four, Gal 6:2; 1Cor 9:21b; Rom 3:27b; and Rom 8:2a—Paul employs the term *nomos* in a "general" way to refer to a norm or a manner of life that is in some setting appropriate or customary.[3] That is the interpretation proposed, for example, by H. Räisänen in his influential book *Paul and the Law*.[4]

About Gal 6:2, Räisänen says, "The 'law' of Christ is not literally a law … *Nomos* is being used in a loose sense … To fulfill the *nomos* of Christ is simply to live the way a life in Christ is to be lived" (80–81). Similarly, in 1Cor 9:21b, as in Gal 6:2: "the talk of 'the law of Christ' refers simply to the way of life characteristic of the church of Christ" (82). Regarding Rom 3:27b, he says, "[Here] *nomos* must be metaphorical; the new 'order of faith' is being referred to" (52). And in Rom 8:2a Paul is not referring literally to Law; he "is speaking of the 'order' of the Spirit" (52).

In a separate philological study Räisänen collected a great number of Greek texts, from Hesiod to Gregory of Nyssa and Theodore of Mopsuestia, in which *nomos* is used in a general sense to speak of what is customary in some setting, that setting often being indicated by an accompanying genitive noun (νόμος πολέμου ["the rules of war"] is frequent).[5]

---

[2] See, e.g., E. Lohse, "ὁ νόμος τοῦ πνεύματος τῆς ζωῆς: Exegetische Anmerkungen zu Röm 8,2," *Neues Testament und christliche Existenz*, ed. H. D. Betz and L. Schotroff (Tübingen: Mohr-Siebeck, 1973) 279–287; P. von der Osten-Sacken, "Befreiung durch das Gesetz," *Richte unsere Füsse auf den Weg des Friedens*, ed. A. Baudis et al. (München: Kaiser, 1979) 349–360; H. Hübner, *Das Gesetz bei Paulus* (Göttingen: Vandenhoeck & Ruprecht, 1980) 118–129. Cf. more recently the interpretation of Rom 3:27b, Rom 8:2a, and Gal 6:2 in J. D. G. Dunn, *The Theology of Paul the Apostle* (Eerdmans: Grand Rapids, 1998): The Law of faith is the Law that calls for and facilitates "the same sort of trust in God as that out of which Abraham lived" (641); the Law of the Spirit is "the positive side of the divided law" (646); in the locution the Law of Christ we see "that Jesus himself provided Paul with a model for the conduct prescribed by the law" (657).

[3] The general denotation is, in fact, the earliest meaning of the term *nomos*; see n. 5 below.

[4] *Paul and the Law* (Tübingen: Mohr-Siebeck, 1983). E. P. Sanders finds the general meaning ("principle") in Rom 3:27b and Rom 8:2a, but the Torah in Gal 6:2 (*Paul, the Law, and the Jewish People* [Philadelphia: Fortress, 1983] 15 n. 26, 97–98). See also M. Winger, "Meaning and Law," *JBL* 117 (1998) 105–110, where an impressive linguistic analysis leads to the conclusion that "the burden of proof rests with those who argue that *nomos* in Paul's letters always refers to Jewish *nomos*" (110; see further nn. 7, 11, and 23 below).

[5] "Sprachliches zum Spiel des Paulus mit *nomos*," *Glaube und Gerechtigkeit: In Memoriam Rafael Gyllenberg*, ed. J. Kiilunen, et al. (Helsinki: Kirjapaino, 1983) 131–154. One does well to speak in this connection of a general employment of the term *nomos*, rather than to refer to it as a metaphorical or figurative use. For the history of the term shows

Polyaenus [Historicus], for example, speaks of walking νόμῳ πομπῆς, meaning to walk in a procession (*Strategemata* 5.5.2). And to Räisänen's labors we can add the observation that Josephus and Philo use the locution sometimes specifically to refer to the Torah ("the Laws of Moses" are "the Law of God;" Josephus, *Ant.* 11.121, 124, 130) and sometimes generally to speak of what is proper in a certain setting: παρὰ τὸν τῆς ἱστορίας νόμον refers to the rules of historiography (Josephus, *B.J.* 1.11); οἱ σωφροσύνης νόμοι are the rules of modesty (Philo, *Spec. Leg.* 4.96).[6] Might not the same be true of Paul? On the theoretical level that question is surely to be answered in the affirmative.

The Underlying Problem

Unease about this reading begins to creep in, however, with two observations. First, all of the Pauline texts for which the so-called "general" reading is usually proposed are positive references to *nomos*.[7] We are entitled to wonder whether the interpretation of *nomos* plus genitive is being unduly influenced by an implicit assumption regarding Paul's theology: If one considers the apostle's attitude toward the Torah to be fundamentally negative (2 Corinthians 3 is often cited), then one may conclude that these positive references must speak of something other than the Torah. The final sentence of Räisänen's collection of comparative texts is indeed telling. Noting that in Rom 8:2 ὁ νόμος τοῦ

---

that its earliest denotation was that of a general reference to what is customary (e.g., Hesiod, *Works and Days* 276–78: Zeus gave one *nomos* to human beings, another to animals that eat one another). In short, in the history of Greek literature the movement is from general to specific, rather than the reverse.

[6] Lacking in Räisänen's extensive collection—and in all of the lexica—are extra-Pauline texts in which a general use of *nomos* is employed to form a contrast with a specific use. See comments on Rom 8:2 below.

[7] There is a significant exception: In a private communication M. Winger has kindly explicated his study mentioned in n. 4 above, emphasizing that he considers the word *nomos* to have its general reference in *all* Pauline instances of *nomos* plus genitive noun. The genitive noun, then, answers the question "Which *nomos*?" It is a strong argument that would be yet stronger if we could assume that the history of *nomos* in Paul's vocabulary was similar to the history of the term in Greek literature (nn. 3 and 5 above), the general meaning preceding the specific reference to the Torah. Surely the reverse is true. In his childhood Paul will have *first* heard in the term *nomos* a weighty reference to the incomparable and transcendent Law of God, whether in his parents' use of the term or in readings from the scriptures. Moreover, in the holy text, constructions with the genitives κυρίου, θεοῦ, or Μωϋσέως emphasize what is already clear: *the* Law is God's Law, the Law of Moses (cf. the frequent use of תורת משֶׁה in rabbinic formulations).

πνεύματος τῆς ζωῆς ("the *nomos* of the Spirit of Life") is the subject of
the weighty verb ἠλευθέρωσεν ("has liberated"), Raisanen comments:

> In the thought of Paul it is inconceivable that such an active role should
> be given to the Torah, regardless of how the Torah is understood.[8]

But, as Paul's understanding of the Law is precisely the question to
be investigated, theological conclusions must be found rather than imposed. Moreover, as many of the apostle's contemporaries discerned,
what seems inconceivable proves in some instances to be exactly what,
after the advent of Christ, Paul held to be true (see, for example Gal
2:19). We should do well to consider the possibility that *in a quite unexpected way* Paul's use of *nomos* plus genitive offers an important clue to
a truly strange view of the Law. And pondering that possibility, we can
gladly accept Räisänen's admirable philological labor *as* we proceed
with further exegetical analysis of the Pauline texts. Considering the
strong bond between philology and exegesis, we may also recall—and
slightly amplify—a bon mot dear to Abe Malherbe's heart from Nathan
Söderblom:

> Philology [that serves our exegetical labors] is the eye of the needle
> through which every theological camel must pass in order to get into
> the heaven in which there is actual knowledge of God.[9]

A second ground for unease with the "general" reading of *nomos* in Gal
6:2; 1Cor 9:21b; Rom 3:27b; and Rom 8:2a lies in the wording of the
last of these texts. Having cried out for the one who will bring about
redemption from the body of death (Rom 7:24–25), Paul continues:

> There is therefore now no condemnation for those in Christ Jesus. For
> *the law of the spirit of life in Christ Jesus* (ὁ νόμος τοῦ πνεύματος τῆς ζωῆς ἐν
> Χριστῷ Ἰησοῦ) has liberated you from *the law of sin and death* (ὁ νόμος τῆς
> ἁμαρτίας καὶ τοῦ θανάτου, Rom 8:2).

Why, in formulating this emphatic declaration, does Paul use the term
nomos twice? Those who favor the "general" interpretation of the first—
and positive—use of our locution tend to answer by saying that the
declaration is polemical.[10] In order emphatically and polemically to

---

[8] "Sprachliches zum Spiel," 154: "Eine derart aktive Rolle ist für die wie auch
immer verstandene Tora im Denken des Paulus unvorstellbar."

[9] "Die Philologie [das die exegetische Arbeit bedient] ist das Nadelöhr, durch das
jedes theologische Kamel in den Himmel der Gottesgelehrtheit eingehen muss." From
A. J. Malherbe, "Through the Eye of the Needle: Simplicity or Singleness?" *ResQ* 5
(1961) 119–129 (119).

[10] See, e.g., Räisänen, *Paul and the Law*, 52.

insist that the new *order* of things has replaced the old *nomos* (with the specific meaning Torah), Paul speaks of that new order as itself a *nomos*, using the term in its "general" denotation to mean nothing more than "*order*." R. Gyllenberg was dramatically bold: The phrase νόμος τοῦ πνεύματος is simply "a rhetorical paraphrase for Spirit."[11] But is this a strong reading of Rom 8:2?

Reconsidering Romans 8:2

We ponder first the possibility virtually suggested by Gyllenberg that, forgoing a rhetorical flourish, Paul could easily have worded the emphatic declaration of Rom 8:2 without using the term *nomos* twice. He could have spoken directly and effectively of the Spirit's act of liberation. And pondering this possibility, we are led to compare Rom 8:2 with Gal 5:16.

Romans 8:2 and Galatians 5:16

Both texts speak about Sin (Gal 5:16 specifies Sin as the Impulsive Desire of the Flesh, the יֵצֶר [*yêṣer*]).[12] Both refer to liberation from Sin, linking that liberation with the Spirit. And both speak explicitly or implicitly about the Law of Moses. Gal 5:16 is a promise that serves as a correction to another promise. The evangelists who have invaded Paul's Galatian churches are telling the Galatians that the Mosaic Law is the God-given antidote to Sin (again, specifying Sin as the Impulsive Desire of the Flesh). In his correction, presupposing a lethal alliance between Sin and the Law, Paul issues a very different promise. Paraphrasing, we can render Gal 5:16 as follows:

> As Sin and the Law are involved in a secret and lethal alliance, it is crucial for you to know that the God-given antidote to Sin is not the Law. The antidote to Sin is the Spirit. The true promise, then, is this:

---

[11] "Eine rhetorische Umschreibung für Geist." Gyllenberg is quoted by Räisänen, "Sprachliches zum Spiel," 151. See also the analysis of M. Winger, *By What Law? The Meaning of Nomos in the Letters of Paul* (Atlanta: Scholars Press, 1992): In Rom 7:22–25 "each genitival expression with *nomos* [is] a genitive of source, identifying the power whose control is in turn identified by the term *nomos*. [It is likely, then, that the same principle operates in Rom 8:2a] ὁ νόμος τοῦ πνεύματος τῆς ζωῆς is ... not Jewish *nomos*, but a metaphorical expression, similar to those in 7:23 and 25, for a power, the power τὸ πνεῦμα τῆς ζωῆς" (195).

[12] Regarding the conceptual link between ἐπιθυμία τῆς σάρκος and *yêṣer*, see Martyn, *Galatians* (AB 33A; Doubleday: New York, 1997) 492–493.

> Lead your daily life guided by the Spirit, and, in this way, you will not end up carrying out the dictates of Sin.[13]

The difference between the two promises involves Paul in a sharp and polemical polarity between πνεῦμα ("Spirit") and *nomos*.

Returning to Rom 8:2, we are virtually compelled, then, to press the question about the double use of the term *nomos*. If Paul were wording Rom 8:2 as a simple recollection of Gal 5:16—as Gyllenberg very nearly suggested—he should emphasize the contrast between πνεῦμα and *nomos*, employing the latter term only once. He should say,

> There is therefore now no condemnation for those in Christ Jesus. For the πνεῦμα of life in Christ Jesus has liberated you from the νόμος that is an ally of Sin.

Why, instead, does he ascribe liberation to the *nomos* of the Spirit of life in Christ Jesus?

Romans 8:2 and 7:7–25

A convincing answer begins to emerge when, turning for a moment from the positive instances of *nomos* plus genitive, we ask about an emphatically negative one, ὁ νόμος τῆς ἁμαρτίας ("the *nomos* of Sin;" Rom 7:23b, 25b; 8:2b).[14] How is this expression to be interpreted in its context? We note first that, before introducing it in Rom 7:23b, Paul has prepared the way for it in 7:7–13. In that earlier part of Romans 7, Paul faces explicitly the issue of the relation between ὁ νόμος and ἡ ἁμαρτία ("Sin"). They are by no means the same (7:7!), but between the two there is a close relationship (reflected already in Galatians, as we have

---

[13] The exegetical case for this rendering is given in Martyn, *Galatians*, 492, 524–536.

[14] Here and in subsequent references to Romans 7, I draw largely on the classic study of P. W. Meyer, "The Worm at the Core of the Apple: Exegetical Reflections on Romans 7," *The Conversation Continues; Studies in Paul and John in Honor of J. Louis Martyn*, ed. R.T. Fortna and B.R. Gaventa (Nashville: Abingdon, 1990) 62–84. For three different and instructive analyses see M. Winger, *By What Law?*, especially 43–44, 159–196; Stanley K. Stowers, *A Rereading of Romans* (New Haven: Yale University Press, 1994) 258–284; Troels Engberg-Pedersen, "The Reception of Greco-roman culture in the New Testament: The Case of Romans 7:7–25," *The New Testament as Reception*, ed. M. Müller and H. Tronier (London: Sheffield Academic Press, 2002) 32–57. The "I" in Rom 7 may well reflect Paul's use of "speech in character," as Stowers has strongly argued, significantly enriching the reading of Kümmel. This fictive "I" nevertheless provides a retrospective that *includes* Paul (*pace* Stowers, *Rereading*, 264), just as does the Adamic picture of Rom 5:12–21, in which the power called Sin is as universal to the human race as is the power called Death.

seen). Now, employing ἡ ἐντολή ("the commandment") as a synonym (by synechdoche) for ὁ νόμος, Paul develops at some length the picture in which Sin uses the Law/commandment to deceive him, indeed to slay him (climactically 7:11). B. Byrne's comment is on target: "By hijacking the law … by using something essentially good—and God-given—to bring death to the human race, sin revealed the magnitude … of its own evil."[15] Here, *nomos*—specified as ἡ ἐντολή against coveting (v. 8)—is a specific reference to the Mosaic Law (with no indication, incidentally, that it is part of the Law, in terms of its ethnic elements or boundary markers). This Law taken in hand by Sin, and employed by Sin to deceive and kill, is nothing other than the holy and spiritual Law of God (Rom 7:12). It is God's own Law corrupted by Sin, indeed conscripted by Sin into a lethal alliance with Sin.[16]

A History of God's Nomos?

It is a short step, then, from this horrifying picture in Rom 7:7–13 to the expression ὁ νόμος τῆς ἁμαρτίας in 7:23b. For a major use of the genitive case is simply to indicate possession. When Paul speaks of ὁ νόμος τῆς ἁμαρτίας, he refers to the Law of God as it has fallen into the hands of Sin. Using the term *nomos* to refer specifically to the Torah, Paul presupposes an *event* in what would appear to be a history of the Law. Are there, then, junctures in Paul's letters at which he clearly speaks of the Law's history? There are, indeed, two.

Romans 5:20

In the opening part of Romans 5:12–21 Paul refers to the Lawless period between Adam and Moses (v. 13). Several pagan poets, philosophers, and historians also speak of a primal period when there was no law, sometimes finding in it an age of injustice necessitating the establishment of law, sometimes seeing in it, by contrast, the golden age of truth

---

[15] B. Byrne, *Romans* (Collegeville: Glazier, 1996) 220. Interpreting Rom 7:21–23 and 8:2, however, Byrne says that Paul "used *nomos* in the generic sense of anything serving to control human behavior" (235). See now also Byrne, "The Problem of Nomos and the Relationship with Judaism in Romans," *CBQ* 62 (2000) 294–309.

[16] One of the major points of Meyer's study of Romans 7 ("The Worm at the Core," 80) is given in the reference to the maxim *corruptio optimi pessima*, "the worst evil consists in the corruption of the highest good." Following Meyer, then, I have used the verb "to corrupt," surely preferable to "pervert."

and justice in which law was superfluous (for example, Ovid, *Metamor-phoses* 1.89–92).[17] Paul's picture is both different and similar. When he speaks of a time before the Law, he means specifically the time prior to Moses, for with Moses the history of God's Law commenced (cf. Gal 3:17, 19). That prior period was scarcely a golden age of justice. On the contrary, deepening the portrait of a time of injustice, Paul pictures an epoch universally dominated by the cosmic power called Sin. Note especially Rom 5:20, about which M. C. de Boer perceptively remarks:

> The Law ... "came in alongside," παρεισῆλθεν ... a situation [already] determined not by willful human transgression but by the twin cosmological powers of sin and death. [The effect of the Law], Paul now asserts without elucidation, was not to ameliorate that situation but to make it worse ...[18]

Some pagans knew quite well that, rather than leading to justice, law could become an instrument of tyranny (e.g., Tacitus, *Annals* 3.26–28), with the multiplication of law being the mark of a degenerating and corrupt society (e.g., Isocrates, *Areopagiticus* 40 and Tacitus, *Annals* 3.27). Thus, far from deterring crime, law could even provide a stimulus to evil (e.g., Seneca, *De clementia* 1.23.1: parricide began with the law against it, and the punishment of crime only served to increase its occurrence). Similar, but also more dramatic, is the event in which a *Pharisee*, fully observant of the Law and profoundly thankful to God for it, comes to believe that, from its beginning, God's Law increased the universally lethal reign of Sin, becoming for that reason—and immediately—ὁ νόμος τῆς ἁμαρτίας.

Tracing Paul's thought, then, we see yet again the disastrous alliance between the Law and Sin, the latter being the senior partner. Thus allied with ἁμαρτία, the Law led—from its inception—not to ζωή ("life"), but to θάνατος ("death;" cf. Rom 7:10 with 7:9 and 5:20).

---

[17] I have drawn the references to Ovid here, as well as those to Isocrates, Tacitus, and Seneca employed below, from K. Haacker, "Der 'Antinomismus' des Paulus im Kontext antiker Gesetzestheorie," *Geschichte-Tradition-Reflexion:Festschrift für Martin Hengel*, ed. H. Cancik et al. (Tübingen: Mohr-Siebeck, 1996) 3.387–404, esp. 398–400.

[18] M. C. de Boer, *The Defeat of Death* (Sheffield: Sheffield Academic Press, 1988) 166–167. A fundamentally different interpretation of Rom 5:12–21 (esp. 5:20) is proposed by Stowers (*Rereading*, 253–55): what is increased by the advent of the Law is *Gentile* liability.

Galatians 5:14 and 6:2

Seized by Sin, the Law was immediately off to a bad start, but that event was not the last in the Law's history. If we translate the verb πεπλήρωται in Gal 5:14 as a simple perfect passive, with Christ as the implied subject ("the whole of the Law has been brought to completion [by Christ]"), we find Paul saying that the climactic event in the Law's history was Christ's bringing it to restorative completion.[19] And with that reading, we have the key to the expression ὁ νόμος τοῦ Χριστοῦ ("the Law of Christ") in Gal 6:2. Paul coins that expression in order to speak of the Law as it has been taken in hand by Christ, thus being delivered from its lethal alliance with Sin and made pertinent to the church's daily life.[20]

God's Nomos *Restored and Made Redemptively Powerful*

For a final time we return to Rom 8:1–2. Having cried out for the one who will bring about redemption from the body of death—the body characterized by service to the Law as it has fallen into the hands of Sin (Rom 7:24–25)—Paul continues:

> There is therefore now no condemnation for those in Christ Jesus. For the Law in the hands of the Spirit of life in Christ Jesus (ὁ νόμος τοῦ πνεύματος τῆς ζωῆς ἐν Χριστῷ Ἰησοῦ) has liberated you from the Law in the hands of Sin and death (ὁ νόμος τῆς ἁμαρτίας καὶ τοῦ θανάτου).

If we ask yet again why in wording this declaration Paul should employ the word *nomos* twice, we may see that a convincing answer has emerged from Rom 7:7–25, Rom 5:20, Gal 5:14 and Gal 6:2. The Law of God—the Torah—has a history; and there are in that history two decisive events, its falling under the power of Sin, so that it leads to death, and its being taken in hand by the Spirit in Christ, so that it leads to life. Thinking of both of these events, and especially of the second, Paul can even allow the word *nomos* to be the subject of the verb ἠλευθέρωσεν ("has liberated"), thus qualifying his denial in Gal 3:21 that

---

[19] The exegetical basis of this reading is given in Martyn, *Galatians*, 486–491.

[20] *Ibid.*, 554–558. We might be tempted to think of the Law's collision with Christ (Gal 3:13) as the second of three events in the Law's history. When it pronounced a curse on God's Messiah, however, the Law only demonstrated climactically the effect of its having been taken in hand at its origin by Sin.

there has ever been a Law that has the power to make alive.[21] In short, the restorative effect of Christ on the Law is so profound as to cause that restored Law—ὁ νόμος τοῦ πνεύματος τῆς ζωῆς ἐν Χριστῷ Ἰησοῦ— to be God's appointed means for liberating the human race from the Law in the hands of Sin and Death.[22]

Without thinking that we have discovered the whole of Paul's view of the Law—surely a large and complex matter!—we come to a modest but perhaps basic conclusion in three parts. (a) Paul's use of the locution *nomos* plus genitive shows that fundamentally he thinks of the Law neither exclusively in negative terms nor exclusively in positive ones. (b) With this locution he does not employ the term *nomos* sometimes as a specific reference to the Torah and sometimes as a general reference to a way of life (in contrast to Josephus and Philo). (c) On the contrary, in every instance Paul refers to the Torah itself, presupposing that God's own Law has a history.[23] Through the whole of that history, the crucial

---

[21] That the Law has the power to make alive, indeed to free, is a central tenet in many strains of Jewish tradition (see the final section of the present study). For Paul that power lies only with the Law as it has been taken in hand by Christ. Immediately after he has attributed liberation to Christ's Law in Rom 8:2, he refers in 8:3 to the impotence of the Law as it had fallen into the hands of Sin (τὸ ἀδύνατον τοῦ νόμου [τῆς ἁμαρτίας]).

[22] Räisänen focuses his chief polemic on the reading of Rom 8:2 by U. Wilckens, *Der Brief an die Römer* (EKK; Köln: Benziger, 1978–81). At one point he quotes Wilckens: "Striking is the absence of references in which different, contrasting 'orders' or 'norms' are designated by the locution *nomos* plus genitive." Answering the challenge, Räisänen then continues, "Indeed so! But where are the references in which different aspects of a law in the 'strict' sense are designated by that locution, being thus placed in contrast with one another?!" ("Sprachliches zum Spiel," 153 n. 75). I have argued, of course, that, holding the Law of God to have had a complex history, Paul speaks in Rom 8:2 precisely of different and contrasting faces had by the Law in the course of its history.

[23] There is a sense in which substantively this three-part conclusion is not far removed from the analysis of M. Winger mentioned in nn. 4, 7, and 11 above. For Winger the genitive noun answers the question "Which law?" In my analysis, the genitive nouns in Rom 8:2, e.g., answer the questions "The Law in which of its epochs?" and "The Law in the hands of which power?" Thus, in Rom 3:27 Paul contrasts the Torah as it is observed (νόμος τῶν ἔργων) with the Torah as it exists newly in the epoch of faith (νόμος τῆς πίστεως; cf. Gal 3:23) where, in the strict sense, it is not *observed*. The expression ἔννομος Χριστοῦ in 1 Cor 9:21b is surely to be taken together with ὁ νόμος τοῦ Χριστοῦ of Gal 6:2, the Law as it has been taken in hand by Christ. For it is now Christ's Law that is the Law of God, as the parenthesis in the middle of 1 Cor 9:21 shows. The denotations of the term *nomos* in Rom 7:21, 23a are not easily grasped, but the reading given by P. W. Meyer ("The Worm at the Core," 78–79) is convincing: "[About 7:21] it strains credulity to read Paul's definite noun [τὸν νόμον] in this context as 'a law' (RSV) in the sense of a perceived regularity of experience ... [As an adverbial accusative of respect] it must instead refer to the same law that is called a

question about the Law is the identity of the power that has it in hand. And the number of such powers is limited to two, first Sin, then Christ. It follows that the climactic event in the Law's history is the foundation of Paul's confident declaration in Rom 8:2. In the hands of Christ, the Law itself has undergone such change as to make it our liberator from the Law in the hands of Sin.

Some Final Reflections

With this conclusion we are reminded that exegesis is a dangerous discipline, one that can lead us along a path not of our choosing. To be sure, some Christian interpreters may be pleased to find Paul identifying as the crucial event in the Law's history its being taken in hand by Christ. But what is one to say about Paul's portrait of the earlier part of that history? On the one hand, that part presumably included Moses and the priests and prophets of ancient Israel, the elect people to whom the oracles of God were entrusted (Rom 3:2; 9:4–5). On the other hand, that was the part in which, prior to being seized by Christ, the Law was so thoroughly allied with Sin as to lead not to life, but rather to death! Presenting an apparent incoherence, lessened only partially in Romans 9–11, does not this picture render impossible all attempts to formulate a Biblical theology drawn from both testaments? And does it not preclude our inviting the Apostle to the table at which modern Jews and Christians enter into dialogue marked by mutual respect and by genuine reverence for the scriptural canons of both groups?

These questions cannot be directly addressed in the present essay. They can be helpfully sharpened, however, when we recall the multi-faceted Jewish tradition in which the Law is emphatically said to lead not to death, but rather to life. Consider the Psalmist's words,

> I will never forget your precepts,
> for by them you have given me life (119:93).

'different' law, or 'the law of sin' in v. 23. But what law is that? The polarized duality of 'laws' at the end of chap. 7 provides the bridge to chap. 8, and this 'different law' must be the same as 'the law of sin and death' in 8:2. But the transitional verses in 8:1–2 also serve as a parenthesis with 7:6b to enclose the whole of our passage. The phrase 'the law of sin and death' in 8:2 can only be intended as a shorthand summary of the whole point of 7:7–25: It is the *law* that has been used by *sin* to produce *death*. But that means that not only the 'law of God' (v. 22) but also this 'different law' (v. 23) [this 'law of sin and death'] is the Mosaic law!".

Think also of passages in which life is identified as the goal that the Law actually accomplishes, having been given by God for that purpose. Hillel is credited with the saying, "The more study of the Law the more life" (*m.'Abot* 2:7). And in order to accent the salvific connection between the Law and life, Sirach employs precisely the locution studied in the present essay, speaking of the Law emphatically as the "law of life" (νόμος ζωῆς, 45:5; cf. 4 Ezra 14:30).

Paul was well acquainted with the riches of this tradition, having enjoyed a blameless life as he followed the precepts of the God-given Law (Phil 3:6). Indeed he refers explicitly to this tradition when he says that the commandment had life as its goal (Rom 7:10).

As he now looks back, however, Paul sees a radically different picture, the one in which Sin plays its awesome role as the cosmic power that has turned the Law into its junior ally. For, noting Sin's role as a spoiler, Paul quickly adds that sin employed the commandment to deceive and kill him (Rom 7:11). As I have indicated, we cannot here consider all of the dimensions of this emphatically dark and tragic picture. We can say, however, that, addressed single-mindedly to the church, it is clearly a retrospective spoken neither to nor about the synagogue.

We can also say that this nomistic retrospective is indelibly connected with Paul's unchosen experience of dying with Christ. For the Christ with whom Paul was himself crucified is the Christ who died under the curse of the Law (Gal 3:13), and thus the Christ who, calling Paul into his service, caused him to suffer the loss of the nomisitc life he had previously known and treasured (Gal 2:19; 3:21; 6:14–15; Phil 3:7–8). On the positive side, it was precisely when he was lethally deprived of his ante-Christum nomistic life that Paul discovered the locus of what he now came to identify as true life. For, sending his messianic son into a Sin-imprisoned cosmos, the God of Israel had done something so radically new as to have consequences for nothing less than the basic elements of that cosmos (Gal 4:3–11). It is thus hardly surprising that, transforming the cosmic elements themselves, this radically new deed of God fundamentally affected the relationship between the Law and life. God remained the giver of life, but God's gift of life could now be found only in his son, the crucified Messiah, and thus, as regards the Law, only in the Law taken in hand by that crucified Messiah.

In the victorious note of Rom 8:2 we do not hear, therefore, the voice of the imperial church of Constantine, the powerful ecclesiastical establishment that unfortunately learned century after century how to speak in a destructively denigrating manner of and to the synagogue. On the contrary, we hear the voice of the weak and suffering apostle, plagued with afflictions and perplexities that arise in part from his having lost the monolithic guidance of the Sinaitic Law, commandeered as it was by the greater power of Sin.[24] He can now rejoice in God's gift of life, but he knows that life only in the form of daily death. Paraphrasing his own words, and accenting yet again that the Law has now been taken into what he could very well have referred to as "nail-scarred hands" (cf. the στίγματα τοῦ Ἰησοῦ or "marks of Jesus" of Gal 6:17), we hear Paul saying that, as he preaches the circumcision-free gospel, he is himself struck down but not destroyed, for he is always carrying in his body the putting-to-death of Jesus, so that the life of Jesus may be made visible in that same body (2 Cor 4:10).

---

[24] Drawing more on Galatians than on Romans, I have elsewhere sketched a somewhat different view of the Law's history, suggesting that, far from considering the Law a monolith, Paul hears in it two quite different voices. Spoken by God directly to Abraham, the scriptural Law voiced an evangelical promise (Gal 3:8; 4:21b; Rom 4:13). Later, given by angels through Moses at Sinai, it acquired a universally cursing voice with which it uttered a false promise (Gal 3:10, 12; 4:21a; Rom 4:15). Still later, its two voices were climactically distinguished from one another (Gal 4:21; Rom 10:4–8), the cursing voice being borne by Christ and the promissory and guiding voice being brought to completion by him. See Martyn, *Galatians*, 502–514.

HOUSEHOLD RULES AT EPHESUS

GOOD NEWS, BAD NEWS, NO NEWS

Benjamin Fiore, S.J.

Household Rules in Ephesians: tradutori traditori

Editors and translators of the text of the New Testament have been inconsistent as to where the household rules section in Eph 5 actually begins, as the following sampling demonstrates.

The Vulgate translation places 5:21 (*subjecti invicem in timore Christi*) at the end of the section on "walking as children of the light" (5:8–21). The translation of the participle ὑποτασσόμενοι as *subjecti* is repeated at 5:24. The translator at 5:22 uses the Latin *subditae sint* to render the same verb, thus creating a break between 5:21 and 22; therefore, a new section on "the order of the Christian household" begins at v. 22. The 1886 Latin edition of Theodore Beza, however, gives *subjicite vos* in v. 22. Like the Vulgate, Beza separated 5:21 from v. 22 with a period and a paragraph break.

Following the Vulgate's lead, the Douay-Rheims version links 5:21 "being subject to one another" to 5:20 with a colon between the two verses. In verse 5:22, similar to Beza, the translator uses the same word, but reverts to the 3rd person form, thus "let women be subject," like the Vulgate.

Contemporaneous with the Douay-Rheims version, the King James Version largely does the same thing, joining 5:21 to v. 20 with a semicolon and joining 5:22 to v. 23 with a comma. This punctuation basically followed that of the 1550 Greek edition of Stephens, which was then deemed the standard English edition of the *textus receptus*.[1] The KJV translator chooses "submitting yourselves" in 5:21 and "submit yourselves" in 5:22, while using "subject" in 5:24, but the Greek word is the same. The imperative form (2nd person) in 5:22 comes from the presence of ὑποτάσσεσθε in the *textus receptus*.

---

[1] The Greek text here has a medial stop between 5:20 and 21, a full stop after v. 21, and a medial stop between between 5:22 and 23; also a medial stop between 5:23 and 24.

The ninth edition of the Greek text by Augustine Merk, S.J. (1964) joins 5:21 and 5:20 with a comma. He emends 5:22 with ὑποτασσέσθω-σαν, following Sinaiticus and Alexandrinus, among other manuscripts, and thereby has a finite verb to complete the sense of 5:22–23.[2] In his Latin translation, however, he separates 5:21 from 5:20 both with a period and with a title "*Officia domestica*," which clearly indicates that 5:21 introduces the household rules section rather than closes the section on Christian holiness. He translates the verb in 5:22 as *subditae sint*, following the Vulgate, although he translates the same verb in 5:21 and 5:24 as *subjecti* and *subjecta est* respectively.

The first edition of the New American Bible (1970) follows the pattern in the Vulgate by separating 5:21 from 5:22 and making 5:21 the concluding thought in the section on the "Duty to Live in the Light" (NAB). Moreover, the translator has chosen to emphasize the difference by translating the participle in 5:21 as "defer," while using "let wives be submissive" (3rd person imperative) in 5:22 and 5:24 for the same verb.

The first to print the Greek text without a finite verb in 5:22 was Tischendorf (1850 edition); this reading was followed by Westcott and Hort (1885).[3] Even so, both editions give a full stop (and a wide gap) after 5:21, while placing commas between vv. 20 and 21 and between vv. 22 and 23. This form of the text was followed in the Nestle-Aland 17th–21st editions (1941–52) on the strength of the readings of 𝔓46, Vaticanus, and Claromontanus; thus, the text has no finite verb in 5:21–23, only the participle (ὑποτασσόμενοι) in 5:21.[4] Based on the N-A text, the RSV[1] (1946) uses "be subject" in 5:21, 22, and 24, consistent with the same Greek verb in 5:21 and 24. Oddly, the paragraphing of the RSV[1] keeps 5:21 together with 5:22, in a section headed "The Christian Household," even though it places a period between the two verses and adds a finite verb in 5:22. In some editions of the RSV[2] (1971), however, the text reverts to a paragraph break between 5:21 and 22, in keeping with the first edition of the United Bible Societies text (1966). This is

---

[2] The variant reading ὑποτασσέσθωσαν (3rd person imperative) was also given in the critical apparatus of the *textus receptus* beginnng with Lachman (1842–50) and Traggelles (1857–72).

[3] Whereas Tischendorf gives ὑποτάσσεσθε in the critical apparatus, Westcott-Hort give ὑποτασσέσθωσαν, in keeping with their preference for the "Western" text.

[4] Compare the edition of Alexander Souter (1st ed. 1910; 2nd ed. 1947) which places a comma at the end of 5:20, a full stop and paragraph break after v. 21, and a medial stop after v. 22, with no finite verb in the verse.

the form continued in the RSV [2.2] (1973), which also includes a section heading "Wives and Husbands," again following the UBS.[5]

The Nestle-Aland 26th (1979) and 27th (1993) editions punctuate the Greek text differently by separating 5:20 from v. 21 with a period and joining v. 21 v. 22 with a comma. With this punctuation, and the absence of a finite verb in 5:22, the Greek clearly affirms that mutual subjection (v. 21) is introductory to the specific rules for husband and wife.

On the whole, however, the English translations have continued the tradition of seeing 5:21 as a conclusion to the previous section, at least until recently. The revised translation of the New American Bible (1986) follows the paragraphing of N-A[26·27], although it punctuates 5:21 as a declarative sentence separated from 5:22 by a period. It translates the verb ὑποτάσσειν the same way in both 5:21 and 22 "be subordinate" and 5:24 "is subordinate." The New Revised Standard Version (1989) also uses the same word ("be subject") to translate the verb and punctuates 5:21 as a separate sentence. NRSV then prints 5:21 as a one-sentence paragraph between 5:15–20 and 5:22–33, with no section titles to interrupt the text.[6] As a result, the NRSV, like the NAB and most others, is still forced to add a finite verb ("be subject, subordinate") in 5:22.

All of this analysis points to the fluidity of the punctuation and paragraphing of 5:21 as well as to varied translations and emendations of the word ὑποτάσσειν. As a participle, ὑποτασσόμενοι in 5:21 could reasonably be interpreted as the last in a series of nominative plural participles from 5:18–21 (λαλοῦντες, ᾄδοντες 5:19, εὐχαριστοῦντες 5:20, and ὑποτασσόμενοι 5:21). On the other hand, the verb ὑποτάσσεται is used at 5:24. If 5:22–23 is separated from the participial phrase in 5:21, there would be no finite verb, but the one implied, as the translators have largely agreed, would be ὑποτάσσειν anyway. Moreover, the section from 5:22–33 is united by the theme "relations between husbands and wives." It

---

[5] This reading is continued in the second (1968) and third (1975) editions of the UBS text, with a period and paragraph break between 5:21 and 5:22, but deleting the finite verb (ὑποτασσέσθωσαν or ὑποτάσσεσθε) from 5:22. For Bruce Metzger's emphatic conclusion that 5:22 (beginning with Aἱ γυναῖκες) is a "new sentence," even though it contains no verb, see *A Textual Commentary on the Greek New Testament* (London / New York: United Bible Societies, 1971) 608. In the UBS 4th edition (1983), the punctuation and paragraphing is brought into conformity with the Nestle-Aland 26th edition (1979), discussed below.

[6] In this, the NRSV follows the pattern of the New English Bible (1961; 2nd ed. 1970).

is thus likely that the participial construction of 5:21 provides a frame-work within which to understand the particular recommendations to husbands and wives in 5:22–23. The original text seems, therefore, to be a single sentence from 5:18–23, and the string of nominative par-ticiples invoke aspects of communal paraenesis introduced by "but be filled with the Spirit" (ἀλλὰ πληροῦσθε ἐν πνεύματι, 5:18). With ὑπο-τασσόμενοι in 5:21, this paraenesis then concludes by also drawing in spousal realtionships (5:22–23). Thus, I suspect that the call to mutual submission at 5:21 was separated from the rules for spousal relationships for reasons beyond grammar and text criticism, just as their reintegra-tion in more recent times can be seen as consistent with the critique of patriarchy both in scriptural studies and in society at large.

Comparison with Colossians' Household Rules: What's the Real Issue?

The relationship between Colossians and Ephesians has been long discussed.[7] I will assume that Ephesians has made use of Colossians, eliminating references to particular difficulties such as the lure of an alternative religious philosophy. My interest is to see what the author of Ephesians has done to the rules for spousal behavior. In Colossians 3 the rules for wives and husbands occupy two verses (18–19):

> [18] Wives, be subordinate (ὑποτάσσεσθε) to your husbands, as is proper in the Lord. [19] Husbands, love your wives, and avoid any bitterness toward them.[8]

The regulations of wives' submission receives the backing of community standards of behavior.[9] The husbands' rule seems to stand on its own but more likely shares the backing of community standards with the first rule. In each of the three pairs of rules, the first consistently receives a Christological motive while the third pair has the motive for both, and it is the same for both, i.e. serving the Lord. It is likely that the motivation expressed, some form of deference toward the Lord, is applicable to both sides of each pair but is mentioned only for the first one. Verse 17 prefixes the applicability of the Christological motivation to three cases that follow.

---

[7] Markus Barth, *Ephesians 1–3* (AB 34; Garden City: Doubleday, 1974) 21–22.
[8] This is the reading of NAB[2]; the RSV[2] and NRSV have "be subject," and the KJV has "submit."
[9] Eduard Lohse, *Colossians and Philemon*, trans. W.R. Poehlmann and R.J. Karris (Hermeneia; Philadelphia: Fortress, 1971) 157–158

Whereas Colossians has two verses, Ephesians gives these rules in 13 verses, 3.5 relating to wives and 8.5 to husbands with one introductory verse. The Christological motivation from Colossians is explicit throughout and on both sides and the letter adds ecclesiastical comparisons. Moreover, a closer look at the rules in 5:21–33 reveals[10] that while 5:22–24 (rules for wives) and 5:25–28a (rules for husbands) parallel the form in Colossians, the next section (5:28b–33) seems to repeat the admonitions to the husbands and depart from the form of subordinate/master. Then, too, the admonition to wives in 5:22 is repeated at 5:24b and that to husbands in 5:25a is repeated at 5:28a. These verses bracket the references to the Christ/Church relationship (5:23–24a and 5:25b–27). The reverse is true from 5:28b–33 where the Christ/Church relationship (5:29b–30 and 5:32) brackets the material on the marital relationship (5:31). Verses 5:28b–29a are repeated at 5:33a and present a summary of the admonition to husbands, while 5:33b summarizes the admonitions to wives. Marital relations are clearly the focus of the section.

Scriptural Quotation and the Debate about Marriage & Divorce: Proof Texts

To support the admonitions to husbands and wives, the author of Ephesians also adds a quotation of Gen 2:24 LXX at 5:31. The author has changed the introductory formula in the LXX from ἕνεκεν τούτου to ἀντὶ τούτου; this change yields the resultant meaning "as a result" or "therefore," a sense parallel to διὸ λέγει in 5:14, where the author inserts another Old Testament quotation. Quotations from the Old Testament in Ephesus are a feature of the letter which is the subject of Thorsten Moritz's monograph *A Profound Mystery: The Use of the Old Testament in Ephesians*.[11] Moritz's analysis of Old Testament quotations and allusions leads him to conclude that the author of Ephesians is correcting misinterpretations of and misuses of the Old Testament by contemporary Rabbinic teachers. Moritz offers the following translation of verses 29–32, following Coppens:[12]

---

[10] Thorsten Moritz, *A Profound Mystery: The Use of the Old Testament in Ephesians* (Leiden: Brill, 1996) 133.

[11] Cited in the previous note.

[12] Moritz, *A Profound Mystery*, 138.

No-one ever hated his own flesh; instead one nourishes and cherishes it, just as Christ does the church. After all, we are members of his body and it is because of what Christ the head has illustrated through his relationship with the church *that man leaves his parents.*

Moritz next surveys the meaning of this verse in Jewish tradition. First, with regard to Genesis 2:24 itself, he concludes with Westermann that "the main significance of this verse lies precisely in that it differs from current conceptions by pointing to the inherent strength of the love bond between husband and wife."[13] Human marriage is clearly rooted in "God's order of creation," although it would be anachronistic to institutionalize this bond.

The Essenes, who seem to have favored celibacy (Josephus *War* 2.8; 2.121), are also known to have discussed matters of intermarriage (*CD* 16.3–4 and *Jub* 20.4; 22.20; 25.1; 27.10; 30.1–15).[14] Thus there seems to have been a diversity of practice among them. In any case, polygamy and divorce appear to be out of the question (*CD* 4.20–5.1). Genesis 1:27 (*CD* 4.21) and Deut 17:17 (*CD* 5.2) rather than Gen 2:24 are their proof texts for this position and it appears that the Essenes disagreed with their Jewish co-religionists on the issues of marriage and divorce (*CD* 5.6ff).

Other uses of the text vary and include Philo's.[15] He allegorizes Gen 2:24 in *Leg. alleg.* 2.49 to express the relationship between sense perception and the mind. The Rabbinic texts, on the other hand, avoid allegorization and find in the passage verification for the view that humans had been originally a bisexual being who, once separated by the creation of woman, seeks to be reunited with his other half (*Midr.R.Gen* 8.9; 22.2). Otherwise, the Rabbis concern themselves with legal matters rather than the love bond suggested in Gen 2:24.

In the Rabbinic texts, very little is made of Gen 2:24 with respect to the binding character of the marital union. While marriage was considered to be a divine command, a major issue was the grounds and procedures for divorce. In this discussion, appeal is seldom made to Gen 2:24. It was primarily brought to bear on the question of legitimacy for offspring. Otherwise, the discussion of marriage focuses on divorce and its grounds. Gen 2:24 was actually brought in to demonstrate cases in which divorce is called for (*Sanh.* 58). The divorce text

---

[13] *Ibid.*, 121.
[14] *Ibid.*, 122–23.
[15] *Ibid.*, 123–29.

(Deut 24:1) is cited ten times more than the "marriage text" Gen 2:24 in the Mishnah and Talmud. Although Gen 2:24 implies that marriage should be indissoluble because of its grounding in the original order of creation, this had little impact on the Rabbinic discussion of marriage. Instead Gen 1:28 ("be fruitful and increase in number") emerges as the first scriptural command whose fulfillment at times involves divorce and remarriage (*Sanh.* 58) or even polygamy.

Elsewhere in the New Testament the portrayal of Jesus' disputes with the Pharisees over marriage, divorce and remarriage echo what has been noted in the previous paragraphs.[16] Mark 10:1–12 (Matt 19:1–9) narrates Jesus' handling of the question of the legitimacy of divorce. The Pharisees' query about the permissibility of dismissing one's wife uses terminology (ἀπόλυσαι) from Deut 24.1–3. Jesus' response refers both to Gen 1:27 and Gen 2:24, setting the Genesis references against the Mosaic law's tolerance of a writ of divorce. Mark 10:8–9 thereby seems to be reclaiming Gen 2:24 from its association with divorce in Rabbinic applications.

Paul at 1 Cor 7:10 also claims that the Lord is at the origin of his teachings on marriage and so he cites Gen 2:24 (at 1 Cor 6:16, albeit in the case of relations with a prostitute), as in Mark, to underscore the union in one flesh. Paul, like the author of Ephesians, goes on to relate the union in one flesh with a spiritual union in the body of Christ.

Divorce thus seems to have been as serious a matter of concern in mid-first century Judaism as it is today. The Rabbis sought ways to legitimate it, as texts from Qumran as well as Rabbinic literature suggest. On the Christian side of the debate about marriage and divorce both Mark 10:1–12 (and Matt 19:1–9) and Paul use the Genesis texts to assert the permanence of the marital bond. The use of Gen 2:24 in 1 Corinthians and the consistency with the gospels of Paul's teachings about the permanence of marriage indicate that the opinion on divorce in the first-century Diaspora Judaism paralleled that of the Homeland, and probably holds true for Asia just as it does for Greece. This debate about marriage and divorce is a plausible background for the treatment of spousal relations in Eph 5:21–33.

Eph 5:32 is traditionally thought[17] to be a clarification of the quotation of Gen 2:24 in the preceding verse (5:31). Moritz contends that

---

[16] *Ibid.*, 129–30.

[17] J. H. Houlden, *Paul's Prison Letters* (Pelican New Testament Commentaries; Harmondsworth: Penguin, 1970) 335.

the whole of verses 30–32 is the author's justification for using the Christ/Church relationship to elaborate on Christian marriage.[18] He goes on to argue that since the overall thrust of the section 5:21–33 is to give rules for spousal behavior, and since the material related to the husband extends from 25–33a (with the admonitions repeated and elaborated), then the apparent digression 5:30–32 refers to the husbands' responsibility to love their wives.[19] The author is either breaking new ground here and/or is reclaiming Gen 2:24 in its original meaning for the Christian community.

The Christ/church relationship is the model which undergirds wives' submission to their husbands (5:23–24), and so, too, it determines the husband's relationship to their wives (5:25–33a).[20] As noted above, the explanatory digression at 5:30–31 finds support in the Christ/church analogy, which brackets it at 5:29 and 32. The husband's union in one flesh with his spouse is related to the example of Christ's relation with the church. By reason of that relationship (ἀντὶ τούτου), the marital oneness of husband and wife is verified. The author of Ephesians established Christ at the ethical model at 5:1. The model is here applied to husbands in a particular way. The Pentateuchal insight that men and women form a union of one flesh receives a new dimension from the Christ event and the ongoing love of Christ for his church. The basis of marriage in natural attraction (Gen 2:23–24) is amplified by Christ's love for the church which marriage is expected to reiterate.

What's the Big Secret?

At 5:32, the author says τὸ μυστήριον τοῦτο μέγα ἐστίν. First of all, it might best be translated "this mystery is great" (NEB) rather than "this is a great mystery" (NAB, RSV). The emphasis thus falls not on the mysteriousness but on its magnitude.[21] But which mystery is the author talking about? The mystery might be that the husband/wife relationship can be seen as parallel to the relationship between Christ and the church, and further that marriage in Christ is not just founded on natural sexual attraction (Gen 2:23–24) but also on being found in Christ. Verses 29–30 remind husbands of their responsibility to love

---

[18] Moritz, *A Profound Mystery*, 134.
[19] *Ibid.*, 136–37.
[20] *Ibid.*, 138–40.
[21] *Ibid.*, 142–46.

their wives in view of their being loved themselves by Christ, who loves his church (see 5:1–2). Verse 31 makes the connection explicit by noting the oneness of husbands and wives which parallels that of Christ and the members of his body, the church. Existence in Christ undergirds the ethical paraenesis throughout the letter and, in the case of marriage, makes it more likely that husbands will love and fulfil their wives as they have experienced these benefits from their relationship with Christ.

At 3:8–9 and 6:19 the mystery is connected with the gospel. It is common[22] to explain the mystery in terms of the unity of Jews and Gentiles (3:3–12), a central concern of the gospel preached by Paul. That, however, is to overlook the application of the mystery of the gospel in chapters 5 and 6 to the household relationships of wives and husbands (chapter 5), children and parents, and slaves and masters (chapter 6). As noted above, the motivation behind the admonitions to all three pairs is Christological, their existence in Christ. Even the connection of the mystery of the gospel with the ethnic union of the Jews and Gentiles flows directly into an acknowledgment of God "the Father, from whom every family in heaven and on earth is named," and the call that the faithful be rooted and grounded in "the love of Christ which surpasses knowledge" (3:14–19). Similarly, the peace which abolishes the wall of enmity between Jews and Gentiles also brings the newly reconciled into the household of God, which has Jesus as its capstone (2:11–22). This "manifold wisdom of God" (NAB) even affects the heavenly powers and principalities (1:21; 2:2; 3:10; 6:12). Consequently, 5:32 applies the mystery of the gospel to marriage as earlier the author applied it to the inclusion of Gentiles into the community of the faithful along with the Jews. The mystery is that a new dimension has been introduced into married life, as yet another practical ramification of being a member of the body of Christ.

At 5:32b the author acknowledges giving an alternative interpretation (ἐγὼ δὲ λέγω). The formula is familiar from Jesus' pronouncements in the Sermon on the Mount where he proposes his own interpretations of Jewish Law and practice. But to what does the author of Ephesians propose an alternative? It is not apparent that there are opponents in the intended audience of the letter or as the occasion for the letter. It has already been seen above that the letter proposes an interpretation of the stability of the marriage bond on the basis of Gen 2:24 that the

---

[22] Markus Barth, *Ephesians 4–6* (AB 34A; Garden City: Doubleday, 1974) 807.

Jewish neighbors might not hold. Ephesians thus goes farther to locate that binding character of marriage in the believers' new existence in Christ. Moritz renders verse 32 as "I use these words to say something about the relevance of the Christ-church relationship for marriage."[23]

Household Do's and Don'ts

In the preceding discussion, the author of Ephesians was seen to have introduced Pentateuchal material into the first part of an expanded version of the *Haustafel* from Colossians.[24] The same holds true for the rest of the *Haustafel*, *i.e.* 6:2 provides an expanded version of Exod 20:12, and 6:9 is similar to Lev 25:43. At the same time, the author provides a Christological framework for the ethical paraenesis, e.g. 5:30 and 6:1. The decalogue in Exod 20 refers not just to family members but to neighbors and slaves, which are the personnel of a typical *Haustafel* list (and see Philo *Hypothetica* 14; *De decal.* 165–167; *De Spec. leg.* 2.225–235 for a similar influence in the pairing of subjects from the decalogue at Exod 20). The lower order is expected to honor the higher in the strict subordination of Eph 6:1–9 and also Philo *Hypothetica* 7.3; Josephus *C. Ap.* 2:24, 199 and Aristotle *Polit.* 1.1253; 1.1259. While the wives' submission and respect are required at 5:21–33, mutual submissiveness is also stressed. Moreover, Ephesians cushions the wives' submissiveness, as was shown above, by insisting that husbands love their wives. Furthermore, the subservience of children and slaves finds expression with the verb ὑπακούειν, but the author uses ὑποτάσσεσθαι in regard to the wives. It appears that Philo and Josephus, while inspired by Exod 20, follow the Graeco-Roman household ethics traceable to Aristotle. The author of Ephesians, however, shows some independence from Graeco-Roman ethics.

Which Way is the Enemy?

4 Macc 2:10–13 represents the Hellenistic Jewish ethical tradition.[25] With its pairings (parents, spouses, friends), it is closer to Ephesians than the more widely ranging Graeco-Roman Haustafel parallels— viz. Epictetus (*Diss.* 2.17.31) who treats only one party in the relation-

---

[23] Moritz, *A Profound Mystery*, 148.
[24] *Ibid.*, 153–61.
[25] *Ibid.*, 162–70.

ship. 4 Maccabees seems to represent an effort of a Jewish philosopher in a Greek philosophical context to deal with ethical libertinism in Graeco-Roman life in Asia Minor. As such it argues that just as reason should be "master of the passions," (κύριός ἐστιν τῶν παθῶν, 2:7) so also "being a citizen to the law" (τῷ νόμῳ πολιτευόμενος, 2.8) has the same benefit, since "being mastered by the Law on account of reason" (ὑπὸ τοῦ νόμου κρατεῖται διὰ τὸν λογισμόν, 2:9) produces virtuous action. This contrasts with the stronger Stoic formulation that reason should eliminate passion,[26] but the theme of "mastery of the passions" is reiterated in 5:23. Moritz points to many allusions to Pentateuchal texts in 4 Macc 2.4–10:[27] The main point seems to be that the Law (and specifically the Decalog) provides a superior way for reason to rule the passions.

Rabbinic law also shows the precedence of law over passions (= benevolence to parents, see *Yebam.* 5b; *Qidd.* 32a). Compare Jesus' criticism of the Law of *korban* at Mark 7:12. Here Mark quotes Exod 20 in this dispute over lax interpretation of the requirements of Mosaic Law. The argument over a similar laxity with respect to marriage and divorce at Mark 10:7 quotes Gen 2:24. The same two Pentateuchal texts are quoted in Eph 5:31 and 6:2 where a comparable debate over ethical laxity makes use of the same scriptural references.

Whereas the Colossians *Haustafel* relates the community to its Graeco-Roman environment, the adaptation of it in Ephesians seems to focus on the relationship of those in Christ to the tradition of Israel.[28] Philo makes use of the Decalog to defend Judaism against the Graeco-Roman charge of immorality in household matters. Ephesians uses it and Pentateuchal texts to demonstrate the continuity between the new community and its Jewish antecedents by highlighting the ethical benefits of living "in Christ," much as 4 Maccabees had touted living "under the Law."

Ephesians, while continuing a patriarchal system, nonetheless goes a long way toward improving the situation of women within it. The women are not to be easily dismissed by their husbands because they are in a one-flesh union. The husbands are also to model their treatment of their wives upon their own experience of being cared for by

---

[26] John M. Rist, "The Stoic Concept of Detachment," in *The Stoics*, ed. J.M. Rist (Berkeley: University of California Press, 1978) 260, 269.

[27] Moritz, *A Profound Mystery*, 161.

[28] Cf. Eph 2:14–15, noting the use of "mystery" in this context, much as in 5:32.

Christ as members of the church. And so love is a requirement for
husbands within the marriage and the requirement is given not just a
Christological motivation but also an assurance of its possibility as an
offshoot of the love shown by Christ to members of his body. At the
same time, the letter is directing its focus on the Jewish context of the
community and not its Graeco-Roman neighbors, unlike Colossians.

A Big Change at Ephesus—Bad News
in 1 Timothy: Beware of the Jewish Teachers

As the Christian community at Ephesus grew in numbers and prominence, attention began to be paid to the way the household of God was
viewed in the Graeco-Roman community. At the same time, a decided
distance from the Jewish community is expressed. One consequence of
this new state of affairs is a decrease in the orbit of women's activity
within the church.

The letter to Titus most clearly puts Jewish teachers at a distance.
They are rebels, idle talkers and deceivers (1:10); they must be silenced
because otherwise they upset whole households (1:11); they peddle Jewish myths and regulations for gain and have repudiated the truth (1;14);
their applications of law to life reveal their own sinfulness and godless-
ness (1:15–16). 1 Timothy is less overtly hostile but shows similar disdain
for "teachers of the law" who concern themselves with "myths and
genealogies" and "meaningless talk" (NAB), but without any understanding of what they claim to know and teach (1:4–7; Tit 3:9). The
letter records "Paul's" self-criticism as a one-time "blasphemer" who
acted in ignorance before his call to Christianity (1:13–14).

1 Timothy also carries a rejection of asceticism at 4:3–4; 5:23. In this
it echoes Eph 5:29 but once again goes farther in its explicit hostility
against those who advance ascetical practices in their teachings. As
before, these teachers might well be Jewish in that abstinence from
certain foods receives particular refutation (4:3–4; cf. Tit 1:15). If so,
it seems that the Pastoral Epistles are engaged in a controversy with
Jewish teachers over the interpretation and application of Law. The
Pastoral Epistles uphold prohibitions inspired by the Decalog (1:9–11) as
they imply misinterpretation of the Law by false teachers. In this they
resemble the letter to the Ephesians. But whereas Ephesians speaks of
the mystery of the gospel which effected a reconciliation of Jews and
Gentiles, the Pastoral Epistles seem largely to reject Jewish traditions
along with their proponents.

Nonetheless, the Pastoral Epistles express an awareness of the language and content of Jewish teaching in the first century.[29] In this, they echo what was noticed in the letter to the Ephesians. What differs is that there is little interest in the Pastoral Epistles to continue a dialogue with those holding erroneous views, for they, like the former Paul, are arrogant, sinful and ignorant (1:13, 15) and are to be separated from the community (1:20; Tit 1:10–11; 3:9–11).

At the same time, the Graeco-Roman world looms large in these letters as the community's reputation in the wider community takes a place of prominence in the letters' injunctions (e.g. 1 Tim 3:7; 5:14, 24–25; 6:1; Titus 2:5, 8, 10). The *Haustafeln* now often follow the Graeco-Roman models, and no longer arrange the subjects in pairs, e.g., 1 Tim 2:8–15, husbands and wives, but 3:1–13, bishops and deacons, both male and female; 5:1–2, older men, younger men, older women, younger women; 5:3–17, widows; 5:17–20, elders; 6:1–2, only slaves; 6:9–10, 17–19, the rich; Tit 2:3–6, older women, younger women, younger men, slaves.[30] Only 1 Tim 2:8–15 suggest reciprocal relationships among those addressed.

The aim of the *Haustafeln* is also different. Moritz, taking his cue from the reference to the Decalog's command to "honor your father and mother" with its promise "so that it may go well with you and you may have a long life on earth," concludes that the purpose, both in Exodus and in Ephesians, is the expectation of the children's willingness to receive and obey the community traditions (see Eph 6:4b).[31] In the Decalog, the support of elderly parents by the children is also in view, but Ephesians focuses rather on the continuity of tradition, which is already present when the promise for following the fifth (fourth) commandment is reiterated at Deut 5:32–33. Unlike 1 Timothy and Titus, or even its parallel and probable source Colossians there is no mention in Ephesians of outsiders nor concern expressed for the Christians' standing in the Graeco-Roman context.

Once the latter concern emerges, the lists of household duties take on a new tone. 1 Tim 2:8–15 departs from earlier usage in the Pauline churches and places husbands in honorable positions and in the public

---

[29] For example βεβήλοις ("profane") at 1 Tim 1:9 reflects Hellenistic Jewish usage. Compare 3 Macc 4:16 = 1 Tim 6:20; 2 Tim 2:16; 3 Macc 2:2 = 1 Tim 1:9 and 1 Tim 4:7, 3 Macc 2:14 = Philo *Spec leg* 1.102.

[30] As noted above, in Ephesians, following Jewish practice, the household admonitions are given in pairs of dominant/subservient; Moritz *A Profound Mystery*, 167.

[31] *Ibid.*, 168–70.

sphere while at the same time it removes women to the areas of social
shame and into the domestic sphere.[32] Women house church leaders
such as Corinth's Chloe, Prisca, and Phoebe, Philippi's Lydia (Acts 16),
and Colossae's Apphia, are not envisioned here, nor are the women's
prophetic contributions to worship which Paul mentions without comment at 1 Cor 11:5 and even 1 Cor 14:26–33a, 37–40, where 33b–36 is
either an interpolation or a reference to speech other than prophetic
speaking.

Women's foibles, commonly assumed and criticized in Graeco-Roman literature, such as a tendency toward extravagant adornment and
gullibility toward teachers of exotic and erroneous beliefs, are assumed
here by the author of 1 Timothy, who prescribes against them (1 Tim
2:9, 11 and 14 and compare 5:11–13). Finally, attention to domestic
duties and the goal of child bearing offer women the path to salvation
(1 Tim 3:15 and compare 5:10) while at the same time placing the Christian community squarely on the side of the Augustan reforms aimed at
shoring up family life. The *Haustafel* in Colossians 3:18–4:1, while not
as elaborate as that at 1 Timothy, moves in its this direction by separating the spouses into dominant and submissive, a separation which
Ephesians was seen above to have turned into a direction of mutuality.

This recourse to a more restrictive view of women's roles in the
household and the house church in the direction of the prevailing views
of Graeco-Roman society runs parallel to the increased hostility toward
Jewish tradition and its interpreters. This is even more surprising in that
the turn has taken place in Ephesus, the city identified with the letter
bearing its name and the location of Timothy's ministry (as outlined in
1 Timothy).

The *Haustafel* at 1 Peter 2:18–3:9 follows the pattern of the Graeco-
Roman model also followed in the Pastoral Epistles. Concern is for
good report among the Gentiles (2:12–15) and obedience to earthly
authority aims to "silence the ignorance of foolish people." Thus slaves
are given prescriptions, then wives and husbands (in a pairing), and
then everyone. In the wife/husband pairing, the subordination of wom-
en and the curtailment of their expenses and spheres of activity as the
"weaker" sex echo those in 1 Timothy.

Likewise in agreement with the Pastoral Epistles, 1 Peter has the

[32] Karen Jo Torjesen, *When Women Were Priests: Women's Leadership in the Early Church and the Scandal of Their Subordination in the Rise of Christianity* (San Francisco, Harper San Francisco, 1993) 135–52.

Christian community supplant the Jewish community. The letter is addressed to Diaspora Christians in, among other places, Asia. The letter takes over the designation of Diaspora Jews and applies it to Christians, thereby pushing the Jews out of the picture. The displacement of Jews continues in 2:4–10 where the Christian community is seen to be the temple as well as the "chosen race, a royal priesthood, a holy nation, a people of his (God's) own," no longer "no people" but now recipients of God's mercy in the place of those who have stumbled on the rock of faith in Jesus (2:8).

In effecting this displacement, 1 Peter, like the Pastoral Epistles, retains connections with Judaism by taking over these designations for Israel and the biblical sources where they are found, such as Exod 19:6; Ps 118:22; Isa 8:14; 28:6; 61:6; Hos 1:6, 9; 2:25. The Christian women who are subservient to their husbands are children of Sarah who called Abraham "lord." The Christians saved by baptism are the antitype of Noah and his family, saved "through" the waters of the flood (3:20, Gen 7:7 and 17). So in 1 Timothy, the author declares to "know that the law is good" when properly understood. That letter also makes use of Deuteronomic regulations in discussing the treatment of elders both exemplary and faulty (Deut 25:4, 17:6, 19:15).

The question arises as to why the striking change of attitude toward Jews occurred in Ephesus. One possible explanation for the deterioration of relations between the Christian community and the community of its religious antecedents might be the consequences of the Jewish revolt in 66–74.[33] In the first place, it would not be surprising that in the Graeco-Roman world, a great deal of animus would be felt toward the Jews who disturbed the peace of the Roman empire. The Christians at Ephesus, who previously were at odds with the Jews over some matters of teaching and practice, as these are expressed in the letter to the Ephesians, might have thought it better to dissociate themselves from the Jews to escape being linked together with them in this atmosphere of blame. Thus the Pastoral Epistles and 1 Peter might be attempts by the Christian community to demonstrate to their Graeco-Roman neighbors that their community accepts and advances Roman cultural aims. This scenario would have the letter to the Ephesians appear before the full effects of the Jewish revolt would have been felt in Asia. The Pastoral Epistles and 1 Peter would be epistles written after the revolt and

[33] Walter Bauer, *Orthodoxy and Heresy in Earliest Christianity* (Philadelphia: Fortress, 1979) 77–94.

in consequence of its effects. The letters of Ignatius (*To the Magnesians* 10–11, *To the Ephesians* 9, 18, 20) exhibit a stance against Jews which echo that in the Pastoral Epistles.

Walter Bauer detected a possible tendency toward gnosticism in the false teachers of the Pastorals, as in the Ephesus-centered letters of John and the letters of Ignatius.[34] To pursue this would divert this paper from its course. Suffice it to say that the deliberate distancing of the Christian community from Jewish and/or Jewish-Christian teaching might be explained by events in Israel and their consequences throughout Asia Minor. The consequences of this turn of events is a greater embrace of Graeco-Roman social and cultural values and a concomitant lessening of the place of women in the Pauline churches.

No News is not Necessarily Good News

Contemporary, feminist-inspired critics[35] of the household rules in all of the letters discussed above start their departure from the emancipatory baptismal confession in Gal 3:27–28: "For all of you who were baptized into Christ have clothed yourselves with Christ. There is neither Jew nor Greek, there is neither slave nor free person, there is not male and female; for you are all one in Christ Jesus." The presumption is that as eschatological urgency waned, the church began to acculturate itself socially with the Graeco-Roman environment. As a result, married women are seen to be subordinate in Colossians and this subordination is even justified Christologically in Ephesians. The revolutionary fact proclaimed in Gal 3:28 had political and social implications. The eschatological reality was put into practice at the community dinners (Gal 2:11–21) as a symbol that the eschatological hope had been realized. In the letter to Philemon, Paul suggests everyday practical applications of this new reality for the social and legal relationships within the community between Philemon, Onesimus, Paul, and the other believers at Colossae. When Colossians links the household code to the baptismal formula at 3:11, the author of the letter introduces a qualitative change; now slaves, formerly pronounced on a par with the free, are to be submissive, without the modifications introduced by Paul into the master/slave relationship. Furthermore, in calling for wives to be sub-

---

[34] *Ibid.*, 78; cf. Moritz (*A Profound Mystery*, 170) sees a similar situation for Ephesians.

[35] David L. Balch and Carolyn Osiek, *Families in the New Testament World: Households and House Churches*, (Louisville: Westminster/John Knox, 1997) 120–121, 178–179.

ordinate to husbands at Col 3:18, the author has omitted the "neither male and female" clause of Gal 3:28, as Paul himself did at 1 Cor 12:13.

There is a change here from earlier Christology, ritual and ethics. The Graeco-Roman household ethic blunts earlier Christian theology and practice.[36] Unlike Paul's references to his churches, the author of Ephesians refers to the cosmic body of Christ over which Christ is the head (1:2–22). Colossians uses the word church to refer to the local house church (4:15), the church of a city (4:16), and the cosmic body of Christ (1:18, 24). Christ as the head is a source of power and growth (Col 2;19; Eph 4:16). The body must submit to the head and this leads to the ethics of the household codes which reflect a Stoic social order that mirrors the social and status distinctions in the Graeco-Roman households.

What Distinctions were being erased in Gal 3:28?

It is important to notice that the conjunction in the three sets of pairs changes from "neither … nor" in the first two (Jew/Greek, slave/free) to "and" in the third (male and female). Matera[37] explains that the third formula seems to reflect Gen 1:27 "male and female he created them." The first two pairs refer to social distinctions and the eschatological formula erases these. The third pair addresses sexual differences but not the gender roles attached to them by society. Paul, at 1 Cor 11:2–16, gives no indication of sweeping these away. Moreover, the fact that marriage will become irrelevant in the eschaton (1 Cor 7), which echoes the gospel explanation that "they neither marry nor are given in marriage, but they are like the angels in heaven" (Mark 12:25, Matt 22:23–33), also suggests the implications of the Galatians baptismal formula. The explanation of the formula at 3:28d, "for you are all one in Christ Jesus," describes the new ontological status Christologically, since they are incorporated into the one Christ. Yet, the formula as it apears in 1 Cor 12 omits the male/female reference entirely.[38]

In view of the preceding discussion of the baptismal formula, it is hard to see it as expressing a reality from which Ephesians, or even Colossians, the Pastorals, and 1 Peter depart. Moreover, one is led to

---

[36] Balch and Osiek, *Families in the New Testament World*, 179, 183.
[37] Frank J. Matera, *Galatians* (SacPag 9; Collegeville: Liturgical, 1992) 142–143,146–147.
[38] Cf. Balch and Osiek, *Families in the New Testament World*, 178.

recall that the same Christological incorporation expressed here as the basis of eschatological unity, finds itself used by the author of Ephesians to modify the behavior of the husband toward his wife in view of their new relationship in Christ. Both letters use Christology for the same purpose.

Second, it does not seem to be a lessening of eschatological expectation that has caused changes in the expressions of the letters in question. Where those changes are verified, i.e. Colossians, the Pastorals, 1 Peter, historical circumstances can explain them. Again, to reiterate the point made previously, the new eschatological reality of the Christian speaks to sexual differences but not to gender roles.

The letter to the Colossians does indeed subordinate women to men but this subordination ought not be confused with what is said about husbands and wives in Ephesians. The exposition in the second part of this study has tried to establish that far from giving *carte blanche* to social inferiority and exploitation of women, Ephesians has ventured into a creative reexamination of spousal roles. Furthermore, the author of the letter does not use Christology as a tool to nail the doors shut on the women's quarters but rather to pry open the hearts of men not only to love their wives but even to submit to them in mutuality.

The issue of slavery is, of course, too large for us to treat in any detail, but the development of the *Haustafel* demands some attention. The assumption that the letter to Philemon demonstrates the emancipation of slaves might well be questioned, for Paul seems not to be suggesting freedom for Onesimus as much as to be afforded his service, however implicitly he expresses this.[39] Moreover, he asks for a welcome reception back into the household of this "now useful" Christian slave but with new standards of treatment. These considerations indicate that Paul himself understood the equality expressed in the baptismal formula at Gal 3:28 as less than absolute.

More directly on the point of gender distinctions, it is true that 1 Cor 12 does not focus on the head because it focuses on the need to accommodate the humbler, less gifted members. 1 Corinthians 11:3, on the other hand, does refer to Jesus as the head of every man in a section where he argues in favor of gender distinctions.

One wonders too whether the Pastoral Epistles' recommendation that women's way to salvation is through childbearing need bear the

---

[39] Houlden, *Paul's Prison Letters*, 226.

additional burden of being characterized as "heretical."[40] Greek moralists such as Maximus of Tyre (*Or.* 36.6b) express the view that marriage is for procreation and others even go so far as to cast a jaundiced eye on sexual pleasure even between spouses (Musonius Rufus fr. 12 and Seneca, *De matrimonio* fr.). And so this would satisfactorily explain how the Pastorals, in their attempt to present the Christian community's best face toward the Graeco-Roman world, would stress childbearing of women within marriage. On the other hand, Philo and Josephus both offer negative evaluations of pleasure within marriage and, in doing so, they seem to be following the lead of Hellenistic moralists.[41] Jewish texts, such as the *Testament of the Twelve Patriarchs*,[42] while expressing a similar denigration of sexual pleasure, stress the Law's emphasis on sexual relations to procreate offspring, as do Philo and Josephus. If this view of procreation as fulfilling the expectations of the Law is fundamental to the Jewish view of the effects of marriage, then it is not necessarily true that the prescription in 1 Tim 2:15 is an invention of the author in view of the Augustan moral reform efforts. Rather it could very well be an example of the letter's claim to know and follow the Law in its best aspects (1 Tim 1:8).

The contemporary critique of the household rules in these letters is, therefore, not news, in that it does not present a consistently accurate interpretation of the texts adduced in the argument. The situation is more nuanced as this study has tried to show. The earlier emancipatory declarations of Paul are not necessarily that emancipatory, nor are the later patriarchal texts necessarily all that patriarchal. Just as the traditional punctuation and translation of Eph 5:21–24 seems to have been influenced by concerns external to textual criticism and accuracy, so too at least some of the criticism against the same text in contemporary quarters. But this is not news either, inasmuch as each generation views the texts through lenses of assumptions and hermeneutical methods that reflect the cultural concerns of that age. The effort of scriptural interpreters, then, is to detect these assumptions and methodological preferences, and in doing so to understand where the text leaves off and the assumptions and preferences begin.

---

[40] So Balch and Osiek, *Families in the New Testament World*, 123.

[41] Marinus de Jonge, "Rachel's Virtuous Behavior in the *Testament of Issachar*," in *Greeks, Romans and Christians: Essays in Honor of Abraham J. Malherbe*, ed. D.L. Balch, E. Ferguson, and W.A. Meeks (Minneapolis: Fortress, 1990) 340–52, esp. 346–50.

[42] *Ibid.*, 340–46.

THE WASHING OF ADAM IN THE ACHERUSIAN LAKE (GREEK *LIFE OF ADAM AND EVE* 37.3) IN THE CONTEXT OF EARLY CHRISTIAN NOTIONS OF THE AFTERLIFE

Marinus de Jonge
and
L. Michael White[1]

Introduction

The last section of the Greek *Life of Adam and Eve*[2] (consisting of chapters 31–43) tells about events surrounding the deaths of Adam and Eve. In chapters 31–37 Adam, penitent and humble, departs to meet his Maker. Immediately after his death the angels and even the sun and the moon offer incense and prayers to God that he may have mercy on Adam (33, 35). The events are observed by Eve and Seth by means of a vision (34–36). Eve questions what she sees, but Seth explains why the sun and the moon, who are also praying over Adam's body, look like "black Ethiopians," since they are not able to shine before the "Father of Lights."[3] After this we read in chapter 37:

> (1) While Seth was saying this to his mother Eve, an angel sounded the trumpet and all the angels who were lying on their faces stood up and cried with a fearful voice, saying: (2) "Blessed be the glory of the Lord on the part of his creatures, for he has had mercy on Adam, the work of his hands." (3) When the angels had cried these words, one of the

---

[1] This essay started as a commentary on the Greek *Life of Adam and Eve* (*GLAE*) 37.3 by Marinus de Jonge in which he tried to demonstrate the Christian origin of the text. To this end, J. Tromp and R. Buitenwerf provided helpful discussion of some difficult passages. It then led Michael White to investigate further the Greek traditions concerning the Acherusian Lake (and the river Acheron) and the different forms in which this motif was taken up in Early Christianity. In its present form this contribution is offered as a joint tribute to Abe Malherbe, eminent scholar of Early Christianity in its Hellenistic environment, a good and mutual friend.

[2] The work is still often called the "Apocalypse of Moses," but this is a misnomer (found in earlier editions of the work) based on the wording in a "preface" that was added to the Greek text. This preface introduces the text as "The narrative and life of Adam and Eve ... *revealed to Moses* by God."

[3] Cf. Jas 1:17.

seraphs with six wings came, seized Adam and carried him off to the
Acherusian Lake; he washed him three times (καὶ ἀπήγαγεν αὐτὸν εἰς τὴν
Ἀχερουσίαν λίμνην καὶ ἀπέλουσεν αὐτὸν τρίτον) and brought him in the
presence of God. (4) He lay there for three hours. After that the Father
of all, sitting on his throne, stretched out his hand, raised Adam up, and
handed him over to the archangel Michael, saying to him: (5) "Take him
up to Paradise, to the third heaven, and leave him there till that great
day when I shall establish order in the world." (6) Then Michael took
Adam away and left him where God had told him. And all the angels
sang an angelic hymn, marveling at the pardon granted to Adam.

The washing of Adam in the Acherusian Lake comes as a surprise.
Known from Greek sources, including Homer and Plato, the Acherusian Lake was a principal landmark in the mythical landscape of Hades,
the realm of the dead. Hence, the question arises what the presence of
such a typically Greek notion tells us about the background and the
origin of the pseudepigraphic tradition in the *Life of Adam and Eve*. To
answer this question we shall have to look for parallels in Jewish and
Christian writings. Before that, however, we shall have to consider some
basic facts about the *Life of Adam and Eve* in its different versions, and to
refer to some recent studies.[4]

The Different Versions of the Life of Adam and Eve

For a long time only three main versions (Greek, Latin, and Slavonic)
were known for this text. To these have recently been added an Armenian one, entitled *The Penitence of Adam*[5] and a Georgian *Book of Adam*.[6]
These five versions now have to be studied alongside one another. G.
A. Anderson and M. E. Stone have brought them together in *A Synopsis of the Books of Adam and Eve*, an indispensable tool for all study of
the writing.[7] Unfortunately we still do not have a new critical edition of

---

[4] Helpful introductions are M. E. Stone, *A History of the Literature of Adam and Eve*
(SBLEJL 3; Atlanta: Scholars, 1992) and M. de Jonge and J. Tromp, *The Life of Adam and
Eve and Related Literature* (Sheffield: Sheffield Academic Press, 1997).

[5] M. E. Stone, *The Penitence of Adam* (CSCO 429–30; Louvain: Peeters, 1981). The
Penitence is not to be confused with an Armenian version (already known for some time)
that is generally regarded as a secondary witness to the Greek text.

[6] C. Kʻurcʻikidze, "Adamis apokripʻuli cʻxovrebis kʻartʻuli versia," *Pʻilologiuri dziebani*
1 (1964) 97–136. A French translation is given in J.-P. Mahé, "Le livre d'Adam géor-
gien," *Studies in Gnosticism and Hellenistic Religions* (Festschrift G. Quispel), ed. R. van den
Broek and M. J. Vermaseren (EPRO 9; Leiden: Brill, 1981) 227–260.

[7] *A Synopsis of the Books of Adam and Eve* (SBLEJL 5; Atlanta: Scholars, 1994), now in
a second, revised edition (SBLEJL 17; Atlanta: Scholars, 1999).

the Greek, although M. Nagel did much useful preparatory work and supplied abundant information on the Greek manuscripts.[8] The situation with regard to the Latin is even worse, given the very great number of textual witnesses, often differing considerably among themselves. *Mutatis mutandis* the same applies to the Slavonic.

The relationships between these versions have been a matter of much discussion. In a recent article M. de Jonge has argued that the Greek version presents the oldest attainable form of the writing.[9] Among the Greek manuscripts three (DSV) generally give the shortest and the oldest form of text. A second group of Greek manuscripts (ATLC) presents a text with a number of significant additions. Though secondary, this text must also be relatively old because all other versions show familiarity with the extra materials found in it. It can, by and large, be found in the text supplied by Nagel for A.-M. Denis's *Concordance grecque des pseudépigraphes d'Ancien Testament*,[10] and used in the Anderson-Stone *Synopsis*.

The Armenian and the Georgian versions go back to a common ancestor, and this family of texts may be situated between the Greek and the Latin. Comparison with the Greek text shows a number of secondary readings in Arm.-Georg. Next, they add to the beginning a long story about the penitence of Adam and Eve after their expulsion from Paradise (and some other themes), which is also found in the Latin version. This material is probably old, but not an original part of the oldest version of the *Life of Adam and Eve*.

The Latin version provides a considerably shortened and heavily redacted account of the death and burial of Adam and Eve. The Slavonic version is related to two Greek mss. (R and M) which give (among other things) a much shorter version of the repentance of Adam and Eve, after their expulsion from Paradise has been mentioned in chapter 29. Here, and elsewhere, the Slavonic very much goes its own way.

---

[8] *La vie d'Adam et d'Eve (Apocalypse de Moïse)*, vols. 1–3 (Lille: Service de réproduction, Université de Lille III, 1974). J. Tromp is currently working on a new edition.

[9] See "The Literary Development of the Life of Adam and Eve," *Literature on Adam and Eve. Collected Essays*, ed. G. A. Anderson, M. E. Stone and J. Tromp (SVTP 15; Leiden: Brill, 2000) 239–49. See earlier De Jonge and Tromp, *The Life of Adam and Eve*, 28–44. For a contrasting view, see G. A. Anderson, "The Original Form of *The Life of Adam and Eve*: A Proposal," in *Literature on Adam and Eve*, 215–31.

[10] Louvain-la-Neuve: Institut Orientaliste, 1987. The text is found on 815–8.

As far as chapter 37 in the Greek version is concerned, we find the following picture. There are a number of variant readings (including omissions) in the Greek mss., but it is not difficult to reconstruct the oldest attainable text. This restored original formed the basis for the translation given above. It is supported by the Georgian version (with some minor variants). The chapter is not found in the Armenian, which omits the whole of 33.1–38.1. Because Georgian is present here, we may be sure that it existed in the common ancestor of the Armenian and the Georgian. The Slavonic section corresponding to the chapter 37 in the Greek follows at a greater distance, but mentions the threefold washing in the Acherusian Lake. The Latin version presents a complicated picture. Meyer's edition gives an abbreviated story.[11] Michael tells the mourning Seth that God has had mercy on Adam. All angels sound the trumpet blessing God for his mercy on his creature. Then Seth sees the extended hand of God, delivering Adam over to Michael with the words:

> Let him be in your custody until the day when I shall establish order in punishment (*usque in diem dispensationis in suppliciis*),[12] until the last years when I will turn his sorrow into joy. Then he shall sit on the throne of him who overthrew him.[13]

One Latin manuscript, Paris BNF, lat. 3832, recently published by J. Pettorelli, has a longer text, nearer to the Greek.[14]

> *pone eum in paradiso in tertio caelo, usque in diem dispensationis qui dicitur economia, quando faciam omnibus misericordiam per dilectissimum filium meum.*

---

[11] See W. Meyer, "Vita Adae et Evae," *Abhandlungen der königlich bayerischen Akademie der Wissenschaften, Philosophische-philologische Klasse* 14 (Munich: Verlag der K. Akademie, 1878). Meyer's text is reprinted in Stone and Anderson, *Synopsis of the Books of Adam and Eve*.

[12] 47.3 in the Latin *Vita*. The text and translation are uncertain. M. D. Johnson (*The Old Testament Pseudepigrapha*, ed. by J. H. Charlesworth [2 vols.; Garden City: Doubleday, 1985] 2.290) translates this phrase "until the day of dispensing punishment." J. Tromp (orally) points to a variant word order in the edition of J. H. Mozley, "The Vita Adae," *JTS* 30 (1929) 121–49: *in suppliciis usque ad diem dispensacionis*. Because it is strange that Adam should be continually punished after God has shown his mercy on him, Tromp suggests that *supplicium* (above translated "punishment") should be taken in the sense of *supplicatio* ("entreaty, humble prayer"), referring to Adam's state while in Michael's custody.

[13] The end of this passage from "when I will turn ..." onwards, has a parallel in *GLAE* 39:2.

[14] "Vie latine d'Adam et d'Ève. La recension de Paris, BNF, lat. 3832," *Archivum Latinitatis Medii Aevi* 57 (1999) 5–52.

This is much closer to the Greek than the text found in the other Latin witnesses. It is particularly close to the Georgian, which reads: "Take him to the third heaven, to the Garden, and leave him before the altar until the day of the *oikonomia* which I contemplate concerning all the fleshly (beings) with my well-beloved son" (trans. Stone/Anderson). The new manuscript also has an equivalent of Gr. 37.3, in which we read: "*Ecce subito uenit seraphim sex alas habens et rapuit Adam, duxitque eum in stanno cerosio, ibique eum baptizauit. Deinde eum adduxit in conspectu domini dei.*" Here *stannum* will stand for *stagnum* ("pool, pond"); *cerosio* is unattested and must go back to a misreading at some stage of *Acheron* (or perhaps one of its cognate forms, e.g., *Acheros* or *Acherusia*).[15]

Chapters 31–37: Their Literary Context in the Greek Version

From here on we shall concentrate on the Greek *Life of Adam and Eve* in its oldest form (hereafter cited as *GLAE*). The first question to be asked concerns the place and function of chapters 31–37 in this version.

The first major part of *GLAE* is the so-called "Testament of Eve" in chapters 15–30. Its contents and function are summed up in the final verse: "Now then, children, I have shown you the way in which we were deceived. But take heed that you yourselves do not forsake the good" (30.1). Eve's testament is preceded by a short overall introduction (chs. 1–4), a brief account by Adam of the events in Paradise (chs. 5–8), and a story of a failed attempt by Eve and Seth to get the "oil of mercy" from the Garden in order to alleviate Adam's pains (chs. 9–13). Because Adam is unable to relate the full story of deception and sin in Paradise, Eve tells it (14.1–2; 31.1).

Eve's story is concerned with the events narrated in Genesis 3. It dwells on the actions of the serpent as an instrument of Satan, the archenemy of humankind. He tries to deceive Eve and Adam through her; of course, he ultimately succeeds (chs. 15–21, cf. Gen 3:1–7). Immediately after this, God descends to Paradise and pronounces judgment (chs. 22–29, cf. Gen 3:8–24). The sin of Adam and Eve consists in their transgression of God's commandment (14.3; 24.1, 4;

---

[15] We should note that four of the Greek manuscripts omit the initial "A;" the Georgian version speaks of "the lake of cheron" and the Slavonic, the "sea of gerusia" (so Anderson and Stone, *Synopsis*[2], 82). Compare also the orthographic variant *Acerosius*, found in a Latin ms. of the *Apocalypse of Paul*, discussed below at n. 34.

25.1). Eve is particularly to blame, as she acknowledges (25.1, 3), but Adam is also responsible, as he explicitly confesses (27.2–3).

Adam's confession of sin (followed by that of Eve in 32.2) is accompanied by a request for forgiveness. In his righteousness God punishes Adam, refuses him access to the tree of life, and expels him from Paradise (27.4–28.3; cf. 29). At the same time, however, he tells him: "If you, after your departure from Paradise, guard yourself from all evil, prepared (rather) to die (than to transgress), I shall raise you at the time of the resurrection. From the tree of life will be given you, and you will be immortal for ever" (28.4).

This promise points to all that will be narrated in the final chapters (beginning at 31) that follow Eve's testament. Neither the promise nor the scene narrated in chapters 31–43 is found in Genesis 3; therefore, it may be argued that in *GLAE* the emphasis falls on these final chapters. The *GLAE* wants to show that God the Creator, who brought the protoplasts into being and put them in the Garden of Eden, is righteous and merciful toward all who, like Adam and Eve, repent wholeheartedly when they sin and who are prepared to live henceforth in accordance with his commandments.[16]

The same emphasis on God's righteousness and mercy vis-à-vis Adam and Eve (and their offspring) is found in interpretations of Genesis 3 in several important Christian apologists of the later second century CE (Theophilus of Antioch and Irenaeus) and beginning of the third century (Tertullian). These interpretations were part of their defense of the Old Testament against all those in their time who, like Marcion and his followers, maintained that Genesis spoke of a different God, weak, inconsistent, and malignant. The parallel approach to Genesis 3 employed in *GLAE* and in these early Christian authors provides a strong argument for a Christian origin of the former.[17]

The final section of *GLAE*, consisting of chapters 31–43, is very complex—too complex to be analyzed here in detail.[18] For the purpose of the present essay it is sufficient to note that two related but

---

[16] Cf. M. Meiser, "Sünde, Buße und Gnade in dem Leben Adams und Evas," in Anderson, *Literature on Adam and Eve*, 297–313.

[17] See, in more detail, M. de Jonge, "The Christian Origin of the Greek Life of Adam and Eve," in Anderson, *Literature on Adam and Eve*, 347–63.

[18] For what follows see the analysis in J. Tromp, "Literary and Exegetical Issues in the Story of Adam's Death and Burial (*GLAE* 31–42)," *The Book of Genesis in Jewish and Oriental Christian Interpretation*, ed. J. Frishman and L. Van Rompay (Traditio Exegetica Graeca 5; Louvain: Peeters, 1997) 25–41.

distinct vignettes are combined. One is about Adam's heavenly afterlife, in a Paradise located in heaven. It ends in 37.6, and is followed
by another account of the burial of Adam in the earthly Paradise, that
emphasizes the promise of an eschatological resurrection (38.1–42.2).
The transition between the two is rather clumsy. After a request by
Michael concerning Adam,[19] God again descends to earth, where the
body of Adam still lies (ch. 38). He next addresses Adam's body about
the latter's disobedience to his commandment, but promises him that
he will be brought back to his dominion and will sit on the throne of
the devil (ch. 39). Then, the angels Michael, Gabriel, and Uriel prepare Adam's body for burial. They simultaneously prepare Abel's body,
which still lies unburied since his murder by Cain (ch. 40). Once again
God calls to Adam's body, which answers: "Here I am, Lord" (cf. Gen
3:8). God now promises Adam's own resurrection and that of all people
(ch. 41, cf. earlier 10.2; 28.4). Finally, God seals Adam's grave, and all
the heavenly beings return to their abode (42.1–2).

Despite the clumsiness, there is no reason to suppose that there ever
existed a form of the *GLAE* (older than the present Greek version)
that contained only one of these two vignettes. In both vignettes the
central issue is the future fate of Adam, and no clear distinction is
made between Adam's body and his spirit. Death is regularly said to
come about when Adam leaves his body,[20] and the surviving part of
Adam is called spirit in some passages,[21] but soul in others.[22] At the
same time Adam's body is said to lie down (33.3; 37.4; cf. 35.2), and
we hear how it is washed (37.3). Earlier, Seth was portrayed as kneeling
over his father's body in grief (34.2; 35.1). Finally Michael brings him
into the third heaven to Paradise (37.5–6), and yet there is a body still
to be buried (38–41).

Adam in the heavenly Paradise awaits the day of the final judgement
(37.5), elsewhere called the day of the resurrection (10.2, cf. 28.4; 41.3
and also 39.2–3). Meanwhile, Adam's body is buried in the earthly

---

[19] The most original Greek text of 38.1 probably has to be understood as follows:
"After the future joy of Adam (had thus been announced), Michael cried to the
Father concerning (the body of) Adam." The first clause is omitted by a number of
manuscripts which clearly did not know what to make of it. Ms. B, often very free,
gives an obviously secondary version of the entire verse. Surprisingly it is followed by a
number of modern translators (see Tromp, "Literary and Exegetical Issues," 27–28).

[20] So 31.1, 4; 32.4: cf. earlier 13.6 and later 42.8, speaking about the death of Eve.

[21] In 31.4 and 32.4.

[22] In 13.6; cf. 43.3.

Paradise; and so dust returns to dust (40.6–41.2, cf. Gen 3:19). Not only the surviving part of Adam in heaven, but also the body that will be raised can be designated as Adam (38.1; 40.3, 5, cf. 42.3–4). God addresses the body as "Adam" and it is able to answer (41.1). The final chapters of the *GLAE* are concerned with Adam, as well as Eve and her burial (particularly in 42.3–43.4), and, through them, with the future fate of all human beings. These chapters are not interested, however, in any precise anthropology, or in the location(s) of Paradise.

The Acherusian Lake in Jewish and Christian Literature

In a very informative article Erik Peterson has gathered most of the important parallels to the passage concerning the Acherusian Lake (*GLAE* 37.3) and discussed them in detail.[23] In particular, he was trying to trace this motif back to Jewish origins. No one can afford to neglect this study, though there is room for criticism of his overall approach to the matter.

The Apocalypse of Peter

The first text to be mentioned is at the beginning of *Apocalypse of Peter* 14. Since the *Apocalypse of Peter* is twice quoted by Clement of Alexandria,[24] it must therefore have been written in the second century C.E. The text is only preserved otherwise in an Ethiopic version translated from a Greek original. Parts of this Greek original are known from a fragmentary papyrus ms. from Akhmim.[25] The passage relating to the Acherusian Lake is also known in Greek from the so-called Rainer fragment (from the third or fourth century).[26] The Greek reads:

> I will give to my called and my elect whomever they request of me from out of punishment. And I will give them a beautiful baptism in salvation

---

[23] "Die 'Taufe' im Acherusischen See" *VC* 9 (1955), 1–20, reprinted in the collection of his essays *Frühkirche, Judentum und Gnosis* (Rome, Freiburg, Vienna: Herder, 1959) 310–32. The reprint was used in the preparation of this study.

[24] *Eclog.* 41.2 and 48–49. There is also a possible allusion to the text in Theophilus of Antioch, *Ad Autolycum* 2.19, which, if true, would push the *terminus ante quem* some twenty years or so earlier.

[25] Which includes the section quoted by Clement in *Eclog.* 41.2.

[26] For a survey of witnesses, see J. K. Elliott, "The Apocalypse of Peter," *The Apocryphal New Testament* (Oxford: Clarendon, 1993) 593–612, and C. Detlef G. Müller, "Offenbarung des Petrus," *Neutestamentliche Apokryphen*, ed. E. Hennecke and W. Schneemelcher (fifth edition; 2 vols.; Tübingen: Mohr, 1989) 2:562–78.

from the Acherusian Lake which is said to be in the Elysian field (καὶ δώσω αὐτοῖς καλὸν βάπτισμα ἐν σωτηρίᾳ Ἀχερουσίας λίμνης ἣν καλοῦσιν ἐν τῷ Ἠλυσίῳ πεδίῳ), a share in righteousness with my saints. And I and my elect will go, rejoicing with the patriarchs into my eternal kingdom, and I will fulfill for them my promises which I and my Father in heaven promised them.[27]

We note that the righteous elect are allowed to make intercession for others who after being saved by a baptism in the Acherusian Lake (situated in the Elysian field) are allowed to enter into the heavenly bliss with the holy ones.

The Sibylline Oracles

A similar picture is found in *Sib. Or.* 2.330–338, where we read:

> To these pious ones the imperishable God, the universal ruler, will also give another thing. Whenever they ask the imperishable God to save men from the raging fire and deathless gnashing, he will grant it, and he will do this. For he will pick them out again from the undying flame and set them elsewhere and send them on account of his own people to another eternal life with the immortals in the Elysian plain where are the long waves of the deep perennial Acherusian Lake (ὅθι οἱ πέλε κύματα μακρὰ λίμνης ἀενάου Ἀχερουσιάδος βαθυκόλπου).[28]

Books 1 and 2 of the *Sibylline Oracles* belong together and are generally considered Christian.[29] J. K. Elliott, following the example of M. R. James, includes a translation of the entire section of *Sib. Or.* 2.190–338 as an appendix to the *Apocalypse of Peter* on the grounds that the former seems to be dependent on the latter.[30] Again the emphasis is on the prayer of the righteous for (an unspecified category of) sinners who are

---

[27] Here following the translation by D. D. Buchholz, *Your Eyes Will Be Opened. A Study of the Greek (Ethiopic) Apocalypse of Peter* (SBLDS 97; Atlanta: Scholars, 1988) 345. See also Elliott, *The Apocryphal New Testament*, 609 n. 40, who adapts the translation of M. R. James in "The Rainer fragment of the Apocalypse of Peter," *JTS* 32 (1931) 270–9. The Ethiopic text is here clearly secondary; so, in particular, Buchholz, *Your Eyes Will Be Opened*, 342–62.

[28] Translation by J. J. Collins in *The Old Testament Pseudepigrapha*, 1:352 (slightly altered).

[29] See E. Schürer, G. Vermes, F. Millar, and M. Goodman, *The History of the Jewish People in the Age of Jesus Christ (175 B.C.-A.D. 135)* (4 vols.; Edinburgh: T & T Clark, 1986) 3.1:645; A. Kurfess and J. D. Gauger, *Sibyllinische Weissagungen* (Düsseldorf/Zürich: Artemis und Winkler, 1998) 418–9. Collins, *Old Testament Pseudepigrapha*, 1:330 regards *Sib. Or.* 1–2 as Jewish, with interpolations by a Christian redactor.

[30] Elliott, *The Apocryphal New Testament*, 613 referring to M. R. James, *The Apocryphal New Testament* (Oxford: Clarendon, 1924) 521–4. Peterson ("Die 'Taufe' im Acherusis-

thereby saved from punishment and receive eternal life with God's people. One should note, however, that this passage in the Sibyllines speaks
of a raging fire and an undying flame, and that it does not mention an
ablution in the Acherusian Lake; we hear only of its "great/long billow-
ing waves" (κύματα μακρά) and its location in the Elysian field. Other
passages within the Sibylline Oracles, including one clearly Jewish passage, mention an alternative name, the river Acheron.[31]

The Apocalypse of Paul

A third passage which mentions the Acherusian Lake is *Apocalypse of
Paul* 22–23. Of its many versions the longer form of the Latin (L1), also
called the *Visio Pauli*, is generally regarded as the earliest one, translated
from a second edition of the now lost Greek original (dating to the
mid-third century).[32] In the passage concerned, an accompanying angel
conducts Paul to a river of which the waters are "whiter than milk"
(*super lac*).[33] The angel tells him:

---

chen See," 311) agrees: "Bekanntlich hat das zweite Buch der Oracula Sibyllina grosse
Teile der Petrus-Apokalypse poetisch wiedergegeben."

[31] *Sib. Or.* 1.283–306 describing the sixth generation, "a good, an excellent one,"
tells that the "happy men to whom Sabaoth gave a noble mind," will "go away to
Acheron, in the halls of Hades, and there they will have honor" (1.304, cf. 302). In *Sib.
Or.* 5.484–485, a Jewish passage quoted by Clement of Alexandria (*Protr.* 4.50.3), the
Sibyl addresses Isis as "thrice-wretched goddess, you will remain by the streams of the
Nile alone, a speechless maenad on the sands of Acheron." In the latter, the poetic
parallelism seems to equate the traditional Egyptian symbol of burial as "crossing the
Nile" with crossing the Acheron in Hades. For the name of the river, Acheron, as part
of the landscape of Hades see also below.

[32] See Elliott, "The Apocalypse of Paul," *The Apocryphal New Testament*, 616–44;
H. Duensing and A. Aurelio de Santos Otero, "Apokalypse des Paulus," *Neutestamentliche
Apokryphen* 2, 644–75. See now T. Silverstein and A. Hilhorst, *Apocalypse of Paul. A New
Critical Edition of three Long Latin Versions* (COr 21; Genève: P. Cramer, 1997). According to
these two authors (*ibid.*, 11–21) the longer Latin recension (L1 and L3, preserved in the
four earliest Latin mss.; see the next note) represent a version made between 450 and
530 from a "second edition" of the apocalypse in Greek to be dated in the beginning
of the fifth century C.E. Silverstein and Hilhorst think that the lost "first edition" of
the Greek must have existed in Egypt around the middle of the third century C.E. A
different view of the dating and the transmission is suggested by C. Carozzi, *Eschatologie
et au-delà: Recherches sur l'Apocalypse de Paul* (Aix-en-Provence: Université de Provence,
1994) 165–6.

[33] We shall return to this passage in the concluding section of this study. The text
of the *Apocalypse of Paul* is difficult to establish. The longer Latin version is preserved in
four mss. which Silverstein and Hilhorst consider to be the most important witnesses to
the text. They include the mss. from Paris and St. Gall (designated L1), which were used
in the older editions, including those of Carozzi and Deunsing-Otero in *Neutestamentliche*

This is the Acherusian Lake where is the City of Christ, but not every man is permitted to enter that city; for this is the journey which leads to Christ (two mss.: to that city). And if anyone is a fornicator and impious, and is converted and will repent and bear fruits worthy of repentance, at first when he has gone out of the body, he is brought and worships God (two mss. omit: he is … God) and thence, by command of God (the Paris ms. only), he is delivered to the angel Michael, and he baptizes him in the Acherusian Lake (*et baptizat eum in Acerosium lacum*). Then he leads him into the City of Christ alongside those who have never sinned.[34]

The angel, standing on the Acherusian Lake, provides a golden ship to take Paul to the City of Christ. Three thousand hymn-singing angels accompany Paul, until he arrives in the city. A little later (chap. 31) the angel and Paul return by the same route and again cross the Acherusian Lake.[35] We note that nothing is said about intercession by the righteous, but that the conversion, repentance, and acts of penitence of the sinner get much attention. It is interesting that Michael is the one who baptizes the repentant sinner in the Lake.[36]

Apokryphen. These have now been supplemented by two other mss. from the Escorial (classed with L1) and Arnhem (designated L3) in the edition of Silverstein and Hilhorst. Both Carozzi and Silverstein-Hilhorst also print the text of a shorter Latin recension (L2) known from three mss. of Vienna, Graz, and Zurich; however, on the whole these are not very helpful for establishing the earliest text. At present there is no critical edition of the *Apocalypse of Paul*, so readings must take account of variations in the four main mss. (see next note). See also the review of Silverstein and Hilhorst by J. Tromp in *VC* 52 (1998) 213–17.

[34] Here we have adapted Elliott's translation in *The Apocryphal New Testament*, 629–30 on the basis of the Latin texts in the edition of Silverstein and Hilhorst. The manuscript from the Escorial does not mention the baptism in the Lake; it is clearly confused towards the end: "… at first when he has gone out of the body, he is led to that city by angels and delivered to the archangel Michael." The spelling varies; The St. Gall ms. reads *Acherusius/-m* consistently, while the Paris (Fleury) ms. reads *Aceriosus* in the first instance and *Acerosium* in the second. The first should be taken as metathesis, so that the proper nominative should be *Acerosium* in the orthography of the Fleury ms. This form also occurs at the beginning of chap. 23 in this ms. using the spelling *Acerosium [lacum]*. The Arnhem ms. has *Acerusius/o/um* three times and the Escorial ms. twice, using the orthography *Agerusius* and *Agerosium*. The latter also confuse *locus* for *lacus*.

[35] The Acherusian Lake is also mentioned at these same two points in the text of a (later) Greek version published by C. Tischendorf, *Apocalypses Apocryphae* (Leipzig: H. Mendelssohn, 1866; repr. Hildesheim: G. Olms, 1966) 34–69, the passage is on 51–52. It has a slightly different version and leaves off the latter part of chap. 22, even though the mention of the Acherusian Lake is clearly preserved. The second reference, parallel to the Latin given above, reads: ὅταν δὲ μετανοήσῃ καὶ μεταστᾰθῇ τοῦ βίου, παραδίδοται τῷ Μιχαήλ, καὶ βάλλουσιν αὐτὸν εἰς τὴν ἀχέρουσαν λίμνην.

[36] In the two manuscripts which have this detail, the soul is brought to worship God before being handed to Michael.

The Book of the Resurrection of Christ

There is yet another Christian text that deserves our attention, the *Book of the Resurrection of Jesus Christ by Bartholomew the Apostle*.[37] Here we find a sort of excursus (chapters 21–22) that explains why Thomas was absent during the meeting of the risen Christ with the apostles (cf. John 20:24). Thomas had received news of the death of his son Siophanes. When he arrives, his son has already been buried, but Thomas raises him from the dead. Siophanes tells him about all he saw in heaven after his soul had left his body. He was conducted by Michael, who made him cross a river of fire and ascend to heaven; there he brought him to the Lake of Acheron,[38] and submerged him three times in the water (21.5–6). Directly afterwards he was admitted to the heavenly Paradise.

Other Christian Parallels

Peterson mentions two further texts. Around 400 C.E. Prudentius speaks in his *Cathemerinon*, hymn 5 (*ad incensum lucernae* or "at lamp lighting") about "that night in which the holy God returned from the waters of Acheron to those living on earth" (5.127–8: *illa nocte, sacer qua rediit Deus stagnis ad superos ex Acherunticis*). That night, just before Easter, the spirits of those who sinned and suffer punishment, enjoy a brief rest and reprieve (cf. 5.125–36).[39] Quite different is a Coptic magical text preserved in London *ms. Or.* 5987.[40] Here seven important spirits are said to dwell near Antioch, at a place called "Acherusian Lake," flowing from underneath the throne of Jao Sabaoth (lines 18–24). The editor of this text thinks that the places mentioned here are located in heaven.[41]

---

[37] Now to be consulted in J.-D. Kaestli and P. Chérix, *L'évangile de Barthélemy d'après deux écrits apocryphes* (Turnhout: Brepols, 1993). The second section (143–241) is devoted to the Coptic *Book of the Resurrection*, which is dated by its translators in the fifth or sixth century CE (so esp. 170, 172).

[38] Note that in this text the name of the river has become that of the lake, see below.

[39] See text, translation and note in M. Lavarenne, *Prudence I, Cathemerinon Liber (Livre d'heures)*, (Collection Budé; Paris: Les Belles Lettres, 1943) 30–1.

[40] The text was edited and translated by A. M. Kropp, *Ausgewählte Zaubertexte* (2 vols.; Bruxelles: Fondation Égyptologique Reine Elisabeth, 1931) 1:22–28 and 2:149–160.

[41] In passing I note that *3 Ap. Bar.* 10 speaks about a great lake in the third (fourth) heaven where the souls of the righteous assemble. This clearly resembles the Acherusian Lake, but it is not called by that name. See D. C. Harlow, *The Greek Apocalypse of Baruch (3 Baruch) in Hellenistic Judaism and Early Christianity* (SVTP 12; Leiden: Brill, 1996) 142–6. Harlow interprets this apocalypse as both a Jewish and a Christian text.

The uncertainties, in some cases, surrounding their transmission notwithstanding, the first four texts mentioned in this section, with all their differences, show several features which seem to be consistent with all of them. These shed light on the following points in *GLAE* 37: Adam's repentance, the intercessory prayers in heaven, the cleansing—three times—by an angel in the Acherusian Lake, and the admission to Paradise in heaven. What these texts leave unclear is how one goes from the earth to Acherusian Lake, traditionally located in the underworld, to the Paradise in heaven. The geography of the afterlife has not yet been fully mapped out.

Peterson[42] notes these parallels when he looks for possible Jewish conceptions behind the apocalypses of Peter and Paul. He has to admit, however, that *GLAE* 37 is not free from Christian redaction, and he is not able to find any clearly Jewish text which mentions the Acherusian Lake.[43] The obvious conclusion is that all the texts discussed so far, including the *GLAE*, represent early *Christian* appropriations of the Greek traditions about the Acherusian Lake. In support of this, it may be useful to look for a moment at the Greek sources for this tradition, especially Plato's *Phaedo*, before turning to some commentaries by early Christian authors.

The Acherusian Lake: from Homer to Plato

Plato's statements about the Acherusian Lake are found in a long disquisition of Socrates (*Phaedo* 107c–115a; cf. 80e–82b) on the future destination of the soul. The tradition of the Acherusian Lake, however, goes back to Homer, where it became well known as one of the key elements of the landscape of Hades. In Homeric tradition Hades, the realm of the dead, was separated from the world of the living by a kind of no-man's land. The shades of the dead haunt this no-man's land until proper burial has occurred, and then—and only then—are they allowed to cross the body of water (either lake or river) which marks the entrance into Hades proper.[44] The body of water is simply

---

[42] See especially "Die 'Taufe' im Acherusischen See," 319–23.

[43] Note, however, the anomalous reference to Acheron in *Sib. Or.* 5.484–485, which Peterson does not seem to have known. See above n. 31.

[44] This summary of the early Greek tradition, is based on the recent, in-depth study of C. Sourvinou-Inwood, *'Reading' Greek Death to the End of the Classical Period* (Oxford: Clarendon, 1995) 61–3, and the extensive bibliography provided. A useful survey of the views of afterlife in Greek and Roman tradition is also given by Alan E. Bernstein,

called "river" (ποταμός) in *Iliad* 23.71–4, but is identified as the Styx in *Iliad* 8.369. In *Odyssey* 10.508–15 (cf. 11.155–9) the rivers have multiplied to include Oceanus, Styx, Pyriphlegethon, Cocytos, and Acheron. Oceanus marks the boundary to Hades' house. On the other side stands the grove of Persephone with its trees and vegetation. The four rivers are there: Cocytus is designated as a branch of the Styx; Cocytus and Pyriphlegethon are said to flow into the river Acheron; and a large boulder stands at this confluence of the rivers. This proliferation of names and details corresponds with an elaboration of the underworld landscape already at work in the later Archaic period.[45] By the fifth century BCE, one finds an even more extensive geography, but now it is the river Acheron and/or the lake, Acherusia, that usually mark the border, where one must board the ferry of Charon to make the crossing.[46]

In the Classical period, a *nekyomanteion* (an oracle or evocation of the shades of the dead) became a regular feature of the crossing into Hades. It was particularly associated with the Acherusian Lake and probably helps explain why this name became the most prominent.[47] Hence, a key feature of the Greek conception of the rite of passage from life to death included an appearance of the shade(s) at the Acherusian Lake. Eventually, this mythical landscape, conceived as a parallel "world" to the land of the living above, was the source of further commentary and interpretation down into Hellenistic and Imperial times.[48] The most

---

The Formation of Hell: Death and Retribution in the Ancient and Early Christian Worlds (Ithaca: Cornell Univ. Press, 1993) 21–129. The study of Emily Vermeule, *Aspects of Death in Early Greek Art and Poetry* (Berkeley: Univ. of California Press, 1979) remains very useful as well. Also for a review essay on earlier studies of death and afterlife in the Greek world see Peter Green, "On the Thanatos Trail," in *Classical Bearings: Interpreting Ancient History and Culture* (London: Thames and Hudson, 1989) 63–76.

[45] Sourvinou-Inwood, *'Reading' Greek Death*, 61.

[46] Compare Aeschylus, *Sept. contra Theb.* 856; Theocritus 17.47; Pausanias 10.28.4; Euripides, *Alcest.* 252–3; 443; 900–2; Aristophanes, *Ranae* 181–3; 193; 471; Sophocles, *Elec.* 137–8; Aeschylus, *Agam.* 1160; Thucydides 1.46; Xenophon, *Anab.* 6.2.2. The names Acheron and Acherusia are not always given.

[47] So Porphyry's commentary on a reference in Sophocles *Polyxena*. See the discussion of this period in Sourvinou-Inwood, *'Reading' Greek Death*, 307–8.

[48] Compare Cicero, *Tusc. disp.* 1.16.37; 1.21.48; Vergil, *Aen.* 6. 298–304; 384–94; *Anthol. Pal.* 5.240; 7.67–68; 7.365; Apuleius, *Metam.* 6.18; Lucian, *Dial. mort.* 20.1; *Necyomantia* 10; *Contemplantes* 7; *De luctu* 3. In the Latin tradition the name Styx, used both of the river and the lake, sometimes holds the place of Acheron in Plato's account. In *Aeneid* book 6, where Aeneas makes his journey to the underworld, Acheron is mentioned clearly as a part of the realm dominated by the geography of the Styx.

influential of these was Plato's, who concluded that the river Acheron flowed into the lake Acherusia, which then lay at the edge of the Elysian fields, the realm of the blessed. Of the four rivers[49] of Hades, Acheron and the lake into which it feeds, are clearly the most benign (*Phaedo* 112e–113a). So we turn to the disquisition of Socrates.

Socrates remarks: "It is right to think then, gentlemen, that if the soul is immortal, it requires our care not only for the time we call life, but for the sake of all time, and that one is in terrible danger if one does not give it that care (107c)."[50] The disquisition takes the form of a myth, a travelog of the underworld. Of this Socrates says:

> No sensible man would insist that those things are as I have described them, but I think it is fitting for a man to risk the belief—for the risk is a noble one—that this, or something like this, is true about our souls and their dwelling places, since the soul is evidently immortal, and a man should repeat this to himself as if it were an incantation, which is why I have been prolonging my tale.[51]

In order to describe the destination of the departed souls Plato gives an elaborate picture of the entire cosmos, which is much vaster than humans on earth can perceive. The subterranean world is surrounded by the waters of Oceanus, while the different realms of Hades are defined by the four rivers, Acheron, Pyriphlegethon, Cocytus, and Styx (112e–113c). Most of the dead wind up at the shores of the Acherusian Lake (113a). The worst go to Tartarus, the pit of Hades full of fire and torment which is fed by the two raging rivers Pyriphlegethon[52] and Cocytus (113b–c). Criminals and scoundrels are hurled into Tartarus

---

[49] So 112e–113c, but in actuality there are five named by Plato; he mentions Oceanus separately and treats Cocytus only in conjunction with the Styx (the fourth), even though both are named.

[50] Here and elsewhere we follow the translation of G. M. A. Grube, *Plato's Phaedo* (Indianapolis: Hackett, 1977), unless otherwise noted.

[51] *Phaedo* 114d. See Dorothea Frede, "Der Mythos vom Schicksal der Seelen nach dem Tod," *Platons 'Phaidon'* (Darmstadt: Wiss. Buchgesellschaft, 1999) 152–67. Elsewhere, for instance in *Gorgias* 523a–527a, *Resp.* 614a–621b and *Phaedrus* 245b–249d, Plato uses other myths in discussing similar subject matter. Cf. also P. Habermehl's treatment of the Greek "Klassische Zeit" (278–82) in C. Colpe, E. Dassmann, J. Engemann, P. Habermehl, and K. Hoheisel, "Jenseits (Jenseitsvorstellungen)," *RAC* 17 (1996) 246–407.

[52] Plato is also interested in "scientific" explanations of natural phenomena that can be correlated with this map of the cosmos. So for example, the third river, Pyriphlegethon (which means "blazing with fire"), is said to run at times close to the surface of earth and is the source of volcanic activity, since "offshoots of it are the lava flows that spout forth wherever they happen on the earth" (113b).

never to emerge from it (113e). Only those who have led eminently pious lives make their way, presumably passing by the Acherusian Lake, to a pure dwelling place above and dwell upon the earth (114b). Among these, the ones who have further purified themselves by philosophy will live without a body, in "even more beautiful abodes" which cannot be described (114c).

It is in connection with the souls of the majority of people, those who have lived an average life, that Plato first mentions the Acherusian Lake (112e–113b). To it "the souls of the majority come after death and, after remaining there for a certain appointed time, longer for some, shorter for others, they are sent back to birth as living creatures" (113a). In a second passage Plato mentions "vessels" or "boats" (ὀχήματα), undoubtedly based on the image of Charon's skiff,[53] to transport the dead down the river Acheron to the lake:

> Now when the dead have come to the place where each is led by his genius (δαίμων), first they are judged, those who have lived good and uprightly lives and those who have not. And those who seem to have lived intermediately (οἳ μὲν ἂν δόξωσι μέσως βεβιωκέναι) [i.e., neither fully good nor fully bad] go upon the Acheron, embarking on vessels provided for them, and are borne in these (vessels) to the lake, and there they dwell; and, if they have done any wrong, being purified (καθαιρόμενοι) of wrongs by paying a penalty (διδόντες δίκας), they are redeemed (ἀπολύονται), while for their benevolent deeds they acquire honors (τῶν τε εὐεργεσιῶν τιμὰς φέρονται), according to the merits of each.[54]

Very interesting is what he says next about "those who are deemed to have committed great but curable crimes ... but who have felt remorse for the rest of their lives" (113e). They must be thrown into Tartarus, but every year the underworld rivers Cocytus and Pyriphlegethon carry them past the Acherusian Lake, where the rivers run near by but do not merge (cf. 113b).[55] As those in torment pass by they are able to cry out across the expanse to the ones they have killed or otherwise maltreated, asking them to forgive them. If their supplications are successful their punishment comes to an end. If not, they are taken back into Tartarus and have to try again at a later time (114a–b). So now we learn that

---

[53] The figure of Charon was actually a later entry into the picture of the underworld's operations, introduced perhaps in the early Classical period from Magna Graecia; cf. Green, "On the Thanatos Trail," 68, and n. 66 below.

[54] 113d–e. The translation has been adapted to bring out the phrasing of the Greek.

[55] Notice that this is quite different than the picture of the rivers in *Od.* 10.508–15; see above at nn. 44–45.

their victims, like most others, also dwell at the Acherusian Lake. In the Greek geography of Hades, it must be remembered, the underworld was the final abode of both good and bad. Only the exceptionally good, as we saw, had prospects of a better abode somewhere beyond. Yet that "place" remained unspecified, at least in Plato, and could only be accessed by journeying first through Hades.

Early Christian Commentary on Plato's Description

At the beginning of the third century CE Clement of Alexandria refers to several passages of Plato, when he argues that the notion of chastisement after death and punishment through fire was taken over by Greek poets and philosophers from the philosophy of the non-Greeks, including the Jews.[56] One of the passages discussed in this regard is *Phaedo* 112–113, taken up in the context of the immortality of the soul by correlation with a quotation from Ps. 104:4 (103:4 LXX):

> As it says, "*the one who makes his angels spirits and the flaming fires his ministers*" (τοὺς λειτουργοὺς αὐτοῦ πῦρ φλέγον). It follows then that the soul is immortal. For that which is punished or corrected (κολαζόμενον ἢ παιδευόμενον) with sensation, inasmuch as he is said to suffer, is alive. What then? Did not Plato know both the rivers of fire and the depths of the earth (καὶ πυρὸς ποταμοὺς καὶ τῆς γῆς τὸ βάθος), poetically naming Tartarus what is called Gehenna by the barbarians, as well as the Cocytus, the Acheron, and the Pyriphlegethon, even introducing them as some punishments for chastening to correction (καὶ τοιαῦτά τινα εἰς τὴν παίδευσιν σωφρονίζοντα παρεισάγων κολαστήρια)?[57]

One of the key points of Clement's argument is the correlation between fire and punishment, thus allowing him an easy connection to Gehenna in the Jewish tradition.[58] It is interesting to note that for Clement the most important element of the passage is the corrective function of the

---

[56] *Strom.* 5.90.4–91.5; cf. 5.90.1 and 1.15. For this argument compare also Arnobius, *Adv. Nationes* 2,14. The basic argument, of course, goes back to early Hellenistic-Jewish apologetic, especially Artapanus and Philo.

[57] *Strom.* 5.90.6–91.2. In this passage, some mss. of Clement read "prophetically" for "poetically," but the latter is supported by Eusebius' quotation of this passage, to be discussed below.

[58] So, it should be noticed that the long rhetorical question regarding the passage from Plato is a chiasm which makes explicit the following equations: "the depths" (βάθος) = Tartarus = Gehenna, while "the rivers of fire" = Cocytus, Acheron, and Pyriphlegethon. For Gehenna as the place of fiery punishment, see *inter alia* Matt 5:22; 18:9; 23:33.

different forms of punishment in conjunction with the immortality of the human soul. This is why the angels "seize and punish the wicked."[59]

About a century later Clement's remarks would be taken over by Eusebius of Caesarea in his *Praeparatio Evangelica*. First, in *Praep. Ev.* 11.38 he quotes *Phaedo* 113a–114c *verbatim*. Here he wants to show how Plato, in accordance with the Hebrew Scriptures, mentions divine judgement, the different dwelling places of the pious, and the various punishments of the ungodly. Eusebius also quotes a number of passages from the scriptures to show the correlation with the sacred word. In 11.38.9 the life of the pious without bodies (ἄνευ σωμάτων) of *Phaedo* 114c is altered—without comment—to a life "without troubles" (ἄνευ καμάτων).[60] Eusebius is also eager to interpret the vessels used on the Acheron and the lake (ὀχήματα in *Phaedo* 113d) as the bodies (σώματα)[61] in which the souls receive punishment, according to the rules of the Hebrews (11.38.10). Then in *Praep. Ev.* 13.13.6 he quotes the passage from Clement (given above). Eusebius next returns to *Phaedo* 113d and 114c in *Praep. Ev.* 13.16.14–15 at the end of a critical discussion of Plato's ideas about the soul.

The use of the *Phaedo* passage clearly became standard in early Christian efforts to prove that Plato, too, spoke about a future judgement and places of chastisement. Theodoretus of Cyrus (†466), in his *Graecarum affectionum curatio* 11.19–24, quotes the same passage as Eusebius (parts of which are only summarized).[62] He criticizes Plato for having the souls chastised without a body, and for his theory of the transmigration of souls. All this, he says, has more to do with the teaching of Pythagoras than that of the apostles (11.33–39).

The way the *Phaedo* passage functions in early Christian apologetic differs considerably from the use of the tradition of the Acherusian Lake in the *Greek Life of Adam and Eve* and other apocalyptic writings

---

[59] *Strom.* 5.90.6.

[60] See G. Favrelle's commentary on this passage in G. Favrelle and É. des Places, *Eusèbe de Césarée, La préparation évangélique. Livre XI* (SC 292; Paris: Cerf, 1982) 382–385.

[61] Eusebius' alterations here reflect differing interpretations and usages of the day. For example, in a variation on the saying of Plato, the fifth cent. CE neoplatonist Hierocles calls the "body the paltry vessel of the soul" (σῶμα ... ψυχῆς λεπτὸν ὄχημα), so the *Carmen Aureum* 26, in *Fragmenta Philosophicorum Graecorum*, ed. by F. Mullach (3 vols.; Paris: Didot, 1861–81) 1:478m. Compare the usage of the term also by the neoplatonist Proclus, *Inst.* 205–210 which says that each different type of soul has its own particular kind of "vessel" (ὄχημα), a conveyance for its ability to descend and ascend into the divine realm, but these "vessels" are not material (208).

[62] He follows Eusebius's reading in *Phaedo* 114c.

discussed in the previous section of this essay. Both types of texts show, however, that this section of the *Phaedo* (together with other Greek traditions about Hades) played an important role in early Christian theological reflection on life after death.

Shifting Sands on the Acherusian Shores

Since we have earlier argued that the passage in *GLAE* 37.3 already reflects Christian origins, we may now suggest some possibilities regarding the changing lines at work here. Let us begin by dividing the traditions into two distinct groups. Group 1 comprises what we shall call the *apocalyptic tradition* and is represented by the passages in *GLAE* 37.3, *Apocalypse of Peter* 14, and its close parallel in *Sib. Or.* 2.330–338.[63] Group 2 comprises a *platonizing tradition* seen chiefly in Clement and Eusebius, and, as we shall see, the *Apocalypse of Paul*.[64]

Chronologically all three texts in Group 1 seem to come from the second century CE. One emphasis within this group of texts is bodily resurrection as a way of conceptualizing the afterlife. It is worth noting, therefore, that one of the contemporary Christian apologists, Theophilus of Antioch, explicitly refuted Plato's belief in the immortality of the soul from the *Phaedo*.[65] We noted the emphasis on resurrection especially in conjunction with the story of Adam's washing in the Acherusian Lake in parallel with the preparation of his body for burial. Only now the angels have replaced Hermes and Charon as the guides for the dead. Even so, the washing scene has strong resonances of ancient mortuary ritual,[66] but in earlier Christian usage, of course, washing, burial, and resurrection were all symbolized in baptism.

---

[63] The passage noted above from the *Book of the Resurrection of Christ* may well reflect later lines of this tradition, but the sparing usage of others is less clearly so.

[64] The passage noted above from Theodoret of Cyrus also marks this trajectory.

[65] *Ad Autolycum* 3.7; cf. 2.38; the former may be a direct allusion to the argument of the *Phaedo* (see esp. 80d, 81e–82a, and 88d; the first and the last are closely tied to the passage in 112–114).

[66] As Sourvinou-Inwood (*'Reading' Greek Death*, 62–4) shows, the mapping out of Hades corresponded to the gradual reconciliation of burial ideas and practices with a growing notion of the afterlife. In the later Classical traditions, she also shows (308–20) that Charon is understood as a benign figure, whose role is to ease the transition to (and thereby alleviate fear of) the underworld. Hermes led the souls down to Charon, who welcomed them (in friendly or familial manner) and ferried them across. The sealing of the tomb at the completion of the mortuary ritual was thought to signal the beginning of this final passage.

Whether there is a more direct literary connection between *GLAE* and the other two texts cannot presently be demonstrated. It may be suggested, however, that the introduction of the Acherusian Lake into the scene derives in some measure from midrashic expansions (or corrections) to 1 Enoch's tours of Sheol, where the fallen angels and the souls of the dead await the final judgment.[67] Secondary harmonization of 1 Enoch to the Greek tradition in Christian texts is also suggested by the allusion in 2 Pet 2:4: ὁ θεὸς ἀγγέλων ἁμαρτησάντων οὐκ ἐφείσατο ἀλλὰ σειραῖς ζόφου ταρταρώσας παρέδωκεν εἰς κρίσιν τηρουμένους ... ("God did not spare the angels when they sinned but having cast them into Tartarus he delivered them to chains of gloom for keeping until judgment ...").[68] The texts of Group 1 show a significant correlation of the traditional apocalyptic elements with the Greek tradition also reflected in Plato; however, lacking in these texts is any direct indication of the discussion of the Acherusian Lake in *Phaedo* 112–13.[69]

At the same time, it must also be remembered that the text of *Apocalypse of Peter* was known both to Clement of Alexandria and to Eusebius, who picked it up from Clement if not other sources.[70] Clement also shows an awareness of the *Sibylline Oracles* and even quotes from it one of the passages on the river Acheron.[71] With these trajectories in mind we may turn to Group 2. Despite their clear awareness of the apocalyptic tradition (Group 1), the documents in Group 2 (chiefly Clement and Eusebius) show a markedly different interest in the Acherusian Lake tradition. Focusing explicitly on the passage from Plato (esp. *Phaedo* 112e–114a) their interest is, as we have seen, more with the immortality of the soul, punishment for sin, and the passage of the soul into heaven. There is likely a point of intersection between these two trajectories,

---

[67] So 1 Enoch 17:4; 21:7; 22:4–6. Note also 22:7 where Abel's spirit wanders in Sheol.

[68] We should perhaps also give attention to the parallel in Jude 6: ἀγγέλους τε τοὺς μὴ τηρήσαντας τὴν ἑαυτῶν ἀρχὴν ἀλλὰ ἀπολιπόντας τὸ ἴδιον οἰκητήριον εἰς κρίσιν μεγάλης ἡμέρας δεσμοῖς ἀϊδίοις ὑπὸ ζόφον τετήρηκεν ("And the angels who did not keep their own position, but left their proper dwelling, he has kept in *eternal* chains in deepest darkness for the judgment of the great day."). Here also we may mention the passage in Ignatius, *Eph.* 19:3.

[69] One feature that may suggest a direct awareness of the platonic tradition is the intercession of the angels (or the elect in *Apoc. Peter*) for the dead, which vaguely resembles the appeal of those in torment to the ones they have harmed in *Phaedo*, 114a.

[70] See above n. 24; for Eusebius see *H.E.* 6.14.1; cf. 3.3.2; 3.25.4.

[71] See above n. 31. Lactantius (*Inst. div.* 7.18.2–4), which cites passages from the Corpus Hermeticum and from books 3, 4, 5, and 8 of the Sibyllines, also includes a passage with similarities to that in *Sib. Or.* 2.330–338 (although attributed to Hystaspes).

but over time the *apocalyptic tradition* receded while the *platonizing tradition* continued and, to some extent, subsumed the former. So it must be noted that Eusebius, in contrast to Clement, seems to resist some elements of Plato's immortal soul "without body" in the afterlife even while retaining the *Phaedo* passage transmitted by Clement. This trend is even more explicit in the passage noted above from Theodoret of Cyrus. Augustine and others, however, would eventually seek a different solution in explaining the body-soul relationship in afterlife.[72] Generally, this platonizing turn dates from the third century CE and later, at least for the texts we know. Whether this more traditionally Greek element entered the Christian tradition earlier is impossible to determine with any precision.[73]

In this light we may conclude by looking again at the passage in the *Apocalypse of Paul* (quoted above), since it may well reveal a point of intersection between the two trajectories. It is worth remembering that this text dates from the mid-third century CE[74] but clearly continued in wide ms. circulation, both Greek and Latin (much wider than *GLAE* or *Apocalypse of Peter*) in the fourth to seventh centuries CE. Augustine (*Ench.* 112–3) seems to know its images,[75] at just about the same time as the passage quoted above from Prudentius. The Latin version, the *Visio Pauli*, comes only slightly later. The *Apocalypse of Paul* clearly preserves elements of the apocalyptic tradition of the Acherusian Lake (Group 1), notably the emphasis on repentance, the delivery to the angel (Michael), the *baptism* in the Acherusian Lake, and the passage into Paradise.[76] On the other hand, there is no mention of intercession

---

[72] Cf. Bernstein, *Formation of Hell*, 313–333 and P. Fredricksen, "Beyond the Body/Soul Dichotomy: Augustine's Answer to Mani, Plotinus, and Julian," in *Paul and the Legacies of Paul*, ed. by W. S. Babcock (Dallas: Southern Methodist University Press, 1990) 227–50, both with ample bibliography.

[73] These and similar Greek traditions on the geography of Hades might now be profitably explored in future studies of other early Jewish and Christian texts, including, *inter alia*, Wis 2:1; 16:13; 17:14; 4 Macc 13:14–17; and Luke 16:23–27 (parable of Lazarus and Dives). R. F. Hock ("Lazarus and Micyllus: Greco-Roman Background to Luke 16:19–31," *JBL* 106 [1987] 447–63) discusses the history of scholarship on this passage and argues persuasively for a hitherto unrecognized classical background to the parable. Cf. Bernstein, *Formation of Hell*, 239–45.

[74] If one were to follow the second century dating of Carozzi (*Eschatologie et au-delà*, 165) then some modification of this scheme would be required, but it seems unlikely.

[75] Even though Augustine elsewhere dismisses the *Apocalypse of Paul* as apocryphal (*In Iohan. Tract.* 98), the passage in the *Enchiridion* shows a much more positive use of the traditions developed in it regarding the afterlife.

[76] Bernstein, *Formation of Hell*, sees the *Apocalypse of Peter* as the stark extreme of the

in this passage, and there is more stress on the soul "leaving the body" (so 22.3: *exierit de corpore*) to make the journey. All in all, notions of resurrection seem less in evidence.

At the same time, the passage mentions some unusual features which may only come from Plato or other Greek traditions, as picked up in the Christian commentary tradition of Group 2. Here we note in particular the "golden ship" (like the vessels in Plato) by which Paul sails across the river into the City of Christ, which is said to be beside the Acherusian Lake. The latter may be taken as an equation of Paradise with the Elysian fields. It appears, therefore, that *Apocalypse of Paul*, like Clement before, was consciously harmonizing the earlier apocalyptic tradition to that of Plato.[77]

This impression is strengthened further when one looks carefully at the geography of Paradise in the *Apocalypse of Paul*. Now we discover that the Acherusian Lake is in the lower heavens, or more precisely in the space just below the gates of heaven.[78] Here Paul is led on a tour

----

apocalyptic tradition (282–291); he takes it as the principal source for the *Apocalypse of Paul*, even though the latter takes a different view (299–305).

[77] So note *Strom.* 5.11.77, which quotes from the *Apocalypse of Zephaniah* (so O. Wintermute in *Old Testament Pseudepigrapha* 1:508). The discussion here by Clement directly correlates the teaching of Plato with that of the prophets. G. Steindorff (*Die Apocalypse des Elias, eine unbekannte Apocalypse und Bruchstücke der Sophonias-Apocalypse* [TU 17.3a; Leipzig: Hinrichs, 1899]) had identified the *Apocalypse of Zephaniah* as the likely source for the passage on "the Acherusian river" as found in *Apocalypse of Paul*. So, too James (*Apocryphal New Testament*, 538 n. 1; cf. 527 n. 1) mentioned both the *Apocalypse of Zephaniah* and the *Apocalypse of Elijah* as sources for the *Apocalypse of Paul*. According to James *Apoc. Zeph.* has the departed embark on a boat accompanied by a myriad chorus of angels. This passage is found in the Sahidic fragment of *Apoc. Zeph.* and is, in fact, quoted in the Coptic version of the *Apoc. Paul* (fol. 35b); so Wintermute in *Old Testament Pseudepigrapha* 1:508 n. B.c. Duensing and Santos Otero (*Neutestamentliche Apokryphen* 2:645–6) agree that both *Apoc. Peter* and *Apoc. Zeph.* were sources for the *Apoc. Paul*. The rest of the Sahidic fragment as restored by Wintermute, however, does not contain the reference to a boat. On the other hand, the longer Akhmim fragment of *Apoc. Zeph.* does contain the reference to the boat in what appears to be the parallel passage to that of the Sahidic (chap. 8.1; cf. 7.9). While these relationships do indicate that Clement knew an earlier Greek version of the *Apocalypse of Zephaniah*, the later Coptic versions may derive additional materials from other sources; so Wintermute (*Old Testament Pseudepigrapha*, 499–500), who follows Steindorff in dating the Akhmimic frag. to the end of the fourth cent. CE, and the Sahidic to the early fifth cent. CE. Both Coptic mss. also contained fragments of the *Apocalypse of Elijah*. So it must be remembered that both the *Apocalypse of Paul* and the *Apocalypse of Peter* were similarly preserved in Egyptian versions of comparable date and provenience. (See above nn. 24–26; 32.) What this suggests about the trajectory of discussion on heavenly judgment tradition in early Egyptian (Coptic) Christianity perhaps deserves further study.

[78] *Apoc. Paul* 21.2–3: after Paul has just come back down from the third heaven,

of the heavenly Paradise and the pits of Tartarus.[79] The angelic guide
first brings Paul to the river Oceanus, "which irrigates [*var.*, is above]
the whole earth" (21.2), and they cross into the land of promise which
is lit by the lights of heaven (21.3). Paul sees "a river flowing with milk
and honey" (*flumen currentem lac et mel*) along whose banks grow many
lush trees (22.1).[80] Next they come to the milk-white waters which the
angel identifies as the Acherusian Lake (22.5). Here, he is told, is where
the good are brought to be baptized by Michael before entering into
the City of Christ. After crossing the lake on the golden boat (23.1),
Paul sees the great city, which is surrounded by four rivers: honey, milk,
wine, and oil (23.3). Each river stands on one side of the city, and next
Paul is taken on a tour of the regions of the four rivers, each of which
is inhabited by specific types of individuals who are on their way into
the city (25–28). In chapters 29–30 Paul is shown the city itself and its
inhabitants, before he is taken back to the entrance by the same route
(31.1). When they once again cross beyond the river Oceanus, Paul now
finds himself in a realm without light, and there begins his tour of the
rivers of fire and the pits of Tartarus, also called the Abyss (31.3–34).
While the number of rivers now seems to have multiplied further, the
basic geography is that of Oceanus and the four rivers of Hades known
to us from Homer and Plato.

One seemingly unusual detail is the description of the Acherusian
Lake, whose waters are said to be "exceedingly white, whiter than milk"
(*cuius erant aquae candidae valde super lac*, 22.5).[81] Apparently it flows from
the "river of milk and honey" (22.1; cf. 31.1). In effect, this seems to be
the river Acheron, which flows into the Acherusian Lake. In the Latin,

the angel leads him "up to the gates of heaven" (*duxit super ianuas caeli*—all mss. but
Arnhem), while the St. Gall ms. (followed closely by the Escorial ms.) adds *deduxit me in
c[a]elum [a]lium* ("and led me to another heaven"). See next note.

[79] The narrative of Paul's tour of heaven and hell is based on the reference to being
"caught up into the third heaven" (ἁρπαγέντα … ἕως τρίτου οὐρανοῦ) and "caught up
into paradise" (ἡρπάγη εἰς τὸν παράδεισον) in 2 Cor 12:2–4. *Apocalypse of Paul* turns this
into three distinct tours: chapters 11–20 describe his tour through the three levels of
heaven; chapters 21–31, the tour of the subheavenly Paradise; and chapters 32–45, the
tour of Tartarus. Yet it will be seen that the second and third are connected by the
traditional Greek geography of Hades.

[80] Cf. *Od.* 10.509–10; Rev. 22:1–2.

[81] The text is somewhat difficult here. Only the Paris ms. gives this precise reading,
which Silverstein and Hilhorst emend by reading *eius* for *cuius*. But the sense is clearly
supported by the Escorial and Arnhem mss.: *et vidi (f)lumen aqu(a)e candidum valde super
lacte* (Arnhem). Only the St. Gall ms. omits the more direct connection with the river
and removes the comparison to milk, thus: *Aqua candida vidi desuper lacum.*

of course, "milk" (*lac*) and "lake" (*lacus*) form a natural wordplay.[82] So, too, the ideal of "whiteness" in relation to baptism is perhaps a natural symbolism, but there may be more at work in this subtle detail. None of the texts in Group 1 mention the river Acheron or being conveyed by it to the lake. This aspect seems to come directly from Plato and sources of the classical period on which he was drawing.

While in *Apocalypse of Paul* the river is not explicitly called Acheron, the identification is assured both by its traditional Greek geography (flowing into the Acherusian Lake) and its description as "milk-white." For what we have here is an attribute derived from the place name. The name Acheron is etymologically connected to the name of a tree (the Ἀχερωίς), called the "white poplar" (sometimes just called λευκή, "white") for its distinctive color.[83] It appears in Homer (*Il.* 13.389; 16.482). The etymological connection is explicated by Pausanias: "Heracles found the white poplar growing on the banks of the Acheron, the river in Thesprotia, and for this reason it is called Ἀχερωίδα by Homer" (5.14.2). Heracles is said to have brought it to Greece. Pausanias adds that Heracles preferred to sacrifice to Zeus by burning the thighbones of his victims only over this particular wood. The mention of Heracles' exploits reminds us of another connection to Hades myths, since his journey to the underworld to retrieve Alcestis took him to the Acherusian Lake (Euripides, *Alcestis* 443; cf. 252–3; 900–2).[84] For readers steeped in classical mythology, allusions to a "milk-white" river in the world of the dead are hard to miss.[85]

Even so, there may be yet another allusion at work here. The phrasing of the preserved Latin version, "exceedingly white, more than milk" (*candidae valde super lac*, 22.5) may preserve in vaguer form another wordplay carried over from the Greek original. In ancient Greek the word milk was γάλα (still used today), of which the genitive form is γάλακτος. Thus its stem [*Grundform*] is γλακ-, which also becomes the direct etymological root of both *lac* (gen. *lactis*) and *glacies* in Latin.[86] In Greek

---

[82] This may well explain the alteration of the text in the St. Gall ms.; see note above.

[83] The poplar is still called λεύκη in modern Greek.

[84] Interestingly, in *Od.* 10.510, the trees said to line the grove of Persephone on the shores of Oceanus are said to include the "black poplar" (αἴγειροι).

[85] We must note that there is also a "river of milk" (*flumen lactis*, 23.3; *fluvius lactis*, 26) among the four rivers that surround the city. This is probably not to be equated directly with the "river of milk and honey" (22.1) or the "milk-white" Acherusian Lake (22.5); however, it may be surmised that these four rivers somehow flow from the lake. The reason for the names of the four rivers will be discussed below.

[86] So Hjalmar Frisk, *Griechisches Etymologisches Wörterbuch* (2 vols.; Heidelberg: Carl

usage, the forms γαλακτίας and γαλαξαῖος, especially when combined with κύκλος ("circle"), became the designation for the astronomical formation which still bears this ancient symbolic name, the "Milky Way." From this common usage[87] came the derived nominal form, γαλαξίας (from which we get "galaxy"), specifically to mean the Milky Way and thereby to signify the heavenly realm.[88] Assuming that the Greek original of the *Apocalypse of Paul* used a similar formulation in 22.5, as seems likely,[89] then the symbolism of the passage takes on new dimensions.

While such symbolism does not appear in the Plato passage itself, it had become part of the pagan discussion of the afterlife by the first century BCE. So, we see it explicitly in Cicero's discussion of the soul in his "Dream of Scipio," in part his commentary on Plato's *Republic*. Cicero certainly knew of the role of the Acherusian Lake in interpretations of the afterlife from Homer to Plato and beyond, even though the name is not used in this instance.[90] So, in the dream, Cicero reports Scipio's conversation with his departed ancestors; Scipio

---

Winter Universitätsverlag, 1960) 1:293–4 (s.v. γάλα); cf. Pierre Chantraine, *Dictionaire étymologique de la Langue Grecque: Histoire des mots* (4 vols.; Paris: Editions Klincksieck, 1968) 1:206–7.

[87] See Aristotle, *Mete.* 345a.25. A variant form is also worth noting: ἐς βάθος κύκλου ("out of the depths of the [heavenly] circle") in Aristophanes, *Aves* 1715; cf. Sophocles, *Ajax* 672. The form γαλακτίας alone came to have this meaning; so Ptolemy, *Syntaxis mathematica* 8.2.

[88] Cf. Diodorus Siculus, *Hist.* 5.23; Lucian, *Ver. hist.* 1.16; Manetho, *Astrol.* 2.116. Latin *galaxies* (var. *galactites*) also derives later as a Greek loan word, cf. Macrobius, *Somn. Scip.* 1.4.

[89] The original wording of the Greek for the phrase preserved in the Latin (*candidae valde super lac*) might have been something like λευκοτητὰ [? λαμπροτητὰ] τοῦ γάλακτος, or perhaps ὑπὲρ γαλαξαῖον, but it is impossible to know for sure. The later Greek version (ed. Tischendorf, *Apocalypses Apocryphae*, 51), thought to be secondary to the shorter Latin versions, does not include this detail at 22.5, so we cannot compare the precise rendering of this motif in Greek. That it was in the Greek original, however, is indicated by the fact that the other references to a "river of milk" are retained in the later Greek version at 23.5 (καὶ ποταμοὶ τέσσαρες ἐκύκλουν αὐτήν, ῥέοντες μέλι καὶ γάλα καὶ ἔλαιον καὶ οἶνον [Tischendorf, 52]). At 26 (Tischendorf, 54) the full phrase ὁ ποταμὸς τοῦ γάλακτος is preserved at precisely the same locus in the text where the Latin reads *fluvius lactis*. Consequently, we can be confident that some form of this word play was in the Greek original.

[90] See esp. Cicero's *Tusc. disp.* 1.16.37; 1.21.48 where Acheron is used explicitly. In the first passage he quotes (in Latin) a passage from an unknown author which he links by direct reference to the pivotal passage in Homer (*Od.* 11), the *nekyomanteion* of the shades before Odysseus. In the latter, he is poking fun at other interpretations of these older myths, notably those of Epicurus. Also in 1.17.39 he mentions the views of Plato, still hard to go wrong with, he would say, but he suggests that newer ideas that place the earth in the middle of the cosmos (the Ptolemaic theory) call for further thought.

discovers they are still "alive" in a world beyond (*De re publ.* 6.14.14). What follows is Cicero's disquisition on the immortality of the soul. Next (6.16.16), the younger Scipio is exhorted by his dead father to live a worthy life so that he might obtain the same reward:

> "But Scipio, thus imitate your grandfather here; imitate me, your father; love justice and duty (*justitiam cole et pietatem*) which are indeed strictly due to parents and kinsmen, but most of all to your fatherland. Such a life is the way into the heavens (*ea vita via est in caelum*) to that gathering of those who have completed their earthly lives and have been loosed from the body (*corpore laxati*) and who live in that place you see [yonder],"—it was the circle of light which blazed most brightly among the other flames [of the sky][91]—"which you folks [pl.] call, as you got it from the Greeks, the Milky Circle[92] (*quem vos, ut a Graiis accepistis, orbem lacteum nuncupatis*)."

Now the heavenly reward is equated with the "milk-white" way through the stars.[93] This notable shift may help understand why in the *Apocalypse of Paul*, and later Christian tradition, the journey of the soul to the afterlife goes first through the heavens, where the Acherusian Lake is now located, before some are sent from there down into the pits of Hades.[94] The geography of the afterlife has taken a new turn.

The conscious harmonization to biblical Paradise myths is explicit in *Apocalypse of Paul*, such as when the Acheron is said to "flow with milk and honey."[95] Parallel to Plato's description of Hades, Paradise (Christ's City) is said to be vast and surrounded by "four rivers" (cf. *Phaedo* 112e), but now they are named according to the rivers of Eden (23.3; cf. Gen 2:11–14). So, we learn that the "river of milk" is named Euphrates.[96] When Paul is once again brought out beyond Oceanus, he discovers a dark and shadowy realm, where there is a "river burning with fire"

---

[91] The phrase here is: *erat autem is splendidissimo candore inter flammas circus elucens.* So compare "Paul's" description of the heavenly city (*Apoc. Paul* 23.2): *Et erat lumen eius super aeris lumen, lucens mundi huius super numerum et modum* ("Its light was brighter than that of the heavenly light, illuminating beyond the number and manner of those of the world.") This passage is not included in all the mss. of *Apoc. Paul*; however, note the use of *candor* in Cicero and *candidus* in *Apoc. Paul* 22.5.

[92] Here the Latin (*orbem lacteum*) is a direct translation of the usual form of the Greek: κύκλος γαλαξαῖος or γαλαξίας κύκλος.

[93] In *Apoc. Paul* 21.3 Oceanus, the entry into paradise, is said to be "the light of heaven which gives light to the whole land" (St. Gall: *quod lumen caeli est quod lucet omni terre illic*); cf. 31.2.

[94] So *Apoc. Paul* 31–36.

[95] 22.1: *currentem lac et mel*; 31.1: *flumen lactis et mellis.* Cf. Exod 3:8; Lev 20:24.

[96] 23.3: *flumen lactis [dicitur] Eufrat(es)*, and this may be why the name Acheron was intentionally dropped in the earlier scene, even though the symbolism is retained.

which is reserved for the lukewarm, i.e., those who pray like Christians but sin like pagans (31). Another river of fire (32) looms over a deep abyss, Tartarus (34);[97] it is reserved for the worst sinners (in a later interpolation, including errant churchmen). The pits of hell lie under Oceanus. Others whom Paul sees during his tour of the heavenly city fare far better. Some are constantly abasing themselves for their pride and sins on earth to improve their lot. In its derived Latin version, at least, the *Apocalypse of Paul* promotes the ascetic life; those who practice chastity and asceticism are said to be welcomed at the river of milk (22; 26).

It is not likely that all of these features belong to the Greek original of the *Apocalypse of Paul*; however, they do reflect at least an extension of basic elements derived from the *platonic tradition* of the afterlife; to some extent, these "platonizing" elements were already at work in the earlier stages of the text quite apart from those conveyed by the *apocalyptic tradition* that were also there. In late antiquity, the image of the Acherusian Lake may have served as a mythic axis for the synthesis of an older apocalyptic eschatology (as seen in the Greek *Life of Adam and Eve*) with Platonic notions of afterlife, now equated with the heavenly Paradise—a synthesis that would eventually come to dominate the new Christian worldview.[98]

---

[97] Note here the equation of Tartarus with the "exceedingly deep pits" (Latin *foveas profundo valde*, 32.1) and the "abyss" (*abyssus*, 32.2). Both formulations seem to be rendered with βάθος in the abbreviated form of this passage in the later Greek version (Tischendorf, *Apocalypses Apocryphae*, 58). The same equation is made by Clement, see note 58 above.

[98] Cf. T. Silverstein, "Did Dante know the Vision of St. Paul?" *Harvard Studies and Notes in Philology and Literature* 19 (1937) 231–47.

LAST WILLS AND TESTAMENTS
IN GRAECO-ROMAN PERSPECTIVE

John T. Fitzgerald

During the Graeco-Roman period, both Jews and Christians produced a number of works that either bear the title of "testament" (such as the *Testaments of the Twelve Patriarchs* and the *Testament of Job*) or have distinct testamentary features, such as the farewell discourses of Jesus in the Gospels of Luke (22:21–38) and John (13:1–17:26), Paul's farewell address at Miletus (Acts 20:17–38), and the pseudonymous letters attributed to both Peter (2 Peter) and Paul (2 Timothy). All of these documents and others like them have been thoroughly scrutinized from the perspective of the literary traditions of which they are a part,[1] but only rarely have they been analyzed in the light of actual last wills and testaments written by Greeks and Romans. Furthermore, biblical scholars have done little in the way of examining the *mentalité* of those who chose to make wills rather than simply die intestate.[2] The purpose of this essay is to provide an overview of Greek and Roman wills, giving emphasis to those features of will-making that appear to be most relevant to the testamentary literature produced by Jews and Christians living in

---

[1] The secondary literature on testaments, farewell discourses, and documents with a pronounced testamentary character is vast. For a survey of scholarship to 1994, see Martin Winter, *Die Vermächtnis Jesu und die Abschiedsworte der Väter: Gattungsgeschichtliche Untersuchungen der Vermächtnisrede im Blick auf Joh. 13–17* (FRLANT 161; Göttingen: Vandenhoeck & Ruprecht, 1994) 9–37. For a more recent study of the testament as a literary genre, see Rosa M. Boixareu i Vilaplana, *El gènere literari dels testaments dels dotze patriarques* (Collectània lecció Sant Pacià 66; Barcelona: Edicions de la Facultat de Teologia de Catalunya, 1999) (in Catalan). A helpful up-to-date overview of testamentary literature is provided by Marinus de Jonge in his article on "Testamentenliteratur" in the *TRE* 33:1–2 (2001) 110–13. I wish to thank Professor de Jonge for supplying me with a pre-publication copy of his article.

[2] There were important differences between Greeks and Romans in regard to laws of succession and testamentary practice, and wills made in places such as Egypt sometimes reflect the influence of local native law as well as Hellenistic and/or Roman law and testamentary formulas. Yet the perspectives of Greeks, Romans, and others on wills and many of their practices in formulating wills were either the same or quite similar, especially during the Graeco-Roman period. In this essay I shall focus on what they had in common, not their differences, and thus I shall draw freely upon both Greek and Roman wills to illuminate these shared aspects of testamentary perspective and practice. I shall give greater attention, however, to Roman wills.

the Graeco-Roman world. I shall pay particular attention to the way in which Hellenistic philosophers and other moralists understood the process of testation.[3]

Theories of Testation

Of the various views of wills and aspects of testation that we find in the Graeco-Roman period,[4] seven merit mention in this sur-

---

[3] At the outset of this discussion, I wish to acknowledge my great debt to the work of Edward Champlin. His treatment of Roman testaments is absolutely indispensable for any investigation of wills in the Graeco-Roman world. See esp. his *Final Judgments: Duty and Emotion in Roman Wills, 200 B.C.—A.D. 250* (Berkeley: University of California Press, 1991). See also "Miscellanea testamentaria I–III," *ZPE* 62 (1986) 247–55; "Miscellanea testamentaria IV–VII," *ZPE* 69 (1987) 197–206; "The Testament of the Piglet," *Phoenix* 41 (1987) 174–83; "*Creditur vulgo testamenta hominum speculum esse morum*: Why the Romans Made Wills," *CP* 84 (1989) 198–215; "The Testament of Augustus," *Rheinisches Museum für Philologie* N.F. 132 (1989) 154–65.

[4] The making of wills by Greeks and Romans began long before the Graeco-Roman period. Among the Greeks, the testament is first mentioned in connection with Solon (ca. 638–ca. 559 B.C.E.), who enacted a law that allowed a man without male legitimate children to dispose of his property by will as he saw fit. See Solon, *Leg.* frg. 49a–d Ruschenbusch (= Eberhard Ruschenbusch [ed.], *ΣΟΛΩΝΟΣ ΝΟΜΟΙ: Die Fragmente des solonischen Gesetzeswerkes mit einer Text- und Überlieferungsgeschichte* [Historia 9; Wiesbaden: Steiner, 1966], 86–87). It is generally agreed that the law was concerned with adoption, providing a means whereby a man could secure an heir for himself if he were either completely childless or were the father of daughters but no legitimate sons. As such, "the law did not disturb, and indeed implicitly reaffirmed, the most fundamental rule of the traditional system of inheritance, that a man's natural son inherits his estate" (Michael Gagarin, *Early Greek Law* [Berkeley: University of California Press, 1986], 109). On other points there is less scholarly agreement. Some scholars, for example, believe that Solon's law was concerned with adoption *inter vivos*, whereas others contend that it created testamentary adoption. Still others argue that the testament already existed prior to Solon and that his law was designed to correct abuses in testamentary practice. For some of the issues in this debate, see esp. Louis Gernet, "La création du testament: Observations sur une loi de Solon," *REG* 33 (1920) 123–68, 249–90, and the revised version of this article printed in Gernet's *Droit et société dans la Grèce ancienne* (Publications de l'Institut de droit romain de l'Université de Paris 13; Paris: Recueil Sirey, 1955) 121–49, and Eberhard Ruschenbusch, "ΔΙΑΤΙΘΕΣΘΑΙ ΤΑ ΕΑΥΤΟΥ: Ein Beitrag zum sogenannten Testamentsgesetz des Solon," *Zeitschrift der Savigny-Stiftung für Rechtsgeschichte* (Romantische Abteilung) 79 (1962) 307–11. For the Thirty's removal of the qualifications that were part of Solon's law, see Aristotle, *Ath. Pol.* 35.2. For an attempt to trace the early history of the Greek will and a study of the various meanings of the word διαθήκη, see Frederick O. Norton, *A Lexicographical and Historical Study of ΔΙΑΘΗΚΗ from the Earliest Times to the End of the Classical Period* (Historical and Linguistic Studies in Literature Related to the New Testament, Second Series: Linguistic and Exegetical Studies 6; Chicago: University of Chicago Press, 1908). See also Eberhard F. Bruck, *Die Schenkung auf den Todesfall im griechischen und römischen Recht, zugleich ein Beitrag*

zur Geschichte des Testaments (Studien zur Erläuterung des bürgerlichen Rechts 31; Breslau: Marcus, 1909). On testate and intestate succession in classical Athens, see A. R. W. Harrison, *The Law of Athens* (2 vols.; Oxford: Clarendon, 1968–1971; 2nd ed. with a foreword and updated bibliography by D. M. MacDowell; Indianapolis: Hackett, 1998) 1.122–62; W. K. Lacey, *The Family in Classical Greece* (Aspects of Greek and Roman Life; Ithaca: Cornell University Press, 1968) 131–37; Douglas M. MacDowell, *The Law in Classical Athens* (Aspects of Greek and Roman Life; London: Thames and Hudson, 1978) 92–108; and S. C. Todd, *The Shape of Athenian Law* (Oxford: Clarendon, 1993) 216–227. Attitudes about wills at Athens are surveyed by Wesley E. Thompson, "Athenian Attitudes Toward Wills," *Prudentia* 13 (1981) 13–23. See also Thompson's study of the legal battles over Hagnias' estate (the subject of Isaeus, *Hagnias* [= *Or.* 11] and Ps.-Demosthenes, *Macartatus* [= *Or.* 43], a family squabble that lasted for half a century: *De Hagniae hereditate: An Athenian Inheritance Case* (Mnemosyne 44; Leiden: Brill, 1976). For a wide-ranging study of inheritance practices among the Athenians and other Greeks, see Robin Lane Fox, "Aspects of Inheritance in the Greek World," *History of Political Thought* 6 (1985) 208–32. For an attempt to correlate Greek testamentary practices with their social and political contexts, see David Asheri, "Laws of Inheritance, Distribution of Land and Political Constitutions in Ancient Greece," *Historia* 12 (1963) 1–21, esp. 6–14.

The origins of testation at Sparta are obscure, though native tradition may have sought to link the practice to the legendary Lycurgus and his purported distribution of Laconian land into 30,000 equal lots and the transmission of those lots from father to son (Plutarch, *Ag. Cleom.* 5.1; *Lyc.* 8.1–4). The historicity of this tradition is sharply debated, however, and even if true, the succession may have been largely or wholly intestate. The entire situation is made even more uncertain by the ambiguity of Aristotle's reference to "the lawgiver" (*Pol.* 2.6.5, 1269b20) who first authorized a man, if he so desired, to give or to bequeath his estate to someone other than his son (*Pol.* 2.6.10, 1270a20–22). Some scholars contend that Aristotle (whether rightly or wrongly) attributes this law to Lycurgus, whereas others argue that Aristotle is thinking of the Spartan ephor Epitadeus and only mentions Lycurgus parenthetically in *Pol.* 2.6.7 (1270a6–8). As for Epitadeus, his name appears in conjunction with the first unambiguous reference to Spartan testation. According to Plutarch (*Ag. Cleom.* 5.2), Epitadeus' *rhētra* ("law") enabled individuals to give their house and lot to anyone they desired while they were alive or to do the same by bequest in their wills. Although some scholars have argued that this *rhētra* marks the creation of the testament in Sparta, it is much more likely that it represents an expansion of existing testatory rights. The inception of testation at Sparta would most likely fall in the period between Lycurgus and Epitadeus, with the latter's *rhētra* greatly increasing the likelihood of testation. Both the historicity of this *rhētra* and its date, however, are contested, with those who accept its historicity usually dating it to either the late fifth century or, more likely, the early fourth century B.C.E. Whatever the date, the chief beneficiaries of this change in Spartan law were women, much to Aristotle's chagrin (*Pol.* 2.6.11, 1270a23–24). For differing views of this matter, see Douglas M. MacDowell, *Spartan Law* (Scottish Classical Studies 1; Edinburgh: Scottish Academic Press, 1986) 89–110; Stephen Hodkinson, "Land Tenure and Inheritance in Classical Sparta," *CQ* 36 (1986) 378–406; and J. F. Lazenby, "The *Archaia Moira*: A Suggestion," *CQ* 45 (1995) 87–91.

vey.[5] First, a will was widely believed to be self-revelatory. That is, to make a will was to disclose both who one was and what one valued. This idea appears, for example, at the beginning of one of Pliny the Younger's letters, where he states that a person's will was popularly believed (*creditur vulgo*) to be a mirror (*speculum*) of his or her character (*morum*).[6] It is also reflected in the fanciful etymological attempts by Roman jurists to derive the word *testamentum* from *(con)testatio* ("giving testimony") and *mens* ("mind").[7] For example, Servius Sulpicius

---

The right of testamentary disposition had not yet developed in Crete when the Gortyn law code (deriving largely from at least the sixth century) was inscribed (ca. 450 B.C.E.), though freedom of choice in adoption had evolved. For the law code's treatment of inheritance and adoption, see Ronald F. Willetts (ed. and trans.), *The Law Code of Gortyn* (Kadmos 1; Berlin: de Gruyter, 1967) 12, 20–22, 30–31, 67. For the principles used in arranging the code, see Michael Gagarin, "The Organization of the Gortyn Law Code," *GRBS* 23 (1982) 129–46.

Among the Romans, the Twelve Tables (ca. 450 B.C.E.) not only mention disposition by will (V.3) but also treat intestate succession (V.4–5). For text, translation, and detailed discussion of the Twelve Tables, see M. Hubert, A. D. E. Lewis, and M. H. Crawford, "Twelve Tables," in *Roman Statutes* (ed. M. H. Crawford; 2 vols.; Bulletin of the Institute of Classical Studies Supplement 64; London: Institute of Classical Studies, University of London, 1996) 2.555–721. For a brief discussion of succession in the Twelve Tables, see Alan Watson, *Rome of the XII Tables: Persons and Property* (Princeton: Princeton University Press, 1975) 52–70.

For succession and testation in Egypt during the Graeco-Roman period, see Vincenzo Arangio-Ruiz, *La successione testamentaria secondo i papiri greco-egizii* (Regia Università di Napoli, Testi di laurea 8; Naples: L. Piero, 1906); Hans Kreller, *Erbrechtliche Untersuchungen auf Grund der graeco-aegyptischen Papyrusurkunden* (Leipzig: Teubner: 1919); and Raphael Taubenschlag, *The Law of Graeco-Roman Egypt in Light of the Papyri: 332 B.C.–640 A.D.* (2nd ed.; Warsaw: Państowe Wydawnictwo Naukowe, 1955) 181–222.

[5] For collections of testaments and/or treatments of them (in addition to the studies of Champlin given in note 3 above), see esp. Friedrich Kraus, *Die Formeln des griechischen Testaments* (Borna-Leipzig: Norske, 1915); B. Kübler, "Testament" and "Testamentvollstrecker," PW, 2nd series, 5:1 (1934) 966–1010 and 1010–1016; Orsolina Montevecchi, "Ricerche di sociologia nei documenti dell'Egitto greco-romano, I: I testamenti," *Aeg* 15 (1935) 67–121; Mario Amelotti, *Il testamento romano attraverso la prassi documentale*, I: *Le forme classiche di testamento* (Studi e testi di papirologia 1; Florence: Le Monnier, 1966); W. Clarysse (ed.)., *The Petrie Papyri: Second Edition (P. Petrie²)*, I: *The Wills* (Collectanea hellenistica 2; Brussels: Comité Klassieke Studies, Subcomité Hellenisme, Koninklijke Akademie voor Wetenschappen, Letteren en Schone Kunsten van België, 1991); Livia Migliardi Zingale, *I testamenti romani nei papiri e nelle tavolette d'Egitto: Silloge di documenti dal I ad IV secolo d.C.* (3d ed.; Torino: G. Giappichelli, 1997).

[6] *Ep.* 8.18.1. For explication of this idea, see esp. Champlin, "*Creditur*," and *Final Judgments*, 1–28.

[7] For the widespread use of Stoic linguistic theory and etymology by Roman jurists, see Franz Wieacker, *Römische Rechtsgeschichte: Quellenkunde, Rechtsbildung, Jurisprudenz und Rechtsliteratur* (Handbuch der Altertumswissenschaft 10:3:1; Munich: Beck, 1988) 653–57. See also Fritz Schulz, *History of Roman Legal Science* (2nd ed.; Oxford: Clarendon, 1953)

Rufus (ca. 105–43 B.C.E.),[8] whom Aulus Gellius describes as "the most learned man of his time," writes in Book 2 of his *On the Annulling of Sacred Rites* (*De sacris detestandis*)[9] that "*testamentum* is a compound word, … made up of *mentis contestatio*, that is, 'an attesting of the mind.'"[10] The same idea appears several centuries later in the *Epitome of Ulpian* (late third – early fourth century C.E.), which states that "a *testamentum* is a legal affirmation (*contestatio*) of our mind (*mentis*)."[11] A similar

---

67 and 336 (Note L). On the definitions of legal terms by Roman jurists, see esp. Remo Martini, *Le definizioni dei giuristi romani* (Università di Milano pubblicazioni della Facoltà di Giurisprudenza, Series 2: Studi di diritto romano 3; Milan: Giuffrè, 1966).

[8] On Servius Sulpicius, see F. P. Bremer (ed.), *Iurisprudentiae antehadrianae* (2 vols. in 3; Teubner; Leipzig: Teubner, 1896–1901) 1.139–242; P. E. Huschke (ed.), *Iurisprudentiae anteiustinianae* (5th ed.; Teubner; Leipzig: Teubner, 1886) 91–94; Otto Lenel (ed.), *Palingenesia iuris civilis* (2 vols.; Leipzig: Tauchnitz, 1889) 2.321–34; H. Malcovati (ed.), *Oratorum romanorum fragmenta* (2 vols.; 4th ed.; Corpus Scriptorum Latinorum Paravianum; Torino: Paravia, 1976) 1.376–79 (§118); Martini, *Definizioni*, 102–12; and Wieacker, *Römische Rechtsgeschichte*) 602–7 and 656 n. 93 and 97.

[9] The meaning of the title is disputed. It probably refers to the abjuring of family *sacra* ("sacred rites") by a person about to be adopted, esp. in the process known as *adrogatio*. See esp. Aulus Gellius, *Noct. att.* 15.27.3, where the *sacrorum detestatio* is mentioned in connection with the making of wills, and *Noct. att.* 5.19 and Gaius, *Instit.* 1.98–99 for adoption by *adrogatio*. See also Servius, *Comm. Aen.* 2.156 and the *Oxford Latin Dictionary*, 530, s.v. *detestatio* (3b) and *detestor* (4b). On the importance of the *sacra privata* see Cicero, *Leg.* 2.9.22; 2.19.48. For discussion, see Bremer, *Iurisprudentiae antehadrianae*, 1.224–25; E. C. Clark, *History of Roman Private Law* (3 vols; Cambridge: Cambridge University Press, 1906–1919) 3.444; Adolf Berger, "Encyclopedic Dictionary of Roman Law," *Transactions of the American Philosophical Society* n.s. 43 (1953) 434; Wieacker, *Römische Rechtsgeschichte*, 605 n. 63; and René Marache (ed. and trans.), *Aulu-Gelle, Les Nuits Attiques* (3 vols.; Budé; Paris: Les Belles Lettres, 1967–89) 3.174 n. 3. For a dissenting view, see F. Daverio, "*Sacrorum detestado,*" *Studia et documenta historiae et iuris* 45 (1979) 530–48, who denies any connection to *adrogatio* and links it with the announcement made in the presence of witnesses by a person who was in charge of the *sacra privata*.

[10] Servius Sulpicius Rufus, frg. 5 Bremer (*Iurisprudentiae antehadrianae*, 1.225) = frg. 3 Huschke (*Iurisprudentiae anteiustinianae*, 92) = frg. 9 Lenel (*Palingenesia*, 2.324) = Aulus Gellius, *Noct. att.* 7.12.1–2; for a brief discussion, see Martini, *Definizioni*, 107 and 355 n. 578. Unless otherwise indicated, the translations are those of the LCL, which is here slightly modified.

[11] *Epitome Ulpiani* 20.1 Huschke (*Iurisprudentiae anteiustinianae*, 593) (my translation). The *Epitome Ulpiani*, also known as the *Tituli Ulpiani* (or *Tituli ex corpore Ulpiani*), is an epitome of the *Liber singularis regularum* (= *Regulae* or *Rules*) attributed to Ulpian (= Domitius Ulpianus), on whom see esp. Tony Honoré, *Ulpian* (Oxford: Clarendon, 1982). Whether Ulpian (d. 223 oe 228 C.E.) wrote such a work is fiercely debated (see esp. Honoré, *Ulpian*, 106–11; see also H. F. Jolowicz and Barry Nicholas, *Historical Introduction to the Study of Roman Law* [3rd ed.; Cambridge: Cambridge University Press, 1972], 458, and Wieacker, *Römische Rechtsgeschichte*, 153 n. 47a and 154 n. 54), with Fritz Schulz (ed.), *Die Epitome Ulpiani des Codex Vaticanus Reginae 1128* (Bonn: Marcus, 1926), arguing that the author of the *Liber singularis regularum* "was certainly not Ulpian but an unknown lawyer of the third or the beginning of the fourth century. His main source was the *Institutes*

explanation is found even later in the *Institutes* of the emperor Justinian
(527–565 C.E.), where the word *testamentum* is etymologically explained
as a *testatio mentis*, that is, "a testament is so called because it is evidence
of a person's state of mind" (2.10).[12] Although Aulus Gellius recognized
that this derivation was false,[13] he was still prepared to say that the idea

---

of Gaius in the form in which they have reached us" (*Roman Legal Science*, 181). On
the other hand, H. L. W. Nelson, *Überlieferung, Aufbau und Stil von Gai Institutiones* (Studia
Gaiana 6; Leiden: Brill, 1981) 80–96, has argued forcefully that the *Epitome Ulpiani* is not
dependent on Gaius (second century C.E.), thus strengthening the arguments that the
work is in fact an epitome of Ulpian's *Regulae*. In any case, the *Liber singularis regularum*
appears to have been written between 211 and 262 (Nelson, *Überlieferung*, 91). Honoré,
Ulpian, 107, dates the *Epitome Ulpiani* to the third century, whereas Schulz, *Epitome*, 8–9,
assigns it to the period 320–342 C.E.

[12] The translation is a modified version of that given by R. W. Lee, *The Elements
of Roman Law, with a Translation of the Institutes of Justinian* (4th ed.; London: Sweet &
Maxwell, 1956) 191. Ancient ingenious ancient etymology for *testamentum* is given by
Isidore of Seville in his *Etymologies* (= *Origines*). Inspired by Heb 9:17 ("a will takes
effect only at death, since it is not in force as long as the one who made it is
alive"), Isidore says that "it is called a testament because it has no validity until after
the tomb of the testator (*testatoris monumentum*) (is erected)" (*Ety.* 5.24, my translation).
That is, he derives *testamentum* from **testa**toris monu**mentum**. See Jose Oroz Reta and
Manuel-A. Marcos Casquero (ed. and trans.), *San Isidoro e Sevilla, Etimologías* (2 vols.;
Biblioteca de autores cristianos 433–434; Madrid: Editorial Catolica, 1982–1983) 1.518
n. 17. Elsewhere Isidore makes a connection between *testis* and *testamentum*; see *De eccles.
Offic.* 1.11; *Ety.* 5.23; 10.265; and note 14 below.

[13] Modern scholars usually derive *testamentum* from either the verb *testari* ("to invoke
as witness") or the noun *testis* ("testimony"); for the former, see Kübler, "Testament,"
985, and for the latter, see A. Ernout and A. Meillet, *Dictionnaire étymologique de la langue
latine* (4th ed. by Jacques André; Paris: Éditions Klincksieck, 1985) 689: "*Testamentum* is
used in the sense of 'testament,' literally, 'taken as a witness,' the testament being at
first an oral declaration made to the *comitia calata* [a convocation of the people] with the
assembly of the people as a witness, and, later, the testament *per aes et libram* [by bronze
and scales] requiring the support of witnesses" (my translation). For a different view, see
Emil Goldmann, "Das Alter des römischen Testaments," *Zeitschrift der Savigny-Stiftung
für Rechtsgeschichte* (Romantistische Abteilung) 51 (1931) 223–28, who, linking the Oscan
word *tristaamentud* with the Latin *testamento* (see the *Oxford Latin Dictionary*, 1932, s.v., *testis*),
argues that the Oscans borrowed the term when it was originally *tristamentom*. If correct,
this analysis would place the origin of the Roman testament at the very beginning of
Roman history. For criticism of this proposal, see Jean Perrot, *Les dérivés latins en -**men**
et -**mentum**: Recherches de linguistique descriptive et historique* (Études et Commentaries 37;
Paris: Klincksieck, 1961) 24.

   There are at least two modern views of the function of the Latin suffix *-mentum*
in *testamentum*. In his massive study, Perrot argues that the suffix functions to form
substantives denoting a thing or a concept, with the sense either instrumental or
resultative. He classifies *testamentum* as an abstract notion with a resultative sense (*Les
dérivés latins*, 259). William M. Gordon, by contrast, argues for the instrumental sense:
"The suffix *-mentum* is not derived from *mens* ('mind'), but refers to instrumentality
in a concrete sense, so that the will is the means by which the deceased makes a

was "neither inappropriate nor unattractive" (*Noct. att.* 7.12.4), doubtless because it accorded well with the widespread belief that the testator's intention was the paramount issue in interpreting a will.[14]

Bad wills, therefore, were widely believed to reveal vile people, and good wills to reveal virtuous ones. Cicero tells Atticus that he has learned of Calva's will, and that it reveals the latter as "a mean, contemptible creature" (*Att.* 15.3.1).[15] Pliny, by contrast, argues that Domitius Tullus' will proves that he was better in death than in life (*Ep.* 8.18.1). In books 15 and 16 of his *Annals*, Tacitus focuses on the wills that various people made at a time of personal crisis, using them as a means of demonstrating whether those individuals' final acts were consonant with their professed values and public reputations.[16] In short, last wills and testaments were not viewed merely as legal documents with large or small economic implications; they were regarded as moral media, as instruments that disclosed a person's true character.[17]

A corollary of this conviction was that good wills merit praise and bad ones condemnation. Diogenes Laertius, for instance, concludes his

---

declaration of his wishes before witnesses." See his "Succession," in *A Companion to Justinian's Institutes* (ed. E. Metzger; London: Duckworth, 1998) 84.

[14] See *Dig. justin.* 28.1.1, where Book 2 of the *Pandectae* (*Encyclopedia*) of Herennius Modestinus (first half of the third century C.E.) is quoted as follows: "A will is a lawful expression of our wishes (*uoluntatia*) concerning what someone wishes to be done after his death." Similarly, Javolenus Priscus (mid-first – early second century C.E.) gives the following quotation from the *Posteriores* (*Posthumous Works*) of M. Antistius Labeo (mid-first century B.C.E. – early first century C.E.): "I think that we should take the natural, not the legal implication of the testator's wishes (*mentem*)" (*Dig. justin.* 35.1.40.3). For Labeo, moreover, the validity of a will depends on the testator's soundness of mind (*integritas mentis*), not physical health (*Dig. justin.* 28.1.2), and statements in extant wills that the testator is "sane and in his right mind" (νοῶν καὶ φρονῶν) reflect the widespread conviction about the necessity of that criterion; see, for instance, P.Oxy. 104.4; 105.2. Concern for the testator's intention is doubtless what motivated Servius Sulpicius to offer his etymology, as Elizabeth Rawson, *Intellectual Life in the Late Roman Republic* (London: Duckworth, 1985) 11, suggests. (The translations of *Digesta justinianus* are those of Alan Watson [trans.], *The Digest of Justinian* [4 vols.; Philadelphia: University of Pennsylvania Press, 1985].)

[15] Unless otherwise indicated, the translations of Cicero's *Epistulae ad Atticum* are those of D. R. Shackleton Bailey (trans.), *Cicero's Letters to Atticus* (7 vols.; Cambridge Classical Texts and Commentaries 3–9; Cambridge: Cambridge University Press, 1965–1970).

[16] See esp. James Keenan, "Tacitus, Roman Wills, and Political Freedom," *BASP* 24 (1987) 1–8.

[17] It is in keeping with Tacitus' interest in the moral implications of wills that he exhibits little or no interest in the economic content of the wills that he mentions; see Keenan, "Tacitus," 8.

treatment of the Peripatetic philosopher Lyco (c. 300 – c. 225 B.C.E.) by first quoting his will, then making the following comment: "Thus while his shrewdness is seen in all his actions, in his teaching, and in all his studies, in some ways his will is no less remarkable for carefulness and wise management, so that in this respect also he is to be admired."[18] In a marble inscription from the first century B.C.E., the will of a twice-married woman by the name of Muridia is praised by a son from her first marriage. Muridia had made all her sons equal heirs, given a bequest to her daughter that was equivalent to what the sons received,[19] and provided a fixed sum for her second husband, the first having preceded her in death. Because of the way she disposed of her estate, the son says that she deserves post-mortem honor and praise "since the division of her estate indicated her grateful and honourable intentions towards her husbands, her fairness to her children, and the justice shown by her sincerity."[20] In a similar way, Pliny the Younger not only praises the will of Ummidia Quadratilla as "excellent" (*honestissimo*: *Ep.* 7.24.2), but he also defends the will of Domitius Tullus as marked by "duty (*pietas*), honesty (*fides*), and propriety (*pudor*)" (*Ep.* 8.18.7).[21]

Testation as Moral Obligation

Second, to make a will was viewed by both Hellenistic moralists and Roman jurists as a moral obligation. For that reason, wills were the subject not only of regular judicial deliberations[22] and rhetorical decla-

---

[18] Diogenes Laertius, *Lives of Eminent Philosophers* 5.74.

[19] The bequest was a *legatum partitionis hereditatis*, which probably was designed to circumvent the *lex Voconia*'s stipuation that no woman could be heir to estates that exceeded a certain amount. For the *lex Voconia* of 169 B.C.E., see Alan Watson, *The Law of Succession in the Later Roman Republic* (Oxford: Clarendon, 1971) 29–31; on its applicability to Muridia's will, see Suzanne Dixon, *The Roman Mother* (Norman: University of Oklahoma Press, 1988) 69. On the circumvention of this law, see esp. Dixon's "Breaking the Law To Do the Right Thing: The Gradual Erosion of the Voconian Law in Ancient Rome," *Adelaide Law Review* 9 (1983–1985) 519–34.

[20] *CIL* VI.10230 = *ILS* 8394 (= H. Dessau [ed.], *Inscriptiones latinae selectae*). The translation is that of Mary R. Lefkowitz and Maureen B. Fant, *Women's Life in Greece & Rome: A Source Book in Translation* (2nd ed.; Baltimore: Johns Hopkins University Press, 1992) 18. The son also defends the fact that his mother had bequeathed him certain property, saying that she did so "not in order to wound my brothers by preferring me to them," but in remembrance of her deceased husband's prior actions.

[21] The translation is that of Champlin, *Final Judgments*, 18.

[22] In classical Athens, the orator Isaeus appears to have specialized in inheritance law, with all of his complete surviving speeches dealing either directly or indirectly with issues involving succession. The circumstance that had occasioned Solon's law

on testaments was that of a man dying without a surviving son, and it was this same circumstance that was generative of most Athenian court cases involving succession. Indeed, as Lane Fox, "Inheritance," 209, notes, "All our Attic speeches which contest inheritances concern disputes over estates whose owner had died without surviving sons." Battles over succession broaden in the Hellenistic period, with family members named explicitly as heirs now engaging in legal disputes; see Lane Fox, "Inheritance," 210.

At Rome, court battles involving succession were often fierce. As John A. Crook, *Law and Life of Rome* (Aspects of Greek and Roman Life; London: Thames and Hudson, 1967) 118, points out, "Out of the fifty books of the *Digest* [of Justinian], eleven are occupied by the law of succession, lovingly elaborated by the lawyers; one must admit that in will-making the idiosyncrasies of humanity are at their most abundant and generate a lot of law." Discussions of wills began early in the history of Roman jurisprudence. According to Alan Watson, *Law Making in the Later Roman Republic* (Oxford: Clarendon, 1974) 145, 163–66, book one of Quintus Mucius Scaevola's (d. 82 B.C.E.) eighteen books on the civil law was devoted to wills, and the second of P. Alfenus Varus' (consul in 39 B.C.E) forty *digesta* was on wills and legacies. During the Empire, Roman jurists who wrote works entitled *On Wills* and *On Undutiful Wills* include Iulius Paulus (late second – early third century C.E.) and Modestinus (see Watson, *The Digest of Justinian*, lxvii–lxix). Needless to say, many of the statutes (*leges*) passed by assemblies of the Roman people either mention testaments or deal explicit with different aspects of them. The word *testamentum* appears, for example, in two statutes for which there is epigraphic evidence, viz., the *lex agraria* of 111 B.C.E. (line 23) and the *lex Tarentina* (col. 2, line 34). For *leges* known from literary sources, testaments are mentioned or discussed in the *lex Tullia de ambitu* of 63 B.C.E. (see Cicero, *Vat.* 37), the *lex Falcidia* of 40 B.C.E. (see Gaius, *Inst.* 2.227 and Peter Stein, "*Lex Falcidia*," *Athenaeum* 75 [n.s. 65] [1987]: 453–57), and the *lex Iunia Vellaea* of ca. 28 C.E. (see Gaius, *Inst.* 2.134 and Peter Stein, "*Lex Iunia Vellaea*," *Athenaeum* 75 [n.s. 65] [1987]: 459–64). For the texts of the preceding statutes, see M. H. Crawford (ed.), *Roman Statutes* (2 vols.; Bulletin of the Institute of Classical Studies Supplement 64; London: Institute of Classical Studies, University of London, 1996) 1.39–63, 113–80, 301–12; 2.761–62, 779–80, 811–12. See also the *lex Cornelia* mentioned by Cicero, *Verr.* 2.1.108 (on which see J. A. Crook, "*Lex Cornelia 'de falsis*," *Athenaeum* 75 [n.s. 65] [1987]: 163–71), and the numerous *leges* mentioned by Gaius in his *Institutes*, such as the *lex Iunia* (1.22–23; 3.56), *lex Furia* (2.225; 4.23, 109; see also Cicero, *Verr.* 2.1.109), *lex Fufia Canina* (1.42; 2.228; see also Cicero, *Verr.* 2.1.109), and *lex Voconia* (2.226; see also Cicero, *Verr.* 2.1.104–112). Finally, for a brief survey of Roman statutes and decrees affecting succession on intestacy, see David Cherry, "Intestacy and the Roman Poor," *Tijdschrift voor Rechtsgeschiedenis* 64 (1996) 163–64.

mations[23] but also of occasional fables[24] and philosophical reflection.[25] Valerius Maximus, for example, compiled his *Memorable Doings and Sayings* with the moral aim of providing his readers with guidance in applied ethics, citing numerous instances of both virtue and vice. He devoted three sections to wills,[26] "which for most Romans must have been one of the main opportunities to apply moral criteria in practice."[27] Galen, moreover, wrote a treatise entitled *On Making Wills* (*Libr. propr.* 13 [19.46 Kühn]), a work which, unfortunately, is no longer extant. But the lamentable fact that there are apparently no surviving moralist works devoted solely to the subject of testation should not lead us to infer that it was viewed as morally or socially insignificant.[28] On the contrary, the implicit and explicit moralist assumption throughout the Graeco-Roman period is that the making of a valid will was a duty, an *officium*, owed to loved ones.[29] Cicero, for example, refers to the tes-

---

[23] See, e.g., the Elder Seneca, *Cont.* 3.9; Quintilian, *Inst.* 7.1.38; 7.4.39; *Decl. min.* 264; 268; 308; 332; 380. The authorship of the *Declamationes minores* ascribed to Quntilian is debated.

[24] See Ben E. Perry (ed.), *Aesopica*, I: *Greek and Latin Texts* (Urbana: University of Illinois Press, 1952) nos. 42 (p. 338) and 703 (pp. 696–97), and Phaedrus, *Fab.* 4.5, on which see John Henderson, "The Law Is Not Mocked: Straightening Out a Crooked Will (Phaedrus 4.5)," in *Thinking Like a Lawyer: Essays on Legal History and General History for John Crook on His Eightieth Birthday* (ed. P. McKechnie; Mnemosyne Supplements 231; Leiden: Brill, 2002) 213–30.

[25] See, for instance, Plato, *Leg.* 922b–926d. Furthermore, the making of a will was primarily of interest to the affluent, esp. property owners, who named an heir in order to facilitate the transmission of property and other assets. Inasmuch as the practice was thus important to those who had sufficient wealth to pursue the study of philosophy, it is not surprising to find ancient philosophers giving attention to various aspects of testation.

[26] Valerius Maximus, *Mem.* 7.7.1–7 ("Of Wills That Were Rescinded"); 7.8.1–4 ("Of Wills That Remained Valid, Though with Reasons for which They Might Have Been Rescinded"); 7.8.5–9 ("Wills That Had Heirs Contrary to General Expectation").

[27] Clive Skidmore, *Practical Ethics for Roman Gentlemen: The Work of Valerius Maximus* (Exeter: University of Exeter Press, 1996) 72, who also suggests that "besides advising those making wills, he may also have in mind those faced with the duty of adjudicating on them." For the moral purpose with which Valerius Maximus writes, see pp. 53–82. For property-owners as those among his anticipated readers, see p. 103.

[28] *Contra* David Daube, "The Preponderance of Intestacy at Rome," *Tulane Law Review* 39 (1964–1965) 262, who makes the unfounded claim that "none of the countless texts in Roman literature dealing with ethical or civic duties hints at the making of a will." Daube is followed in this regard by Watson, *Succession*, 175.

[29] Fritz Schulz, *Principles of Roman Law* (Oxford: Clarendon, 1936) 156: "to make a will was as much the duty of every self-respecting Roman as to keep proper accounts." See also Andrew Wallace-Hadrill, "Family and Inheritance in the Augustan Marriage Laws," *Proceedings of the Cambridge Philological Society* 207 (1981) 66–70, esp. 67: "The will in fact expressed one's pattern of obligations. The first duty was of course to the

tamentary provisions made by the dying Epicurus, noting his "observance of these solemn duties (*summorum officiorum*) with his last breath"
and praising "so strong a sense of duty (*tanta officia*) in a dying man"
(*Fin.* 2.99). Elsewhere, he tells Atticus that his uncle, Quintus Caecilius,
did his duty by him in the matter of his inheritance (*Att.* 3.20.1).[30] By the
end of the Roman republic, moreover, "the principle that the descendants … of a testator … had a legitimate expectation of acquiring a
share of his estate"[31] became a part of Roman law with the institution
of "the complaint of the undutiful will" (*querela inofficiosi testamenti*).[32] The
latter was an action that "children who were disinherited or otherwise
unfairly treated" might take, "the basis of which was that the testator
had offended against the duty to respect the family, the *officium pietatis*."[33]

From a philosophical perspective, to die intestate or without a valid
will was not simply socially unacceptable; more important, it was morally reprehensible.[34] It was a grave error, for it meant that one had failed

---

family; but the testator should also remember anyone to whom he was bound by ties
of *officium*." That testation was regarded as a duty is implicit even in the treatment of
soldiers' wills. Roman citizens who were soldiers had the right to make a will that was
free (*libera testamenti factio*) from formal legal requirements, but such wills were valid only
for a year after they left military service. If they failed to make a new will during this
grace period, they could be regarded as negligent. See J. B. Campbell, *The Emperor and
the Roman Army: 31 B.C. – A.D. 235* (Oxford: Clarendon, 1984) 215.

[30] See also Cicero, *Fam.* 6.19.1.

[31] David Johnston, *The Roman Law of Trusts* (Oxford: Clarendon, 1988) 3.

[32] See esp. E. Renier, *Etude sur l'historie de la querela inofficiosi en droit romain* (Liége:
Vaillant-Carmanne, 1942). For this legal action at the time of Diocletian (284–305 C.E.),
see Olga E. Tellegen-Couperus, *Testamentary Succession in the Constitutions of Diocletian*
(Zutphen: Terra, 1982) 155–72. On the frequency of these complaints, see *Dig. justin.*
5.2.1.

[33] Champlin, *Final Judgments*, 15. For Pliny the Younger's account of two such complaints, see his *Ep.* 5.1 and 6.33; for discussion, see esp. J. W. Tellegen, *The Roman Law of
Succession in the Letters of Pliny the Younger* (Studia Amstelodamensia ad epigraphicam, ius
antiquum et papyrologicam pertinentia 21; Zutphen: Terra, 1982) 83–94, 110–18. See
also Ditlev Tamm, *Roman Law and European Legal History* (Copenhagen: DJØF, 1997) 185.
The making of a will was not only a moral obligation but also an exercise of power
(*potestas*) by the *paterfamilias*. In addition to being a violation of familial piety, therefore,
the unjust treatment of family members was viewed as an inappropriate, even immoral
exercise of the power by which he dominated and controlled members of his family.

[34] See, e.g., Fronto, *Ant. Imp.* 2.1.2 van den Hout (= *M. Caes.* 2.16 Naber). For literature dealing with intestacy and intestate succession in ancient Greece, see J. C. Miles,
"The Attic Laws of Intestate Succession," *Hermathena* 75 (1950) 69–77, and Evanghe-
los Karabélias, "La succession *ab intestat* en droit attique," *Journal of Juristic Papyrology*
20 (1990) 55–74. For the modern debate about the prevalence of testacy among the
Romans–with the debate centering on the accuracy of Sir Henry Maine's famous claim
that Romans had a "passion for Testacy" and a corresponding "horror of Intestacy"

in one's duty to one's loved ones. As Juvenal says at *Sat.* 3.272–274, the individual who dies intestate runs the risk of being deemed both slothful (*ignavus*) and thoughtless (*improvidus*). This moralist sentiment helps to explain the attitude of Cato the Elder, who, according to Plutarch (*Cat. Maj.* 9.6), had occasion to repent just three times in his life; one of these times was when he was ἀδιάθετος for a single day, that is, either "without a will, or (more likely) with one that had been for some reason invalidated."[35] It also helps to explain Juvenal's vicious attack in *Satire* 1

(*Ancient Law* [3rd ed.; London: J. Murray, 1866; repr. with an introduction by D. J. Scala; New Brunswick: Transactions, 2001], 222–23)—see esp. Daube, "Preponderance," 253–62, and *Roman Law: Linguistic, Social, and Philosophical Aspects* (Edinburgh: Edinburgh University Press, 1969) 71–75; Watson, *Succession*, 175–76; John Crook, "Intestacy in Roman Society," *Proceedings of the Cambridge Philological Society* 199 [n.s. 19] (1973) 38–44; J. Duncan Cloud, "Satirists and the Law," in *Satire and Society in Ancient Rome* (ed. S. H. Braund; Exeter Studies in History 23; Exeter: University of Exeter, 1989) 57–59; Champlin, *Final Judgments*, 42–46; and Cherry, "Intestacy," 155–73. In general, it appears that the rich made wills and the poor did not, though there are many important exceptions to this generalization. A number of propertied individuals died intestate—Cicero names six such people in his writings and the *Digesta justinianus* mention some 15 cases of intestacy. At the other end of the economic scale, an ex-slave by the name of Tiberius Claudius Alexander (134 C.E.) instituted his concubine as his heir (P.Oxy. 2857). The size of the estate is unclear, but it is not likely to have been large. No slaves are manumitted, no specific property is mentioned, and only two legacies are given, each just 100 drachmas. To cite an example from Latin literature, when Umbricius in Juvenal's third satire (272–274) decries the folly of not making a will, he "has in mind the poor, not the rich citizen, one who cannot afford a proper lantern (286–7) and is accused by a mugger of stuffing himself on beans, vinegar and a boiled sheep's head in a cobbler's company (292–4);" this indicates that, from the perspective of Umbricius, "the poor as well as the rich were expected to make a will" (Cloud, "Satirists," 58). And it is clear from surviving evidence that people of rather moderate means did indeed make wills (see esp. Crook, "Intestacy," 39, and his review of Champlain, *Final Judgments*, in *JRS* 82 [1992]: 233–34; and Cherry, "Intestacy," 169–70), likely influenced in that regard by the attitudes and practices of the upper classes. On this last point, see esp. Susan D. Martin's review of Champlin's *Final Judgments* in *CP* 88 (1993) 179; see also Cherry, "Intestacy," 171, who mentions the influence of the upper classes on the practices of the lower ones but does not invoke this as a factor to explain testacy among those with moderate assets. Even some slaves made wills, which, though lacking validity under Roman law, were treated as valid by certain masters (Pliny, *Ep.* 8.16.1–2). Furthermore, some slaves were dues-paying members of funerary clubs; the latter, it is clear, anticipated that such slaves would die with wills having been made, but they were prepared to conduct the funeral and inter the body even if the slave should die intestate (*CIL* XIV.2112 = *ILS* 7212). Unfortunately, the statistical percentage of testators is impossible to determine, either for Roman society as a whole or for its various classes. In any case, philosophers and other moralists took a rather dim view of intestacy, and it is this perspective that is in view here.

[35] Champlin, *Final Judgments*, 41; see also 21 n. 70. The alternative interpretations of ἀδιάθετος advanced by Daube ("Preponderance," 261, and *Roman Law*, 73) and

on a patron who, rather than dine with clients of long standing (1.132: *veteres clientes*),[36] chooses to eat alone,[37] reclining by himself on a couch adjacent a splendid, antique round table (1.136–138).[38] In solitude he feasts on "the finest produce of sea and woodland" (1.135),[39] especially boars (1.141)[40] and peacocks (1.143).[41] The dinner (*cena*: 1.133), so "central to the operation of *amicitia*"[42] ("friendship"), becomes here the occasion for solitary self-indulgence. Although the boar is "an animal born for parties" (*convivia*: 1.141)[43] and dinner is a time for being together and for

---

R. Flacelière ("Le troisième remords de Caton," *REG* 80 [1967]: 195–97) have been persuasively refuted by Crook ("Intestacy," 39–41).

[36] See also Juvenal, *Sat.* 5.64; compare "old friend(s)" at 3.1; 6.346 and 6.O 30 (line 30 of the Oxford MS of *Sat.* 6).

[37] See the anticipation of this aspect of the vignette in Juvenal, *Sat.* 1.94–95: "Which of our grandfathers built so many villas, or dined off seven courses, alone (*secreto*)?"

[38] See also Juvenal, *Sat.* 1.75; 11.117–129. For the obsession of affluent men for fine tables, see Pliny the Elder, *Nat.* 13.91–95, and John E. B. Mayor (ed.), *Thirteen Satires of Juvenal* (2 vols.; London: Macmillan, 1900–1901) 1.149–50. Contrast Seneca's statement about his frugality in regard to tables (*Tranq.* 1.7) with the claim of Cassius Dio (*Hist.* 61.10.3) that Seneca owned "five hundred tables of citrus wood with legs of ivory, all identically alike."

[39] Unless otherwise indicated, translations of Juvenal are those in Niall Rudd (trans.) and William Barr, *Juvenal, The Satires* (Oxford: Clarendon, 1991).

[40] See also Juvenal, *Sat.* 5.115–116; Horace, *Sat.* 2.2.89–92; 2.4.40–42; 2.8.6–9; Martial, *Epig.* 7.59; Petronius, *Saty.* 40; Pliny the Elder, *Nat.* 8.210; Plutarch, *Ant.* 28.3; and Suetonius, *Tib.* 34.

[41] See Cicero, *Fam.* 9.20.2; Horace, *Sat.* 1.2.116; Petronius, *Saty.* 55.2; and Mayor, *Thirteen Satires of Juvenal*, 1.154–55.

[42] Susanna Morton Braund (ed.), *Juvenal, Satires, Book I* (Cambridge Greek and Latin Classics; Cambridge: Cambridge University Press, 1996) 305.

[43] Juvenal uses here the widely held view that pigs existed simply for human consumption, but he emphasizes a communal context for that consumption. See esp. Porphyry, *Abst.* 1.14.3: "Pigs are not useful for anything except for eating," and 3.20.1,3: "the pig … was born for nothing but to be sacrificed, and God added soul to its flesh like salt, to make it tasty for us. … Now the pig is brought into being by nature to be slaughtered and devoured; so in experiencing this it achieves the end for which it is naturally suited, and it benefits." The translations of Porphyry are those of Gillian Clark (trans.), *Porphyry, On Abstinence from Killing Animals* (Ithaca: Cornell University Press, 2000) 36 and 91. See also Varro, *Rust.* 2.4.10: "There is a saying that the race of pigs is expressly given by nature to set forth a banquet (*ad epulandum*); and that accordingly its soul was given it just like salt" (LCL, modified). The idea that pigs exist for sacrifice was supported in antiquity by the etymological claim that the Greek word for "pig" (ὗς or σῦς) was originally θῦς, which either was derived from θύειν ("to sacrifice") or connected with θυσία ("sacrifice"); see Varro, *Rust.* 2.4.9; Athenaeus, *Deipn.* 9.401c; and Clement of Alexandria, *Strom.* 2.105.2. See also Cicero, *Nat. d.* 2.160; *Fin.* 5.38; Pliny the Elder, *Nat.* 8.207; Plutarch, *Quaest. conv.* 685c and frg. 193 Sandbach (= Porphyry, *Abst.* 3.20); Clement of Alexandria, *Strom.* 7.33.3; Aelian, *Var. hist.* 10.5; and Galen, *De alimentorum facultatibus* (= *On the Powers of Foods*) 3.1.2 *CMG* (= *Corpus Medicorum Graecorum*),

eating and drinking together (*convivia*, **συμ**πόσια),[44] the stingy patron prefers μονοφαγία, eating alone.[45] That this is sheer gluttony[46] is made emphatic by Juvenal's use of *gula* ("gullet"). "What size of gullet," he asks, "could order a whole boar for itself?" (1.140–141).[47] Only an oxymoron can capture the magnitude of the patron's outrageous behavior: it is "niggardly excess" (*luxuriae sordes*: 1.140).[48] Through his unrestrained consumption, he and other patrons like him "gobble up (*comedunt*)[49] their ancestors' wealth (*patromonia*) at a single sitting" (1.138).[50]

But the patron will soon pay the penalty (*poena*) for his crimes (1.142). Shifting suddenly in diatribe fashion to the second person singular,[51] the

---

who argues that "of all foods, therefore, pork is the most nutritious" (see also 3.18.2 and Clement of Alexandria, *Strom.* 7.33.5 for the same sentiment). The translation of Galen's text is that of Mark Grant (trans.), *Galen on Food and Diet* (London: Routledge, 2000) 154. For Clement of Alexandria's attack on pork as food "orchestrated for people of luxury," see *Strom.* 2.105.1 and compare 5.51.3.

[44] For this emphasis, see esp. E. Courtney, *A Commentary on the Satires of Juvenal* (London: Athlone, 1980) 112. See also Braund, *Juvenal*, 104. Note esp. Cicero, *Sen.* 45: "For our fathers did well in calling the reclining of friends at feasts a *convivium*, because it implies a communion of life, which is a better designation than that of the Greeks, who call it sometimes a 'drinking together' and sometimes an "eating together,' thereby apparently exalting what is of least value in these associations above that which gives them their greatest charm."

[45] The recognition that Juvenal is depicting the patron as a μονοφάγος is at least as old as the nineteenth century. See Karl Friedrich Heinrich (ed.), *D. Iunii Iuvenalis Satirae* (ed. K. B. Heinrich; 2 vols.; Bonn: A. Marcus, 1839) 1.81, and Ludwig Friedländer (ed.), *D. Junii Juvenalis, Saturarum Libri V* (2 vols.; Leipzig: S. Hirzel, 1895) 1. 149–50, 156. The practice was viewed as anti-social and widely condemned. See, for example, Epicurus, frg. 542 Usener, quoted approvingly by Seneca, *Ep.* 19.10: "A dinner of meats without the company of a friend is like the life of a lion or a wolf." See also Cicero, *Pis.* 67.

[46] For the connection between solitary dining and gluttony, see esp. 4Macc 1:27 (pleasure in the body is exhibited in "indiscriminate eating, gluttony, and solitary gormandizing") and 2:7 ("someone who is habitually a solitary gormandizer, a glutton, or even a drunkard"). See also Pliny the Younger, *Pan.* 49.6 and compare Plutarch, *Luc.* 41.2–6.

[47] Like μονοφαγία, *gula* connotes gluttony; compare Martial, *Epig.* 5.70.5: "How large a gullet to eat ten million [*sesterces*]!"

[48] The translation is mine. Compare Pliny the Younger, *Ep.* 2.6.6: "this novel association of extravagance and meanness" (*luxuriae et sordium novam societatem*), and *Ep.* 2.1.1: "a sort of stingy extravagance" (*sordidum simul et sumptuosum*).

[49] See also Juvenal's use of *vorabit* ("devours") in *Sat.* 1.135; as Braund, *Juvenal*, 105, notes, both terms are stronger than simple *edo* ("eat").

[50] A common accusation by moralists and others: see Athenaeus, *Deipn.* 4.165d; 166b–d; Cicero, *Fin.* 2.23; *Sest.* 110–111; Seneca, *Ben.* 1.10.2. It is disputed whether *mensa* in 1.138 should be translated "sitting" or "table."

[51] Compare the change from the singular *rex* in *Sat.* 1.136 to the plural in 1.137–138, and the shift to the plural at the beginning of 1.144 (*subitae mortes*).

satirist first addresses the patron, then ends the vignette:

> When you strip and, within that bloated body,
> carry an undigested peacock into the bath-house,
> death steps in, too sudden for old men to make wills.
> At once the joyful news goes dancing around the dinners.
> The funeral cortège departs to the cheers of indignant friends (1.142–
> 46).[52]

Whereas Romans usually bathed before dinner,[53] this patron does so after stuffing himself with peacock.[54] He does so because peacocks were widely regarded as indigestible[55] and hot baths were believed to "cook" food that had been consumed, thus aiding digestion.[56] But the patron becomes apoplectic and dies suddenly (1.144: *subitae mortes*, "sudden deaths"),[57] without time to make a will (*intestata*).[58]

---

[52] The translation is that of Rudd, *Juvenal*, 7, except for the latter part of line 144, where I use the translation of Rolfe Humphries (trans.), *The Satires of Juvenal* (Bloomington: Indiana University Press, 1958) 22.

[53] Noted by several commentators, including J. D. Duff (ed.), *D. Ivnii Ivvenalis Saturae XIV: Fourteen Satires of Juvenal* (Cambridge: Cambridge University Press, 1900) 131, and Pierre de LaBriolle and François Villeneuve (8th revised and corrected printing; Budé; Paris: Les Belles Lettres, 1964) 11.

[54] The patron's action was typical behavior for gormandizers and gluttons; see esp. Plutarch, *Tu. san.* 128b: "but much more is it a shame to bear indigestion, overloading, and overfullness in a body which is dragged to the bath like a rotten and leaky boat into the sea." See also Lucretius, *De rerum natura* 6.799–800 and Cicero, *Deiot.* 21.

[55] Courtney, *Commentary*, 113. See esp. Galen, *De alim. fac.* 3.18.3 *CMG*, who in his discussion of various kinds of fowl gives the peacock as the most difficult to digest: "The flesh of peacocks is even harder, more difficult to digest and more fibrous than these (other birds)." The translation is that of Grant, *Galen*, 171. See also Cicero, *Fam.* 9.18.3–4, where mention of the consumption of peacocks is followed by a reference to possible death by indigestion (*cruditate*).

[56] See esp. Pliny the Elder, *Nat.* 29.8.26: "broiling baths, by which they have persuaded us that food is cooked (*coqui*) in our bodies." As the LCL notes, Pliny is making a pun on *coquere*: "to cook" and "to digest." For the extremely high heat of Roman baths, see Seneca, *Ep.* 86.10–11 and Petronius, *Saty.* 72. The dry heat of sweat-chambers was used for the same purpose; see Celsus, *Med.* 2.17.1 and esp. Columella, *Rust.* 1. Prooemium 16: "we steam out our daily indigestion in sweat-baths."

[57] For the danger of bathing after overindulgence or when suffering from indigestion, see Lucretius, *De rerum natura* 799–802; Pliny the Elder, *Nat.* 14.28.139; Celsus, *Med.* 2.17.2; and Plutarch, *Tu. San.* 124c.

[58] The text of line 144 is *hinc subitae mortes atque intestata senectus*, lit., "hence sudden deaths and intestate old age." The logic of the line is sequential: sudden death is the result of the patron entering the *calidarium* in his bloated condition, and intestacy is the result of the sudden death. The same connection between a sudden death and dying intestate appears in *Sat.* 3.272–274: "You may well be regarded as slack, and heedless of sudden (*subiti*) disaster, if you fail to make your will (*intestatus*) before going out to dinner." The only additional element that appears in *Sat.* 1.144 is old

In short, the patron dies as he had lived, with thoughts only for himself and in total disregard for the past, the present, and the future. With no regard for what his ancestors accumulated in the past, he devours his patrimony in the same manner that he does the food on his luxurious table (1.135–138). With no regard for family and friends in the present, he dines alone (1.136), willfully oblivious to the needs and desires of others.[59] With no regard for the future, he dies intestate, making no provision for those who had been faithful to him for a long time. His client-"friends" (*amicis*)[60] gather for the funeral procession, not to lament (*plangendum*) in grief as true friends typically did at such times,[61] but in anger to jeer and applaud (*plaundendum*:

age. For this interpretation, see J. E. B. Mayor, "Notes on Plin. *Ep.* I 5 3 and on Juvenal I 144–6," *Journal of Philology* 13 (1885) 231–32; Friedländer, *Juvenalis Saturarum Libri V*, 1.158; S. G. Owen, "On Some Passages in Juvenal *Satires* I. and III.," *Classical Review* 11 (1897) 400; Champlin, *Final Judgments*, 21; Cloud, "Satirists," 58; and Braund, *Juvenal*, 106. For a different interpretation of *intestata*, see A. E. Housman, "Juvenal I 132–146," *Classical Review* 13 (1899) 432–34, and *D. Ivnii Ivvenalis Saturae* (corrected ed.; Cambridge: Cambridge University Press, 1931) 6; John Ferguson (ed.), *Juvenal, The Satires* (New York: Macmillan, 1979; repr. Bristol: Bristol Classical Press, 1996) 122, and Niall Rudd in Rudd and Edward Courtney, *Juvenal, Satires I, III, X* (1st ed. 1977; 2nd ed. with revised and updated bibliography; Bristol: Bristol Classical Press, 1996) 46. Two emendations have been proposed: *infestata* and *intentata* (= *intemptata*). For the former, see Johan N. Madvig, *Adversaria critica ad scriptores graecos et latinos* (3 vols.; Hauniae: Librariae Gyldendalianae [F. Hegel], 1871–84) 3.249–50; and the critical apparatus of J. R. C. Martyn (ed.), *D. Ivni Ivvenalis Satvrae* (Amsterdam: Hakkert, 1987). For the latter, see E. C. Corelli, "On Juvenal, *Sat.* i.144," *Classical Review* 19 (1905) 305; Courtney, *Commentary*, 114, and *Juvenal, The Satires: A Text with Brief Critical Notes* (Instrumentum litterarum 1; Rome: Edizioni dell'Ateneo, 1984) 12 and 14.

[59] Juvenal describes the clients as wretches (*miseris*) who are weary and without hope (1.132–134). The only thing that they receive from the patron is the daily dole (*sportula*: 1.128), which consisted of 100 *quadrantes* (= 25 *asses* = 6 *sesterces*; see 1.120–121). But because they are not invited to dinner, they are forced to use at least a portion of that money to purchase (*emendus*) cabbage and kindling (1.134), leaving little or nothing for other necessities (1.119–120). As Duff, *Juvenal*, 131, points out, *emendus* is emphatic. See Seneca, *Ep.* 20.3: "see … whether you treat yourself lavishly and your family meanly."

[60] The use of *amicis* in 1.146 is ironic, as are all instances of *amicus* and *amicitia* in Juvenal's *Satires*; see Richard A. LaFleur, "*Amicitia* and the Unity of Juvenal's First Book," *ICS* 4 (1979) 158–77, esp. 158. As LaFleur (160) perceptively points out, "*Amicis* is the satirist's last word; and it is delayed, like *amici* in verse 33 and *amicus* throughout Book One, to final position in the line, where the *para prosdokian* [an idea that is contrary to expectation] is specially accentuated."

[61] In his *Commentary on Isaiah*, Theodoret says that laments are made by friends, not by enemies. The comment is made at the end of his remarks on Isa 1:3 and in anticipation of his quotation of Isa 1:4; see Jean-Noël Guinot (ed. and trans.), *Théodoret de Cyr, Commentaire sur Isaïe* (3 vols.; SC 276, 295, 315; Paris: Cerf, 1980–1984) 1.152, section 1, line 83.

1.146).[62] Because their patron had died intestate, they received none of the legacies that patrons normally included in their wills, and with intestate succession, only members of the family received a share in the inheritance, not friends.[63] It thus comes as no surprise that they are angry and cheer their patron's death,[64] and that the whole sorry affair becomes a dinner-table joke (1.145).

That Juvenal here both exaggerates and distorts the historical patron-client relationship is not relevant for our purposes.[65] What is relevant is the kind of person whom Juvenal depicts as dying intestate. He is an ogre, a totally odious person, so self-absorbed that his failure to make a will is not at all shocking. Such are the kinds of people—at least in Juvenal's social circle—who do not make wills.[66]

The morally scrupulous person, therefore, tried to avoid dying without a will. One of Martial's epigrams depicts a dying man who begs the Fates for time to apportion his property among his friends and is mercifully granted his request:

> When Vestinus was ill, spending his final hours, on the point of passing through the waters of Styx, he begged the Sisters as they unwound the last threads to delay a little in drawing the black strands[67] while, already dead to himself, he lived for his dear friends. So unselfish a prayer moved

---

[62] Another instance of *para prosdokian*, as Braund, *Juvenal*, 146, notes.

[63] For regulations affecting intestate succession, see Gaius, *Inst.* 3.1–87.

[64] On anger in Juvenal, see esp. S. H. Braund, *Beyond Anger: A Study of Juvenal's Third Book of Satires* (Cambridge: Cambridge University Press, 1988), and on anger in general, see now William V. Harris, *Restraining Rage: The Ideology of Anger Control in Classical Antiquity* (Cambridge: Harvard University Press, 2001).

[65] See, in general, S. C. Fredericks, "Irony of Overstatement in the Satires of Juvenal," *ICS* 4 (1979) 178–91, and on the client-patron relationship in particular, Duncan Cloud, "The Client-Patron Relationship: Emblem and Reality in Juvenal's First Book," in *Patronage in Ancient Society* (ed. A. Wallace-Hadrill; London: Routledge, 1989) 205–18.

[66] As several commentators point out, Juvenal's "death in the bath" scene was inspired by Persius, *Sat.* 3.98–106. See, for example, Braund, *Juvenal*, 105, and Guy Lee (trans.) and William Barr, *The Satires of Persius* (Latin and Greek Texts 4; Liverpool: Francis Cairns, 1987) 115. Given this connection, it is important to emphasize a key difference between these two texts. Whereas Juvenal depicts the patron as having died intestate, Persius portrays the deceased as having died testate; the latter is carried out to burial by "new Romans" with covered heads (line 106), that is, by ex-slaves who had been manumitted in the man's will and who are wearing the *pilleus* as a sign of their newly attained freedom. See J. R. Jenkinson, *Persius, The Satires* (Warminster: Aris & Phillips, 1980) 82.

[67] The image of the Fates spinning out the threads of a person's life and cutting them to bring about death is Homeric in origin (*Il.* 24.209–210) and used by Martial not only here but also at *Epig.* 4.54.5–10; 6.58.7–8; and 11.36.3–4.

the grim goddesses.[68] Then, having divided his ample wealth, he left the light, believing that this done he was dying an old man (*Epig.* 4.73).[69]

Deathbed Testation

Third, although the very scrupulous (such as Cato the Elder) tended to make their wills early in life and keep them up-to-date by adding codicils or writing new wills,[70] most people in the ancient world postponed the making of their wills until they were either ill or in danger, thus regarding death as imminent. Therefore, the fact that the Vestinus of Martial's epigram left the making of his will to the last minute is not in the least surprising. His behavior was quite typical. Indeed, the postponement of testation until the end of life was so widespread in classical Athens that Plato can simply assume that wills are made at the point of death (*Leg.* 922b–923a). Furthermore, "Plato's tacit assumption that in general wills are made on a sick bed or in fear of immediate death agrees with the allusions in the orators, who often mention illness or some dangerous expedition in connexion with testaments."[71] As one might anticipate, soldiers, because of the danger of death in battle,

---

[68] This comes as a pleasant surprise in light of Martial's statement at *Epig.* 4.54.5–6: "To no man's prayers has it fallen to move the three wool-spinning maids; they observe their appointed day."

[69] For brief explanatory comments on this epigram, see Ludwig Friedländer, *M. Valerii Martialis Epigrammaton Libri* (2 vols.; Leipzig: S. Hirzel, 1886) 1.376–77.

[70] A Ptolemaic officer by the name of Drytōn (second century B.C.E.) made at least three wills—the first when he was a young man (176/175), the second after his marriage to his second wife (between 151 and 145), and the third after the births of his five daughters (126). See P.Batav. 4 and P.W. Pestman, "Copie d'un testament de Drytôn," in E. Boswinkel and P.W. Pestman (eds.), *Textes grecs, démotiques et bilingues* (Papyrologica Lugduno-Batava 19; London: Brill, 1978) 30–37. Not to keep one's will up-to-date meant that it might no longer express one's wishes and intentions; see the observations of Pliny the Younger, *Ep.* 8.18.5, on a will that was eighteen years old.

[71] William Wyse, *The Speeches of Isaeus with Critical and Explanatory Notes* (Cambridge: Cambridge University Press, 1904) 249. For Greek wills made during illness (as in the case of Martial's Vestinus), see Apollodorus, *Neaer.* 55–57 (= Ps.-Demosthenes, *Or.* 59.55–57); Demosthenes, *2 Aphob.* 15 (= *Or.* 28.15); *Pro Phorm.* 7 (= *Or.* 36.7); *Spud.* 17–18 (= *Or.* 41.17–18); Diogenes Laertius, *Lives of Eminent Philosophers* 4.43–44; 5.69; Isaeus, *Menecles* 14 (= *Or.* 2.14); Isocrates, *Aeginet.* 19.11–12 (= *Or.* 19.11–12); and Lysias, *Aristophanes* 41 (= *Or.*19.41). For Roman deathbed testaments in the time prior to the Twelve Tables, see Watson, *Rome of the XII Tables*, 62. For other examples of Greek and Roman deathbed testaments, see Aristophanes, *Vesp.* 583–584; Lysias, *Agoratus* 41–42 (= *Or.* 13.41–42); Cicero, *Fin.* 2.99; 3.65; Seneca the Elder, *Cont.* 2.7.7; Martial, *Epig.* 4.70; Apuleius, *Apol.* 97.2; 99.3 Hunink; Plutarch, *Nic.* 30; P.Ryl. II.153.45; *Inst. justin.* 2.25 (on which see Champlin, "Miscellanea Testamentaria I–III," 249–51); John Malalas, *Chron.* 18.23 (439 Dindorf); and Crook, *Law*, 116.

often made wills when departing for military service[72] or before enter-ing the fray.[73] According to Plutarch, "It was a custom with the Romans of that time [ca. 490 B.C.E.], when they were going into action, and were about to gird up their cloaks and take up their bucklers, to make at the same time an unwritten will (διαθήκας ἀγράφους), naming their heirs in the hearing of three or four witnesses" (Cor. 9.2).[74]

The deathbed or imminent death testament was thus as common in the ancient world as deathbed confessions are in our own time.[75] Usually these testaments were written, but at other times they had to

---

[72] See Isaeus, *Philoctemon* 5 (= *Or.* 6.5); *Apollodorus* 9 (= *Or.* 7.9); *Astyphilus* 14 (= *Or.* 9.14); Lysias, *Diogeiton* 5 (= *Or.* 32.5; see also Dionysius of Halicarnassus, *Lys.* 21 and 25). See also Isaeus, *Hagnias* argument and 8 (= *Or.* 11. argument and 8). Testamentary adoption appears to have been the strategy adopted by young or middle-aged men without a legitimate male heir. When faced with a military call-up or some other danger, they made a will in which they named an heir in the event of their death. Such a contingency strategy may also have been employed by an older or ill man whose only son was going into battle or another similar life-threatening situation. See Thompson, "Athenian Attitudes," 16; Lane Fox, "Inheritance," 224; Todd, *Shape*, 223–24; and esp. Lene Rubinstein, *Adoption in IV. Century Athens* (Opuscula Graecolatina 34; Copenhagen: Museum Tusculanum Press, University of Copenhagen, 1993) 14, 22–25, 56–57.

[73] See Julius Caesar, *Bell. gall.* 1.39.

[74] The technical term for this kind of will was *testamentum in procinctu*; see Berger, "Dictionary," 733. It appears to have become obsolete by the late Republic (Cicero, *Nat. d.* 2.9; Gaius, *Inst.* 2.101–103), but Julius Caesar revived its original intention by giving soldiers the right to make a will that was free from formal legal requirements, and this right was confirmed and extended for a variety of reasons by a number of early emperors (*Dig. justin.* 29.1.1). For references to the old *testamentum in procintu* ("battle-line testament"), see Arthur Stanley Pease (ed.), *M. Tvlli Ciceronis de natvra deorum* (2 vols.; Cambridge: Harvard Univesity Press, 1955–1958), 2.570–71. For the soldier's will (*testamentum militis*) in imperial Rome, see Juvenal, *Sat.* 16.51–54; Gaius, *Inst.* 2.114; *Inst. justin.* 2.2.11; *Dig. justin.* 29.1; Berger, "Dictionary," 734; Charles S. Rayment, "An Ancient G I Benefit," *CJ* 47 (1951–1952) 110–12; Crook, *Law*, 110–11, 128–29; Tellegen-Couperus, *Testamentary Succession*, 44–48; Champlin, *Final Judgments*, 51, 56–58, 60–61, 144; and esp. Campbell, *Emperor*, 210–29. It is in keeping with the constant danger of death and the diminished legal requirements that "the incidence of attested testation [for soldiers] is strikingly higher than that found among civilians" (Champlin, *Final Judgments*, 39).

[75] It was so common that the deathbed is the *Sitz im Leben* of the fable of "The Farmer's Bequest to His Sons" (Perry, *Aesopica*, no. 42, p. 338) and at least a portion of Varro's *Testamentum* (one of the books of his *Menippean Satires*). In the latter Varro makes use of this common practice to represent a testator (almost certainly Varro himself) on his deathbed, giving instructions concerning his unborn children. See Varro, frg. 543 Astbury (= Aulus Gellius, *Noct. att.* 3.16.13), and the quite different interpretations of this fragment proposed by Joel C. Relihan, *Ancient Menippean Satire* (Baltimore: Johns Hopkins University Press, 1993) 28 and 60–61, and Jean-Pierre Cèbe (ed. and trans.), *Varron, Satires Ménippées*, XII: *Sexagessis–Testamentum* (Collection de l'École française de Rome 9; Paris: École française de Rome, 1998) 2026–29.

be done orally.[76] For illustrative purposes I shall give five examples of imminent death testaments. The first is that of Valerius Aion, a centurion, who in making his will adds to the conventional testamentary formula "if some mortal event should befall me" the quite personal statement "in the very serious illness that has attacked me."[77] The second is that of Herod the Great, who revised his will twice in his final days. According to Josephus, Herod "fell ill and wrote a will."[78] Later, after his illness grew worse and "he had not the slightest hope of being restored to health,"[79] he altered his will a final time before expiring.[80] The third example is that of the poet Horace. According to Suetonius, Horace "named Augustus as his heir by word of mouth, since he could not make and sign a will because of the sudden violence of his ailment" (*Vita Horati* 76–77 Rostagni).[81]

The fourth example is one of the most ingenious oral wills of antiquity, and, unfortunately, one with tragic consequences. It is the oral testament of the Roman soldier Artorius, who found himself trapped by flames in a portico of the Jerusalem temple in 70 C.E.:

> Among those enveloped in the flames one, Artorius, saved his life by an artifice. Calling at the top of his voice to Lucius, a fellow-soldier with whom he shared a tent, "I leave you," he said, "heir to my property if you come and catch me." Lucius promptly running up, Artorius plunged down on top of him and was saved; while he who received him was dashed by his weight against the pavement and killed on the spot.[82]

The fifth example is the most humorous example of testation from the Graeco-Roman world. A parody of the military will,[83] it is known

---

[76] See, e.g., Demosthenes, *Spud.* 16 (= *Or.* 41.16), with the comments of Harrison, *Law*, 1.153, and Lysias, *Agoratus* 41–42 (= *Or.* 13.41–42), with the comments of Rubinstein, *Adoption*, 85.

[77] SB XII.11042 = P.Col. VII.188. See also Roger S. Bagnall and Klaas A. Worp, "Three Papyri from Fourth-Century Karanis," *Chronique d'Égypte* 59 (1984) 307–10.

[78] Josephus, *A.J.* 17.146 (LCL, modified); see also Josephus, *B.J.* 1.646.

[79] Josephus, *A.J.* 17.172. For Josephus' graphic depiction of Herod's agonizing final illness, see *A.J.* 17.168–170; *B.J.* 1.647, 656; and Eusebius, *Hist. eccl.* 1.8.5–16.

[80] Josephus, *A.J.* 17.188; see also *B.J.* 1.664.

[81] The *Vita Horati* (*Life of Horace*) is part of Suetonius' *De poetis* (*On the Poets*), which itself is part of his *De viris illustribus* (*On the Lives of Illustrious Men*). For a brief treatment of Suetonius' *Vita Horati*, see Barry Baldwin, *Suetonius* (Amsterdam: Hakkert, 1983) 394–96. For oral wills made by nomination (*nuncupatio*) of someone as heir to the entire estate (*universitas*), see *Dig. justin.* 28.1.21, and Rayment, "G I Benefit," 111.

[82] Josephus, *B.J.* 6.188–189; for a brief discussion, see Campbell, *Emperor*, 210–11.

[83] For other ancient parodies of wills, see Varro, frgs. 540–543 Astbury, with the commentary of Cèbe, *Varron*, 2018–29; Petronius, *Saty.* 71 (Trimalchio's will) and 141.2–4

as the *Testamentum Porcelli*, "The Testament of the Piglet."[84] Possibly written as early as the time of Augustus though likely much later,[85] this hilarious testament was still recited in Jerome's time by laughing schoolboys.[86] The last will and testament of a certain M. Grunnius Corocotta (Marcus Grunter Hyena) the piglet begins as follows:

> M. Grunter Hyena the piglet has made this will. As I cannot write myself, I have dictated it. Butcher the cook said: "Come here, destroyer of the house, digger up of the soil, runaway, piglet, and today I take your life."[87] Hyena the piglet said: "If I have done anything, if I have sinned in any way, if I have broken some little vases with my feet, I petition you, master cook, I ask my life, grant it to the petitioner." Butcher the cook said: "Come here, boy, hand me the knife from the kitchen in order that I may make a bloody end of this piglet." The piglet is seized by the assistants, led off on the fifteenth day before the end of the Herbal Month,[88] when herbage is plentiful, in the consulship of Roastingtin and

---

(Eumolpus' will); and Tertullian, *Apol.* 15.1 (*The Reading of the Will of Jupiter the Deceased*).

[84] The text of the *Testamentum Porcelli* is printed in Franz Buccheler (ed.), *Petronii Satvrae* (8th ed.; Berlin: Weidmann; Zürich: Max Niehans, 1963) 346–47. For an insightful analysis, see Champlin, "Testament of the Piglet."

[85] The will presupposes Augustus' concession that a Roman soldier who was still a *filius familias* (under the authority of a *paterfamilias*) could dispose of his *peculium castrense* (his camp property, consisting of everything that he had acquired during his military service) by testament (*Inst. justin.* 2.12). There is also another possible connection with the time of Augustus: the piglet is named Corocotta, possibly after an infamous Spanish bandit of Augustus' time (Cassius Dio, *Hist.* 56.43.3). Yet the term *corocotta*, in addition to being either a synonym of "hyena" (Porphyry, *Abst.* 3.4.5) or closely linked to the hyena (Aelian, *Nat. an.* 7.22), is more likely a pun on *coerococta*, "roast pig." For this suggestion, see Graham Anderson, "The Cognomen of M. Grunnius Corocotta: A *Dissertatiuncula* on Roast Pig," *AJP* 101 (1980) 57–58. For the date of the work, compare Daube, *Roman Law*, 77–78, who thinks that it might be prior to Hadrian, and Champlin, "Testament of the Piglet," 179–83, who assigns it to the fourth century C.E.

[86] Jerome mentions the *Testamentum Porcelli* in two places: the Preface to chapter 12 of his *Commentary on Isaiah* and *Ruf.* 1.17. As Champlin points out ("Testament of the Piglet," 176 n. 8), Jerome's pejorative pseudonym for Rufinus was "Grunnius" ("Grunter"), one of the piglet's names. Jerome has doubtless derived this pseudonym from the *Testamentum Porcelli*, which he viewed with utter disdain. For *grunnire* ("to grunt," "to oink") as the voice of the pig, see Giuseppiana Barabino, "Le *voces animalium* in Nonio Marcello," *Studi Noniani* 3 (1975) 33–36, cited by Champlin, "Testament of the Piglet," 176 n. 9.

[87] The piglet is being executed for military crimes, especially being a deserter ("runaway"). Roman law still permitted such individuals to make a will (*Dig. justin.* 29.1.11). See Daube, *Roman Law*, 79 n. 2 and Champlin, "Testament of the Piglet," 179.

[88] The day of the piglet's death will thus be "December 17th, the first day of the Saturnalia, when the end of autumn was celebrated by the eating of pork." So Champlin, "Testament of the Piglet," 176, citing I. Mariotti, "Kalendae lucerninae," *Rivista di Cultura classica e medioevale* 20 (1978) 1021–25.

Peppersauce. And as he saw that he was going to die, he asked for an
hour's reprieve and petitioned the cook in order to be able to make a
will.[89]

Given his momentary stay of execution, the piglet proceeds, first, to
apportion his possessions to his father, mother, and sister, and then,
foreshadowing the modern living will, to donate his various organs to
those who would want them, including the cobblers, brawlers, deaf,
pleaders and prattlers of tongue, sausage-makers, stuffing-experts,
women, boys, girls, catamites, runners and hunters, robbers, and, of
course, the cook who is about to roast him.[90] Signed at the end by seven
piggy witnesses,[91] the piglet's will is ended, and so is his life. As humorous as this parody of a soldier's will is, one should remember that it is
grounded in the social reality that testation was most often among the
last actions taken by individuals living in the Graeco-Roman world.

Testation as Gratitude

Fourth, one of the reasons why testation was deemed a duty was
that it was widely viewed as an appropriate time to express gratitude
for services that had been rendered by family, friends, servants, and
others.[92] At Athens, the philosopher Lyco, who had headed the Lyceum
for some forty-four years, bequeathed certain items to a young couple,
saying, "that, so far as I have the means of recompensing them, I
may not prove ungrateful."[93] In Mysia, King Attalus III of Pergamum
(d. 133 B.C.E.) may have granted freedom to the city of Ephesus in
testamentary gratitude to his former teacher, a native Ephesian.[94] In
Egypt, a woman by the name of Taharpaesis expressed gratitude to her

---

[89] The translation is that of Daube, *Roman Law*, 78–79.

[90] *Ibid.*, 79–80.

[91] As translated by Daube, *Roman Law*, 81, they are Bacony, Morselly, Spicy, Sausage-
lump, Porkrind, Charles Lamb, and Weddingpig.

[92] The corollary is that those in despair often die intestate, having no gratitude to
express. See, e.g., Ps.-Quintilian, *Decl. maj.*19.16, where a father who had tortured his
son to death says, "I am now able to die, already deep in despair. … I do not write my
testament. I do not entrust my last words to a will. I will also die in my own kinds
of torment." Translations of Ps.-Quintilian's *Declamationes majores* are those of Lewis
A. Sussman (trans.), *The Major Declamations Ascribed to Quintilian: A Translation* (Studien
zur klassischen Philologie 27; Frankfurt am Main: Peter Lang, 1987).

[93] Diogenes Laertius, *Lives of Eminent Philosophers* 5.72. See also Isocrates, *Aeginet.* 11–12
(= *Or.* 19.11–12).

[94] For this hypothesis, see Kent J. Rigsby, "The Era of the Province of Asia," *Phoenix*
33 (1979) 39–47.

husband in her will, including him because "he was always good to me and gave me much joy."[95] Similarly, a resident of Hermopolis gave his maternal cousin the right to live in his new house, rent-free for life, because the latter "has shown himself well disposed towards me and my father Ammonius on many occasions, and has been of service in our affairs and useful to us on the occasion of our absence abroad and to my father Ammonius when he was living at home, and to whom I owe much gratitude."[96]

At Rome, "the use of the testament to acknowledge *officia*" was quite likely "a traditional custom, dating back long before the arrival of Greek wealth and corruption," with the latter helping to transform it in certain socio-economic circles "from a token gesture of respect to a real financial benefit."[97] During both the Republic and Empire freedmen were not only encouraged to include their former masters in their wills in gratitude for emancipating them, but they were also required by law to do so.[98] In one particular case, they were even

---

[95] SB X.10500.14. The translation follows that of D. Klamp, "Das Testament der Taharpaesis," *ZPE* 2 (1968) 93 and 121.

[96] P.Ryl. II.153.10–13.

[97] Wallace-Hadrill, "Family and Inheritance," 69–70.

[98] See esp. Cassius Dio, *Hist.* 51.15.7; Gaius, *Inst.* 3.39–54; *Epitome Ulpiani* 29.1–7 Huschke; *Dig. justin.* 38.2; J. T. Abdy and Bryan Walker (trans.), *The Commentaries of Gaius and Rules of Ulpian* (2nd ed.; Cambridge: Cambridge University Press, 1874) 447–49; A. M. Duff, *Freedmen in the Early Roman Empire* (Oxford: Clarendon, 1928) 43–44; Alan Watson, *The Law of Persons in the Later Roman Republic* (Oxford: Clarendon, 1967) 228–229, and *Roman Slave Law* (Baltimore: Johns Hopkins University Press, 1987) 35–45; Crook, *Law*, 50–55; Susan Treggiari, *Roman Freedmen During the Late Republic* (Oxford: Clarendon, 1969) 78–80. See also Lewis A. Sussman, *The Declamations of Calpurnius Flaccus: Text, Translation, and Commentary* (Mnemosyne 133; Leiden: Brill, 1994) 136, and Jane F. Gardner, *Family and Familia in Roman Law and Life* (Oxford: Clarendon, 1998) 55–67. On the general relationship between freedmen and their patrons, see esp. Georges Fabre, *Libertus: Recherches sur les rapports patron-affranchi à la fin de la République romaine* (Collection de l'Ecole française de Rome 50; Rome: École française de Rome, 1981). That the freedman was compelled in his will to express gratitude to his former owner reflects the growing problem of the "ungrateful freedman" (*ingratus libertus*), a problem that received immense attention during the late Republic and early Empire as freedmen increased dramatically in number and acquired enormous wealth and power (see, e.g., Plautus, *Pers.* 838–840; Suetonius, *Claud.* 25.1; Cassius Dio, *Hist.* 60.28.1; Tacitus, *Ann.* 13.26–27; Duff, *Freedmen*, 40–43; Fergus Millar, *The Emperor in the Roman World (31 BC – AD 337)* [Ithaca: Cornell University Press, 1977], 69–83; Jane F. Gardner, *Being a Roman Citizen* [London: Routledge, 1993], 41–48; Donna W. Hurley [ed.], *Suetonius, Divvs Clavdivs* [Cambridge Greek and Latin Classics; Cambridge: Cambridge University Press, 2001], 172–73). The seriousness of the problem is reflected in the fact that, from a legal standpoint, an ungrateful freedman was deemed worse than an undutiful one (*Dig. justin.* 37.14.1). To address the problem while the freedman was alive, the *lex Aelia*

required to do so before they died.[99] Even where there was no legal compulsion to express gratitude in one's will, many did so. Augustus felt very strongly about this aspect of testation; indeed, he "was a fanatical believer in *post-mortem* benevolence to friends, and he had more friends than anyone."[100] Pliny the Younger praises the will of Domitius Tullus because "in it Tullus shows his gratitude (*gratia*) to all his relatives in return for their services (*officio*) to him," especially those rendered to him by his wife.[101] He is distressed, on the other hand, that Gaius Fannius "had the misfortune to die without making a new will, when the old one leaves out some of his dearest friends and benefits people who had become his enemies."[102] The same sentiment about testamentary gratitude is expressed by Apuleius, who says that his recently deceased stepson Pontianus spoke of him most dutifully and

---

Sentia was passed in C.E. 4. This law gave patrons the right to bring an accusation of ingratitude against a freedman (*accusatio ingrati liberti*); see *Dig. justin.*40.9.30 and 50.16.70 for discussion of this right, and for other provisions of the *lex Aelia Sentia*, see S. Riccobono (ed.), *Acta Divi Avgvsti* (Rome: Regia Academia Italica, 1945) 205–19. Romans viewed a freedman's failure to include his patron in his will as both unjust and inequitable (Gaius, *Inst.* 3.40–41). They took two key steps to address the problem legally, so that the law not only changed over time but also exempted both freedmen and freedwomen under certain conditions. The first step was the praetor's Edict, which was issued between 118 and 74 B.C.E. (Treggiari, *Roman Freedmen*, 79). According to Ulpian (*apud Dig. justin.* 38.2.1), this Edict was "put forward by the praetor for the purpose of regulating the gratitude (*gratia*) that freedmen are to show their patrons," and it did so by entitling the patron to half of his freedman's estate. The next step was the *lex Papia Poppaea* of 9 C.E., which extended the patron's rights against rich freedmen who had estates of 100,000 *sesterces* or more, giving him a proportional share even if there were two surviving natural (i.e., not adopted) children. By establishing and specifying the freedman's testamentary obligations, these two laws functioned to protect the patron at the freedman's expense. Other laws functioned to protect the freedman at the patron's expense; for these, see Treggiari, *Roman Freedmen*, 68–81. For a failed attempt by the daughter of a freedman to prove that her father's will was forged and disproportionately benefited the patron, see *Dig. justin.* 48.10.24 with the commentary of Champlin, "Miscellanea Testamentaria IV–VII," 198–99. For the testamentary situation of freedmen in classical Athens, see Harrison, *Law*, 1.148–49, 153.

[99] Following Marc Antony's death, Octavian "ordered Antony's freedmen to give at once to Iullus, the son of Antony and Fulvia, everything which by law they would have been required to bequeath him at their death" (Cassius Dio, *Hist.* 51.15.7). The law referred to is the praetor's Edict (see the preceding note).

[100] Champlin, "Testament of Augustus," 160. See pp. 161–63 for Champlin's estimates regarding the value of the legacies given to Augustus' friends and relatives after his death.

[101] Pliny the Younger, *Ep.* 8.18.7, with the LCL translation slightly modified.

[102] Pliny the Younger, *Ep.* 5.5.2; see also 8.18.5.

respectfully (*officiosissime et honestissime*) in his unfinished will and points to "what gratitude he would have expressed to me ... in his will" (*quas ... in testamento gratias*).[103] Similarly, Seneca in his *On Benefits* asks,

> Why is it that we wish to be grateful (*grati*) at the hour of death, that we carefully weigh the services of each one, that, with memory as judge of the whole of our life, we try to avoid the appearance of having forgotten the service of any? Nothing then is left for us to hope for; nevertheless, as we pause upon the threshold, we wish to appear as grateful (*gratissimi*) as possible at the end of our departure from human affairs (*Ben.* 4.22.1).

Given Seneca's convictions, it was tragic that, according to Tacitus, he was denied the opportunity of expressing his gratitude to his last companions by adding a final codicil to his will.[104] When the orders came for him to commit suicide, he "asked for the tablets containing his will. The centurion refusing, he turned to his friends, and called them to witness that 'as he was prevented from showing his gratitude (*gratiam*) for their services, he left them his sole but fairest possession— the image of his life.'"[105]

A final indication of how firmly gratitude was established as a moral and cultural norm is that, according to Suetonius, two or three first-century emperors invoked its absence as the pretext for rescinding wills

---

[103] Apuleius, *Apol.* 97.2 and 96.5; see also 96.3. The translation is that of H. E. Butler (trans.), *The Apologia and Florida of Apuleius of Madaura* (Oxford: Clarendon, 1909; repr. Westport, CT: Greenwood, 1970) 148. As Vincent Hunink (ed.), *Apuleius of Madauros, Pro se de magia (Apologia)* (2 vols.; Amsterdam: Gieben, 1997) 2.237, rightly notes, "this is no rhetorical exaggeration. Roman wills often contained unofficial elements, like an expression of thanks." For Apuleius' knowledge of Roman law in regard to testate and intestate succession, see Fritz Norden, *Apulejus von Madaura und das römische Privatrecht* (Leipzig: Teubner, 1912) 140–55.

[104] In a codicil previously appended to his will, he had already given instructions about the cremation of his body; see Tacitus, *Ann.* 15.64.4. In contrast to what happened to Seneca, his brother Annaeus Mela was able to update his will by adding a codicil and possibly a postscript to the codicil (though the postscript may have been forged); see Tacitus, *Ann.* 16.17.5–6 and the commentaries of Henry Furneaux (ed.), *Cornelii Taciti annalium ab excessu divi Augusti libri* (2nd ed. revised by H. F. Pelham and C. D. Fisher; 2 vols.; Oxford: Clarendon, 1896–1907) 2.449–50, and Erich Koestermann, *Cornelius Tacitus, Annalen* (4 vols.; Wissenschaftliche Kommentare zu griechischen und lateinischen Schriftstellern; Heidelberg: Carl Winter, 1963–1968) 4.369–70.

[105] Tacitus, *Ann.* 15.62.1. On this passage, see Furneaux, *Tacitus*, 2.399; N. P. Miller, *Tacitus, Annals XV* (London: Macmillan, 1973; repr. Bristol: Bristol Classical Press, 1994) 115, and esp. Koestermann, *Tacitus*, 4.301.

and confiscating property.[106] The first to do this was Caligula:[107] "If
any chief centurions since the beginning of Tiberius' reign had not
named that emperor or himself among their heirs, he set aside their
wills on the ground of ingratitude (*ingrata*)." Similarly, he also set aside
"the testaments of all others, as null and void, if anyone said that they
intended to make Caesar their heir when they died," yet failed to do
so.[108] Nero, building on the precedent established by Caligula, enacted
a law "that the estates of those who were ungrateful (*ingratorum*) to
their emperor should belong to the privy purse, and that the advocates
who had written or dictated such wills should not go unpunished,"
i.e., because they had failed to make their clients aware of this law.[109]
Finally, Domitian, after initially following Augustus' example of refusing
to accept inheritances from those who had surviving children, appears
later to have totally abandoned ingratitude as a pretext for his actions.
He confiscated the estates not only of those who were alleged to have
said or done anything derogatory to his majesty (*maiestas*) but also of
those who supposedly indicated that the emperor was to be their heir.[110]
That the latter group included total strangers was proof to many of
his rapacious avarice.[111] It was no wonder, then, that Pliny the Younger
praised Trajan for abandoning this practice and thus giving security to
wills:

[106] On the topic of ungrateful testaments, see esp. Jean Gaudemet, "'Testamenta
ingrata et pietas Augusti': Contribution à l'étude du sentiment impérial," *Stvdi in onore
di Vincenzo Arangio-Ruiz* (ed. Mario Lauria et al; 4 vols.; Naples: Jovene, 1953) 3.115–37.

[107] Compulsion rather than choice in regard to naming the emperor as an heir
appears to have originated, not with Caligula, but with Tiberius in the latter part
of his reign; see Suetonius, *Tib.* 49.1; Cassius Dio, *Hist.* 58.4.5; 58.16.2. For Tiberius'
practice in regard to inheritances earlier in his reign, see Tacitus, *Ann.* 2.48; Cassius
Dio, *Hist.* 57.17.8. For a brief discussion, see Gaudemet, "Testamenta," 119–20, and
Millar, *Emperor*, 155.

[108] Suetonius, *Cal.* 38.2. See also Cassius Dio, *Hist.* 59.15.1–2.

[109] Suetonius, *Nero* 32.2. Nero is also alleged to have murdered his aunt Domitia and
suppressed her will in order to acquire her entire estate (Suetonius, *Nero* 34.5; Cassius
Dio, *Hist.* 62.17.1). For other alleged Neronian atrocities involving wills, see Tacitus,
Ann. 14.31; Cassius Dio, *Hist.* 62.11.2–3; and compare *Ann.* 16.11. For an assessment
of the historicity of the ancient tradition of Nero's avarice and rapacity, see Keith
R. Bradley, *Suetonius' Life of Nero: An Historical Commentary* (Collection Latomus 157;
Brussels: Latomus, 1978) 185–92.

[110] Suetonius, *Dom.* 9.2; 12.2. For a brief treatment, see Brian W. Jones (ed.), *Suetonius,
Domitian* (Bristol: Bristol Classical Press, 1996) 80–81, 102. See also Tacitus, *Agr.* 43.4,
who indicates that his father-in-law Agricola only named Domitian as co-heir to protect
the rest of the estate.

[111] The charge that someone had profited from the will of a total stranger was an old
one, applied already against Marc Antony by Cicero (*Phil.* 2.40–42).

You are not named as heir because someone else has given offence, but on your own merits, set down by your personal friends and passed over by strangers. … If someone dies now without showing gratitude (*gratus*), still he leaves heirs to his property, and nothing comes to you but an increase in reputation (*gloria*): for generosity may be more fortunate when it receives gratitude (*gratus*), but it is more glorious when there is ingratitude (*ingratus*).[112]

Testation as Consolation

Fifth, to make a will was not only an obligation owed to family and friends but also a solace (*solacium*) for oneself, as noted in the *Declamationes minores* attributed to Quintilian.[113] Although the testator receives no posthumous benefit from the gifts he bestows in his will, he has the great personal satisfaction of knowing that he is providing benefits and making provisions for loved ones. That is the point emphasized by Seneca in *On Benefits*:

> And tell me, when we have reached the very end of life, and are drawing up our will, do we not dispense benefits that will yield us nothing? How much time is spent, how long do we debate with ourselves to whom and how much we shall give! For what difference does it make to whom we give since no one will make us any return? Yet never are we more careful in our giving, never do we wrestle more in making decisions than when, with all self-interest banished, only the ideal of good remains before our eyes; we are bad judges of our duties (*officiorum*) only so long as they are distorted by hope and fear and that most slothful of vices, pleasure. But when death has shut off all these, and has brought us to pronounce sentence as incorrupt judges, we search for those who are most worthy to inherit our possessions, and there is nothing that we arrange with more scrupulous care than this which is of no concern to ourselves. Yet, heavens! the great joy (*voluptas*) that comes to us as we think: "Through me this man will become richer, and I, by increasing his wealth, shall add new lustre to his high position." If we give only when we may expect some return, we ought to die intestate! (*Ben.* 4.11.4–6).

In penning these words, Seneca was drawing on the philosophical (especially Stoic) tradition that saw in "the careful preparation of wills"

---

[112] Pliny the Younger, *Pan.* 43.1–2, 4 (LCL, modified).
[113] See Quintilian (?), *Decl. min.* 308.1. For a discussion of this declamation, see Michael Winterbottom (ed.), *The Minor Declamations Ascribed to Quintilian* (Texte und Kommentare 13; Berlin: de Gruyter, 1984) 449–52.

a proof of the immortality of the soul.[114] Cicero, who represents this tradition, asks, after mentioning the making of a will, "What better type of human nature can we find among human beings than those people who regard themselves as born into the world to help and guard and preserve their fellows?"[115] In short, according to this viewpoint, the act of testation not only fulfills a moral obligation and expresses gratitude to others but also brings pleasure and comfort to the testator who seeks to assist others through a final benefaction.

Testation as Moral Judgement of Others

Sixth, to make a will is also to express a judgment about one's family and associates. The will, precisely because it is a "last will and testament," gives the testator's final verdict in regard to these people. Indeed, many Romans used the phrase *supremum iudicium* to designate the will, doing so to indicate that it contained the testator's "final judgment."[116] Thus, in a declamation defending a blind son against the charge of parricide, the defense attorney can point to the father's designation of the son as his sole heir, offering that as evidence of the deceased's affection for the accused: "If you want to know what the old man's attitude towards him was, you can go and examine his will."[117] Roman testaments typically contained clauses that summed up a person's character and provided the reason for his or her inclusion or exclusion from the inheritance, with a special clause known as the *elogium* sometimes giving the basis for the inheritance,[118] but more often the reason for the disinheritance.[119] To be named an heir or to be given a legacy was, in general, an honor and a sign of genuine merit;[120] to

---

[114] Cicero, *Tusc.* 1.31; see also *Fin.* 2.99–103, where Cicero argues that Epicurus' careful preparation of a will was inconsistent with his tenets as a philosopher.

[115] Cicero, *Tusc.* 1.32 (LCL, modified).

[116] See, e.g., Apuleius, *Apol.* 70.8; 96.5 Hunink, and the texts in Justinian's *Digest* cited by Norden, *Apulejus*, 141 n. 2. Champlin entitled his monograph *Final Judgments* to make precisely this point (see esp. pages 16–17).

[117] Ps.-Quintilian, *Decl. maj.* 1.2.

[118] See, e.g., Seneca the Elder, *Cont.* 2.7: "The trader died, leaving her all his wealth in his will, to which he added the clause (*elogium*) 'I found her chaste.'"

[119] See, e.g., Cicero, *Clu.* 135: "I mean the clause (*elogium*) which you quote from the will of the elder Egnatius … stating that he disinherited his son for taking a bribe" (LCL, modified). See also Apuleius, *Apol.* 99.4 Hunink; Petronius, *Satyr.* 53; Quintilian, *Inst.* 7.4.20; Augustine, *Serm.* 355.2. See the *TLL* 5:2.405 (s.v., *elogium*) and Champlin, *Final Judgments*, 12.

[120] See, e.g., Pliny the Younger, *Ep.* 10.94.2, who asks Trajan to grant his childless

be disinherited,[121] given a niggardly amount,[122] or simply passed over in silence[123] was a disgrace.[124] In short, wills were an important part of the honor-shame culture of the ancient Mediterranean world,[125] and not only people such as Cicero[126] and Pliny the Younger[127] took a keen

---

friend Suetonius (the imperial biographer) the *ius trium liberorum* (the status granted to parents of three children), thus making it easier for Suetonius' friends in their wills "to express effectively their recognition of his merits" (*promeretur*). There are, of course, exceptions to the generalization that inheritances and legacies are recognitions of merit. The testator could also insult the people whom he named as heirs or legatees; see, e.g., *Dig. Justin.* 28.5.49.1: "Let my most undutiful son, ill-deserving of anything from me, be heir."

[121] The disowning and disinheriting of sons is a fairly common topic in Latin rhetorical declamations. See, e.g., Ps.-Quintilian, *Decl. maj.* 2; 9; and esp. 17, in which a father makes a charge of attempted parricide against a son whom he had three times unsuccessfully attempted to disinherit. In numerous cases, exheredation was intended as a punishment. In many cases, however, testators actually disinherited their children in order to circumvent Roman testamentary law and/or to spare them the burdens of being an heir. In order to ensure that the disinherited children would receive the estate, such testators typically appointed a friend as heir, charging him with the duty of tranfering the inheritance to the children. See Champlin, *Final Judgments*, 108–11, and David Johnston, *Roman Law In Context* (Key Themes in Ancient History; Cambridge: Cambridge University Press, 1999) 45. The situation in classical Athens was quite different, for the testator could neither legally disinherit his son in his will nor deprive his daughter of her status as an *epiklēros* ("heiress"). He could, however, use other means to exclude his son from his share of the inheritance. And inasmuch as Solon's law gave greater weight to the personal wishes of the deceased than to the rights of his surviving relatives under intestate succession, a childless testator could functionally disinherit a hostile relative by adopting a son and making him the heir of his estate. See Harrison, *Law*, 1.75; MacDowell, *Law*, 100; and Thompson, "Athenian Attitudes," 20–21. As far as Sparta is concerned, Plutarch insinuates that Epitadeus' motive in giving Spartans the power of free testamentary bequest was his vindictive desire to disinherit his own son, with whom he was angry as the result of a nasty quarrel (*Ag. Cleom.* 5.2–3).

[122] See, e.g., *Dig. Justin.* 32.37.2: "To Maevius my freedman, who has deserved nothing from me, one hundred and fifty jars of the oldest wine." Maevius had earlier, before his fall from favor, been named as heir to half of the testator's estate!

[123] In a Roman civilian will, the testator's omission of children was insufficient to disinherit them. In a Roman soldier's will, by contrast, not to mention existing children was to disinherit them, unless it could be established that the omission was purely accidental. See Rayment, "G I Benefit," 111–12, and Campbell, *Emperor*, 222–23.

[124] Norden, *Apulejus*, 143.

[125] On the social function of legacies to various groups of people, see Laurent Boyer, "La fonction sociale des legs d'après la jurisprudence classique," *Revue historique de droit français et étranger* 43 (1965) 333–408.

[126] For Cicero's interest in wills, which was partly financial, see *Att.* 7.2.7; 7.3.9; 15.2.4; 15.3.2; 15.26.5.

[127] Pliny gives the witnessing of will as part of his daily routine (*Ep.* 1.9.2); compare Seneca, *Ep.* 8.6.

interest in wills, but also emperors,[128] especially Augustus. Indeed, "the will for Augustus, as for Romans long before, was the final and decisive judgement of how valuable your friends had been to you,"[129] and of how valuable you had been to them. According to Suetonius, Augustus

> demanded of his friends affection on their part, both in life and after death. For though he was in no sense a legacy-hunter, and in fact could never bring himself to accept anything from the will of a stranger, yet he was highly sensitive in weighing the death-bed utterances of his friends, concealing neither his chagrin if he was left a niggardly bequest or one unaccompanied with compliments, nor his satisfaction, if he was praised in terms of gratitude (*grate*) and affection.[130] Whenever legacies or shares in inheritances were left him by men of any station who had offspring, he either turned them over to the children at once, or if the latter were in their minority, paid the money back with interest on the day when they assumed the gown of manhood or married.[131]

In most cases, the people named as primary and secondary heirs were being rewarded and honored for their services or affection. For example, Pliny the Younger notes that when Ummidia Quadratilla named her grandson Ummidius Quadratus as her primary heir, she was bestowing an honor (*honore*) on an excellent young man.[132] And to name relatives, friends, or prominent individuals as tertiary heirs was purely

---

[128] See Robert S. Rogers, "The Roman Emperors as Heirs and Legatees," *TAPA* 78 (1947) 140–58; Millar, *Emperor*, 153–58; and Champlin, *Final Judgements*, 203–4. Legacies to the emperor were "an extension of the Republican practice whereby politicians made bequests to political friends and allies" (B. H. Warmington [ed.], *Suetonius, Nero* [Bristol: Bristol Classical Press, 1977], 89).

[129] Wallace-Hadrill, "Family and Inheritance," 68.

[130] Among those who included Augustus in their wills was Herod the Great, who also made provision for Augustus' wife, children, friends, and freedmen; see Josephus, *A.J.* 17.146, 190; *B.J.* 1.646, 669, and Millar, *Emperor*, 153.

[131] Suetonius, *Aug.* 66.4. For Augustus' treatment of inheritances and legacies that he received from those with surviving children, see also Cassius Dio, *Hist.* 56.32.3; 56.41.8; and, in regard to Herod's surviving children, Josephus, *A.J.* 17.322–323. Although not mentioned by Suetonius in this section of his work, an additional reason for Augustus' keen interest in wills was financial. As John M. Carter (ed.), *Suetonius, Divus Augustus* (Bristol: Bristol Classical Press, 1982) 189, correctly notes, "The reader gains the impression from this passage that Augustus had little interest in the money. In fact his finances depended on it." Carter notes that while Augustus in his will boasts of having received 1.4 billion *sesterces* in testamentary bequests in the final twenty years of his life (Suetonius, *Aug.* 101.3), he says in his *Res gestae* (16–17) that he spent 1.3 billion on pensions and land for veterans and on funding the *aerarium militare*. See also Millar, *Emperor*, 154–55, and Champlin, *Final Judgments*, 152–53.

[132] Pliny the Younger, *Ep.* 7.24.8. For a helpful discussion of this letter, see A. N. Sherwin-White, *The Letters of Pliny: A Historical and Social Commentary* (Oxford: Clarendon, 1966) 430–34.

honoris causa, as was the case in Augustus' will, for some of those named may not even have been liked by the testator and the likelihood of such people succeeding to the inheritance was remote.[133] By naming such notables, the testator was not only bestowing honor but also heightening his own prestige.[134] In certain cases, however, the testator was deliberately insulting various individuals, by either omitting mention of them altogether or by giving them a contemptuous inheritance or legacy. When Junia, the sister of Brutus and widow of Cassius, died in 22 C.E., she left legacies to almost all the eminent men at Rome— except Tiberius. Because her omission of Tiberius was so conspicuous, it engrossed the public conversation.[135] More blatant in this regard was the insult depicted in an epigram of Martial (*Epig.* 4.70), who has Ammianus' dying father leave him nothing in his will but a dry rope; the father is telling the son in no uncertain terms to hang himself.[136] Testamentary acts of this type were typically attributed to the anger of the testator.[137]

Yet the expression of negative testamentary judgments about people was risky, for if testators erred in their judgments and showed themselves ungrateful for the services rendered them by others, their wills were a self-indictment. Because they had failed properly to discharge their duty, shame fell on them, not on those maligned or neglected in the will.[138] Such wills were not only immoral but could also lead to pub-

---

[133] Suetonius, *Aug.* 101.2; Tacitus, *Ann.* 1.8 (who notes that Augustus thought that some of those named in his will were obnoxious individuals); and Champlin, "Testament of Augustus," 159.

[134] Champlin, "Testament of Augustus," 165.

[135] Tacitus, *Ann.* 3.76.1–2. For discussion of this episode and the subsequent non-exhibition of the images of Cassius and Brutus during her funeral procession, see Koestermann, *Tacitus*, 1.566–67, and esp. Robert S. Rogers, "An Incident of the Opposition to Tiberius," *CJ* 47 (1951–1952) 114–15.

[136] Similarly, in the *Testamentum Porcelli* the piglet leaves his soup-ladle and pestle to "the unmentionable cook," with instructions to wear them around his neck, viz., as a rope. See *Dig. justin.*28.2.3 for the insult involved in not mentioning the heir's name (cited by Daube, *Roman Law*, 80 n. 4) and Champlin, "Testament of the Piglet," 177.

[137] See, for example, Isaeus, *Cleonymus* 3, 10, 43 (= *Or.* 1.3, 10, 43); Plato, *Leg.* 922c–e; Josephus, *A.J.* 17.148; and Fronto, *Ant. Pium* 3; 4; 7.

[138] Valerius Maximus, for example, says that Tettius was unjust to disinherit his infant son, that a son who had disinherited his father and seven brothers had acted impiously, and that Septicia had offended Equity herself by omitting her sons from her will (*Mem.* 7.7.3–5). He regards Septicia's action as so immoral that he addresses her with the following words: "So thus conducting yourself, even down in the underworld you were blasted by a celestial thunderbolt" (*Mem.* 7.7.4). See also 7.8.8, where he imagines the dying T. Barrus attacked by his conscience for omitting his best friend from his will:

lic outrage. For example, as Edward Champlin points out, "Valerius Maximus devotes a lively and highly disapproving section [*Memorable Doings and Sayings* 7.8.5–9] to a series of bad examples—testators who should have rewarded a relative or a friend or a patron, yet who shocked society by ignoring them in their wills."[139] His first example of an immoral (*taetrioris*) will (7.8.5) is that of the knight Q. Caecilius, the uncle of Cicero's friend Atticus:

> Q. Caecilius had attained a respectable status and ample wealth by the ready patronage and unstinted generosity of L. Lucullus. He had always given out that Lucullus was his sole heir and on his deathbed gave him his signet rings. In his will, however, he adopted Pomponius Atticus and left him heir to all he possessed. But the Roman people put a rope around the neck of the treacherous deceiver and dragged his corpse through the streets. So the villain had the son and heir he wanted, but funeral obsequies such as he deserved.[140]

Cicero, for his part, denounces Lucius Rubrius Casinas because he, in naming Marc Antony as his heir, had passed over his brother's son, "the son of Quintus Fufius, a most honorable Roman knight, and his own very dear friend, whom he had always openly proclaimed his heir, he does not even name." Addressing Antony, he continues: "you whom he had never seen, or at any rate never visited, he made heir" (*Phil.* 2.41). Immoral wills were denounced not only in retrospect but also in prospect, and attempts were made to prevent such testaments from being made. For instance, Cicero was utterly distraught about the testament that his estranged wife Terentia was in the process of drawing up shortly before their divorce.[141] He apparently feared that she would treat their children unfairly, especially their daughter Tullia:

> This poor child's long-suffering affects me quite beyond bearing. I believe her like on earth has never been seen. If there is any step in my power which might protect her in any way, I earnestly desire you [Atticus]

"For he breathed his last just as he was meditating upon his wicked deceit and ingratitude. It was like a torturer tormenting his mind within, as he saw that his passage from life to death was hateful to the gods above and would be detestable to those below."

[139] Champlin, *Final Judgments*, 14.

[140] Contrast Cicero's letter of congratulations to Atticus on his being named heir (*Att.* 3.20), in which Cicero says that Caecilius has done his duty (*officio*) in the matter of his will; for a brief discussion of this letter, see Shackleton Bailey, *Cicero's Letters to Atticus*, 2.156–57.

[141] The letters in which Cicero mentions the will date from the summer of 47 B.C.E., with the divorce taking place during the winter of 47/46 B.C.E.

to suggest it. I realize there is the same difficulty as formerly in giving advice. Still, this causes me more anxiety than everything else put
together.[142]

Therefore, he wrote to Atticus, asking him to intercede:

> The last thing I have to beg you is, if you think it right and it is something
> you feel you can undertake, to talk to Camillus with a view to your both
> admonishing Terentia about her will. The signs of the times are plain
> to read. She should see that she does justice where it is due. One has
> heard from Philotimus that she is doing some wicked things. It is hardly
> credible; but certainly, if there is anything else that can be done, steps
> should be taken in time.[143]

Unfortunately, the outcome of these efforts is as unknown as the details
of Terentia's prospective will.[144]

Those who made immoral wills, therefore, were justly blamed and
received the same kind of censure as those who forged wills.[145] On the

---

[142] Cicero, *Att.* 11.25.3; see also 11.23.3; 11.24.2.

[143] Cicero, *Att.* 11.16.5; see also 11.21.1; 11.22.2; 11.23.1.

[144] Shackleton Bailey, *Cicero's Letters to Atticus*, 5.287–88. Inasmuch as Tullia died in 45
B.C.E. with her mother still alive, Terentia's testamentary treatment of her daughter
soon became legally irrelevant.

[145] Forged wills were a serious and widespread problem in the ancient world. The
speeches of Athenian orators frequently contain attacks on allegedly forged wills; see,
e.g., Demosthenes (?), *Stephanus I* (= *Or.* 45), and Isaeus, *Astyphilus* (= *Or.* 9) and
Nicostratus (= *Or.* 4). As a result of both actual cases of forgery and allegations of forgery,
Athenian juries were highly suspicious of contested wills and frequently invalidated
them, deciding in favor of relatives rather than those named in the will as beneficiaries
(see esp. Aristophanes, *Vesp.* 583–587; Ps.-Aristotle, *Prob.* 29.3, 950b5–8; and Isaeus,
Cleonymus 41 [= *Or.* 1.41]). At Rome, the *lex Cornelia testamentaria* (ca. 78 B.C.E.) made
forged wills (as well as suppressing or tampering with genuine ones) the subject of one of
the nine permanent courts (Cicero, *Verr.* 2.1.109; Crook, "*Lex Cornelia*," 163–71, and *Law*,
270), with Cicero calling the forging of wills a daily occurrence (*Nat. d.* 3.74; see Joseph
B. Mayor, *M. Tulli Ciceronis de natura deorum libri tres* [3 vols.; Cambridge: Cambridge
University Press, 1880–1885], 3.156–57, and Pease, *Cicero*, 2.1162–64). The heinousness
of this act is evident in the crime lists in which it appears, where it is mentioned
together with assassination, poisoning, theft, and embezzlement (Cicero, *Nat. d.* 3.74;
Off. 3.36, 73). The charge of forging a will or profiting by one often appears in ancient
invective. For instance, Cicero accuses Crassus and Hortensius of profiting by a will
that they strongly suspected was forged (*Off.* 3.73–75, on which see Andrew R. Dyck,
A Commentary on Cicero, De Officiis [Ann Arbor: University of Michigan, 1996], 587–93),
and he refers to "the many forged wills" in a list of Crassus' crimes (*Parad.* 46). Trials
involving allegations of testamentary forgery could attract widespread attention; for one
such case, see Pliny the Younger, *Ep.* 7.6.8–13 (on which see Champlin, "Miscellanea
Testamentaria I–III," 247–49). On the legal penalties for the falsification of a will,
see Theodor Mommsen, *Römisches Strafrecht* (Systematisches Handbuch der Deutschen
Rechtswissenschaft 1:4; Leipzig: Duncker & Humblot, 1899) 669–72.

other hand, if the testators' final judgments were on target, their wills
were worthy of praise and could serve as compelling evidence about an
individual's character. Apuleius, for example, praises the way in which
Pontianus, his late stepson, treated his wife, the daughter of Apuleius'
opponent Rufinus:

> For Pontianus not only did not leave Rufinus' daughter as his heir—
> he had discovered her evil character—but he did not even make her a
> respectable legacy. He left her by way of insult linen to the value of 200
> denarii, to show that he had not forgotten or ignored her, but that he set
> this value on her as an expression of his resentment (*Apol.* 97.5–6).

The insult lay not simply in the paltry amount (equivalent to eight
hundred *sesterces*) involved—paltry because his wife had brought into
the marriage a dowry of 400,000 *sesterces* (92.2). The real insult lay
in giving the wife linen valued at this amount. As Vincent Hunink
points out, "linen was associated with prostitutes" and "the final blow
is that a supply of linen for two hundred denarii would suffice for at
least *a dozen* cloaks, and so implies extensive activities in the field of
prostitution."[146] Therefore, by citing Pontianus' will, Apuleius is able to
depict his opponent Rufinus as an avaricious legacy-hunter who serves
as his daughter's pimp—one of several vituperative sexual allegations
that are standard in both rhetoric and satire.[147]

The Will as an Occasion for Frank Speech

Seventh, wills were an occasion for speaking the truth, once and for
all time. According to Lucian's Nigrinus, the "sons of Rome speak the
truth only once in their lives (meaning in their wills), in order that they
may not reap the fruits of their truthfulness" (*Nigrinus* 30). The Romans
prized this freedom, and though it was occasionally abused, they generally resisted efforts to curtail this testamentary frank speech. In fact,
early in the days of the Empire, Augustus "vetoed a law to check freedom of speech in wills."[148] Indeed, in his own will Augustus made use of

---

[146] Hunink, *Apuleius*, 239, who is dependent for this insight on Norden, *Apulejus*, 144.

[147] For sexual innuendo as part of the arsenal against legacy-hunters, see Juvenal,
Sat. 1.37–41 (legacy-hunting gigolos); 1.55–57 (a voyeuristic husband acting as pimp for
his wife); and Quintilian (?), *Decl. min.* 325 (a wife sues her pandering husband, claiming
that her lover had left her a trust that her husband controlled and was withholding from
her). See also Juvenal, *Sat.* 10.236–239 for an old man instituting a veteran prostitute as
his heir because of the services (*fellatio*) that she had rendered him.

[148] Suetonius, *Aug.* 56.1.

this freedom to make it clear that Tiberius was heir to two-thirds of his estate only because "a cruel fate has bereft me of my sons Gaius and Lucius."[149] Although this was not quite an unambiguous public denigration of the new emperor,[150] it was hardly a ringing endorsement of Tiberius as his successor.[151] Tiberius, for his part, did nothing to prevent less ambiguous assaults; he even had a testamentary attack on him by Fulcinius Trio read to the Senate, an attack that the testator's sons had feared to make public.[152] These testamentary attacks were so widespread by the time of Nero that a praetorian senator named Fabricius Veiento, an insider who "knew his way too well round the court of Nero,"[153] used the form of a will as a cloak to attack both senators and priests in a series of scandalous pamphlets. The objects of his exposé were not amused, regarding the pamphlets as libelous. Nero responded by exiling him in 62 C.E. and ordering copies of his imaginary *Wills* burned, promptly sending the market value of the banned books into the stratosphere and multiplying their readership.[154] One of the most celebrated instances of actual testamentary frankness of speech (παϱϱησία)[155] during Nero's reign was the will of Petronius, who eschewing "the routine death-bed flatteries of Nero, … wrote out [in codicils to his will] a list of Nero's sensualities—giving names of each male and

[149] Suetonius, *Tib.* 23. For Augustus' will, see also Suetonius, *Aug.* 101; Tacitus, *Ann.* 1.8; and Cassius Dio, *Hist.* 56.32–33.

[150] For the thesis that Augustus' will casts no aspersions on Tiberius, see B. M. Levick, "*Atrox Fortvna*," *Classical Review* 86 (1972) 309–11.

[151] Note Suetonius' (*Tib.* 23) comment: "These words in themselves added to the suspicion of those who believed that he had named Tiberius his successor from necessity rather than from choice, since he allowed himself to write such a preamble." That August in his will does in fact malign Tiberius is argued persuasively by Champlin, "Testament of Augustus," 156–58.

[152] Cassius Dio, *Hist.* 58.25.2–3; Tacitus, *Ann.* 6.38.2–3 (on which see Koestermann, *Tacitus,* 2.332). See also Tiberius' civil response to Junia's omission of him from her will as well as his decision to allow her funeral to be conducted without interference (Tacitus, *Ann.* 3.76.1–2).

[153] Sherwin-White, *The Letters of Pliny,* 300. On Fabricius Veiento, see Juvenal, *Sat.* 3.185; 4.113, 123–129; 6.113; Pliny the Younger, *Ep.* 4.22.4; Cassius Dio, *Hist.* 61.6.2; and the discussions of Courtney, *Commentary,* 221–22, and Ronald Syme, *Tacitus* (2 vols.; Oxford: Clarendon, 1958) 2.633.

[154] Tacitus, *Ann.* 14.50.1–2. On this passage, see Furneaux, *Tacitus,* 294; E. C. Woodcock (ed.), *Tacitus, Annals XIV* (Methuen's Classical Texts; London: Methuen, 1939; repr. Bristol: Bristol Classical Press, 1992) 136; and esp. Koestermann, *Tacitus,* 4.120–21.

[155] For some recent treatments on candid speech, see John T. Fitzgerald (ed.), *Friendship, Flattery, and Frankness of Speech: Studies on Friendship in the New Testament World* (NovTSup 82; Leiden: Brill, 1996).

female bed-fellow (*exoletorum feminarumque*)[156] and details of every lubri-
cious novelty—and sent it under seal to Nero."[157] Most Romans were,
of course, not so bold, for they recognized that their surviving loved
ones could pay the price for their candor. Wills were, in short, "vessels
of truth,"[158] but the full contents of those vessels were seldom poured
out when the welfare of survivors was at stake.

To summarize the preceding discussion, the making of a will was,
as Valerius Maximus says, an activity requiring special care (*praecipuae
curae*) and one's final hours (*ultimi temporis*).[159] Wills, accordingly, were
usually either made or revised when the testator was near death or in
serious danger of dying, and in them people saw a reflection of the
testator's character. The making of a will was undertaken with the
understanding that it was a moral duty as well as an opportunity to
express gratitude for services rendered. To discharge that duty brought
joy and comfort to the testator. The making of a will also entailed the
necessity of making a final judgment about the worthiness of potential
beneficiaries of one's will, so that it provided the opportunity to speak
the truth once and for all.[160]

---

[156] Compare Suetonius' (*Tib.* 43.1) description of Tiberius' sexual partners: *puellarum
et exoletorum greges*, and the interpretation proposed by Jean-G. Préaux, "Tacite, *Annales*,
XVI, 19," *Latomus* 15 (1956) 369. For Tiberius' alleged sexual exploits at Capri, see
Tacitus, *Ann.* 6.1; Suetonius, *Tib.* 43–45; *Vit.* 3; Cassius Dio, *Hist.* 58.22.1.

[157] Tacitus, *Ann.* 16.19.3; the translation is that of Michael Grant (trans.), *Tacitus, The
Annals of Imperial Rome* (rev. ed.; New York: Penguin, 1985) 390. On this passage, see
esp. Keenan, "Tacitus," 6–8. See also Pliny the Elder, *Nat.* 37.20: "When the ex-consul
Titus Petronius was facing death, he broke, to spite Nero, a myrrhine dipper that had
cost him 300,000 sesterces, thereby depriving the Emperor's dining-room table of this
legacy."

[158] Champlin, *Final Judgments*, 10.

[159] Valerius Maximus, *Mem.* 7.7. praef.

[160] Earlier versions of part of this essay were read at the SBL International Meeting
in Krakow, and in seminars and symposia at Brown University, the University of
Texas, and Union Theological Seminary in New York. I wish to thank all those who
responded to these presentations with various suggestions.

INDEX OF ANCIENT SOURCES

Citations and abbreviations for ancient authors and sources generally follow the SBL guidelines as published in *JBL* 107 (1988) 579–96. For other ancient sources where there is no SBL recommendation, we use the standard form in *LSJ* and *OLD*. Because there is some variation among the articles in the use and rendering of English titles for Classical and Early Christian works, we have employed as far as is possible the Latin titles as found in the Loeb Classical Library and J. Quasten's *Patrology* (3 vols.; Utrecht-Antwerp: Spectrum, 1962–66). Pseudonymous works are listed, in general, under the supposed author.

A. Biblical Books with Apocrypha
B. Dead Sea Scrolls and Related Literature
C. Rabbinic Materials: Mishnah, Talmud, and Related Literature
D. Philo, Josephus, and Other Ancient Jewish Writers
E. Pseudepigrapha and Nag Hammadi Tractates
F. New Testament
G. Other Early Christian Literature (to the IVth cent. CE)
H. Classical, Late Antique, and Byzantine Sources
I. Inscriptions
J. Papyri
K. Medieval Literature

Biblical Books with Apocrypha

Gen	432	5:5	92–93
1–2	245–247	6:4	92
1–3	540	7:4	90
1:27	239, 594–595, 605	7:7	603
1:28	595	7:11	92
2:11–14	634	7:12	90
2:17	92–93	7:16	445
2:23	596	7:17	90, 603
2:24 [LXX]	593–597, 599	8:3–4	90
3	614–615	8:10, 12	90
3:8–24	613	8:21	77
3:1–7	613	9:1, 13	445
3:14	91	11:6	413
3:16	535, 539	12:12, 14	435
3:18	445	13:12	435
3:19	616	14:13	435
4:21	423	15:17–18	88
4:26	92	22:21	435
5:1–20	91	25:2	108
5:3	445	25:20	435

26:1	93
29:14	91
31:27	411
41:1	91
41:45	433, 435
41:50–52	433
42:11	394
46–49	442
49:3	104

Exod — 432, 601

1	435, 437
1–2	449
1–15	442
1:7–8	434
1:12–22	434
1:22	443
2	445
2:1–10	442
2:6	434
2:7	443
2.11	443–444
3:7	444
3:8	634
3:14–15	444–445
3:18	445
4:22	114
12:1–20	444
12:3	445
12:27	445
12:29–36	115
13:2	104
13:2–16	116
13:5	444
13:10	90
15:1–21	420–422
15:27	443
19:6	603
20	598–599
20:12	598
22:28	113
22:29	114
23:16	114
23:19	103, 105, 113–114, 116
25:2	103
25:3	113

30:23–33	87
32:6, 17–19	408
34:22	114, 116
34:26	105, 114
36:6	103
39:21	114

Lev

2:14	114
19:18	206
20:24	634
22:12	103
23:14	116
23:17, 20	114
25:29	90–91
25:43	598
27:26	128
27:26 27	116

Num

3:44–51	116
5:9	104
5:18	249–251, 256
6:5	249
13:20	114
15	77
15:18–21	108, 111
15:20–21	121
18:1	114
18:3–4	127–128
18:5–7	128
18:8–12	104
18:12	114, 116, 127
18:13	114, 116
18:13–17	116
18:15	104
24:20	116
27:1–11	183
28:26	114
28:26–27	116
28–29	77
35:30	292
36:7–9	183

Deut

5:32–33	601
8:8	117

10:16	454	1 Kgs	
12:6, 11	103	10:4	114
12:16[17]	114	10:21	91
12:17	103	17	486
14:23–26	116, 128	11:42	91
16:9–12	116		
17:6	603	2 Kgs	432
17:17	594	4:42	114
18:4	103–104, 116	5	486
19:15	292, 603	15:29	91
21:12	250	18:2	93
21:15–17	183	18:13–19:36	93
21:17	104	19:37	92
24:1–3	595	20:1	92–93, 98
24:17–22	195	20:6	93
25:4	603	20:12	93
25:6	104	25:27	93
26:2	103–104, 117		
26:10	103–104, 113	Isa	487
27:26, 32	127	1:3	652
28:13	248	6:9–10	475, 480
32:1–43	416, 420	[LXX]	
32:21	466	7:20	250
		8:14	465, 603
Josh		19:13	435
6	118	27:9	467–468
		28:6	603
Judg		28:16	465
17:10	90	36:1–37:37	93
19:2	90–91	37:38	92
		38:1	92
1 Sam		38:6	93
1:19–28	69	39:1	93
1:21	90	49:6	475
2	420	58:6	486
2:19	90	59:20	468
3:1	92	61:1–2	486
3:2–20	69	61:6	603
9:5–10	69	65:1–2	479
10:4	113		
15:21	116	Jer	
20:6	90	1:4	69
27:7	90, 92	2:3	115–116
28:1	92	2:16	435
		25:20	94
2 Sam		31:9	114
10:4	250	49:35	116

Ezek

20:25–26	116
20:31	114
30:13, 15	435
38:17	92
44:30	103, 105, 116
45:13–16	104
48:12	114

Hos   394

1:6, 9	603
2:25	603
9:6	435

Amos

6:6	116

Nah

3:12	105
4:9	105

Ps

45:9	87
48:2	530
51:5 [Vulgate 50:7]	537
78:51 [LXX 77:51]	103, 115, 129
102:3 [LXX 101:3]	91–92
104:4 [LXX 103:4]	625
105:36 [LXX 104:36]	103, 115, 129
118:22	603
119:93	585

Job

1:13, 18	104
18:13	114

Prov

3:9	114
3:9–10	116
7:17	87
24:70	104
25:13	91, 93

Song (or Cant)

1:12	87
4:12	87
4:14	87
5:5, 13	87
7:10	539

Esth   483

8:17	459

Dan

1:1	94
10:1	94
10:2–3	90

4 Ezra

14:30	586

Neh

10:36 [LXX 10:35]	116
10:37 ff	104

1 Chr

19:4	250

2 Chr

30:24	114
31:6	127
35:7–9	114

3 Kgdms

10:21	91
14:25	94

1 Esdr

2:12	94
1:8	94

2 Esdr

7:1	94

2 Macc   483, 487

1:10	448
1:30	415
13:11	434

3 Macc
2:2, 14	601
2:29	437
4:16	601

4 Macc 381
1:10–13	598
1:27	650
2:4–10	599
5:23	599
13:14–17	629

Sir
5:9–13	324
6:5–17	323
7:31	116

24:15	74, 77, 83, 86
24:23	75
25.24	535
39:13	75
45:5	586
45:20	116
50:15	75

Tob
1:7	128

Wis   323
2:1	629
16:13	629
17:14	629

Dead Sea Scrolls and Related Literature

CD
4.20–5.2	594
5.6ff	594
16.3–4	594
4Q169	105

1QS
6.5–6	116

1QSa
2.18–19	116

4QpNah   105

4QTLevi
9:7, 14	116

11QT
60:3–4	127–128

Rabbinic Texts: Mishnah, Talmud, and Related Literature

Tg. Yer. 2:3	116

Midr. R. Gen.
8.9	594
22.2	594

Mishnah
'Abot
2.7	586

Ber.
6.4	117

Bik.
1.3, 9	117

2.1, 4, 10	117
3.2	117
Ma'as. 5.6	117
Pe'a 1.1	117
Qidd. 32A	599
Sanh. 58	594–595
Sota 5.4	421
Yebam. 5B	599

Talmud
b. Ber. 24A	421
b. Sota 48A	421

Philo, Josephus, and Other Ancient Jewish Writers

Aristeas   430, 450, 483
   158   116

Aristobulus   10, 430, 432, 447,
       456–457, 487,
       492
   frg. 2–3   448–450
   4   450–451
   5   449

Artapanus   10, 430, 432, 456
   frg. 1   434–435, 437
   2.1   434
   2.3   435
   2.4   437
   3.1–3   434–435, 437
   3.6   436
   3.8   435
   3.10   436
   3.12, 17   435
   3.19   436
   3.21–22   434, 436
   3.31–37   434
   3.35   435

Cleodemus   430
   Malchus

Demetrius the   10, 430, 432, 434,
   Chrono-   456–457
   grapher
   frg. 2.7   433
   2.12, 9, 18, 16   432
   3–6   432
   5   433

[Ps] Eupolemos   429–430, 483

Ezechiel the   10, 430, 432, 456–
   Tragedian   457
   Exagoge   443
     frg. 1   443
     2   443, 446
     9   444
     13–14   444, 446

   15   445
   16–17   443

Ps-Hecataeus   10, 430, 432, 438–
       439, 451, 456–
       457
   On the Jews   437
   1.186   439
   1.189   439
   1.190   442
   1.192   440
   1.194   440
   2   441

Josephus   5, 10, 13, 15, 62,
       129, 380, 429,
       441–442, 584,
       607
   Antiquitates Judaicae
   2.224   443
   3.180   57
   3.235, 250–   117
     251
   3.317–319   57
   3.320   57
   4.70   116–118
   4.71   118
   4.226   117
   5.26   118
   7.103   95
   7.378   117
   9.273   116–117
   10.268   56
   11.121, 124,   577
     130
   12.50   118
   15.371–379   56
   16.173   118
   17.146   656, 666
   17.148   667
   17.168–170   656
   17.172, 188   656
   17.190   666
   17.322–323   666
   17.385   99

18.1–2   99
18.26   99
18.53–89   100–101
19.345   55
20.267   101
Bellum Judaicum
1.646   666
1.646–647   656
1.656, 664   656
1.669   666
2.8   594
2.121   594
2.454   459
2.463   459
6.188–189   656
Contra Apionem   437
1.232   55
1.279   57–58
2:24   598
2.162–163   57
2.199   598

Justus of   430
  Tiberius

Orphica   430

Philo the Epic   430, 442, 457
  Poet

Philo of   5, 9–10, 13, 15,
  Alexandria   22, 37, 39, 129,
     290, 295, 302,
     305, 323, 360,
     366, 372, 375,
     378, 380, 385,
     387–388, 391,
     395–396, 398,
     404, 426, 429,
     451, 457, 499,
     584, 607
[NB: citations of Philo's works
generally follow the titles and
numbering of the Cohn-Wend-
land ed. as used in the LCL, with
the traditional chapter numbers
given in square brackets.]

De Abrahamo
[17]77   415
[26]135   255
[29]148,   411
  150
[35]196   117
[41]243   270
De aeternitate mundi
[2]4   415
De agricultura
[8]35   411
[12]51   270
[17]79   408
[17]79–   422
  [18]82
[17]80   413
[31]136–   408–409
  139
[31]139   393
De cherubim
[7]23   415
[17]57   249, 251
[27]93   409
[30]105   409–410
[31]110   412, 415
De confusione linguarum
[5]15   413
[7]21   413
[10]35–36   421
[11]41   394
[11]43   413
[13]55   413
[13]56   414
[13]58   413
[18]83   413
[19]150   413
[23]108   413
[28]149   415
[25]124   117
De congressu   256
  quaerenda
  eruditionis
  gratia
[4]15–18   409
[4]16   410
[9]46   393
[10]51   415

[14]74–76   408–409
[17]89   392
[18]98   117
[21]115   417
[23]124   252
[25]142   408–409
[25]144   393

De decalogo

[9]33   425
[25]132   254
[30]159   408
[31]165–   598
    167

De ebrietate

[19]79   421
[23]94   425
[24]95   408
[27]105   408
[28]110   408
[29]111   421
[29]112   418
[30]115   408
[30]116–   412–413
    117
[31]121   408, 418
[43]177   407
[51]212   246

De fuga et inventione

[3]22   411, 423
[20]110   249

De Iosepho

[7]31   254
[20]107   251
[42]253   416
[42]257   251

De migratione Abrahami

[8]39   393
[18]104   412, 418
[20]113   416
[21]120   393
[28]157   415
[32]178   415

De mutatione nominum

[11]80   409
[13]87   394
[19]111   255
[20]115   415

[21]122   394
[24]139   394
[25]143   420
[26]146   409
[34]182   421
[34]184   411
[36]200   270
[37]201   251
[39]217   251

De opificio mundi

[1]3   254
[15]48   392
[17]54   415
[25]78   414–415
[31]96   392
[37]107–   392
    110
[42]126   409, 423
[40]119   248
[46]134–   246
    150
[47]136–   247
    170
[52]149–   246
    151
[53]151–   247
    152
[54]154   386

De plantatione

[2]10   414
[7]29   415
[9]39   415
[12]48   421
[14]59   421
[30]126   425
[30]129   408
[31]131   416
[33]135   408, 417
[38]159   411, 414

De posteritate Caini

[15]53   248
[24]88   412
[31]103–   424
    104
[31]104   410
[32]105–   423–424
    108, 111

[35]121	421	
[43]142	393	
[45]155	393	
[47]163	407	
[48]167	421	
[53]181	251	

De praemiis et poenis

[16]97	251
[18]108	254
[20]125	248

De providentia

[2]20	394

De sacrificiis Abelis et Caini

[4]18	423
[5]22, 29	393
[5]26f	252
[7]37	393
[21]72	105
[21]74	117, 393
[28]107– 109	121
[31]117	121
[37]136	117

De sobrietate

[3]10, 13	421
[5]25	254
[8]36	410, 423
[11]58	416

De somniis

1.[5]28	410
1.[6]35	425
1.[6]35–[7]37	415
1.[22]145	248
1.[35]205	410
1.[43]256	416–417
2.[4]27–28	410
2.[5]34	416
2.[5]38	408, 416
2.[11]77	117
2.[32]184	246
2.[33]191	421
2.[37]245– 246	415
2.[41]268	408
2.[41]269	421
2.[41]270	413

2.[42]272	117

De specialibus legibus

1.[5]28–29	410–411
1.[6]34	415
1.[18]61	415
1.[19]102	601
1.[26]138	270
1.[27]132–134	121
1.[35]193	416
1.[41]224	416
1.[50]271–272	425
1.[53]294	365
1.[59]320	365
1.[61]336	409
1.[62]342	410, 424
1.[62]343	409–410
2.[17]75	365
2.[18]82	365
2.[25]125	256
2.[25]129–30	254
2.[25]134	115
2.[25]138	117
2.[27]148	417
2.[28]157	394
2.[31]188, 192	408
2.[32]193	411
2.[32]199	416
2.[32]200	392
2.[33]209	417
2.[35]216	417
2.[38]225–235	598
2.[40]230	409
2.[44]246	394
2.[44]247	365
2.[47]259	394
3.[4]25	252
3.[6]36–51	255
3.[7]37–50	247, 252–253
3.[7]38	253
3.[8]48	255
3.[9]51	252

3.[10]56–   252
  60
3.[10]60   249, 254
3.[20]112   254
3.[20]115   248
3.[22]125   408
3.[30]166   365
3.[31]172–   256
  173
3.[31]176   255
3.[31]169,   253
  171, 173
3.[33]184   248
4.[13]75   365
4.[16]96   577
4.[17]102   394
4.[24]177   416
4.[25]134   412
4.[26]140   251
4.[34]178   417
4.[34]180   111, 120
De virtutibus
[11]72–75   416, 421
[11]74   414
[18]95   117, 417
[22]111   249, 252
[25]133   365
[27]145   394
De vita contem-   255, 420
plativa
[3]25   415
[3]29   410, 419
[4]35   424
[6]52   253
[7]63   247
[10]80   419
[11]83–85,   419
  87–88
De vita Mosis
1.[4]15   443
1.[5]21–24   409–410
1.[6]29   412
1.[8]48   254
1.[14]84   251
1.[28]161   251
1.[32]180   421
1.[38]212   415

1.[46]255   416
1.[51]284   408
2.[1]7   412
2.[5]30   249
2.[24]120   270
2.[31]162   408
2.[43]234   252
2.[43]235   564
2.[43]239   417
2.[46]256–   422
  257
2.[49]271   415
2.[409]270   408
Hypothetica (Apologia pro Iudaeis)
[7]3, 14   598
In Flaccum
[10]85   407
[14]121–   418
  122
Legatio ad   382
  Gaium
[1]5   251
[2]12   408
[4]92   248
[7]42   407
[11]75   394
[13]96   408
[36]276   251
[36]293   251
[44]352   251
[45]367   55
Legum allegoriae
1.[5]14   423
1.[22]70, 71   248
1.[30]94   393
2.[3]7   393
2.[7]21   393
2.[8]26   393
2.[9]31   246
2.[14]49   594
2.[15]56   425
2.[18]75   407, 411, 423–424
2.[21]82   407
2.[25]102–   421
  [26]103
3.[8]26   417
3.[14]44   425

3.[18]57 393
3.[34]105 421
3.[39]116 248
3.[41]121 393
3.[41]122 410
3.[78]221 411, 423

Quaestiones et solutiones in Genesim

1.25 247
1.31 246
2.3 424
2.7 246
3.3 414–415, 424
3.27 254
3.54 255
4.27 392
4.29 394
4.76 394
4.110 411
4.196 394

Quaestiones et 420
solutiones in
Exodum

2.20 412
2.38 417
2.120 417
2.38 411

Quis rerum divinarum heres

[4]14–15 425
[22]110– 417
111
[23]113– 114
116
[26]128 252
[38]183 270
[51]253 117, 126

Quod deterius potiori insidiari solet

[9]18 393

[21]75 393
[30]114 421
[33]125 415
[34]126 425
[34]130 425
[41]150 364–365
[43]156 365
[43]156– 364
158
[43]157 407
[43]158 365
[45]163, 364, 365
166

Quod Deus immutabilis sit

[6]24–25 412, 424
[16]74 415
[19]88 249
[31]147 365

Quod omnis probus liber sit

[7]49 394
[8]51 394
[12]87 251
[21]157 394

[Ps-Philo]
On Jonah 381

Ps-Phocylides 251
Sententiae
70–75 270

Thallus 430

Theodotus 430, 442, 457
frg. 4 459

Theophilus 430

Pseudepigrapha and Nag Hammadi Tractates

Acta Pilati A		*3 Baruch*	620
2.1	459		
		Book of Adam	See *Vita Adam et*
Acta Pauli (et	74		*Evae*
Theclae)			
		Discourse on the	425
Apocalypsis Baruch	See *3 Baruch*	*Eighth and*	
		Ninth	
Apocalypsis Eliae	630		
		1 Enoch	
Apocalypsis Mosis	See *Vita Adam et*	17:4	628
	Evae	21:7	628
		22:4–7	628
Apocalypsis (Visio)	613, 627, 629		
Pauli		*Jubilees*	
21–31	631	20.4	594
21:2–3	630–631	22.20	594
21:3	634	25.1	594
22	635	27.10	594
22:1	631–632, 634	30.1–15	594
22–23	618	32:2	128
22:3	630, 632, 634	32:15	127
22:5	631–634		
23:1	631	*Oracula Sibyllina*	13, 618
23:2	634	1–2	617
23:3	631	1.283–306	618
25–30	631	2.190–338	617
26	633, 635	2.330–338	627–628
31	619	3–5	628
31:1	634	5.484–485	618, 621
31:1–34	631	8	628
31–36	634–635		
31:2	634	*Penitence of Adam*	See *Adam and Eve*
32–45	631		
32:1–2	635	*Psalms of Solomon*	
		15:3	117
Apocalypsis Petri	617–618, 628–630		
14	616, 627	*The Resurrection of*	627
		Jesus Christ by	
Apocalypsis Sophoniae		*Bartholomew*	
7:9	630	21:5–6	620
8:1	630	21–22	620
		Testament of Job	637

Testaments of	637	31–37	613
the Twelve		31–43	609, 614
Patriarchs		32:2	614
T. Iss.		32:4	615
5:6	116	33:1–38:1	612
T. Judah		33:3	615
21:5	116	34:2	615
		35:1–2	615
Vita Adam et Evae	611, 626, 628–	37	612, 621
	629, 635	37:3	12, 609, 616, 627
1–13	613	37:3–6	610, 615
10:2	615	37:6	615
13:6	615	38:1	616
14:1–3	613	38:1–42:2	615
15–21	613	39	615
22–29	613	39:2	612
24:1, 4	613	39:2–3	615
25:1, 3	614	40–41	615
27:2–3	614	40:3, 5	616
27:4–28:4	614	40:6–41:2	616
28:4	615	41:1	616
29	614	41:3	615
29:6	87	42:1–2	615
30:1	613	42:3–4	616
31–43	614	42:3–43:4	616
31:1	613, 615	42:8	615
31:4	615	43:3	87, 615

New Testament

Matt		13:8	527
2	528	14:1	95
2:1	4, 89, 93, 95–97,	17:9	96
	100	18:9	625
2:14–23	97	19:1–9	595
3:1	4, 89, 96–98, 101	19:3–9	532
4:2	94	22:16	515
5–7	572	22:20	95
5:3–7:27	567	22:23–33	605
5:22	625	23:33	625
5:44–45	566	24:37	95
6:16	567	24:38	94
6:30	566		
6:34	94	**Mark**	
11:20	95	2:20	94
11:25	95	3:6	515
12:1	95	7:12	599

9:9	96	9:25	192
10:1–12	595	11:49–51	477
10:7	599	12:1	183
12:13	515	12:13–34	46, 195, 573
12:25	605	12:15	194
15:16–32	81	12:16–20	6
		12:42–46	186
Luke	10, 431, 500	13:1	95, 101
1:5	95, 99	15:2	486
1:7	94	15:11–32	186, 567, 573
1:8	96	15:20–24	184
1:18	94	15:25–31	184
1:24	96	16:1–8	186
1:26	96, 98	16:19–31	182, 192–193
1:39	96	16:23–27	629
1:57	98	18.1–5	186
1:80	98	18:12	128
2:1	4, 89, 98	18:30	95
2:1–6	100	20:9–16	186
2:2	95	21:20–24	477
2:13	182–183	21:22	96
2:13–34	181	21:23	95–96
2:14–15	183	22:21–38	637
2:15	181	23:7	96
2:16	185	23:27–31	477
2:16–20	181–182, 184, 189, 192	23:29	540
2:17–19	186–187, 190	24:18	96
2:19	185		
2:20	193–194	John	25n
2:21	194	2:1–11	15n
2:22, 39	486	12:3, 7	87
2:36	94	13:1–17:26	637
3:1	94–95	19:39	87
3:2	95, 99	20:24	620
3:38	494		
4	487	Acts	10, 25, 39, 431, 458, 472, 500
4:2	96	1:3	57
4:18	486	1:5	96
4:19–20	98, 486	1:6	95
4:21, 24	486	1:8	477
6:12	96	2:9–11	487
6:24–26	192	2:47	486
6:20–49	567	3:24	96
9:11	486	5:14	486
9:21–18:34	183	5:17–42	96
9:28–36	96	5:36	96

6:1	96	18:8	479
6:7	486	18:9–11	478
6:11, 13–14	486, 500	18:12–17	476, 479
7:41	95	19:8–10	478–479
9:15	476, 480	19:20	486
10	487	19:22–23	95
10:28	499	19:23–41	478
10:35	486	20:17–38	637
11:24	486	20:18–21	478–479
11:26	515	20:26	478
11:26–27	96	21:10, 15	96
11:28	95	21:21	486, 500
11:30	95	21:31–36	476
12:1	95	21:38	96
12:22–23	494	22:17–21	480
12:24	486	22:28	499
13	477	23:11	478
13–28	476	24:1–21	296
13:1	515	24:2	243
13:2	475	25:23–26:32	477
13:5	475–476	26:15–18	480
13:45	480	26:18	481
13:46	479–480	26:23	124
13:46–48	476–477	26:26	44, 483
13:50	479	26:28	515
14:1–2	479–480	27:23–25	478
14:5, 19	479	28	487
14:15	494	28:23–31	475–476, 479
14:27	100, 477	28:30	485–486
15	462, 477		
15:5	486	Rom	9, 131–132, 154, 351
15:23, 28	499		
16:13–14	479–480	1–2	512
16:16–24	478	1:4	216, 230
16:16–40	479	1:5	454
16:30–34	480	1:8–15	165
16:32	515	1:10	341
17:1–4	479–480	1:13	244, 455, 458
17:5	480	1:14	455, 457
17:6, 9	335	1:16	451, 455, 463, 479
17:10–12	479–480	1:18	474
17:17	477, 479	1:18–32	219, 223, 367
17:22	243	1:18–2:16	366
17:27–28	494	1:20	474
18:4	480	1:24, 26	250
18:6	476–477, 480	1:26–27	239, 251
18:7	480	1:29–32	228

1:32–2:3   367
2:1–16   367
2:1–29   357–358, 362
2:1–4:2   352, 361
2–4   365
2:9–10   45[1], 455
2:14   455
2:17   461
2:17–24   452
2:18–20   219
2:24   454
2:25–27   453
2:25–29   45[2], 454, 457
3:1   363–364, 453
3:1–9   365
3:2   585
3:9   45[1], 455
3:21–26   229
3:27   575–576, 578, 584
3:29   45[1]–45[2]
3:30   229, 45[2]–453, 455
4:9–12   453
4:11–12   469
4:13   587
4:17–18   455
5–8   216
5:5   216
5:12   534–535
5:12–21   229, 5[12], 580–582
5:20   582–583
5:68   210
6:1–23   216
6:3–9   231
7   358, 366
7:2   575
7:6   216
7:7–25   580–583, 585
7:7–8:2   352–353, 362, 366–367
7:10–11   586
7:21–23   58[1], 584
7:22   39, 575, 579, 58[5]
7:23   580–581, 585
7:23–25   219, 575, 578–579, 583
8   229
8:1–3   230, 583, 585

8:2   217, 575–582, 584 586
8:3   584
8:4–5   217
8:5   220
8:5–8   230
8:6   220
8:7   220, 575
8:9   217
8:11   230
8:14–16   217, 230
8:19–23   463
8:23   108–109, 111–112, 121, 124–125
8:26   217
8:27   220, 230
8:29   230
9:1   217
9–11   10, 462–464, 467, 469–470, 475–476, 478, 585
9:1–5   463
9:3   453
9:4–5   43[1], 479, 585
9:6   453
9:6–11:32   464
9:7   468
9:8–29   465
9:21–24   469
9:24   45[1]–45[2], 455
9:27   453
9:30–31   453
9:31   575
9:31–33   465
10:1   463
10:4–8   587
10:12   45[1], 455
10:19   453, 455, 466
10:20–21   479
10:21   453
11:1   465
11:4   480
11:2, 7   453
11:7–10   465
11:11   480
11:11–12   455, 466–467

11:13	219, 454, 462, 466, 477	15:1–7	229
		15:5–6	173, 220
11:14	462, 466, 477	15:8	453, 455
11:16	103, 108–109, 111–112, 121–122, 129, 466	15:9	455
		15:9–12	454
		15:13	173, 218
11:17	481	15:14	165–166
11:17–32	464, 467–468	15:14–33	164, 461
11:19	360, 367	15:16–18	454
11:20	220	15:17	166
11:25	220, 453, 455, 479	15:19	472
11:26	453, 466, 474	15:19–31	458
11:29	431	15:26	473
11:30	480	15:27	454
11:30–31	466	15:31	458, 473
12:1–2	217, 219–221, 223, 227, 511–513	15:33	172
		16:2	335
12:1–6	225	16:4	454–455, 458
12:1–5:12	230	16:5	111, 121, 124
12–14	216, 229, 231	16:6, 12	335
12:2	231, 234	16:20	172
12:3	220, 222–224, 227	16:26	454
12:3–13:14	218		
12:4–5	227, 233	1 Cor	231
12:6	224	1–4	143, 242, 250, 277–278, 302–303
12:6–8	226		
12:8	335, 342		
12:10–13	217	1:1	473
12:11	218	1:2	473–474
12:11–5:6	197	1:10–11	241, 244, 294
12:12	232	1:17	280
12:16	207, 220, 233	1:17–2:5	295
12–15	206	1:18–31	288
13:8–10	231	1:18–2:16	232
13:13	342	1:22–24	451, 455
13:13–14	228, 231, 233	1:23	470
14:1	226	2	8
14:1–15:12	218	2:1	280
14:2	227–228	2:1–5	280–281, 290
14:5	227	2:3	288
14:6	220	2:6–16	242, 280–282
14:7–9	227–228	2:16	234–235
14:10	474	2:16–3:4	245
14:14–15	228–229	3:1–5	241
14:17	218	3:3	342
14:18	227	3:16	242
14:22–23	227	3:23	245, 247

4:1–3	241	9:1–12	302
4:6	292, 302	9:3	301–302
4:8	241	9:9	575
4:12	335	9:14	242
4:14–21	165	9:15–18	295
4:16	334	9:19–22	232, 242, 472
4:21	300	9:20	451
4:23–24	334	9:21	575–576, 578, 584
4:33	172	9:23	472
5:1	294, 455	10:1	244, 474
5:1–13	241–242, 244	10:1–13	242
5–16	143	10:4	248
5:9	154–155, 241	10:14–22	471
6:1	294	10:16–17	227, 242
6:1–6	517	10:18	453
6:1–7:40	241	10:23–24	204, 241
6:3, 5	242, 250	10:24	197, 199, 205
6:7	232, 242	10:31–11:1	232
6:9	242	10:32	451, 455, 474
6:9–11	471	10:33	197, 204–205, 236, 289
6:12	294		
6:12–20	246	11:2–16	6, 237, 239, 242– 243, 245–247, 256–257, 605
6:12–7:40	244		
6:15–20	227		
6:16	595	11:2–26	243
6:16–17	245	11:2–14:40	241–242
7	532, 605	11:3	246–249, 606
7:1	144, 155, 241, 244, 294	11:3–16	244–245
		11:4	239
7:1–7	242	11:4–6	243, 250, 254, 256
7:10	242, 595	11:4–16	245, 249
7:10–13	531	11:5	602
7:18–19	453, 471	11:7–9	244, 250
7:19	456	11:7–12	245
7:20	471	11:11	238
7:25	294	11:12	244
7:29	168	11:16	238, 240, 474
7:40	167	11:17–34	243
8:1	294	11:18	294
8–9	45	11:22	241, 243, 253, 474
8:1–11:1	241	11:23–29	232, 243, 245
8:6	242, 244–245, 247–248	11:27–34	242
		12	605–606
8:10	471	12:1	244, 294, 471
8:11	228, 242	12:2	455, 471
8:11–13	232, 242	12:2–4	631
9	278, 295	12:7	289

12:12–31	227
12:13	246, 451, 455, 605
13:1–7	232
13:4–5	205
13:5	197, 236
13:13	527
13:47	205
14:1–5	232
14:7	425
14:11	456
14:26–33	602
14:26–36	242
14:33	474
14:33–36	237, 242, 244, 250, 253
14:37–40	602
14:40	243
15	242
15:3–5	245
15:9	76, 473
15:10	335
15:12	294
15:13	207
15:20	108–109, 112, 121–124, 129
15:23	112, 121–124, 129
15:28	249
15:44–49	245
15:53–54	228
16:1	294–295, 473
16:3	458
16:6	335
16:12	292, 294, 302, 335
16:15	109, 111, 121, 124
16:16	335
16:17–18	241
16:22	242
16:23	169
2 Cor	8, 21n, 80–81, 132, 142, 306, 317, 479
1–13	143
1:1	474
1:1–7:16	71
1:2–2:13	147
1:8	244
1:12	167
1:16	458
1:22	125
2	300
2:1	473
2:4	154–155
2:10–12	20
2:14	72–79, 82, 87
2:14–15	71, 77
2:14–16	74–75, 78
2:14–17	4, 79, 83, 88
2:14–6:13	147
2:14–7:4	71, 75
3	577
3:7, 13	453
3:12–16	471
4:6–7	83
4:7–15	232, 290
4:10	87, 587
5:3	228
5:10	161
5:14	82
5:16–21	232
5:20	341
6:1–10	290
6:6–7	325
6:11	458
6:14–7:1	71
7:2–16	143
8–9	71
8:4	341, 473
8:7–8	342
8:9	232
9:2	458
9:4	458, 473
10:1	328
10–13	71, 146, 154, 281–282, 289, 301, 305, 325–326
10:3–6	292
10:7	290
10:10	278, 292, 295
11	300
11:6	278, 288, 292, 295
11:16–12:13	288
11:22	452
11:23–28	19, 461

11:24	451, 472	3:1	318, 330–332
11:26	454	3:1–5	325–328, 330–333, 337, 342, 346
12:1–11	290		
12:14	292	3:1–22	344
12:16–17	278, 295	3:6–29	333
12:19	288, 300–301, 303	3:8	454, 587
13:1	292	3:10, 12	587
13:2–30	300	3:13	583, 586
13:1–4	288	3:14	454
13:3–10	232	3:17, 19	582
13:11	168, 172	3:21	583, 586
13:13	169, 473	3:23	584
		3:23–4:7	337
Gal	6, 38, 232, 470	3:26–29	334
1–2	310	3:27	228, 604
1:6	325–328, 332–333, 346	3:28	239, 245–246, 451, 455, 604–606
1:6–10	324, 330–331, 337, 342	4	457
		4:1–7	344
1:6–11	344	4:1–11	333
1:7	327, 346	4:3	334
1:13	68, 76, 452, 473	4:3–11	586
1:14	342, 452	4:8–9	334
1:15	461	4:8–11	325, 336–338, 340–341, 343, 471
1:16	454, 461		
1:17–18	458		
1:21–2:3	472	4:8–20	345
1:22	454, 458	4:12–20	8, 38, 165, 307–312, 323–326, 336–343
1:23	76		
2	462		
2:1	458	4:15	330
2:1–10	337	4:15–16	314, 318, 322, 327–328
2:3	453, 455		
2:7	453	4:20	318
2:7–9	454–455	4:21	587
2:9	330, 463	4:21–31	309
2:11	332	4:25–26	458
2:11–15	325, 327, 330, 342	5:1	309
2:11–21	604	5:1–4	345
2:12	454–455	5:1–13	337, 342
2:14	334, 452, 455, 459–460	5:1–6:18	346
		5:2	164
2:14–15	451	5:2–4	330
2:15	455–456	5:2–11	453
2:19	578, 586	5:6	456
2:19–20	208	5:7–12	341
2:23	452	5:8	326, 333

5:10	165	5:29	600
5:10–12	327	5:29–32	594
5:13–26	206	5:30	598
5:13–6:5	234–235	5:31	599
5:14	197, 583	5:32	597–598, 599
5:15	205	6:1–9	598
5:16	579–580	6:2	599
5:16–26	206, 325	6:4	601
5:20, 22	205	6:11	228
6:1–5	325	6:12	597
6:2	575–576, 578, 583–584	6:14	228
		6:19	597
6:12–13	453	6:24	169
6:14–15	586	8:5	593
6:15	456		
6:15–16	453	Phil	131, 154, 158–161, 206, 232, 479, 570
6:16	474		
6:16–18	330		
6:17	587	1:1	473
6:18	169	1:1–3:1	157, 161–162, 167
		1:4	169, 174, 232
Eph	606	1:7	301
1:4	125	1:10	161
1:2–22	605	1:11–3:21	176
1:21	597	1:18	169,174
1:23	257	1:19	233
1:24	605	1:25	169, 174
2:2	597	1:27	303
2:11	454	2:1	161, 233
2:11–22	597	2:1–18	303
2:12	453	2:2	169, 174, 232
2:14–15	599	2:3	207, 232
3:5	493	2:4	6, 197–199, 202–204, 207–209, 212, 214
3:3–12	597		
3:14–19	597	2:5	235
4:4	227	2:5–11	210, 233–234
4:15	227, 605	2:12	167, 208
4:16	605	2:14	209
4:24	228	2:14–18	161–162, 169, 174
5	12	2:16	335
5:1	596–597	2:17	210
5:2	78, 597	2:19–30	161, 163–165, 167, 171, 174, 177, 234
5:8–21	589		
5:15–20	591–592		
5:19	417	2:19–3:1	162–163, 169, 171
5:21–24	589–592, 607	2:21	197, 202–203
5:21–33	593, 595–596, 598		

2:24	163, 165–167		3:12	228
2:25–30	157–169, 171		3:15	227
2:27	202		3:17–19	592
2–14	175		3:18	605
3:1	152, 157, 161, 163, 167–171, 174, 177		3:18–4:1	602
			4:11	453
			4:16	152
3:1–17	234		4:18	169
3:2–21	170		5:22	257
3:2–4:4	157, 161, 167, 171, 177			
			1 Thess	44, 46, 131, 154
3:2–4:9	172		1:1	458
3:3	454, 474		1:5	170
3:5	452–453, 455		1:9	471, 481
3:6	342, 473, 586		2	42
3:7–8	586		2:1–2, 5, 9, 11	170
3:15	232		2:13	451
3:17	167		2:13–16	458, 470
3:19	232		2:14	451
3:20	458		2:16	455
4:1	167, 169, 174		2:17–3:13	165
4:1–3	172–173		3:10	341
4:2	232		3:11	172
4:4	169, 174		4:1	168
4:4–9	157, 161–162, 167, 171–173		4:1–2, 6	170
			4:5	455–456
4:8	167–168		4:9–12	556, 570
4:10	169, 174, 232		4:13	244
4:10–20	157, 173–177		5:2	170
4:11	46		5:8	228
4:15	458		5:12	335
4:18	78		5:21	198
4:21–23	157, 162, 167		5:23	172
4:22	473		5:27	151
4:23	169		5:28	169
Col	598–599, 606		2 Thess	
1–3	592		2:13	109, 111, 121, 124
1:18	124, 249, 257		2:16	173
2:1	244		3:1	168
2:10	249, 257		3:18	169
2:11	453			
2:15	72		1 Tim	
2:19	605		1:5	535
3:10	228		1:4–7	600
3:11	246, 451, 453, 455–456, 604		1:8	607
			1:9, 13, 15, 20	601

2:8–15	601		21	166
2:9, 11, 14	602, 240		21–22	164
2:15	607		25	169
2:16	601			
3:1–13	601		**Heb**	
3:5	335		1:2	96
3:7	601		7:3	570
3:15	602		9:17	642
4:3–4	600			
4:7	601		**Jas**	
5:1–20	601		1:1	458
5:10	602		1:17	609
5:11–13	602		1:18	108–109, 111–112, 121, 124
5:14	601			
5:23	600		1:26–27	512
5:24–25	601		1 Pet	605
6:1–2	601		1:1	458
6:4	505		2:4–10	603
6:9–10	601		2:12–15	602
6:17–19	601		2:18–3:9	602
6:20	601		3:20	95, 603
2 Tim	637		4:14–15	516
2:14	505		2 Pet	637
4:2	44		1:4	53
			2:4	628
Tit			1–3 John	604
1:10	453			
1:10–11	601		**Jude**	
1:10–16	600		6	628
2:3–6, 5, 8, 10	601			
3:9	600		**Rev**	
3:9–11	601		1:5	124
			2:13	95
Phlm	132, 604, 606		5:9	126
5	473		9:6	95
7	168, 174		14:4	109–112, 121, 125–126
19	164		22:1–2	631
20	165			

Other Early Christian Literature (to the IVth cent. CE)

Ambrose of   540
  Milan
  Apologia prophetae David
    1.11.56   537
  De Abrahamo
    1.4.25–26   529
  De viduis
    13.81   538
  De virginibus
    1.6.25–27   539

Ammianus Marcellinus
    15.5.31   515
    27.3.13   515

Arnobius of Sicca
  Adv. nationes
    2.14   625

Athenagoras   42

Augustine of   7, 11, 526
  Hippo
  Confessionum
    2.3.7   528
    8.7   525
  Contra Faustum
    22.30–31   540
  Contra Iulianum
    3.21.43   533–534
  De adulterinis coniugiis
    1.4.3   531
    1.4.4–5   532
    2.2.2   531
    2.8.7–8   540
    2.20.21   533
  De bono coniugali
    6.6   540
    11–12   534
    13.15   535
    17.19   530
  De civitate Dei
    7.17   503
    10.27   14
    15.16.3   535

    15.26   527
    22.22   546
  De doctrina christiana
    4.21.49–50   240
  De moribus ecclesiae catholicae et
    Manichaeorum
    1.30.63   535
  De nuptiis et concupiscentia
    1.10.11   530
    2.27.45   535
  De sancta virginitate
    6.6   537
  Enarrationes in Psalmos
    50.10   537, 546
    90.2.6   533–534
    143.6   540
  Enchiridion
    112–113   629
  Epistula
    2.4   536
    104.3   14
    137.12   14
    153.14   17
    258.5   14
  In Evangelii Iohannis Tractates
    98   629
  Retractationes
    2.48.1   540
  Sermones
    9.3–4   528
    9.18   530
    39   532
    51.13.22   530
    82.11   528
    153.5.5–6   528
    165   546
    224.3   528
    278.9.9   530
    318.2   534
    332.4.4   540
    355.2   664
    392.4   540

Barnabae Epistula
    1:7   III, 121, 124, 126

Clement of   39, 375, 378, 385,
   Alexandria   388, 429, 446,
     448–449, 627–
     629

Eclogae
   41.2, 48–   616
     49
Protrepticus
   4.50.3   618
Stromateis   442
   1–3   387
   1.23.155.1   430
   2.105.1   650
   2.105.2   649
   4.26   265
   5.1.15   625
   5.8   415
   5.11.77   630
   5.51.3   650
   5.90.4–91.5   625
   5.90.6   626
   7.33.3   649
   7.33.5   650

Clement of   (see *1 Clement*)
   Rome

Constitutiones Apostolicae
   8.40.2   116

Correspondence   19
   Between Paul
   and Seneca

Didache   385
   13:3–7   103, 111, 116, 121,
     127–129

Eusebius of   60, 429, 434–435,
   Caesarea   443, 445, 448–
     449, 518, 627
   Chronica [apud Jerome]
     Olymp.   430
     151
   Historia Ecclestica
     1.8.5–16   656
     3.3.2   628

   3.25.4   628
   6.14.1   628
   7.13.1   519
   7.23   519
   10.5.21   513
   Praeparatio evangelica
     4.13   425
     9   442
     9.24.1   430
     11.38   626
     13.13.6   626
     13.16.14–15   626
   Vita Constantini
     4.32   14

1 Clement
   9.4   262, 271
   11.2   271
   19.1–3   271–272
   20.1–8   272
   20.3   7, 259–260, 271–
     273
   20.8–11   262, 271–272
   20.12   272
   21.1   271, 273
   24.1   121–122, 124, 129
   29.3   111, 121
   30.3   271
   42.4   111, 121, 124
   63.2   271, 273
   65.1   271, 273

Gregorius of Nazianzus
   Orationes
     40.27   74
     (712d)

Gregorius of   576
   Nyssa
   Vita Mosis   41

Ignatius of   516
   Antioch
   Ephesians
     9, 18   604
     19:3   628
     20   604

Magnesians
    10–11   604

Irenaeus   614

Isidorus of Seville
  De ecclesiasticis officiis
    1.11   642
  Etymologiae
    5.23–24   642
    10.265   642
  Origines   See *Etymologies*

Jerome   11, 525–528, 530,
             536, 540
  Adversus Iovianum
    1.32   537
  Commentarii in 657
    Isaiah
  De viri illustribus
    12   17
  Epistulae
    53.7   14
    79.8   534
    108.4   538
    130.8   535
  Adversus Rufinum
    1.17   657

John Chryso-   7, 74, 78, 383, 526
  stom
  Commentary on Galatians
    1:1   343
    3:1   328, 331, 332
    4:11–13   340
    4:11–20   343
    4:16   338–339

Lactantius
  De mortibus persecutorum
    15.7   515
    34   519
    34.1   513
    34.4   515
  Institutiones Divinae
    5.5   14
    7.4   14

    7.18.2–4   628

Melito of Sardis
  Peri Pascha
    7.18.2–5   381

Origen   366
  Contra Celsum
    1.1   520
    3.26   68
    4.23   514
  Homilies   381

Palladius
  Historia Lausiaca
    45.1   95

Pollentius   531–532

Prudentius 371
  Clemens,
  A.
  Cathemerinon
    5.125–136 620, 629

Tertullian, Q. 614
  Septemius
  Florens
  Apologia
    15.1   657
    38.1   513
  De anima
    20   17
  De praescriptione hereticorum
    7   1

Theodore of 576
  Mopsuestia
  Adversus allego- 383
    ricus

Theodoretus of 74, 629
  Cyrus
  Commentarium 652
    in Isaiah

Graecarum affectionum curatio (*Thera-peutica*)
  11.19–24   626
  11.33–39   626

Classical, Late Antique, and Byzantine Sources

Achilles Tatius
  Leucippe et Clitophon
    5.17.2–10   186
    6.9.2   183

Aelianus
  De natura animalium
    3.9   262
    7.22   657
    12.2   262
  Varia historia
    4.17   61
    10.5   649

Aelius Aristides   7, 260, 263–264,
                    269–270, 279,
                    284, 315
  Orationes
    5.31.13   61
    5.33.3–5   61
    6   380–381
    10–11   58
    13   59
    13.174   58
    20   59, 271
    23.76–77   266–267
    26.64   499
    31   321
    33   321
    33.24–25   304
    43   321
    54.152.8   59

Aeschines
  Against Ctesiphon
    21–22   363–364
  Timarchus
    29   365

Theophilus of   614
  Antioch
  Ad Autolycum
    2.19   616
    2.38   627
    3.7   627

Aeschylus
  Agamemnon
    1160   622
  Septem contra Thebas
    856   622

Aesop   373

Aesopica   646
    42   655

Alciphron   134
  Epistulae
    2.11   190
    2.3.3   185
    3.19.7   190
    4.18.5   190

Alexander   429–430, 442–
  Polyhistor   443, 459

Alfenus Varus, P.
    2   645

Ammonius
  De adfinium voc. diff.
    208   322

Anacharsis   133
  Epistologra-
  phus

Anastasius Sinaita
  Hexaemeron
    12   74
  Vita Amphi-   74
    lochii

Anthologia Palatina
  5.240   622
  7.67–68   622
  7.365   622

Antiphon   264, 273

Aphthonius Rhetor
  Progymnasmata 184–185
    1   194
    8   191
    10   188
    11   187

Apollodorus [Ps-Demosthenes 59]
  In Neaeram 654
    55–57

Apollonius Para- 68
  doxographus,
  Mirabilia 3

Apollonius   80
  Rhodius,
  Argonautica
  2.904

Apollonius   49, 50
  Tyanensis
  De sacrificiis 425
  Epistula 17   58

Apuleius   83, 665
  Apologia
    69   528
    70.8   664
    92.2   670
    96.3   661
    96.5   661, 664
    97.2   654, 661
    97.5–6   670
    99.3   654
    99.4   664
  Florida   661
  Metamorphoses
    6.18   622
    11   509

    11.7   80
    11.9   81–82

Aratus   448, 451

Archestratus   396

Archytas   410, 414

Arion   296

Aristeas   68

Aristides Quintilianus Musicus
  2.3.55   408
  2.4.55–56 400, 402
  2.6.61   397, 401, 406
  2.8.66–68 414
  2.8.66–   411
    2.19.92
  2.14.79–82 414
  2.14.80   401
  2.16.84–89 414
  2.19.91f   423
  3.6.102–103 414
  3.7.105   414
  3.9.107–   403, 414
    27.133
  3.12.112   414
  3.20.120   414
  3.23.124–125 414

Aristophanes
  Aves
    1715   633
  Nubes   286
  Ranae
    181–183 622
    193   622
    471   622
  Vespae
    583–584 654
    683–587 669

Aristophanes Byzantinus
  Nomina aetatum
    15.5   261

279.5	261	6.9.4	222
		6.10.2	224
Aristotle	6, 61, 112, 132,	6.11.4, 6	223
	263, 269, 282,	6.13.4–7	223
	367, 375–377,	6.13.7	224
	399, 411, 489,	8.1.7	568
	571	8.2.1–4	568
Athenaion Politeia		8.3.1–2, 6	568
35.2	638	8.4.6	568
De anima		8.6.2	568
420B–	424–425	8.7.1–6	568
421A		8.11	119
421A7–	85	(1160A)	
422A7		8.12.8–	568
421A11–13	85	8.13.1	
421A28–	85	8.13.2–	568
421B4		9.1.8	
424B4–19	85	9.2.1–	568
428B10–25	86	9.2.10	
De caelo		9.3.1–5	569
290B	414	9.4.1–9.6.4	568
De generatione animalalium		9.9.1–10	569
788A	424	9.10.1–6	568
De sensu		9.11.1–6	568
2,438B16–	85	10.8.3	222
28		1098B	190
5,441B26–	86	1117B.13	221
445B1		1155A34	281
5,443B20–	86	*Metaphysica*	
27		345A.25	633
Ethica Nicoma-	229, 231, 235	1004B25	285
chea		*Politica*	
1.13.20	222	1.1253	598
2.5–6	221	1.1259	598
2.6.15	221, 224	1269B20	639
2.6.17	224	[2.6.5]	
3.3.10–11	222	1270A6–8	639
6.2.2–3	224	[2.6.7]	
6.3.1–12	225	1270A20–	639
6.5.1–4	222	22	
6.5.5	224	[2.6.10]	
6.5.6	222–223	1270A23–	639
6.6.2	223	24	
6.8.1	224	[2.6.11]	
6.8.3	223–224	1339A	406
6.8.4	224	1339B	408, 423
6.8.5, 9	223	1340A-B	410

1341A-B   423
Rhetorica
  1.3   372
  1.6.3–17   190
  1.9.35   315
    (1368A)
  2.4.10–11   374
  2.4.30–32   322
  2.20.1–8   373
  2.20.6–7   374
  2.26.1   561
  3.2.8–9   374
  3.4.3   373
  3.10.2–3   374
  3.13.5   384
  3.19.5   373
  16   384
Rhetorica ad   190
Alexandrum
  1422A
Sophistici   285
elenchi
  165A22

[Ps-Aristotle]
  De mirabilibus auscultationibus
    147 (845A-   78
      B)
  De mundo   263–264, 267, 270
    396B   268
    397A.23   268
    399A   421
  Problemata
    906A21–   86
      907B19
      [12]
    907B21–   86
      909A10
      [13]
    [19.27]   404
    [19.39]   422, 424
    950B5–8   669
      [29.3]

Aristoxenus   412
  Musicus
  Elementa harmonica

  2.31.15–30   401
  2.32.2–10   424
  2.44.20ff   410
  3.1   410

Arrian   500
  Anabasis   485–487
  Alexandri
    1.11.5   488
    1.16.7   488
    2.3.6   488, 493
    2.7.4–6   488, 490
    2.12.5   488
    2.14.7   488
    3.4.5   489, 493
    3.9.6   489
    3.15.2–3   489
    3.23.8   489
    4.4.2   489
    4.8–14   489
    4.11   489
    4.15.5–6   490, 494
    5.3.1–4   491
    5.25.2   490
    5.26.1–2   490, 494
    6.7.3   489
    6.29.8   488
    7.1.3   495
    7.1.4   491, 494
    7.4.4   490
    7.6.1   490
    7.11.6, 8–9 490
    7.15.4–5   492, 494
    7.19.6   494
  Indica
    5.8–13   491
    20.2   491
    35.2–8   491

Athenaeus, *Deipnosophistae*
    4.165D   650
    4.166B-D   650
    6.267B   262
    8.355B   190
    9.401C   649
    14.617B-F   80
    620A–631C   397

623F–624A   402, 410

Athenodorus   67

Augustus   657, 667, 670–671
  Res gestae
    2.8   98
    16–17   666

Aulus Gellius, *Noctes Atticae*
   3.16.13   655
   5.19   641
   7.12.1–2   641
   7.12.4   642–643
   15.27.3   641
   17.21.1   316

Caecilius   377

Callisthenes   487, 489, 494

Cassius Dio   7, 260
  Historia Romana
    51.15.7   659–660
    53.12   98
    53.22.5   99
    54.7.4–5   99
    56.32.3   666
    56.32.33   670
    56.41.8   666
    56.43.3   657
    57.17.8   662
    57.18.5a   100
    58.4.5   662
    58.16.2   662
    58.22.1   672
    58.25.2–3   671
    59.15.1–2   662
    60.17.4–8   499
    60.28.1   659
    61.6.2   671
    61.10.3   649
    62.11.2–3   662
    62.17.1   662
    73.16   119

Cato Major   648, 654

[Ps-]Cebes,   17, 22n, 24n
  Tabula
    7–8   321
    8.1   328
    14.3   328
    19.1–5   67, 366
    22.2–23.1   67
    26.2–3   67
    28.2   366

Celsus   43, 514
   2.17.1–2   651

Chariton
  De Chaerea et Callirhoe
    1.12.8   186
    2.3.1   186, 189
    3.8.2–9   186
    5.1.4–7   188

Chrysippus   262
  Fragmenta logica et physica
    389   255
    601   266

Cicero, M.   5–6, 131, 153–155,
  Tullius   282, 285, 357,
         367, 369, 376,
         379, 530

  Ad Atticum   135–140
    3.20   668
    3.20.1   647
    7.2.7   665
    7.3.9   665
    8.9   149
    8.9.1–4   150–151
    8.11   152
    8.11–12   151
    8.15   151
    8.91–   152
      92[3a]
    9.6–7   151
    9.7   151
    9.10.4–10   152
    9.11   151–152
    9.13   151–152
    9.14   143

9.15	143	1.3.4	136, 146–147
10.8–9	151	1.4.1–3a	146–147
11.16.5	669	1.4.3b–6	146–147
11.21.1	669	1.6.4	145
11.22.2	669	1.15.1–13	149
11.23.1, 3	669	1.16	148
11.24.2	669	1.17	144, 148
11.25.3	669	1.18	148
12.5	139	2.1–5	135
14.13	151–152	*Ad Quintum*	135–136
14.17	151	*fratrem*	
15–16	140	1.1	134
15.2.4	665	1.3	174
15.3.1	643	2.4	137
15.3.2	665	2.5	137
15.26.5	665	3.1.1–25	144
16.5.5	134	3.5	138
16.16	151–152	3.7	137
Ad familiares	137–138	*De finibus*	197, 210
1.4.3	170	2.23	650
1.9	134	2.99	647, 654
1–8	136	2.99–103	664
2.1–7	142	3.65	654
2.4.2	170	5.38	649
2.13	142	*De inventione*	373, 376–377
3.1–13	141	*De legibus*	
6	141	1.8.25	239
6.19.1	647	2.9.22	641
8.6.1–5	141	2.19.48	641
9.18.3–4	651	*De natura deorum*	
9.20.2	649	2.3.154	265
9–16	136	2.9	655
12.25.1–5	147	2.101	271
12.25.6	147	2.160	649
13	135	3.74	669
13.2.2	142	*De officiis*	
13.4.5	142	1.17.54	535
13.8.10	142	3.36	669
13.9.3	142	3.73–75	669
15.21.4	149	*De oratore*	373, 376
Ad M. Brutum	138	3.19–37A	278
1.1–18	135–136	3.38.155–	377
1.2.1–3	136, 145	172	
1.2.1–6	146	3.39.158	377
1.2.2	145	52–95	278
1.2.(3)4–6	145	*De res publica*	
1.3.1–3	136, 146–148	6.14.14	634

6.16.16	634
6.18–19	414
De senectute	
45	650
Paradoxa Stoicarum	
46	669
Philippics	
2.7	150
2.40–42	662
2.41	668
In Pisonem	
67	650
Pro Caelio	533
Pro Cluentio	
135	664
Pro Ligario	
3.9	361
Pro Rege Deiotaro	
21	651
Pro Sestio	
110–111	650
Tusculanae disputationes	
1.16.37	622, 633
1.17.39	633
1.21.48	622, 633
1.31–32	664
2.9.21	539
Verrines	
2.1.104–112	645
2.1.109	669

Cleanthes	379, 396, 405
Clitarchus	487
Corpus Medicorum Graecorum	649, 651
4.175–178	66
10.5	66
11.1.1	66
Columella	
De re rustica	
I	651

Cornelius Nepos	
De viris illustribus	
25.16.3	135
Cornutus, L. Annaeus	
Theologiae Graecae compendium	380
Corpus Hermeticum	628
1.31	425
13.7	39
13.18–19	425
Crates Thebanus [Ps-Crates]	133
Epistulae	
3	193
7	195
10:3	193
Ctesias	
Persica	
13	73
58	73
Curtius Rufus, Q.	
Historiae Alexandri Magni	487
3.1.6	493
3.10.5	493
4.4.19, 21	493
4.6.7	491
4.7.26	493
4.11.13–15	493
6.2.1–3	496
6.2.13	496
6.3.8–11	496
7.14.5	496
8.5.5–24	489
8.7	489
8.7.12	496
8.7.12–15	494
8.8.13–15	494

9.1.3 490
9.2.10–11 490
9.2.26, 28 490
9.3.7–8 490
9.3.10 496
9.7.15 497
9.7.15–26 496
10.1.17–19 495
10.3.5 497
10.3.10–13 498
10.5.33 497
10.8.3–4 493

Damascius 96

Damon 395, 401, 406

Ps-Demetrius of 343
Phaleron
Epistolary Types
2 334
3 329
4 327
6 328, 331
7 327
20 327
De Elecutione 373
223 132
77–78, 80 375
272–274 375

Democritus 400
frg. 68B21 54

Demosthenes 185, 259, 273, 377
Orationes
18 [De 281
corona]
28.15 [2 654
Aphob.]
36.7 [Pro 654
Phorm.]
41.16 656
[Spud.]
41.17–18 654
45 [Stepha- 669
nus I]

Ps-Demosthenes
Orationes
43 [Macar- 639
tatus]
59.55–57 654
[Neaer.]

Dio Chrysostom 7, 39n, 260, 263–
264, 268–269,
271, 273, 278–
280, 282, 516
Orationes
1.7 489
2.16, 73 489
4.19–23 489
7 289
7.105 348
12 289
12.15 313
13 290, 313
13.12, 22, 289
28
16.10 365
17 181
24.42 266
26 289
30.30 265
31 315
31.95–97 349
32 315
32.2 288
32.11–12 289
32.22 313
33.15 313–314
33.44 314
33.61 239–240
34.2–4 313–314
35.2–4 313–314
35.11–12 313
36 380–381
36.34 54
37 8, 292 [see Favo-
rinus]
38 312, 314
38.1–3 286, 313
38.4 315
38.6–11 265, 286

38.22	322
38.28	315
38.38	264, 315
40.35	265
40.36–37	266
47.1, 8	304
48.14	264
53.1	54
53.6	54
64	316, 321 [see Favorinus]
77–78.32–39	322

Diodorus Siculus	15
4.3.1	80
4.66.5	119
5.23	633
17	487
17.1.4	493
17.51.1–2	493
17.54.4–5	493
17.93.4	494
17.100	485
17.100–101	496
17.113.2	492, 494
18.4	495
18.4.4	496

Diogenes Babylonius	395–396, 399–402

Diogenes Laertius	209

De clarorum philosophorum vitis

1.114	68
3.80	190
3.80–81	191
4.43–44	654
5.30	190, 193
5.69	654
5.72	658
5.74	643–644
7.106	190
7.119	58
8.41	52

9.42	67
10.35–135	133
10.120	406

Diogenes of Oenoanda	133

Ps-Diogenes [Cynicus]
Epistulae

1.25	239
6.26	239
7.11	239
16.25	239

Dionysius of Halicarnassus	20, 117, 126, 288, 483

Antiquitates Romanae — 10

1.60.3	487
1.89.1–3	484, 486–487
1.89–90	486
1.90.2	484
2.11.3–4	484
2.15–17	484
2.15.4	484
2.16.3	484, 486
2.17.1	484, 486
2.63.3	59
3.10.4–6	484–486
3.11.3–4	486
3.11.7–8	484
4.2.2	61
7.70–73	486
7.72.15	119
11.3	485

Opuscula
De Lysia

21, 25	655

De Thucide

37	355, 359

On Literary Composition [*Comp.*]

3	117

Ps-Ecphantus	
frg. 81	262

Empedocles	68

Epictetus   7, 17, 20, 43, 260,
                     366, 381, 568
  Dissertationes   380, 564, 567
    1.2.29   365
    1.2.36–37   190
    1.3.5   365
    1.7.31   365
    2.14.12   239
    2.6.16, 21–   364
      22
    3.1   278
    3.1.1, 7–9   286
    3.1.14–15   240, 287
    3.1.31   286
    3.1.34–36   287
    3.1.42–45   240
    3.7.2   190
    3.20.4   364
    3.20.9–10   364
    3.22.10, 30   240
    3.22.50   313
    3.23   277, 287
    4.1.115   240
    4.5.35   263
    4.12   328
    17.31   598

Epicurus   68, 285, 400, 402,
                     406, 633, 647,
                     664
  Epistulae
  Ad Pythocles
    10.84–116   133
  Fragmenta
    542   650

Epimenides   67–68

Eratosthenes   491

Eunapius
  Vitae sophistarum
    454   60
    491–492   60

Euripides
  Alcestis
    252–253   622, 632
    443   622, 632
    900–902   622, 632
  Hippolytus
    1391   74
  Ion
    327   119
    401–402   110, 119
  Laodameia
    Frg. 565   299
  Orestes
    96   108, 118
  Phoenissae
    857   119
    1524   119

Favorinus of   8, 39, 278–279,
  Arelate   287–288, 291,
                     295, 300, 303–
                     304, 306, 324,
                     326, 331
  De exilio   316
    11.8ff   298
    12.39ff   298
    14.39ff   298
  Orationes [Ps-Dio]
    37 [*Korin-*   301, 316, 343
      thiakos]
    37.1   317, 347
    37.1–19   296–297
    37.7   322, 347
    37.8   293, 317, 347–348
    37.9   294, 318, 323, 340,
                       347
    37.10   293
    37.10–21   318
    37.11   347
    37.15–16   348
    37.18–20   322
    37.19–23   348
    37.20–47   296–297, 319, 321
    37.21   298
    37.22   293
    37.23   317
    37.28   293

37.35   322, 348
37.36   320
37.37   298, 320, 348
37.44   298
37.46   294, 347
37.46–47   320, 349
37.47   299, 322, 348
64 [*De*   321
  fortuna]

Festus, S. Pompeius
  De verborum   503
    significatu

Fronto, M. Cornelius
  Epistulae
  Ant. Imp.
    2.1.2   547
  Ant. Pium
    3–4   667
    7   667

Gaius
  Institutiones 642
    1.22–23   645
    1.42   645
    1.98–99   641
    2.101–103   655
    2.114   655
    2.225–228   645
    3.1–87   653
    3.39–54   659
    3.40–41   660
    3.56   645
    4.23, 109   645

Galen of Pergamon
  De alimentorum facultatibus
    3.1.2   649
    3.18.2   650
    3.18.3   651
  De pulsuum differentiis
    2.4   516
    3.3   516
  De sanitate tuenda
    1.8   68
  Libr. propr. 13 646

On making   See *Libr. propr.*
  wills
Opt. doctr.   292

Hecataeus of   439
  Abdera
On the   438
  Egyptians

Heliodorus   332
  Aethiopica
    3.16.4   55

Heraclitus [Ps?] 133
  Quaestiones Homericae
    22   379–380
    22.8   269
    32.4   269
    69.8   269

Ps-Heraclitus
  Epistulae   43
    4.3   19

Herennius   645
  Modestinus
  Encyclopaedia See *Pandectae*
  Pandectae
    2   643

Hermogenes Rhetor
  Progymnasmata 184
    1   194
    3   185
    6   562
    7   191
    9   187
    11.28–30   562

Herodianus
  1.10.5–7   80

Herodotus   296
  1.92   105, 119
  4.71   119
  8.98   322

Hesiodus   363, 378, 448,
                              450–451, 576
  Opera et dies
     276–278   577
     763–764   299

Hierocles   564
  Carmen aureum
     26   626

Hippocrates   4
  Epistulae
     1   64
     1–21   63
     2.48ff   62, 64–67
     3.50.1–2   69
     3.50.6–8   68
     3.50.14–15   67
     5   64
     11   64

Homeric Hymns
     2.277 [*Deme-*   82
        ter]
     7.36–37   82
        [*Dionysus*]

Homer   54, 94, 299, 354,
                              448, 450–451,
                              457, 610, 621
  Ilias
     1.320–348   188
     8.639   622
     10.508–515   622
     11.155–159   622
     13.389   632
     15.346–349   355
     16.482   632
     23.71–74   622
     24.209–210   653
  Odyssea
     2.222   347
     10.508–515   624
     10.509–510   631–632
     11   633
     14.422   119
     17.218   281

     22.347–348   67

Horace   656
  Saturae
     1.2.116   649
     2.2.89–92   649
     2.4.40–42   649
     2.8.6–9   649

Iamblichus
  De vita Pythagorica
     31   60
     65   55
     142   67

Isaeus
  Orationes
     1 [*Cleonymus*]
        1.3, 10   667
        1.41   669
        1.43   667
     2.11 [Ha-   639, 655
        gnias]
     2.14 [Me-   654
        necles]
     4 [Nico-   669
        stratus]
     6.5 [Philo-   655
        ctemon]
     7.9 [Apol-   655
        lodorus]
     9 [Asty-   669
        philus]
     9.14   655

Isocrates   273, 314
  Orationes
     19.11–12   654, 658
        [*Aegi-*
        net.]
     40 [*Aeropa-*   582
        giticus]
     69 [*Archi-*   119
        damus]
     105   170
        [*Philip.*]

Julius Paulus   645

Javolenus Pri-   643
  scus [apud
  Justinian,
  Dig.]

Joannes Doxapatres
  Hom. in Aphth.   185
    3

Joannes Sard.
  Comm. in   185
    Aphth. 3

Julius Caesar
  Commentarii de Bello Gallico
    1.39   655

Justinian
  Digesta   645, 648
    5.2.1   647
    25.2.17   531
    28.1.1   643
    28.1.2   643, 656
    28.2.3   667
    28.5.49.1   665
    29.1.1   655
    29.1.11   657
    30   532
    29.1.12
    32.37.2   665
    35.1.40.3   643
    37.14.1   659
    38.2   659
    38.2.1   660
    40.9.30   660
    48.10.24   660
    50.16.70   660
  Institutes   643
    2.2.11   655
    2.10   642
    2.12   657
    2.25   654

Juvenal
  Saturae
    1.37–41   670
    1.55–57   670
    1.75   649
    1.119–120   652
    1.132–133   649
    1.132–134   652
    1.135–138   649–650, 652
    1.140–142   650
    1.141–143   649
    1.142–146   651
    1.144   650–651
    1.145–146   653
    1.146   652
    3.1   649
    3.185   671
    3.272–274   648, 651
    3.286–287   648
    3.292–294   648
    4.113, 123–   671
      129
    5.115–116   649
    5.64   649
    6.113   671
    6.346   649
    10.236–239   670
    11.117–129   649
    16.51–54   655

Labeo, M. Antistius
  Posteriores   643
    [apud
    Justinian,
    Dig.]

Legatum partitionis 644
  hereditatis

Lex Aelia Sentia   659–660

Lex agraria   645

Lex Cornelia   645

Lex Cornelia 669
  testamentaria

Lex Falcidia 645

Lex Fufia Canina 645

Lex Furia 645

Lex Iunia Vellaea 645

Lex Papia Poppaea 660

Lex Tarentina 645

Lex Tullia de 645
  ambitu

Lex Voconia 644–645

Libanius 383, 485

Ps-Libanius
  Epistolary Types
    3   329
    4.1   329
    4.3–13   329
    4.26ff   329
    5   329
    6   327
    6.11   329
    9   327
    13   327
    17   327
    32   327, 331
    34   327, 331
    53   327
    56   327
    60   327
    64   327–328, 336
    79   327, 331, 341
    81   327, 331

Linus 448

Livy
  1.1.30–31 528

    1.58   528
    27.15   97
    26.11.9 119
    29.11.7 77

Longinus 356
  On the sublime 373
    27.1–2   355
    32.3–7   377

Longus
  Daphnis et Cloe
    1.2.1–3.2 183
    1.7.1–2   192
    1.12.8   186
    1.16.4   185
    2.12.1   185
    2.15.1   183
    3.21.1   185
    3.25.4   185
    4.11.1   185
    4.13.1–2   186
    4.23.2–24.2 184
    4.24.3–4   184
    13.2   185
    26.4   185
    33.4   185

Lucan [M. Annaeus Lucanus]
  Pharsalia (Bellum Civile)
    4.819–820 142

Lucian of 383
  Antioch

Lucian of Samo- 26, 260
  sata
  Alexander
    38   516
    60   64
    61   58
  Cataplus
    8   194
    11   193–194
    23–29   195
  Contemplantes
    7   622

17   193
De luctu
    3   622
De morte peregrini
    11   516
    32   19
Dialogi mortuorum
    1.3   193
    20.1   622
Necyomantia
    10   622
Nigrinus
    30   670
Philopseudes
    21   68
Somnium
    1   287
Verae historiae
    1.16   633
Vitarum auctio
    26   190

Lucretius
De rerum natura
    5.13–54   68
    6.799–802   651

Lycurgus   54, 57, 639

Lysias
    6.13   200
    13.41–42   654, 656
    [*Agoratus*]
    19.41 [*Aristo-*   654
       phanes]
    25.13   202
    32.5 [*Dio-*   655
       geiton]

Macrobius
Somnium Scipionis
    1.4   633

Malchion of   383
    Antioch

Manetho
    Astrologia 2.116   633

Marcus Aurelius   270
    Meditationes
    5.30   269
    11.3.2   516

Martial
    Epigrammata
    4.54.5–10   653–654
    4.70   654
    4.73   653–654
    5.70.5   650
    6.58.7–8   653
    7.59   649
    11.36.3–4   653

Maximus of Tyre
    Orationes   564, 567–568
    13.5   67
    36.6B   607

Menander
    Frg. 763K   291, 299

Musonius Rufus   264, 391, 393, 564
    Dissertationes   567–568
    2, 5   392
    6   67, 392
    8   263
    12   607
    14   240
    17   58, 239

Nicolaus
    Progymnasmata   184
    8   191

Nicomachus Gerasenus Mathemati-
    cus
    Harmonicum Enchiridium
    2.240.20ff   424
    3.241–242   414

Ps-Ocellus Lucanus
  De universi natura
    frg. 1   261

Olympiodorus   96

Ovid
  Amores
    1.2.27–30   82
    2.12   82
  Ars amatoria
    1.189   82
  Fasti
    5.376   74
    2.520   119
  Metamorphoseon libri
    1.89–92   582
    8.274   119

Pausanias
    5.14.2   632
    7.3.1   119
    10.28.4   622

Persius
  Saturae
    3.98–106   653

Petronius   671
  Cena Trimal-   See *Satyricon*
    chionis
  Satyricon   657, 667
    40   649
    53   664
    55.2   649
    71   656
    72   651
    141.2–4   656
  Testamentum   See *Satyricon*
    Porcelli

Phaedrus
  Fabulae 4.5   646

Pherecydes   67

Philodemus   9, 262, 285, 288,
                      325, 391, 409,
                      411, 426, 567–
                      568
  De musica
    1, 3   396
    4   395–407
    7.90   396
    7.187   398, 401
    7.190   396
    8.7   396, 401
    8.9   400
    8.17   402
    8.22   396
    8.142   396
    8.148   406
    8.154   405
    9.64   399
    9.69–70   396, 401–402
    9.73   398
    11.72   398
    11.80   396, 398
    11.82   402
    11.88   397
    11.89, 92   396
    85.28   270
  De Oeconomia [*Peri oikonomias*]
    12.28   569
  De Libertate dicendi [*Peri parresias*]
    53, 56   563
    67   563
    70, 74   563
    81   563
    84–85   563
    81.1–9   562–563
    88   563
    253–258   569
    275–283   569
  De poemata
    4   400
  Volumina rhetorica
    2   283–284

Philostratus   279
  Vita Apollonii   50
    1.2   59
    1.4–6   61–62

1.11   67
3.42–43   59
4.34   269
5.21   397
5.41   269
7.38   59
8.5   60
8.7.7–9   59
8.13   60
Vitae sophistarum   291
1.8 (489–492)   316
1.8.4   286
521   60
532   183
552–554   61
570   61

Photius Lexicographus
Bibliotheca
p.7b   95
p.60a   96
p.340b   96

Pindar   68, 404
Nemean Odes
1.8   53
6.4–5   53
Olympian Odes
2.2   53
2.86–88   53
3.40–43   53
9.28–29   53
9.100–102   53
9.110   53
11.10   53
Pythian Odes
1.25–28   53
1.41–42   53
5.25   53

Plato   12, 62, 132–133, 190–191, 263, 375, 377, 384, 386, 405, 448, 450, 457, 610, 622, 630–631
Alcibiades I
103A6   201
Apologia
22C   54
Gorgias
453A   284
462B3–465E6   285
501–502   406
523A–527A   623
Ion
533D–534C   54
542A   54
Laches
188D   412
Leges
1.642D   52
2.657–659   406
2.669   423
2.669–670   399, 401, 410
2.673A   423
3.691E   54
3.696B   54
7.701A-B   413
7.790E–791B   423
7.795D   398
7.800–802   416
7.802   406
7.803   399
7.812D-E   408
11.922B–923A   654
11.922B–926D   646
11.922C-E   667
Meno
99C   52
99C-E   54

100B	54
Phaedo	629
80D	627
80E–82B	621
81E–82A	627
85–86	410
86	393
88D	627
107C	623
107C–115A	621
112–113	625, 628
112E	634
112E–113C	623–624
112E–114A	628
113A–114C	626
113E	624
114A	628
114A-C	624
114D	623
Phaedrus	
233B	200
245B–	623
249D	
247A	415
Philebus	
25B7	202
51E	84
Protagoras	
326A-B	410
343B	108
Res publica	633
329A	281
347E2	202
366C	58
397A	423
398	410
398D	423
399C-E	423
400A-D	423
401D	408, 410
410	398
424C	413
431	411
432–433	403
439–441	411
441–442	398
441–444	403

530D–	413
531B	
584B	84
588D–	39
589B	
614A–621B	623
Sophista	285
Symposium	
175E7–9	201
195B	281
189C–	247
193D	
Timaeus	
34B–36D	413
66D–67A	84

Plautus, T. Maccius
| *Persa* | |
| 838–840 | 659 |

Pliny the Elder	503
[G. Plinius	
Secundus]	
Historia Naturalis	
8.207, 210	649
12.26.42	87
12.33–35	87
12.66–71	87
13.2	87
13.91–95	649
14.28.139	651
18.2.8	119
18.8	119
18.30.119	119
29.8.26	651
37.20	672

Pliny the Younger [G. Plinius Caecilius Secundus]
Epistulae	
1.9.2	665
2.1.1	650
2.6.6	650
4.22.4	671
5.1	647
5.5.2	660
6.33	647

INDEX OF ANCIENT SOURCES 717

7.6.8–13	669
7.24.2	644
7.24.8	666
8.16.1–2	648
8.18.1	640, 643
8.18.5	654, 660
8.18.7	644, 660
10	134
10.94.2	664
10.96.7	516
Panegyricus	
49.6	650

Plutarch 10, 23, 62, 260, 332, 365, 516

Vitae parallelae
Agis-Cleomenes

5.1–2	639
5.2–3	665
5.3	263
Alexander	487
9.3	486
18.2	493
27.6–7	493
30.5	57–58
31.6	493
34.1	488
47.2	490
Antonius	
28.3	649
Brutus	
22.4	148
53.6–7	148
Caesar	
22.6	494
23.2–3	494
32.7	494
58.6–7	494
Cato Major	
9.6	648
Cicero	
7.6	459
45.2	148
Cleomenes	
39.1–2	58
Coriolanus	
9.2	655

Lucullus	
41:2–6	650
46	58
Lycurgus	
8.1–4	639
Nicias	
30	654
Numa	
1.1	94
Romulus	
1.1	484
4.2	485
6.3–4	485–486
7.1	485–486
9.2–3	485–486
14.2	485
16.2, 5	485
20.1	485
25.1	485
Theseus	
13.1	485
24.1	485
25.1	485
16.2	119
32.1	485
36.1	485
38D	74
Moralia	22, 564, 567–568

Anime an corporis affectionis sint peiores

501B–502A	68
501E–502A	264

Coniugalia praeacepta

139C	240

De capienda ex inimicis utilatate

86C	322
91B	322

De fraterno amore

478F–479A	263

De invidia et odio

536C–538E	322

De Iside et Osiride

357B	74, 82

De Pythiae oraculis
  401E   105
  401F–   120
    402A
De recta ratione audiendi
  40B   108
De se ipsum citra invidiam laudando
20
  539A–547F   321
  542E   288
De tuenda sanitate praecepta
  124C   651
  128B   651
*Maxime cum principibus philosopho
  esse disserendum*
  777C   39
*Non posse suaviter vivi secundum
  Epicurum*
  1095C–   406
    1096C
Quaestionum convivialium
  676C   278
  685C   649
  frg. 193   649
Quaestiones Graecae
  298F   105
  298F–   120
    299A
*Quomodo adolescens poetas audire
  debeat*
  19E   380
*Quomodo adulator ab amicis inter-
  noscatur*
  53D   342
  54C   342
  69E-F   328, 331
*Quomodo quis suos in virtute sentiat
  profectus*
  74A   326

Ps-Plutarch
  De musica
    Mor. 1131D   409, 424
    Mor.   400
      1136.B
    Mor.   397, 399, 408
      1140B-F

Mor. 1142D   410
Mor. 1143F   424
Mor. 1144A   410
Mor. 1144F   424
Mor. 1146D   410
Mor.   398
  1146E-F
Mor. 1447A   413
Vita Homeri   380

M. Antonius   279, 287–288, 291,
  Polemo   316–317
  *Scriptores physiognomonici Graeci et
    Latini*
    1.93–294   292

Polyaneus
  Strategemata
    5.5.2   577

Polybius   15, 20
  2.40.1   261
  3.3.7   261
  4.46.7   261
  23.11.7   261
  42.6   261

Porphyry   622
  Comm. in Aristotelis Categorias
    56–57   414
    61   425
  De abstinentia
    1.14.3   649
    2.34   425
    3.4.5   657
    3.20.1, 3   649
  Vita Pythagorae
    20   68
    30   55

Posidonius
  frg.
    247F   261, 263

Pratinas [apud   80
  Athenaeus,
  Deip.]

Proclus
  Institutio 626
    Theologica
    205–210

Propertius
  2.14 82
  3.1 82

Ptolemaeus 487, 492
  Harmonica
    1.20.9 424
    3.4.95 413
    3.5.96– 401
      3.7.100
    3.5.97–98 403
    3.7.100 399
    3.8.100–111 403
    30–31 410
  Syntaxis mathematicae
    8.2 633

Pythagoras 67–68, 423–424,
      448, 457, 567–
      568, 626
  Golden verses
    5–8 570–571
    9–20 571–572

Quintilian 367, 369
  Institutio 362, 373, 377
  oratoria
    1.8.3 353–354
    1.8–9 384
    3.8.51 187
    5.10.20 562
    5.10.119– 305
      125
    5.11.17–19 378
    7.1.38 646
    7.4.20 664
    7.4.39 646
    8.6.4–6, 19 378
    8.6.44, 47, 379
      52
    9.2.7 361
    9.2.30 361

9.2.30–33 357–359
9.2.32, 36 360
9.2.37 355–356, 360
9.2.38 361
10.1.71 187

Ps-Quintilian
  Declamationes majores
    1.2 664
    2 665
    9 665
    17 665
    19.16 658
  Declamationes minores
    264, 268 646
    308 646
    308.1 663
    325 670
    332, 380 646
  Rhetorica ad 373
  Herennium
    1.8–9 384
    2.1–4 376
    2.27–30 376
    4.34 376

Sapho 349

Scaevola, Q. 645
  Mucius

Scriptores Historiae Augustae

Aurelian 20.5 511

Seneca the Elder [L. Annaeus
  Seneca]
  Controversiae
    2.7 664
    2.7.7 654
    3.9 646
  Suasoriae 1 490

Seneca the 365
  Younger
  [L. Annaeus
  Seneca]

De beneficiis
  1.10.2   650
  4.11.4–6   663
  4.22.1   661
Consolatio ad Helviam matrem
  16.3–4   528
De anima
  20   1
De clementia   17
  1.23.1   582
De matrimonio 607
De tranquillitate animi
  1.7   649
Epistulae   133–34
  8.6   665
  19.10   650
  20.3   652
  75   239
  84.9   421
  85.26–27 19
  85.41   19
  86.10–11 651
  94.26   529
  101.4–9   193

Servius, M., *Commentarium Aeneidae*
  2.156   641

Severus of   188
  Alexandria

Sextus Empi- 279, 288
  ricus
Adversus mathematicos
  2 (= *Adv.*   283
    Rhetores)
  2.11   286
  2.16–19   284
  2.20–42   284
  2.43   284
  6   395
  6.1   404
  6.7–9   423
  6.18   399
  6.19–20   400
  6.21–24   396
  6.23   423

  6.27–28   406
  6.30, 37   403
  6.38   396
  6.39–51   397
  11.45–46 190

Simonides   404

Solon   296, 66

Leges frg. 49A-D 638

Sophocles   105
  Ajax
    624   93
    672   633
    1308–1314 201
    1313   200
  Electra
    137–138 622
  Oedipus   372
    Coloneus
  Oedipus Tyrannus
    298   52n
  Polyxena (apud 622
    Stobaeus)
  Trachiniae 539
    183   119
    761   119

Soranus (Medi- 66, 68
  cus), *Vita*
  Hippocratis

Statius, P. Papi- 14
  nius
  Silviae 2.1.86– 539
    87

Stobaeus, Joan- 22, 209
  nes
  2.67–68   58
  Anthologia 564
    4.24A.14
  Eclogae 1.13.2 261
  Florilegium
    4.7.64   262

4.7.67   263

Strabo 6.11   495
7.3.8   94

Suetonius   503, 656, 665
  De poetis   656
  De viris illustri-   656
    bus
  Vita Horati
    76–77   656
  Vita Caesarum   672
    Augustus
      56.1   670
      66.4   666
      101   670
      101.2   667
      101.3   666
    Caligula   662
      38.2
    Claudius   659
      25.1
    Domitian
      9.2   662
      12.2   662
    Julius 49   533
    Nero
      16.2   516
      25.1   515
      25.2   81
      32.2   662
      34.5   662
    Tiberius
      23   671
      34   649
      36   100
      43.1   672
      43–45   672
      49.1   662

Sulpicius Rufus, Servius
  De sacris   641
    detestandis 2
  Iurisprudentiae antehadrianae
    1.225   631
  Iurisprudentiae anteiustinianae
    92   641

Palingenesia
  2.324   641

Stoicorum Veterum Fragmenta
  2.601   266
  2.1076.9–10   263
  3.94   255
  3.292.9   262
  3.353.2   262
  3.625.3   262
  3.625–636   197
  3.630–631   209, 262
  3.661.17   262

Tacitus, Corne-   503
  lius
  De vita Iulii   662
    agricolae
    43.4
  Annales
    1.8   667, 670
    1.566–567   667
    2.48   662
    2.85   100
    3.76.1–2   671
    3.26–28   582
    3.48   99
    3.76.1–2   667
    6.1   672
    6.38.2–3   671
    11.23.3–4   498
    11.24   499
    13.26–27   659
    14.15.5   515
    14.31   662
    15–16   643
    15.44.3   516
    15.62.1   661
    15.64.4   661
    16.11   662
    16.17.5–6   661
    16.19.3   672

Theocritus 17.47   622

[Aelius] Theon
  Progymnasmata   184, 360, 561

8	191
10	187
20–22	362
106.5–6	562
119.7–14	562

Theon of   270
  Smyrna
  De utilitate mathematicae
    12.16–24   269

Theophrastus   377, 410, 425

Theopompus   61

Thucydides, *Historia*
   1.46   622
   3.85   119
   5.84–85   355

Twelve Tables   654
   3–5   640

Ulpianus, Domi- 660
  tius
  Epitome Ulpiani
    8–9   642
    20.1   641
    29.1–7   659
  Liber singularis   641–642
    regularum
  Regulae   See *Liber singularis*
         regularum
  Tituli ex corpore See *Epitome*
    Ulpiani   *Ulpiani*

Valentinus   388

Valerius Flaccus, 80
  Argonautica
   3.538

Valerius Maximus

Factorum et   300
  dictorum
  memora-
  bilium
   7.7   672
   7.7.1–7   646
   7.7.3–5   667
   7.8.1–4   646
   7.8.5–9   646, 668
   7.8.8   667

Varro, M. Terentius
  Antiquitates rerum divinarum
   frg. 204   503
  De lingua latina 119
   6.16
  Fragmenta
   540–543   656
   543   655
  Res rusticae   649
   2.4.9–1
  Saturae Menip- 655
   pea 12

Vergilius Maro, P.
  Aeneid   14
   2.29   356
   2.342   97
   6.298–304   622
   6.384–394   622
   6.801   80
  Eclogues
   4.4–5   14

Verrius Flaccus   503

Xenocrates   287

Xenophon   377
  Anabasis
   6.2.2   622
  Oeconomicus
   1.1.1–2   192
   1.13, 23   190
   2.1.2   186
   2.1.4   192
   2.5.6–7   188

3.5	185	Xenophon of Ephesus	
5.4	190	*Ephesiaca*	191
5.5.5	188		
12.7	190	Zeno	190
17.6	185		
20.1–2	185	Zosimus, *Historia*	502–503
21.9	185		

Inscriptions

CIL

		IG	
6.355	80	12[8].273,	108
6.10230	644	280, 283,	
6.18280	542	285	
6.26112	547		
6.26115	547	*IGUR*	
6.26473	547	160	514
9.3144	80		
9.5179	80	*ILS*	
11.695	80	2683	99
11.5737	510	3004	99
14.2112	648	6095	99
		7212	648
ICUR		8150	99
2.4165	544	8394	644
2.4226	545	9502–9503	99
2.4249	543		
2.4827	543	*SIG*	
3.7445	543, 546	18.51	108
3.7770	544	19.8	108
3.9673	542, 546	83.55	119
3.9759	544	200.10	119
4.9415	547	455.2	119
4.9422	547	502.40	119
4.9762	547	529.21, 35–38	110
4.10953	543	739.5	119

Papyri

𝔓⁴⁶ (*P. Chester*   219, 336, 338, 345,   58.29–30   170
    Beatty II + *P.*   590   483.3ff   174
    Mich. 6238)   512.6   164

P. Bologna 5   329   *P. Oslo Inv.*
                                                         1475.11   168
P. Col.
    3.6.14–15   168   *P. Oxy.*
    7.188   656   1.119.8.8, 13   168
                                                         2.300.3ff   167
P. Elephant.   4.709.12   168
    13.2–3   174   12.480.13   168
                                                         12.1481.7–9   173
P. Fay.   12.1488.3ff   167
    113.3–4   167   17.2149.5   168
                                                         17.2154.15   168
P. Giss.   48.3400   168
    21.3–4   174   48.3408.19   168
                                                         65   55
PGM   104.4   643
    iv.220   62   105.2   643
                                                         113.27–28   164
P. Hib.   297.3–4   170
    41.2ff   167   1068.4–5   170
    66.4ff   164   1160.12–13   170
                                                         1216.17ff   164
P. Herc.   395   1293.4–5, 23–   167
    176   133   24
    1497 (*De*   395–407   1666.11–14   164–165
        musica)   1757.19   170
                                                         2857   648
P. Lond.   3119   517
    42.7ff   174   3035   517
    43.3–4   174
                                                     P. Par.
London ms. *Or.*   620   43.4   164
    5987.18–24
                                                     P. Ryl.
P. Mich.   2.153.10–13   659
    8.481.5ff   167   2.153.45   654
    8.481.14–15   165
    8.490.5ff   167   *P. Taur.*
    8.499.12–14   167   1.7.10   108
    10.13–14   164
    36.1–2   170

P. Teb.
  316.10J   108

P. Tebt.
  747.16–17   164

PSI
  5.500.8–9   168
  841.2ff   167

Stud. Pal. 4.72J   108

Medieval Literature

Aquinas, Thomas
  Summa theologica
    ii.ii.47.10   236
    ii.ii.52.1–2 236

Dante
  Inferno   14

Purgatorio
  22.64–73   14

Dies irae   13

Petrarch   136

INDEX OF MODERN SCHOLARS

Abdy, J. T., 659n
Aland, B., 111n
Aland, K., 23n, 109, 111, 123n, 200, 219, 590–591
Albertz, M., 104–105
Alexander, L., 159–160, 168, 173
Alexandre, Jr., M., 305n, 387n
Alford, H., 77n
Allo, E. B., 76n
Alon, G., 128n
Ameling, W., 189n
Amelotti, M., 640n
Amquist, H., 23n
Anderson, G. A., 279, 610–611, 612n, 613, 614n, 657n
Anderson, Jr., R. D., 8, 277–278, 285, 305n, 351–352, 354, 356–358, 359n, 360–362, 367–368, 371n, 565n
Anderson, W. D., 395n, 401n, 402n, 410n
André, J., 642n
Angeli, A., 133n
Annemiek, J., 565n
Arangio-Ruiz, V., 640n, 662n
Armstrong, D., 555n
Arndt, W. F., 111, 516n
Artz, P., 173
Asheri, D., 639n
Asmis, E., 395n, 569n
Astbury, R., 656n
Attridge, H. W., 4
Aune, D. E., 5, 159n, 381n

Baasland, E., 126n
Babbitt, F. C., 120
Babcock, W. S., 629n
Badian, E., 489n, 490n, 491n, 495n
Baer, R., 246n, 247n
Baeumer, M. L., 556n, 570n
Bagnall, R. S., 656n
Bahr, G. J., 143

Bailey, D. R. S., 135, 137, 138n, 139n, 140, 141n, 142n, 144n, 145n, 148n, 149, 150n, 151, 643n, 668n, 669n
Baird, W., 15n, 16n, 18n
Balch, D. L., 10, 71n, 176n, 190n, 210n, 233n, 305n, 371n, 604n, 605n, 607n
Baldwin, B., 656n
Barabino, G., 657n
Barclay, J., 430, 431, 456
Bardy, G., 259n
Barigazzi, A., 297n, 298n
Barker, A., 392n, 394n, 399n, 401n, 406n, 411n
Bar-Kochva, B., 437–438, 439n
Barnes, J., 85n
Barnett, P., 71n, 77n
Baron, F., 18n
Barr, J., 29–30
Barr, W., 649n, 653n
Barrett, C. K., 76n, 476n
Barth, M., 592n, 597n
Barton, S., 505n
Bassler, J. M., 170n
Batav, P., 654n
Baudis, A., 576n
Bauer, B., 19
Bauer, W., 21n, 109–112, 123n, 516n, 603n, 604
Baur, F. C., 9
Beare, J. I., 86n
Beaujeau, J., 136n
Beck, C. H., 184n
Beck, R., 510n
Beger, A., 641n
Behr, C. A., 61n, 267n
Bélis, A., 412n
Bell, R. H., 462n, 466n
Berger, K., 25, 38n, 64n, 655n
Bernstein, A. E., 621n, 629n
Berry, K. L., 175n, 176

Betz, H. D., 7, 24–26, 38n, 50, 134n,
    301–302, 308–309, 310n, 311,
    312n, 318n, 320n, 322n, 323,
    324n, 330n, 331n, 332n, 333n,
    334n, 335n, 336n, 339, 341n,
    342n, 344n, 460n, 474n, 512–513,
    567n, 572n, 576n
Beyer, E., 22n
Bieler, L., 62n
Billerbeck, P., 22, 30–31
Bjerkelund, C. J., 172n
Black, C. C., 277n
Black, D. A., 199n
Blank, D., 283n, 284n
Blank-Sangmeister, U., 145n
Bliss, M. T., 565n
Bloennigen, C., 372n
Blomqvist, K., 279
Bloomquist, G. L., 159n, 160, 161n,
    162n, 163n, 164n, 165n, 166n,
    168n, 170n
Boixareau i Vilaplana, R. M., 637n
Bonhöffer, A., 20n
Bonnard, P., 307n, 528n
Bookidis, N., 505n
Borgen, P., 49n
Boring, M. E., 25, 38n, 64n
Borkowski, J.-F., 133n, 292n
Bornkamm, G., 71n, 131n
Bornscheuer, L., 570n
Boswinkel, E., 654n
Bosworth, A. B., 488n, 489n, 490n,
    491n, 494n, 495–496
Boulanger, A., 264n
Bovini, G., 518n
Bovon, F., 182n, 183n, 184n, 187n,
    194n, 195n
Bowersock, G., 286n
Boyer, L., 665n
Bradley, D., 557–560, 572n
Bradley, K. R., 662n
Brainard, P., 81n
Brashear, W. M., 509n, 520n
Braund, S. H., 648n, 650n, 652n,
    653n
Braund, S. M., 332n
Brawley, R. L., 476

Bremer, F. P., 641n
Brerewood, E., 504n
Breuer, D., 556n
Breytenbach, C., 7, 75n, 260n, 263n,
    264n, 267n, 273n
Bromiley, G. W., 29n, 109n, 220n
Brown, C., 105
Brown, P., 527n
Brown, R. E., 385n
Bruce, F. F., 76n, 81, 308n
Bruck, E. F., 638n
Brucker, R., 64n
Brunt, J., 559
Brunt, P. A., 487n, 489n, 491n, 494,
    495n
Bücheler, F., 21n
Buchholz, D. D., 617n
Büchner, K., 134n, 148n
Budde, L., 80n
Buecheler, F., 657n
Buffière, F., 380n
Buitenwerf, R., 609n
Bultmann, R., 20, 22, 24, 73–74, 77n,
    215n, 381n
Bunyun, J., 17
Burkert, W., 35n, 118n, 521n
Burstein, S. M., 495n
Burton, E. W., 308n, 339n
Bury, R. G., 281n, 284n
Butler, H. E., 353–354, 661n
Byrne, B., 581

Cairns, H., 84n, 85n
Calvin, J., 17
Camerarius, J., 17
Campbell, J. B., 647n, 655n, 656n
Campbell, J. Y., 501n
Cancik-Lindemaier, H., 134n, 582n
Caplan, H., 376n
Capps, E., 317n, 347n
Caragounis, C. C., 23n
Cardauns, B., 503n
Carozzi, C., 618n, 619n, 629n
Carroll, J. T., 198n
Carter, J. M., 666n
Cary, E., 483n
Cary, M., 145n

Casaubon, I., 35
Casquero, M.-A. M., 642n
Cavarzere, A., 141n
Cèbe, J.-P., 655n, 656n
Chadwick, H., 372n, 384n
Champlin, E., 12, 638n, 640n, 647n,
    648n, 652n, 654n, 655n, 657n,
    660n, 664n, 665n, 666n, 667n,
    668n, 669n, 671n, 672n
Chance, J. B., 182n
Chantraine, P., 633n
Charlesworth, J. H., 429n, 612n
Chérix, P., 620n
Cherry, D., 645n, 648n
Christiansen, I., 372n
Clark, E. A., 240n, 251n, 526n, 527n,
    530n, 531n, 536n, 540n
Clark, E. C., 641n
Clark, G., 649n
Clarysse, W., 640n
Clauss, M., 510n
Clay, D., 26n
Cloud, J. D., 648n, 652n, 653n
Cochrane, C. N., 1n,
Cohen, N. G., 372n
Colish, M., 17n, 34n
Collange, J.-F., 75n, 76n, 77n
Collins, A. Y., 26n, 71n, 134n
Collins, J. J., 13n, 617n
Collins, R. F., 240n, 280n
Colpe, C., 25, 38n, 64n, 623n
Colson, F. H., 22, 248n, 386n
Conley, T. M., 360, 375n
Conybeare, F. C., 60n, 418n
Conzelmann, H., 123n, 238n
Cope, L., 238n
Corbett, E. P. J., 566n
Corelli, E. C., 652n
Corrington, G. P., 49n
Cosgrove, C. H., 198n
Cothenet, É., 75n
Court, J. M., 128
Courtney, E., 650n, 651n, 652n, 671n
Cozijnsen, B., 25n
Cranfield, C. E. B., 125n
Cratander, A., 136
Crawford, M. H., 498n, 640n, 645n

Cremer, H., 29
Crenshaw, J. L., 465n
Crook, J. A., 644n, 645n, 646n,
    648n, 655n, 659n, 669n
Crosby, H. L., 317n, 319n, 320n,
    348nn, 349n
Crossan, J. D., 184n
Cugusi, P., 135n
Culpepper, R. A., 165
Cumont, F., 24
Currie, S. D., 43
Curtius, E. R., 556, 560, 565

Dahl, N. A., 43, 199n
Dähne, A. F., 430
Danker, F. W., 21n, 31n, 111, 281,
    333n, 336, 342n, 516n
Darwin, C., 36
Dassmann, E., 623n
Daube, D., 372n, 646n, 648n, 657n,
    658n
Dautzenberg, G., 72–73, 74n, 79
Daverio, F., 641n
Davies, P. R., 419n
Dawson, D., 372n, 382n, 385, 386n,
    387, 388n
de Boer, M. C., 143n, 582
de Budé, G., 348n
de Jonge, M., 12, 14n, 15n, 18n, 21n,
    87n, 607n, 609n, 610n, 611, 614n,
    637n
de LaBriolle, P., 651n
de Robertis, F., 517n
de Romilly, J., 260n
de Rossi, G-B., 517, 541n
de Santos Otero, A. A., 618n, 630n
Deissman, A., 15n, 21, 23, 36, 132,
    516
Delacy, P. H. & E. A., 284n
Delling, G., 15n, 23n, 24, 25n, 72,
    75n, 104–105, 109–110, 113, 119n,
    372n, 381n
Dembitz, L. N., 421n
Deming, W., 575n
Demke, C., 131n
Denis, A.-M., 611
Denniston, J. D., 200–202

Derrett, J. D. M., 100n
des Places, É., 626n
Dessau, H., 99n
Detienne, M., 87n
DiCicco, Mario, 281, 282n
Dickie, M. W., 299n, 332n
Didot, F., 106
Diels, H., 54n, 64, 68n
Dihle, A., 27n, 512, 572n
Dillon, J., 375n
Dindorf, L., 106–107, 654n
Dindorf, W., 106–107, 266n,
 267n
Dittenberger, W., 110n
Divjak, J., 536n
Dixson, S., 644n
Dolan, W., 495n
Dölger, F. J., 24, 33–34
Donaldson, T. L., 461n, 464n, 465n,
 467n, 468n
Donfried, K. P., 467n
Doty, W. G., 159n, 160, 161n, 162n,
 164n, 165n, 168n, 172n, 174n,
 560n
Downey, G., 385n
Drew, 272n
du Toit, D. S., 49n, 50–52, 54n, 55–
 57, 59n, 60
Dubnow, S., 430
Duensing, H., 618n, 630n
Duff, A. M., 659n
Duff, J. D., 651n, 652n
Duff. P. B., 75n, 80–83
Dunbabin, K. M. D., 299n
Dunn, J. D. G., 215n, 220n, 226n,
 231n, 308, 330n, 339n, 474n,
 576n
Dyck, A. R., 669n

Ebeling, G., 131n
Edelstein, L., 66n, 261n, 263n
Edmonds, J. E., 349n
Egan, R. B., 73n
Eggenberger, C., 259n
Ehrhardt, A., 517n
Elliott, J. K., 616n, 617, 618n,
 619n

Ellis, E. E., 234n, 242n, 244n
Emperius, A., 348n
Engberg-Pedersen, T., 6, 27n, 29n,
 32n, 45, 233n, 238n, 244n, 352n,
 366n, 367, 420n, 580n
Engermann, J., 623n
Eno, R. B., 536n
Epp, E. J., 3, 26n, 45
Epstein, I., 421n
Erasmus, 17
Eriksson, A., 242n, 371n
Erler, M., 395n, 400n, 401n, 402n
Ernout, A., 642n
Esler, P. F., 308n
Eyben, E., 529n
Eynickel, E., 113, 129

Fabre, G., 659n
Fant, M. B., 644n
Farmer, W.R., 164n
Farquharson, A. S. L., 269n
Fassler, M., 71n, 81n
Favrelle, G., 626n
Fee, G., 123n, 157n, 175n, 176, 238n,
 281n
Feil, E., 504n
Feldman, L. H., 392n, 409n, 410n,
 417n, 421n
Ferguson, E., 9, 35, 41–42, 44, 46,
 67n, 176n, 190n, 210n, 233n,
 270n, 305n, 371n, 387n, 426n,
 483n, 607n, 652n
Ferrua, A., 541n
Filson, F., 27–28, 35n, 77n
Findlay, G. G., 80n
Finney, P. C., 36n
Fiore, B. J., 12
Fischel, H., 27
Fisher, C. D., 66n
Fitzgerald, J. T., 1, 3, 12, 17n, 18n,
 20, 22n, 26n, 29n, 31n, 46, 49n,
 67n, 71n, 75n, 87n, 131n, 157n,
 175n, 176, 183n, 209n, 233n,
 295n, 305n, 312n, 314n, 321n,
 323n, 325n, 329n, 395n, 396n,
 483n, 525n, 532n, 555n, 569n,
 671n

Fitzmyer, J. A., 182n, 183n, 184n, 185n, 189n, 192n, 194n, 195, 220n, 221n, 226n, 231n, 247n, 465n
Flacelière, R., 649n
Fleury, A., 19
Foley, E., 426n
Fornberg, T., 23n, 46
Forster, E. S., 86n
Fortna, R. T., 45, 309n, 580n
Foucart, P., 501n
Fournet, J. L., 362n
Fowl, S., 231n
Fox, R. L., 294n, 518, 639n, 645n, 655n
François, L., 264n
Frede, D., 623n
Fredericks, S. C., 653n
Fredrickson, E., 314n, 325n
Freese, J. H., 373n
Freudenthal, J., 27n
Fridrichsen, A., 23
Friedländer, L., 650n, 652n, 654n
Friesen, S., 264n, 319n
Frishman, J., 614n
Frisk, H., 632n
Fuhrmann, M., 150n
Fung, R., 308n
Funk, R. W., 162n, 164n, 165n, 173n, 560n, 570n
Furneaux, H., 661n, 671n
Furnish, V. P., 71n, 77n
Fyfe, W. H., 355n, 377n

Gagarin, M., 638n, 640n
Galinsky, K., 14n
Gamble, H., 168
Gardner, J. N., 659n
Garland, D. E., 131n, 157n, 169n, 171n, 172n, 173n
Garret, J. L., 42
Gaston, L., 467n, 468n
Gaudemet, J., 662n
Gauger, J. D., 617n
Gaventa, B. R., 45, 309, 580n
Gempf, C., 98n
Geoffrion, T. C., 157n
Georgi, D., 71n, 431n

Gernet, L., 638n
Gershevitch, I., 489n
Giebel, M., 145n
Gigante, M., 395n
Gill, C., 332n
Gill, W. J., 98n
Gingrich, F. W., 111, 516n
Giversen, S., 49n
Glad, C. E., 26n
Glare, P. G. W., 107n, 108n
Gleason, M., 279, 287, 294n, 297, 299, 316n, 317, 319n, 320n, 321n
Gnilka, J., 131n
Goldin, J., 421n
Goldman, E., 642n
Goodman, M., 617n
Gordon, W. M., 642n
Gottschalk, H. B., 264n
Goudge, H. L., 77n
Graf, D. F., 488n
Granfield, P., 42
Grant, R. M., 126n, 240n, 382, 650n, 651n, 672n
Grasser, E., 234n
Green, J. B., 185n, 195n
Green, P., 622n, 624n
Greenfield, S. N., 371n, 379n
Greer, R. A., 534n
Grese, W. C., 25
Griffiths, J. G., 372n, 509n
Grimm, C. L. W., 108
Grobel, K., 215n
Grotius, H., 18, 35
Grözinger, K. E., 392n, 426n
Grube, G. M. A., 375n, 623n
Gruen, E., 431, 456
Grundmann, W., 182n, 184n, 190n, 192n
Guinot, J.-N., 652n
Gulley, N., 133n
Gurlitt, L., 135n, 148–149
Gutbrod, W., 451
Gyllenberg, 579–580

Haacker, K., 582n
Haase, K. B., 106

Haase, W., 45
Habermehl, P., 623n
Haenchen, E., 476n
Hafemann, S., 75n, 78n
Hahm, D. E., 263n
Hahn, H. J., 502n
Hall, R., 310n
Hamilton, E., 84n, 85n
Hansen, R. P. C., 380
Hansen, W. G., 310
Harder, R., 26n
Harlow, D. C., 620n
Harmer, J. R., 126n
Harnack, K. G. A. von, 32–33,
    272n
Harris, B. F., 264n
Harris, W. V., 653n
Harrison, A. R. W., 638n, 665n
Harrison, J. R., 521n
Harrison, P., 504n
Harrisville, R. A., 74n
Hartman, L., 46
Hauser, A. J., 371n
Hauspie, K., 113, 129
Hausrath, A., 146n
Havelaar, H. W., 25n
Hawthorne, G. F., 157n
Hay, D. M., 372n, 420n
Hayes, J. H., 16n, 18n
Hays, R. B., 229n, 365
Hayward, R., 116n
Hedrick, C. W., 185n, 189n, 192n
Heininger, 184n, 187n, 193n, 194n
Heinrich, K. B., 650n
Heinrici, C. F. G., 19–21, 77n
Hellemo, G., 81n
Hellholm, D., 46
Henderson, J., 646n
Henderson, M., 145n
Hengel, M., 27n
Hennecke, E., 616n
Hense, O., 262n, 263n
Hermann, G., 22n
Herter, H., 253n
Herzfeld, L., 430
Hester, J., 310
Hilhorst, A., 618n, 619n, 631n

Hill, E., 535n
Hillard, T. W., 520n
Hinks, D. A. G., 380n
Hock, R. F., 6, 182n, 184n, 629n
Hodkinson, S., 639n
Hoffmann, G., 292n
Hoggarth, W. D., 498n
Hoheisel, K., 623n
Holford-Strevens, L., 298n
Holladay, C. R., 10, 55n, 429n, 431n
Holland, G., 26, 281, 295n, 325n,
    395n
Holmes, M. W., 126n
Holson, F. H., 382n
Honoré, T., 641n, 642n
Hooke, S. H., 182n
Hooker, M. D., 234n
Hooker, R., 504n
Horbury, W., 431
Horsley, G. H. R., 31n, 508, 510n,
    511n, 522
Horsley, H., 254n
Horsley, R. A., 282n
Hort, F. J. A., 590
Houlden, J. H., 595n, 606n
Housman, A. E., 652n
Hubert, M., 640n
Hübner, H., 576n
Heugenot, F., 35
Hughes, 77n
Hulbert-Powel, 16n
Humphries, R., 651n
Hunger, H., 184n, 186n, 188n, 191n
Hunink, V., 661n, 664n, 670
Hunter, D. G., 531n, 532n, 537n
Hunter, L., 557n
Hurd, J. C., 165n, 310n
Hurley, D. W., 659n
Huschke, P. E., 641n, 659n
Hutchinson, G. O., 141n, 142n, 150n,
    153n
Hvalvik, R., 126n

Innes, D. C., 375n

Jacobson, H., 442n
Jaeger, W., 7, 259–260, 272

Jal, P., 260n
James, M. R., 617, 630n
Jehn, P., 556n, 565n
Jenkinson, J. R., 653n
Jeremias, J., 182, 194
Jervell, J., 43, 477n, 480n
Jervis, L. A., 71n, 245n, 246n
Johnson, E. E., 198n
Johnson, L. T., 220n, 229n
Johnson, M., 262n, 612n
Johnson, T., 6, 206n, 511n
Johnston, D., 647n, 665n
Jolowicz, H. F., 641n
Jones, B. W., 662n
Jones, C. P., 264n, 286n, 289n, 304n,
    312n, 313n, 315n
Jones, H, S., 107, 108
Jordan, D. R., 332n
Joubert, S., 336n, 337n
Jowett, B., 85n
Judge, E. A., 10, 24n, 31n, 33n, 34n,
    294, 301, 502n, 514n, 518n, 520n,
    521n
Jungmann, J., 42

Kaesemann, E., 220n, 221n, 226n,
    227n
Kaestli, J.-D., 620n
Kalms, J. U., 56n
Kampmann, U., 264n
Kantorowicz, E., 81n
Karabélias, E., 647n
Karadimas, D., 279, 284
Karnthaler, Fr. P., 188n
Karpp, H., 517n
Karris, R. J., 592n
Kasten, H., 139n, 141n, 145n, 149n
Kaster, R. A., 297n
Kayser, C. L., 286n
Kearney, R., 531n, 537n
Keck, L.E., 10, 41, 46, 229n, 476n
Keenan, J., 643n, 672n
Keil, J., 266n, 267n
Kelly, J. N. D., 526n, 537n
Kemke, I., 395n, 396n, 397n,
    398n, 399n, 400n, 401n, 405n,
    406n

Kennedy, G. A., 277n, 281n, 291n,
    309–311, 560–561, 565n
Kent, J. H., 278n
Kerferd, G. B., 285n
Kern, P. H., 310n, 311
Kidd, B. J., 261n, 263n
Kienast, D., 491n
Kiilunen, J., 576n
Kinoshita, J., 132n
Kinzig, W., 521n
Kipling, G., 81n
Kirchmaier, G. W., 15n
Kittel, G., 29, 29n, 30n, 109n
Kittel, R., 29n
Klamp, D., 659n
Klauck, H.-J., 5, 39n, 131n, 132n,
    323n, 324
Klauser, T., 24, 33, 34n
Klinzing, G., 511n
Kloppenborg, J. S., 520n
Klostermann, E., 23
Knaach, G., 491n
Knopf, R., 259
Knox, P. G., 77n
Koester, H., 45, 53n, 254n, 255n,
    264n, 333n
Koesterman, E., 661n, 667n, 671n
Kögel, J., 29n
Kollmann, B., 50n
König, J., 319n
Konstan, D., 26n, 29n, 312n, 555n,
    563n, 564n
Koskenniemi, E., 49n, 50
Kraft, R. A., 126n
Kranz, W., 54n, 68n
Kraus, F., 640n
Kreller, H., 640n
Krentz, E., 7, 315n
Kreyher, J., 19
Kropp, A. M., 620n
Kübler, B., 640n, 642n
Kudlien, F, 64
Kühn, C. G., 646n
Kümmel, W. G., 16n, 18n, 73, 76n,
    580n
Kunkler, S., 18n
Künzel, E., 76n, 80n

Kurcikidze, C., 610n
Kurfess, A., 171n, 617n
Kurz, W. S., 233n

Lacey, W. K., 639n
Lachman, L., 590n
LaFleur, R. A., 652n
Lakoff, G., 262n
Lampe, G. W. H., 55n
Lapidge, M., 263n, 271n
LaPorte, J., 408n
Larsen, E. M., 301n
Lasserre, F., 63n
Lauria, M., 662n
Lausberg, H., 243n, 359, 560–561, 565
Lavarenne, M., 620n
Lazenby, J. F., 639n
Lee, R. W., 642n
Lefkowitz, M. R., 644n
Leipoldt, J., 22
Lemche, N. P., 445n
Lenel, O., 641n
Leon, H. J., 515n
Levick, B. M., 497n, 498n, 671n
Lewis, A. D. E., 640n
Lewis, L. G., 44
Liddell, H. G., 107
Liebenberg, J., 262n
Lieberman, S., 27n
Liebeschuetz, J. H. W. G., 383n, 510n
Lietzmann, H., 21, 33n, 73, 74n, 75n, 77n, 83n, 142, 143n
Lightfoot, J. B., 30,126n, 271n,
Lindemann, A., 122, 126n, 272n
Lindsay, W. M., 503n
Link, H.-G., 105
Llewelyn, S. R., 514n
Lloyd, G. E. R., 383n
Lohmeyer, E., 74n
Lohse, E., 576n, 592n
Lona, H., 271n, 272n
Longenecker, R. N., 132n, 310, 339n
Lonsdale, M., 82n

Louw, J., 112, 114, 115n, 123n, 125n, 126n
Luck, U., 221n
Ludolph, M., 134n
Lührmann, D., 46
Lumpe, A., 511n
Lung-kwong, L. O., 46
Luschnat, O., 67n
Lust, J., 113, 128
Lutz, C., 392n
Lyons, J., 51

MacDowell, D. M., 639n, 665n
Mack, B. L., 559n
Mack, B., 372n
MacMullen, R., 510
MacRae, G. W., 3, 26n, 44–45
Macro, A. D., 264n
Madvig, J. N., 652n
Magill, F. N., 43
Mahé, J.-P., 610n
Maine, H., 647n
Malalas, J., 654n
Malcovati, H., 641n
Malherbe, A. J., 2, 3, 15n, 26, 29n, 36n, 37–38, 41, 46, 131n, 133n, 158n, 175n, 176n, 181, 183, 189n, 190n, 193n, 195, 197–198, 210n, 215n, 229n, 233n, 239n, 260n, 277n, 292, 305n, 311n, 327n, 329n, 334n, 335n, 351, 371, 381n, 392, 483n, 502n, 508n, 555n, 556–557, 560n, 564n, 567n, 568n, 569n, 570n, 573n, 578n, 609n
Manson, T. W., 75n
Marache, R., 641n
Marcello, N., 657n
March, W. E., 43
Marcus, R., 394n, 411n
Marg, W., 52n
Mariotti, I., 657n
Marrou, H. I., 408n
Marshall, H., 182n, 189n, 241n
Marshall, P., 76n, 83n, 324, 326, 331n, 334n, 337n
Martin, J., 56n
Martin, S. D., 648n, 649n

Martini, R., 641n

Martyn, J. L., 11, 45, 132n, 308,
309n, 330n, 333n, 334n, 339n,
469, 474n, 476n, 579n, 580n,
583n, 587n

Martyn, J. R. C., 652n

Maser, S., 21n, 46

Mason, H., 299n

Mastrangelo, M., 371n

Matera, F. J., 605n

Matthews, C., 359n

Matz, F., 80n

Mayor, J. E. B., 649n, 652n, 669n

McCall, Jr., M. H., 373n, 376–377

McCormick, M., 81n

McDonald, J. I. H., 381n

McKechnie, P., 646n

McKenzie, R., 107, 108

McKim, D. K., 26n, 371n

McKinnon, J. W., 418n, 426n

McLean, B. H., 165n, 310n, 514n

McNamara, M., 421n

McNeil, B., 131n

Measell, J. S., 383n

Meeks, W. A., 36n, 41, 43, 45, 176n,
190n, 199n, 210n, 229n, 233n,
239, 245n, 246n, 247n, 305n,
334n, 371n, 534n, 607n

Meier, J. P., 385n

Meillet, A., 642n

Meiser, M., 614n

Melanchthon, P., 7

Mendelson, A., 409n

Mendelssohn, H., 619n

Mengel, B., 157n

Merk, A., 590

Mertner, E., 565n

Messing, G. M., 192n

Metzger, B. M., 35n, 36n, 45, 591n

Metzger, E., 643n

Meyer, B. F., 44, 351n

Meyer, H. A. W., 21n, 75n, [612???]

Meyer, M. W., 508n

Meyer, P., 465n, 580n, 581n, 584n

Meyer, T., 509n, 510n

Miles, J. C., 647n

Milgrom, J., 116n

Millar, F., 617n, 659n, 662n, 666n

Miller, N. P., 661n

Milligan, G., 21n, 31n, 73, 74n, 110,
113, 341n

Mitchell, E., 241n, 242n

Mitchell, M. M., 2, 26n, 71n, 278,
325n

Mitchell, S., 264n, 519n

Mitthof, F., 510n

Moessner, D. P., 2

Moles, J. L., 289n

Momigliano, A., 498n

Mommsen, T., 531n, 669n

Montevecchi, O., 640n

Montgomery, H., 332n

Moo, D. J., 217n, 220n, 221n, 226n

Moran, R., 374n

Moritz, T., 593–595, 596n, 597,
599n, 601, 604n

Mortley, R., 375n

Moulakis, A., 260n, 262n

Moule, C. F. D., 165n

Moulton, J. H., 21n, 31n, 73, 74n,
110, 113, 341n

Moxnes, H., 185n, 240n, 250n

Mozley, J. H., 612n

Mueller, H.-F., 529n

Mullach, F., 626n

Müller, C. D. G., 616n

Müller, K., 22n

Müller, M., 580n

Mullins, T. Y., 162n, 165n, 168n,
170n, 172n, 558–559

Mumprecht, V., 60n

Munck, J., 282n

Muraoka, T., 105n

Murphy-O'Connor, J., 239, 247n,
251n

Murray, O., 505n

Müseler, E., 133n

Mussies, G., 4, 25, 100n

Mussner, F., 474n

Nagel, M., 611

Nagel, T., 6, 198, 212–214

Najman, H., 254n

Naldini, M., 518n

Nanos, M. D., 311n
Nanos, M., 466n, 468n
Nelson, H. L. W., 642n
Nesselrath, H.-G., 279n
Nestle, E., 200, 219, 590–591
Neubecker, A. J., 395n, 396n, 397n,
    398n, 399n, 400n, 401n, 402n,
    403n, 404n, 405n, 406n, 407n
Neyrey, J. H., 570n
Nicholas, B., 641n
Nichols, R., 80n
Nickelsburg, W. E., 44
Nida, E. A., 112, 114, 115n, 123n,
    125n, 126n
Niebuhr, R. R., 165n
Niederwimmer, K., 128n
Nielsen, H. S., 11
Nock, A. D., 24, 26, 35, 334n, 485n
Nolland, J., 183n, 195n
Norden, E., 7, 20
Norden, F., 661n, 664n, 665n, 670n
Norris, F. W., 41, 483n, 508n
Norton, F. O., 638n
Nygren, A., 29n

O'Brien, J. M., 491n
O'Brien, P. T., 157n, 199n
O'Neil, E. N., 184n
O'Neill, J. C., 132n, 431n
Obbink, D., 26, 283n, 295n, 325n,
    395n
Oepke, A., 307
Olbrechts-Tyteca, L., 374n
Olbricht, T. H., 9, 26n, 158n, 277n,
    281n, 371n, 375n, 386n
Oldfather, W. A., 286n
Olearius, G., 286n
Oliver, J. H., 499n
Olson, S. N., 163, 166
Oltramare, A., 568n
Orton, D. E., 565n
Orton, D., 359n
Osiek, C., 604n, 605n, 607n
Oster, R., 239
Owen, S. G., 652n

Page, D. L., 80n

Patzer, H., 53n
Paulsen, H., 126n
Pearson, B. A., 45
Pease, A. S., 655n, 669n
Pelham, H. F., 661n
Pelikan, J. J., 1n, 14n
Pépin, J., 372n
Perelman, C., 374n
Perkins, J., 182n
Pernot, L., 555n, 556n, 560n, 561n,
    565n, 566n, 569n
Perriman, A. C., 247n
Perrin, B., 120, 484n, 487n
Perrot, J., 642n
Perry, B. E., 646n, 655n
Pestman, P. W., 654n
Peter, H., 134n, 148n
Peterson, E., 34n, 616
Petit, P., 188n
Pettorelli, J., 612
Petzke, G., 24n
Philippson, R., 63, 64n
Pickering, S. R., 518n
Pilgaard, A., 49n, 50
Plummer, A., 77n, 123n
Poehlmann, W. R., 592n
Pogoloff, S. M., 241n, 278n
Pohlenz, M., 239n
Poland, F., 514n, 517
Pomeroy, S. B., 495n
Porod, R., 497n
Porter, S. E., 26n, 158n, 188n, 277n,
    281n, 310n, 311n, 360n, 375n,
    381n
Praechter, K., 22n
Préaux, J.-G., 672n
Preisker, H., 23n
Price, S. R. F., 264n
Prieur, A., 475n
Purser, L. C., 137n, 138n, 146n, 147n,
    150n

Quasten, J., 383
Quilligan, M., 379n

Rabe, A., 194n
Rackham, H., 210n, 221n

Räisänen, H., 11, 576–578, 579n, 584n
Rawson, B., 545n
Rawson, E., 643n
Rayment, C. S., 655n, 656n, 665n
Reardon, B. P., 134n
Reed, J. T., 157n, 159n, 168, 169n, 170, 171n, 174n
Rehkopf, F., 114n
Reisner, R., 498n
Reitzenstein, R., 24
Relihan, J. C., 655n
Rendtorff, T., 501n
Renier, E., 647n
Reta, J. O., 642n
Reumann, J., 175n
Riaud, J., 418n
Riccobono, S., 513n, 660n
Richard, E. J., 131n
Richardson, P., 71n
Ridley, R. T., 503n
Riedweg, C., 375n
Rigsby, K. J., 658n
Rigsby, R. O., 116n
Rist, J. M., 263n, 599n
Ritchl, A., 22n
Robbins, V. K., 216n, 559n
Roberts, J. T., 495n
Roberts, W. R., 375n
Robertson, A., 123n
Roetzel, C. J., 463n, 465n
Rogers, R. S., 666n, 667n
Rohde, E., 188n
Rohde, J., 307n
Rolfe, J. C., 487n
Rordorf, W., 128n
Rorty, A. O., 374n
Ros, J., 15n
Rubinstein, L., 655n, 656n
Rücker, A., 33n
Rudd, N., 649n, 651n, 652n
Ruete, E., 146n, 148n
Ruschenbusch, E., 638n
Russel, R., 160, 161n, 162n, 165n
Russell, D. A., 289
Rutgers, L. V., 25n

Sachs, M., 27n
Saenger, P., 353n, 362n
Sakalis, D. T., 62n, 63n
Salles, C., 135n
Sampley, J. P., 198–199, 204, 207, 233n, 325–326, 330
Sand, A., 103–105
Sandbach, F. H., 649n
Sanders, E. P., 31, 44, 351n, 463, 464n, 576n
Sanders, J. T., 172n, 471–472, 477n
Sanders, L., 259, 271
Sandmel, S., 30n
Scala, D. J., 648n
Schaff, P., 525n
Schanze, H., 556n
Schäublin, C., 385n
Scheffler, S., 6, 198, 211–214
Scheid, J., 513n, 514n
Schekenveld, D. M., 375n
Schenk, W., 172n, 173n
Schlarb, E., 21n, 46
Schlatter, A., 56, 77n
Schleier, R., 17n
Schlier, H., 307, 339n
Schlosser, J., 135n
Schmidt, O. E., 147, 149
Schmidt, P., 136n
Schmidt, T. E., 81n
Schmithals, W., 131n, 132n
Schmitz, T., 279n
Schneemelcher, W., 616n
Schnelle, U., 25
Schnider, F., 165n
Schniewind, J.,, 23n
Schoedel, W. R., 1n
Schofield, M., 265n
Schönegg, B., 134n
Schoon-Janssen, J., 158n
Schotroff, L., 576n
Schöttgen, J. C., 30n
Schrage, W., 243n, 245n
Schroeder, F. M., 29n
Schubert, P., 476n
Schueller, H. M., 392n
Schultz, F., 640n, 641n, 646n
Schürer, E., 430, 617n

Schüssler-Fiorenza, E., 241n, 243n, 244n
Schwerdtfeger, G. E., 18n
Scott, R., 107
Scroggs, R., 238, 245n, 247n
Segal, A., 31, 32n
Segovia, F., 233n
Selby, G. S., 281
Sellew, P., 158n, 186
Sellin, G., 131n
Sevenster, J. N., 17n, 75n
Shaw, B. D., 526n, 528n, 529n, 530n, 534n, 535n, 540n
Shaw, T., 530n, 536n
Sheppard, A. R. R., 264n
Sherwin-White, A. N., 498–499, 666n, 671n
Shive, W., 2
Shorey, P., 84n, 281n
Showalter, D., 319n
Siebeck, M., 157n
Sieffert, F., 339n
Siegert, F., 56n, 381, 414n
Silvagni, A., 541n
Silverstein, T., 618n, 619n, 631n, 635n
Singer, I., 421n
Skidmore, C., 300n, 646n
Slingerland, H. D., 499n
Sly, D., 251n, 252, 255n
Smallwood, E. M., 498n
Smith, E. W., 25n
Smith, J. A., 85n, 418n
Smith, J. Z., 34, 35n, 36
Smith, M. F., 133n
Smith, R. W., 382
Smith, W. C., 502n
Smith, W. D., 62n, 63n, 64n, 66n, 68n, 133n
Smith, W. S., 426n
Smyth, H. W., 192n
Sokolowski, F., 505–506, 508–509, 521
Sourvinou-Inwood, C., 621n, 622n, 627n
Souter, A., 590n
Spicq, C., 75n, 77n, 113

Spiess, E., 19
Städele, A., 133n
Stamps, D. L., 375n
Stange, E., 21n
Starr, J., 53n
Steck, R., 19
Steen, H. A., 162n, 172n
Stegner, W. R., 381n
Stein, E., 372n
Stein, P., 645n
Steindorff, G., 630n
Stendahl, K., 44
Stengel, P., 118n, 119n
Stenger, W., 165n
Sterling, G. E., 26n, 39n, 244n, 245n, 248n, 371n, 431
Stern, M., 516n
Sternkopf, W., 136n
Stewart, J. A., 384n
Stewart, Z., 24n, 334n
Stewart-Sykes, A., 132n
Stirewalt, M. L., 165n
Stock, C., 106n
Stone, M. E., 13n, 610–611, 612n, 613
Stoneman, R., 490n, 491n, 495n
Stowers, S. K., 8, 20n, 159n, 170, 175n, 176, 221, 225n, 229n, 243n, 352–353, 357, 365n, 371n, 381n, 462n, 463n, 465n, 508, 580n, 582n
Strack, H. L., 22n, 30–31
Strecker, G., 25
Stroux, J., 498n
Strugnell, J., 446n
Sumney, J., 241n
Sussman, L. A., 658n, 659n
Swain, S., 279, 287n
Syme, R., 497n, 671n
Szesnat, H., 255n

Tamm, D., 647n
Tarn, W. W., 26n
Tarn, W., 490n
Taubenschlag, R., 640n
Taylor, J. E., 419n
Tellegen, J. W., 647n

Tellegen-Couperus, O. E., 647n, 655n

Temkin, O., 66n, 68n

Teske, R. J., 530n, 533n

Teugs, L., 25n

Thayer, J. H., 19n, 108–109, 111

Thime, O., 52n

Thom, J. C., 11, 26n, 567n, 570n, 571n, 572n, 573n

Thomas, C., 319

Thomassen, E., 332n

Thompson, A. A., 107n, 108n

Thompson, W. E., 639n, 665n

Thomsom, J. W., 6, 41, 483n, 508n

Thraede, K., 165n

Thrall, M., 71n, 73n, 75n, 76n, 77, 78n, 79n, 81n, 168

Thurén, L., 359n

Thyen, H., 381n

Tibiletti, G., 518n

Tischendorf, C., 339n, 590, 619n, 633n, 635n

Todd, S. C., 639n, 655n

Tomson, P., 244n

Torjesen, K. J., 602n

Tosi, R., 491n

Tracey, D., 382

Traggelles, T. R., 590n

Trask, W. R., 556n

Travis, R., 372n

Treggiari, S., 530n, 659n, 66on

Tromp, J., 609n, 610n, 611n, 614n, 615n, 619n

Tronier, H., 580n

Tsevat, M., 104n, 105n

Tsouna, V., 555n

Tuilier, A., 128n

Turcan, R., 77n, 8on

Turner, M., 262n

Tyrell, R. Y., 137n, 138n, 146n, 147n, 150n

Tyson, J. B., 477n, 480n

Überlacker, W., 371n

Ueding, G., 64n

Ulansey, D., 510n

Usener, H., 21n

Usher, S., 363n

Valloza, M., 64n

van de Sandt, H., 243n, 244n

van den Broek, R., 610n

van den Hout, 647n

van der Horst, P. W., 16n, 22n, 24–25, 27n, 31n, 25in, 270n

van Halsema, J. D. F., 277n

van Harnack, A., (see Harnack)

van Rompay, L., 614n

van Unnik, W. C., 7, 23n, 24–26, 27n, 75n, 260, 272

Vermaseren, M. J., 24, 510n, 610n

Vermes, G., 617n

Vermeule, E., 622n

Versnel, H. S., 76n, 8on, 332n

Vidman, L., 509

Villeneuve, F., 651n

Vogel, C., 542n

von Albrecht, M., 150n

von Arnim, H., 209, 255n, 282, 289n, 348n, 564n

von der Osten-Sacken, P., 576n

von Dobschütz, E., 21–23

von Fritz, K., 133n

von Lips, H., 558n, 569n

von Martitz, W., 50n

von Rad, G., 445n

von Staden, H., 71n

Wacholder, B. Z., 432n

Wachsmuth, B., 261n

Walker, B., 659n

Walker, J., 315n

Walker, W. O., 238n

Wallace-Hadrill, A., 646n, 653n, 659n, 666n

Wallace-Hadrill, D. S., 383n

Walter, N., 20, 21n, 463n, 468n

Waltzing, J.-P., 517

Wankel, H., 555n, 556n, 562n, 565–566, 567n

Wansink, C., 174

Ware, J., 26n

Warmington, B. H., 666n

Waszink, J. H., 33n

Watson, A., 640n, 643n, 644n, 645n, 646n, 648n, 654n, 659n
Watson, D. F., 5, 152n, 158n, 281n, 310n, 371n, 462n
Watts, W. S., 137n, 138n, 140, 141n, 144n, 149n
Weaver, P., 545n
Webb, R., 332n
Weima, J. A. D., 172n, 174n
Weiss, J., 20, 123n
Weitlin, E. G., 1n
Wellborn, L., 278
Welles, C. B., 487n, 493n
Wendland, P., 22n, 23, 76n
Wenger, L., 33n
West, M. L., 396n, 408n, 418n, 421n
Westcott, B. F., 590
Westermann, W. L., 509n, 594
Wettstein, J. J., 15, 16, 19, 21, 23–25, 27n, 75n, 78n, 93
Wevers, J. W., 435n
Whitaker, G. H., 248n
White, J. L., 159, 161n, 162n, 163–165, 166n, 167n, 168n, 169n, 170n, 172n, 173, 174, 175, 310
White, L. M., 2–3, 8, 12, 14n, 17n, 22n, 26n, 29n, 32n, 33n, 37n, 39n, 45, 49n, 71n, 82n, 131n, 175n, 199n, 210n, 233n, 234n, 243n, 264n, 286n, 292n, 319n, 321n, 333n, 334n, 505n, 508n, 510n, 519n, 525n, 527n, 534n, 538n, 609n
Whitman, J., 380n
Wieacker, F., 640n, 641n
Wilburn, J. R., 44
Wilckens, U., 486n, 584n
Wilcox, C. T., 531n
Wilke, C. G., 7, 108
Wilken, R. L., 1n, 383n
Wilkinson, L. P., 401n, 402n, 404n

Will, G. F., 237n
Willcock, M. M., 146n
Willets, R. F., 640n
Williams, R., 384n
Williams, W. G., 141n, 145n
Williamson Jr., L., 72–73, 76n
Wilson, S. G., 521n
Wilson, W. T., 217n, 218n, 221n, 225n
Windisch, H., 21, 23, 77n
Winger, M., 576n, 576n, 579n, 580n, 584n
Winter, B. W., 7, 277–278, 282n, 286n, 290n, 317n, 381–382, 483, 501n, 637n
Winterbottom, M., 663n
Wintermute, O. S., 630n
Wipszycka, E., 518n
Wire, A., 246n, 250n
Wisse, J., 277n, 285
Wissowa, G., 119n
Wistrand, E., 528n
Witherington III, B., 243n, 302
Wohl, V., 133n
Woodcock, E. C., 671n
Wordsworth, 77n
Worp, K. A., 656n
Worstbrock, F. J., 136n
Wright, G. E., 27, 28n
Wright, N. T., 470n
Wuellner, W., 560
Wyse, W., 654n

Yarbrough, O. L., 45, 199n, 334n, 534n
Young, F. M., 378n, 383–384, 385n

Zeller, D., 4, 67n, 133n, 431n
Zelzer, M., 135n
Ziebarth, E., 517
Zingale, L. M., 640n

SUPPLEMENTS TO NOVUM TESTAMENTUM

ISSN 0167-9732

2. Strobel, A. *Untersuchungen zum eschatologischen Verzögerungsproblem auf Grund der spätjüdi-sche-urchristlichen Geschichte von Habakuk 2,2 ff.* 1961. ISBN 90 04 01582 5

16. Pfitzner, V.C. *Paul and the Agon Motif.* 1967. ISBN 90 04 01596 5

27. Mussies, G. *The Morphology of Koine Greek As Used in the Apocalypse of St. John.* A Study in Bilingualism. 1971. ISBN 90 04 02656 8

28. Aune, D.E. *The Cultic Setting of Realized Eschatology in Early Christianity.* 1972. ISBN 90 04 03341 6

29. Unnik, W.C. van. *Sparsa Collecta.* The Collected Essays of W.C. van Unnik Part 1. Evangelia, Paulina, Acta. 1973. ISBN 90 04 03660 1

31. Unnik, W.C. van. *Sparsa Collecta.* The Collected Essays of W.C. van Unnik Part 3. Patristica, Gnostica, Liturgica. 1983. ISBN 90 04 06262 9

34. Hagner, D.A. *The Use of the Old and New Testaments in Clement of Rome.* 1973. ISBN 90 04 03636 9

37. Reiling, J. *Hermas and Christian Prophecy.* A Study of The Eleventh Mandate. 1973. ISBN 90 04 03771 3

43. Clavier, H. *Les variétés de la pensée biblique et le problème de son unité.* Esquisse d'une théologie de la Bible sur les textes originaux et dans leur contexte historique. 1976. ISBN 90 04 04465 5

47. Baarda, T., A.F.J. Klijn & W.C. van Unnik (eds.) *Miscellanea Neotestamentica.* I. Studia ad Novum Testamentum Praesertim Pertinentia a Sociis Sodalicii Batavi c.n. Studiosorum Novi Testamenti Conventus Anno MCMLXXVI Quintum Lustrum Feliciter Complentis Suscepta. 1978. ISBN 90 04 05685 8

48. Baarda, T., A.F.J. Klijn & W.C. van Unnik (eds.) *Miscellanea Neotestamentica.* II. 1978. ISBN 90 04 05686 6

50. Bousset, D.W. *Religionsgeschichtliche Studien.* Aufsätze zur Religionsgeschichte des hellenistischen Zeitalters. Hrsg. von A.F. Verheule. 1979. ISBN 90 04 05845 1

52. Garland, D.E. *The Intention of Matthew 23.* 1979. ISBN 90 04 05912 1

53. Moxnes, H. *Theology in Conflict.* Studies in Paul's Understanding of God in Romans. 1980. ISBN 90 04 06140 1

56. Skarsaune, O. *The Proof From Prophecy.* A Study in Justin Martyr's Proof-Text Tradition: Text-type, Provenance, Theological Profile. 1987. ISBN 90 04 07468 6

59. Wilkins, M.J. *The Concept of Disciple in Matthew's Gospel, as Reflected in the Use of the Term 'Mathetes'.* 1988. ISBN 90 04 08689 7

64. Sterling, G.E. *Historiography and Self-Definition.* Josephos, Luke-Acts and Apologetic Historiography. 1992. ISBN 90 04 09501 2

65. Botha, J.E. *Jesus and the Samaritan Woman.* A Speech Act Reading of John 4:1-42. 1991. ISBN 90 04 09505 5

66. Kuck, D.W. *Judgment and Community Conflict.* Paul's Use of Apologetic Judgment Language in 1 Corinthians 3:5-4:5. 1992. ISBN 90 04 09510 1

67. Schneider, G. *Jesusüberlieferung und Christologie.* Neutestamentliche Aufsätze 1970-1990. 1992. ISBN 90 04 09555 1

68. Seifrid, M.A. *Justification by Faith.* The Origin and Development of a Central Pauline Theme. 1992. ISBN 90 04 09521 7

69. Newman, C.C. *Paul's Glory-Christology*. Tradition and Rhetoric. 1992. ISBN 90 04 09463 6
70. Ireland, D.J. *Stewardship and the Kingdom of God*. An Historical, Exegetical, and Contextual Study of the Parable of the Unjust Steward in Luke 16: 1-13. 1992. ISBN 90 04 09600 0
71. Elliott, J.K. *The Language and Style of the Gospel of Mark*. An Edition of C.H. Turner's "Notes on Marcan Usage" together with other comparable studies. 1993. ISBN 90 04 09767 8
72. Chilton, B. *A Feast of Meanings*. Eucharistic Theologies from Jesus through Johannine Circles. 1994. ISBN 90 04 09949 2
73. Guthrie, G.H. *The Structure of Hebrews*. A Text-Linguistic Analysis. 1994. ISBN 90 04 09866 6
74. Bormann, L., K. Del Tredici & A. Standhartinger (eds.) *Religious Propaganda and Missionary Competition in the New Testament World*. Essays Honoring Dieter Georgi. 1994. ISBN 90 04 10049 0
75. Piper, R.A. (ed.) *The Gospel Behind the Gospels*. Current Studies on Q. 1995. ISBN 90 04 09737 6
76. Pedersen, S. (ed.) *New Directions in Biblical Theology*. Papers of the Aarhus Conference, 16-19 September 1992. 1994. ISBN 90 04 10120 9
77. Jefford, C.N. (ed.) *The Didache in Context*. Essays on Its Text, History and Transmission. 1995. ISBN 90 04 10045 8
78. Bormann, L. *Philippi – Stadt und Christengemeinde zur Zeit des Paulus*. 1995. ISBN 90 04 10232 9
79. Peterlin, D. *Paul's Letter to the Philippians in the Light of Disunity in the Church*. 1995. ISBN 90 04 10305 8
80. Jones, I.H. *The Matthean Parables*. A Literary and Historical Commentary. 1995. ISBN 90 04 10181 0
81. Glad, C.E. *Paul and Philodemus*. Adaptability in Epicurean and Early Christian Psychagogy. 1995. ISBN 90 04 10067 9
82. Fitzgerald, J.T. (ed.) *Friendship, Flattery, and Frankness of Speech*. Studies on Friend-ship in the New Testament World. 1996. ISBN 90 04 10454 2
83. Tilborg, S. van. *Reading John in Ephesus*. 1996. 90 04 10530 1
84. Holleman, J. *Resurrection and Parousia*. A Traditio-Historical Study of Paul's Eschatology in 1 Corinthians 15. 1996. ISBN 90 04 10597 2
85. Moritz, T. *A Profound Mystery*. The Use of the Old Testament in Ephesians. 1996. ISBN 90 04 10556 5
86. Borgen, P. *Philo of Alexandria - An Exegete for His Time*.1997. ISBN 90 04 10388 0
87. Zwiep, A.W. *The Ascension of the Messiah in Lukan Christology*. 1997. ISBN 90 04 10897 1
88. Wilson, W.T. *The Hope of Glory*. Education and Exhortation in the Epistle to the Colossians. 1997. ISBN 90 04 10937 4
89. Peterson, W.L., J.S. Vos & H.J. de Jonge (eds.) *Sayings of Jesus: Canonical and Non-Canonical*. Essays in Honour of Tjitze Baarda. 1997. ISBN 90 04 10380 5
90. Malherbe, A.J., F.W. Norris & J.W. Thompson (eds.) *The Early Church in Its Context*. Essays in Honor of Everett Ferguson. 1998. ISBN 90 04 10832 1
91. Kirk, A. *The Composition of the Sayings Source*. Genre, Synchrony, and Wisdom Redaction in Q. 1998. ISBN 90 04 11085 2
92. Vorster, W.S. *Speaking of Jesus*. Essays on Biblical Language, Gospel Narrative and the Historical Jesus. Edited by J. E. Botha. 1999. ISBN 90 04 10779 7
93. Bauckham, R. *The Fate of Dead*. Studies on the Jewish and Christian Apocalypses. 1998. ISBN 90 04 11203 0

94. Standhartinger, A. *Studien zur Entstehungsgeschichte und Intention des Kolosserbriefs.* 1998. ISBN 90 04 11286 3

95. Oegema, G.S. *Für Israel und die Völker.* Studien zum alttestamentlich-jüdischen Hintergrund der paulinischen Theologie. 1999. ISBN 90 04 11297 9

96. Albl, M.C. *"And Scripture Cannot Be Broken".* The Form and Function of the Early Christian *Testimonia* Collections. 1999. ISBN 90 04 11417 3

97. Ellis, E.E. *Christ and the Future in New Testament History.* 1999. ISBN 90 04 11533 1

98. Chilton, B. & C.A. Evans, (eds.) *James the Just and Christian Origins.* 1999. ISBN 90 04 11550 1

99. Horrell, D.G. & C.M. Tuckett (eds.) *Christology, Controversy and Community.* New Testament Essays in Honour of David R. Catchpole. 2000. ISBN 90 04 11679 6

100. Jackson-McCabe, M.A. *Logos and Law in the Letter of James.* The Law of Nature, the Law of Moses and the Law of Freedom. 2001. ISBN 90 04 11994 9

101. Wagner, J.R. *Heralds of the Good News.* Isaiah and Paul "In Concert" in the Letter to the Romans. 2002. ISBN 90 04 11691 5

102. Cousland, J.R.C. *The Crowds in the Gospel of Matthew.* 2002. ISBN 90 04 12177 3

103. Dunderberg, I., C. Tuckett and K. Syreeni. *Fair Play: Diversity and Conflicts in Early Christianity.* Essays in Honour of Heikki Räisänen. 2002. ISBN 90 04 12359 8

104. Mount, C. *Pauline Christianity.* Luke-Acts and the Legacy of Paul. 2002. ISBN 90 04 12472 1

105. Matthews, C.R. *Philip: Apostle and Evangelist.* Configurations of a Tradition. 2002. ISBN 90 04 12054 8

106. Aune, D.E., T. Seland, J.H. Ulrichsen (eds.) *Neotestamentica et Philonica.* Studies in Honor of Peder Borgen. 2002. ISBN 90 04 126104

107. Talbert, C.H. *Reading Luke-Acts in its Mediterranean Milieu.* 2003. ISBN 90 04 12964 2

108. Klijn, A.F.J. *The Acts of Thomas.* Introduction, Text, and Commentary. Second Revised Edition. 2003. ISBN 90 04 12937 5

109. Burke, T.J. & J.K. Elliott (eds.) *Paul and the Corinthians.* Studies on a Community in Conflict. Essays in Honour of Margaret Thrall. 2003. ISBN 90 04 12920 0

110. Fitzgerald, J.T., T.H. Olbricht & L.M. White (eds.) *Early Christianity and Classical Culture.* Comparative Studies in Honor of Abraham J. Malherbe. 2003. ISBN 90 04 13022 5

111. Fitzgerald, J.T., D. Obbink & G.S. Holland (eds.) *Philodemus and the New Testament World.* 2003. ISBN 90 04 11460 2